Microsoft®

Visual Studio® 2015

UNLEASHED

20 Ansari Road, Darya Ganj, New Delhi-110002

FIRST EDITION 2016

ISBN : 978-81-8333-417-4

Reprinted in India under arrangement with Pearson Education Inc., USA

Authorized reprint from the English language edition, entitled MICROSOFT VISUAL STUDIO 2015 UNLEASHED, 3rd Edition, 9780672337369 by POWERS, LARS; SNELL, MIKE, published by Pearson Education, Inc, publishing as Sams Publishing, Copyright © 2016 Pearson Education, Inc.

LIMITS OF LIABILITY AND DISCLAIMER OF WARRANTY

The author and publisher of this book have tried their best to ensure that the programmes, procedures and functions described in the book are correct. However, the author and the publishers make no warranty of any kind, expressed or implied, with regard to these programmes or the documentation contained in the book. Although every precaution has been taken in the preparation of this book, the publisher and author assume no responsibility for errors or omissions. The author and publisher shall not be liable in any event of any damages, incidental or consequential, in connection with, or arising out of the furnishing, performance or use of these programmes, procedures and functions. Product name mentioned are used for identification purposes only and are the trademarks of their respective companies/owners and are duly acknowledged.

Distributors:

COMPUTER BOOK CENTRE
12, Shrungar Shopping Centre,
M.G.Road, Bengaluru–560001
Ph: 25587923/25584641

MICRO BOOKS
Shanti Niketan Building,
8, Camac Street, Kolkata-700017
Ph: 22826518/22826519

DECCAN AGENCIES
4-3-329, Bank Street,
Hyderabad-500195
Ph: 24756967/24756400

MICRO MEDIA
Shop No. 5, Mahendra Chambers,
150 DN Rd. Next to Capital Cinema,
V.T. (C.S.T.) Station, Mumbai-400 001
Ph: 22078296/22078297

BPB BOOK CENTRE
376 Old Lajpat Rai Market,
Delhi-110006
Ph: 23861747

INFOTECH
G-2, Sidhartha Building,
96, Nehru Place,
New Delhi -110019
Ph: 41619735, 26438245

BPB PUBLICATIONS
20, Ansari Road, Darya Ganj
New Delhi-110002
Ph: 23254990/23254991

Published by Manish Jain for BPB Publications, 20, Ansari Road, Darya Ganj, New Delhi-110002 and Printed at Akash Press, New Delhi.

Contents at a Glance

Table of Contents

About the Authors

Mike Snell spends his work life helping teams build great software that exceeds the expectations of end users. He runs the Solutions division at CEI (www.ceiamerica.com). Mike and his team deliver architecture, consulting, and mentoring to clients looking for help with enterprise projects, commercial software, mobile applications, or cloud-based solutions. He is also a Microsoft Regional director.

Lars Powers is currently the director of application development at Newgistics, Inc. Prior to Newgistics, he held various technical management positions at 3M and spent many years with Microsoft as a platform evangelist focused on emerging technologies.

Dedication

To my wife, Carrie Snell. Thank you.

Mike Snell

To Cheryl, once again.

Lars Powers

Acknowledgments

Mike Snell:

I would like to thank all the fine people involved with the making of this book. This includes the team at Pearson: Joan Murray, Mark Renfrow, Elaine Wiley, and Christophe Nasarre-Soulier. I would also like to thank the team of developer-architects at CEI for acting as a sounding board for so many topics. Of course, I'm also grateful to my co-author, Lars Powers, for the many years of collaboration.

Lars Powers:

Nothing of consequence is delivered without team work. This book is no exception. I'd like to acknowledge the Pearson team who did all the hard work to get this book into your hands. Joan Murray alternately cajoled, supported, and pushed us along. Mark Renfro and Elaine Wiley stitched all the pieces together for us. And Christophe Nasarre-Soulier ensured we stayed on the mark for technical accuracy.

And to my co-author, Mike: as always, projects are easier with you on board.

We Want to Hear from You!

As the reader of this book, *you* are our most important critic and commentator. We value your opinion and want to know what we're doing right, what we could do better, what areas you'd like to see us publish in, and any other words of wisdom you're willing to pass our way.

We welcome your comments. You can email or write to let us know what you did or didn't like about this book—as well as what we can do to make our books better.

Please note that we cannot help you with technical problems related to the topic of this book.

When you write, please be sure to include this book's title and author as well as your name and email address. We will carefully review your comments and share them with the author and editors who worked on the book.

Introduction

Visual Studio 2015 is Microsoft's first, big release since moving to a more open-source approach for .NET and related technologies. This includes the new Roslyn compiler for C# and Visual Basic, the .NET Core Framework, ASP.NET itself, and more. The result is enabling a wider reach for .NET applications, including both building and deploying on Mac, Linux, and Windows.

Microsoft has also worked to integrate Visual Studio with community-driven, open source JavaScript frameworks, package managers, and UI kits. The ASP.NET 5 model simplifies modern web development using frameworks such as Bootstrap, AngularJS, Knockout, Gulp, and many more.

Visual Studio 2015 supports the new, Universal App model for building on Windows. These applications can be written once and adapted to desktop, tablet, and phone. This includes upcoming support for Windows 10 development.

Cross-platform mobile development is also supported. Microsoft has provided project templates for the open-source Apache Cordova. This enables developers to build a mobile application that runs on iOS, Android, and Windows Phone using familiar web technologies of Hypertext Markup Language (HTML), Cascading Style Sheets (CSS), and JavaScript.

This latest version of Visual Studio unlocks productivity across platforms and application types. And this book is meant to help you unlock the power behind Visual Studio so that you can realize productivity gains and greater reach for your applications.

Who Should Read This Book?

Developers looking to use Visual Studio (Community, Professional, or Enterprise) to build great apps for users will want to read this book. Of course, established .NET developers who rely on Visual Studio to get work done will also want to read this book to ensure they are getting the most out of their chosen toolset. This book covers both using the IDE and building most of the many types of applications Visual Studio supports. It covers all of the following key topics:

- Writing code using Visual Basic and C#
- Understanding the basics of solutions, projects, editors, and designers
- Writing IDE extensions and add-ins
- Writing unit tests to verify your code works as designed
- Debugging code with the IDE
- Refactoring your code
- Building websites using the new ASP.NET 5 (and MVC 6) model, which includes support for Bower client-side package management and the new .NET Core 5 for running ASP.NET applications on Windows, Mac, and Linux
- Using JavaScript and the many client-side frameworks such as Knockout, AngularJS, and Bootstrap to create great web experiences
- Developing service-based solutions for web and mobile clients using ASP.NET Web API and Windows Communication Foundation (WCF)
- Creating Windows desktop and Store applications using Windows Presentation Foundation (WPF)
- Working with data and databases and leveraging LINQ and Entity Framework to build data-centric applications
- Using Microsoft Office and Visual Studio to create enterprise solutions based on common office tools (Word, Excel, and so on)
- Creating Windows Azure applications that live in the cloud
- Developing applications for Windows Phone
- Building cross-platform mobile applications that run on iOS, Android, and Windows Phone using Apache Cordova and related tools

This book has one primary focus: detailing and explaining the intricacies of the Visual Studio 2015 IDE to enable developers to be work faster and, ultimately, work smarter. Although we do provide a language primer, those just starting out with Visual Basic or C# may want a companion book that focuses solely on their language of choice. If you can write C# or Visual Basic code, this book will radically help you optimize your productivity with Visual Studio.

This book focuses primarily on Visual Studio 2015 Professional edition (which also covers the Community edition). There are additional features in Visual Studio Enterprise. However, those are mostly not covered by this book. Instead, we dedicate space to the version of the product used by the majority of .NET developers all over the world.

How Is This Book Organized?

You can read this book cover to cover, or you can pick the chapters that apply most to your current need. We sometimes reference content across chapters, but for the most part, each chapter can stand by itself. This organization allows you to jump around and read as time (and interest) permits. There are seven parts to the book; each part is described next.

Part I: Introducing Visual Studio 2015

The chapters in this part provide an overview of what to expect from Visual Studio 2015. This includes a tour of using the IDE to build various types of applications. In addition, we cover the new C# and Visual Basic language enhancement for the 2016 and the .NET Framework 4.6. Finally, we conclude this part with a language primer for those just getting started with .NET development. Readers who are familiar with prior versions of Visual Studio will want to review these chapters for the new additions in 2015.

Part II: An In-Depth Look at the IDE

This part covers the core development experience relative to Visual Studio. It provides developers with a base understanding of the rich features of their primary tool. The chapters walk through the many menus and windows that define each tool. We cover the base concepts of projects and solutions, and we explore in detail the explorers, editors, and designers.

Part III: Working with the Visual Studio Tools

Part III is the largest section of the book; it unlocks many of the powerful productivity features of Visual Studio 2015. These chapters investigate the developer productivity aids that are present in the IDE and discuss how to best use Visual Studio for testing, refactoring, debugging, and deploying your code. This part also covers building applications in Azure. The section concludes with a chapter dedicated to using Visual Studio to work with databases.

Part IV: Extending Visual Studio

For those developers interested in customizing, automating, or extending the Visual Studio IDE, these chapters are for you. We explain the automation model and then document how to use that application programming interface (API) to automate the IDE through macros. We also cover how you can extend the IDE's capabilities by writing your own add-ins.

Part V: Building Web Applications

Part V is for web developers. We cover building applications with the new ASP.NET 5 (and MVC 6) model. This section also covers JavaScript and related client-side frameworks for building responsive, highly interactive client-side solutions. The section concludes with coverage on writing and consuming services using Web API and Windows Communication Foundation (WCF).

Part VI: Building Windows Client Apps

This section is targeted at developers looking to build applications for Windows. This includes the class Windows Forms. We also cover the powerful WPF and building Universal Application. Finally, this part includes a chapter dedicated to building custom solutions on Microsoft Office.

Part VII: Creating Mobile Apps

Here we cover creating mobile application for Windows Store, Windows Phone, and cross-platform (iOS, Android, and Windows Phone). This part is targeted at the mobile developer looking to either build on Windows or use the hybrid mobile technology, Apache Cordova.

Conventions Used in This Book

The following typographic conventions are used in this book:

Code lines, commands, statements, variables, and text you see onscreen appears in a `monospace` typeface.

Placeholders in syntax descriptions appear in an *`italic monospace`* typeface. You replace the placeholder with the actual filename, parameter, or whatever element it represents.

Italics highlight technical terms when they're being defined.

A code-continuation icon is used before a line of code that is really a continuation of the preceding line. Sometimes a line of code is too long to fit as a single line on the page. If you see ➥ before a line of code, remember that it's part of the line immediately above it.

The book also contains Notes, Tips, and Cautions to help you spot important or useful information more quickly.

Source Code

You can download all the source code associated with this book from the book's website: www.informit.com/title/9780672337369

CHAPTER 1

A Quick Tour of Visual Studio 2015

IN THIS CHAPTER

- The Visual Studio Product Line
- Languages and Frameworks
- The Many Faces of a .NET Application
- Developing Windows 8/10 Clients
- Creating Web Applications with ASP.NET 5
- Coding for Azure
- Working with Data
- Writing Mobile Apps

Visual Studio 2015 and the latest version of the .NET Framework introduce new features that address modern, mobile-first/cloud-first development concerns such as cross-platform development, adoption of open standards, and transparency through open source. This latest version also continues to improve on existing developer experiences when writing code for the web, Windows, Office, database, and mobile applications. The 2015 product allows developers to really increase their range when building modern applications that users demand. Some highlights for the 2015 release include the following:

- Developer productivity enhancements in the code editor, including touch support
- Cross-platform mobile development for Windows, iOS, and Android
- Modern, unified web development with ASP.NET 5
- Cloud-ready integration to ease development and deployment
- Integration of the new, open source "Roslyn" compiler for VB, C#, and now TypeScript
- Easier, faster data development across web, Windows, Windows Phone, and Windows Store using Entity Framework 7
- Shared projects for C# and JavaScript to make sharing code between applications easier
- Redesigned version of Blend for creating beautiful user interfaces (UIs) with XAML

- Enhanced IDE support for building JavaScript solutions with object-oriented TypeScript language (a superset of JavaScript itself)
- Open source of many .NET elements including the compiler, the .NET Core, TypeScript, ASP.NET, and more

This chapter covers the core makeup and capabilities of Visual Studio 2015. We first help you sort through the product choices available to .NET developers. We then compare the .NET programming languages. The remaining sections of the chapter cover the many possibilities open to .NET programmers, including building web, Windows, cloud, data, and mobile applications. Our hope is to give you enough information in this chapter to get the full picture of what is available to you when you build solutions using Visual Studio.

NOTE

Part I, "Introducing Visual Studio 2015," is broken into three chapters. This chapter provides a snapshot of all things Visual Studio. Chapter 2, "The Visual Studio IDE," is an introduction to getting the tool installed, running it, and creating a first project. It also familiarizes you with the basics of the IDE. Chapter 3, "The .NET Languages," is a quick primer on coding constructs in Visual Basic and C#. It also covers general programming against the .NET Framework.

The Visual Studio Product Line

There are three primary editions of the Visual Studio product: Community, Professional with MSDN, and Enterprise with MSDN. Development teams need to understand which tool they need for their development projects and price point. At a high level, the primary tool editions are differentiated as follows.

- **Visual Studio Community**—A free, full-featured version of the development tool for building Web, Windows, Desktop, and mobile applications. This new version of the tool is targeted at developers learning to code, doing open source projects, and taking academic courses.
- **Professional with MSDN**—Includes the core features of the IDE to build applications of all types on all .NET languages. Targets professional developers and team looking to build commercial or enterprise software. Includes support for writing, debugging, and testing code.
- **Enterprise with MSDN**—Formerly the Ultimate edition, the Enterprise edition includes the core IDE features along with many advanced tools for building applications. It builds on the Professional edition to add additional load testing support, architecture tools, lab management, release management, and more.

NOTE

You can see a detailed product comparison at https://www.visualstudio.com/products/compare-visual-studio-2015-products-vs.

There is a peripheral version of the Visual Studio product called Test Professional. It is a tool targeted directly at testers. You will learn more about all this product in the coming sections.

VISUAL STUDIO CODE

Microsoft released another development tool alongside Visual Studio 2015. This tool is called Visual Studio Code. It is a free tool that allows developers to write web applications on Windows, Mac, and Linux. The .NET Framework went cross-platform; this is the tool that allows developers to work on these other platforms. You can find more information at https://code.visualstudio.com//.

Community Edition

The new Visual Studio Community 2015 edition is a full-featured IDE similar to Professional but targeted toward students, small groups of developers, and open source contributors (and not enterprise teams). This version is free and available for immediate download. Note that Microsoft has also release a Visual Studio Community 2013 edition.

The former Express editions have been retired. These editions were also free, but they were feature limited. Community, student, and entrepreneurial developers should be pleased to know this new edition is nearly the same as Professional but just has licensing restrictions.

Being based on Professional opens community developers to all types of applications using the great productivity tools built in Visual Studio. Just as significant, it ensures the Community Edition supports Visual Studio plug-ins (more than 5,000 in existence) for using community extensions targeted at increasing productivity. It also allows developers to target multiple different platforms with this single tool.

The primary difference between the editions Community and Professional (outside of licensing and costs) are a few project types Microsoft has decided not to include with the Community Edition. These project types are targeted squarely at enterprise developers. They include SharePoint, Office, LightSwitch, and Cloud Business Apps. These type of solutions are outside the bounds of the solutions Microsoft sees students, hobbyists, and small groups needing to create.

NOTE

For more information about the Visual Studio Community Edition (including licensing restrictions) or to download, you can visit the Microsoft site: https://www.visualstudio.com/products/visual-studio-community-vs.

Professional Edition

Visual Studio Professional is the base entry for most developers who make a living writing code. Visual Studio Professional gives you all the language support (including VB, C#, F#, TypeScript, C++); the capability to write all types of applications, including cross-platform mobile, web and JavaScript, console, Windows, cloud, database, Office, SharePoint; and more. This edition gives access to the tools that are key to building professional applications. The following are important features that ship with Visual Studio Professional (and higher):

- Unit testing and test-driven development
- Code analysis and code metrics
- Developing all application types, including Windows, web, mobile, Office, SharePoint, Cloud, SQL, and more
- CodeLens to provide quick, detailed information including references, linked items such as bugs, and changes on your code right in the IDE
- Performance and diagnostics hub
- Blend tool for building XAML UIs
- Server Explorer
- Refactoring in C# and Visual Basic
- SQL Server Data Tools (SSDT) for database development
- Code review tools (when working with Team Foundation Server, or TFS)
- Much more

NOTE

This book targets Visual Studio Professional only. A quick perusal of the book will allow you to see the depth and breadth of what you can do with this powerful edition of the tool.

Enterprise

Visual Studio Enterprise 2015 is targeted toward professional developers who build both corporate and commercial applications. It includes all the features inside Professional plus tools that help developers verify, test, and check their code against common issues. It also includes debugging tools designed to eliminate the "can't reproduce" bugs. It provides architecture tools for creating UML models and exploring code visually. This version of the product is the everything-but-the-kitchen-sink option in a single package. The following list highlights the features of Enterprise:

- Advanced performance and code profiling
- Code Clone tool for finding and eliminate duplicate code

- Unit test code coverage analysis and fakes
- Coded UI testing
- Test case management and exploratory testing
- Test lab management tools
- Historical debugging with IntelliTrace (including in production)
- Unified Modeling Language (UML) support for use case, class, sequence, component, and activity diagrams (including generating sequence diagrams from code)
- Architecture Explorer, for coming up to speed on and examining the structure of a code base
- Web, load, and performance testing

MSDN

Developers with Professional and Enterprise typically also have a related MSDN subscription. This subscription gives you development access to Microsoft tools such as TFS or Visual Studio Online (VSO). MSDN benefits are different between Professional and Enterprise. The latter provides developer access to nearly all Microsoft software and operating systems including SharePoint, Exchange, Office, Dynamics, BizTalk, and more. Professional with MSDN, however, only provides access to TFS, Windows Server, and SQL Server.

MSDN subscribers also have training benefits, access to deployment planning services, and monthly credits to allow Azure application hosting ($50 / month Azure credit for Professional subscribers and $150 / month for Enterprise). In addition, there is a new e-learning benefit for MSDN subscribers that includes access to a number of great learning solutions and instructional videos.

NOTE

The MSDN benefit is vast, check out the following link for full details: https://www.visualstudio.com/products/visual-studio-with-msdn-overview-vs.

TFS and Related Tools

A key component of most professional development teams includes the application lifecycle management environment, TFS. This tool allows teams to manage and track work. It provides the hub for collaboration between developers, project managers, testers, and those providing feedback. This section includes a brief overview of TFS and the related products: Team Explorer and Visual Studio Test Professional (also known as Microsoft Test Manager).

TFS

Application Lifecycle Management (ALM) is a broad term applied to the concept of continuous delivery of software through a set of integrated tools and processes. Microsoft uses this term often to refer to its collective group of developer tools. This collection includes Visual Studio editions, TFS, Test Professional, and related ancillary tools. TFS is the central hub that provides the integrated ALM experience around the various tools and their associated disciplines.

VISUAL STUDIO ONLINE (VSO)

TFS comes in two versions: on-premises-hosted TFS and the online-only version called Visual Studio Online (VSO). MSDN subscribers have access to both.

The versions are similar, and Microsoft is working to make them nearly the same. However, at the time of writing this, VSO has fewer features than TFS; these missing features include the following: SharePoint integration, process template and work item customization, data warehouse, and related reporting. This latter item is the most notable missing element.

Of course, there are advantages to VSO. First, it is online and therefore more easily accessible and lower overall maintenance. Second, it automatically updates versions, patches, and service packs. It also supports cloud load testing and a few other VSO-specific items. For more information on VSO relative to TFS, see the link: https://www.visualstudio.com/en-us/products/what-is-visual-studio-online-vs.aspx.

The first version of TFS was delivered with the release of 2005. This included source control, a centralized project management system, build automation, and reporting. By all accounts, these tools have been a great success over the past 10 years. Microsoft continues to build upon this with the release of TFS 2015.

TFS is at the center of development and ALM coordination. The following list highlights the many services provided by TFS:

- **Process guidance/template**—TFS includes three process templates out of the box: Microsoft Solutions Framework (MSF) for CMMI Process Improvements, MSF for Agile Software Development, and Microsoft Visual Studio Scrum. All provide a set of work items, workflows, and reports that are uniquely crafted with regard to their specific methodology. They also offer guidance to the team for executing key activities on the project (such as requirements management or build automation).
- **Project management**—TFS enables project managers to define their projects in terms of iterations and functional areas. It provides work items that are used to define, assign, and track work on the project. A work item can be a task on the project, a requirement, a bug, a test scenario, and so on. In general, a work item represents a generic unit of work on the project. Of course, work items are customizable and can have states, new fields, and business rules associated with them. TFS also includes a task board for easily viewing, working with, and tracking items in a collaborative way. Work items play a central part in ensuring project team communication and reporting. Project managers can use the TFS website along with the Excel and Project add-ins to Office to manage the work items on a project.

- **Requirements management**—TFS provides specific work items for managing requirements. Work items are hierarchical, which means you can create work item children. For example, you might create a requirement work item and then define the tasks required to build that requirement. You might also define the test cases that will be used to verify the requirement. In this way, TFS enables rich reporting through the aggregation of the child work item data (such as tests passing for a requirement or work remaining at the requirement level).
- **Test case management**—TFS and Test Professional enable work items specific to test planning and test case management. You can define a set of test cases for a given requirement. Each test case can define the steps required to execute the test case along with the expected results.
- **Version control**—The source control features in TFS include enterprise-class features such as change sets, shelving, automatic build rules, the capability to associate work items to changed source, parallel development, a source control policy engine, branching, checkpoints, and more. There are powerful tools included for visualizing branch and changeset relationships.
- **Build automation**—The TFS build tools allow for automatic, scheduled, and on-demand builds. Builds are reported against, documented, automatically tested, and analyzed for code coverage and churn (as an example). The build engine is written using Windows Workflow Foundation (WWF). TFS provides a build template you can use as the basis for creating custom build processes.
- **Release management**—TFS includes the Release Management tool for managing software releases from your environments such as development to test to staging to production. This tool allow you to track a release and assign approvers for various stages of that release.
- **Reporting**—TFS provides a rich set of reports for tracking statistics and the overall health of your project. Reports include those built on SQL Reporting Services (that are accessible from the IDE, the Web, and SharePoint) as well as a new set of Excel reports for working directly with the data.
- **Collaboration**—TFS includes Web Portal for teams collaborating on iterations, requirements, and the related project task. This consists of a project home page for quick health check, a team room for discussions, and task boards for updating status. Web Portal also provides web-based access to source code, builds, and tests.
- **Integration with other IDEs**—TFS is accessible from Visual Studio, Office, SharePoint, and the Web. In addition, there is Team Explorer Everywhere for accessing the TFS features using other IDEs running on operating systems outside Windows. This includes the Eclipse IDE and the Mac Xcode IDE.

Team Explorer

Some team members will not have a development tool such as Visual Studio or Test Professional that provides access to TFS. In this case, they can get full access through Team Explorer. Team Explorer is targeted at project managers, business analysts, directors, and others on the team who need to access TFS but do not do direct development. This tool is purchased as a client access license (CAL). It includes a basic explorer, the Excel and Project add-ins, full access to Web Portal, and reporting.

Test Professional (or Test Manager)

Visual Studio Test Professional 2015 provides test planning, test case management, and manual testing for those people dedicated to the testing role. This is a separate tool that should seem comfortable and familiar to testers. Test plans are created based on application requirements (to provide traceability). Test cases are created and tracked as work items.

When testers run a test plan, they work through each test case and each step in the test case. They indicate the success or failure of the given test. For failures, they can log bugs (also work items). The bugs can automatically include things such as diagnostic trace information, event log data, network information, and even video recording of the steps the tester was executing when the bug was found.

Test Professional also enables testers to create action recordings of their steps. These recordings can be played back to execute the same steps again. This helps automate many portions of manual tests.

In addition, Test Professional includes lab management, which is a suite of tools for provisioning test environments from a template. These environments are virtual machines that are meant to be set up and torn down as needed for testing. You also can create checkpoint environments for various builds.

Test Professional enables automated web, load, and stress tests. You can run these automated tests directly from Visual Studio on your local machine to simulate smaller user loads. However, if you want to collect data on multiple machines and test against a higher user load, you can leverage a test controller along with test agents. The test controller serves as the central data collector and manages the test agents. Test agents are then installed on both the servers under test and multiple client computers. This allows the servers under test to send back important data such as IntelliTrace information. The multiple client agents are used to simulate increased load and collect data from the client perspective. Finally, the centralized controller aggregates the resulting data for reporting.

Languages and Frameworks

Programming in Visual Studio and with the .NET Framework means you have a variety of languages from which to choose. Coding against the framework means selecting from C#, Visual Basic .NET (VB.NET), F#, or C++. The Framework itself is common to all three. Once compiled and deployed, applications written against .NET are similar in runtime execution. In fact, the new, open source .NET Compiler Platform ("Roslyn") is now the shared compiler for both VB and C#.

Microsoft is now delivering the .NET Core as an open source stack to be run on multiple operating systems including Linux, Windows, and Mac. It joins other .NET open source products from Microsoft including ASP.NET itself, the .NET Framework reference source,

Entity Framework, and more. Together, these initiatives enable developers to write, run, and host web and client applications on all three platforms.

Programming Language Choices

What should be important to developers is selecting a language that enables you to be productive and has a high degree of support inside the IDE. Productivity is about developing with syntax that is familiar and logical to you. IDE support means the tools can generate code, help you write code, and provide features and artifacts that accelerate your coding. This is where many third-party (non-Microsoft-supported) languages often fall short. It takes a lot to provide IDE support to build the many application types Visual Studio enables.

The following list is an overview of the Microsoft-supported languages for .NET development with Visual Studio:

- C#—C# is a programming language designed for those who are familiar and comfortable programming in C-style languages (such as C, C++, and Java). C# is type safe, object oriented, and targeted for rapid application development. C# developers tend to spend more of their time inside the Visual Studio code editor and less time with the designers.
- **Visual Basic .NET**—VB.NET is about productivity. Developers can rapidly build type-safe, object-oriented applications. Although VB developers have full access to all code constructs in .NET, they tend to use VB.NET because of the productivity features inside the IDE, and they are already familiar with it from past experience with VB (or a similar language built on Basic).
- C++—With C++, developers can build .NET managed applications. However, they can also create Windows-based applications that do not rely on .NET. Most C++ developers have a C background and are therefore more comfortable inside the C++ world than they are with other languages. A C++ developer also has access to build against Active Template Library (ATL), the Microsoft Foundation Class (MFC) libraries, and the C Runtime (CRT) library.
- **Visual F#**—The F# language is said to be multiparadigm because it allows for functional, object-oriented, and imperative programming. It brings .NET developers a solution to many difficult programming problems. There are several features of F#, including lightweight function types, functions as values, function composition and pipelining, recursive functions, and lambda expressions, to name a few. F# makes for simpler programming of math, scientific, engineering, and symbolic analysis (such as machine learning) problems. Visual Studio 2015 introduces F# 4.0 developed by both Microsoft and the open source community.
- **TypeScript**—Visual Studio 2015 includes support for TypeScript. TypeScript is an answer to the many developers writing more and more JavaScript on a daily basis but longing for more of the language and IDE features they are accustomed to from other languages. TypeScript is a strongly typed superset of JavaScript. It allows JavaScript developers to write JavaScript in a faster, cleaner, and more productive

way. The language syntax is JavaScript. The compiler outputs TypeScript to plain JavaScript that can be run in any browser on any platform.

NOTE

The basics of programming the languages of .NET are covered in Chapter 3.

NOTE

If you are familiar with one language but need to program in another (or translate), search for "Keywords Compared in Various Languages" on MSDN (last updated for the 2010 version but still useful).

The .NET Framework

The .NET Framework represents, in addition to the managed runtime, the base classes, libraries, and useful functions that make programming in .NET so productive. The classes and functions found in the .NET Framework offer the majority of common features you need as a developer. Thanks to the Common Type System (CTS), each language can take advantage of this single Framework of functionality. Framework features include file I/O, web, workflow, collections, Windows, communication, and much, much more.

Of course, as the .NET languages evolve, so does the Framework. However, to maintain backward compatibility, each version of the Framework remains as a separate entity. There are now many versions of the .NET Framework: 4.6, 4.5.2, 4.5.1, 4.5, 4.0, 3.5, 3.0, 2.0, 1.1, and 1.0.

NOTE

See Chapter 2 for details on how you can target a specific version of the .NET Framework inside Visual Studio 2015.

The .NET Core

The new .NET Core is an open source version of the framework designed to help you build cross-platform web and client solutions. It is also meant to be easy to deploy and can be deployed with your application. Because it is open source, you can edit the .NET Core to meet specific needs if required.

The .NET Core shares the same family (and much of the source code) as the full .NET Framework but is without a few features such as code access security and application domains. Thus, it also has a smaller footprint. It does have the base class libraries, JIT, and GC.

Microsoft is shipping the .NET Core for Windows, Linux, and Mac. It intends to update the .NET Core in cycle with the .NET Framework. The first major product to adopt the .NET Core runtime is ASP.NET 5.

The Many Faces of a .NET Application

.NET has become the standard when building applications targeting the Microsoft Windows client, server products, Windows Phone, Windows Store apps, websites, and more. Windows programming and .NET programming are now synonymous.

Many of the user applications we interact with have some if not all of their code base in .NET. This includes rich clients built on Windows, solutions built on Office (including parts of Office itself), mobile apps that also work with web services, web applications that run in a browser and execute on a Windows server, product extension solutions such as those written for SharePoint and BizTalk, and Windows Store applications targeting Windows 8/10.

The good news is that the .NET developer is in high demand, and you can leverage your skills to target a wide audience across an array of user experiences.

Figure 1.1 shows the New Project dialog in Visual Studio; it serves as an example of the myriad user solutions that are possible with .NET. This graphic cannot fit all the possibilities available to you, but it does illustrate that Windows, web, Office, and many other project types are within the reach of .NET developers working with Visual Studio.

FIGURE 1.1 The many application faces made possible by Visual Studio 2015.

As discussed, you have many project templates available for your next solution. What is needed, however, is some sort of road map with respect to user experience. Choosing the right project template is an important part of making the delivery of your solution successful. The following is a high-level overview of the core presentation technologies available to the .NET developer. (There are more, but these are the common ones.)

NOTE

Visual Studio provides many UI platform options. Many are highlighted here; for in-depth coverage, see their specific chapters in this book: Chapter 17, "Building Modern Websites with ASP.NET 5," Chapter 18, "Using JavaScript and Client-Side Frameworks," Chapter 20, "Building Windows Forms Applications," Chapter 21, "Building WPF Applications," Chapter 22, "Developing Office Business Applications," Chapter 23, "Developing Windows Store Applications," Chapter 24, "Creating Windows Phone Applications," and Chapter 25, "Writing Cross-Platform Mobile Applications with Apache Cordova."

Windows

- **Windows Forms application (WinForms)**—Windows form applications are used to deliver business applications and tools built on the Windows platform. You typically select a WinForms application template when you need to build a solution that leverages the resources on the user's machine. This means the application is installed and users expect it to run more responsively than the typical web application. WinForms applications can be standalone or data driven (often client-server). WinForms applications might connect to web services and work in both connected and unconnected scenarios.

NOTE

Microsoft has deemphasized building applications with WinForms. If you're building a new business application, you should consider Windows Presentation Foundation (WPF) because you can create a more modern user experience with it. A WPF application can also be built as a Universal application that runs on various Windows devices such as desktop, phone, and tablet.

- **WPF application**—WPF leverages XAML to allow you to create the richest, most full-featured client solution that runs on Windows. You choose WPF when you need to deliver a modern visual experience for your Windows application by taking advantage of vector-based scaling, 3D, and the benefits of using XAML markup.
- **Office and SharePoint**—Visual Studio enables you to build solutions based on the Office productivity tools, including Excel, Word, Project, Visio, Outlook, and PowerPoint. Choose an Office project when you want to write a business-productivity application centered on, and running within, one of the Office applications or documents (such as an Excel template or spreadsheet). You can also develop SharePoint applications for delivering functionality through the collaboration portal.

Web

- **ASP.NET**—ASP.NET has evolved for 2015 and is now a unified, lean stack that allows developers to create all types of web applications. The latest version of ASP.NET is primarily focused on ASP.NET Model-View-Controller (MVC) and web application programming interface (API) applications. These solutions typically run inside a user's browser but communicate with a web server for application processing. They use Hypertext Markup Language (HTML), Cascading Style Sheets (CSS), and JavaScript on the client but communicate across Hypertext Transfer Protocol (HTTP) to a server for centralized processing of code and data storage and retrieval. There are many project templates outside the defaults that are based on MVC. These enable various JavaScript-first solutions based on single-page application concepts (see the later bullet) as well as other web development types. The core, however, is a single ASP.NET stack to run it all.

NOTE

Microsoft deemphasizes the older style of web development based on web forms. Web forms are still in the current version of Visual Studio for backward compatibility. However, if you are building modern applications, you should consider MVC or one of the SPA templates. This gives you better separation of code, greater testability, and a simplified programming model based on open standards.

- **Web API**—Nearly all devices speak HTTP. As a result, web services are the ubiquitous means for communicating from device to server. This is true for desktop, phone, tablet, and all manners of applications. ASP.NET speaks HTTP very well and has thus been extended to allow developers to create services similar to the way you create other ASP.NET MVC solutions. The ASP.NET web API is now unified with MVC for a single programming model.
- **Single page applications (SPAs)**—Users are demanding richer client applications in the browser that often work like native applications running on an operating system. Developers have turned to JavaScript to make this work. Many JavaScript frameworks, such as jQuery, exist to make developing rich applications easier. Larger "frameworks" have created a whole new web client programming paradigm. Take AngularJS as an example. It allows developers to code using an MVC style on the client; the code runs in the user's browser versus ASP.NET running on a server. These frameworks and application types are known as SPAs. A user hits a single page in his web browser, and that page works like an application behind the scenes serving up requests and updating the UI. This is in contrast to a website that moves from page to page with full browser refresh.

Mobile

- **Windows Store application (Universal Apps)**—Visual Studio 2015 allows developers to create applications that target the Windows 8/10 store for desktops, tablets, and phones. The new universal app model (and project templates) allows developers to create a single application that targets Windows and Windows phone at the same time.

- **Cross platform mobile applications**—Visual Studio Tools for Apache Cordova support building mobile applications that target Android, iOS, Windows, and Windows Phone from a single project. This includes a new Visual Studio Emulator for Android. Of course, the Windows and Windows phone emulators already exist. You can also debug an iOS version of an app from Visual Studio when it is deployed to the iOS Simulator or a connected device. Apache Cordova is an open source set of device APIs that allow device access from JavaScript. This allows developers to create native device apps using HTML, CSS, and JavaScript.

Visual Studio supports each of these UI delivery technologies. With them, you have many options for creating great user experiences on .NET. The sections that follow highlight a number of these technologies for building both Windows and web solutions.

Developing Windows 8/10 Clients

Today's users demand a rich, interactive experience when they work with software. The line between what a web-based client can do versus one that runs on Windows has blurred thanks to many UI advancements, technologies, and tools, which can make it difficult to choose the right UI delivery for your next application. It also means that if you do decide to write a Windows-based client, you need to be sure you take full advantage of having the desktop resources at your disposal. Your application should perform well, look great, provide a high degree of interactivity, be able to work with larger data sets at any given time, and more. Here we look at the Windows-based client options for Visual Studio and creating smart, rich applications using WinForms, WPF (and the Universal App model), and Microsoft Office.

Windows (WinForms)

Visual Studio provides a mature, feature-rich set of tools for the rapid development of Windows applications that includes a drag-and-drop form designer and many controls inside the form toolbox. With these tools, developers can quickly lay out a Windows application that includes menus, toolbars, data access, tabs, resizing support, common controls for working with and printing files, and much more.

You create a Windows application by selecting the Windows Forms Application project template in the New Project dialog. This type of application is also called a WinForms application because it is based on the WinForms technology in Visual Studio and the .NET Framework.

The first step in a WinForms application is determining the layout of your form. You might decide to create a document-centric application (such as Word or Excel), a single utility application (such as Calculator or Disk Defragmenter), or some other type of application. Whatever your choice, layout is typically controlled through the docking of controls to the form (through the Properties dialog) and the use of Panel controls.

For example, Figure 1.2 shows a possible line-of-business application. A MenuStrip and ToolStrip control are docked to the top of a Windows Form, a StatusStrip is docked to the bottom of the form, and a TreeView and a Tab control occupy the center.

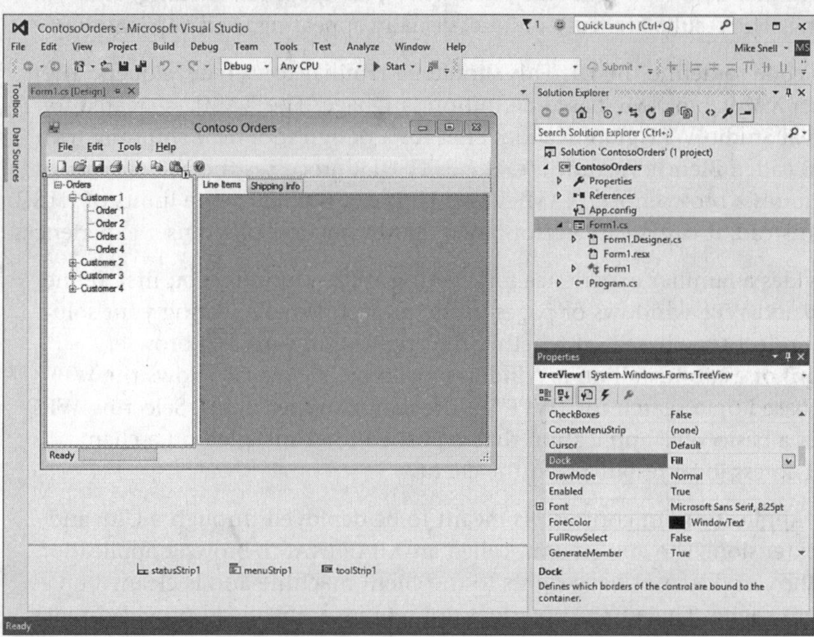

FIGURE 1.2 Building a WinForms application inside Visual Studio 2015.

Containing both the TreeView and the Tab control is a SplitContainer control, which allows two panels to size relative to one another using a splitter bar. Together, these controls define the layout of the main, interactive section of the form. In this case, a user can select records to view in the TreeView control and have a DataGrid within the Tab control automatically populate with the required information. Each control is added to the appropriate area of the form and then configured via the Properties window.

You can start to see that the initial layout and definition of a WinForms application is a rapid experience. You first need to decide your form layout. The tools make it easy from that point forward.

As with all .NET programming, you create the visual design and layout of your user interface and then write code to respond to events. The WinForms application has a standard model that includes such events as Load, Closing, and Closed. You also respond to the events triggered by the controls on the form. For more detailed information about building WinForms applications, see Chapter 20.

Windows Presentation Foundation (WPF)

WPF is a set of classes, tools, and controls with which developers can create even richer, more dynamic client solutions for Windows. This includes developing user experiences that combine traditional data view and entry with video, 3D graphics, shading, and vector-based scaling. The results are truly unique, visually appealing, rich applications.

WPF uses markup code to define the UI. This should be familiar to web developers. The markup is based on XAML, an XML-based definition language. The XAML is created for you using the Visual Studio WPF graphical designer (or a design tool now shipping with Visual Studio 2015 called Blend). At runtime, the .NET CLR processes the XAML. Unlike for HTML that requires a browser, the XAML-based UI is not bound by the limits of HTML inside a browser. Instead, it can create vector-based, hardware-accelerated user experiences.

Visual Studio provides a familiar experience for creating WPF solutions. You first define a WPF project and add WPF windows or pages to the project. When creating your solution, you select a project type based on whether the application runs as a browser add-in (uncommon) or as an install on a Windows machine. Figure 1.3 shows the WPF project templates based on a search for "WPF" in the dialog (upper right). Selecting WPF Application creates a basic WPF application that is pushed to or installed on a client machine. It might access local resources on the client.

The WPF Browser Application, in contrast, is meant to be deployed through a URL and run as a browser extension. The application, called an XBAP (XAML browser application), runs inside a sandbox. It does not have rights to the client machine and is cleaned up as part of the browser's cache. The application does not require a download provided that users have the right version of the .NET Framework on their machine. It can work with the browser's cookies and is supported by both IE and Firefox on Windows. (It does not run on other operating systems.)

Note that the other two application types in Figure 1.3 are WPF User Control Library and WPF Custom Control Library. Both are for creating reusable controls for WPF applications.

The next step in building your WPF window is to simply open it and drag and drop UI controls onto a design surface. One big difference for developers used to building WinForm applications, however, is that you now have control over the layout code (or XAML), which is more akin to designing a web form with Visual Studio. Figure 1.4 shows the XAML designer in action using the sample application built later in Chapter 21.

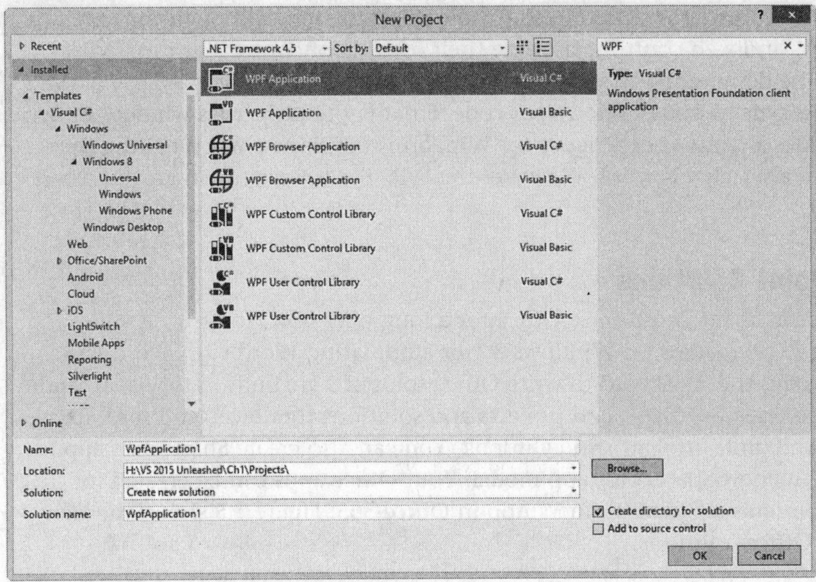

FIGURE 1.3 Creating a new WPF project.

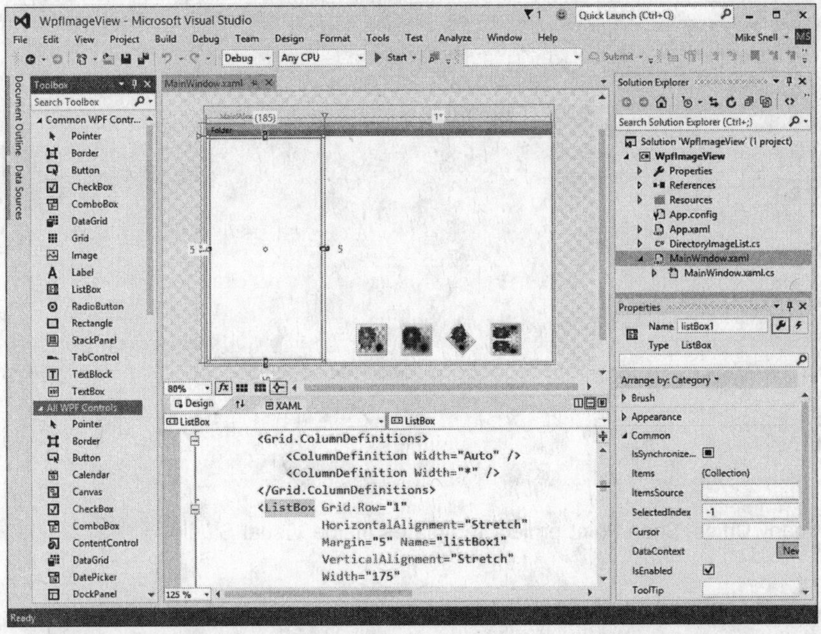

FIGURE 1.4 Designing a WPF window.

Notice that the WPF controls are listed in the Toolbox on the left. Although they are similar to Windows and web controls, they are their own set of controls just for WPF. Also, notice how the designer has a split view between the design surface and the XAML. These views stay in sync as you develop your code. Finally, the properties window shown on the right provides a familiar experience for WinForms developers when editing the many properties of a selected control. We cover the WPF Form Designer in greater detail in Chapter 21.

Office/SharePoint Solutions

Developers have been able to customize Office for a long time now; some of us still remember writing Excel macros on Windows 3.1 or automating Word with Word Basic. Thankfully, these days the tools used to write Office solutions are built in to Visual Studio. With them, you can create Office-based projects and solutions that leverage Word, Excel, Project, Visio, PowerPoint, InfoPath, and Outlook. You can also create SharePoint applications following the new SharePoint app model. Your Office apps can be created for desktop installation or as a Cloud Business App in Office 365. Figure 1.5 shows the New Project dialog for Office solutions.

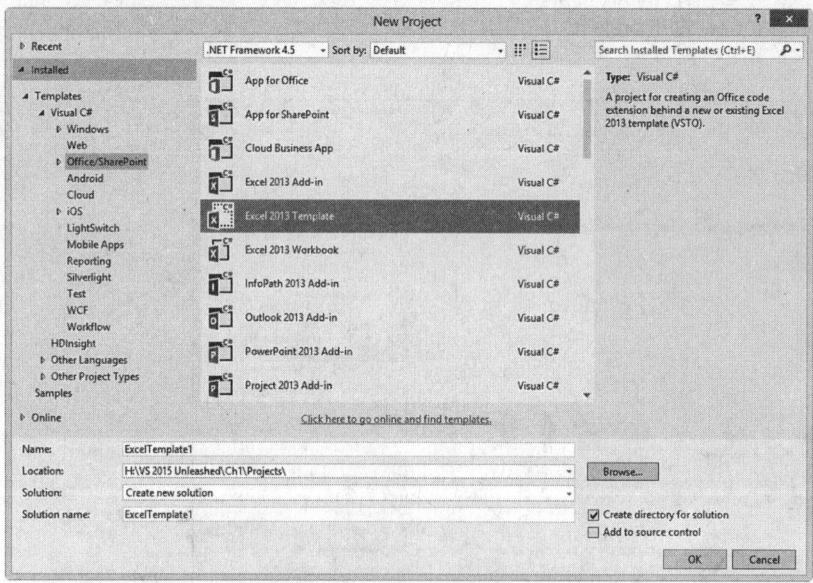

FIGURE 1.5 The many Office/SharePoint project templates inside Visual Studio.

There are a few scenarios that might lead developers to create an application based on Office. The most common is when you need to extend a line-of-business (LOB) application to provide functionality inside the common, information-worker productivity tools of Office. This type of solution typically combines structured, corporate data with a business process workflow that's centered on a document (such as an invoice or a purchase request).

For example, suppose you work with a financial, manufacturing, or payroll application. Each of these fills a specific need. However, users might need to work with the data that is housed inside the application and make key decisions that feed back into these systems. This work is often done through cut and paste and is not captured by the systems. Users lose productivity switching back and forth between the Office tools and the LOB application. This is precisely where you should consider creating an Office application to help bridge this gap.

NOTE

The Office templates in Visual Studio 2015 cover both Office 2010 and Office 2013. The same is true for the SharePoint templates.

Develop Documents, Templates, and Add-Ins

Notice the many templates in Figure 1.5. There are three separate templates for Excel, for example. Each of these templates provides a specific purpose. Office application templates allow you to create solutions built on a single document, a document template, or as an add-in to the given Office application. The following list provides a brief overview of these three project subtypes:

- **Document (Workbook in Excel)**—Document projects allow you to build a solution based on a specific document. There are typically not multiple instances of the document. As an example, suppose you have an Excel workbook that needs to read and write project resource billing information from and to an enterprise resource planning (ERP) system. This document might be updated weekly as part of a resource meeting. The data should be up-to-date and changes should feed the billing system. In this instance, you would create a solution based on this single document.
- **Template**—An Office Template project is one that is based on an Office template file (an Excel .xltx, for example). Creating a solution based on an Office template file gives you the flexibility to provide users with assistance when creating a new instance of a given template. You might push common document templates out to your users. When a user creates a new instance, the template might reach into data housed in other systems to help the user fill out the details of the document. You might then, in turn, capture the results in a database after routing the template through a basic SharePoint workflow.
- **Add-in**—An Add-in project allows you to extend the features and functionality of a given Office application. You create add-ins to offer additional productivity and solutions inside a given application. You might, for example, write an Outlook add-in that allows users to more easily file and categorize their email.

Whichever template you choose, Visual Studio provides a rich, design-time experience for building your Office solution. For example, Figure 1.6 shows the Visual Studio design experience building a solution for a Word 2013 template. In this example, a user is creating a quote for training. The fields in the document pull from a line of business (LOB) application database that includes customer information, resource data, and common pricing.

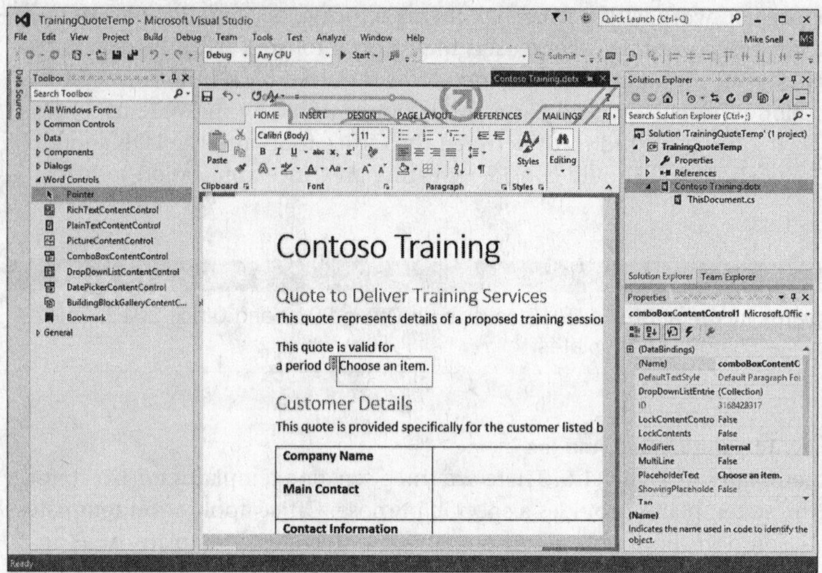

FIGURE 1.6 Designing a Word Template project in Visual Studio.

Create SharePoint Solutions

Although SharePoint is not a true Windows client, SharePoint and Office have become nearly synonymous. They share the same release cycle, and companies are urged to keep versions of Office and SharePoint in synch. Companies leverage SharePoint for knowledge management, collaboration, and business process automation. Of course, this inevitably means customization and extension by developers.

Visual Studio presents a rich toolset for SharePoint developers. With it, you can create SharePoint workflows and build Web Parts based on ASP.NET. You can also take advantage of the new app model for SharePoint 2013. In addition, the debug experience when building SharePoint solutions is what developers have come to expect. SharePoint development is a first-class consideration inside the IDE. This allows developers to more easily extend SharePoint to meet the business demand this collaboration product has generated.

Creating Web Applications with ASP.NET 5

Nearly every business application written today involves some level of web development. This includes full-blown websites, native mobile application talking to web services, a desktop application working with service layers, or those applications that run natively but are written using the HTML, CSS, or JavaScript open standards. Web development is ubiquitous. Microsoft has invested heavily in this area, and Visual Studio 2015 represents the convergence of those investments.

ASP.NET 5 (previously referred to as vNext) includes enhancements to every aspect of web development. In fact, this is the first release that also includes many enhancements written by open source contributors. A lot has changed, but developers will still feel comfortable in ASP.NET 5. This release makes modern web apps easier to develop. Highlights for what's new include the following:

- The ASP.NET Core 5.0 framework that can install with your application and allow it to run on multiple devices and platforms (Mac, Linux, Windows and not just a web server). Developers can also now develop on all these devices using other tools such as Sublime Text.
- Unified project templates for building web applications.
- New and improved cloud tools in Visual Studio and Azure for deployment, tracing, debugging, and editing in the cloud.
- Auto compile of changes (no compile feature) saving precious seconds every time you make a code change and need to view it in the browser.
- Improved browser development tools in IE.
- Development support for multiple web form factors to render responsive user interfaces to desktops, tablets, and phones.
- Integrated web API as a single project model for building web back ends.
- Rich support for server-side and client-side frameworks such as jQuery, Ember.js, and AngularJS.
- Support for community tools like Grunt and Bower that plug directly into Visual Studio.
- Improved NuGet support through the references dialog (no more referencing DLLs in your projects), including IntelliTrace for NuGet packages.
- More...

Visual Studio provides an array of web development templates from which to choose. This section presents many of these possibilities.

NOTE

We cover numerous aspects that follow in greater detail in Part V of this book, "Building Web Applications."

Building Websites with Web Forms

For many years, ASP.NET has been evolving website development with a rich set of server-side controls that do a lot of the client-server communication and HTML rendering tough stuff on the developer's behalf. Visual Studio 2015 continues to enable developers to take advantage of this design-time richness and productivity. However, modern, responsive UIs that leverage the many JavaScript frameworks often require more direct access to the HTML and CSS than what is available when the HTML is emitted on your behalf (as it is in Web Forms). For this reason, Web Forms have diminished in popularity (for new development) in favor of ASP.NET MVC and SPAs. That said, there are still many business applications taking big advantage of the developer productivity of drag-and-drop, an event-driven model, and the overall simplicity Web Forms has to offer.

Developers building with Web Forms do so because Web Forms include the productivity-enhancing, rich set of design-time controls. These controls make handling and binding to data easier. They allow for validation, viewstate, and postback. They emit HTML on the developer's behalf. And, of course, they make coding with them on server side much easier. Figure 1.7 shows just some of the controls (and control groups) that are available to Web Forms developers. The Standard group is shown as icons only to help you get a feel for the volume of controls.

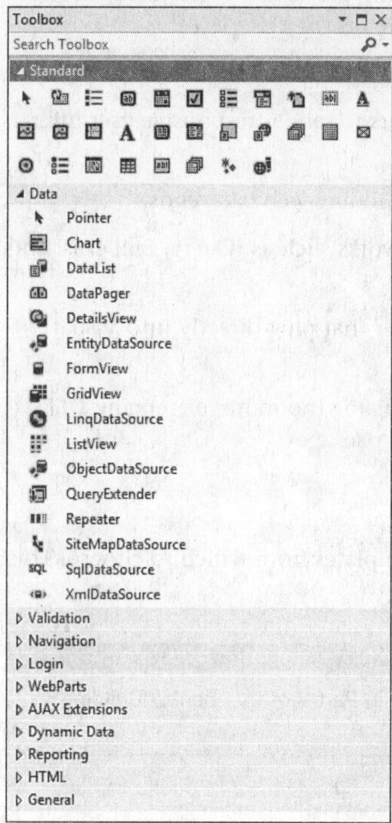

FIGURE 1.7 The rich set of server-side controls for building Web Forms websites.

Develop and Design at the Same Time

You develop ASP.NET Web Forms pages by designing with controls and connecting code to those controls. The code for the design is referred to as markup. This is XHTML that defines the controls, their layout, and their look on your page. The Web Forms tools include both a markup editor and a visual WYSIWYG designer for laying out your page. You can switch between the source (XHTML) and the design (WYSIWYG) view of a web form many times during development. The source view allows you full access to editing the XHTML of the page. Design view lets you see the page develop and gives access to the many shortcuts attached to controls in the designer. Visual Studio makes switching between these views simple. It also provides a split view. With it, you can see both the XHTML and the visual designer. Figure 1.8 shows an example.

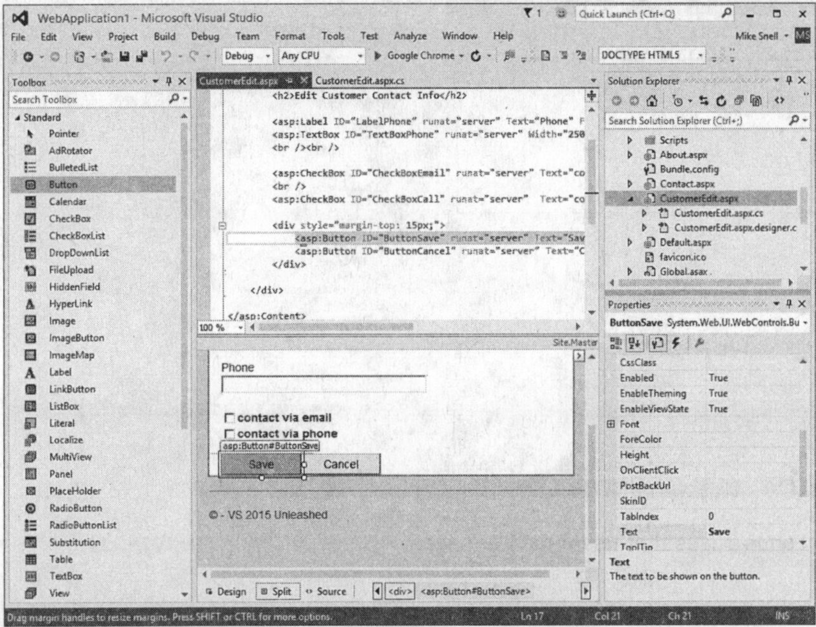

FIGURE 1.8 The Web Forms designer split view.

Split view tries to keep both the source and the design in sync. This works when you drag items from the Toolbox to either the source or the design view panes. However, the design view can get out of sync when you are doing a lot of edits to your source. In these cases, the design view indicates that it is out of sync. Click on the designer, and everything is back in sync.

Centrally Manage Navigation and Design

Visual Studio 2005 first introduced the capability to create master pages. These pages centralize the management of a site's design and navigation elements. In addition, master pages are supported by the designer, which allows for a richer design experience. A developer can see the page in the context of the site's central design while in design mode.

You create a master page by selecting the Master Page template from the Add New Item dialog. You then define your site navigation, header and footer information, styles, and anything else that should apply to each page in the site (or subarea of a site). After you define the navigation, you can create new web forms that provide specific content that should be enclosed inside a master page. Figure 1.9 shows an example of working with a web form whose outer header content is based on a master page.

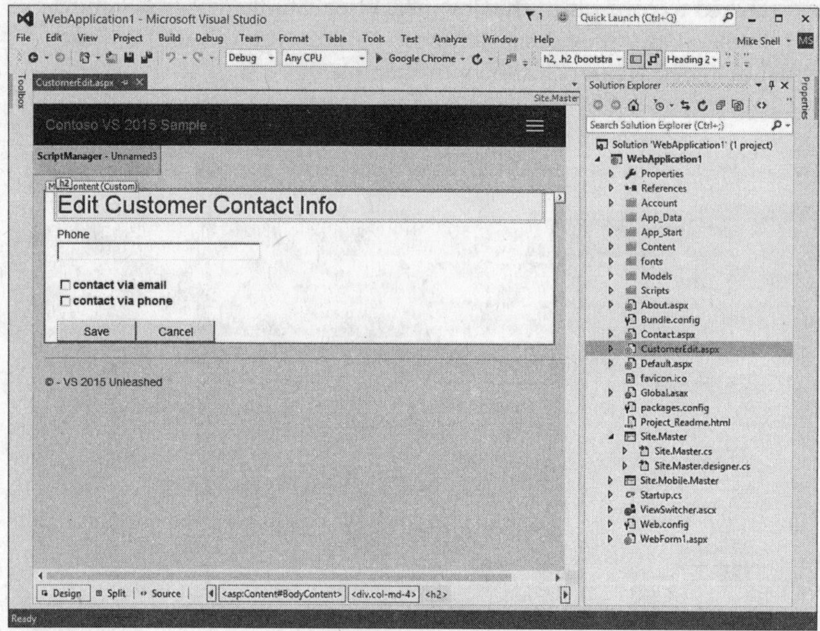

FIGURE 1.9 Web Forms pages that use a master page.

Developing with MVC/Razor

Visual Studio supports an alternative to building your application using Web Forms. This alternative is based on the Model-View-Controller (MVC) design pattern and the Razor syntax. The purpose of this pattern is to separate the application's logic and data (model), its user interface display (view), and the code that helps the user interact with the UI and the data (controller).

Developers choose MVC because it gives them direct access to the HTML and CSS, allowing them to more easily work with responsive design and JavaScript frameworks. MVC also better supports test-driven development because the views are just markup, and all their logic is in controller classes that can be tested independently of the view markup.

You create a new MVC site by first selecting ASP.NET Web Application from the New Project dialog. This launches the unified New ASP.NET Project dialog. From here you can select Web Forms, MVC, Single Page Application, Web API, and more. Of course for MVC, select the template titled “MVC.” Figure 1.10 shows an example of the ASP.NET MVC site template inside Visual Studio. See Chapter 17 for a detailed discussion of ASP.NET MVC.

NOTE

Project templates do not preclude you from writing any type of ASP.NET code you like. That is, you can mix MVC with Web Forms, Web Pages with Razor, SPA, or any combination that makes your website work the way that makes sense to you. In fact, the New ASP.NET Project dialog now allows you to create one type of web application (such as MVC) but choose the references and core folders required of another (such as Web Forms and Web API).

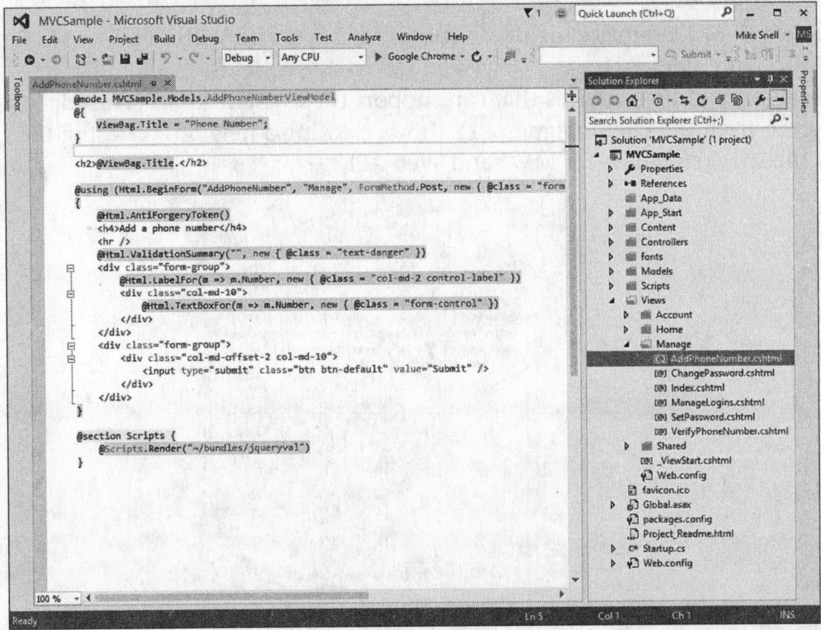

FIGURE 1.10 An ASP.NET MVC project structure (see Solution Explorer) and simple HTML markup (see AddPhoneNumber.cshtml).

NOTE

Visual Studio allows developers to also create websites built on just the Razor syntax. This is helpful for simple websites that do not need Web Forms or MVC but can take advantage of the easier syntax of working with HTML. It can serve as a nice basis for SPA applications. (See the next section.)

Creating a Single Page Application (SPA)

Visual Studio supports development of an application that leverages HTML5 and rich client-side JavaScript known as a SPA. Like MVC, a SPA allows you to write web applications using the open standards of HTML, CSS, and JavaScript. However, the key tenant of a SPA application is that it leverages the ubiquity of JavaScript to build highly interactive, desktop-like applications that run in browsers on any device type and operating system. JavaScript is what makes it work. A SPA loads a single page and then uses JavaScript to talk to the server and update portions of the page. Your site is not bound to a single page, however. It is just that a lot happens in a single before you might transition to another page (and set of features).

Writing all that JavaScript is a huge task. Thankfully, SPA applications are built using common JavaScript frameworks that make development easier and more consistent. These frameworks help with styling and page-to-server asynchronous communication.

The Visual Studio default SPA template includes support for MVC and Web API. The MVC support allows you to write your web page views and server-side code using a familiar model. Web API is about building services that can support the asynchronous JavaScript to server communication from the client. Figure 1.11 shows creating a new project using the SPA template and the core references for MVC and Web API.

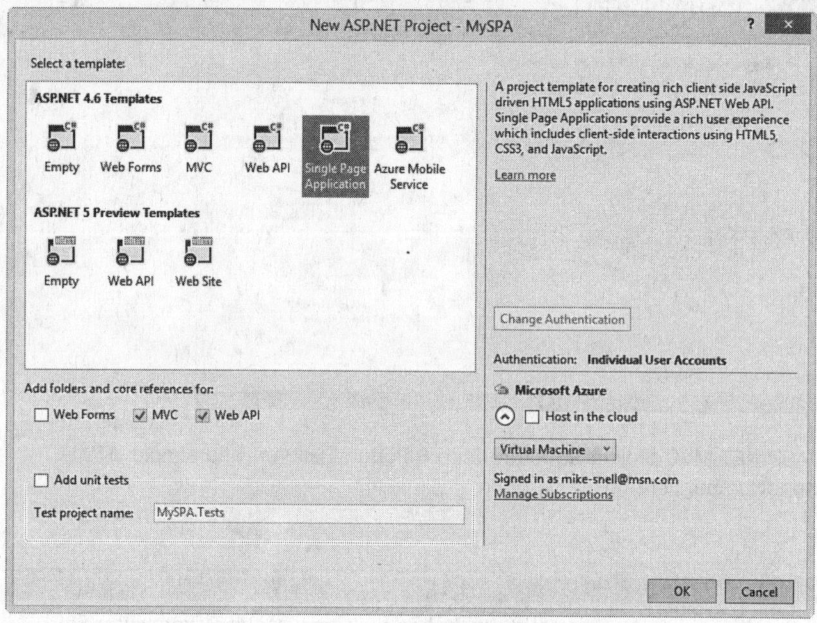

FIGURE 1.11 Creating a new SPA project in Visual Studio.

The default SPA template in Visual Studio is configured by default to support a few JavaScript frameworks. These include Bootstrap, Knockout, and jQuery. Together, these frameworks allow developers to create a SPA application using ASP.NET standards (MVC and Web API) and established JavaScript frameworks. These frameworks are described as follows:

- **Bootstrap**—Bootstrap (also called Twitter Bootstrap) is used for building responsive, mobile-first web applications using HTML, CSS, and JavaScript. This enables your web application to render correctly on various device sizes like phones, tablets, and desktops without a ton of extra work.
- **Knockout**—Knockout (also called knockout.js) is used to bind data from your model to your DOM elements (views) and get an automatic refresh from client to server. It leverages the Model-View-View Model (MVVM) design pattern to make development a familiar experience.
- **jQuery**—The jQuery library is the basis for handling JavaScript and client HTML manipulation. It allows developers to create events, do server-side communication, and animate the user interface.

NOTE

Visual Studio supports SPA templates that go far beyond the default template. This includes support for building with the even more popular SPA frameworks of Ember.js and AngularJS. In fact, there are community-created and supported SPA templates available for download. These templates simplify using these JavaScript frameworks and combination of frameworks. Of course, you can always skip the template and start with an empty project. In that case, you could use NuGet to add components as you need them.

Coding Web Services with Web API

Most organizations have multiple systems, each designed for a specific purpose. They might have systems for finance, HR, order management, inventory, customer service, and more. Each application houses specific business processes. However, most organizations need to unlock these business processes from their applications and reuse them as part of a different solution. These include providing employees, customers, vendors, and partners access via mobile devices. This is where service-oriented solutions help. By exposing an application's business process as a service, multiple clients can take advantage of that process.

The promise of code reuse has been with us a long time. However, service-oriented code reuse became popular with the advent of Web Services. The ubiquitous nature of HTTP (and port 80), JavaScript, and JSON/XML data structures allows for a new level of communication between application boundaries. We can now write services that wrap business functions and call them from multiple clients devices on multiple operating systems.

Web API services are designed to embrace the web standards of HTTP and JavaScript. Building on HTTP allows creating REST (Representational State Transfer) services that use the standard HTTP methods of GET, POST, PUT, and DELETE to communicate back to the server. JavaScript allows that communication to be asynchronous You can send data directly to the client formatted as JSON or XML and then process those results in a client-side, JavaScript function to update the user's browser.

You create a Web API project in Visual Studio by adding a new item to your project. Web API files are built as controllers in MVC. Therefore, you right-click the Controllers folder in the Solution Explorer and choose Add, New Item. This brings up the Add New Item dialog in the correct context, as shown in Figure 1.12. We discuss creating, hosting, and consuming services in detail later in this book in Chapter 19, "Building and Consuming Services with Web API and WCF."

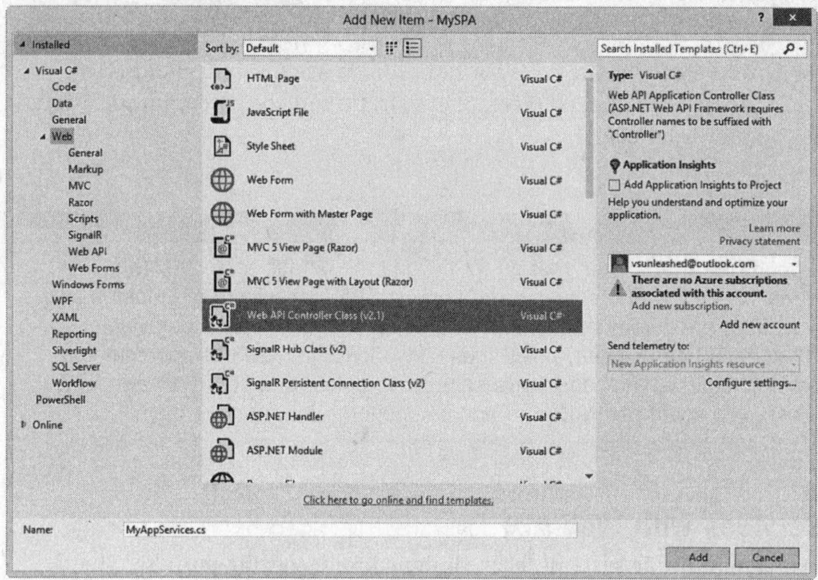

FIGURE 1.12 Add a web API as a controller to your MVC application.

NOTE

Visual Studio still allows developers to write service-oriented solutions using Windows Communication Foundation (WCF). However, these solutions are much more complex to create and consume correctly. Business and mobile application developers greatly prefer services based on HTTP, JSON, and REST.

Coding for Azure

Most of the distributed applications we write are deployed onto one or more servers for hosting and delivery out to the user base. This hosted environment might contain multiple web servers, a database server, and other servers as necessary. The environment then needs to be monitored and managed either internally or through a hosting provider. The management of this environment can be costly. Servers require repair and updates; as the demand for your application increases, you often have to add new hardware to scale with the demand.

Cloud computing is meant to help address these issues. In its basic form, cloud computing represents a hosting environment for your entire application (user interface, logic, database, and so on). The environment is meant to automatically scale with your demand and free you from hardware management and monitoring tasks. This is accomplished through massive amounts of distributed, automatically managed computing power.

Visual Studio developers that want to take advantage of cloud computing can do so via Microsoft Azure. You can think of this technology as the server operating system for hosting your application. The difference is that Azure is not a single server operating system you install; rather, it is an operating system that sits atop massive amounts of shared computing power. You can develop, deploy, manage, and scale your application using the Microsoft Azure cloud as the single host for your application. Adding scale to that host is then simply a configuration change.

Creating a Cloud Application

Microsoft Windows Azure continues to mature and offers many scenarios for developers, including data storage, service bus solutions, mobile web services, websites, and much more. Visual Studio is built to integrate with Azure. You get started by downloading and installing the Azure SDK for .NET (VS 2015) 2.5. This includes Visual Studio 2015 tools and project templates along with various Azure emulators.

NOTE

You can download the Azure SDK for Visual Studio 2015 from the site: http://azure.microsoft.com/en-us/downloads/

You can work directly with Azure inside of Visual Studio by selecting the Host in the Cloud option from the new ASP.NET Project dialog as shown back in Figure 1.11 (bottom right). When you select this option, you must log into an Azure account (or create a new one) to set up hosting. In this case, Visual Studio sets up your project and creates an Azure website. You still develop locally but are able to determine when to deploy your project to Azure.

NOTE

MSDN subscribers have up to $150/month in Azure benefits for development, testing, and production. Use the link that follows to find out your benefit level or search for "MSDN subscribers Azure benefit": http://azure.microsoft.com/en-us/pricing/member-offers/msdn-benefits-details

The Azure SDK also enables a number of QuickStart templates for building various Azure solutions. You can access these through the New Project dialog, as shown in Figure 1.13. Here you can quickly create a media service, storage queue, service bus messaging application, and more. Selecting a QuickStart template creates an application already configured for the given task you are trying to accomplish.

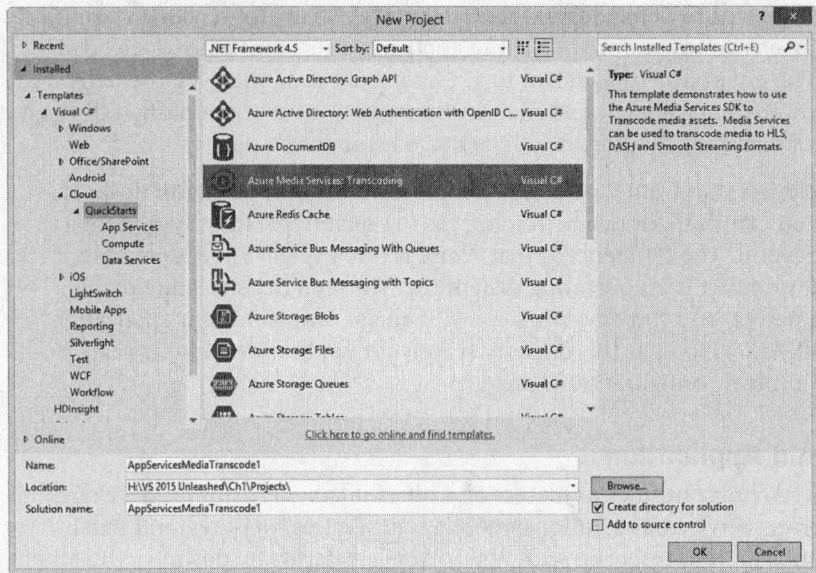

FIGURE 1.13 The Azure SDK QuickStart templates.

Publishing to Azure

When you are ready to push your application into Azure, you can do so directly within Visual Studio. For example, when you create your site and choose hosting in Azure, Visual Studio creates the site locally and works with Azure to establish a hosting area, uniform resource locator (URL), and configuration. It also creates a publishing script in your project. This script enables publishing and configuration of that publishing. However, Visual Studio does not deploy the site at the time of creation or when you run your application. Instead, you choose when to deploy.

To deploy, you can right-click your website and choose Publish, or you can use the Web Publish Activity window (View, Other Windows, Web Publish Activity). This launches the Publish Web dialog as shown in Figure 1.14.

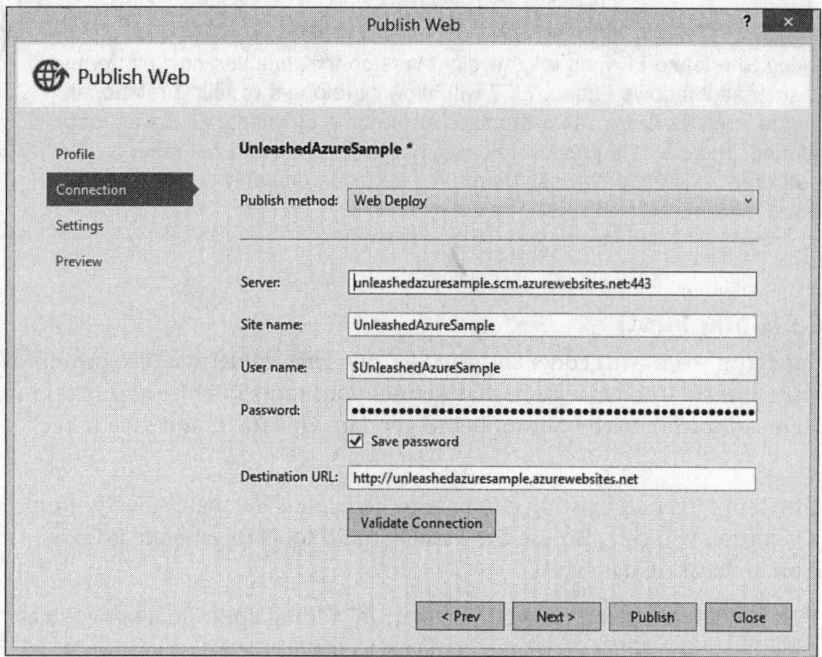

FIGURE 1.14 The Azure Publish Web dialog allows you to publish your project directly to Azure.

After deployment, you can start, suspend, configure, or upgrade the application from the Microsoft Azure management site. Of course, you can also now access your site directly from its temporary URL.

Working with Data

Data is the domain of the business developer. It makes sense then that the number one tool and framework for business development continues to provide new and better ways of accessing and exposing that data. Data access is everywhere inside Visual Studio and the .NET Framework. Here we highlight some of the things you encounter when working with data inside Visual Studio.

Visual Studio allows developers to access their data in a multitude of ways. However, the most popular development technique for the modern .NET developer is leveraging the Entity Framework (EF). This framework eliminates the repetitive code that used to be required for working with data. A developer can now write clean, straightforward models and code that make it easy to access data. The framework handles the repetitive and clutter-filled database communication and configuration stuff on behalf of the developer.

ENTITY FRAMEWORK 7

Microsoft is working to release EF 7 as a lightweight version that enables new platforms and data stores such as Windows Phone. EF 7 will allow developers to target relational or nonrelational data such as Azure Table Storage. At the time of writing, EF 7 was just getting off the ground. There was a preview release, but the team could not mark it beta because it was still very much in progress. Therefore, we focus primarily on the latest version of EF: 6.x.

Model as Code (Code First)

Developers often prefer to work with code, and the EF Code First model is a recognition of that fact. Code First allows you to write code that defines your model (tables and relationships). You can then easily work with your model to get data, update it, and save it back to the database.

Code First can be used to target an existing database or generate a database directly from the code model. Of course, you can also use the Visual Studio tools to generate a Code First model based on an existing database.

To write a Code First model in a given project, you start by adding appropriate references to Entity Framework or use the NuGet package manager to install the latest version of EF and add it to your project. Once your project is set up, you start by defining simple classes called plain old CLR objects (POCOs) that represent your database entities. You then create a database context object that uses EF to communicate to your database via your model classes. The following is an example.

Generate Code First from Existing Database

EF 6.1 introduced the ability to generate Code First from an existing database. To get started, you add a new ADO.NET Entity Data Model to your application by right-clicking your project and choosing Add, New Item and selecting the Data template group. This launches the Entity Data Model Wizard, as shown in Figure 1.15. Here you select Code First from Database to generate a Code First model based on existing database entities.

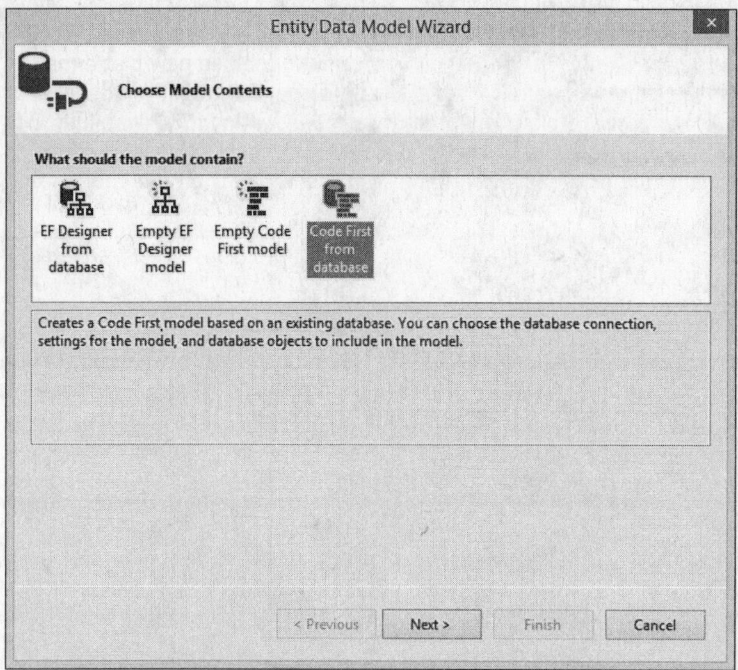

FIGURE 1.15 The Entity Data Model Wizard simplifies the creation of Code First and Model First EF development.

The next step in the wizard is to define a connection string to your database. This connection string will be stored for you inside your application configuration file. The final step is to select the tables for which you want the wizard to generate Code First access. Figure 1.16 shows an example where Customers and Orders are selected from a database.

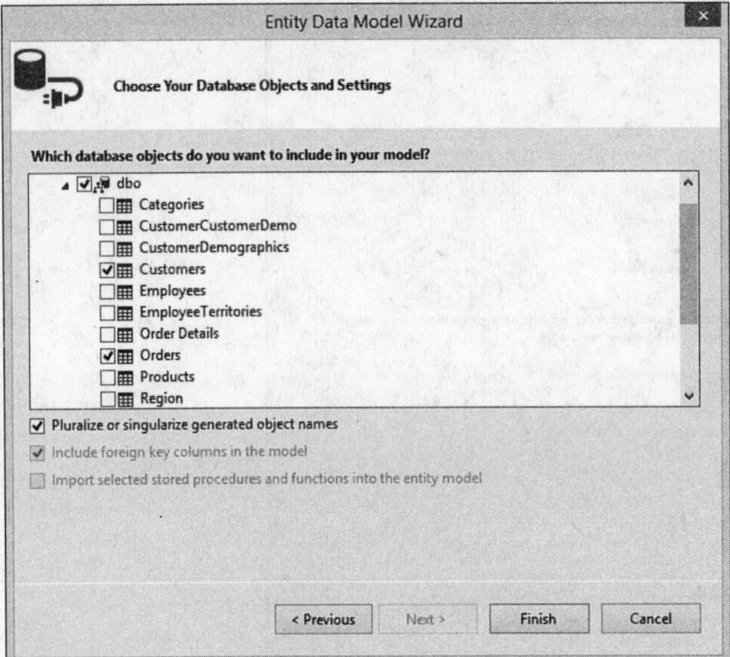

FIGURE 1.16 Use the Entity Data Model Wizard to select tables to target for Code First development.

The Visual Studio Wizard then generates a database context class and simple classes to represent each of your database tables. The database context class (derived from `System.Data.DbContext`) defines objects (of type `DbSet<TEntity>`) that you use to work with your data. The `DbContext` classes knows how to get a connection to your database and read and write data. Figure 1.17 shows an example of this class in the code editor.

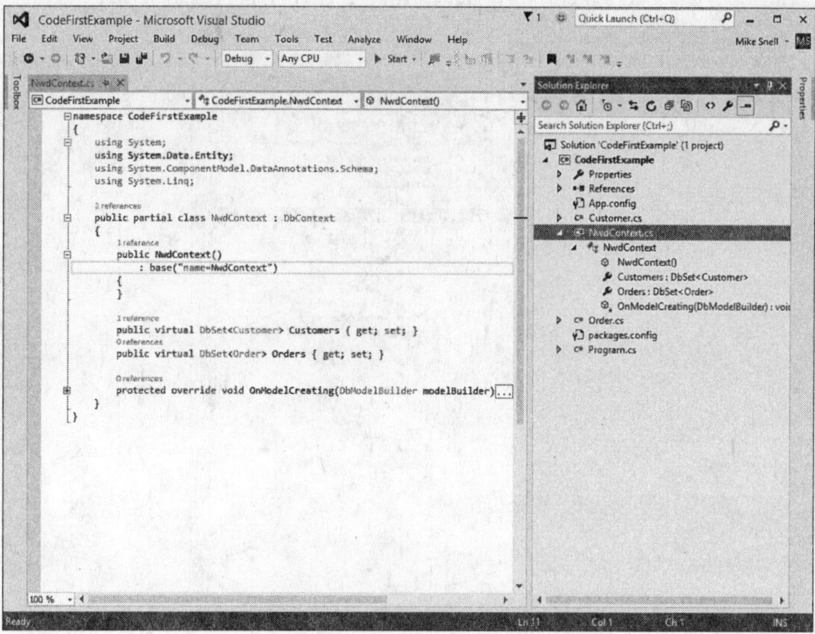

FIGURE 1.17 The Code First DbContext object provides access to database tables as objects.

The simple POCO classes that the wizard generates contain properties that represent fields on your database. These classes have no dependency on EF. You use attributes to set rules for your data validation, such as required fields and maximum string lengths. Figure 1.18 shows the `Customer` class generated by the wizard.

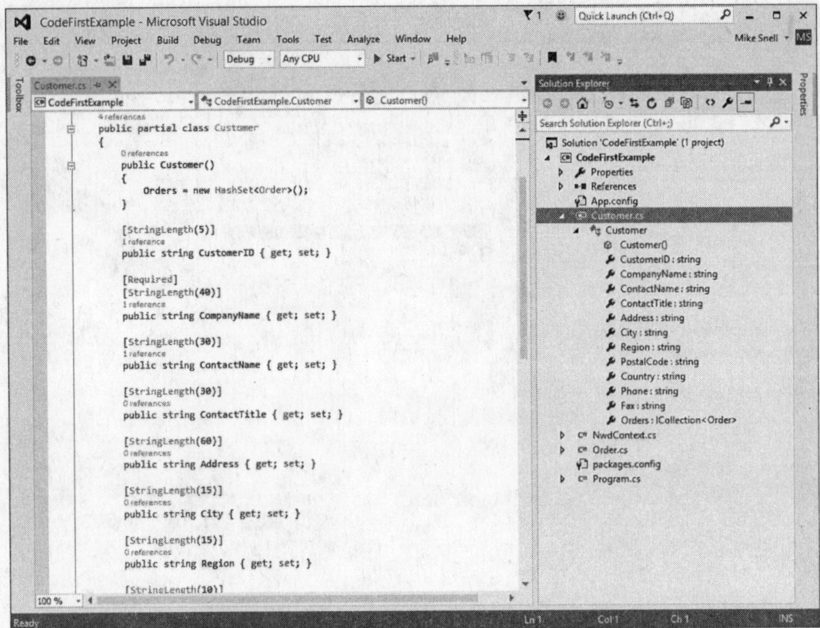

FIGURE 1.18 The wizard can generate your Code First POCO classes on your behalf.

The last step is to write code to read data into your Code First model, use it, and write data back to the database if required. Entity Framework makes this an easy process for developers. You access the data by creating a new instance of your `DbContext`. You then can create a LINQ query to access that data using your `DbContext` and `DbSet` collections. You can also add items to your `DbSet` collections and tell the context to save your changes. Figure 1.19 shows an example of querying the Customer table inside a console application.

NOTE

Visual Studio, the .NET Framework, and even EF provide many additional ways to work with your data. This includes EF model first development, data synchronization, data sets, and others. Data access and development is covered in detail in Chapter 13, "Working with Databases."

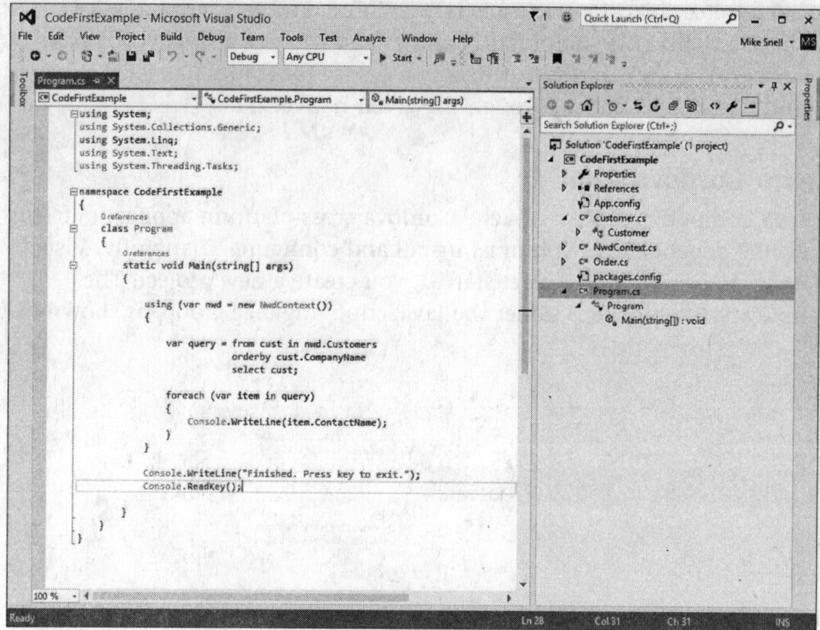

FIGURE 1.19 Use the DbContext object to access data from your database.

Writing Mobile Apps

Visual Studio allows developers to target mobile devices in many ways. You can create websites that use the SPA template to be adaptive to various device sizes. Of course, Visual Studio enables native Windows Phone and Windows Store applications. New to Visual Studio 2015 is the ability to write native, cross-platform applications using Visual Studio Tools for Apache Cordova.

NOTE

Apache Cordova (http://cordova.apache.org/) is an open source project that provides an application wrapper and device APIs for accessing native features on Mac, Windows, and Linux.

The Apache Cordova tools allow you to build and debug apps that target iOS, Android, Windows, and Windows Phone from a single Visual Studio project. You can run and test your applications using Windows Phone emulator, the new Visual Studio Emulator for Android, or by connecting a device (such as an iPad) to your development computer.

You install the Apache Cordova tools from a secondary installer for Visual Studio. This will set up the various emulators and give you the SDKs for building cross-platform mobile applications.

Your Apache Cordova applications are written as HTML5, CSS, and JavaScript applications wrapped in a native shell. This combination allows you to write a single code base to target all these devices. You gain access to the native device for things like local storage, camera functions, and barcode scanning through the given native shell.

Create an Apache Cordova App

There are many, many components of an Apache Cordova cross-platform application. This includes more than nine dependencies you must install and configure. Thankfully, Visual Studio makes this easier for developers. To get started, you create a new project. The Apache Cordova application template is under the JavaScript language group, as shown in Figure 1.20.

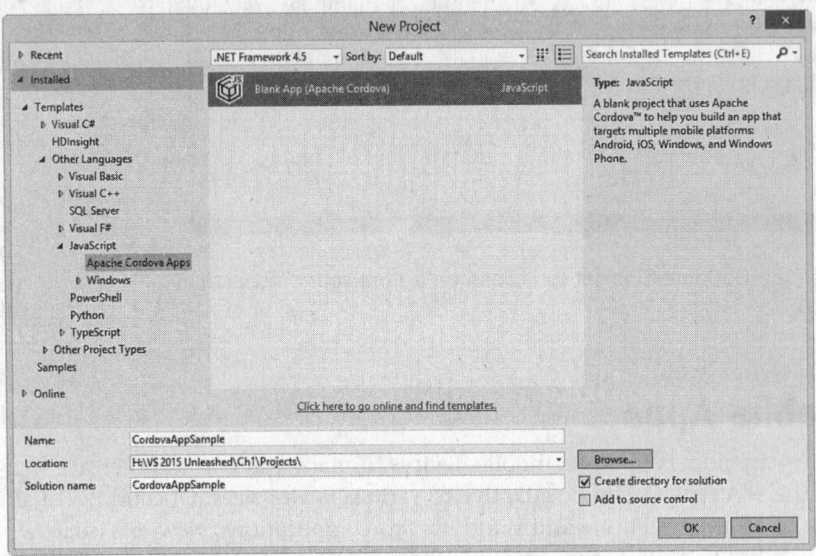

FIGURE 1.20 You can find the Apache Cordova project template under the JavaScript templates.

The project template should be familiar to web developers. It includes the core web folders css, images, and scripts. Your screens are written as HTML pages (see index.html in Figure 1.21). The merges and res folders are Cordova-specific; the merges folder is for platform-specific overrides to your code; the res folder is for icons and splash screens specific to a given platform. Figure 1.21 shows the Solution Explorer view of a Cordova application.

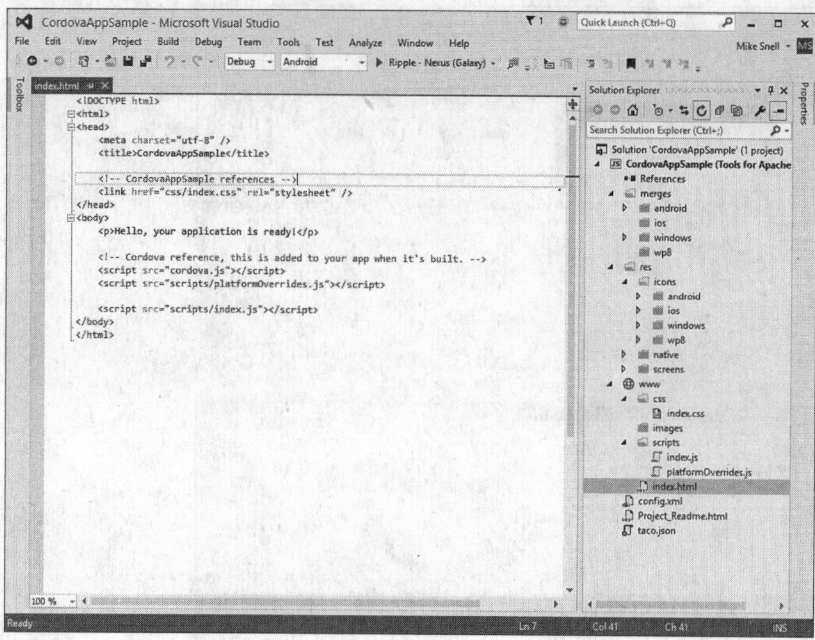

FIGURE 1.21 The Apache Cordova project structure should be familiar to web developers.

You write Cordova screens using standard HTML, CSS, and JavaScript. Again, this should be familiar to web developers. You can run and preview your application directly from Visual Studio. To do so, you select your platform in the toolbar (see Android in Figure 1.21) and then select the device emulator (see Ripple – Nexus (Galaxy) in Figure 1.21). From there, you press the green run (or play) button. This builds your application and launches the appropriate emulator. It also give you access to the DOM explorer from Visual Studio. Figure 1.22 shows a simple example of a Cordova application running in the Ripple emulator/debugger and Visual Studio controlling the debug process.

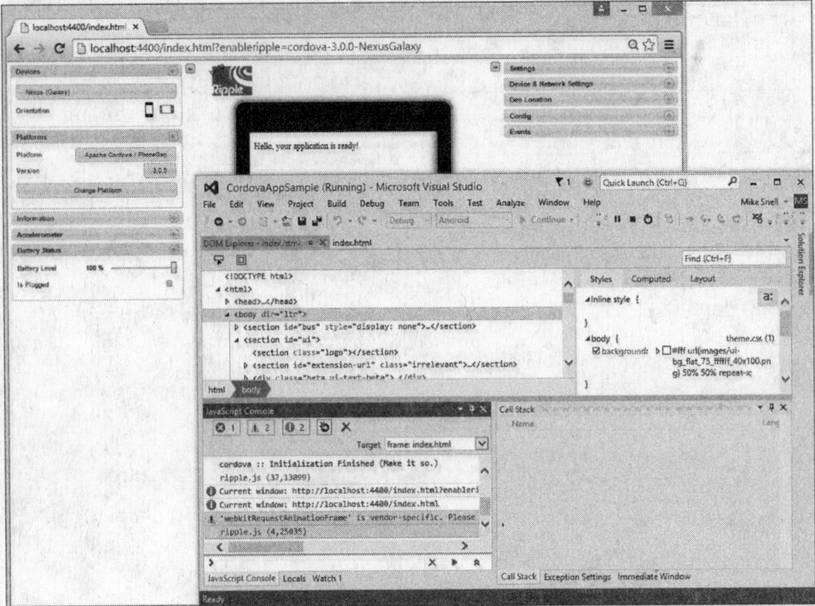

FIGURE 1.22 A sample application being debugged in the Apache Ripple Android emulator.

NOTE

Mobile applications are covered in Part VII of the book, "Creating Mobile Apps." This includes Windows Phone/Store applications and cross-platform applications built on Apache Cordova.

Summary

A new release of Visual Studio means a lot to all the various development camps out there. Visual Studio touches developers who write code in C++, C#, Visual Basic .NET, and many other languages. Millions of developers boot and launch their favorite tool every day. They spend the majority of their working hours, days, weeks, and months architecting and building solutions with the tool. We hope this chapter oriented you to the many possibilities available for building your next application.

CHAPTER 2

The Visual Studio IDE

IN THIS CHAPTER

- Installing Visual Studio
- Managing Your IDE Settings
- Getting Started
- Creating Your First Project
- Navigating the IDE
- Managing the Many Windows of the IDE
- Providing Feedback on Visual Studio

When you're traveling over new ground, it's often wise to consult a guide. At a minimum, a quick check of the map is in order before you set out for new adventures. The same holds true for approaching a new development tool the size and breadth of Visual Studio 2015. It is wise to familiarize yourself a bit with the tool before starting that first project off on the wrong foot.

This chapter is your quick, to-the-point guide. It serves to orient you before you set out. We cover the basics of installation; configuration; booting the IDE; and getting to know the layout of the tool in terms of projects, menus, tools, editors, and designers. We also point out what's new and improved for 2015. Let's get started.

Installing Visual Studio

The installation of Visual Studio 2015 remains similar to that of earlier versions. The application plays host to many tools. Depending on your purchase, a subset of these items is available during install. (See Chapter 1, "A Quick Tour of Visual Studio 2015," for a comparison of Visual Studio editions.) If you are fortunate enough to own Visual Studio Enterprise, you are presented with the full set of options for installation. For those with Visual Studio Professional, however, you can choose between the types of applications you intend to build such as Microsoft Office Developer Tools, Microsoft Web Developer Tools, Cross Platform Mobile Development, Universal Windows App Development tools, and more. Figure 2.1 shows the setup options selection page for Visual Studio Professional 2015.

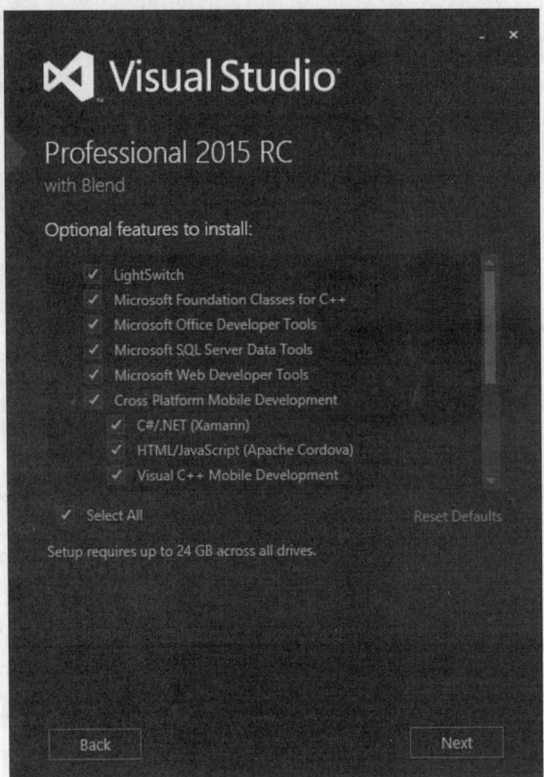

FIGURE 2.1 Visual Studio 2015 Professional basic installation options.

Setting up your development machine should be relatively straightforward. We suggest that most developers install the core set of tools they intend to use. For example, if you are a web developer, you want the Microsoft Web Developer Tools; if you intend to build applications for Windows Phone, you want the Windows 8.1 and Windows Phone 8.0/8.1 Tools; and so on. You can, of course, install everything the product offers. Some people prefer this approach; others find it just clutters their environment.

TIP

You might change your mind about your installation selections at a later date. In this case, you can always go back and rerun setup. Rerunning setup gives you the Add or Remove Features, Repair/Reinstall, and Uninstall options.

Installing Optional Features

Visual Studio 2015 includes a number of options features as a secondary dialog in the installation process. After hitting the Next button shown in Figure 2.1, the installer will launch a secondary selection for optional features. Many of these features are shown in

Figure 2.2. Notice these include many optional items required for doing cross-platform mobile development such as Xamarin or the Android SDK and emulator. Most cross platform mobile developers (using Xamarin or Cordova) will want to install these optional items.

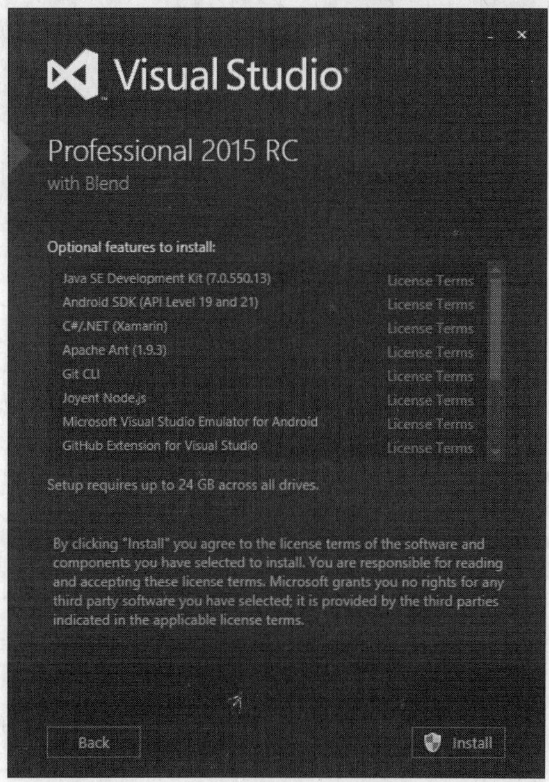

FIGURE 2.2 Use the Visual Studio 2015 installer to set up and configure optional frameworks and templates for things like cross-platform mobile development.

Signing In to Visual Studio

Visual Studio gives developers with MSDN the option to sign in to their MSDN account directly from within the IDE. This verifies your license to use the software and allows you to store development settings (such as colors, key bindings, and more) in a central place between computers and versions. Signing in also gives you access to Visual Studio Online (TFS in the cloud) if you are using that for source control and project tracking. It also links you to an Azure account if you leverage that for hosting. Of course, logging in requires that you have an Internet connection. Figure 2.3 shows how you access the sign in process for Visual Studio directly from within the IDE.

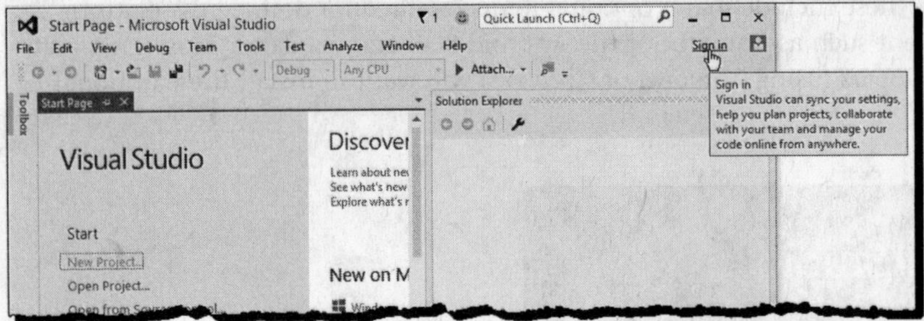

FIGURE 2.3 You can sign into your MSDN account directly from within the IDE.

Clicking the Sign in link as shown in Figure 2.3 will launch a Visual Studio sign in dialog. Here you enter your email address and then link to the appropriate ID that you use to maintain your credentials for MSDN. You can have multiple accounts inside Visual Studio. We will look at that scenario in an upcoming section.

Managing Your IDE Settings

On subsequent visits to Visual Studio (post-sign in), you go straight to the tool, and Visual Studio automatically signs you in. This way, on your behalf, Microsoft stores any customizations you make around development settings such as keyboard shortcuts or user interface (UI) themes. Settings are stored locally on your machine (c:\users\[user]\documents\visual studio 2015\settings) and synched in the cloud against your profile. This allows you to sign in from a different device and maintain your settings without doing additional customizations. Visual Studio also allows you to manually move setting files from one device to another (or share them with your co-workers). This section explores managing some of the key IDE settings.

Specify Stored and Synchronized Settings

Visual Studio stores and synchronizes all your development settings (and modifications to those settings) by default. This includes the theme, fonts and colors, keyboard shortcuts, start-up settings, and text editor options. You can use the options dialog (Tools, Options) to find these many settings and change them (discussed later in this chapter). You can also use this dialog to enable (or disable) synchronized settings between machines. Figure 2.4 shows the Synchronization Settings option.

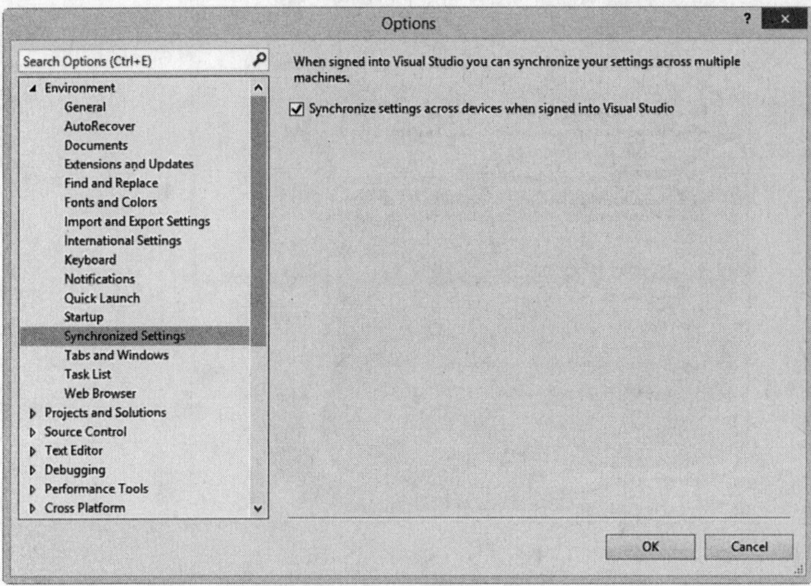

FIGURE 2.4 Use the Synchronized Settings option under Environment to specify if you wish to synch settings between machines.

Change Color Theme

You can switch your selected theme or your default settings post initial setup. To change your theme, you launch the Options dialog from the Tools menu, as shown in Figure 2.5. You select the Environment category from the tree view on the left side of the dialog. Under Environment you choose the General options. This gives you access to the color theme (see top right-side of Figure 2.5). The Visual Studio theme options are Light, Blue, and Dark. This book uses the Light theme. The Dark theme provides a high-contrast visual theme (black background with brighter text). The Blue theme looks similar to prior versions of Visual Studio.

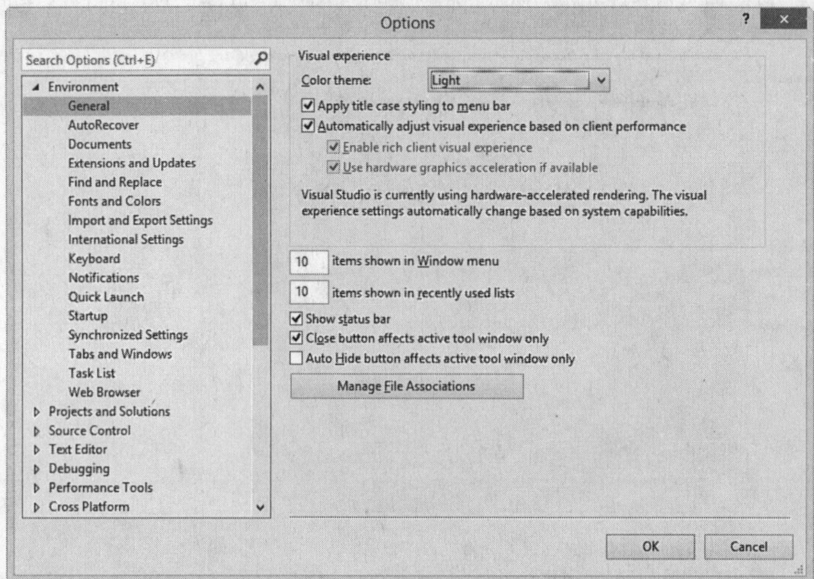

FIGURE 2.5 The Environment category General option allows you to change the color theme applied to your IDE.

Manually Import/Export and Change Default IDE Settings

You can also switch your full environment settings from one type of developer to another. The developer settings collections reset your IDE and related dialogs (such as New Project) to highlight items most relevant to a given developer type (such as Web, C#, or Visual Basic). Resetting your IDE default settings collection is useful if you do a lot of switching from one language to another or if you switch roles. For example, C# developers might use the C# development settings most of the time. They might then toggle to another collection of settings when switching to Visual Basic or developing a web-only application.

You manage your environment settings from the Tools menu's Import and Export Settings option. Figure 2.6 shows the first screen in this wizard. This screen enables you to choose to execute a settings export, import, or total reset. First, we focus on resetting the IDE to one of the Visual Studio defaults (by choosing Reset all settings).

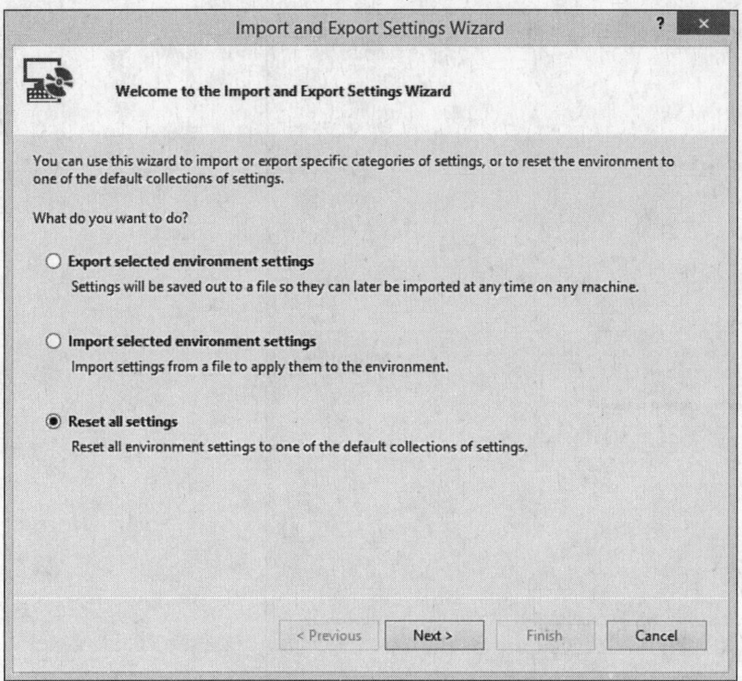

FIGURE 2.6 Use the Import and Export Settings Wizard to reset your settings back to the Visual Studio default options.

The next step in the Wizard when resetting your settings is an option to save any current settings. Figure 2.7 shows how you can store your current settings locally before resetting. This allows you to use the same tool to import this settings file back to your IDE if you need to use them again. You can use this same file to share these saved settings if needed.

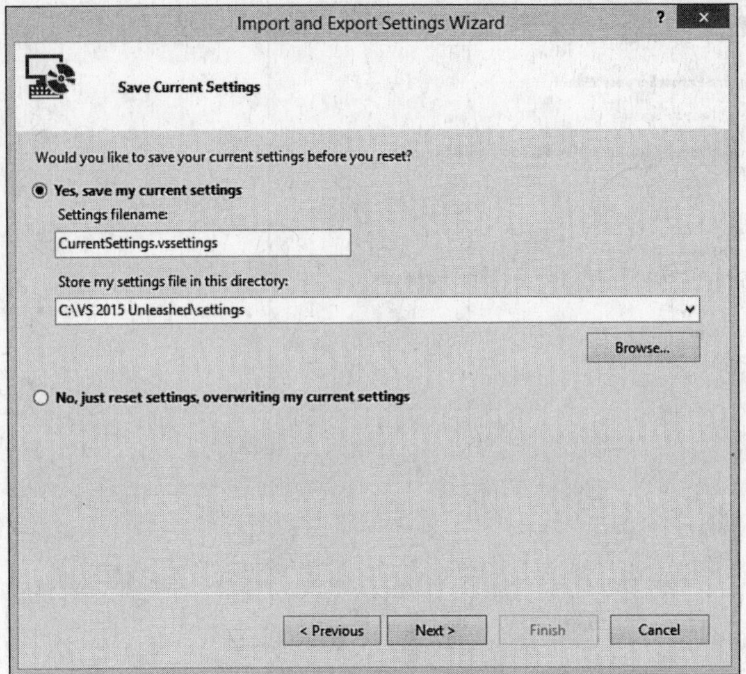

FIGURE 2.7 You can export/save your settings prior to resetting.

The last step when resetting is to select a default collection of settings to import. Figure 2.8 shows the available collections from which to choose. These settings are based on language selection and development style.

The other two options in the wizard are used to export and import settings (see Figure 2.6). In both cases you select which settings you want to export and which you plan to import. For example, you might love the way a friend has configured her code editor in terms of font and contrasting colors, but you do not want all her other settings, such as her keyboard configurations. You can accomplish this by selecting to import only her code editor settings. Figure 2.9 provides a glimpse at the granular level to which you can manage your environment settings during import and export.

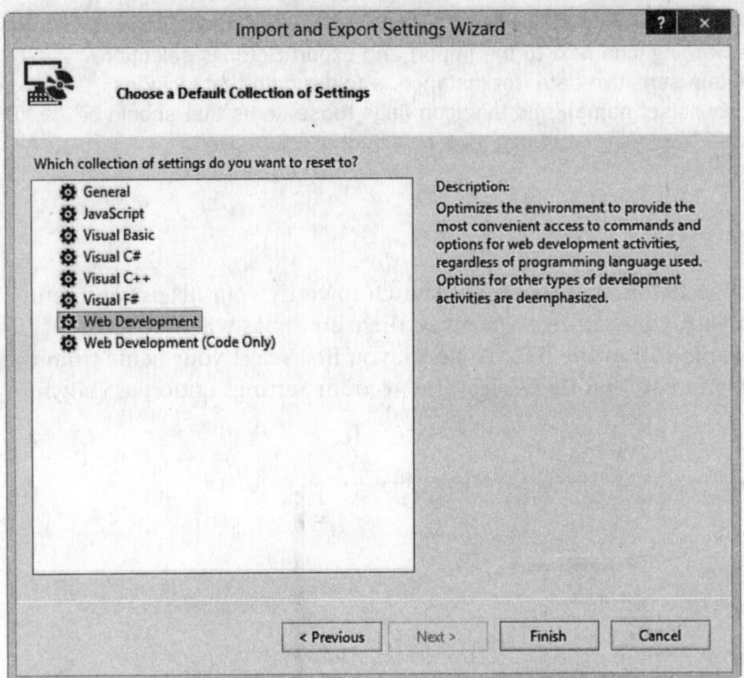

FIGURE 2.8 You can reset to one of the default settings collections in Visual Studio.

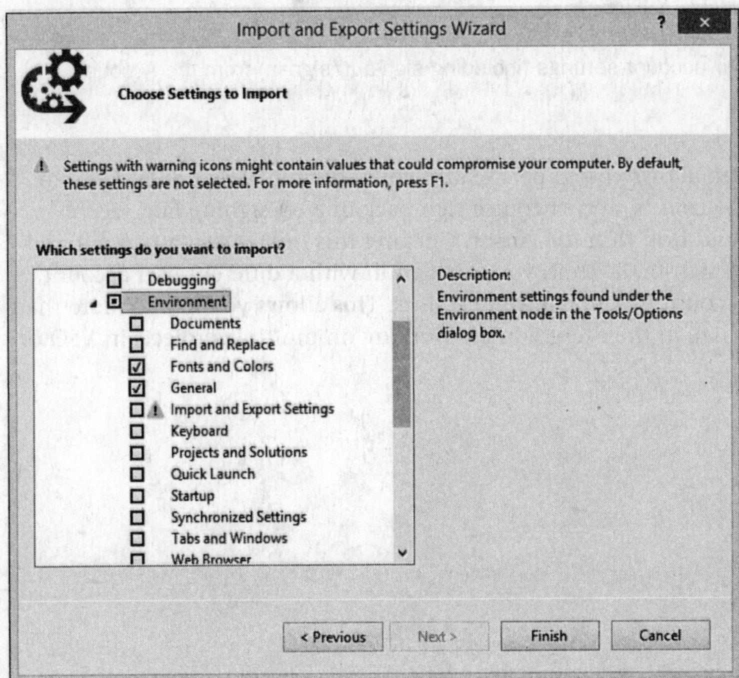

FIGURE 2.9 You can specify exact settings to import and export.

TIP

In Figure 2.9, note the warning icon next to the Import and Export Settings selection. Some settings may contain sensitive data (for instance, a folder path that includes domain information or your user name), and this icon flags those items that should be treated with care to avoid disclosing what might be confidential information.

Switch IDE User

Visual Studio 2015 asks you to log in at the initial launch to verify your license and setup storage/synchronization with your settings. However, there are times you may have to switch users or user accounts within the IDE. To do so, you first select your name from the upper-right side of the menu bar. You then select the Account Settings option as shown in Figure 2.10.

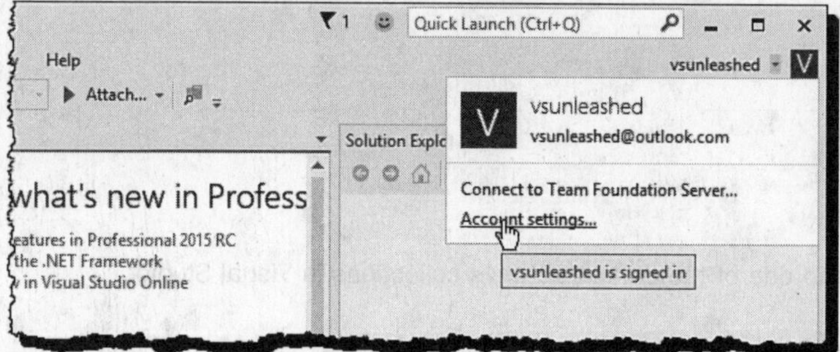

FIGURE 2.10 Access your account settings (including sign-out/sign-in) from the Account settings option.

The Account Settings form allows you to personalize your account. It also allows you to sign out, add additional accounts, and of course sign back in after signing out. Figure 2.11 highlights the sign-out link with the cursor. Clicking this link will sign you out and provide a new button for sign-in. With it, you can sign in with a different user account. Notice too the Add an account link under All Accounts. This allows you to add more than a single account to your IDE in the event you are working on multiple projects in VSO or Azure.

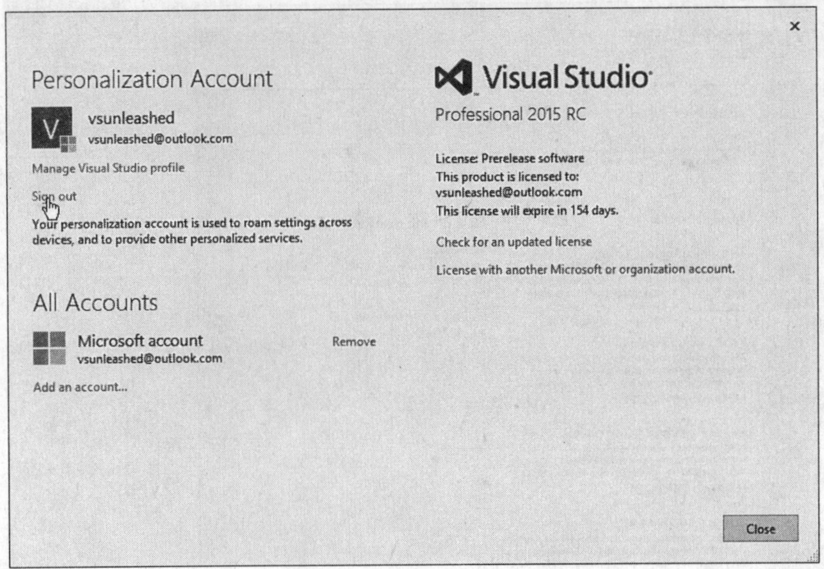

FIGURE 2.11 The Visual Studio account page allows you to sign out and back in using different user profiles.

Getting Started

When you first launch Visual Studio 2015, you are presented with the Start Page for the IDE (see Figure 2.12). The Start Page contains a number of useful links to get you moving quickly. Starting from the upper left, you have three primary options: New Project, Open Project, and Open from Source Control. You also can launch a recent project from the left side of the screen. The centermost real estate is used for providing access to the latest learning links and videos relevant to your development choices.

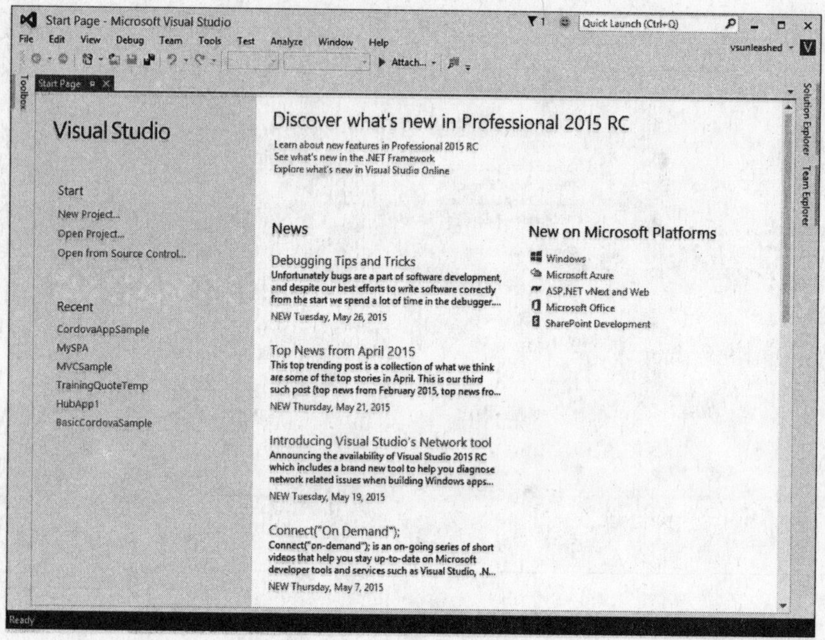

FIGURE 2.12 The Visual Studio Start Page.

TIP

You can highlight a project under the Recent list and pin it to ensure it stays in the list. You can also right-click to easily remove a project from this list.

Startup Options

If you just don't like the Start Page, want to create your own, or prefer to launch directly into the project you'll be spending the next few months of your life working on, you can customize what happens when the IDE boots. From the Options dialog box (Tools, Options), choose the Environment node and then the Startup leaf. Figure 2.13 shows some of the options available to you at startup.

TIP

You may like to briefly scan the Start Page but want it to disappear after you load a project. This option is available to you as a check box at the bottom left (scroll all the way down) of the Start Page.

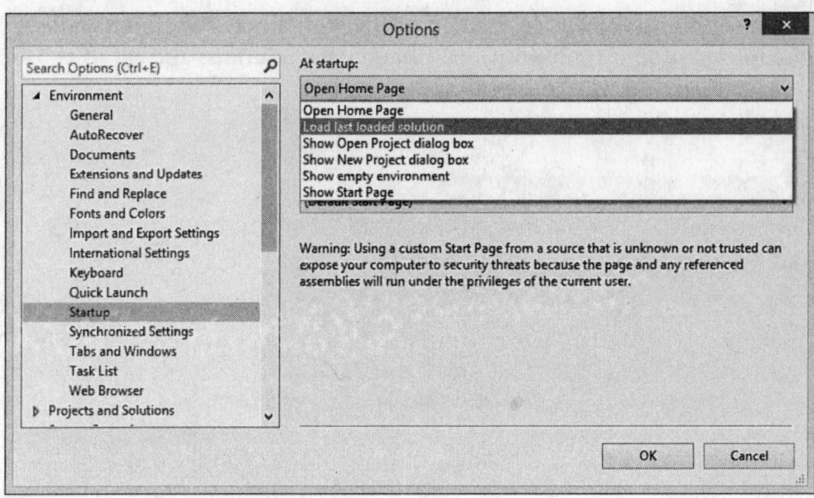

FIGURE 2.13 Startup/Start Page options.

You can also use the At Startup option to tell the environment to load the last solution, show the new or open project dialog boxes, open a custom Start Page, or do nothing (show an empty environment). You can also configure how often Start Page content is automatically refreshed from the server. (This is hidden under the drop-down in Figure 2.13.) Finally, you have the option here to use a custom Start Page.

NOTE

To see how you can create and use a custom Start Page for Visual Studio, search "Customizing the Start Page for Visual Studio" on msdn.microsoft.com.

Creating Your First Project

The next, natural step is to create your first project. You might have an existing project you want to open, or you might be starting fresh. In either case, creating or opening a project quickly exposes you to some of the basic project and file management features within the IDE.

To get started, you can click the File menu or the New Project link on the Start Page. Assuming you are using the File menu, you see the options to create a new project or a website under the New submenu. Projects are simply templates that group files for Windows, Office, web, and similar applications. Visual Studio supports web projects as templates-driven web applications and websites as a set of files that are promoted and managed to your web server as files. You might also have multiple projects grouped together to form a single application. In this case, each project might be grouped under a single solution. Figure 2.14 shows an example of the New Project dialog box. Notice that a

Visual C# ASP.NET Web Application is being created, along with a new solution to house the project. For more information on solutions, see Chapter 4, "Solutions and Projects."

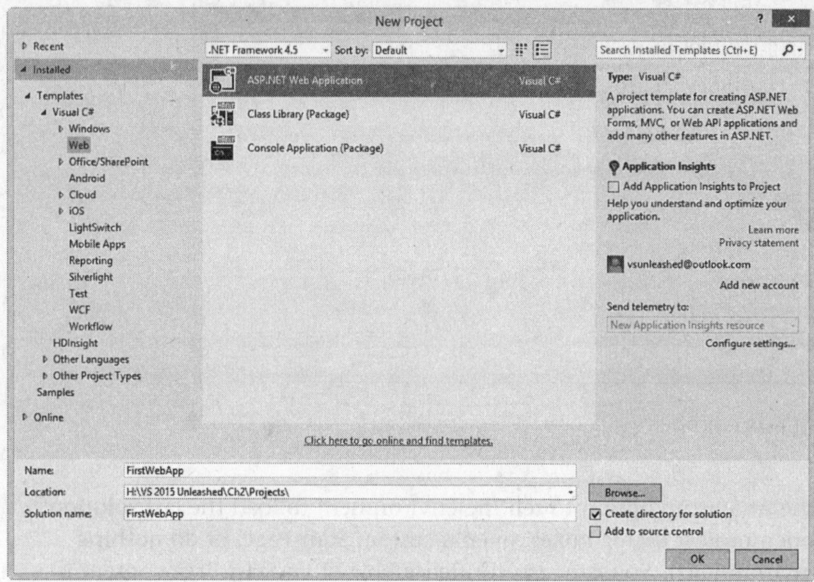

FIGURE 2.14 Creating a new project as a C# web application.

Targeting Your Environment

Many of us work in environments that include applications built on various versions of the .NET Framework. You might be building your new applications on .NET 4.6 but still need to support one or more .NET 3.5 applications. Of course, this becomes even more prevalent as more versions of the framework are released. You do not, however, want to have to keep multiple versions of Visual Studio on your machine. Instead, you should be able to target the version of the Framework for which the application is written. This way you can work in a single IDE and take advantage of the latest productivity enhancements.

Visual Studio 2015 supports the ability to target a specific version of the .NET Framework for an application. This means you can use a single tool to develop against many applications built on various .NET Framework flavors. Setting the .NET Framework version of an application appropriately sets the toolbox, project types, available references, and even IntelliSense inside the IDE to be in sync with the chosen .NET Framework version. Figure 2.15 shows the New Project dialog box again; this time, the .NET Framework version selection (top center) has been highlighted.

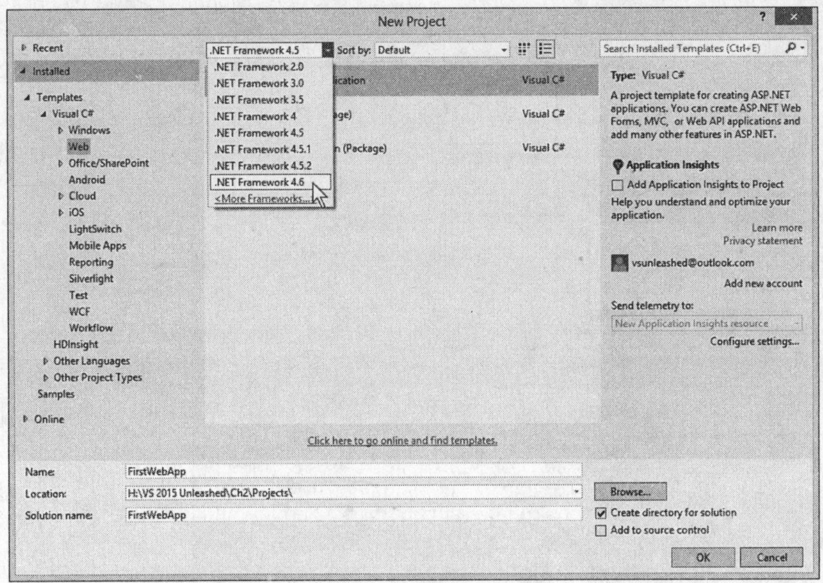

FIGURE 2.15 Setting your new project to target a specific version of the .NET Framework.

After you select a Framework version, the IDE automatically adjusts the available project types, IntelliSense, referenceable libraries, and similar features. For instance, if you choose to add a reference to your project, only those libraries from the target version of the Framework are available to you in the Add Reference dialog box.

You can also decide to move your application to a different (hopefully newer) version of the .NET Framework at a later date. You can do so inside the Project Properties dialog box. (Right-click your project file inside of Solution Explorer and select Properties.) Figure 2.16 shows an example of the properties for an ASP.NET MVC application. Notice the Target Framework drop-down. You can change this, and the IDE then resets IntelliSense, references, your toolbox, and more to the newly selected target framework.

NOTE

The Framework setting is per project. Therefore, you can create a single solution that contains multiple projects, and each can target a different version of the .NET Framework.

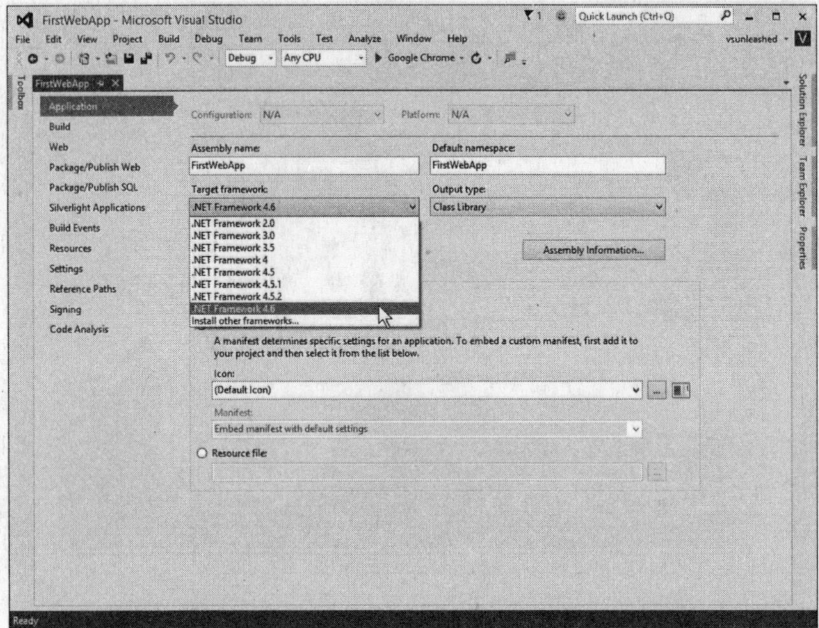

FIGURE 2.16 Resetting the target Framework of a web application.

Of course, you can use Visual Studio 2015 to open an existing application built on an earlier version of Visual Studio and the .NET Framework. When doing so, you have the option of upgrading or keeping it tied to its current framework version.

Navigating the IDE

After you've created your first project, you should get started adding features to your application. This, of course, requires that you have some basic understanding of the many components of the IDE. Figure 2.17 shows a sample website inside the IDE. Notice that the IDE layout is relatively generic: Toolbox on the left, Solution Explorer on the right, and code in the middle. You should expect a similar experience for your applications (at least until you've customized things).

Getting around inside the IDE is the first step to being productive. The following sections break down the many items shown in Figure 2.17; it might be useful to refer back to this graphic to provide overall context as given item is discussed.

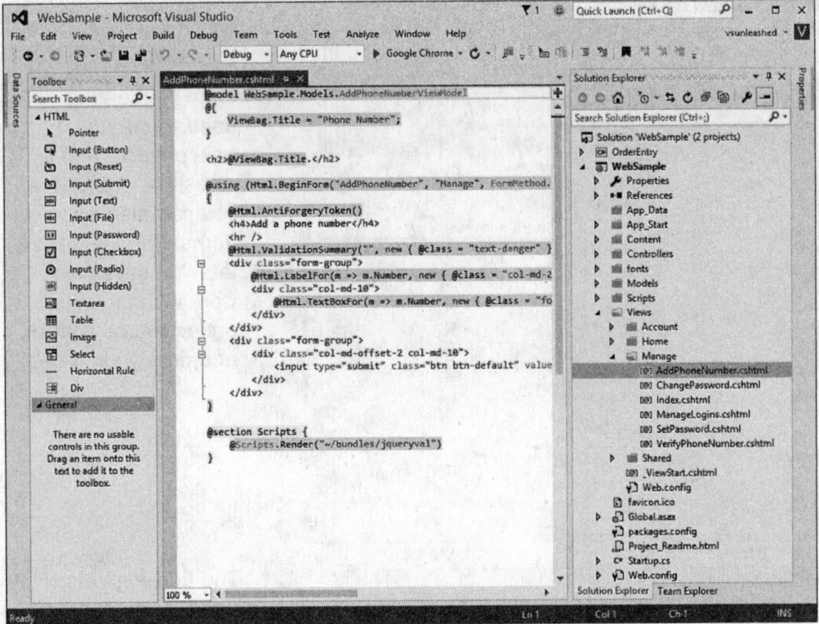

FIGURE 2.17 The standard layout of an application inside the IDE.

The Menus

If you've been working with earlier versions of Visual Studio, you should find the Visual Studio 2015 menu bar to be standard fare. It is intuitive; options are where you would expect them; and new menus appear depending on your place within the IDE, the tools you've chosen to install, and your default programming language. For example, the Build menu shows up when you have a project open.

Table 2.1 lists (from left to right across the IDE) some of the more common menus, along with a description of each.

TABLE 2.1 Visual Studio 2015 Menus

<table>
<tr><th>Menu</th><th>Figure</th><th>Description</th></tr>
<tr><td>File</td><td>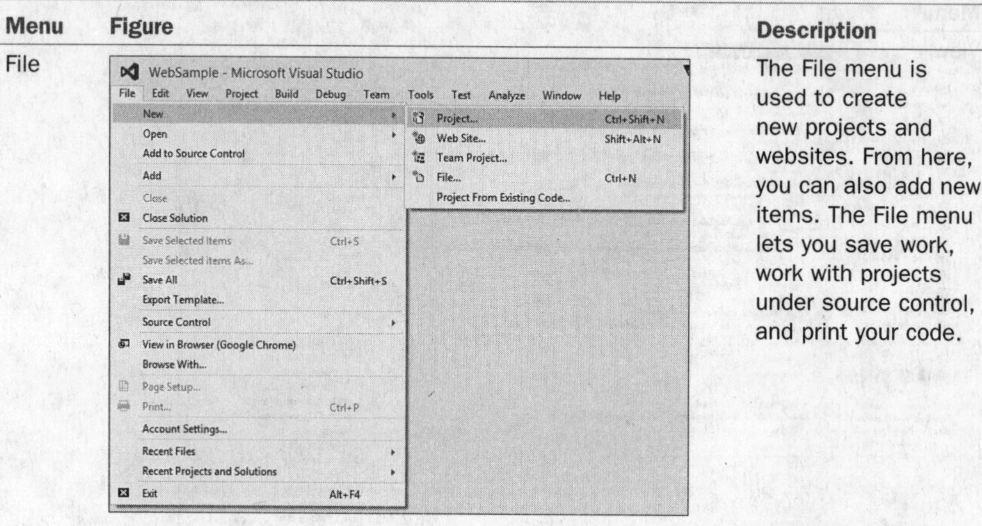
</td><td>The File menu is used to create new projects and websites. From here, you can also add new items. The File menu lets you save work, work with projects under source control, and print your code.</td></tr>
<tr><td>Edit</td><td>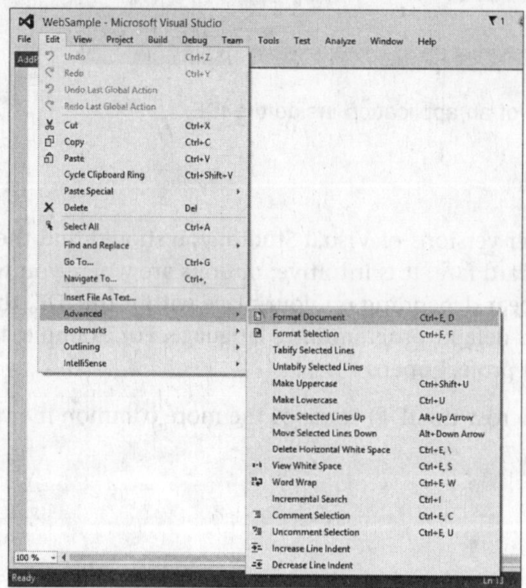
</td><td>The Edit menu is used for managing items on your Clipboard and fixing mistakes with Undo and Redo. In addition, the Edit menu provides access to important tools such as Find and Replace and IntelliSense. The fly-out menu in the graphic shows some of the advanced options available from the Edit menu, such as Format Document, which is useful to apply your formatting settings to the code you are working with.</td></tr>
</table>

Menu	Figure	Description
View		The View menu provides access to the multitude of windows available in Visual Studio. If you lose your way (or window) in the tool, the View menu is the best place to look to find your bearings. From here, you can access the Server Explorer, Solution Explorer, Task List, and other key windows of the IDE. The fly-out menu shows the Other Windows option (the many, many windows of Visual Studio 2015).
Website	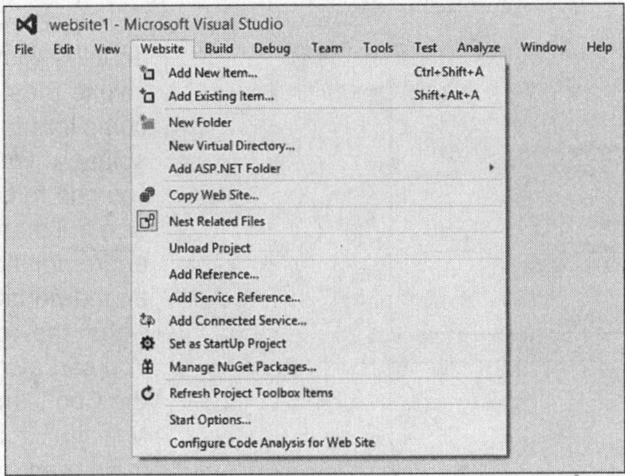	The Website menu is available only when you're working with websites (and not web applications or other project types). It provides access to add new items, add references, copy your website to a deployment location, and work with project dependencies. You can also set the Start Page for the application and access ASP.NET configuration options for the given website.

Menu	Figure	Description
Project		The Project menu is similar to the Website menu but is available to both web and non-web-based projects. From here, you can add new items and references to your projects, set the startup project, and change the build order for projects in your solution. In addition, you can access the properties for a given project. This enables you to set things such as the version of the .NET Framework you are targeting and the default namespace.
Build	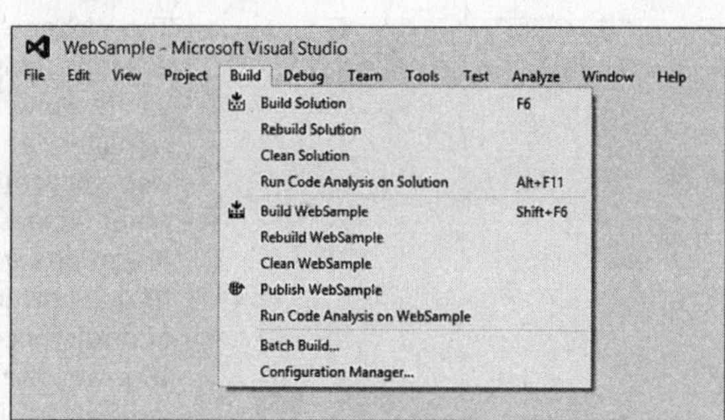	The Build menu enables you to invoke the given compilers for your solution. From here, you can force a build or rebuild on the entire solution or an individual project within the solution. You can also access the Configuration Manager from the Build menu. This dialog box enables you to control your target build in terms of debug versus release, central processor unit (CPU), and so on.

Menu	Figure	Description
Debug	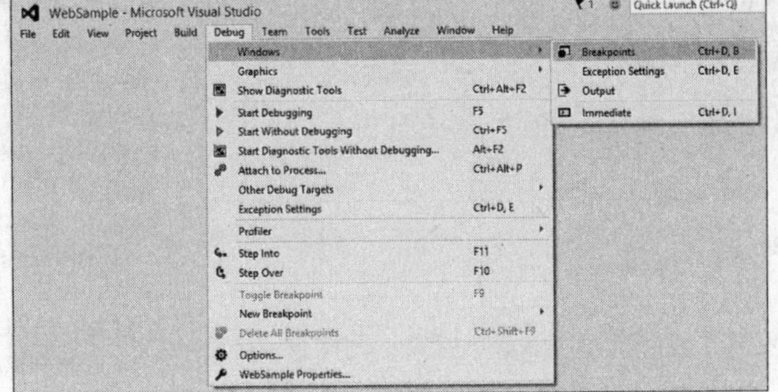	The Debug menu provides developers access to the debug commands for Visual Studio. These commands include options for starting your project inside a debugging session and attaching a new debug session to an existing, executing process. In addition, you can manage debug breakpoints and define how the debugger handles exceptions from this menu. The fly-out menu shows some of the other debug windows available from this menu. For more information, see Chapter 10, “Debugging Code.”
Tools	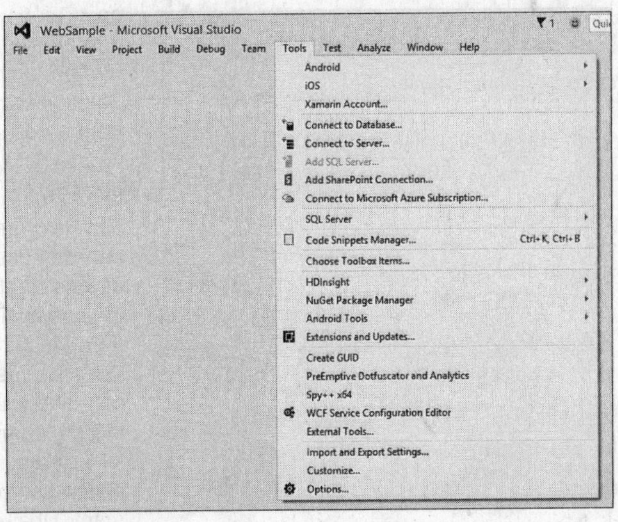	The Tools menu provides access to many of the tools that ship with Visual Studio. This includes managing Visual Studio add-ins and macros that extend your environment (see fly-out menu). You can also access tools for connecting to other servers and applications and for managing your IDE settings. The items in this tool menu are covered in depth throughout the book.

Menu	Figure	Description
Test	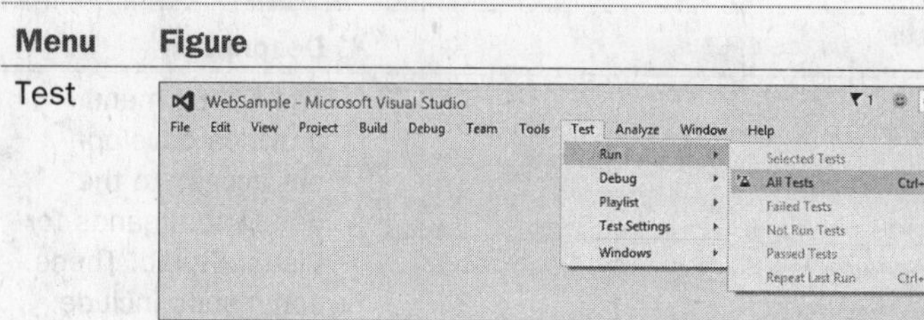	The Test menu enables you to manage tests in Visual Studio. For example, you can use options on this menu to create a new unit test, manage existing tests, and measure test effectiveness. You can also launch test runs from here.
Analyze	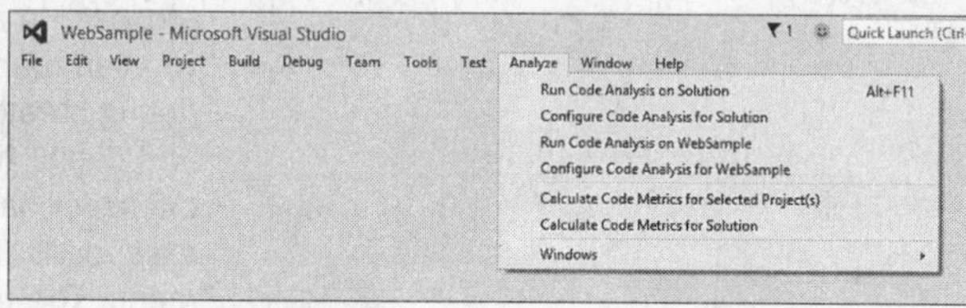	The Analyze menu gives you access to all the static code analysis, performance profiling, and code metrics tools available in Visual Studio 2015 Professional.
Window	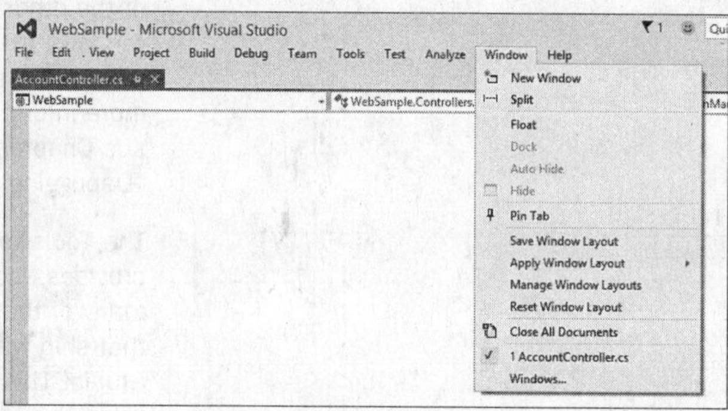	The Window menu enables you to manage the open windows in the IDE. You can hide windows, close all open windows, and turn an existing window such as the Solution Explorer from a docked window into a tabbed document.
Help	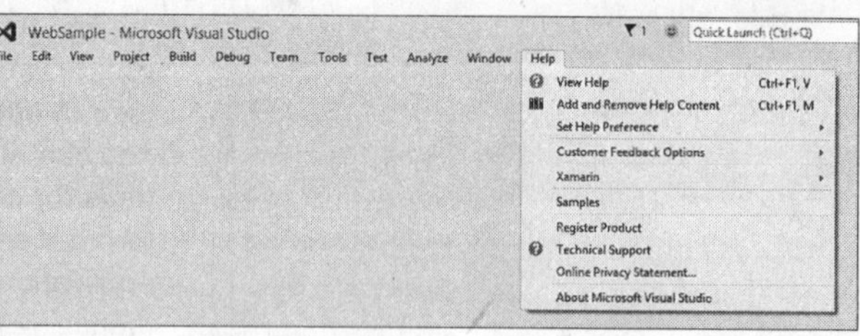	The Help menu provides direct access to all the help options available from Visual Studio. The Help menu can take you to the MSDN forums and let you report a bug, review samples, and more. Finally, you can check for updates from here and, of course, access the help documentation.

NOTE

Note that each menu screenshot in Table 2.1 was taken using the C# menu default settings. In each case, Visual Basic has an equivalent, albeit slightly different, menu. The keyboard shortcut callouts in the menu items are also those of default C#. Visual Basic developers should recognize a lot of them as the same. All menus can be customized to an individual developer's preference. You can also use the Keyboard options (Tools, Options, Environment, Keyboard) to apply specific keyboard mapping schemes.

The Many Toolbars

Visual Studio 2015 includes close to 30 toolbars in just the professional edition. If you use a set of commands often, there is a good chance that there is a matching toolbar to group those commands. As a result, a large percentage of the toolbars are highly specialized. For example, if you are working with the Class Designer, you use the Class Designer toolbar to manage classes or change screen magnification. Or if you are building a SQL Query, you use the Query Designer toolbar. We do not cover each of these toolbars here because they are highly specialized. Instead, we stick to a quick tour to cover the common ground.

The Standard Toolbar

The Standard toolbar is present at all times during your IDE sessions (unless, of course, you customize things or turn it off). It provides quick access to all the commands you use over and over. The standard commands are on the top left: Back and Forward, Create New Project, Open File, Save, and Save All. These are followed by Undo and Redo. Figure 2.18 shows the Standard toolbar in the IDE.

FIGURE 2.18 The Standard toolbar in Visual Studio 2015.

TIP

We suggest you learn the keyboard equivalents for such standard commands as cut, copy, paste, undo, and the like. In fact, most standard toolbar items have a shortcut you should learn. You can then remove many of these toolbar icons from the toolbar to save precious screen real estate for commands that have you reaching for the mouse anyway (and have harder-to-remember shortcut keys). Keep in mind that toolbars can, and will, change configurations depending on the project type currently loaded in the IDE.

The button to the right of the undo/redo commands allow you to set your build type (Debug or Release). The next button allows you to configure your build by CPU. The button with the green start arrow is often called the Debug or Play button. This button looks different depending on your project type (in this case, a web project). This initiates a build of your project and launches it under the debugger control. In the example shown in Figure 2.18, you also have the option to select the default, debug browser (Chrome in this case). The last button on the right provides an option for initiating a search within your code files. This capability can be handy for quickly finding the place where you left off or the place you are looking for. Finally, to the right of this is a drop-down that enables you to add buttons to or remove them from the Standard toolbar. As you will see later, you can, in fact, customize any of the toolbars in the IDE.

Customizing Toolbars

If the standard toolbars that ship with Visual Studio don't meet your needs, you can create custom toolbars that do. Select the Tool menu's Customize item or right-click a toolbar in the IDE and select Customize to launch the Customize dialog box shown in Figure 2.19.

The Toolbars tab allows you to select which toolbars to show. It also allows you to dock the toolbar in a different location in the IDE (top, bottom, left, and right). The Commands tab allows you to customize the menus, toolbars, and context menus (right-click). Figure 2.19 shows the Commands tab for working with the Standard toolbar.

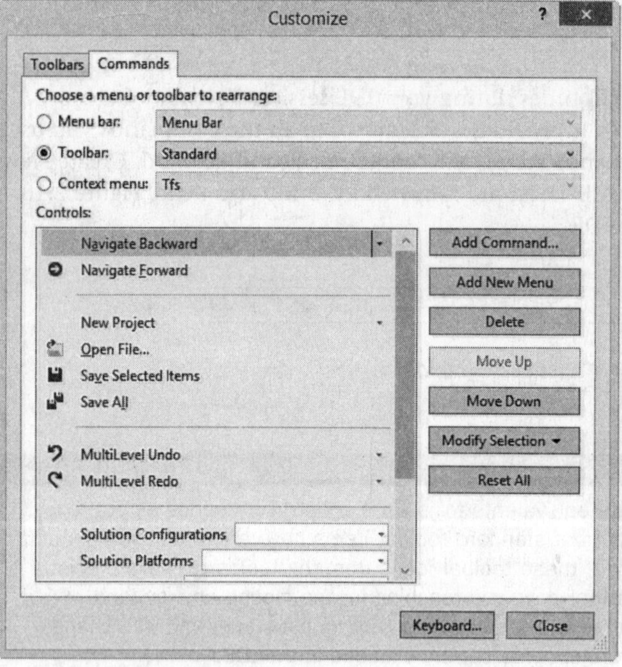

FIGURE 2.19 The Customize dialog box allows you to select and customize menus and toolbars in the IDE.

You make customizations to the toolbar by selecting an item and choosing one of the option buttons on the right (move up, move down, delete, and so on). If things get messed up, you can use the Reset All button for a selected toolbar to revert to the default state.

Create a New Toolbar

The Toolbars tab on the Customize dialog box enables you to select which toolbars are visible. This dialog box also includes the New button, which enables you to create new toolbars to group existing commands. This gives you a great deal of customization options. After you've clicked the New button, you name your new toolbar. You then switch to the Commands tab and select the toolbar.

To add items to your new toolbar, you select the Add Command button, as shown in Figure 2.19. Figure 2.20 shows the Add Command dialog. Here you can access commands by categories. You select a command you want to add and click the OK button to complete the operation. You repeat this process until you have created your custom toolbar.

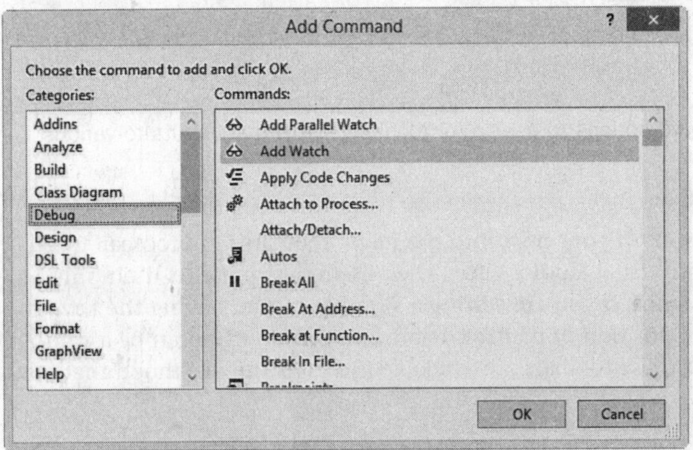

FIGURE 2.20 Create a custom toolbar and add commands.

Assign Keyboard Shortcuts

You can also configure your keyboard shortcut combinations from the Customize dialog box. Use the Keyboard button (the bottom of Figure 2.19) to bring up the Options dialog box to the environment's keyboard options screen. Figure 2.21 shows an example. First, you find a command from the list of hundreds; next, you set your cursor in the Press Shortcut Keys text box and press a shortcut key to map (or remap) a combination.

In Figure 2.21, the `Build.Compile` command is selected. The user is trying to assign the Ctrl+F10 shortcut key to the command (under "Press shortcut keys"). However, notice that Visual Studio lets you know that the Ctrl+F10 shortcut is already assigned to `Debug.RunToCursor`. Reassigning this shortcut is possible but may not be your intent.

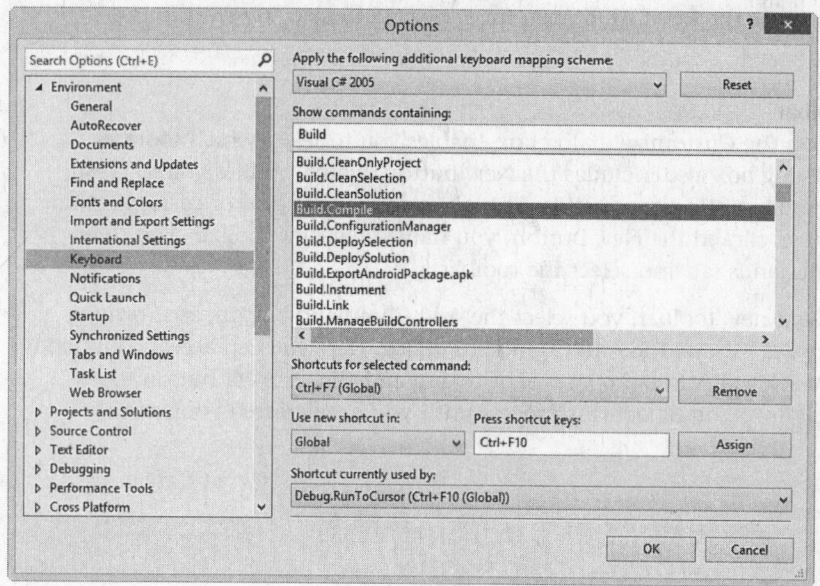

FIGURE 2.21 Use the Keyboard options to assign (or modify) keyboard shortcuts to various IDE commands.

You should do some exploration of your own into the many toolbars (and toolbar customization options) within Visual Studio. Often their usefulness presents itself only at the right moment. For instance, if you are editing a Windows form, having the Layout toolbar available to tweak the position of controls relative to one another can be a valuable timesaver. Knowing that these toolbars are available increases the likelihood that you can benefit from their value.

The Solution Explorer

The Solution Explorer enables you to group and manage the many files that make up your application. A solution simply contains multiple projects (applications or assemblies). A project groups files related to its type. For instance, you can create a website, Windows Forms application, class library, console application, and more. The files inside the project containers represent your code in terms of web pages, forms, class files, XML, and other related items.

Figure 2.22 shows the Solution Explorer undocked from the IDE. The solution contains two applications (called projects). There is a Windows Forms application (OrderEntry) and a web application (WebSample).

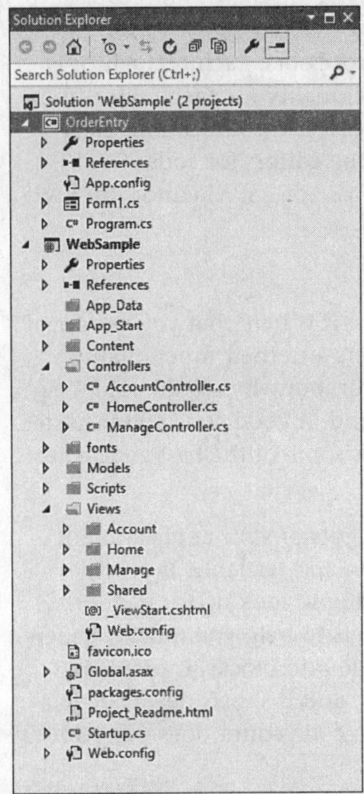

FIGURE 2.22 The Visual Studio 2015 Solution Explorer with two projects loaded.

You use the Solution Explorer to navigate the many items in your projects. You can access an item by first selecting it and then double-clicking it. Solution Explorer opens the given designer or editor associated with the type of file you request. For example, opening a file with the extension `.cs` opens the C# code editor. You can also add a new item (class, image, form) to your application from here by right-clicking a project or folder and selecting the Add menu. Finally, you can use the Solution Explorer during source control scenarios to check items in and out of source control. The Solution Explorer is covered in depth in Chapter 4.

TIP

You can select an item in the Solution Explorer (single-click) to view its contents without actually opening the file for edit (double-click). In this scenario, Visual Studio shows you the file, and you are able to browse its contents. However, if you select another file, the previous file does not remain open, and you are not responsible for closing it. Note that you can leave it open in the IDE by pressing the Keep Open tiny icon at the right of the filename.

The Text Editors

Visual Studio 2015 has several text editors or word (code) processors. Each text editor is based on a common core that provides the basic set of functionality for each editor, such as the selection margin, the capability to collapse nested items, and colorization. Each editor derives from this core and is customized to give you the editors for code (C#, Visual Basic, and so on), the XML editor, the XAML editor, the HTML (or ASPX) editor, the style sheet editor, and more.

The Code Editors

The code editor, for our money, is where the magic happens. It is here that you get down to business leveraging your favorite language to define objects and their functionality. Of course, you can write code outside the Visual Studio editor, but why would you? You can also write a novel using Notepad or do your taxes by hand. A good code editor means higher productivity, plain and simple. And Visual Studio has some of the best code editors around.

The code editor is front and center when you're writing the guts of your application. It handles indentation and whitespace to make your code clean and readable. It provides IntelliSense and statement completion to free you from having to look up (or memorize) every object library and keyword. It provides shortcut snippets to help you quickly generate common code such as property definitions. It groups code into blocks, it provides color codes for keywords and comments, it highlights errors, and it shows new code relative to previously compiled code. All in all, the Visual Studio code editor does quite a bit to keep you focused, organized, and productive.

The C# Code Editor

Figure 2.23 shows the C# code editor with a controller open from the ASP.NET MVC template. Some items to note include the following:

- The code is grouped into logical sections along the left side. You can use the minus signs to close a whole class, method, property, or similar group. This capability enables you to hide code you are not working on at the moment. You can also create your own custom, named regions to do the same thing.
- Code lines are numbered along the left edge of the editor. You can turn this feature on or off for different code editors in the tool.
- New code is signaled inside the section groups with a colored line. Yellow is used for new code that has yet to be saved. The highlighted line turns green after a save and disappears after you close and reopen the file. This feature enables you to track where you have made changes to code during your current session.
- The name of the open code file is listed as the code window's tab across the top. The asterisk indicates that the code has changed since the last time it was saved.
- IntelliSense is invoked as you type. You can use the arrow keys to quickly find the item in the list. Hovering over the item shows details for the given item (tip text to the right). You can press the Tab key to complete the item from IntelliSense. Note that the completion also occurs after you press SPACE.

- The code is highlighted in various colors. By default, keywords are navy blue, comments are green, text is black, types you create are light blue, string values are red, and so on.
- The three drop-downs at the top of the code editor enable you to navigate between projects (left-most side), between the classes in the file (middle drop-down) and methods, fields, and properties within a given class (right-side drop-down).

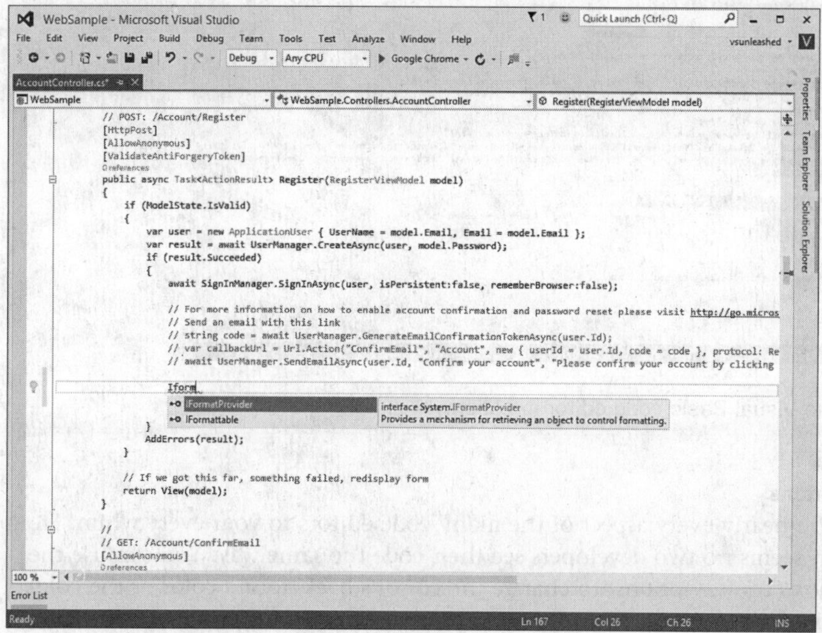

FIGURE 2.23 The C# code editor in action.

The Visual Basic Code Editor

The Visual Basic code editor works much the same way as the C# editor. Figure 2.24 shows the code editor, this time with a Visual Basic file loaded. Over time, these editors have become more and more similar. The primary difference currently (outside the language syntax) is the horizontal lines used to separate methods and properties within the editor.

Of course, Visual Studio contains many more text editors. There are other language editors (C++ and F#), XML editors, XHTML editors, and more. Each has similar features to the two code editors shown here.

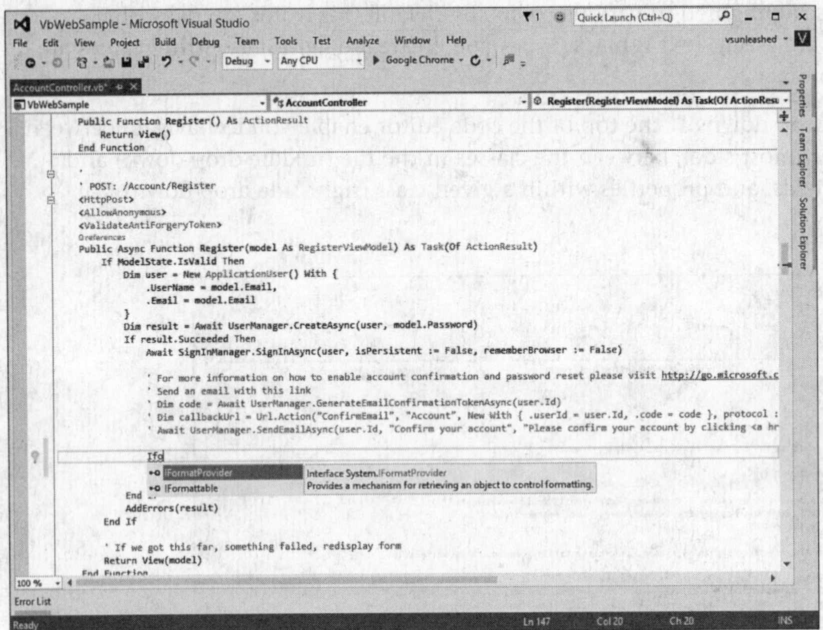

FIGURE 2.24 The Visual Basic code editor in action.

Editor Customizations

You can customize nearly every aspect of the many code editors to your every whim. From our experience, it seems no two developers see their code the same way. You can use the Options dialog box (Tools, Options) to change the editor's background color or the color and font of various text elements within the editor. You can also turn on line numbering and manage indenting (tabs) and whitespace. You can set options based on language and editor. The full list of customizations for the editors is large.

Figure 2.25 shows the Options dialog box set for Fonts and Colors. From here, you can tweak the many display items in the editor in terms of their color, font, and font size.

If you look a little closer at the Options dialog box, you come across the Text Editor node as a topmost element in the option tree. From here, you can manipulate even more settings for the text editor in general for language-specific editors. For example, you can remove the horizontal procedure separators in the Visual Basic editor or turn off the automatic reformatting of code by the editor.

One common change we see developers make is controlling how the editor automatically formats code inside the C# editor. It seems granular control of curly braces is a big deal to those who look at code all day. For instance, you might like to see all your curly braces on separate lines, or you might prefer them to start on the line that starts the given code block. Fortunately, you can control all of that from the Options dialog box. Figure 2.26 shows some of these options available for formatting C# inside the editor. Notice how the option also shows an example of how the editor formats the code.

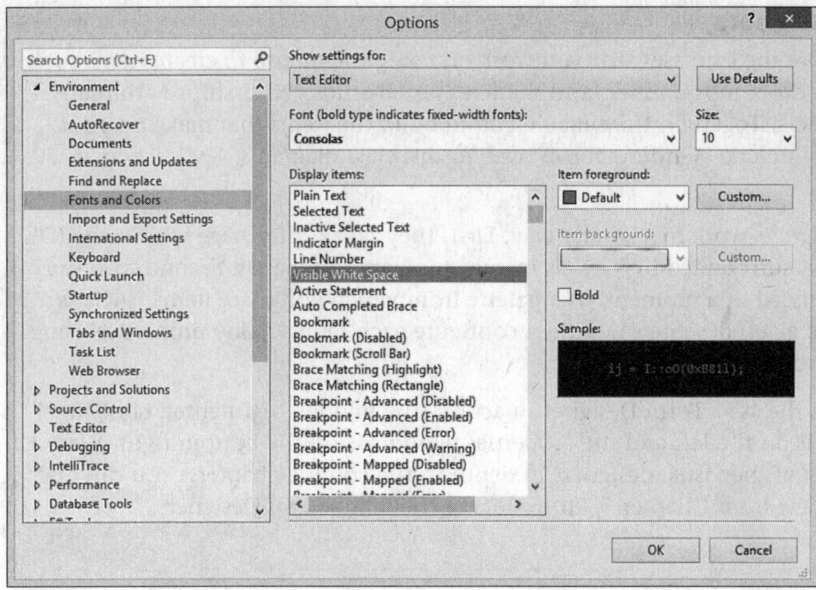

FIGURE 2.25 Use the Options dialog box to set Fonts and Colors of the text editors.

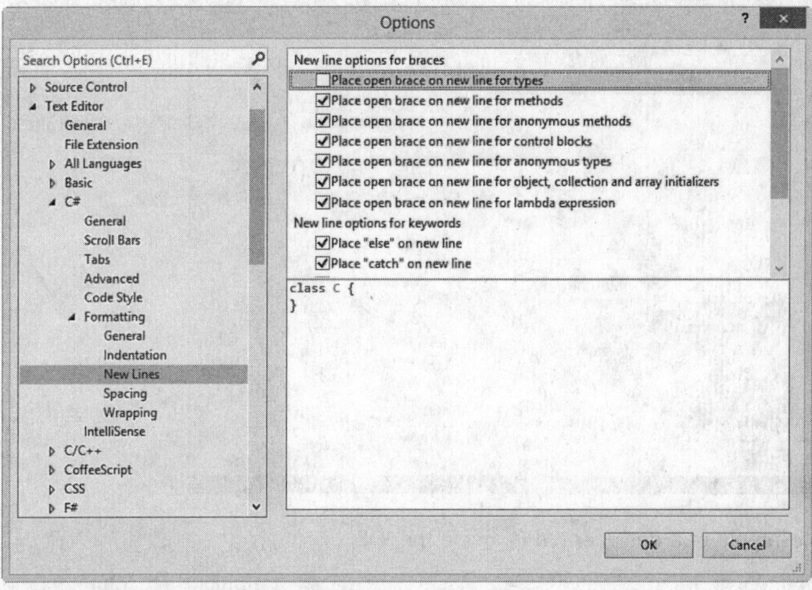

FIGURE 2.26 Use the Options dialog to control how code is formatted by the editor.

The Visual Designers

Visual Designers are the canvases that you work on using the mouse to create items such as forms via drag, drop, move, resize, and the like. Visual Studio 2015 ships with many such visual designers. Together, they enable you to build the items that make up your application. Items include Windows forms, web forms, class diagrams, XML schemas, and more.

All the visual designers work in a similar way. First, they take center stage within the IDE as tabbed windows surrounded by various menus, toolbars, and panes. Second, you use the Toolbox (discussed in a moment) as a palette from which you place items (such as controls) onto the given designer. You then configure each item's many properties using the Properties window.

Figure 2.27 shows the WPF Form Designer in action (the middle, highlighted tab). Note that the Toolbox is on the left and the Properties window is on the bottom right. We cover the majority of the visual designers in depth in the coming chapters. You can also get a better overview from Chapter 6, "Introducing the Editors and Designers."

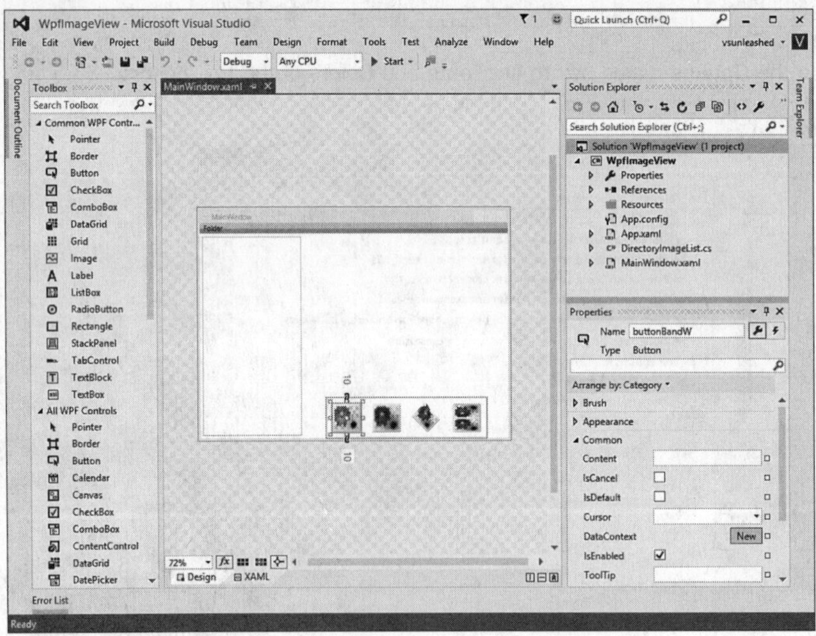

FIGURE 2.27 An example of a designer (WPF) inside the IDE.

The Toolbox

The Visual Studio 2015 Toolbox provides access to the many controls when you're building web and Windows forms. It also provides access to nearly anything that can be dragged onto one of the numerous designers used for creating forms, XML schemas, class diagrams, and more. As an example, if you are building a web form, the Toolbox provides the many controls, grouped for easier access, that can be added to the form. Furthermore, if you are working with a text editor, the Toolbox enables you to save clips of text for quick access.

Figure 2.28 shows the Toolbox in a standard configuration (undocked from the IDE) for building a web form. The many controls inside this Toolbox and those inside other Toolbox dialogs are covered throughout the rest of the book in their respective chapters.

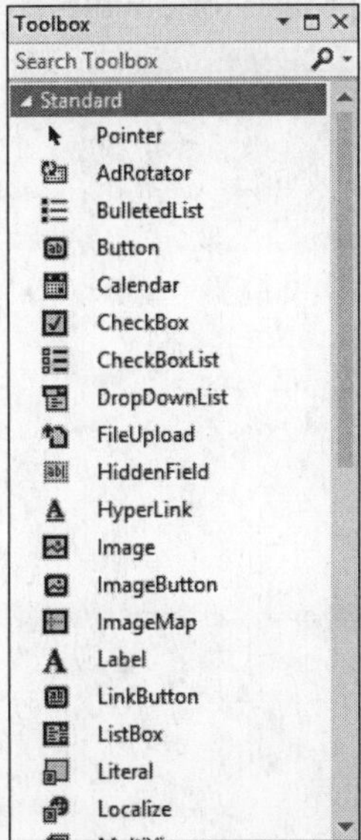

FIGURE 2.28 The Visual Studio Toolbox used to add controls to a form (in this case, a web form).

TIP

You can customize the Toolbox to your liking. For example, you can add your own groups (called tabs). You can also configure the Toolbox to show more icons on the screen at a time. As you familiarize yourself with the various standard controls, you can turn off their text descriptions and simply show them as icons. To do so, right-click the control group (tab) and uncheck List View.

The Properties Window

The many tools, controls, and rich designers that free us from repetitive code also require our attention in the form of maintenance. This work is typically done through the manipulation of the hundreds of properties that work in concert to define our application. This is where the Properties window comes into play. It enables us to control the size, appearance, and behavior of our controls. Furthermore, the Properties window groups common properties into sets for easier access. Finally, the Properties window gives us access to connecting the events for a given control to the code inside our application.

Figure 2.29 shows the Properties window (undocked from the IDE) for a web form button control. Note that the window can group similar properties into sections via banded categories, such as Appearance. You can also list properties in alphabetic order by clicking the AZ icon on the Properties window toolbar. Another item worth noting is the lightning bolt icon on the toolbar. This gives you access to the events for the given control. From the list of events, you can select an event and wire it to code in your project (or double-click it to generate an event handler).

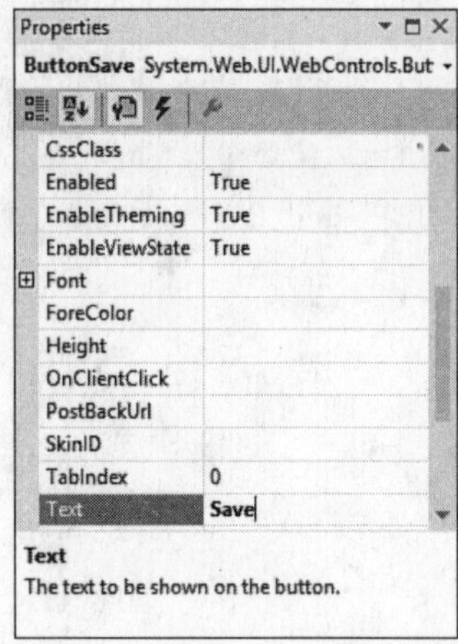

FIGURE 2.29 A save button inside the Properties window.

Managing the Many Windows of the IDE

To round out our whirlwind tour, we thought it important to provide you with guidance on customizing and managing the plethora of windows available within the IDE (lest they leave you with a postage-stamp-size window in which to write your code). To manage these windows, you really need to know only two skills: pinning and docking. In addition, Visual Studio 2015 brings you custom window layouts for saving and applying different layouts.

Pinning

Pinning refers to the process of making a window stick in the open position. It is called pinning in reference to the visual cue you use to perform the act: a pushpin. Pinning is a key concept because you sometimes want full-screen real estate for writing code or designing a form. In this case, you should unpin (auto hide) the various extraneous windows in your IDE. Figure 2.30 shows the mouse cursor over the pin of the Solution Explorer window. Note that this window is currently pinned open. You would push this pin to unpin the window.

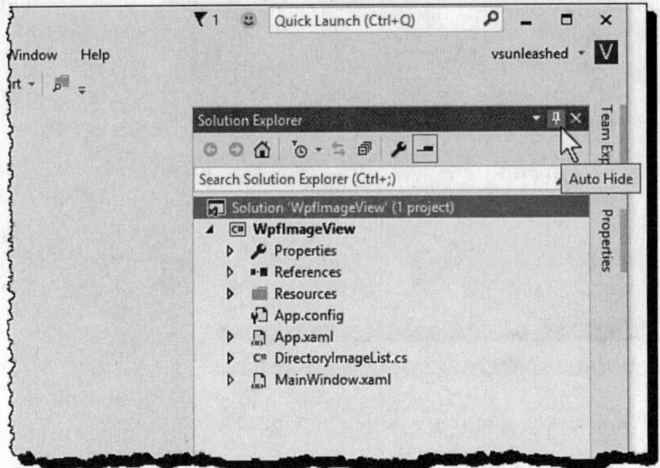

FIGURE 2.30 Pinning and unpinning windows in the IDE.

An unpinned window slides the window closed but keeps it accessible to you (versus closing it altogether). When a window is unpinned, a vertical tab represents the window. The Toolbox and Properties tabs on the far left and right of Figure 2.30 are examples. Clicking on this tab results in the window unfolding for your use. After you use it, however, it goes back to its hiding spot.

Docking

Docking is the process of connecting windows to various sticky spots within the IDE. Typically, this means docking to the left, top, right, or bottom of the IDE. For example, the Toolbox is, by default, docked to the left side of the IDE. You might prefer to put it at the bottom of the screen, docked below the active designer. You might also want to dock the Solution Explorer to the top of the screen and then unpin it for quick access. You can see an example of this docking approach in Figure 2.31.

You can also dock windows to one another. For example, you might want to dock the Properties window below the Solution Explorer. Or you might want the Properties window to be a tab within the same window to which the Solution Explorer is docked. Figure 2.32 shows an example of the Properties window being docked to the bottom of the Solution Explorer window.

To help with docking, Visual Studio 2015 has provided visual cues and helpers. First, click and hold the title bar with the mouse, and then drag the window to where you want to dock it. Visual Studio displays some docking icons.

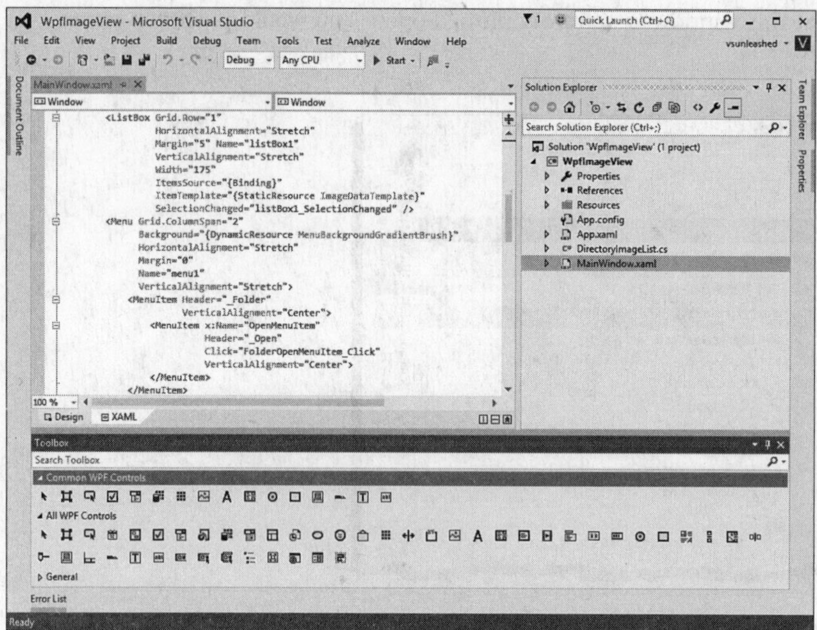

FIGURE 2.31 Horizontally docking windows in the IDE.

Four icons are at the edge of the IDE, one each at the left, top, right, and bottom. These icons are used for docking the window at the given edge of the IDE. Using these icons results in the window being docked across the full length (or width) of the IDE. Figure 2.32 shows each of these icons as the Properties window is being docked.

There is also an icon that shows over the top of a window to which you might want to dock. This icon is used for docking the selected window relative to another window in the IDE. For example, you might want to dock the Properties window under the Solution Explore window (as shown in Figure 2.32). You do so with the bottom icon inside this icon group.

Of course, you can also undock items. This is simply the process of floating windows off by themselves (outside, or on top of, the IDE). To do so, you simply grab (click with the mouse) a window by the title bar and move it off to the side of the IDE or just don't choose a docking icon.

Finally, when working with a window, you can right-click the title bar and tell Visual Studio how the window should behave. Figure 2.33 shows the available options. The down-arrow icon on the window title bar provides access to the same features. The Float option indicates that the window floats wherever you put it, on top of the IDE. This can be useful if you find yourself moving windows about or need to use multiple monitors. You turn off this option by choosing Dock. You can also use the Dock as Tabbed Document option to add a window to the center of your IDE (just like the default positioning of a designer or code editor).

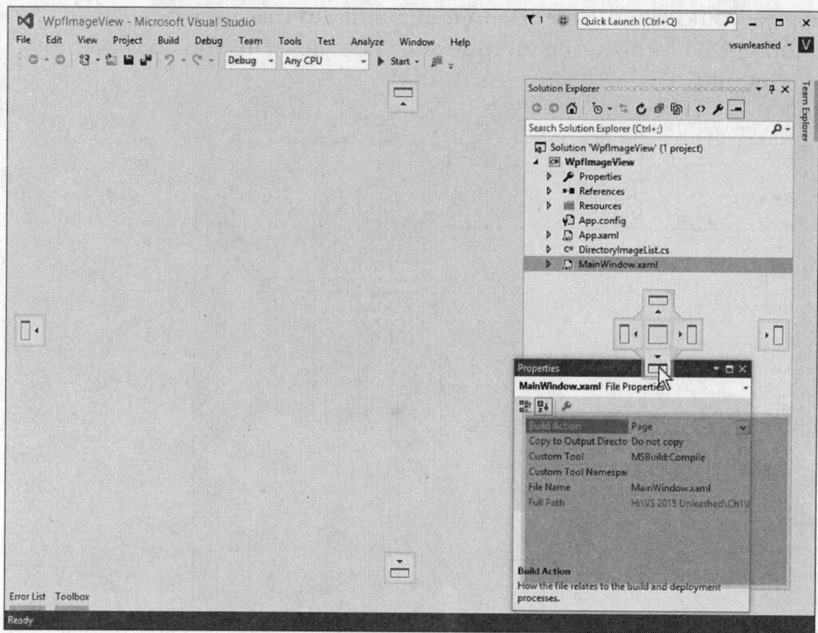

FIGURE 2.32 Docking one window to another in the IDE.

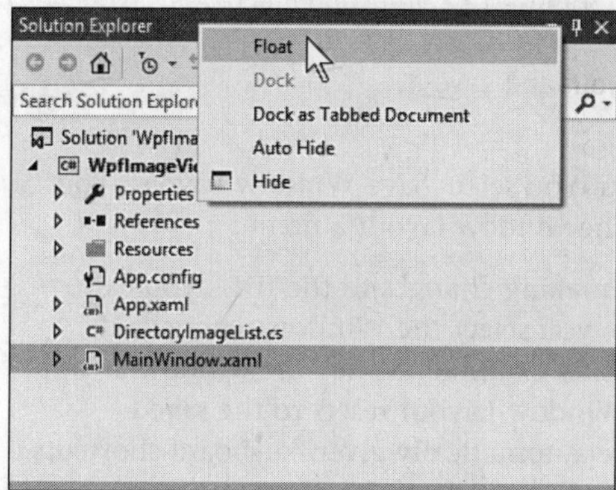

FIGURE 2.33 The float and docking options of a window in the IDE.

Custom Window Layouts

Visual Studio 2015 provides support for saving your custom window layouts. This allows you to tweak your IDE for different functions such as C# coding versus XAML layout activities. You can then save your window layout with a name and apply it when the time is right.

As an example, suppose you configure the IDE to look similar to that shown in Figure 2.34. This layout is optimized for focusing on code and code files. The Toolbox and properties windows are unpinned.

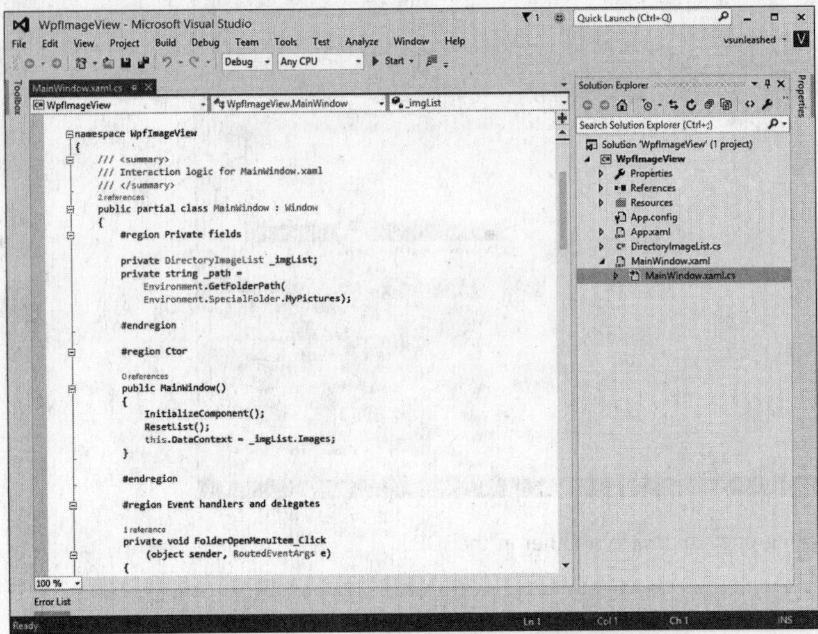

FIGURE 2.34 You can create a custom window layout and save it.

You can save this layout from the Window menu. You select Save Window Layout. You are then presented with a simple dialog to give the window layout a name.

When your IDE activity changes (or you end up making changes to the IDE), you can easily apply your saved window layout. To do so, you select the Window menus and choose Apply Window Layout. Figure 2.35 shows an example. Notice the window layout behind the menu has changed. Clicking Apply Window Layout resets to the saved layout. Also, notice that your window layouts are automatically given keyboard shortcuts (Ctrl+Alt+1). This makes switching between layouts even easier.

Finally, Visual Studio also allows you to manage your saved windows. You do so from the Windows menu, Manage Window Layouts. Figure 2.36 shows an example. Here you can rename a layout, delete it, or move it up and down in the sequence (and thus change the keyboard shortcut associated with the layout).

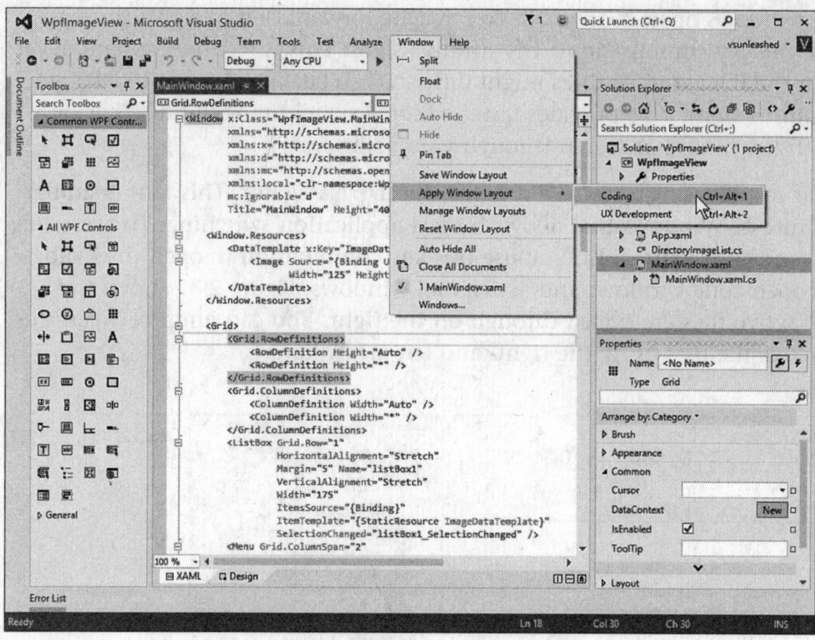

FIGURE 2.35 You can apply a custom window layout to your IDE.

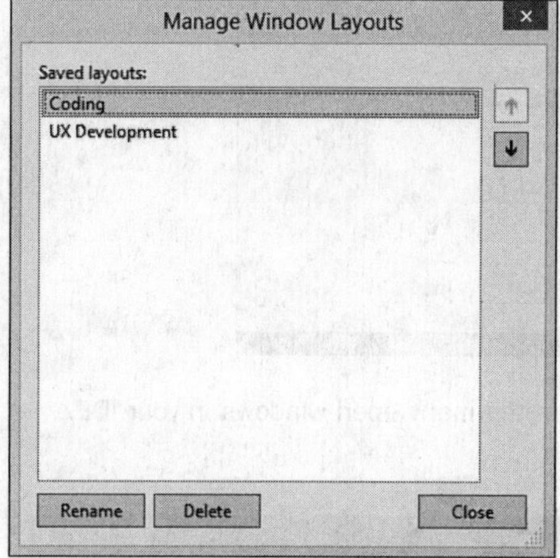

FIGURE 2.36 Manage custom window layouts.

Navigating IDE Windows

You can navigate open windows in the IDE without touching a mouse. This keeps your fingers on the keyboard and can lead to greater productivity. Visual Studio 2015 provides a couple of options here. The first is a simple window-switching hotkey. Suppose you have a number of code windows open in the IDE. To navigate forward (left to right) through them, you can use the key combination Ctrl+- (minus sign). This is for the standard development settings in the IDE; your settings might differ. To go backward (right to left), you use Ctrl+Shift+- (minus sign). This provides faster window switching without requiring that you scroll with the mouse or search through your solution.

You can get similar results using a visual aid called the IDE Navigator. This tool is similar to the Alt+Tab feature of Windows that allows for fast application switching. To access it, you use Ctrl+Tab (and Ctrl+Shift+Tab). You use this key combination to open the dialog box and navigate open code windows and active tool windows. Figure 2.37 shows the result. Notice that active files are cycled through on the right. You can jump between the active tools and active file lists using the right- and left-arrow keys.

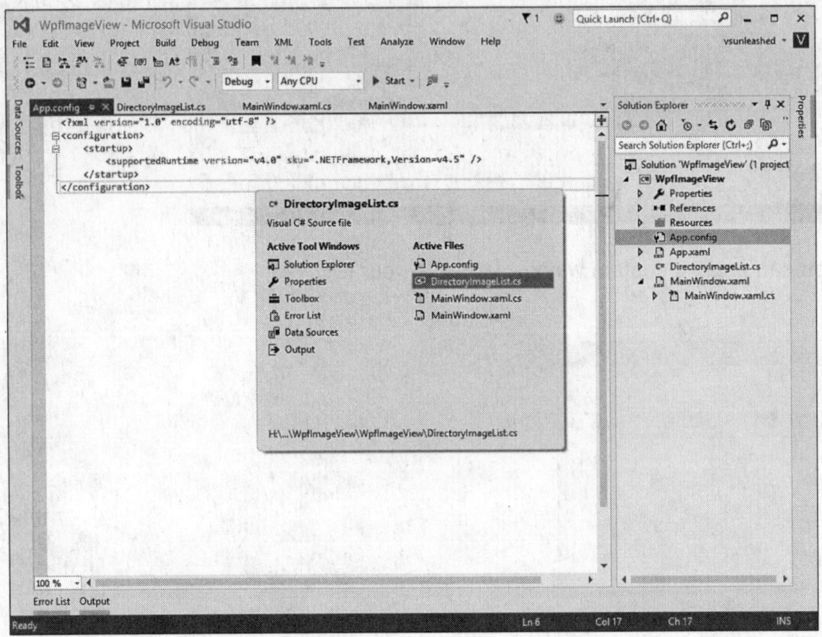

FIGURE 2.37 Use the IDE Navigator to jump between the many open windows in your IDE.

NOTE

To change the keyboard combinations assigned to the IDE navigator, select the menu option Tools, Options. Under the Environment node, select Keyboard. Here you can set keyboard shortcut keys. The settings to change are as follows: Window.NextDocumentWindowNav and Window.PreviousDocumentWindowNav.

Touch Support

Visual Studio 2015 introduces touch support to the code editor. Developers with touch monitors, touch laptops, or coding on a Surface will find this useful. You likely will still type with your keyboard. However, you can use basic gestures in the code editor to simplify a few key tasks including these:

- ▶ Scroll via tapping and dragging on the code editor
- ▶ Zoom and shrink via the pinch and expand gesture
- ▶ Select a link of text by tapping in the margin of the editor
- ▶ Select a single "word" of code by double-tapping the word
- ▶ Press and hold your finger on the editor to open the context (right-click) menu

Customize Your IDE Font

You can change the font that your IDE uses for menus and related items. To do so, you open the Options dialog from the Tools menu. You first select the Environment node and the Fonts and Colors subnode. At the top of the options for fonts and colors is a drop-down for selecting where you wish to modify the Fonts and Colors (for example, the Text Editor, Output Window, All Text Tool Windows, and more). You can also use this drop down to set the font for the entire IDE to the selection of your choice. Figure 2.38 shows selecting this option (Environment Font) and changing the font from Automatic to Arial Narrow.

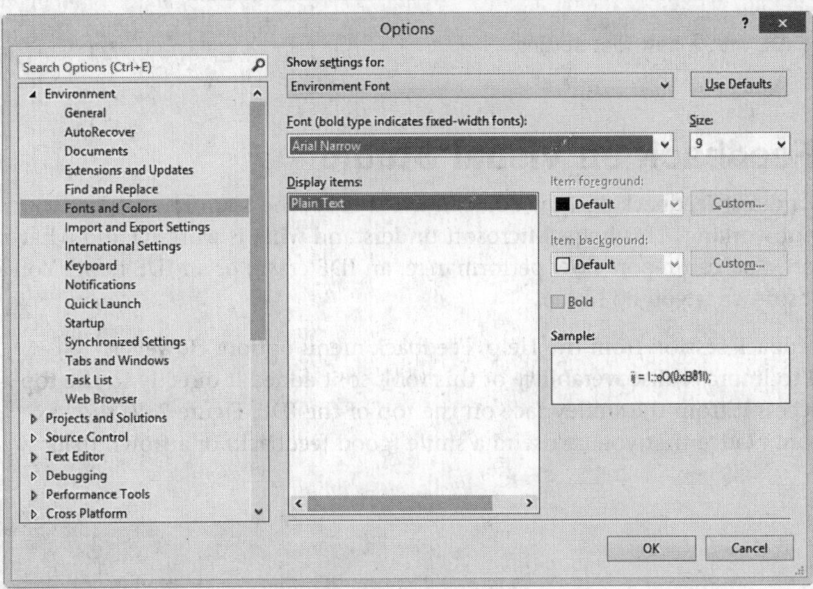

FIGURE 2.38 Changing the font for your IDE.

Figure 2.39 shows the results. Notice the menu items and Solution Explorer are now using the new font choice. Other items such as the Toolbox, Server Explorer, and dialogs (like New Project) will pick up this same setting. If you do not like your change, you can always change it back the same way by selecting Automatic as your font choice.

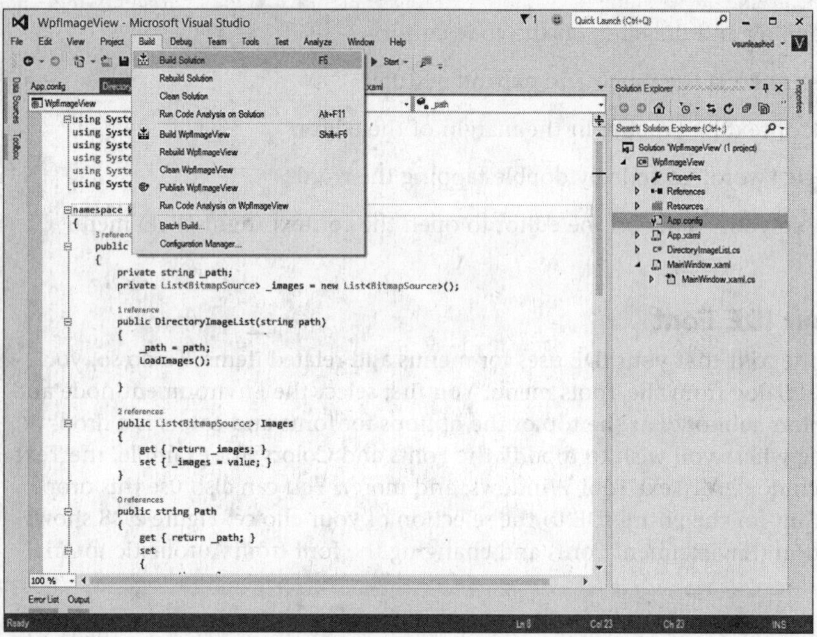

FIGURE 2.39 The IDE with a new font setting.

Providing Feedback on Visual Studio

Visual Studio has a direct feedback option. You can use it to let the team know what you like and what is not working. This helps Microsoft understand what is working and what it needs to work on. You can report slow performance, an IDE crash, or an IDE hang. You can also tell Microsoft what you do like.

You can start a feedback session from the Help, Feedback menu option. However, Microsoft wanted to improve discoverability of this tool, so it added it directly to the top of the IDE. You access it from the smiley face on the top of the IDE. Figure 2.40 shows this menu in action. Notice that you can send a smile (good feedback) or a frown (bad feedback).

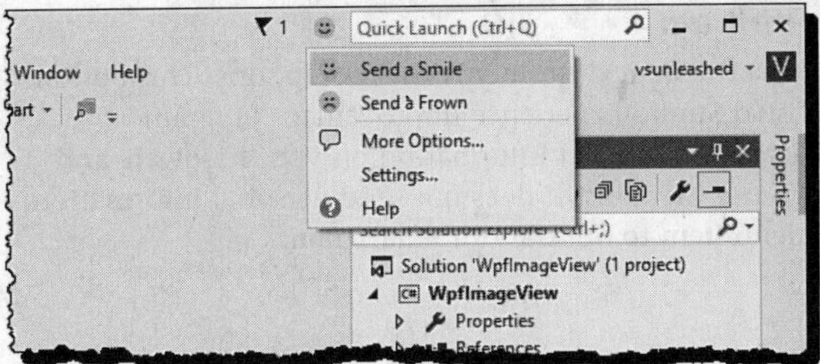

FIGURE 2.40 Use the smiley face to send good and bad feedback on the IDE directly to Microsoft.

Clicking the More Options menu item shown in Figure 2.40 takes you to the Visual Studio connect site. Here you can log a bug, submit an ideal, or ask a question.

Starting a feedback session launches the send feedback dialog, as shown in Figure 2.41. The tool automatically captures a screenshot on your behalf. You can then write Microsoft a note describing your feedback. Your email is included (optional) if Microsoft contacts you about the feedback.

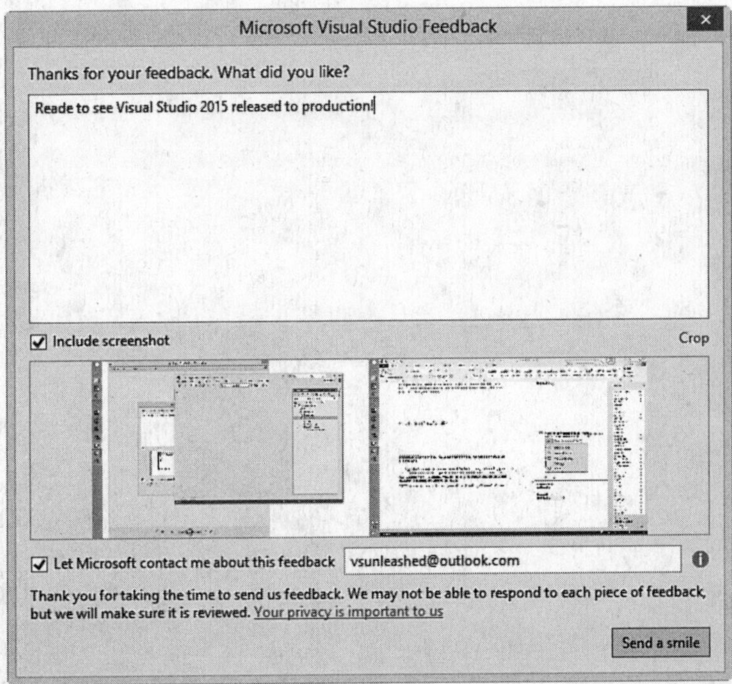

FIGURE 2.41 The Visual Studio Feedback dialog.

The Customer Experience Program

The Visual Studio help menu includes the item Customer Feedback Options. This option enables you to participate in the Visual Studio Experience Improvement Program. Choosing to participate enables Microsoft to collect information on your hardware and software configuration and how you use the tools. It does not send personal information. Of course, you can use this same menu item to opt out of the program.

Summary

The whirlwind tour is over. We've covered the basics of installation, creation of your first project, and the standard items you encounter when journeying out on your own. You should now be oriented to the basic set of menus, toolbars, settings, and window management inside Visual Studio. With your bearings in place, you can push onward.

CHAPTER 3

The .NET Languages

IN THIS CHAPTER

- What's New in C# 6.0 and VB 14
- Language Primer
- Language Features
- Asynchronous Programming
- The .NET Framework

Unlocking the productivity promises of the Visual Studio IDE is at the heart of this book. The IDE, of course, also ships from Microsoft in concert with new versions of the .NET languages and Framework. You need to have a solid grasp of programming the Visual Basic or C# language using the .NET Framework to take advantage of everything Visual Studio has to offer. Of course, you may also need to know many other things such as XAML, Hypertext Markup Language (HTML), Cascading Style Sheets (CSS), TypeScript, JavaScript (and related frameworks), C++, F#, and LightSwitch. Today's developer likely does not code in a single language syntax. However, VB and C# are still at the core of most Visual Studio development.

In this chapter, we set aside the IDE (for the most part) and focus on the foundations of .NET programming in C# and Visual Basic. We start by highlighting new features of the languages for those who are already familiar with C# and VB. We then include a language primer as a review of some basic .NET programming tasks. We then cover some more in-depth programming features, enhancements to C# 6.0 and VB 14, and language-related IDE enhancements. The chapter concludes with an overview and map of the .NET Framework class library.

What's New in C# 6.0 and VB 14

This section is for developers looking for highlights on what's new about the C# and Visual Basic languages. For those who need the basics (or a refresher), we suggest you start by reading the "Language Primer" section a little later in this chapter. You can then return here to see what additions exist to the primer.

In general, the language changes are small additions that help you write cleaner code. They simplify coding by eliminating unnecessary, repetitive code. The changes also make the code easier to read and understand.

NOTE

You can examine much of the code in this section by downloading the code files associated with this book.

Null-Conditional Operators

One of the most repetitive tasks you do as a programmer is to check a value for null before you work with it. The code to do this checking is typically all over your application. For example, the following verifies whether properties on an object are null before working with them. (For a more complete discussion of all operators, see the section "Understanding Operators" later in this chapter.)

C#

```
public bool IsValid()
{
    if (this.Name != null &&
        this.Name.Length > 0 &&
        this.EmpId != null &&
        this.EmpId.Length > 0)
    {
        return true;
    }
        else
    {
        return false;
    }
}
```

VB

```
Public Function IsValid() As Boolean
    If Me.Name IsNot Nothing AndAlso
        Me.Name.Length > 0 AndAlso
        Me.EmpId IsNot Nothing AndAlso
        Me.EmpId.Length > 0 Then

        Return True

    Else
        Return False
    End If
End Function
```

Both C# 6.0 and VB 14 now allow automatic null checking using the question mark dot operator (`?.`). This operator tells the compiler to check the information that precedes the operator for null. If a null is found in an `If` statement for example, the entire check is considered false (without additional items being checked). If no null is found, then do the work of the dot (`.`) to check the value. The code from earlier can now be written as follows:

C#

```
public bool IsValid()
{
    if (this.Name?.Length > 0 &&
        this.EmpId?.Length > 0)
    {
        return true;
    }
    else
    {
        return false;
    }
}
```

VB

```
Public Function IsValid2() As Boolean
    If Me.Name?.Length > 0 AndAlso
        Me.EmpId?.Length > 0 Then

        Return True

    Else
        Return False
    End If
End Function
```

NOTE

The `?.` operator is referred to as the Elvis operator because you can see two dots for the eyes and the question mark as a swoop of hair.

The null-conditional operator cleans up code in other ways. For instance, when you trigger events, you are forced to copy the variable and check for null. This can now be written as a single line. The following code shows both the old way and the new way of writing code to trigger events in C#.

C#

```
//trigger event, old model
{
  var onSave = OnSave;
  if (onSave != null)
  {
    onSave(this, args);
  }
}

//trigger event using null-conditional operator
{
  OnSave?.Invoke(this, args);
}
```

ReadOnly Auto Properties

Auto properties have been a great addition to .NET development. They simplify the old method of coding properties using a local variable and a full implementation of `get` and `set`. See "Creating an Automatically Implemented Property" in the later section "Language Features."

However, up until 2015, auto properties required both a getter and a setter; this makes it hard to use them with immutable data types. The latest release now allows you to create auto properties as read only (with just the `get`). A read-only backing field is created behind the scenes on your behalf. The following shows an example of a full property, a standard auto property, and the new read-only auto property.

C#

```
Public class Employee
{
    //full property
    private string name;
    public string Name
    {
        get { return name; }
        set { name = value; }
    }

    //standard auto property
    public string Address { get; set; }

    //read-only auto property
    public string EmpId { get; }
}
```

VB

```
Public Class Employee

    'full property
    Private _name As String
    Public Property Name() As String
        Get
            Return _name
        End Get
        Set(ByVal value As String)
            _name = value
        End Set
    End Property

    'standard auto property
    Public Property Address As String

    'read-only auto property
    Public ReadOnly Property EmpId As String

End Class
```

Read-only auto properties can be assigned from the constructor. Again, they have a hidden backing field. The compiler knows this field exists and thus allows this assignment. The following shows a constructor inside the `Employee` class shown above assigning the read-only `EmpId` property. Notice that, in Visual Basic, the Sub New constructor must be used to assign a read-only property.

C#

```
public Employee(string id)
{
    EmpId = id;
}
```

VB

```
Public Sub New(ByVal id As String)
    EmpId = id
End Sub
```

You can also initiate read-only auto properties at the time of their creation (just like the field that backs them), as shown next. Note that if you were to combine this assignment with the previous constructor code (that initialized the read only property), the object creation would happen first. Thus, the constructor init would take precedence.

C#

```
public string EmpId { get; } = "NOT ASSIGNED";
```

VB

```
Public ReadOnly Property EmpId As String = "NOT ASSIGNED"
```

NameOf Expression

You now have access to the names of your code elements, such as variables and parameters. The .NET languages use the `NameOf` expression to enable this feature.

Prior to 2015, you often had to indicate the name of a program element by enclosing it in a string. However, if the name of that code element changed, you had an error lurking in your code (unless you managed to remember to change the string value). For example, consider the following code that throws an instance of `ArgumentNullException`. This class takes a string as the name of the argument. It then uses the string value to find your program element; it's not strongly typed programming at all.

C#

```
public void SaveFeedback(string feedback)
{
    if (feedback == null)
    {
        //without nameOf
        throw new ArgumentNullException("feedback");
    }
}
```

VB

```
Public Sub SaveFeedback(ByVal feedback As String)
    If feedback Is Nothing Then
        'without nameOf
        Throw New ArgumentNullException("feedback")
    End If
End Sub
```

The `NameOf` expression eliminates this issue. You can use the expression along with your actual, scoped code element to pass the name of your code element as a string. However, `NameOf` uses the actual type to reference the name. Therefore, you get compile-time checking and rename support. The following shows an example of throwing the same exception as used earlier but using `NameOf`.

C#

```
throw new ArgumentNullException(nameof(feedback));
```

VB

```
Throw New ArgumentNullException(NameOf(feedback))
```

Using (Imports) Statics

The using statement (Imports in VB) allows developers to declare namespaces that are in scope; thus, classes in the namespace do not need to be fully qualified inside your code. (See "Organizing Your Code with Namespaces" later in this chapter.) You can now use the same statement with static classes. To do so, in C# you must include the static keyword as in "using static." In Visual Basic, you simply use Imports and then specific the static library.

The ability to indicate using (Imports in VB) with a static class tells the compiler that the class and its members are now in scope. This allows you to call a method of the static class without referencing the namespace or even the class name inside your code.

As an example, consider the static class `System.Math`. You could add a using statement to the top of your code file. In that case, calls to the static methods would no longer need to be qualified by namespace and class. Instead, you could call the method directly. The following shows the difference between the two approaches.

C#

```
using static System.Math;
...

//use the static method, round without using
return System.Math.Round(bonus, 0);

//use the static method
return Round(bonus, 0);
```

VB

```
Imports System.Math
...

'use the static method, round without imports
Return System.Math.Round(bonus, 0)

'use the static method
Return Round(bonus, 0)
```

String Interpolation

The .NET languages allow you to replace portions of a string with values. To do so, you use `String.Format` or `StringBuilder.AppendFormat`. These methods allow you to use placeholders as numbers inside curly braces. These numbers are replaced in series by the values that follow. This is cumbersome to write and can lead to confusion.

In 2015, the code editor allows you to put the variable right in the middle of the string. You do so using the format that starts the string with a dollar sign ($) as an escape character. You can then add curly braces within the string to reference variables, as in `{value}`. The editor gives you IntelliSense for your values, too. The call to `String.Format` then happens for you behind the scenes. The example that follows shows how the previous use of `String.Format` is now simplified with enhanced string literals.

C#

```
//old style of String.Format
return String.Format("Name: {0}, Id: {1}", this.Name, this.EmpId);

//string interpolation style
return ($"Name: {this.Name}, Id: {this.EmpId}");
```

VB

```
'old style of String.Format
Return String.Format("Name: {0}, Id: {1}", Me.Name, Me.EmpId)

'string interpolation style
Return $"Name: {Name}, Id: {EmpId}"
```

Lambda Expressions as Methods (C# Only)

Methods, properties, and other bits of code can now be assigned using lambda expression syntax (in C# only). (See "Write Simple Unnamed Functions Within Your Code (Lambda Expressions)" later in this chapter.) This makes writing and reading code much easier. The following shows a full method implementation as a lambda and a single expression. Notice that we use the string interpolation discussed in the prior section.

C#

```
public override string ToString() => $"Name: {this.Name}, Id: {this.EmpId}";
```

Index Initializers (C# Only)

Prior language editions brought developers the concept of creating an object and initializing its values at the same time. (See "Object Initializers" later in this chapter.) However, you could not initialize objects that used indexes. Instead, you had to add one value after another, making your code repetitive and hard to read. C# 6.0 supports index initializers. The following shows an example of creating a `Dictionary<string, DateTime>` object of key/value pairs and initializing values at the same time.

C#

```
var holidays = new Dictionary<string, DateTime>
{
```

```
    { "New Years", new DateTime(2015, 1, 1) },
    { "Independence Day", new DateTime(2015, 7, 4) }
};
```

Language Primer

You have a few language choices available to you as a .NET programmer: Visual Basic, C#, C++, or F# are at the core. There are also user interface (UI)-specific languages and markup syntax, such as JavaScript, HTML, and XAML. Which core language you choose is typically a result of your history, style, and intent. Developers who have worked with past incarnations of Visual Basic or another basic language will find they are at home inside Visual Basic. The language (including templates, tools, wizards, and so on) is all about developer productivity. Developers whose roots are in a C-based language (C++, Java, and so on) and who want similar productivity in a straightforward way gravitate toward C#. Of course, some developers will just want to stay in C++ even for their .NET applications.

Visual Studio 2010 saw the introduction of the F# language. Now part of the full Visual Studio product line, F# 4.0 targets enterprise developers. Similar to other .NET languages, F# supports object-oriented programming. What makes it different is that it is also a functional programming language. Functional programming elevates functions to first-class values. (The *F* in F# is for functional.) For example, a functional language allows you to easily pass functions as parameters, return functions as the result of a function, chain functions together to create new functions, create recursive functions, and more. These powerful features in F# allow you to more easily tackle complex algorithms with less code (and often less pain) than it would take with the standard object-oriented (OO)-only languages of Visual Basic and C#. Having F# inside of Visual Studio also means that you can leverage the .NET Framework, get the benefits of the Common Language Runtime (CLR) (including calling to and from other .NET code), and have debugging and other related tools support.

NOTE

F# is both a new language and a new way of programming. You need to spend time to be able to "think" in F#. There is not room in this book to present the language. In addition, most .NET developers still write nearly all their code in Visual Basic or C#. Therefore, we focus on those two languages throughout this book.

Programming Objects

Programming in .NET is an object-oriented experience. You write your own classes and leverage those created by Microsoft (forms, controls, and libraries). In fact, every .NET application has at least one class, and more often it has hundreds. You can extend classes with new functionality (inheritance), define classes based on a contract (interface), and override the behavior of existing classes (polymorphism). This section looks at defining objects with .NET code.

Classes

Think of classes as the container for your code. Classes define how you hold data (properties) and perform actions (methods); they communicate how your class works after it's created (instantiated). When you create an instance of the class, it is an object and can actually maintain its own state and execute code to update and give access to it.

You define a class using the `Class` keyword. The following shows an example.

C#

```
public class Employee
{
}
```

VB

```
Public Class Employee

End Class
```

Fields and Properties

You add code to a class to define its data and behavior. Data for your class can be stored in fields or properties. Fields and properties are similar; both define data that is contained in the class. The difference is that properties can provide a means to protect the access (setting and getting) to field data. Fields are typically private variables defined by the class, accessible only from the class code, and defined as follows.

C#

```
public class Employee
{
  private string _name;
}
```

VB

```
Public Class Employee
  Private _name As String
End Class
```

You can define public fields on your class to make them accessible from any other class code. However, it is a best practice to encapsulate public data inside a property. This way you can control whether to expose the ability to read or write the value of a property. Properties are typically backed by an internal, private field. This is called data hiding and is implemented with the `Private` keyword. For example, the previously defined field can be encapsulated into a property as follows.

C#

```
public class Employee
{
  private string _name;

  public string Name
  {
    get { return _name; }
    set { _name = value; }
  }
}
```

VB

```
Public Class Employee
    Private _name As String

    Public Property Name() As String
        Get
            Return _name
        End Get
        Set(ByVal value As String)
            _name = value
        End Set
    End Property
End Class
```

You can also create read-only properties. This is useful when you want to reserve the writing of the property's value to code running inside the class. You create a read-only property by not implementing the `set` statement in the property definition. In Visual Basic, you also have to add the `ReadOnly` keyword. For example, suppose you want to add an `Id` property to the `Employee` class defined previously. This `Id` can be read by anyone, but its value (backed by `_Id`) is only set by internal class code. You could implement a read-only property as follows.

C#

```
private int _id;

public int Id
{
  get { return _id; }
}
```

VB

```
Private _id As Integer
```

```
Public ReadOnly Property Id() As Integer
  Get
    Return _id
  End Get
End Property
```

Methods

Methods represent the blocks of code in your class that, when called, perform some specific action. This action could be reading or writing from a database, calling other methods, calculating a value, processing some business rules and returning a result, or whatever you need your code to do.

Methods are defined by their names and access levels; see the next section for more details on access levels. In Visual Basic, you also need to add the `Sub` keyword to define a method that does not return a value. In C#, this is done by indicating the return type of `void` before the method name. For example, if you were to add a `Save` method to the `Employee` class previously defined, the code would look like this.

C#

```
public void Save()
{
  //implementation code goes here
}
```

VB

```
Public Sub Save()
  'implementation code goes here
End Sub
```

Methods often return values to the code that called the method. To define a method that returns a value, you must indicate the method's return type (the class type of the returned data). In Visual Basic, you also use the keyword `Function` (instead of `Sub`). You use the `Return` keyword to indicate the value to return from your code. For example, if you were to add a method to calculate an employee's remaining sick day, you would do so as follows.

C#

```
public int GetRemainingSickDays()
{
  int _sickDays = 0;

  //calculate remaining sick days

  return _sickDays;
}
```

VB

```
Function GetRemainingSickDays() As Integer

  Dim _sickDays As Integer = 0
  'code to calculate remaining sick days

  Return _sickDays
End Function
```

In this example, note the return type defined in the method signature (first line of the method). Also note the use of the keyword `Return` to return a value from the method. In this case, that value is stored inside a variable defined as internal to the method.

Member Accessibility

The properties, fields, and methods in your application are referred to as class members. Each member in your class is defined to have a specific access level. As you've seen, if you want other classes to be able to access a member, you must declare that member as public. If you want to reserve the member for accessibility only within the class, you declare it as private. These are two of the member accessibility levels available to you. The full complement of accessibility levels is described in Table 3.1.

TABLE 3.1 Member Accessibility Level in .NET

Level	Description
Public	Indicates that a member is publicly available to any code outside of the class.
Private	Indicates that the member is hidden and private to the class that contains the member. No code outside the class can directly access members defined as private.
Protected	Protected is similar to private. It indicates that the member is not exposed publicly. Rather, it is private to the class. However, protected members are also made available to any class that derives from the class that contains the protected method. (See the "Inheritance" section for more details.)
Internal	Indicates that a member is available to all code within the assembly that contains it. This means other classes within a compiled `.dll` or `.exe` can access the member. However, other assemblies that reference a given `.dll` cannot access its internal members.
Protected Internal	Indicates that the member is accessible by all code within an assembly and any code that derives from a class that contains the given member.

In addition to class-member accessibility, classes themselves use the same accessibility levels. You can declare a class as public, private, protected, and so on to define your intended usage. You want to make many classes private or protected to the class and deriving types. The classes you make public define the functionality you want to expose to other code.

Constructors

A constructor is code that is called when a new instance of your class is created. This code is used to define how you want your class instance initialized, typically by setting default values or some related setup code. You create a constructor as you would a method. The difference is that you give the constructor the same name as the class; you also do not need to prefix the method with void in C#. In Visual Basic, you can use the `Sub New` statement to create a default constructor for the class. This can be useful if you are initializing read-only properties. The following code shows an example for the `Employee` class.

C#

```
public Employee()
{
  //init default values of an empty employee object
}
```

VB

```
Public Sub New()
  'init default values of an empty employee object
End Sub
```

A class can have multiple constructors to change the way in which the object is initialized. In these cases, each constructor is defined with a different set of parameters. In C#, the version of the constructor that does not take parameters is referred to as the default constructor. In Visual Basic, the Sub New construct is used to define the default constructor. The following shows a couple additional constructors added to the `Employee` class. One initializes an `Employee` object based on the calling code passing in an `id` parameter; the other uses the employee's email address to initialize the object.

C#

```
public Employee(int id)
{
  //init default values for the employee defined by the given ID
}

public Employee(string emailAddress)
{
  //init default values for the employee defined by the given email
}
```

VB

```
Public Sub Employee(ByVal id As Integer)
  'init default values for the employee defined by the given ID
```

```
End Sub

Public Sub Employee(ByVal emailAddress As String)
  'init default values for the employee defined by the given email
End Sub
```

Static (Shared in VB) Members and Objects

Sometimes you do not want the full behavior of a class for all your methods. Instead, you might want to define certain methods that are not part of an instance of the class. These methods often retrieve information or calculate values but are not part of a specific object. In these cases, you can create entire classes or just specific methods of a class as static (or shared in Visual Basic).

The `Shared` and `static` keywords, when applied to a method, indicate that the method can be called without creating an instance of the class that contains it. `Shared` and `static` can also be defined at the class level. In this case, you are indicating that the class only contains shared and static methods, and you cannot create an instance of it. For example, you might add a static helper method to the `Employee` class to check to see whether an employee is active in the system before you create an instance. This declaration would look like this.

C#

```
public static bool IsActive(string emailAddress)
{
  //check to see if an employee has been added to the system
}
```

VB

```
Public Shared Function IsActive(ByVal emailAddress As String) As Boolean
  'check to see if an employee has been added to the system
End Function
```

Enumerations

Enumerations enable you to create a group of named values that help improve your code readability. Each item in an enumeration is a unique numerical value (`byte`, `sbyte`, `short`, `ushort`, `int`, `uint`, `long`, or `ulong`). Note that the default is `int`. You can pass around the enumeration value as a name rather than an actual value. In this way, your code doesn't rely on arbitrary, "magic" numbers. Instead, the code is sensible and readable.

You create an enumeration using the `enum` keyword. For example, you might add an enumeration to the `Employee` class to store the employment status of an employee. This would enable you to make decisions in your code based on the specific status of an employee. To define this enumeration, you add code as follows to the `Employee` class.

C#

```
enum EmploymentStatus
{
  Salaried,
  Hourly,
  Contract,
  Other
}
```

VB

```
Enum EmploymentStatus
  Salaried
  Hourly
  Contract
  Other
End Enum
```

Inheritance

You can define a new class based on an existing class, which is called inheritance. You use inheritance to extend (or add to) the functionality of a base class. Classes that extend a base class are said to derive their functionality from another class. That is, they contain all the functionality of the base class plus any additional functionality added to the new class.

You indicate inheritance in Visual Basic by using the `Inherits` keyword; in C# you add a colon and the base class name following the name of the new class. For example, suppose you implement a `Manager` class that derives from `Employee`. The `Manager` class contains all the members of an `Employee` but might add special properties and methods specific to a `Manager`. You define this new class as follows.

C#

```
class Manager: Employee
{
}
```

VB

```
Public Class Manager
  Inherits Employee

End Class
```

Note that you can actually define a base class that cannot be created. Instead, it only exists to form the basis for a new class. Other classes can derive from it, but you cannot create a direct instance of just the base class. This is done by adding the `MustInherit` (VB) or `abstract` (C#) keyword in front of the class definition. The keyword `NotInheritable` (VB) or `sealed` (C#) indicates that the class cannot be used as the basis for a new class.

NOTE

.NET programmers can only derive from a single class. They cannot inherit from multiple base classes. However, they can implement multiple interfaces (as discussed next).

Overriding Behavior

When you design your classes, consider how other developers might extend them. Your classes might serve as the base class for future derived classes. If this is the case, you might also consider which (if any) features of your base class you want to allow a derived class to override. The derived class may then implement a new version of one of your base methods, for example. This process is often referred to as polymorphism in OO programming.

To change the data or behavior of a base class, you can either add to the base class or override an existing member of the base class. Doing the latter gives you alternate behavior for the same function in your new class. You decide which members of your base class are available for override. You do so by marking them as virtual (Overridable in VB) members; this indicates that a derived class may override your base class functionality.

For example, suppose that you want to enable the `CalculateYearlyCost` method of the `Employee` class to be overridden when the `Employee` is used as the base for the `Manager` class. In this case, the calculation for a `Manager` is different for that of an `Employee`. You therefore mark the method inside the `Employee` class as `virtual` (C#) or `Overridable` (VB), as follows.

C#

```
public class Employee
{
  public virtual float CalculateYearlyCost()
  {
  }
}
```

VB

```
Public Class Employee
  Public Overridable Function CalculateYearlyCost() As Single

  End Function
End Class
```

You can then override this method in the derived class. You do so using the override (C#) or Overrides (VB) keyword. You can still call the method on the base class if you need to by using the base (C#) or MyBase (VB) keyword. The following shows an example.

C#

```
class Manager : Employee
{
  public override float CalculateYearlyCost()
  {
    //add new functionality, access underlying method using base keyword
  }
}
```

VB

```
Public Class Manager
  Inherits Employee

  Public Overrides Function CalculateYearlyCost() As Single
    'add new functionality, access underlying method using MyBase
  End Function

End Class
```

Hiding Members

There is a second way you can override the functionality of a base class. It involves using the keyword new (C#) or Shadows (VB) to redefine the base method. Overriding in this manner hides the base class members. However, the base class member is still called if an instance of the derived class gets downcast to an instance of the base class. This type of overriding is referred to as hiding by name. For example, you could replace the C# keyword override with new or the VB Overrides with Shadows to implement this type of behavior.

You need to be careful about hiding members versus overriding because downcasting can occur often. For example, you might be working with a collection of Employee objects (some of type Manager and some of type Employee). If you iterate over the list using the base class (for each employee), you get a different method called on the Manager class depending on whether you hid the member (in which case, the base class method is called) or overrode the member (in which case, the derived class method is called).

Overloading Members

You can also create multiple versions of the same procedure. All versions of a procedure can be defined inside the same class, or you can have a few versions in a base class and yet other versions in a derived class. This is useful when you need to preserve the name of the procedure but need to create different versions that each take different parameters.

Creating multiple versions of a procedure is called overloading or hiding by signature (as in the method's calling signature).

Overloading a method must follow rules designed to make each overload somehow different from all the others. Of course, each overload has the same name. However, you must change either the number of parameters the method accepts, the data type of one or more of those parameters, or the order of the parameters. You create a valid overload by changing one or more of these items to make the overload signature unique. Note that changing the return type, if the method returns a value, is not sufficient to create an overload; nor is changing just a parameter modifier.

For example, suppose you were creating a method to return the number of vacation days left for an employee. You might allow the users of this method to get the vacation days left for the current year, a supplied month, or a supplied month and year. In this case, the users of your method see a single method with multiple overloads. You implement this overloading similar to the following code.

C#

```
public short GetVacationUsed()
{
  //returns all vacation used in the current year
}

public short GetVacationUsed(short monthNumber)
{
  //returns all vacation used in the given month of the current year
}

public short GetVacationUsed(short monthNumber, short year)
{
  //returns all vacation used in the given month and year
}
```

VB

```
Public Function GetVacationUsed() As Short
  'returns all vacation used in the current year
End Function

Public Function GetVacationUsed(ByVal monthNumber As Short) As Short
  'returns all vacation used in the given month of the current year
End Function

Public Function GetVacationUsed(ByVal monthNumber As Short, ByVal year As Short) _
  As Short
  'returns all vacation used in the given month and year
End Function
```

Defining Interface Contracts

An interface is used to define a class contract. An interface does not contain any actual functioning code. Rather, it indicates a common structure for code that must be implemented by another class. This enables you to create common contracts and use those contracts across multiple objects. You can then trust that each class that implements the interface does so completely, following the outline of the interface.

An interface can define different types of class members, including properties, methods, events, and the like, but not fields or constructors. To create an interface, you use the `Interface` keyword. For example, suppose you want to define a basic interface for a person. The `Employee` class might then be required to implement this interface. Other classes (such as `User` and `Customer`) might also implement the same interface. The following shows an example of how you might define this interface.

C#

```
interface IPerson
{
  string Name { get; set; }
  DateTime DateOfBirth { get; set; }
  string EyeColor { get; set; }
  short HeightInInches { get; set; }
}
```

VB

```
Public Interface IPerson
  Property Name As String
  Property DateOfBirth As DateTime
  Property EyeColor As String
  Property HeightInInches As Short
End Interface
```

You implement the interface by adding the interface to the class definition on the class where you intend to implement the interface. In Visual Basic, this is done by adding the `Implements` keyword under the class definition (similar to inheritance). In C#, you add the interface to the class definition the same way you would indicate a base class (using a colon). You can separate multiple implemented interfaces by a comma.

NOTE

You implement an interface when you want to define the structure of a base class but do not intend to implement any base functionality. If you have common base functionality for which you provide for extension, you should consider using inheritance and abstract base class.

Creating Structures

So far we have talked about programming classes. There is another kind of type available to .NET programmers called a structure. Structures are similar to classes; they can contain properties, fields, enumerations, and methods. They can implement interfaces and can have one or more constructors. The main differences lie in how structures are managed by .NET.

Structures are considered value types. This means that when structures are used, the entire class instance is passed around as a value and not a reference. A class is a reference type. When you use a class instance and pass it around your application, you are actually passing a reference to a class instance. Not so with a structure. This also changes how .NET manages the memory used for structures and classes. Structures use stack allocation, and classes are managed on the heap by the Garbage Collector. To put this in perspective for .NET developers, imagine you have an instance of an `Employee` class. This instance might be created inside one object and passed to another object's method. If the second object makes a change to the `Employee` instance, this change is reflected inside all objects that maintain a reference to the instance. If this were a structure, however, there would be copies of that object passed around, and changes would be isolated to each copy.

There are other differences between classes and structures. For one, structures are sealed; that is, they cannot be inherited from. They also have an implicit public constructor that cannot be redefined. For these reasons, structures are best used when you need a lightweight container for data values and do not need the features of a reference type. Structures are often used to define small custom data types, reducing the odds to trigger a garbage collection.

You define a structure much like you define a class. In place of the `class` keyword, however, you use `struct` (C#) or `Structure` (VB). For example, imagine you want to define a data type that represents a paycheck. You could create a structure to hold this information. The following shows an example.

C#

```
public struct PayCheck
{
  private double _amount;

  public double Amount
  {
    get { return _amount; }
  }

  //add additional structure elements ...
}
```

VB

```
Public Structure Paycheck

  Private _amount As Double
  Public ReadOnly Property Amount() As Double
    Get
      Return _amount
    End Get
  End Property

  'additional structure elements ...

End Structure
```

Organizing Your Code with Namespaces

A namespace is used to group code that is specific to a company, an application, or a given library. Namespaces help .NET programmers overcome naming conflicts for classes and methods. For instance, you cannot have two classes with the same name in the same namespace because it would confuse the .NET runtime and developers. Instead, your class names are unique inside your namespace.

You declare a namespace at the top of your code using the keyword `namespace`. Alternatively, you can set the default namespace inside your project properties. In this way, you do not have to see the outer namespace definition inside each code file. A common practice for defining namespaces includes using your company name followed by the application being written and then perhaps the library to which the code belongs. For example, you might define the namespace grouping for the `Employee` class as follows.

C#

```
namespace MyApplication.UserLibrary
{
  public class Employee
  {
  }
}
```

VB

```
Namespace MyApplication.UserLibrary

  Public Class Employee

  End Class

End Namespace
```

You do not have to add this namespace information at the top of every code file in your project. This can become redundant and is error prone because a developer might forget to include the namespace definition. As an alternative, you can set the root namespace for your entire project using the project properties window. (Right-click the project file and choose Properties.) Figure 3.1 shows an example. This is a similar experience in both C# and VB. Note that you can define a root namespace here and still add additional namespace groupings in your code as necessary. Of course, those additional namespace definitions fall inside the root namespace.

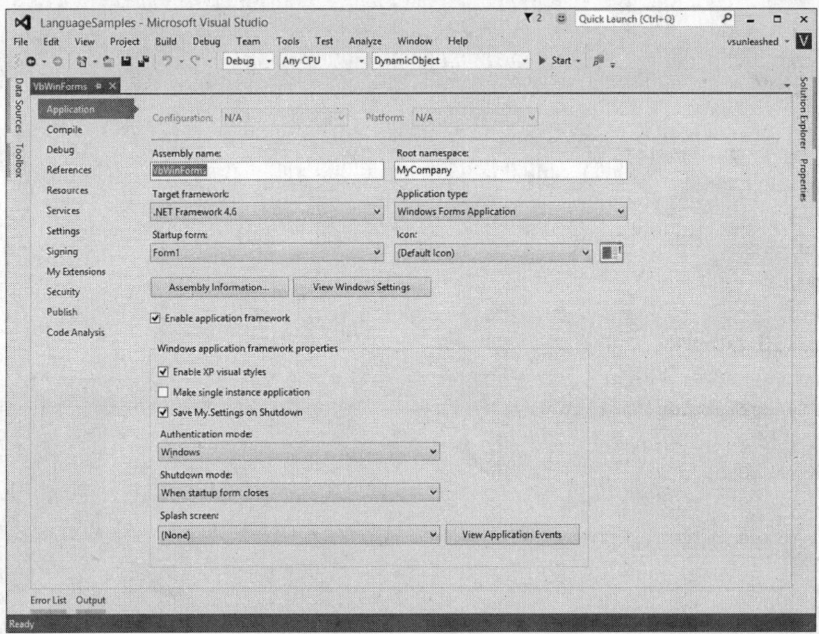

FIGURE 3.1 Use the application properties to set the root namespace at the project level.

You access code inside a namespace by using the fully qualified definition of the namespace. For example, the .NET root namespace is `System`. If you were to access the `String` class, you would do so by using `System.String`. This is true for your code, too. To access the `GetVacationUsed` method, you might call out as follows.

```
MyCompany.MyApplication.UserLibrary.Employee emp =
  new MyCompany.MyApplication.UserLibrary.Employee();
short usedVaca = emp.GetVacationUsed();
```

As you can see, accessing code using the fully qualified namespace can be cumbersome in terms of typing and reading your code. Thankfully, you can import (with the `using` statement in C#) a namespace inside your code. This frees you from having to fully qualify each type you use. Instead, the compiler resolves class names based on your imported namespaces. Of course, the namespaces themselves are still required to prevent ambiguity in the compiler. Importing namespaces also help trim IntelliSense to those imported libraries.

In most cases, you do not get conflicts with imported namespaces. Type names are typically different enough in a given library that they do not overlap. If names do overlap, you can add qualification to eliminate the conflict.

You import namespaces using the `using` statement (C#) or `Imports` (VB) keyword. For example, the following shows namespaces imported into a class file for a Windows Forms application. The code includes the `import` statements for referencing the `Employee` class library.

C#

```
using System;
using System.Collections.Generic;
using System.ComponentModel;
using System.Data;
using System.Drawing;
using System.Linq;
using System.Text;
using System.Threading.Tasks;
using System.Windows.Forms;
using MyCompany.MyApplication.UserLibrary;

namespace TestHarnessCSharp
{
  public partial class Form1 : Form
  {
    public Form1()
    {
      InitializeComponent();
    }

    private void Form1_Load(object sender, EventArgs e)
    {
      Employee emp = new Employee();
      //do work
    }
  }
}
```

VB

```
Imports MyCompany.MyApplication.UserLibrary

Public Class Form1
```

```
    Private Sub Form1_Load(sender As Object, e As EventArgs) _
        Handles MyBase.Load

        Dim emp As New Employee()

        'do work ...

    End Sub

End Class
```

Notice in the preceding example that the C# code has a number of additional `using` (or `imports`) statements at the top of the file. This is because VB files automatically import many of the default namespaces in .NET. The latest version of the IDE indicates which `using` statements are not necessary by fading their color. The IDE also provides a quick action to remove these if you want. Figure 3.2 shows an example.

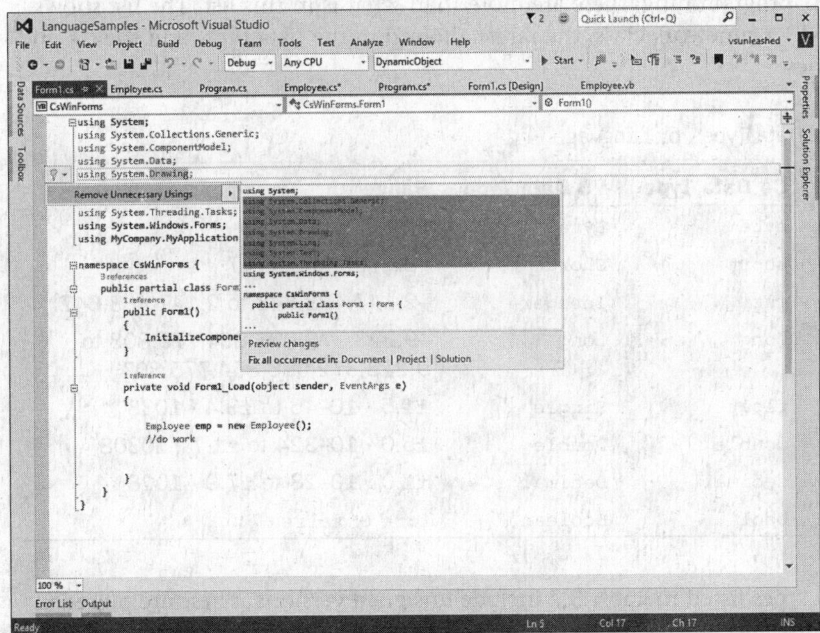

FIGURE 3.2 You can easily eliminate unnecessary `using` statements in your code.

Types, Variables, and Constants

All classes, structures, and interfaces you create in .NET are considered types. That is, they define a specific type of data. The underlying .NET Framework Base Class Library also provides strong types. In fact, the .NET languages of both C# and VB are based on strongly typed objects. This means when you define a variable you create an instance of a strongly typed class. The .NET runtime can then rely on this type information for handling casting, comparisons, and other rules.

Data Types

A number of built-in types (classes) are used for common programming needs. These built-in types are referred to as data types and represent things such as a string of characters or a numeric value. You work with these data types like you would any structure or class. You can declare a variable of a certain type, create a new instance, or execute a method off of the type.

Most of the simple data types you use are value types (structures). There are a couple simple data types that are reference types (classes). These are string (`System.String`) and object (`System.Object`). Recall that value types store data (and copies of data) and that reference types instances store a reference to underlying data: this is important in terms of performance (cost of duplication with value types instances and cost of garbage collections induced by the reference type instances). Table 3.2 lists many of the common value types used in .NET programming; there are more than what is in this list. The list shows the underlying .NET Framework class, the range allowed in the data type, and the C# and VB data type names.

TABLE 3.2 Value Data Types by Language

.NET Framework	C# Data Type	VB Data Type	Range
`System.Byte`	`byte`	`Byte`	0 to 255
`System.Int16`	`short`	`Short`	–32,768 to 32,767
`System.Int32`	`int`	`Integer`	–2,147,483,648 to 2,147,483,647
`System.Int64`	`long`	`Long`	–9,223,372,036,854,775,808 to 9,223,372,036,854,775,807
`System.Single`	`float`	`Single`	±1.5 · 10–45 to ±3.4 · 1038
`System.Double`	`double`	`Double`	±5.0 · 10–324 to ±1.7 · 10308
`System.Decimal`	`decimal`	`Decimal`	±1.0 · 10–28 to ±7.9 · 1028
`System.Boolean`	`bool`	`Boolean`	`true` or `false`

Many of the data types listed in Table 3.2 include unsigned versions. These are preceded with a *u* (as in ulong and uint). The `System.Byte` data type is the exception. It is unsigned. The signed version is called `sbyte`. Signed values include both the negative and the positive numbers in their range. Unsigned value types start at zero and include only positive numeric values.

Declaring Variables

When you declare a variable using a simple type, you typically want to declare the variable using the type that represents the lowest possible range for your situation. For example, if you were to define a variable to hold the month value, you might use

System.Byte. If you were to define the year, you might use System.Int16. In this way, the lowest possible memory overhead is used for these types.

You declare a variable in C# by preceding the name of the variable with its type. In Visual, you use the Dim statement. The type then comes after the variable's name. The following code shows an example of declaring variables in each language.

C#

```
byte month;
short year;
float paycheckAmount;
```

VB

```
Dim month As Byte
Dim year As Short
Dim paycheckAmount As Single
```

Of course, you can also define variables of other (more complex) types in the .NET Framework or types defined in your own class libraries. When you declare a variable, you can also assign it a default value or instantiate a new instance. The following shows an example.

C#

```
byte month = 1;
short year = 2015;
float paycheckAmount = 0;
string name = "test";
Employee emp = new Employee();
```

VB

```
Dim month As Byte = 1
Dim year As Short = 2015
Dim paycheckAmount As Single = 0
Dim name As String = "test"
Dim emp As Employee = New Employee()
```

Type Conversion

Again, both VB and C# are strongly typed languages. Therefore, the variables you declare cannot be reused by assigning different type values. Rather, they must always represent the underlying type to which they were declared or a type deriving from the variable type. This can be problematic. Sometimes, for instance, you have an integer that you need to pass to a method that only accepts a string. Or you need to parse a string value into an integer for a calculation. These are all instances in which you need to convert one type to another.

There are two conversions that you can make: implicit and explicit. An implicit conversion happens when you pass a smaller value type into a larger type that can contain the smaller value. In this case, if no data is lost, the conversion is allowed. For example, you can pass a short into a long without issue. However, passing a float (or double) into an integer might result in data loss and is thus not allowed as an implicit conversion; you need to explicitly convert. For example, the following code converts an integer value to a double. This code does not throw a type conversion error. Rather, it converts using implicit conversion.

C#

```
int intVal = 100;
double doubleVal = intVal;
```

VB

```
Dim intVal As Integer = 100
Dim doubleVal As Double = intVal
```

If there is a chance that the conversion results in data loss, you must explicitly indicate your intention to convert types. This is called casting. You can also cast values that might otherwise be implicitly converted. In fact, this often makes your code more readable.

In C#, you cast a variable to another type by putting the type to which you are casting in parentheses in front of the type (or value) being cast, as in the following.

C#

```
double doubleVal = 12.345;
int intVal = (int)doubleVal;
```

In Visual Basic, you cast a variable to another type using conversion keywords. These keywords have a *C* (for cast) in front of them followed by the type to which you are casting. For example, you can cast to an integer using `CInt`, a double using `CDbl`, or a string using `CStr`. The following shows an example.

VB

```
Dim doubleVal As Double = 12.345
Dim intVal As Integer = CInt(doubleVal)
```

There are times when you have a string value and need to convert it into a numeric. This cast is not allowed. However, most of the numeric types include the method `Parse` that enables you to parse a string into a numeric value. There is also `TryParse`, which returns a Boolean indicating whether the parse will work. It is recommended to use the latter for performance sake because with `Parse`, an exception is thrown if the parsing fails. The following code shows an example.

C#

```
string stringVal = "1234";
int intVal;
intVal = int.Parse(stringVal);
```

VB

```
Dim stringVal As String = "1234"
Dim intVal As Integer
intVal = Integer.Parse(stringVal)
```

The framework also includes the `Convert` class, which enables you to convert one type to almost any other (including strings). This class is available to both Visual Basic and C# programmers.

Defining Constants

You might need to define values in your application that will not (and cannot) change during the execution of the application. In this case, you need to declare a constant. A constant in .NET is said to be an immutable value. That is, a constant cannot change values. You declare a constant in your code (typically at the class level) using the keyword `const`. Like a field, a constant can be private or public. The following shows an example.

C#

```
private const int CompanyTaxNumber = 123456;
```

VB

```
Private Const CompanyTaxNumber As Integer = 123456
```

Understanding Operators

Operators are indicators in your code that express an operation to perform. An operator might be an assignment from one variable to another, a comparison between two values, or a mathematical calculation among values. There are many operators available to .NET programmers. We do not cover them all here, but many of the more common operators are discussed in the following sections.

Assignment

Assignment operators are used to assign one variable or value to another. The most simple example is the equal (`=`) operator. This simply assigns the value on the right of the operator to the variable on the left side of the assignment (as in `x = y`). Other operators enable you to do assignment with addition (`+=`), assignment with subtraction (`-=`), assignment with multiplication (`*=`), and assignment of a string value with concatenation (`&=`). There are also assignment operators for division, arithmetic shifting, and more. The following shows a few assignment code examples.

C#

```
public double CalculatePaycheck(double gross, double commission,
  double deductions)
{
  double paycheck = gross;  //define paycheck as gross pay
  paycheck += commission;   //add commission
  paycheck -= deductions;   //subtract deductions

  return paycheck;
}
```

VB

```
Public Function CalculatePaycheck(ByVal gross As Double, _
  ByVal commission As Double, ByVal deductions As Double)

  Dim paycheck As Double = gross  'define paycheck as gross pay
  paycheck += commission          'add commission
  paycheck -= deductions          'subtract deductions

  Return paycheck
End Function
```

Arithmetic

The arithmetic operations enable you to perform calculations on variables and using values. For example, you can use the multiplication operator (`*`) to multiply two numbers (`x * y`). All the operators you expect are available, such as addition (`+`), subtraction (`-`), division to return an integer (\), division to return a floating point (/), multiplication (`*`), and dividing for remainder (`mod` in VB, `%` in C#). There are other less common operators, too.

You typically use assignment with arithmetic operators, as in `x = y * z`. However, you can use the value of the calculation when making decisions in your code (without first assigning it to a variable); there's more on this in the coming sections. As an example of basic arithmetic in code with assignment, the following code shows how you might calculate an employee's accrued vacation days at any given point in the year. (The `AccrualRate` is either a constant or a set based on the number of days of vacation an employee has.)

C#

```
double accruedVacation = DateTime.Today.DayOfYear * AccrualRate;
```

VB

```
Dim accruedVacation as Double = DateTime.Today.DayOfYear * AccrualRate
```

Comparison

The comparison operators enable you to determine whether values are equal to, greater than, or less than one another. You typically use these operators comparing two variables, values, or expressions. The results of the comparison indicate whether or not (`true` or `false`) the comparison is valid (as in is `x > y`). The comparison operators include less than (`<`), less than or equal to (`<=`), greater than (`>`), greater than or equal to (`>=`), equal (`=` in VB and `==` in C#), and does not equal (`<>` in VB and `!=` in C#). The following shows an example of assigning a variable of type Boolean to a comparison result.

C#

```
bool check = accruedVacation > vacationTakenToDate;
```

VB

```
Dim check As Boolean = accruedVacation > vacationTakenToDate
```

You can also do type comparison to check whether two objects point to the same reference (or not). In C#, this type of comparison is still done with the equal (`==`) and not equal (`!=`) operators. In Visual Basic, you use the keywords `Is` and `IsNot`, as in `check = Employee1 Is Employee2`.

NULL COMPARISON

See the earlier section "Null-Conditional Operators" under "What's New in C# 6.0 and VB 14" to see how you can now use `?.` to check for nulls.

Concatenation

The concatenation operations enable you to combine string values. In Visual Basic, the concatenation operator is an ampersand (`&`) sign used with two string variables or values. In C#, the plus (`+`) sign is used. Note that for performance sake, it is recommended to call `string.Format` or use a `StringBuilder` if you need to create large strings. The following shows an example.

C#

```
string fullName = firstName + " " + lastName;
```

VB

```
Dim fullName as String = firstName & " " & lastName
```

Logical and Conditional

The logical and conditional operators enable you to combine comparisons in different ways to help make decisions in your code. (See the next section for even more details.) For example, you might combine two comparisons to make sure they are both `true`. Alternatively, you might need to determine if at least one of the two comparisons is `true`.

You can do this and more with the logical operators. Table 3.3 lists many of the logical operators. (For code examples, see the next section.)

TABLE 3.3 Logical and Conditional Comparison Operators

Purpose	**C#**	**VB**	**Pseudo Code Example**
Join two Boolean expressions and get the result, as in the result is `true` if both this and that are `true`. Note that both operands are evaluated.	`&`	`And`	VB: `check = (x>Y) And (x>0)` C#: `check = (x>Y) & (x>0)`
Negate a Boolean value or expression, as in the results equal the opposite of an evaluation.	`!`	`Not`	VB: `check = Not someVal` C#: `check = !someVal`
Choose between one or another values, as in the result is `true` if this or that is `true`. Note that both operands are evaluated.	`|`	`Or`	VB: `check = (x>y) Or (x>0)` C#: `check = (x>y) | (x>0)`
Two values must evaluate to opposite values, as in the result is `true` if this is `true` and that is `false`.	`^`	`Xor`	VB: `check = True Xor False` C#: `check = true ^ false`
A short-circuited version of `And` in which, if the first condition does not pass evaluation, the second condition is not executed.	`&&`	`AndAlso`	VB: `check = (x>Y) AndAlso (x>0)` C#: `check = (x>Y) && (x>0)`
A short-circuited version of `Or` in which, if the first condition does not pass evaluation, the second condition is not executed.	`||`	`OrElse`	VB: `check = (x>y) OrElse (x>0)` C#: `check = (x>y) || (x>0)`

Making Decisions and Branching Code

You can use the operators discussed previously to test for specific conditions in your code. These tests are then evaluated so you can make a decision on what code to execute or where to branch off in your application. There are three primary decision structures in .NET programming: `If...Then...Else`, `Select...Case`, and `Try...Catch...Finally` (as covered in the "Exception Handling" section later in this chapter).

`If...Then...Else`

You can use the `If` syntax in your code to test one or more conditions. Based on the results of your test, you might decide to execute one set of code if the condition proves `true` and another set of code if the condition proves `false`. You can also get into more complex scenarios by nesting `If` statements and using the logical operators discussed in the prior section.

In Visual Basic, you use the explicit `If...Then` statements nested with `End If`. In C#, you put your `if` conditions inside parentheses and the statements nested inside brackets. For example, the following shows code to determine whether an employee can get her vacation request approved. In this code, there is a nested `if` statement and an example of combining two conditions with and.

C#

```
public bool CanApproveVacationRequest(int daysRequested, int daysTaken,
  int daysAllowed, int daysAccruedToDate)
{
  //rule: employee can take vacation if it is accrued and not used
  if ((daysRequested < daysAllowed) && (daysTaken < daysAllowed))
  {
    if ((daysTaken + daysRequested) < daysAccruedToDate)
    {
      return true;
    } else {
      return false;
    }
  } else {
    return false;
  }
}
```

VB

```
Public Function CanApproveVacationRequest(ByVal daysRequested As Integer,
  ByVal daysTaken As Integer, ByVal daysAllowed As Integer,
  ByVal daysAccruedToDate As Integer) As Boolean

  'rule: employee can take vacation if it is accrued and not used
  If daysRequested < daysAllowed And daysTaken < daysAllowed Then
    If (daysTaken + daysRequested) < daysAccruedToDate Then
      Return True
    Else
      Return False
    End If
  Else
    Return False
  End If
End Function
```

Note that in Visual Basic if you have a single line that executes based on an `if` condition you can write that as a single line of code, as in `If x > 500 Then doSomething`. In C#, if you have a single line that executes, you can eliminate the need for the braces, and the statement following the `if` condition is executed based on the condition's evaluation.

Select...Case (Switch)

The `Select...Case` (`switch` in C#) code construct enables you to evaluate a single statement for a value. Based on this condition, you then can execute blocks of code depending on the value.

In C#, you define the condition inside parentheses following the keyword `switch`. You then define each case block with the keyword `case`, the value you are checking on, and a colon. You must then add a `break` statement at the end of the `case` to indicate the end of the `case`. You can use the `default` keyword to execute code if no case was realized. The following code shows an example.

C#

```
private void CalculateAdditionalCompensation()
{
  switch (this.Status)
  {
    case EmploymentStatus.Contract:
      //code for contract employees
      break;
    case EmploymentStatus.Hourly:
      //code for hourly employees
      break;
    case EmploymentStatus.Salaried:
      //code for salaried employees
      break;
    case EmploymentStatus.SalariedCommissioned:
      //code for commissioned employees
      break;
    case EmploymentStatus.Other:
      //code for other employees
      break;
    default:
      //code that runs if bad status was set
      break;
  }
}
```

In Visual Basic, you write case `Select...Case` statements using the keyword `Select` followed by `Case` followed by the condition. Each condition is then preceded with `Case`. You can use `Case Else` to run code when no other condition value evaluates. Here is a code example.

VB

```
Private Sub CalculateAdditionalCompensation()

  Select Case Me.Status
    Case EmploymentStatus.Contract
```

```
    'code for contract employees

  Case EmploymentStatus.Hourly
    'code for hourly employees

  Case EmploymentStatus.Salaried
    'code for salaried employees

  Case EmploymentStatus.SalariedCommissioned
    'code for commissioned employees

  Case EmploymentStatus.Other
    'code for other employees

  Case Else
    'code that runs if bad status was set

 End Select

End Sub
```

Looping

There are many times in your code when you need to execute a set of statements more than once. In these cases, you need to create a loop. The most common scenarios are looping through code a set number of times, looping until a condition becomes `true` or `false`, or looping through code once per element in a collection of objects. (See the section "Working with Groups of Items" later in this chapter.)

`For...Next`

The `For...Next` construct enables you to execute a block of code statements a set number of times. This is accomplished through a counter that increments a set number of steps each time the loop executes. After the counter has reached a max value, the looping completes.

In C#, you write a `for` statement inside parentheses. The `for` statement has three parts: counter declaration, condition for the counter, and counting step. Each part is separated by a semicolon. The following code shows an example of executing a code block once for each employee's direct report.

C#

```
for (int i = 0; i < numDirectReports; i++)
{
  //update employee based on num of direct report
}
```

In Visual Basic, your For statement is a little more readable. You indicate the counter, the initial value, and the To value. Optionally, you can add the Step keyword to indicate how many times you want to increment the counter each time through the loop. Here is a code example:

VB

```
For i As Integer = 1 To numDirectReports
  'update employee based on num of direct reports
Next
```

For...Each (Iterators)

Like For...Next, the For...Each construct enables you to execute a group of statements. However, For...Each executes once for each element in a group of elements (or a collection). For instance, if you add a block of code to the Employee class that needs to execute once for each DirectReport, you could do so using the For...Next (as shown previously) and then execute based on the count of DirectReports. However, using For...Each allows you to iterate over each object in a collection. As you do, you get a reference to the given object that you can use in your code. This makes coding a little easier to write and to understand.

You implement For...Each similar to For...Next in both C# and Visual Basic. The following shows code that executes once for each Employee instance inside the collection DirectReports.

C#

```
foreach (Employee emp in DirectReports)
{
  //execute code based on each direct report
  //  using the item as in emp.Name
}
```

VB

```
For Each emp As Employee In DirectReports
  'execute code based on each direct report
  '  using the item as in emp.Name
Next
```

Do...While/Until

Sometimes you need to repeat a block of code as many times as required until a condition evaluates to true or false. You might be looking for a specific value or might be using a counter that increments based on logic (instead of standard steps). In these cases, you can use a Do...While or a While loop. A Do...While loop executes once before the condition is evaluated to determine whether it should execute a second time. A While loop evaluates the condition first and then only executes if the condition evaluates to true.

In C#, you can create Do...While loops using the do keyword followed by your block of code in braces. The while statement is written at the end of the code block indicating that the statements are executed once before looping. (Use a while loop to evaluate a condition before looping.) The following shows an example.

C#

```
do
{
  //get next project and calculate commission
  projectCommission = GetNextProjectCommision(empId);
  calculatedCommission += projectCommission;
  if (projectCommission == 0)
  break;
} while (calculatedCommission < MaxMonthlyCommission);
```

Notice in this code the use of the break keyword. This indicates that the code should break out of the Do...While loop. You can also use the continue keyword to skip remaining code in your code block and jump right to the while statement to force a condition evaluation (and possible another loop).

In Visual Basic, you can define the While (or until) statement at the top or bottom of the loop. If defined at the top, your statement is evaluated before the loop executes once. If at the bottom, the loop executes at least once before the statement is evaluated. The While keyword indicates that you want to loop while a condition is true (until it becomes false). The Until keyword allows you to loop until a condition evaluates to true (while it is false). The following shows an example.

VB

```
Do
  'get next project and calculate commission
  projectCommission = GetNextProjectCommision(empId)
  calculatedCommission += projectCommission
  If projectCommission = 0 Then Exit Do
Loop While calculatedCommission < MaxMonthlyCommission
```

As mentioned before, there is also the basic While loop (without do). This simply loops a block of code while a condition evaluates to true. Also, like all looping constructs, you can nest Do...While loops to handle more complex situations.

Working with Groups of Items

A common scenario in computer programming is managing a group of similar items. For example, you might need to work with a set of values, such as ZIP Codes to which a sales representative is assigned. Alternatively, you might need to work with a group of objects such as the paychecks an employee has received in a given year. When you need to work with a group of elements, you can do so using an array or a collection class. The former is great for working with a set sequential list of items of the same type. The latter is more applicable for managing a variable-sized group of objects.

Arrays

An array is a group of items of the same type (either value or reference types). For instance, you might create an array that contains all integer values or all string values. You also have to define the number of elements contained in your array when you first initialize it. There are ways to expand or contract this size, but these typically involve copying the array into another array. If you need the flexibility of adding and removing items in a group, you want to use a collection class and not an array.

When you define an array's size, you need to know that they are zero-based arrays. That is, the first element in the array is item zero. Each item is contiguous and sequential. This enables you to set and access items quickly using the items index.

NOTE

When dimensioning the size of array in C# you get the actual number of items indicated in the definition. Therefore, the declaration `short[] myArray = new short[6]` yields six items in the array (items 0–5). In Visual Basic, however, a similar call to `Dim myArray(6) As Short` yields seven items in the array (items 0–6).

The typical array you create is one dimensional, meaning that it contains a single group of indexed items. You declare this type of an array by indicating the number of elements in the array either on the declaration of the variable or before the array's first use. There are a few valid syntaxes for defining an array. The standard way in C# is to use the `new` keyword to set the size of the array. In Visual Basic, you can set the size of the array without using the keyword `new`. The following shows an example.

C#

```
short[] salesRegionCodes = new short[numRegions];
```

VB

```
Dim salesRegionCodes(numRegions) As Short
```

You access an array through its index value. Array objects inherit for the `System.Array` class. This gives you a number of properties and methods you can use, including getting the total number of elements in all dimensions of an array (`Length`) and getting the upper-bound value for a single dimension (`GetUpperBound`). The following code shows an example of using this last method and accessing an array through its index.

C#

```
for (int i = 0; i < salesRegionCodes.GetUpperBound(0); i++)
{
```

```
  short code = salesRegionCodes[i];
  //additional processing ...
}
```

VB

```
For i = 0 To salesRegionCodes.GetUpperBound(0)

  Dim code As Short = salesRegionCodes(i)
  'additional processing ...
Next
```

You can also initialize the values in an array inside the declaration statement. In this case, the number of elements you define sets the size of the array. The following is an example.

C#

```
double[] salesFigures = new double[] {12345.98, 236789.86, 67854.12};
```

VB

```
Dim salesFigures() As Double = {12345.98, 236789.86, 67854.12}
```

You can define arrays that have more than a single dimension (up to 32). A common scenario is a two-dimensional array in which one dimension is considered rows and the other columns. You can use the `Rank` property to determine the number of dimensions in an array.

For an example of a multidimensional array, consider one that contains sales figures for each sales representative (rows) in each region (columns). You might define this array as follows.

C#

```
double[,] salesByRegion = new double[6, 5];
```

VB

```
Dim salesByRegion(6, 5) As Double
```

Note that an array can also contain other arrays. These type of arrays are called jagged arrays (or arrays of arrays). They are considered jagged because each element in the array might contain an array of different size and dimension; therefore, there might be no real uniformity to the array.

Collection Classes and Generics

A collection class can give you more flexibility when working with objects. For example, you can have objects of different types in a single collection; collections can be of varying lengths; and you can easily add and remove items in a collection.

The standard collection classes are defined inside the `System.Collections` namespace. The classes in this namespace include a base class for creating your own, custom collections (`CollectionBase`) and more specific collections such as `ArrayList`, `Stack`, `SortedList`, `Queue`, and `HashTable`.

For example, you might create a simple, dynamic `ArrayList` to contain a set of sales figures. The following code shows how you can create a new `ArrayList`, add items to it, and loop through those items.

C#

```
ArrayList salesFigures = new ArrayList();

salesFigures.Add(12345.67);
salesFigures.Add(3424.97);
salesFigures.Add("None");

for (int i = 0; i < salesFigures.Count; i++)
{
  object figure = salesFigures[i];
  //process figures ...
}
```

VB

```
Dim salesFigures As New ArrayList()

salesFigures.Add(12345.67)
salesFigures.Add(3424.97)
salesFigures.Add("None")

For i As Integer = 0 To salesFigures.Count - 1
 Dim figure As Object = salesFigures(i)
 'process sales figure data ...
Next
```

Of course, many additional properties and methods are available to you through the `ArrayList` and related collection classes. You should explore these for your specific scenarios.

Notice in the preceding code that the collection class has two types of objects inside it: double and string. This can be problematic if you need to rely on a collection of objects all being of the same type. For example, you might want all your sales figures to be of type `double`; or you might want a collection of only `Employee` objects. In these cases, you need a strongly typed collection class. You can create these by coding your own, custom collection classes (inheriting from `CollectionBase` and implementing the interfaces specific to your needs). However, .NET also provides a set of classes called generics that allow for strongly typed groups of objects.

Generic collections can be found inside the `System.Collections.Generic` namespace. A generic collection class enables you to define the type that the class contains when you initialize it. This then restricts what types the class can contain. You can rely on this information within your code.

You define a generic list in C# using angle brackets (`<>`) with the type defined inside those brackets. In Visual Basic, you define the generic type inside parenthesis using the `Of` keyword. For example, the following defines a simple, generic list of items that can only include values of type double.

C#

```
List<double> salesFigures = new List<double>();
```

VB

```
Dim salesFigures As New List(Of Double)
```

There are many generic collection classes available to you, including `Dictionary`, `HashSet`, `LinkedList`, `List`, `Queue`, `SortedList`, `Stack`, and more. You can also write your own generic collection classes.

Tuple

The `System.Tuple` class enables you to create a set, ordered list of items and work with that list. After you've created the list, you cannot change it. This makes for easy storage (and access) of sequential items.

For example, if you wanted to create a `Tuple` to store the month names in the first quarter, you could do so using the static member `Tuple.Create`. Each item you want to add to the list you add inside parentheses (and separated by commas). You can then access the items in your `Tuple` using the `Item1`, `Item2`, `Item3` syntax. Note that the `Tuple` only exposes item properties for the number of items that exist inside the group. The following code shows an example.

C#

```
var q1Months = Tuple.Create("Jan", "Feb", "Mar");
string month1 = q1Months.Item1;
```

VB

```
Dim q1Months = Tuple.Create("Jan", "Feb", "Mar")
Dim month1 As String = q1Months.Item1
```

The `Tuple` class is based on generics. You define the type of object you enable for each member in the list. The `Create` method shown infers this type for you. However, you might want to be explicit. In this case, you can declare your types using the constructor as follows.

C#

```
Tuple<int, string, int, string, int, string> q1MonthNumAndName =
        Tuple.Create(1, "Jan", 2, "Feb", 3, "Mar");
```

VB

```
Dim q1MonthNumAndName As Tuple(Of Integer, String, Integer, String,
                                Integer, String) =
  Tuple.Create(1, "Jan", 2, "Feb", 3, "Mar")
```

Programming with Attributes

Sometimes you need to provide metadata about the capabilities of your code. This metadata is meant to tell other code that is inspecting your code (through reflection) specific things about what the code might do. This includes information for the .NET runtime, such as how you want your code compiled. There are many attributes available in the .NET Framework. You can also create your own, custom attributes to be applied to your code. In this case, you can write code to examine the metadata about your own application.

Declarative attributes can be applied to classes, properties, methods, parameters, and other elements inside your code. You can apply a single attribute or multiple attributes to an application. Some attributes also might take parameters to indicate additional information to the attribute code.

Note that, by convention, all attributes end with the word `Attribute` in their names, such as `SerializableAttribute`. You typically leave the word *attribute* off your declaration, however, because it is not required.

In C#, attributes are placed on code using square brackets (`[]`). For example, you can use the `ConditionalAttribute` to indicate to the compiler which code should be compiled based on environment variables or command-line options. You would apply this attribute to your code as shown.

C#

```
[System.Diagnostics.Conditional("DEBUG")]
public void EmployeeCalculationsTestMethod()
{
  //code that compiles in the debug version of the assembly
}
```

In Visual Basic, you decorate your code elements with an attribute by putting the attribute in angle brackets (`<>`) in front of the code element, as follows.

VB

```
<Conditional("DEBUG")> Public Sub EmployeeCalculationsTestMethod()
  'code that compiles in the debug version of the assembly
End Sub
```

Exception Handling

A lot of programming time is spent eliminating exceptions from our code. However, you can't always eliminate all scenarios that might cause an exception. In these cases, you need a way to anticipate the exception and then, if possible, handle the exception in your code. There is where the `Try...Catch...Finally` construct comes into play.

You put a `Try` statement around a block of code you expect might cause an exception. You typically do so if you intend to handle the error. If you are not intending to handle the error, you can let the error bubble up to the calling code. Of course, you need to have an outer-error handler (or manager) inside your outer code to prevent errors from bubbling up to users in nasty ways.

When an exception actually occurs inside your `Try` block, execution is immediately passed to a `Catch` block. This might be a general catch of all errors or a catch meant for a specific exception type. The code inside the `catch` block is then meant to handle the error. Handling an error might include logging the error, sending it to a message system, or actually trying something different (or trying again using a `jump` statement) as the result of the error.

The following shows a basic example. Inside the `Try` block is a calculation that does division. This `Try` block has the possibility of raising an exception in the case where the division is done by zero. This condition raises the specific exception `DivideByZeroException`. There is a `Catch` block that consumes this (and only this) type of exception. You can add code to the `Catch` block to either eat the exception (do nothing) or process it somehow. Also, if you want to rethrow the exception after handling it, you can do that, too.

C#

```
try
{
  averageSales = salesToDate / avgRate;
}
catch (System.DivideByZeroException e)
{
  //handle the exception ...
  // if rethrowing use: throw;
}
```

VB

```
Try
  averageSales = salesToDate / avgRate

Catch ex As System.DivideByZeroException
  'handle the exception ...
  ' if rethrowing use: Throw
End Try
```

You can have multiple `Catch` blocks that are both specific and generic. Note that if no exception type is found in a `Catch` block, the exception is actually not handled but is bubbled up to the calling code (or to the runtime).

Note that you can also rethrow the error from your `Catch` block using the `Throw` keyword. If you do not rethrow the exception, the runtime assumes you have handled the error and moves on. You can also use throw anywhere in your application where you want to raise an exception.

There is also a `Finally` block that you can write. This bit of code goes after your `Catch` blocks and runs regardless of whether an exception is raised. That is, it will always run after the code execution path exits the try block, either as a normal exit, after an exception is raised, or a call has been made to return. In all cases, the `Finally` block will execute. It is useful for cleaning up any resources that might have been allocated inside the `Try` block.

EXCEPTION FILTERING

Both Visual Basic 14 and C# 6.0 now allow exception filtering during your catch blocks. This allows you to interrogate properties of the exception and only enter the `catch` block if a condition is met. You implement this approach using an `if` statement at the end of your `catch`.

Creating and Raising Events

There is not much functionality you can build using the .NET languages without events. Events enable one piece of code to notify another bit of code that something has just happened. Code that raises events is said to publish an event, and code that receives the event notice is said to subscribe to events. A simple example is when you write a user interface for the Web or Windows. In these cases, you are consistently adding code that subscribes to events published by the UI, such as a user clicking a button control. Of course, an event may have more than a single subscriber, and subscribers may subscribe to multiple events.

Define an Event

When you define an event you need to determine whether you need to pass custom data to the subscribers. This custom data is referred to as event arguments (or args). If you do not need to pass custom data, you simply declare the event using the keyword event and the existing delegate `EventHandler`. For example, if you were to define a simple event that you would raise when an `employee` class is updated, you might define that event as follows.

C#

```
public event EventHandler EmployeeUpdatedEvent;
```

VB

```
Public Event EmployeeUpdatedEvent As EventHandler
```

By declaring the event, you have effectively published it. Subscribers who have a reference to your class can then set up a subscription to your event. You then need to raise the event in the same class where you published it. This notifies the subscribers that the event has fired.

It is slightly more complicated to define events where you need to pass custom data. In this case, you must first create a custom class to maintain your event data. This class must inherit from the `EventArgs` base class. For example, you might create a custom event arguments class to contain the employee ID for the employee-updated event. In this case, your custom class contains a property to hold the `Id` value and a constructor for passing in this value, as in the following code.

C#

```
public class EmployeeUpdatedEventArgs : EventArgs
{
  public EmployeeUpdatedEventArgs(string id)
  {
    _id = id;
  }

  private string _id;
  public string EmployeeId
  {
    get { return _id; }
  }
}
```

VB

```
Public Class EmployeeUpdatedEventArgs
  Inherits EventArgs

  Public Sub New(ByVal id As String)
    _id = id
  End Sub

  Private _id As String
  Public ReadOnly Property EmployeeId() As String
    Get
      Return _id
    End Get
  End Property

End Class
```

When you use a custom event argument, you need to declare your event to use the custom event argument class. You can do so using the version of the `EventHandler` class that is defined as generic. In this case, you indicate the class that contains the argument as part of the generic definition of `EventHandler`. This class also automatically contains the sender argument (typically a copy of the object publishing the event). The following shows an example of defining this custom event handler.

C#

```
public event EventHandler<EmployeeUpdatedEventArgs> EmployeeUpdatedCustomEvent;
```

VB

```
Public Event EmployeeUpdatedCustomEvent As _
  EventHandler(Of EmployeeUpdatedEventArgs)
```

Raise an Event

You raise the event in the same class where the event is defined. An event is raised as the result of some action. In the case of the example, the action in the employee class has been updated. To raise the event, you simply call it in the right spot and pass the appropriate parameters. In the case of the employee-updated custom event, you pass an instance of the `employee` class as the sender and then the employee `Id` as part of an instance of the `EmployeeUpdatedEventArgs`, as shown here.

C#

```
public void UpdateEmployee()
{
  //do work to update employee ...

  //raise event to notify subscribers of the update
  EmployeeUpdatedCustomEvent(this, new EmployeeUpdatedEventArgs(this.Id));
}
```

VB

```
Public Sub UpdateEmployee()
  'do work to update employee ...

  'raise event to notify subscribers of update
  RaiseEvent EmployeeUpdatedCustomEvent(Me, _
    New EmployeeUpdatedEventArgs(Me.Id))
End Sub
```

Subscribe to and Handle an Event

The final step is to actually listen for (or subscribe to) the event. Here, you need to do two things. First, you must write a method that mimics the signature of the event. The content of this method is yours to write. It is called when the event fires. The following shows an example of a method (inside a class that subscribes to the `employee` class) that is called when the event fires. Notice how this method uses the custom event type and must therefore match that signature.

C#

```
private void OnEmployeeUpdate(object sender, EmployeeUpdatedEventArgs e)
{
  //do something in response to employee update
  string empId = e.EmployeeId;
}
```

VB

```
Private Sub OnEmployeeUpdate(ByVal sender As Object, _
  ByVal e As EmployeeUpdatedEventArgs)

  Dim empId As String = e.EmployeeId
  Console.WriteLine("Event Fired: id=" & empId)
End Sub
```

Second, you must register your event handler with the actual event. You do this by adding a pointer to the event using the `+=` (C#) or `AddHandler` (VB) syntax. You typically add your handlers inside the subscribing class's constructor or initialization code. The following shows code to connect the `OnEmployeeUpdate` handler to the `EmployeeUpdatedCustomEvent` event.

C#

```
Employee _emp = new Employee();
_emp.EmployeeUpdatedCustomEvent += this.OnEmployeeUpdate;
```

VB

```
AddHandler _emp.EmployeeUpdatedCustomEvent, AddressOf OnEmployeeUpdate
```

When the code is run, you undoubtedly access features of the class that fire the event (in this case, `Employee.UpdateEmployee`). When you hit a method that triggers the event, your subscribing code is called accordingly. When you don't need to listen to the event, you must remember to unsubscribe your handler from the event. If you forget to do so, the garbage collector might not be able to free the memory used by the listener object.

Language Features

Thus far, you've looked at the basics of programming with the .NET languages, including building objects and solving common coding issues with respect to looping, handling logic, and creating and consuming events. This section points out some additional elements that make the .NET languages special. Many of these items are not necessarily things you might use every day; however, they can provide you with additional skills when writing code and better understanding when reading it. The .NET language features covered here include the following:

- Local type inference (also called implicit typing)
- Object initializers
- Collection initializers
- Extension methods
- Anonymous types
- Lambda expressions
- Partial methods
- Language Integrated Query (LINQ)
- Friend assemblies
- XML language support
- Unused event arguments
- Automatically implemented properties
- Implicit line continuation in VB
- Work with dynamic language/objects
- Covariance and contravariance
- Intrinsic support for async operations
- Type equivalence support

Infer a Variable's Data Type Based on Assignment

In the later versions of Visual Basic and C# (2008 and later), you can define variables without explicitly setting their data type. And, when doing so, you can still get the benefits of strongly typed variables (compiler checking, memory allocation, and more). The compilers actually infer the data type you intend to use based on your code. This process is called local type inference or implicit typing.

For example, consider the following lines of code. Here you create a variable of type `String` and assign a value.

C#

```
string companyName = "Contoso";
```

VB

```
Dim companyName As String = "Contoso"
```

Now, let's look at the same line of code using type inference. You can see that you do not need the `string` portion of the declaration. Instead, the compiler is able to determine that you want a string and strongly types the variable for you. In C#, this is triggered by the keyword `var`. This should not be confused with the `var` statement in languages such as JavaScript. Variables defined as `var` are strongly typed. In Visual Basic, you still simply use the `Dim` statement but omit the data type.

C#

```
var companyName = "Contoso";
```

VB

```
Dim companyName = "Contoso"
```

These two lines of code are equivalent in all ways. Although in the second example no data type was declared, one is being declared by the compiler. This is not a return to a generalized data type such as `Variant` or `Object`. Nor does this represent late-binding of the variable. Rather, it is simply a smarter compiler that strongly types the variable by choosing a data type based on the code. You get all the benefits of early-bound variables while saving some keystrokes.

For example, take a look at Figure 3.3. This is the C# compiler in action. (The Visual Basic compiler does the same thing.) You can see that even at development time, the compiler has determined that this variable is of type `System.String`.

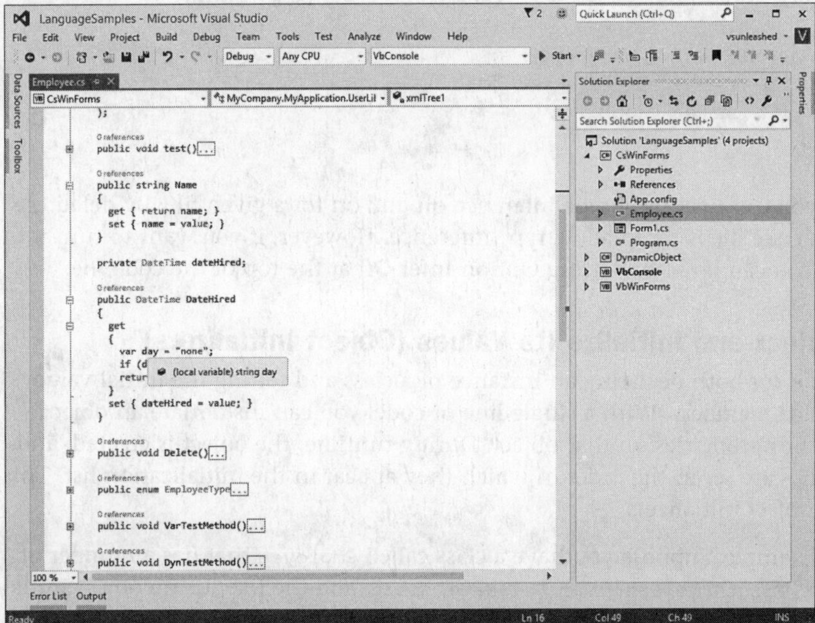

FIGURE 3.3 Type inference in action inside the IDE.

There are a few things for you to be aware of when using type inference. The first is that it requires your local variable to be assigned a value to do the compiler typing. This should not be a big deal because if your variable is not assigned, it is not used.

The second item you should consider is that type inference works only with local variables. It does not work with class-level variables (also called fields) or static variables. In these cases, using local type inference results in the compiler throwing an error in C#. In Visual Basic, you would get the same error provided that Option Strict is set to On. If you are not using Option Strict in your Visual Basic code, the variable is not strongly typed. Instead, the variable is assigned the generic `Object` data type.

Local type inference can be useful in other declaration scenarios as well. This includes defining arrays, creating variables during looping, defining a variable inside a `Using` statement, and defining a variable that contains the result of a function call. In each of these cases, the compiler can infer your data type based on the context of the code.

As another example, the following code creates a `Using` statement and infers the type of the variable `cnn` (as a `SqlConnection` object). Note that a `Using` block defines a block of code for which a given resource is being used. The use of a `Using` block guarantees that the runtime disposes of the used object (in this case, the database connection) when done.

C#

```
using (var cnn = new System.Data.SqlClient.SqlConnection()) {
  //code to work with the connection
}
```

VB

```
Using cnn = New System.Data.SqlClient.SqlConnection
  'code to work with the connection
End Using
```

In Visual Basic, you can turn local type inference off and on for a given file. By default, a new Visual Basic code file is set to allow type inference. However, if you want to turn it off at the file level, you can do so by setting Option Infer Off at the top of the code file.

Create an Object and Initialize Its Values (Object Initializers)

There is a shortcut for both declaring an instance of a class and setting the initial value of all or some of its members. With a single line of code, you can instantiate an object and set a number of properties on that object. During runtime, the object is created, and then the properties are set in the order in which they appear in the initialization list. This feature is called object initializers.

Let's look at an example. Suppose you have a class called `Employee` that has a number of properties such as `FirstName`, `LastName`, `FullName`, `Title`, and the like. Using object initialization, you can both create an instance of this class and set the initial values of some (or all) of the `Employee` instance's properties. To do so, you first construct the object. In Visual Basic, you follow this construction with the `With` keyword. (C# does not require an equivalent indicator.) You then place each property initialization inside a set of curly braces. Examples are as shown here.

C#

```
Employee emp = new Employee { FirstName = "Joe",
  LastName = "Smith", Title = "Sr. Developer" };
```

VB

```
Dim emp As New Employee With {.FirstName = "Joe", _
  .LastName = "Smith", .Title = "Sr. Developer"}
```

This single line of code is the equivalent of first creating an `Employee` class and then writing a line of code for each of the listed properties. Notice that in Visual Basic, you access each property using a dot. In C#, you do not need the dot.

Of course, you can also use object initialization with parameterized constructors. You simply pass the parameters into the constructor as you normally would. You then follow the constructor with the initialization. For example, suppose that the `Employee` class had a constructor that took the first and last name, respectively. You could then create the object with the parameters and use object initialization for the `Title`, as shown here.

C#

```
Employee emp = new Employee("Joe", "Smith")
  { Title = "Sr. Developer" };
```

VB

```
Dim emp As New Employee("Joe", "Smith") With _
  {.Title = "Sr. Developer"}
```

Object initialization also enables you to write some code in the initialization. In addition, with Visual Basic you can use properties of the object you are initializing to help initialize other properties. This is not valid in C#. The C# compiler does not allow you to access the variable until the assignment is complete. To see an example of this, the following code initializes an `Employee` object and sets the `Employee.FullName` property by concatenating the first and last names. Notice that the Visual Basic code uses the object itself.

C#

```
Employee emp = new Employee { FirstName = "Joe",
  LastName = "Smith", FullName = "Joe" + " Smith"};
```

VB

```
Dim emp As New Employee() With {.FirstName = "Joe", _
  .LastName = "Smith", _
  .FullName = .FirstName & " "" & .LastName}
```

You can also nest object initialization. That is, if a given property represents another object, you can create the other object as part of the initialization. You can also nest an initialization of the other object within the initialization of the first object. A simple example makes this clear. Suppose that the `Employee` class has a property called `Location`. The `Location` property might point to a `Location` object that includes the properties for `City` and `State`. You could then create the `Employee` object (along with the nested `Location` object), as shown here.

C#

```
Employee emp = new Employee { FirstName = "Joe",
  LastName = "Smith", Location = new Location
  { City = "Redmond", State = "WA" } };
```

VB

```
Dim emp As New Employee() With {.FirstName = "Joe", _
  .LastName = "Smith", _
  .Location = New Location With _
  {.City = "Redmond", .State = "Washington"}}
```

Define a Collection and Initialize Its Values

You can now define a collection class or an array and, at the same time, set the initial values in your object. This turns multiple lines of code calling simple add methods into a single line. This is especially useful if you have a list of items that your application works with and you need to both declare the list and initialize these values.

For example, you might need to define an array to contain the geographic locations for your sales office. You could define this array and initialize it as follows.

C#

```
string[] salesGeos = {"South", "Mid Atlantic", "Mid West"};
```

VB

```
Dim salesGeos() As String = {"South", "Mid Atlantic", "Mid West"}
```

You can use similar syntax to define and initialize a collection class, including those based on a generic. For example, the following defines a list of `Employee` objects and adds two new `Employee` classes to that list. Note that the Visual Basic code requires the `From` keyword.

C#

```
List<Employee> empList = new List<Employee>
  {new Employee("1234"), new Employee("3456")};
```

VB

```
Dim empList As New List(Of Employee) From _
  {New Employee("1234"), New Employee("3456")}
```

Creating an Instance of a Nonexistent Class

The .NET languages enable you to create an object that does not have a class representation at design time. Instead, an unnamed (anonymous) class is created for you by the compiler. This feature is called anonymous types. Anonymous types provide crucial support for LINQ queries. With them, columns of data returned from a query can be represented as objects (more on this later). Anonymous types are compiled into class objects with read-only properties.

Let's look at an example of how you would create an anonymous type. Suppose that you want to create an object that has both a `Name` and a `PhoneNumber` property. However, you do not have such a class definition in your code. You could create an anonymous type declaration to do so, as shown here.

C#

```
var emp = new { Name = "Joe Smith",
  PhoneNumber = "123-123-1234"};
```

VB

```
Dim emp = New With {.Name = "Joe Smith", _
  .PhoneNumber = "123-123-1234"}
```

Notice that the anonymous type declaration uses object initializers (see the previous discussion) to define the object. The big difference is that there is no strong typing after the variable declaration or after the `New` keyword. Instead, the compiler creates an anonymous type for you with the properties `Name` and `PhoneNumber`.

There is also the `Key` keyword in Visual Basic. It is used to signal that a given property of an anonymous type should be used by the compiler to further define how the object is treated. Properties defined as `Key` are used to determine whether two instances of an anonymous type are equal to one another. C# does not have this concept. Instead, in C# all properties are treated like a Visual Basic `Key` property. In Visual Basic, you indicate a `Key` property in this way.

```
Dim emp = New With {Key .Name = "Joe Smith", _
  .PhoneNumber = "123-123-1234"}
```

You can also create anonymous types using variables (instead of the property name equals syntax). In these cases, the compiler uses the name of the variable as the property name and its value as the value for the anonymous type's property. For example, in the following code, the `name` variable is used as a property for the anonymous type.

C#

```
string name = "Joe Smith";
var emp = new {name, PhoneNumber = "123-123-1234" };
```

VB

```
Dim name As String = "Joe Smith"
Dim emp = New With {name, .PhoneNumber = "123-123-1234"}
```

Add Methods to Existing Classes (Extension Methods)

You can add custom features to an existing type as if the type always had the custom features. In this way, you do not have to recompile a given class, nor do you have to create a second derived class to add these features. Rather, you can add a method to an existing class by using a compiler feature called extension methods.

Adding methods varies between Visual Basic and C#. In Visual Basic, you first import the `System.Runtime.CompilerServices` namespace into your code file. Next, you mark a given `Sub` or `Function` with the `ExtensionAttribute` directive. Lastly, you write a new `Sub` or `Function` with the first parameter of the new method being the type you want to extend. The following shows an example. In this example, we extend the `Integer` type with a new method called `DoubleInSize`. The compiler knows we are extending the `Integer` class because this method is marked as `Extension`, and the first parameter in the method takes an `Integer` value.

VB

```
Imports System.Runtime.CompilerServices

Public Module IntegerExtensions
  <Extension()>
  Public Function DoubleInSize(ByVal i As Integer) As Integer
    Return i + i
  End Function
End Module
```

The C# compiler does not require the same import or method attribute. Instead, you first create a static class. Next, you create a static method that you intend to use as your extension. The first parameter of your extension method should be the type you want to extend. In addition, you apply the `this` modifier to the type. Notice the following example. In it, we extend the `int` data type with a new method called `DoubleInSize`:

C#

```
namespace IntegerExtensions
{
  public static class IntegerExtensions
  {
```

```
    public static int DoubleInSize(this int i)
    {
      return i+i;
    }
  }
}
```

To use an extension method, you must first import (using in C#) the new extension class into a project. You can then call any new method as if it had always existed on the type. The following is an example in both Visual Basic and C#. In this case, a function called `DoubleInSize` that was defined in the preceding example is being called from the `Integer` (`int`) class.

VB

```
Imports IntegerExtensions

Module Module1
  Sub Main()
    Dim i As Integer = 10
    Console.WriteLine(i.DoubleInSize.ToString())
  End Sub
End Module
```

C#

```
using IntegerExtensions;

namespace CsEnhancements
{
  class Program
  {
    static void Main(string[] args)
    {
      int i = 10;
      Console.WriteLine(i.DoubleInSize().ToString());
    }
  }
}
```

Add Business Logic to Generated Code (Partial Methods)

A partial method (like a partial class) represents code you write to be added as a specific method to a given class upon compilation. This enables the author of a partial class to define an empty method stub and then call that method from other places within the class. If you provide implementation code for the partial method stub, your code is called when the stub would be called (actually the compiler merges your code with the partial class into a single class). If you do not provide a partial method implementation, the compiler goes a step further and removes the method from the class along with all calls to it. This is why such as partial method returns `void` and cannot take `out` parameters.

The partial method (and partial class) was created to aid in code generation and should generally be avoided unless you are writing code generators or working with them because they can cause confusion in your code.

Of course, Visual Studio has more and more code generation built in. Therefore, it is likely you will run into partial methods sooner or later. In most cases, a code generator or designer (such as LINQ to SQL) generates a partial class and perhaps one or more partial methods. The `Partial` keyword modifier defines both partial classes and partial methods. If you are working with generated code, you are often given a partial class that allows you to create your own portion of the class (to be merged with the code-generated version at compile time). In this way, you can add your own custom business logic to any partial method defined and called by generated code.

Let's look at an example. The following represents an instance of a partial class `Employee`. Here there is a single property called `Salary`. In addition, there is a method marked `Partial` called `SalaryChanged`. This method is called when the value of the `Salary` property is modified.

C#

```
partial class Employee {

  double _salary;

  public double Salary {
    get {
      return _salary;
    }
    set {
      _salary = value;
      SalaryChanged();
    }
  }

  partial void SalaryChanged();
}
```

VB

```
Partial Class Employee

  Private _salary As Double

  Property Salary() As Double
    Get
```

```
      Return _salary
    End Get
    Set(ByVal value As Double)
      _salary = value
      SalaryChanged()
    End Set
  End Property

  Partial Private Sub SalaryChanged()
  End Sub

End Class
```

The preceding code might represent code that was created by a code generator. The next task in implementing a partial method then is to define another partial `Employee` class and provide behavior for the `SalaryChanged` method. The following code does just that.

C#

```
partial class Employee
{
  partial void SalaryChanged()
  {
    double newSalary = this.Salary;
    //do something with the salary information ...
  }
}
```

VB

```
Partial Class Employee
  Private Sub SalaryChanged()
    Dim newSalary As Double = Me.Salary
    'do something with the salary information ...
  End Sub
End Class
```

When the compiler executes, it replaces the `SalaryChanged` method with the new partial method. In this way, the initial partial class (potentially code generated) made plans for a method that might be written without knowing anything about that method implementation. If you decide to write it, it is called at the appropriate time. However, it is optional. If you do not provide an implementation of the partial method `SalaryChanged`, the compiler strips out the method and the calls to the method (as if they had never existed). This provides similar services to the `virtual/override` mechanisms presented earlier in this chapter.

Access and Query Data Using the .NET Languages

Visual Studio 2008 introduced the language feature set called LINQ. LINQ is a programming model that takes advantage of many of the features discussed in this section. It provides language extensions that change the way you access and work with data. With it, you can work with your data using object syntax and query collections of objects using Visual Basic and C#.

You can use LINQ to map between data tables and objects. (See Chapter 13, "Working with Databases.") In this way, you get an easier, more productive way to work with your data. This includes full IntelliSense support based on table and column names. It also includes support for managing inserts, updates, deletes, and reads.

The last of these, reading data, is a big part of LINQ in that it has built-in support for easily querying collections of data. Using LINQ features, you can query not only your data but also any collection in .NET. There are, of course, new keywords and syntax for doing so. Query operators that ship with Visual Basic, for example, include `Select`, `From`, `Where`, `Join`, `Order By`, `Group By`, `Skip`, `Take`, `Aggregate`, `Let`, and `Distinct`. The C# language has a similar set of keywords. And, if these are not enough, you can extend the built-in query operators, replace them, or write your own.

You use these query operators to query against any .NET data that implements the `IEnumerable` or `IQueryable` interface. This may include a `DataTable`, mapped SQL Server objects, .NET collections (including Generics), `DataSets`, and XML data.

Let's look at an example. Suppose you had a collection of employee objects called `employees` and you wanted to access all the employees at a specific location. To do so, you might write the following function.

C#

```
public static IEnumerable<Employee> FilterEmployeesByLocation
  (IEnumerable<Employee> employees, string location)
{
  //LINQ query to return collection of employees filtered by location
  var emps = from Employee emp in employees
             where emp.Location.City == location
             select emp;

  return emps;
}
```

VB

```
Public Shared Function FilterEmployeesByLocation(
  ByVal employees As IEnumerable(Of Employee),
  ByVal location As String) As IEnumerable(Of Employee)

  'LINQ query to return collection of employees filtered by location
  Dim emps = From Employee In employees
```

```
            Where Employee.Location.City = location

    Return emps

End Function
```

Take a look at what is going on in the previous listing. The function takes a list of employee objects, filters it by a region passed to it, and then returns the results. Notice that to filter the list we create a LINQ in-memory query called `emps`. This query can be read like this: Looking at all the employee objects inside the employees collection, find those whose city matches the city passed into the function. Finally, we return emps as an IEnumerable<T> to allow the calling client to cycle through the results.

This is just a brief overview of LINQ. There are many things going on here, such as compile-time checking and schema validation (not to mention the LINQ language syntax). You will undoubtedly want to spend more time with LINQ.

Write Simple Unnamed Functions Within Your Code (Lambda Expressions)

The latest versions of the .NET languages (2008 and later) enable you to write simple functions that might or might not be named, execute inline, and return a single value. These functions exist inside your methods and not as separate, standalone functions. These functions are called *lambda expressions*. It's useful to understand lambda expressions because they are used behind the scenes in LINQ queries. However, they are also valid outside of LINQ.

Let's take a look at an example. Suppose that you want to create a simple function that converts a temperature from Fahrenheit to Celsius. You could do so within your Visual Basic code by first using the keyword `Function`. Next, you could indicate parameters to that function (in this case, the `Fahrenheit` value). Lastly, you could write an expression that evaluates to a value that can be returned from the lambda expression. The syntax is as follows.

VB

```
Dim fahToCel = Function(fahValue As Integer) ((fahValue - 32) / 1.8)
```

The C# syntax is a bit different. In C#, you must explicitly declare a delegate for use by the compiler when converting your lambda expression. Of course, you declare the delegate at the class-level scope. After you have the delegate, you can write the expression inside your code. To do so, you use the `=>` operator. This operator is read as "goes to." To the left side of the operator, you indicate the delegate type, a name for the expression, and then an `=` sign followed by any parameters the expression might take. To the right of the `=>` operator, you put the actual expression. The following shows an example of both the delegate and the expression.

C#

```
//class-level delegate declaration
delegate float del(float f);

//lambda expression inside a method body
del fahToCel = (float fahValue) => (float)((fahValue - 32) / 1.8);
```

Notice that in both examples, we assigned the expression to a variable `fahToCel`. By doing so, we have created a delegate (explicitly converting to one in C#). We can then call the variable as a delegate and get the results, as showh here.

C#

```
float celcius = fahToCel(-10);
```

VB

```
Dim celcius As Single = fahToCel(70)
```

Alternatively, in Visual Basic, we could have written the function inline (without assigning it to a variable). For example, we could have written this.

VB

```
Console.WriteLine((Function(fahValue As Integer) ((fahValue - 32) / 1.8))(70))
```

Notice in this last example that the function is declared and then immediately called by passing in the value of 70 at the end of the function.

The C# language has its own quirk, too. Here you can write multiple statements inside your lambda expression by putting the statements inside curly braces and setting off each statement with a semicolon. The following example has two statements inside the lambda expression. The first creates the new value; the second writes it to a console window. Notice, too, that the delegate must be of type `void` in this instance and that you still must call the lambda expression for it to execute.

C#

```
//class level delegate declaration
delegate void del(float f);

del fahToCel = (float fahValue) => { float f =
  (float)((fahValue - 32) / 1.8); Console.WriteLine(f.ToString()); };
fahToCel(70);
```

Lambda expressions are used in LINQ queries for things such as the `Where`, `Select`, and `Order by` clauses. For example, using LINQ, you can write the following statement.

C#

```
var emps = from emp in db.employees
  where emp.Location == "Redmond"
  select emp;
```

VB

```
Dim emps = From emp In db.employees
  Where(emp.Location = "Redmond")
  Select emp
```

This LINQ code gets converted to lambda expressions similar to this.

C#

```
var emps = from emp in db.employees
  where (emp => emp.Location == "Redmond")
  select (emp => emp);
```

VB

```
Dim emps = From emp In db.employees.Where(Function(emp) emp.Location = _
  "Redmond").Select(Function(emp) emp)
```

Splitting an Assembly Across Multiple Files

The 2005 version of C# introduced the concept of friend assemblies; the feature was added to Visual Basic in 2008. It enables you to combine assemblies in terms of what constitutes internal access. That is, you can define internal members but have them be accessible by external assemblies. This capability is useful if you intend to split an assembly across physical files but still want those assemblies to be accessible to one another as if they were internal.

NOTE

Friend assembles *do not* allow for access to private members.

You use the attribute class `InternalsVisibleToAttribute` to mark an assembly as exposing its internal members as friends to another assembly. This attribute is applied at the assembly level. You pass the name and the public key token of the external assembly to the attribute. The compiler then links these two assemblies as friends. The assembly containing `InternalsVisibleToAttribute` exposes its internals to the other assembly (and not vice versa). You can accomplish the same thing by using the command-line compiler switches.

Friend assemblies, like most things, come at a cost. If you define an assembly as a friend of another assembly, the two assemblies become coupled and need to coexist to be useful. That is, they are no longer a single unit of functionality. This can cause confusion and increase management of your assemblies. It is often easier to stay away from this feature unless you have a specific need.

Working with XML Directly Within Your Code (VB Only)

You can embed XML directly within your Visual Basic code. This can make creating XML messages and executing queries against XML a simple task in Visual Basic. To support this feature, Visual Basic enables you to write straight XML when using the data types called `System.Xml.Linq.XElement` and `System.Xml.Linq.XDocument`. The former enables you to create a variable and assign it an XML element. The latter, `XDocument`, is used to assign a variable to a full XML document.

Writing XML within your Visual Basic code is a structured process and not just simple strings assigned to a parsing engine. In fact, the compiler uses LINQ to XML behind the scenes to make all this work. Let's look at a simple example. The following code creates a variable `emp` of type `XElement`. It then assigns the XML fragment to this variable.

VB

```
Dim emp As XElement = <employee>
                          <firstName>Joe Smith</firstName>
                          <title>Sr. Developer</title>
                          <company>Contoso</company>
                          <location>Redmond, WA</location>
                      </employee>
```

You can create a similar fragment to an `XDocument`. You simply add the XML document definition (`<?xml version="1.0"?>`) to the header of the XML. In either scenario, you end up with XML that can be manipulated, passed as a message, queried, and more.

Visual Basic enables you to write XML inside your code. The two objects (`XElement` and `XDocument`) are still important to C# developers. However, C# developers work with the properties and methods of these objects directly and do not rely on the editor to parse XML directly within a code window. The following shows the same code sample written using C#. (You need the `using` statement `using System.Xml.Linq;`.)

C#

```
XElement xmlTree1 = new XElement("employee",
    new XElement("firstName", "Joe Smith"),
    new XElement("title", "Sr. Developer"),
    new XElement("company", "Contoso"),
    new XElement("location", "Redmond, WA")
);
```

In most scenarios, however, you do not want to hard-code your XML messages in your code. You might define the XML structure there, but the data comes from other sources (variables, databases, and so on). Thankfully, Visual Basic also supports building the XML using expressions. To do so, you use an ASP-style syntax, as in `<%= expression %>`. In this case, you indicate to the compiler that you want to evaluate an expression and assign it to the XML. For XML messages with repeating data, you can even define a loop in your expressions. For example, let's look at building the previous XML using this syntax. Suppose that you have an object `e` that represents an employee. In this case, you might write your `XElement` assignment as shown here.

VB

```
Dim e As Employee = New Employee()
Dim emp As XElement = <employee>
                        <firstName><%= e.FirstName %></firstName>
                        <lastName><%= e.LastName %></lastName>
                        <title><%= e.Title %></title>
                        <company><%= e.Company %></company>
                        <location state=<%= e.Location.State %>>
                            <%= e.Location.City %>
                        </location>
                      </employee>
```

Removing Unused Arguments from Event Handlers (VB Only)

Visual Basic now enables you to omit unused and unwanted arguments from your event handlers. The thought is that this makes for code that reads more cleanly. In addition, it enables you to assign methods directly to event handlers without trying to determine the proper event signature.

For example, suppose you had the following code to respond to a button click event.

```
Private Sub Button1_Click(ByVal sender As System.Object, _
  ByVal e As System.EventArgs) Handles Button1.Click

  'your code here

End Sub
```

You could remove the arguments from this code (or never put them in). Your new code functions the same and looks like this.

```
Private Sub Button1_Click() Handles Button1.Click
  'your code here
End Sub
```

Creating an Automatically Implemented Property

C# and Visual Basic allow for a simplified property declaration called auto-implemented properties. With this feature, you can declare a property without having to declare a local private field to back the property. Instead, the compiler does this for you. This can be useful when you do not need logic inside the property's assessors.

For example, suppose you want to define the property `Name` on the `Employee` class. You can declare this property without setting a private field variable, as shown here.

C#

```
public string Name { get; set; }
```

VB

```
Public Property Name As String
```

Notice that there is no logic in the `get` or `set` statements. Instead, the compiler creates an anonymous field to back the property for you.

Dropping the Underscore in VB for Line Continuation

Visual Basic added a feature in 2010 for implicit line continuation. This enables you to drop the need for the underscore (_) commonly used to indicate line continuation. For example, the following code shows a valid method signature without the need for the underscore required for line continuation.

```
Private Sub OnEmployeeUpdate(ByVal sender As Object,
  ByVal e As EmployeeUpdatedEventArgs)
```

There are many places in Visual Basic where you can eliminate the underscore and instead allow the compiler to use implicit continuation. These include after commas, after an open parenthesis, after an open curly brace, after concatenation, and more.

TIP

Visual Basic 14 (for Visual Studio 2015) now allows for multiline string literals.

Working with Dynamic Languages/Objects

Most .NET development is about working with strongly typed objects where the compiler knows in advance the properties and methods that a given class exposes. However, there are objects (and languages) out there that do not have a static structure against which you can program. Instead, they are designed to get their information at runtime based on data inside an HTML form, a text file, XML, a database, or something similar. These objects and languages are said to be dynamic in that they get their structure only at runtime. Dynamic support was added to .NET for the purpose of simplifying the access to dynamic application programming interfaces (APIs) provided by languages such as IronPython and IronRuby or even those found in Office Automation.

The Dynamic Data Type

The C# language has a new data type called `dynamic`. This type is similar to `object` in that it might contain any actual type. In fact, in Visual Basic you simply use `object` to get dynamic-like behavior. The difference in C#, however, is that any value defined as dynamic only has its actual type inferred at runtime (and not at compile time). This means you do not have type checking against valid methods. That is, the compiler does not stop you from writing code against methods or properties it cannot see at design time. Instead, type checking is only done when the code executes. Of course, this means that your dynamic type should be the right type at the right time or you get errors.

You can define dynamic fields, properties, variable, or return types of methods. For example, the following shows a property defined as a dynamic.

```
public dynamic DyProperty { get; set; }
```

At first glance, it would seem that the `dynamic` keyword simply makes the type behave like types declared as objects. In fact, the differences are so slight that Visual Basic combines the concept of object and dynamic. However, in C#, the keyword `dynamic` indicates that the property can contain any value and that no type checking is done at compile time regardless of what the code looks like that uses the property. That is in contrast to types declared as objects, in which the compiler evaluates expressions that use the type and prevents certain code (such as doing arithmetic with objects). Dynamic types do not get this scrutiny by the compiler and therefore either execute properly or throw an error if a problem exists.

Dynamics are useful for dealing with types and code outside of .NET, such as IronPython. However, you have to be careful when using them for your own needs. Because no resolution is done until runtime, you do not get strong type checking by the compiler or with IntelliSense. There is also a slight memory and performance penalty to pay at runtime for dynamic objects.

Figure 3.4 shows an example of the experience inside Visual Studio. There are two methods here. The first, `VarTestMethod`, uses the `var` statement to create an instance of the `Employee` class. Notice an attempt to call the nonexistent property `NewName` is type-checked as an error. The second method, `DynTestMethod`, declares a `dynamic` instance of `Employee`. In this case, a call to `emp.NewName` does not get a compile time error. The compiler allows this call, but an exception will be thrown at runtime if you get it wrong.

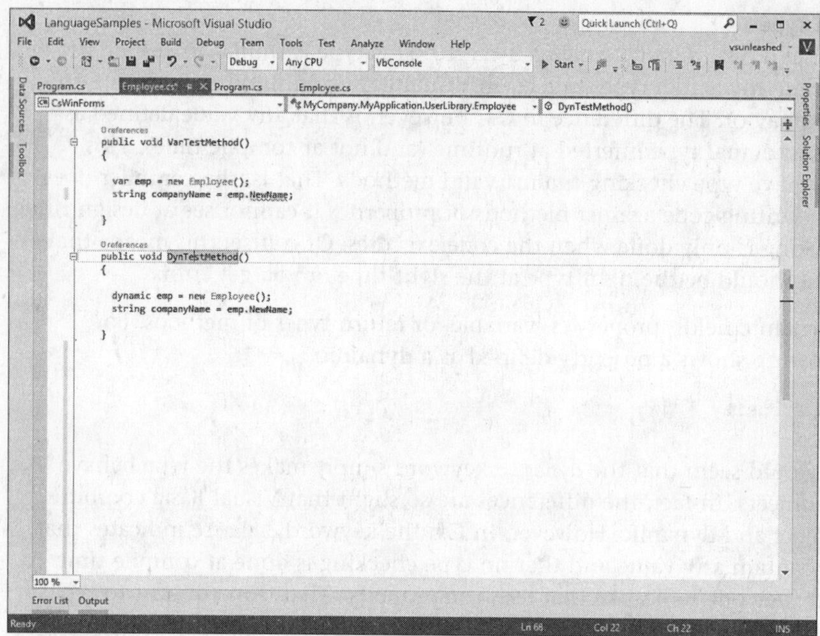

FIGURE 3.4 Using dynamics means no type checking even in IntelliSense.

Creating a Custom Dynamic Object

A dynamic object is one that gets its type information for things such as properties and methods at runtime. This is typically due to the fact that the object is meant to represent dynamic information such as that contained in an HTML or XML script file. In both cases, the underlying HTML and XML files you create are unique to your needs. Therefore, you cannot code directly against these models. Instead, you often have to code against static objects and write syntax such as `MyXml.GetElement("EmployeeId")`. In this example, the `GetElement` method then searches for the given XML element and returns the same. With a dynamic object, the object can be written to interrogate your XML (or similar data) and enables developers to code against the dynamic object as if it contained the `EmployeeId` property. For example, developers could use your dynamic object to write their code as `MyXml.EmployeeId`. The dynamic object still has to interrogate the underlying structure for an `EmployeeId`, but this does simplify the coding for those working with your object and a dynamic structure such as XML or HTML.

You can create dynamic objects using either Visual Basic or C#. To do so, you inherit from the `DynamicObject` class inside the `System.Dynamic` namespace. You then override the members inside this class. These members serve as the basis for your dynamic items. For example, you can override the `TrySetMember` and `TryGetMember` to indicate the code that should be run when a user attempts to set or get a dynamic property on your object (such as calling `MyXml.EmployeeId`). In this case, if a user is trying to return a dynamic property, the `TryGetMember` method is called. Your code then determines how to return information for the dynamic property. (You might interrogate a file, for instance.)

There are many members on DynamicObject for which you can provide functionality. In addition to the two aforementioned members, the other notables include TryInvokeMember for invoking dynamic methods and TryCreateInstance for creating new instances of a dynamic object.

You might also add your own methods and properties to a dynamic object. In this case, the dynamic object first looks for your property or method before calling out to the appropriate Try member.

Let's look at an example. Suppose that you were to write a dynamic object to represent an Employee. In this case, perhaps you get data scraped from a web page or inside an XML file. You therefore want to convert this data to an object for easier programming. In this case, you can create a new class called Employee and make sure it inherits from DynamicObject. In our example, we use a simple Hashtable of key value pairs to simulate the employee data. When a user creates an instance of this class, he is expected to pass the employee data to the dynamic class in the constructor. The skeleton of this class might then look like this.

C#

```
class Employee : System.Dynamic.DynamicObject
{
  Hashtable _memberData;

  public Employee(Hashtable employeeData)
  {
    _memberData = employeeData;
  }
}
```

VB

```
Public Class Employee
  Inherits System.Dynamic.DynamicObject

  Dim _memberData As Hashtable

  Public Sub New(ByVal employeeData As Hashtable)
    _memberData = employeeData
  End Sub

End Class
```

The next step is to override one or more of the Try members of DynamicObject to add our own functionality. In this simple example, we override the TryGetMember method to provide functionality for reading a property and add it to the Employee class created earlier. This method takes two parameters: binder and result. The binder parameter is an object that represents the dynamic call made to your object (such as its name). The result parameter is an outbound parameter of type `object`. You use it to pass back any value you intend to pass as the property read. Finally, the method returns a `bool`. This indicates `true` if the member was determined to exist; otherwise, you return `false`.

In the example, we simply look inside the `Hashtable` for a given key (based on the `binder.Name` property). If it exists, we set the result to its value and return `true`. Otherwise, we set the result to `null` and return `false`. The following shows the code for this additional member of our `Employee` class (assumes you're `using` [`imports` in VB] `System.Dynamic`).

C#

```
public override bool TryGetMember(
  GetMemberBinder binder, out object result)
{
  if (_memberData.ContainsKey(binder.Name))
  {
    //set the out parameter results to the value in the
    //  hash table for the given key
    result = _memberData[binder.Name];

    //indicate that member existed
    return true;
  }
  else
  {
    //property does not exist in hash table
    result = null;
    return false;
  }
}
```

VB

```
Public Overrides Function TryGetMember(ByVal binder As GetMemberBinder,
  ByRef result As Object) As Boolean

  If _memberData.ContainsKey(binder.Name) Then
    'set the out parameter results to the value in the
    '  hash table for the given key
    result = _memberData(binder.Name)

    'indicate that member existed
    Return True
  Else
    'property does not exist in hash table
    result = Nothing
    Return False
```

```
    End If

End Function
```

NOTE

Note that classes that inherit from `DynamicObject` can be passed as instances to other languages that support the dynamic interoperability model. This includes IronPython and IronRuby.

Using the Dynamic Object

You use a dynamic object like you would any other. You can create an instance, call methods and properties, and so on. However, you do not get type checking by the compiler. Again, this is because the object is late bound at runtime. In C#, you indicate a late-bound dynamic object using the keyword `dynamic`. In Visual Basic, you simply declare your type as `object`. Visual Basic figures out whether you are using late binding.

For example, suppose that you want to use the dynamic version of the `Employee` class created in the previous section. Recall that this class simulates converting data into an object. In this case, the simulation is handled through a `Hashtable`. Therefore, you need to declare an instance of the `Employee` class as dynamic (or object in VB) and then create an instance passing in a valid `Hashtable`. You can then call late-bound properties against your object. Recall that these properties are evaluated inside the `TryGetMember` method you overrode in the previous example. The following shows a `Console` application that calls the dynamic `Employee` object.

C#

```
class Program
{
  static void Main(string[] args)
  {
    Hashtable empData = new Hashtable();
    empData.Add("Name", "Dave Elper");
    empData.Add("Salary", 75000);
    empData.Add("Title", "Developer");

    dynamic dyEmp = new Employee(empData);

    Console.WriteLine(dyEmp.Name);
    Console.WriteLine(dyEmp.Salary);
    Console.WriteLine(dyEmp.Title);
    Console.WriteLine(dyEmp.Status);

    Console.ReadLine();
  }
```

```
}
```

VB

```
Module Module1

  Sub Main()

    Dim empData As New Hashtable()
    empData.Add("Name", "Dave Elper")
    empData.Add("Salary", 75000)
    empData.Add("Title", "Developer")

    Dim dyEmp As Object = New Employee(empData)

    Console.WriteLine(dyEmp.Name)
    Console.WriteLine(dyEmp.Salary)
    Console.WriteLine(dyEmp.Title)
    Console.WriteLine(dyEmp.Status)

    Console.ReadLine()

  End Sub

End Module
```

All this code passes the compiler's test and executes accordingly. However, the last call to `dyEmp.Status` is not valid. In this case, the dynamic object returns `false` and thus throws an error. Figure 3.5 shows the results, including the Console output and the error message trying to access a bad member.

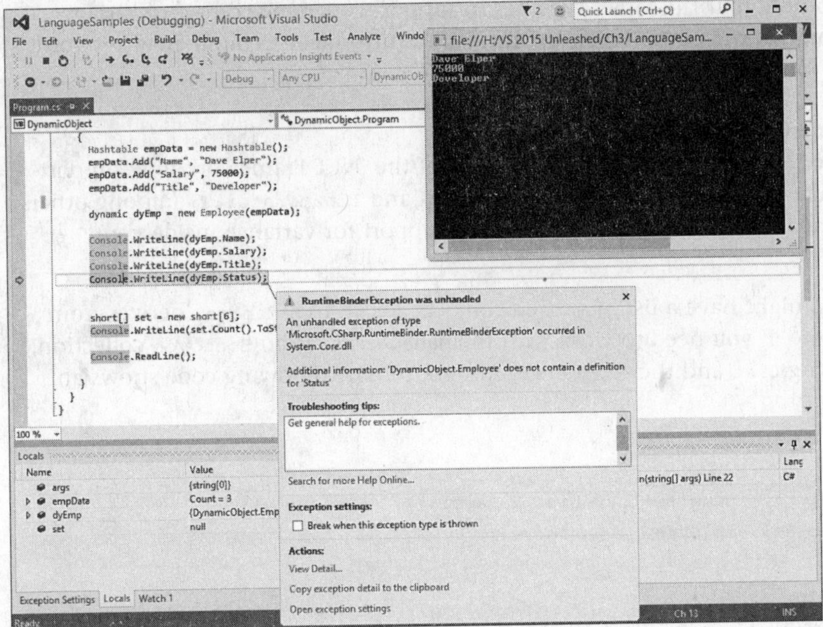

FIGURE 3.5 The dynamic object executing in the `Console` and throwing an error in Visual Studio.

> **TIP**
>
> You can use the features discussed here to load a dynamic language library such as IronPython. In this case, you load the dynamic language library and can then use this library inside your code. For more on this, see "Creating and Using Dynamic Objects (C# and Visual Basic)" inside MSDN.

Covariance and Contravariance

The .NET languages support the concepts of covariance and contravariance. These concepts enable you to reduce restrictions on strong typing when working with delegates, generics, or generic collections of objects. In certain situations, decreasing the type restrictions might increase your ability to reuse code and objects and decrease the need to do a lot of casting or converting to provide the right type to a method.

Covariance is the ability to use a more derived type than that which was originally specified by an interface or function signature. For example, you could assign a list of strings to a generic list that only takes objects if that list supports covariance (because strings inherit from objects and are thus more derived). Contravariance is similar; it is the ability to use a less-derived type for a given parameter or return value. That is, you might assign an object type as the return type for a method that returns a string (provided that method supports contravariance).

It is important to note that the target type has to support covariance or contravariance. This is not a change to the entire language. Instead, it introduces a couple new keywords to allow support for these concepts when appropriate.

Variance in Generic Collections

Many of the generic interfaces in the latest version of the .NET Framework now support variance. This includes the interfaces `IEnumerable<T>` and `IEnumerator<T>` (among others) that support covariance. This means you can have support for variance inside your collections.

For example, you might have a list of `Manager` objects. Recall that `Manager` derives from `Employee`. Therefore, if you need to work with the `Manager` list as an `Employee` collection, you can do so using `List` and the `IEnumerable` interface. The following code shows an example.

C#

```
IEnumerable<Manager> managers = new List<Manager>();
IEnumerable<Employee> employees = managers;
```

VB

```
Dim managers As IEnumerable(Of Manager) = New List(Of Manager)()
Dim employees As IEnumerable(Of Employee) = managers
```

The preceding code compiles and executes because `Manager` inherits from `Employee` and is thus more derived. Using covariance, you can use a list of `Manager` objects with a list of `Employee` objects. For example, you might have a method that takes a list of `Employee` objects as a parameter. Using covariance support, you can pass the `Manager` list instead.

Additional Considerations

Support for variance has additional ramifications for your coding. These include the following:

- **Custom generic classes**—If you create your own custom generic classes, you can declare support for variance. You do so at the interface level using the `out` (covariant) and `in` (contravariant) keywords on generic type parameters.
- **Delegate variance**—Using variance, you can assign methods to delegates that return more derived types (covariance). You can also assign those methods that accept parameters that have a less derived type (contravariance).
- **`Func` and `Action`**—The generic delegates `Func<>` and `Action<>` now support variance. This enables you to more easily use these delegates with other types (and thus increase the flexibility of your code).

Asynchronous Programming

Most of the time, developers write code that processes a series of commands sequentially. For instance, we can envision a simple routine (`TallyExpenseReport`) that accepts an ID, calls a second routine (`GetExpenseReport`) to call a service with that ID to retrieve an expense report, grabs the total dollar amount of the expense report, and then updates a database before finally giving the user a message indicating the status of the operation.

C#

```
public void TallyExpenseReport(string id)
{
    //get the expense report
    ExpenseReport rpt = GetExpenseReport(id);
    UpdateDataStore(id, rpt.TotalAmt);

}

public ExpenseReport GetExpenseReport(string id)
{

    //code to fetch an expense report goes here
    return new ExpenseReport();

}
```

VB

```
Public Sub TallyExpenseReport(id As String)
    'get the expense report
    Dim rpt As ExpenseReport = GetExpenseReport(id)
    UpdateDataStore(id, rpt.TotalAmt)

End Sub

Public Function GetExpenseReport(id As String) As
    ExpenseReport

    'code to fetch an expense report goes here
    Return New ExpenseReport()

End Function
```

But in this top-down sequential process, we have actually sacrificed a bit of the user's experience; because of its sequential nature, each time we make a call, the application is blocked until the call completes. If we are talking to a service, this might be anywhere from fractions of a second to minutes. The same is true when we go to update the database. The entire time that the application is waiting for a task to complete, the application (and the user) cannot do anything else.

A better approach is an asynchronous one: we still issue a request for information from the service, and we still make a call to update the database, but in this case the application makes the call and then continues on its merry way. That, in essence, is an asynchronous application: the application doesn't block any of the calls we chose to make asynchronous. These types of applications are fraught with complexity. But even the syntax to create and work with asynchronous calls has been complex and a tad arcane. The .NET Framework 4.5 added two keywords—`async` and `await`—to both Visual Basic and C# that help make asynchronous programming a bit easier.

`Async` is used as a modifier to indicate that a method is asynchronous. The `await` keyword is used to mark any calls within an async method that should be waited on for completion. For the runtime wiring to work, all your async function calls also need to have their return values modified to `Task<originaltype>` (C#) or `Task(of originaltype)`.

If we were to take another stab at writing our expense report code, we might end up with two routines that look something like this.

C#

```
public async void TallyExpenseReport(string id)
{
    //get the expense report
    ExpenseReport rpt = await GetExpenseReport(id);
    UpdateDataStore(id, rpt.TotalAmt);

}

public async Task<ExpenseReport> GetExpenseReport(string id)
{

    //code to fetch an expense report goes here
    return new ExpenseReport();

}
```

VB

```
Public Async Sub TallyExpenseReport(id As String)
    'get the expense report
    Dim rpt As ExpenseReport = Await GetExpenseReport(id)
    UpdateDataStore(id, rpt.TotalAmt)

End Sub

Public Async Function GetExpenseReport(id As String) As
    Threading.Tasks.Task(Of ExpenseReport)
```

```
    'code to fetch an expense report goes here
    Return New ExpenseReport()

End Function
```

Our "await" call to `GetExpenseReport` will cause the `TallyExpenseReport` routine to block further execution in this method until a value is returned; meanwhile, execution control will be immediately passed back to the original method that called `TallyExpenseReport` in the first place. In other words, the application will continue on, it won't block, and it may elect to do other things such as processing more user input, making additional expense report calls, and so on.

NOTE

Obviously, these simple code examples barely scratch the surface of async programming. For more information, search MSDN for "Asynchronous Programming Patterns." This includes the recommended, task-based asynchronous pattern (TAP) based on the `System.Threading.Tasks` namespace.

The .NET Framework

The .NET Framework continues to evolve. This latest version layers on top of the many earlier versions that brought us support for generics, LINQ, Windows Presentation Foundation (WPF), Windows Communication Foundation (WCF), Windows Workflow Foundation (WF), SQL Synch Services, parallel computing, Dynamic Language Runtime (DLR), asynchronous programming, and more. Version 4.6/5.0 adds features and enhancements to most classes in the framework. It also provides new capabilities.

A Map to the .NET Framework

We cannot begin to cover all the features of the .NET Framework in this limited space. Therefore, we simply highlight some of the key areas that fuel the current version of the .NET Framework. Think of this section as a high-level map to help guide you when exploring the Framework. Many of these items are also covered in more depth throughout the book:

- **`System.AddIn` (add-in framework)**—Provides classes and methods for developers looking to build applications that can be extended based on a common add-in framework. For example, the `AddInStore` class allows for the discovery and management of add-ins. The framework also provides versioning, isolation, activation, and sandboxing. If you are building a new application and hope to allow for add-ins, you should dig deeper on this namespace.
- **`System.CodeDom`**—Includes the classes used to represent the structure of a code file. The classes in this namespace can be used to generate and compile code.

- **System.Collections**—Provides the collection classes inside the Framework, including ArrayList, Hashtable, Queue, Stack, SortedList, and others. It is recommended to use the generic type-safe collections from the System.Collections.Generic namespace instead. This not only gives you type safety but also better performance and memory usage. .
- **System.ComponentModel**—Provides classes used to help with the runtime and design time execution of .NET controls, including data-binding and progress monitoring.
- **System.Configuration**—Provides classes for reading, writing, and managing application configuration information.
- **System.Data (ADO.NET)**—Provides the classes required to work with data and databases. This includes the DataTable and DataSet. There is also the namespace System.Data.SqlClient for working with SQL databases. For more information on working with ADO.NET, see Chapter 21, "Building WPF Applications."
- **System.Diagnostics**—Contains classes for working with diagnostic information about your application. This includes an EventLog and Process class. There is also the EventSchemaTraceListener class to allow for cross-domain, cross-thread, cross-computer, end-to-end, lock-free logging, and tracing.
- **System.Diagnostics.Contracts**—Provides support for code contracts, including preconditions and other data that is not typically defined inside a method signature.
- **System.Drawing**—Provides classes (like Pen, Brush, and Graphics) related to drawing with GDI+.
- **System.Dynamic**—Provides support for dynamic objects that get their members are runtime. (See content earlier in this chapter for more details.)
- **System.EnterpriseServices**—Provides the services architecture for creating serviced components that run under COM+.
- **System.Globalization**—Used to define language and culture information for writing multilingual, multicultural applications.
- **System.IO**—Provides classes for reading and writing file and data streams. This includes classes such as File, Directory, and Stream. Note there is also the System.IO.Pipes namespace that provides support for writing code that communicates at the pipe level across processes and across computers.
- **System.Linq (LINQ)**—Defines standard LINQ query operators and types. The System.Data.Linq namespace holds the connection between databases and the LINQ subsystem. There are more LINQ-related namespaces, too. These include System.Data.Linq.Mapping for handling the O/R mapping between SQL and LINQ and System.Xml.Linq for working between XML and the LINQ subsystem.
- **System.Media**—Used for accessing and playing sounds and music.
- **System.Messaging**—Provides support for working with message queues.

- `System.Net`—Provides support for programming with network protocols, including the Hypertext Transfer Protocol (HTTP), File Transfer Protocol (FTP), and Transmission Control Protocol/Internet Protocol (TCP/IP). It also includes peer-to-peer networking support found in the `System.Net.PeerToPeer` namespace.
- `System.Security`—Provides the classes used to implement security inside the .NET runtime.
- `System.ServiceModel` (WCF)—Encapsulates what is known as WCF. With it you can easily create service-based applications that work across multiple protocols, transports, and message types. WCF is covered more in Chapter 21.
- `System.Threading`—Provides support for writing multithreaded applications. This includes `System.Threading.Tasks`, which provides support for parallel computing on multiple threads and multiple cores. This namespace simplifies the task of writing for these environments.
- `System.Timers`—Allows developers to raise an event on a specified interval.
- `System.Web` (ASP.NET)—Includes many classes and controls. For example, the framework directly supports AJAX programming with the `ScriptManager` and `UpdatePanel` controls. There are also controls for displaying data, such as `ListView`. For more on the ASP.NET framework, see Chapter 17, "Building Modern Websites with ASP.NET 5."
- `System.Windows` (WPF)—Provides the WPF presentation technology for Windows applications. This technology is spread throughout the namespace and includes support for creating Windows applications based on XAML, XBAP, vector graphics, and both 2D and 3D scenarios. For more information, see Chapter 21.
- `System.Workflow.Activities` and `System.Activities` (WF)—Provides classes for writing workflow applications and the custom activities found inside a workflow application.
- `System.Xml`—Provides support for working with XML and XSL.

Summary

This chapter highlighted new programming features and provided a primer on the .NET languages. It should serve to get you running on the many features and programming constructs made possible by these languages. Our intent is to help you write more and better code during your development day. This chapter also presented a high-level roadmap of the .NET Framework. This Framework is becoming so large that developers (and books) are often forced to specialize in a particular area. We suggest that you look at our list and then jump off to your own specialty area for further exploration.

CHAPTER 4

Solutions and Projects

IN THIS CHAPTER

- ▶ Understanding Solutions
- ▶ Getting Comfortable with Projects

Solutions and projects are the containers Visual Studio uses to house and organize the code you write within the IDE. Solutions are virtual containers; they group and apply properties across one or more projects. Projects are both virtual and physical in purpose. Besides functioning as organizational units for your code, they map one to one with compiler targets. Put another way, Visual Studio turns projects into compiled code. Each project results in the creation of a .NET component (such as a DLL or an EXE file).

This chapter covers the roles of solutions and projects in the development process. You learn how to create solutions and projects, examine their physical attributes, and best leverage their features.

Understanding Solutions

From a programming perspective, everything that you do within Visual Studio takes place within the context of a solution. As mentioned in this chapter's introduction, solutions in and of themselves don't do anything other than serve as higher-level containers for other items. Projects are the most obvious items that can be placed inside solutions, but solutions can also contain miscellaneous files that may be germane to the solution itself, such as "read me" documents and design diagrams. Really, any file type can be added to a solution. Solutions can't, however, contain other solutions. In addition, Visual Studio loads only one solution at a time. If you need to work on more than one solution concurrently, you need to launch another instance of Visual Studio.

So what do solutions contribute to the development experience? Solutions are useful because they allow you to treat different projects as one cohesive unit of work. By grouping multiple projects under a solution, you can work against those projects from within one instance of Visual Studio. In addition, a solution simplifies certain configuration tasks by enabling you to apply settings across all the solution's child projects.

You can also "build" a solution. As mentioned previously, solutions themselves aren't compiled, per se, but their constituent projects can be built using a single build command issued against the solution. Solutions are also a vehicle for physical file management: because many items that show up in a solution are physical files located on disk, Visual Studio can manage those files in various ways (delete them, rename them, move them). So it turns out that solutions are useful constructs within Visual Studio.

The easiest way to explore solution capabilities and attributes is to create a solution in the IDE.

Creating a Solution

To create a solution, you first create a project. Because projects can't be loaded independently of a solution within Visual Studio, creating a project causes a solution to be created at the same time.

NOTE

There actually is a way to create a blank, or empty, solution without also creating a project. While creating a new project, if you expand the Other Project Types node that appears in the Installed Templates list, you will see a category for Visual Studio Solutions. This contains a Blank Solution template. Blank solutions are useful when you need to create a new solution to house a series of already existing projects; the blank solution obviates the need to worry about an extra, unneeded project being created on disk.

Launch the New Project dialog box by using the File menu and selecting the New, Project option (shown in Figure 4.1).

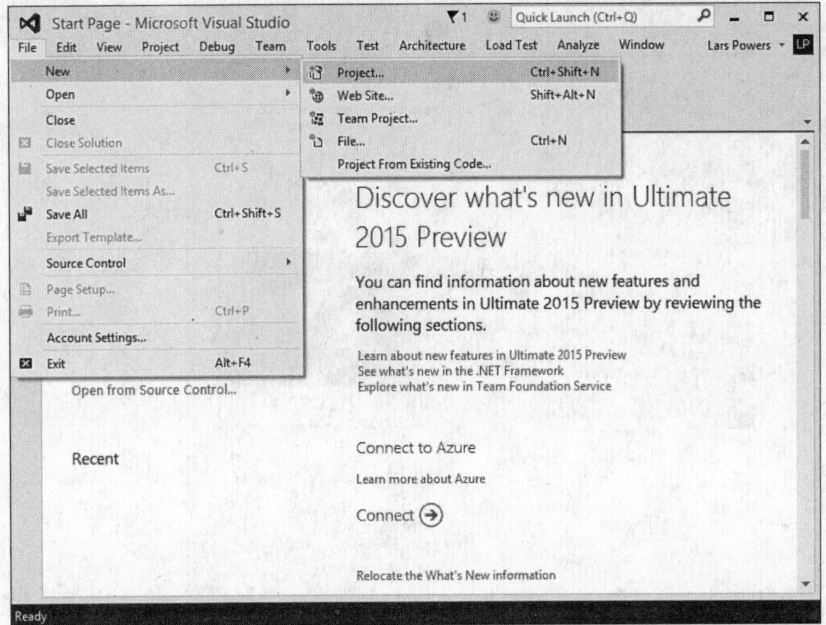

FIGURE 4.1 The File, New, Project menu.

The New Project dialog box is displayed with defaults for the project name, location, and solution name (see Figure 4.2). We take a detailed look at the various project types offered there when we discuss projects later in this chapter. Notice that a Solution Name field is displayed at the bottom of the dialog box. In this field, you can customize the name of your solution before you create it. Clicking OK at this point does two things: a project of the indicated type and name is created on disk (at the location specified), and a solution, with links to the project, is created on disk using the provided name.

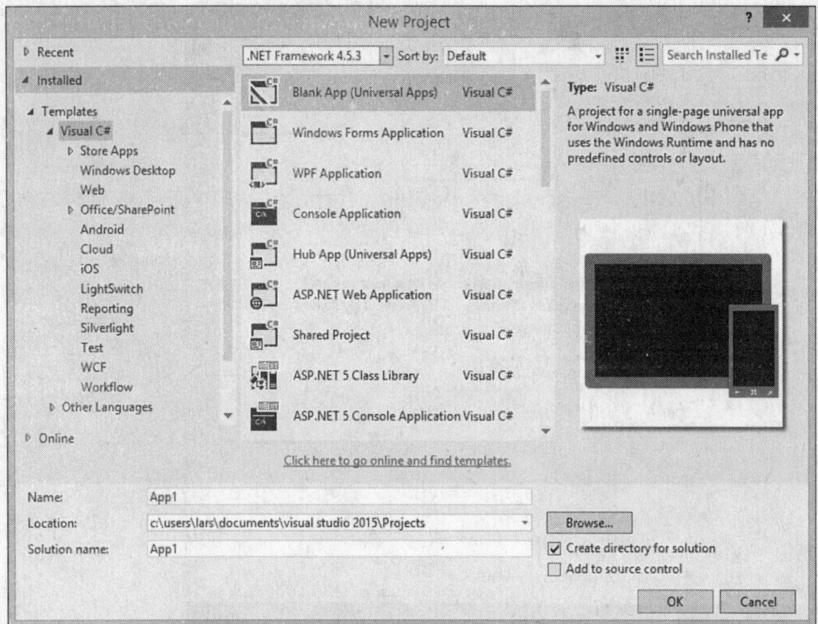

FIGURE 4.2 The New Project dialog box.

If you have selected something other than the Blank Solution project type, Visual Studio now displays the newly created solution and project in the Solution Explorer window. (You will learn about Solution Explorer in depth in Chapter 5, "Browsers and Explorers.") In effect, Visual Studio has created the solution hierarchy shown in Figure 4.3.

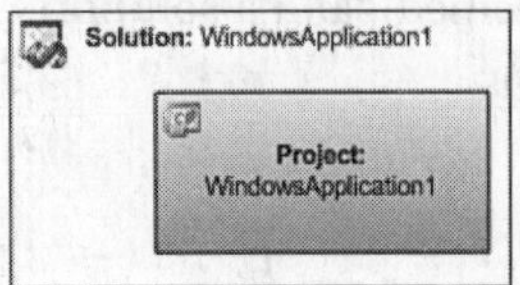

FIGURE 4.3 A simple solution hierarchy.

Assuming that you have accepted the default locations and left the Create Directory for Solution box checked on a Universal App solution, the physical directory/file structure is created, as shown in Figure 4.4.

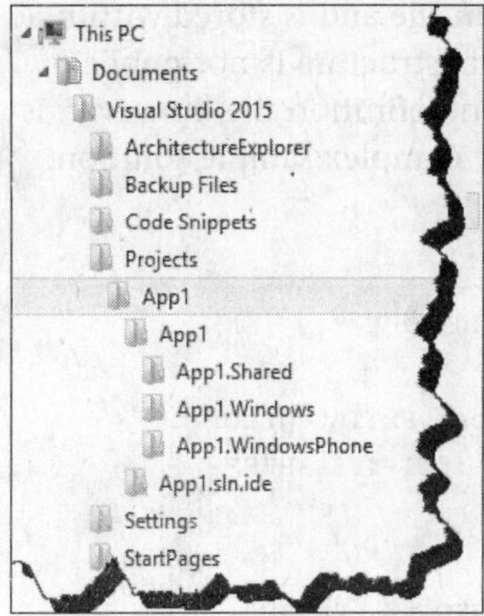

FIGURE 4.4 The solution file hierarchy.

In this example, the first `App1` folder holds the solution file and has a subfolder for each project. The second `App1` folder contains the new project. The source files are placed in this folder, and any compiled output files sit underneath the `bin` directory and then under the specific build configuration (for example, Debug or Release). This particular example is unique to the Universal App project type; each project type can have its own unique approach to structuring its file hierarchy.

CAUTION

By default, the solution is named after the project. There is potential for confusion here because you now have two folders/entities named `App1`. One refers to the solution; the other refers to the project. This is not an ideal way to physically organize your code on disk. It is recommended that you give the solution a unique name during the project creation process by simply overriding the default name given in the Solution Name field (see Figure 4.2).

The Solution Definition File

Visual Studio stores solution information inside two separate files: a solution definition file and a solution user options file. For the preceding example, a solution definition file (`App1.sln`) and a solution user options file (`App1.suo`) were created.

The solution definition file is responsible for actually describing any project relationships in the solution and for storing the various solution-level attributes that can be set. The solution user options file persists any customizations or changes that you, as a Visual Studio user, might have made to the way the solution is displayed within the IDE (such as whether the solution is expanded or which documents from the solution are open in the IDE). In addition, certain source control settings and other IDE configuration data are stored here.

The solution user options file is, by default, marked as a hidden file and is stored within a hidden folder; its content is actually binary. Because its internal structure is not publicly documented, we do not attempt to dissect it here. The solution definition file, however, is simply a text file. Listing 4.1 shows the file content for a fairly complex sample solution.

LISTING 4.1 Sample Solution File

```
Microsoft Visual Studio Solution File, Format Version 12.00
# Visual Studio 14
Project("{FAE04EC0-301F-11D3-BF4B-00C04F79EFBC}") = "Contoso.Fx.Integration",
"ClassLibrary1\Contoso.Fx.Integration.csproj", "{DA0BA585-76C1-4F5E-B7EF-
➥R57254E185BE4}"
EndProject
Project("{FAE04EC0-301F-11D3-BF4B-00C04F79EFBC}") = "Contoso.Fx.Common",
"Contoso.Fx.Common\Contoso.Fx.Common.csproj", "{A706BCAC-8FD7-4D8A-AC81-
➥R249ED61FDE72}"
EndProject
Project("{FAE04EC0-301F-11D3-BF4B-00C04F79EFBC}") = "Contoso.Fx.Analysis",
"Contoso.Fx.Analysis\Contoso.Fx.Analysis.csproj", "{EB7D75D7-76FC-4EC0-
➥A11E-2B54849CF6EB}"
EndProject
Project("{FAE04EC0-301F-11D3-BF4B-00C04F79EFBC}") = "Contoso.Fx.UI",
"Contoso.Fx.UI\Contoso.Fx.UI.csproj", "{98317C19-F6E7-42AE-AC07-72425E851185}"
EndProject
Project("{2150E333-8FDC-42A3-9474-1A3956D46DE8}") = "Architecture Models",
"Architecture Models", "{60777432-3B66-4E03-A337-0366F7E0C864}"
    ProjectSection(SolutionItems) = postProject
        ContosoSystemDiagram.sd = ContosoSystemDiagram.sd
    EndProjectSection
EndProject
Project("{FAE04EC0-301F-11D3-BF4B-00C04F79EFBC}") = "Contoso.UI.WindowsForms.
OrderEntry", "Contoso.UI.WindowsForms.OrderEntry\Contoso.UI.WindowsForms.
OrderEntry.csproj", "{49C79375-6238-40F1-94C8-4183B466FD79}"
EndProject
Project("{2150E333-8FDC-42A3-9474-1A3956D46DE8}") = "Class Libraries", "Class
Libraries", "{E547969C-1B23-42DE-B2BB-A13B7E844A2B}"
EndProject
Project("{2150E333-8FDC-42A3-9474-1A3956D46DE8}") = "Controls", "Controls",
"{ED2D843C-A708-41BE-BB52-35BFE4493035}"
EndProject
Global
    GlobalSection(SolutionConfigurationPlatforms) = preSolution
        Debug|Any CPU = Debug|Any CPU
        Release|Any CPU = Release|Any CPU
    EndGlobalSection
    GlobalSection(ProjectConfigurationPlatforms) = postSolution
```

```
    {DA0BA585-76C1-4F5E-B7EF-57254E185BE4}.Debug|Any CPU.ActiveCfg = Debug|
    Any CPU
    {DA0BA585-76C1-4F5E-B7EF-57254E185BE4}.Debug|Any CPU.Build.0 = Debug|
    Any CPU
    {DA0BA585-76C1-4F5E-B7EF-57254E185BE4}.Release|Any CPU.ActiveCfg = Release
    |Any CPU
    {DA0BA585-76C1-4F5E-B7EF-57254E185BE4}.Release|Any CPU.Build.0 = Release|
    Any CPU
    {A706BCAC-8FD7-4D8A-AC81-249ED61FDE72}.Debug|Any CPU.ActiveCfg = Debug|
    Any CPU
    {A706BCAC-8FD7-4D8A-AC81-249ED61FDE72}.Debug|Any CPU.Build.0 = Debug|
    Any CPU
    {A706BCAC-8FD7-4D8A-AC81-249ED61FDE72}.Release|Any CPU.ActiveCfg = Release
    |Any CPU
    {A706BCAC-8FD7-4D8A-AC81-249ED61FDE72}.Release|Any CPU.Build.0 = Release
    |Any CPU
    {EB7D75D7-76FC-4EC0-A11E-2B54849CF6EB}.Debug|Any CPU.ActiveCfg = Debug| Any
    CPU
    {EB7D75D7-76FC-4EC0-A11E-2B54849CF6EB}.Debug|Any CPU.Build.0 = Debug|
    Any CPU
    {EB7D75D7-76FC-4EC0-A11E-2B54849CF6EB}.Release|Any CPU.ActiveCfg =
    Release |Any CPU
    {EB7D75D7-76FC-4EC0-A11E-2B54849CF6EB}.Release|Any CPU.Build.0 = Release
    |Any CPU
    {98317C19-F6E7-42AE-AC07-72425E851185}.Debug|Any CPU.ActiveCfg = Debug|
    Any CPU
    {98317C19-F6E7-42AE-AC07-72425E851185}.Debug|Any CPU.Build.0 = Debug|
    Any CPU
    {98317C19-F6E7-42AE-AC07-72425E851185}.Release|Any CPU.ActiveCfg =
    Release |Any CPU
    {98317C19-F6E7-42AE-AC07-72425E851185}.Release|Any CPU.Build.0 = Release
    |Any CPU
    {49C79375-6238-40F1-94C8-4183B466FD79}.Debug|Any CPU.ActiveCfg = Debug|
    Any CPU
    {49C79375-6238-40F1-94C8-4183B466FD79}.Debug|Any CPU.Build.0 = Debug|
    Any CPU
    {49C79375-6238-40F1-94C8-4183B466FD79}.Release|Any CPU.ActiveCfg =
   Release |Any CPU
    {49C79375-6238-40F1-94C8-4183B466FD79}.Release|Any CPU.Build.0 =
    Release |Any CPU
EndGlobalSection
GlobalSection(SolutionProperties) = preSolution
    HideSolutionNode = FALSE
EndGlobalSection
GlobalSection(NestedProjects) = preSolution
    {ED2D843C-A708-41BE-BB52-35BFE4493035} = {E547969C-1B23-42DE-B2BB-
```

```
        ➥A13B7E844A2B}
        {EB7D75D7-76FC-4EC0-A11E-2B54849CF6EB} = {E547969C-1B23-42DE-B2BB-
        ➥A13B7E844A2B}
        {A706BCAC-8FD7-4D8A-AC81-249ED61FDE72} = {E547969C-1B23-42DE-B2BB-
        ➥A13B7E844A2B}
        {DA0BA585-76C1-4F5E-B7EF-57254E185BE4} = {E547969C-1B23-42DE-B2BB-
        ➥A13B7E844A2B}
        {98317C19-F6E7-42AE-AC07-72425E851185} = {ED2D843C-A708-41BE-BB52-
        ➥35BFE4493035}
    EndGlobalSection
EndGlobal
```

At the beginning of the file are references to the projects that belong to the solution. The references contain the project's name, its globally unique identifier (GUID), and a relative path to the project file itself (more on project files in a bit):

```
Project("{FAE04EC0-301F-11D3-BF4B-00C04F79EFBC}") = "Contoso.Fx.Integration",
"ClassLibrary1\Contoso.Fx.Integration.csproj",
➥"{DA0BA585-76C1-4F5E-B7EF-R57254E185BE4}"
EndProject
```

You can also see some of the various configuration attributes applied to the solution; the Debug and Release settings, for instance, show up here. Note that this project contains several solution folders: Architecture Models, Class Libraries, and Controls. They are represented in the solution file in much the same way as projects. In fact, the only difference is that they do not have a relative file path associated with them.

Working with Solutions

After you have created a solution, the primary vehicle is in place for interacting with your code base. In essence, this boils down to controlling the way its constituent projects and files are built and deployed. Solutions also provide functionality outside the scope of projects. The primary tool for manipulating solutions and projects is the Solution Explorer. This tool is discussed in depth in Chapter 5. Here, we look at the general procedures used to manage solutions by using the menu system in Visual Studio; keep in mind that most of the commands and actions discussed here can be initiated from the Solution Explorer.

Solution Items

In practice, the content you add most often to a solution is project related. But items can be added directly to a solution as well. Collectively, the term *solution items* refers to any non-project file that is attached to a solution. Because a solution can't be compiled (only its projects will), it stands to reason that files added at the solution level serve no practical purpose from a compilation perspective. There are various reasons, however, that you might want to add solution items to your solution. For instance, adding solution items to your solution is a convenient way to store documentation that applies to the solution as a whole. Because you can add any type of file to a solution, this could take the form of documents, notes to other developers, design specifications, or even source code files from other solutions that could have some effect or bearing on the work at hand.

By default, Visual Studio supports a few types of solution items that can be created directly from within the IDE. They are grouped within three categories. Within each category are various file types that can be generated by Visual Studio. Table 4.1 shows the supported General types.

TABLE 4.1 File Types Supported Within a Solution by Add New Item

Category	Item Type	File Extension
General	Text file	.txt
	Style sheet	.css
	XML schema	.xsd
	Bitmap file	.bmp
	Cursor file	.cur
	Visual C# class	.cs
	Visual Basic class	.vb
	HTML page	.html
	XML file	.xml
	XSLT file	.xsl
	Icon file	.ico
	SQL file	.sql
	F# Script file	.fsx
	F# Source file	.fs
	Shader file	.hlsl
	Directed Graph Document	.dgml
	Native resource template	.rct

NOTE

Keep in mind that you are in no way limited as to the type of file you can add to a solution. Even though Visual Studio supports only a limited number of file types that can be created within the IDE, you always have the option of creating a file *outside* the IDE and then adding it to a solution by using the Add Existing Item command.

Figure 4.5 shows the Add New Item - Solution Items dialog box that appears when you try to add a new item to a solution.

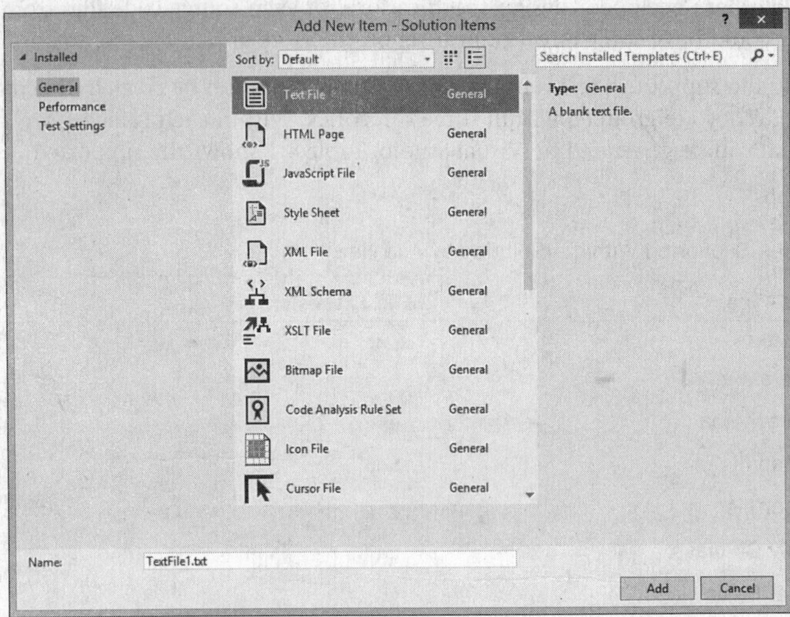

FIGURE 4.5 Adding a new solution item.

Solution Folders

To assist in organizing the various files in your solution, you can use solution folders. Solution folders are virtual folders implemented entirely within Visual Studio. Creating a solution folder does not cause a physical file folder to be created on disk; these folders exist solely to provide another grouping level within the solution. Solution folders can be nested and are especially useful in large solutions that contain many different projects and miscellaneous files. For example, you might want to group all your web service projects under a single solution folder called Services and group the Windows forms elements of your solution under a user interface (UI) folder. On disk, files added to a virtual folder are physically stored within the root of the solution directory structure.

NOTE

Visual Studio creates solution folders automatically if you add a nonproject item to a solution. For instance, if we want to add a text file to the current solution, Visual Studio automatically adds a solution folder titled Solution Items to contain the text file. Similarly, you might see a `Misc Files` folder in some solutions. This is simply a solution folder.

Beyond providing a way to visually group items, solution folders allow you to apply certain commands against all the projects contained within an individual folder. For example, you can "unload" all the projects within a virtual folder by issuing the unload command against the virtual folder. (This makes the projects temporarily unavailable within the solution; they can be useful when trying to isolate build problems or solution problems.) After unloading the projects in a solution folder, another right-click on the same solution folder allows you to reload the projects.

Solution Properties

You can set several solution-level properties from within the IDE. The Solution Property Pages dialog box gives you direct access to these properties and enables you to do the following:

- Set the startup project of the solution. (This project runs when you start the debugger.)
- Manage interproject dependencies.
- Specify the location of source files to use when debugging.
- Control static code analysis settings.
- Modify the solution build configurations.

You launch this dialog box by clicking the solution in the Solution Explorer window and then clicking View, Property Pages, or right-clicking the solution in the Solution Explorer and selecting Properties. On this dialog box, the property page categories are represented in a tree view to the left; expanding a tree node reveals the individual property pages available.

Specifying the Startup Project Figure 4.6 shows the Startup Project property page. The Startup Project property page indicates whether the startup project should be the currently selected project, a single project, or multiple projects.

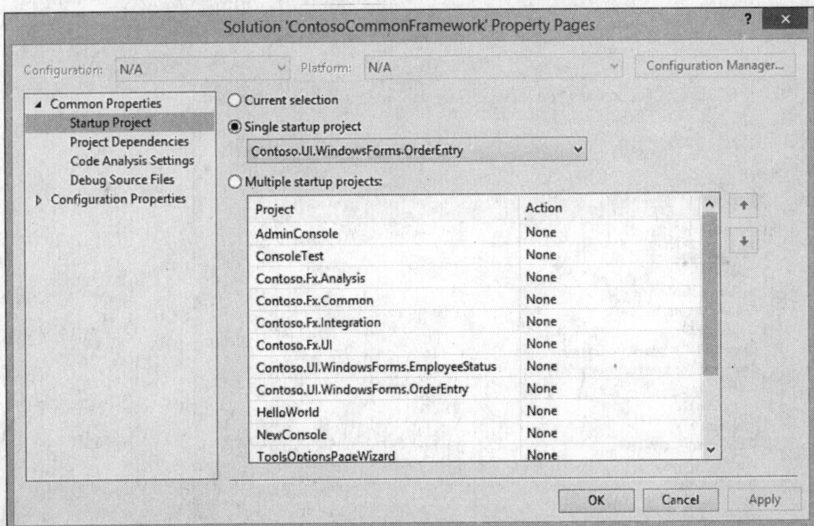

FIGURE 4.6 The Startup Project property page.

The default, and most typically used option, is to specify a single startup project. The project to run is specified in the drop-down box. If Current Selection is selected, the project that currently has focus in the Solution Explorer is considered the startup project. Also note that as soon as you switch from one file of a project to another file of another project, the latter project becomes the current project: no need to click on the project in the Solution Explorer!

You can also launch multiple projects when the debugger is started. Each project currently loaded in the solution appears in the list box with a default action of None. Projects set to None are not executed by the debugger. You can also choose from the actions Start and Start Without Debugging. As their names suggest, the Start action causes the indicated project to run within the debugger; Start Without Debugging causes the project to run, but it is not debugged.

Setting Project Dependencies If a solution has projects that depend on one another—that is, one project relies on and uses the types exposed by another project—Visual Studio needs to have a build order of precedence established among the projects. For example, consider a Windows application project that consumes types that are exposed by a class library project. The build process fails if the class library is not built first within the build sequence.

Most of the time, Visual Studio is able to determine the correct sequence based on the references added to the different projects. You might need to manually indicate that a project is dependent on other specific projects. For instance, a UI project might depend on another class library project. To supply this information, you use the Project Dependencies property page (see Figure 4.7). By selecting a project in the drop-down, you can indicate which other projects it depends on by placing a check mark on any of the projects shown in the Depends On list.

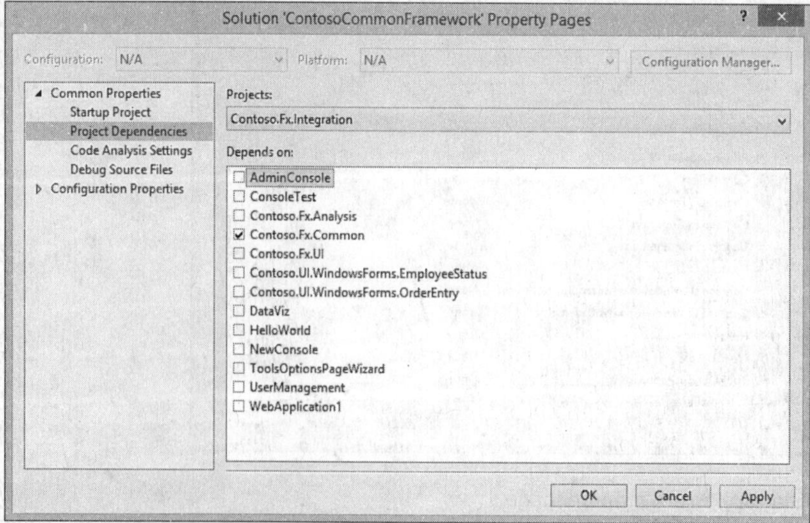

FIGURE 4.7 Project dependencies.

Code Analysis Settings Visual Studio has a built-in capability to perform static code analysis. Put simply, this allows the IDE to analyze and report on the health of your code with regard to how well it follows a set of best practices and guidelines. Microsoft provides multiple rules libraries that can be executed against your code. These range from globalization rules to security rules to basic design guideline rules. The Code Analysis Settings property page (see Figure 4.8) is used to specify which rule set should be run against which project in your solution. Chapter 9, "Refactoring Code," covers more of the features of static code analysis.

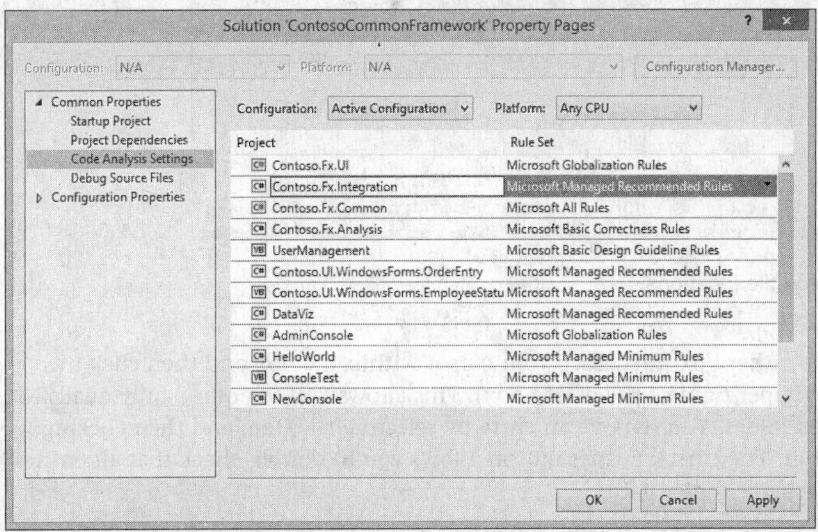

FIGURE 4.8 Code analysis settings.

Source File Location for Debugging In certain situations, you might need to explicitly point the Visual Studio debugger at source files to use when the debugger executes. One such scenario occurs when you are trying to debug a solution that references an object on a remote machine. If the source is not available locally for that remote object, you can explicitly point Visual Studio at the source files.

The Debug Source Files property page (see Figure 4.9) has two different list boxes. The top box contains a list of folders that hold source code specific to your debugging scenario. The bottom list box enables you to indicate specific files that the debugger should ignore (that is, should not load) when debugging. This last option is useful when you may not have all the source code files on your local machine; you can simply tell Visual Studio to ignore files that aren't available to the debugger.

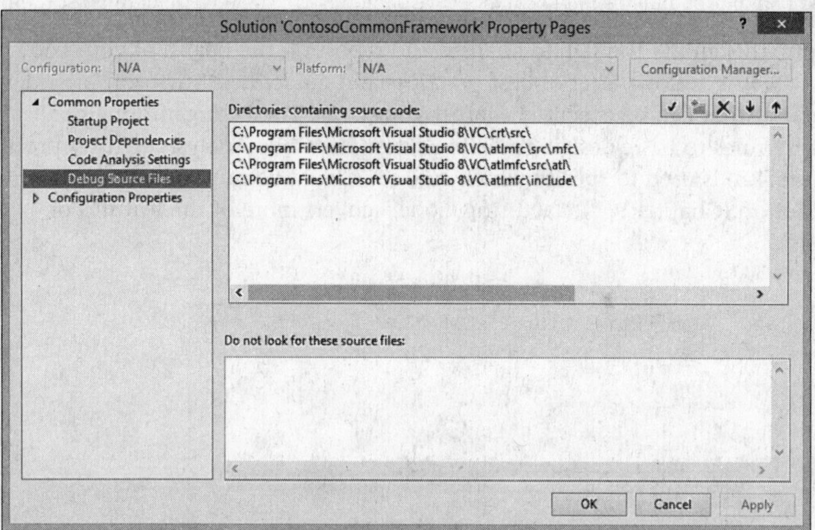

FIGURE 4.9 Source file locations.

To add an entry to either box, first place your cursor within the box and then click the New Line button (upper right of the dialog box). This allows you to enter a fully qualified path to the desired folder. You remove an entry by selecting the item and then clicking the Cut Line button. The Check Entries button allows you to double-check that all entries point to valid, reachable folder paths.

If the loaded solution has any Visual C++ projects, you probably see several items already added into the Directories Containing Source Code list box.

Build Configuration Properties Build configurations are covered in depth in Chapter 10, "Debugging Code." On the Build Configuration property page (see Figure 4.10), you indicate how Visual Studio builds the projects contained within the solution. For each project, you can set a configuration (Release or Debug by default) and platform (AnyCPU, x86, x64 or any specific target) value. In addition, a check box allows you to indicate whether to build and deploy a particular project.

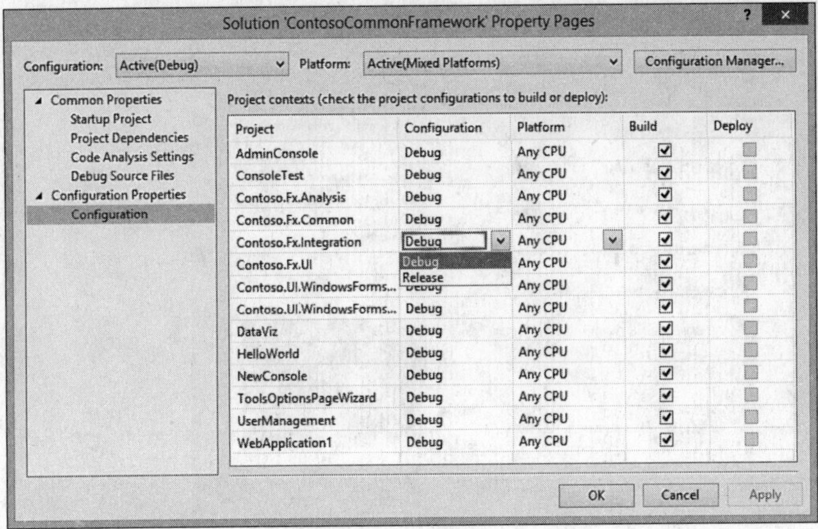

FIGURE 4.10 Build configuration properties.

See Chapter 10 for information on how to effectively use build configurations in your development.

Now that we have covered the concept of a solution in depth, let's examine the role of projects within Visual Studio.

Getting Comfortable with Projects

Projects are where all the real work is performed in Visual Studio. A project maps directly to a compiled component. Visual Studio supports various project types. Let's reexamine the project creation process.

Creating a Project

As you saw earlier during the solution creation discussion, you create projects by selecting the New, Project option from the File menu. This launches the New Project dialog box (see Figure 4.11).

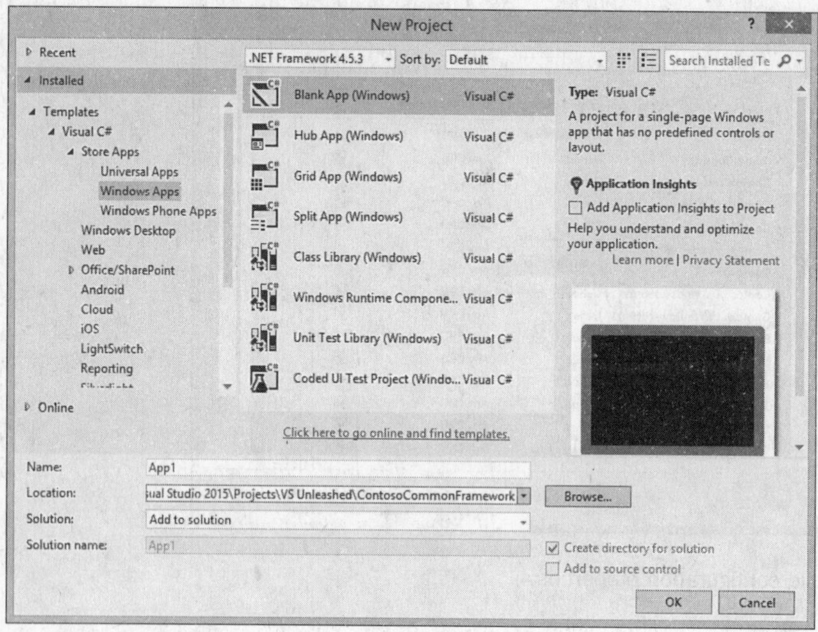

FIGURE 4.11 Adding a project to the current solution.

Table 4.2 shows some of the various project types supported in Visual Studio out of the box.

NOTE

Visual Studio supports the capability to create new project types and templates. Because Visual Studio is extensible in this fashion, the list of project types that you see in your particular copy of Visual Studio can vary greatly depending on the Visual Studio SKU you have installed and any add-ins, extensions, or "starter kits" you have installed on your PC.

For example, the Windows Azure software development kit (SDK), when downloaded and installed, adds project types under the Cloud category.

TABLE 4.2 Supported Project Types

Category	Project Type
Other Languages/SQL Server	SQL Server Database Project
Office	App for Office
	Cloud Business App
	Excel Add-In
	Excel Template

Category	Project Type
	Excel Workbook
	InfoPath Add-In
	Outlook Add-In
	PowerPoint Add-In
	Project Add-In
	Visio Add-In
	Word Add-In
	Word Document
	Word Template
Test	Unit Test Project
Web	ASP.NET 5 Class Library
	ASP.NET 5 Console Application
	ASP.NET Web Application
Windows Desktop	Class Library
	Class Library (Portable)
	Console Application
	Empty Project
	Shared Project
	Windows Forms Application
	Windows Forms Control Library
	Windows Service
	WPF Application
	WPF Browser Application
	WPF Custom Control Library
	WPF User Control Library

NOTE

Project types are dependent on a specific version of the .NET Framework. Changing the selected entry in the framework version drop-down that you see at the top of Figure 4.11 will filter the list of project types accordingly.

As outlined previously, creating a new project also creates a new containing solution. However, if you are creating a project and you already have a solution loaded in the IDE, the New Project dialog box offers you the opportunity to add the new project to the existing solution. Compare Figure 4.11 with Figure 4.2; notice that there is a new option in the form of a drop-down box that allows you to indicate whether Visual Studio should create a new solution or add the project to the current solution.

Website Projects

Developers have two different ways to create web projects within Visual Studio 2015. Web application projects are created using the New Project dialog that we just discussed. Website projects are created in a slightly different fashion. Instead of selecting File, New, Project, you select File, New, Web Site. This launches the New Web Site dialog box (see Figure 4.12).

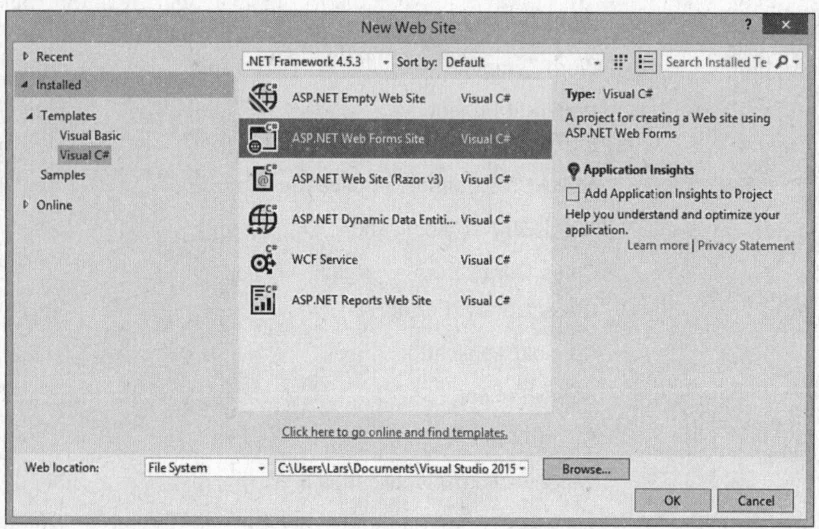

FIGURE 4.12 Creating a new website project.

As with other project types, you initiate website projects by selecting one of the predefined templates. In addition to the template, you select a target source language and the location for the website. The location can be the file system, an HTTP site, or an FTP site. Unlike other project types, websites are not typically created within the physical folder tree that houses your solution. By default, even selecting the file system object places the resulting source files in a Web Sites folder under the Visual Studio 2015 projects folder.

NOTE

The *target source language* for a website project simply represents the default language used for any code files. It does not constrain the languages you can use within the project. For instance, a website project created with C# as the target language can still contain Visual Basic code files.

After you have created the website, you manage and maintain it just like the other project types within the IDE.

You might be wondering about the difference between a web application project and a website project. One key difference is the way that these two different project types are built. Web application projects use the same build model as the other .NET project types; that is, all the code in the project is compiled into a single assembly. Website projects, however, support a dynamic build model in which the code for a particular page is generated at runtime the first time a user hits the page. In this model, each page has its own assembly. There are many other differences between the two project types, as discussed in Part V, "Building Web Applications."

Working with Project Definition Files

As with solutions, projects maintain their structure information inside a file. These files have different extensions depending on their underlying language. For instance, Visual Basic project files have a `.vbproj` extension, and Visual C# project files have a `.csproj` extension.

Each project definition file contains all the information necessary to describe the source files and the various project properties and options. This includes the following:

- Build configurations
- Project references and dependencies
- Source code file locations/types

Visual Basic and Visual C# project definition files are based on the same schema. Listing 4.2 contains a snippet from a Visual C# project definition file.

LISTING 4.2 Contents of a Visual C# Project Definition File

```
<?xml version="1.0" encoding="utf-8"?>
<Project ToolsVersion="4.0" DefaultTargets="Build"
➥xmlns="http://schemas.microsoft.com/developer/msbuild/2003">
  <Import Project="$(MSBuildExtensionsPath)\$(MSBuildToolsVersion)\
➥Microsoft.Common.props"
Condition="Exists('$(MSBuildExtensionsPath)\$(MSBuildToolsVersion)\
➥Microsoft.Common.props')" />
  <PropertyGroup>
    <Configuration Condition=" '$(Configuration)' == '' ">Debug</Configuration>
    <Platform Condition=" '$(Platform)' == '' ">AnyCPU</Platform>
    <ProjectGuid>{65C9998A-C3F7-4299-B91E-030499362F80}</ProjectGuid>
    <OutputType>WinExe</OutputType>
    <AppDesignerFolder>Properties</AppDesignerFolder>
    <RootNamespace>WindowsFormsApplication1</RootNamespace>
    <AssemblyName>WindowsFormsApplication1</AssemblyName>
    <TargetFrameworkVersion>v4.5</TargetFrameworkVersion>
```

```
    <FileAlignment>512</FileAlignment>
  </PropertyGroup>
  <PropertyGroup Condition=" '$(Configuration)|$(Platform)' == 'Debug|AnyCPU' ">
    <PlatformTarget>AnyCPU</PlatformTarget>
    <DebugSymbols>true</DebugSymbols>
    <DebugType>full</DebugType>
    <Optimize>false</Optimize>
    <OutputPath>bin\Debug\</OutputPath>
    <DefineConstants>DEBUG;TRACE</DefineConstants>
    <ErrorReport>prompt</ErrorReport>
    <WarningLevel>4</WarningLevel>
  </PropertyGroup>
  <PropertyGroup Condition=" '$(Configuration)|$(Platform)' == 'Release|AnyCPU' ">
    <PlatformTarget>AnyCPU</PlatformTarget>
    <DebugType>pdbonly</DebugType>
    <Optimize>true</Optimize>
    <OutputPath>bin\Release\</OutputPath>
    <DefineConstants>TRACE</DefineConstants>
    <ErrorReport>prompt</ErrorReport>
    <WarningLevel>4</WarningLevel>
  </PropertyGroup>
  <ItemGroup>
    <Reference Include="System" />
    <Reference Include="System.Core" />
    <Reference Include="System.Xml.Linq" />
    <Reference Include="System.Data.DataSetExtensions" />
    <Reference Include="Microsoft.CSharp" />
    <Reference Include="System.Data" />
    <Reference Include="System.Deployment" />
    <Reference Include="System.Drawing" />
    <Reference Include="System.Windows.Forms" />
    <Reference Include="System.Xml" />
  </ItemGroup>
  <ItemGroup>
    <Compile Include="Form1.cs">
      <SubType>Form</SubType>
    </Compile>
    <Compile Include="Form1.Designer.cs">
      <DependentUpon>Form1.cs</DependentUpon>
    </Compile>
    <Compile Include="Program.cs" />
    <Compile Include="Properties\AssemblyInfo.cs" />
    <EmbeddedResource Include="Properties\Resources.resx">
      <Generator>ResXFileCodeGenerator</Generator>
      <LastGenOutput>Resources.Designer.cs</LastGenOutput>
      <SubType>Designer</SubType>
```

```
    </EmbeddedResource>
    <Compile Include="Properties\Resources.Designer.cs">
      <AutoGen>True</AutoGen>
      <DependentUpon>Resources.resx</DependentUpon>
    </Compile>
    <None Include="Properties\Settings.settings">
      <Generator>SettingsSingleFileGenerator</Generator>
      <LastGenOutput>Settings.Designer.cs</LastGenOutput>
    </None>
    <Compile Include="Properties\Settings.Designer.cs">
      <AutoGen>True</AutoGen>
      <DependentUpon>Settings.settings</DependentUpon>
      <DesignTimeSharedInput>True</DesignTimeSharedInput>
    </Compile>
  </ItemGroup>
  <ItemGroup>
    <None Include="App.config" />
  </ItemGroup>
  <Import Project="$(MSBuildToolsPath)\Microsoft.CSharp.targets" />
  <!-- To modify your build process, add your task inside one of the targets below
➥and uncomment it.
       Other similar extension points exist, see Microsoft.Common.targets.
  <Target Name="BeforeBuild">
  </Target>
  <Target Name="AfterBuild">
  </Target>
  -->
</Project>
```

This project definition file would look relatively the same as a Visual Basic project.

Working with Projects

As source code containers, projects principally act as a settings applicator. They are used to control and organize your source code files and the various properties associated with the whole build and compile process. (You learn about the build process in depth in Chapter 11, "Deploying Code.") As with solutions, projects can contain various items that are germane to their development. Projects are language specific. You cannot mix different languages within a specific project. There is no similar limitation with solutions: a solution can contain many projects, each one in a different language.

Project Items

After a project is created, by default it contains one or more project items. These default items vary depending on the project template you selected and on the language of the project. For instance, creating a project using the C# Windows Forms application template results in the formation of a `Form1.cs` file, a `Form1.Designer.cs` file, and a `Program.cs` file. Projects are also preconfigured with references and properties that make sense for the given project type: the Windows Forms application template contains a reference to the `System.Windows.Forms` assembly, whereas the class library template does not.

Projects, like solutions, can have subfolders within them that you can use to better manage and group project items. Unlike solutions, the folders you create within a project are physical; they are created on disk within your project directory structure. These are examples of physical project items. Source code files are also physical in nature.

Projects can contain virtual items (items that are merely pointers or links to items that don't actually manifest themselves physically within your project structure). They are, for example, references to other assemblies, database connections, and virtual folders. (Virtual folders are described in Chapter 5.) Figure 4.13 illustrates a fully described solution and project.

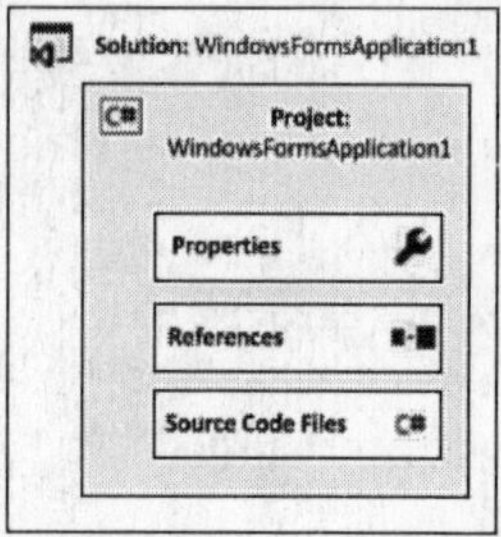

FIGURE 4.13 Project structure.

Project Properties

Like solution properties, project properties are viewed and set using a series of property pages accessed through the Project, Properties menu. These property pages are hosted within a dialog box referred to as the Project Designer. Figure 4.14 shows the Project Designer that is displayed for a sample Visual Basic class library project. Different languages and different project types actually surface different property pages within the Project Designer. For instance, the Application property page for a Visual Basic project looks different and contains slightly different information than an identical Visual C# project (although the basic intent of the page remains unchanged).

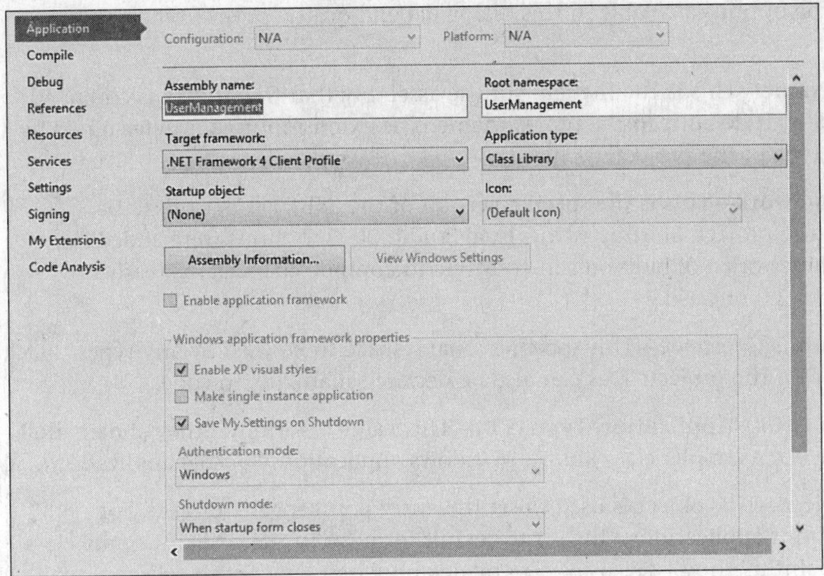

FIGURE 4.14 Setting properties using the Project Designer.

In general, you use project properties to control the following:

- General project attributes such as the assembly name and project type
- The way the project is built/compiled
- Debugger configuration for the project
- Resources used by the project
- Signing and security settings

NOTE

The Project Designer is easily accessed from the Solution Explorer pane. For C# projects, you can double-click the Properties item under the project. Visual Basic projects have a My Project item that does the same thing. And, of course, you can always right-click the project name and then select Properties from the pop-up menu.

Let's examine some of the more common project property pages and discuss briefly the options that can be set on each.

Application The Application property page allows you to set the assembly name, root/default namespace, application/output type, and startup object. For Windows Forms applications, authentication modes and visual styles are also controlled via this property page. Note that the options available in this dialog depend on the project type and the chosen language:

- **Assembly Name**—This is the filename of the assembly that the project is compiled into. Typically, it defaults to the project name. The extension used is determined by the output type of the project.
- **Target Framework**—This is the specific version of the .NET Framework to be targeted by the project. Starting with Visual Studio 2012, options were added here for .NET Framework 4.5, but you can continue to compile code against earlier versions from 2.0 onward.
- **Root/Default Namespace**—This specifies a namespace to be used by any types declared within the project. This can also be declared manually in code.
- **Output Type (C#)/Application Type (VB)**—This value determines the fundamental project type (for example, class library, Windows application, console application).
- **Startup Object**—This object is used to set the entry point for the project. For Windows Forms applications, this is the default form (or in the case of C#, the class and entry point method—`Program.Main` by default when [Not Set] is selected) that should be launched when the application is executed. For console applications, the startup object is the method that Windows calls after the console has been created—also `Program.Main` by default when (Not Set) is selected. Class library projects do not have an entry point and will be set to (Not Set) for C# projects, and (None) for Visual Basic projects.
- **Icon**—This is the icon to associate with the assembly and visible from the Windows Explorer. It is not pertinent to class library or web projects.
- **Resource File**—This text box can be used to specify a path and filename for a Win32 resource file. Resource files contain nonexecutable content, such as strings, images, or version information, that is embedded within the compiled assembly. Note that by default for .NET projects, version information is generated based on the `AssemblyInfo` file that contains specific attributes.
- **Windows Application Framework Properties**—Visual Basic provides a series of properties that apply specifically to Windows application projects. These properties allow you to set the splash screen associated with the project, enable or disable support for XP themes/visual styles, set the authentication mode supported by the project (Windows or application-defined), and set the shutdown mode of the project. The shutdown mode specifies whether the application should shut down when the initial form is closed or when the last loaded form in the application is closed.

Build (C# Only) The Build property page is used with Visual C# projects to tweak settings associated with build configurations. Using this dialog box, you can select whether the

DEBUG and TRACE constants are turned on, and you can specify conditional compilation symbols. Settings that affect the warning and error levels and the build output are also housed here. For more exploration of the options available here, see Chapter 10.

Build Events (C# Only) Visual Studio triggers a prebuild and postbuild event for each project. On the Build Events page, you can specify commands that should be run during either of these events. This page also allows you to indicate when the post-build event runs: always, after a successful build, or when the build updates the project output. Build events are particularly useful for launching system tests and unit tests against a project that has just been recompiled. If you launch a suite of, say, unit tests from within the postbuild event, the test cycle can be embedded within the build cycle.

NOTE

If you specify commands in the prebuild or postbuild events, Visual Studio creates a batch file for each event and places it into the `bin/debug` directory. These files, `PreBuildEvent.bat` and `PostBuildEvent.bat`, house the commands you enter on the Build Events property page. In the event of an error running the build event commands, you can manually inspect and run these files to try to chase down the bug.

Compile (VB Only The Compile property page is used by Visual Basic projects to control which optimizations are performed during compile and control general compilation options for the output path and warnings versus errors raised during the compilation process. It is analogous to the C# Build property page:

- **Compile Options**—You use the Option Strict, Option Explicit, and Option Infer drop-downs to turn on or off these settings. You can also control whether the project performs binary or text comparisons with the Option Compare drop-down.
- **Compiler Conditions**—Visual Basic allows you to customize the level of notification provided upon detecting any of a handful of conditions during the compilation process. For instance, one condition defined is Unused Local Variable. If this condition is detected in the source code during the compile, you can elect to have it treated as a warning or an error or to have it ignored altogether.
- **Build Events**—Visual Basic allows you to access the Build Events property page (see the preceding section for an explanation) via a Build Events button located on this screen.
- **Warning configurations**—You can choose to disable all compiler warnings, treat all warnings as errors, and generate an XML documentation file during the compile process. This results in an XML file with the same name as the project; it contains all the code comments parsed out of your source code in a predefined format.

Debug The Debug property page allows you to affect the behavior of the Visual Studio debugger:

- **Start Action**—You use this option to specify whether a custom program, a URL, or the current project itself should be started when the debugger is launched.
- **Start Options**—You use this option to specify command-line arguments to pass to the running project, set the working directory for the project, and debug a process on a remote machine.
- **Enable Debuggers**—You use the check boxes in this section to enable or disable such things as support for debugging unmanaged code, support for SQL stored procedure debugging, and use of Visual Studio as a host for the debugger process.

Publish The Publish property page enables you to configure many ClickOnce-specific properties. You can specify the publish location for the application, the install location (if different from the publish location), and the various installation settings, including prerequisites and update options. You can also control the versioning scheme for the published assemblies.

References (VB Only) The References property page is used within Visual Basic projects to select the assemblies referenced by the project and to import namespaces into the project. This screen also allows you to query the project in an attempt to determine whether some existing references are unused. You do this by using the Unused References button.

Reference Paths (C# Only) The Reference Paths property page allows you to provide path information meant to help Visual Studio find assemblies referenced by the project. Visual Studio first attempts to resolve assembly references by looking in the current project directory. If the assembly is not found there, the paths provided on this property page are used to search for the assemblies. Visual Studio also probes the project's `obj` directory, but only after attempting to resolve first using the reference paths you have specified on this screen.

Resources Resources are items such as strings, images, icons, audio, and files that are embedded in a project and used during design and runtime. The Resources property page allows you to add, edit, and delete resources associated with the project.

Security For ClickOnce applications, the Security property page allows you to enforce code access security permissions for running the ClickOnce application. Various full-trust and partial-trust scenarios are supported.

Settings Application settings are dynamically specified name/value pairs that can be used to store information specific to your project/application. The Settings property page allows you to add, edit, and delete these name/value pairs.

Each setting can be automatically scoped to the application or to the user and can have a default value specified. Applications can then consume these settings at runtime.

Signing The Signing property page allows you to have Visual Studio code sign the project assembly (and its ClickOnce manifests) by specifying a key file. You can also enable Delay Signing from this screen.

Summary

Solutions and projects are the primary vehicles within Visual Studio for organizing and managing your code. They allow you to divide and conquer large solutions, and they provide a single point of access for various settings (at both the solution and project levels). Solutions are the top-level container and the first work item that Visual Studio creates when creating a new code project.

In this chapter, you learned the following about solutions:

- Solutions can be built (triggering a build of each of its projects) but cannot be compiled.
- Visual Studio can load only one solution at a time; to work on multiple solutions concurrently, you must have multiple copies of Visual Studio running.
- You can create folders within a solution to help group its content; these folders are virtual and do not represent physical folders on disk.
- Solutions are primarily used to group one or more projects. Projects within a solution can be a mix of the various supported languages and project types.
- Solutions cannot contain other solutions.
- Besides projects, solutions can contain miscellaneous files (called solution items) that typically represent information pertinent to the solution (readme files, system diagrams, and the like).

Although solutions are an important and necessary implement, it is the Visual Studio project that actually results in a compiled .NET component. Projects are created and based on templates available within the IDE that cover the various development scenarios, ranging from web application development to Windows application development to smart device development.

In this chapter, you learned the following about projects:

- Projects exist to compile code into assemblies.
- Projects are based on a project template; project templates define the various artifacts, references, and so on that make sense for the project's context.
- Like solutions, projects support subfolders to help you better organize your code. These folders are actual physical folders that are created on disk.
- Projects contain project items. They can be source code files, references, and other items such as virtual folders and database connections.

You have seen how solutions and projects are physically manifested; the next chapter covers the primary Visual Studio tools used to interact with solutions and projects.

CHAPTER 5

Browsers and Explorers

IN THIS CHAPTER

- Leveraging the Solution Explorer
- Class View
- Server Explorer
- Object Browser
- Document Online

Visual Studio provides a cohesive and all-encompassing view of your solutions, projects, and types within your projects through windows called browsers and explorers. These windows (which are confusingly also referred to as view windows) attempt to provide a visually structured representation of a large variety of elements (some code based, others not).

In general, you access and display these windows through the View menu. Some of these windows, such as the Solution Explorer and Class View, are staples of a developer's daily routine. Others touch on elements that are used during specific points within the development cycle or by more advanced Visual Studio IDE users.

This chapter examines each of the basic browser and explorer windows in detail.

Leveraging the Solution Explorer

The Solution Explorer is the primary tool for viewing and manipulating solutions and projects. It provides a simple but powerful hierarchical view of all solution and project items, and it enables you to interact with each item directly via context menus and its toolbar.

Using Solution Explorer, you can launch an editor for any given file, add new items to a project or solution, and reorganize the structure of a project or solution. In addition, the Solution Explorer provides instant, at-a-glance information as to the currently selected project; the startup project for the solution; and the physical hierarchy of the solution, its projects, and their child items.

The Solution Explorer is simply a window hosted by Visual Studio. It can be docked, pinned, and floated anywhere within the Visual Studio environment. It is composed of a title bar, a toolbar, and a scrollable tree-view region (see Figure 5.1).

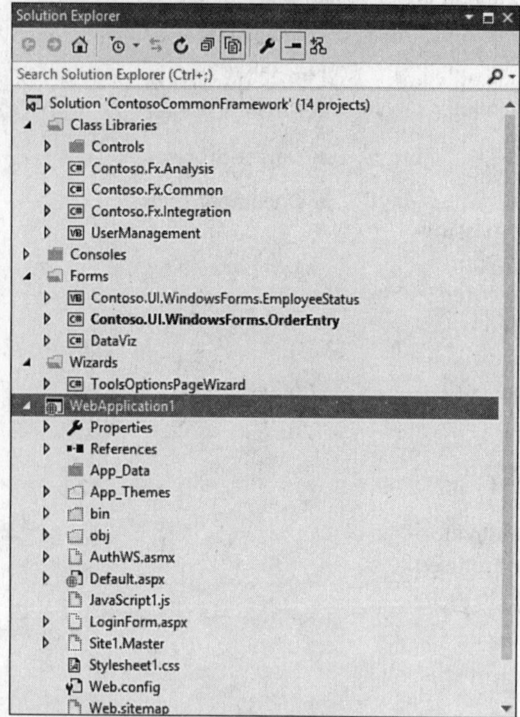

FIGURE 5.1 The Solution Explorer.

The tree view provides a graphics- and text-organizational view of the currently loaded solution. Figure 5.1 shows all the various items and projects represented for a 14-project solution loaded in the IDE.

Visual Cues and Item Types

Each item in the Solution Explorer is represented by a name and by an icon. Table 5.1 shows which icon is used to represent the supported item types.

TABLE 5.1 Solution Explorer Item Types and Icons

Icon	Item	Notes
	ASP.NET Web Site	The root node for an ASP.NET website project
	Bitmap File	
	Custom Control	
	DataSet	
	Folder	Solution folders or project folders
	HTML Page	
	Icon File	
	Interface	
	Master Page	Web projects only
	Module	Visual Basic only
	My Project File (VB) / Properties Folder (C#)	
	Project Reference	Visual C# only
	Site Map	Web projects only
	Skin File	Web projects only
	Solution	The topmost root node visible within Solution Explorer
	Style Sheet	
	Text File	
	User Control	Any class that inherits directly from the `UserControl` class
	VBScript/JScript File	
VB	Visual Basic Source File	
	Visual Basic Project	The root node for a Visual Basic project
	Visual C# Project	The root node for a Visual C# project
C#	Visual C# Source File	
	Web Configuration File	
	Web Form (`.aspx`)	
	Web Project	
	Web Service	
	Windows Form	Refers to a file containing a class that implements the `Form` class
	XML File	
	XML Schema File	
	XSLT File	

NOTE

The icons shown in Table 5.1 are a representative list of icons that correspond to specific project and solution items within the IDE. Other files added to a project or solution are represented by the icon associated with their file types. For example, a Word document is represented by the standard Word document icon in the Solution Explorer.

Version Control and Item Status

To provide a visual cue about the status of a particular item, the Solution Explorer overlays an additional graphical element on the item icon. These overlays are called signal icons. For example, when source code control is enabled, the Solution Explorer visually indicates whether an item is checked out via a graphical overlay. Table 5.2 describes the version control signal icons used by the Solution Explorer to indicate the current version control status of the item. Note that the version control state of an item is dependent on the actual version control system you are using (for instance, Git or Team Foundation Version Control).

TABLE 5.2 Version Control Signal Icons

Icon	Description
	Checked in. The item is under source code control and is currently checked in.
✔	Checked out (to you). The item is under source code control and is currently checked out by you.
	Checked out (by someone else). The item is under source code control and is currently checked out by someone else.
	Excluded. The item has been specifically excluded from version control.
	Pending Add. The item is scheduled to be added to the source control system during the next check-in.

Interacting with Items

The Solution Explorer supports different management actions depending on whether you are currently interacting with a solution or a project. In fact, supported commands might vary by project type as well. As an example, the Copy Web Project command button is available for web projects but not class library projects, whereas the Properties command button is available for all item types.

There are two primary interfaces for interaction within Solution Explorer: the toolbar and the context menu. Let's review the primary features.

Table 5.3 shows the various buttons hosted in the Solution Explorer's toolbar, along with their specific scope.

TABLE 5.3 Solution Explorer Toolbar Buttons

Icon	Context	Description
	All	Back button. Moves to the prior filtering scope.
	All	Next button. Moves to the next filtering scope.
	All	Home button. Removes any existing filtering scope.
	All	File filter. Allows you to show only files that are open in an editor, or only files that have pending changes. You select between the two different modes (open files versus pending changes) by using the drop-down, and then you turn on or turn off the filter by toggling the button.
	All	Synch with active document. Selects the file in Solution Explorer that is open in the current/active designer/editor window.
	All	Refresh. Refreshes the contents of the Solution Explorer window.
	All	Collapse all. Collapses any currently expanded trees within the Solution Explorer.
	Project	Show all files. Collapses any currently expanded trees within the Solution Explorer.
	Project	Nest related files. The Solution Explorer window has the capability to group certain project item constructs. This is most commonly done with items such as code behind files. Clicking this toggle button "on" causes related files to be nested underneath the "parent" file. Clicking it "off" causes all files to show up at the same level under the project.
	Code file	View code. Opens the currently selected item in a code editor window.
	All	Properties. Opens the Properties dialog, or shows the properties window, for the currently selected item.
	All	Preview selected item. Toggles the item preview feature of Visual Studio. With preview turned on, just selecting/single-clicking an item in the Solution Explorer will cause the item to immediately load in an editor/designer tab.

Managing Solutions

Clicking the solution in Solution Explorer immediately exposes all the valid management commands for that solution. As stated earlier, you access these commands through either the Solution Explorer toolbar or the context menu for the solution (which you access by right-clicking the solution). Through the toolbar and the solution's context menu, the Solution Explorer allows you to do the following:

- View and set the properties for a solution
- Build/rebuild a solution
- Directly launch the configuration manager for a solution
- Set project dependencies and build order

- Add any of the various Visual Studio-supported solution and project items
- Run code analysis against all the files in the solution
- View code metrics for all the files in the solution
- Add the solution to the source control

You can initiate some of these actions by using the Solution Explorer toolbar; you can access the balance in the context menu for a solution, as shown in Figure 5.2.

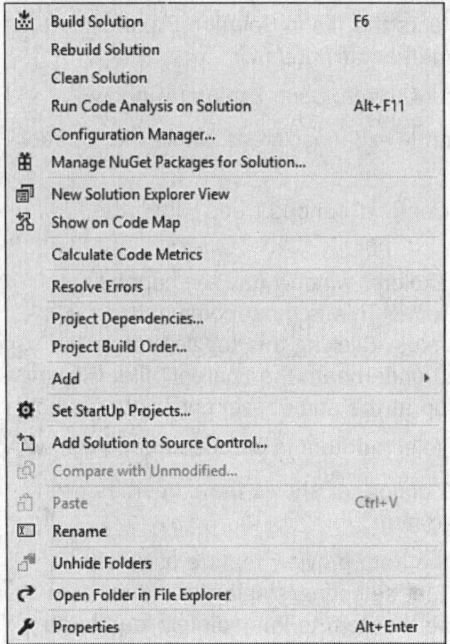

FIGURE 5.2 The solution context menu.

Managing Projects

Just as with solutions, Solution Explorer provides various ways to manage projects within a solution, including the following:

- Opening a project item
- Building or rebuilding a project
- Adding items to a project
- Adding a reference to a project
- Cutting, pasting, renaming, or deleting a project within the solution tree

- Editing project properties
- Running code analysis against all the files in the project
- Viewing code metrics for all the files in the project
- Unloading a project
- Limiting the scope of the Solution Explorer to a single project
- Launching a separate instance of the Solution Explorer window scoped to a single project

NOTE

The current startup project for a solution is indicated with a bold font (as is the `OrderEntry` project in Figure 5.1). If multiple projects are selected as startup projects, the solution name is instead bolded.

Figure 5.3 shows the project context menu for a class library project.

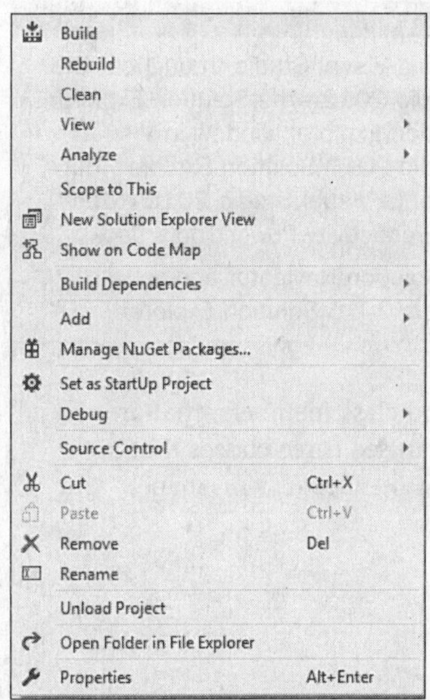

FIGURE 5.3 The project context menu.

The default action when you double-click an item is to open it within its default editor or designer. Multiple select and drag-and-drop operations are also supported. For instance, multiselecting several code files allows you to open them simultaneously in their editor windows either by right-clicking or typing the Enter key.

You can move and copy items within a solution, within a project, or between projects through the standard drag and drop using the left mouse button. You can also drag certain items from within a project and drop them onto a suitable designer surface. This is an easy way, for instance, to add classes to a class diagram: simply highlight the code files that contain the types you want to add and drag them onto the class diagram designer window.

Inspecting Objects

Visual Studio 2015 implements several improvements to the Solution Explorer from earlier versions that directly improve your ability to find and interact with objects within a solution. For instance, although the top-level hierarchies shown within the Solution Explorer are based on physical files (for example, solution files that reference project files that reference C# code files), you can also drill down directly into object definitions.

NOTE

A quick historical note: for those of you who have been using Visual Studio throughout the years, you may have noticed that—starting with Visual Studio 2012—the Solution Explorer window changed significantly over prior versions. The Solution Explorer window in Visual Studio 2012 is actually not a refinement of the Visual Studio 2010 Solution Explorer, but rather is a refinement of the popular Solution Navigator tool (a Visual Studio 2010 extension made available for download by Microsoft within the Productivity Power Tools pack).

If you need to still work in Visual Studio 2010, using the Solution Navigator add-on will give you nearly 100% of the functionality of the Visual Studio 2015 Solution Explorer.

Figure 5.4 illustrates how we can directly access a class, and class members, that are implemented within a specific code file. In this case, we can see three classes that are all implemented within the `Integration.cs` code file: `MessageMapper`, `MessageBus`, and `ContextToken`.

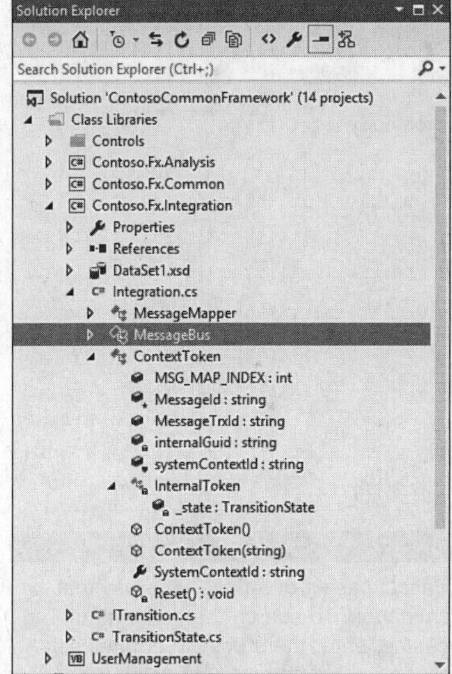

FIGURE 5.4 Examining class members.

Further expanding a class shows its properties, private fields, methods, and nested classes. If you click any of these, a code editor window opens, and you will be placed directly within the class on that specific line of code.

NOTE

The Visual Studio 2015 Solution Explorer provides an improved and speedier way to open items in an editor window. "Item Preview" mode let's you open the editor for any item in the project by simply clicking on the item; there's no need to double-click or select and then press Enter. This mode is enabled by default, but can be turned on and off by using the Preview Selected Item button at the top of the Solution Explorer window.

Searching the Solution

The Solution Explorer search box allows you to quickly locate files and code based on simple string searches. Just type your search string into the box (using the Ctrl+; hotkey combination will get you there quickly), and as you type Solution Explorer automatically starts filtering the contents of the window to only those items that match your string.

Search can be limited to just filenames or to files and their content/code. It will even search files that are external to the solution (for example, external dependencies). The option of what to search is controlled by the search box drop-down (see Figure 5.5).

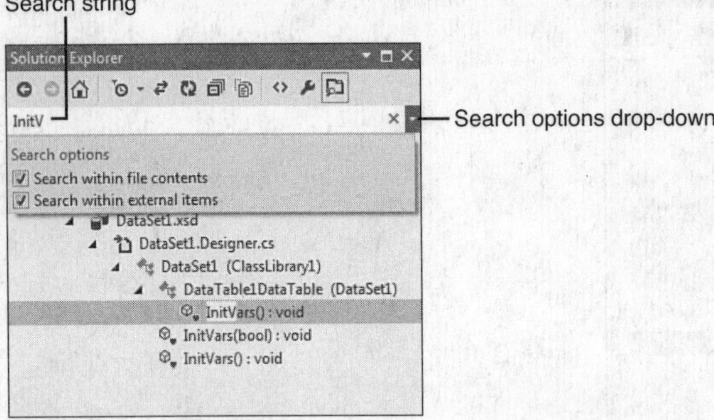

FIGURE 5.5 Searching the solution.

TIP

The search box directly supports camel casing and Pascal casing of strings. The way that it works is subtle and could be missed on initial examination. To search the contents of the solution for matches based on exact character casing, enter the string cased precisely the way that you want. For example: a class called `AboutBox` would be found using the search string `AboutB`. If you type in a search string without casing, camel casing will not be used and the search algorithm will ignore the casing entirely. Typing in `aboutb`, for example, would also locate that same `AboutBox` class.

The search box also supports Pascal-casing breaks. This allows you to type `AB` and get any element Pascal cased with a capital *A* followed by a capital *B*. The `AboutBox` class name fits this pattern and as a result would be returned by a search of `AB`.

Using View Scopes and Additional Windows

Search is one way to limit the scope of what is displayed in the Solution Explorer window. There are also three other mechanisms for filtering the contents of the window to only those things you care about. By right-clicking any project or project item, you can select Scope to This in the context menu and filter the contents of the window to only that item or the things that the item contains. Scoping to a project will only show that project and its content, and scoping to a code file will only show that code file and its methods/ properties (and so on, and so forth). Every time you scope to a different item within the window, it is just as if another view of the Solution Explorer were added as a "page." You can then use the Back, Forward, and Home buttons on the Solution Explorer toolbar to move through these scope pages or bring you back to home, which essentially removes all scopes and shows you the entire solution again.

The second way to constrain the list of items shown in the solution explorer is via the files filter. This is toggled using the filter button on the Solution Explorer toolbar. You can select from three modes: the Pending Changes filter will show only those files that have uncommitted changes; the Open Files filter will show only those files that are currently open in the IDE; and the Errors filter will show only those files that have current compile errors associated with them.

Finally, you can also scope to an element and launch that view within a completely separate, new Solution Explorer window. This is done by right-clicking an item (for instance, a project) and then selecting New Solution Explorer View. This is a great productivity feature if you have a lot of screen real estate on your monitor or if you have multiple monitors. You can take a complex solution, grab the project or class that you want to focus on, and create a new Solution Explorer view, which can be floated anywhere on your screen or docked within the IDE. Figure 5.6 shows two Solution Explorer windows, one docked and one floating, existing side by side.

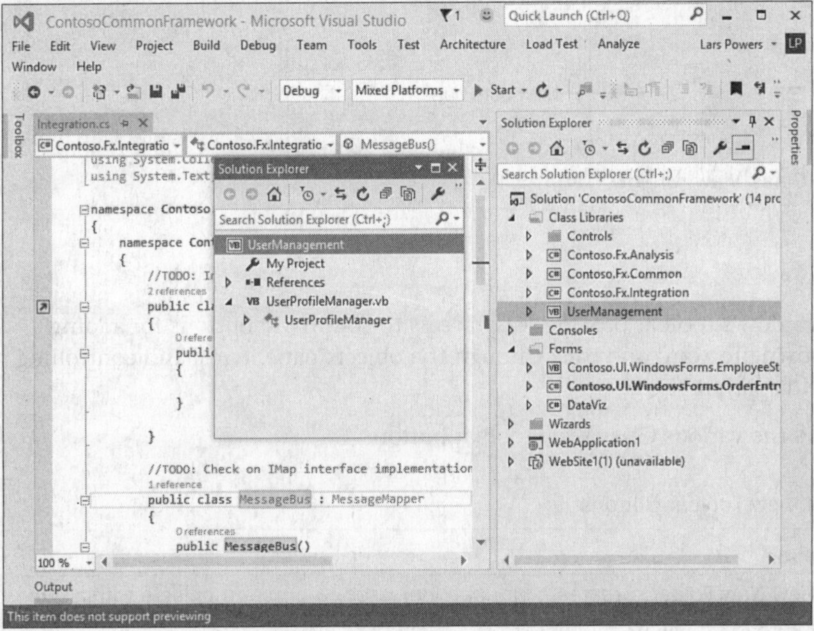

FIGURE 5.6 Creating a new Solution Explorer view.

Class View

The Class View window is similar in design and function to the Solution Explorer window. It, too, provides a hierarchical view of project elements. However, the view here is not based on the physical files that constitute a solution or project; rather, this window provides a logical view based on the relationships of the various namespaces, types, interfaces, and enums within a project.

The Class View window is composed of four major visual components: a toolbar, a search bar, a tree view of types (called the objects pane), and a members pane, as shown in Figure 5.7.

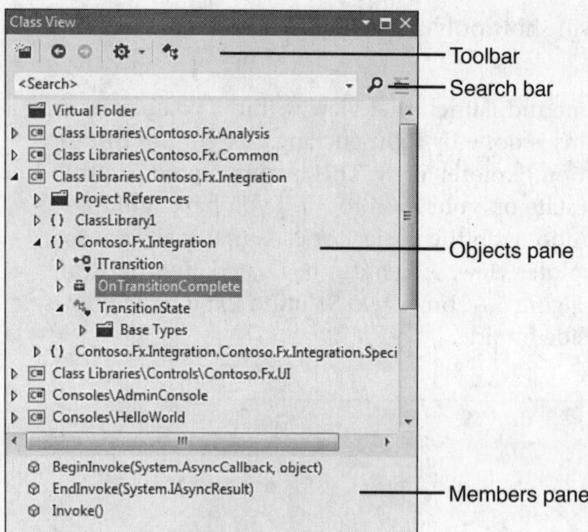

FIGURE 5.7 The Class View window.

Toolbar

The Class View window's toolbar provides easy access to command buttons for adding virtual folders, moving forward and back through the objects pane items, and controlling which objects are displayed.

Table 5.4 describes the various Class View toolbar buttons.

TABLE 5.4 Class View Toolbar Buttons

Icon	Description
	Class View New Folder. Creates a virtual folder used to organize objects within the objects pane.
	Back. Causes the previously selected item to become the currently selected item.
	Forward. Causes the most recently selected item to become the currently selected item. This button is available only after you've used the Back button.
	Class View Settings. Displays a drop-down that allows selection of object types to display within the objects pane and the members pane. The available options include these: Show Base Types, Show Project References, Show Hidden Types and Members, Show Public Members, Show Protected Members, Show Private Members, Show Other Members, and Show Inherited Members.
	View Class Diagram. Creates a class diagram project item and launches the viewer for that item. All the types contained within the project are automatically added to the diagram.

Search Bar

The search bar is a drop-down text box that provides a quick and easy way to filter the objects shown in the objects pane. When a search term (such as type name or namespace name) is entered, the Class View window clears the objects pane and then repopulates it with only those objects that match the search term. Figure 5.8 shows the results of a search for ITransition.

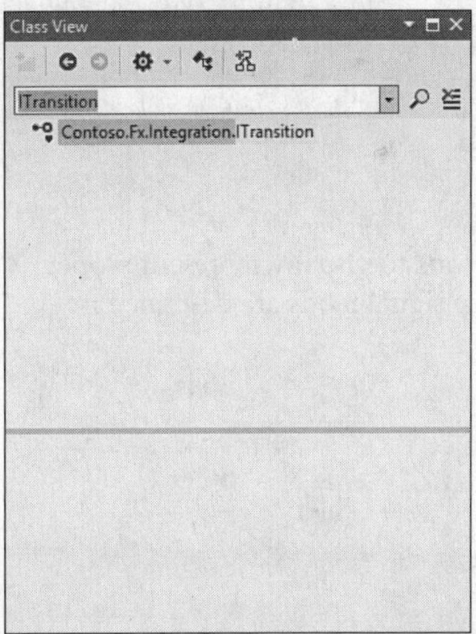

FIGURE 5.8 Filtering the objects pane.

To restore the Objects pane and remove the filter, click the Clear Search button to the right of the Search button.

Recent search terms are saved for reuse in the drop-down list.

Objects Pane

The objects pane encloses a tree of objects grouped, at the highest level, by project. Each object is identified by an icon and by its name. Expanding a project node within the tree reveals the various types contained within that project. Further parent-child relationships are also visible, such as the namespace-to-class relationship and the type-to-parent-type relationship.

Table 5.5 shows the icons used in the Objects pane.

TABLE 5.5 Objects Pane Icons

Icon	Description
	Class/struct
	Delegate
	Enum
{}	Namespace
	Module
	Interface

Certain signal images are also overlaid on top of these icons to visually represent scope and access information for each object. These access type signal icons are described in Table 5.6.

TABLE 5.6 Scope/Access Signal Icons

Icon	Description
Padlock	Private
Shield	Internal/friend
(None)	Public
Star	Protected

The depth of the various levels shown for each object is dictated by the view settings in place at the time. For example, turning on the Show Base Types option appends an additional base type level to the tree for each type. The objects pane's principal duty is to allow quick and easy navigation back and forth through the object tree for each project. It exposes, in other words, an object-oriented view of each project.

Right-clicking within the objects pane displays the shortcut menu, which is useful for quickly re-sorting and organizing items in the Class View window. These are the Sort/Group options available:

- **Sort Alphabetically**—The projects, namespaces, and types in the objects pane are sorted in ascending, alphabetic order.
- **Sort by Object Type**—The types in the objects pane are alphabetically sorted by their general classification (for example, in the following order: classes, enums, interfaces, structs).
- **Sort by Object Access**—The members are sorted by their access modifiers (public, private, protected, and so on).

- **Group by Object Type**—Another folder level is added to the tree for each distinct object type present. For example, if a project contains both class and interface types, a class folder and an interface folder are displayed in the objects pane tree, with their correlated types contained within.

Members Pane

The members pane reacts to the selections made in the objects pane by displaying all the members (properties, events, constants, variables, enums) defined on the selected type. Each member has a distinctive icon to immediately convey information such as scope and type; even member signatures show up here. (Note that the same signal icons used by the objects pane, and documented in Table 5.7, are used here as well.)

TABLE 5.7 Members Pane Icons

Icon	Description
	Constant
	Method/function
	Property
	Field

The members pane is ideal for quickly visualizing type behavior and attributes: Just select the class/type in the objects pane and browse its members in the members pane.

NOTE

Many developers find that the bulk of their development tasks are more easily envisioned and acted on within the Class View window rather than in the Solution Explorer window. The available actions among the two are virtually identical, but the Class View window provides a much more code-focused perspective of your projects. Developers can spelunk through inheritance trees and see, at a glance, other various members implemented on each defined type within their projects. The downside to using the Class View is that source code control information is not visually surfaced here.

The members pane also exposes the ability to immediately view the definition code for a member, to find every code location where the selected member is referenced, and to launch the Object Browser with the primary node for the member already selected for you.

The capability to alter the filter and display settings is also presented here. Figure 5.9 illustrates all the available commands on this menu.

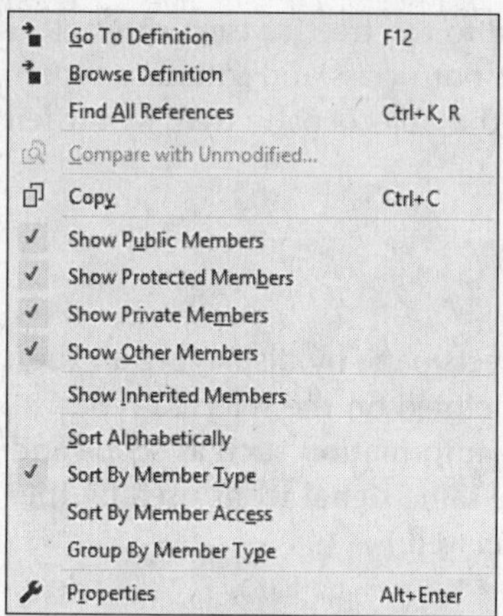

FIGURE 5.9 The members pane context menu.

Server Explorer

The Server Explorer window serves two purposes: it exposes various system services and resources that reside on your local machine and on remote machines, and it provides access to data connection objects. This tool also allows for direct management of Azure cloud-based resources and services and SharePoint instances.

As with the other Visual Studio explorer windows, the systems, services, resources, and data connections are viewed in a graphical tree format. Systems appear under a top-level Servers node (your local machine shows up by default), data connections appear under a top-level Data Connections node, Azure resources appear under an Azure node, and so on.

NOTE

The Server Explorer window content and configuration are not specific to a solution or project. Server Explorer settings are preserved as part of the IDE environment settings and are thus not subject to change on a per-solution (or project) basis.

The toolbar at the top of the Server Explorer window provides one-click access for adding a data or server connection or connecting to your Azure subscription (see Figure 5.10). You can also force a refresh of the window contents. (A button is provided to cancel the refresh because querying remote machines might be a lengthy process.)

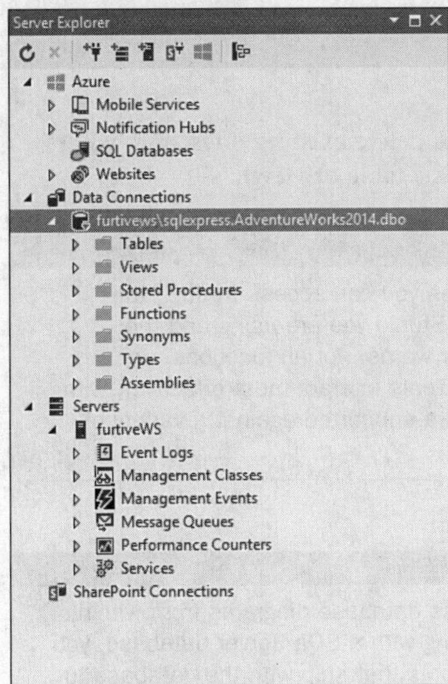

FIGURE 5.10 The Server Explorer window.

Data Connections

Data connections represent a physical connection to a local or remote database. Through an established connection, you can gain access to and manipulate the various objects within a database. Each category of object shows up as a folder node under the Data Connections node. The tree items under each node allow you to directly interact with their physical database counterparts through a suite of designers and editors. These tools are covered in depth in Chapter 13, "Working with Databases."

In Figure 5.10, we have connected to a SQL Server 2014 database and have access to the following objects within Server Explorer:

- Tables
- Views
- Stored procedures
- Functions
- Synonyms

- Types
- Assemblies

In general, you can create new database objects, edit or delete existing ones, and, where appropriate, query data from a database object (such as a table or view).

NOTE

The level of functionality and the number of object types you can access through the Server Explorer depends on both the version of Visual Studio you are using and the version of the database you are connecting to. In other words, not all functions are supported across all databases. The Visual Database Tools interact most effectively with Microsoft SQL Server, although most basic functions are supported against a variety of other relational databases.

NOTE

In prior versions of Visual Studio, you could also access database diagrams from within Server Explorer. This is no longer true. If you are working with a SQL Server database, you will need to use the SQL Server Management Studio tools that ship with the database to edit diagrams outside of Visual Studio.

Server Components

The Servers node in Server Explorer exposes various remote or local services and resources for direct management or use within a Visual Studio project. In essence, it is a management console for server-based components. By default, your local machine is visible here as a server; to add other servers, right-click the Servers node and select Add Server or click the Connect to Server button in the Server Explorer toolbar. A dialog box prompts you for a computer name or IP address for the server; this dialog box also supports the capability to connect via a different set of credentials.

Under the Servers node, the following component categories appear as child nodes:

- Event Logs
- Management Classes
- Management Events
- Message Queues
- Performance Counters
- Services

Other component categories might also choose to register for display under the Servers node; the preceding list, however, represents the default, out-of-the-box functionality provided by Visual Studio 2015.

Event Logs

Under the Event Logs node, you can administer the separate application, security, and system event logs for the connected server. This includes clearing event log entries or drilling into and inspecting individual event log entries. Highlighting an event log or event log entry causes its properties to display in the Visual Studio property window, enabling you to view and edit their values. If you drag and drop one of the event logs into a project, a System.Diagnostics.EventLog or System.Diagnostic.EventLogEntry component instance is automatically created.

Management Classes

The items under the Management Classes node represent various Windows Management Instrumentation (WMI) classes. Each of these classes maps to a logical or physical entity associated with a server. The available classes are shown in Table 5.8.

TABLE 5.8 WMI Management Class Nodes

Title	WMI Class
Desktop Settings	`Win32_Desktop`
Disk Volumes	`Win32_LogicalDisk`
My Computer	`Win32_ComputerSystem`
Network Adapters	`Win32_NetworkAdapter`
Network Connections	`Win32_NetworkConnection`
NT Event Log Files	`Win32_NTEventLogFile`
Operating Systems	`Win32_OperatingSystem`
Printers	`Win32_Printer`
Processes	`Win32_Process`
Processors	`Win32_Processor`
Services	`Win32_Service`
Shares	`Win32_Share`
Software Products	`Win32_Product`
System Accounts	`Win32_SystemAccount`
Threads	`Win32_Thread`

A thorough discussion of WMI is beyond the scope of this chapter and this book; in summary, however, each of these nodes exposes various WMI class property groups (such as precedents, antecedents, settings, dependents, and so on), and, in turn, each of these property groups exposes a span of commands, enabling you to directly affect a resource on the server.

One simple example of how you might use this capability is to set access information for a share exposed on a remote server. When you expand nodes in the Server Explorer down to the share (via the Disk Volumes node), access to the share information is gained via the shortcut menu on the share. In this example, you would select the SetShareInfo action, which initiates a WMI dialog box allowing you to change various share attributes such as the description and maximum allowed users.

Management Events

The Management Events node contains a list of event queries; essentially, these are "listeners" that you establish to periodically poll the WMI event system on the server. These event queries are established through a dialog box. (See Figure 5.11; you launch the dialog box by selecting Add Event Query on the shortcut menu.) When an event is created, a child node to the Management Events node is created, and under this node, actual event instances appear.

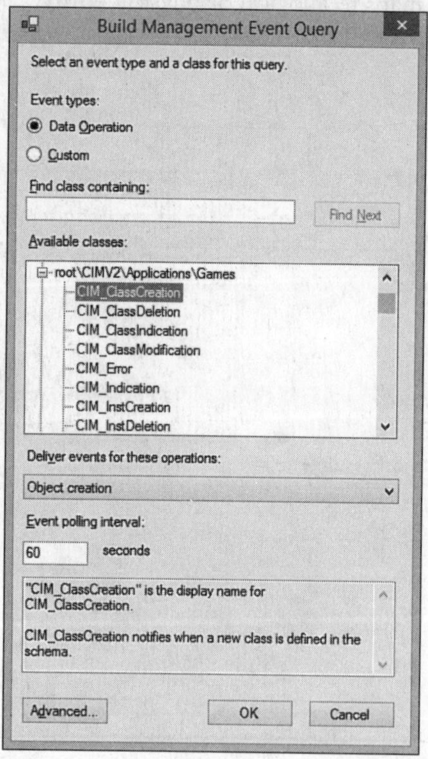

FIGURE 5.11 Creating a Management Event query.

Message Queues

If message queuing is installed on the target server, the Message Queues node displays all the available message queues, along with any messages currently residing in each queue.

Performance Counters

You can view every performance counter installed on the target computer in the Performance Counters node. Each performance counter is displayed within its category. Performance counter instances, if available, are also displayed.

Services

Each installed service is enumerated under the Services node.

Programming with Server Explorer

Beyond enabling you to examine and manipulate data connections and server resources, the Server Explorer serves another task: by dragging and dropping items from the Server Explorer onto a Visual Studio design surface, you can quickly create components in code that directly reference the item in question. For example, dragging the Application Log node (from Servers, Event Logs) onto an existing Windows form creates a System. Diagnostics.EventLog component instance that is preconfigured to point to the application log. You can then immediately write code to interact with the event log component. You can use the same process to quickly embed message queue access into your application or read from/write to a performance counter. Table 5.9 lists the various possible drag-and-drop operations, along with their results.

TABLE 5.9 Server Explorer Drag and Drop

Under This Node	Dragging This	Does This
Event Logs	Event Log Category (for example, Application or System)	Creates a System.Diagnostics. EventLog component instance, configured for the appropriate event log
Management Classes	Management Class instance	Creates the appropriate WMI/CIMv2 component instance
Management Events	Management Event Query	Creates a System.Management. ManagementEventWatcher component instance
Message Queues	Message Queue instance	Creates a System.Messaging. MessageQueue component instance for the selected queue
Performance Counters	Performance Counter or counter instance	Creates a System.Diagnostics. PerformanceCounter component instance, configured for the appropriate counter
Services	Service	Creates a System.ServiceProcess. ServiceController, provisioned for the indicated service

NOTE

Data connection items in the Server Explorer cannot be dragged onto a design surface. For more information regarding drag-and-drop development of database solutions, see Chapter 13.

Azure

The Azure node in Server Explorer is a central place for managing all the resources associated with your Azure subscription accounts. If you have a valid Azure account, connecting to it from Server Explorer will give you quick access to edit and configure your cloud-based databases, websites, and other services.

For example, editing the HTML for an Azure hosted web page is as simple as connecting to your subscription, expanding the websites node, and then double-clicking on the web page to load it into Visual Studio. Figure 5.12 shows a simple "about" page being edited within Visual Studio.

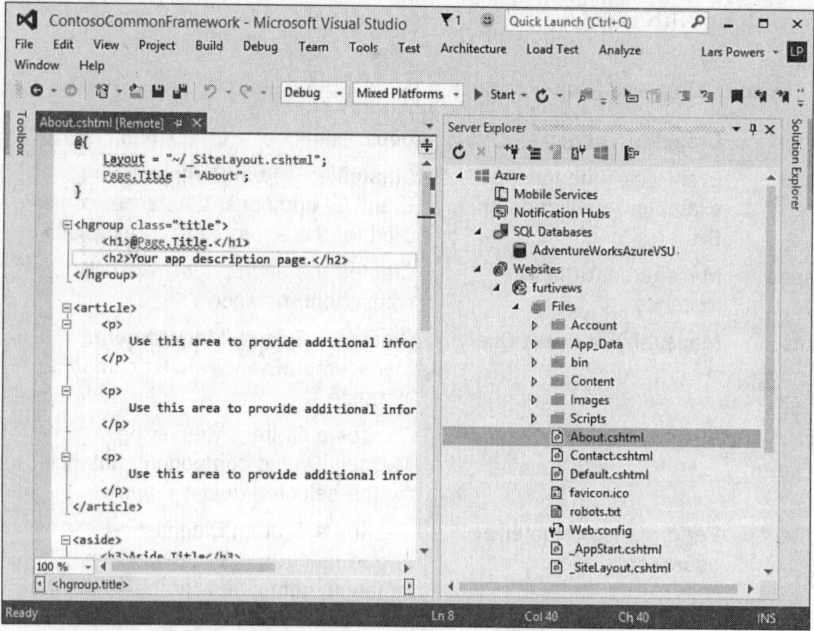

FIGURE 5.12 Editing an Azure web page.

Server Explorer provides other useful ways to interact with Azure resources. You can view an Azure website in your browser, attach a debugger to a web page or Azure service, or directly launch the Azure management portal. These actions are available by right-clicking an item under the Azure node. Figure 5.13 shows the context menu available for an Azure website.

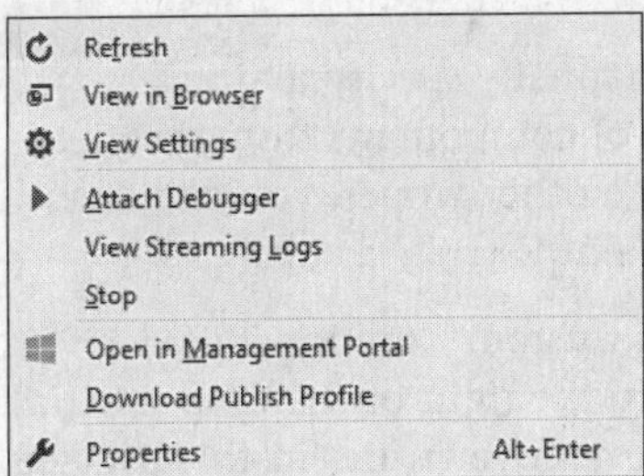

FIGURE 5.13 Options for interacting with an Azure website.

We dig into much more detail on the Azure development front within Chapter 12, "Developing Applications in the Cloud with Windows Azure."

Object Browser

The Object Browser is similar in functionality and look and feel to the Class View window. It provides a hierarchical view of projects, assemblies, namespaces, types, enums, and interfaces. Unlike the Class View window, however, the Object Browser is capable of a much wider scope of objects. In addition to the currently loaded projects, the Object Browser can display items from the entire .NET Framework, up to and including COM components and externally accessible objects. This is a great tool for finding and inspecting types, regardless of where they are physically located.

Changing the Scope

You can use the toolbar's Browse drop-down to filter or change the scope of the objects displayed within the Object Browser. The scoping options offered are shown in Table 5.10.

TABLE 5.10 Object Browser Scoping Options

Scope	Effect
All Components	This is a superset of the other scopes offered. Selecting this shows all types and members within the .NET Framework, the current solution, any libraries referenced by the current solution, and any individually selected components.
.NET Framework	Shows all objects within a specific version of the .NET Framework (for example, .NET Framework 2.0, .NET Framework 3.0).
My Solution	Shows all objects with the currently loaded solution, including any referenced components.
Custom Component Set	Shows any objects specifically added to the custom component set.

Editing the Custom Component Set

A custom component set is a list of components that you manually specify. Using a custom list might be useful when you want to browse a list of components from a variety of different "buckets." Instead of wading through each of the other scopes, you could include only those types that you care about in the component list.

You add to the custom component list by selecting the Edit Custom Component Set option in the Browse drop-down or by clicking the ellipsis to the right of the drop-down. This launches an editor dialog box in which you can add or remove entries in this list (see Figure 5.14).

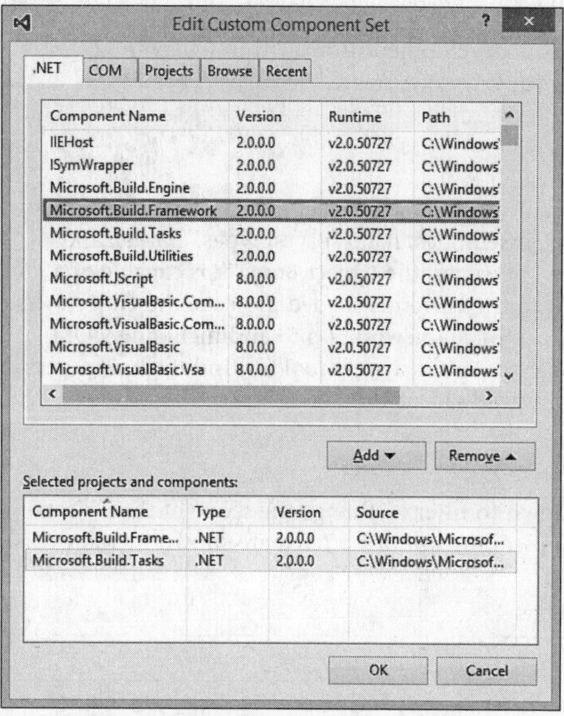

FIGURE 5.14 Editing the custom component set.

Adding a component to the set is as easy as selecting from one of the prepopulated object lists (available via the .NET, COM, or Projects tabs) or by browsing directly to the container assembly via the Browse tab. You can select an object or objects and then click the Add button. The current set members show up at the bottom of the dialog box. You can also select a current member and remove it from the list by clicking the Remove button.

Browsing Objects

The Object Browser consists of a toolbar and three different panes: an objects pane, a members pane, and a description pane. Again, the similarity here to the Class View window is obvious. The toolbar, objects pane, and members pane function identically to the Class View objects pane and the members pane. You click down through the tree view to view each object's members; the toolbar aids in navigating deep trees by providing a Forward and Back button. Figure 5.15 shows the Object Browser in action.

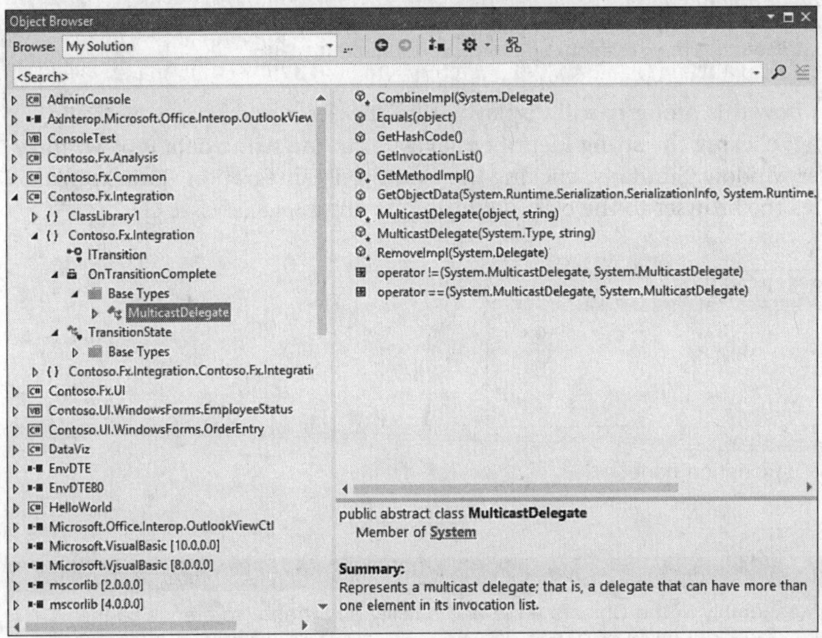

FIGURE 5.15 The Object Browser.

The hierarchical relationships, icons, and actions possible within the panes are the same (therefore, we won't rehash them here). The description pane, however, is a new concept.

> **NOTE**
>
> You can quickly access the MSDN help topic for any given object or member by selecting an item in the members pane and then pressing the F1 key.

Description Pane

When an item is selected in either the Object Browser's objects pane or the members pane, the description pane provides detailed information about the selected item. The data provided is quite extensive and includes the following:

- The name of the selected object
- The name of the parent of the selected object
- Code comments and inline help associated with the selected object

Where possible, the description pane embeds hyperlinks within the data that it displays to enable you to easily navigate to related items. For example, a declared property of type string might show the following description:

```
public string SystemContextId { set; get; }
   Member of Contoso.Fx.Integration.Specialized.ContextToken
```

Figure 5.16 shows how this property will display within the description pane. Note the use of hyperlinking: clicking the string identifier navigates to the string data type within the Object Browser window. Similarly, clicking the Contoso.Fx.Integration.ContextToken hyperlink navigates the browser to the class definition for the `ContextToken` class.

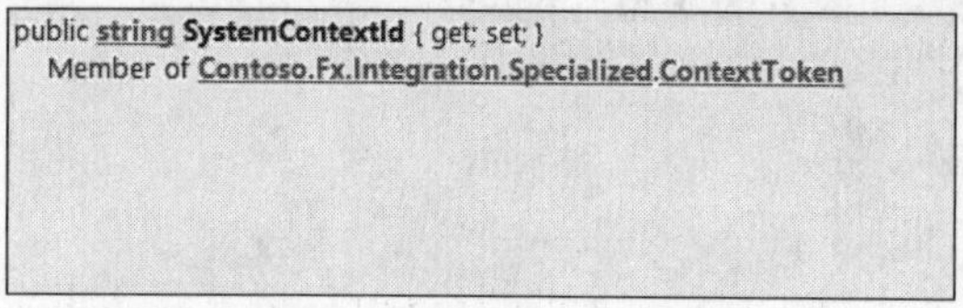

public **string** **SystemContextId** { get; set; }
Member of **Contoso.Fx.Integration.Specialized.ContextToken**

FIGURE 5.16 The description pane.

TIP

You can click an assembly in the Objects pane and quickly add it as a reference to the current project by clicking the Add to References button located on the Object Browser's toolbar.

Document Outline

The Document Outline window (opened from the View, Other Windows menu) exposes a hierarchical view of elements residing on a Windows form, a web form, or a Windows Presentation Foundation (WPF) window. This is a fantastic tool for "reparenting" form items or changing the z-order of a control within its parent. In addition, it assists with understanding the exact logical structure of a form that might have a lot happening on it from a visual perspective.

Figures 5.17 and 5.18 show the Document Outline windows for a simple web form and a slightly more complicated WPF window.

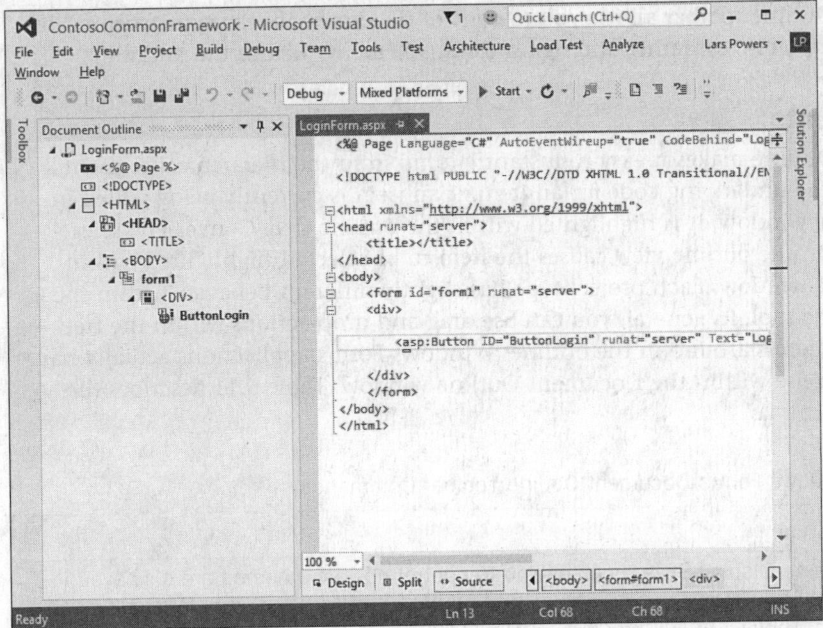

FIGURE 5.17 A web form.

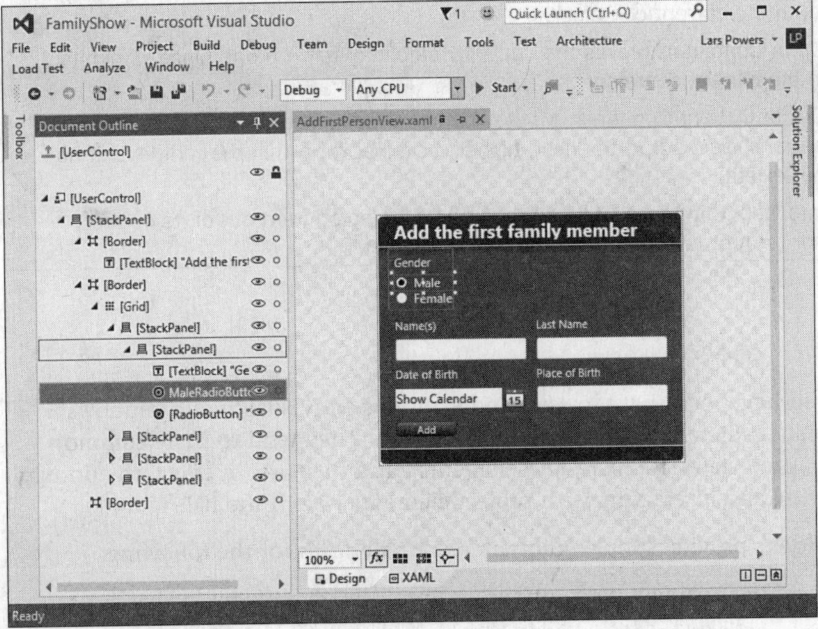

FIGURE 5.18 A WPF form.

The Document Outline toolbar allows you to control the display of the types within the tree view and facilitates reordering and repositioning elements within the outline.

Editing Elements

The Document Outline makes it easy to instantly jump from the hierarchical element view directly to the underlying code for an item. If an item is currently being edited in the designer/code window, it is highlighted within the outline tree. Conversely, selecting an item within the outline view causes the item to be selected/highlighted within the designer/code window. Each project type has slightly different behavior within the Document Outline tool. In general, you can use drag-and-drop actions within the tree view to move elements around in the outline. Windows Forms applications actually have a toolbar you can use within the Document Outline window. Table 5.11 describes the toolbar buttons.

TABLE 5.11 Windows Forms Document Outline Toolbar Commands

Icon	Description
	Type Name Display Style. Enables you to control how type names are displayed in the tree view: None (no type names are displayed); Short (the local, unqualified type name is displayed); Full (the fully qualified type name is displayed).
+	Expand All. Causes all the parent nodes to expand.
	Collapse All. Causes all the parent nodes to collapse.
↓	Move Down in Container. Moves the currently selected item down one place within its order in the current container.
↑	Move Up in Container. Moves the currently selected item up one place within its order in the current container.
←	Move Out of Current Container. Moves the currently selected item out of its current container and places it in the next, higher container (or within the root level if no container exists).
→	Move into Next Container. Moves the currently selected item out of its current container (or root level) and into the next container.

Summary

In this chapter, you have seen that browsers and explorers are Visual Studio windows that typically provide a hierarchical view of their content. They tend to share common interface elements (tree views, toolbars, and elements), and they are, in effect, the primary means for visualizing and interacting with project elements within the IDE.

Browsers and explorers provide simple point-and-click interfaces for the following:

- Visualizing and organizing your solutions and projects on a file-by-file basis
- Visualizing and organizing your projects on a type-by-type, class-by-class basis

- Querying and interacting with server resources such as databases, performance counters, Azure resources, and message queues
- Browsing through type libraries

Although certain browsers/explorers touch underlying concepts that are fairly deep and complicated (WMI, for instance), they are all geared toward a common goal: extending the reach of the IDE as a rapid application development tool for tasks beyond simple code file editing.

CHAPTER 6

Introducing the Editors and Designers

IN THIS CHAPTER

- Getting Started with the Basics
- Coding with the Code Editor
- Creating and Editing XML Documents and Schema
- Working with Cascading Style Sheets
- Developing Windows Client Applications
- Developing Web Forms
- Authoring WinForms Components and Controls
- Creating Classes with the Class Designer

Although Visual Studio provides an impressive array of functionality for nearly all areas of the development process, its editors and designers are the real heart of the IDE. They are the bread-and-butter tools of the programmer: they enable you to write code, edit resources, design user interfaces, and construct schemas. And, of course, each of these tools has key features designed to boost your productivity and the quality of your output.

This chapter is squarely focused on using these editors and designers to create solutions within the IDE.

Getting Started with the Basics

Broadly speaking, a Visual Studio editor is a text editor (think word processor) that enables you to write specific output efficiently (Visual Basic code, Hypertext Markup Language [HTML], XAML, and so on). A designer, in contrast, is a visual editor that enables you to work directly with visual concepts instead of text. Many document types are supported by both designers and editors: you can build a form, for instance, by using the drag-and-drop convenience of the Windows Forms Designer or by handcrafting the code within a text editor; or you can build an XML file using the same mechanisms.

The Visual Studio text editor provides the core text-editing functionality for all the editors. This functionality is then inherited and added upon to create editors specific for a given document type. Thus, you have a code editor for source code files, an XML editor for markup, a Cascading Style Sheets (CSS) editor for style sheets, and so on.

Likewise, designers manifest themselves in ways specific to their roles. The HTML designer is part text editor and part graphical tool, and the Windows and web forms designers are superb what-you-see-is-what-you-get (WYSIWYG) form builders.

The Text Editor

There are a few text-editing features that we all take for granted: selecting parts of an existing body of text, inserting text into a document, copying and pasting text, and so on. As you would expect, the text editor window supports all these features in a way that is familiar to anyone who has used a Windows-based word processor.

You select text, for instance, by using the following familiar actions:

1. Place the cursor at the start of the text you want to select.
2. While holding down the left mouse button, sweep the mouse to the end of the text you want to select.
3. Release the left mouse button.

In addition to this "standard" selection method, the Visual Studio text editor supports "column mode" selection. In column mode, instead of selecting text in a linear fashion from left to right, line by line, you drag a selection rectangle across a text field. Any text character caught within the selection rectangle is part of the selected text. This is called column mode because it allows you to create a selection area that captures columns of text characters instead of just lines. The procedure is largely the same:

1. Place the cursor at the start of the text you want to select.
2. While holding down the Alt key *and* the left mouse button, expand the bounds of the selection rectangle until it includes the desired text.
3. Release the left mouse button and the Alt key.

After you've selected text, you can copy, cut, or drag it to a new location within the text editor. As with text selection, the commands for cutting, copying, and pasting text remain unchanged from their basic standard implementations in other Windows applications: you first select text, and then you cut or copy it using the Edit menu, the toolbar, or the text editor's shortcut menu. You can also quickly copy an entire line within the editor by positioning your cursor anywhere on the line and, with nothing selected in the editor, use Ctrl+C.

By dragging a text selection, you can reposition it within the current text editor, place it in a previously opened text editor window, or even drag the selection into the command or watch windows. Moving lines of code around the editor is also accomplished with the Alt+Up Arrow or Alt+Down Arrow keys; these will move the current line up or down within the editor.

Line Wrapping and Virtual Space

The default behavior of the text editor is not to automatically wrap any text for you. In other words, as you type, your text or code simply keeps trailing on to the right of the editor. If you exceed the bounds of the currently viewable area, the editor window scrolls to the right to allow you to continue typing. However, the text editor window can behave more like a word processor, in which the document content is typically constrained horizontally to its virtual sheet of paper.

TIP

With word wrapping turned on, Visual Studio automatically wraps your text onto the next line. You can also have the IDE place a visual glyph to indicate that a wrap has taken place. Both of these options are controlled on the Options dialog box, under the Text Editor, All Languages, General page (shown in Figure 6.1).

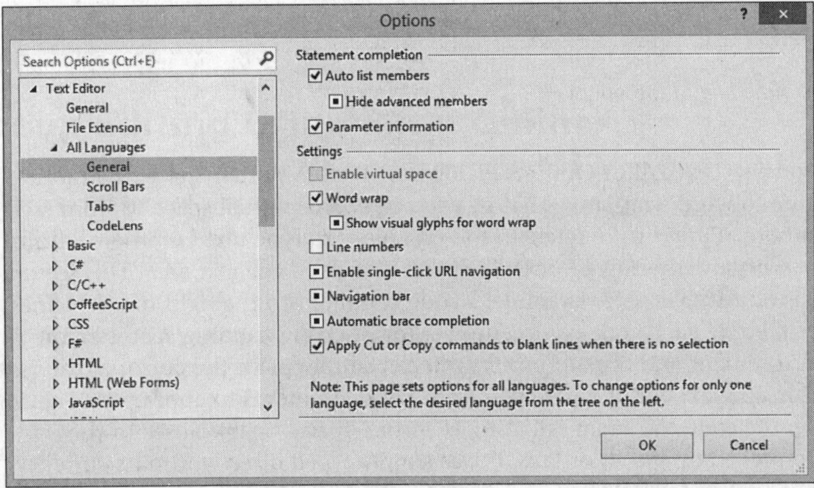

FIGURE 6.1 Editor Options dialog box.

If you override the default behavior, turn wrapping on, and then type a line of code that exceeds the editor's width, you can see that the editor window (see Figure 6.2) automatically wraps the source to fit within the boundaries of the window and provides an icon to the far right of the editor to indicate that a wrap has taken place. Word wrapping is useful for keeping all your code in plain sight (without the need for scrolling horizontally).

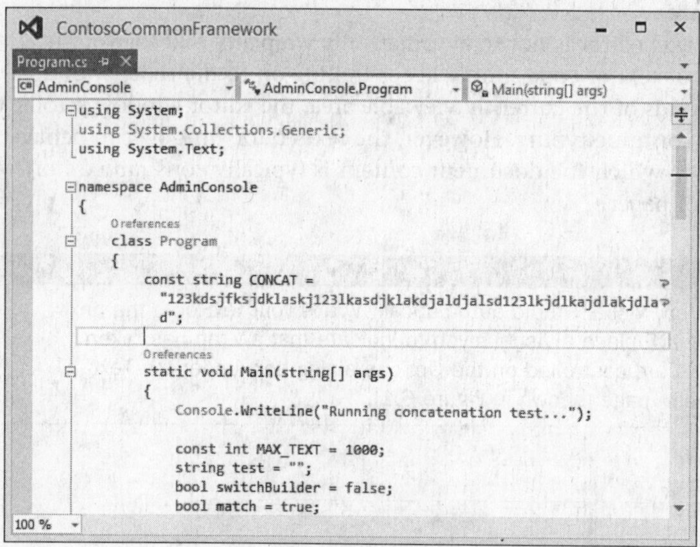

FIGURE 6.2 Word wrapping in the editor.

The other option on the Text Editor Options dialog box, Enable Virtual Space, is a mutually exclusive feature to word wrapping. That is, you can enable virtual space or word wrapping, but not both. *Virtual space* refers to the capability to type text anywhere within the editor window without entering a bunch of spaces or tabs in the text area. This feature is useful when you want to place, for example, a code comment to the right of a few lines of code. Instead of tabbing each code comment over (or inserting padding spaces before them) to get them to indent and line up nicely, you can simply place the cursor at the exact column within the text editor where you want your comments to appear. See Figure 6.3 for an example; the code comment "floating in virtual space" that you see in the screenshot is not preceded by spaces or tabs. It was simply typed directly into its current position.

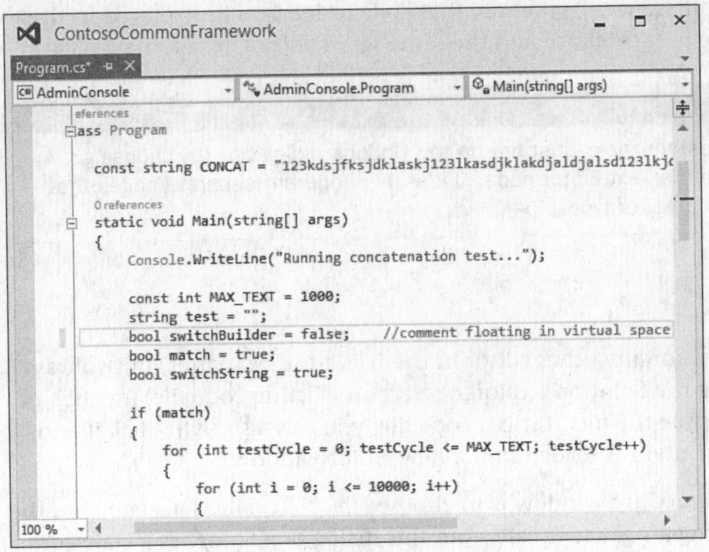

FIGURE 6.3 Virtual spacing in the editor window.

Visual Studio Designers

Designers are much more visual in nature than the text editors within Visual Studio; they provide a graphical perspective of a particular solution artifact. Thus, a form appears within a designer just as it would to the end user, as visual constructs made up of buttons, borders, menus, and frames. The code to implement the items shown in a designer is actually written by Visual Studio.

Like the various editors, the designers are similar in form and function. They occupy space within the tabbed documents area of the IDE (just as the editors do). They might take on different behaviors depending on their target use. The Windows Forms Designer and the component designer appear nearly the same, but there are subtle differences in their uses.

Coding with the Code Editor

Writing code and creating other syntax-based files is really all about typing text. The text editor window is the Visual Studio tool directly on point for creating source code text files. It is the keystone of development inside the IDE. It supports text entry and basic text operations such as selecting text regions, dragging and dropping text fragments, and setting tab stops. With basic text features alone, the editor would be sufficient to code with. However, it is the advanced features layered on top for debugging, code formatting, code guidance, and customization that really make this tool shine.

As we mentioned previously, the text editor actually has a few different personalities within the IDE. The code editor is designed to support creating and editing of source code files, the XML editor is targeted at XML files, and the CSS editor is targeted at CSS files.

Although there are subtle differences in the way that code or markup is displayed in these windows, they all share the user interface and the same set of editing functionality.

TIP

Each editor type is fully customizable. Just fire up the Options dialog box (by choosing Tools, Options) and locate the Text Editor node. Under this node are separate pages that allow customization of each editor type.

Opening an Editor

You can launch a text editor (or any other editor in the IDE, for that matter) in two ways. The first way involves using the Solution Explorer: select an existing code file, text file, or other type file and double-click the file. If it is a code file, you can also right-click it and select View Code. The file content is loaded into a new editor window.

The second way to launch an editor window is to choose File, New, File. This launches the New File dialog box. Selecting a code template from this dialog box launches a code editor prefilled with the initial code stubs relevant to the template selected.

TIP

The text editor windows live as tabbed windows front and center within the IDE. If multiple code editors are open, they are each accessible by their tabs. If several editors are open at one time, finding the window you are looking for by cycling through the tabs can be cumbersome. There are four ways to quickly locate and select a code editor window. First, you can use Solution Explorer. Double-clicking the code file again within the Solution Explorer selects and displays the associated code editor window. Second, you can use the Window menu. Each open code editor window is shown by name in the windows list under the Window menu. Third, to the far right of the editor tabs, right next to the Close icon, is a small drop-down button in the image of an arrow. Clicking the arrow drops down a list of all open editor windows, allowing you to select one at will. Finally, Visual Studio has its own version of the Windows switcher: Hold down the Ctrl key and tap the Tab key to cycle through a list of all windows open in IDE.

Writing Code in the Code Editor

Because the code editor's primary purpose is "word processing" for source code, let's first look at writing the simplest of routines, a "Hello, World" function, from the ground up using the code editor.

Figure 6.4 shows a code editor with an initial stubbed-out console file. This was produced by creating a new Visual C# Console project using the Solution Explorer. Double-clicking the `Program.cs` file within that new project displays the source code for this console application.

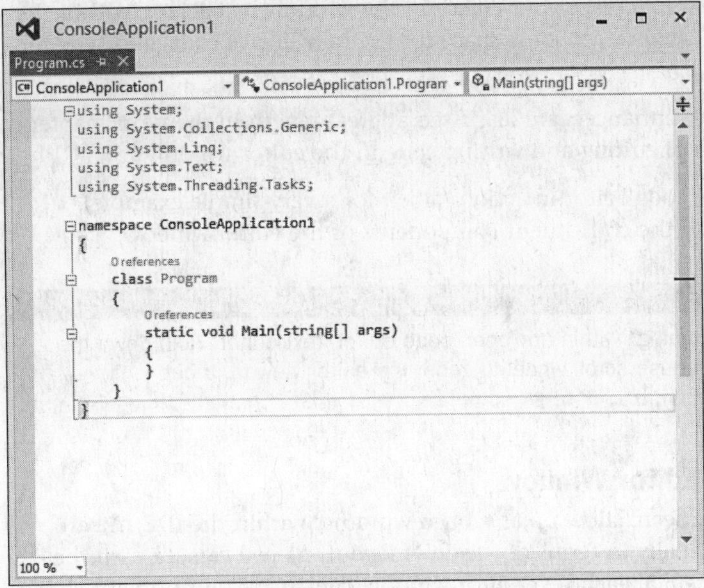

FIGURE 6.4 Code template for a Console code file.

As you can see, Visual Studio, as a result of the template used for creating the project, has already filled in some code.

```
using System;
using System.Collections.Generic;
using System.Linq;
using System.Text;
using System.Threading.Tasks;


namespace ConsoleApplication1
{
    class Program
    {
        static void Main(string[] args)
        {
        }
    }
}
```

To demonstrate the code editor in action, write the code that outputs the `"Hello, World!"` string to the Console window.

Within the `Main` routine, add the following.

```
Console.WriteLine("Hello, World!");
```

To begin writing the code, simply place your cursor in the window by clicking within the `Main` routine's braces, press Enter to get some space for the new line of code, and type the `Console.WriteLine` syntax.

These and other productivity enhancers are discussed at great length in the next chapter. Here, we focus on the basics of editing and writing code in the editor window.

Now that you have seen the code editor in action (albeit for a very simple example), you're ready to dig more into the constituent components of the editor window.

TIP

Visual Studio supports "zooming" within any open code editor/text editor. Hold down the Ctrl key and then use the mouse scroll wheel to zoom the editor view in or out.

Anatomy of the Code Editor Window

Editor windows, as you have seen, show up as tabbed windows within the IDE and are typically front and center visually in terms of windows layout. As you can see with the code editor window in Figure 6.5, each text editor window consists of four primary regions: a code pane, a selection margin, an indicator margin, and scrollbars.

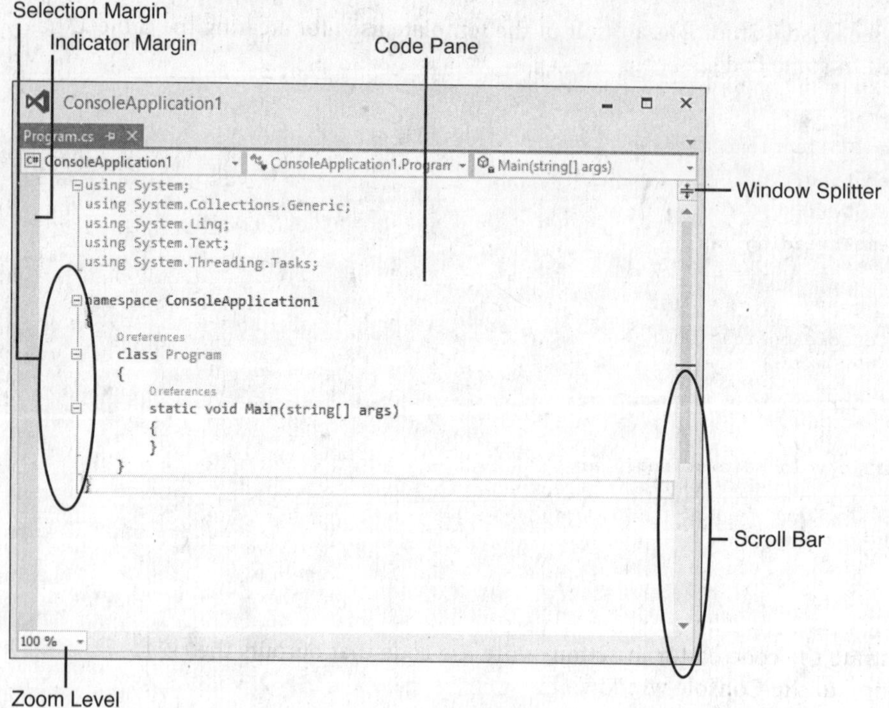

FIGURE 6.5 The components of the code editor window.

These regions and their functionality remain the same for all editor types within the IDE.

The code editor for C# files also adds a set of user interface (UI) elements that are not present with the other language editors: three drop-down boxes at the top of the code editor window enable you to quickly navigate through source code by selecting a loaded project in the leftmost drop-down, a type contained within that project in the middle drop-down, and a specific type member (property, field, function, and so on) in the right drop-down for the selected type. This jogs the current cursor location directly to the indicated type.

The Code Pane

The code pane is the place where the document (source code, XML, and so on) is displayed and edited. This region provides basic text-editing functionality, in addition to the more advanced productivity features of the editor, such as IntelliSense.

Right-clicking within the code pane provides a shortcut menu (see Figure 6.6) that includes standard cut, copy, and paste tools along with an assortment of other handy editing actions.

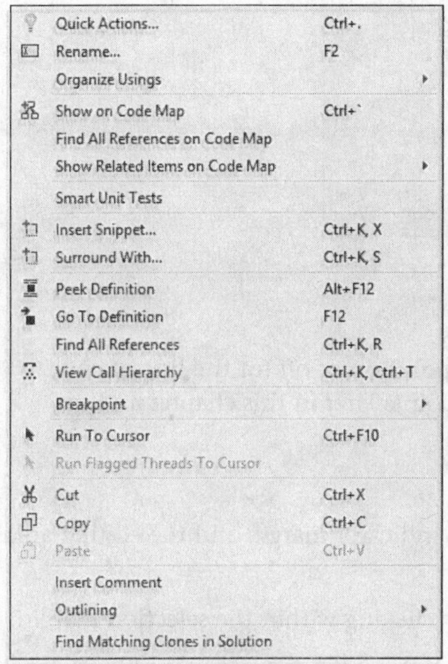

FIGURE 6.6 Code editor shortcut menu.

The Indicator Margin

The indicator margin is the slim gray-colored margin to the far left of the editor. This margin area is used to mark a line of code that contains a breakpoint or bookmark.

Figure 6.7 shows the `"Hello, World"` example with a bookmark placed on the `Main` routine and a breakpoint placed on the `Console.WriteLine` command.

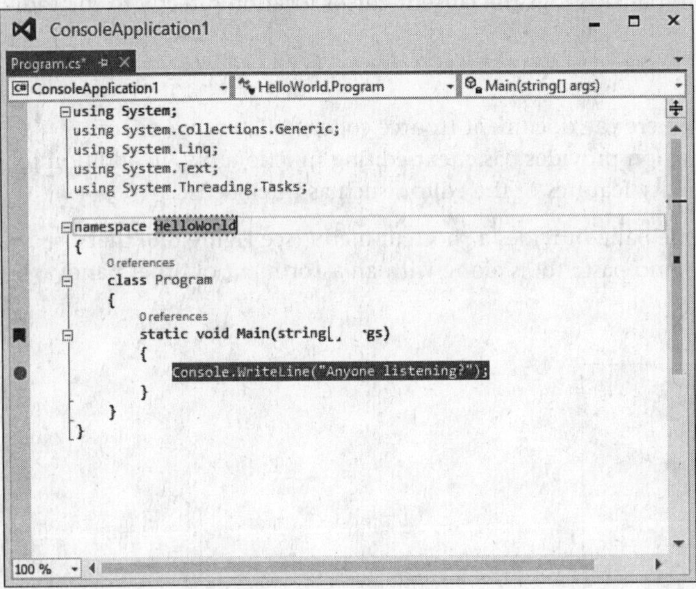

FIGURE 6.7 A bookmark and a breakpoint.

Clicking within the indicator margin toggles a breakpoint on or off for the line of code you have selected. (You will learn more about breakpoints later in this chapter and in Chapter 10, "Debugging Code.")

The Selection Margin

The selection margin is a narrow region between the indicator margin and the editing area of the code pane. It provides the following:

- The capability to select an entire line of text by clicking within the selection margin.
- A visual indication, via colored indicator bars, of those lines of code that have changed during the current editing session.
- Line numbers (if this option has been turned on). See the following section in which we discuss customizing the text editor's behavior.

You can clearly see the "changed text" indicator and line numbers in action in Figure 6.8.

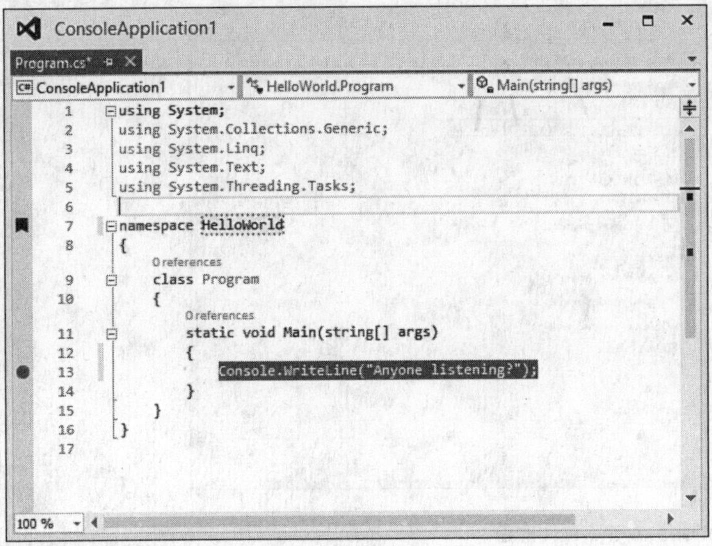

FIGURE 6.8 Changed text indicators and line numbers.

TIP

Visual Studio provides a dedicated toolbar for the text editor. You can view this toolbar by selecting View, Toolbars, Text Editor. It exposes buttons for the Member List, Quick Info, Parameter List, and Word Completion IntelliSense features, in addition to indenting buttons, commenting buttons, and bookmark navigation buttons. The navigation buttons are arguably the most useful because they provide easily accessible forward and back navigation through your code.

The Vertical Scrollbar

In addition to performing the obvious function of allowing you to scroll vertically within the code editor, Visual Studio can overlay various pieces of information onto the scrollbar. The options of what can be shown on the scrollbar are controlled on the Options dialog in the Scroll Bars section (see Figure 6.9). The following annotations can be added:

- **Changes**—Any unsaved edits made to the code
- **Marks**—Breakpoints and bookmarks
- **Errors**—Current compile errors in the code
- **Caret position**—The current cursor location within the file

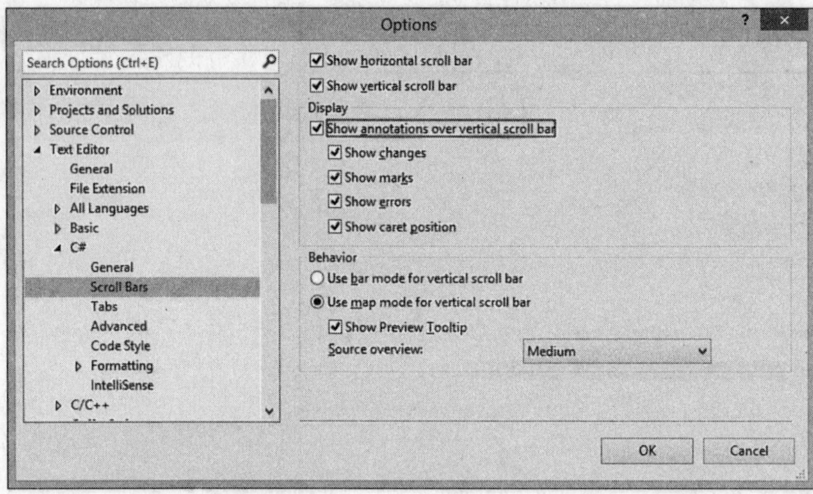

FIGURE 6.9 Adding annotations to the scrollbar.

Figure 6.10 shows an example of a more complicated code set within the window. Note the annotations on the vertical scrollbar.

```
ContosoCommonFramework
ExpenseReportOps.cs*
Contoso.Fx.Common | Contoso.Fx.Common.ExpenseReportOp | TallyExpenseReport(string id)

using System.Text;
using System.Threading.Tasks;

namespace Contoso.Fx.Common
{
    0 references
    class ExpenseReportOps
    {
        0 references
        public async void TallyExpenseReport(string id)
        {
            // get the expense report
            ExpenseReport rpt = await GetExpenseReport(id);
            UpdateDataStore(id, rpt.TotalAmt);
            UpdateDataStore(id);

        }

    1 reference
    public async Task<ExpenseReport> GetExpenseReport(string id)
    {
        //TODO: code to fetch an expense report
        return new ExpenseReport();
    }
100 %
```

FIGURE 6.10 Scrollbar annotations.

There is also an alternate "map mode" visualization that can be enabled for the vertical scrollbar. In map mode, a thumbnail visual of the code file is shown, along with all the annotation marks. This is a great way to instantly determine where you are within a large code file; and, if you hover your pointer over a line within the scrollbar, you can actually preview the code within a small inset window (see Figure 6.11). You can select between wide, normal, or narrow width for this map mode area in the same Scroll Bars section of the Options dialog.

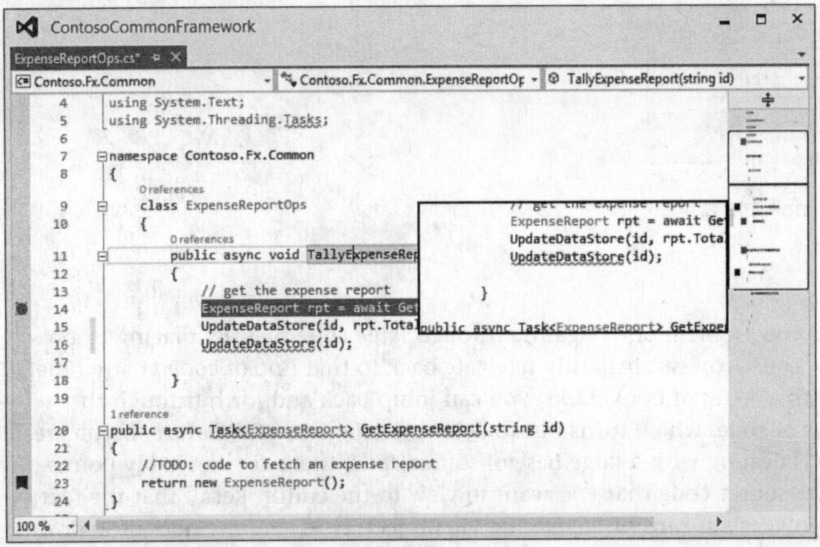

FIGURE 6.11 The vertical scrollbar in map mode.

Code Navigation Tools

As the lines of code in any given project increase, effectively navigating through the code base (that is, quickly and easily finding lines of interest among the potentially thousands or even millions of lines of code) becomes an issue.

The text editor comes equipped with several tools to help you mark lines of code, search and replace text across source files, and, in general, maintain your situational awareness from within a long code listing.

Line Numbering

As mentioned in the discussion of the text editor's selection margin, you can enable line numbering for any given document loaded into an editor. This option is controlled in the Options dialog box within the Text Editor, All Languages, General page, or selectively under the individual languages and their General page.

By themselves, line numbers would be fairly useless. The capability to immediately jump to a line of code completes the equation and provides some real benefit from a navigation perspective. While within a text editor, press Ctrl+G to jump to a line of code. This triggers the Go To Line dialog box (see Figure 6.12), which provides a text box for specifying the line number to jump to and even indicates the valid "scope" for the jump by providing a line number range for the current document. Entering a valid line number here moves the cursor position to the start of that line.

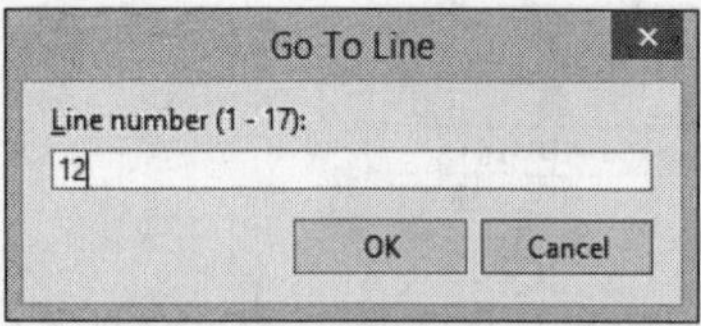

FIGURE 6.12 Jumping to a line.

Bookmarks

Bookmarks tackle the problem of navigating through large code files. By placing a bookmark on a line of code, you can instantly navigate back to that line of code at any time. When dealing with a series of bookmarks, you can jump back and forth through the bookmarked lines of code, which turns out to be a surprisingly useful feature. If you are a developer who is dealing with a large base of source code, there are inevitably points of interest within the source code that you want to view in the editor. Recall that the text editor window provides a means of navigating via project, type, and member drop-downs; these are not, however, the best tools for the job when your "line of interest" is an arbitrary statement buried deep within a million lines of code.

Bookmarks are visually rendered in the indicator margin of the text editor. (Refer to Figure 6.8; a bookmark appears on line 7.)

To add a bookmark or navigate through your bookmarks, you use either the text editor toolbar or the Bookmarks window.

You can view the Bookmarks window, shown in Figure 6.13, by choosing View, Other Windows, Bookmark Window. Notice that this window provides a toolbar for bookmark actions and provides a list of all available bookmarks, along with their actual physical location (filename and line number within that file).

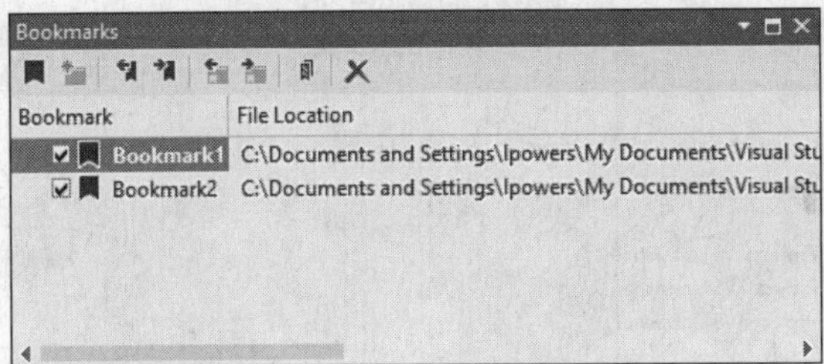

FIGURE 6.13 The Bookmarks window.

To toggle a bookmark for a given line of code, you first place your cursor on the desired line within the text editor and then click the Toggle Bookmark button. The same process is used to toggle the bookmark off. Using the Forward and Back buttons within the bookmarks window jumps the text editor's cursor location back and forth through all available bookmarks.

TIP

Use the Bookmarks window to navigate through code across projects. You are not limited to bookmarks placed within a single code file; bookmarks can, in fact, be in `any` loaded code file. The list of bookmarks in this window is also a useful mechanism for quickly toggling a bookmark on or off (via the check box next to the bookmark) and for assigning a meaningful name to a bookmark. Right-clicking a bookmark allows you to rename it something more meaningful than Bookmark7.

Bookmark Folders One interesting feature with the Bookmarks window is the capability to create a bookmark folder. This is an organizational bucket for related bookmarks. For instance, you might want to place bookmarks for a specific math algorithm under a folder called `MathFuncs`. To do this, you first create a folder by using the New Folder button on the toolbar. You can rename the folder to whatever makes sense for your particular scenario. Then you can create a bookmark and drag and drop it into the folder.

See Figure 6.14 for a look at a populated Bookmarks window. Note that two folders are in use, in addition to bookmarks being shown for various source code files.

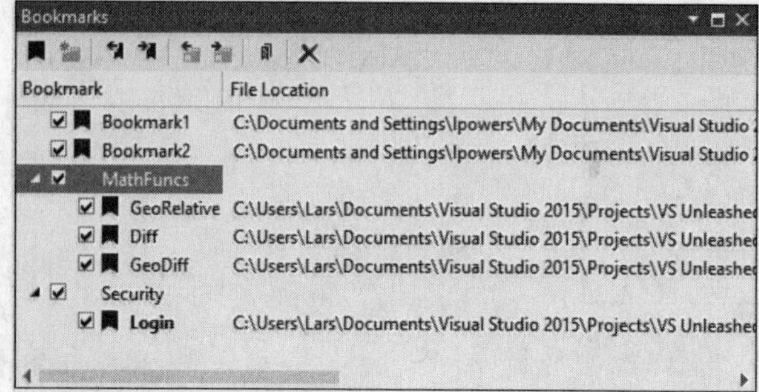

FIGURE 6.14 The Bookmarks window with folders.

Call Hierarchy

The Call Hierarchy window is yet another way to navigate through your projects. This window lets you easily follow the calls to and from every method, property, or constructor. With the code editor open, just right-click the member name and select View Call Hierarchy. This launches the Call Hierarchy window. The member name appears in a tree view in the left pane of this window; this tree view itemizes the various calls made to and from the member. If you click one of the calling sites, you can then view the calls to and from that method and so on.

Figure 6.15 shows an example of this iterative information displayed for successive callers. Clicking any of the caller or callee nodes shows you the specific location of that code in the right pane, and double-clicking that information in the right pane immediately jumps the code editor to that line of code.

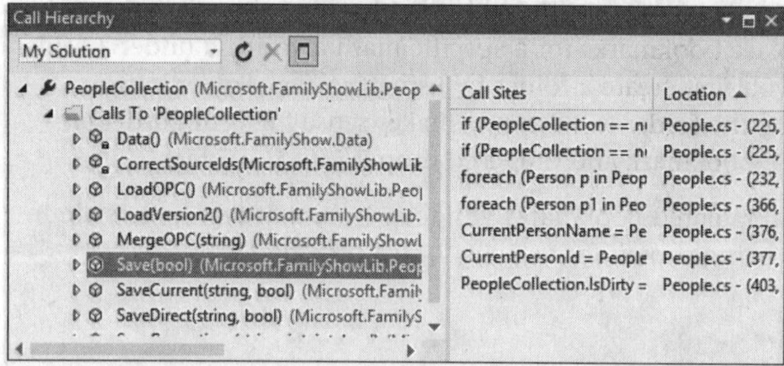

FIGURE 6.15 Using the Call Hierarchy window to explore code relationships.

NOTE

Starting with Visual Studio 2012, the Call Hierarchy window works with both Visual Basic and C# code. In earlier versions, only C# code was supported.

The usefulness of this tool doesn't stop at caller/callee information. If you right-click any node in the tree, you can jump directly to the code that implements the method/property, find all references to the selected method/property within your code, or even directly copy the code content represented by the node. All these commands and more are available right from a node's right-click pop-up menu.

Searching Documents

The text editor window provides an extensive search-and-replace capability. Two primary methods of searching are supported: Quick Find (ideal for finding text fragments within the current document or set of open documents) and Search in Files (ideal for finding text in a file residing anywhere within a folder structure). All these search mechanisms are triggered through the Edit, Find and Replace menu (and more commonly, through their hotkeys).

Each search mode is also capable of doing replacement operations. That makes a total of four different functions:

- Quick Find
- Quick Replace
- Find in Files
- Replace in Files

Let's take a closer look at each of the two search-and-replace modes individually.

Quick Find/Quick Replace

Figure 6.16 shows the Quick Find window in its native position to the top right of the text editor window. Its minimalist UI allows you to quickly start your search process by typing directly into the search box.

```
namespace Contoso.Fx.Analysis
{
    public class CustomAnalyzer
    {
        public CustomAnalyzer()
        {
        }

        public string ComputeGeoDiff()
        {
            return "";
        }
```

FIGURE 6.16 The Quick Find tool.

The search box drop-down holds the last 20 strings used in a find operation, making it easy to reuse a previous search. Just select the string from the list.

Fine-Tuning Your Search The Quick Find window also hosts options for fine-tuning your search via a small toolbar at the bottom edge of the Find window:

- Match Case causes the search to be executed against the exact case you used in the Find What drop-down.
- Match Whole Words forces the search to match on the entire string as entered in the Find What drop-down.
- Use Regular Expression changes how the search engine performs matching on the string you have entered into the search box. A standard search does a character match for the target string. By selecting this option, however, you can instead use a full-blown regular expression to perform even more intricate searches. For instance, checking this box and then entering `\b[0-9]{9}\b` would return all matches for a nine-digit number.
- Scope alters the area that the search operation functions over. Your selections in the drop-down here include the currently selected block of code, the current document, all open documents, all documents in the current project, and all documents in the entire solution.

NOTE

Although a complete discussion of regular expressions is beyond the scope of this book, you should note that the Replace With box is capable of supporting tagged expressions. For more information on how you might use this to your advantage during replace operations, consult a regular expression reference manual and look at the MSDN Regular Expressions help topic for Visual Studio.

Finding Search Results After you have specified all the criteria for your search, the right-arrow button (or F3 as a shortcut) to the right of the search box will find the next match to the search or Shift+Ctrl F3 for the previous match. Any matches within the scope specified are highlighted for you within the document and will be scrolled into view. Subsequent clicks on the Find Next button move to the next match until no more matches are found.

The Find Next button also functions as a drop-down that lets you perform a Find Previous or a Find All action.

Replacing Text The arrow to the left of the search box will expand the Quick Find window to show a Replace text box: Type in the replacement string here, and then use one of the two buttons to the right of the box to replace either the next matching string or all matching strings with the new text (see Figure 6.17).

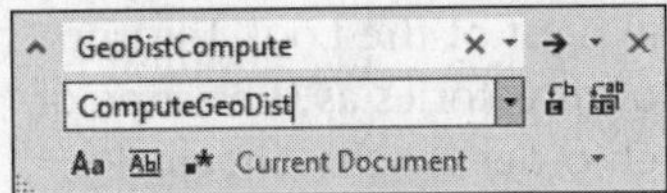

FIGURE 6.17 Expanding the Quick Find window to do a replacement.

Note that any replacements you make can always be undone via the Undo command under the Edit menu.

Find in Files/Replace in Files

Figure 6.18 shows the Find in Files tool. This tool is similar to Quick Find, with two minor additions. You still have to specify the "what" (search string) and the "where" (scope) components of the search. And you still can fine-tune your search using regular expressions and by matching on case or whole word. But you also have the option of creating a custom search scope. The way that the search results are displayed is via a separate window instead of within the code/text editor window.

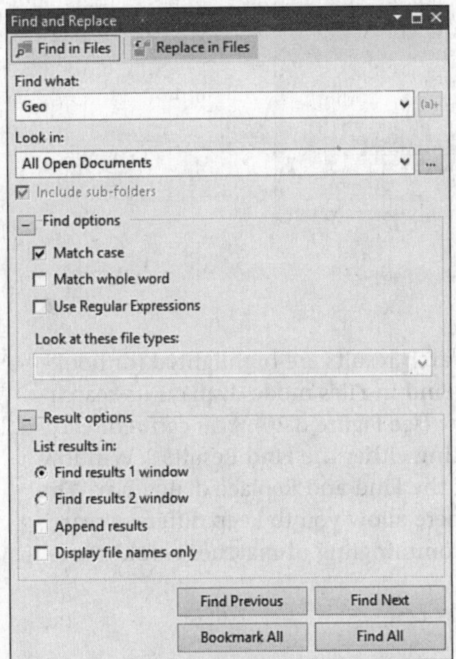

FIGURE 6.18 Find in Files.

Let's look at these two differences in turn.

Building Search Folder Sets Clicking the ellipses button to the right of the Look In drop-down launches a dialog box that allows you to build up a set of directories as the scope of the search. You can name this folder set and even set the search order for the directories. Figure 6.19 captures this dialog box as a search set called `ClassLibCode` is built. You can see that two directories have been added to the set. You can add more by simply browsing to the folder with the Available Folders control and adding them to the Selected Folders list.

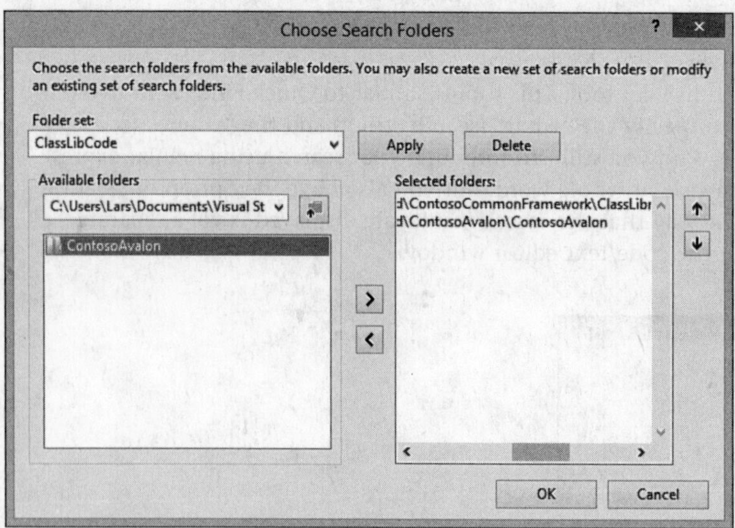

FIGURE 6.19 Building a Search Folder set.

The Find Results Window With Quick Find, the search results are highlighted (or bookmarked) right within the text editor window. The Find in Files mode displays its search results in a separate, dedicated Find Results window (see Figure 6.20). You can redirect the output to one of two results windows by selecting either the Find Results 1 Window or Find Results 2 Window option at the bottom of the Find and Replace dialog box. The two windows are identical; two options provided here allow you to keep different search results separate and avoid the confusion that the commingling of matches would cause if you were constrained to just one output window.

```
Find all "Geo", Match case, Subfolders, Find Results 1, Entire Solution, ""
  C:\Users\Lars\Documents\Visual Studio 2015\Projects\VS Unleashed\ContosoCommor
  C:\Users\Lars\Documents\Visual Studio 2015\Projects\VS Unleashed\ContosoCommor
  C:\Users\Lars\Documents\Visual Studio 2015\Projects\VS Unleashed\ContosoCommor
  Matching lines: 3    Matching files: 1    Total files searched: 159
```

FIGURE 6.20 The Find Results window.

In Figure 6.20, you see the results of a simple search conducted across all the files in a solution. The contents of the Find Results window provide the following information:

- A description of the search performed (for example, Find all "Geo," Subfolders, Find Results 1, "Entire Solution").
- The matches returned from the search. Match information includes the file path and name, the line number within the file, and a verbatim repeat of the line of code containing the match.
- A summary of the find results, including the number of matching lines of code, the number of files containing matches, and the total number of files searched.

Double-clicking one of the results lines in the window jogs the cursor location directly to the matching line within the editor. Note that this window has a toolbar. From left to right, the buttons on this toolbar allow you to do the following:

- Jump to the matched line of code within the text editor. (First place your cursor on the match inside the Find Results window and then click the Go to the Location of the Current Line button.)
- Move back and forth through the list of matches. Each matched item is highlighted in the Find Results window and in the Text Editor window.
- Clear the Find Results window.
- Clear the selected result window.
- Cancel any ongoing searches.

Replacing in Files Just as with Quick Find, there is a way to perform replacements using the Find in Files tool. This mode is entered by clicking the Replace in Files button at the top of the search window (see Figure 6.21).

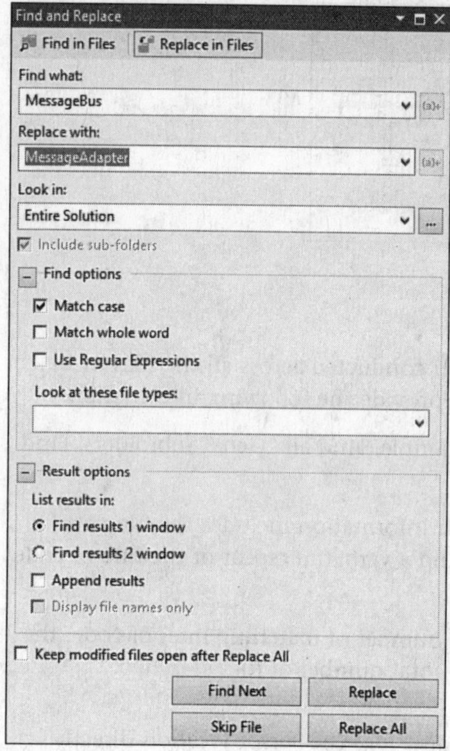

FIGURE 6.21 Replace in Files mode.

We've already covered the Replace and Replace All functions. Each file that matches the search phrase is opened in a separate text editor window, and the replacements are made directly in that window. If you're performing a Replace All, the replacements are made and then saved directly into the containing file. You also have the option, via the Keep Modified Files Open After Replace All check box, to have Visual Studio keep any files touched open inside their respective text editors. This allows you to selectively save or discard the replacements as you see fit.

You can elect to skip files during the search-and-replace process by using the Skip File button. This button is available only if more than one file has been selected as part of the search scope. Clicking this button tells the search engine to skip the current file being processed and continue with the next in-scope file.

Incremental Search

Incremental Search is a special case function that works with the Quick Find window. With a text editor open, select Edit, Advanced, Incremental Search (or press Ctrl+I). While Incremental Search is active, you will see the Quick Find window and a special visual pointer cue composed of binoculars and a down arrow. If you start typing a search string, character by character, the first match found is highlighted within the text editor window. With each successive character, the search string is altered and the search itself is re-executed. The current search string and search scope is displayed on the Visual Studio status bar and brought to view in the Editor. Figure 6.22 illustrates an Incremental Search in progress; the characters MESS have been entered, and you can see the first match flagged within the text editor.

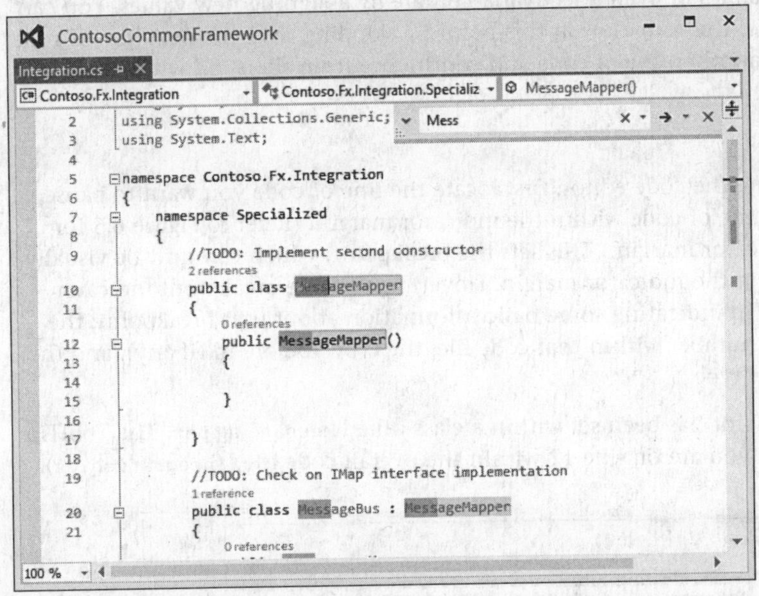

FIGURE 6.22 Incremental Search.

By default, the search function works from the top of the document to the bottom and from left to right. You can reverse the direction of the search by using the Ctrl+Shift+I key combination.

To jump to the next match within the document, use the Ctrl+I key combination.

Clicking anywhere within the document or pressing the Esc key cancels the Incremental Search.

NOTE

Incremental Searches are always performed in a manner that is not case sensitive and will always match on substrings.

Debugging in the Text Editor

The text editor (more specifically, the code editor) has several interactive features that facilitate the code-debugging process. Debugging activities within the text editor primarily center on breakpoints and runtime code control. We cover general Visual Studio debugging in greater detail in Chapter 10.

A breakpoint is simply a location (a line of code) that is flagged for the debugger; when the debugger encounters a breakpoint, the currently executing program is paused immediately before executing that line of code. While the program is in this paused state, you can inspect the state of variables or even affect variable state by assigning new values. You can also interactively control the code flow at this point by skipping over the next line of code or skipping directly to another line of code and continuing from there, all without actually leaving the IDE.

Setting a Breakpoint

To set a breakpoint using the code editor, first locate the line of code you want to pause on and then click that line of code within the indicator margin. (Refer to Figure 6.5 for the location of the indicator margin.) This sets the breakpoint, which can now be visually identified by a red ball in the indicator margin. Hovering over the breakpoint indicator margin displays a ToolTip indicating some basic information about that breakpoint: the code filename, the line number within that code file, the type you are in (if any), and the line number within that type.

In Figure 6.23, a breakpoint has been set within a class called `MessageMapper`. The ToolTip information shows that you are on line 12 within the overall code file (`Integration.cs`).

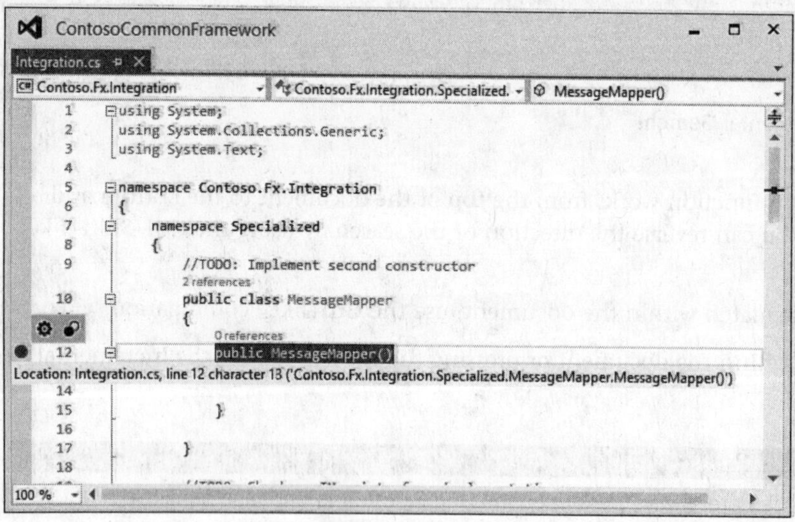

FIGURE 6.23 Setting a breakpoint.

Clicking the breakpoint again removes it.

The breakpoint we have set is a simple one in that it suspends the program on that line of code without regard for any other variable or factor. Simple breakpoints are, however, only the tip of the iceberg. Breakpoints support an extensive set of conditions used to fine-tune and control what will actually trigger the breakpoints. For instance, you can set a breakpoint to print a message, and you can specify different conditions for firing the breakpoint.

Configuring a Breakpoint

If you refer to Figure 6.23, you will see that, in addition to presenting a tooltip window with information about the breakpoint, there is a small, simple toolbar exposed directly above the breakpoint symbol. This toolbar has two buttons that allow you to configure the breakpoint or enable/disable the breakpoint. (Disabled breakpoints appear as empty red circles; enabled breakpoints appear as solid red circles.)

If you elect to configure the breakpoint, its settings will show directly within the code editor window. You can set a condition for the breakpoint (in other words, when should the breakpoint fire?) and tweak what exactly happens during the breakpoint triggering process. (This is referred to as an action.) In Figure 6.24, we have configured a breakpoint to fire on a specific conditional expression and break count.

TIP

Disabling a breakpoint, rather than deleting it, will preserve its locations and all of its settings in case you ever need to enable it again.

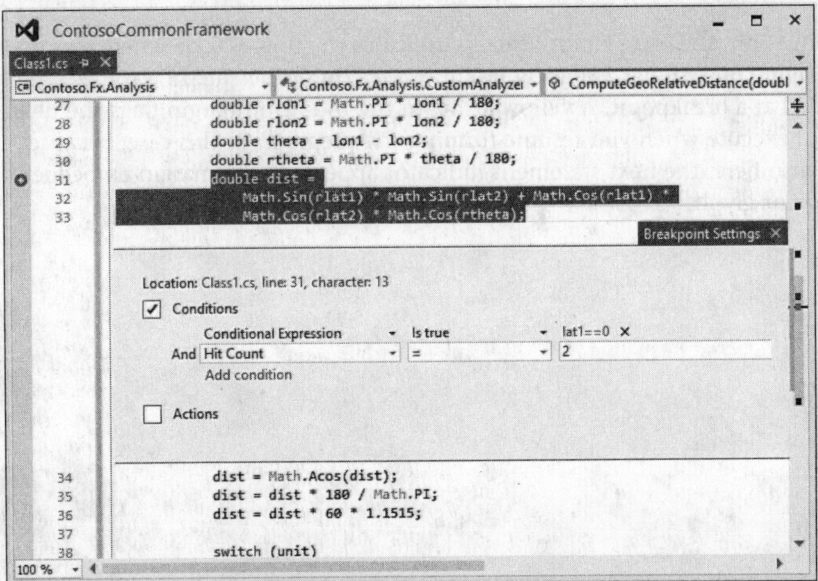

FIGURE 6.24 Configuring a breakpoint directly within the code editor.

You can also access breakpoint settings by right-clicking the breakpoint indicator to show the context menu.

TIP

Visual Basic actually provides a command word that allows you to programmatically trigger a breakpoint within your code. The `Stop` statement, like a breakpoint, suspends execution of the executing code. This capability is useful when you're running the application outside the IDE. Any time a `Stop` statement is encountered during runtime, the Visual Studio debugger launches and attaches to the program.

Although C# doesn't have an internal, equivalent statement to Visual Basic's `Stop` command, you can use the `Debugger` class to achieve the same thing: simply call `Debugger.Break` to force a breakpoint programmatically. You can even write code that will run only when under debugger control by checking the Debugger.IsAttached property. The `Debugger` class lives in the `System.Diagnostic` namespace.

Controlling the Flow of Running Code

When a program is run within the IDE, it continues along its path of execution through the code base until it hits a breakpoint or `Stop` statement, is paused manually, or terminates either by reaching the end of its code path or by being manually stopped.

TIP

The DVR-like controls and their shortcut keys (available under the Debug menu or on the Debug toolbar) are, by far, the easiest way to start, pause, or stop code within the IDE.

When a breakpoint is hit, the code editor visually indicates the line of code where execution has paused. Figure 6.25 shows a slightly modified version of the `"Hello, World"` program, suspended at a breakpoint. A yellow arrow in the indicator margin flags the next statement that will execute when you resume running the program. In this case, because the breakpoint is also here, the next statement indicator appears in the margin embedded within the breakpoint glyph.

```
using System;
using System.Collections.Generic;
using System.Linq;
using System.Text;
using System.Threading.Tasks;

namespace HelloWorld
{
    0 references
    class Program
    {
        0 references
        static void Main(string[] args)
        {
            for (int i=0; i<=5; i++)
            {
                Console.WriteLine("Hello, World! try={0}", i);
            }

            Console.WriteLine("Anyone listening?");
```

FIGURE 6.25 Stopping at a breakpoint.

When execution is paused, you can change the next line of code to be executed. By default, of course, this is the line of code where operations were paused. (Recall that execution stops just before running the line of code matched with the breakpoint.) But you can manually specify the next line of code to run by dragging the yellow "next statement" arrow to any other executable line within the code editor.

In Figure 6.26, this feature has been used to jump out of the `WriteLine` loop. Normal flow through the code has been circumvented, and instead of continuing to spin through the `for` loop, the program immediately executes the line of code just after the loop. You can see the arrow and highlighting that show the next line of code and the breakpoint are no longer at the same location within the code file.

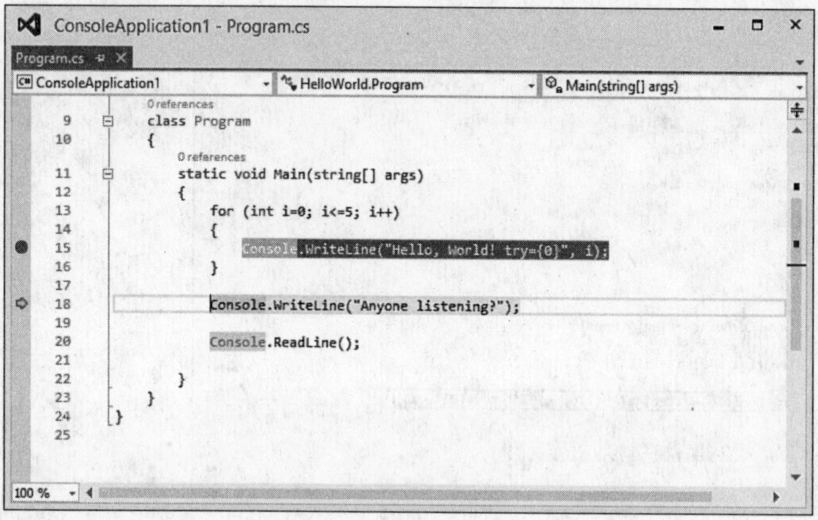

FIGURE 6.26 Setting the next `Run` statement.

You can also create a sort of virtual breakpoint by right-clicking on an executable line within the code editor window and selecting Run to Cursor from the editor's context menu. This causes the program to run until it hits the line of code that you have selected, at which point it pauses much as if you had set a breakpoint there.

Printing Code

To print the current text editor's contents, select Print from the File menu. The Print dialog box is fairly standard, allowing you to select your printer and set basic print properties. Two Visual Studio-specific options bear mentioning here. The Print What section in this dialog box controls whether line numbers are produced in the printout and whether collapsed regions are included in the printed content.

Colors and Fonts

By default, the font colors and markup that you see in the text editor window are sent to the printer as is (assuming that you are printing to a color printer). If you so desire, you can tweak all these settings from the Environment, Fonts and Colors page in the Options dialog box (see Figure 6.27).

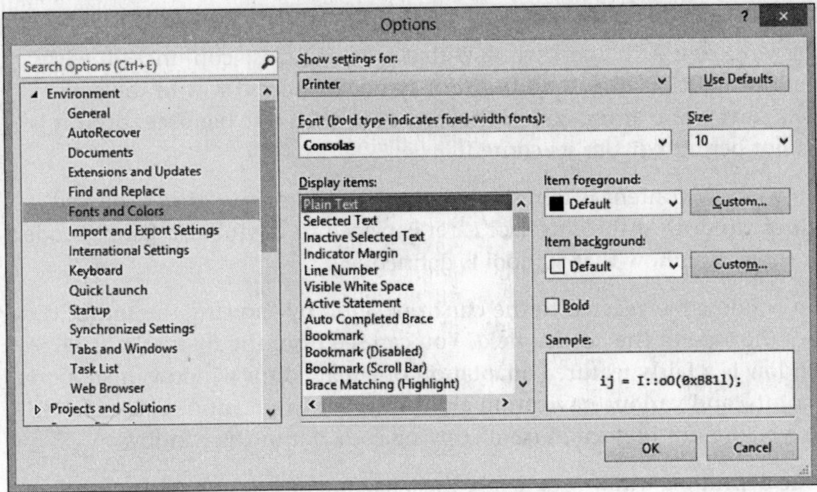

FIGURE 6.27 The Fonts and Colors Options dialog box.

This is the same dialog box used to control font and color settings for many of the IDE's constituent parts. You access the printer settings by selecting Printer in the Show Settings For drop-down at the top of the dialog box.

Figure 6.28 provides a snapshot of output produced by printing a code file.

```
...ojects\ConsoleApplication1\ConsoleApplication1\Program.cs                1
using System;
using System.Collections.Generic;
using System.Linq;
using System.Text;
using System.Threading.Tasks;

namespace HelloWorld
{
    class Program
    {
        static void Main(string[] args)
        {
            for (int i=0; i<=5; i++)
            {
                Console.WriteLine("Hello, World! try={0}", i);
            }

            Console.WriteLine("Anyone listening?");

            Console.ReadLine();

        }
    }
}

```

FIGURE 6.28 Code printout.

Using the Code Definition Window

The code definition window is a "helper" window that works in close conjunction with the code editor window by displaying definitions for symbols selected within the code editor. It is actually a near clone of the code editor window, with one big exception: It is read-only and does not permit edits to its content.

The code definition window content is refreshed anytime the cursor position is moved within the code editor window. If the cursor or caret is placed in a symbol/type, the code definition window shows you how that symbol is defined.

The code definition window has reacted to the cursor position by showing the source code that actually defines the type of the `_state` field. You can see from the figure that the code definition window is a fairly featured adaptation of a text editor window: it supports bookmarks, breakpoints, and various navigation aids. Although you cannot edit code using this window, you are not prevented from copying code out of the window.

You can open a code definition window by using the View menu.

> **TIP**
>
> The code definition window also works well with the Class View window. If you single-click a class within the Class View window, the code definition window refreshes to show you the code implementation for that class.

Visual Studio 2015 also has an alternate, and quicker way, of getting to the definition of a particular type, method, or property. It's called peek definition. To see this in action, put your cursor over a type or member within the editor window, right-click, and then select Peek Definition. A small editing window will open within the parent code editor window. The advantage to this is that you don't need to switch your attention away from the code at hand, and you can edit the definition code directly (unlike the Code Definition window). See Figure 6.30 for an example of peek definition in action.

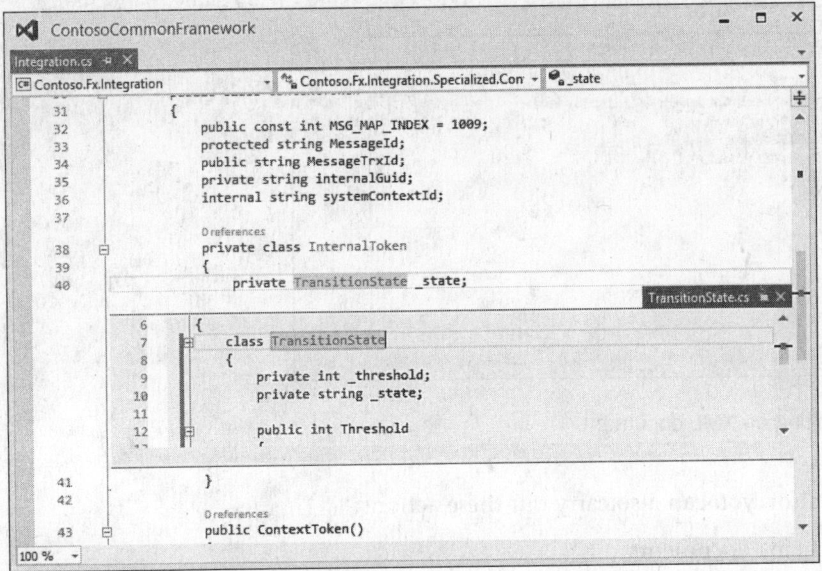

FIGURE 6.29 Using Peek Definition.

Creating and Editing XML Documents and Schema

The text editor is equally adept, and just as productive, at editing documents with XML content, including XML schemas. The XML editor is launched whenever you open a file with the `.xml` extension inside of Visual Studio. It is also launched for `.xsl` files and `.config` files and is always available when you use the Open With command in the Solution Explorer against any item in a project.

Because XML documents contain structured content involving the concepts of nodes and tags, attributes, and node containership, the XML editor supports document outlining in a similar fashion to the code editor: you can expand or collapse nodes within the editor to expose or hide a node's content (see Figure 6.30). And just as with the code editor, syntax checking and IntelliSense are fully supported by the XML editor. The XML editor is aware of the syntactical requirements for the current document and provides appropriate IntelliSense and formatting help where possible.

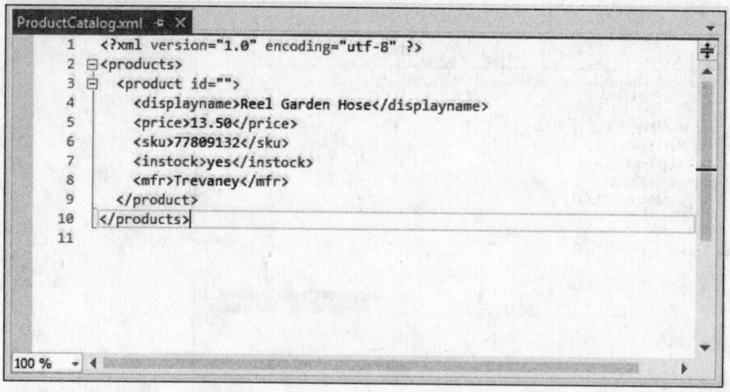

ProductCatalog.xml

```
<?xml version="1.0" encoding="utf-8" ?>
<products>
  <product id="">
    <displayname>Reel Garden Hose</displayname>
    <price>13.50</price>
    <sku>77809132</sku>
    <instock>yes</instock>
    <mfr>Trevaney</mfr>
  </product>
</products>
```

100 %

FIGURE 6.30 Editing an XML document.

Using the XML editor, you can also carry out these actions:

- Edit XSD schema documents
- Generate a schema document from an XML document
- Edit XSLT style sheets
- Edit Document Type Definition (DTD) documents and XML-Data Reduced (XDR) documents
- Insert XML snippets

For a proper treatment of the various editing, validation, and productivity aids available in this editor, see Chapter 7, "Working with Visual Studio's Productivity Aids." Here, let's explore two of the core XML functions: schema generation and EXtensible Stylesheet Language Transformations (XSLT) style sheet editing.

Inferring Schema

The XML editor can automatically generate an XML schema document (XSD) based on a valid XML document. While the XML document is open, select Create Schema from the XML main menu. This creates an XSD document and opens it in the XML Schema Designer (more on this in the next section). From there, you can make any necessary changes to the XSD document and save it to disk. You can also include it in your project at this point.

NOTE

If you run the Create Schema command against an XML document that already contains a DTD or XDR schema, the XML inference algorithm uses these schemas as the basis for the conversion as opposed to the actual data within the XML document.

Designing XML Schemas

Visual Studio has made huge strides over the years in its support for XML schema design. This is evident right off the bat when you open an XML schema file (`.xsd`). A visual design window and an XML Schema Explorer window, working in tandem, quickly allow you to inspect, edit, and build out your schema. Figure 6.31 shows the same schema we just inferred from our simple "product catalog" XML file opened in the Visual Studio IDE. Note the schema explorer to the right and the schema designer to the left. Let's examine the various views in detail.

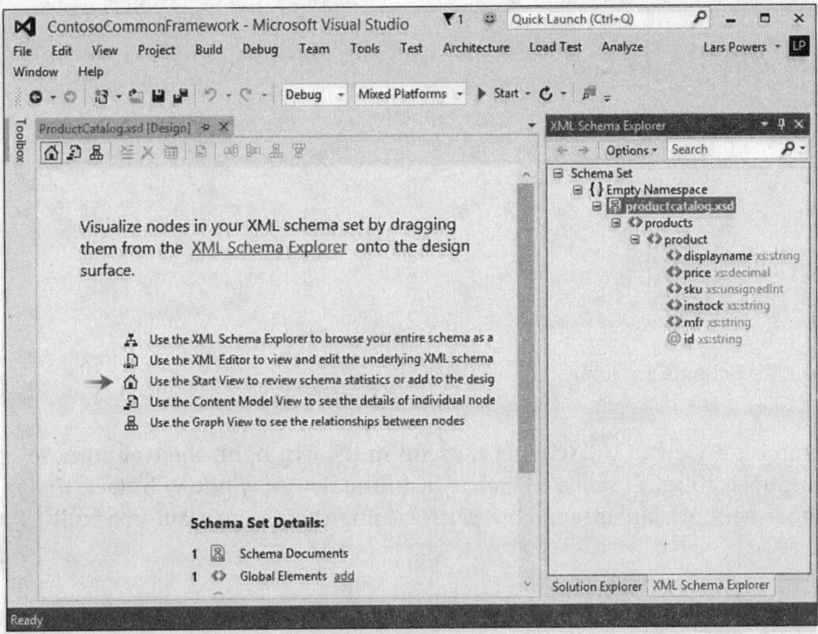

FIGURE 6.31 Editing a simple XML schema.

Schema Views

Visual Studio provides five different ways to visualize/edit the information in an XML schema, delivered by three different tools. We have already covered the XML editor. Because XML schemas are verbalized using XML, the editor's functions apply just as well to schema editing as they do to document editing.

That leaves us with four remaining views implemented using two tools: the XML Schema Explorer and the XML Schema Designer. Just as you have come to expect with most explorer/designer pairs in the IDE, these two tools work hand in hand.

The XML Schema Explorer

The Schema Explorer exposes a tree-view representation of schema content (see Figure 6.32). Using this explorer, you can expand any of the schema container elements to view their child elements. The toolbar on this explorer window lets you search for schema elements and change the sort order.

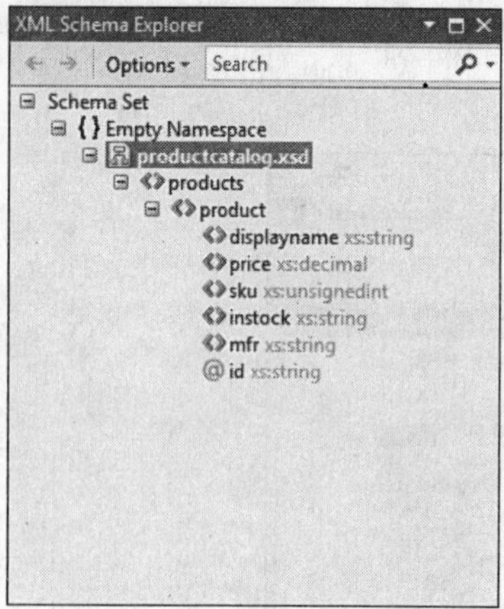

FIGURE 6.32 The XML Schema Explorer.

Although this hierarchical view of the schema is useful in its own right, the real purpose of the explorer window is to select items to view/edit in the design window. In fact, the explorer and designer windows are inseparable pairs: closing the designer automatically closes the explorer.

The XML Schema Designer

The schema design window is where all the schema editing takes place. You can edit or view a schema (or set of schemas) by dragging items from the XML Schema Explorer window onto the XML Schema Designer surface.

After you have added the schema to the design surface, the schema design window provides three different views into the schema's structure and content:

- The Start View is the default view. As its name implies, this is a launching page into the other views. The Start View also provides summary statistics for the XML schema (such as a count of the global elements, attributes, and types) and provides a quick and easy way to add these items to the design surface.
- The Graph View is a 2D view of the nodes and node relationships within a schema. The Graph View is primarily useful in visualizing the complexity and types of relationships within a schema. You can't use this to directly edit the nodes or node relationships. Use the toolbar buttons at the top of the designer to change the way

that the graph is displayed: left to right, right to left, top to bottom, or bottom to top. Double-clicking a node opens the schema's XML in the XML editor, with the XML for that node highlighted. See Figure 6.33 for a picture of the Graph View with a more complex schema file loaded. This schema file represents a data model of pet types. In this example, we have a base pet entity that implements base-level attributes, and we have two other entities, dog and cat, that derive from the base entity. This relationship is clearly depicted in the graph view.

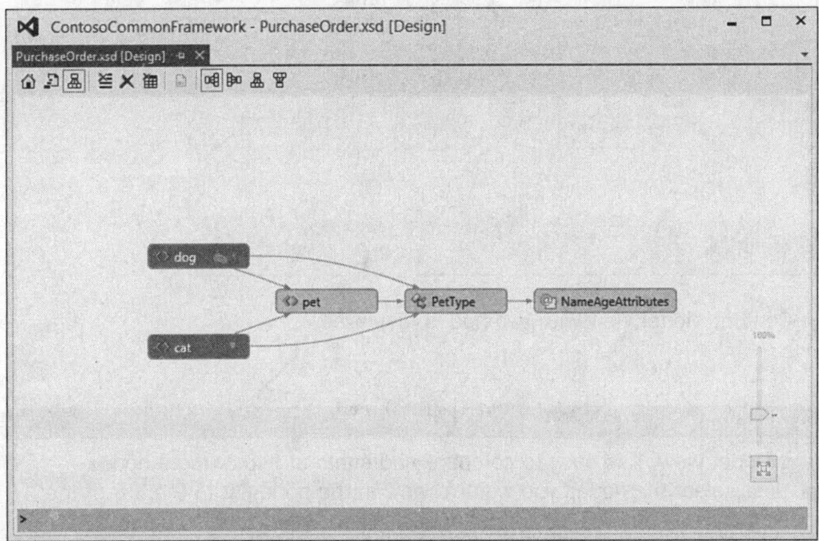

FIGURE 6.33 Using the Schema Designer's Graph View.

- The Content Model View is a graphical, hierarchical view of the nodes and node elements, attributes, types, and groups. This view is particularly useful if you are trying to understand the details of a particular portion of the schema. For instance, by double-clicking a type, you can quickly gain a fairly complete understanding of that type's schema, including elements, attributes, types, and groups (in addition to any constraints or relationships that are defined in the schema). This view also provides a simple way to select nodes: an A-Z list of all nodes within the schema appears in the list box to the left of the design surface. Clicking the node in this list displays the node details on the design surface (see Figure 6.34).

You can switch among these views by using the options on the start page or by using the toolbar at the top of the designer window.

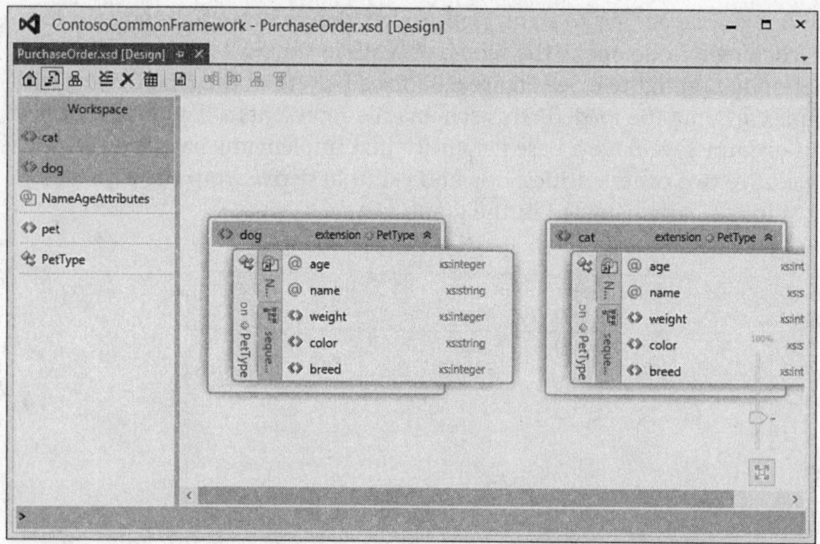

FIGURE 6.34 The Content Model View with two nodes displayed.

> **TIP**
>
> Using the Content Model View, it is easy to compare and contrast two or more nodes within a schema. Just select the nodes you want to view in the node list to the left of the design surface (using Ctrl+Left to add additional nodes to your selection). You can then use the design surface's image scaler to get a high-level view of the nodes or to zoom in on specific details.

Editing XSLT Style Sheets

XSLT files are XML files, so the process of editing an XSLT style sheet is the same as that described for editing an XML document. There are, however, a few additional features specific to XSLT documents. First, keywords are recognized and shaded appropriately in the editor just as with a code document. Second, the XML editor automatically processes the current state of the document against the standard schema for XSLT style sheets and shows any validation errors to you directly. Finally, Visual Studio is fully aware of any script embedded in an XSLT document. You can set breakpoints within a script block, and there is full debug support for scripts, enabling you to step through code, see the current state of variables, and so forth. Figure 6.35 shows an XSLT style sheet with a breakpoint set within a section of embedded script.

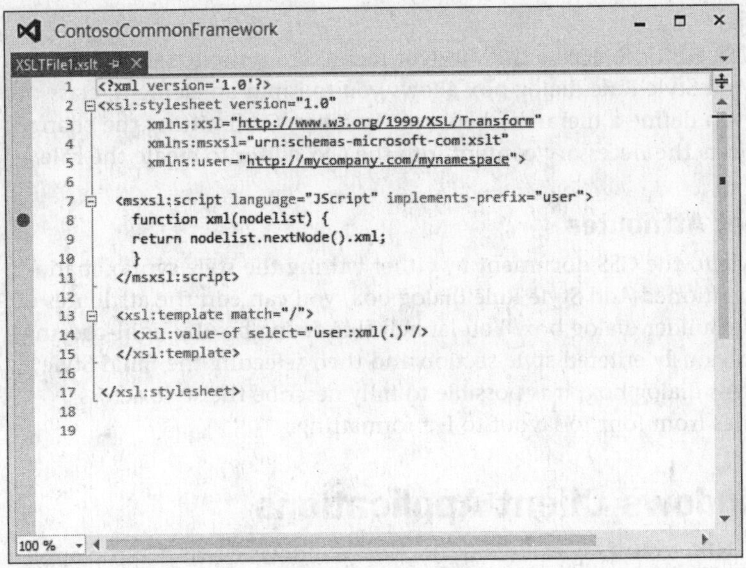

ContosoCommonFramework

XSLTFile1.xslt

```
<?xml version='1.0'?>
<xsl:stylesheet version="1.0"
      xmlns:xsl="http://www.w3.org/1999/XSL/Transform"
      xmlns:msxsl="urn:schemas-microsoft-com:xslt"
      xmlns:user="http://mycompany.com/mynamespace">

  <msxsl:script language="JScript" implements-prefix="user">
    function xml(nodelist) {
    return nodelist.nextNode().xml;
    }
  </msxsl:script>

  <xsl:template match="/">
    <xsl:value-of select="user:xml(.)"/>
  </xsl:template>

</xsl:stylesheet>
```

100 %

FIGURE 6.35 Debugging script embedded into an XSLT document.

Running XSLT Against XML

After a style sheet has been created and attached to an XML document, you can execute that XSLT style sheet and view the output within a new editor window. To attach the XSLT sheet to the XML document, use the Properties window for the XML document and set the `Stylesheet` property. Entering the full path and filename of the XSLT in this property attaches the style sheet. Alternatively, you can manually code the style sheet into the XML document's prolog section by typing an `xml-stylesheet` Processing Instruction prolog into the document, like this:

```
<?xml-stylesheet type='text/xsl' href='myxsl.xsl'?>
```

When a style sheet is associated, selecting the Show XSLT Output option from the XML menu runs the transforms against the XML document and shows you the results in a separate editor window.

Working with Cascading Style Sheets

The CSS editor allows you to build and edit cascading style sheet documents. Because CSS documents are, at their core, text documents, the editor doesn't need to provide much more than standard text-editing features to be effective. However, a few built-in tools available from the editor enable you to add style rules and build styles using dialog boxes as opposed to free-form text entry.

Adding Style Rules

Right-click within the CSS editor to access the shortcut menu. From there, select the Add Style Rule option. The Add Style Rule dialog box allows you to input an element, class name, or class ID and even define a hierarchy between the rules. Committing the change from this dialog box injects the necessary content into the CSS editor to create the rule.

Defining Style Sheet Attributes

After you've added a style to the CSS document by either writing the style syntax manually or using the aforementioned Add Style Rule dialog box, you can edit the attributes of that style using the Style Builder dialog box. You launch this dialog box by right-clicking anywhere within the previously entered style section and then selecting the Build Style option. When you use this dialog box, it is possible to fully describe the style across several different categories from font to layout to list formatting.

Developing Windows Client Applications

There are two principal .NET technologies used to develop Windows client desktop applications: Windows Forms (WinForms) and Windows Presentation Foundation (WPF). Both of these technologies are essentially a set of classes and user interface controls exposed by the .NET Framework that enable developers to quickly build out applications that are installed, and run, under the Microsoft Windows operating system.

NOTE

With Windows 8, Microsoft has introduced a third client application stack. These are so-called "modern UI" applications that run on top of the Windows runtime. Although we don't cover building Windows client applications for the Windows runtime in this chapter, we do cover those tools and technologies in depth in Chapter 23, "Developing Windows Store Applications."

WPF is unique when compared to the older Windows Forms technology because it uses a markup language called XAML to describe application objects, property values, and behavior. In this respect, it is similar to a web application that uses HTML to describe the various elements of a web page. WPF as a technology heavily leverages vector graphics and graphics hardware acceleration to display an application's user interface.

Regardless of the type of client application you need to build, the process is much the same: both the WinForms designer and the WPF designer enable drag-and-drop development, and both have project templates available in Visual Studio.

Creating a Windows Forms Project

The process of building a Windows Forms application starts the same as all other project types within Visual Studio: you select the Windows Application project template from the New Project dialog box and set up the location for the application's source. From there, Visual Studio stubs out an initial project, and the Windows Forms Designer loads, as shown in Figure 6.36.

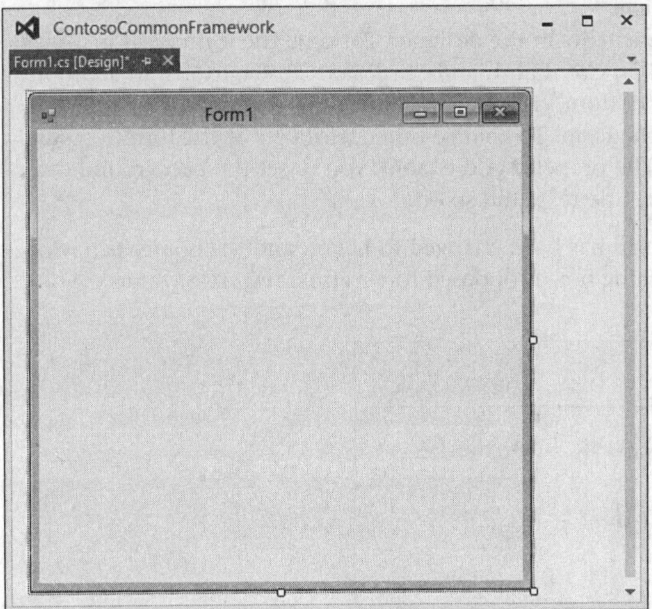

FIGURE 6.36 Initial form in the Windows Forms Designer.

As you can see from the figure, a design-time mock-up of the actual form is visible within the designer. This is the canvas for your user interface. Using this canvas, you can add controls and visual elements to the form, tweak the look and feel of the form itself, and launch directly to the code that is wired to the form.

To investigate how the designer works, start with a simple design premise: Suppose, for instance, that you want to take the blank form that Visual Studio generated for you and create a login dialog box that allows users to input a name and password and confirm their entries by clicking an OK button. A Cancel button should also be available to allow users to dismiss the form.

NOTE

Don't get confused about the various representations that a form can have, such as message box or dialog box. From a development perspective, they are all windows and are therefore all forms.

The designer in this exercise allows you, the developer, to craft the form and its actions while writing as little code as possible. Using drag-and-drop operations and Property dialog boxes, you should be able to customize the look and feel of the application without ever dealing with the code editor.

Customizing the Form's Appearance

There are a few obvious visual elements in the designer. For one, the form itself is shown complete with its borders, title bar, client area, and Min/Max/Close buttons. In addition, you can see grab handles at the bottom, right, and bottom-right corner of the form. The grab handles are used to resize the form. To change other attributes of the form, you use the property grid for the form. The property grid enables you to set the background color, border appearance and behavior, title text, and so on.

In Figure 6.37, the title of the form has been changed to Login, and the border behavior has been changed to match a dialog box as opposed to a normal resizable window.

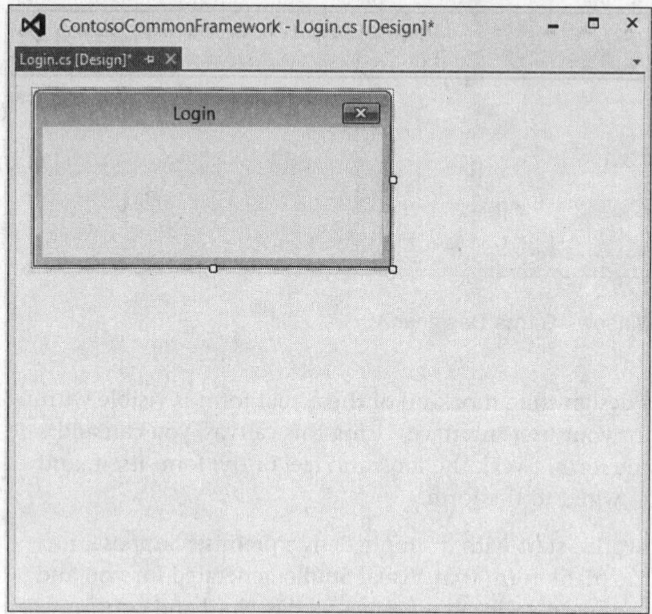

FIGURE 6.37 Editing the form's size, border, and title.

Adding Controls to a Form

Controls are adornments to a form that have their own user interface. (There is such a thing as UI-less controls; we cover such controls later in this chapter in the section "Authoring WinForms Components and Controls.") They provide the principal interaction mechanism method with a form. Put another way, a form is really just a container for the various controls that implement the desired functionality for the form.

You can add controls to a form quite easily by dragging and dropping them from the Toolbox. Continuing the metaphor of the designer as a canvas, the Toolbox is the palette.

The Toolbox The Toolbox is a dockable window within the IDE; it is viewable only when you are editing a project element that supports Toolbox functionality. To make sure that the Toolbox is visible, select it from the View menu (or use the Ctrl+W, X shortcut).

The Toolbox groups the controls in a tabbed tree. Expand the tab grouping (such as Common Controls or Menus & Toolbars), and you see a list of the available controls. In this case, you want two text box controls to hold the login ID and password text, a few label controls to describe the text box controls, and the OK and Cancel buttons to commit or cancel the entries. You can find all these controls under the Common Controls tab (see Figure 6.38).

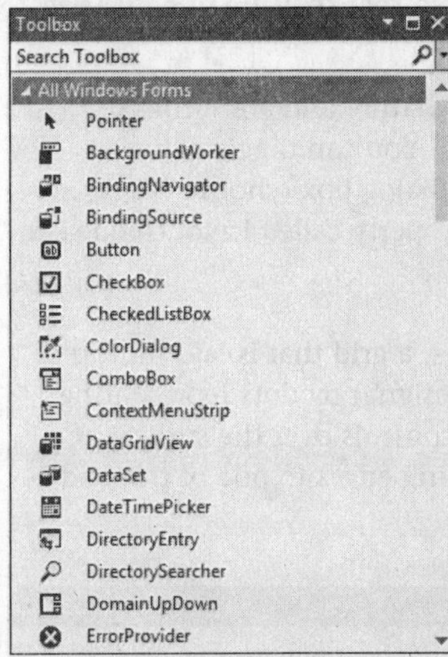

FIGURE 6.38 The WinForms Toolbox.

To place a control on the form, drag its representation from the Toolbox onto the form. Some controls, referred to as components, don't actually have a visual user interface. The timer is one example of a component. When you drag a component to a form, it is placed in a separate area of the designer called the component tray. The component tray allows you to select one of the added components and access its properties via the Properties window.

TIP

The Toolbox is customizable in terms of its content and arrangement. You can add or remove tabs from the Toolbox, move controls from one tab to another through simple drag and drop, and even rename individual items within the Toolbox. To perform many of these actions, bring up the Toolbox context menu by right-clicking a tab or an item.

Arranging Controls When you are designing a form, control layout becomes an important issue. You are typically concerned about ensuring that controls are aligned either horizontally or vertically, that controls and control groups are positioned with equal and common margins between their edges, that margins are enforced along the form borders, and so on.

The designer provides three distinct sets of tools and aids that assist with form layout. First, you have the options available to you under the Format menu. With a form loaded in the designer, you can select different groups of controls and use the commands under the Format menu to align these controls vertically or horizontally with one another, standardize and increase or decrease the spacing between controls, center the controls within the form, and even alter the controls' appearance attributes so that they are of equal size in either dimension.

The other layout tools within the designer are interactive in nature and are surfaced through two different modes: snap line and grid positioning. You can toggle between these two modes via the Windows Forms Designer Options dialog box (choose Tools, Options and then the Windows Forms Designer tab). The property called LayoutMode can be set to either SnapToGrid or SnapLines.

Using the Layout Grid The layout grid is, as its name implies, a grid that is laid on top of the form. The grid itself is visually represented within the designer by dots representing the intersection of the grid squares. As you drag and move controls over the surface of the grid, the designer automatically snaps the control's leading edges to one of the grid's square edges.

TIP

Even with the grid layout turned on, you can circumvent the snapping behavior by selecting a control, holding down the Ctrl key and using the arrow keys to move the control up, down, right, or left one pixel at a time.

The size of the grid squares (and thus the spacing of these guide dots) is controlled by the GridSize property (also located in the Options dialog box). A smaller grid size equates to a tighter spacing of guide dots, which in turns equates to more finely grained control over control placement.

Figure 6.39 shows the login form with the layout grid in evidence. Note that the grid was used to confirm the following:

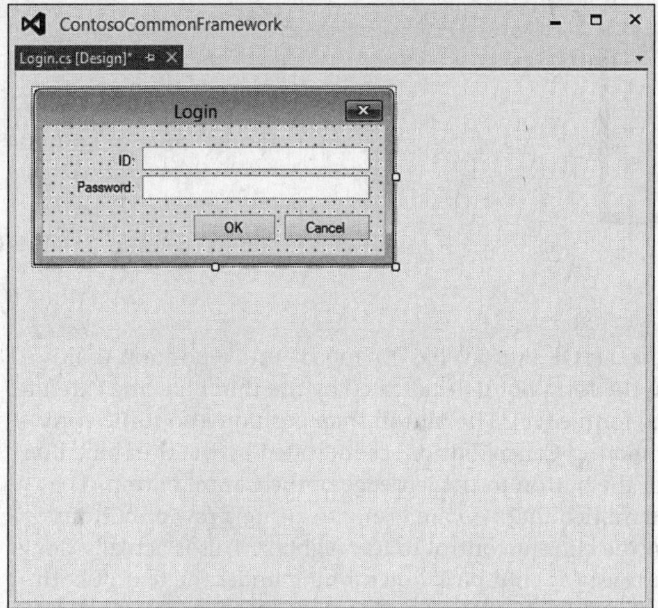

FIGURE 6.39 The layout grid.

- The text boxes are aligned with one another (and are the same length).
- The labels are aligned vertically with the text boxes and horizontally with each other.
- The buttons are aligned vertically and have an appropriate buffer area between their control edges and the form's border.

Using Snap Lines Snap lines are a slightly more intelligent mechanism for positioning controls. With snap lines, no grid is visible on the form's surface. Instead, the designer draws visual hints while a control is in motion on the form.

Figure 6.40 illustrates snap lines in action; this figure shows the process of positioning the OK button.

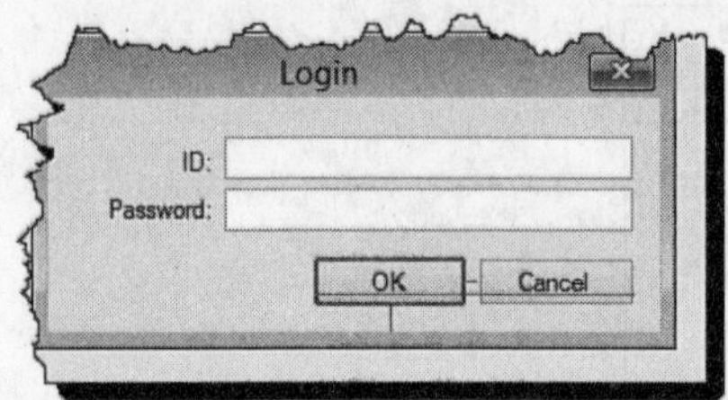

FIGURE 6.40 Using snap lines.

Note that the control (in this case, an OK button) has "snapped" into a position that is located a set distance away from the form border (indicated by the thin blue line extending down from the button to the form edge). The button snap position also sufficiently spaces the control from its neighboring Cancel button, as indicated by the thin blue line extending from the right edge of the button to the left edge of the Cancel button. The snap line algorithm has also determined that you are trying to create a row of buttons and thus need to vertically align the current control to its neighbor. This is actually done using the interior text of the buttons; the thin pink line running under the text of both buttons clearly shows that they are perfectly aligned.

The snap line algorithms automatically take into account the recommended margins and spacing distances as discussed in the Windows User Interface Guidelines written and adopted by Microsoft. This feature takes the guesswork out of many layout decisions and helps to ensure some commonality and standards adherence within the Windows Forms applications.

NOTE

Changes made to the layout modes of the designer typically do not take effect immediately. You might need to close the designer and reopen it after making a change (such as switching between SnapLine mode and SnapToGrid mode). If you have multiple designer windows open, you may need to close them all before your layout mode changes take effect.

Resizing Controls and Editing Attributes

When a control is in place on its parent form, you can interact with the control in various ways. You can set control properties using the Properties window. You also can alter the sizing and shape of the control by dragging the grab handles on the sides of the control.

Writing Code

Although the designer excels at enabling developers to visually construct a user interface, its capability to actually implement behavior is limited. You can use the designer to place a button, but responding to a click of a button and reacting in some way are still the domain of code.

At the code level, a form is simply a class that encapsulates all the form's behavior. For simplicity and ease of development, Visual Studio pushes all the code that it writes via the designer into clearly marked regions and, in the case of Windows forms, a separate code file. The file is named after the primary form code file like this: `FormName.Designer.language_extension`. As an example, the login form is accompanied by a `Login.Designer.cs` file that implements the designer-written code.

Listing 6.1 shows what Visual Studio has generated in the way of code to implement the changes made through the designer.

LISTING 6.1 Windows Forms Designer–Generated Code

```
namespace Contoso.UI.WindowsForms.OrderEntry
{
    partial class Login
    {
        /// <summary>
        /// Required designer variable.
        /// </summary>
        private System.ComponentModel.IContainer components = null;

        /// <summary>
        /// Clean up any resources being used.
        /// </summary>
        /// <param name="disposing">true if managed resources should be disposed;
        /// otherwise, false.</param>
        protected override void Dispose(bool disposing)
        {
            if (disposing && (components != null))
            {
                components.Dispose();
            }
            base.Dispose(disposing);
        }

        #region Windows Form Designer generated code

        /// <summary>
        /// Required method for Designer support - do not modify
        /// the contents of this method with the code editor.
        /// </summary>
        private void InitializeComponent()
        {
            this.label1 = new System.Windows.Forms.Label();
            this.label2 = new System.Windows.Forms.Label();
            this.textBoxID = new System.Windows.Forms.TextBox();
            this.textBoxPassword = new System.Windows.Forms.TextBox();
```

```
this.buttonCancel = new System.Windows.Forms.Button();
this.buttonOk = new System.Windows.Forms.Button();
this.SuspendLayout();
//
// label1
//
this.label1.AutoSize = true;
this.label1.Location = new System.Drawing.Point(61, 23);
this.label1.Name = "label1";
this.label1.Size = new System.Drawing.Size(17, 13);
this.label1.TabIndex = 0;
this.label1.Text = "ID:";
//
// label2
//
this.label2.AutoSize = true;
this.label2.Location = new System.Drawing.Point(26, 46);
this.label2.Name = "label2";
this.label2.Size = new System.Drawing.Size(52, 13);
this.label2.TabIndex = 1;
this.label2.Text = "Password:";
//
// textBoxID
//
this.textBoxID.Location = new System.Drawing.Point(85, 20);
this.textBoxID.Name = "textBoxID";
this.textBoxID.Size = new System.Drawing.Size(195, 20);
this.textBoxID.TabIndex = 2;
//
// textBoxPassword
//
this.textBoxPassword.Location = new System.Drawing.Point(85, 46);
this.textBoxPassword.Name = "textBoxPassword";
this.textBoxPassword.Size = new System.Drawing.Size(195, 20);
this.textBoxPassword.TabIndex = 3;
//
// buttonCancel
//
this.buttonCancel.DialogResult =
   System.Windows.Forms.DialogResult.Cancel;
this.buttonCancel.Location = new System.Drawing.Point(205, 72);
this.buttonCancel.Name = "buttonCancel";
this.buttonCancel.Size = new System.Drawing.Size(75, 23);
this.buttonCancel.TabIndex = 4;
this.buttonCancel.Text = "Cancel";
//
```

```
            // buttonOk
            //
            this.buttonOk.Location = new System.Drawing.Point(124, 72);
            this.buttonOk.Name = "buttonOk";
            this.buttonOk.Size = new System.Drawing.Size(75, 23);
            this.buttonOk.TabIndex = 5;
            this.buttonOk.Text = "OK";
            //
            // Login
            //
            this.AcceptButton = this.buttonOk;
            this.AutoScaleDimensions = new System.Drawing.SizeF(6F, 13F);
            this.AutoScaleMode = System.Windows.Forms.AutoScaleMode.Font;
            this.CancelButton = this.buttonCancel;
            this.ClientSize = new System.Drawing.Size(292, 109);
            this.Controls.Add(this.buttonOk);
            this.Controls.Add(this.buttonCancel);
            this.Controls.Add(this.textBoxPassword);
            this.Controls.Add(this.textBoxID);
            this.Controls.Add(this.label2);
            this.Controls.Add(this.label1);
            this.FormBorderStyle =
                System.Windows.Forms.FormBorderStyle.FixedDialog;
            this.MaximizeBox = false;
            this.MinimizeBox = false;
            this.Name = "Login";
            this.ShowInTaskbar = false;
            this.SizeGripStyle = System.Windows.Forms.SizeGripStyle.Hide;
            this.Text = "Login";
            this.ResumeLayout(false);
            this.PerformLayout();

        }

        #endregion

        private System.Windows.Forms.Label label1;
        private System.Windows.Forms.Label label2;
        private System.Windows.Forms.TextBox textBoxID;
        private System.Windows.Forms.TextBox textBoxPassword;
        private System.Windows.Forms.Button buttonCancel;
        private System.Windows.Forms.Button buttonOk;
    }
}
```

Creating a Windows Presentation Foundation Project

Windows Presentation Foundation (WPF) projects behave much like WinForms projects do. In fact, one of the design goals for the WPF Designer and editor was to act in ways that would be familiar to developers who are used to Windows Forms development. Just as we previously did with our WinForms project, we start the development and design process by selecting a template (WPF Application) from the File, New Project dialog.

Two XAML files are automatically created within the project: `MainWindow.xaml`, which represents the main window for the app; and `App.xaml` (`Application.xaml` in Visual Basic), which represents the application itself. These are analogous to the `Form1.cs`/`Form1.vb` and `Program.cs`/`Module1.vb` files created in a new Windows Forms project.

The first difference you notice with WPF projects is that, by default, you are presented with two different panes. In one pane, you see the design surface for the window, and in another you see an editor that contains the XAML declarations for the form. This design view is actually the same that is used for web applications (which we investigate as part of the next topic). See Figure 6.41 for a look at the `Window1.xaml` file loaded in the IDE.

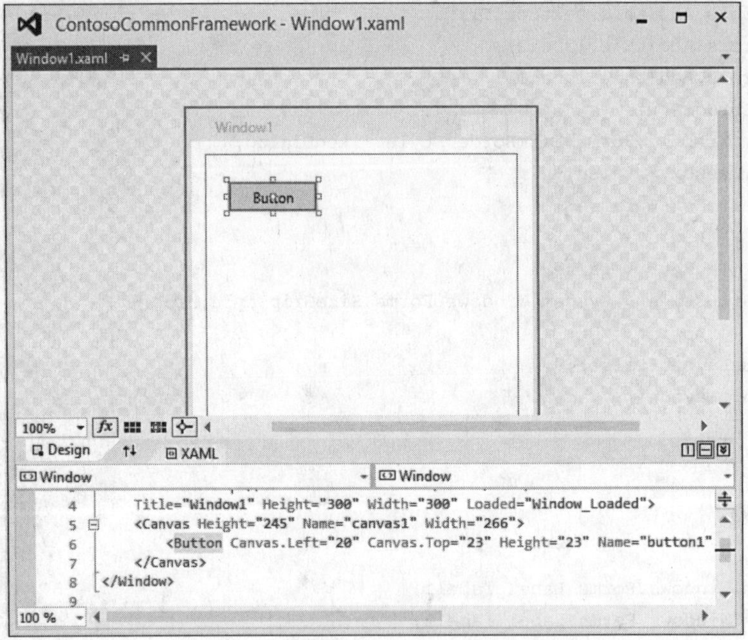

FIGURE 6.41 The initial window in the WPF Designer.

Each of these panes is simply a different view of the same window: a visual view and a text/XML view. I can add a button to the window, for example, by dragging it from the Toolbox onto the design surface or by typing the XAML declaration directly into the XAML pane like this:

```
<Button Height="25" Name="button1" Width="75">Button</Button>
```

Both the design and the XAML view are kept in sync with one another automatically.

Because WPF is based on vector graphics, you can zoom in and out in the designer using the combo-box control in the lower left of the designer. Note that you can hold down the Ctrl key and use the mouse scroll wheel to control the zoom level directly. Figure 6.42 shows the Window1 content, with a button, zoomed in at 10x.

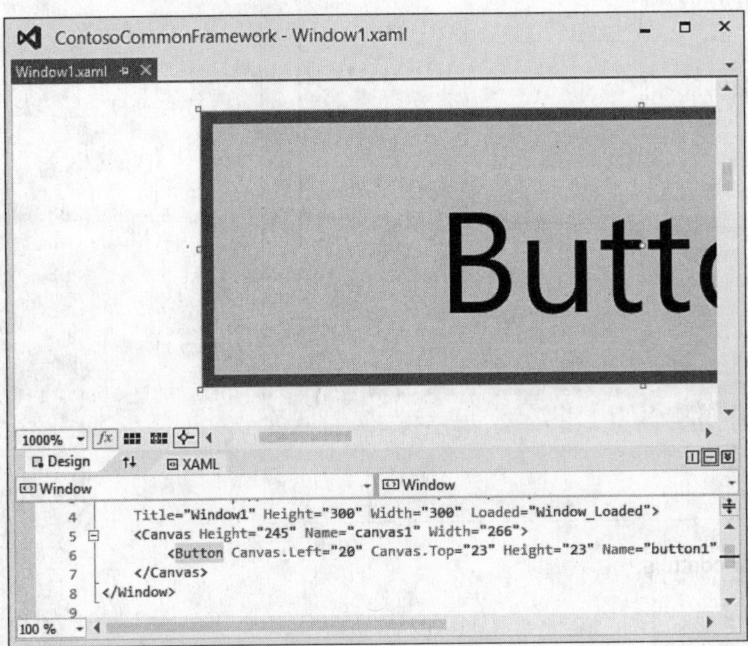

FIGURE 6.42 Ten times magnification in the WPF designer.

Using the Split Panes

You have control over how the design and XAML panes are displayed and positioned within the IDE. There is a small button flagged with two-way arrows that, when pressed, swaps the position of the two panes. You can also change the panes from a horizontal to a vertical orientation (or vice versa) by clicking the Horizontal Split or Vertical Split button. Finally, you can collapse either pane by clicking the Collapse/Expand Pane button.

A cluster of controls situated on the border between the design and XAML editor panes control zooming, pane management/arrangement, and other functions (see Figure 6.43).

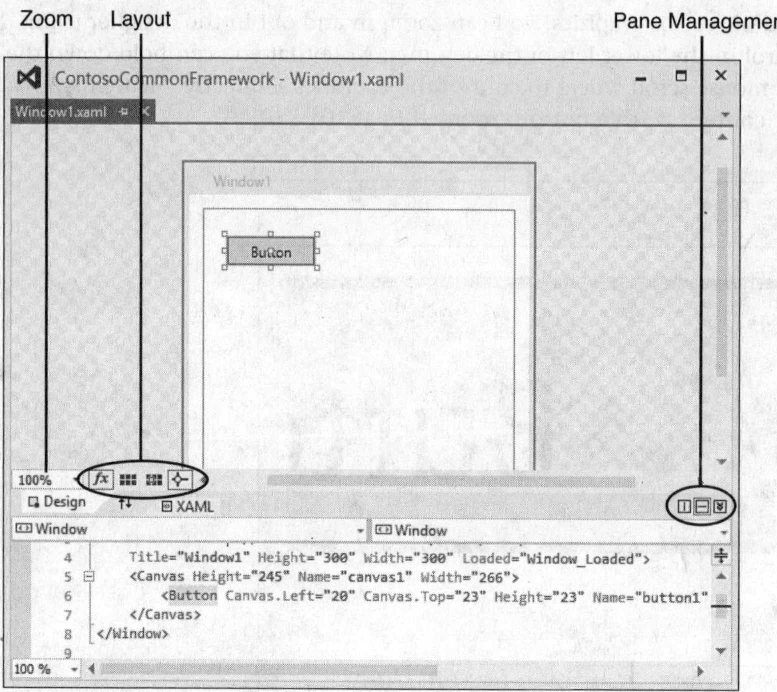

FIGURE 6.43 WPF editor controls.

Adding Controls

WPF windows are populated with controls by using the same drag-and-drop action from the Toolbox that is used with Windows Forms and web forms development. Control positioning and sizing are aided through snap lines, grid lines, and sizing boxes that look a bit different than their WinForms counterparts but perform the same tasks (see Figure 6.44).

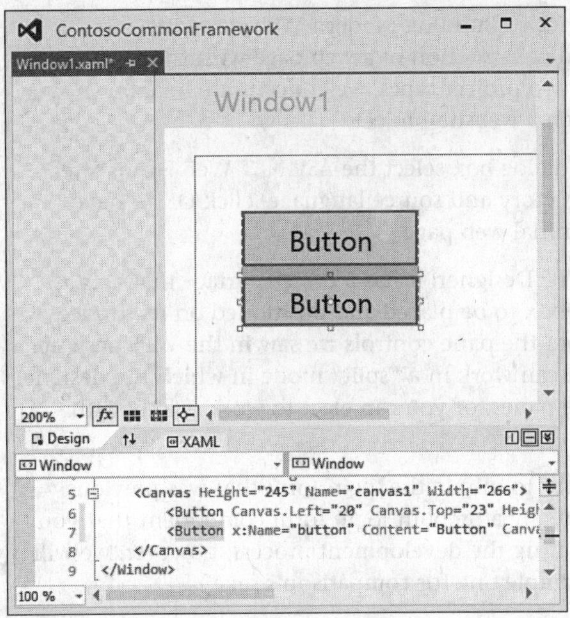

FIGURE 6.44 Positioning controls in the WPF Designer.

We cover WPF development in more detail in Chapter 21, "Building WPF Applications."

Developing Web Forms

Web forms represent the user interface element to a web application. Traditionally with .NET, the term *web form* is used to refer specifically to pages processed dynamically on the server (using ASP.NET). We use a broader definition here and use the term to refer to any web page, static or dynamic, that can be developed and designed within the Visual Studio IDE.

The HTML designer (also referred to as the web designer) is the sister application to the Windows Forms and WPF designers; it allows you to visually design and edit the markup for a web page. As with the two client application designers, it works in conjunction with the HTML designer and source view to cover all the bases needed for web page design. We cover the entire web application development process in depth in Part V, "Building Web Applications"; the following sections cover the basics of the web designers and editors.

Designing a Web Form Application

Web page design starts with a web project. As previously discussed, there are two different ways for you to construct a web page or website with Visual Studio. Both of these approaches are represented by their own unique project templates. Specifically, we are talking about "web application" versus "website" projects. In Chapter 4, "Solutions and Projects," we broached some of the core differences between these two project types; even more detail is waiting for you in Chapter 17, "Building Modern Websites with ASP.NET 5." However, because the actual construction of a web page with the web designer remains the same between the two project types, we concentrate here on illustrating our points by walking through a website project.

Select File, New Web Site, and from the dialog box select the ASP.NET Web Forms Site option. After you set the source code directory and source language, click OK to have Visual Studio create the project and its initial web page.

The web designer looks similar to the WPF Designer; it has a design surface that acts as a canvas, allowing objects from the Toolbox to be placed and positioned on its surface. Although they look slightly different from the pane controls we saw in the WPF designer, they have the same basic functions. You can work in a "split" mode in which the designer and markup editor are visible in separate panes, or you can elect to work strictly with either the designer or the editor open.

Now examine what happens when you try to mimic the login form that was previously built using Windows forms. (There is actually a prebuilt login form component that you could use here; for the sake of demonstrating the development process, however, we will go ahead and cobble together our own simple one for comparison's sake.)

Adding and Arranging Controls

The process of adding and arranging controls doesn't change from the Windows Forms or WPF Designer process. Simply drag the controls from the Toolbox onto the designer's surface. In this case, you want two labels, two text boxes, and an OK button (because this isn't a dialog box, you can dispense with the Cancel button). Changing control properties is handled the same way via the Properties window. You can select the labels and command buttons and set their text this way.

NOTE

As you add controls to a web page, note that the default layout mode is relative. That is, controls are not placed at absolute coordinates on the screen but instead are placed relative to one another. Absolute positioning is accommodated via style sheets. For instance, you can select a label control, edit its style properties, and select Absolutely Position as the position mode. This will now allow you to range freely over the form with the control.

A formatting toolbar is provided by default; it supplies buttons for common text formatting actions such as changing font styles, colors, paragraph indenting, and bulleting.

To line up control edges the way you want, you can press Shift+Enter to insert spacing between the controls as necessary. (This generates a break tag, `<br>`, in the HTML.) In this case, a break was added between the first text box and the second label and between the second text box and the first button. Figure 6.45 shows the design in progress. The text boxes don't line up, and you probably want to apply a style for the label fonts and buttons; but the general layout and intent are evident. Note that the designer provides a box above the currently selected control that indicates both the control's type and the instance name of the control on the page.

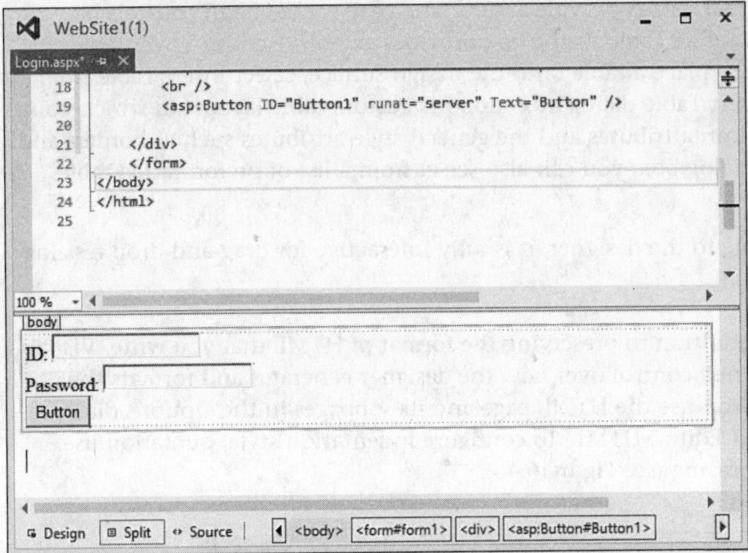

FIGURE 6.45 Creating a web form.

TIP

As a further aid for control alignment, be sure to turn on the ruler, the positioning grid, or both; they are accessed from the View menu under Ruler and Grid.

Editing Markup

As controls and other elements are added and manipulated on the designer's surface, HTML is created to implement the design and layout. As a designer or developer, you are free to work at either the visual level with the designer or the text/source level with the HTML source editor. Like the other editors within Visual Studio, the HTML source editor supports IntelliSense and other interactive features for navigating and validating markup.

Looking back at Figure 6.42, you can see the markup generated by the designer when the controls were added to the login page.

As with the other designer/editor pairs, you can write your own HTML and see it implemented immediately in the design view. The HTML editor has a toolbar as well: the HTML source editing toolbar provides quick access to code "forward and back" navigation, commenting, and schema validation options. (We discuss schema validation in the later section "Browser Output and Validation.")

One key feature realized with the HTML editor is source format preservation. The HTML source editor works hard to respect the way that you, the developer, want your markup formatted. This includes the placement of carriage returns and whitespace, the use of indentation, and even how you want to handle word and line wrapping. In short, Visual Studio never reformats HTML code that you have written.

Working with Tables HTML tables provide a quick and easy way to align controls on a web page. A dedicated Insert Table dialog box provides extensive control over table layout and appearance. To place a table onto the design surface, select Insert Table from the Table menu. The Insert Table dialog box supports custom table layouts in which you specify the row and column attributes and the general style attributes such as borders and padding. Through this dialog box, you can also select from a list of preformatted table templates.

After you've added a table to the designer, it is fully interactive for drag-and-drop resizing of its columns and rows.

Formatting Options In addition to preserving the format of HTML that you write, Visual Studio provides fine-grained control over how the designer generates and formats the HTML that it produces. You use the HTML page and its subpages in the Options dialog box (Tools, Options, Text Editor, HTML) to configure indentation style, quotation use, word wrapping, and tag casing (see Figure 6.46).

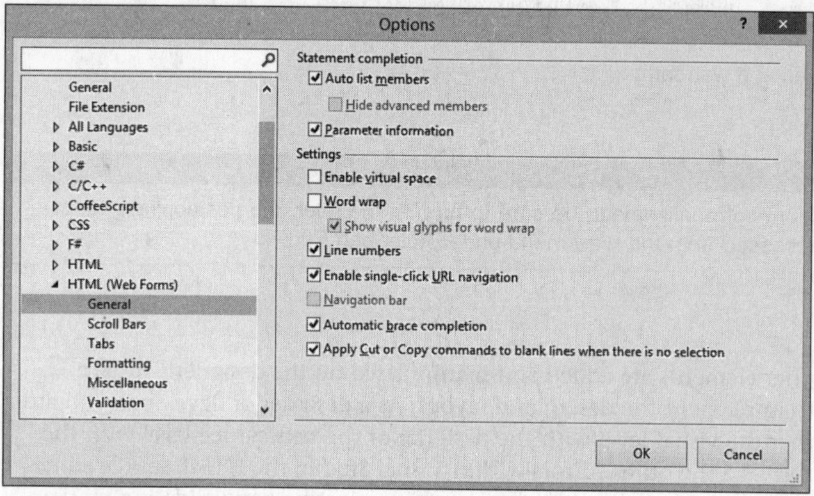

FIGURE 6.46 HTML formatting options.

Settings can be applied globally for all markup, or you can set options on a per-tag basis by clicking the Tag Specific Options button (Text Editor, HTML, Format). For example, this level of control is useful if your particular coding style uses line breaks within your table column tags (`<td>`) but not with your table row tags (`<tr>`). In Figure 6.47, the `tr` tag is being set to support line breaks before and after the tag, but not within the tag.

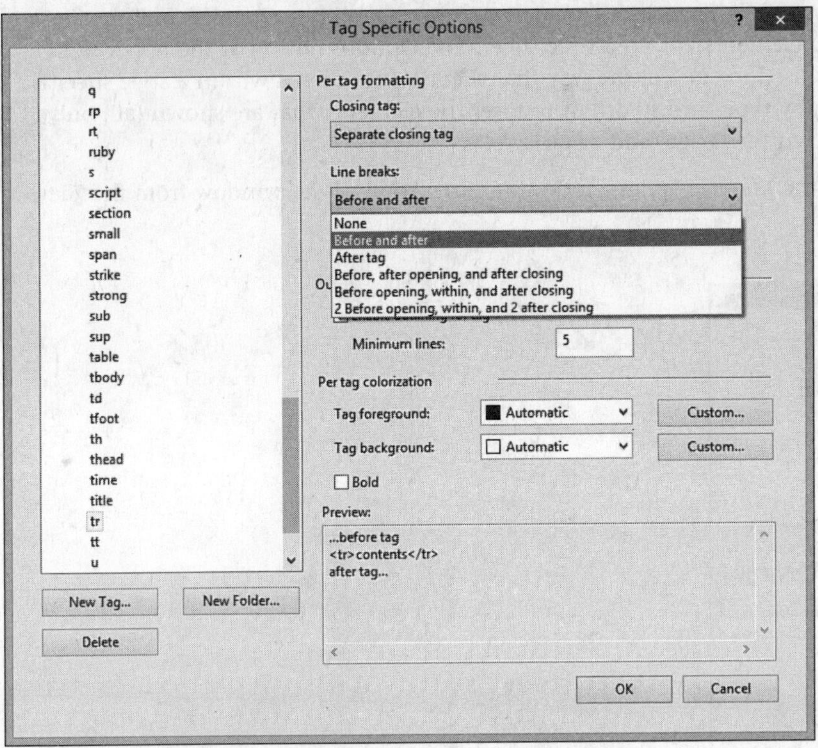

FIGURE 6.47 Setting HTML formatting options at the tag level.

Managing Styles and Style Sheets

Visual Studio has a complete set of tools for managing styles and cascading style sheets. The Manage Styles and Apply Styles windows are both used to perform common style editing tasks, including applying a style to the current HTML document or attaching/detaching a cascading style sheet file to/from the current HTML document. The third tool, the CSS Properties window, enumerates all the CSS properties for the currently selected page element, allowing for quick changes for any of the property values.

A typical workflow for editing styles might look like this:

1. Open a web page.
2. Define a new style.
3. Apply the style.
4. Tweak the style.

Figure 6.48 shows the Manage Styles window and its capability to itemize and preview any of the formatting elements within a style sheet. The Options button at the upper right of the window is used to control the way that the list of elements within a style sheet is shown (by order, by type, and so on) or to filter the elements that are shown (all, only those used in the current page, and so on).

You access both the Manage Styles window and the Apply Styles window from the View menu.

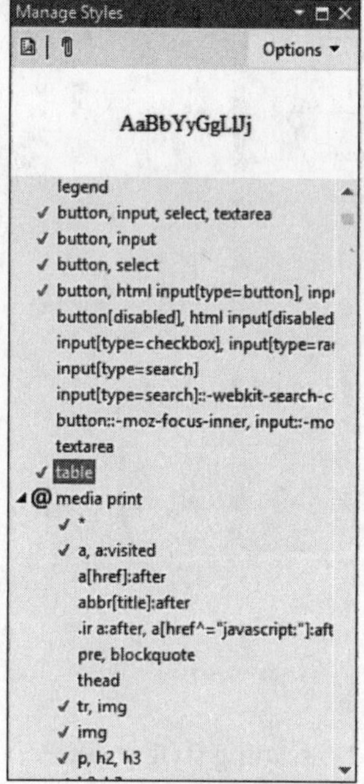

FIGURE 6.48 The Manage Styles window.

Browser Output and Validation

The result of all the design effort put into an HTML document is its final rendering within a browser. With various flavors of browsers in use supporting various levels of HTML specifications (including XHTML), it is difficult to ensure that the page's design intent actually matches reality. Visual Studio's browser target settings help with this problem by enabling you to easily target a specific HTML standard or browser. As you type HTML into the source editor, Visual Studio validates the syntax on the fly against your selected browser target. If a piece of markup violates the rules of your particular validation target, it is flagged by the familiar red squiggly line (complete with a ToolTip explaining the exact violation), and the error is listed within the Task List window.

The target can be selected on the HTML designer or source editor toolbar; just pick the target from the drop-down.

NOTE

The validation rules for a given browser or standard can actually be customized to support targets that do not ship out of the box with Visual Studio.

Standards Compliance The HTML code generated by the HTML designer is, by default, XHTML compliant; tags, for instance, are well formed with regard to XHTML requirements. Using the various XHTML validation targets helps to ensure that the code you write is compliant as well.

Visual Studio also focuses on providing compliance with accessibility standards (those standards that govern the display of web pages for persons with disabilities). You launch the Accessibility Checker by using the Check Page for Accessibility button on the HTML Source Editing or Formatting toolbars. (Note that this button is not added by default on those toolbars; you'll have to use the "add or remove buttons" feature to add it.)

Figure 6.49 shows the Accessibility Validation dialog box. You can select the specific standards you want to have your HTML validated against. You can also select the level of feedback that you receive (errors, warnings, or a text checklist). Each item flagged by the checker appears in the Task List window for resolution. For more details on the two standards supported here (WCAG and Access Board Section 508), see their respective websites: http://www.w3.org/TR/WCAG10/ and http://www.access-board.gov/508.htm.

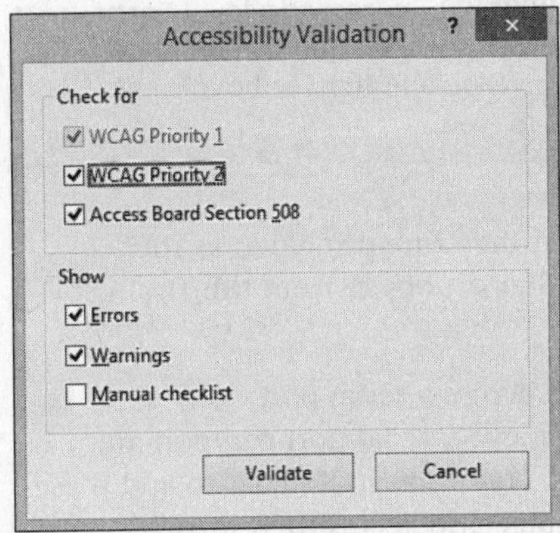

FIGURE 6.49 Setting accessibility validation options.

Authoring WinForms Components and Controls

Referring to our earlier discussion of Windows forms, components are nonvisual controls or classes. This is a good generic definition, but a more specific one is this: a component is any class that inherits from `System.ComponentModel.IComponent`. This particular interface provides support for designability and resource handling. If you need a designable control that does not have a user interface of its own, you work with a component. Controls are similar in function but not form; a control is a reusable chunk of code that does have a visual element to it.

Because Visual Studio provides a dedicated design surface for creating Windows Forms components, we cover this separately in this section. WPF projects also allow for custom controls and components, but in a fashion that is much more streamlined and integrated with the overall development of forms in the WPF world. We cover some of that content in our WPF chapter later in the book (Chapter 21).

Creating a New Component or Control

Starting from an existing WinForms project, you kick off the process of authoring a component by using the Add New Item dialog box (from the Project menu). Selecting Component Class in this dialog box adds the stub code file to your current project and launches the component designer. To start control development, you use the Add New User Control dialog box.

NOTE

Two different "types" of WinForms controls can be authored within Visual Studio: custom controls and user controls. Custom controls inherit directly from the `System.Windows.Forms.Control` class; they are typically code intensive because you, the developer, are responsible for writing all the code necessary to render the control's visual portion. User controls (sometimes called *composite controls*) inherit from the `System.Windows.Forms.UserControl` class. User controls are advantageous because you can build them quickly by compositing other controls together that are already available in the Toolbox. These controls already have their user interface portion coded for you.

Both the control and the component designers work on the same principles as the Windows Forms Designer: The designers allow you to drag an object from the Toolbox onto the design surface.

Assume that you need a component that sends a signal across a serial port every *x* minutes. Because Visual Studio already provides a timer and a serial port component, which are accessible from the Toolbox, you can use the component designer to add these objects to your own custom component and then leverage and access their intrinsic properties and methods (essentially, using them as building blocks to get your desired functionality).

Figure 6.50 shows the component designer for this fictional custom component. Two objects have been added: a process component and a timer component.

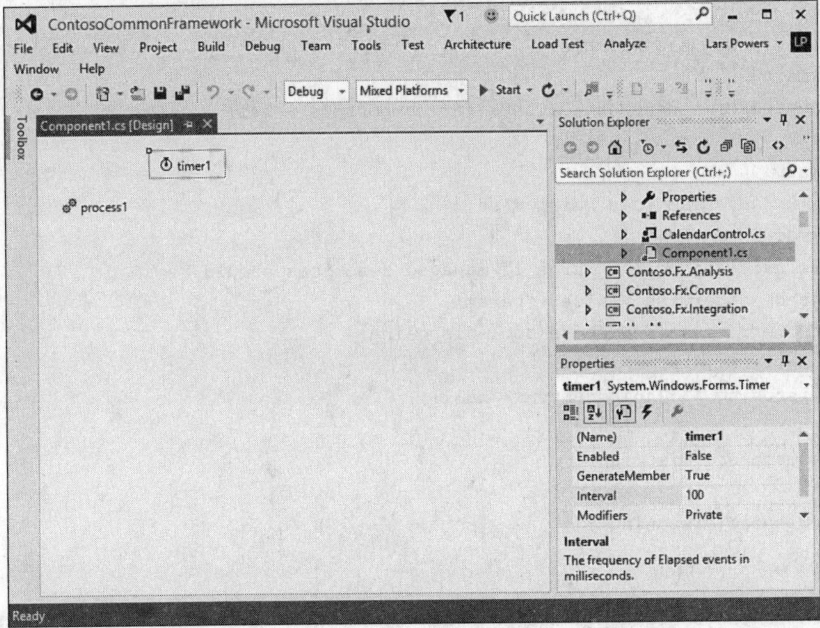

FIGURE 6.50 The component designer.

A similar scenario can be envisioned with a user control. You can take the example of a login "form," consisting of two text boxes, two labels, and two buttons, and actually make that a control (one that can be easily included in the Toolbox and dropped onto a Windows form or web form).

Further Notes on Writing Component Code

Because the component has no visual aspect to it, you don't have the layout and formatting features that you see with the Windows Forms Designer. However, the concept of drag-and-drop programming is alive and well. Visual Studio, behind the scenes, injects the code to programmatically add the given class to the component's container. From there, you can edit the various objects' properties, double-click an object to get to its code, and so on.

When you drag the timer and process objects over from the Toolbox, Visual Studio aggregates these objects into the component by automatically writing the code shown in Listing 6.2.

LISTING 6.2 Component Designer–Generated Code

```
namespace Contoso.UI.WindowsForms.OrderEntry
{
    partial class Component1
    {
```

```
        /// <summary>
        /// Required designer variable.
        /// </summary>
        private System.ComponentModel.IContainer components = null;

        /// <summary>
        /// Clean up any resources being used.
        /// </summary>
        /// <param name="disposing">true if managed resources should be
        /// disposed; otherwise, false.</param>
        protected override void Dispose(bool disposing)
        {
            if (disposing && (components != null))
            {
                components.Dispose();
            }
            base.Dispose(disposing);
        }

        #region Component Designer generated code

        /// <summary>
        /// Required method for Designer support - do not modify
        /// the contents of this method with the code editor.
        /// </summary>
        private void InitializeComponent()
        {
            this.components = new System.ComponentModel.Container();
            this.timer1 = new System.Windows.Forms.Timer(this.components);
            this.process1 = new System.Diagnostics.Process();

        }

        #endregion

        private System.Windows.Forms.Timer timer1;
        private System.Diagnostics.Process process1;


    }
}
```

Writing code "behind" one of the objects placed on the component designer canvas is easy: double-click the object's icon, and the code editor is launched. For instance, double-clicking the timer icon on the designer surface causes the `timer1_Tick` routine to be created and then launched in the code editor.

Creating Classes with the Class Designer

The final designer we cover in this chapter is the class designer. The class designer, via its class diagram, allows you to get a view of your code as it exists statically (or at rest). You also get real-time synchronization between the model and the actual code. You should think of the class designer more as a visual code editor and less like a diagram. If you make a change to code, that change is reflected in the diagram. When you change the diagram, your code changes, too.

Creating a Class Diagram

There are a couple of ways to create a class diagram. The first is to add a class diagram to your project from the Add New Item dialog box. Here, you select a class diagram template (`.cd`) and add it to the project. You can then add items to this diagram from the Toolbox or from existing classes in the Solution Explorer.

The second way to add a class diagram to a project is to choose View Class Diagram from the context menu for a given project. In this way, Visual Studio generates a class diagram from an existing project. This option is shown in Figure 6.51.

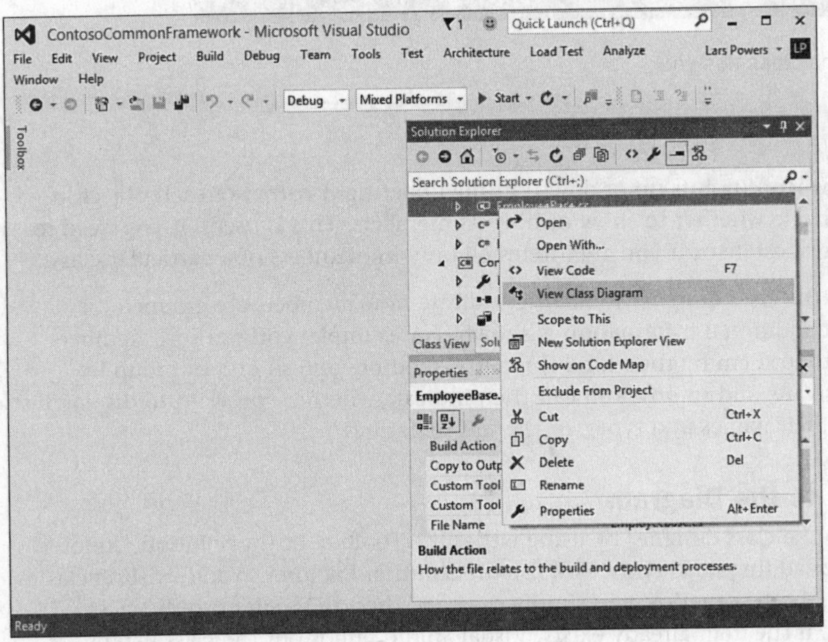

FIGURE 6.51 Launching the class designer.

In either case, you end up with a `.cd` file in your project that represents the visual model of your classes. Clearly, the View Class Diagram option saves you the time of dragging everything onto the diagram. Figure 6.52 shows an example of the class designer file. We cover each window shown in this designer.

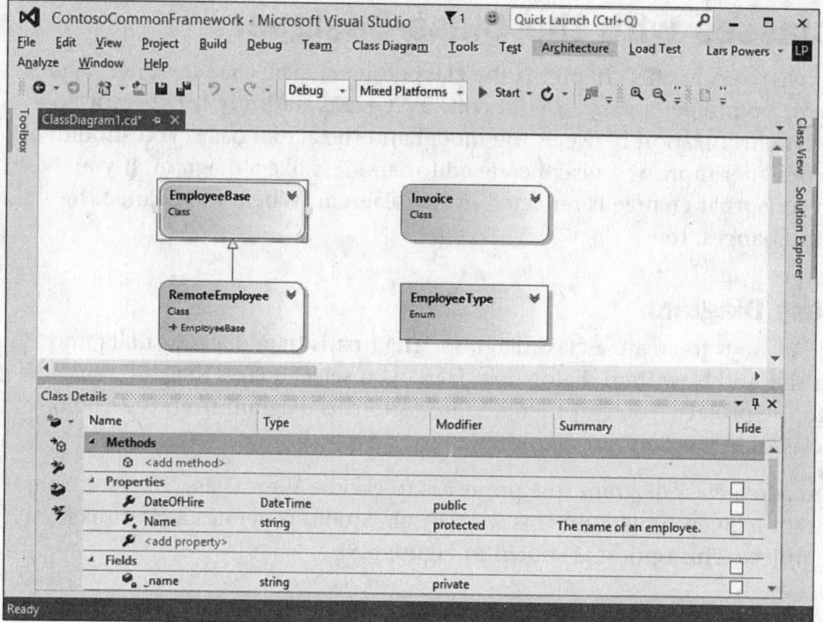

FIGURE 6.52 The class designer.

Displaying Members

You use the arrow icon (points up or down) in the upper-right corner of each object in the designer to toggle whether to show or hide its members. This is useful if you need to conserve screen real estate or if you are interested only in members of a particular class.

You can also use the class designer toolbar to indicate how members are grouped for display and what additional information is shown. For example, you can sort members alphabetically, group them by their kind (property, method, and so on), or group by access (public, private, and so on). You can then indicate whether you want to display just member names, their names and types, or the full signatures.

Adding Items to the Diagram

You add items to the class designer by using either the Toolbox or the Solution Explorer. The Toolbox is for adding new items. You use the Solution Explorer to add existing classes to the diagram. In both scenarios, you simply drag and drop the item onto the class designer window. If the item already exists, Visual Studio builds out the class details for you. In fact, if the class file contains more than one class, each class is placed as an object on the diagram.

Figure 6.53 shows an example of the class designer Toolbox tools. Notice that you can define all object-oriented concepts here, including classes, interfaces, and inheritance.

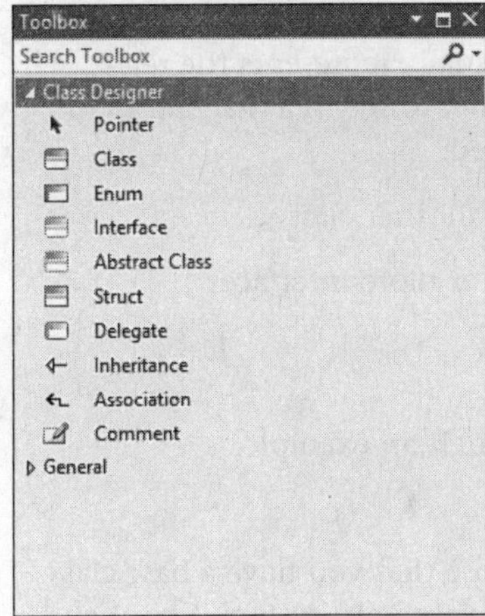

FIGURE 6.53 The class designer Toolbox.

When you add a new item such as a class or struct to the designer, the designer prompts you for the item's name and location. You can choose to generate a new file to house the item or place it in an existing file. Figure 6.54 shows the New Class dialog box. Here, you can give the class a name, set its access modifier, and indicate a filename.

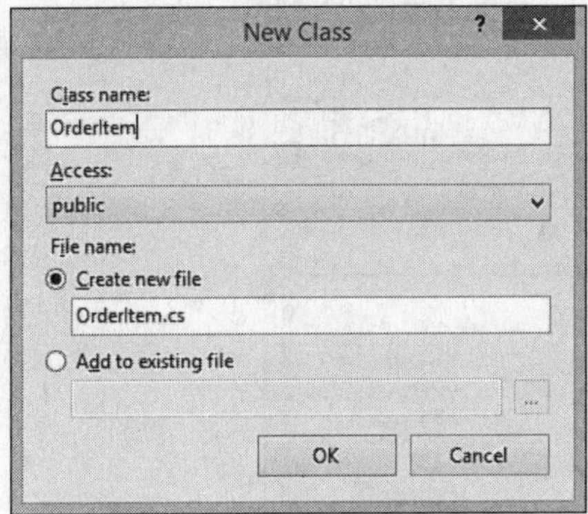

FIGURE 6.54 Adding a new class to the class designer.

TIP

The class designer can automatically add related classes to the diagram. For example, suppose you add a class from the Solution Explorer. If you want to show classes that inherit from this class, you can right-click the class and choose Show Derived Classes. This adds to the model all classes that derive from the selected class.

Defining Relationships Between Classes

One of the biggest benefits of the class diagram is that it visually represents the relationships between classes. These relationships are much easier to see in a diagram than through code. The following relationships can be represented:

- **Inheritance**—Indicates whether a class inherits from another class
- **Interface**—Indicates whether a class implements one or more interfaces
- **Association**—Indicates an association between classes

Let's look at implementing each of these relationships through an example.

Inheritance

First, let's look at inheritance with the class designer. Suppose that you have a base class called `EmployeeBase`. This class represents a generic employee in your system. You then want to create a concrete `RemoteEmployee` class that inherits from `EmployeeBase`. If you look back at Figure 6.52, you can see that both of these classes are connected with an arrow leading from the implementing class to the base or parent class. This is simply a visualization of the inheritance that we had already set up in our code. But you can also wire classes together through inheritance by using the class diagram window and the class designer Toolbox. Select the Inheritance tool from the class designer Toolbox, click the inheriting class (in this example, `Employee`), and then extend the line up to the base class and click it. And just like that, you have inherited a class, with Visual Studio writing the code for you. Figure 6.55 shows the two classes being connected via the Inheritance tool.

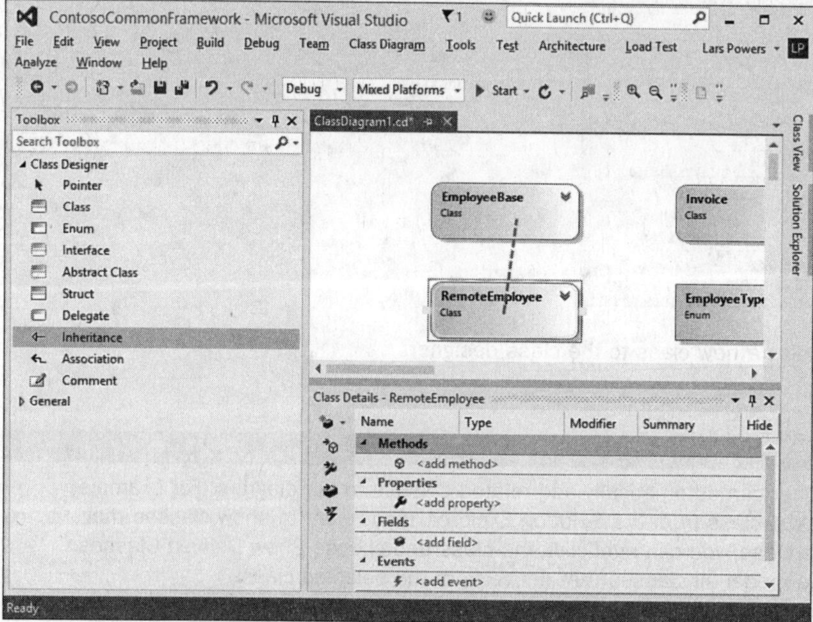

FIGURE 6.55 Class inheritance.

Interface

The next visual relationship we look at is an interface. For this example, suppose that all the business entities in your system implement a similar contract. This contract might define properties for ID and name. It also might define methods such as `Get`, `Delete`, and `Save`.

To implement this interface, you again use the Inheritance tool from the class designer Toolbox. You drag it from the class doing the implementation toward the interface. Figure 6.56 shows the result of an implemented interface. Notice the lollipop icon above the `Customer` class; it denotes the interface implementation.

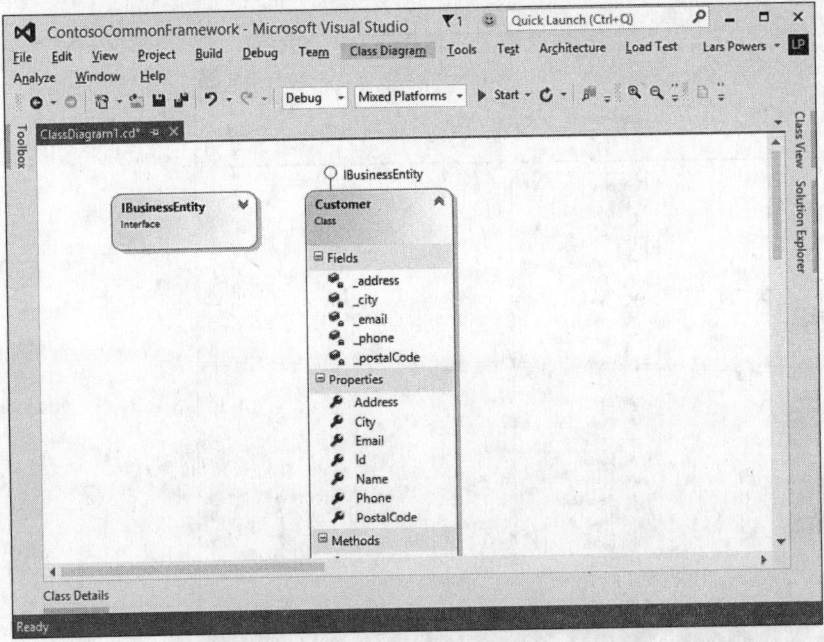

FIGURE 6.56 Implementing an interface.

Association

The final relationship to look at is association. This relationship is typically a loose one in the Unified Modeling Language (UML) world. However, in the class designer, an association is very real. Typically, this means that two classes have an association through the use of one of the classes. This relationship is also optional in terms of viewing. It can exist, but you do not have to show it in the diagram.

For example, suppose that you have an `Order` object. This object might expose an `OrderStatus` property. Suppose that it also has a property for accessing the `Customer` record associated with the order. These two properties are associations. You can leave them as properties, or you can choose to show them as associations.

You can also draw these property associations on the diagram. To do so, you select the Association tool from the Toolbox. This tool has the same icon as Inheritance. You then draw the association from the class that contains the association to the class that is the object of the association. You can also right-click the actual property that represents the association and choose Show as Association from the context menu (or Show as Collection Association for associations that are part of a collection).

The result is that the association property is displayed on the association arrow. This indicates that the class from which the association originates contains this property. (It is shown only on this line, however.) Figure 6.57 illustrates an association between Order and OrderStatus, and Order and Customer.

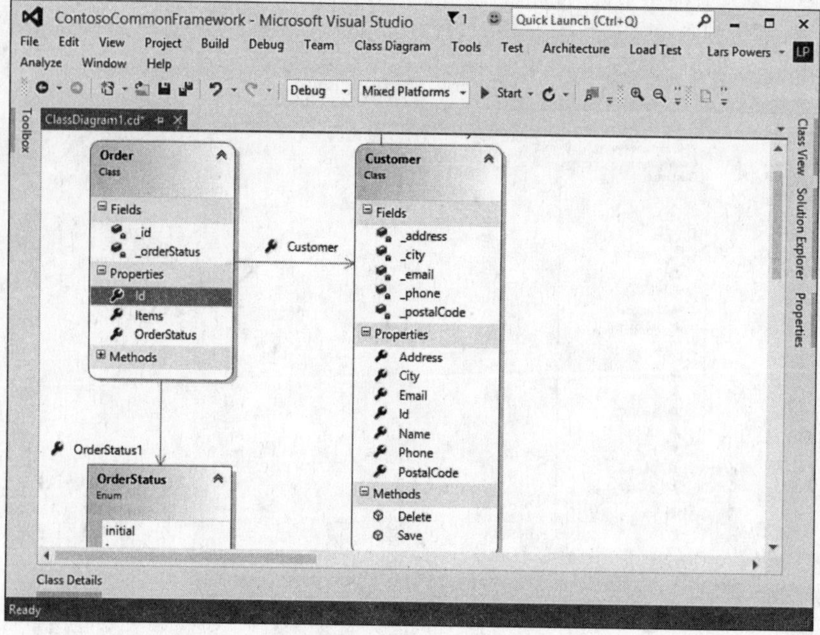

FIGURE 6.57 Creating an association.

Defining Methods, Properties, Fields, and Events

The most exciting part of the class designer is that it allows you to do more than define classes and relationships. You can actually stub out code and do refactoring. (See Chapter 9, "Refactoring Code," for details.)

There are two ways to add code to your classes, structs, interfaces, and the like. The first is to type directly into the designer. For example, if you are in the Properties section of a class, you can right-click and choose to add a new property. This places the property in your class and allows you to edit it in the diagram. This method works for other class members as well. It does have a couple of drawbacks, however. You can't, for instance, define a full method signature or indicate access levels. For that, you need the Class Details window.

The Class Details window allows you to fully define methods, fields, properties, and events for a class. It also works with other constructs such as interfaces, delegates, and enums. To use this window, right-click a class and choose Class Details from the context menu. Selecting this menu item brings up the Class Details editor for the selected class. Figure 6.58 shows the Class Details window in action.

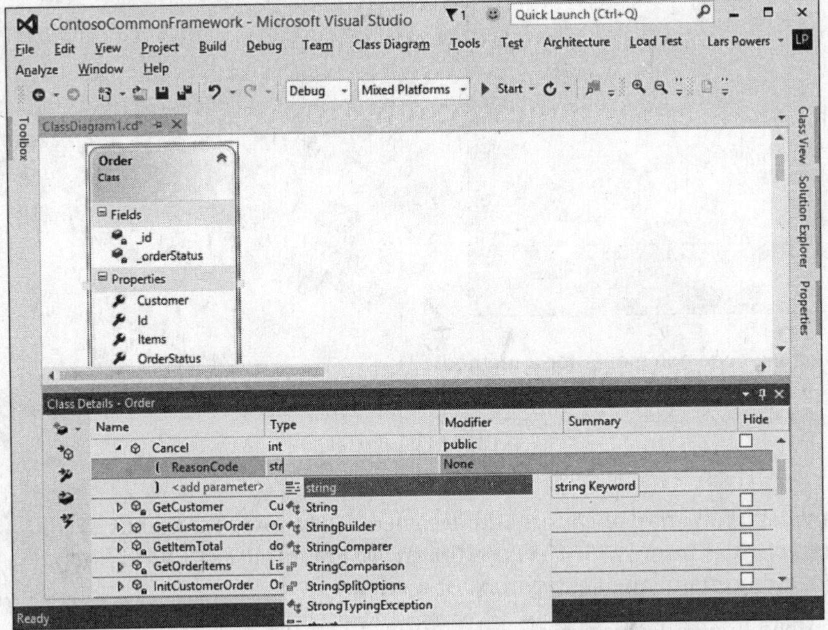

FIGURE 6.58 Creating a method in the Class Details window.

Notice that when working in the Class Details window, you still get IntelliSense. In this example, the `Cancel` method is being added to the `Order` class. You can indicate a return type for the method with the Type column. You can define the access modifier with the Modifier column. You can also set the parameters of the method. In this case, the method takes the string parameter `ReasonCode`.

Finally, there are Summary and Hide columns. The Hide column indicates whether you want to show an item on the diagram. This capability allows you to hide various members when printing or exporting as an image. The Summary column allows you to add your XML documentation to the class. Clicking the ellipsis button (not shown) in this field brings up the Description dialog box. Here, you can enter your XML summary information for the given member. Figure 6.59 shows an example for the Cancel method.

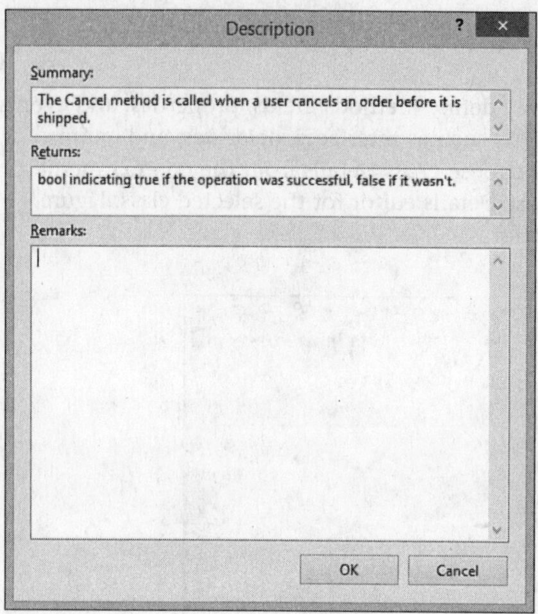

FIGURE 6.59 Creating code comments for a method.

Summary

Visual Studio provides a full array of editors and designers. They cover the gamut of solution development activities from WYSIWYG positioning of graphical controls to finely tuned text editing for a certain language, syntax, or markup.

This chapter described how to leverage the basics within these editors and designers. It also described how the editor and designer relationship provides two complementary views of the same solution artifact, in effect working together to provide you, the developer, with the right tool for the right task at hand.

In subsequent chapters, we look at the more advanced options and productivity features available within these tools and even look at end-to-end development efforts involved in building a web application with ASP.NET or Silverlight and building a Windows application using Windows Forms or WPF.

CHAPTER 7

Working with Visual Studio's Productivity Aids

IN THIS CHAPTER

- Basic Aids in the Text Editor
- Outlining and Navigation
- Smart Tasks and Light Bulbs
- IntelliSense
- The Task List

In Chapter 6, "Introducing the Editors and Designers," we discussed the basic capabilities of the designers and editors in Visual Studio 2015. In this chapter, we delve a bit deeper into their capabilities and those of other Visual Studio tools by examining the many productivity aids that the IDE provides. Many of these productivity enhancers are embedded within the text editors. Others are more generic in nature. But they all have one common goal: helping you, the developer, write code quickly and correctly.

If you recall from Chapter 6, in our coverage of the editors, we used a basic code scenario: a console application that printed `"Hello, World!"` to the console. In Figure 7.1, you see what the final code looks like in the code editor window.

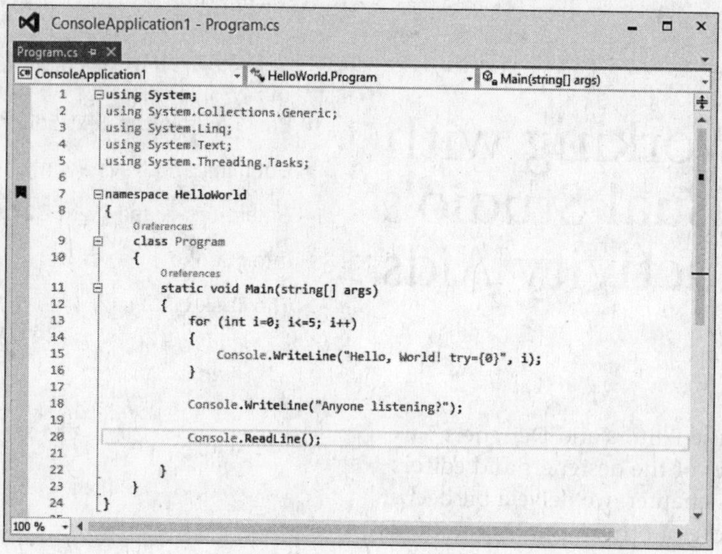

ConsoleApplication1 - Program.cs

Program.cs

ConsoleApplication1 | HelloWorld.Program | Main(string[] args)

```
using System;
using System.Collections.Generic;
using System.Linq;
using System.Text;
using System.Threading.Tasks;

namespace HelloWorld
{
    0 references
    class Program
    {
        0 references
        static void Main(string[] args)
        {
            for (int i=0; i<=5; i++)
            {
                Console.WriteLine("Hello, World! try={0}", i);
            }

            Console.WriteLine("Anyone listening?");

            Console.ReadLine();

        }
    }
}
```

100 %

FIGURE 7.1 `"Hello, World"` in the code editor.

If you have followed along by re-creating this project and typing the `"Hello, World!"` code in Visual Studio, you have noticed that the productivity features of the code editor have already kicked into gear.

First, as you start to type, the code editor has tabbed in the cursor for you, placing it at a new location for writing nicely indented code.

Second, as you type your first line of code, Visual Studio reacts to your every keystroke by interpreting what you are trying to write and extending help in various forms (see Figure 7.2). You are given hints in terms of completing your in-progress source, provided information on the members you are in the process of selecting, and given information on the parameters required to complete a particular method. These features are collectively referred to as IntelliSense, and we explore its forms and functions in depth in this chapter.

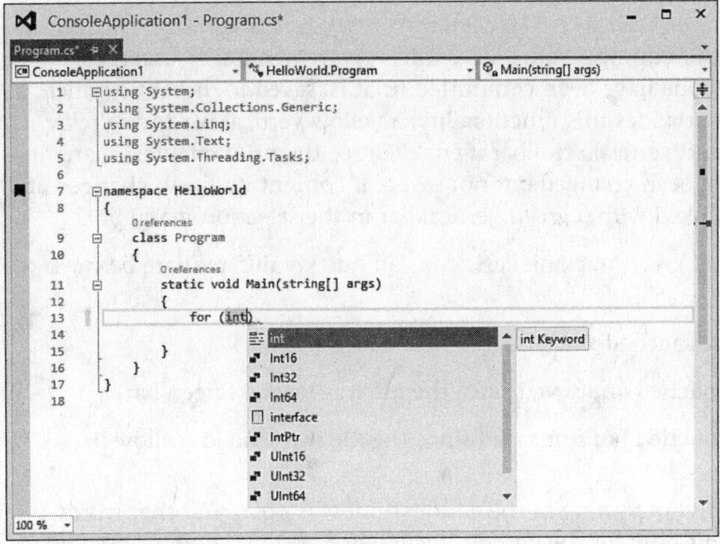

FIGURE 7.2 IntelliSense in action.

As you type, the IDE is also constantly checking what you have written with the compiler. If compile errors exist, they are dynamically flagged for you in the code editor with a red underline.

So for this one simple line of code, Visual Studio has been hard at work improving your coding productivity by doing the following:

- Intelligently indenting the code
- Suggesting code syntax
- Displaying member descriptions to help you select the correct code syntax
- Visually matching delimiting parentheses
- Flagging code errors by constantly background compiling the current version of the source code

These features subtly help and coach you through the code-writing process and accelerate the act of coding itself.

Basic Aids in the Text Editor

The text editor user interface has several visual constructs that help you with common problem areas encountered during the code-writing process. These basic aids provide support for determining what has changed within a code document and what compile problems exist in a document. In addition, the discrete syntax elements for each language are visually delineated for you using colored text.

Change Tracking

When you are in the midst of editing a source code file, it is tremendously useful to understand which lines of code have been committed (that is, saved to disk) and which have not. Change tracking provides this functionality; a yellow vertical bar in the text editor's selection margin (and vertical scrollbar if enabled; see the prior chapter) spans any lines in the editor that have been changed but not saved. If content has been changed and subsequently saved, it is marked with a green vertical bar in the selection margin.

By looking at the yellow and green tracking bars, you can quickly differentiate between the following:

- Code that hasn't been touched since the file was loaded (no bar)
- Code that has been touched and saved since the file was loaded (green bar)
- Code that has been touched but not saved since the file was loaded (yellow bar)

Change tracking is valid only for as long as the editor window is open. In other words, change tracking is significant only for the current document "session"; if you close and reopen the window, the track bars disappear because you have established a new working session with that specific document.

Figure 7.3 shows a section of a code file displaying the change tracking bars.

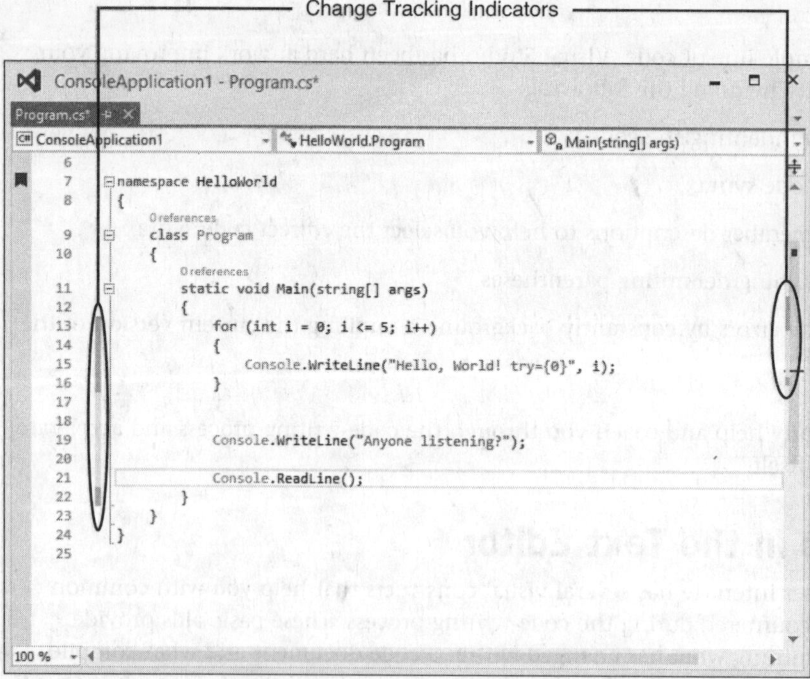

FIGURE 7.3 Change tracking.

Coding Problem Indicators

The Visual Studio compiler works in conjunction with the code editor window to flag any problems found within a source code document. The compiler can even work in the background, enabling the editor window to flag problems as you type (as opposed to waiting for the project to be compiled).

Coding problems are flagged using "squiggles" (wavy, color-coded lines placed under the offending piece of code). These squiggles are the same mechanism Microsoft Word uses to flag spelling and grammar problems. The squiggle colors indicate a specific class of problem. Table 7.1 shows how these colors map to an underlying problem.

TABLE 7.1 Coding Problem Indicator Colors

Color	Problem
Red	Syntax error; the code will not compile because of the syntax requirements and rules of the language.
Blue	Semantic error; this is the result of the compiler not being able to resolve the type or code construct within the current context. For instance, a type name that doesn't exist within the compiled context of the current project is flagged with a blue squiggle. Typically, these are good indicators for typos (for example, misspelling a class name).
Purple	Warning; the purple squiggle denotes code that has triggered a compiler warning.

Hovering the mouse pointer over the problem indicator reveals the actual compiler error or warning message, as demonstrated in Figure 7.4. You will also be presented with a list of potential fixes to the issue. Note the hyperlink in the message box: `Show potential fixes`. Clicking on this will provide access to a number of refactoring options that could solve the code issue. For example, perhaps you are trying to reference an object type that doesn't exist. This could be a simple typo, or you could be attempting to refer to an object that you haven't defined yet. In the latter case, this "potential fixes" refactoring window can inject the code necessary to create a stub of the object and will even show you a small preview of what that code looks like (Figure 7.5).

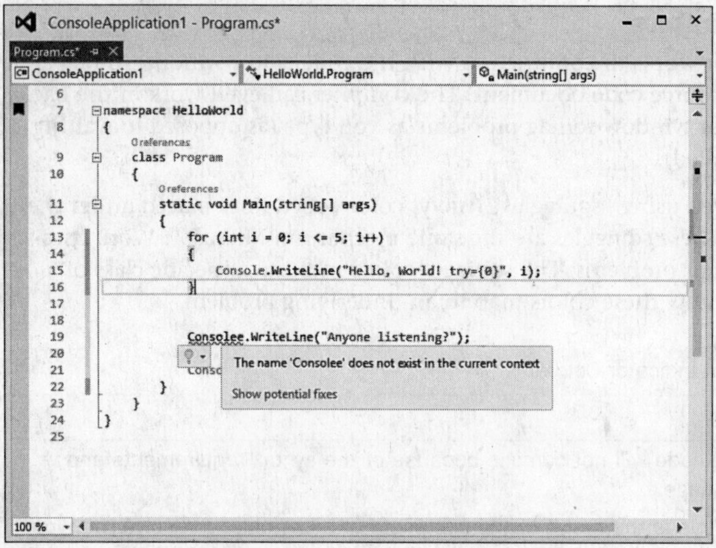

FIGURE 7.4 Code problem indicators.

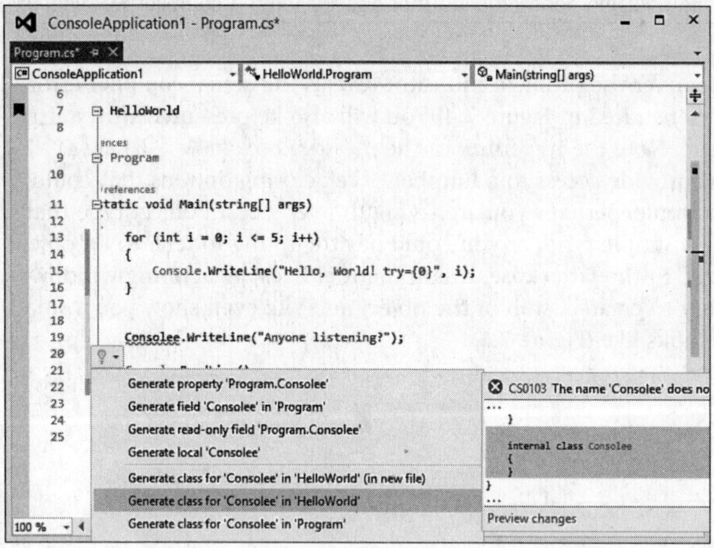

FIGURE 7.5 Refactoring a coding issue.

Active Hyperlinking

Text editors support clickable hyperlinks within documents; clicking a link launches a browser redirected at the URL. One great use of this feature is to embed URLs for supporting documentation or other helpful reference information within code comments.

Syntax Coloring

The text editor can parse and distinctly color different code constructs to make them that much easier to identify on sight. As an example, the code editor window, by default, colors any code comments green. Code identifiers are black, keywords are blue, strings are red, and so on.

In fact, the number of unique elements that the text editor is capable of parsing and coloring is immense: the text editor window recognizes more than 100 different elements. And you can customize and color each one of them to your heart's content through the Fonts and Colors section, under the Environments node in the Options dialog box. Do you like working with larger fonts? Would a higher contrast benefit your programming activities? How about squeezing more code into your viewable screen real estate? These are just a few reasons you might stray from the defaults with this dialog box.

Figure 7.6 shows the Fonts and Colors page in the Options dialog box that allows you to specify foreground and background colors for code, Hypertext Markup Language (HTML), Cascading Style Sheets (CSS), or other elements. Select the element in the Display Items list and change its syntax coloring via the Item Foreground and Item Background drop-downs.

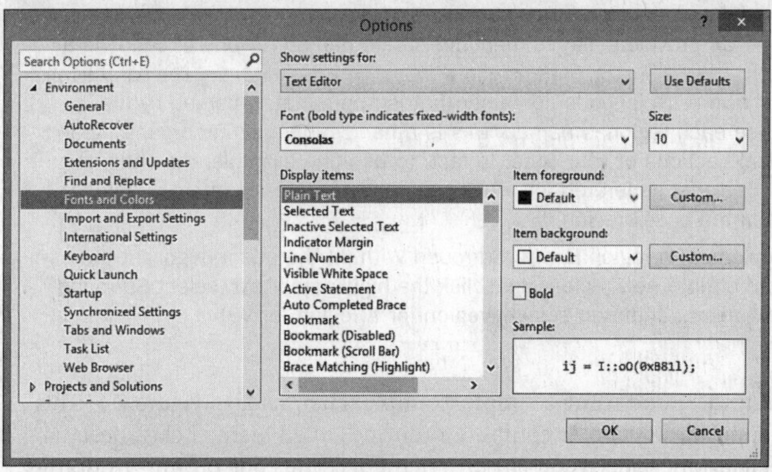

FIGURE 7.6 Setting font and color options.

NOTE

We first explored this dialog back in Chapter 2, "The Visual Studio IDE." The dialog box shown in Figure 7.6 enables you to control much more than the syntax coloring for the text editor; you can change the coloring schemes used in all the different windows within Visual Studio. The item you select in the Show Settings For drop-down determines the portion of the IDE you are customizing and alters the list of items in the Display Items list.

You can always click the Use Defaults button at the upper right of the dialog box to restore the default coloring schemes.

Outlining and Navigation

Certain documents, such as source code files and markup files, have a natural parent-child aspect to their organization and syntax. XML nodes, for instance, can contain other nodes. Likewise, functions and other programming language constructs such as loops and `try/catch` blocks act as a container for other lines of code. Outlining is the concept of visually representing this parent-child relationship.

Code Outlining

Code outlining is used within the code editor; it allows you to collapse or expand regions of code along these container boundaries. A series of grouping lines and expand/collapse boxes are drawn in the selection margin. These expand/collapse boxes are clickable, enabling you to hide or display lines of code based on the logical groupings.

TIP

Both Visual Basic and C# provide a way to manually create named regions of code via a special region keyword. Use `#region/#endregion` (`#Region` and `#End Region` for Visual Basic) to create your own artificial code container that is appropriately parsed by the code outliner. Because each region is named, this is a handy approach for organizing and segregating the logical sections of your code. In fact, to use one example, the code that the Windows Forms Designer generated for you is automatically tucked within a "Windows Forms Designer generated code" region.

One quick way to implement a region is with Surround With. In the editor, highlight the code that you want to sit in a new region, right-click the highlighted text, select Surround With from the context menu, and then select #region (or #Region for VB).

Code outlining is best understood using a simple example. First, refer to Figure 7.1. This is the initial console application code. It contains a routine called Main, a class declaration, a namespace declaration, and several `using` statements. The code outline groupings that you see in the selection margin visually indicate code regions that can be collapsed or hidden from view.

Because the class declaration is a logical container, the selection margin for that line of code contains a collapse box (a box with a minus sign). A line is drawn from the collapse box to the end of the container. (In this case, because you are dealing with C#, the class declaration is delimited by a curly brace.) If you click the collapse box for the class declaration, Visual Studio hides all the code contained within that declaration.

Figure 7.7 shows how the editor window looks with this code hidden from view. Note that the collapse box has changed to a plus sign, indicating that you can click the box to reshow the now-hidden code and that the first line of code for the class declaration has been altered to include a trailing box with an ellipsis.

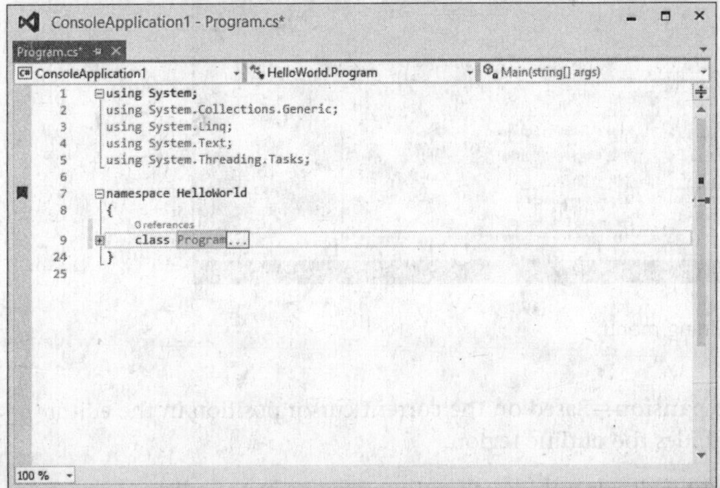

FIGURE 7.7 A collapsed outline region.

The HTML Editor also supports outlining in this fashion. HTML elements can be expanded or collapsed to show or hide their containing elements.

Using the Outlining Menu

Several code outlining commands are available under the Edit, Outlining menu (see Figure 7.8):

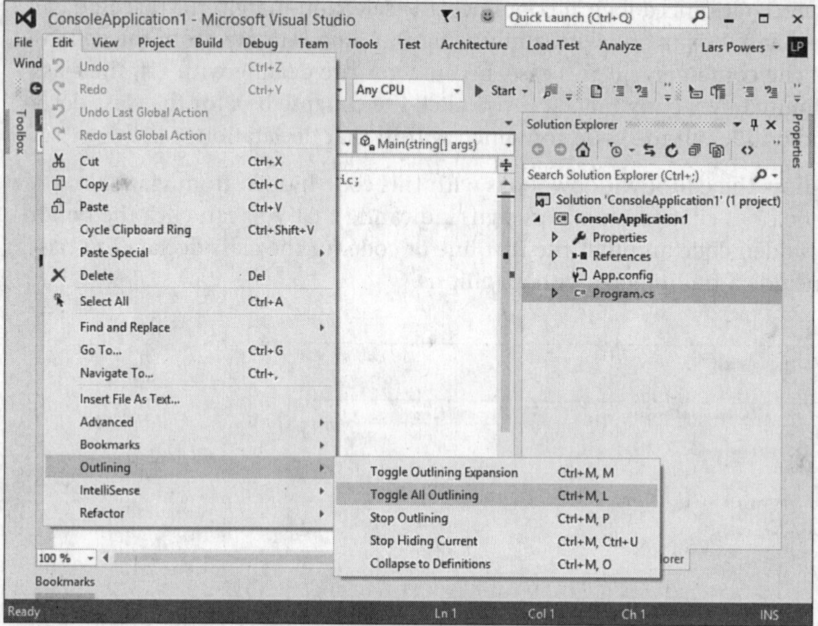

FIGURE 7.8 The Edit, Outlining menu.

- **Toggle Outlining Expansion**—Based on the current cursor position in the editor window, hides or unhides the outline region.
- **Toggle All Outlining**—Hides or unhides all outline regions in the editor.
- **Stop Outlining**—Turns off automatic code outlining (any hidden regions are expanded). This command is available only if automatic outlining is turned on.
- **Stop Hiding Current**—Removes the outline for the currently selected region. This command is available only if automatic outlining has been turned off.
- **Collapse to Definitions**—Hides all procedure regions. This command is useful for distilling a type down to single lines of code for all its members.
- **Start Automatic Outlining**—Enables the code outlining feature. This command is available only if outlining is currently turned off.

Code outlining is a convenience mechanism: by hiding currently irrelevant sections of code, you decrease the visible surface of the code file and increase code readability. You can pick and choose the specific regions to view based on the task at hand.

TIP

If you place the mouse pointer over the ellipsis box of a hidden code region, the contents of that hidden region are displayed to you in a ToolTip-style box; this is done without having to expand and reshow the code region.

Tag Navigation

One problem with large or complex markup files, be they web forms, XAML files, or XML documents, is navigation through the multiple levels and layers of nested tags. Envision a web page containing a button within a table within a table within a table. When you are editing the HTML (through either the designer or the editor), how can you tell exactly where you are? Put another way, how can you tell where the current focus is within the markup hierarchy?

Using the Tag Navigator

The tag navigator is Visual Studio's answer to this question. The navigator appears as a series of buttons at the bottom of the XAML, web, and XML Schema designers. A breadcrumb trail of tags is shown that leads from the tag that currently has focus all the way to the outermost tag. If this path is too long to display within the confines of the editor window, it is truncated at the parent tag side; a button enables you to display more tags toward the parent.

Figure 7.9 shows the tag navigator as implemented by the web designer. While you're editing the OK button in the sample login page, the tag navigator shows the path all the way back to the parent enclosing <html> tag.

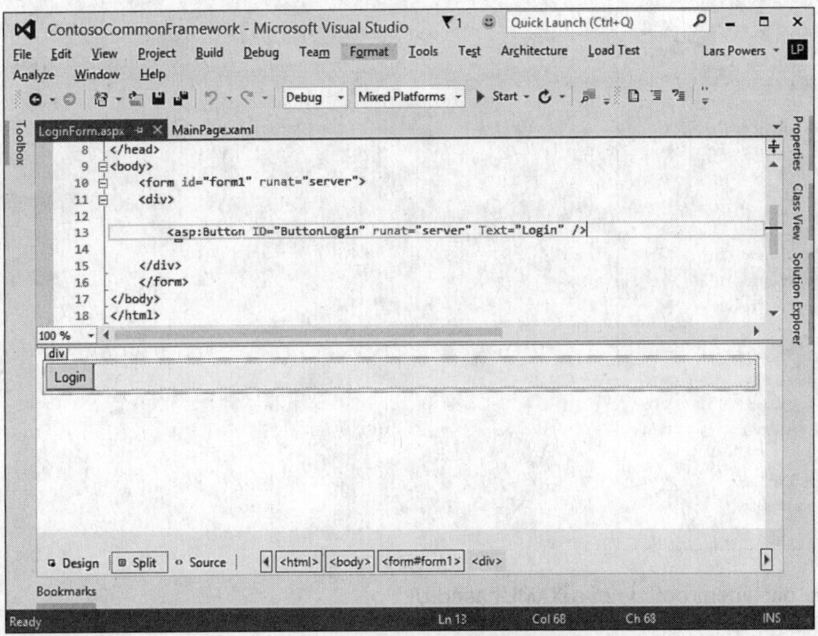

FIGURE 7.9 The web designer's tag navigator in action.

Each tag button displayed by the navigator can be used to directly select the inclusive or exclusive contents of that tag. A drop-down triggered by the tag button contains options for selecting the tag or selecting the tag content. The former causes the tag itself, in addition to all of its enclosed content, to be selected. The latter excludes the tag begin and end but still selects all its enclosed content.

The navigator is a great mechanism for quickly moving up and down within a large tag tree.

Using the Document Outline Window

The document outline window displays a tree-view representation of the elements on a web page, XAML window, or Windows form. This hierarchical display is a great navigation tool because it enables you to take in the entire structure of your document in one glance and immediately jump to any of the elements within the page.

To use the document outline window, choose Document Outline from the View, Other Windows menu. Figure 7.10 shows a sample outline for a window constructed with XAML.

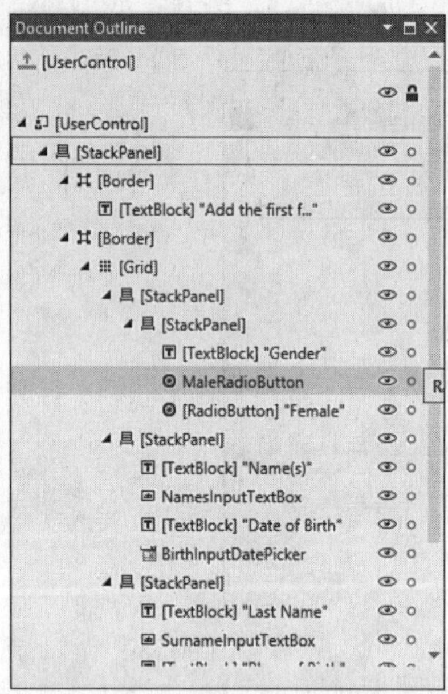

FIGURE 7.10 The document outline of a XAML-based UI.

Clicking an element navigates to that element (and selects it) within the designer window, and, of course, you can expand or collapse the tree nodes as needed.

NOTE

The features and look and feel of the document outline window change by document type. For instance, the XAML document outline shows a thumbnail image of the UI element when you hover over the node in the outline window. It also toggles visibility of any line item by clicking the "eye" icon located to the right of every line in the outline. The Windows Forms outline window actually allows you to move and reparent items within the form. Using just the outline window, you could move a button from within one tab container and place it within another by dragging the corresponding node to the new parent in the outline.

Smart Tasks and Light Bulbs

Smart tasks and light bulbs (a new addition to Visual Studio starting with version 2015) are menu- or IntelliSense-driven features for automating common control configuration and coding tasks within the IDE. Both designers and editors implement these features in different ways. In the following sections, we examine a few of the ways that these IDE aids make your life easier, starting with smart tasks and designers.

HTML Designer

As controls are placed onto the HTML designer, a pop-up list of common tasks appears. These tasks, collectively referred to as *smart tasks*, allow you to "set the dials" for a given control to quickly configure it for the task at hand.

You use the common tasks list to quickly configure a control's properties as well as walk through common operations you might perform with it. For example, when you add a GridView control to a web page, a common task list appears that allows you to promptly enable sorting, paging, or editing for the GridView. When you add a TextBox control to a web page, a common task list appears that enables you to rapidly associate a validation control with the control.

The Windows Forms Designer also plays host to smart tags.

Windows Forms Designer

With the Windows Forms Designer, the functionality of smart tasks remains consistent; they do, however, take a slightly different form. A form control that supports this functionality shows a smart tag glyph somewhere within its bounds (typically to the top right of the control). This glyph, when clicked, opens a small drop-down of tasks. Figure 7.11 contains a snapshot of the smart tag in action for a tab control.

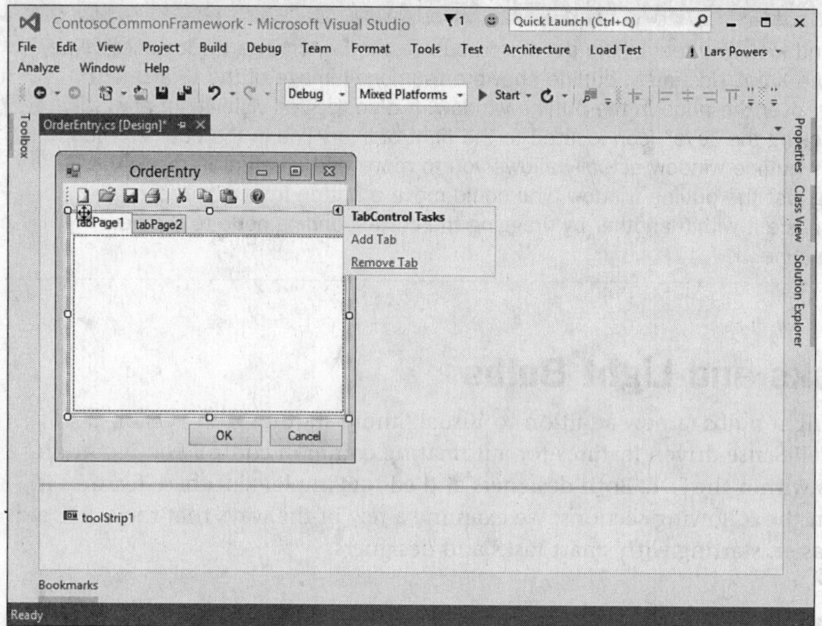

FIGURE 7.11 The smart tag on a tab control.

Code Editor

The Code Editor is where productivity really starts to come into its own with the concept of light bulbs. Light bulbs (which in prior incarnations of Visual Studio were called Smart Tags) pull together the collective intelligence of the IDE into one central, inline spot where code fixes, refactorings, and code completion suggestions can be provided and acted on quickly and easily.

A good example of the light bulb in action can be found when trying to implement an interface. Normally, implementing an interface is a fairly code-intensive task. We have to individually create a member within the implementing class to map to each member defined on the interface. With the light bulb concept, we can let the code editor itself do a lot of the work for us. To implement our interface on an existing class, we would add the "implements" syntax like this.

```
class Program : IContosoConsole { }
```

As we type this into the code editor, Visual Studio's IntelliSense (more to come on this technology in a bit) will automatically flag the interface name with a red underline indicating that potential problems exist. This is because we have not yet followed through on the requirements of the interface. In other words, we have established the "this class implements a specific interface" syntax, but we haven't actually gone ahead and implement the interface members. Figure 7.12 shows our initial syntax along with the IntelliSense underline/highlight.

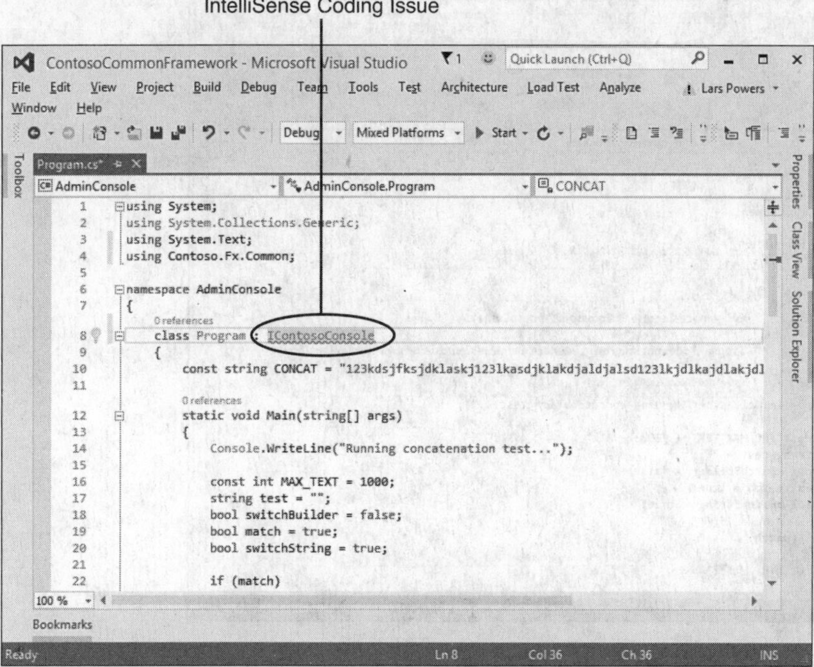

FIGURE 7.12 The Code Editor catching potential issues with an interface implementation.

If we now hover our cursor over the interface name that has been highlighted for us, we will get a brief summary of what the code editor has identified issue wise, along with the light bulb icon to the left of the issues window (see Figure 7.13). In this case, the editor has correctly identified that our implementing class does not (yet) implement all the required interface members.

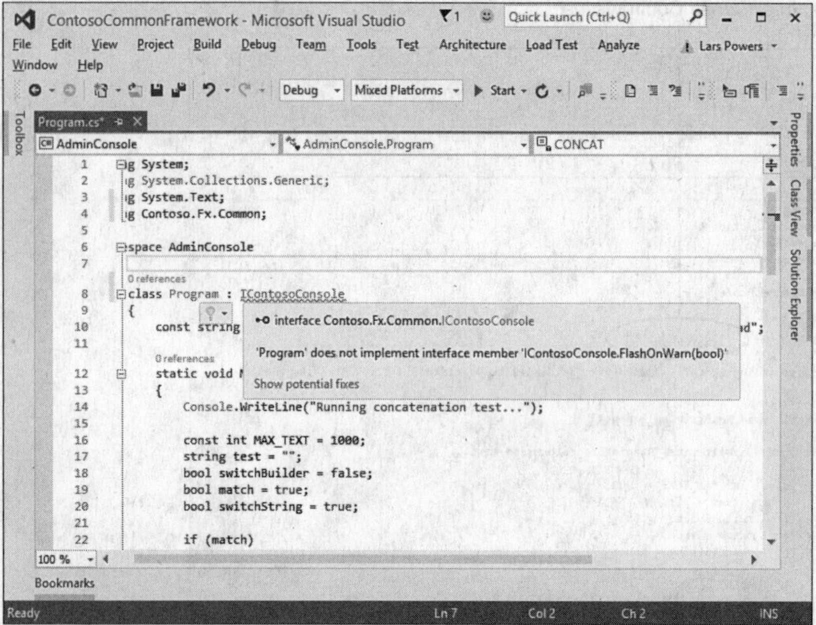

FIGURE 7.13 An issue identified with the light bulb.

If we click on the light bulb or select the `Show potential fixes` link within the issues window, we will have a set of actions that Visual Studio recommends to fix the identified issue.

NOTE

The light bulb indicator is also accessible in the left margin of the code editor. It works the same way there that it does when you hover over a flagged coding problem: it produces a drop-down list of issues and fixes when you click on it.

In this case, the actions are Implement Interface and Implement Interface Explicitly.

These two options will essentially write the code for us necessary to implement our interface using either an implicit or an explicit style:

- **Implement interface**—Member names do not reference the name of the derived interface.
- **Implement interface explicitly**—Members are prefixed with the name of the derived interface.

In fact, fixes are visually presented to you within the editor, allowing you to get an actual preview of the code changes that will happen if you select one of the options. See Figure 7.14 to view the light bulb in action.

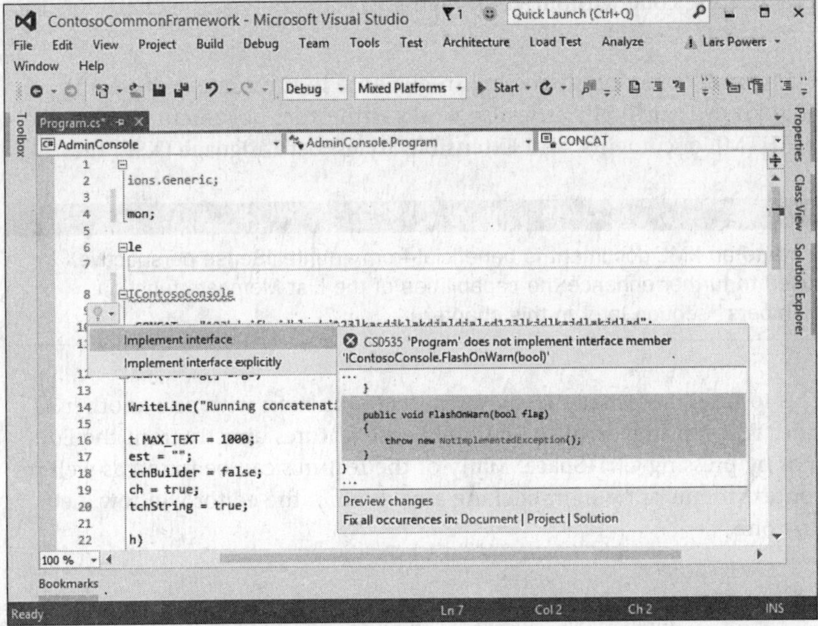

FIGURE 7.14 Code fixes with in-line preview using the light bulb.

This type of fix is known as a "Generate from Usage" scenario. It's meant to solve a fairly common workflow issue: with certain development styles (especially, test-driven development or TDD), it is often the case that you are referencing members and types that have not yet been created. In the preceding example, this is an interface, but it could just as easily be another class, a property, or a method.

Light bulbs are a common aid for any type of coding issue ranging from actual syntax errors in the code to refactoring to missing references to more involved usage scenarios (such as the one we just discussed).

IntelliSense

IntelliSense is the name applied to a collection of different coding aids surfaced within the text editor window. Its sole purpose is to help you, the developer, write a syntactically correct line of code *quickly*. In addition, it tries to provide enough guidance to help you write lines of code that are correct *in context* (that is, code that makes sense given the surrounding lines of code).

As you type within the text editor, IntelliSense is the behind-the-scenes agent responsible for providing a list of code fragments that match the characters you have already entered, highlighting/preselecting the one that makes the most sense given the surrounding context, and, if so commanded, automatically inserting that code fragment in-line. This saves you the time of looking up types and members in the reference documentation and saves time again by inserting code without your having to actually type the characters for that code.

We spend a lot of time in this section discussing IntelliSense in the context of editing code, but you should know that IntelliSense also works with other document types such as XML documents, HTML documents, and Extensible Stylesheet Language (XSL) files.

TIP

Attaching a schema to an XML document is beneficial from an IntelliSense perspective. The schema is used to further enhance the capabilities of the List Members function. (See the "List Members" section later in this chapter.)

Many discrete pieces to IntelliSense seamlessly work in conjunction with one another as you are writing code. You can trigger all these IntelliSense features directly from the Edit, IntelliSense menu or by pressing Ctrl+Space. Many of the features can be found as well on the text editor's context menu or by right-clicking anywhere in the editor window. Let's look at them one by one.

Complete Word

Complete Word is the basic timesaving kernel of IntelliSense. After you have typed enough characters for IntelliSense to recognize what you are trying to write, a guess is made as to the complete word you are in the process of typing. This guess is then presented to you within a list of possible alternatives (referred to as the *completion list*) and can be inserted into the code editor with one keystroke. This is in contrast to your completing the word manually by typing all its characters.

Figure 7.15 illustrates the process. Based on the context of the code and based on the characters typed into the editor, a list of possible words is displayed. One of these words is selected as the most viable candidate; you may select any entry in the list (via the arrow keys or the mouse). Pressing the Tab (or the Enter) key automatically injects the word into the editor for you.

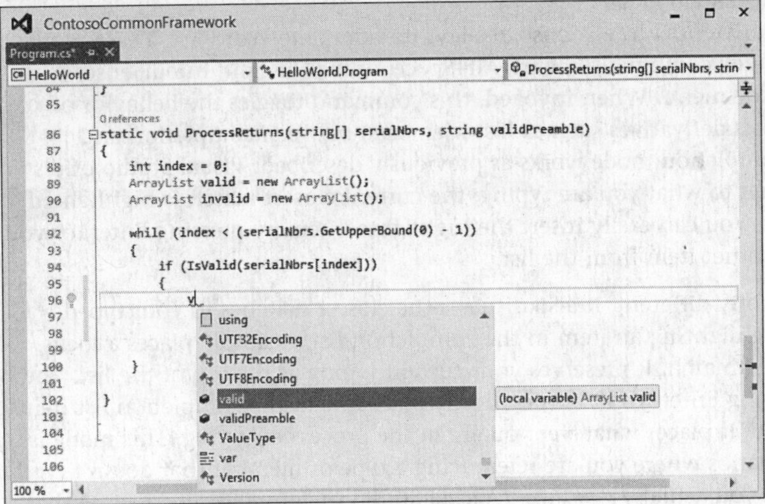

FIGURE 7.15 IntelliSense: Complete Word.

NOTE

Complete Word takes the actual code context into account for various situations. For instance, if you are in the midst of keying the exception type into a `try/catch` block, IntelliSense displays only exception types in the completion list. Likewise, typing an attribute triggers a completion list filtered only for attributes; when you're implementing an interface, only interface types are displayed; and so on.

This IntelliSense feature is enabled for all sorts of content. Beyond C# and Visual Basic code, IntelliSense completion works for other files as well, such as HTML tags, JavaScript, XAML, CSS style attributes, `.config` files, and HTML script blocks, just to name a few. Visual Basic offers functionality with Complete Word that C# does not: it provides a tabbed completion list, in which one tab contains the most commonly used syntax snippets, and the other contains *all* the possible words.

You can manually invoke Complete Word at any time by using the Ctrl+Space or Alt+right-arrow key combinations.

TIP

Holding down the Ctrl key while the completion list is displayed makes the list partially transparent. This is useful if, during the process of selecting an item from the list, you need to see any of the lines of code that are hidden behind the list.

Completion Versus Suggestion Mode

Two different modes drive how IntelliSense displays its Complete Word list. These modes are toggled with a hotkey combination, Ctrl+Alt+Space, or via the Edit, IntelliSense, ToggleCompletionMode menu. When invoked, this command toggles the behavior of Complete Word (and its derivatives such as List Members) between completion and suggestion modes. Completion mode works as previously described: Visual Studio offers you the closest matches to what you are typing; the current closest match is highlighted in the completion list. You can easily insert the highlighted item by pressing Enter, or you can select to insert another item from the list.

Suggestion mode is subtly different. It also displays the closest matches to your typed text, but instead of highlighting an item in the completion list, it simply places a focus rectangle on the closest match. It preserves your current typing at the top of the list. The net result is that pressing Enter won't automatically place one of the completion list items into your code; instead, it places whatever you are in the process of typing. This mode is meant to cater to scenarios where you are referencing a type or member that doesn't (yet) exist. In this scenario, you actually *don't want* Visual Studio to automatically assume that you are trying to reference a code construct that currently exists. In this mode, you have the explicit option to select an existing code element or to continue typing and enter the name for a code element that has yet to be created. This gives you more flexibility while sacrificing a bit of the speed of standard mode. (If you are referencing an existing item, consume-first mode requires an extra mouse click to insert the item because it won't be highlighted in the completion list.)

Quick Info

Quick Info displays the complete code declaration and help information for any code construct. You invoke it by hovering the mouse pointer over an identifier; a pop-up box displays the information available for that identifier.

Figure 7.16 shows Quick Info being displayed for the `Console.WriteLine` function. You are provided with the declaration syntax for the member and a brief description of the member. The description that shows up in the Quick Info window also works for code that you write. If you have a code comment associated with a member, IntelliSense parses the comment and uses it to display the description information.

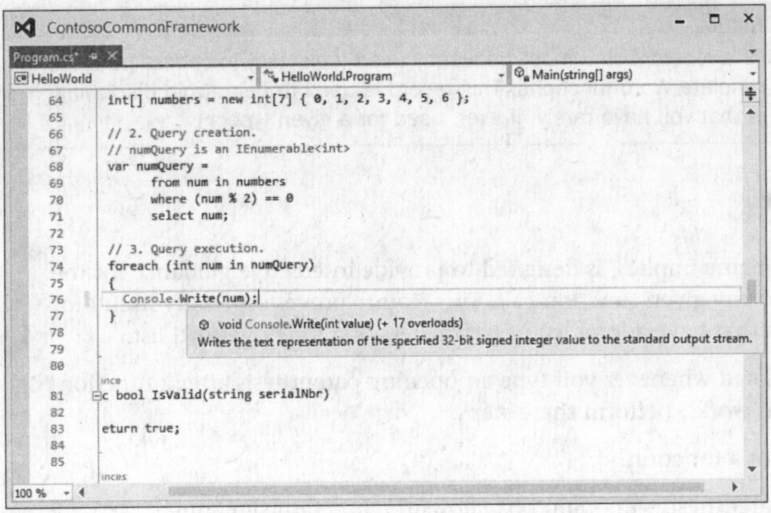

FIGURE 7.16 IntelliSense: Quick Info.

List Members

The List Members feature functions in an identical fashion to Complete Word; for any given type or namespace, it displays a scrollable list of all valid member variables and functions specific to that type. To see the List Members function in action, perform the following steps in an open code editor window:

1. Type the name of a class. (Ctrl+Space gives you the IntelliSense window with possible class names.)
2. Type a period; this indicates to IntelliSense that you have finished with the type name and are now "scoped in" to that type's members. The list of valid members is displayed.
3. Manually scroll through the list and select the desired member at this point, or, if you are well aware of the member you are trying to code, simply continue typing until IntelliSense has captured enough characters to select the member you are looking for.
4. Leverage Complete Word by pressing the Tab key to automatically insert the member into your line of code (thus saving you the typing effort).

This feature also operates in conjunction with Quick Info: as you select different members in the members list, a Quick Info pop-up is displayed for that member.

As noted earlier in our discussion of Complete Word, List Members can function in either standard or consume-first modes.

NOTE

IntelliSense maintains a record of the most frequently used (selected) members from the List Members and Complete Word functions. This record is used to help avoid displaying or selecting members that you have rarely, if ever, used for a given type.

Parameter Info

Parameter Info, as its name implies, is designed to provide interactive guidance for the parameters needed for any given function call. This feature proves especially useful for making function calls that have a long list of parameters or a long overload list.

Parameter Info is initiated whenever you type an opening parenthesis after a function name. To see how this works, perform these steps:

1. Type the name of a function.
2. Type an open parenthesis. A pop-up box shows the function signature.
3. Scroll through the different signatures by using the small up- and down-arrow cues if there are multiple valid signatures (for example, multiple overloaded versions of this function). Select the desired signature.
4. Start typing the actual parameters you want to pass in to the function.

   As you type, the parameter info pop-up continues coaching you through the parameter list by bolding the current parameter you are working on. As each successive parameter is highlighted, the definition for that parameter appears. If the function in question has multiple overloads, the pop-up box will contain up and down arrows that can be used to cycle between the different parameter definition sets.

In Figure 7.17, we are entering a parameter for the `Console.ReadKey` method. Note that we are using an overload of this function and the presence of the up and down arrows for cycling between the two defined function definitions for `ReadKey`.

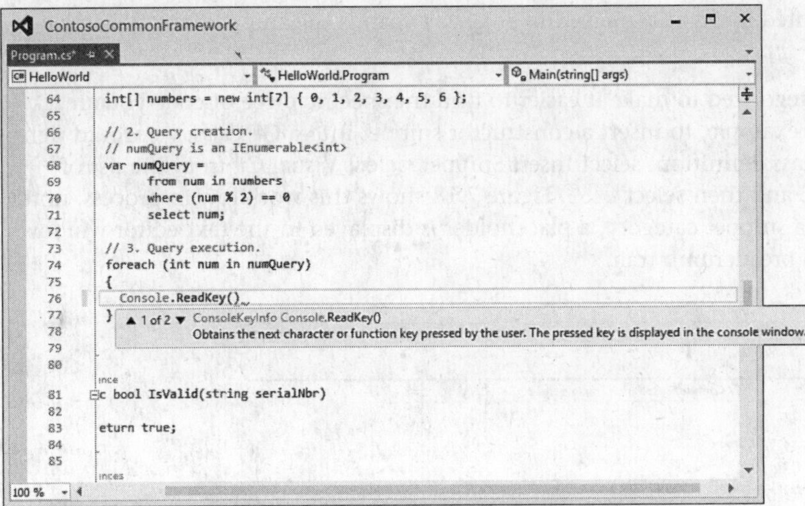

FIGURE 7.17 IntelliSense: parameter info.

Organize Usings

Organize Usings is a C# and Visual Basic IntelliSense item. It provides three separate functions: Remove Unnecessary Usings/Imports, Sort Usings/Imports, and Remove and Sort Usings/Imports (which combines the first two actions into one). All three commands live under the Organize Usings menu item on the editor shortcut menu or under the main Edit, IntelliSense menu.

The Remove Unused Usings/Imports function is a great aid for uncluttering your code. It scans through the current body of code and determines which Using/Import statements are necessary for the code to compile; it then removes all others. The Sort command is straightforward as well; it simply rearranges all your Using/Import statements so they appear in *A–Z* alphabetic order by namespace.

Code Snippets and Template Code

Code snippets are prestocked lines of code available for selection and insertion into the text editor. Each code snippet is referenced by a name referred to as its alias. Code snippets are used to automate what would normally be non-value-added, repetitive typing. You can create your own code snippets or use the default library of common code elements that Visual Studio provides.

Using the Code Snippet Inserter

You insert snippets by right-clicking at the intended insertion point within an open text editor window and then selecting Insert Snippet from the shortcut menu. This launches the Code Snippet Inserter, which is a drop-down (or series of drop-downs) that works much like the IntelliSense Complete Word feature. Each item in the inserter represents a snippet, represented by its alias. Selecting an alias expands the snippet into the active document.

Each snippet is categorized to make it easier to find the specific piece of code you are looking for. As an example, to insert a constructor snippet into a C# class, we would right-click within the class definition, select Insert Snippet, select Visual C# from the list of snippet categories, and then select `ctor`. Figure 7.18 shows this workflow in process; note that as you select a snippet category, a placeholder is displayed in the text editor window to help establish a breadcrumb trail.

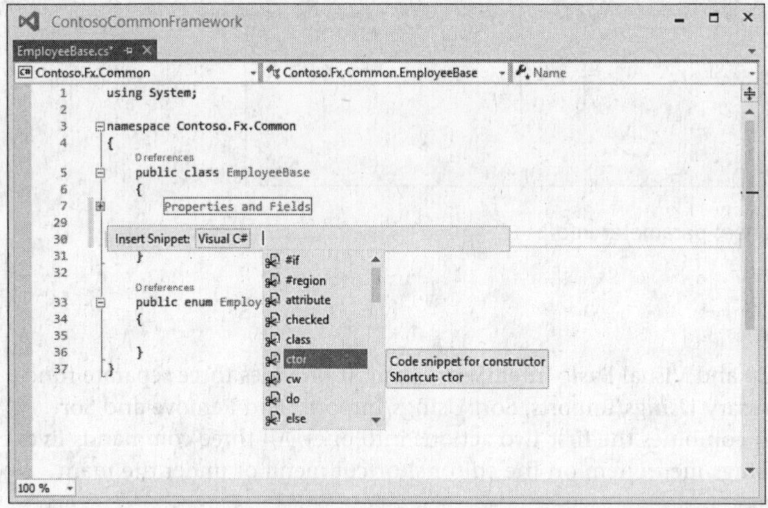

FIGURE 7.18 The C# `ctor` code snippet.

After the constructor snippet is expanded into the text editor, you still, of course, have to write meaningful code inside the constructor; but, in general, snippets eliminate the process of tedious coding that really doesn't require much intellectual horsepower to generate.

Figure 7.19 shows the same process being followed for a Visual Basic code window. The process is identical with the exception that Visual Basic makes more extensive use of categories.

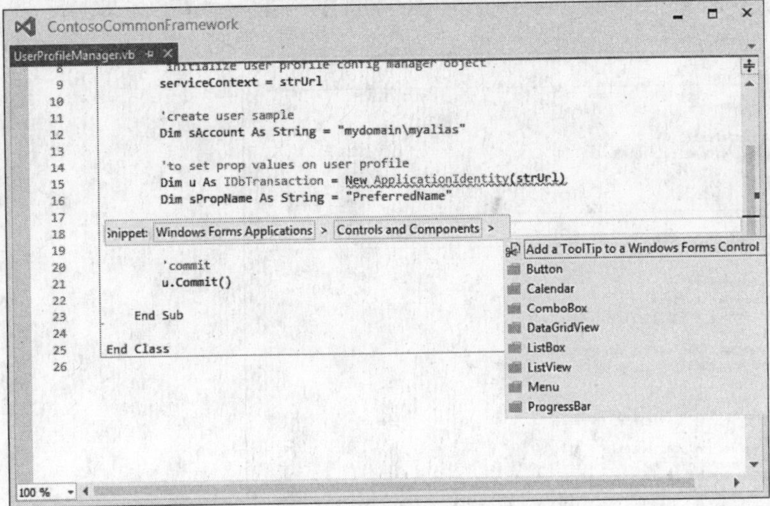

FIGURE 7.19 Inserting a Visual Basic code snippet.

TIP

If you are coding in Visual Basic, a quick, alternative way to display the Code Snippet Inserter is to type a question mark and then press the Tab key.

Visual Basic also exhibits slightly different behavior than C# after a snippet has been expanded into the code window. Figure 7.20 shows the results of drilling down through multiple categories and, in this example, selecting the Create Transparent Windows Form snippet. Notice that the inserter has injected the template code into the Visual Basic code for you, but the inserter (at least in this case) wasn't intelligent enough to know the name of the form you are trying to make transparent.

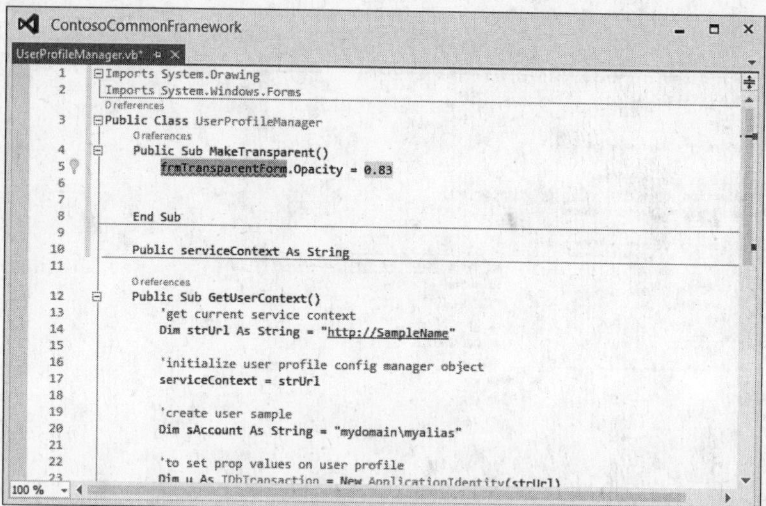

FIGURE 7.20 A Visual Basic form transparency code snippet.

The snippet code has the form name filled in with a default, dummy name that is already highlighted. You merely start typing the form name you need, and it replaces the dummy name. The opacity value is also a dummy value that you can quickly correct at this time.

TIP

Snippets may have one or more placeholder values: fragments of code that you will want and probably need to change. You can cycle through each of the placeholder values by pressing the Tab key. When a placeholder is highlighted (in blue), you can start typing to replace the syntax with something that makes sense for your specific code context.

Surrounding Code with Snippets

C# and XML documents have one additional style of code snippets that bears mentioning: Surround With snippets. Surround With snippets are still snippets at their core (again, these are simply prestocked lines of code), but they differ in how they are able to insert themselves into your code.

Using a Surround With snippet, you can stack enclosing text around a selection with the text editor. As an example, perhaps you have a few different class declarations that you would like to nest within a namespace. Using the Surround With snippet is a simple two-step process: highlight the class definitions and fire up the Code Snippet Inserter. This time, instead of selecting Insert Snippet from the shortcut menu, you select Surround With. The insert works the same way but this time has applied the snippet (in this case, a namespace snippet) in a different fashion. Compare the before and after text shown in Figures 7.21 and 7.22. We have encapsulated the class definitions within a new namespace that sits within yet another namespace (all with just a few mouse clicks).

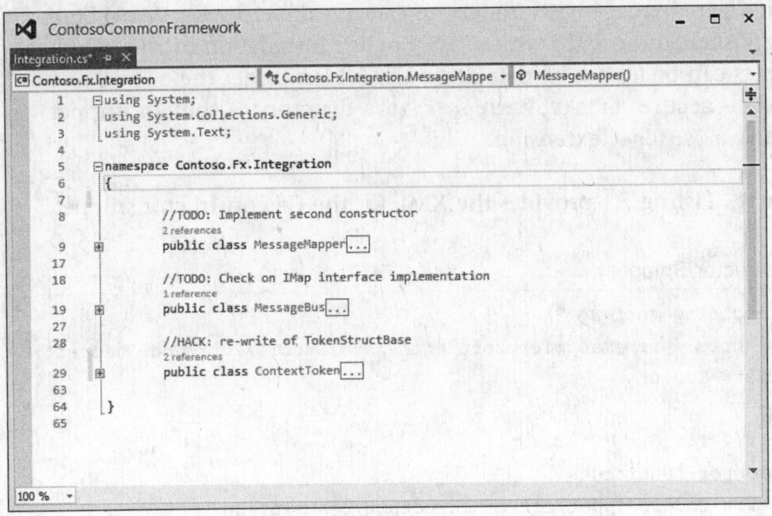

FIGURE 7.21 Before inserting a Surround With snippet.

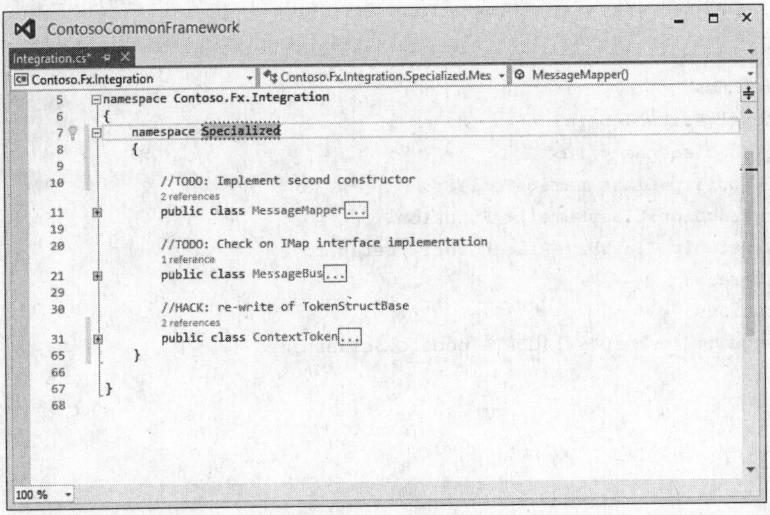

FIGURE 7.22 After inserting a Surround With snippet.

Creating Your Own Code Snippets

Because code snippets are stored in XML files, you can create your own snippets quite easily. The key is understanding the XML schema that defines a snippet, and the best way to do that is to look at the XML source data for some of the snippets included with the IDE.

Snippets are stored on a per-language basis under the `install` directory for Visual Studio. For example, running Visual Studio 2015 with a U.S. English installation of x86 Windows, the Visual Basic snippets can be found, by default, in the folders under the `C:\Program Files\Microsoft Visual Studio 14.0\Vb\Snippets\1033` directory. Although snippet files are XML, they carry a `.Snippet` extension.

The XML Snippet Format Listing 7.1 provides the XML for the C# constructor snippet.

LISTING 7.1 C# Constructor Snippet

```
<?xml version="1.0" encoding="utf-8" ?>
<CodeSnippets  xmlns="http://schemas.microsoft.com/VisualStudio/2005/CodeSnippet">
    <CodeSnippet Format="1.0.0">
        <Header>
            <Title>ctor</Title>
            <Shortcut>ctor</Shortcut>
            <Description>Code snippet for constructor</Description>
            <Author>Microsoft Corporation</Author>
            <SnippetTypes>
                <SnippetType>Expansion</SnippetType>
            </SnippetTypes>
        </Header>
        <Snippet>
            <Declarations>
                <Literal Editable="false">
                    <ID>classname</ID>
                    <ToolTip>Class name</ToolTip>
                    <Function>ClassName()</Function>
                    <Default>ClassNamePlaceholder</Default>
                </Literal>
            </Declarations>
            <Code Language="csharp"><![CDATA[public $classname$ ()
    {
        $end$
    }]]>
            </Code>
        </Snippet>
    </CodeSnippet>
</CodeSnippets>
```

The basic structure of this particular snippet declaration is described in Table 7.2. A more complete schema reference is available as part of the Visual Studio Microsoft Developer Network (MSDN) library; it is located under Visual Studio 2015, Reference, XML Schema References, Code Snippets Schema Reference.

TABLE 7.2 XML Snippet File Node Descriptions

XML Node	Description
`<CodeSnippets>`	The parent element for all code snippet information. It references the specific XML namespace used to define snippets within Visual Studio.
`<CodeSnippet>`	The root element for a single code snippet. This tag sets the format version information for the snippet. Although multiple `CodeSnippet` elements are possible within the parent `<CodeSnippets>` element, the convention is to place one snippet per file.
`<Header>`	A metadata container element for data that describes the snippet.
`<Title>`	The title of the code snippet.
`<Shortcut>`	Typically, the same as the title, this is the text that appears in the code snippet insertion drop-downs.
`<Description>`	A description of the snippet.
`<Author>`	The author of the snippet.
`<SnippetTypes>`	The parent element for holding elements describing the snippet's type.
`<SnippetType>`	The type of the snippet: Expansion, Refactoring, or Surrounds With. You cannot create custom refactoring snippets. This property is really used to tell Visual Studio where the snippet can be inserted within the editor window: Expansion snippets insert at the current cursor position, whereas Surrounds With snippets are inserted before and after the code body identified by the current cursor position or selection.
`<Snippet>`	The root element for the snippet code.
`<Declarations>`	The root element for the literals and objects used by the snippet.
`<Literal>`	A string whose value can be interactively set as part of the snippet expansion process. The Editable attribute on this tag indicates whether the literal is static or editable. The `ctor` snippet is an example of one without an editable literal; contrast this with the form transparency snippet that you saw (an example of a snippet with an editable literal that allows you to set the form name as part of the snippet insertion).
`<ID>`	A unique ID for the literal.
`<ToolTip>`	A ToolTip to display when the cursor is placed over the literal.
`<Function>`	The name of a function (see Table 8.3) to call when the literal receives focus. Functions are available only in C# snippets.
`<Default>`	The default string literal to insert into the editor.
`<Code>`	An element that contains the actual code to insert.

The trick to writing a snippet is to understand how literals and variable replacement work. Suppose, for instance, that you want to create a C# snippet that writes out a simple code comment indicating that a class has been reviewed and approved as part of a code review process. In other words, you want something like this.

```
// Code review of ContextToken.
//   Reviewer: Lars Powers
//   Date: 12/1/2015
//   Approval: Approved
```

In this snippet, you need to treat four literals as variable; they can change each time the snippet is used: the classname, the reviewer's name, the date, and the approval. You can set them up within the declarations section like this:

```
<Declarations>
    <Literal Editable="False">
        <ID>classname</ID>
        <ToolTip>Class name/type being reviewed</ToolTip>
        <Function>ClassName()</Function>
        <Default>ClassNameGoesHere</Default>
    </Literal>
    <Literal Editable="True">
        <ID>reviewer</ID>
        <ToolTip>Replace with the reviewer's name</ToolTip>
        <Default>ReviewerName</Default>
    </Literal>
    <Literal Editable="True">
        <ID>currdate</ID>
        <ToolTip>Replace with the review date</ToolTip>
        <Default>ReviewDate</Default>
    </Literal>
    <Literal Editable="True">
        <ID>approval</ID>
        <ToolTip>Replace with Approved or Rejected</ToolTip>
        <Default>Approved</Default>
    </Literal>
</Declarations>
```

Notice that you are actually calling a function to prepopulate the class name within the snippet. Functions are available only with C#; they are documented in Table 7.3. The rest of the literals rely on the developer to type over the placeholder value with the correct value.

TABLE 7.3 Code Snippet Functions

Function	Description
`GenerateSwitchCases (enumliteral)`	Creates the syntax for a switch statement that includes a case statement for each value defined by the enumeration represented by `enumliteral` (C#/J#).

Function	Description
`ClassName()`	Inserts the name of the class containing the code snippet (C#/J#).
`SimpleTypeName(typename)`	Takes the type name referenced by `typename` and returns the shortest name possible given the using statements in effect for the current code block. For example, `SimpleTypeName(System.Exception)` would return `Exception` if a `using System` statement is present (C#).
`CallBase(parameter)`	Is useful when stubbing out members that implement or return the base type. When you specify `get`, `set`, or `method` as the parameter, a call will be created against the base class for that specific property accessor or method (C#).

You should also provide some basic header information for the snippet.

```
<Header>
    <Title>review</Title>
    <Shortcut>review</Shortcut>
    <Description>Code review comment</Description>
    <Author>L. Powers</Author>
    <SnippetTypes>
        <SnippetType>Expansion</SnippetType>
    </SnippetTypes>
</Header>
```

The last remaining task is to implement the `<Code>` element, which contains the actual text of the snippet and references the literals that we have previously defined.

```
<Code Language="csharp">
    <![CDATA[// Review of $classname$
    //   Reviewer: $reviewer$
    //   Date: $currdate$
    //   Approval: $approval$]]>
</Code>
```

When you put all this together, you end up with the custom snippet shown in Listing 7.2.

LISTING 7.2 A Custom C# Snippet

```
<?xml version="1.0" encoding="utf-8" ?>
<CodeSnippet Format="1.0.0">
    <Header>
        <Title>review</Title>
        <Shortcut>review</Shortcut>
        <Description>Code review comment</Description>
        <Author>L. Powers</Author>
```

```
    <SnippetTypes>
      <SnippetType>Expansion</SnippetType>
    </SnippetTypes>
  </Header>
  <Snippet>
    <Declarations>
      <Literal Editable="False">
        <ID>classname</ID>
        <ToolTip>Class name/type being reviewed</ToolTip>
        <Function>ClassName()</Function>
        <Default>ClassNameGoesHere</Default>
      </Literal>
      <Literal Editable="True">
        <ID>reviewer</ID>
        <ToolTip>Replace with the reviewer's name</ToolTip>
        <Default>ReviewerName</Default>
      </Literal>
      <Literal Editable="True">
        <ID>currdate</ID>
        <ToolTip>Replace with the review date</ToolTip>
        <Default>ReviewDate</Default>
      </Literal>
      <Literal Editable="True">
        <ID>approval</ID>
        <ToolTip>Replace with Approved or Rejected</ToolTip>
        <Default>Approved</Default>
      </Literal>

    </Declarations>
                        <Code Language="csharp">
      <![CDATA[// Review of $classname$
  //    Reviewer: $reviewer$
  //    Date: $currdate$
  //    Approval: $approval$]]>
    </Code>
                </Snippet>
      /CodeSnippet>
</CodeSnippets>
```

When the code snippet is executed, our literals (bracketed by the $ symbols in the preceding code) are replaced by their specified default values and are highlighted to allow the snippet user to easily replace them after they are in the editor. Our `$classname$` literal is a bit different in that it places a call to the `ClassName()` function to get the name of the current, enclosing class.

At this point, the snippet is syntactically complete. Although this snippet is writing comments into the editor, the same process and structure applies for emitting code into the editor. If you want to write a Surround With snippet, you change the `<SnippetType>` to `SurroundsWith`.

Now you need to make Visual Studio aware of the snippet.

Adding a Snippet to Visual Studio You can use Visual Studio's own XML editor to create the XML document and save it to a directory. (A big bonus for doing so is that you can leverage IntelliSense triggered by the XML snippet schema to help you with your element names and relationships.) The Visual Studio installer creates a default directory to place your custom snippets located in your `Documents` folder: `user\Documents\Visual Studio 2015\Code Snippets\Visual C#\My Code Snippets`. If you place your XML template here, Visual Studio automatically includes your snippet for use.

TIP

If you have placed your snippet file in the correct folder and it still doesn't show up within the Code Snippets Manager dialog box, you probably have a syntax error within the file. A good way to check this is to try to import the snippet file using the Import button. Visual Studio immediately tells you whether the snippet file is valid.

The Code Snippets Manager, which is launched from the Tools menu, is the central control dialog box for browsing the available snippets, adding new ones, or removing a snippet (see Figure 7.23). As you can see, the review snippet shows up under the `My Code Snippets` folder.

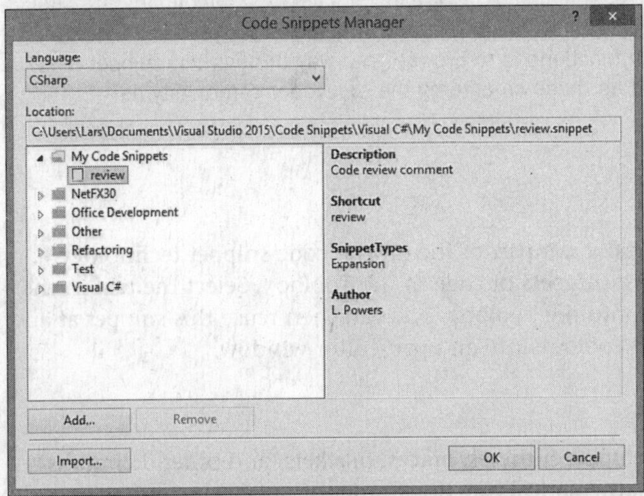

FIGURE 7.23 The Code Snippets Manager.

You can also opt to include other folders besides the standard ones. To do so, click the Add button to enter additional folders for Visual Studio to use when displaying the list of snippets.

Figure 7.24 shows the results of the custom snippet.

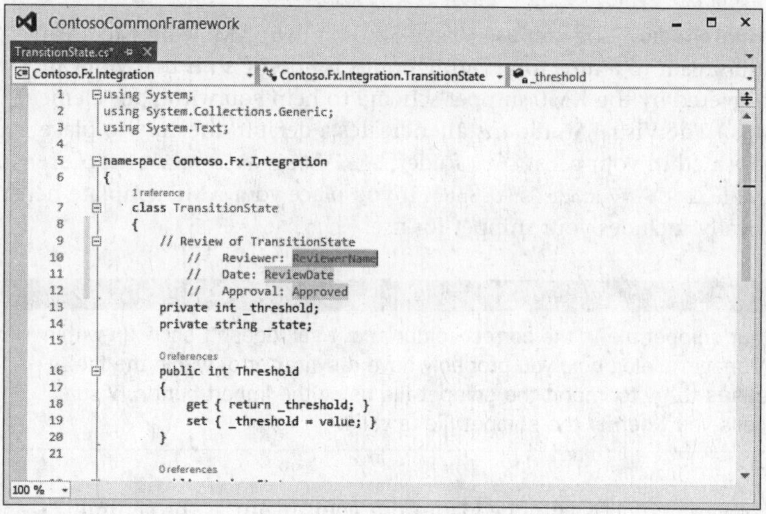
ContosoCommonFramework
TransitionState.cs*
Contoso.Fx.Integration
Contoso.Fx.Integration.TransitionState
_threshold
using System;
using System.Collections.Generic;
using System.Text;
namespace Contoso.Fx.Integration
{
1 reference
class TransitionState
{
// Review of TransitionState
// Reviewer: ReviewerName
// Date: ReviewDate
// Approval: Approved
private int _threshold;
private string _state;
0 references
public int Threshold
{
get { return _threshold; }
set { _threshold = value; }
}
0 references
100 %

FIGURE 7.24 The results of a custom code snippet in C#.

TIP

Snippets can also be browsed and shared online. A great way to further your understanding of code snippet structure and functions is to browse your way through the snippet files included in Visual Studio, as well as those created by the developer community as a whole.

Snippets in the Toolbox

Although this capability is technically not part of the official code snippet technology within Visual Studio, you can store snippets of code in the Toolbox. Select the text in the editor and then drag and drop it onto the Toolbox. You can then reuse this snippet at any time by dragging it back from the Toolbox into an open editor window.

Brace Matching

Programming languages make use of parentheses, braces, brackets, and other delimiters to delimit function arguments, mathematical functions/order of operation, and bodies of code. It can be difficult to visually determine whether you have missed a matching delimiter—that is, if you have more opening delimiters than you have closing delimiters—especially with highly nested lines of code.

Brace matching refers to visual cues that the code editor uses to make you aware of your matching delimiters. As you type code into the editor, any time you enter a closing delimiter, the matching opening delimiter and the closing delimiter are briefly highlighted. In Figure 7.25, brace matching helps to indicate the matching delimiters for the interior `for` loop.

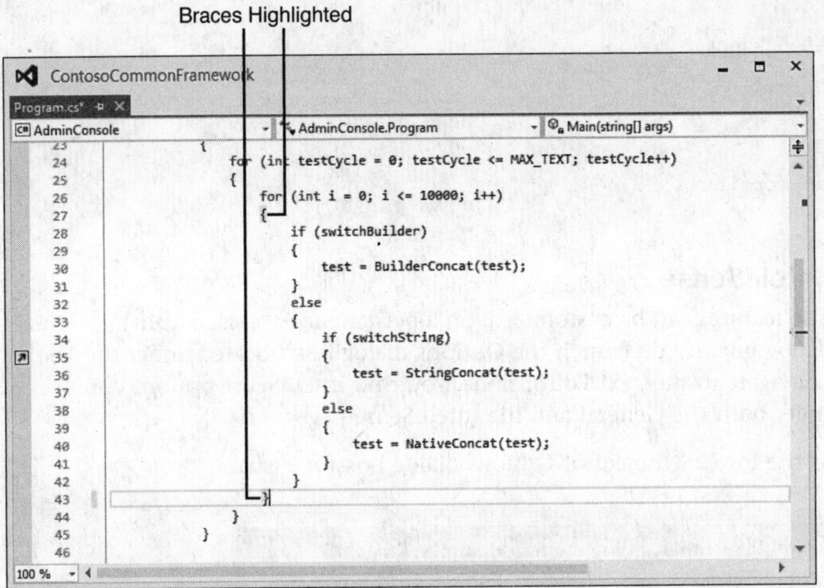

FIGURE 7.25 Brace matching.

TIP

You also can trigger brace matching simply by placing the cursor directly to the left of an opening delimiter or the right of a closing delimiter. If you are browsing through a routine congested with parentheses and braces, you can quickly sort out the matching pairs by moving your cursor around to the various delimiters. If you want to move to the second member of a pair, you can press Ctrl+^.

Although this feature is referred to as brace matching, it actually functions with the following delimiters:

- Parentheses: `()`
- Brackets: `[]`, `<>`
- Quotation marks: `""`
- Braces: `{}`

In the case of C#, brace matching also works with the following keyword pairs (which essentially function as delimiters using keywords):

- `#region, #endregion`
- `#if, #else, #endif`
- `case, break`
- `default, break`
- `for, break, continue`
- `if, else`
- `while, break, continue`

Customizing IntelliSense

Certain IntelliSense features can be customized, on a per-language basis, within the Visual Studio Options dialog box. If you launch the Options dialog box (located under the Tools menu) and then navigate to the Text Editor node, you find IntelliSense options confusingly scattered under both the General and the IntelliSense pages.

Figure 7.26 shows the IntelliSense editor Options dialog box for Visual C#.

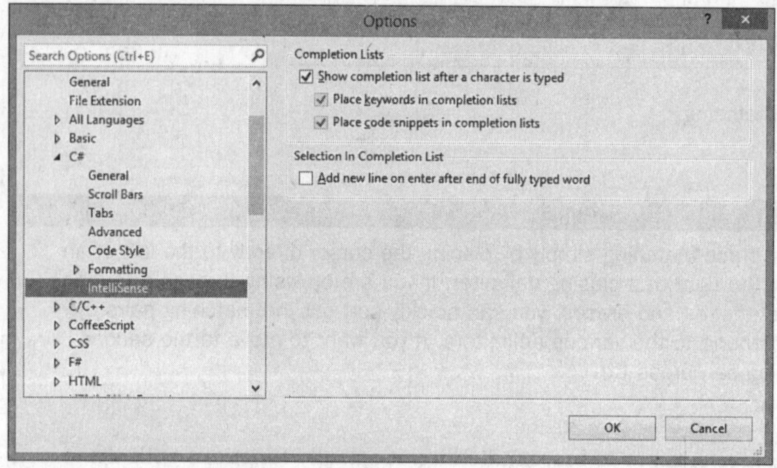

FIGURE 7.26 IntelliSense options.

Completion Lists in this dialog box refer to any of the IntelliSense features that facilitate autocompletion of code, such as List Members and Complete Word. Table 7.4 itemizes the options available in this dialog box.

TABLE 7.4 IntelliSense Options

Option	**Effect**
Show Completion List After a Character Is Typed	This causes the Complete Word feature to automatically run after a single character is typed in the editor window.
Place Keywords in Completion Lists	If this box is checked, language keywords are displayed within the completion list. As an example: for C#, this would cause keywords such as class or string to be included in the completion list.
Place Code Snippets in Completion Lists	Checking this box places code-snippet alias names into any displayed completion lists.
Add New Line on Enter After End of Fully Typed Word	Checking this box causes the cursor to advance down an entire line if you fully type a word in the IntelliSense list box. This is useful for those scenarios in which fully typed keywords are unlikely to be followed on the same line with other code.

The Task List

The Task List is essentially an integrated to-do list; it captures all the items that, for one reason or another, need attention and tracking. The Task List window then surfaces this list and allows you to interact with it. To show the window, select the View menu and choose the Task List entry. Figure 7.27 illustrates the Task List window displaying a series of user tasks. Tasks belong to one of three categories: comment tasks, shortcut tasks, and user tasks. Only one category can be displayed at a time.

Task List

Description	Project	File	Line	Col
TODO: this is something you have to do...	AdminConsole	Program.cs	51	15
TODO: Implement second constructor	Contoso.Fx.Integration	Integration.cs	9	11
TODO: Check on IMap interface implementation	Contoso.Fx.Integration	Integration.cs	19	11
UNDONE: MessageBus ctor	Contoso.Fx.Integration	Integration.cs	24	19
HACK: re-write of TokenStructBase	Contoso.Fx.Integration	Integration.cs	29	11
TODO: Customize the application's assembly information in the "Application" pane of the project	Contoso.UI.WindowsFor...	AboutBox1.vb	13	11
TODO: Login routine	Contoso.UI.WindowsFor...	CommonFuncs.vb	15	11

FIGURE 7.27 The Task List window.

You can sort the tasks by any of the columns shown in the list. Right-clicking the column headers provides a shortcut menu that allows you to control the sort behavior as well as which columns (from a list of all supported columns) should be displayed. This shortcut menu is also how you will delete, cut, copy, or paste tasks from the list.

Shortcut Tasks

Shortcut tasks are similar to user tasks. But shortcut tasks are directly tied to a line of code, and they are added by putting your cursor on the line of code you want to associate with the task and then selecting Edit, Bookmarks, Add Task List Shortcut. (We covered the similar concept of bookmarks back in Chapter 6.)

In addition to the description, completion indicator, and priority indicator columns, shortcut tasks show the file and line number for the shortcut. Double-clicking the shortcut task opens the associated file and puts your cursor back on the associated line of code.

Comment Tasks

Comment tasks, like shortcut tasks, are associated with lines of code. But unlike shortcut tasks or user tasks, comment tasks are created by placing a code comment with a special string literal/token in a code file. There are three tokens defined by default by Visual Studio: HACK, TODO, and UNDONE.

There is no check box in the Task List to mark a comment task as complete. Instead, you simply remove the comment token from your code to remove the task from the list.

For example, the following C# code results in four different comment tasks in the Task List.

```
namespace Contoso.Fx.Integration.Specialized
{
    //TODO: Implement second constructor
    public class MessageMapper : IMessageSink
    {
        public MessageMapper()
        {
        }
    }

    //TODO: Check on IMap interface implementation
    public class MessageBus : MessageMapper
    {
        public MessageBus()
        {
            //UNDONE: MessageBus ctor
        }
    }

    //HACK: rewrite of TokenStruct
    public class ContextToken
    {
        public ContextToken()
        {
        }
```

```
        public ContextToken(string guid)
        {
        }
    }
}
```

Double-clicking the comment task takes you directly to the referenced comment line within the editor window.

Custom Comment Tokens

If needed, you can add your own set of tokens that are recognized as comment tasks. From the Tools, Options dialog box, select the Task List page under the Environment section; this dialog box provides options for adding, editing, or deleting the list of comment tokens recognized by the Task List.

TIP

The UI for adding a comment task token is not that intuitive. To add a token, you first type in a name for the token using the Name text box. At this point in time, the Add button becomes enabled. Click the Add button to add the token to the list, and then you can edit its priority and so on. Similarly, if you want to change a token's name or priority, you would select the token, make the change to either the priority or name, and then click the Change button to commit the change to the list.

In Figure 7.28, a Review token has been added to the standard list. Note that you can also set a priority against each of the tokens and fine-tune some of the display behavior by using the Task List Options check boxes, which control whether task deletions are confirmed, and by setting whether filenames or complete file paths are displayed within the task list.

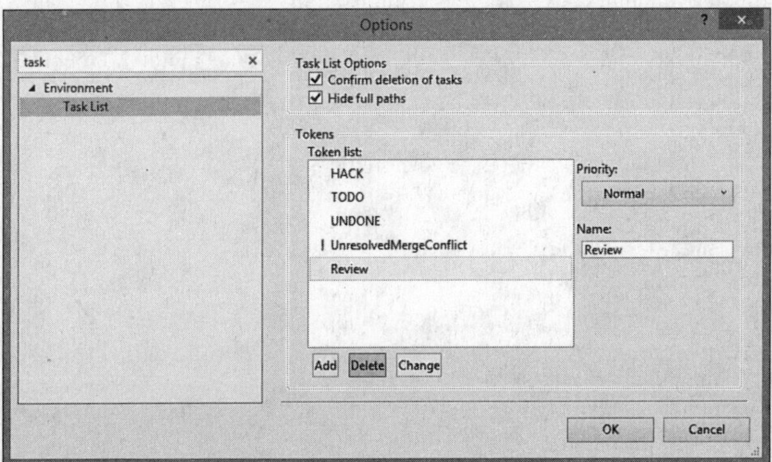

FIGURE 7.28 Adding a custom comment task token.

NOTE

Visual Studio's automation model provides complete control over task lists. Using the exposed automation objects such as `TaskList` and `TaskListEvents`, you can, for example, programmatically add or remove tasks from the list; respond to a task being added, edited, or even selected; and control the linking between a task and an editor.

Summary

Visual Studio carries a staggering number of features designed to boost your productivity. This chapter described the many facets of the IntelliSense technology, ranging from statement completion to the new light bulb tool, and you learned how to work with the various IntelliSense features to both write code faster and improve the quality of your code.

We covered how to navigate and browse through sometimes complicated and congested code files.

We also introduced code snippets and discussed the different types of code snippets and their usefulness.

Finally, we covered how to use the Task List window to its fullest potential to help organize and track the various to-do items inherent with any programming project.

From a productivity standpoint, Visual Studio truly is more than the sum of its parts. In synergy with one another, each of these features knocks down substantial hurdles and eases pain points for developers, regardless of their backgrounds, skill levels, or language preferences.

CHAPTER 8

Testing Code

IN THIS CHAPTER

- ▶ Unit Testing Basics
- ▶ The Unit Testing Framework
- ▶ Testing Web Applications
- ▶ Creating Ordered Tests

Developers have always been responsible for testing their code before it is released to testers or users. In years past, this meant walking through every line of code in the debugger (including all conditions and errors). To do so, you often had to create test-harness applications that mimicked the functionality required to execute your code. Stepping through all your code in a debugger made for a fine goal but was not always realized (and was difficult to verify). In fact, the entire exercise was often skipped during code changes and updates. In addition, this process made it difficult to see if your code changes affected other parts of the system. The result was lower-quality builds sent to testers and users and thus higher defect rates and wasted time going back and forth between developers and testers.

The unit test framework in Visual Studio provides a robust, automated means for developers to test code as they write it. Tests are saved and run again if any code changes. This helps with regressions and increases confidence in last-minute fixes, refactoring, and late additions.

This chapter covers the basics of unit testing and the details of the unit test framework. With this information in hand, you are on your way to realizing the benefits of automated, developer testing, including fewer bugs, easier to understand code, and additional confidence in code changes.

INTELLITEST

Visual Studio 2015 introduces IntelliTest. This feature examines your code and generates a suite of unit tests and even test data on your behalf. This is especially useful for developers that work with an existing code base that does not have an associated set of unit tests. IntelliTest will explore your code and analyze every conditional branch for a possible test.

IntelliTest is part of Visual Studio Enterprise 2015 and not Professional (the focus of this book). You can learn more at: https://msdn.microsoft.com/en-us/library/dn823749.

Unit Testing Basics

Unit testing in Visual Studio is about creating tests methods that run the code inside the working layers of your application and validate the expected results—even thrown exceptions. This includes testing the many classes that make up your business and data domain. The user interface domain is typically just markup (depending on your architecture approach), and the markup is tested manually (or through tools such as CodedUI which is in Visual Studio Enterprise). The focus of unit tests is writing code to test the functional code you write. In this section, we cover the basics of writing unit tests. We drill in on these basics in coming sections.

NOTE

Visual Studio Enterprise includes additional testing tools targeted at the test team. These include tools for creating and tracking test plans, test cases, and bugs. They also include tools for testing the user interface and doing performance and load testing.

Creating a Test Project

Your unit tests must exist inside a test project. This is a project that has the right references to the unit testing framework and the configuration required to be run via the test tool built inside Visual Studio. There are two primary ways you can initiate the creation of a unit test project: You can create an empty test project from scratch, or you can automatically generate unit tests into a new test project for existing code. We start with the first option.

The Test Project Template

You create a new test project in Visual Studio through the Add New Project dialog box (File, New, Project). Inside this dialog box, you navigate to the Test node under your preferred language, as shown in Figure 8.1. Notice that you can put your test project inside a new solution or an existing solution. In most cases, you add test projects to existing solutions because they must reference the projects within your solution.

The recommended naming convention for test projects is to end the project name with "Test" as in `BusinessDomainUnitTests`. This also helps you recognize your unit tests versus other project types or even other test project types such as Coded UI Tests. This is useful not only in Solution Explorer but as part of the TFS build setup configuration; there, you select test projects for the build process to execute automatically as part of the build.

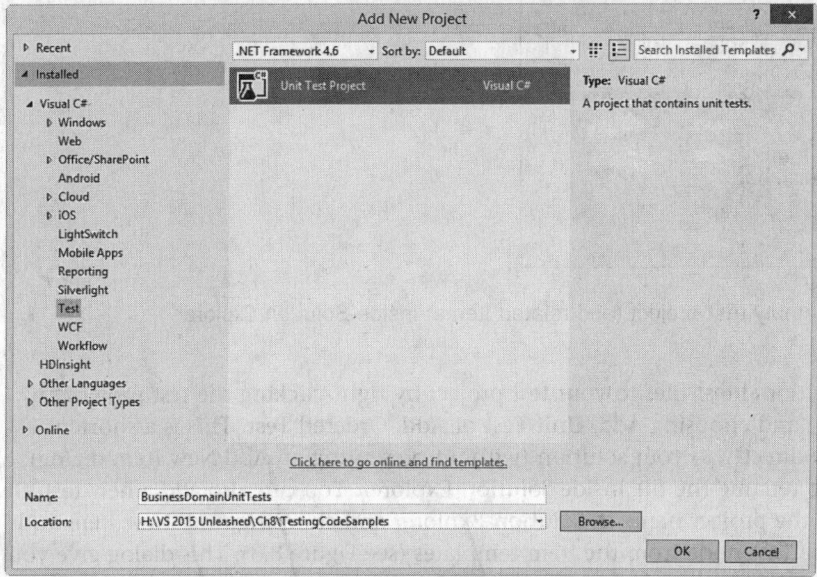

FIGURE 8.1 Add a new test project to your solution using the Add New Project dialog.

TIP

You should define a policy on how many test projects you want to create for your solution. Typically, you create a test project as a one-to-one ratio with a project you want to test. For example, if you have a project for your business objects and another project for your data services, you might create two test projects (one for each). This is not required; it just makes for an easily understood organization of your code.

A similar approach holds true for test classes. You should create a single test class for each class you have in your target project you want to test. For example, if you are creating a test project for your business domain objects that includes a `Customer` and an `Order` object, you should create a `CustomerTest` and `OrderTest` class. Again, this is not required; rather, it makes for a good, logical organization of your code.

The Test Project

Visual Studio sets a reference to the unit test framework (`Microsoft.VisualStudio.QualityTools.UnitTestFramework`) when you create a new test project. In addition, it creates a test class for you that encapsulate your unit tests. Figure 8.2 shows the default project files included in the unit test project along with the key references.

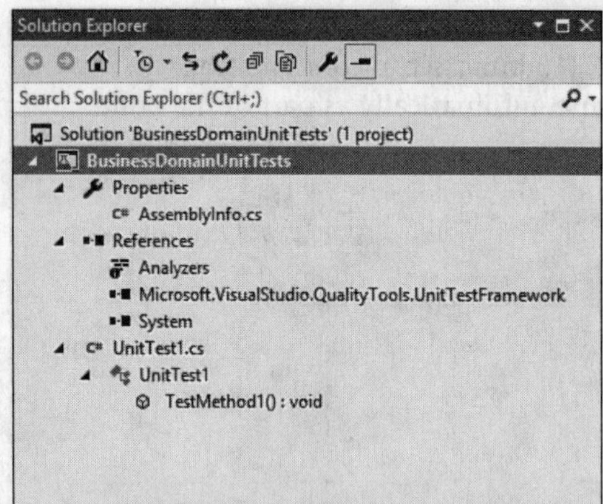

FIGURE 8.2 An empty test project (and related items) inside Solution Explorer.

You can add additional test files to your test project by right-clicking the test project in Solution Explorer and choosing Add, Unit Test or Add, Ordered Test. This is a shortcut that adds the file directly to your solution (without presenting an Add New Item dialog). You then have to rename the file inside Solution Explorer. You can also add a new test file by right-clicking the project name in Solution Explorer and choosing Add, New Item and then selecting the Test node from the item templates (see Figure 8.3). This dialog give you three test type choices:

- **Basic Unit Test**—This template creates a unit test class that is almost a blank file. It includes just the basic lines of code required to get started (`using` statement, namespace definition, class definition, and blank test method.
- **Ordered Test**—This template enables you to create a sequential list of tests to be executed as a group. (See "Creating Ordered Tests" later in this chapter.)
- **Unit Test**—This template creates a unit test class that includes stubbed out methods for managing a `TestContext`, calling various test startup and clean up events, and more (including comments).

The Test Menu The Test menu and the test toolbar access the common testing features, including running tests, managing test settings, and accessing the Test Explorer window. Figure 8.4 shows the Test menu open in the IDE. We touch on the details of all these actions shortly. But first, let's explore how to create tests.

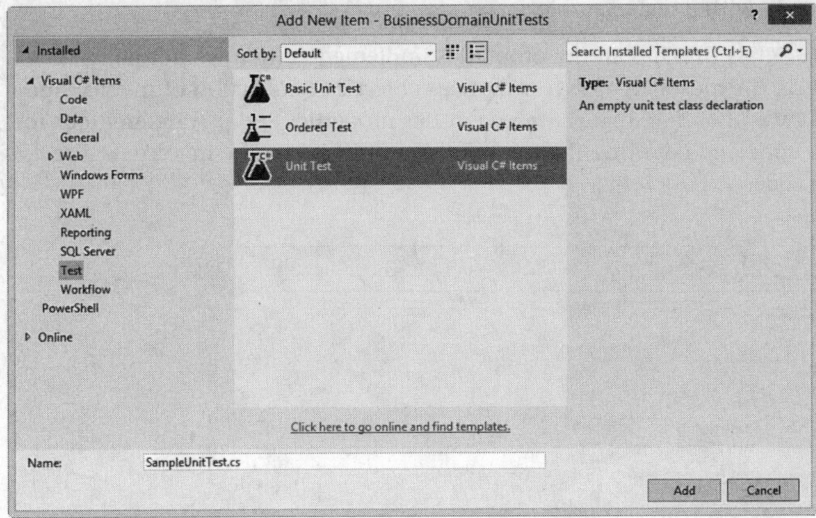

FIGURE 8.3 Add new unit test (test class) to your project.

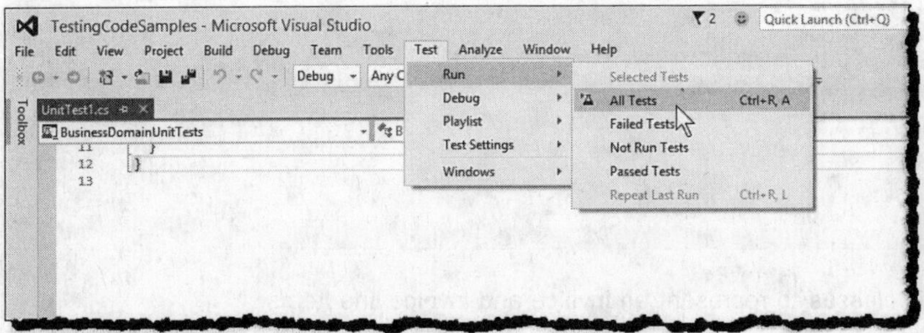

FIGURE 8.4 Use the Test menu to access developer testing features.

Writing a Unit Test

Recall that a unit test is simply test code you write to call your application code. This test code asserts that various conditions are either `true` or `false` as a result of the call to your application code. The test either passes or fails based on the results of these assertions. If, for example, you expect an outcome to be `true` and it turns out to be `false`, that test would be a failed test.

In broad strokes, there are three steps to creating a typical unit test:

1. Apply the `TestMethod` attribute to the method you want to be treated as a test.
2. Write code in your test method to execute the code you want to test, passing in known values if there are parameters.
3. Write assertions in your test code to evaluate the results of your test.

Let's look more closely with a real example.

Consider an `Invoice` class that has all the properties implemented that we normally associate with an invoice. It exposes an `InvoiceLineItem` object as a collection of invoice line items (represented by a `List<InvoiceLineItem>`). It has properties and private methods for getting the invoice total and counting the total number of items on the invoice. Figure 8.5 shows this sample code.

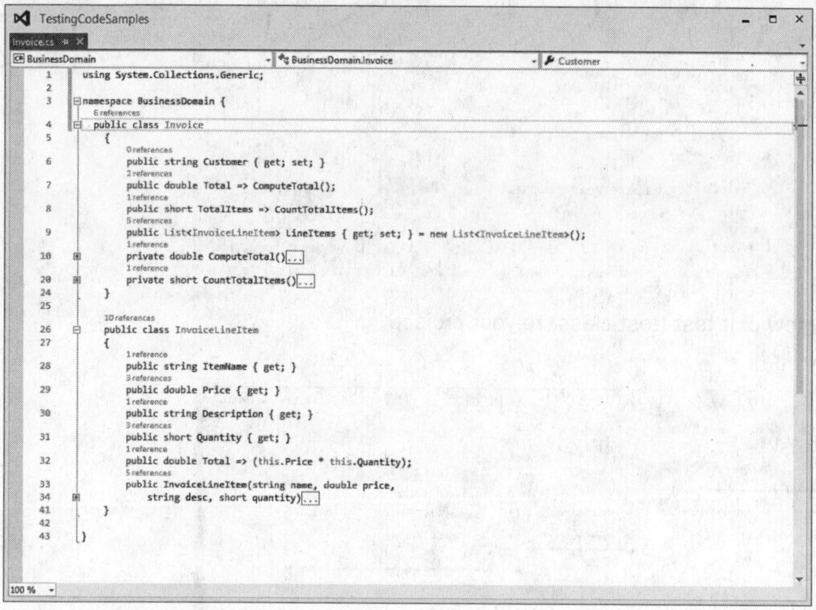

```
using System.Collections.Generic;

namespace BusinessDomain {
    public class Invoice
    {
        public string Customer { get; set; }
        public double Total => ComputeTotal();
        public short TotalItems => CountTotalItems();
        public List<InvoiceLineItem> LineItems { get; set; } = new List<InvoiceLineItem>();
        private double ComputeTotal()...
        private short CountTotalItems()...
    }

    public class InvoiceLineItem
    {
        public string ItemName { get; }
        public double Price { get; }
        public string Description { get; }
        public short Quantity { get; }
        public double Total => (this.Price * this.Quantity);
        public InvoiceLineItem(string name, double price,
            string desc, short quantity)...
    }
}
```

FIGURE 8.5 Basic classes to represent an invoice and invoice line items.

NOTE

The code for this chapter is available for download from the website associated with this book: informit.com/title/9780672337369.

Let's dig into the `ComputeTotal` method. This method cycles through the line items on the invoice and calculates a total price for the invoice (without shipping and tax, of course).

```
private double ComputeTotal()
{
    double total = 0;
    foreach (InvoiceLineItem item in LineItems)
    {
        total += item.Price * item.Quantity;
    }
        return total;
}
```

Now let's see how we can add a unit test that will validate whether the invoice total property returns correctly when accessed. To do that, we create a new unit test project, as previously discussed. We then add a reference to the project containing the `Invoice` object. (Right-click the References folder under the unit test project, select Add Reference, and then pick the project containing the invoice class from within the list of projects; in this case, the project assembly name is `BusinessDomain`.)

NOTE

You don't need to have access to a target object's project or source code to write a unit test. You can add a reference instead to an assembly that implements the code you want to test.

With the initial structure set up, now we can actually write the unit test. One approach to organizing a unit test is to use the arrange, act, and assert (AAA) pattern. This pattern advocates a code structure that initializes the necessary objects and fields (arrange), calls the method that you want to test (act), and finally verifies that everything has worked as expected (assert). Listing 8.1 shows our test method, organized with the AAA pattern.

LISTING 8.1 Testing `Invoice.Total` with a unit test

```
using System;
using Microsoft.VisualStudio.TestTools.UnitTesting;
using BusinessDomain;

namespace BusinessDomainUnitTests
{
    [TestClass]
    public class InvoiceTests
    {
        [TestMethod]
        public void ComputeTotalTest()
        {
            //arrange-------------------
            Invoice invoice = new Invoice();

            //note: could store prices and quantities as variables in our code
            //      and then calculate the total here to make tests safer
            double expectedTotal = 12;

            //act-----------------------
            invoice.LineItems.Add(new InvoiceLineItem(
                "Prod 1", 1.75, "First item description", 1));
```

```
            invoice.LineItems.Add(new InvoiceLineItem(
                "Prod 2", 5.25, "Second item description", 1));

            invoice.LineItems.Add(new InvoiceLineItem(
                "Prod 3", 2.50, "Third item description", 2));

            //assert-------------------
            Assert.AreEqual(expectedTotal, invoice.Total,
                "Total invoice not computed correctly.");
        }
    }
}
```

Notice that there is nothing special with respect to this code. It looks like any other method that you would craft with C#. This is because unit testing with Visual Studio is attribute driven. What distinguishes your unit test code and signals it as an actual unit test to Visual Studio are the attributes (`TestClass` and `TestMethod`) added at the class and method levels. These attributes are automatically added for you when you create a unit test project, but there is nothing stopping you from writing a unit test class from the ground up and just adding the attributes manually.

The test as written should pass, as you will see in the next section. However, we will look at additional tests a developer might write to ensure their code passes other conditions, such as when the invoice list does not contain items or is null.

Running Your Tests

As you saw back in Figure 8.4, the Test menu is used to run your unit tests. There are many options here. You can select individual tests to run, or you can run them all. You can also choose to run only failed tests, passed tests, tests not yet run, or just rerun your last run tests.

The Debug selection on the Test menu will run tests with the debugger activated. This allows you to break into the debugger if a test fails and is useful if you are actively troubleshooting code through tests.

NOTE

When you run a test project, any referenced projects are recompiled along with your test project.

Viewing Test Results

When you run your tests, the results are shown in the Test Explorer window. The Test Results window provides an overview of which tests passed and which failed. Figure 8.6 shows the results of running our unit test of `Invoice.Total`: It passed!

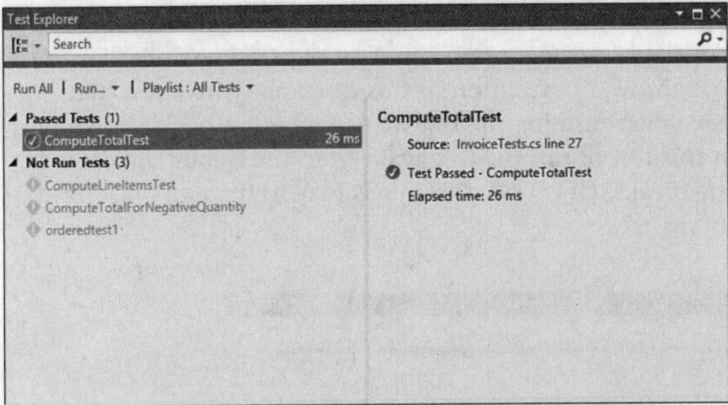

FIGURE 8.6 The Test Explorer window showing the test passed.

Note that the Test Explorer window is not only a tool for exploring test results; it is also the primary way within Visual Studio to categorize/organize tests. It can also directly run tests (arguably an easier way to execute tests than using the Test menu). For example, you can use the Group By button (second from left on the toolbar, upper right) for showing tests by class, outcome, project, and more.

To see the outcome of a given test, you just click on it from the left side of Test Explorer. This is useful if you are managing a lot of test results. You can see information regarding the test name, whether it passed or failed, the duration of the test, and the start and end time. The results pane also shows you the stack trace for any failed unit test code and includes a link to the unit test source code file.

Working with a Failed Test

The previous test succeeded. However, good developers will write multiple tests to verify their code meets other conditions, such as what happens when you pass null values, large values, negative values, and so on. For example, consider the following test added to the `InvoiceTests` class.

```
[TestMethod]
public void ComputeTotalForNegativeQuantity()
{
    Invoice invoice = new Invoice();

    invoice.LineItems.Add(new InvoiceLineItem(
        "Prod 1", 1.75, "First item description", -1));

    Assert.AreEqual(0, invoice.Total,
        "Total invoice not computed correctly.");
}
```

This test passes a negative quantity for the invoice line item. If your code is working correctly, suppose the line item should calculate zero based on our business rules for this example (alternatively, we could throw an exception in this case and write a test that expects an exception). However, when running the test we expose an error, as shown in Figure 8.7. We can track down this test or run the test again from the Debug option to be taken right to the spot our code breaks. Of course, this bug is easy to fix, and once fixed you can rerun the test to verify the fix.

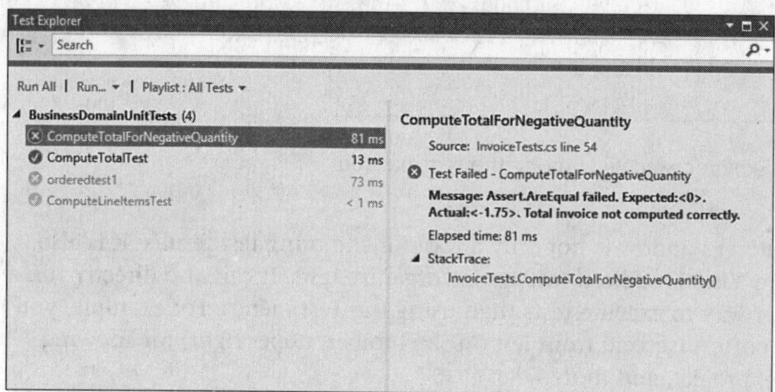

FIGURE 8.7 One passed and one failed test (and 2 not run) in Test Explorer.

Controlling Test Settings

Previous editions of the test framework used a `.testsettings` file to manage advance test settings such as deploying test data along with your tests. However, in 2012 Microsoft introduced a newer version of the test framework and mostly did away with the `.testsettings` files. You can still use them, but if you do, your tests will be run under the old unit test framework (and thus execute more slowly; also, the older test framework does not allow tests from third-party frameworks).

The recommended solution is to use the default configuration of your unit tests whenever possible. If you need to use test configuration files, you can add them to your project from the Test menu (Test, Test Settings, Select Test Settings File). You can then set the Copy to Output property for those settings files. You can also use `DeploymentItemAttribute` on a method you want to use to make your deployments. There are also many setup and teardown attributes you can use to configure your tests. (See the next section, "The Unit Testing Framework.")

NOTE

Visual Studio 2015 allows you to use `.runsettings` to configure things like code coverage (Enterprise only) analysis and deployment directories. For more information on how to use these advanced settings files, search MSDN for "Specifying Test Settings for Visual Studio Tests."

The Unit Testing Framework

The unit testing framework is part of Visual Studio (and not the .NET Framework itself). Unit testing in Visual Studio includes a set of framework classes, the tools, and the execution host. You can find the namespace that contains the unit testing framework classes at `Microsoft.VisualStudio.TestTools.UnitTesting`. Developers are most interested in the attribute classes and the `Assert` class in this namespace. This section highlights the core usage scenarios for both the attribute and the assertion classes (among others).

NOTE

The namespace for unit testing is `Microsoft.VisualStudio.TestTools.UnitTesting`. However, you set a reference to the assembly `Microsoft.VisualStudio.QualityTools.UnitTestFramework`.

The `TestContext` Class

The unit test framework contains a class that is used to store information pertaining to executing tests. This class is called `TestContext`. You use the properties of this class to get information about your running tests, including the path to the test directory, a URL to the executing test (in the case of ASP.NET unit tests), and data-binding information such as the data connection or the current row of data for the executing test class. There are also a couple useful methods of this class for things like writing trace messages. The test context information is stored inside properties of this class. The key properties and methods are defined inside Table 8.1.

TABLE 8.1 `TestContext` Key Properties and Methods

Property / Method	Description
`CurrentTestOutcome`	Enables you to determine the outcome of the last test that executed. This is useful inside methods marked as `TestCleanup`. (See "The Test Attribute Classes.")
`DataConnection`	Enables you to view the connection string used by any data-driven unit tests. (See "Creating Data-Driven Unit Tests.")
`DataRow`	Enables you to access columns in a row of data when working with data-bound unit tests. (See "Creating Data-Driven Unit Tests.")
`RequestedPage`	Provides access to the `Page` object for the requested page in an ASP.NET unit test. (See "Unit Testing ASP.NET Pages.")
`TestRunDirectory`, `DeploymentDirectory`, `TestResultsDirectory`	The `TestRunDirectory` gets the path to the top-level directory containing your deployed test files and results. `DeploymentDirectory` takes you directly to the directory where your test run files are deployed. `TestResultsDirectory` is a subdirectory of `DeploymentDirectory`.

Property / Method	Description
`TestRunResultsDirectory`, `ResultsDirectory`	`TestRunRusultsDirectory` gets the path to the top-level directory where your test results are written. `ResultsDirectory` is a subdirectory where your actual results are stored.
`TestName`	Enables access to the name of the currently executing test.
`WriteLine()`	Use this method to write trace messages from your unit tests to your test results information.
`AddResultFile`	This method allows you to add additional files to the results of your test execution. This is useful if you need these external files to better evaluate your results after execution.
`BeginTimer() / EdnTimer()`	Use these methods to set time information for executing the code called by the unit test. These transaction times can then be output as part of load test results (load testing is an Enterprise feature).

`TestContext` is not accessible to your code by default. You access `TestContext` by first defining a field and a property named `TestContext`. The unit test framework automatically creates an instance of a `TestContext` object when it runs your tests. It then looks for a `TestContext` property in your source code. If it finds it, the framework assigns an instance of `TestContext` to your property. You can then use your property to access information about the executing test context. The following code shows how you might define the `TestContext` property in a C# unit test.

```
private TestContext testContextInstance;

public TestContext TestContext {
  get
  {
    return testContextInstance;
  }
  set {
    testContextInstance = value;
  }
}
```

NOTE

Some attribute classes require that you define a parameter of type `TestContext` to your decorated method. This is true for `ClassInitialize` (as discussed later). In this case, the unit test framework automatically passes an instance of a `TestContext` object to your method when it executes.

The Test Attribute Classes

The unit tests you write are run by Visual Studio using the unit test execution host. This host has to examine your code and find the unit tests within it and run them accordingly. To do so, the host relies on attributes. Recall that an attribute is used to provide metadata about your code. Other code (such as the unit test host) can use reflection to determine various bits of information about your code.

As you've seen in the brief samples thus far, you signify unit tests by decorating your code with the attribute classes defined inside the unit testing namespace. For example, a test class has the `TestClass` attribute; a test method is indicated using the `TestMethod` attribute. Table 8.2 presents a list of the most common attribute classes found in the unit testing namespace.

TABLE 8.2 Visual Studio Test Attribute Classes

Test	Description
`AssemblyCleanup`	Used to define a method that should be run after all the tests in a given assembly have been executed by the framework. This is useful if you need to clean up resources after all tests have executed. Note that only one method in a given assembly can contain this attribute.
`AssemblyInitialize`	Used to define a method that should be run before any tests in a given assembly have been executed by the framework. This is useful if you need to initialize resources for all tests in an assembly. Note that only one method in a given assembly can contain this attribute.
`ClassCleanup`	Used to indicate a method that should be run once after all tests are executed in a given test class. This can be useful if you need to reset the system state (such as a database) after your tests have completed.
`ClassInitialize`	Used to indicate a method that should be run once by the test execution host before any other tests are run in the given test class. This can be useful if you need to reset a database or execute any code to prepare the test environment. Requires that your method take a parameter of type `TestContext`.
`DataSource`	Used to provide connection information for a data-driven unit test. (See "Creating Data-Driven Unit Tests.")
`DeploymentItem`	Used to indicate any additional files (`.dll`, `.txt`, or otherwise) that need to be deployed to the folder in which your tests run.
`ExpectedException`	Used to indicate that a certain exception is supposed to be thrown by the code called within the test method. This type of test method is considered successful if the given exception type is received as part of the test execution; otherwise, the test fails. This capability is useful for testing expected error conditions in your code. (See "Testing Your Exceptions.")

Test	Description
`HostType`	Used if you want to override the default test host (Visual Studio). In most test scenarios, you do not need to use this attribute. If, however, you write tests to run in another host process (such as ASP.NET), you can use this attribute (along with `UrlToTest` and `AspNetDevelopmentServerHost`).
`Ignore`	Added to a `TestMethod` to indicate that method should not be run by the test execution host.
`TestClass`	Used to indicate that a given class is a test class that contains one or more unit tests (test methods).
`TestCleanup`	Used to indicate a method that should be run once after each test method is executed. You can use this method to do any cleanup after each test method runs in a given test class. Cleanup at the class level can be done via the `ClassCleanup` attribute.
`TestInitialize`	Used to indicate that a given method should be run once before each test method is executed. This capability is useful if you need to reset the system state before each test method within a given test class. If you only need to initialize for all the methods in a given test class, use `ClassInitialize`.
`TestProperty`	Used to define a property (name and value pair) attribute to a test method. This property information can be read inside the code of the test method.
`TestMethod`	Used to decorate a method as a unit test inside a test class. Test methods must have no return value (void). They succeed or fail based on error conditions and assertions. Test methods cannot take parameters because the host cannot pass parameters to the method. There are ways to simulate parameters, however. See "Creating Data-Driven Unit Tests" for more information.
`Timeout`	Used to indicate a timeout (in milliseconds) for a given test method. If the test exceeds this timeout period, it is stopped and considered failed.

You can see from Table 8.2 that a number of attribute classes give you control over your unit tests. Figure 8.8 shows our `InvoiceTests` unit test class with a few additions. We have created a `TestContext` instance. We have also stubbed out code for initializing the test class and cleaning up following the test run. The next step is to write code inside each of these test methods.

Unit Test Setup and Teardown

A good practice for your unit tests is to write them for a known state of the system; this includes the database, files, and anything that makes up the entire system. This ensures that developers can rely on these items being there when they write their tests. Of course, the tests themselves often disrupt this state. You might have a test that deletes data, changes it, adds new records, and the like. In this case, you need to be able to reinitialize the state of the system prior to executing your tests (or after executing your tests) to ensure both a steady state to test against and a one-click test run experience for developers (another good practice for unit testing).

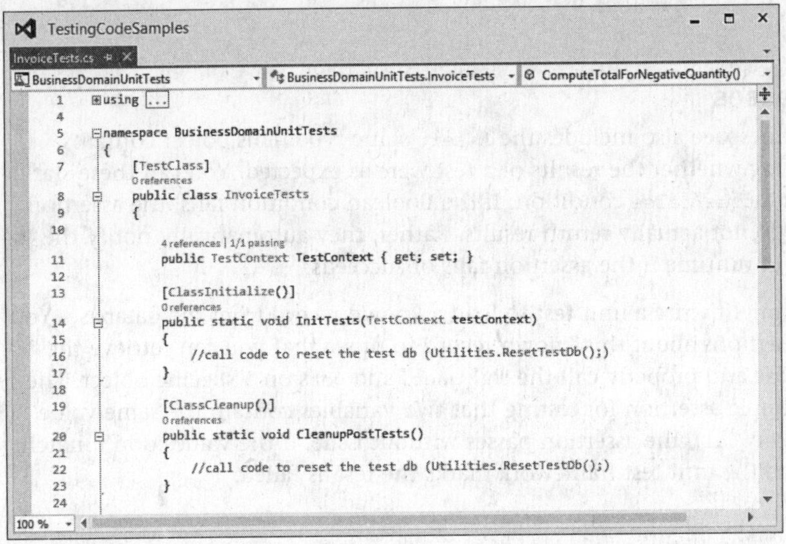

TestingCodeSamples

InvoiceTests.cs

BusinessDomainUnitTests | BusinessDomainUnitTests.InvoiceTests | ComputeTotalForNegativeQuantity()

```
using ...

namespace BusinessDomainUnitTests
{
    [TestClass]
    0 references
    public class InvoiceTests
    {

        4 references | 1/1 passing
        public TestContext TestContext { get; set; }

        [ClassInitialize()]
        0 references
        public static void InitTests(TestContext testContext)
        {
            //call code to reset the test db (Utilities.ResetTestDb();)
        }

        [ClassCleanup()]
        0 references
        public static void CleanupPostTests()
        {
            //call code to reset the test db (Utilities.ResetTestDb();)
        }

```

100 %

FIGURE 8.8 The invoice test class with stubbed out methods for class initialize and cleanup.

You typically need to write code to keep your system in a steady state. This code might copy a known good test database down to the `test` directory (you could also do this with a `DeploymentItem` attribute); reset your database using SQL; use a data generation plan to create your database; copy files; or verify other deployment items.

The code to reset your system is specific to your environment. However, to ensure this code is called when your tests run, you have a few attribute classes with which to work: `ClassInitialize` and `ClassCleanup`, or `TestInitialize` and `TestCleanup`. The former set are run at the start (or end) of a test run in the entire unit test class. The latter are run before (or after) each test executes in a given test class.

In most cases, you run initialize and cleanup at the class level. As an example, if you had a `Utilities` class that included a method to reset your database, you could ensure it is called by marking a method as `ClassInitialize`. Note that this method takes a `TestContext` object (which is passed to it by the unit test framework). A good practice is to reset the system again after the unit tests execute. The following code shows an example of two test methods doing both setup and cleanup.

```
[ClassInitialize()]
public static void InitTests(TestContext testContext)
{
  Utilities.ResetTestDb();
}
```

```
[ClassCleanup()]
public static void CleanupPostTests()
{
  Utilities.ResetTestDb();
}
```

The `Assert` Classes

The `UnitTesting` namespace also includes the `Assert` static type. This object contains methods for evaluating whether the results of a test were as expected. You call these static methods and expect a `true/false` condition. If the Boolean condition fails, the assertion fails. The assertions do not actually return results. Rather, they automatically notify the unit test framework at runtime if the assertion fails or succeeds.

As an example, you might write a unit test to load a known record from the database. You would then write assertions about this known record to prove that you can retrieve the data from the database and properly call the right `sets` and `gets` on a specific object. The following shows a simple assertion for testing that two variables contain the same value. If the values match (`AreEqual`), the assertion passes without issue. If the values don't match, the assertion fails and the unit test framework marks the test as failed.

```
Assert.AreEqual(cust.Id, customerId);
```

The `AreEqual` method is just one example of the many assertion methods available to you from the `Assert` class. For the most part, these assertion methods are variations on a concept: compare two values and determine the results. Table 8.3 provides a more complete list.

TABLE 8.3 Test Assertions

Test	Description
`AreEqual/AreNotEqual`	Used to test whether two values are equal to one another.
`AreSame/AreNotSame`	Used to test whether two objects' variables specify the same object.
`Equals`	Used to determine if two objects are equivalent.
`Fail`	Used to fail a condition without doing an evaluation. This might be useful if your evaluation is based on logic and you get to a point in your code where the logic represents a failed test.
`Inconclusive`	Used to indicate that a given test has not failed or succeeded (but has inconclusive results).
`IsInstanceOfType/ IsNotInstanceOfType`	Used to determine whether an object is of a specified type.
`IsNull/IsNotNull`	Used to test whether an object contains a null reference.
`IsTrue/IsFalse`	Used to test whether a condition is `true`.

Each assertion method has a number of overloads. These overloads enable you to compare various data types, such as strings, numeric values, objects, and generic collections of objects, to one another. In addition, there are overloads that enable you to simply do the assertion and those that both do the assertion and enable you to enter a message that is displayed when the assertion fails.

The `Assert` class also contains a version of the `AreEqual/AreNotEqual` methods that use a generic data type. These methods enable you to compare two generic types against one another for equality. In this case, you indicate the generic type using standard generic notation, `<T>` (or `(of T)` in VB), and pass the two generic types you want to compare. The following shows an example.

```
Assert.AreEqual<Invoice>(cust1, cust2);
```

Verifying Collections of Objects (CollectionAssert)

The `UnitTesting` namespace also contains the assertion classes, `CollectionAssert`. With it, you can verify the contents of collection classes. For instance, you can call the `Contains` method to assert whether a given collection contains a specific element (or `DoesNotContain`). You can use `AllItemsAreInstancesOfType` to check that a collection only contains like instances. You can compare two collections to see if they are equal (`AreEqual/AreNotEqual`) or simply equivalent; they have the same elements but might be in a different order (`AreEquivalent/AreNotEquivalent`).

Verifying Strings (StringAssert)

The `StringAssert` class contains methods for verifying strings and portions of strings. For example, the `Contains` method enables you to check that a string contains a specific substring. You can use the `StartsWith` method to assert whether a string begins with a certain set of characters or use `EndsWith` to check the ending of a string. Finally, the `Matches/DoesNotMatch` methods enable you to check whether a string matches a regular expression you define.

Testing Your Exceptions

You should write unit tests to verify your code behaves as expected in both positive and negative conditions. The positive conditions can be verified using the `Assert` methods, as discussed previously. However, many times you want to verify that your code returns the correct exception when you call or use it in a certain manner. In this case, you can decorate a test method with the `ExpectedException` attribute to test for specific error conditions.

The attribute takes the type of expected exception as a parameter. If the test method results in an exception being thrown and the type of that exception is as you defined in the attribute, the test is considered a success. If an exception is not thrown or an exception of a different type is thrown, the test is considered to have failed.

As an example, suppose that you want to test what happens when you try to create a new invoice that has incomplete details. In this case, your code might be written to throw a custom exception of type `InvalidInvoiceException`. You would then decorate your test method as follows.

```
[TestMethod()]
[ExpectedException(typeof(InvalidInvoiceException),
  "The Invalid Invoice Exception was not thrown.")]
public void Invoice_Is_Valid() {

  //create a bad, new invoice instance to test against
}
```

Notice that, in this code, if the exception is not thrown, there is an error message provided as the result of the test (`The Invalid Invoice Exception was not thrown`). This error message is an optional parameter of the `ExpectedException` attribute.

You can combine assertions with the `ExpectedException` attribute. In this case, both the assertions need to pass, and the exception needs to be thrown for the test method to be considered passed.

NOTE

The resulting exception must be of the same type as the expected exception. The resulting exception cannot, for instance, inherit from the expected exception. In this case, the test is considered to have failed.

Creating Data-Driven Unit Tests

Let's build on our knowledge of both basic unit testing concepts and the unit testing framework attribute classes and examine how to create a unit test that feeds off of a data source.

Looking back at Listing 8.1, you recall we had to manually define a few invoice objects in the "arrange" section of the test. This works out fine for the limited data we are dealing with here but would quickly become unmanageable if we wanted or needed a more expansive data set. In other words, instead of just testing with a scenario of adding two invoice lines, what if we wanted to add hundreds? And what if we wanted to dynamically populate those line items instead of hard-coding them in the test method? In these cases, you want to author the unit test in such a way that it derives its values from an actual data source.

The basic process for authoring the unit test remains the same, with the following tweaks:

1. Create the data source that will store the values to inject into the unit test.
2. Add a `TestContext` property (public) to the unit test class.
3. Add a reference to `System.Data` from the unit test project.
4. Add a `DataSource` attribute to the method to wire the data to the unit test method.

Let's put the data-driven scenario into action by adding another unit test method. This one tests whether the `InvoiceLineItem` object is successfully producing line item totals (that is, the product of the price and the quantity of each line). The test will be executed for each line item we add to the invoice via the data source.

Adding a Data Source

Any .NET accessible data source will work: a table in SQL Server, an object collection, an Excel file, a CSV file, an XML file, and so on. Because it is quick and easy to implement, let's store our invoice test data in a CSV file.

First we add a text file to the test project (right-click the project, select Add New Item, and then select the Text File item template); we name the file `InvoiceTestData.csv`.

Next, we enter the following values and save the file. Each line in the file represents an invoice line item. Fields are separated by commas, as in name, description, quantity, and price. Remember, you can download the code for this chapter from the website associated with this book: informit.com/title/9780672337369.

```
"Prod 1","line 1",2,2.50
"Prod 2","line 2",0,100
"Prod 3","line 3",10,1.25
"Prod 4","line 4",3,3.33
"Prod 5","line 5",1000,10
"Prod 6","line 6",2,5
"Prod 7","line 7",1,9.10
"Prod 8","line 8",5,5
"Prod 9","line 9",8,9.75
"Prod 10","line 10",20,2000
```

Because we have chosen to use a file to store our test data, we want to make sure that the file is deployed along with the unit test binaries as part of any build. The CSV file needs to be marked as `content`, and it needs its build action set to `Copy Always` or `Copy if newer`. To do this, right-click the file in the Solution Explorer window, and use the property window to change the Build Action and Copy to Output Directory values to the mentioned values.

With the file setup complete, let's write the data source attribute. The `DataSource` attribute class has three overloads. The first simply takes a single parameter: `dataSource-SettingName`. In this case, you are expected to pass the name of the data source settings as defined inside a configuration file. The second overload takes both a `connectionString` and a `tableName`. In this case, you pass a valid connection string to the `DataSource` and indicate the name of the table you intend to bind to the unit test. The final overload takes `providerInvariantName`, `connectionString`, `tableName`, and `dataAccessMethod`. The provider name is used to indicate the type of provider, such as a CSV provider, SQL Server, or similar. The connection string is based on your chosen provider and indicates how you access the data. The table name is the name of the table (or file) that contains your data. Finally, the data access method determines how your data is bound to the unit test: sequentially or randomly. The following shows an example for our CSV file.

```
[DataSource("Microsoft.VisualStudio.TestTools.DataSource.CSV",
   "InvoiceTestData.csv", "InvoiceTestData#csv",
   DataAccessMethod.Sequential)]
```

NOTE

The first parameter is using the built-in CSV data source parser that exists in the unit testing framework. The way you configure this data source for other sources, such as SQL tables or even Excel files, will vary. You should consult the Microsoft Developer Network (MSDN) documentation to determine exactly how to construct this attribute for your data source.

Notice that in the preceding code example, the first parameter of the `DataSource` attribute constructor defines the CSV provider. The next parameter is a connection string to the actual data file. The third parameter (`InvoiceTestData#csv`) simply indicates that the table name does not exist; it is the filename. The last parameter, the enumeration `DataAccessMethod.Sequential`, indicates that each row should be bound to the unit test in sequential order.

Because we are deploying a file as a data source here, we need one additional attribute, `DeploymentItem`, to tell the unit testing framework what specific deployed file it should seek. That brings us to three attributes for this test method, as follows.

```
[TestMethod]
[DataSource("Microsoft.VisualStudio.TestTools.DataSource.CSV",
   "InvoiceTestData.csv", "InvoiceTestData#csv",
   DataAccessMethod.Sequential)]
[DeploymentItem("InvoiceTestData.csv")]
```

With the attributes in place, we can write our test method. See Listing 8.2 for our final product. Each row within our data source is accessed via the `TestContext` property, which we added to our unit test class. Because we have attributed our method correctly, it will be called once for every row in our data source.

We extract the values from the row (item number, description, quantity, and price) within the “arrange” section, and then we create a new `InvoiceLine` object using those values. Within the “act” section, we create the `LineItem` instance and store off the line item total that it produced. Finally, in the “assert” section, we compare the total from the `LineItem` object with the total that we manually computed. If they are equal, our code has passed the unit test. Note, you might also put the expected value directly in your test data.

LISTING 8.2 Driving a Unit Test Using a CSV File

```
[TestMethod]
[DataSource("Microsoft.VisualStudio.TestTools.DataSource.CSV",
   "InvoiceTestData.csv", "InvoiceTestData#csv",
   DataAccessMethod.Sequential)]
[DeploymentItem("InvoiceTestData.csv")]
```

```
public void ComputeLineItemsTest()
{

    //arrange ---------------------------
    string name = Convert.ToString(TestContext.DataRow[0]);
    string desc = Convert.ToString(TestContext.DataRow[1]);
    short qty = Convert.ToInt16(TestContext.DataRow[2]);
    double price = Convert.ToDouble(TestContext.DataRow[3]);

    double expected = qty * price;

    //act
    InvoiceLineItem line = new InvoiceLineItem(name, price, desc, qty);
    double actual = line.Total;

    //assert ---------------------------
    Assert.AreEqual(expected, actual, "Line total is incorrect.");

}
```

Figure 8.9 shows the results of newly minted unit tests. Notice the data-driven unit tests are executed once for every row in the data source CSV file.

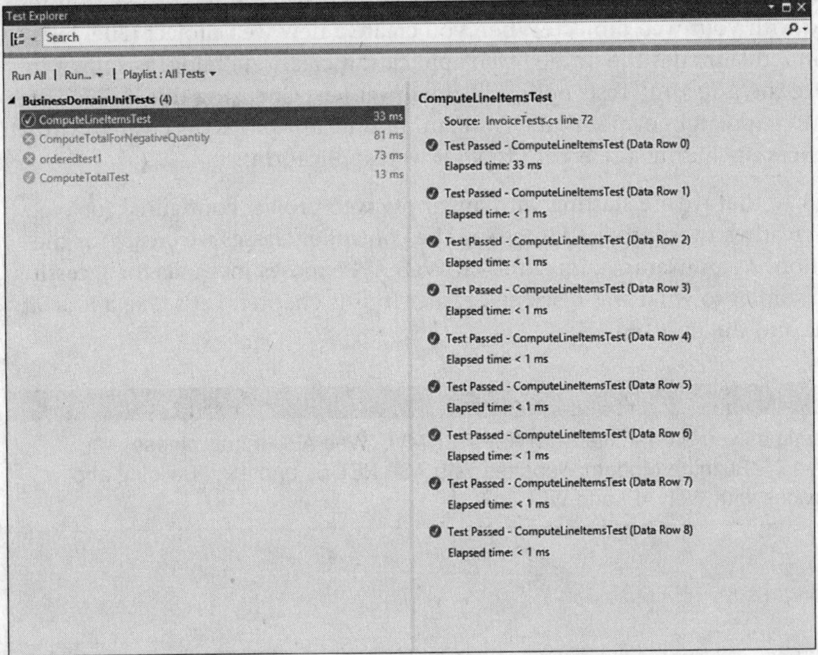

FIGURE 8.9 Data-drive unit tests results in Test Explorer.

NOTE

You may want to store your data source connection in a configuration file (`App.config`). The unit test framework supports this scenario. For a walkthrough, see "Using a Configuration File to Define a Data Source" inside MSDN.

Testing Web Applications

Modern web applications separate user experience markup from the code that responds to requests and serves views to the user. This separation makes web code much more testable (as opposed to code files mixed with markup and server-side code). As an example, the ASP.NET Model-View-Controller (MVC) and web application programming interface (API) models use controllers as C# classes to respond to Hypertext Transfer Protocol (HTTP) requests and return results. This structure makes writing unit tests against controller classes a straightforward process.

There are times, however, when you need to write tests against actual pages running on the web server. Visual Studio supports this scenario, too, allowing you to write tests that have access to the server state, such as Page and Session. This section takes a look at both scenarios. For more information on writing web applications, see Part V of this book, "Building Web Applications."

Unit Testing MVC and Web API Projects

The ASP.NET MVC and Web API project templates include the option to create a unit test project associated with your web project. When you create a new web project (File, New Project), Visual Studio launches the unified web application creation dialog, as shown in Figure 8.10. Notice the Add Unit Tests option in the lower left. Checking this box for the MVC and Web API templates ensures that a companion unit test project is created with all the proper references (including a reference to your web application).

Notice in Figure 8.10 that we are starting with an empty web project configured for Web API. We are also creating a test project for testing the controller classes we create for the Web API application. As an example, imagine our Web API exposes methods for accessing an invoice object similar to what was discussed earlier in this chapter. Let's take a look at the Web API code and the unit test.

NOTE

This section assumes you are familiar with ASP.NET MVC/Web API. If not, please check Chapters 17, "Building Modern Websites with ASP.NET 5" and 19, "Building and Consuming Services with Web API and WCF."

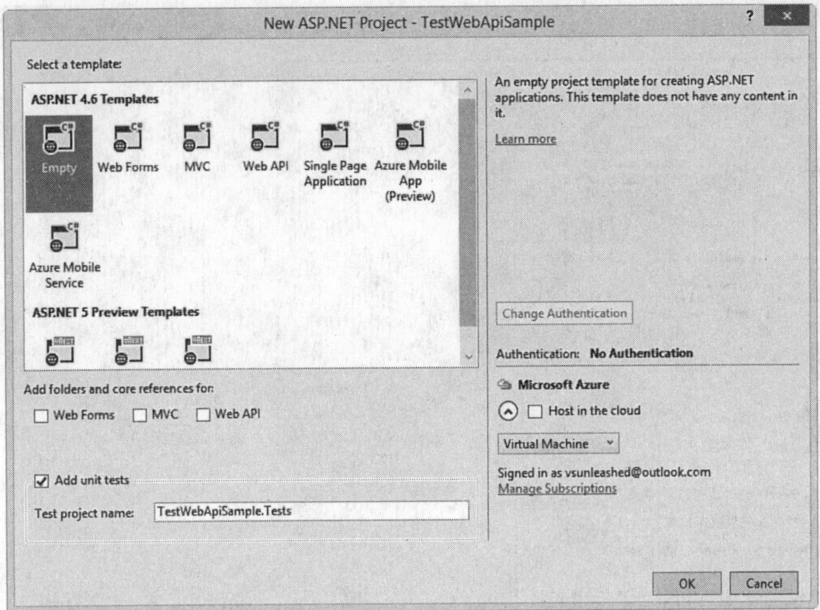

FIGURE 8.10 You can include a unit test project with your ASP.NET application.

The Web API Model and Controller

Before writing the unit test, we must have something to test. In this example, we get started by adding a model to the Web API project. You can do so by navigating to the project in Solution Explorer and right-clicking the `Models` folder. Here we choose Add, New Item. From the New Item dialog, we select a class and name it `Invoice`. We then write code to represent the invoice object and invoice line items as shown in Figure 8.11. (You can get this code as a sample from the book download.)

The next step is to write a controller for serving up HTTP web services around the invoice model. The public members of this controller will be exposed as services for HTTP clients such as browsers, mobile devices, and desktop applications.

To get started, inside Solution Explorer, right-click the Controllers folder and choose Add, Controller. This will launch the Add Scaffold dialog; from here, we choose the Web API empty controller. This will create a simple controller class that inherits from `System.Web.Http.ApiController`.

We now need to add HTTP services for accessing the invoice. In this example, we will create two services: `GetInvoice` and `GetInvoiceLineItems`. Both services use an internal method to simulate (with a `switch` statement) looking up these domain items from a database. Figure 8.12 shows the two services and the stubs for the private lookup methods. These are typical, albeit simple, web services you would create using Web API. (Again, see Chapter 19 for details.)

```
using System;
using System.Collections.Generic;
using System.Linq;
using System.Web;

namespace TestWebApi.Models
{
    public class Invoice
    {
        public int Id { get; set; }
        public string Customer { get; set; }
        public double Total { get; set; }

        public Invoice(int id, string customer, double total)...
    }

    public class InvoiceLineItem
    {
        public string ItemName { get; set; }
        public double Price { get; set; }
        public short Quantity { get; set; }
        public double LineTotal { get; set; }

        public InvoiceLineItem(string name, double price,
            short quantity)...
    }

}
```

FIGURE 8.11 The `Invoice` model used by the sample Web API application.

```
using System.Collections.Generic;
using System.Web.Http;
using TestWebApi.Models;

namespace TestWebApi.Controllers {
    public class InvoiceController : ApiController
    {

        public IHttpActionResult GetInvoice(int invoiceId)
        {
            Invoice invoice = LookupInvoice(invoiceId);
            if (invoice == null)
            {
                return NotFound();
            }
            return Ok(invoice);
        }

        public IEnumerable<InvoiceLineItem> GetInvoiceLineItems(int invoiceId)
        {
            return LookupInvoiceLineItems(invoiceId);
        }

        //simulate looking up an invoice from the db
        private Invoice LookupInvoice(int invoideId)...

        //simulate looking up invoice line items from the db
        private List<InvoiceLineItem> LookupInvoiceLineItems(int invoideId)...
    }
}
```

FIGURE 8.12 The `Invoice` model used by the sample Web API application.

The Controller Unit Test

Before we can create a unit test for the Web API controller, we must install and reference key components of the Web API. Visual Studio did not automatically do these tasks for us in the version of the project we created (Empty, Web API + unit tests). We can accomplish this task through NuGet.

Right-click Reference under the unit test project inside Solution Explorer and choose Manage NuGet Packages. This will launch the NuGet Package Manager as shown in Figure 8.13. Here we search for the Web API package by typing `asp.net web api` into the search box (upper-right of Figure 8.13). Next, select `Microsoft.AspNet.WebApi.Core` and choose Install.

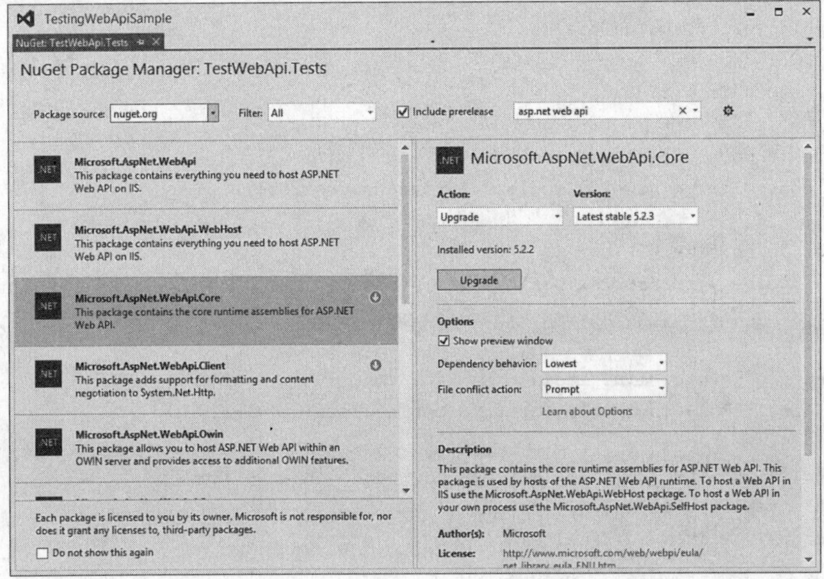

FIGURE 8.13 Install `AspNet.WebApi.Core` inside the unit test project from NuGet.

We can verify the installation by confirming the new references were added to the project. Notice that most of these reference match those in the Web API project. This ensures you can create a client that accesses the same types the controller uses. We use NuGet (versus setting Framework references) to get a matching version of the Web API libraries installed in the test project. For instance, if you right-click a reference and look at the Properties dialog, you will notice that version numbers match between the two projects.

The test method can now be written. In this example, we first rename the test class to `WebApiInvoiceTest`. Next, we add a `using` statement to the top of the class for `System.Web.Http.Results`. This allows us to use the `OkNegotiatedContentResult` class when calling `GetInvoice`. It also allows us to strongly type the results to the `Invoice` class from the model. We access these results through the object's `Content` property (as shown in the final assertion in Listing 8.3).

LISTING 8.3 The Unit Test Method for Testing the Web API Controller

```
using System;
using System.Web.Http;
using Microsoft.VisualStudio.TestTools.UnitTesting;
using System.Web.Http.Results;

namespace TestWebApi.Tests
{
    [TestClass]
    public class WebApiInvoiceTest
    {
        [TestMethod]
        public void VerifyInvoiceTotal()
        {
            int invoiceId = 1500;

            //create controller instance for testing
            var controller = new Controllers.InvoiceController();

            //get an invoice
            var invoice = controller.GetInvoice(invoiceId) as
                OkNegotiatedContentResult<Models.Invoice>;

            //get the invoice line items
            var lineItems = controller.GetInvoiceLineItems(invoiceId);

            //verify the invoice total matches the total of line items
            double verifyTotal = 0;
            foreach (var item in lineItems)
            {
                verifyTotal += item.Price * item.Quantity;
            }

            //assert results of test
            Assert.AreEqual(invoice.Content.Total, verifyTotal);
        }
    }
}
```

Notice that the `TestMethod` works the same as the other unit test methods we wrote earlier in the chapter. The big wrinkles here are using the Web API core for creating the client to access the controller and the objects inside `System.Web.Htttp.Results` for dealing with HTTP results from the service. Figure 8.14 shows the results of the test running inside Visual Studio.

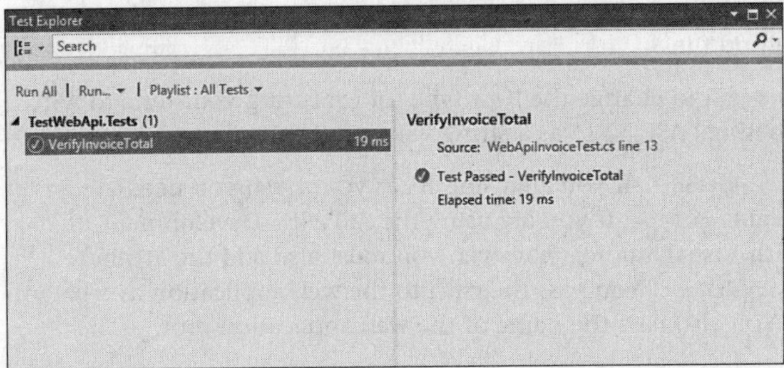

FIGURE 8.14 The test method calling the Web API controller and succeeding.

Unit Testing ASP.NET Pages

You may need to create a unit test that calls older web code (code that is not segmented like MVC or Web API). You might also just want to create tests that call specific web pages and validate the results. Sometimes you need access to Page and Session objects in your tests, for example. In this case, you can create an ASP.NET unit test. These tests are configured to be hosted by a web server (local or IIS) and can call directly into your pages and ASP.NET environment.

To get started, add a new test project to your web solution (or create a new solution and project designed to test your website). You will also need the attribute classes found in the `Microsoft.VisualStudio.TestTools.UnitTesting.Web` namespace. No need to change your references in the unit test project. You simply need to add this `using` statement (imports in Visual Basic) to your test class file. You should now have two `using` statements related to testing, as shown here.

```
using Microsoft.VisualStudio.TestTools.UnitTesting;
using Microsoft.VisualStudio.TestTools.UnitTesting.Web;
```

Next, you may want to set a reference from your unit test application to your website application. This ensures you can access the classes defined within the site. This includes the pages themselves and any other class files you might have in the `App_Code` directory or elsewhere.

You will also want to set a reference to `System.Web`. This exposes the ASP.NET components such as `Page` and `Session`.

You define three primary attributes when creating ASP.NET unit tests: `UrlToTest`, `HostType`, and `AspNetDevelopmentServerHost`. These attributes are defined as follows:

- `UrlToTest`—This allows you to indicate a page that should be called for the execution of the given unit test. This page is called by the test framework, and the context of that web request is available to your unit test (via the `Page` object). You can code against the ASP.NET environment inside your unit test as if you were writing code in a web page's code-behind file.

- `HostType`—This allows you to change the host type for executing your tests to ASP.NET. You do so by passing "ASP.NET" as a string value to the attribute.
- `AspNetDevelopmentServerHost`—If you are using IIS as your host, you need only set `UrlToTest` and `HostType`. If you are using the ASP.NET Development Server (that works with Visual Studio), however, you must also add the attribute `AspNetDevelopmentServerHost`. You pass the path to the web application as a parameter of the attribute. You also pass the name of the web application root.

Listing 8.4 shows an example of using all three attributes to define an ASP.NET unit test that runs against a local development server. Notice that you obtain a reference to the ASP.NET objects from the `TestContext` object's `RequestedPage` property. You can use this property to cast directly to the type of the requested page (in this case, `ShoppingCartPage`). Of course, the `RequestedPage` property is of type `System.Web.UI.Page` and therefore gives you access to objects such as `Server`, `Session`, `Request`, and `Response`.

LISTING 8.4 An ASP.NET Unit Test

```
using System;
using Microsoft.VisualStudio.TestTools.UnitTesting;
using Microsoft.VisualStudio.TestTools.UnitTesting.Web;
using System.Web.UI;
using AspNetHostedTestSample;

namespace AspNetHostedTests
{
   [TestClass]
   public class ShoppingCartTests
   {
       public TestContext TestContext { get; set; }

       [TestMethod()]
       [HostType("ASP.NET")]
       [AspNetDevelopmentServerHost("%PathToWebRoot%",
           "/AspNetHostedTestSample")]
       [UrlToTest("http://localhost:15279/ShoppingCart")]
       public void AddShoppingCartItemTest()
       {
           // **** README: change UrlToTest to your localhost to run ****

           //get the requested page
           Page reqPage = TestContext.RequestedPage;
           Assert.IsTrue(reqPage.Title == "Shopping Cart",
               "Page title does not match.");
```

```
            //cast to actual page type
            ShoppingCart actualPage = (ShoppingCart)reqPage;
            Assert.IsNotNull(actualPage.Cart, "There is no cart on the page.");

            //validate cart usage
            actualPage.Cart.Add("Product 1");
            actualPage.Cart.Add("Product 2");
            Assert.IsTrue(actualPage.Cart.Count == 2,
                "Item count does not match.");
        }
    }
}
}
```

Creating Ordered Tests

Visual Studio enables you to group unit tests, set their sequence of execution, and treat the results as if a single test was run. This can be useful if you need to write unit tests that are dependent on one another. For example, you might insert a record in one test and rely on that record being there in a later test. Of course, this goes against a good practice for unit testing; each test should be able to execute independently. Thankfully, you can create an ordered test that groups the individual unit tests into a new, self-contained test.

You add an ordered test to your test project by right-clicking the unit test project and selecting Add, Ordered Test. You can also select the Ordered Test template from the Add New Test dialog box.

An ordered test is simply an XML file based on the `OrderedTest` schema. You do not, however, need to hand-edit the XML. Instead, Visual Studio gives you the ordered test designer to help you. Figure 8.15 shows an example of this designer.

The left side of the dialog box is where you find all your tests in your solution. Tests are shown by test name. You select individual tests from the left side and use the arrow (>) in the middle to include the tests in your ordered test. You can use the up and down arrows on the right side to change the order in which your tests execute.

The ordered test becomes its own test within your test project. You can then run it by itself or as part of a larger group. When run, Visual Studio executes each unit test in the order you defined. If any fail, the entire ordered test fails unless you have checked the Continue After Failure check box (located on the bottom of the dialog in Figure 8.15). You can view the details of the failed ordered test to see which tests passed and which failed. Figure 8.16 shows the ordered test inside the Test Explorer being run. Notice the first item (compute for negative) failed, so the other two tests in the ordered test were not run.

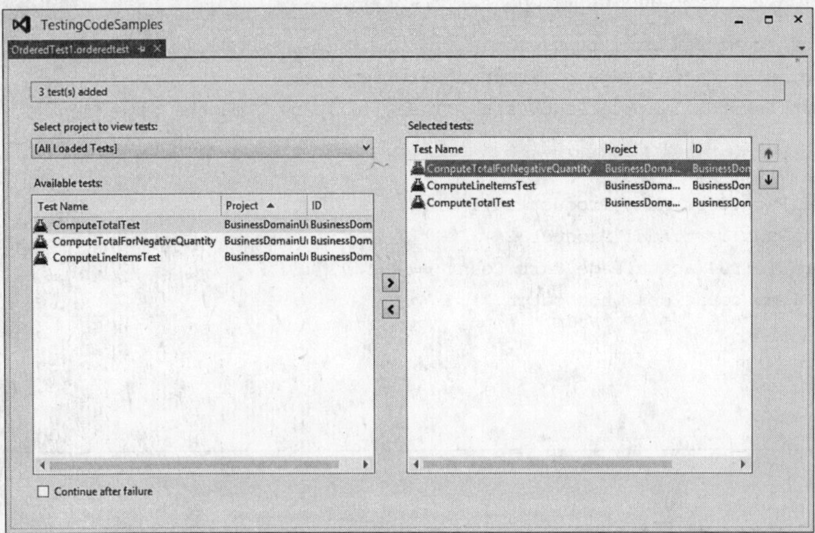

FIGURE 8.15 You add existing unit tests to an ordered test to create a new test that executes two or more tests in a specific order.

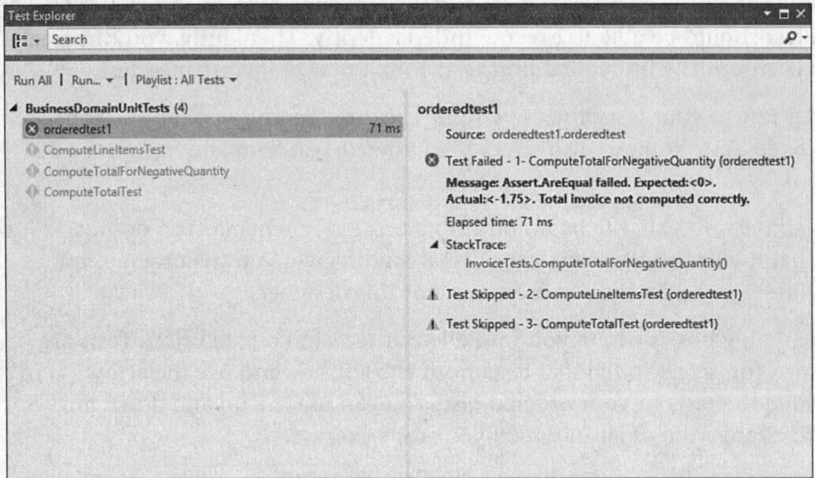

FIGURE 8.16 The ordered test results inside Test Explorer.

Summary

This chapter showed how you can use the unit test framework to define test projects and create test class files using the `TestClass` attribute. Each test method should include the `TestMethod` attribute. You can also data-bind unit tests using the `DataSource` attribute class.

You can write unit tests to verify ASP.NET MVC and Web API controller classes. When doing so, you need to ensure the unit test project references the core client objects required to easily communicate with ASP.NET MVC.

You can also create unit tests that run inside of ASP.NET (either in IIS or the Visual Studio development server). An ASP.NET unit test uses the `TestContext` object to access information about the ASP.NET environment, including the executing page, session, and server variables.

Writing unit tests can lead to fewer issues found in production. Having a suite of tests for your code makes that code easier to understand and more reliable. You will also gain confidence with code changes because you will be able to tell what code was broken as a result of a change.

CHAPTER 9

Refactoring Code

IN THIS CHAPTER

- Visual Studio Refactoring Basics
- Renaming Code
- Refactoring Variable Assignments
- Extract Method
- Extract Interface
- Change Signature
- Encapsulate Field

Whether or not you realize it, if you are like most developers, you are always refactoring code. Every time you change your code to reduce duplication or rename items for the sake of clarity, you are refactoring. Refactoring is simply putting a name to a common development task. The strict definition of the term is "a change made to the internal structure of software to make it easier to understand and cheaper to modify without changing its observable behavior." That is, refactoring does not add features to the application. Instead, it improves the general maintenance of the code base.

The time to refactor your code is as you are building it. This is when you are closest to the code and thus able to quickly make these maintenance-type changes. It is much harder to let the problems linger and come back to them later. Refactoring should be part of your everyday development approach.

Refactoring is also a key tenet of modern, agile development where your code base builds feature by feature to satisfy a series of tests. This can result in code that works wonderfully but does not look as though it was designed as a cohesive unit. It can create maintenance issues, duplicate code, poor conventions, and other issues. To combat these problems, you would be wise to go over the code base at frequent intervals after everything works fine. The goal is to improve the general quality of the code (remove duplication, create common interfaces, rename items, put things into logical groups, and so on) without risk.

Refactoring has been moved inside the code editor for 2015. It presents itself in the margin of the editor as a light bulb appearing as you need it. Refactoring has also been extended beyond C# to Visual Basic. These tools let you make changes to the code base without the concern of creating more problems than you are solving.

NOTE

There are a couple of features built in to Visual Studio for refactoring database elements. We cover these in Chapter 13, "Working with Databases."

Visual Studio Refactoring Basics

The Visual Studio refactoring tools work to ensure that you see the promises of refactoring: increased reuse of your code, fewer rewrites, reduced duplication, and better readability. These tools work to instill confidence in the edits they make to your code. They do so by using a common refactoring engine based on the new .NET compiler platform ("Roslyn") rather than string matching and search-and-replace. The engine and compiler work together to cover the entire code base (and its references) to find all possible changes that need to be made as part of a given Refactor operation. The engine even searches out code comments and tries to update them to reflect new type names. In addition, you can preview changes to your code before they happen. This adds further to your comfort level with the modifications these tools are making to your code.

Table 9.1 presents a high-level overview of the many Refactoring operations that are possible with the code editor. We cover each of them in detail in the coming sections. First, however, we cover some of the common elements of the refactoring process. These elements include both invoking a refactoring tool inside Visual Studio and previewing the refactoring changes as they happen.

TABLE 9.1 Refactoring Operations Inside the Visual Studio Code Editor

Tool	Description
Rename	Renames fields, properties, namespaces, methods, types, and local variables
Extract Method	Creates a new method using existing code within an existing method
Introduce Constant	Converts a "magic" number or string in your code to a constant
Introduce Local	Creates a local variable from an inline expression in your code
Inline Temporary Variable	Converts a local variable to an inline expression (opposite of introduce local)
Change Signature (Reorder/Remove Parameters)	Allows you to reorder/remove parameters for a given method and updates all callers
Encapsulate Field	Quickly creates a property from an existing field
Extract Interface	Creates an interface from an existing class or structure

Invoking the Refactoring Tools

The refactoring tools are available directly inside the code editor. You can invoke them in several ways. First, if your cursor is positioned near code that Visual Studio thinks could or should be refactored, you will see a light bulb in the left margin of the code editor (called the Quick Actions menu). You can click on this to see your options unfold in a context-sensitive, refactoring menu. Second, you can always access Quick Actions from the editor using the shortcut "control dot" (Ctrl+.). A right-click inside your code will also take you to Quick Actions from the context menu. Finally, the Visual Studio class designer supports edits that work as refactoring.

NOTE

Visual Studio has done away with the Refactoring menu that used to appear at the top of the tool in favor of the Quick Actions menu directly inside the code editor.

Using the Quick Actions Menu

Figure 9.1 shows the Quick Actions menu being invoked via the keyboard shortcut (Ctrl+.) or a right-click on the method signature (and choosing Quick Actions from the context menu). Notice the light bulb on the left and the menu that unfolds. The options in the menu are context sensitive to actions you could take on the highlighted code. In this case, the only option is to change the method signature (reorder the parameters) within the selected constructor for the `InvoiceLineItem` class.

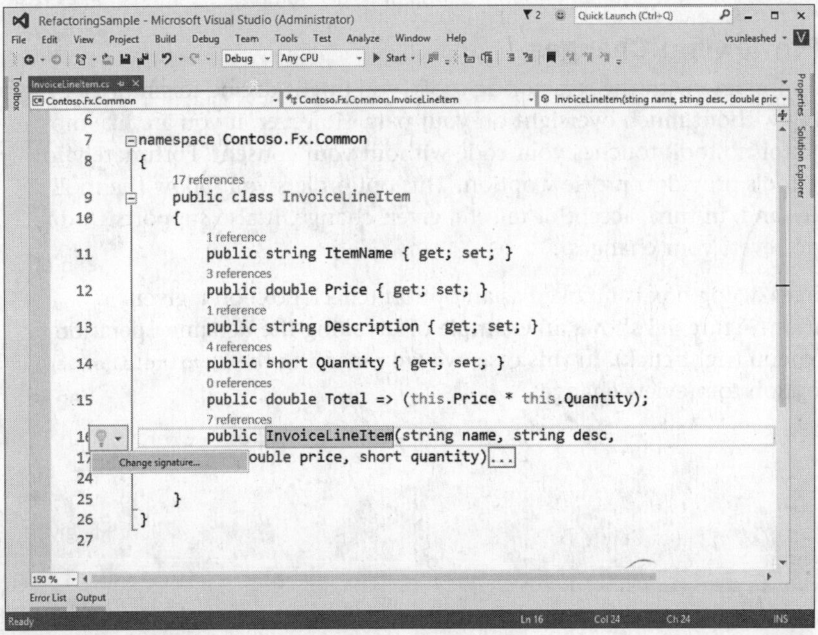

```
namespace Contoso.Fx.Common
{
    17 references
    public class InvoiceLineItem
    {
        1 reference
        public string ItemName { get; set; }
        3 references
        public double Price { get; set; }
        1 reference
        public string Description { get; set; }
        4 references
        public short Quantity { get; set; }
        0 references
        public double Total => (this.Price * this.Quantity);
        7 references
        public InvoiceLineItem(string name, string desc,
            double price, short quantity)...

    }
}
```

FIGURE 9.1 Use Ctrl+. to access the Quick Actions menu to refactor your code.

Notice in Figure 9.1 that there is no preview of your possible changes. This is because the Change Signature refactor option has too many options, and it would be confusing to put all of them in the preview window. To finish invoking this refactor, click on the Change Signature menu item next to the light bulb. This brings up the Change Signature dialog as shown in Figure 9.2. From here you can chance the order of parameters (move up/down buttons with arrows) and remove parameters.

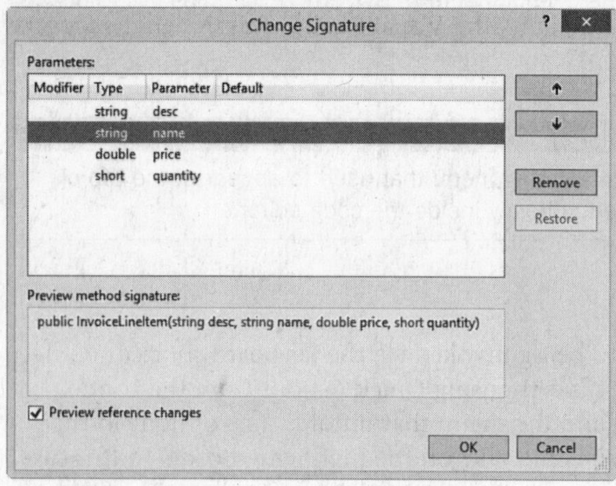

FIGURE 9.2 Use the Change Signature dialog to modify your method signature.

Making (and Previewing) Changes

As you become comfortable with the refactoring tools, you might decide to simply let them do their thing without much oversight on your part. However, if you are like most developers, no one (or no tool) touches your code without your consent. Fortunately for us, the refactoring tools provide a preview option. This option lets you follow the tool through its changes and, in turn, accept or reject a given change. It also supports Undo should you want to revert your changes.

The Preview Changes dialog box is invoked as an option (check box) on a given Refactoring operation. Figure 9.3 shows an example of invoking the Rename operation from the context menu (right-click). In this case, we are renaming the `InvoiceLineItems` class. Notice the option to preview changes.

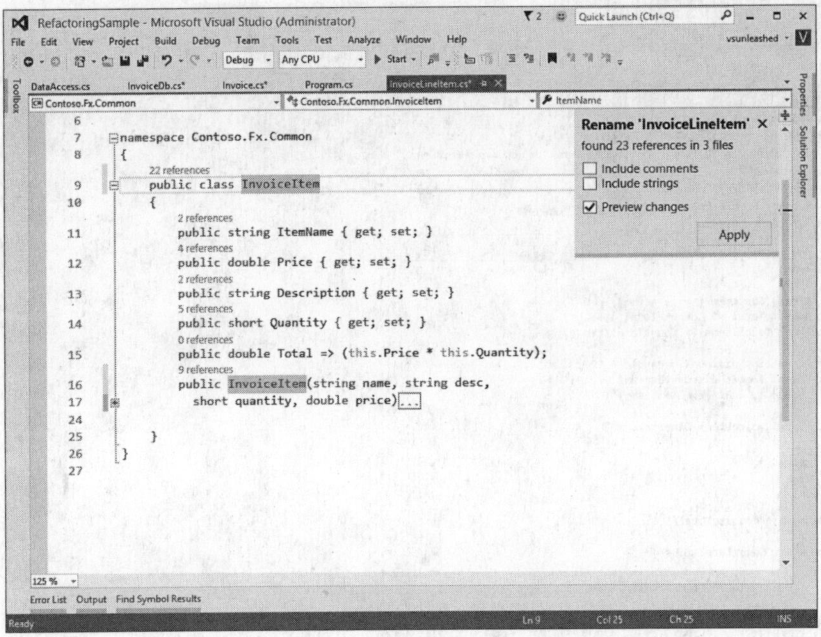

FIGURE 9.3 A Rename operation with Preview Changes selected.

To complete this refactor, you first rename the class inside the code editor. You then click Apply on the small Rename dialog shown in Figure 9.3 (upper right). Provided you have enabled Preview Changes, Visual Studio will open the Preview Changes dialog, as shown in Figure 9.4. The top portion of this dialog box lists all the changes that the given Refactor operation intends to make. This list is presented as a tree, with the outer branch representing where you intend to originate the change. All the leaves under this branch are files where changes happen. Nested beneath the filenames are the actual places within the code where a change is made. You use this list to select each item you would like to preview. You can review each change, select/unselect those to apply, and ultimately apply changes to your code (or cancel the operation).

As each item in the Preview Changes tree is clicked, the corresponding code is displayed below the tree in the Preview Code Changes section of the dialog box. This enables developers to quickly review where changes are being made. To prevent a given change, you can simply uncheck the item in the tree view. Of course, you can prevent entire file changes by unchecking further up in the hierarchy at the file level. When you are finished with your preview and satisfied with the proposed changes, you simply click the Apply button to commit the changes to your code.

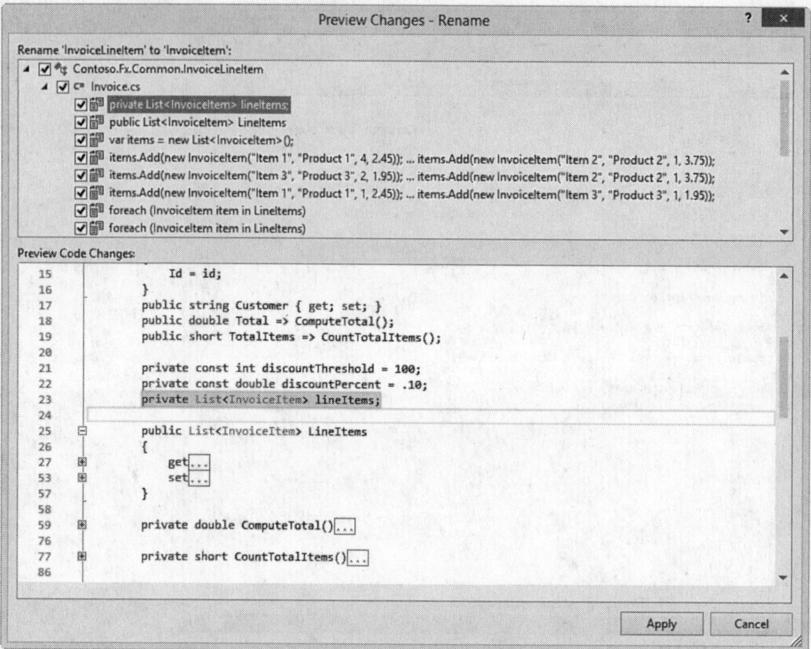

FIGURE 9.4 Previewing the changes of a Rename operation.

Using the Class Designer to Refactor

The class designer enables you to view the contents of your classes and their relationships. It can also be used as a productivity tool: you can create new classes and modify existing ones directly within the designer.

NOTE

The class designer is covered in Chapter 6, "Introducing the Editors and Designers."

The class designer also supports refactoring. For example, you can rename elements within your classes or change their signature and the operation will use the compiler to update references accordingly. Figure 9.5 shows renaming a class directly within the diagram. Hitting enter after this rename will update references.

NOTE

In the current build at time of writing (2015 RC), the Visual Studio class designer exposes the refactoring tool as a context menu from items within the class. However, the items in the menu are currently not implemented and throw an error. Microsoft may fix this in future builds. That said, refactoring by just editing the items in the diagram is very much operational.

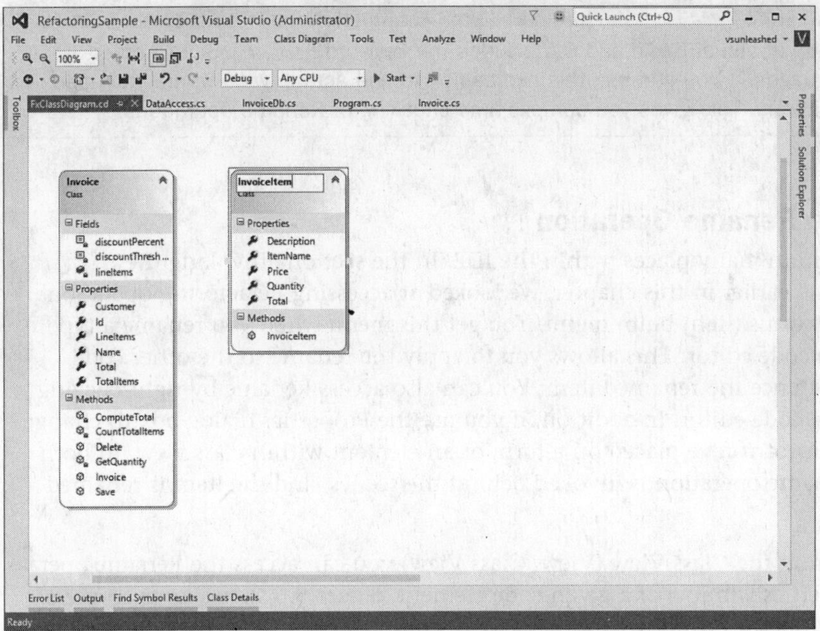

FIGURE 9.5 Refactoring within the Visual Studio class designer.

Renaming Code

Renaming code elements is the most common Refactoring operation. Visual Studio supports Rename operations in Visual Basic, C#, C++, database schemas, and other code elements. Thankfully, all these Rename operations work in a similar fashion.

Most developers do not wait until the code base is operational and say to themselves, “Okay, now I will go back and rename items for clarity.” The more likely scenario is that as you build your application, you consistently rename items to correct mistakes or make things clearer and more readable. Of course, as the code base builds, it becomes more and more difficult to rename classes, methods, fields, and the like without introducing new bugs into your code.

The capability to rename items with the confidence that you are not introducing bugs into your code is paramount. With the Visual Studio editor, you can rename all relevant code items including namespaces, classes, fields, properties, methods, and variables. The compiler helps make sure that your code does not get broken and that all source code references are found. In fact, the Rename operation can even search through your code comments and strings and update them accordingly.

TIP

The 2015 version of Visual Basic and C# includes the keyword `nameOf`. (See Chapter 3, "The .NET Languages.") You can use this expression to use actual types where you need to pass string literals. This gives you compile-time checking of Rename operations.

Accessing the Rename Operation

You can rename from many places within the IDE. In the section "Invoking the Refactoring Tools," earlier in this chapter, we looked at accessing Refactoring operations from the Quick Actions (light bulb) menu. You get this menu when you rename a type or method in the code editor. This allows you to apply the rename to the other code elements that reference the renamed item. You can also access Rename by right-clicking an element in the code editor. In addition, if you use the Properties dialog box to change the name of a control you've placed on a form or an element within class view. In both instances the Rename operation is invoked behind the scenes, and the item is renamed appropriately.

As an example, from the Class View (View, Class View) you can access the Rename operation via the Properties window of a given code element. Figure 9.6 shows an example of the Class View, Properties window, and Rename operation working together. Renaming an item here invokes the full rename for all code that references the given element being renamed (without preview).

You can also rename directly within Solution Explorer for a filename that equates to a class name. For instance, suppose you have a file named `Customer` and you want to change the class name and filename to `Shopper`. You do so by right-clicking and choosing Rename. Visual Studio enables you to rename the file. When you do so, it prompts you to see whether you also want to rename the class. If you choose yes, Visual Studio refactors your code on your behalf. So if you have a `Customer` class and a `Customer.cs` file, a Rename operation to `Shopper` will rename the file as well as the class if you give it permission to (and will refactor all references to the previous class name).

NOTE

Although an undo on the Rename operation rolls back a change, in the case of a filename change, Undo reverts the code but does not change the filename back to its original name.

Rename Keyboard Shortcuts

You can access the Rename operation from keyboard shortcuts. Rename is a popular task, so Visual Studio has provided its own shortcut key: F2. Previous versions of Visual Studio required you to invoke rename via the shortcut "chord," Ctrl+R, R (where you continue to hold Ctrl when pressing the second R). Pressing this combination in sequence still brings up the Refactoring, Rename operation relative to the code element behind your cursor. Figure 9.7 shows an example of using the shortcut key to rename the `Customer` class.

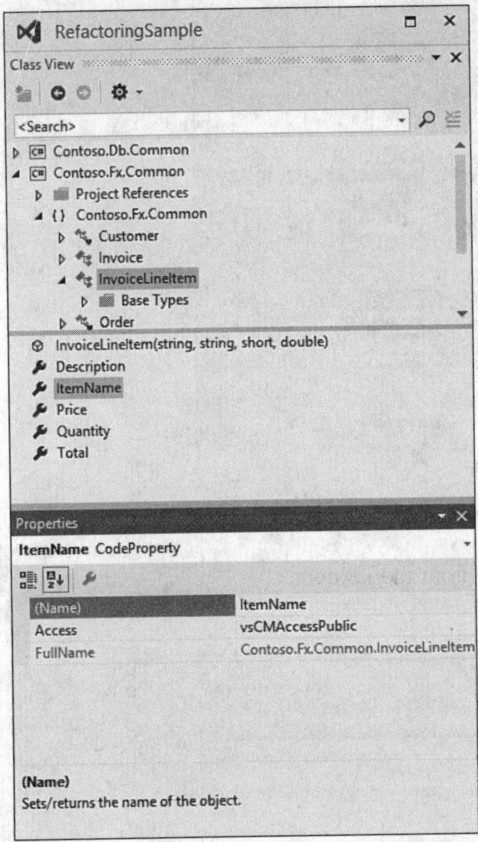

FIGURE 9.6 You can access Rename from the Class View and Properties window.

Notice the editor highlights the item being renamed. You now simply type the new name in the editor and hit the Apply button as shown.

Rename from Quick Actions

You can also invoke rename directly from the Quick Actions menu. As an example, suppose we are trying to rename an enum from `OrderStatus` to `OrderState`. Typing over the old name in the code editor invokes the light bulb menu, as shown in Figure 9.8. Notice that directly from this light bulb menu you can choose to apply the rename or execute the rename with preview. Notice also the squiggled line shown over `OrderStatus` above, showing a compile error relative to the element being renames. Figure 9.9 shows the Preview dialog after selecting the operation from the light build menu.

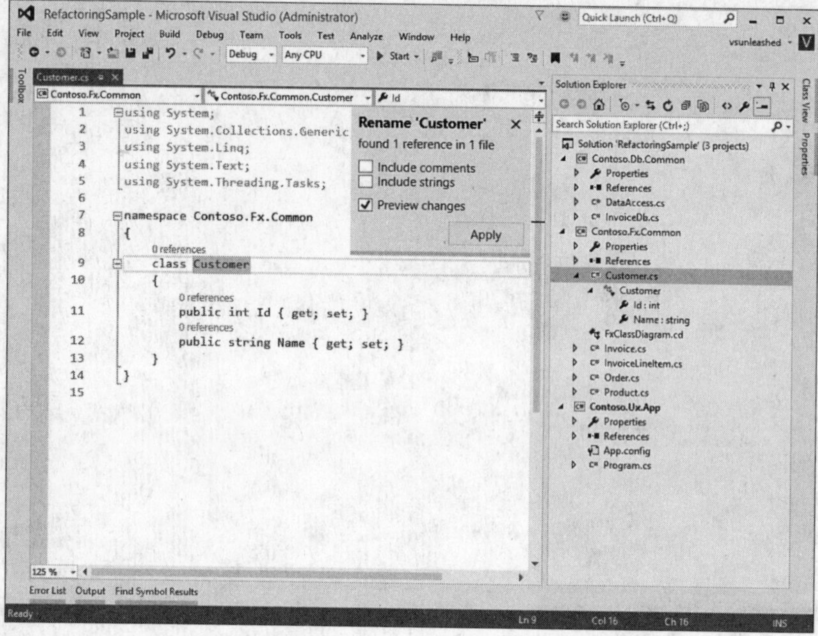

FIGURE 9.7 Use F2 or Ctrl+R, R to invoke rename from the keyboard.

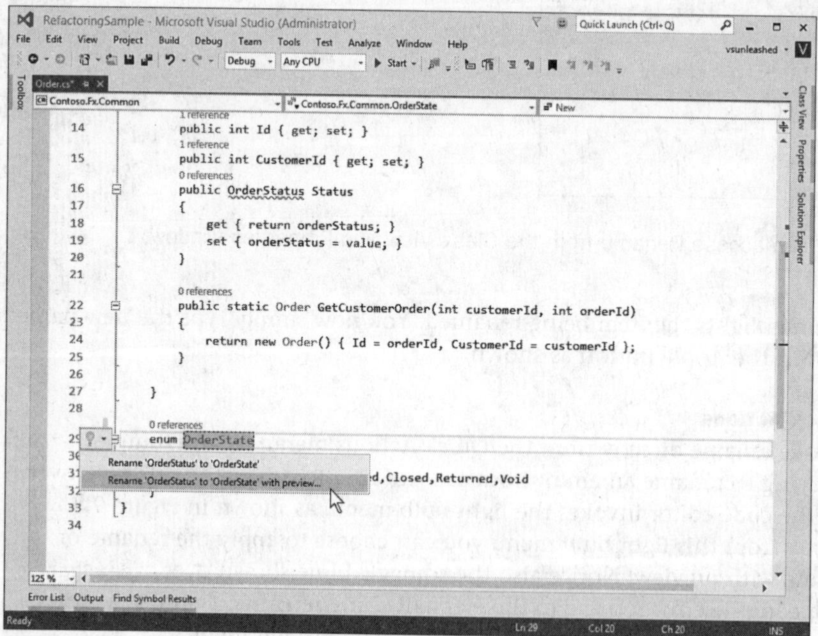

FIGURE 9.8 Renaming an element in the code editor invokes the light bulb menu.

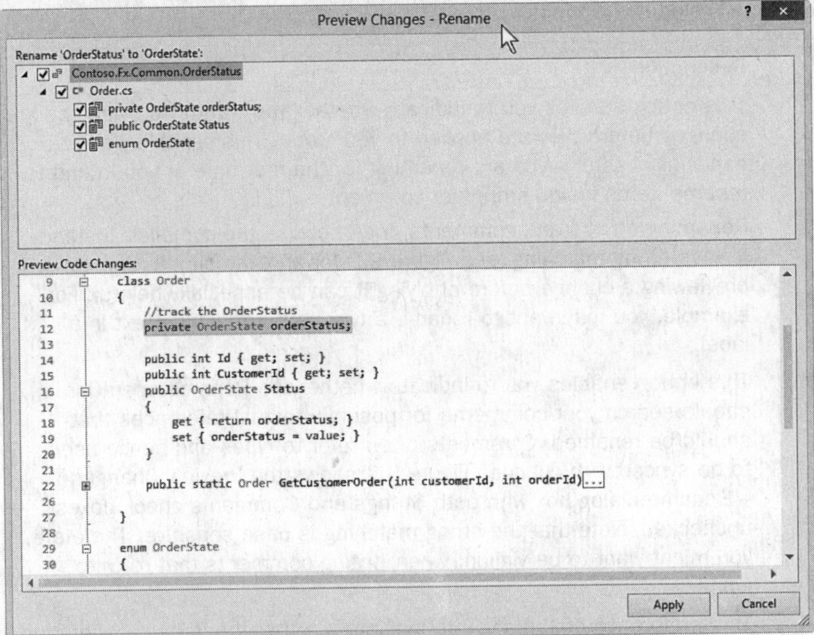

FIGURE 9.9 Previewing rename changes including comments and strings.

NOTE

Using the light bulb menu to rename does not give you the option to choose to rename comments or strings. You would need to invoke from the keyboard or shortcut menu to get that option.

Working with the Rename Dialog Box

The Rename dialog that appears in your code editor enables you to specify a few options when invoking a given Rename Refactor operation. Recall that you get the small Rename dialog from either F2 or Ctrl+R, R. Refer to Figure 9.7 for an example. The dialog presents developers with a few options when doing a rename. The three check boxes enable you to set the options described in Table 9.2.

TABLE 9.2 The Rename Dialog Box Options

Option	Description
Preview Changes	This option enables you to indicate whether you want to preview the changes before they are applied to your code. This capability can be especially useful if you are renaming for the first time or you intend to rename items inside strings or comments. Renaming strings and comments does not use the compiler. Instead, it uses string matching (see Figure 9.9 for an example). In this case, previewing a change before applying it can be especially helpful. For example, you may want to rename a type, but not similar text in a label.
Include Comments	This option enables you to indicate whether the Rename operation should search your comments for possible textual references that should be renamed. Comments often refer to types and hence need to be synced with changes.Figure 9.7 shows the Preview Changes – Rename dialog box with both Strings and Comments check boxes unchecked. Note that the string matching is case sensitive. Therefore, you might want to be vigilant when writing comments that refer to types.
Include Strings	This preference enables you to indicate whether the Rename operation should search inside your literal strings for references to a given item name. String literals include constants, control names, form names, and so on. This capability is most useful if there is a tight coupling between your code and the elements within your user interface. Again, this too is case sensitive.

Refactoring Variable Assignments

Some common refactoring opportunities found during code reviews are "magic numbers" that should be variables or constants, code that should assigned a variable to allow clarity and re-use, and variables that could more easily be expressed as inline code. Visual Studio 2015 allows you to quickly refactor to take advantage of these opportunities.

Introduce Constant

The new code editor allows you to do away with magic numbers passed as parameters, in conditional statements, or lurking elsewhere in your code. It allows you to at least push these numbers into constant variables. That way if the number changes, you only need to change the constant and not hope you find all occurrences of the magic number in your code. (Of course, it would be even better if you externalized the value so you did not have to recompile your code to change a number.)

Let's look at an example. Figure 9.10 shows code for a discount rule on an invoice. The rule states that if the order is greater than $100, then a 10% discount should be applied. However, both 100 and .10 are represented as magic numbers in the code. Selecting the value in the editor and then invoking the light bulb menu (Ctrl+.) presents you with options to introduce a constant instead of these numbers. Notice that the resulting changes are previewed right in the IDE. The example shown in Figure 9.10 will create a new variable (V) and assign it the constant value of 100.

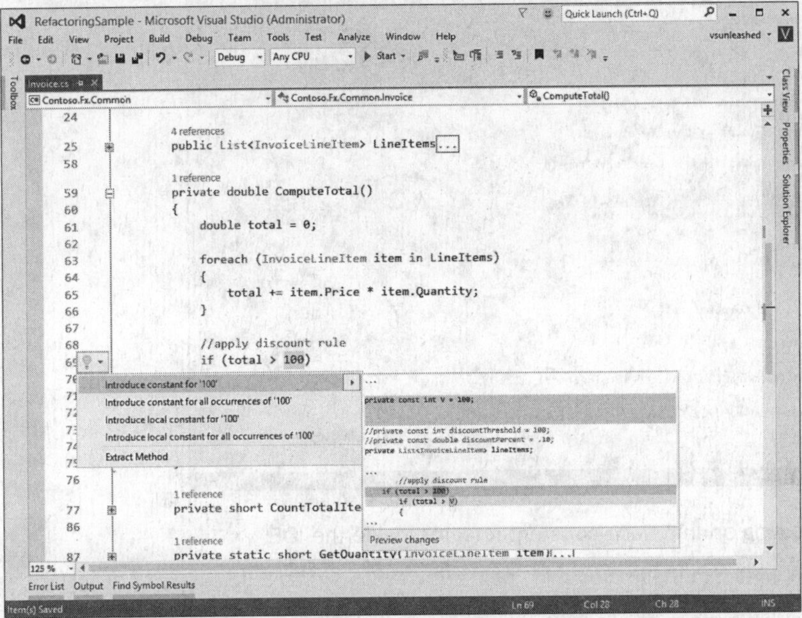

FIGURE 9.10 Convert a "magic number" in your code to a constant.

You apply the change by clicking on the menu item representing the version of the refactor you want to execute. This makes the change but also brings up the small refactor menu to allow you to apply the change to strings and comments (see Figure 9.11). Notice, too, in Figure 9.10 that you can click on Preview Changes directly from the light bulb foldout menu. Figure 9.11 shows the change being made. Notice as you name the constant the references are updated also.

The Introduce constant refactor gives you a few options (see Figure 9.10). The first option, Introduce Constant For, creates a standard constant scoped at the class level. The Introduce Local Constant For option creates a constant inside your method (or whatever type of code you are referencing in the editor). The options that include All Occurrences are going to search outside the selected magic number and find other uses of that number (and replace them with the constant variable).

Introduce Local

The Introduce local refactor allows you to convert an expression of code to a local variable within your method (or similar). This can make your code easier to read. It is also useful if you plan to reuse the result of the expression multiple times. Figure 9.12 shows converting the discount amount (total * .10) to a local variable.

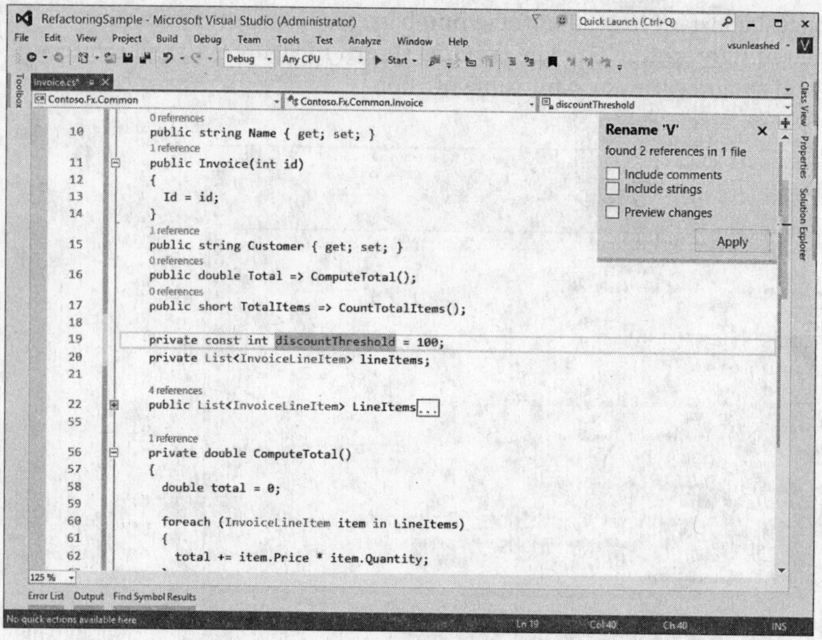

FIGURE 9.11 Executing an Introduce constant refactor inside the IDE.

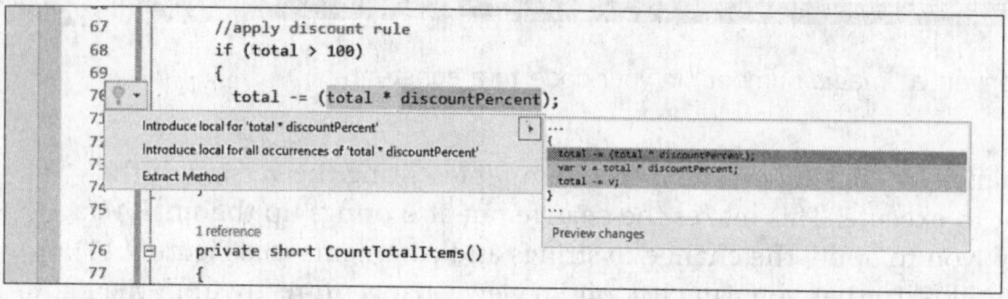

FIGURE 9.12 Use Introduce Local to move code expressions into local variables.

The result of the Refactor operation is a variable to represent the discount. You can now change the code to make it more readable, as follows.

```
//apply discount rule
if (total > discountThreshold)
{
    var discount = total * discountPercent;
    total = total - discount;
}
```

Inline Temporary Variable

The Inline temporary variable refactor allows you to remove temporary variables from your code and replace them with actual code expressions assigned to the temporary variable. Think of this as the opposite of Introduce Local. For example, Figure 9.13 shows how you can turn the `discount` variable back into inline code.

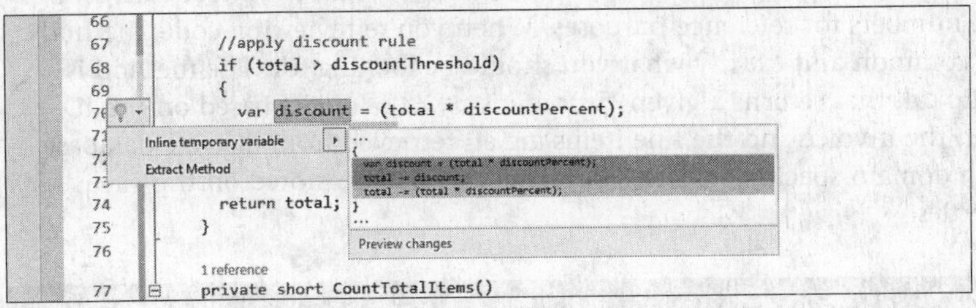

FIGURE 9.13 Use the Inline temporary variable to turn temporary variables into inline code.

The result of this Refactor operation is the removal of the temporary variable. The use of the temporary variable is then replaced by inline code, as the following shows.

```
//apply discount rule
if (total > discountThreshold)
{
    total = total - total * discountPercent;
}
```

Extract Method

When developers go back and take a look at their code, perhaps during a periodic code review or after a particularly long session of heads-down development, they often find methods that are too long or coarse grained, contain duplicate code, or are just poorly organized. A common thing to do is pass over the code and create fine-grained, discrete methods to reduce these issues and make for a more readable, reusable, and maintainable code base.

The problem, of course, is that doing this is time consuming and often introduces bugs into the code. The code editor in Visual Studio provides an Extract Method refactoring tool to ensure a quick, bug-free experience when you're working to better organize your code. With this tool, you can create a new method using existing code.

Accessing the Extract Method Refactor

To access the Extract Method Refactor operation, you first must select a portion of code to refactor. You then invoke the light-bulb menu either through a right-click or the keyboard shortcut (Ctrl+.).

Extracting Methods

With the Extract Method operation, you can create (or extract) a new method from multiple lines of code, a single line, or an expression within a given line of code. In each case, the method is created immediately following the method from which the code was extracted. The extracted code is replaced by a call to the new method.

Listing 9.1 provides an example of a method (`GetFullInvoice`) that is unnecessarily long. We've added line numbers for reference purposes. When you're reviewing code, methods such as these are common and exactly what you should be looking for. The method is designed as a static call that returns a given customer's `Invoice` object based on the ID number. However, the invoice and the line items are all retrieved from discrete database calls and stored in domain-specific objects. These objects are then stored on the `Invoice` instance as properties.

NOTE

If you would like to follow along in your code editor, download the sample code from the website associated with this book: informit.com/title/9780162337369.

LISTING 9.1 A Long Static Method

```
public class InvoiceDb
{
  public static Invoice GetFullInvoice(int id)
  {
    //get invoice table data
    DataTable dtOrder = DataAccess.GetTableData("Invoice", id);

    //validate invoice against id
    if (id != (int)dtOrder.Rows[0]["id"])
    {
      throw new ApplicationException("Invalid invoice.");
    }

    //create empty invoice object based on id
    Invoice invoice = new Invoice(id);

    //get invoice items
    List<InvoiceLineItem> items = new List<InvoiceLineItem>();
    DataTable invItems = DataAccess.GetTableData("InvoiceLineItems", id);
    foreach (DataRow r in invItems.Rows)
    {
      InvoiceLineItem item = new InvoiceLineItem(
        (string)r["name"], (string)r["description"],
        (double)r["unit_price"], (Int16)r["quantity"]);
      items.Add(item);
```

```
26     }
27     invoice.LineItems = items;
28     return invoice;
29   }
30 }
```

Opportunities for method extraction inside this one method are numerous. Obvious considerations are the code to initialize the `Invoice` instance and the code to get invoice line items. Extracting these two chunks of code into discrete methods would result in better organized code (thus, more readable), more opportunities for reuse, and an easier-to-maintain code base. Let's look at doing these two extractions.

First, let's extract the code that sets up the `Invoice` instance. Knowing what to select for extraction requires a bit of experience with the tool. In this case, we will extract lines 05 through 15 (as numbered in the Listing 9.1), which is the code from the first call to `DataAccess` through the `Invoice` class initialization. Figure 9.14 shows the selected code and related light bulb menu to access the Extract Method refactor.

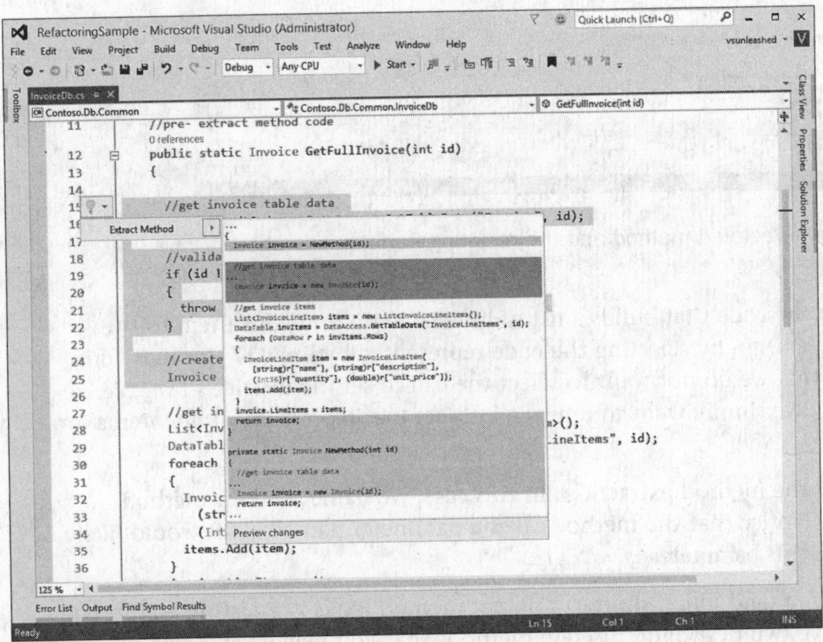

FIGURE 9.14 Select the code to refactor, invoke the light build menu, and choose options to Extract Method.

Invoking the Extract Method refactor creates a new method from your selected code along with the appropriate parameters and return type. It also replaces the extracted code with a reference call to this new method. Finally, Visual Studio invokes the Rename refactor so you can give your new method a name that makes sense. Figure 9.15 shows the extracted method, the call to the extracted method, and the results of renaming the new method inside the IDE.

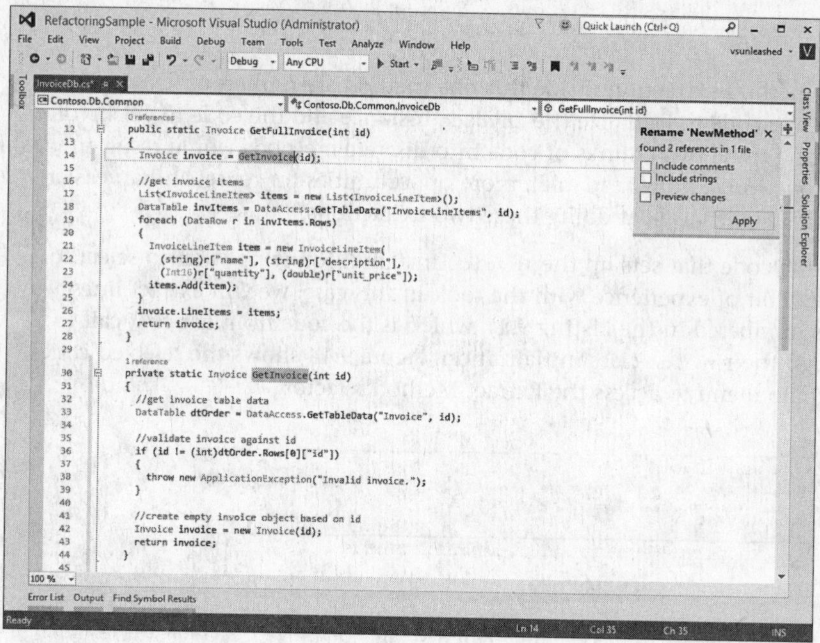

FIGURE 9.15 The refactored method and the resulting Rename operation.

Next, let's extract the code that builds a list of invoice items and adds them to the `Invoice` object. We begin by selecting the code represented by lines 17 through 26 in Listing 9.1. Note that we do not want to select the call to set the invoice's `LineItems` property (line 27); we simply want to return an object that represents all line items for a given invoice.

Figure 9.16 shows the method extraction. In this case, we name the new method `GetInvoiceItems`. Notice that the method takes a parameter named `id`. It would likely be helpful to rename this parameter `invoiceId`.

The newly organized (and much shorter) original method looks like Listing 9.2. In addition, you now have two new tight, discrete methods that you may be able to reuse in the future (and perhaps make public). These new methods are in Listing 9.3.

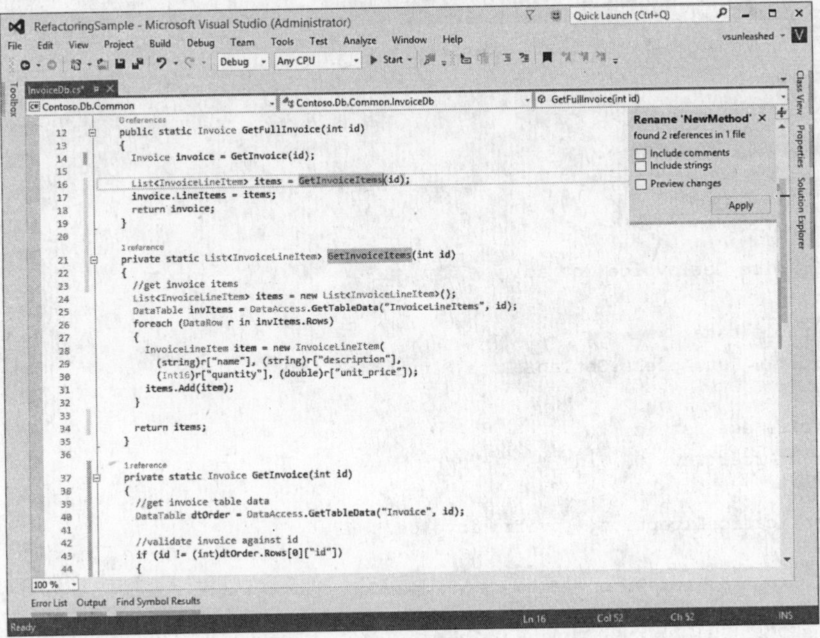

FIGURE 9.16 The code after refactoring the call to get invoice line items.

LISTING 9.2 The Original Long Static Method After the Extractions

```
public static Invoice GetFullInvoice(int id)
{
  Invoice invoice = GetInvoice(id);

  //get invoice items
  List<InvoiceLineItem> items = GetInvoiceItems(id);
  invoice.LineItems = items;

  return invoice;
}
```

LISTING 9.3 The Extractions

```
private static List<InvoiceLineItem> GetInvoiceItems(int invoiceId)
{
  List<InvoiceLineItem> items = new List<InvoiceLineItem>();
  DataTable invItems = DataAccess.GetTableData("InvoiceLineItems", invoiceId);
  foreach (DataRow r in invItems.Rows)
  {
    InvoiceLineItem item = new InvoiceLineItem(
```

```
        (string)r["name"], (string)r["description"],
        (double)r["unit_price"], (Int16)r["quantity"]);
      items.Add(item);
    }

    return items;
  }

private static Invoice GetInvoice(int id)
{
  //get invoice table data
  DataTable dtOrder = DataAccess.GetTableData("Invoice", id);

  //validate invoice against id
  if (id != (int)dtOrder.Rows[0]["id"])
  {
    throw new ApplicationException("Invalid invoice.");
  }

  //create empty invoice object based on id
  Invoice invoice = new Invoice(id);
  return invoice;
}
```

NOTE

The Extract Method does not allow you to choose where to put the extracted method. Many times, you might find a bit of code that really needs to be extracted into a method of another, different class. For this, you have to extract the method and then move things around manually.

Extracting a Single Line of Code

Sometimes you want to extract a single line of code or a portion of a line of code as its own method. For example, you might have a calculation that is done as part of a line of code but is common enough to warrant its own method. Alternatively, you might need to extract an object assignment to add additional logic to it. In either case, the code editor supports this type of extraction.

Let's look at an example. Suppose you have the following line of code that calculates an invoice's total inside a loop through the invoice items list.

```
total += item.Price * item.Quantity;
```

You might want to extract just the portion of the assignment that calculates a line item's total (price * quantity). To do so, you select the portion of code and invoke the Extract

Method refactor using the Quick Actions (light bulb) via Ctrl+. or from the context menu. Figure 9.17 shows this operation in action for the selected code.

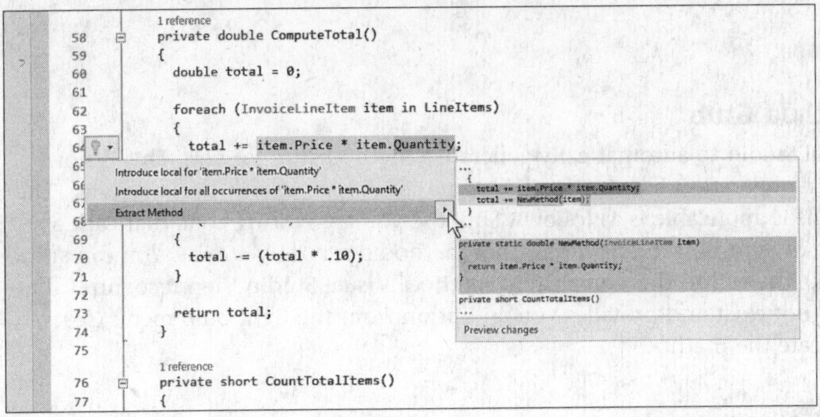

FIGURE 9.17 You can extract a single line (or portion of a line) to its own method.

Notice that, by default, the new method would like an instance of `InvoiceLineItem`. You might prefer to pass both quantity and unit price instead. You would have to make these changes manually. Alternatively, if quantity and unit price were assigned to variables before the extraction was done, you would get a new method that accepted these parameters (instead of an `InvoiceLineItem` instance). Figure 9.18 demonstrates this fact.

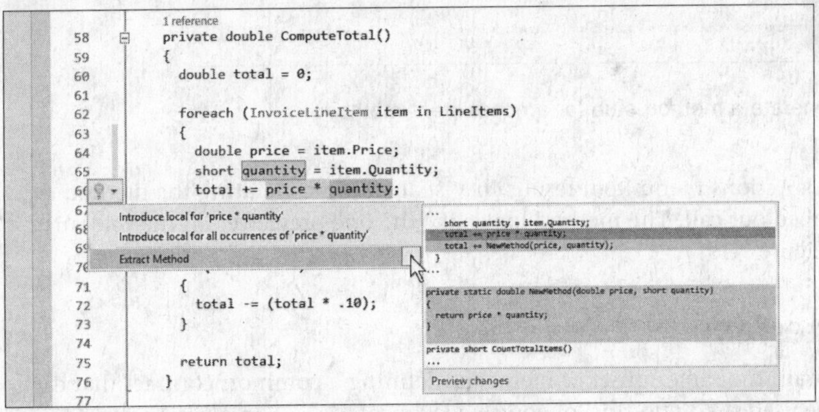

FIGURE 9.18 An alternate view of extracting a portion of code using variables.

The resulting refactor replaces a portion of the line of code with the following.

```
total = total + GetItemTotal(price, quantity);
```

It also adds the new method, as follows.

```
private static double GetItemTotal(double price, short quantity) {
  return price * quantity;
}
```

Generate Method Stub

You can get Visual Studio to automatically generate a method stub for you. This is not strictly a refactoring operation but can provide some similar increases in productivity. The scenario where this is applicable is as follows. Suppose you are writing code that calls a method from one of your objects. However, that method does not yet exist. You can still write code to make the call to the nonexistent method. Visual Studio then recognizes that this method does not exist and provides you an option from the light bulb menu (see Figure 9.19) to create the method.

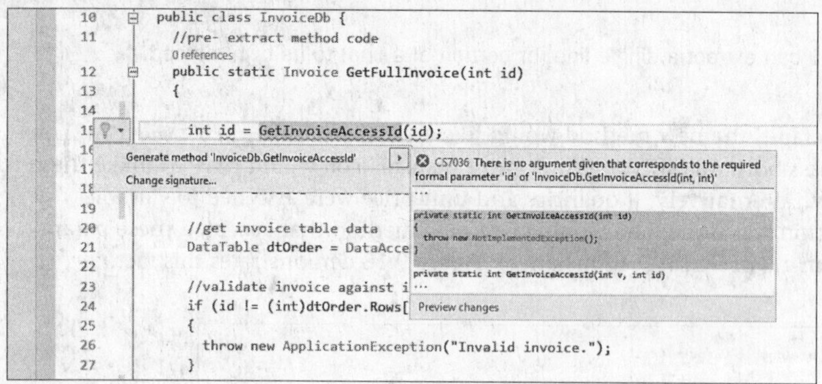

FIGURE 9.19 Generate a method stub for a nonexistent method.

Clicking the Quick Actions menu item results in Visual Studio generating the method based on the stubbed out call. The method looks like the one previewed in the foldout menu shown in Figure 9.19.

Extract Interface

When classes contain the same subset of members, defining a common contract that each class shares can be useful. You do this, of course, via an interface. Some basic advantages to defining interfaces are that your code becomes more readable, is easier to maintain, and operates the same for like members. However, developers often don't realize the commonality between their classes until after those classes are coded. This sometimes makes creating interfaces painful.

The Visual Studio code editor provides the Extract Interface refactoring operation to make this process easier. It enables you to take an existing class or struct and automatically generate a matching interface that the existing class then implements.

Accessing the Extract Interface Refactor

To access the Extract Interface refactor operation, you first must position your cursor on a class, a struct, or another interface definition that contains the members you want to extract into a new interface. You then can use the Quick Actions menu (Ctrl+.) to execute an Extract Interface refactor.

TIP

To invoke the Extract Interface operation from the keyboard, first position your cursor on the class, struct, or interface definition that contains the members you want to extract. Next, play the keyboard shortcut chord Ctrl+R, I.

Extracting Interfaces

To better understand the Extract Interface operation, let's look at an example. Suppose you review your code and notice that a number of your domain objects share similar properties and methods. Let's say the objects `Invoice`, `Order`, and `Product` all contain properties for `Id` and `Name` and methods for `Save` and `Delete`. In this case, you should consider extracting this commonality into a standard interface that each of your domain objects would implement. Let's look at how the Extract Interface refactoring operation aids in this regard.

First, you position your cursor on the target class whose members you want to extract. In the example, choose the `Invoice` class and position the cursor on the class name. Then press Ctrl+. to show the light bulb. From here choose Extract Interface. Invoking the Extract Interface operation presents a dialog box named the same. Figure 9.20 shows this dialog box relative to the example.

Notice that you first define a name for the interface. By default, the tool names the interface with the name of the class preceded by the letter *I* for *interface* (in this case, `IInvoice`). Of course, we are going to use our interface across our domain, so we change this to `IBusinessEntity`.

The Extract Interface dialog box also shows the generated name and the new filename for the interface. The generated name is simply the fully qualified name of the interface. This is used by the class for implementation of the interface. The New File Name text box shows the filename for the interface. All extracted interfaces result in the creation of a new file. The tool tries to keep the filename in sync with the interface name.

The last thing to do is select which members of the object you want to publish as an interface. Of course, only public members are displayed in this list. For this example, select the members `Delete`, `Id`, `Name`, and `Save`.

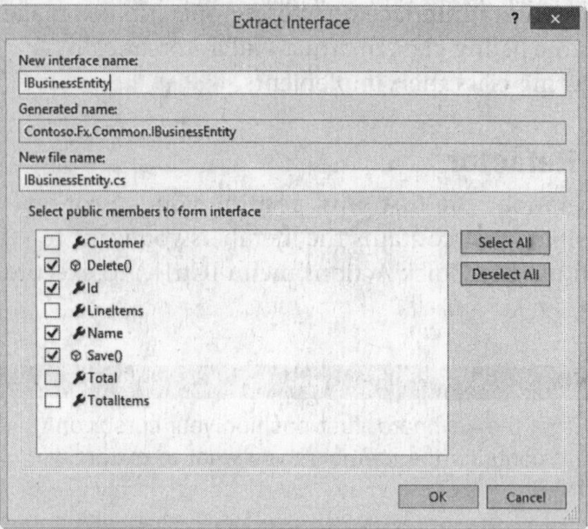

FIGURE 9.20 Use Extract Interface to create an interface based on an existing class.

Clicking the OK button generates the interface. The only change that is made to the `Invoice` class is that it now implements the new interface, as in the following line of code.

```
public class Invoice : IBusinessEntity
```

The interface is then extracted to a new file. Listing 9.4 shows the newly extracted interface.

LISTING 9.4 The Extracted Interface

```
namespace Contoso.Fx.Common
{
  interface IBusinessEntity
  {
    int Id { get; set; }
    string Name { get; set; }
    void Delete();
    void Save();
  }
}
```

The next step in the example is to go out to each domain object and implement the new interface. This is not exactly refactoring, but Visual Studio does help make this easier. Once you indicate that the given object implements an interface, Visual Studio pops up the light bulb in the code editor. This helps implement the interface. Figure 9.21 shows the light bulb that results from typing `IBusinessEntity` after the `Order` class declaration.

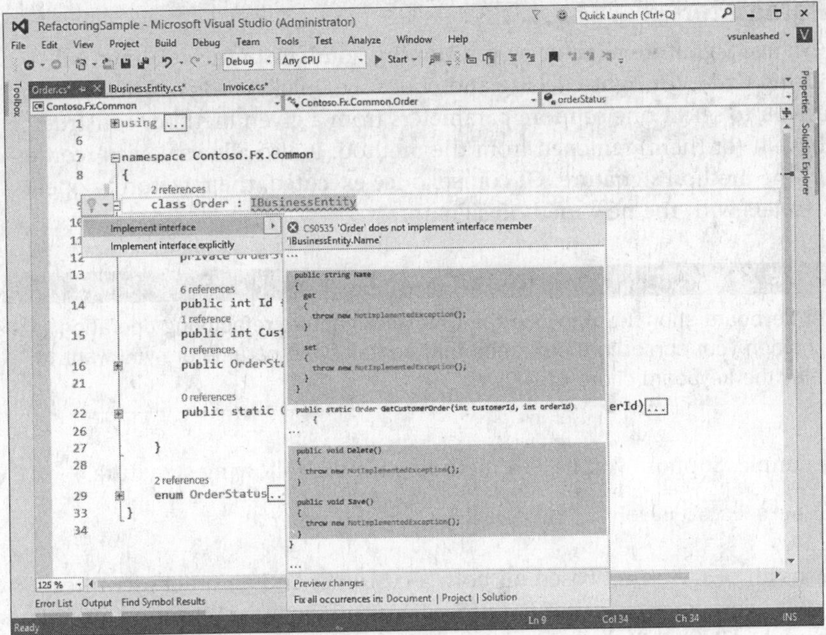

FIGURE 9.21 Implementing an interface with the help of the light bulb.

Notice in Figure 9.21 that you have two options: Implement Interface and Implement Interface Explicitly. The former checks the current class to see whether there are implementations that apply. The latter generates code that explicitly calls the interface items. It puts all this code inside a region for the given interface. This capability can be useful if you're stubbing out a new class based on the interface. The following lines of code provide an example of explicitly implementing the Save method of the interface.

```
void IBusinessEntity.Save() {
  throw new NotImplementedException();
}
```

Change Signature

You sometimes need to change your method signatures by removing an item, by adding a local variable as a parameter, or by reordering the existing parameters. These changes require that all calls to the method also be changed. Doing this manually can introduce new bugs into the code. For example, suppose you want to swap the order of two parameters with the same type (`int`, for example). If you forget to change a call to the method, it might still work; it just won't work right. These bugs can be challenging to find. Therefore, Visual Studio provides refactoring operations for removing and reordering parameters.

Removing a Parameter

You invoke the Change Signature refactor by positioning your cursor inside a method signature and clicking Ctrl+. (or right-clicking and choosing Quick Actions). This Refactor operation enables you to select one or more parameters from a given method, constructor, or delegate and have it (or them) removed from the method. It also allows you to reorder the parameters on the method signature. Of course, once executed, the refactoring operation updates any callers with the new method signature.

TIP

There is another keyboard shortcut to invoke the Change Signature refactoring operation directly. First, position your cursor in the method that contains the parameters you want to remove. Next, play the keyboard chord Ctrl+R, V.

Let's look at an example. Suppose you have a method with the following signature.

```
public static Order GetCustomerOrder(int customerId, int orderId)
```

This method returns an `Order` object based on both a customer and an order identification number. Suppose you determine that the order ID is sufficient for returning an order. In this case, you invoke Change Signature on the method using Ctrl+. and the resulting light bulb. This brings up the Change Signature dialog, as shown in Figure 9.22. To remove a parameter, you simply select it in the dialog and click the Remove button. In this example, the `customerId` parameter is crossed out because it is being removed. If you change your mind, you can use the Restore button to cancel individual parameter removals.

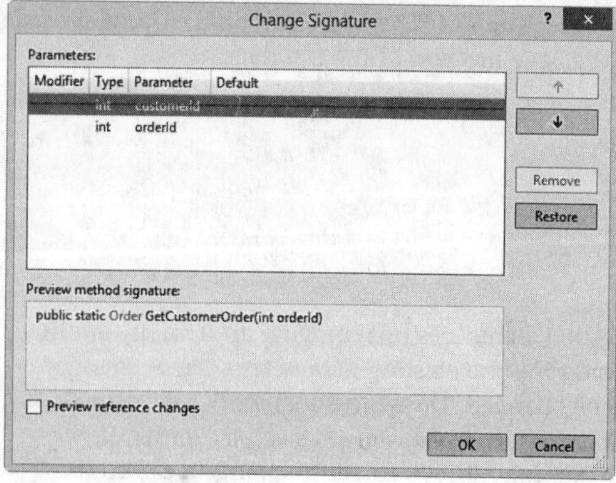

FIGURE 9.22 The Change Signature dialog in action while removing a parameter.

When you are ready to make the removal, you can choose to preview the changes or simply apply them all simultaneously. The Preview option works the same as other previews. It shows you each change in a tree view and enables you to see the details behind the change. You can, of course, also uncheck specific changes. When finished, you apply the final set of removals to your code.

CAUTION

It is common to declare a local variable inside a method and pass that local variable in a call to another method. If you use the refactoring operation to remove the parameter on the method you are calling, the local variable still exists in your calling method. Be careful to make sure that this is what you intended; if not, you have to remove the local variable manually.

Reorder Parameters

You typically move parameters around in a method just for readability and maintenance. You might want the more important parameters to appear first on the method signature, or you might try to keep the order similar across like methods or overloads. You can see from Figure 9.22 that the Change Signature dialog allows you to move around the parameters using the up and down arrows (upper right).

As you change the parameter order, the resulting method signature is displayed below the parameter list (bottom of Figure 9.22). You also have the option to preview any changes that are made to callers of the method. Clicking the OK button applies the changes to both the method and its callers.

Encapsulate Field

It's common to have a private field in your object from which you need to create a property. These fields might have been built as private because they were used only internally to the object. Alternatively, a developer might have simply defined a public field instead of encapsulating it as a property. In either case, if you need to make an actual property out of a field, you can do so with the Encapsulate Field refactor operation.

Accessing Encapsulate Field

The Encapsulate Field operation enables you to quickly generate properties from a given field. Properties, of course, enable you to protect the field from direct access and to know when the given field is being modified or accessed. To encapsulate a field, you position your cursor over the field and again press Ctrl+. to access the light bulb menu. Figure 9.23 shows an example.

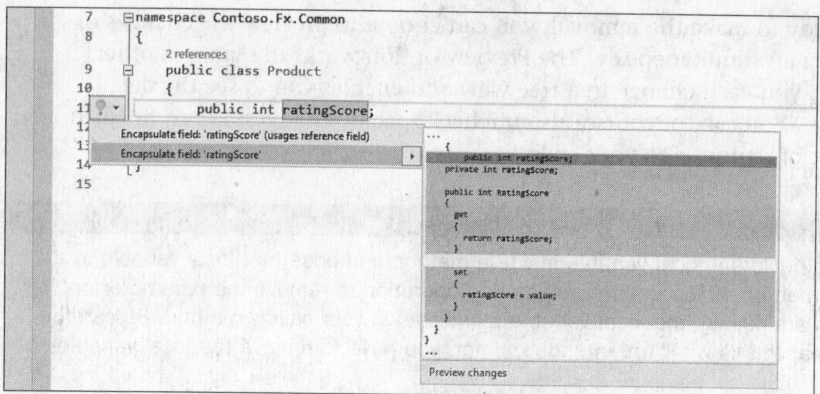

FIGURE 9.23 Encapsulate a field into a property from the Quick Actions menu.

An additional option on the Quick Actions menu for encapsulate field is the choice of the Usages Reference Field. This refers to existing references to the field. Suppose you have a public field. This field might be called both from within the object that defines the field and by other, external objects. You might want to force external callers to use the new property. In this case, you select the Usages Reference Field option.

When you apply the encapsulation, the tool changes your internal field to private (if it was not already private) and then generates a property. The property includes both `get` and `set` accessors for the field. If the field was declared as read-only, the encapsulation generates only a `get` accessor.

Let's look at the code. Suppose you have the following field declaration.

```
public int ratingScore;
```

Suppose you use this field in another assembly, such as this.

```
Product p = new Product();
p.ratingScore = 3;
```

Now suppose you want to encapsulate this public field into a public property (with a private backing field). You would do so by highlighting the field in the code editor and pressing Ctrl+. to get started. You would want to select the Usages Reference Field option from the light bulb menu. Figure 9.24 shows the preview available for this refactor. Notice that the code that uses the current field is also being updated to use the new property.

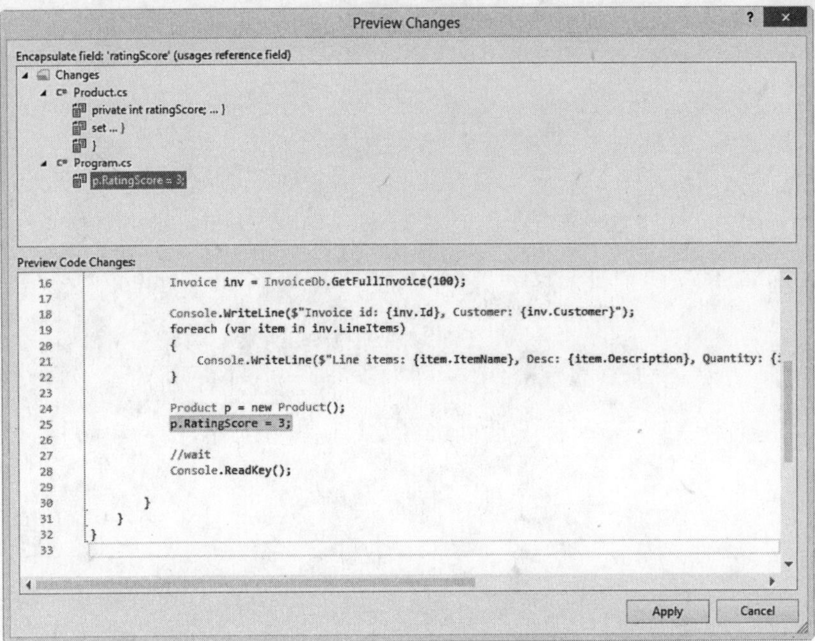

FIGURE 9.24 Preview the encapsulate field changes, including referenced usages.

Summary

This chapter showed how the refactoring tools built in to the Visual Studio code editor can greatly increase productivity and decrease unwanted side effects (bugs) when you're making sweeping changes to your code to improve maintenance, reuse, and readability. The refactoring tools don't simply make changes using text searches and replacements; they use the Visual Studio compiler to make and validate the code changes, and this improves confidence in, and reliability of, the tools.

These tools can be accessed using the keyboard (Ctrl+.), the Quick Actions menu (via a right-click), the class designer, and elsewhere. The refactoring tools enable you to change your code in many ways. You can easily rename items in your code. You can take existing lines of code and extract them to new methods. Your objects can be used as the basis to define new interfaces. You can modify method signatures, including removing and reordering parameters. Finally, you can take existing fields and quickly encapsulate them into properties.

CHAPTER 10

Debugging Code

IN THIS CHAPTER

- ▶ Debugging Basics
- ▶ The Visual Studio Debugger
- ▶ Advanced Debugging Scenarios

Today's developers might spend as much time debugging their code as they do writing it. This is due in some part to the nature of today's highly dependent and distributed applications. These applications are built to leverage existing functionality, frameworks, building blocks, libraries, and so on. In addition, they often communicate with other applications, services, components, databases, and even data exchanges. Developers also demand more assistance from their debugger to help increase their productivity. The Visual Studio debugger addresses these needs by enabling some great debugging scenarios. Some highlights include the following:

- ▶ Breakpoint and tracepoint configuration
- ▶ Visualizers and debugger DataTips
- ▶ Visual diagnostic tools during debug session
- ▶ Edit and Continue
- ▶ Just-my-code debugging
- ▶ The Exception Assistant
- ▶ Debugging support at design time
- ▶ Client-side script debugging
- ▶ Debugging multithreaded and parallel code
- ▶ Remote debugging

We cover all these features and more in this chapter. Of course, if you are just getting started with .NET, more than just this list is new to you. The Visual Studio debugger has been evolving since the first release of .NET, which provided a unified debugger with the capability to debug across languages. In this chapter, we start by covering the basics of debugging an application. We then discuss the Visual Studio debugger in depth.

Debugging Basics

A typical scenario for a developer is to start building a web page or form and build up the code that surrounds it. In addition, the developer might rely on a framework or a few building blocks that provide added functionality. The application might also communicate with a services layer and most often a database. Even the most typical applications have a lot of moving parts. These moving parts make the task of finding and eliminating errors in the code all the more complex. The tools that help you track down and purge errors from your code not only have to keep up with this complexity, but must ease the effort involved with the debugging process. In the following sections, we cover how a developer uses the tools built into Visual Studio to debug a typical development scenario.

The Scenario

We want to define an application scenario that we can use both to introduce the basics of debugging and to function as a base for us to build on throughout the chapter when demonstrating the many features of the debugging tools. In this scenario, imagine you are writing a web application with all the typical moving parts:

- Data for the application is stored in a SQL database.
- A data access library built on Entity Framework code-first abstracts working with the database.
- A variety of different technologies are involved in the solution, including a web-based user interface (UI) built on ASP.NET Model-View-Controller (MVC) using C# controllers and HTML/JavaScript views.

Even though we concentrate on C#, the debugging tools in Visual Studio are equally applicable to Visual Basic development. Everything we discuss here applies to both languages unless specified otherwise.

The Many Phases of Debugging

Nearly every time developers open the IDE, they are in some way debugging their code. The line between debugging and writing code, in fact, is blurred. For example, the code editor helps eliminate errors in your code as you write it. It highlights items where errors are present and enables you to fix them. You are then both writing and debugging simultaneously.

In addition, the compiler acts as another debugging tool. It is constantly compiling your code and checking it. Should you click the Run button, the compiler will report a list of errors for you to fix before continuing. This is debugging. The steps or phases of the debugging process include the following:

- **Coding**—The editor helps you by pointing out issues and possible resolutions using the Quick Actions menu (light bulb) and other visual cues.
- **Compiling**—The compiler checks your code and reports errors you should fix before continuing.
- **Self-checking**—You run the application in debug mode and step through screens and code to verify functionality.
- **Unit testing**—You write and run unit tests to check your application. (See Chapter 8, "Testing Code.")
- **Code analysis**—You run the Static Code Analyzer to verify that your application meets project standards.
- **Code review**—Your code is reviewed by a peer and issues are logged, tracked, and fixed accordingly.
- **Responding to bug**—When a bug has been logged against the code, you must re-create and debug a specific scenario.

In this chapter, we concentrate on two of these phases: self-checking (which may include unit testing) and responding to bugs. These are the two phases in which developers get the most use of the debugging tools built in to Visual Studio. For the purposes of this chapter, we assume that the code is written and that it compiles. Let's start by looking at how to self-check the code.

Debugging the Application (Self-Checking)

In this scenario, you have just started writing a web page to edit a customer's profile. Assume that you've laid out the page, connected to the profile web service, and written the code to save a user's profile to the database. You now need to start self-checking your work to make sure everything operates as you expect.

NOTE

If you want to follow along, the code we have used in this chapter comes predominantly from the Contoso University sample application that Microsoft provides to demonstrate construction of an MVC-based web application. Search for "Contoso University" on the Microsoft Developer Network (MSDN) site to find the download location for the entire Visual Studio solution. We are using the ASP.NET MVC 5 and Entity Framework 6 version.

Note that the site contains the setup instructions for working with the application. You should be using SQL Express LocalDb for development. This site instructs you on installing the database and data. However, you may have to modify the `Web.config` file connection string to point to your instance of LocalDb. The best way to do this is to create a new database with the same name (currently `ContosoUniversity2`) using SQL Server Object Explorer (accessible from the View menu). You can then right-click the database and view properties. Here you can find the right connection string information for the `Web.config` file. You can then install the database schema and related data following instructions.

The first step is to start your application in debug mode. This allows you to break into your code if an error occurs. In development, this is typically your default setting. You first invoke debug mode by clicking the Run (or Start Debugging) button (the green arrow on the Standard toolbar). Figure 10.1 shows the sample application about to be run in debug mode for the first time. Notice that for web applications, you can choose which browser to use out of all the installed browsers on your machine. In this case, we are selecting Internet Explorer.

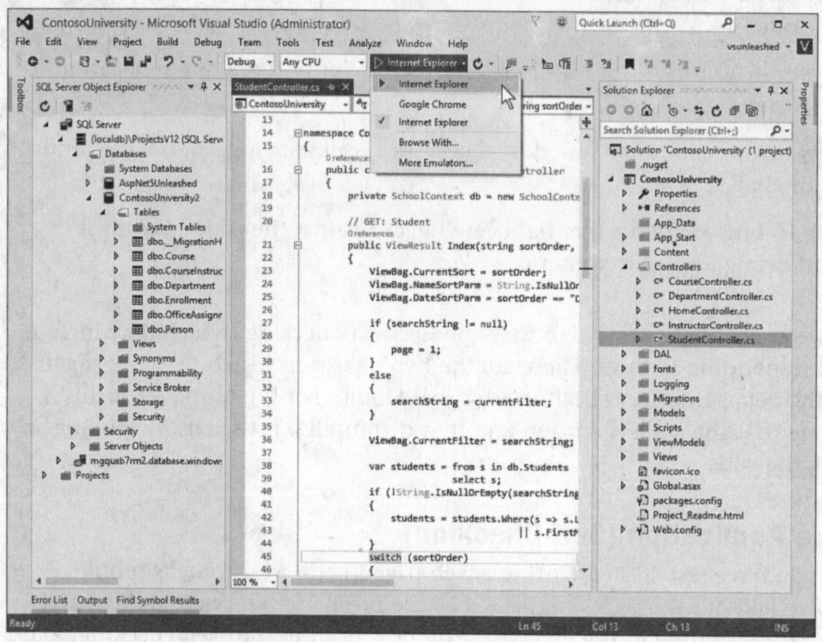

FIGURE 10.1 Use the Start button to debug the application.

Enabling Debugging on a Website

This example is a web application. Therefore, it requires you to set up debugging on server-side code whose errors and information are output to a remote client. Of course, in the majority of cases, developers code and debug on a single development machine. However, sometimes you have to debug a process on a test server.

In either case, you have to enable debugging through a setting in the configuration file (`Web.config`) for your application. The modern, default `Web.config` file has debugging enabled by default. The setting that controls debugging is the compilation element under the system.web node. You set debug equal to `false` (as in off) or `true` (as in on). The following is an example of the XML with debug mode turned on. Again, this is the default setting. Controlling debugging directly with this setting is not recommended. As you will see in a moment, the type of build you target can control this setting.

```
<system.web>
  <compilation debug="true" targetFramework="4.5"/>
    ...
</system.web>
```

The `Web.config` file has multiple subfiles that are used based on the type of build you are creating in Visual Studio. This allows you to define settings for Debug and Release configurations. You do so through XDT (XML-Document-Transform). Figure 10.2 shows the IDE build setting set to Debug (top drop-down menu), the `Web.Release.config` subfile, and the XDT transform that would turn off debugging for a release build. Notice, too, in Solution Explorer the `Web.config` file and the two subfiles: one for debug-specific settings and one for release-specific settings.

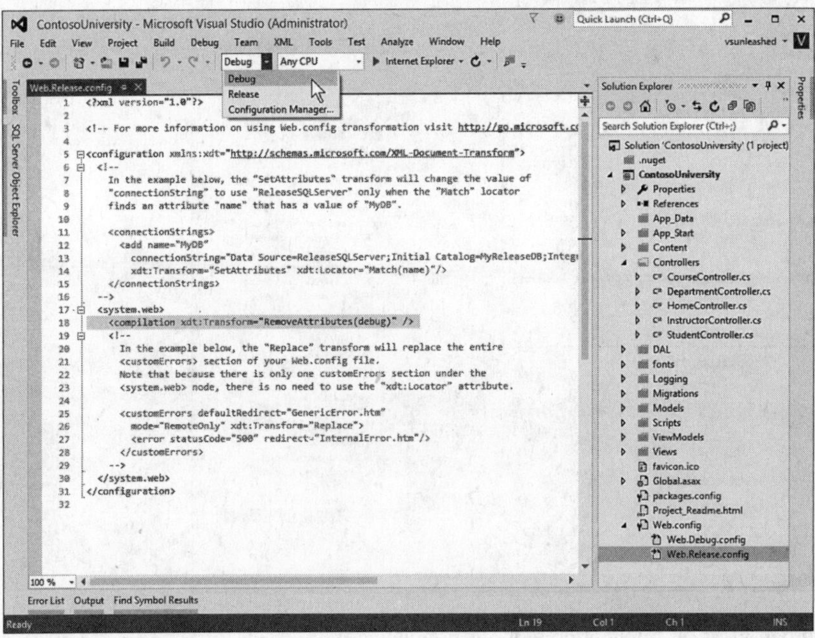

FIGURE 10.2 The `Web.config` files control your debug setting on your website build.

NOTE

It is important that you turn off debugging (by doing a release build) before deploying your web application to production. Having debugging enabled in a production environment is a security risk. With debugging enabled, ASP.NET writes the details of your errors to a web page. These details provide valuable clues to would-be attackers about how your application is put together. In some instances, the error could include user credentials that are being used to access secured resources.

Starting in Debug Mode

The most typical scenario for starting a debug session is just clicking the Start button on the toolbar. This works with all application types, including Windows and ASP.NET. This action instructs Visual Studio to compile the application and bring up the initial form or page.

Applications can also be started without debugging; this includes both Windows and ASP.NET applications. This capability is useful if you simply want to walk through an application as a user might see it (without breaking into the IDE). You use the Debug menu, Start Without Debugging option to start your application without attaching it to the Visual Studio Debugger. Figure 10.3 shows an example of invoking this action.

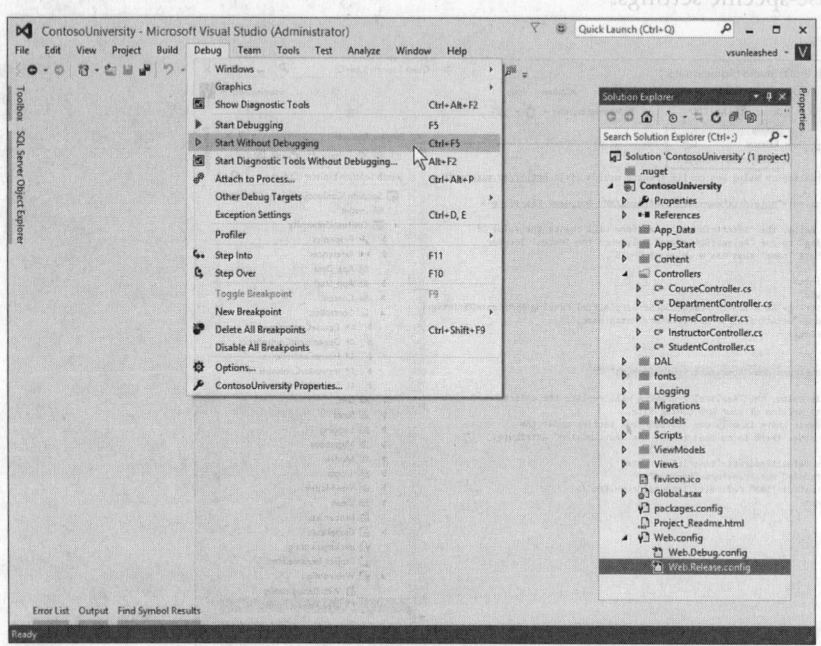

FIGURE 10.3 You can start an application without debugging it.

You can also start a debugging session by stepping into code, line by line. This approach is useful if you want to see all your code as it executes (rather than just errors). You might desire this if you are getting some unexpected behavior. Stepping line by line gives you an exact understanding of what is going on with your code (rather than just your assumed understanding).

Stepping into code on a web form is typically done by first opening the main source. You then right-click and select the Run to Cursor option from the shortcut menu. Figure 10.4 shows an example. This command tells Visual Studio to start debugging the application. When the execution gets to this point, the IDE opens to let you step through each line of code (or continue, and so on).

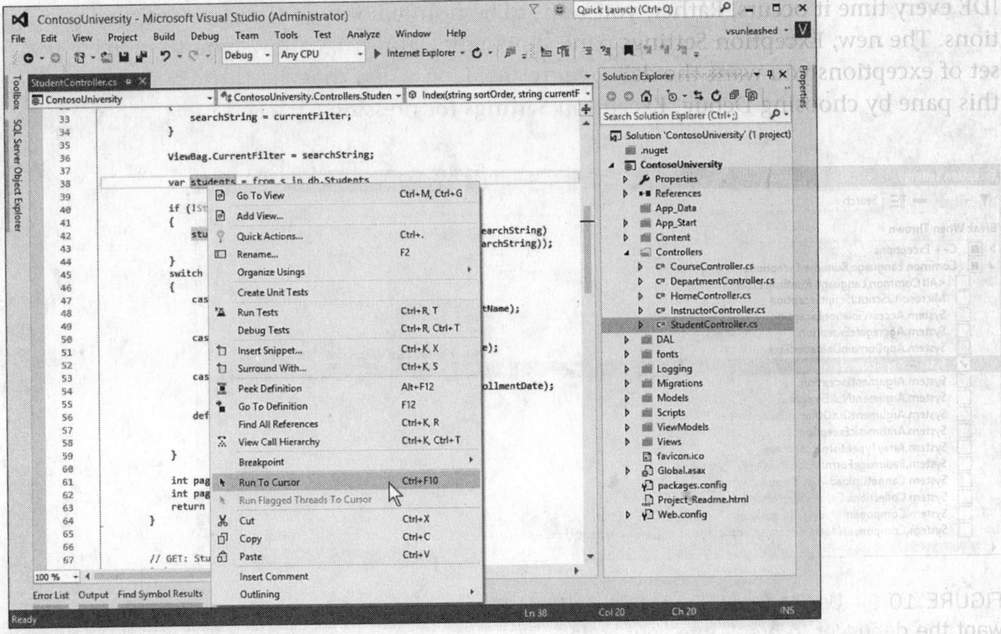

FIGURE 10.4 You can have Visual Studio run your application up to the current line of code and then break into debugging.

Breaking on an Error

Not everything you find in debug mode is an error that results in a break into the code for a debug session. Often, issues arise just because you're looking at the behavior of the application. For example, a control could be out of place, the tab order could be wrong, and so on. For these items, you still have to rely on your eyes. The debugging tools in Visual Studio help you respond to hard errors in your code.

By default, when unhandled exceptions occur in your code, the IDE will break into the debugger and highlight the offending code. The key in that sentence is "unhandled exceptions." They represent places in your code where you do not have `try-catch` blocks to manage an exception. Your code should catch expected exceptions, trace them, and recover from the corresponding error if possible. In this case, you see the following message in the Output pane (but the debugger does not stop on the faulting statement):

A first chance exception of type 'System.ArgumentNullException' occurred in...

Breaking on just unhandled exceptions is typically a good default setting. However, you often need to see handled exceptions as well. This can help you get to the root cause of the error when the exception is thrown rather than when it is caught and dealt with by your code.

Fortunately, the errors that result in a break in the IDE are a configurable set. For example, you might handle a specific exception in your code and not want to be dumped to the

IDE every time it occurs. Rather, you want to be notified only of those exceptional conditions. The new, Exception Settings pane shown by Figure 10.5 allows you to manage the set of exceptions you want the debugger to break on when they are thrown. You access this pane by choosing Debug, Exception Settings (or pressing Ctrl+D, E).

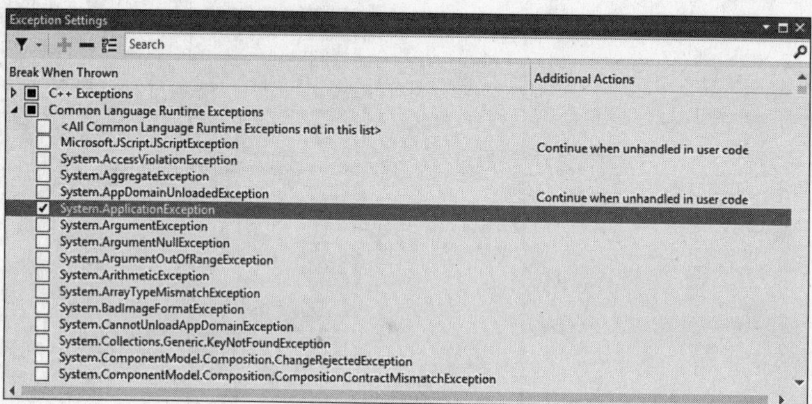

FIGURE 10.5 Use the new Exception Settings pane to select the exceptions on which you want the debugger to break into your code.

In the Exception Settings pane, the various exceptions are categorized by debug engine and sorted by namespace for easy access. There is also a Filter feature on the toolbar. When a box in not checked in the Exception Settings pane, the debugger will only break execution when that exception is thrown and not handled by your code. This is the default setting for the vast majority of exceptions. Checking the box indicates you want the debugger to break execution when the exception is thrown (regardless if it is handled or not). The debugger then reacts by breaking on the line that triggers the exception, before your `catch` handler is called.

The Exception Settings pane also has a context menu (right-click) for exceptions. Here you find the option "Continue when unhandled in user code." This option tells the debugger to ignore this exception even if you are not handling it in your code.

Debugging an Error

The first step in debugging your application is to click the Start button. Your application is then running under the control of the debugger. As it happens, the sample application we discussed in our scenario can throw an exception upon its initial startup provided the database connection string is not set up or the database has not been created. The debugger responds by breaking into the code and showing the offending line (in this case, the call to get students from the database). Figure 10.6 shows a typical view of the editor when it breaks on an error.

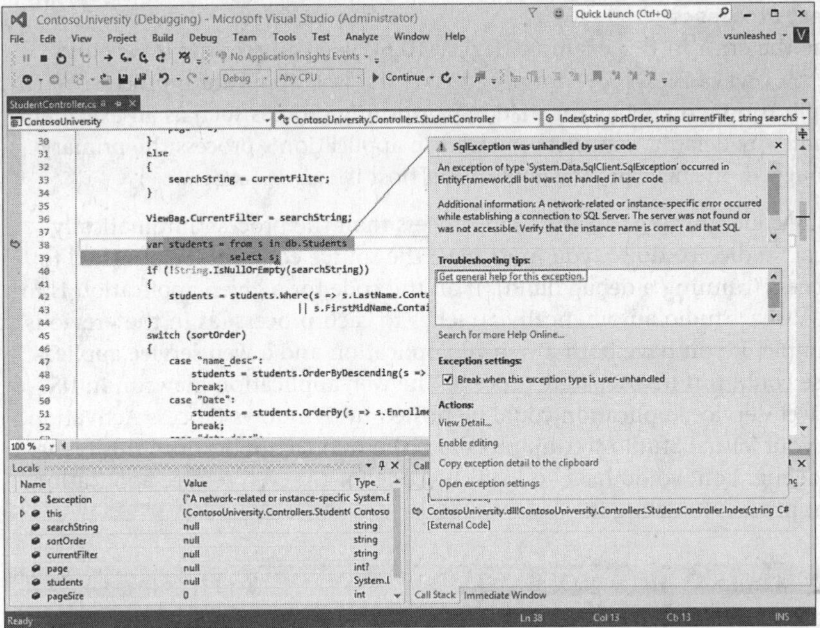

FIGURE 10.6 The Visual Studio debugger breaking on an exception.

There are a few items of interest about the standard debug session shown in Figure 10.6. First, Visual Studio has highlighted the line that has thrown the exception. You can see this clearly by the arrow (left margin) and the highlighted text.

Next, notice the window in the middle right of the image. This is the Exception Assistant. It provides details on the exception and offers tips for troubleshooting and fixing the given issue. From this window, you can access a few actions, including searching online help for more information on the exception.

At the bottom of the screen are a few additional helpful windows. The Locals window on the left automatically shows the value assigned to all variables local to the code in scope where the exception was thrown. This gives you easy access to key information that might be contributing to the issue. Notice that at the bottom of this window is an inactive tab called Watch 1. This is a Watch window; it keeps track of any custom watch scenarios you set up (more on this later).

The window on the bottom right of the screen is the call stack. It shows the order in which various components of an application were called. You can look at the call stack to find out how you got to where you are. You can also use it to navigate to any code referenced in the stack. (See the section "Debugging Multithreaded Applications" later in this chapter for more on the call stack.) Finally, the inactive tab next to this gives you access to the Immediate window. The Immediate window allows you to type in code commands and get the results in the editor (more on this to come).

Debugging Different Processes

After you examine the error in this example (Figure 10.6), you can see that it is being thrown from the `EntityFramework.dll` running inside the web application process. When you debug an application, you debug (or shadow) a running process such as an executable (`.exe`). Visual Studio, by default, considers the startup application's process the primary process being debugged. In this case, the application host is `iisexpress.exe`.

You can also debug code running in a different process than the process automatically launched by Visual Studio. To do so, you must have the source code and be attached to the executing process (running a debug build). If all the code for a given application is in a single solution, Visual Studio automatically attaches to each process (as in the previous example).For example, if you have both a web UI application and a web service application, each of these could run in a separate process. The web application may run in IIS Express, and the web service application could be hosted by Windows Process Activation Service (WAS). If your Visual Studio startup process is the web UI application, this is the process you will debug. You would have to load the code for the web service application and attach to that process to debug it.

NOTE

The debugger does automatically break into the IDE on errors raised outside of the Visual Studio application startup host process. Therefore, an unhandled error raised by code in the startup process would result in a break into the debugger on the offending line of code. An unhandled error raised by code running in another host process will do the same. Visual Studio does respect breakpoints you set inside code executing in other processes. You can also step into code from one process to another inside the debugger.

Sometimes you need to manually attach to an already-running process. You might want to attach the IDE to a running web server, or you might have a web service application to which you want to bind debugging. Whatever the scenario, Visual Studio allows you to attach to the process and begin a debug session. To attach to a running process, such as a web server, you choose the Attach to Process option from the Debug menu. This brings up the dialog box shown in Figure 10.7.

To connect the Visual Studio debugger to a process, you simply highlight it and click the Attach button (as shown in Figure 10.7). Note that any currently attached processes are grayed out. This is a visual indicator that you are already attached to a given process. In the example in Figure 10.7, the application was started without debugging. We then used Attach to process to connect a debug session to the running process.

Setting a Breakpoint

To get the debugger to break into your code when it reaches a specific line of code, you set a breakpoint on that line. You do so by clicking on the indicator bar (far left of the code editor) for the given line. Alternatively, you can right-click on the line and choose Insert Breakpoint from the Breakpoint context menu. Figure 10.8 shows setting a breakpoint from the indicator bar. Just before the line is executed, Visual Studio breaks into the code and allows you to interrogate variable values and step line by line. It also confirms how your code is executing.

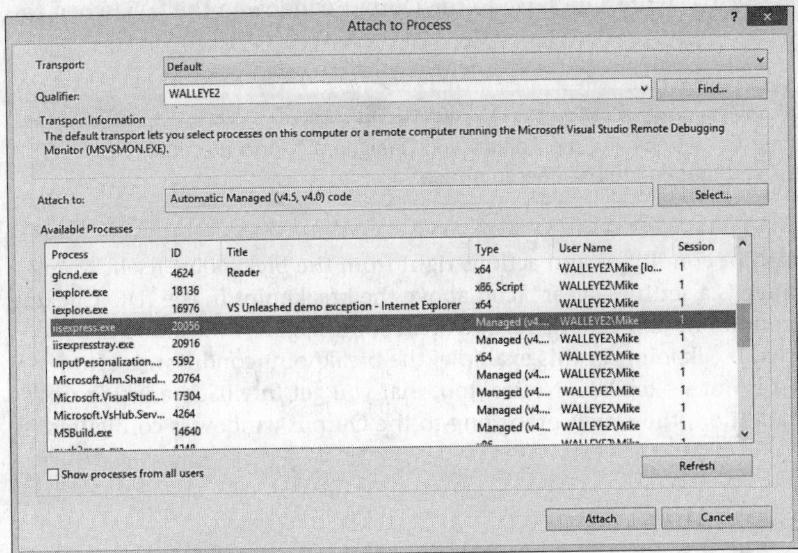

FIGURE 10.7 Use Attach to Process (Debug menu) to attach the Visual Studio debugger to a running process such as a web host application.

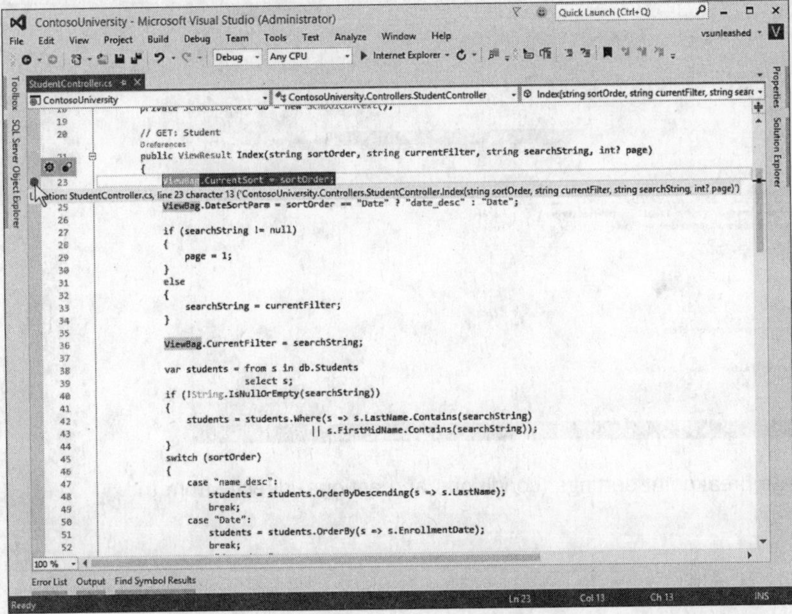

FIGURE 10.8 You can set a breakpoint on a specific line of code.

Breakpoint Conditions and Actions

You can set additional conditions on your breakpoint. This allows you to only break on the given line if a certain condition inside your code is `true`. You can also choose to implement an action, such as write a message to the Output window in the IDE, when the line of code is executed.

> **NOTE**
>
> Refer back to Chapter 6, "Introducing the Editors and Designers," for a discussion of the breakpoint indicator and margin toolbar user interface.

You can access breakpoint conditions and actions right from the breakpoint itself. Notice in Figure 10.8 that there is a settings "gear" icon above the breakpoint in the IDE. Clicking this gear opens the conditions and actions for the breakpoint. Figure 10.9 shows the settings for the selected breakpoint. In this example, the breakpoint condition is set to break if the sort order is not set to Date. Notice, too, that you get IntelliSense inside this settings window. In addition, the action of logging to the Output window is configured in Figure 10.9.

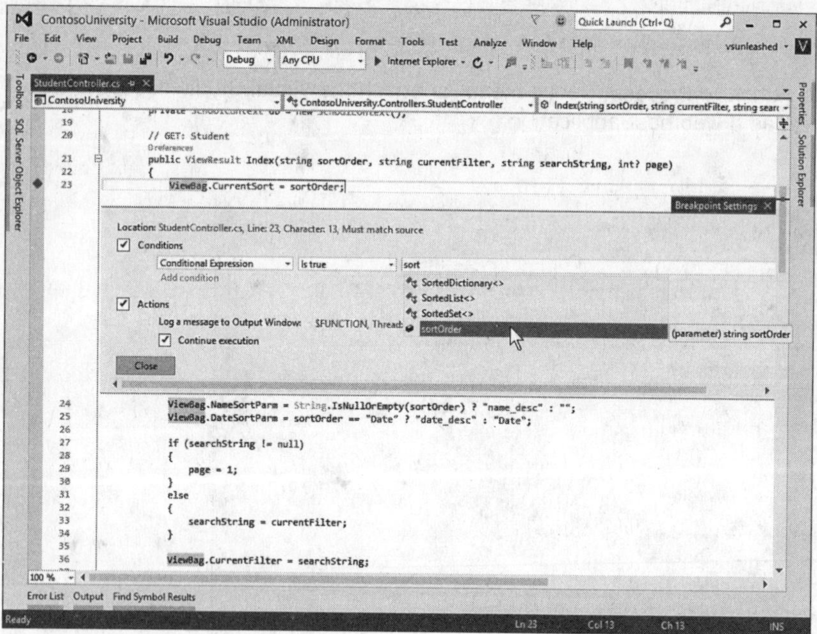

FIGURE 10.9 Manage breakpoint settings (conditions and actions) directly from the code editor.

Continuing Debugging After a Breakpoint

When you hit a breakpoint, you often end up examining running code, code that was run (call stack), and code that will be run. Of course, you also verify variables, check the call stack, look for bugs, and more. Once you are done with the breakpoint, you want to tell Visual Studio to continue executing the code normally (or at least until you hit another breakpoint). You do so by simply hitting the large green arrow button (with the word "Continue" now) again.

It is easy to get lost in a debug session. You often have to navigate off the executing code to find issues. You scroll through the current file and even switch files. It can often be hard to find your way back; the line that was executing could be buried in any one of the open code windows. Thus, Visual Studio provides the Show Next Statement button (gray arrow) on the Debug toolbar to take you back, effectively returning you to the line of code that the debugger broke on. Figure 10.10 shows this button on the toolbar in a debug session. Note you can also get here from a right-click in the code editor.

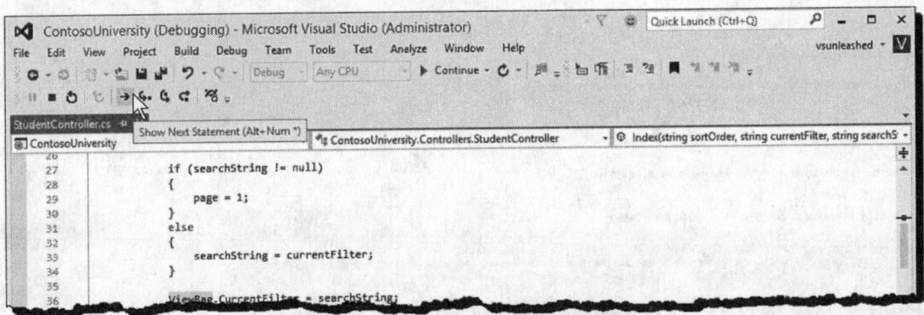

FIGURE 10.10 Show Next Statement takes you back to the code that will execute next in the debug session.

There are times when you are debugging and want to skip lines or sections of your code. In this instance, you can tell Visual Studio the next statement to execute (and thereby skip any code that might have otherwise executed). You do so with Set Next Statement. You can access this option by right-clicking a line of code and selecting Set Next Statement from the context menu.

Stepping Through Code to Find an Error

The debugger breaks execution and steps into code as soon as it hits a breakpoint or an unhandled exception is thrown. This allows you to step through the code. To step line by line through the code, you can click the Step Into button (blue arrow pointing to a dot) on the Debug toolbar or press the F11 function key. This executes the code one line at a time, enabling you to view both execution flow and the state of the application as code executes. You can also exit the current method and return to the calling method using Shift+F11.

In many scenarios, you can make a fix to bugs found during the debug session and continue stepping through or running the code; this is referred to as Edit and Continue.

However, this is not supported in certain scenarios. You cannot invoke Edit and Continue when the debugger has been attached to an already running process, for example.

If you are not using Edit and Continue, you can bookmark the line where you want to make the change using the Text Editor toolbar. You then click the Stop button (red square) on the Debug toolbar to stop the debug session. The code change can now be made. You again use the Text Editor toolbar to return to your bookmark and make your change. Figure 10.11 shows an example of creating a bookmark during a debug session.

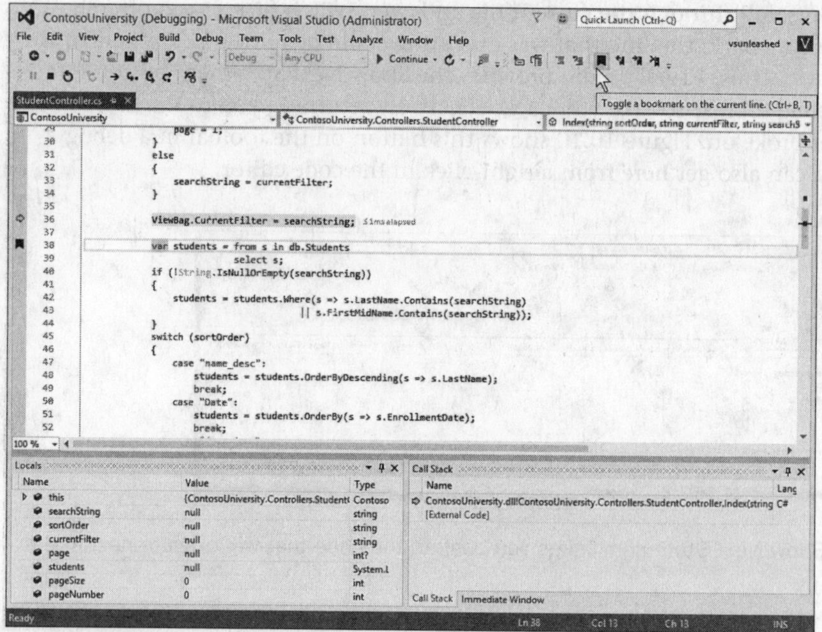

FIGURE 10.11 You can uses bookmarks to flag places in your code you intend to return to following the debug session.

To continue through self-checking following a change, you restart the debugging process. However, before restarting, you might want to clear the breakpoint you set by selecting the Debug menu, Windows, and then Breakpoints. This brings up the Breakpoints window shown in Figure 10.12. From this window, you can view all breakpoints in the application. Here, you select and clear the breakpoint by clicking the Delete button from the toolbar on the Breakpoints pane. Finally, you click the Start button to continue the debug self-check session.

Debugging Basics Summary

This section walked through the many phases of debugging and introduced the basic concepts of executing code line by line inside Visual Studio. If you are familiar with prior IDE versions, you probably noticed a lot of similarities. This section showed the many tools inside the debugging environment, including the Debug toolbar and menu, the Breakpoints window, the Watch window, and so on. Now that you have a grasp of the basics, in the next section we intend to explore these debug elements in greater detail.

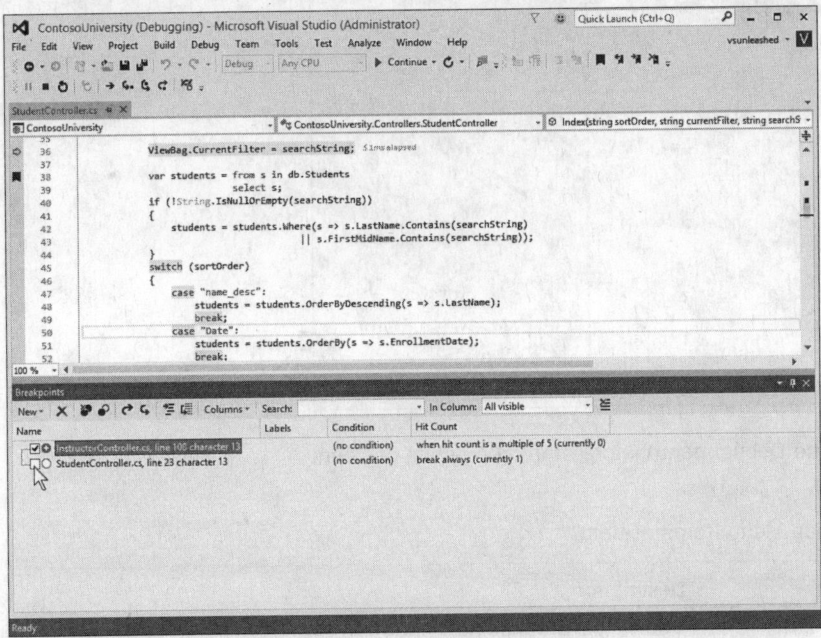

FIGURE 10.12 You can manage your breakpoints using the Breakpoints window.

The Visual Studio Debugger

The debugger built in to Visual Studio 2015 is one of the largest and most complex tools in the IDE. With such a large feature-set area, we cannot possibly cover every scenario you might encounter. In this next section, however, we hope to expose the most commonly applicable features. We touch on advanced features in the next section.

The Debug Menu and Toolbar

The Debug menu and its related toolbar provide your first-level access to starting debug sessions, stepping into code, managing breakpoints, and accessing the many features of debugging with Visual Studio. There are two states to the debug menu: at rest (or inactive) and in debug mode. Figure 10.13 shows the menu in the at-rest state.

In the at-rest state, the Debug menu provides features to start a debug session, attach code to a running process, or access some of the many debug windows. Table 10.1 lists all the features available from the Debug menu at rest.

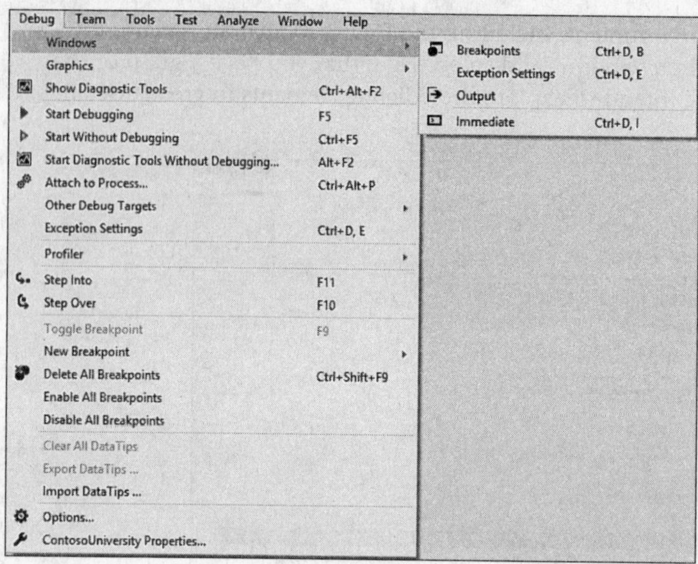

FIGURE 10.13 The Debug menu before starting a debug session.

TABLE 10.1 Debug Menu Items at Rest

Menu Item	Description
Windows, Breakpoints	Opens the Breakpoints window in the IDE. This window provides access to all the breakpoints in the option solution.
Windows, Output	Shows the Output window in the IDE. The Output window is a running log of the many messages that are emitted by the IDE, the compiler, and the debugger and the debugged application. Therefore, the information transcends just debug sessions.
Windows, Immediate	Opens the Immediate window in the IDE. This window allows you to execute commands. For example, during application design, you can call your methods directly from the Immediate window. This will start the application and enter directly into a debug session.
Graphics	Used to debug code running on your graphics processing unit (GPU). Includes options for DirectX.
Show Diagnostic Tools	Shows the new Diagnostic Tools pane for your application running in debug mode. This pane provides information on your running application such as memory and CPU usage.
Start Debugging	Starts to debug your application.
Start Without Debugging	Starts your application without connecting the debugger to the executing process. In this mode, the developer sees what users would see (instead of breaking into the IDE for errors and breakpoints).

Menu Item	Description
Attach to Process	Allows you to attach the debugger to a running process (executable) that contains your code. If, for example, you started the application without debugging, you could then attach to that running process and begin debugging.
Other Debug Targets	Used to start debugging an App Package, Windows Store app, or Windows Phone app.
Exception Settings	Opens the Exception Settings pane that enables you to choose how the debugger breaks on any given exception.
Profiler	Allows you to launch the diagnostic tools without a debug session.
Step Into	For most projects, clicking the Step Into command invokes the debugger on the first executing line of the application. In this way, you can step into the application from the first line.
Step Over	When not in a debugging session, the Step Over command simply starts to debug the application the same way as clicking the Start button would.
Start Windows Phone Application Analysis	Launches the analysis tool for Windows Phone (provided you are creating a Windows phone application).
Toggle Breakpoint	Toggles the breakpoint on or off for the current, active line of code in a text editor. The option is inactive if you do not have a code window active in the IDE.
New Breakpoint, Break at Function	Brings up the New Breakpoint dialog box. This dialog box enables you to indicate a function name to define for which to create a breakpoint. This can be useful if you know a function's name but do not want to search your code files for it.
New Breakpoint, Data Breakpoint	This option is available only for native, C++ applications. It allows you to define a breakpoint that breaks into the IDE when a value in a specific memory location changes.
Delete All Breakpoints	Removes all breakpoints from your solution.
Enable All Breakpoints	Enables all the breakpoints in your solution.
Disable All Breakpoints	Disables (without removing) all the breakpoints in your solution.
Clear All DataTips	Enables you to clear any data tips you might have pinned to the IDE (including comments). See "DataTips" later in this chapter.
Export DataTips	Allows you to export your data tips as an XML file for sharing with other developers. See "DataTips" later in this chapter.
Import DataTips	Allows you to import an XML data tips file for use inside your debug sessions. See "DataTips" later in this chapter.
Options	Brings up the Options dialog box for debugging. See "Debug Options" later in this chapter.
(project) Properties	Brings up the Properties dialog box for the current project.

When the debugger is engaged and you are working through a debug session, the state of the Debug menu changes. It now provides several additional options over those provided by the at-rest state. These options include those designed to move through the code, restart the session, and access even more debug-related windows. Figure 10.14 shows the Debug menu during a debug session.

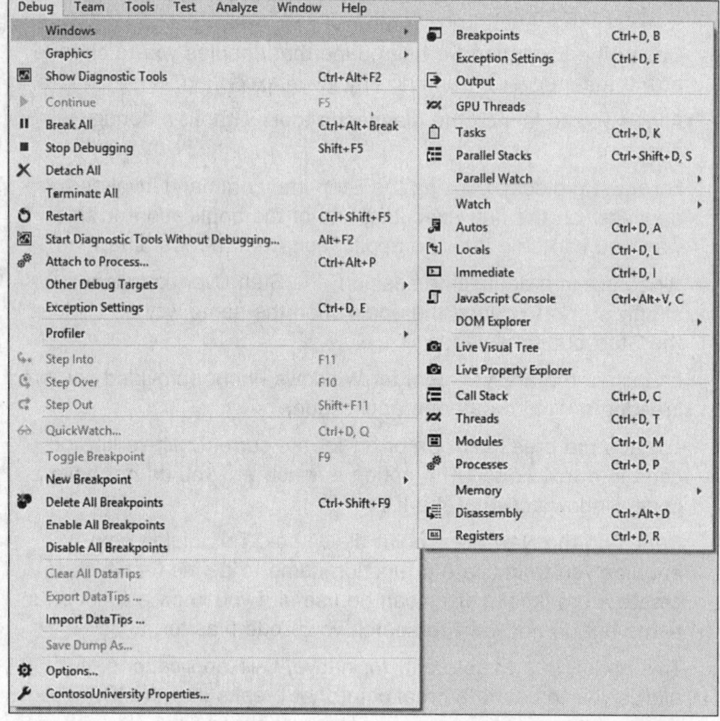

FIGURE 10.14 The Debug menu during an active debug session.

Let's look at the many options provided by the Debug menu during a debug session. Table 10.2 presents the many items available from the debug menu in this state. When reading through the table, refer to the preceding figures to get context on any given item.

TABLE 10.2 Debug Menu Items for an Active Debug Session

Menu Item	Description
Windows, Breakpoints	Allows you to open the Breakpoints window during a debug session.
Windows, Exception Settings	Open the Exception Settings pane for managing when the IDE breaks on specific exceptions.

Menu Item	Description
Windows, Output	Opens the Output window during an active debug session in order to read output messages emitted by the compiler, debugger, and debugged code.
Windows, GPU Threads	Opens a window for inspection of any active GPU threads spawned by your application.
Windows, Parallel Tasks	Enables you to view parallel tasks in a visual window. See "Debugging Parallel Applications" later in this chapter.
Windows, Parallel Stacks	Enables you to view executing threads and tasks in a visual window. See "Debugging Parallel Applications" later in this chapter.
Windows, Parallel Watch	Enables you to evaluate watch expressions spanning multiple or even all available threads.
Windows, Watch	Opens one of many possible Watch windows in the IDE. Watch windows represent items and expressions you are keeping a close eye on through a debug session.
Windows, Autos	Opens the Autos window. This window shows variables (and their values) in the current line of code and the preceding line of code.
Windows, Locals	Opens the Locals window in the IDE. This window shows variables in the local scope (function).
Windows, Immediate	Opens the Immediate window where you can execute a command.
JavaScript Console	Available for web applications, this launches the JavaScript Console window. This console enables you to execute JavaScript against the currently loaded Document Object Model (DOM).
DOM Explorer	Allows you to drill down into the currently loaded Document Object Model (DOM), and easily view property settings at any point within the DOM tree.
Live Visual Tree	Enables a pane that allows you to see the markup tree for running XAML.
Live Property Explorer	Enables a pane for seeing the properties of XAML elements in the visual tree.
Windows, Call Stack	Shows the list of functions that are on the stack. Also indicates the current stack frame (function). This selected item is what defines the content from the Locals, and Autos windows.
Windows, Threads	Shows the Threads window in the IDE. From here, you can view and control the threads in the application you are debugging.
Windows, Modules	Shows the Modules window in the IDE. This window lists the DLLs and EXEs used by your application.
Windows, Processes	Shows the Processes window in the IDE. This window lists the processes to which the debug session is attached.

Menu Item	Description
Windows, Memory	Opens the Memory window for a view at the memory used by your application. This is valid only when address-level debugging is enabled from the Options dialog box.
Windows, Disassembly	Opens the Disassembly window. This window shows the assembly code corresponding to the compiler instructions. This is valid only when address-level debugging is enabled from the Options dialog box.
Windows, Registers	Opens the Registers window so that you can see register values change as you step through code. This is valid only when address-level debugging is enabled from the Options dialog box.
Show Diagnostic Tools	Launches the new Diagnostic Tools pane for tracking information about your running application such as CPU and memory usage over time.
Continue	Continues executing the application after broken into the IDE. The application continues running on the active line of code (the breakpoint, a line that threw an error, or a line set using Set Next Statement).
Break All	Enables you to break the application into the debugger manually (without having to hit a breakpoint) during a debug session. The application breaks on the next line that executes. This capability is useful to gain access to the debug information, such as Watch windows. It can also be used to gain access to the debug session when your application appears to have hung.
Stop Debugging	Terminates the debugging session. It also terminates the process you are debugging, provided that the process was started by Visual Studio.
Detach All	Detaches the debugger from the executing process. This enables your application to continue running after the debugger is through with it.
Terminate All	Stops debugging and terminates all processes to which you are attached.
Restart	Stops the debugging session and restarts it. Similar to clicking both Stop Debugging and Start Debugging in sequence.
Attach to Process	Enables you to attach the active debug session to one or more additional processes such as an executing web server or a Windows service.
Exception Settings	Brings up the Exception Settings pane, which enables you to manage how the IDE breaks on specific exception types in the .NET Framework and other libraries.

Menu Item	Description
Step Into	Advances the debugger a line. If you choose to "step into" a function, the code of the function is shown in the IDE and the debugger move to the first line of code in it. If the current line is not a function, the line is executed.
Step Over	Functions the same as Step Into with one major difference: If you choose to "step over" a function, the line calling the function is executed (along with the function), and the debugger sets the next line after the function call as the next line to be debugged.
Step Out	Tells the debugger to execute the code up to the end of the current function and then break back into debugging at the line that was calling it of the previous method in the callstack. This capability is useful if you step into a function but then want to have that function just execute and yet return you to debug mode when it is complete.
QuickWatch	Brings up the QuickWatch window when the debugger is in break mode. The QuickWatch window shows one variable or expression you are watching and its value.
Toggle Breakpoint	Turns an active breakpoint on or off.
New Breakpoint	Brings up the New Breakpoint dialog box (see Table 10.1 for more information).
Delete All Breakpoints	Deletes all breakpoints in your solution.
Enable All Breakpoints	Enables all breakpoints in your solution.
Disable All Breakpoints	Disables breakpoints in the solution without deleting them. You can also disable individual breakpoints. This capability is very useful if you want to keep the breakpoints around for later but simply don't want to hit that one at the moment.
Clear All DataTips	Allows you to clear any data tips you might have pinned to the IDE (including comments). See "DataTips" later in this chapter.
Export DataTips	Enables you to export your DataTips as an XML file for sharing with other developers. See "DataTips" later in this chapter.
Import DataTips	Enables you to import an XML DataTips file for use inside your debug sessions. See "DataTips" later in this chapter.
Save Dump As	Enables you to save a memory dump for the active debug session.
Options	Brings up the Options dialog box for debugging. See "Debug Options" later in this chapter.
(project) Properties	Brings up the Properties dialog box for the current project.

The Debug Toolbar

The Debug toolbar provides quick access to some of the key items available on the Debug menu. From here, you can manage your debug session. For example, you can start or continue a debug session, stop an executing session, step through lines of code, and so on.

TIP

A variety of buttons aren't visible within the debug toolbar by default. We recommend adding all the available debug commands to this toolbar. There aren't many, and they turn out to be tremendously useful during debugging sessions. You can do so using the down arrow on the end of the toolbar. This brings up the Add or Remove Buttons option for the given toolbar. Even better, learn the keyboard shortcut to become even more productive during a debugging session.

Figure 10.15 presents the Debug toolbar during an active debug session. Be default, the debug menu is hidden by the IDE unless you are debugging. However, you can choose to show it (right-click the toolbar area and select Debug from the list of available toolbars). In design mode a number of these items are disabled; in fact, hitting the green continue arrow in design mode actually starts a debugging session for your application. We have added callouts for each item on the toolbar. You can cross-reference these callouts to Table 10.2 for further information.

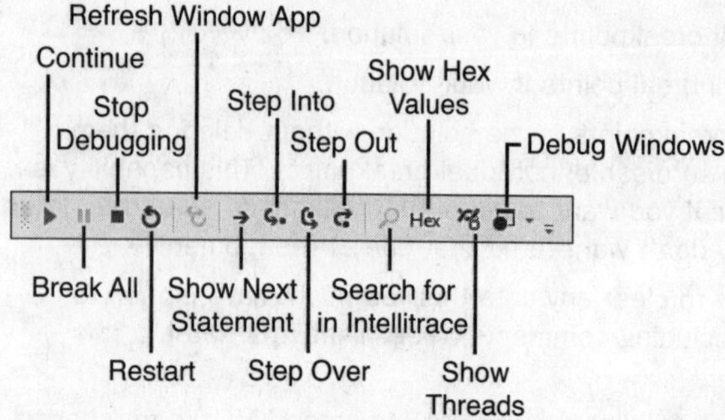

FIGURE 10.15 The Debug toolbar during an active debug session (break mode).

NOTE

In Figure 10.15, the item with the callout, Debug Windows, on the right of the figure is actually is a drop-down menu. This menu provides access to the many debug windows that are available to developers. See Figure 10.13 for a sample of the menus you can access from this toolbar item.

Debug Options

You can control the many debugging options in Visual Studio through the Options dialog box. You can access these options from the Tools menu (Tools, Options) and then select the Debugging node from the left side of the dialog box. Alternatively, you can open the Options dialog right to the Debugging section using the Debug menu (Debug, Options).

Four sets of options are available under the Debugging node:

- **General**—Provides access to the many debugging switches (more than 20) to turn on and off Visual Studio debugging behavior. This includes enabling and disabling breakpoint filters, using just-my-code debugging, enabling the new Diagnostic Tools, creating breakpoint filters, handling warnings, and many other options (see Figure 10.16). Note that the Edit and Continue options have been moved under General for Visual Studio 2015.
- **Just-In-Time**—Enables you to indicate the type of code (managed, native, and script) for which you want to enable or disable Visual Studio debugging (also called just-in-time debugging).
- **Output Window**—Provides management features for the Output window, such as which messages are shown.
- **Symbols**—Enables you to choose which debug symbols are loaded for your debug session. You can also choose additional debug symbol files (`.pdb` and `.dbg`). These files can be helpful if you do not have the source code associated with a particular library you need to debug, such as the .NET Framework itself or a third-party component.

The majority of the settings you manage can be found on the General screen. Figure 10.16 shows the many options for this dialog box. We cover the features behind these options throughout the remainder of this chapter. These many options help you customize your debug experience. However, as we debug code in this chapter, we are assuming the default options for the debugger.

Stepping In, Out, and Over Code

Probably the most common debug operation for developers is stepping through their code line by line and examining the data emitted by the application and the debugger. Code stepping is just that: examining a line, executing the line, and examining the results (and then repeating the process over and over). Because this is such a dominant activity, becoming efficient with the step operations in Visual Studio is important for maximizing the use of your time during a debug session. Here, we cover each of the stepping options and provide examples.

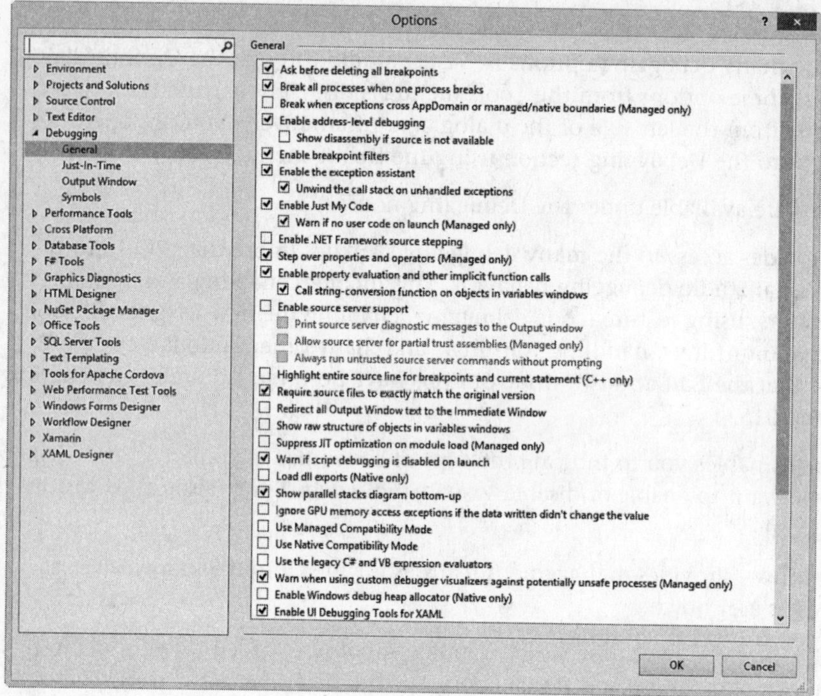

FIGURE 10.16 You can use the Options dialog box to control how Visual Studio behaves during a debugging session.

Start Debugging

The most common way to start a debug session is selecting the Start Debugging option (green "play" arrow) from the Debug menu or the similar arrow on the Standard toolbar. Of course, F5 also does the trick. This starts a debug session but does not break into code unless an exception occurs or a breakpoint is encountered. This is a common operation for developers testing their code without wanting to walk through it or those who use a lot of breakpoints.

The Step Into command is another option available from the Debug menu and toolbar. (You can also press F11 as a shortcut.) Two behaviors are commonly associated with this one command. First, when in an active debug session, Step Into steps into the next line of code and executes it (more on this in a moment). The second behavior is related to when you invoke the command for an application that is not currently running in debug mode. In this case, the application is compiled and started, and the first line is presented to you in the debug window for stepping purposes. This is, in essence, stepping into your application. This works great for Windows, WPF, Console, and similar applications. However, it is not practical for most web applications. If you step into a web application at start time, you are likely stepping into someone else's JavaScript code (and a lot of it).

For web applications, you should start debugging using the Start Debugging option on the Debug toolbar or the Run button on the Standard toolbar. In this case, your web application simply runs in debug mode and only steps into code if you set a breakpoint or an error occurs. You can also choose the line from which you want to start stepping through code using the Run to Cursor option. (See the following section.)

A call to the Step Over command (Debug menu, toolbar, or F10) while your application is at rest results in the same behavior as Step Into. That is, your application is compiled and started in a debug session on the first line of code. (Again, for websites, this is typically a JavaScript file.)

Run to Cursor

One of the more handy (and overlooked) features of the debug toolset is Run to Cursor. This feature works the way it sounds. You set your cursor position on some code in the IDE and invoke the Run to Cursor command (right-click or Ctrl+F10). The application is compiled and run until it hits the line of code where your cursor is placed. At this point, the debugger breaks the application and presents the line of code for you to step through. This capability is especially handy because this is how many developers work. They are looking at a specific line (or lines) of code and want to debug this line. They do not need to start from the first line and might not want to be bothered with breakpoints. The Run to Cursor feature is, therefore, an efficient means to get the debugger on the same page as you.

As an example, suppose we want to get to the first, real meaningful line of our executing code in the Contoso University sample and begin stepping through. We can open the `HomeController.cs` file. Here we will find a method called `Index`. We can put our cursor inside this method and press Ctrl+F10 (or right-click and choose Run to Cursor). This starts the application and breaks on this line of code as shown in Figure 10.17. Notice there is no breakpoint set. From here, we can start stepping through code in our website.

In this example, we would get through the home page controller quickly. The IDE would then start stepping through code in the shared layout file, `_Layout.cshtml`. Eventually, the requested page will render to the browser and no additional executing lines of code will be active in the IDE. Provided you step through each line, however, the IDE still knows you want to step through every line of code. Therefore, a subsequent request from the browser (clicking on the `Students` link, for example) will also break into the IDE (in this case on the `StudentController.cs` class).

Run to Cursor works even if the application user (tester or developer) is required to activate some portion of the code prior to the code's reaching the cursor position. In this way, it acts like an invisible, temporary breakpoint. For instance, consider an example in which users are presented with a default web page. From here, they can select to edit their profiles. If you set the Run to Cursor command on a line inside the code that executes to edit a profile, the debugger still executes the application and waits until the user invokes the given line of code.

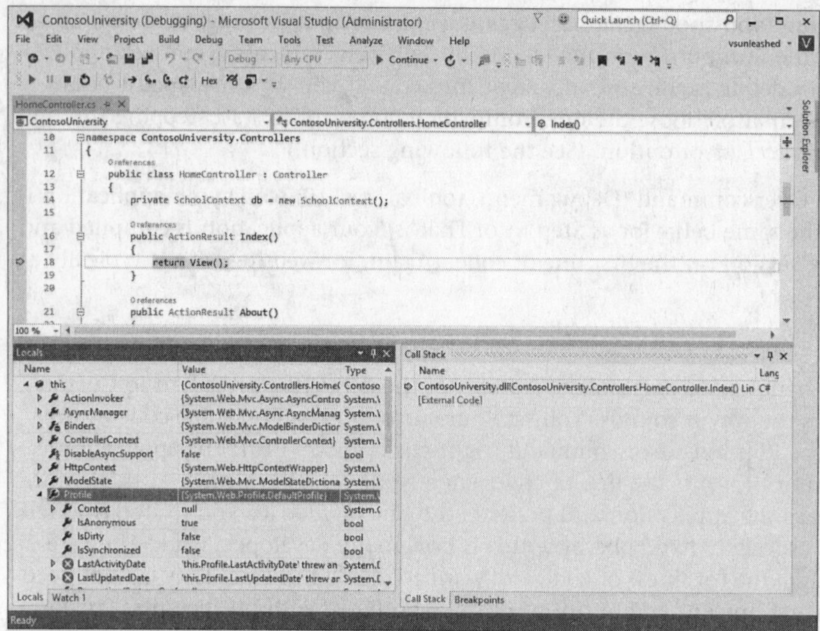

FIGURE 10.17 You can tell the debugger to run to a given line of code and stop before executing it using the Run to Cursor command.

Break All

If your application is already running in a debug session and you want to break into the debugger, you can do so at any time by invoking the Break All command from the Debug menu or toolbar (using the Pause button). (You can also use the keyboard shortcut Ctrl+Alt+Break.) Invoking Break All stops your application on the next executing line and enables you to interrogate the debugger for information. The Break All command is especially useful if you need to break into a long-running process or a loop that seems to have stalled your application.

NOTE

Setting Break All on a web application that is waiting for a user request does not break into any code by default. Instead, you get a message from the IDE indicating that that call stack contains only external code (provided Just My Code is enabled for debugging, which is the default). You would need to click the Continue button (green play arrow) to continue debugging in this scenario.

Step Into

During an active debug session (where the IDE is stopped on a line of code waiting for instructions on how to move forward), you have basically three options for moving through your code. You can step into a line or function, step over a given function, or step out of a function. Let's look at each option.

The Step Into command (F11) enables you to progress through your code one line at a time. Invoking this command executes the current, highlighted line of code and positions your cursor on the next line to be executed. The important distinction between stepping into and other similar commands is how Step Into handles lines of code that contain method calls. If you are positioned on such a line, calling Step Into takes you to the first line inside that method being called.

For example, look at Figure 10.18. It shows an example of a call to present the edit page for a university course. This line of code is calling an internal method, `PopulateDepartmentsDropDownList`, to get all the departments from which to select. A call to Step Into will result in your stepping into the first line of this method.

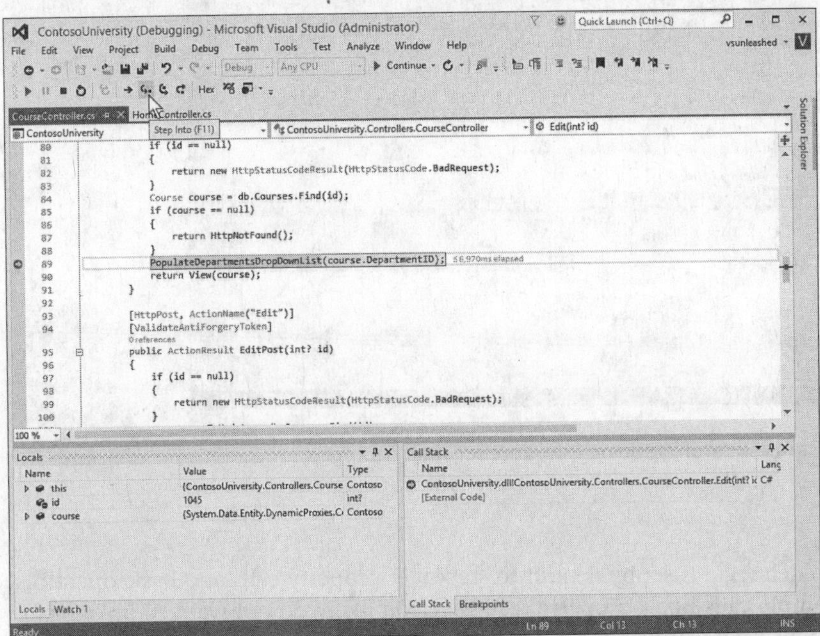

FIGURE 10.18 Stepping into a line of code can take you into another method (or class).

Figure 10.19 shows stepping into this method. Notice that you are now positioned to step line by line through the called method. Of course, when you reach the end of this method, the debugger returns you to the next line in the calling function (back to the next line depicted in Figure 10.18).

NOTE

Visual Studio helps manage the many code windows you step through while in a debug session. It does not fully open them. Instead, it presents them to you and closes each one as it is no longer needed. This prevents you from having a dozen or more code windows open at the end of your debug session.

If you want to keep a code window open, however, you can do so using the Keep Open icon on the Window tab. You can also use the Text Editor toolbar to set flags on certain code elements to return to them later.

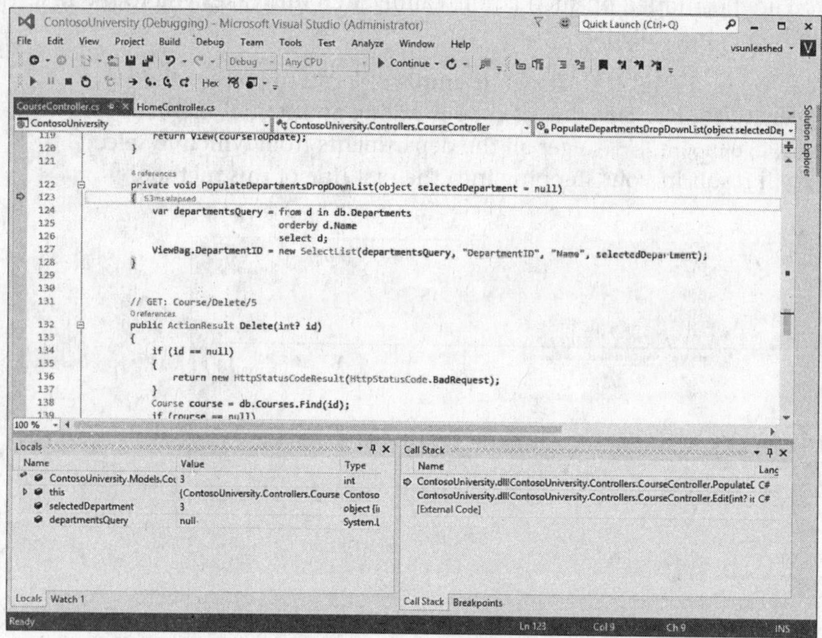

FIGURE 10.19 The results of stepping into another method.

Step Into Specific

The Visual Studio debugger is set by default to step over property calls and basic operators. This eliminates simple calls like a property read that you likely do not want to interrogate line by line. You will get a warning message about this behavior from the IDE the first time you encounter it. You can tell the IDE to stop reminding you about this fact.

There are times, however, when you do want to step into a specific property or operation. To do so, you can right-click the line of code about to be executed and choose Step Into Specific from the context menu, as shown in Figure 10.20. This line of code has two options: call the property getter for the `DAL Student` object, or step into the `Find` code in the `DataSet` class of `System.Data`.

NOTE

You can change this default behavior form the Debugging Options, General settings (Debug menu, Options item). Here you will see the option Step Over Properties and Operators (Managed Only). Unchecking this option will tell the debugger to always step into properties and operators of managed code.

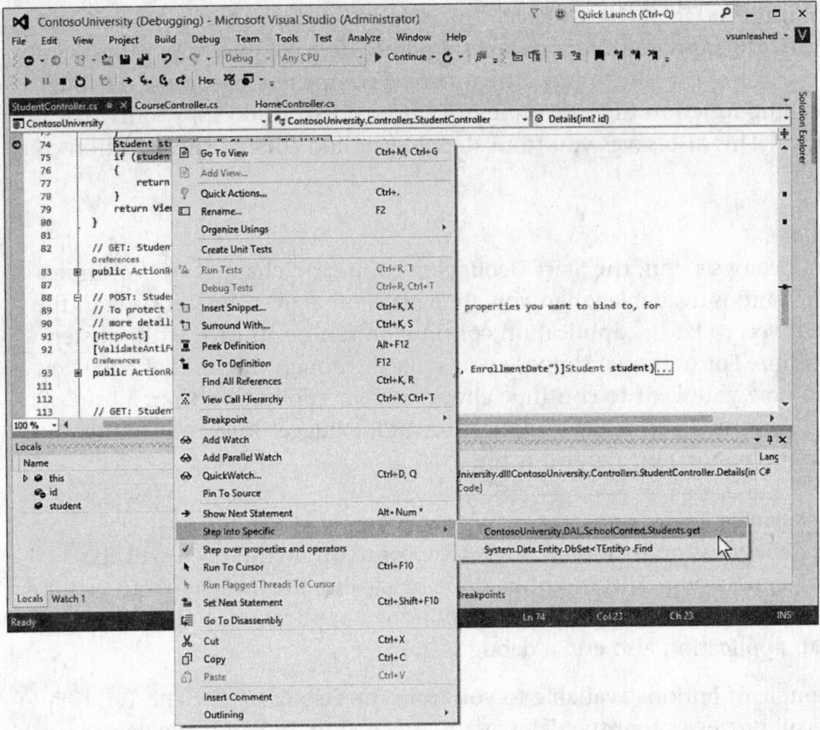

FIGURE 10.20 You can step into a specific property or operator call in the IDE.

Step Over

The Step Over command (F10) enables you to maintain focus on the current procedure without stepping into any methods called by it. That is, calling Step Over executes line by line for the current executing method but does not take you into any function calls, constructors, or property calls outside the executing method.

For example, consider Figure 10.18. Here, the debugger is positioned on the call to `PopulateDepartmentsDropDownList`. If you call the Step Over command, the function executes in its entirety without your stepping through it. Instead, the next line to execute in step mode is the line following the call to `PopulateDepartmentsDropDownList` (`return View(course);`). Of course, any exception thrown by the function you step over (and not handled by your code) results in the debugger breaking into your code (and the function) as normal.

Step Out

The Step Out command (Shift+F11) is another useful tool. It allows you to tell the debugger to finish executing the current method you are debugging but return to break mode as soon as it is finished. This is a great tool when you get stuck in a long method you wish you had stepped over. In addition, you might step into a given function only to debug a portion of it and then want to step back out.

For example, refer again to Figure 10.19. Recall that you stepped into this method from the code in Figure 10.18. Suppose that you start stepping. After you take a look and verify some of the code, you simply want to have the function complete and return to debugging back in the calling function (the next line in Figure 10.18). To do so, you invoke Step Out from the toolbar. This also saves you from stepping should code in this function call other code.

Continuing Execution

When you are in a debug session, the Start Debugging command changes to Continue. The Continue command is available when you are paused on a given line of code in the debugger. It enables you to let the application continue to run on its own without stepping through each line. For example, suppose you walked through the lines of code you wanted to see, and now you want to continue checking your application from a user's perspective. Using Continue, you tell the application and debugger to keep running until either an exception occurs or a breakpoint is hit.

Ending a Debug Session

You can end your debug session in several ways. One common method is to kill the currently executing application. This might be done by closing the browser window for a web application or clicking the Close button of a Windows application. Calls in your code that terminate your application also end a debug session.

You also have a couple of options available to you from the Debug menu. The Terminate All command kills all processes that the debugger is attached to and ends the debug session. There is also the Detach All option. Figure 10.21 shows both options from the Debug menu. Detach All simply detaches the debugger from all running processes without terminating them. This capability can be useful if you've temporarily attached to a running process, debugged it, and want to leave it running.

Indicating When to Break into Code

You control the debugger through breakpoints and tracepoints. With these, you can tell the debugger when you are interested in breaking into code or receiving information about your application. Breakpoints enable you to indicate when the debugger should stop on a specific line in your code. Tracepoints were introduced in Visual Studio 2005. They are a type of breakpoint that enables you to perform an action when a given line of your code is reached. This typically involves emitting data about your application to the Output window. Mastering the use of breakpoints reduces the time it takes to zero in on and fix issues with your code.

The most common method of setting a breakpoint is to first find the line of code on which you want the debugger to stop. You then click in the code editor's indicator margin for the given line of code. Doing so places a red circle in the indicator margin and highlights the line of code as red. Of course, these are the default colors; you can change the look of breakpoints in the Tools, Options dialog box under the Environment node, Fonts and Colors.

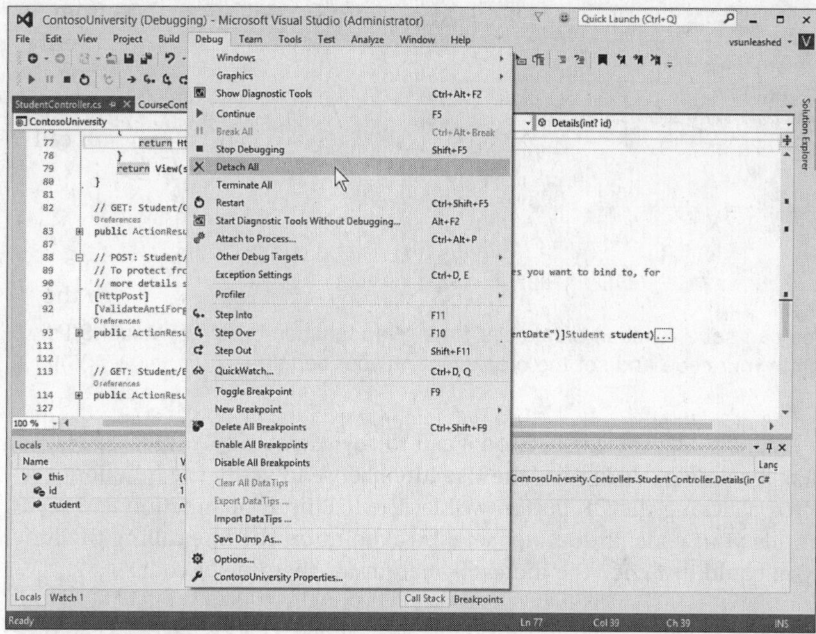

FIGURE 10.21 You can detach from a running process but leave the process running.

There are a few additional ways to set breakpoints. For instance, you can right-click a given line of code and choose Insert Breakpoint from the Breakpoint context menu; this will set a breakpoint using the indicator margin. You can also choose New Breakpoint from the Debug menu (or press Ctrl+D, N) to open the New Breakpoint dialog box, in which you can set a function breakpoint. We cover this in the next section.

Setting a Function Breakpoint

A function breakpoint is just a breakpoint that is set through the New Breakpoint dialog box (see above as to how to invoke). It is called a function breakpoint because it is typically set at the beginning of the function (but does not need to be). From the New Breakpoint dialog box, you can manually set the function on which you want to break, the line of code in the function, and even the character on the line.

If your cursor is on a function or on a call to a function when you invoke this dialog box, the name of the function is automatically placed in the dialog box, or you can type a function name in the dialog box. Figure 10.22 shows the New Breakpoint dialog box in action. Notice that you can manually set the line and even the character on the line where the breakpoint should be placed (for lines of code that include multiple statements).

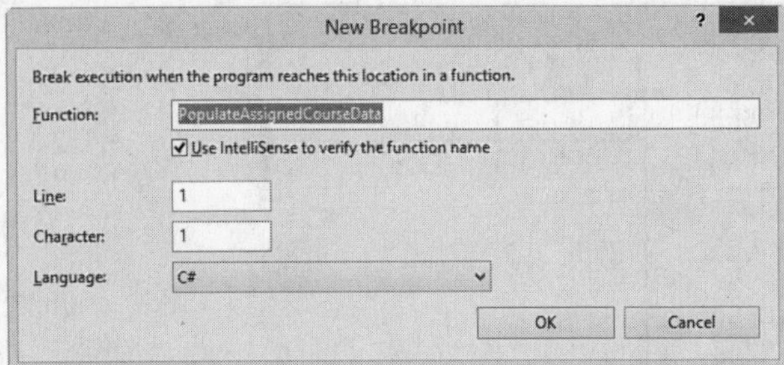

FIGURE 10.22 You can set a function breakpoint for a given function by name; Visual Studio will find the function in your code and set the breakpoint on your behalf.

In the example in Figure 10.22, the cursor is on a call to `PopulateAssignedCourseData`. Notice that the New Breakpoint dialog has the Use IntelliSense to verify the function name option selected. Clicking the OK button will let the IDE find the function and set a breakpoint on it inside your code. It does not set a breakpoint on the line calling the function. To do that, you could just click the indicator margin for that line of code.

NOTE

If you specify an overloaded function in the New Breakpoint dialog box, you must specify the actual function on which you want to break. You do so by indicating the correct parameter types for the given overload. For example, if you have a function called `GetCustomer` that takes a `customerId` parameter (as an `int`) and an overload that also looks up a customer by name (as a `string`), you indicate this overload in the `Function` field as `GetCustomer(string)`.

Recognizing the Many Breakpoints of Visual Studio

Visual Studio has a number of breakpoint icons. These icons enable you to easily recognize the type of breakpoint associated with a given line of code. For instance, a round, filled circle is a common breakpoint, whereas a round, hollow circle represents a common breakpoint that has been disabled. We've provided Table 10.3 for reference purposes. It shows some of the more common icons associated with breakpoints and presents a description of each.

TABLE 10.3 The Breakpoint Icons

Icon	Description
●	This icon indicates a standard, enabled breakpoint. When the debugger encounters this line of code, it stops the application and breaks into debug mode.
◆	This icon indicates a standard tracepoint. When the debugger hits this line of code, it performs the action associated with the tracepoint.
⊕	The plus icon inside the breakpoint indicates an advanced breakpoint that contains a condition, hit count, or filter.

Icon	Description
	The plus icon inside the tracepoint indicates an advanced tracepoint that contains a condition, hit count, or filter.
	An empty or hollow breakpoint indicates a disabled breakpoint. The breakpoint is still associated with the line of code. However, the debugger does not recognize the disabled breakpoint until it has been reenabled.Hollow icons are associated with types of breakpoint icons, such as tracepoints, advanced items, and even breakpoint errors and warnings. In all conditions, the hollow icon indicates that the item is disabled.
	This icon indicates that the breakpoint is also the next line to be executed by Visual Studio (step into).

Working with the Breakpoints Window

The Breakpoints window in Visual Studio provides a convenient way to organize and manage the many conditions on which you intend to break into the debugger. You access this window from the Debug menu or toolbar (or by pressing Ctrl+D, B). Figure 10.23 shows the Breakpoints window inside Visual Studio with a number of active breakpoints.

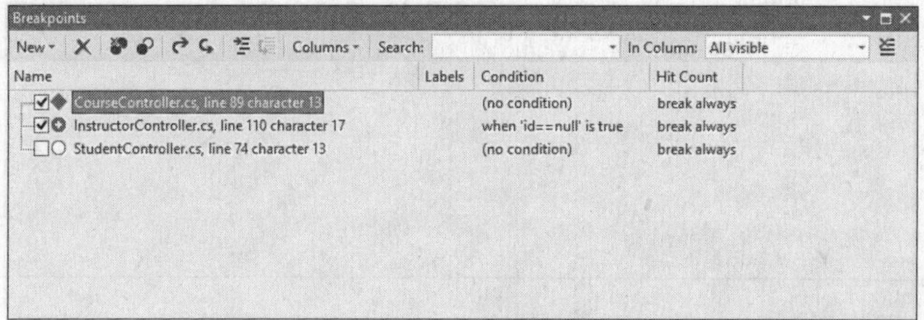

FIGURE 10.23 Use the Breakpoints window to manage the many breakpoints in your debug session.

The Breakpoints window also has its own toolbar (refer to Figure 10.23) that enables you to manage the breakpoints listed in the window. The commands available from the toolbar are described in detail in Table 10.4.

TABLE 10.4 The Breakpoints Window Toolbar

Icon	Description
New ▾ / Break at Function... Ctrl+D, N / New Data Breakpoint...	Brings up the new Breakpoints window, enabling you to set a breakpoint at a function.
	Enables you to delete the selected breakpoint in the list.
	Deletes all breakpoints in the window.

Icon	Description
	Toggles all breakpoints as either on or off. If even one breakpoint in the list is enabled, clicking this icon the first time disables it (and all others that are enabled). Clicking it a second time (or when all breakpoints are disabled) enables all breakpoints.
	Enables you to export your breakpoints to an XML file. This can be useful if you have a lot of breakpoint information you want to share. You can share your breakpoints to allow others to debug your code.
	Enables you to import breakpoints from an XML file.
	Enables you to go to the source code associated with the selected breakpoint.
	Enables you to go to the disassembly information associated with the selected breakpoint.
Columns ▾ ✓ Name ✓ Condition ✓ Labels ✓ Hit Count Filter When Hit Language Function File Address Data Process	Enables you to choose which columns you want to view in the Breakpoints window. Each column provides information about a given breakpoint. For example, you can see information on the condition associated with each breakpoint, the filename, the function, the filter, the process, and so on.

Managing Each Individual Breakpoint

The Breakpoints window also gives you access to each breakpoint. It serves as a launching point for setting the many options associated with a breakpoint. For example, you can disable a single breakpoint by toggling the check box associated with the breakpoint in the list. In addition, you can set the many properties and conditions associated with a breakpoint. Figure 10.24 shows a disabled tracepoint and a disabled breakpoint; it also shows the context menu associated with an individual breakpoint. Notice, too, that this dialog is for an active debug section. The highlighted breakpoint (bold) is the current, active breakpoint in the IDE awaiting instruction from the developer.

Notice that from this context menu for a breakpoint, you can delete the breakpoint and navigate to its related source code (Go to Source Code). More important, however, is the access to setting the conditions and filters associated with the breakpoint. We cover using each of these options next.

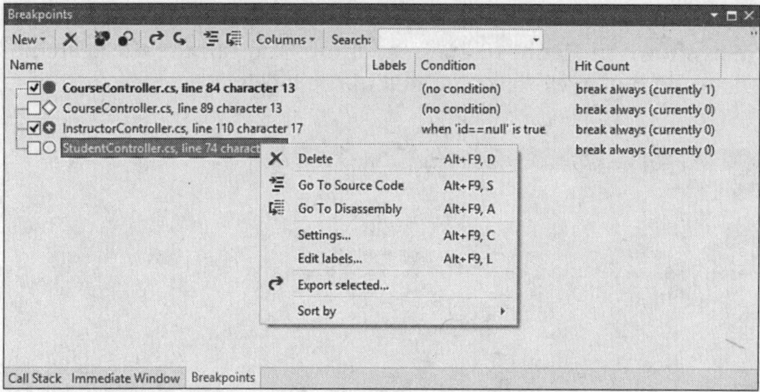

FIGURE 10.24 You can manvage individual breakpoints inside the Breakpoints window.

Labeling Breakpoints You can provide labels for your breakpoints, which enables you to define categories of breakpoints and quickly find them in the Breakpoints window. For example, you might want to set a number of breakpoints and tracepoints related to a specific scenario in your code, such as editing an instructor record or adding a new student. These breakpoints are useful when you need to modify and review this code. However, when you are working on unrelated code, you might want to turn a whole group of breakpoints off. Breakpoint labels support this scenario.

You label a breakpoint by selecting Edit Labels from the breakpoint context menu (refer to Figure 10.24 to see an example). The Edit Breakpoint Labels dialog box opens, as shown in Figure 10.25. Here you can add a new label and apply that label to the selected breakpoint. Alternatively, you can select one or more labels from the existing labels previously defined.

FIGURE 10.25 You can use the Edit Breakpoint Labels dialog box to label breakpoints to make them easier to find and work with as a group.

You can work with the breakpoint labels inside the Breakpoints window. You can sort the list by the Labels column, as shown in Figure 10.26. In addition, you can use the Search feature to find breakpoints based on keywords contained in the labels.

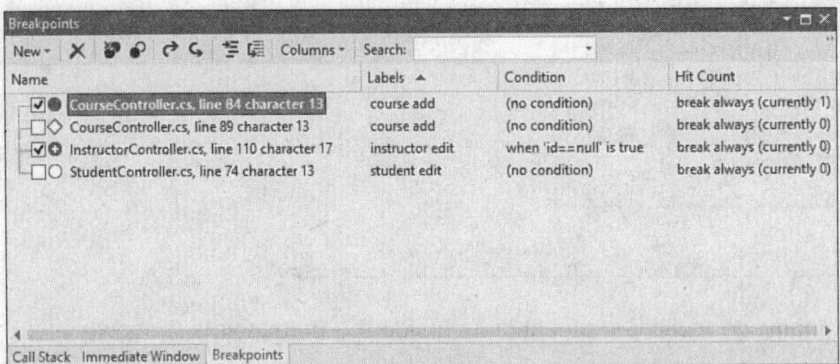

FIGURE 10.26 You can sort or search breakpoints based on their labels.

Breakpoint Conditions and Actions

Often, setting a simple breakpoint is not sufficient (or efficient). For instance, if you are looking for a particular condition to be `true` in your code (a condition that seems to be causing an exception), you would prefer to break based on that condition. This saves the time of constantly breaking into a function only to examine a few data points and determine that you have not hit your condition. You might also want to set an action to execute should the breakpoint be hit (such as logging information to the Output window). The BreakPoint Settings dialog allows you to set breakpoint conditions and actions.

Setting a Breakpoint Condition

A breakpoint condition enables you to break into the debugger or perform an action when a specific condition either is evaluated as `true` or has changed. Often, you know that the bug you are working on occurs only based on a very specific condition. Breakpoint conditions are the perfect answer for troubleshooting an intermittent bug.

There are three types of conditions you typically add to breakpoints: Conditional Expression, Hit Count, and Filter. There are a couple ways to add a condition to your breakpoint: inside the Breakpoints window and using the new breakpoint settings right inside the code editor.

To set a breakpoint condition from within the Breakpoints window, you select the breakpoint on which you want to apply a condition and then right-click it to open the context menu for the given breakpoint. Refer to Figure 10.24 for an example of the context menu; here you would select the Settings option to set a breakpoint condition (or action).

The other option is to launch the breakpoint settings dialog right inside your code editor. You do so by hovering over the breakpoint icon in the indicator margin of the code edit. This will show two icons: breakpoint settings (gear icon) and disable breakpoint (filled circle over an open circle). Figure 10.27 show the results of hitting the first icon: breakpoint settings.

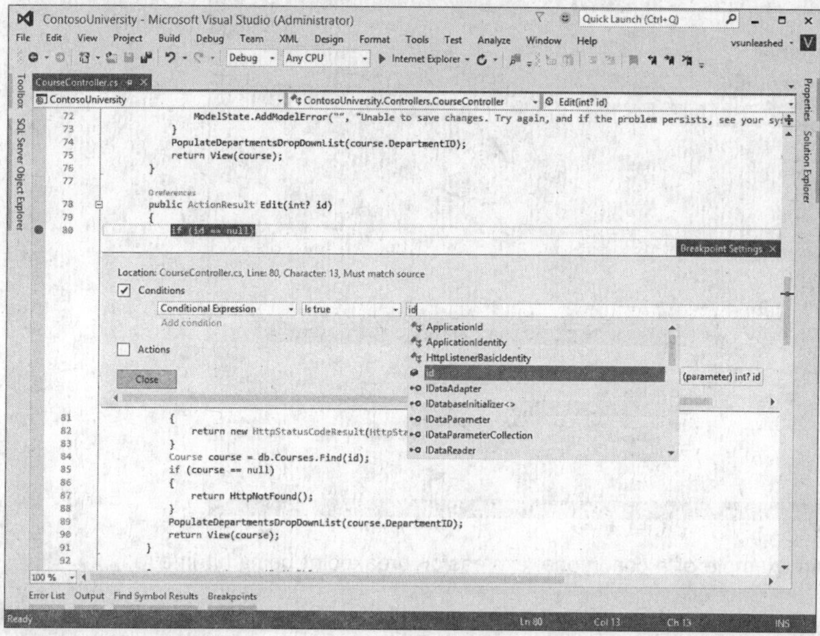

FIGURE 10.27 You can use the Breakpoint Settings dialog box directly in the code editor to set a Boolean code condition that tells the debugger when to stop on your breakpoint.

Notice in Figure 10.27 that, when setting the breakpoint condition, you have access to IntelliSense. After setting the condition using the code editor, the settings window stays visible in your code editor and your breakpoint icon is given a plus sign. You can close this window if it is in your way. You can reopen by again hovering over the breakpoint icon and clicking the gear icon from the indicator margin.

When you set a condition expression as a condition (as shown in Figure 10.27), you have two options: Is True and Has Changed. The Is True option enables you to set a Boolean condition that, when evaluated to `true`, results in the debugger's breaking into the given line of code.

For example, suppose that you are notified of an error that happens when populating a collection of student objects. There are many options where you could set your breakpoint. Suppose you want to walk through code in your view (`.cshtml` page). You could do so by setting a breakpoint in the view and then setting a condition on that breakpoint. Figure 10.28 shows setting a conditional expression `Is True` condition `Model.Count() > 0` to a breakpoint. This tells the debugger not to stop on this line of code unless this condition is met.

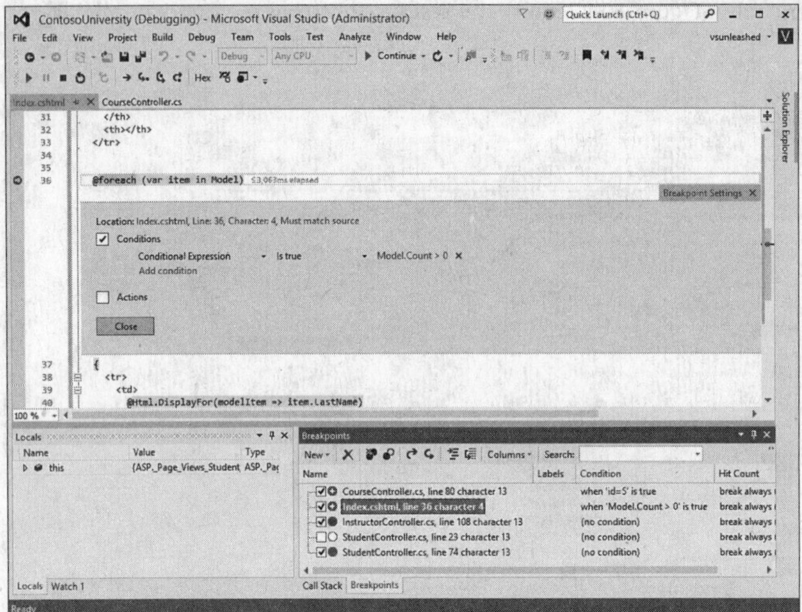

FIGURE 10.28 An example of a conditional expression breakpoint being hit in a debug session.

The other option for Conditional Expression breakpoints is Has Changed. This option tells the debugger to break when the value of an expression changes. The first pass through your code sets the value for the first evaluation. If the value changes after that, the debugger breaks on a given line. This capability can be useful when you have fields or properties with initial values and you want to track when those values are being changed. In addition, Has Changed can be useful in looping and `if...then` scenarios in which you are interested only in whether the results of your code changed a particular value.

TIP

Your breakpoint information is persisted between debug sessions. That is, when you close Visual Studio for the day, your breakpoints are still there when you return. This validates the time you might spend setting some sophisticated debugging options because they can remain in your application and be turned on and off as required. The options can also be exported to a file and shared with other developers or other computers.

Setting a Breakpoint Filter

Breakpoint filters enable you to specify a specific machine, process, or thread on which you want to break. For instance, if your error condition seems to happen only on a certain machine or within a certain process, you can debug this condition specifically with a filter. Filters are most useful in complex debugging scenarios in which your application is highly distributed.

You access this feature by adding a filter condition to a breakpoint from within the code editor window or the Breakpoint Settings dialog accessed via a right-click from the Breakpoints pane. When setting a Filter you can specify the machine by name, the process by name or ID, or the thread by name or ID. You can also specify combinations with `&` (and), `||` (or), and `!` (not). This allows you to get to a specific thread on a specific process on a certain machine. Figure 10.29 shows the Breakpoint Settings dialog box; here we are adding another condition to an existing breakpoint. Notice the Intellisense dropdown; we can use it to stop provided that the running process is the development web server (`ProcessName = "iisexpress.exe"`).

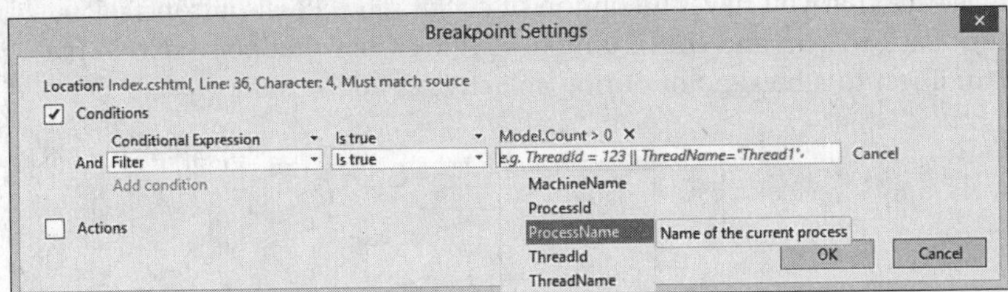

FIGURE 10.29 You can set a breakpoint filter to stop the debugger inside a specific process or thread or on a specific machine.

Using a Hit Count with a Breakpoint

Using Hit Count, you can tell the debugger that you want to break when a given line of code is reached a number of times. Typically, you can find a better condition than breaking based on Hit Count. However, this feature is useful when you can't determine the actual condition but know that when you pass through a function a certain number of times, something bad happens. In addition, the Hit Count option might be more useful in tracepoint scenarios in which you are emitting data about what is happening in your code. You might want to write that data only periodically.

Figure 10.30 shows the Breakpoint Settings dialog box with a Hit Count condition being set.

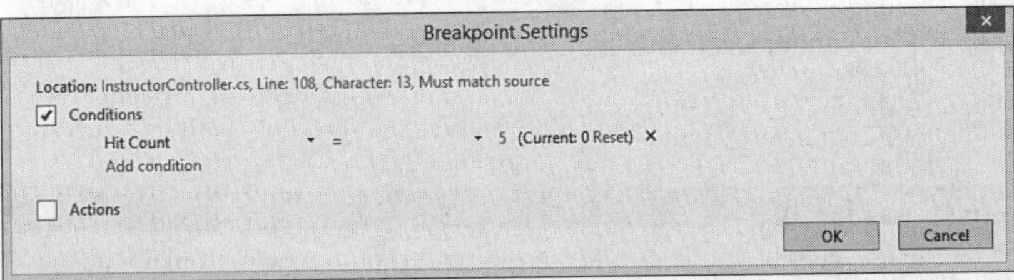

FIGURE 10.30 You can set the debugger to break when it hits a line of code a set number of times.

This dialog box also provides a few options for setting the actual hit count condition. In the drop-down list to the right of Hit Count (Figure 10.30), the following options are available:

- = —Breaks when the hit count is equal to a number
- is multiple of—Breaks when the hit count is a multiple of a certain number
- >= —Breaks when the hit count is greater than or equal to a specified value

Visual Studio breaks into your code when the hit count condition is met. Figure 10.31 shows an example. Notice that you have the option of clicking the Reset button and turning the hit count back to zero and continuing debugging from that point. Note that you can add any condition to a breakpoint during an active debug session.

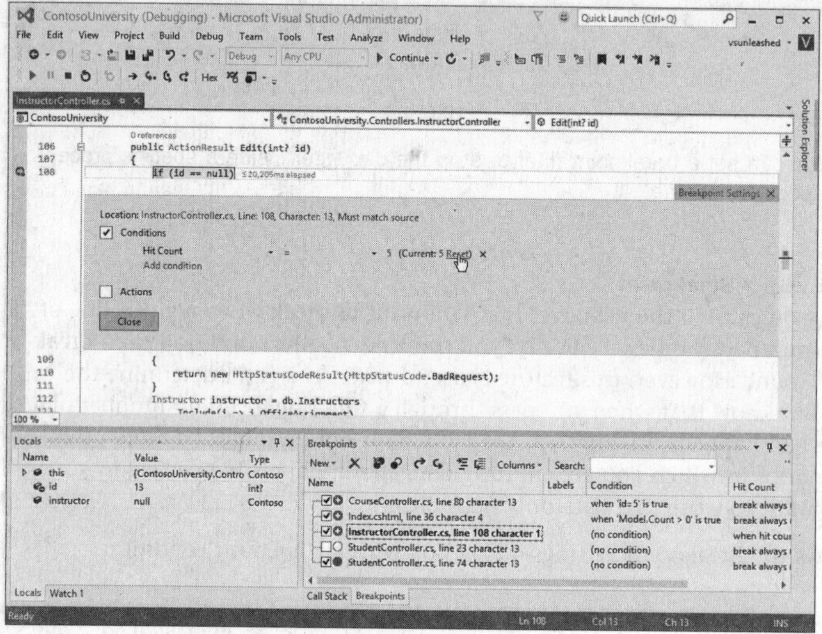

FIGURE 10.31 When the hit count condition is met, you have the option to reset the hit count from the editor.

TIP

You can combine all the breakpoint conditions we've discussed on a single breakpoint. For example, you may add a condition and a filter to a given breakpoint. Doing so allows you to create even more specific scenarios for debugging your application using breakpoints.

Working with Tracepoints (When Hit Option)

Tracepoints enable you to emit data to the Output window or run a Visual Studio macro when a specific breakpoint is hit. You then have the option to break into the debugger (like a regular breakpoint), process another condition, or just continue executing the application. This capability can be useful if you want to keep a running log of what is happening as your application runs in debug mode. You can then review this log to get valuable information about specific conditions and order of execution when an exception is thrown.

You can set tracepoints explicitly by right-clicking a line of code and choosing Insert Tracepoint from the Breakpoint menu (see Figure 10.32). This simply enables the Breakpoint Settings dialog in the code editor and automatically enables an Action. Figure 10.33 shows setting the message for the action inside this editor. You can also enable an Actions option for any given breakpoint. Doing so adds tracking to the breakpoint.

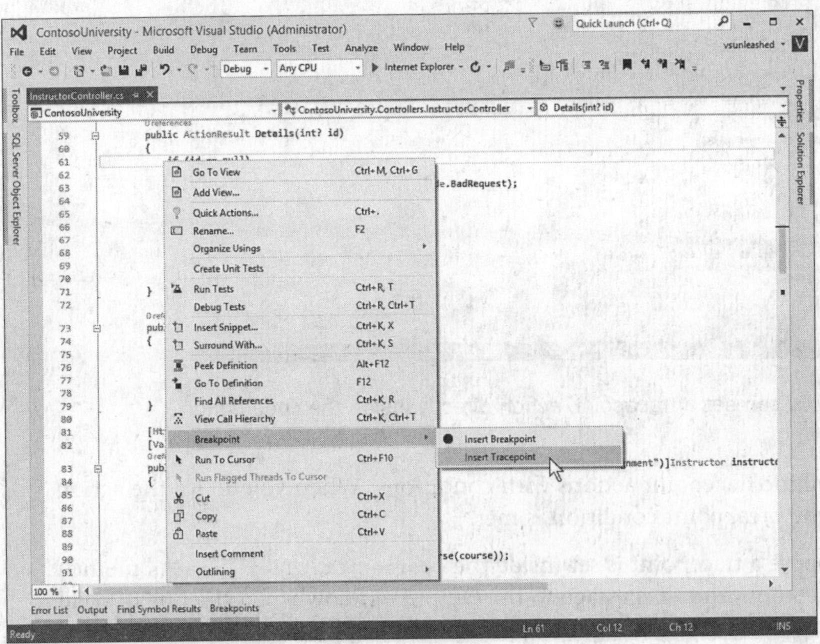

FIGURE 10.32 You can set a tracepoint using the When Breakpoint Is Hit dialog box.

The options available for logging and action include logging a message to the Output window and continuing execution. The first option, logging a message, enables you to output data about your function. You can use a number of keywords to output data, such as `$FUNCTION` for the function name and `$CALLER` for the name of the calling function. Additional keywords include: `$ADDRESS`, `$CALLSTACK`, `$PID`, `$PNAME`, `$TID`, and `$TNAME`. You can also output your specific variable values. You do so by enclosing the variable names in curly braces.

The Continue execution option enables you to indicate whether this is a true tracepoint or a breakpoint that contains a tracing action. If you choose to continue, you get only the trace action (message/macro). If you indicate not to continue, you get the trace action, and the debugger stops on this line of code, just as with a regular breakpoint. This is essentially applying an action to a standard breakpoint.

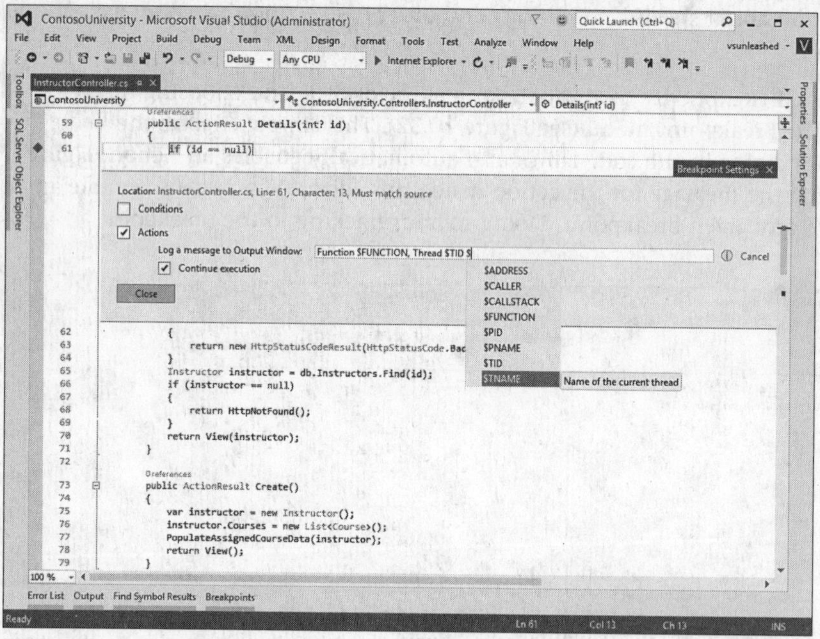

FIGURE 10.33 You can set a tracepoint/action directly inside the code editor.

You can also combine tracepoint actions with conditions. When you do so, the action fires only when the breakpoint condition is met.

For example, suppose a tracepoint is set inside the `CourseController.Details` method. Imagine this tracepoint prints a message to the Output window when the line of code is hit and simply continues executing the application. Imagine, too, you set a condition on the breakpoint to only break when a certain course is being accessed. The message we intend to print is as follows:

```
Function: $FUNCTION, Thread: $TID $TNAME, Id: {id}
```

This message prints the function name, the thread ID and name (if any), and the value of the variable, `id`. Figure 10.34 shows two passes through the tracepoint output in the Output window (Debug, Windows, Output). The message is intermingled with other messages. The first message is at the top of the Output window; the second is highlighted.

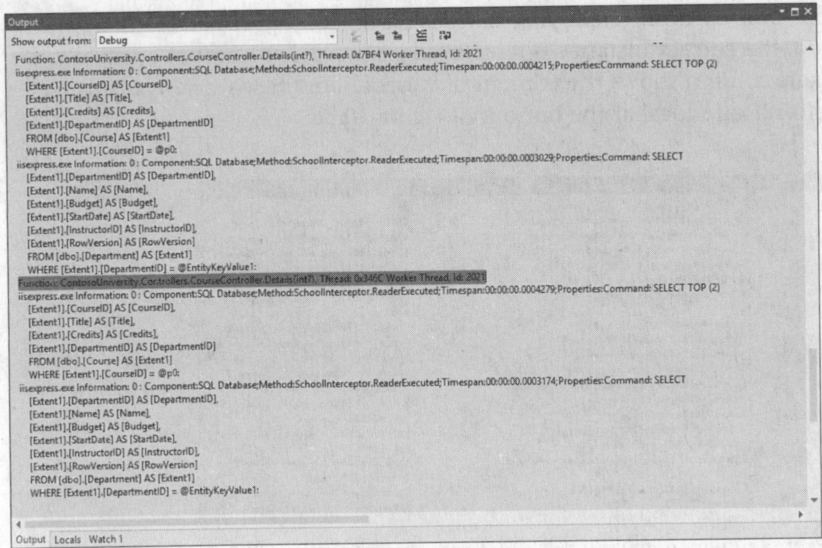

FIGURE 10.34 You can view the results of tracepoints inside the Output window.

Viewing Data in the Debugger

After the debugger has thrown you into break mode, the next challenge is to filter all the data that your application is emitting. Getting to the right data helps you find and fix problems faster. Visual Studio tries to make the data available where you want it. For example, DataTips show you variable values right in the code editor. There are many similar examples in the way Visual Studio shows debugging data when and where you need it, which are covered throughout the following sections.

Watching Variables

A common activity in a debug session is to view the values associated with the many variables in your application. Various windows are available to help you here. The two most obvious are the Locals and Autos windows.

Locals Window The Locals window shows all the variables and their values for the current debug scope, which gives you a view of everything available in the current, executing method. The variables in this window are set automatically by the debugger. They are organized alphabetically in a list by name. In addition, hierarchy is shown with variable members listed as a tree-based structure. When the debugger breaks on an exception, it appears as `$exception` in the list.

Figure 10.35 shows an example of the Locals window. In it, you can see the sample Contoso University application paused while executing a call to get student details for editing. Notice that the `db` object (of type `SchoolContext`) is highlighted and expanded to show the various properties and fields associated with this object. If you break in a nonstatic method, the current instance is referenced by the `this` local that appears expanded. The Value column shows the content of variables and fields, and it turns red when it changes, like the `id` local at the bottom of Figure 10.35.

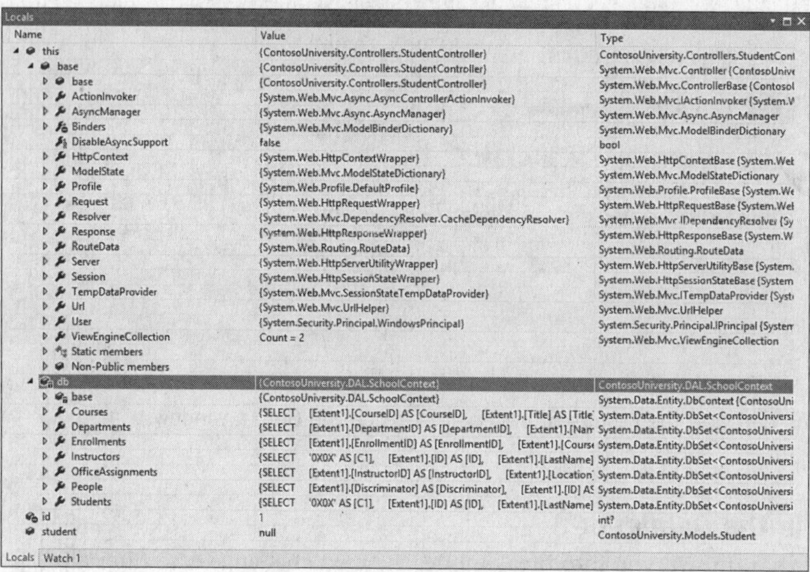

FIGURE 10.35 Use the Locals window to see variable values for the currently executing method.

TIP

You can edit a value in the Locals or Autos window by right-clicking the variable and choosing Edit Value from the context menu. You can then change the value of the variable directly from within the window (similar to changing variable values using the Immediate window).

The Autos Window Often, viewing all the locals provides too many options to sort through. This can be true when there is just too much in scope in the given process or function. To home in on the values associated with the line of code you are looking at, you can use the Autos window, which shows the value of all variables and expressions that are in the current executing line of code or in the preceding line of code. This allows you to really focus on just the values you are currently debugging.

Figure 10.36 shows the Autos window for the same method as was shown in Figure 10.35. Notice there are not a lot of difference in this example. However, the Autos window does show the additional call to `db.Students`, which is the active code in the debug session. The Autos window tries to anticipate the items you might need to review and shows their values.

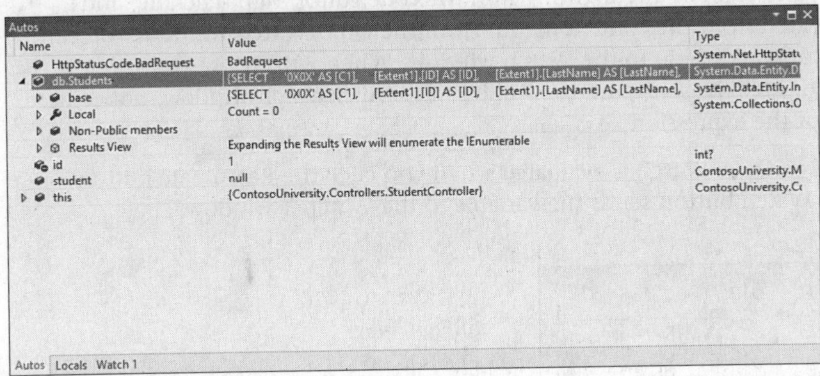

FIGURE 10.36 You can use the Autos window to automatically get VARIABLE values for the last executed and the currently executing line of code.

The Watch Windows The Visual Studio Watch windows enable you to set a custom list of variables and expressions that you want to keep an eye on. In this way, you decide the items in which you are interested. The Watch windows look and behave just like the Locals and Autos windows. In addition, the items you place in Watch windows persist from one debug session to another.

You access each Watch window from the Debug menu (Debug, Windows, Watch) or toolbar during an active debug session. The four Watch windows are named Watch 1, Watch 2, Watch 3, and Watch 4. Having four Watch windows enables you to set up four custom lists of items you want to monitor. This capability can be especially helpful if each custom list applies to a separate scope in your application.

You add a variable or an expression to the Watch window from either the code editor or the QuickWatch window. If you are in the code editor during a debug session, select a variable or highlight an expression, right-click, and choose the Add Watch menu item. This takes the highlighted variable or expression and places it in the Watch window. You can also drag and drop the highlighted item into a Watch window. Also, from the Autos and Locals windows, you can right-click a variable and select Add Watch.

NOTE

Watch windows now support lambda expressions; you can write a lambda expression as a Watch "variable" and monitor the value of the expression within the debug Watch window.

QuickWatch The QuickWatch dialog enables you to quickly view the result of a single variable or expression; you can also add an item from QuickWatch to an existing Watch window.

You set a QuickWatch item by highlighting it in the code editor, right-clicking, and choosing QuickWatch from the context menu. From the QuickWatch window, you can write expressions and add them to the Watch window. When writing your expression, you have access to IntelliSense. Figure 10.37 shows the QuickWatch window; notice here we add a watch for the expression `id != null`.

The item you add to QuickWatch is evaluated when you click the Reevaluate button. Clicking the Add Watch button sends the variable to the Watch 1 window.

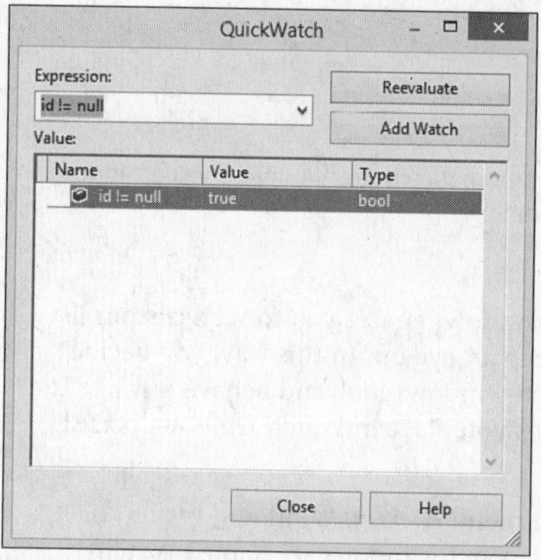

FIGURE 10.37 The QuickWatch window enables you to define expressions and monitor their results during a debug session.

DataTips

DataTips enable you to highlight a variable or an expression in your code editor and get information right in the editor. This feature is more in tune with how developers work. For example, if you are looking at a line of code, you might highlight something in that line to evaluate it. You can do this by creating a QuickWatch. However, you can also simply hover your mouse over the item, and its data is unfolded in a DataTip. In addition, Visual Studio lets you pin your data tips directly to your code window so that they are always visible during a debug session inside your code editor.

Figure 10.38 shows a DataTip active in a debug session. Here, the cursor is positioned over a string variable. If it were a complex object with multiple properties, the IDE would present a plus sign to allow you to expand the variable to unfold the many properties and fields of the object. Notice, too, you can right-click the member and edit its value, copy it, or add it to the Watch window (as shown). Also, notice the magnifying glass icon next to the items in the list; it allows you to select a specific visualizer for a given item (more on visualizers shortly).

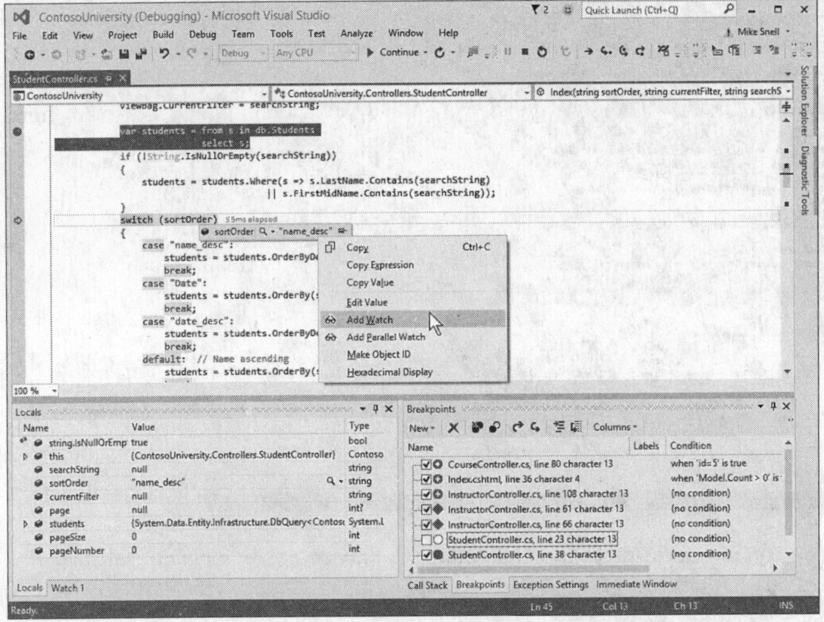

FIGURE 10.38 You can use DataTips to quickly visualize your object data in the debugger.

TIP

The DataTips window can get in the way of viewing code. Sometimes you need to see the DataTips and the code underneath. In this case, pressing the Control (Ctrl) key makes the DataTips window transparent for as long as you hold the key.

Pinning a Data Tip In Figure 10.38, the highlighted member, `sortOrder` has a pin icon on the far right of the window. This icon enables you to pin your DataTip to the code window, which ensures this DataTip is displayed each time you pass through the code in the debugger. This is a faster, more accessible version of a Watch window.

You can pin all sorts of code items as DataTips. You can pin an entire object, or, in the case of the example, a single variable. You can also move pinned DataTips around in the editor to position them accordingly. In Figure 10.39, we have pinned a DataTip to the code editor. Note that when the debug session is over, the indicator margin in the code window includes a pin to indicate there is a DataTip pinned to the given line of code. After a DataTip is pinned, you can highlight it to remove it, unpin it, or add your own comment to the DataTip.

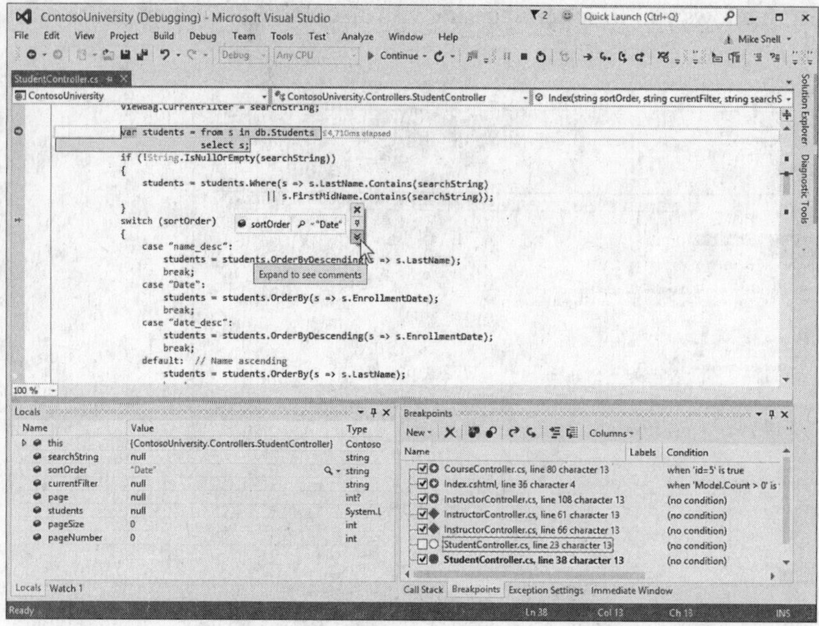

FIGURE 10.39 You can pin DataTips to the code editor to provide easier variable watching during a debug session.

TIP

You can use the Export and Import options from the Debug menu to save your DataTips to an XML file and reuse them on another computer.

PerfTips

The Visual Studio 2015 debugger has added performance information directly inside the code editor. This information is available during an active debug session. To see line by line performance, you can execute a line of code, run to breakpoint, or step over a line; you then simply hover over the line of code that was executed, and you can see the duration of the execution (in milliseconds). This makes recognizing performance issues in your code much easier.

Clicking the performance tip in the code editor brings up the new Diagnostic Tools pane as shown in Figure 10.40. This is the diagnostic information being captured about your running application (more on this in a moment). Here you can use the diagnostic window to see time elapsed between steps in the Debugger (among other things).

Diagnostic Tools

Visual Studio 2015 includes the new Diagnostic Tools window that automatically begins tracking performance information about your running code during a debug session. You access this tool from the Debug menu, Show Diagnostic Tools option (or CTRL+Alt+F2).

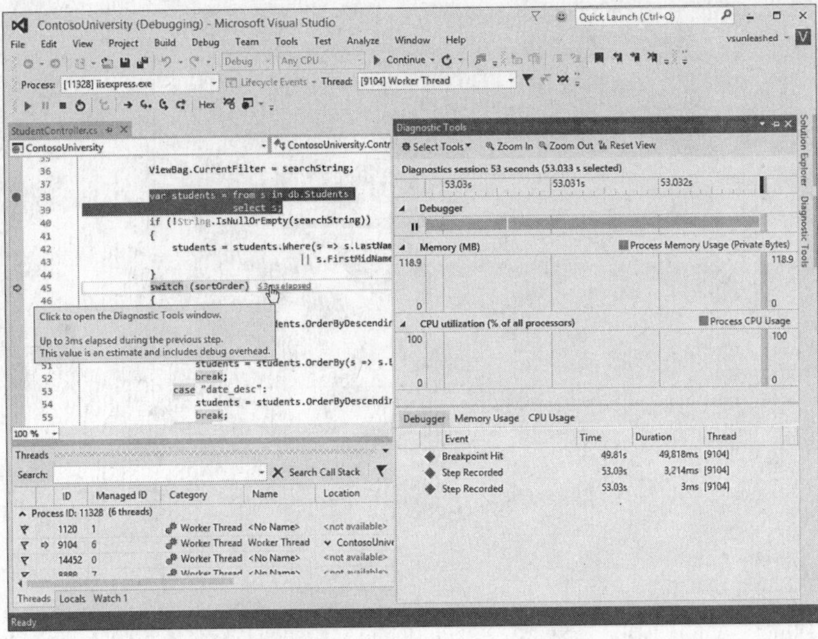

FIGURE 10.40 Select a PerfTip in the editor to bring up diagnostic information about lines of code previously executed.

This Diagnostic Tools window (shown in Figure 10.41) shows running graphs over a timeline at the top of the window and detailed information in tabs at the bottom half of the window. You can use this information to find where your code is using too much memory or CPU. The tool works closely with your debugger to break the graphs into sections based on when you are in the debugger stepping through code versus when you are simply running your application.

There is also a timeline across the top of the window that shows a running time as your application is being debugged. You can use the toolbar in the window to zoom in and out of this timeline. You can also select a section of the timeline and then use slider bars to select a start and end time to zero in on a portion of your data. This can be useful, for example, if you see a spike in memory usage. You can zero in on this portion of the data and then use the Memory Usage tab to take a snapshot of the objects that were running on the heap.

Visualizing Data

When you are looking at variable values, what you really want to get to is the data behind the object. Sometimes this data is obscured by the object model itself. For example, suppose you are looking for the data that is contained in a `DataSet` object. To find it, you have to dig many layers deep in a Watch window or a DataTip. You have to traverse the inner workings of the object model just to get at something as basic as the data contained by the object. If you've spent much time doing this, you know how frustrating it can be.

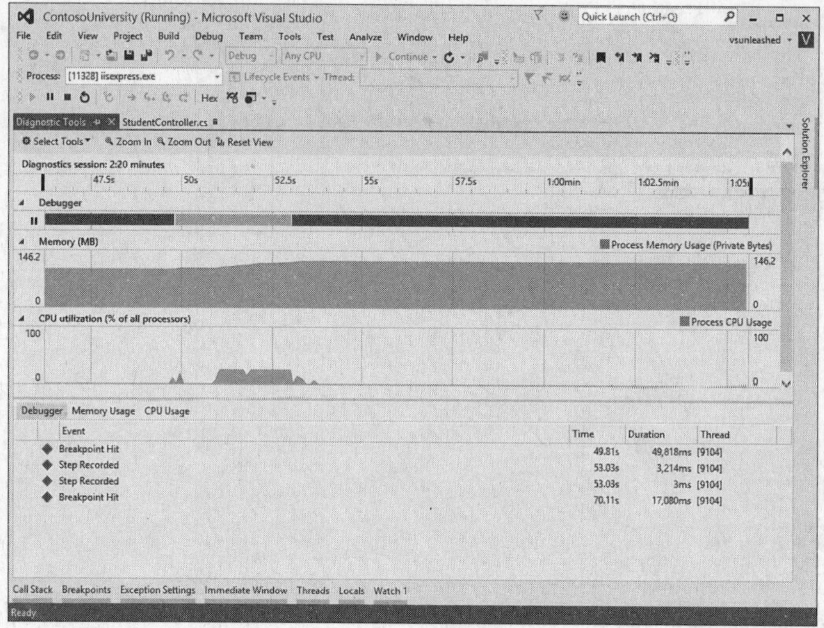

FIGURE 10.41 Visual Studio 2015 provides the Diagnostic Tools window to give you profiling data as your application is being debugged.

Visual Studio offers a quick, easy way to access the data contained in an object. It does so through a tool called a visualizer. Visualizers are meant to present the object's data in a meaningful way.

A number of visualizers ship with Visual Studio by default. The following list highlights many of them:

- **HTML**—Shows a browser-like dialog box with the HTML interpreted as a user might see it.
- **XML**—Shows the XML in a structured format.
- **JSON**—Shows JSON structured results in an easier-to-read format.
- **Text**—Shows a string value in an easy-to-read format.
- **WPF Tree Visualizer**—Enables you to view the WPF application events in a meaningful way. We cover WPF applications in Chapter 21, "Building WPF Applications."
- **DataSet**—Shows the contents of the `DataSet`, `DataView`, and `DataTable` objects.

There is also a framework for writing and installing visualizers in Visual Studio so that you can write your own and plug them into the debugger. You can also download more visualizers and install them. The possibilities of visualizers are many—as many ways as there are to structure and view data. A few ideas might be a tree-view visualizer that displays hierarchical data or an image visualizer that shows image data structures.

You invoke a visualizer from one of the many places you view data values, including Watch windows and DataTips. Visualizers are represented by a magnifying glass icon. Refer to Figures 11.38 or 11.39 to see an example of the magnifying glass icon used to launch a visualizer. As an example, instead of digging through the object hierarchy in a Watch window to get at data, you can invoke the DataSet visualizer right from a DataTip. Figure 10.42 shows the visualizer in action for a string variable named `query`.

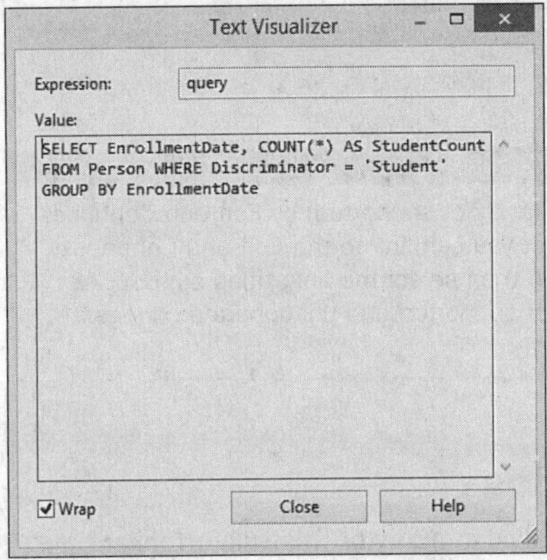

FIGURE 10.42 Use visualizers (magnifying glass icon) such as the Text Visualizer to make data easier to view in the debugger.

Using the Edit and Continue Feature

Edit and Continue enables you to change code as you debug without killing your debug session. You can make a modification to a line of code or even fix a bug and keep working in break mode. Visual Basic developers who worked in versions prior to .NET should recall this powerful tool. Its absence in .NET made it one of the most requested features. The good news is that Edit and Continue was added in 2005 to both Visual Basic and C#. In 2008, this feature was also added to Visual C++. Visual Studio 2015 continues to improve on this feature.

There is no trick to invoking Edit and Continue. You simply make your code change during a debug session and then keep running through your code with a Step command or Continue.

The feature is turned on by default. If it is turned off, you can reenable it using the Options dialog box available from the Tools menu.

Not all code changes you make are eligible for Edit and Continue. In fact, it should be used only in minor fixes. As a best practice, any major additions to your code should not be done in debug mode. If your change is within the body of a method, it has a higher likelihood of passing the Edit and Continue test. Most code changes outside the method body require the debugger to restart. Common changes that are not eligible for Edit and Continue include the following:

- Changing code on the current, active statement
- Changing code on any calls on the stack that lead to the current, active statement
- Adding new types, methods, fields, events, or properties
- Changing a method signature

NOTE

For a more exhaustive list of features supported (and not supported) by Edit and Continue, search MSDN for "Edit and Continue." From there, you can link to the Edit and Continue documentation for your chosen language. You can then select the link, titled `Supported Code Changes`. Here you can review the full list of supported and unsupported changes for your chosen language (C#, VB, C++).

Advanced Debugging Scenarios

Debugging can sometimes be complex. We've looked at many of the straightforward scenarios presented by Windows and web applications. However, the debugging of remote processes, multithreaded applications, and multicore (parallel) applications, for example, presents unique needs in terms of configuration and tools. This section presents a few of the more common, advanced debugging scenarios you will encounter.

Remote Debugging

Remote debugging allows you to connect to a running application on another machine or domain and debug that application in its environment. This is often the only way to experience errors that are occurring on specific hardware. We've all heard this developer's cry: "Works on my machine." Remote debugging helps those developers figure out why their application doesn't work in other environments.

Remote debugging makes a lot of sense in various scenarios, such as debugging SQL server-stored procedures, web services, web applications, remote services or processes, and so on.

The hardest part about remote debugging is getting it set up properly. The actual debugging is no different from the debugging we've discussed thus far. However, the setup requires you to jump through a lot of hoops in terms of installation and security. These hoops are necessary because you do not, by default, want developers to easily connect debug sessions to applications on your servers.

There is some good news. Visual Studio tries to minimize and simplify the setup and configuration of remote debugging. Microsoft has written the Remote Debugging Monitor (`msvsmon.exe`) for this purpose. However, developers still find the setup tasks somewhat arduous (but rewarding when finished). We do not cover the setup in great detail here because it is often environment specific. We suggest querying MSDN for "Remote Debugging" to get the full walk-through and troubleshooting advice for your specific situation.

TIP

You can also remote debug Windows Store apps running on a separate device such as a Windows Surface. See MSDN, "Debug and test Windows Store apps on a remote device from Visual Studio."

We do offer the following, however, as a set of high-level tasks that you need to complete to get remote debugging working:

1. Install the remote debugging monitor (`msvsmon.exe`) on the remote machine being debugged. You install it using the setup application, `rdbsetup.exe`. You can also run it from a file share. You need to select the version that matches the version of Visual Studio you are using and the type of processor on the remote device (x86, x64, ARM).
2. Configure remote debugging permissions. Typically, this means one of two things. First, you can set up identical accounts (username and password) on both machines (debugging and server). The debugging account may be a local or a domain account. However, the server account should be a local account. Second, you can give your user account administrative access to the machine being debugged, but this is often a security risk that you shouldn't take lightly.
3. Run the remote debugging monitor on the remote machine. This is a Windows application (with a GUI). You can also set the monitor to run as a Windows service. This capability can be useful for specific server scenarios and ASP.NET remote debugging.
4. If your debug machine is running XP with SP2, you have to configure your security policy and firewall for remote debugging. (See the MSDN documentation "How to: Set Up Remote Debugging.") If you are running Windows 7 or 8+, you might have to elevate privileges when running Visual Studio (run as Administrator).
5. Run Visual Studio on your debug machine as you would to debug any process. Open the project that contains the source for the process you want to debug.
6. Attach to the running process on the remote machine using Attach to Process. You have to browse to the machine you want to debug and find the process running on that machine.

As you can see, getting remote debugging set up can be a challenge. However, if you have a test environment that you typically debug, the setup should be a one-time operation. From there, you should be able to debug in a more realistic environment as well as walk through SQL-stored procedures.

NOTE

You can set up remote debugging to the Azure cloud. This is actually pretty straightforward. For a detailed walk-through, see MSDN "Debugging a Cloud Service or Virtual Machine in Visual Studio."

Debugging WCF Services

For the most part, you debug a web service (or Windows Communication Foundation [WCF] service) using the same tools and techniques we've discussed to this point. The key to debugging services is properly attaching to them. There are basically two options for this. The first option is to step into a service directly from within code you are debugging (a client calling a service). The second option is to attach to a service that has already been called by a client. Let's look at these options.

Stepping into a WCF Service

You can step directly into a WCF service provided that your calling code (or client) has a two-way contract with the service. This is called a Duplex Contract, and it enables the client and the service to communicate with one another. Each can initiate calls. This is useful when your server needs to call back to the client or raise events on the client. You use the `ServiceContractAttribute` to set this up.

Your client must also be synchronous for this to work. That is, the client cannot make a call to the WCF service asynchronously and then begin doing something else. Instead, it must call and wait.

Attaching to a WCF Service

You can use the Attach to Process option (covered earlier) to debug both WCF and Web Services. In these cases, the service is already running typically in a process outside of your current debug environment. To attach and debug to this process, you must make sure you have the code for the service loaded inside of Visual Studio. Next, the service process must be hosted by IIS or IIS Express for development. Finally, the service must have been invoked by a WCF-based client to gain access to its execution.

Debugging Multithreaded Applications

A multithreaded application is one in which more than a single thread is running in a given process. By default, each process that runs your application has at least one thread of execution. You might create multiple threads to do parallel processing. This can significantly improve performance, especially when run on today's multicore processors and hyperthreading technology. However, multithreading comes at a cost. The code can be more complex to write and more difficult to debug. If you've ever written a multithreaded application, you already know this. For example, just stepping line by line through a multithreaded application to debug it might have you jumping from one thread to another. You would then have to keep track of this flow in your head to make sense of the diagnostic information you see.

Fortunately, Visual Studio provides a few tools that make the job a bit easier. We do not cover coding a multithreaded application here. Instead, we cover the debug options available to you for debugging one, such as the following:

- The ability to view threads in your source during a debug session
- The Debug Location toolbar used to view processes, threads, and flagged threads
- The Thread window used to work with a list of threads in your application
- Breakpoint filters that enable you to set a breakpoint for an individual thread

Let's look at each of these features in more detail.

NOTE

MSDN provides a simple code sample that is useful for working through debugging a multithreaded application. Search for the topic "Walkthrough: Debugging a Multithreaded Application." We use that code sample here to help drive home the key debugging concepts. You can also download this sample from the book's website.

Discovering and Flagging Threads

Visual Studio enables you to visualize the threads in your application in debug mode. When you are stopped on a breakpoint, your application is paused, and all threads in that application are halted. The threads are still there. They are put in a suspended state so you can examine their statuses. They do not continue until you continue the execution of your code. However, in a multithreaded scenario, threads outside the one on which your code broke might not be easily visible in the debugger. To see them in the Debug menu, you can use the Show Threads in Source option from the Debug menu, as shown in Figure 10.43.

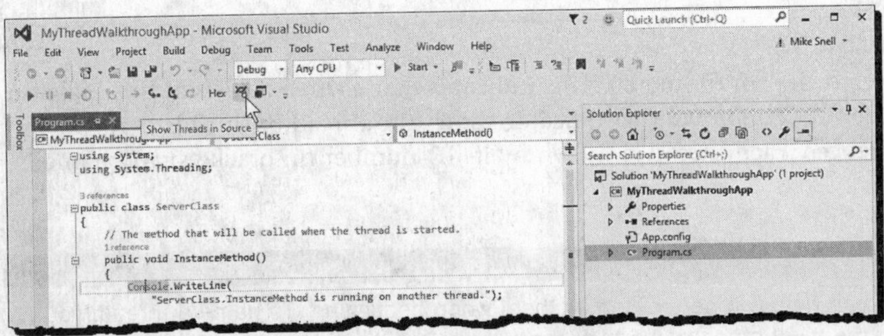

FIGURE 10.43 Select the Show Threads in Source icon from the Debug toolbar to tell Visual Studio to visually display threads in the debug session.

Selecting Show Threads in Source highlights other threads that exist in your code in the indicator margin (or gutter) of the code window during a debug session. The icon used to highlight these items looks like two wavy lines (or cloth threads). Figure 10.44 shows an example of a multithreaded application in a debug session.

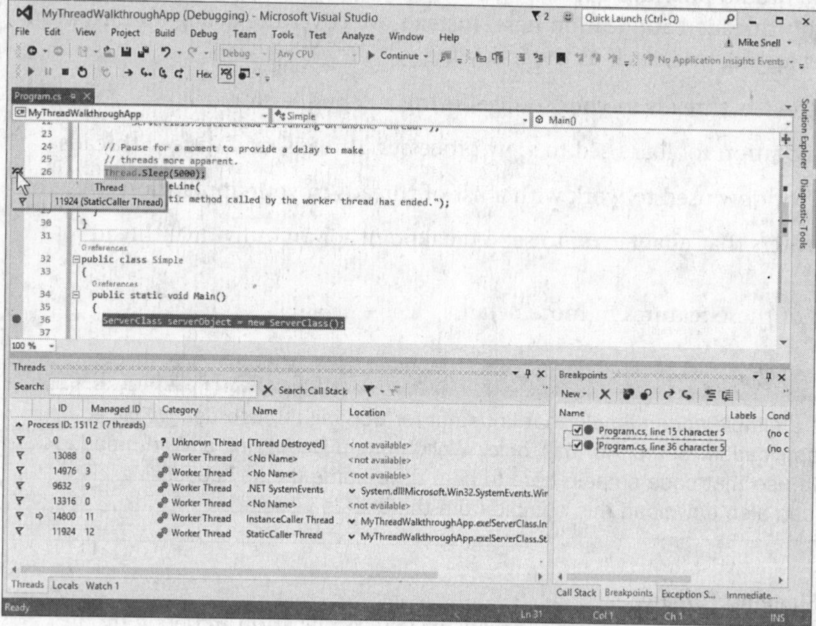

FIGURE 10.44 The thread icon in the indicator margin of the code window indicates that a thread is stopped on a line of code in the debug session.

NOTE

Most debug scenarios are single threaded. Therefore, you will not see another thread executing. You must write an application that uses more than one thread to see the thread icon in the debugger.

Notice the graphic on the left of line 26. This indicates that a thread exists at this location in your source code. Hovering over the indicator shows the thread or threads that the indicator references. Each thread is shown by its ID number (in brackets) and name (if any).

TIP

Naming threads can help you better identify them when debugging. To name a thread, you set the value of the `Name` string property of the `System.Threading.Thread` instance you are interested in. Also, notice that you can't rename the same thread more than once or a `System.InvalidOperationException` is thrown.

Now that you've found a thread, you might want to flag it for further monitoring. This simply helps group it with the threads you want to monitor versus those you do not care about. You can flag a thread right from the indicator margin. To do so, right-click the indicator and choose the Flag option on the context menu. You can see this flag under the cursor shown in Figure 10.44.

Flagged threads show up highlighted (red flag) in the Threads window (Debug, Windows, Threads). This window is shown at the bottom of Figure 10.44. You can use this window to flag or unflag additional threads. Flagged threads provide special grouping in both the Thread window and the Debug Location toolbar. We cover these features next.

Managing Debug Processes and Threads

You can switch between the processes you are debugging and the threads within those processes by using the Debug Location toolbar. (You might have to right-click the toolbar area and add this toolbar to the IDE.) This toolbar is shown in Figure 10.45. On the left is the Process list. Here you can select a process to view details about that process, including executing threads. Many multithreaded applications are run within a single process, however.

FIGURE 10.45 The Debug Location toolbar.

The Thread list drop-down (see Figure 10.45) on the Debug Location toolbar shows a list of threads for the selected process. Notice that the threads are shown with their IDs, names, and flag indicators. You can select a thread in this list to jump to source code associated with the thread. If no source code is associated with a selected thread, the IDE indicates that source code is not available.

You can filter the list to show only flagged threads by toggling the second button to the right of the Thread list (shown with two flags). The first button to the right flags (or unflags) the current, active thread.

You can also manage threads from within the Threads window (Debug, Windows, Threads). Here you see all threads listed for a given process. Figure 10.46 shows an example. Notice that the left of the list shows the flagged status of threads. We have flagged a thread in a sample application. Notice also that these threads can be named. This allows for easy recognition in the Name column.

You have several options available when you right-click a thread in the window, as shown in the context menu in Figure 10.46. Notice the Switch to Thread option, which allows you to switch the active thread being debugged. The active thread is shown with a yellow arrow in the thread list (to the right of the flag). Switching active threads changes the debug context and content in the debug windows. You can also Freeze (or pause) threads using this context menu. (Of course, you can then thaw [or resume] them, too.) Freezing a thread is equivalent to suspending it. The icons for freezing and thawing selected threads are on the far right side of the toolbar in the Threads window. The Threads window has a number of other features. You can use it to search the calls stack group threads by process, ID, category, priority, suspended state, and more.

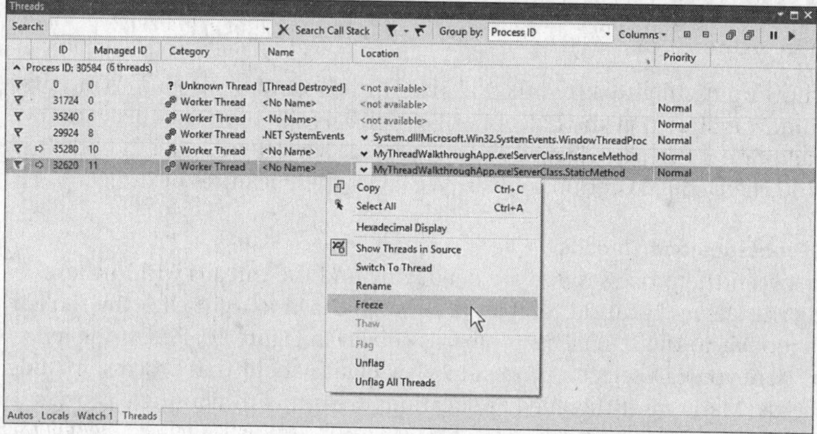

FIGURE 10.46 The Threads window provides total control over the threads in a debug session.

TIP

When debugging multithreaded applications, it's often easier to freeze all but one thread. This allows you to focus on what is happening with the given thread.

Inspecting Individual Threads

When your application hits a breakpoint, all executing threads are paused. This enables you to inspect them individually. As you've seen, you can use the Debug Locations toolbar (refer to Figure 10.45) to change the selected thread in the IDE. Doing so reconfigures the debug windows. This includes the call stack and Watch windows (including Autos and Locals).

For example, imagine you are working on an application that has a main thread of execution. It might then create two additional threads on which it does work. In fact, the sample we started this section with works just like this. We added two lines of code to the sample application (which you can download): one to name each of the threads (`InstanceCaller` thread and `StaticCaller` thread). We then increased the sleep times in each of the methods used as delegates to create and sleep the threads. Finally, we set a breakpoint in the `StaticMethod` on the `Thread.Sleep` line of code.

When you break into the application, you can inspect each of the executing threads. Here you can see the code state for the selected thread (or any of the other threads spawned by the application). Figure 10.47 shows an example. Notice that the `StaticCaller` thread is the active thread in the Debug Locations toolbar (top of the drop-down list). The code is also stopped inside this method.

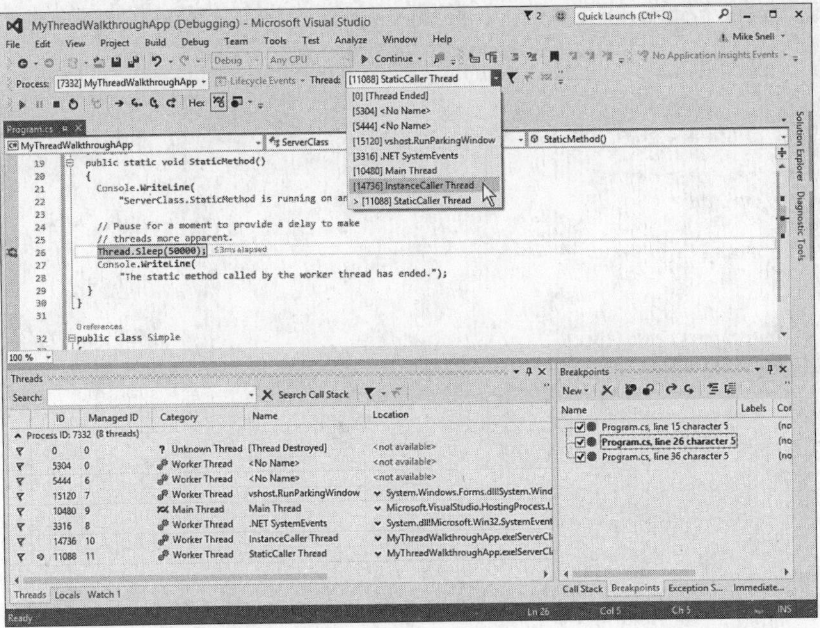

FIGURE 10.47 You can switch to active threads using the Debug Location toolbar. Name your threads to make them easier to work with.

The sample code actually creates the `InstanceCaller` thread first and puts it to sleep to simulate a long-running operation. You can select this thread using the drop-down list shown in Figure 10.47. Figure 10.48 shows this thread selected. Notice that the code window changes to the current line being executed by this thread (`Thread.Sleep`). Because this is not the active thread, this icon in the indicator margin is a different type of arrow, and the selection is a different color (by default). In addition, the Autos window now shows values for this thread, and the call stack shows the lifeline of this code.

Breaking Based on a Specific Thread

You can also break on a line of code when it hits a thread. To do so, set a breakpoint in your code and choose a breakpoint filter (covered earlier). Figure 10.49 shows an example. In this example, the filter is set based on the thread name. You could have multiple threads calling into this method. However, you would only hit the breakpoint when the specific thread hit this method.

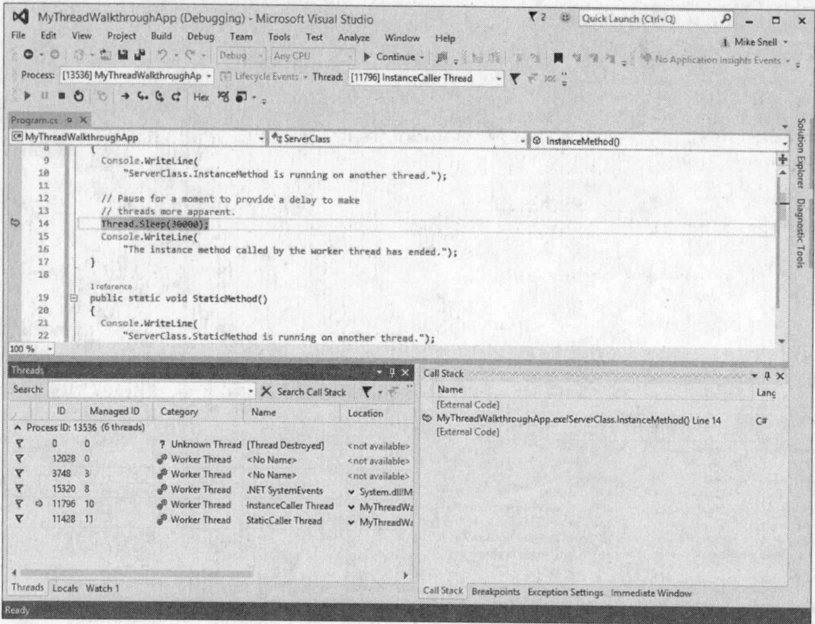

FIGURE 10.48 Selecting another thread in a debug session allows you to view the call stack for that thread and inspect its variables.

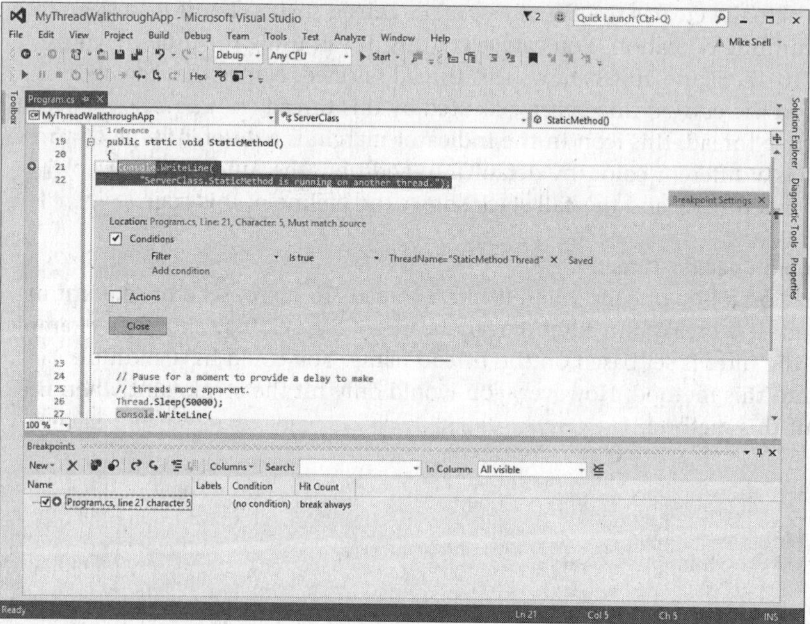

FIGURE 10.49 You can add a breakpoint filter to stop Visual Studio on a specific thread.

Debugging Parallel Applications

A parallel application is one that executes code simultaneously. This includes multithreaded applications. Therefore, the multithreaded debugging discussed thus far is applicable to parallel applications. However, there are additional features of the .NET languages, the framework, and the Visual Studio Debugger to help support parallel coding scenarios. These features are an attempt to take advantage of the recent proliferation of many-core processors. Developers want to take advantage of this computer power, which means they need to begin changing the way they write their applications to take advantage of the multiple cores, each capable of running one or more threads in parallel.

This section covers two of the new debugging features that help support parallel programming: Parallel Stack and Parallel Tasks. Some of these features also apply to multithreaded applications. However, the main focus of these features is parallel applications written for multicore. Recall that parallel programming means task-based programming using features of the .NET 4.0 and above. You can refer to Chapter 3, "The .NET Languages," for a short discussion on parallel programming (`System.Threading.Task`, `Parallel.For`, and so on).

The Parallel Stacks Window

As more cores become available and more programming is done to support those cores, more threads will be executing in parallel. Therefore, you need additional support for debugging the processing complexities of your application. The Parallel Stacks window provides some help. It gives you a view of either all threads or all tasks executing at any given moment in time. The view is a diagram that shows the threads or tasks in your application, how they were created, and full call stack information for each thread or stack.

Parallel Stacks Threads View You access the Parallel Stacks window in an active debug session from the Debug menu (Debug, Windows, Parallel Stacks). This window provides a visual diagram of the threads executing in your application. Figure 10.50 shows an example of the Threads view of the sample application in the Parallel Stacks window.

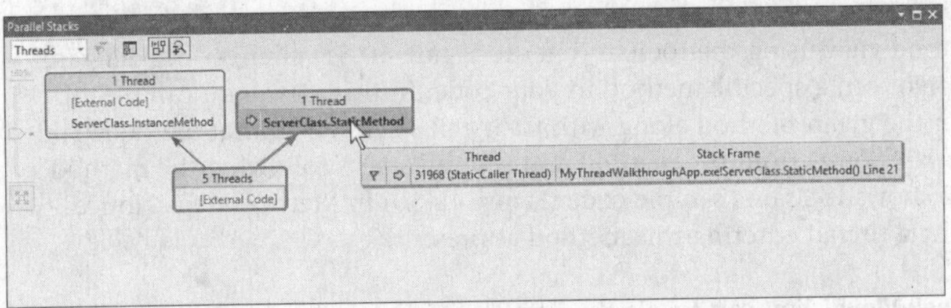

FIGURE 10.50 Use Threads view of the Parallel Stacks window to visualize your threads.

In this example, notice that there are five threads in the application (see bottom box). As you can see, if you hover over one of the thread call stack boxes, you can see the thread IDs and their names (if they have been named). Hovering over the initial grouping (5 Threads) will show all five threads represented by the code in this application.

TIP

You can visualize external code (including that being executed by the framework) in the Parallel Stacks window by right-clicking in the window and selecting Show External Code.

The arrows in the diagram indicate how the threads are spawned within the application and provide information such as the thread ID, name, and call stack. You can use each thread's call stack information to switch to the code associated with a thread (and thus debug its context) by double-clicking.

The Parallel Stacks window has a toolbar at the top. In this case, the Threads option is selected in the first drop-down (as opposed to tasks). You can toggle between tasks (see the next section) and threads using this toolbar. The other options for this toolbar are shown in Figure 10.51.

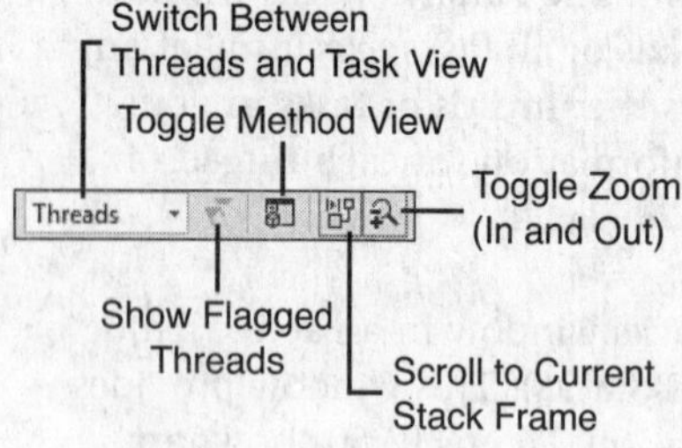

FIGURE 10.51 The toolbar in the Parallel Stacks window.

Switching to Method view using the toolbar (refer to Figure 10.51) changes the diagram to highlight (or pivot on) a specific method in your code. In this view, you can see all threads that enter the given method along with their call stacks up to that method. You can then see the exit points from the method and the call stacks following the method's exit. Figure 10.52 shows the same sample code (Figure 10.50) in Method view. Notice there is only a single thread entering this method at present.

Parallel Stacks Task View You can toggle the Parallel Stacks window to show tasks instead of threads. You can use the drop-down in the toolbar to switch from threads to tasks. You can then use the same diagram tool and related features to visualize tasks as you would threads. Both tasks and threads are joined in this same tool window because they are such similar concepts. Of course, this feature requires that your application is coded to use tasks.

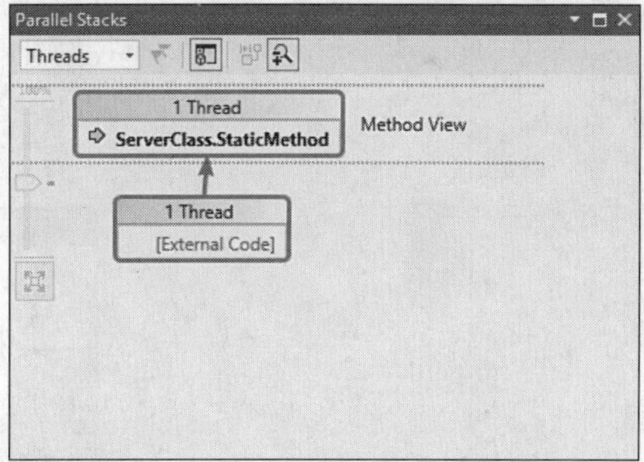

FIGURE 10.52 Use the Method view to show all threads that enter and exit a method along with the related call stack information.

Recall that tasks are bits of work that can be executed in parallel by two or more processor cores. You code tasks using the task scheduling service in the .NET Framework's parallel task library (`System.Threading.Task` namespace). The task scheduler provides a number of services such as managing thread pools on each core and providing synchronization services for your code. This is an additional layer of abstraction over simply managing your own threads or using the `ThreadPool` class. Instead, the framework handles cores and threads. Therefore, trying to debug task-based applications at the thread level is a challenge given the fact that the framework (and not your code) is typically managing the threads.

Visual Studio provides two principal windows for looking at the task-level abstraction of multicore development: Parallel Stacks (in Tasks view) and the Parallel Tasks window. We discuss the latter in a moment. First, let's look at what can be done to view tasks using the Parallel Stacks window.

TIP

If you are debugging unfamiliar-but-parallel code and are unsure if it uses tasks or threads, you can enable external code in the Parallel Tasks window (right-click and select Show External Code). In Threads view, you can see whether there are calls to the `Task` class. This indicates the code was written using multitask (and not simply multithreads).

You switch to Tasks view by selecting Tasks in the drop-down of the Parallel Stacks toolbar. This shows the call stacks for each task being executed. It also shows you the status of the task (waiting, running, scheduled). Figure 10.53 shows you an example of a parallel application running. Note the sample application uses a naming scheme to show how various tasks can execute simultaneously on different processors. Here, we are simply showing you how you can use the tools in your application.

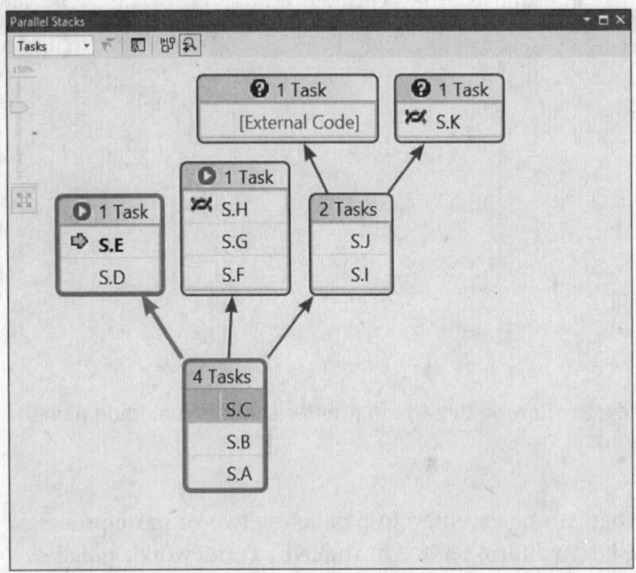

FIGURE 10.53 You can switch the Parallel Stacks window to Tasks view to view the tasks running in your debug session.

NOTE

Like the multithreading sample we suggested you download from MSDN, here we are using a parallel application sample. You can create it, too, by following the MSDN topic "Walkthrough: Debugging a Parallel Application." You can also download this sample from the book's website.

This abstracted view helps you see the tasks in your application without worrying so much about on which processor and thread they are executing. Of course, you can switch to Threads view to see this information, too. Figure 10.54 shows the same sample code as Figure 10.53 at the same breakpoint in the same window but for Threads view. Notice that in this simple example, the parallel framework has created threads that are similar to the tasks (two main threads executing the work). If you start to add a lot more work to this application, however, you see inactive threads that are sitting in the pool waiting to do work. You also start to see a single thread executing larger call stacks (due to reuse) that do not align with your Tasks view.

The Parallel Tasks Window

Another way to look at the tasks running in your application is through the Parallel Tasks window (Debug, Windows, Tasks). This window is actually similar to the Threads window, but it shows the abstraction layer of tasks for those developers doing task-based development.

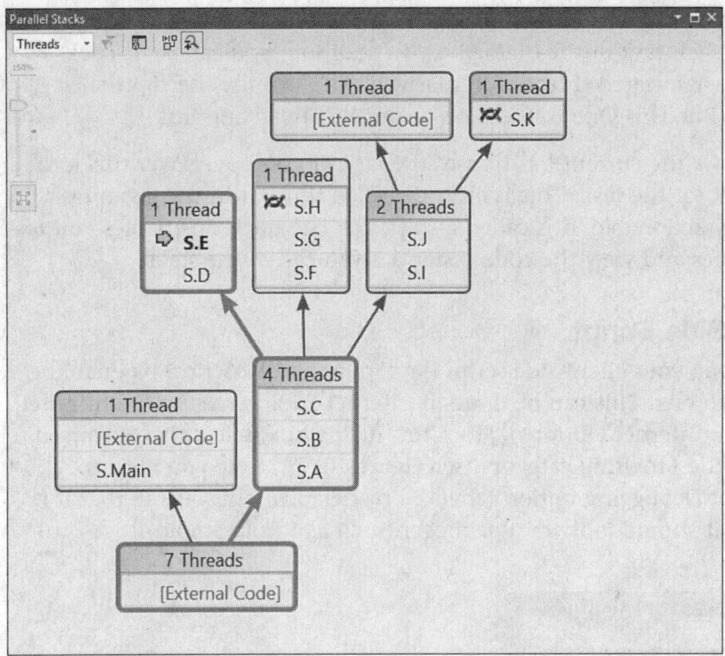

FIGURE 10.54 The Threads view of the same spot in a debug session depicted by the Tasks view shown in Figure 10.53.

Figure 10.55 shows an example of this window running in the same spot as before for the parallel sample application. Notice that for each task (in this case there are four) you can view the task ID, status, location, task (or entry point for the task), thread assignment, and application domain. Note that this example groups the tasks by their status (active, blocked, and so on). This is done by right-clicking the status column and selecting Group by Status from the context menu.

Tasks

ID	Status	Start Tim...	Duration...	Location	Task
Status: Blocked (2 tasks)					
3	Blocked	0.000	357.908	S.J	S.A
4	Blocked	0.000	357.908	S.K	S.A
Status: Active (2 tasks)					
1	Active	0.000	357.908	S.E	S.A
2	Active	0.000	357.908	S.H	S.A

Autos Locals Watch 1 Threads Tasks

FIGURE 10.55 You can use the Parallel Tasks window in a similar manner to the Threads window.

You can also use the Parallel Tasks window to flag tasks for viewing. You do so using the arrows on the left side of each task in the dialog box. In addition, you can right-click a task to freeze or thaw its associated thread. Alternatively, you can use the right-click option Freeze All Threads But This One to focus on a specific thread and task.

The Location column shows the current location of the task. If you hover over this location, you see the call stack for the task. This is all code called thus far in the given task. This mouseover is actually actionable. It is called a stack tip. The stack tip enables you to switch between stack frames and view the code inside a given call in the stack.

Debugging a Client-Side Script

Visual Studio lets you debug your client-side script (JavaScript and VBScript) by enabling script debugging in the browser. This can be done in Internet Explorer using the Internet Options dialog box (Tools, Internet Options). From this dialog box, select the Advanced tab and then navigate to the Browsing category (see Figure 10.56). Here you need to uncheck the Disable Script Debugging option (checked by default). This tells IE that if it encounters a script error, it should look for a debugger (such as Visual Studio).

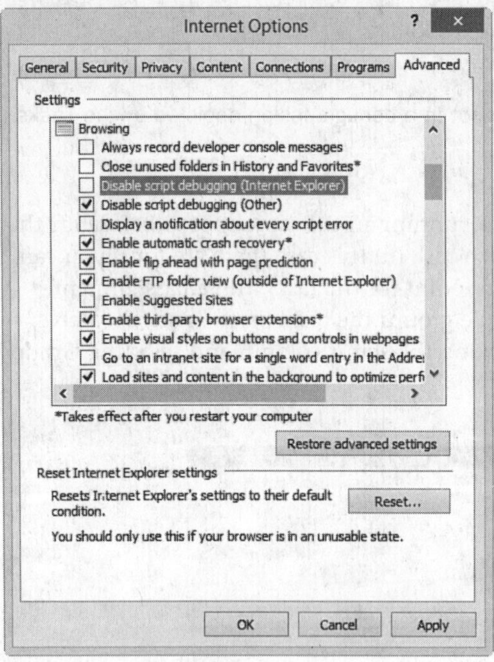

FIGURE 10.56 You can enable client-side script debugging from IE's Options dialog box.

Next, set breakpoints inside your web view files within your `<script>` blocks or inside any JavaScript code file. You can then stop on these lines and debug them with Visual Studio. There are some limitations, however. If you are having trouble, review "Limitations on Script Debugging" in the MSDN documentation.

Debugging Crash Information (Dump Files)

It is often not possible to re-create all environment- or user-specific scenarios in a development environment. Of course, many application bugs or crashes happen without the developer present or a copy of Visual Studio running. In these cases, you can use tools to generate a dump file of the application state at the time of the issue.

Dump files save information about the state of your application. Dump files are typically created in response to a major bug or an application failure (crash). The dump file can then be sent to a developer. A developer can open the file and connect it with the source code and debug symbols to debug the state of the application at the time of the issue.

Dumping Debug Information

You can save running (but paused or on a breakpoint) .NET managed code as dump files. You have a few options for creating these files. In a debugging setting, you can use Visual Studio to create these files and share them with other developers as necessary. Of course, other applications can also create mini dump files, which then can be opened by Visual Studio for debugging. Your options for creating dump files include the following:

- Use the Save Dump As option from the Debug menu in an active debug session of Visual Studio.
- Attach to a running (or crashed) remote process from Visual Studio. (See the information about attaching to a process earlier in this chapter.) You can then break into that process and save the dump file using the Save Dump As option.
- Microsoft provides the utility UserDump as part of its OEM Support Tools. You can use this utility to create dump files that Visual Studio can read.
- Microsoft provides the Autodump+ utility as part of the Microsoft Debugging Tools for Windows. It, too, creates dump files for use by Visual Studio.

We focus on how Visual Studio creates dump files. A quick web search will lead you to the download for other dump-creating utilities.

Using Visual Studio to Create a Dump File

Creating a dump file with Visual Studio is straightforward. You stop (or break into) the application at the point you want to capture. This might be at a place in the testing where there is a known issue. You then select the Save Dump As option from the Debug menu. The Save Dump As dialog box is then displayed, as shown in Figure 10.57.

Notice that when you save a dump file, you can choose between creating the file with heap information and without. The heap information is often not required for many managed code debugging scenarios. Thus, you can save your file without it and conserve hard drive space.

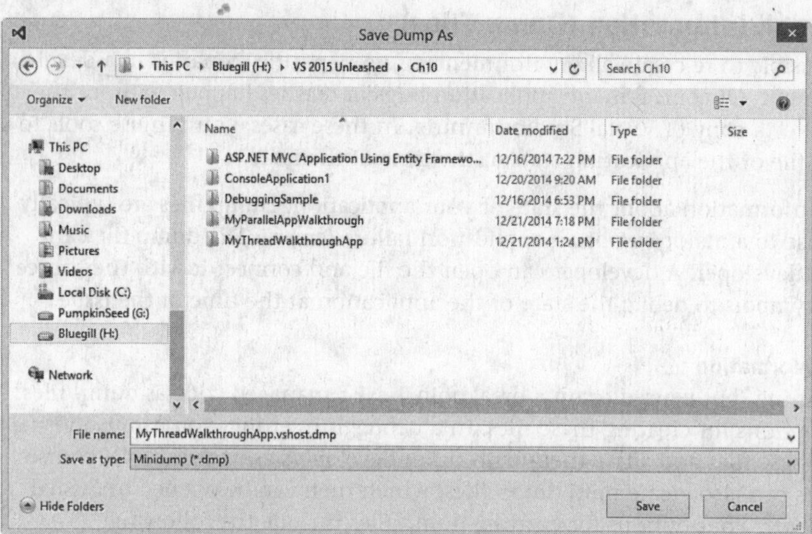

FIGURE 10.57 You can save a mini dump file with or without heap information.

Debugging with a Dump File

The first step to debugging with a dump file is to open the file from the File menu (File, Open, File) or by double-clicking the dump file. When you open a dump file, the new Dump File summary page appears. This page displays information about the dump file, such as when the dump file was created, the version of the OS and CLR that was running when the dump file was written, and the versions of the various other components (modules) that were running at the time. Figure 10.58 shows an example of this summary page. Notice that you can use the Modules search box to determine if a specific `.dll` or `.exe` was loaded at the time of the dump.

The dump summary page provides a few actions. The two that developers use the most are Set Symbol Paths and Debug with Mixed. The Set Symbol Paths option enables you to indicate the paths to the symbol files (`.pdb`) that match the build of the application from which the dump originated. By default, Visual Studio looks for symbol files where your code executed. Therefore, if you dump and open that dump on the same machine, you have nothing more to set up. Visual Studio finds your symbol files. If, however, symbol files are created on a per-build basis and dumps can originate from anywhere, you have to use Set Symbol Paths to indicate where Visual Studio should find your latest symbols.

IMPORTANT

Symbol files (`.pdb`) are important if you intend to debug a built application. For this reason, we recommend you store your symbol files in a safe location along with the compiled versions of your deployed code to make debugging a production issue using a dump much easier. Symbols should also be generated for Release builds.

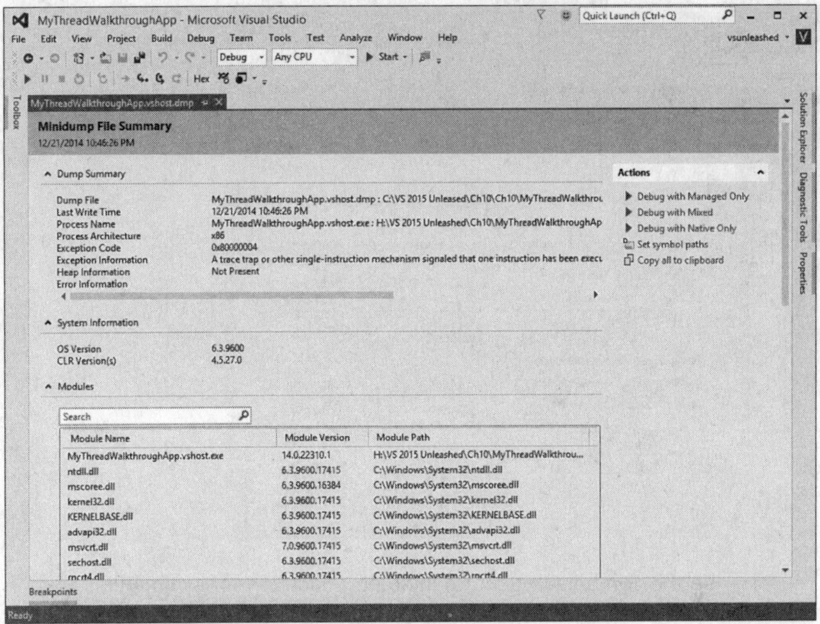

FIGURE 10.58 The mini dump summary page shows you both detailed information and next steps (actions) when you open a dump file.

Figure 10.59 shows an example of the Options, Debugging, Symbols dialog box. In the top part of the dialog box, you can set up a symbol location, which might be a server where builds are dropped or a local folder on your machine. Notice, too, that you can load the Microsoft Public Symbols from their servers. The middle section of the dialog box, Cache Symbols in This Directory, enables you to set up a local folder for caching symbols downloaded from a server, which saves time in that the files can load from a local source. You indicate which modules of your symbol files should be loaded (or excluded) in the last part of the dialog box. You can set this option to All Modules.

The other option available on the mini dump page (refer to Figure 10.58), Debug with Mixed, enables you to start the debugger using the data found in the mini dump file. It is helpful to know that a .NET symbol file (`.pdb`) essentially contains information about your source files path, variable names, and code line numbers. When you debug a dump file, Visual Studio looks at the `.pdb` files it finds (searching your code or your symbol directory) and tries to use this information to find your code files on your machine. If it can locate your code, it opens the code file and gives you a rich debugging experience.

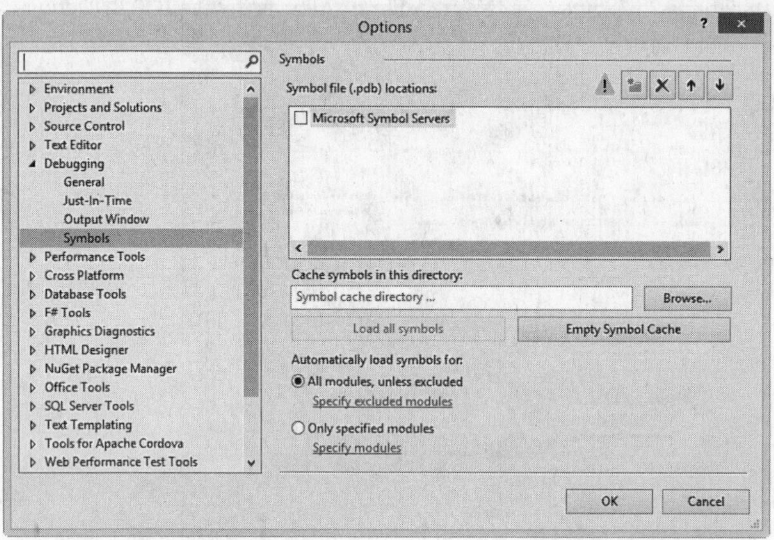

FIGURE 10.59 You can use the Symbols options to indicate a location for symbol files and set up a local cache.

Debugging Windows Store Apps

Windows Store apps can be difficult to debug because they are often started, suspended, and resumed based on user actions. These actions are controlled by the Windows Process Lifetime Management (PLM) environment. When in debug mode, however, these activation events (start, suspend, resume, terminate) are disabled. Fortunately, you can still trigger these events using the debugger.

NOTE

See Chapter 23, "Developing Windows Store Applications," for additional details on creating and debugging Windows Store apps.

You debug a PLM event by first setting a breakpoint in the event handler for the event you want to debug. You then start to debug the application. From there you can use the Debug Location toolbar to fire PLM events to respond to app suspend, resume, suspend and shutdown, and even trigger background tasks.

For example, you may want to save the application state when the user navigates away from your app or the device enters a low power state. To do so, you would write code to handle the `Suspending` event. You might also want to restore your application if the user reopens your application (prior to it being terminated). To do so, you would respond to the `Resuming` event.

Once you've written your event handler, you run the application form the IDE in Debug mode (using the green "play" arrow). You then set a breakpoint inside the given event handler. Finally, you trigger the PLM event by clicking on the Debug Location toolbar and selecting the appropriate event.

Figure 10.60 shows an example; notice the Lifecycle Events option on the Debug Location toolbar. Also, notice the breakpoint set in the event handler, `OnSuspending`. Clicking the Suspend option from the toolbar will fire from inside the IDE the `Suspending` event that will trigger the `OnSuspending` registered handler.

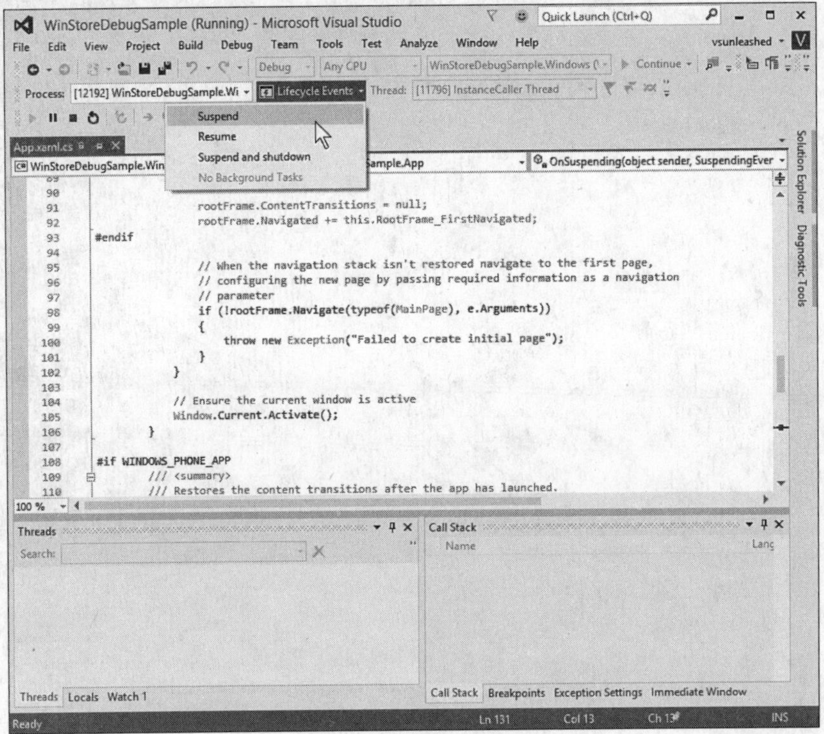

FIGURE 10.60 You can trigger Windows Store PLM events from the debugger.

Summary

This chapter presented the Visual Studio 2015 debugger. We covered setting breakpoints in code as well as setting conditions for when those breakpoints are hit. We discussed stepping through code after hitting that breakpoint. In addition, we presented tracepoints, which perform an action (such as printing a message to the Output window) when a line of code is hit in the debugger. The chapter also examined the many ways you can see the data presented by the debugger, including the Watch windows, visualizers, and DataTips.

The advanced debugging scenarios covered included remote processes, web services, multi-threaded applications, multicore, and client-side script. In this chapter, you also learned how to use the mini dump features to take a snapshot of a running application and debug it at a later time on a different machine. Finally, we covered calling into Process Lifetime Management events for Windows store apps.

Although the debugger itself is large and, in some areas, complicated, mastering its features is a critical skill to have for all Visual Studio developers.

CHAPTER 11
Deploying Code

IN THIS CHAPTER

- An Overview of Client Deployment Options
- Publishing a Project with ClickOnce
- Publishing a Project with InstallShield Limited Edition (forthcoming)
- Publishing an ASP.NET Web Application

PLEASE NOTE

Over the last few revisions of Visual Studio Unleashed, this chapter has traditionally covered all of the core knowledge required to package and deploy applications. This has included coverage of a free add-in from InstallShield called InstallShield Limited Edition. Unfortunately, this time around, a copy of InstallShield Limited Edition for Visual Studio 2015 was not available in time for us to include it in the print version of this book. We've left the section here in this chapter, and will provide content for that section via an electronic, free version of this chapter published online at this book's website when available: www.informit.com/title/9780672337369.

Visual Studio is primarily a coding and development tool. But after you have built an application, the next problem you face is how to get it into the hands of the users. This is not an insignificant problem. Applications can have a variety of prerequisites that need to be verified. Is the right version of the .NET Framework installed? Does the target machine have SQL Server installed? Is a supported operating system detected?

In addition to prerequisites, the actual install process involves myriad variables. Some applications are simple enough to enjoy the ability to do "xcopy deployment." In other words, you just copy the executable to the target machine and away you go. But there are certainly more complicated scenarios as well. For instance, your application might store some data in the Registry and might require Registry values to be set upon install. Or there might be a particular folder structure required. Or maybe a database schema needs to be configured, and data populated, during the deployment process.

In addition to these standard deployment scenarios, Microsoft has been advancing its strategy with respect to application "stores": central locations where developers can publish their applications. We cover these specific flavors of code deployment in Chapters 23, "Developing Windows Store Applications," and 24, "Creating Windows Phone Applications."

In this chapter, we focus on the more traditional code deployment scenarios for .NET client applications and for server-based ASP.NET web applications.

An Overview of Client Deployment Options

Two primary installation and deployment technologies are available within Visual Studio: ClickOnce and InstallShield. Both of these vehicles are similar in that they enable you to move binaries and components from one location and install them onto a target client machine. But there are definitely pros and cons to dealing with each.

Introducing ClickOnce Deployments

ClickOnce was created to try to match the low-deployment factor of web applications. With web applications, users can merely open a browser and click a link to access functionality. In a similar fashion, with ClickOnce, you can publish a set of binaries to a web server or file share, and users can simply click a link to the ClickOnce package to have the application installed onto their machine. The ClickOnce technology is available for Windows Presentation Foundation applications, Windows Forms applications, and .NET console applications.

You can use three methods to deploy any of these flavors of applications using ClickOnce:

- **Web/Share deployment**—In this model, your application executables or DLLs are first published to a web server or network share. You can then provide a link (either a web URL or network path) to binaries. Users can click this link to have the applications automatically installed onto their current machine (thus the moniker *ClickOnce*). No further interaction is required from the user.

- **CD deployment**—With this method, binaries are packaged and copied onto a CD or DVD. Users then browse the content of the media and launch the install process with one click. This method is primarily used when users are isolated and do not have the required Internet access or network access to make the web/share deployment method useful.

- **Web/share execution**—This scenario is nearly identical to the first method discussed. Binaries are published to a web location or network share, and a link to that location is then provided to users. When the user clicks that link, the binaries are immediately copied over and the application starts without making a permanent home for the app on the user's PC. After a user closes the application, it is like it was never there in the first place; all the application binaries are removed, there are no entries placed within the Start menu or within the Add or Remove Programs list in the Control Panel, and so on. To the user, it appears as if the application has been run directly from the Internet (or network share), although in fact the binaries have been cached on to the local machine.

ClickOnce applications are extremely easy to deploy for developers, and they are extremely easy for users to install because little interaction is required and there is little overall footprint on the client. However, this simplicity comes with a price. Generally speaking, ClickOnce deployments cannot do any of the more complicated things we referenced in the introduction to this chapter, such as modifying Registry settings or installing third-party software. If your install scenario is too complicated for ClickOnce to handle, you have to turn to Windows Installer.

Introducing Windows Installer and InstallShield Deployments

InstallShield is an installer technology created by Flexera; Visual Studio 2015 ships with a version of this software called InstallShield Limited Edition. InstallShield generates installation packages (MSI files), which contain all the information that the Windows Installer runtime needs to execute and support the installation process for that particular payload.

The basic process looks like this:

1. InstallShield, based on your input, bundles your application and its resources within a setup package, typically referred to as an MSI file because of its default `.msi` file extension. MSI files are a cohesive unit of deployment that is understood by the Windows Installer runtime.
2. The MSI file is delivered to the end users.
3. Running the MSI file launches a wizard that guides the user through the install process. This typically includes querying for information such as where the software should be installed on the hard drive and specifying various options that the software might support in terms of feature set selection.

NOTE

Earlier versions of Visual Studio offered a dedicated project template for generating MSI packages. With Visual Studio 2012, this approach was deprecated in favor of InstallShield Limited Edition. Even though the InstallShield project template is integrated directly into Visual Studio 2015, you must still register, download, and install the software to use it. If you have Windows Installer setup projects created in earlier versions of Visual Studio, you can import those for use with InstallShield and Visual Studio 2015.

And, as mentioned previously, modern applications are moving more to a store-based publishing ecosystem.

With few limitations, you can craft a setup wizard to handle a variety of situations, including different payloads based on the running operating system (OS) version, adding a shortcut to the Windows startup group, adding Registry entries, and installing device drivers.

NOTE

Certain applications have special deployment requirements. We reexamine the topic of deployment for the other major application types within each chapter that covers those types. For example, for Azure cloud-based applications, read Chapter 12, "Developing Applications in the Cloud with Windows Azure."

Publishing a Project with ClickOnce

You create a ClickOnce install by first configuring the correct "publish" options for your project. These are located on the Project Properties dialog box, under the Publish tab (see Figure 11.1).

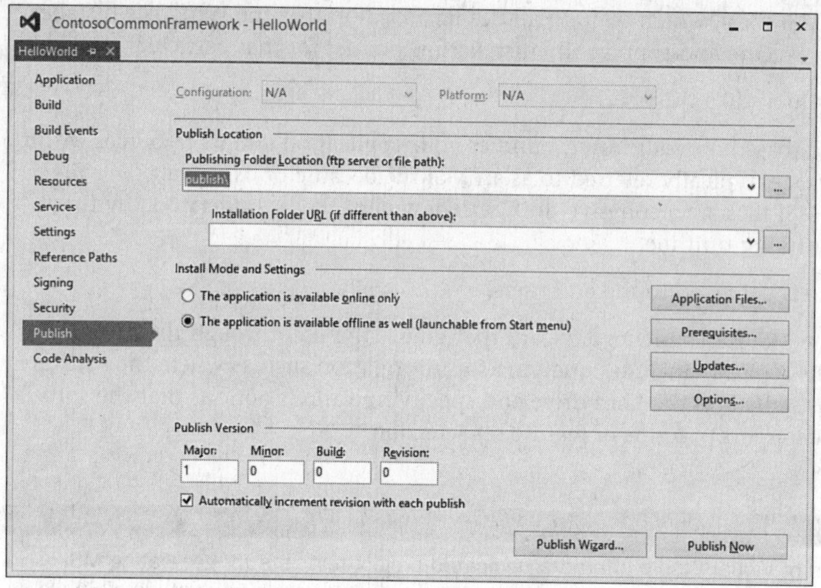

FIGURE 11.1 Setting ClickOnce publication properties.

You can see that this property page holds a variety of settings, including where to host the ClickOnce installation and how we want to handle the offline versus online aspects of ClickOnce. To make things easy for our first deployment, we let the Publish Wizard walk us through setting these options. Click the Publish Wizard button at the bottom of the Publish property page to get started.

The first page of the wizard captures where we want to publish our application. This can be a path to a file share, or it can be a uniform resource locator (URL) pointing to a website or File Transfer Protocol (FTP) site directory (see Figure 11.2).

Page two of the wizard identifies how users install the application. You have three choices here: via a website, via a network share, or from physical media (CD/DVD).

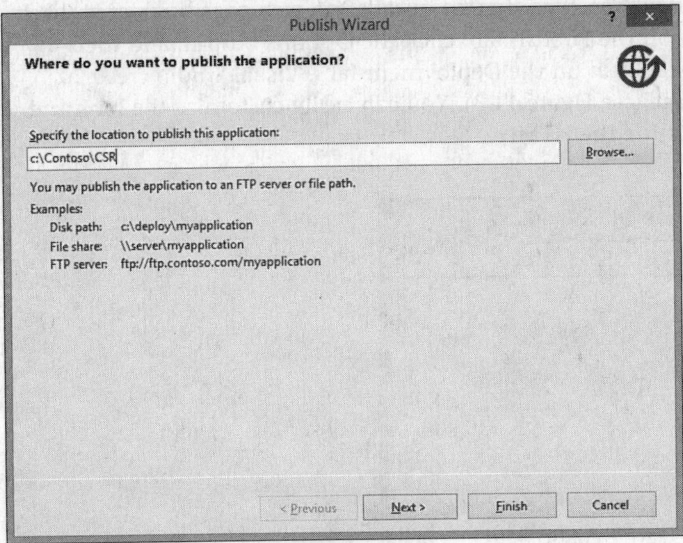

FIGURE 11.2 Setting the install type in the Publish wizard.

The first two options require you to enter the exact location where users can download the software. At first glance, it's not clear what is different about the location specified here and the location specified on page one. Let's clarify what is happening with an example. Let's assume, for instance, that we want users of our application to be able to install the Windows Forms client by visiting a link on the Contoso website. In this scenario, we might end up with the following values:

- **Publishing folder location**—`c:\inetpub\wwwroot\ContosoCSRInstall`
- **Installation folder location**—http://www.contoso.com/CSR/Install.htm

The first path is the physical one that Visual Studio uses to copy the installation files to their home. The second path is the one (in this case, a URL) that the world uses to access those installation files.

The third and final page of the wizard varies slightly depending on the install option we selected on the second page. For website and network share installs, we must indicate whether the application should be available online and offline or just online. Offline capable applications have a shortcut added to the Start menu and can be uninstalled through the normal Add/Remove Programs control panel. Online-only applications are run directly from the `Installation` folder location. If we select the CD/DVD installation option, we have the opportunity to specify whether the application updates itself when online.

After the wizard finishes, the project builds and immediately tries to publish using the information collected. If you have specified that an installation web page be created (back in the Project Properties page, on the Publish tab, click the Options button, and then specify a web page such as Install.htm on the Deployment tab), Visual Studio creates a basic ClickOnce install web page (see Figure 11.3). You can easily customize the look and feel of a ClickOnce page by editing the HTML.

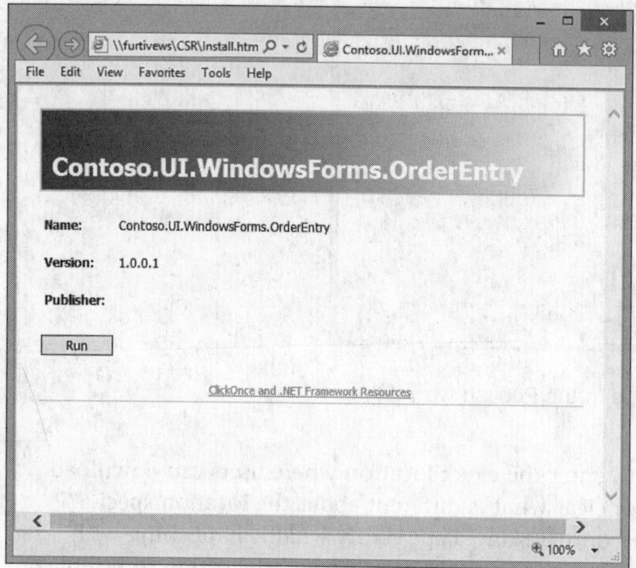

FIGURE 11.3 A ClickOnce install point (web page).

NOTE

You don't need to go through the entire Publish Wizard every time you want to deploy or redeploy your application. After you have the options set the way you want them on the Publish property page, you can republish using those settings by selecting Publish from the Visual Studio Build menu.

Now let's move on and see how to accomplish the same end result using Visual Studio and the Windows Installer technology.

Publishing a Project with InstallShield Limited Edition

Just as with ClickOnce, Visual Studio directly supports deployment of applications using the Windows Installer technology. The approach is different (as are the underlying technologies); Windows Installer deployments are created with the use of a separate project template and application (InstallShield).

Unfortunately, InstallShield Limited Edition for Visual Studio 2015 was not available in time for us to cover the content in this version of our book.

Please keep an eye out for revised content at this book's website (www.informit.com/title/9780672337369); we'll re-publish this chapter in its entirety, including documentation on InstallShield projects.

Publishing an ASP.NET Web Application

Visual Studio provides a dedicated tool/wizard for publishing ASP.NET web applications. Using this tool, you can take an existing web application project, compile it, bundle all the folders, files, settings, and databases that are used by that application into a web package, and then deploy that package to a web server. One advantage to compiling your website before deploying is that the compiler finds compile-time errors for you before deploying onto the target server. Another advantage you gain by compiling your application is increased page performance. Because all the pages within the site are precompiled, the need to compile dynamically during the first page hit is removed.

Let's continue with a brief walk-through of the publishing process. The Web Publish process is kicked off via the Build menu's Publish command (see Figure 11.4) or by right-clicking on the web application project in Solution Explorer and selecting Publish.

The first screen asks for the deployment target to use.

Selecting a Target

The publishing process is driven by a profile. This is a collection of settings that define the parameters of the deployment target. You can either create your own profile (as you would if you were publishing to an internal web server, to your own development machine, or to a corporate IT/enterprise asset), or you can use a profile bundled with Visual Studio (such as Windows Azure) or provided by a third party (as would be the case if you were publishing your web application to a third-party hosting provider).

On this first page of the Publish tool, we have an option to publish to Windows Azure (which we'll cover in-depth in Chapter 12). If you are using a third-party hosting provider, and that provider has a profile file available, you can import it by using the Import option. In this chapter, we'll look at the Custom option that allows us to create our own deployment target (see Figure 11.5).

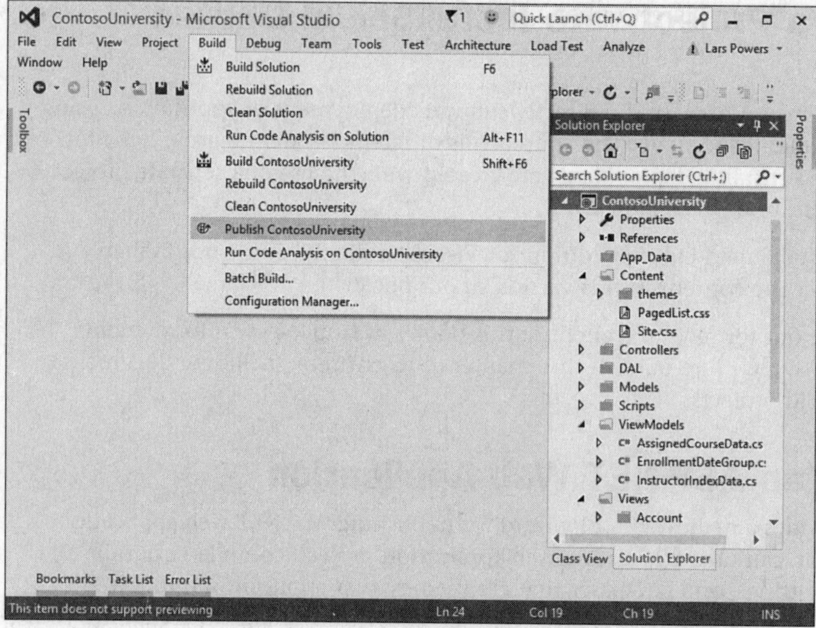

FIGURE 11.4 Launching the Web Publishing tool.

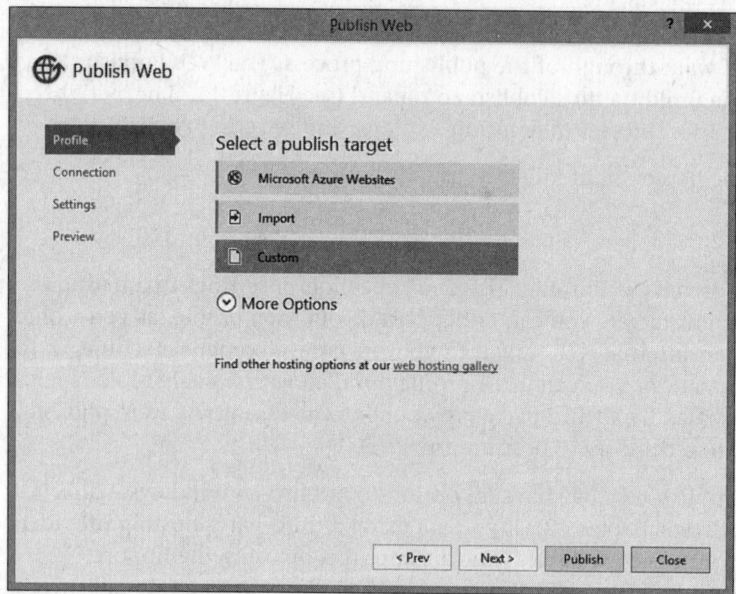

FIGURE 11.5 Selecting a publish target.

When we select the Custom target option, we are prompted to name the profile, and then we need to set the connection parameters for our target.

Configuring a Connection

The next page captures the method of deployment and connection information. The method of deployment is selected by using the Publish Method drop-down. There are four different options here: Web Deploy (formerly known as One-Click Publishing), Web Deploy Package, FTP, and File System. Of all the options available, Web Deploy is the best in terms of leveraging Visual Studio to do the heavy lifting. This method uses Internet Information Services (IIS) remote management services to copy the relevant application files to a remote or local server. As mentioned in the discussion about profile settings, some web hosting providers directly support One-Click Publishing/Web Deploy, which makes this method particularly attractive for targeting offsite web servers that a third party is maintaining.

The rest of the options on this page of the wizard are dynamic and depend on the method you choose. For FTP deployments, for example, you need to provide the appropriate FTP login information. For Web Deploy profiles, you must provide a service URL and an application URL (see Figure 11.6).

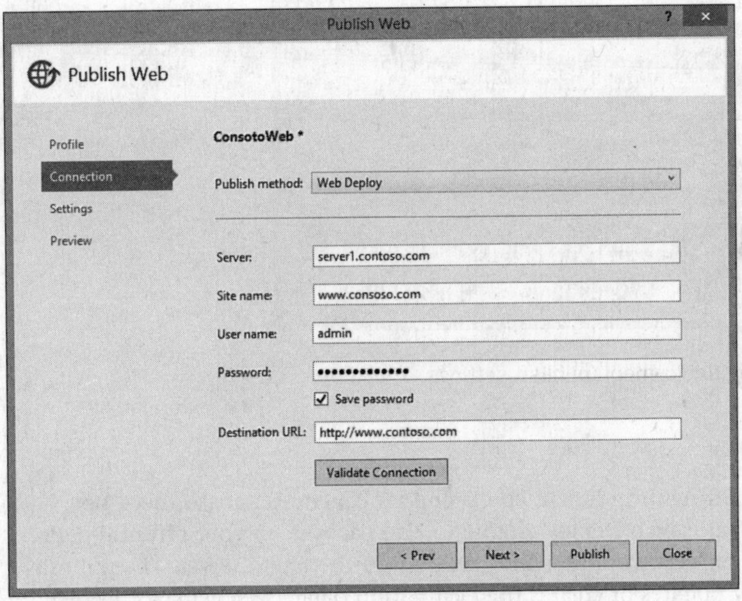

FIGURE 11.6 A One-Click install point (web page).

Configuring Deployment Settings

The next-to-last step in the Publish Wizard captures the build configuration that you want to deploy (for example, Release or Debug). Also, for each database connection used by the web application, it configures the corresponding connection string to use on the target server.

In the Contoso University sample application, two database connections are used: one called `SchoolContext`, and the other called `ApplicationServices`. If you look at Figure 11.7, you can see that the wizard shows us a section for each of these connections. Use the drop-down box to enter the connection string that the application should use on the target server (that is, the server on the receiving end of the publish operation).

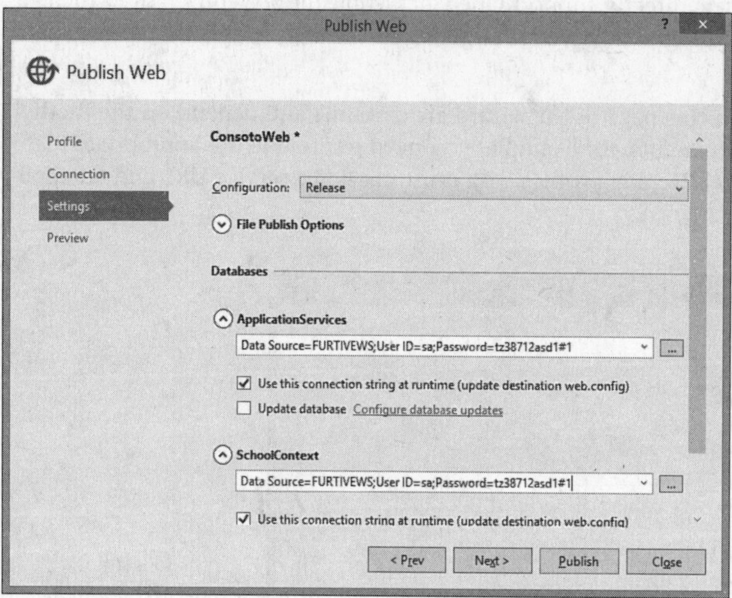

FIGURE 11.7 Configuring deployment/publish settings.

Deploying the Database

Under each Connection String drop-down, you'll find an Update Database check box. Placing a check here tells the Web Deploy engine to also package up your physical database (in this case, a SQL Express database) and deploy it to the target server. The publishing engine automatically updates or creates the destination database schema as needed.

You can also provide custom SQL scripts to be used as part of the deployment process. To do this, click the Configure Database Updates link located to the right of the Update Database check box. In the dialog, click the `Add SQL Script` link at the top (see Figure 11.8).

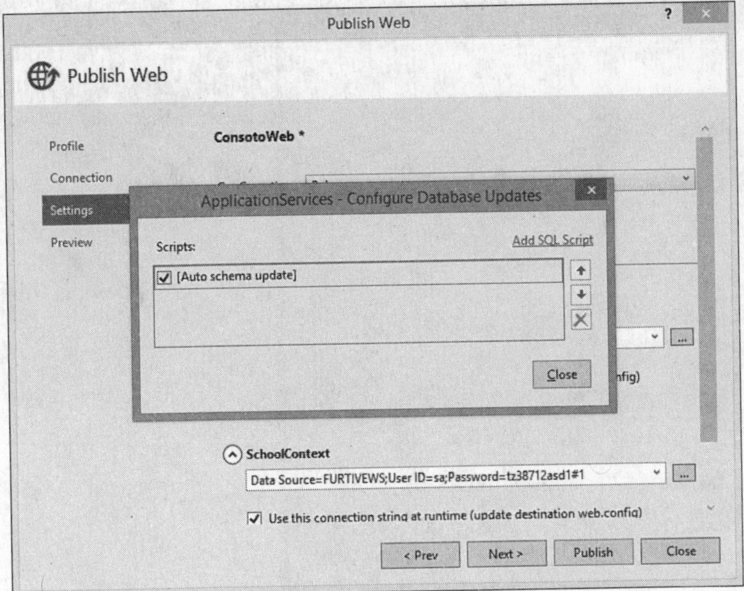

FIGURE 11.8 Deploying referenced databases with custom SQL script.

From there, click the Add Script button, and then navigate to the script file. Notice that there is already a script entry in the list; this is the script that the deployment tool generates based on the settings you have provided. Custom scripts that are added are executed in the order they are listed. For instance, if you need a script to execute *before* the general schema and data script that the tool generates, you add the script to the list and then use the arrow keys to the right of the list to move it above the default script.

Previewing the Publication

After all the required properties and settings have been provided, the final page of the wizard shows you a preview of the actions that will be performed (see Figure 11.9). This is a smart preview and not just a restatement of your earlier settings. In other words, the publishing tool actually reaches out to the target server at this stage and shows you a list of files that will be copied or deleted, database schemas that will be created, and so forth. You can make last-minute changes on this screen by opting to not copy or delete specific files.

If everything looks okay, click the Publish button to initiate the deployment.

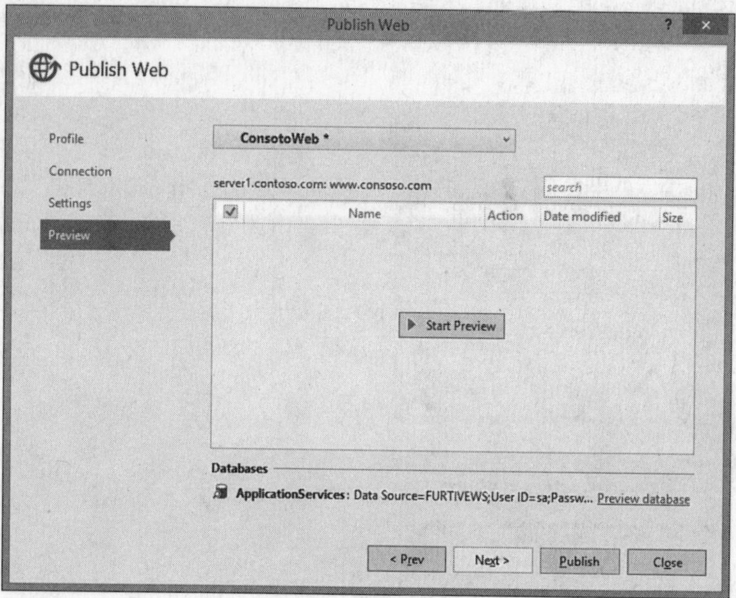

FIGURE 11.9 Previewing the deployment.

Summary

This chapter introduced you to the various tools available within Visual Studio for deploying both client applications and server-side ASP.NET web applications. For client applications, you learned about the two principal deployment technologies (ClickOnce and InstallShield) and the specific reasons you might choose one over the other. This chapter explored these two technologies in depth by examining how to use Visual Studio to publish a WinForms application using both methods.

This chapter also covered the tools available for deploying ASP.NET web applications from a local machine to a web server and demonstrated the tools within the IDE for accomplishing the same.

CHAPTER 12

Developing Applications in the Cloud with Windows Azure

IN THIS CHAPTER

- Create Your Azure Account
- Create and Deploy an Azure Web App in Visual Studio
- Create Your Web App form the Azure Portal
- Monitor and Manage Applications in Azure
- The Azure SDK for Visual Studio 2015
- Azure Cloud Services (PaaS)

Microsoft continues to evolve Azure as a full-service, easy-to-scale, cloud platform for building, testing, and hosting applications. Azure offers website and cloud service hosting, virtual machines, storage, and media services. There are two core concepts of Azure: infrastructure as a service (IaaS) and platform as a service (PaaS). The former allows you to create, host, and manage virtual machines in the cloud. The latter, PaaS, is a hosting platform that is managed and scaled on your behalf. You can take advantage of PaaS directly by creating your own cloud services; alternatively, you can use Azure web apps, a hosting platform already built on PaaS and designed to make your development and deployment easier. The following describes the core Azure offerings across IaaS and PaaS:

- **App**—The Azure platform allows fast and easy deployment and management of websites built on .NET, PHP, Node.js, and other technologies. These websites can take advantage of SQL databases, table storage, blog storage, caching, a content delivery network (CDN), and more. In addition, you can build mobile services for handling iOS, Android, Xbox, and other applications.
- **Compute/networking**—This service allows you to deploy and run virtual machines (VMs) based on Windows Server or Linux. You can then use the machines to custom configure and host your applications. This allows you to deploy existing code without changes and take advantage of custom hosting

configurations. You can also configure hybrid (on-premises to cloud) networked solutions.

- **Storage**—Azure provides SQL and NoSQL database solutions. This includes full power of SQL Server as well as the ability for other storage solutions. It also has data services that allow you to get insight from all your data using HDInsight (Hadoop).
- **And more**—Azure is big and ever-growing; the following are some additional services available to developers: Stream Analytics for processing millions of events per second; Predictive Analytics to use machine learning to mine historical data; identity management, single-sign on, and synch with on-premises directories; BizTalk services and other application integration options; media services to enable content encoding, storage, protection, and delivery; and more.

This chapter focuses on the developer experience with Azure and Visual Studio 2015. We first cover getting started with the Azure management portal; creating, deploying, and debugging your first application in Azure; and using the portal to monitor and manage your application. The chapter then covers the details of the Azure software development kit (SDK) for Visual Studio to make building and scaling cloud applications easier.

NOTE

This chapter is focused on the Azure PaaS offering as related to website hosting and building applications using cloud services. We do not cover Azure IaaS here because that is about setting up and managing virtual machines for your application hosting.

Create Your Azure Account

Visual Studio 2015 has built-in support for many basic Azure functions, such as creating and deploying a website or set of mobile services. These features require an Azure portal account. This section covers the basics of setting up your portal account, linking it to Visual studio, and managing your Azure subscription. The sections that follow cover creating and deploying an Azure application with Visual Studio and using the Azure Portal to monitor and manage your application.

NOTE

Microsoft has also created an Azure SDK for Visual Studio that ships separately. This is covered later in this chapter.

Azure Account Sign-Up

The first step is to set up your Azure account. Microsoft has a lot of ways for you to get started. This includes a free trial, Microsoft Developer Network (MSDN) benefits/credits, BizSpark benefits for start-ups, monthly credits for Microsoft Partners, pay-as-you-go options, spending limits, prepackaged deals, Enterprise Agreements, and more. You will want to visit http://azure.microsoft.com/en-us/pricing/ for details.

To get started, you will want to sign up for Azure using a Microsoft Live ID. If you have an MSDN subscription, you will want to use the same Live ID associated with your subscription to set up your Azure account. If you have a work or school account, you will want to sign in with that ID. Signing in with the right account ensures that you have access to your Azure benefits.

If you do not have an MSDN subscription or want to create a new account, you can sign up for Azure from the website (azure.microsoft.com) by clicking Free Trial or Buy Now. First, you log in with an existing Live ID (or create a new Live ID account). Next, you sign up for your Azure account using your Live ID. Figure 12.1 shows the sign-in process for setting up a free trial account. The free trial does require a credit card to set up. However, this is for verification purposes only. The account automatically expires and has a spending limit of zero (unless you change these options).

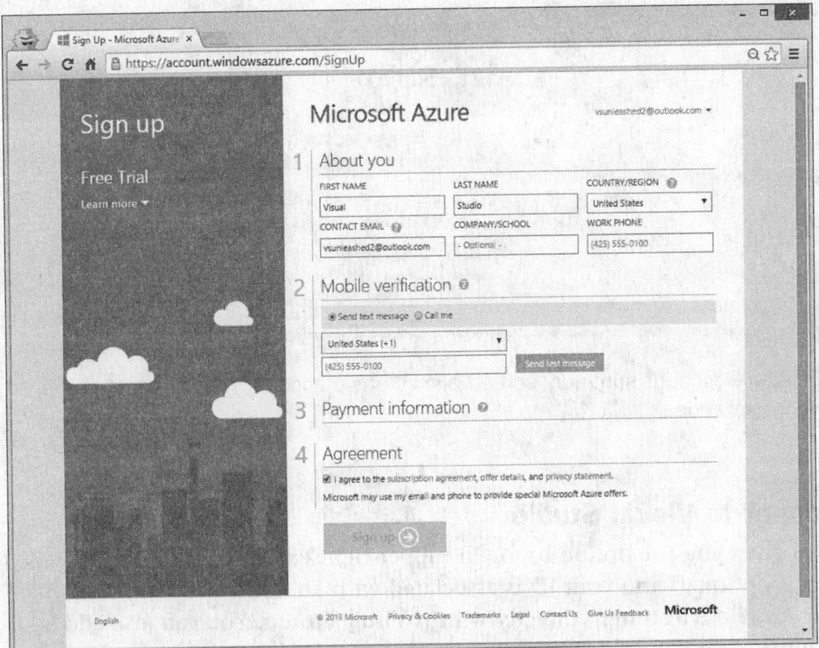

FIGURE 12.1 Sign up for Azure using your MSDN, work, or school account to access related benefits.

Once signed up, you have the option to go to get started with a few video tutorials or go directly to the management portal. When you hit the management portal for the first time, the Azure site will walk you through the basics. More on the management portal later in this chapter.

You can also access a usage a billing summary page for your account directly from the management portal. Figure 12.2 shows the billing summary information for a newly created, free trial account. From here you can see your usage and upgrade your account if necessary. You can also change subscription details, cancel your subscription, modify your payment method, and more. Notice the Portal link in the upper-right corner. This links you back to the Azure management portal for configuring your services.

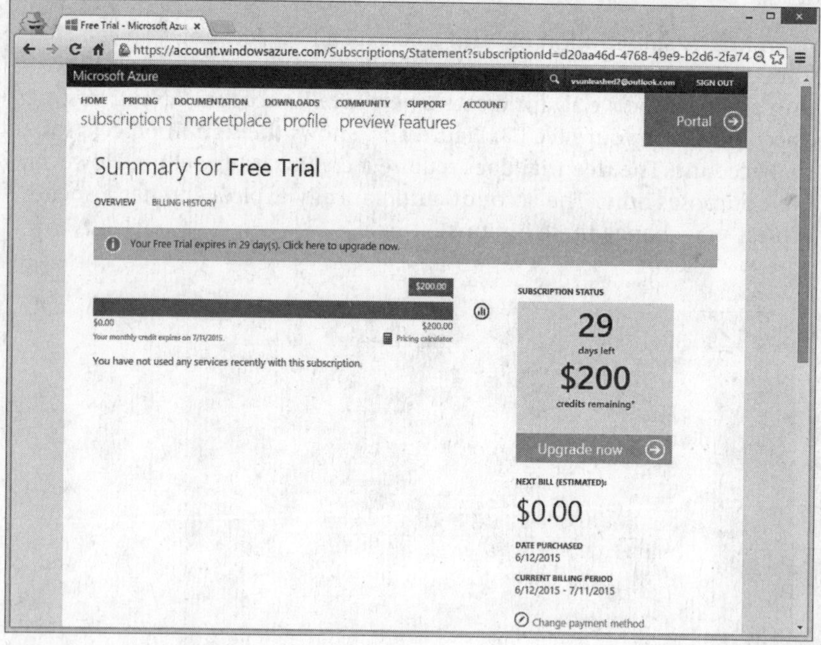

FIGURE 12.2 The Azure account summary screen allows basic account management tasks and provides billing information.

Link Your Account to Visual Studio

Visual Studio 2015 gives you the option to log in (upper-right corner of the IDE). Provided you log in (which is optional) and your ID is associated with an Azure account, you will get access to your Azure environment directly within Visual Studio. You can also add additional Azure accounts to your Visual Studio profile. This enables you to log in to Visual Studio with one account and log in to Azure with a different account. You can also leverage multiple Azure accounts from the same instance of Visual Studio. Let's take a look at how this works.

You navigate your Azure services from the Server Explorer window (View, Server Explorer). Figure 12.3 shows an example. Notice that the window exposes Azure cloud services, mobile services, notification hubs, SQL databases, web apps, and more. The first time you access Azure this way, you may be prompted to log in to an account that works with Azure.

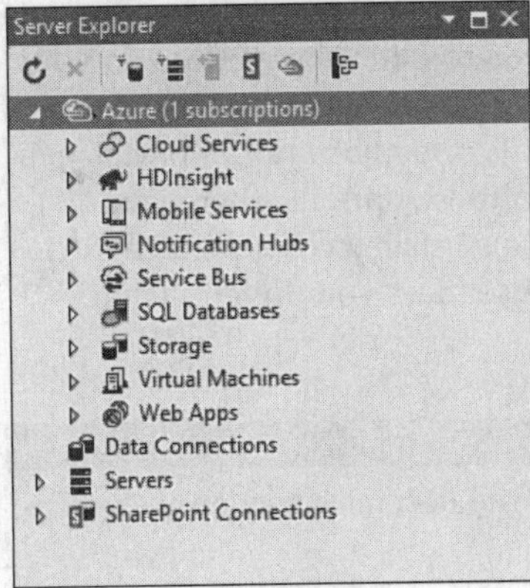

FIGURE 12.3 Server Explorer allows you to navigate and work with the Azure services for your account(s).

Manage Azure Subscriptions

The Azure node in Server Explorer provides access to manage your subscriptions through its context menu by right-clicking and selecting Manage and Filter Subscriptions. Figure 12.4 shows the Manage Microsoft Azure Subscriptions dialog. You can see here that there are three accounts already associated to Visual Studio. You can add additional accounts using the link in the bottom right: `Add an account`. This process simply requires you to log in to your additional account. (See the prior section on setting up that account inside the Azure web app.)

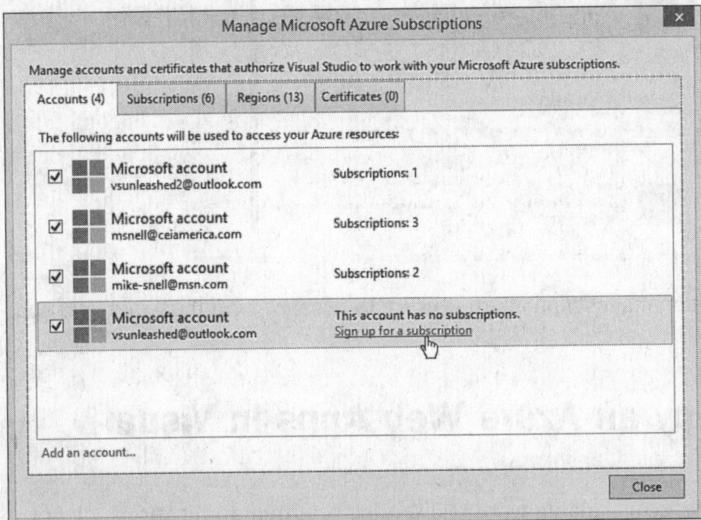

FIGURE 12.4 Visual Studio allows you to manage your Azure subscriptions from within Server Explorer.

Notice that three of the accounts in Figure 12.4 already have Azure subscriptions and one does not. You can use the link `Sign Up for a Subscription` to add subscriptions to your account. An Azure subscription is a usage plan associated with your account. Figure 12.5 shows the current, available options. You can also access this directly from the portal when adding a subscription to your account. In addition to these options, there is the free trial and the standard benefits you get with MSDN (or a similar account/agreement). Subscriptions control how you will likely pay for the Azure services you use and what support agreement you have with Microsoft.

NOTE

You manage your Azure services from the Azure portal. See the upcoming section, "Monitor and Manage Applications in Azure" for details.

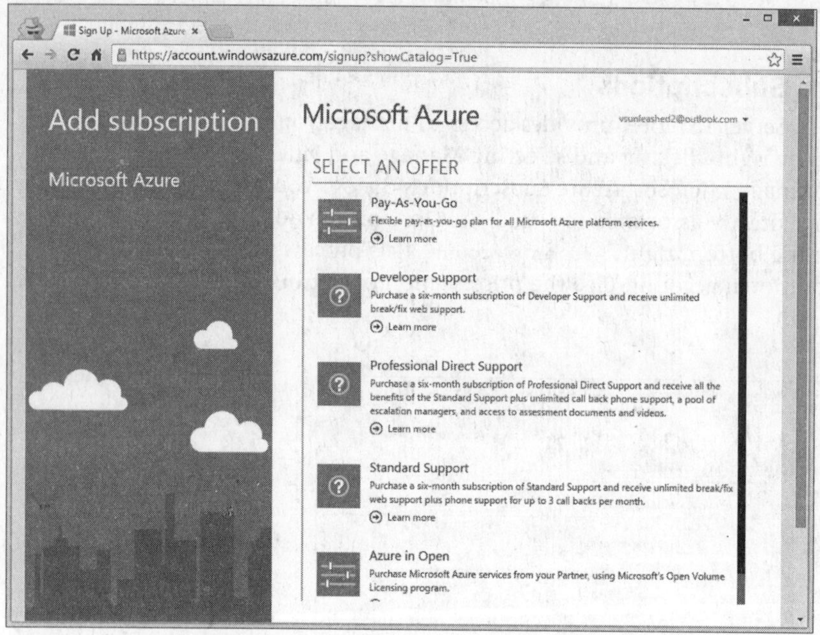

FIGURE 12.5 You add additional subscriptions to your Azure account from the Azure web app.

Create and Deploy an Azure Web Apps in Visual Studio

Azure web apps allow you to host scalable websites, service-oriented applications, dev-ops scenarios, and more. Web apps can be built on .NET, Java, PHP, Node.js, and Python. You can also access your data using SQL databases, MySQL, DocumentDB, Search, and

MongoDB. Azure web apps include support for third-party products designed to help build websites, such as the content management systems (CMS) WordPress, Umbraco, Joomla, and Drupal. In this section, we focus on building and deploying an ASP.NET website to Azure using Visual Studio.

The Azure Hosting Platform

The Azure web apps hosting technology is built on top of the fully managed PaaS environment. The PaaS environment (covered in the upcoming section, "Azure Cloud Services (PaaS)") is a platform on which you can build applications without the overhead of managing the infrastructure on which they run. Azure web apps sit on top of this environment and allow you to leverage Azure cloud services in an easier way for building and hosting your web applications. This includes new applications as well as existing applications. (Even those with sticky sessions can be moved to this environment without changes.)

Azure web apps are run on a set of VMs shared as a resource pool in Azure (on your behalf). You don't have control over these machines, nor do you want it. Instead, Azure takes care of all infrastructure concerns on your behalf (including automatic patching). Your app is isolated and hosted in VMs dedicated to your application. This ensures predictable performance and security isolation.

One of the biggest benefits of Azure hosting (outside of no infrastructure management) is scalability. You can easily scale your application platform to meet demand (and scale down when demand subsides). You do so from the Azure portal; it is as easy as moving a slider control. In fact, Azure has an AutoScale feature that allows you to increase the virtual instances (called nodes) running your application based on CPU consumption. If your application meets a target percentage of CPU consumption (you set the target), you can tell your app to run on additional nodes. Of course, AutoScale will also scale back down.

Create the ASP.NET Application and Azure Hosting

Azure web apps can be created directly from the Azure portal interface (a website) or from within Visual Studio (for ASP.NET solutions). The portal interface allows deploying from a source code provider such as Visual Studio Online, GitHub, TeamCity, Hudson, or BitBucket. You can use these source control providers for continuous deployment during a dev-test scenario. Here, we cover creating directly from Visual Studio. (The portal interface is covered in upcoming sections.)

To get started, we will create a new ASP.NET application linked directly to an Azure web app. This will create the Visual Studio application project (and related source code) locally as well as set up an Azure web app to which we can deploy. You can also link (and deploy) an existing application to an Azure web app; we cover that scenario later in the chapter. The first step is File, New Project, where we select the Web node and an ASP.NET Web Application. Figure 12.6 shows an example of the first step in creating the web application project.

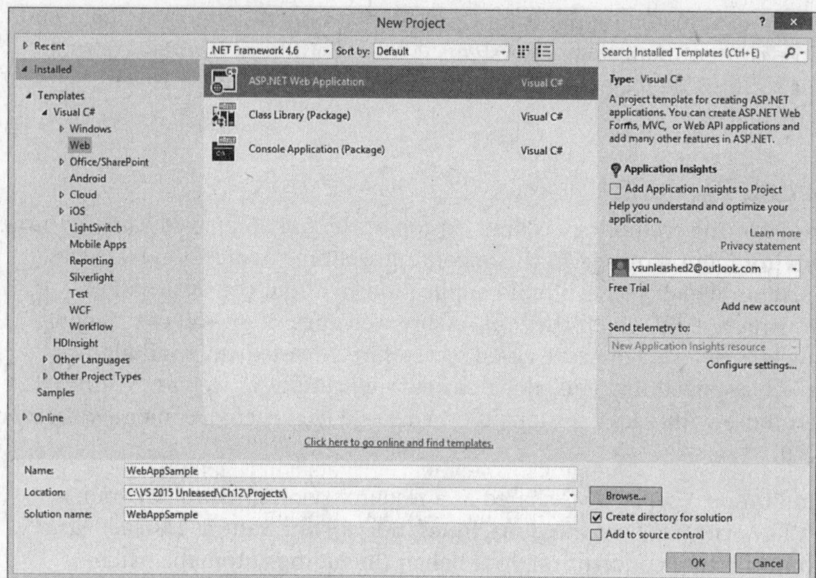

FIGURE 12.6 You create a new Azure web app in Visual Studio the same way you would create any website in Visual Studio.

Visual Studio then brings up the New ASP.NET Project dialog, as shown in Figure 12.7. Notice the bottom-right corner. This is where you choose to automatically set up and link this project to an Azure cloud hosting environment as either a web app or a virtual machine. You can use the Manage Subscriptions link to select the subscription you intend to use by turning off other subscriptions from this dialog (refer to Figure 12.4). If you leave multiple subscriptions active, you are prompted for the subscription under which the web app should be hosted (see Subscription option in Figure 12.8).

Figure 12.8 shows the final step in setting up your Visual Studio project to be hosted by Azure. Here you can configure the basic Azure web app hosting settings. You start by creating a site name which also becomes your temporary URL as [*SiteName*].azurewebsites.net (until you update your DNS to point to an actual URL). You then set an Azure region for hosting the application (typically you select one closest to your users). Finally, you can choose to set up a database to be associated with the site.

The drop-down under Microsoft Azure hosting in Figure 12.6 (set to Website in the figure) includes the alternate choice: Virtual Machine. This allows you to set up your Visual Studio project to be deployed to a VM server that you manage (versus the Azure hosting platform built on PaaS). Figure 12.9 shows the VM setup dialog you receive after selecting this choice. This includes settings for your DNS, the VM location, a username and password, and server sizing. You have a couple dozen choices for VM size based on CPU cores and RAM. (Of course, different pricing applies as you select bigger VMs.)

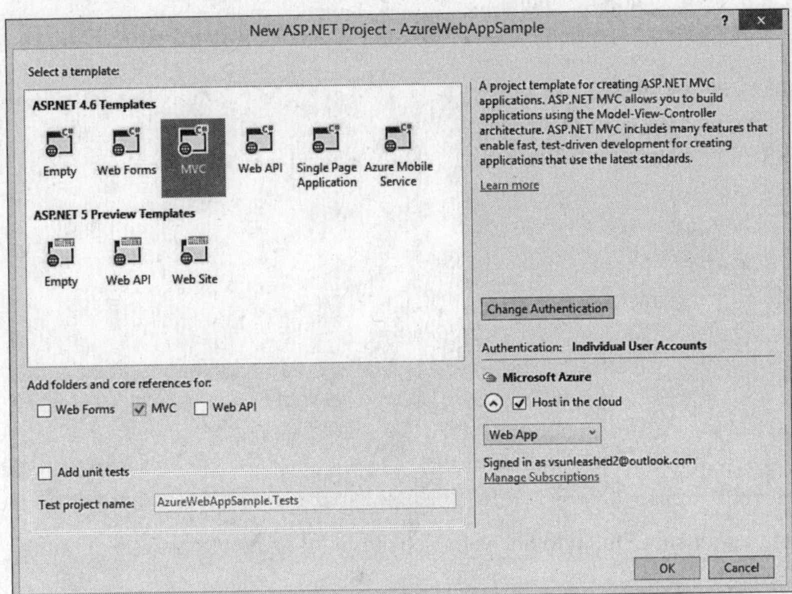

FIGURE 12.7 Use the New ASP.NET Project dialog to link your new project to an Azure website or VM.

FIGURE 12.8 Configure your Azure URL, default hosting region, and database as part of the new project creation process.

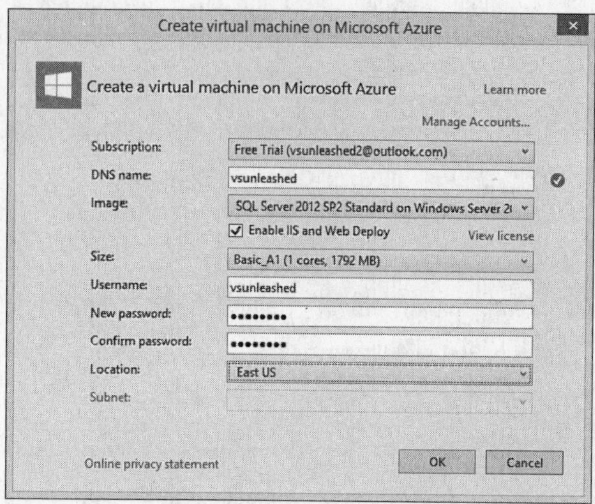

FIGURE 12.9 You can use Visual Studio to link your website to an Azure VM (versus an Azure web app hosted on PaaS).

Clicking the OK button on either Figure 12.8 or 12.9 will create your new project and related Azure hosting infrastructure. (Provision a VM or create an Azure web app.) Visual Studio will also link your project to the given Azure environment to allow for easy deployment (also called publishing by Visual Studio). It can take a few minutes for your provisioning to complete (especially for VMs); however, Visual Studio will notify you when it's complete in both the Output and the Web Publish Activity windows.

Figure 12.10 shows a completed project setup for Azure web apps. (The VM solution looks similar in the end.) Notice the link from Server Explorer to the site. (We cover this in upcoming sections.) Also, notice that the solution inside Solution Explorer now contains a folder called `PublishScripts`. These are the scripts Visual Studio uses to publish your site to Azure. You can add similar scripts to an existing site to connect it to Azure in the same way (more on this to follow).

Deploy/Publish an Application to Azure

You can use Visual Studio to build, run, and debug your application locally (using your localhost server) as you would any application. Visual Studio also simplifies publishing to Azure when you are ready to post the build to a server (typically for testing, but it can also be used for production).

To get started, you can use the Publish link inside the Web Publish Activity (View, Other Windows, Web Publish Activity), as shown at the bottom of Figure 12.10. This dialog makes executing a publish activity quick (using the toolbar) and allows you to see the activity results as they happen. However, the first time you set up your publishing profile, you will want to use the Publish Web Wizard. You typically access this by right-clicking the web application inside Solution Explorer and choosing Publish.

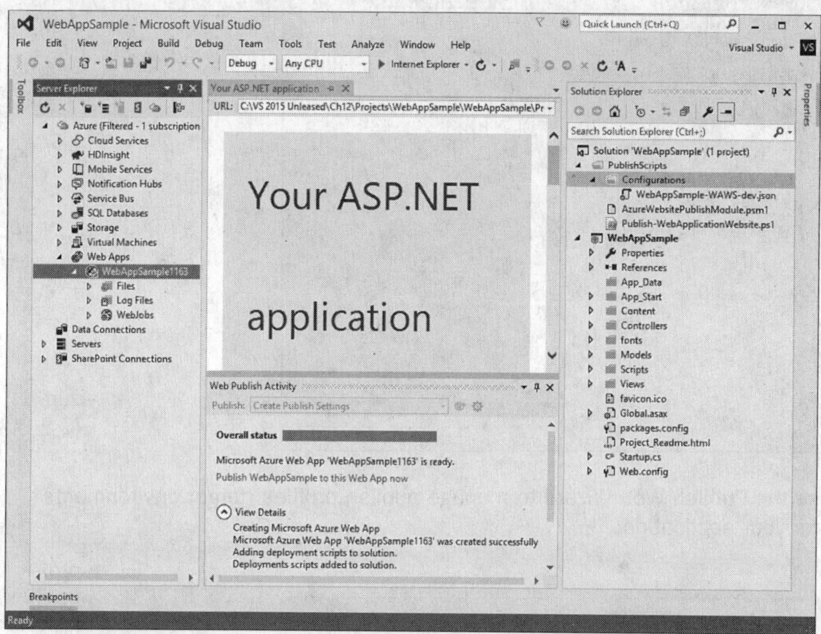

FIGURE 12.10 The Azure hosted website inside Visual Studio.

Figure 12.11 shows the Profile screen inside the Publish Web Wizard. From here you can select which publishing profile you want to configure (using Manage Profiles). Having multiple publishing profiles allows you to deploy the same application to different environments with different settings. Notice, too, that you can select the publish target as an Azure web app or VM. Doing so downloads the configuration from Azure for the given environment.

The next step is to set the Connection information for your selected publishing profile. Most of this information should be configured already by Visual Studio on your behalf. Figure 12.12 shows the Connection information for publishing a website to Azure. The first option, Publish Method, allows you to set the publish method as a web deployment (via HTTP), create a web deployment package (to be deployed by a deployment service), use FTP, or use the file system for deployment. In this case, we have selected Web Deploy.

You will also want to click the Validate Connection button, as shown in Figure 12.12. This ensures your Web Deploy can connect to the environment for deployment.

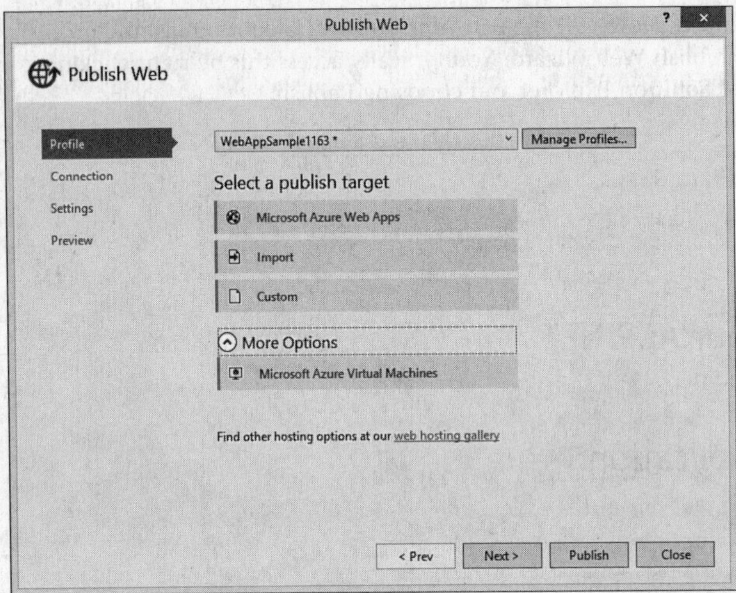

FIGURE 12.11 Use the Publish Web Wizard to manage publish profiles (target environments and configuration) for your application.

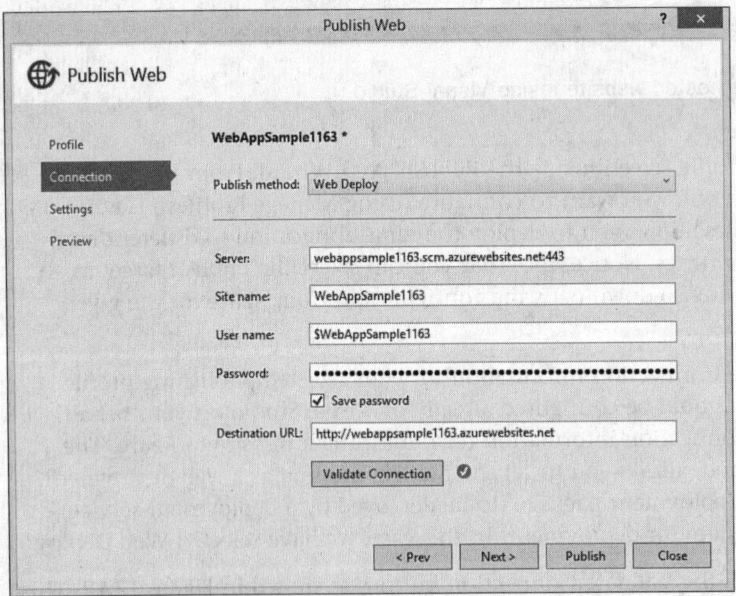

FIGURE 12.12 The Connection tab allows you to choose your deployment method, URL, and other server connection settings.

The next step in the wizard is to configure the deployment settings. Figure 12.13 shows an example. The Configuration drop-down allows you to select a Debug or Release build for the application deployment. This makes sure the appropriate `Web.config` version is published with your web application. (Typically the Debug version points to debug data/server settings and the Release version points to production.) The File Publish Options allow you to set whether files should be removed from the destination, precompiled during publishing (to eliminate "warm-up" for first-time access), or exclude any test data you might have in the `App_Data` folder. Finally, if you have a database associated to the application, you would set that information here, too.

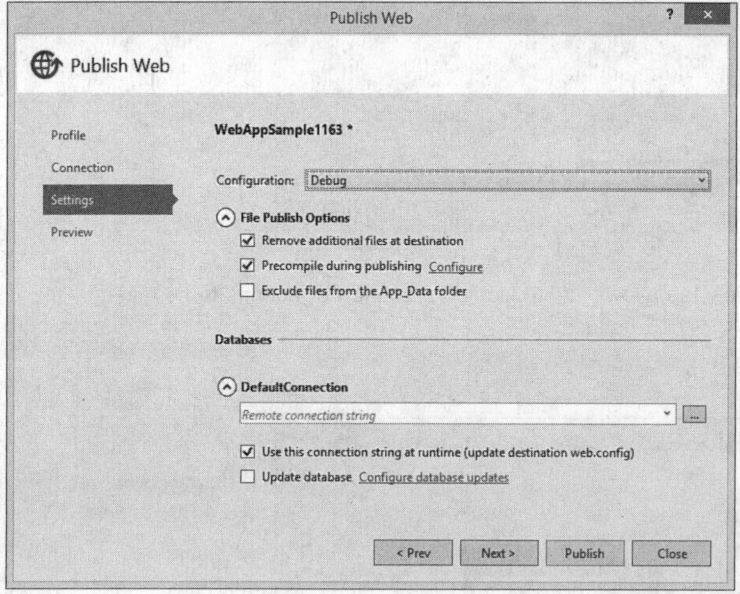

FIGURE 12.13 The Settings tab is used to set a Debug or Release version of the deployment.

The last step in the Publish Web Wizard is shown in Figure 12.14. Here you can create a preview of your deployment. Clicking Start Preview runs the publish profile and determines actions to be taken by file. Figure 12.15 shows the results by file.

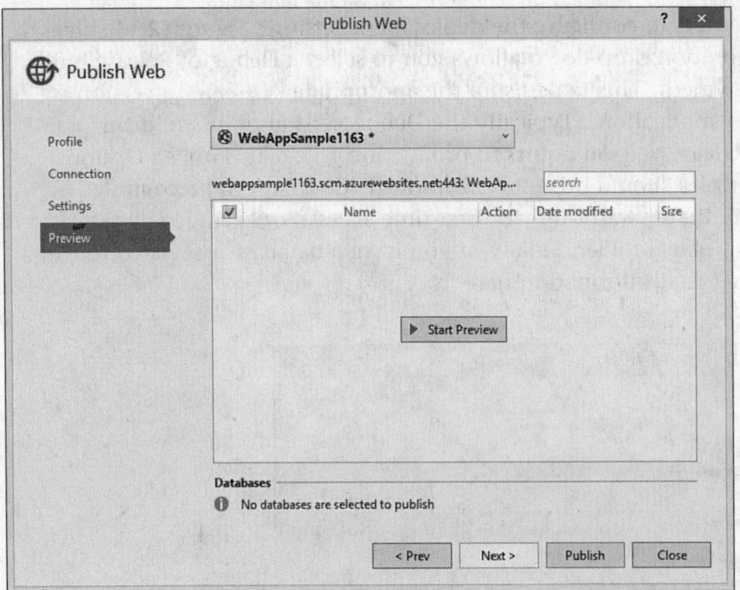

FIGURE 12.14 The Preview tab allows you to kick off a preview of actions to be taken by file as part of the publish process.

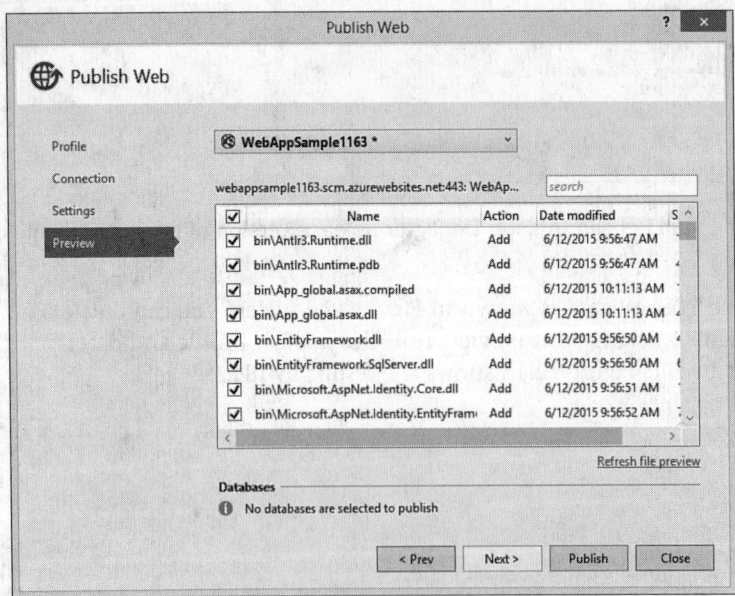

FIGURE 12.15 You can preview each file to be added, updated, or removed as part of the publishing process.

The last step is to click the Publish button. This kicks off the publish activity and shows the results inside both the Output and the Web Publish Activity windows. Once the publish activity has succeeded, Visual Studio will launch your site in a browser for verification. Figure 12.16 shows the site running inside a browser. (Notice the temporary URL.)

NOTE

Subsequent deployments do not need to go through the wizard. Once they're configured, you can kick off another deployment from the Web Publish Activity window using the toolbar at the top of the window. (Refer to Figure 12.10, where the toolbar is grayed out because the profile configuration has yet to be set up.) Here you select a publish profile and click the Publish Web icon next to the selected profile. This will redeploy your site using the same configuration you set up previously.

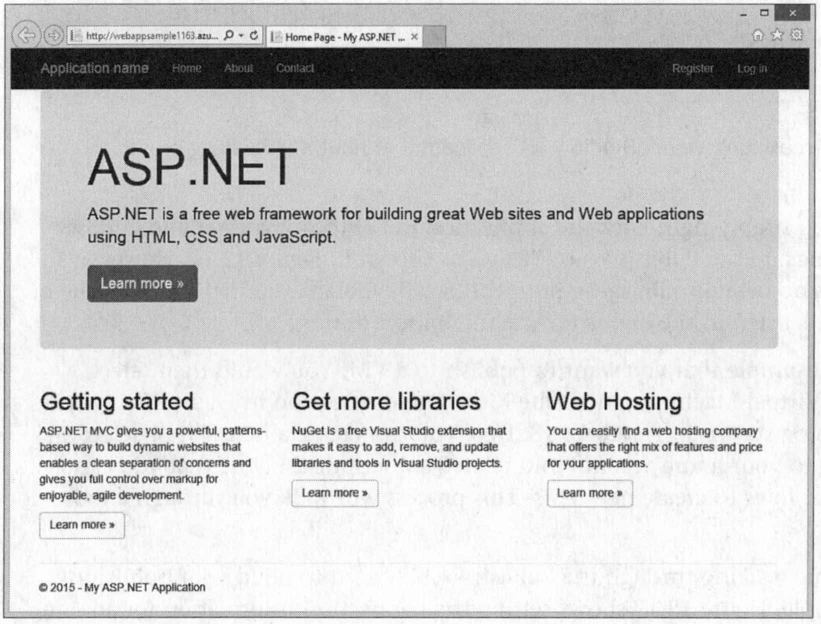

FIGURE 12.16 The Azure web app running in Azure post-publish.

Set Up an Existing Application to Publish to an Azure web app

You can set up an existing application with a publishing profile. You do not have to link your project to Azure at the time of creation (as shown in Figure 12.7). For example, suppose you have an existing application, as shown in the Solution Explorer inside Figure 12.17. Notice there is no publishing profile associated with the solution (as compared to Figure 12.10).

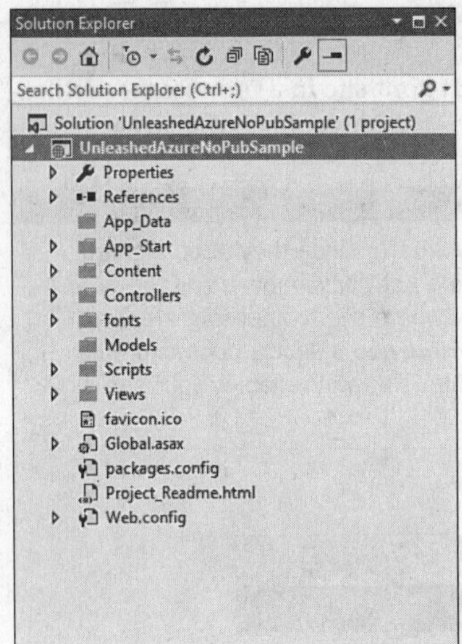

FIGURE 12.17 An existing Visual Studio web application without a publishing profile.

To get started, you simply right-click the application in Solution Explorer and choose Publish. This brings up the Publish Web Wizard, as shown in Figure 12.11. However, in this case, there is no default publishing profile. Instead, you are required to select one of the publish targets listed in the dialog (or use the Import option).

Suppose for this example that you want to publish to a VM. You would then select Microsoft Azure Virtual Machines under the More Options section in Figure 12.11. This brings up the dialog shown in Figure 12.18. Here you can create a new VM or select an existing one tied to your Azure account and related subscriptions. Note that you can also use Server Explorer to create new VMs. This process will walk you through a more in-depth wizard.

You then continue walking through the Publish Web Wizard to build your publishing profile. For example, Figure 12.19 shows setting the connection information for an Azure VM deployment.

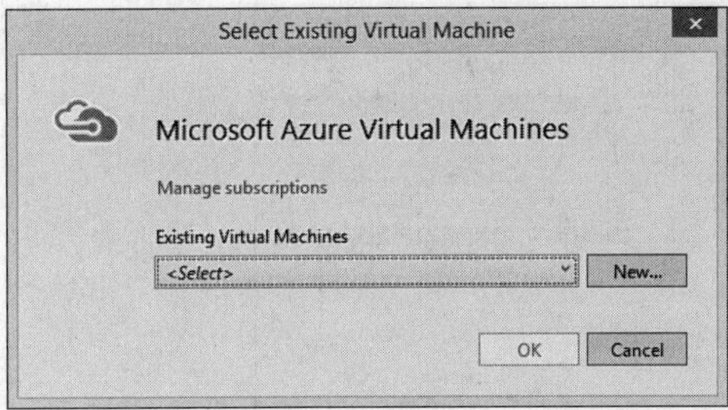

FIGURE 12.18 Select the Azure VM for the publishing profile.

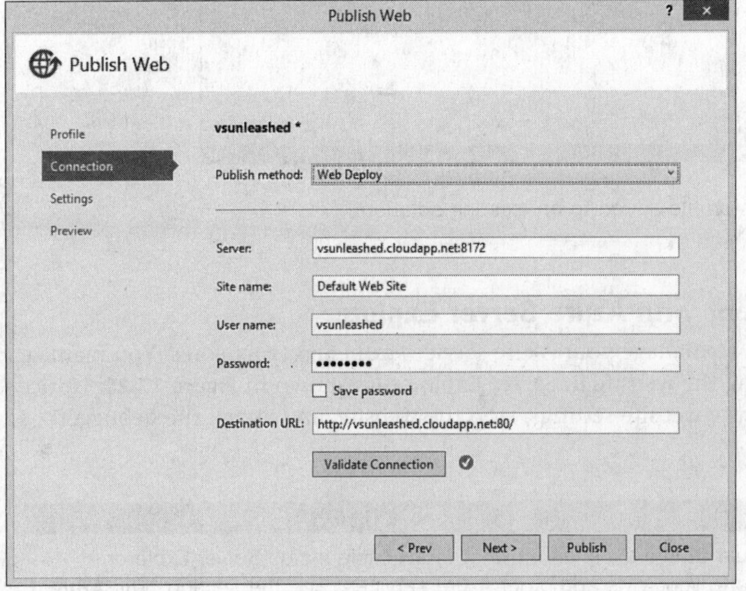

FIGURE 12.19 You can use Publish Web to add a publishing profile to your solution (and to publish to VMs, too).

Your website is deployed upon completion of the wizard. Your Solution is also now updated with a publishing profile, as shown in Figure 12.20. Note that you can use the toolbar in the Web Publish Activity window to both republish your app (globe icon with arrow) and change settings (cog icon) for your publish profile using the Publish Web Wizard.

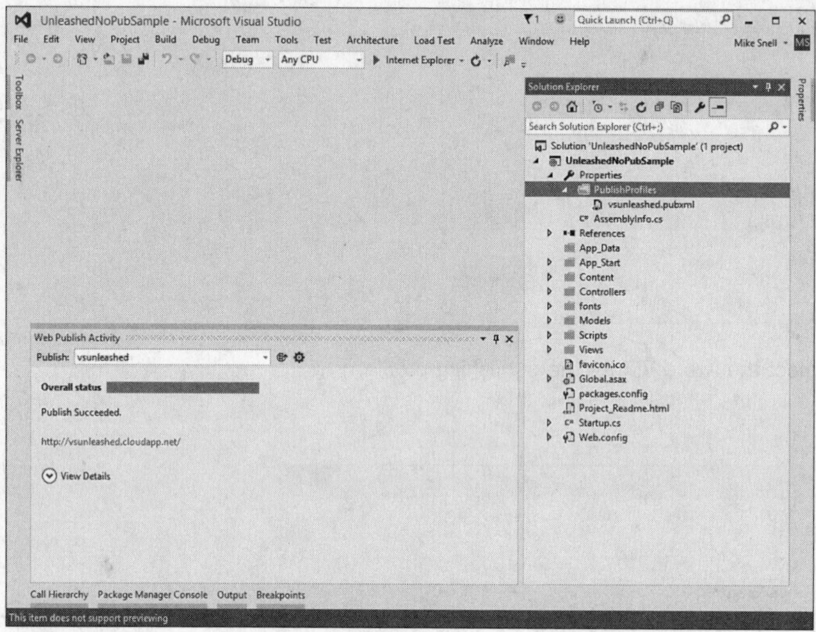

FIGURE 12.20 A publish profile added to an existing solution.

Website Management with Azure Server Explorer

Visual Studio allows you to manage your Azure services from Server Explorer. You manage a website by right-clicking the website in Server Explorer, as shown in Figure 12.21. Notice from here you can view the website settings, stop the website, and attach the debugger (among other things).

> **NOTE**
>
> That Azure SDK for Visual Studio expands on what is available inside Server Explorer, including adding access to your VMs and other Azure services. See the section "The Azure SDK for Visual Studio 2015" for details.

Clicking the View Settings option on your Azure web app in Server Explorer brings up the configuration and logs information for your website. Figure 12.22 shows the configuration information. Notice here you can stop and start (and restart) your website. You can also change settings such as logging and remote debugging. Clicking the link `Full Website Settings` will launch the Azure management portal to the Configure tab. This is used for controlling the many additional settings you might need to access your website.

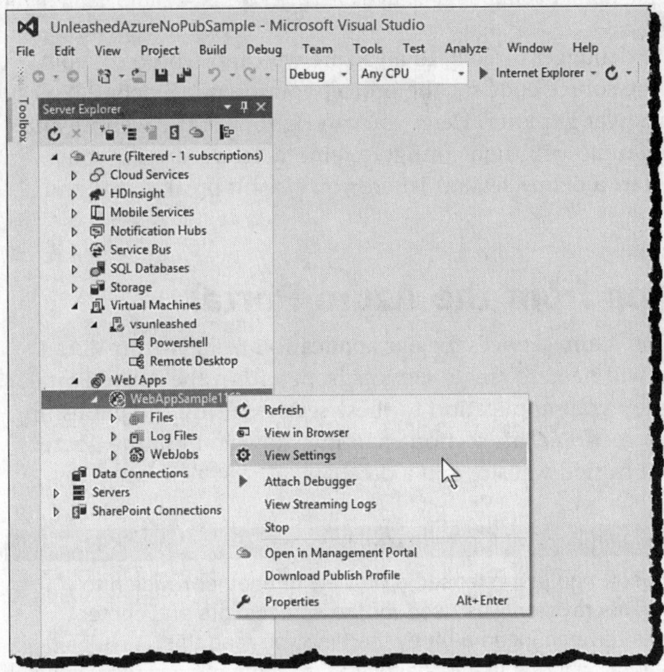

FIGURE 12.21 The Visual Studio Server Explorer allows you to manage your Azure web apps (among other things).

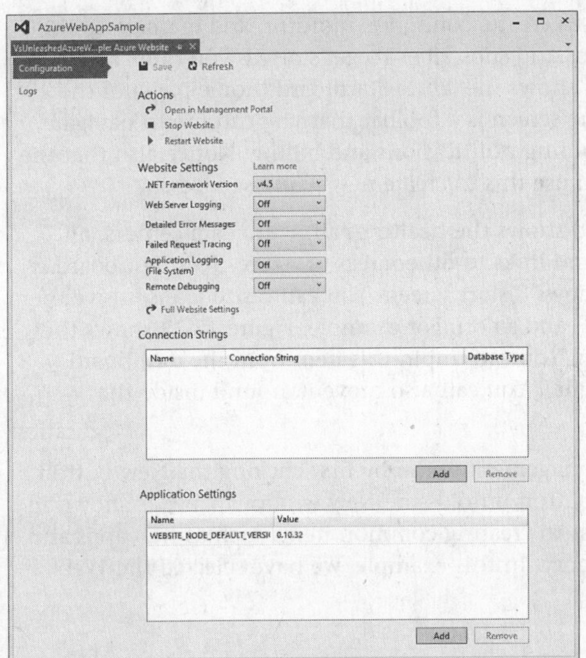

FIGURE 12.22 You manage your Azure web app settings from within Visual Studio.

Debug an Azure web app

You can attach the Visual Studio debugger directly to an Azure web app. To do so, you open the project that contains the source code for the project you intend to debug. You then navigate to the website in Server Explorer. Here, you can right-click the website and choose Attach Debugger. Visual Studio will then configure remote debugging for your site, attach to the process, and start a debug session where you can hit breakpoints and examine values.

Create Your Web App from the Azure Portal

Thus far we have covered creating Azure services for our application from within Visual Studio. However, it is likely you will need to create services from within the Azure Portal itself and then connect and deploy your application to these services using the publishing techniques described in the prior section. This section examines how you use the Azure portal to set up services such as a hosted website and a database.

NOTE

At the time of this writing, Microsoft had just released a preview of another revision to their Azure management portal. This revision was used for the screenshots and content here. Don't be surprised if things have changed a bit by the time you read this.

Create the Application Hosting Environment

The Azure management portal is used to create, configure, monitor, and manage all the Azure services to which you have access and subscribe. To get started, you must first log in (portal.azure.com). Figure 12.23 shows the Azure Startboard (home page) of the management portal. The left side of the screen is a toolbar that you can use to navigate the various sections of the portal, including notifications and billing. Notice also that the bottom left holds the New button; you use this to create new Azure services.

The center area of the portal Startboard shows the health of all Azure data centers, an update on your current billing cycle, and links to other areas of Azure. This dashboard is configurable. Think of it like the Windows 8 start screen. You can resize icons, move them around, pin different ones to this page, and so on. For example, Figure 12.23 shows the right-click action on the Feedback icon. You can unpin this item from the dashboard or customize its size (small, normal, wide). You can also move it around inside the dashboard grid.

You create a new item in the Azure management portal by first clicking the New button (upper left of Figure 12.23). The New button unfolds the New window pane, as shown in Figure 12.24. This provides quick access to creating common items such as web apps and databases. Items are organized by category. In this example, we have selected the Web Apps group.

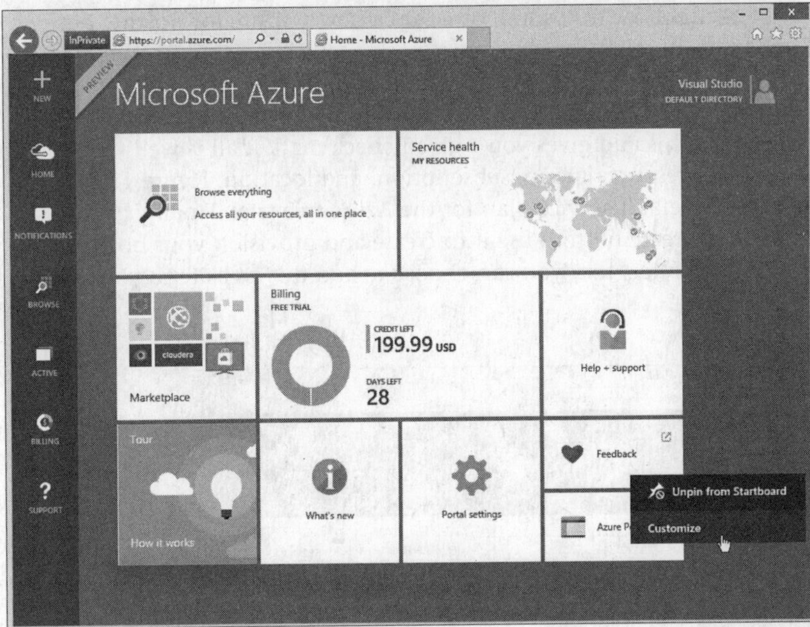

FIGURE 12.23 The Azure portal dashboard is where you go to manage and create sites, services, and storage items.

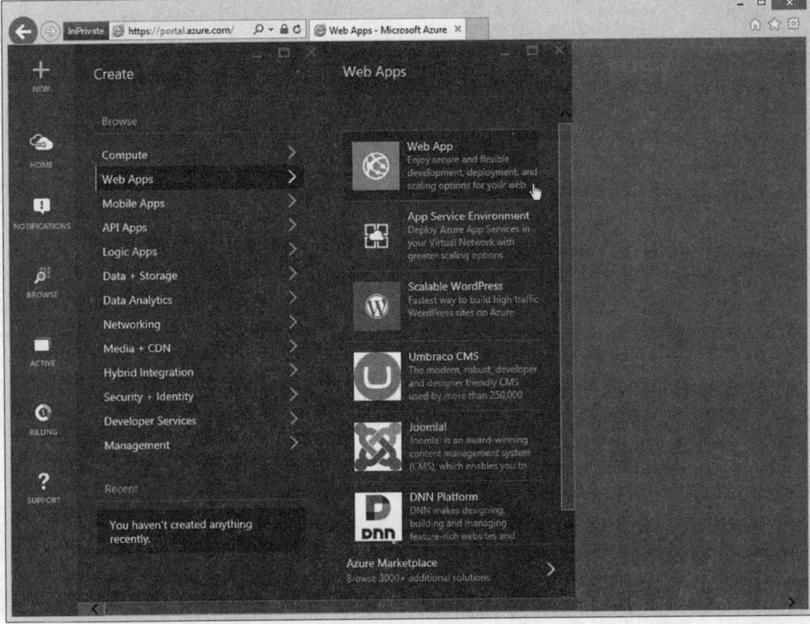

FIGURE 12.24 Use the New button to create a new Azure service, including a web app.

As an example, we will click the Web Aps link to set up a new website for hosting our code. Figure 12.25 shows creating a new web app. You start by choosing a temporary, azurewebsites.net URL. You can configure your domain name system (DNS) later to use your actual domain name. Your temporary domain name must be unique across other Azure sites. The tool verifies this and gives you a green check mark if all is well. You then select your app service plan, resource group, subscription, and location. Figure 12.25 shows selecting the East US default service plan for the Azure free trial. Finally, at the bottom of the screen is the Create button; use it to create and provision your hosting environment for a website. Notice, too, you can choose to add this website to your Startboard (portal home page).

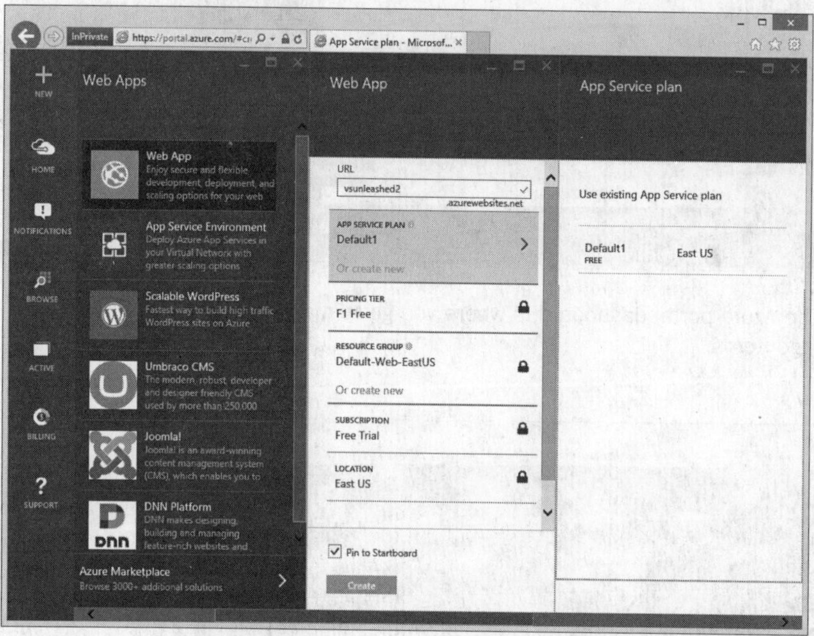

FIGURE 12.25 You create a new Azure new website by indicating a temporary URL, location, and subscription options.

Configuring Your New Azure web app

Azure will return you to the Startboard when you click Create. Here you will see a notification that your website is being created (along with a progress bar). You will also get a notice when Azure is finished. Once it's finished, you can click on the notification or the new Starboard item that represents your website on the home page to open your website. This will open a new window pane that Azure calls a "blade." You can maximize and minimize blades in the portal. Figure 12.26 shows a maximized blade that represents just some of the many options for monitoring and managing your website.

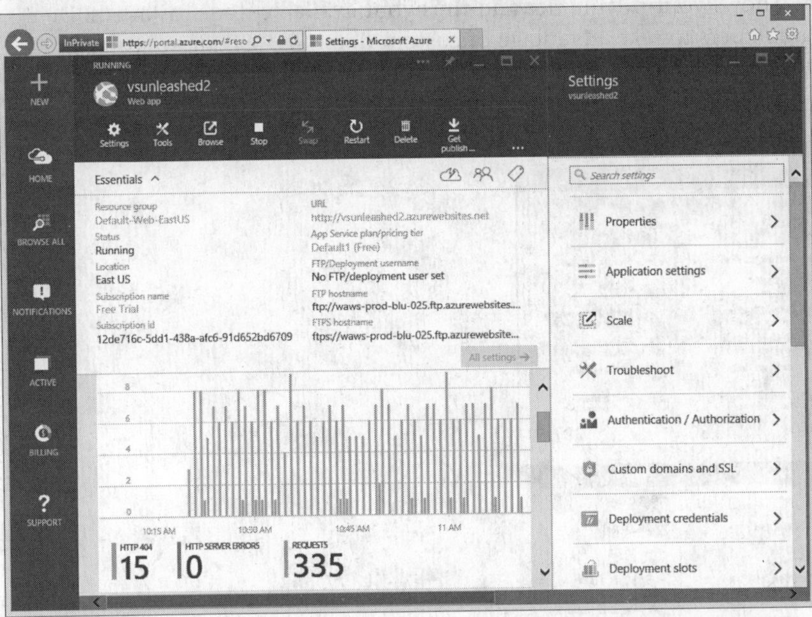

FIGURE 12.26 You can manage, monitor, and configure your website inside an Azure blade window.

The Azure web app blade as shown in Figure 12.26 provides many options for working with your website. Many of these options demonstrate a dashboard-like view. You can also click on each to expose additional details and access other features of each of these items. Some of these options are highlighted here:

- **Monitoring**—Monitor the performance of your application.
- **File System Storage**—Monitor your file system storage inside Azure for your website.
- **Requests and errors**—View requests and errors on your site. You can also access the diagnostics tools from here.
- **Events**—Access error, warning, and informational events for your site.
- **Alert rules**—View, add, and configure alerts for tracking various site conditions such as too many specific occurrences of an error in a given time window.
- **Settings**—Configure the core settings for your website such as properties, scalability, backups, SSL, web hosting, diagnostic logging, users, roles, and more. You can also use the Application settings tab to set .NET Framework version, PHP version, Java version, connection strings, and more.
- **Estimated spend**—Track your Azure spending related to this website.
- **Virtual network**—Configure access to a virtual network from your website.
- **Deployment credentials**—Set credentials used to deploy your application.
- **Quick start**—Access tools and knowledge about getting started with your site and Azure.
- **Deployment**—Set up continuous deployment from a source repository to your website. You can choose deployment from Visual Studio Online, GitHub, and others.

- **Pricing tier**—Shows your pricing tier and thus your available node instances. Here you can upgrade tiers to take advantage of custom domains, SSL, more storage, website staging, and the Auto scale feature. See Figure 12.27 for an example of the Azure web app tiers available and their differences.

FIGURE 12.27 The Azure web app pricing tiers control access to the many features of Azure web apps.

The Website Toolbar

The Azure web app blade contains a toolbar at the top of the page. This is useful for managing your running website. Figure 12.28 highlights this toolbar. You can use the Stop and Start buttons to control if the site is up and running. Restart cycles your website and resets the running instance. The options on the Azure web app toolbar are listed next (from left to right on the toolbar):

- **Settings**—Used to define the many settings of your web app, including authentication, SSL, backups, extensions, and more.
- **Tools**—Used to access tools for working with your site such as Log Stream, Console, Process Explorer, and Troubleshoot.
- **Browse**—Used to browse to your running site.
- **Start**—Used to start your site if it is currently stopped.
- **Stop**—Used to turn off your site.
- **Swap**—Used to swap content and configuration from one Azure site to another. This is useful if you have a dev site you want to promote to staging, for example.
- **Restart**—Used to restart (stop and start) your website hosting process.
- **Delete**—Used to delete the website.
- **Get publish profile**—Used to download your publish profile for import into Visual Studio (or similar tool) for publishing. Note that Visual Studio can also just reach out to your Azure instance and get this information provided you have the right credentials.
- **Reset publish profile**—Used to reset your website publishing profile if information has changed. The publish profile gives tools like Visual Studio all it needs to publish a site directly to your Azure instance.
- **Change app service plan**—Used to upgrade or downgrade your hosting plan. (Refer to Figure 12.27 for web app plans.)
- **Buy Domains**—Used to purchase custom domains and SSL.

FIGURE 12.28 Use the Azure web app toolbar to start and stop your running website.

Creating a Database

The Azure web app blade allows you to easily add a SQL database or a MySQL database to your website. Of course, you can add these and other data storage and access services directly from the Azure home page and then configure their access using the other features of Azure. However, here we will walk through the scenario of adding a SQL database to your Azure web app.

You use the New button on top left of the web app blade (refer to Figure 12.28) to get started adding a SQL database to your web app. This brings up the Create blade where you can select Data + Storage form the available categories. You can then select SQL Database from the possibilities as shown in Figure 12.29.

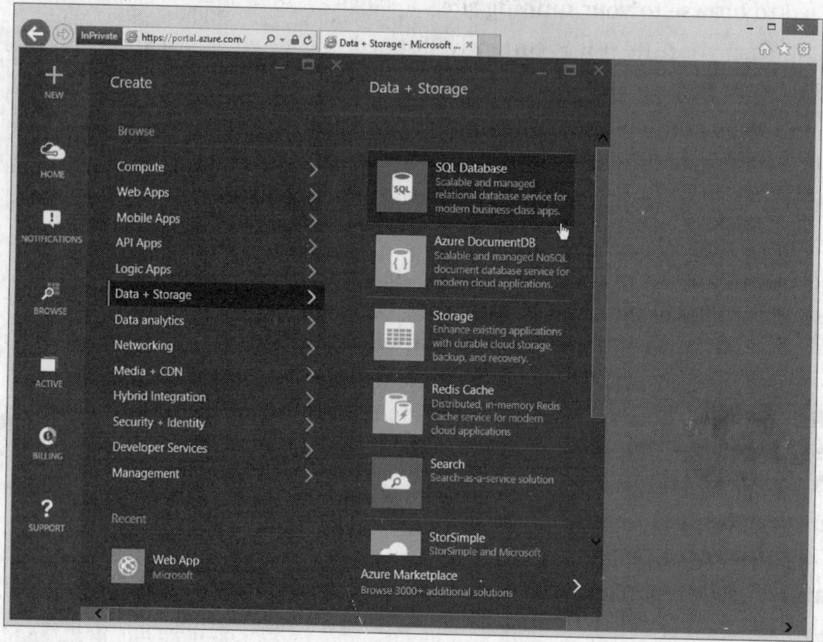

FIGURE 12.29 Use Add from the website toolbar to add a SQL database to your Azure web app.

The next step is to provide additional details about your database. Here you define the name of your database, your pricing tier, resource group, server, and more. Figure 12.30 shows an example. In this case, the database name is set to `vsunleashedDb`; the pricing tier is set to B Basic. Notice too that this database uses the Adventure Works sample database; this sample database is an option inside Azure. Figure 12.31 shows the process of selecting (or in this case, creating) a database server for hosting the database.

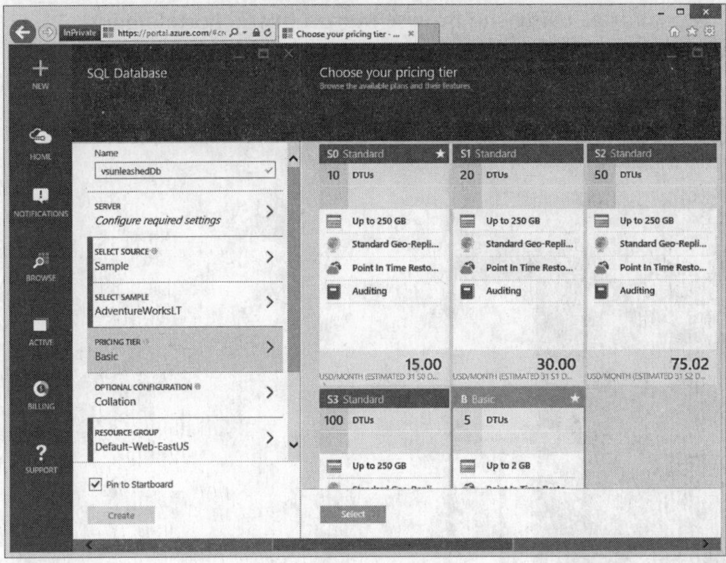

FIGURE 12.30 There are many options required to set up your SQL database.

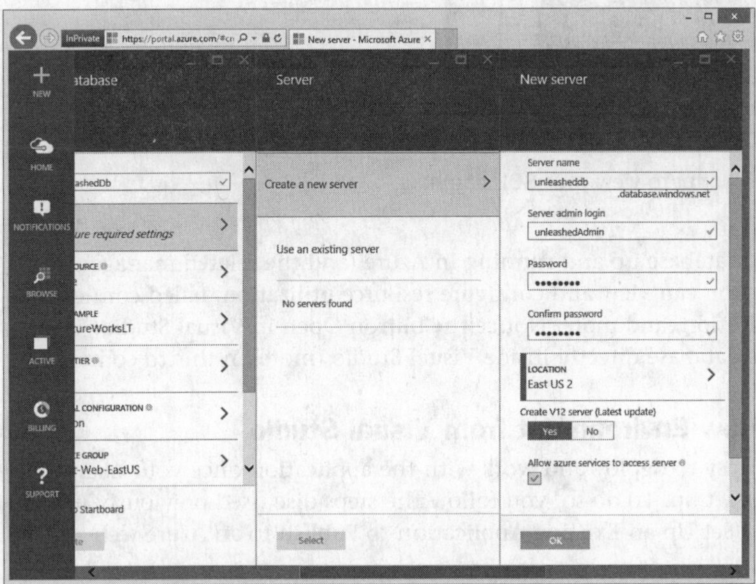

FIGURE 12.31 You can select an existing server or create a new one to host your database.

Azure will now provision your database and link it correctly to your Azure web app. You can view provisioning progress using the notifications from the Startboard. Once it's complete, you can view, monitor, and manage the SQL database from the Azure portal. To do so, you can browse to the database using the Browse button in the portal. Figure 12.32 shows accessing a SQL database from Browse, Recent. You can also filter the browse list by type (such as SQL Server).

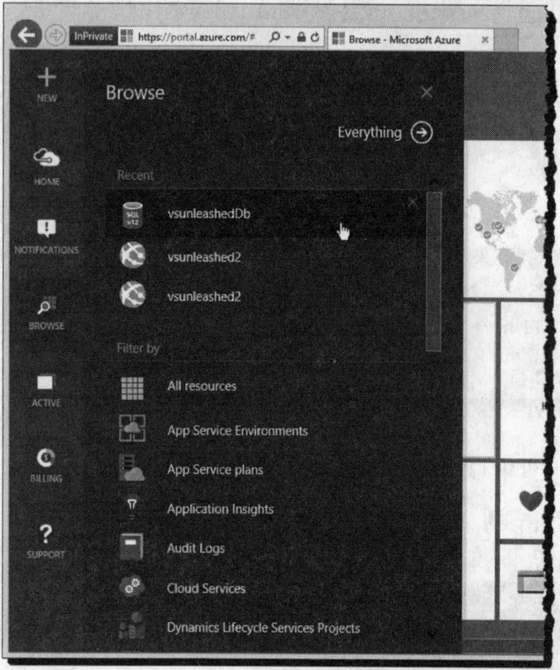

FIGURE 12.32 Use the portal to view your SQL database.

Figure 12.33 shows the database up and running in Azure (and the related management Startboard). From here you can view and configure resource utilization, failed connections, events, alerts, geo replication, and more. Notice the button Open in Visual Studio. This allows you to open the database directly inside Visual Studio (more on this to come).

Deploying to the New Environment from Visual Studio

Visual Studio makes it easy to deploy and work with the application once your Azure hosting environment is set up. To do so, you follow the steps discussed previously in the chapter in the section, "Set Up an Existing Application to Publish to an Azure web app."

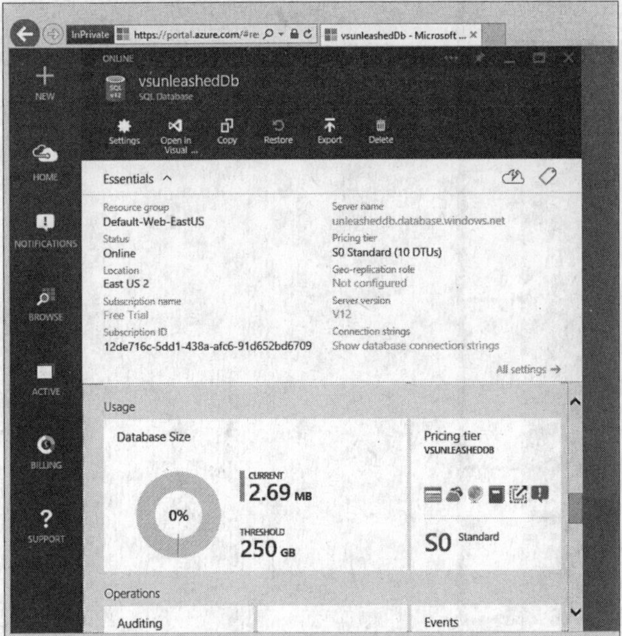

FIGURE 12.33 Manage a SQL database using the Azure portal.

Monitor and Manage Applications in Azure

You monitor and manage your Azure services in the same management portal shown earlier (portal.azure.com). Here you can monitor, stop, and start running services. You can also add new services and delete existing ones. In addition, this is where Azure provides detailed information about things happening in your hosted environment, such as logging, storage usage, and billing. Refer to the section "Configuring Your New Azure web app" for basic information on configuring your website.

Monitor and Manage a Website

Managing your website includes monitoring activity, changing configuration, scaling it, linking other Azure resources, and more. To access website management, you select your site's name from the Browse All option shown on the left toolbar of the portal home page, as shown in Figure 12.34.

Once you select a website, Azure presents you with a Startboard that shows details specific to this site. Figure 12.35 shows an example. The website management Startboard shows essential site details at the top and site monitoring (requests and errors) in the middle of the page. You can scroll down to view usage information, events, alerts, and more. You can also access the many settings for the site by clicking the All Settings link. This provides access to users and roles, scaling options, backups, troubleshooting, and more.

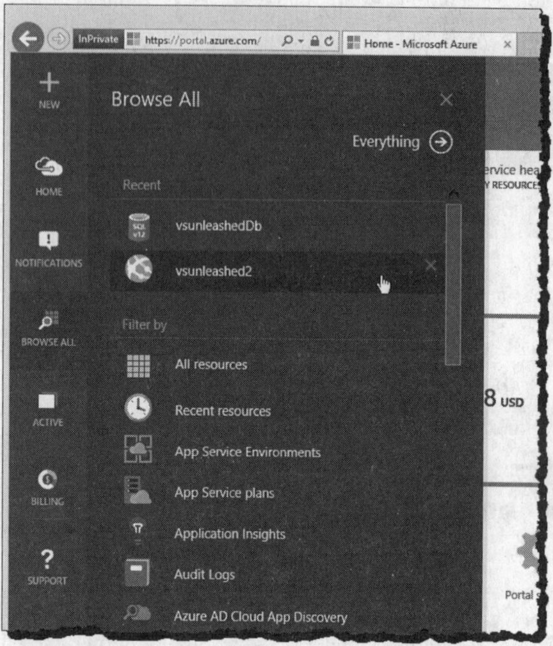

FIGURE 12.34 Use the Browse option to select a service you want to monitor or manage.

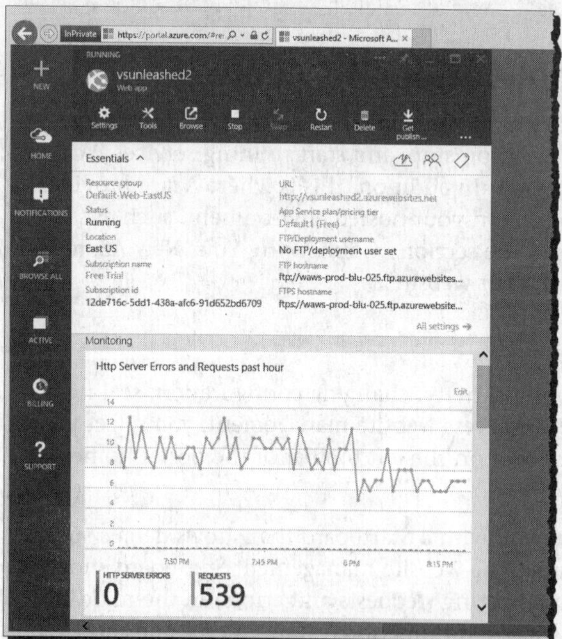

FIGURE 12.35 The management portal provides details on things happening in your site, including information messages, warnings, and errors.

Traffic Monitoring

Azure allows you to view the HTTP traffic hitting your site and capture related metrics about requests, response times, and errors. You get started by clicking the Monitoring blade item from the site Startboard (see Figure 12.35). Doing so opens the Metric blade, as shown in Figure 12.36. Notice that you get a larger view of the data. In this case, the data is showing requests and errors for the past hour. You can scroll this page to also show alerts.

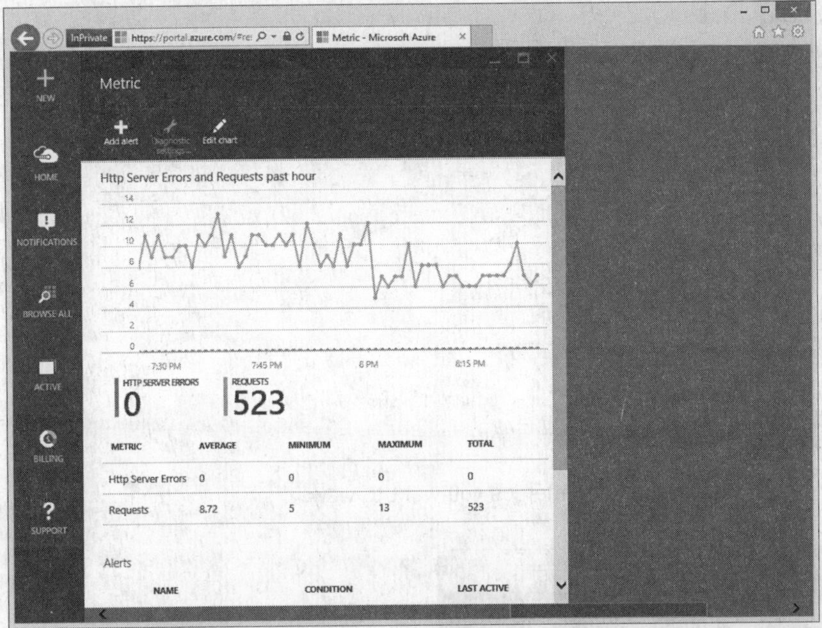

FIGURE 12.36 The Metric blade shows additional detail on web app metrics to help you monitor your application performance and any related issues.

You can edit the metrics shown on this chart and the timeline across which you want to view the information. To do so, you click the Edit chart link in the Metric toolbar (at the top of the page); you can also right-click the chart itself. This brings up your options, as shown in Figure 12.37.

The Edit Chart pane allows you to customize your view of web app metrics. Notice that you can choose the Time Range at the top to show data across the past hour, today, past week, or set a custom range. You can then set information to a bar or line chart. The checkbox items in the list allow you to select what type of metrics you want to see on the chart. For example, if you choose the Http 404 (bad request) option, Azure will include this information in your metric results. Figure 12.38 shows an example of adding 404 errors to the chart and changing the chart type to Bar.

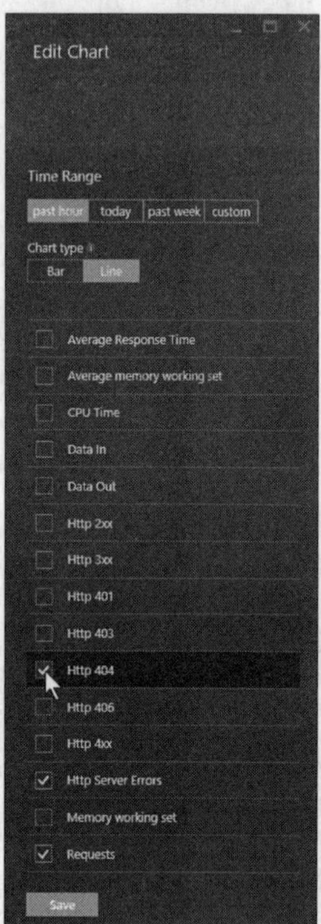

FIGURE 12.37 You can edit the website metrics you want to view.

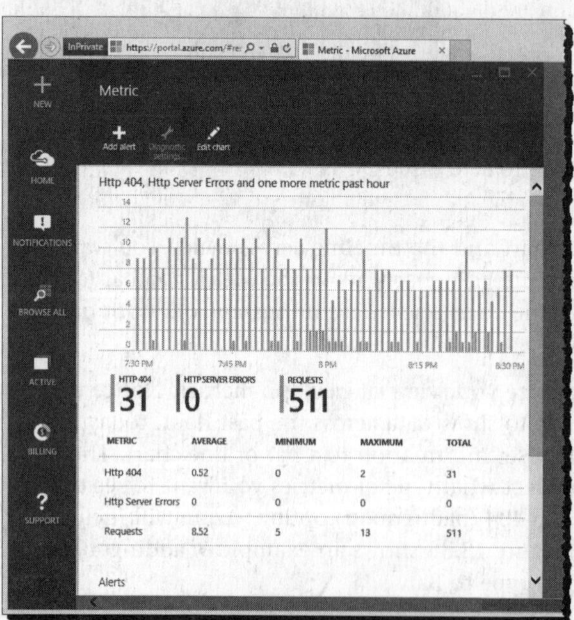

FIGURE 12.38 The metrics window with the additional metric, Http 404 errors added.

Managing Alerts

An alert allows Azure to notify someone should something not go as planned in your website. You can view the alerts configured for your site by scrolling the Metric window (bottom of Figure 12.36). These are alerts specific to metrics around errors, CPU usage, and response time (such as, average response time greater than 1 second). There are also those associated with events (such as website stopped).

You can use the Metrics pane to click on an alert rule and edit it (turn it off, change parameters, or add additional people that need to be notified). You can also click the Add Alert button at the top of Figure 12.36 to create a new metric alert.

Azure also provides the Alert Rules Startboard item for managing all your alerts. This can be accessed from the startboard for your web app. The interface is similar to the one found when editing just metric alerts. Figure 12.39 shows two alerts in the Alert rules blade.

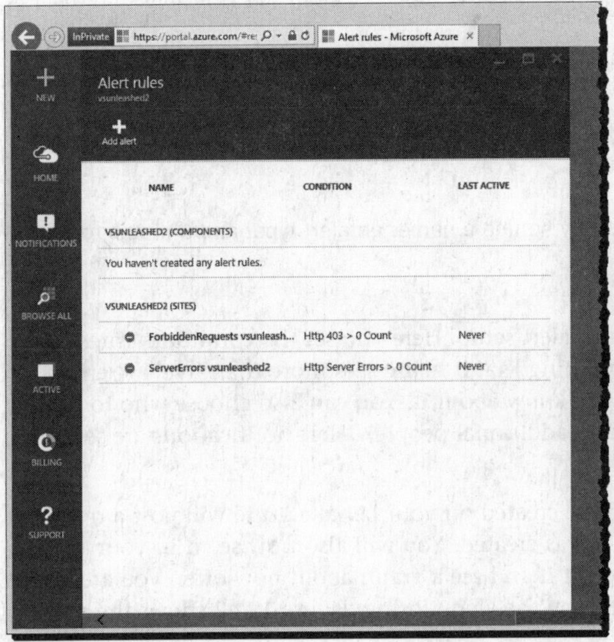

FIGURE 12.39 Use Alert rules to create and edit conditions on which you want Azure to send out notifications.

Clicking an alert from Figure 12.39 will take you to the editing options for the given alert. You can also create a new alert by clicking the Add Alert button at the top of the page. This brings up the blade shown in Figure 12.40. You can see that you first select a resource being monitored; you then set an alert name, description, and alert type (metric or event). In this case, we are creating a metrics alert. You select from an available list of metrics; here we pick the 404 (not found) metric. Notice that Azure shows the recent average for the metric in a graph to help you set your threshold.

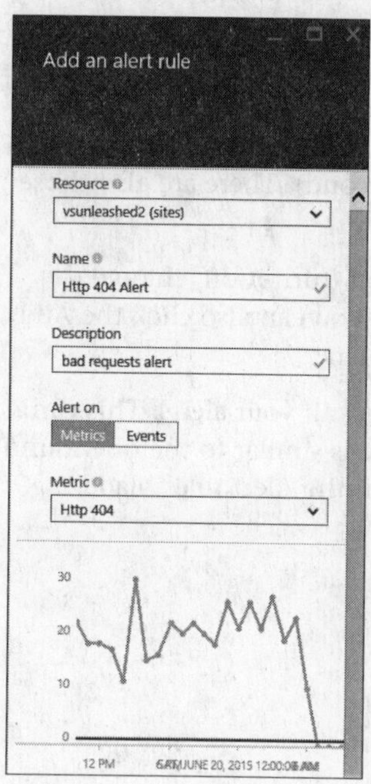

FIGURE 12.40 You create a new alert by setting a name, an alert type, and a metric (or event) choice.

Figure 12.41 shows the rest of the new alert setup. Here you set the condition, threshold, and period. In this case, you are requesting that if Azure sees more than five 404 errors in the course of one hour, you want to know about it. You can also choose who to notify (administrators, co-administrators, and additional people). Alert notifications are sent in the form of an email.

Once you save your new alert, it will be created on your behalf. Azure will post a notification to your portal to let you know it was created. You will also now see it in your alert's list. Clicking the alert allows you to edit it and see a graph about how often you are above the threshold. This allows you to manage the alert closing. Figure 12.42 shows the previously created alert in edit mode.

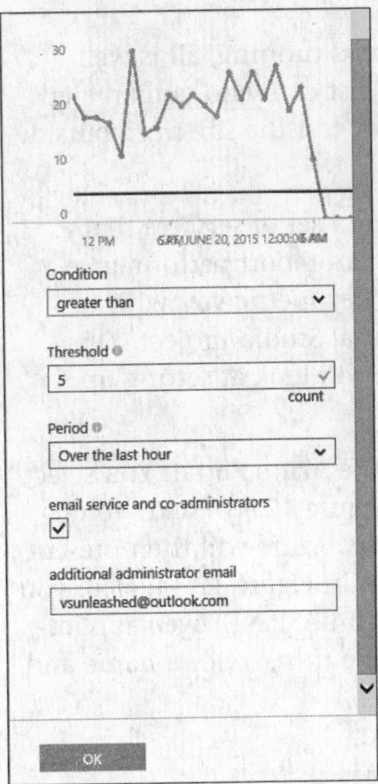

FIGURE 12.41 You finish creating an alert by setting a condition, threshold, and notification options.

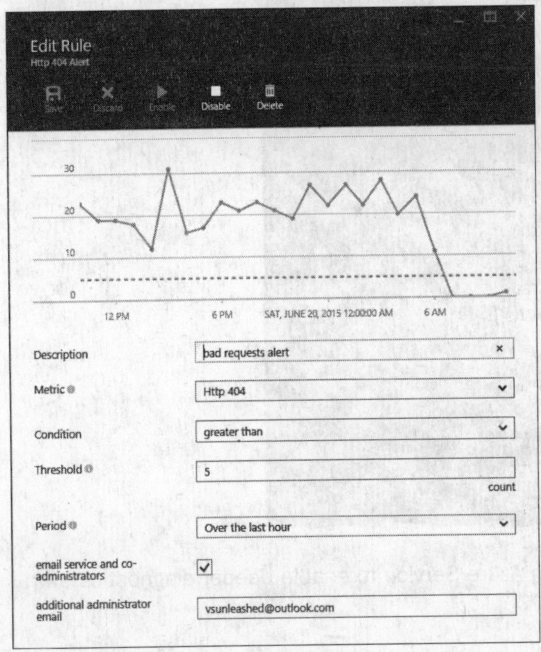

FIGURE 12.42 Use the Edit Rule blade to view how often you hit your threshold and make the necessary edits to the alert.

Application Insights and Web Tests (Outside-In Monitoring)

Azure allows you to create web tests that verify your site is up and running, all is well, and users around the world can access the site. If not, the web test can send you an alert. These type of tests are referred to as outside-in tests because they test the site from outside the environment.

Web tests are a feature of Azure Application Insights. This tool is a set of services that work to monitor your application, IIS server, VM, and more. It can report performance, usage analytics, availability, server diagnostics, and almost any key metric you wish to track. In addition, you can add Application Insights to your Visual Studio project. This is code that will emit data to be managed by the tool. Here, we will look at setting up Application Insights and using just the web tests feature.

To get started, you add Application Insights as a service inside the Azure Portal. You select the New (+ icon) which displays the Create blade as shown in Figure 12.43. Next, you browse to Developer Services and then select Application Insights. Azure will then present the required fields for configuring Application Insights as shown in Figure 12.44. Here you can select the type of application being monitored (in this case, an ASP.NET web application), resource group, subscription, and location. Finally, you give this service a name and hit the Create button.

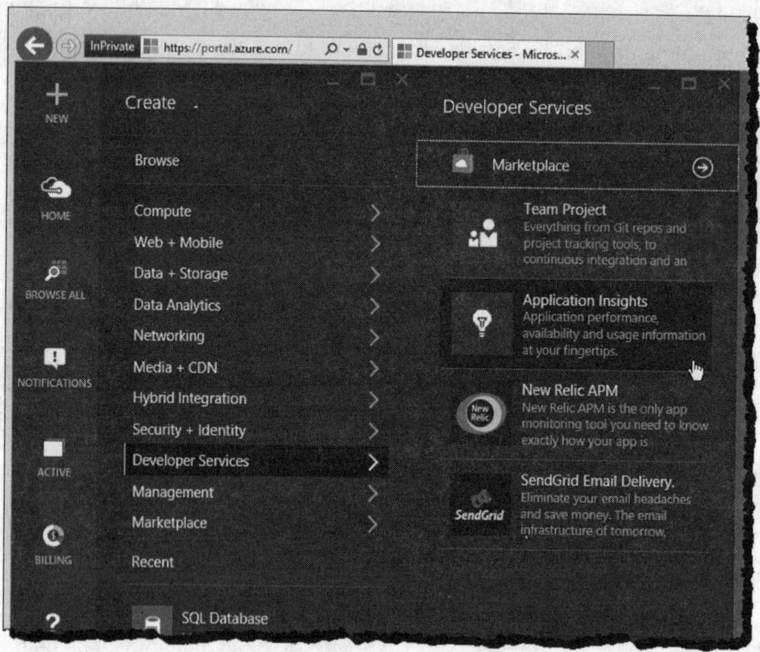

FIGURE 12.43 Add Application Insights as an Azure Service to enable deeper diagnostics and web tests.

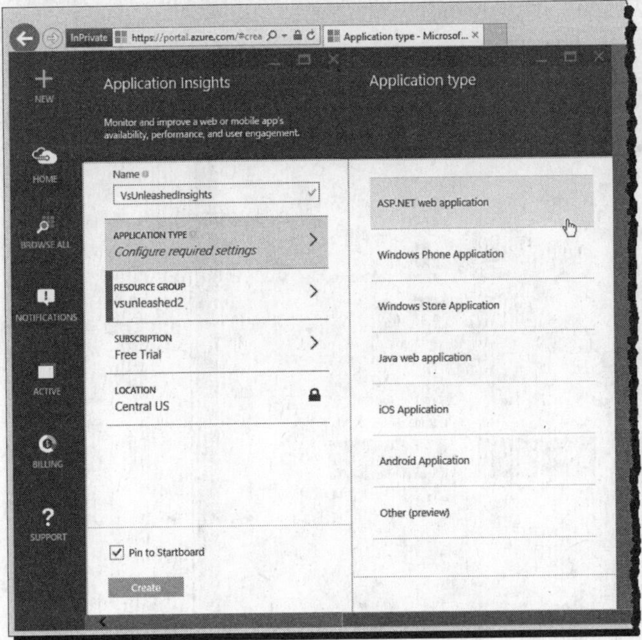

FIGURE 12.44 You can configure Application Insights to work with an ASP.NET web application or a mobile app.

Azure will then work to deploy and configure your Application Insights service. Once complete, you can select it from the Startboard to get started configuring it for your specific scenario. Figure 12.45 shows some of the many configuration options. You select the Availability option to create a web test. This brings up the Web tests blade as shown in Figure 12.46.

You use the Web tests blade to add a new web test to Application Insights. Figure 12.46 shows clicking the Add web test option. Tests are configured to hit certain pages in your site from other Azure locations. Figure 12.47 shows configuration of a standard ping test to verify a site is up and responding okay from Chicago, Illinois; San Jose, California; San Antonio, Texas; Ashburn Virginia; and Miami Florida. This test can be configured as a ping test or a multistep tests that hits multiple pages in your site. You can also have the test check for specific content on the requested page as part of the success criteria. Finally, you can configure alerts to be sent if a test fails or if certain locations fail in a set time period.

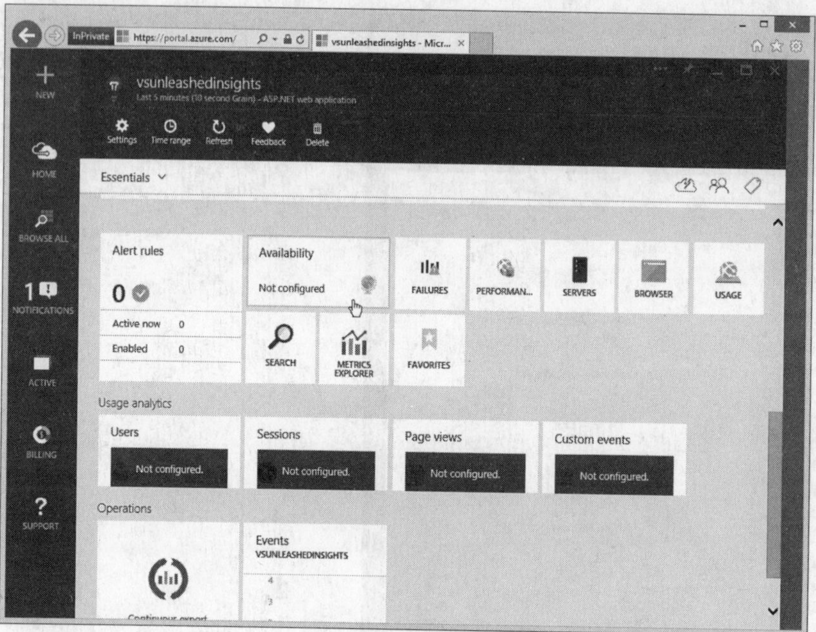

FIGURE 12.45 Use the Application Insights blade to configure the many options for monitoring your application.

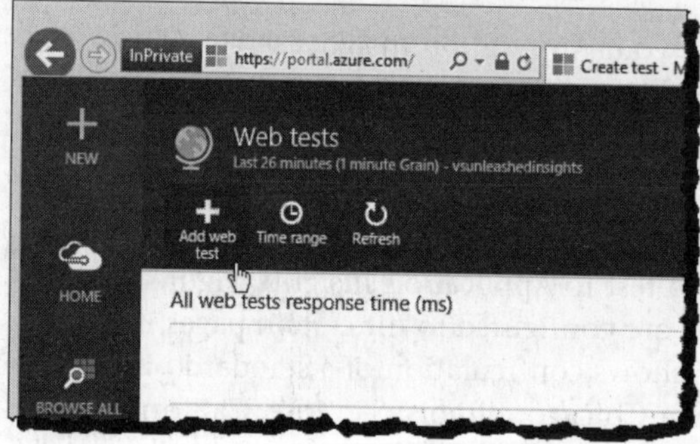

FIGURE 12.46 Use the Add web test option to add a new web test to Application Insights.

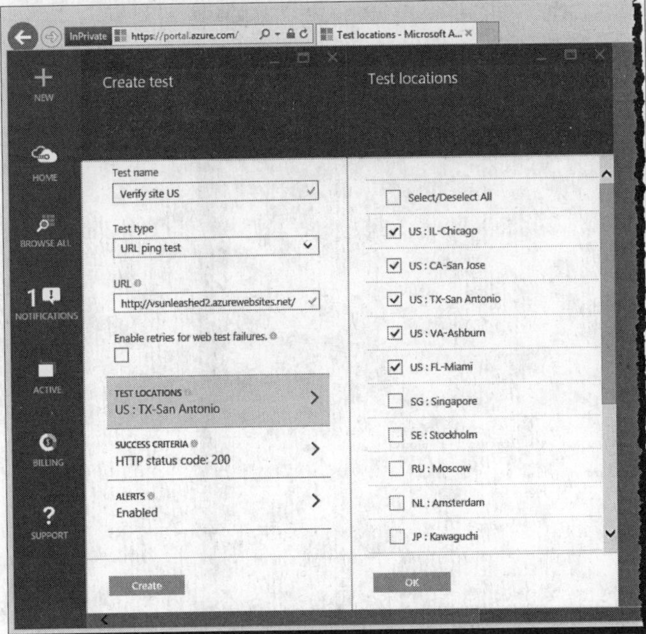

FIGURE 12.47 You can test your site from the outside in using Azure.

You can return to the web tests page once you have configured your tests and they have been up and running for a while. The page will show you a summary view of all your web tests. You can then select an individual web test to see detailed information about that specific test. Figure 12.48 shows the specific web test created previously (Verify site US) and trends over time. You can use the toolbar at the top of the page to edit the test, disable it, set a specific time range, and refresh your results.

Manage Scalability

You manage the elastic scale of your site by clicking the Scale option on the website Startboard (or from All settings, Scale). The Scale page (see Figure 12.49) shows a graph at the top that indicates how Azure has scaled your instances over time—in this case, based on CPU percentage. Notice that this site has never needed to be scaled.

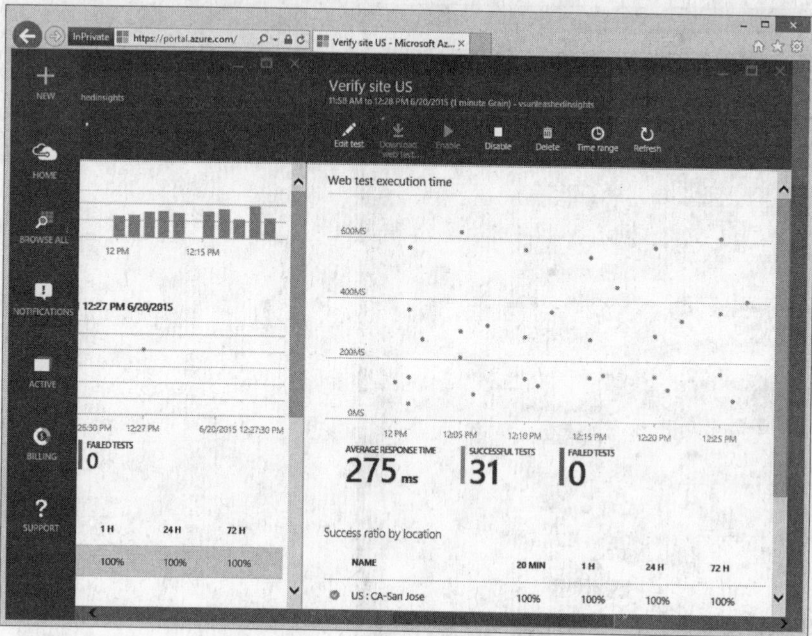

FIGURE 12.48 You can view specific results of your test.

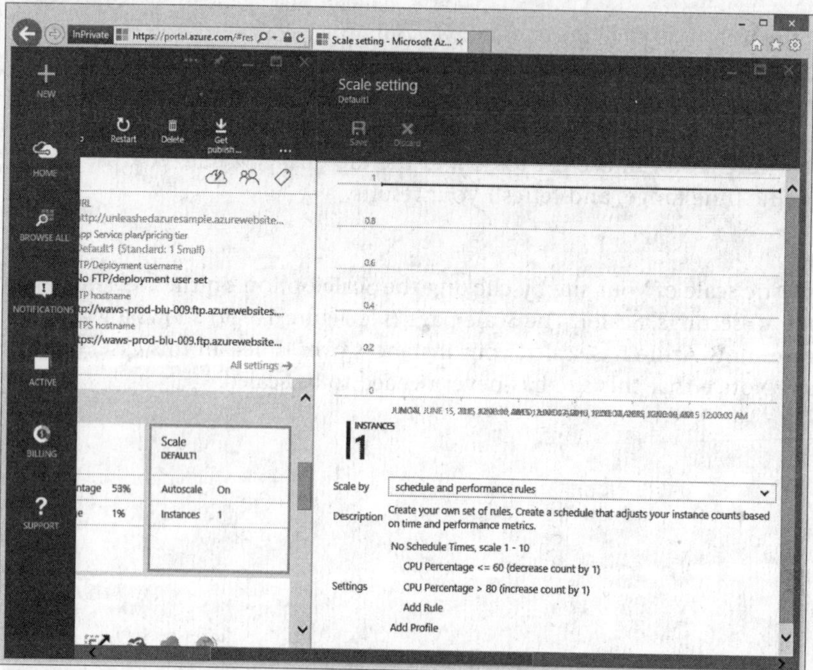

FIGURE 12.49 The Azure scale page shows how Azure has scaled your site up and down over time based on key metrics you control.

NOTE

Your scale options (instances) are restricted by your selected hosting plan. (Refer to Figure 12.27 for details.)

Azure has the Autoscale feature that allows you to automatically scale up and down based on key metrics in your site. Figure 12.49 shows Autoscale set to scale up an instance (to 10 as the max) should the CPU usage be greater than 80%. It then scales down if CPU decreases to 60% or less. You can modify these rules by selecting them. You can also add additional rules using the Add Rule link.

Figure 12.50 shows a simplified version of these rules. You access this by setting the Scale by option to CPU Percentage. Notice that you can set the Instance Range. This is the minimum and maximum number of virtual instances (or nodes) on which your code can execute. Your Azure plan controls the maximum. You then set the scale up and scale down range for CPU usage.

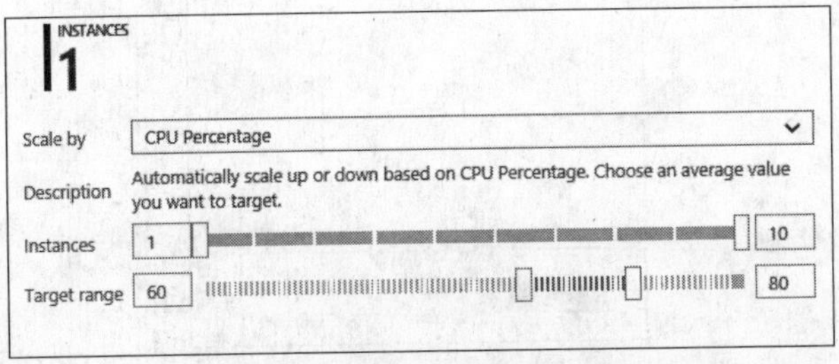

FIGURE 12.50 The Azure Autoscale rules for CPU.

Setting the Scale by to, schedule and performance rules (refer to Figure 12.49), allows you to add specific rules and rule profiles. Clicking the Add Rule link allows you to select a metric on which you want to scale. You have a choice of metrics like CPU usage, memory percentage, and data in/out. Figure 12.51 shows adding a rule to scale by memory usage. Here the environment is set to scale up a node as average memory usage hits 70% usage over the past 15 minutes. You can add another rule then to scale down when the memory usage has a sustained drop below 70%.

Clicking the Add Profile link (bottom of Figure 12.49) allows you to set a custom scaling profile based on a recurrence or a fixed date. You can then add additional rules to this custom profile. Figure 12.52 shows scaling from 1 node to 5 on Monday at 9:00 am through Friday (and back to 1 on the weekends).

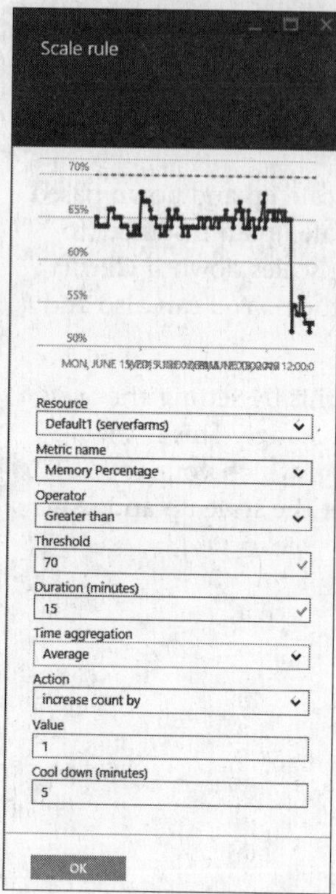

FIGURE 12.51 Adding an Azure Autoscale scale up rule based on memory usage.

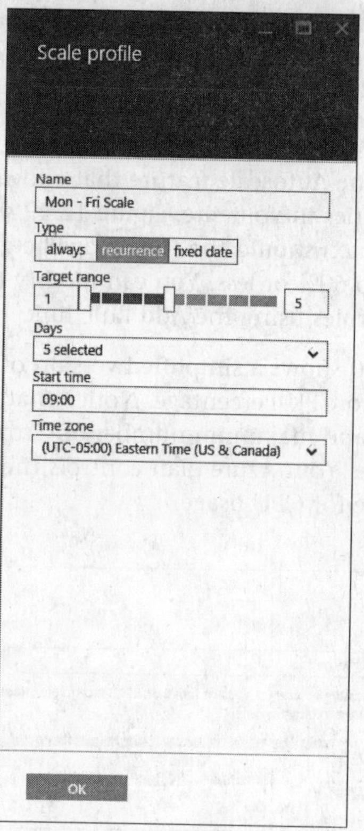

FIGURE 12.52 The Azure Autoscale scale down rules.

Diagnostic Logs

Azure supports diagnostic logging to help you better understand what is happening in your site and to troubleshoot errors. You enable logging via the Settings option from the Startboard. Figure 12.53 shows the settings pane along with the Diagnostics logs option selected.

Notice in Figure 12.53 that you can download and review logs from an FTP site. You can also use the options to turn various logging options on and off. The middle section, Application Logging, is where you set application logging (see Figure 12.54). This allows you to turn on tracing for your application and view the results in the Azure portal. Notice here that you can choose a level (error, warning, or verbose).

NOTE

Application logging (tracing) will automatically turn off in 12 hours if you don't turn it off manually.

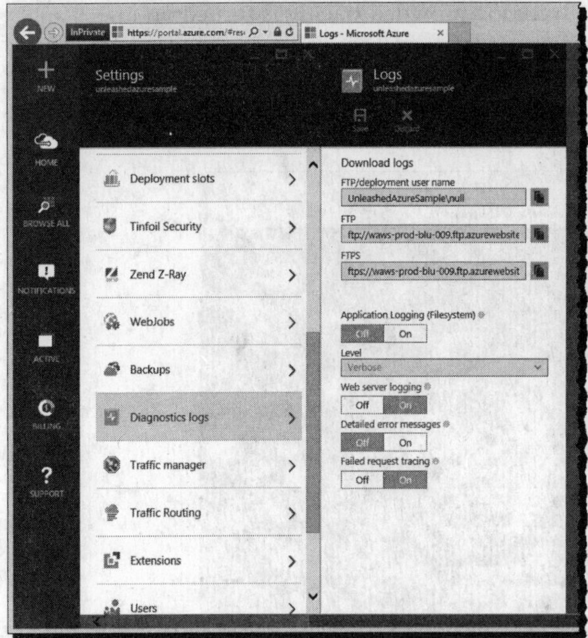

FIGURE 12.53 You enable diagnostic logging from the Settings option in the Azure Startboard for a website.

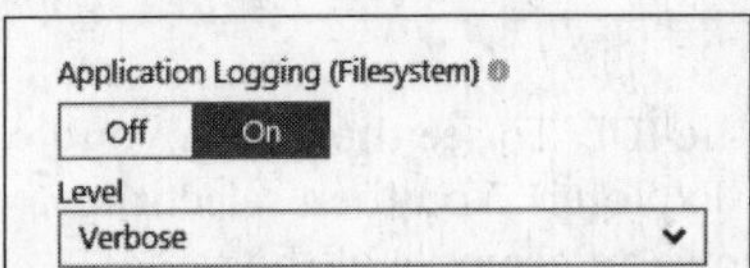

FIGURE 12.54 You can enable application tracing (and thus streaming logs).

Before you use application tracing, you must have trace messages inside your code. The following line of code writes a simple informational message when the site's home page is requested. Of course, you could write a trace message for warnings, errors in your code, and just about anything you want to monitor.

```
System.Diagnostics.Trace.TraceInformation("Home page requested.");
```

These tracing messages will output to a trace log provided tracing is turned on (as discussed previously). You access this trace information from the web app Startboard by selecting the Tools option from the toolbar and then clicking Log Stream. Figure 12.55 shows the output of a few trace messages for a sample application.

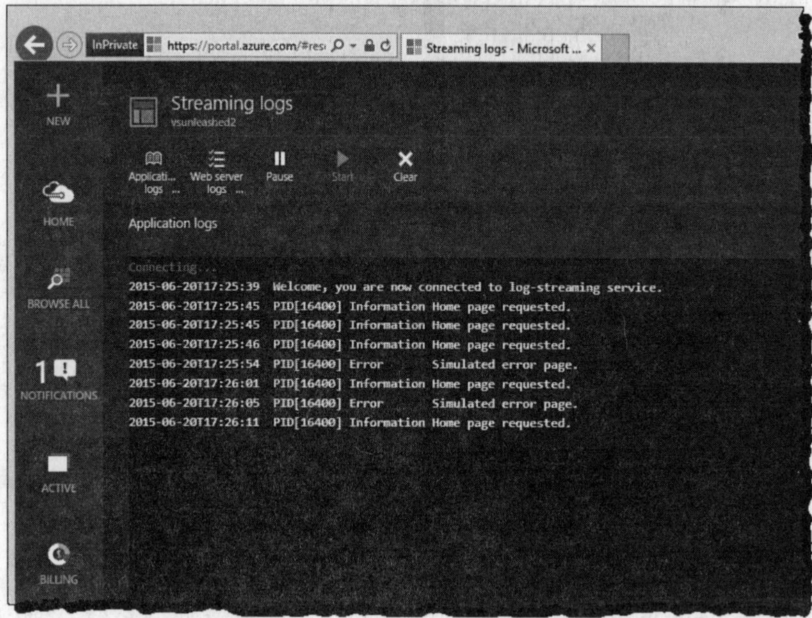

FIGURE 12.55 The application logs (trace messages) from the Azure Streaming logs.

Visual Studio also gives you access to log files directly in the IDE. To see these logs, you can navigate to the Server Explorer window (View, Server Explorer). You then select the Azure node and navigate to your website. Figure 12.56 shows an example of the same trace log shown in Figure 12.55 open inside the IDE. You can also right-click your website in Server Explorer and choose View Streaming Logs to see the logs as they stream (again, similar to Figure 12.55).

Monitor and Manage a SQL Database

You manage your SQL databases in a similar manner to your websites. You can access the Startboard for a database by selecting it from the Browse option (top option back in Figure 12.34). Figure 12.57 shows a standard Startboard for a small SQL database in Azure. You can see resource metrics and set alerts in the same way you would for an Azure web app (see prior section).

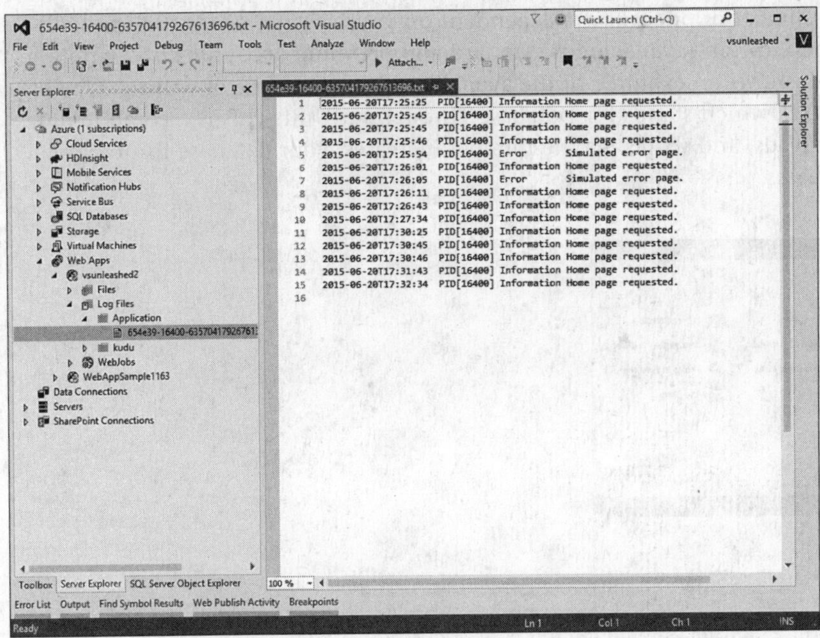

FIGURE 12.56 The application logs open inside Visual Studio Server Explorer.

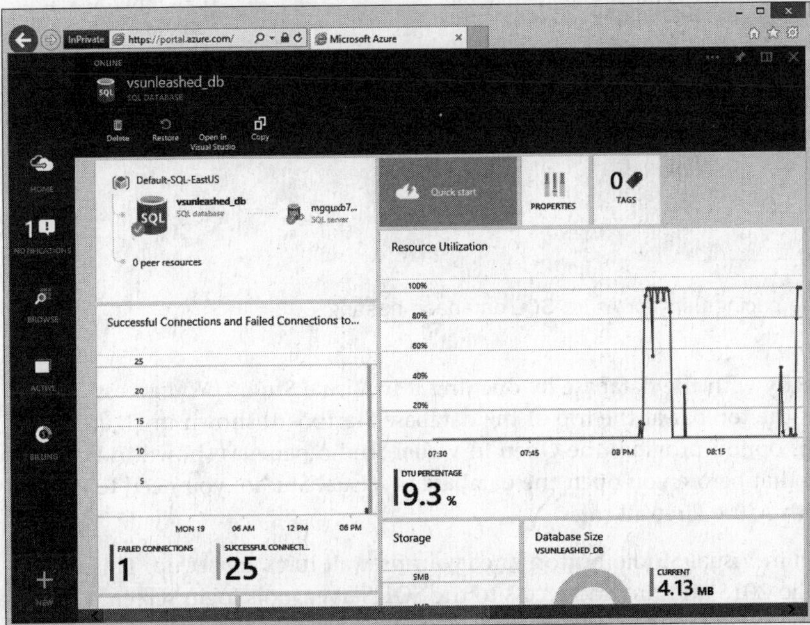

FIGURE 12.57 The Startboard for an Azure SQL database.

Azure provides a number of pricing tiers dependent on your specific needs such as auditing, storage, geo-replication (available for standard and premium accounts only), and more. Figure 12.58 shows an example of the available tiers at the time of writing. One big concern here is DTU, which stands for Database Throughput Unit. This is a combination of CPU, memory, reads, and writes. As the number increases, your database throughput performance increases.

FIGURE 12.58 The pricing tiers for Azure SQL database hosting.

You can work directly with the database by opening it in Visual Studio. You access this option from either the toolbar at the top of the database Startboard shown in Figure 12.57. Clicking this option provides the Open in Visual Studio pane, as shown in Figure 12.59. Notice here that before you open the database in Visual Studio, you need to open your IP address with Azure Firewall rules.

You click the Open in Visual Studio button once your firewall rules are set up. This will launch Visual Studio 2015 and provide access to the SQL Server tools login screen. Once connected, you can execute queries and create new tables, views, and stored procedures as you would with any database. Figure 12.60 shows the database open in SQL Server Object Explorer to a sample, VS Unleashed Feedback database. See Chapter 13, “Working with Databases,” to learn more about these Visual Studio tools.

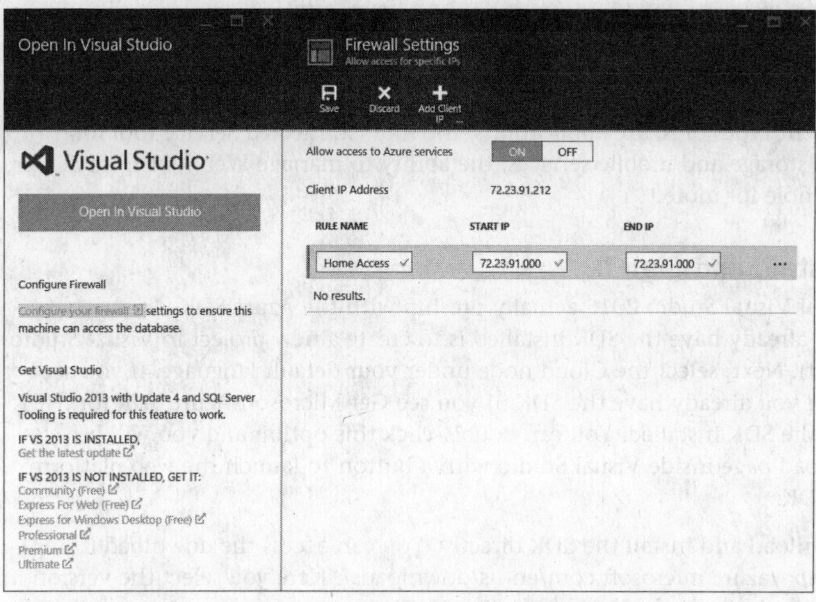

FIGURE 12.59 Open the Azure SQL Database in Visual Studio by adding your IP address in the firewall rules.

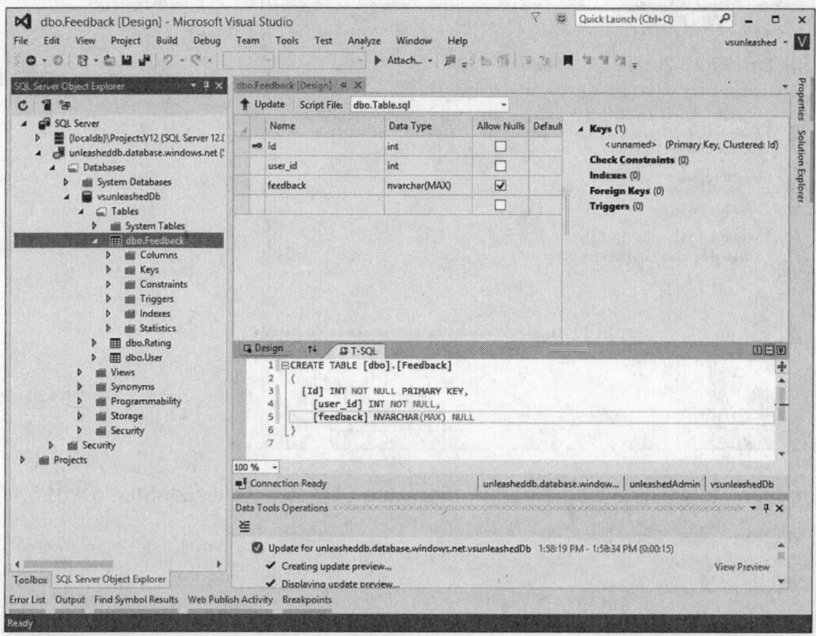

FIGURE 12.60 The Azure SQL database open in Visual Studio.

The Azure SDK for Visual Studio 2015

The Azure SDK for Visual Studio 2015 provides additional tools and platform support for building applications targeted to Azure. This includes the QuickStart project templates for creating different types of Azure applications, the Add Connected Service tool for consuming Azure storage and mobile services, the ability to manage Web Jobs from Server Explorer, and a whole lot more.

Download, Install, and Sign In

Certain versions of Visual Studio 2015 actually preship with the Azure SDK. An easy way to find out if you already have the SDK installed is to create a new project in Visual Studio (File, New, Project). Next, select the Cloud node under your default language. If you see project types then you already have the SDK. If you see Get Microsoft Azure SDK for .NET, you do not have the SDK installed. You can double-click this option and you will be taken to a download page inside Visual Studio with a button to launch the web platform installer for the SDK.

You can also download and install the SDK directly. You can access the download from the Azure site: http://azure.microsoft.com/en-us/downloads/. Here you select the version of the SDK based on the version of Visual Studio (2015). There are also versions available for 2012 and 2013. Figure 12.61 shows the install process screen for the SDK version 2.6 (in this case, the SDK is already installed).

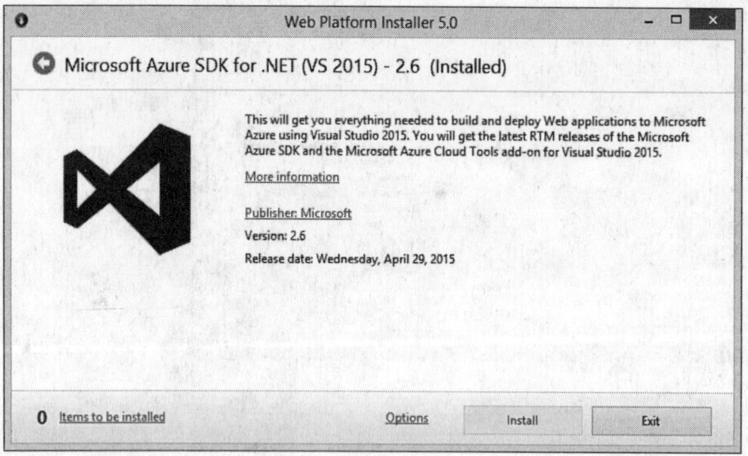

FIGURE 12.61 The many tools installed as part of the Azure SDK 2.5 for Visual Studio 2015.

When you launch Visual Studio after installation of the SDK, you will still sign into the IDE and to Azure the same way, as discussed at the start of this chapter. However, you now have access to many more Azure services directly from Server Explorer. Figure 12.62 shows the support for the many Azure services, including Cloud Services, HDInsight, Service Bug, Storage, and Virtual Machines.

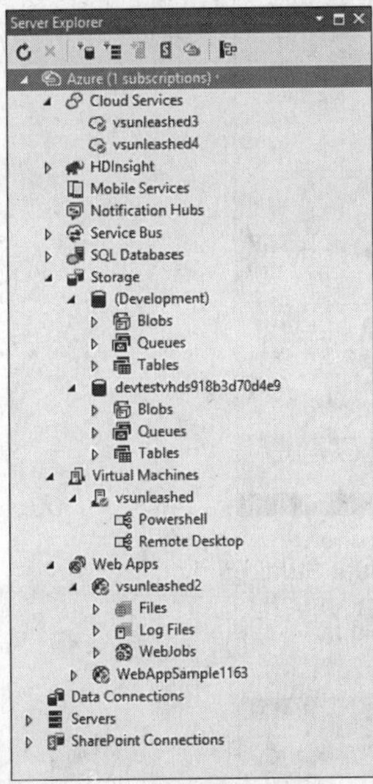

FIGURE 12.62 The Azure SDK expands connectivity from Visual Studio Server Explorer to additional Azure services.

You can select the various nodes shown in Figure 12.62 and begin working with that service right inside the IDE. As an example, you can double-click a VM and be taken to a configuration screen for the VM. Figure 12.63 shows an example. Notice that you can connect to the VM, shut it down, change its size configuration, and more.

QuickStart Templates

The Azure SDK ships with a number of QuickStart templates designed to speed your development of applications that take advantage of the many Azure services. You access these templates from the New Project dialog (File, New, Project) under the Cloud node. Figure 12.64 shows an example of these many project templates.

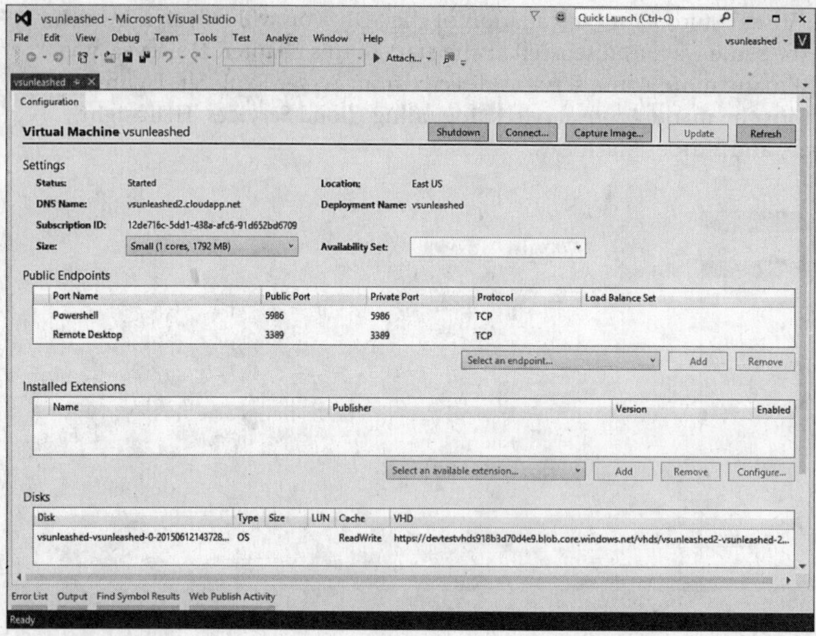

FIGURE 12.63 You can edit VM configuration information from Visual Studio.

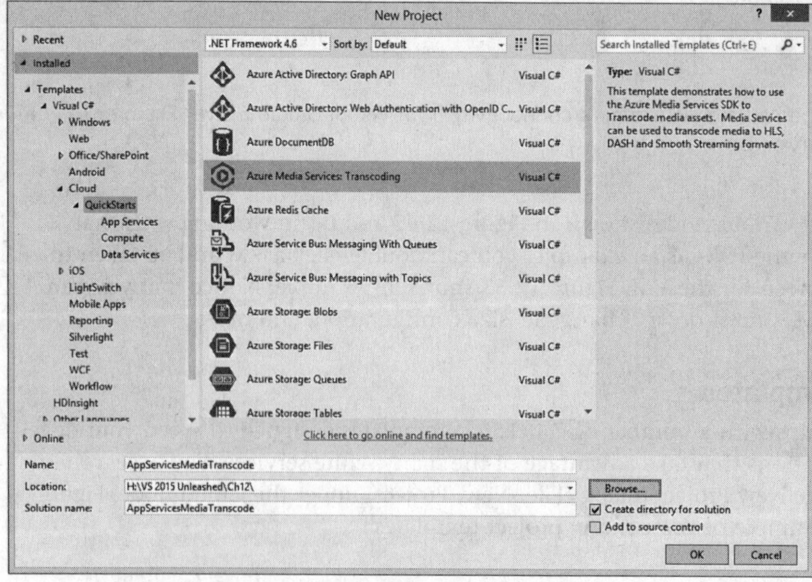

FIGURE 12.64 Use the Azure QuickStart templates to speed development of applications that use Azure services.

The QuickStart templates for Azure provide sample code and configuration for various Azure services. The following outlines the templates available at the time of writing:

- AppServices
    - **Azure Active Directory: Graph API**—Shows how to use the AAD Graph API for working with users, groups, and membership roles
    - **Azure Active Directory: Web Authentication with OpenID Connect**—Shows how to build an application with ASP.NET MVC and use OpenID for Azure AD sign-in
    - **Azure Media Services: Transcoding**—Shows how to use Azure media services to transcode media in various formats for streaming
    - **Azure Service Bus: Messaging with Queues**—Demonstrates using Azure queues for building reliable messaging applications
    - **Azure Service Bus: Messaging with Topics**—Illustrates using Azure Service Bus Topics for distributed messaging applications based on the PubSub pattern
- Compute
    - **Azure WebJobs SDK: Blobs**—Example of creating WebJobs to work with Blob storage
    - **Azure WebJobs SDK: Queues**—Project template for using WebJobs to work with queues
    - **Azure WebJobs SDK: Service Bus**—Shows how to leverage Azure Service Bus with WebJobs
    - **Azure WebJobs SDK: Tables**—Example of WebJobs working with Azure table storage
    - **Deploy and Manage Cloud Services**—Template for creating code to provision (and deprovision) Storage Accounts and Cloud Services
    - **Deploy and Manage Virtual Machines**—Template for creating code to provision (and deprovision) Azure VMs
    - **Deploy and Manage Web Sites**—Example of Azure web app deployments using WAML
- DataServices
    - **Azure DocumentDB**—Allows you to write code that stores JSON messages/documents
    - **Azure Redis Cache**—Shows how you can create an application to move items into and out of the Azure cache service
    - **Azure Storage: Blobs**—Builds an application that uses blog storage for files
    - **Azure Storage: Files**—Builds an application that uses Azure file storage

- **Azure Storage: Queues**—Allows you to work with Azure storage queues (insert, peek, get, delete messages)
- **Azure Storage: Tables**—Helps you work with structured data and Azure table storage
- **Deploy and Manage SQL Database**—Illustrates how to deploy and manage an Azure SQL Database using the management libraries in Azure
- **Deploy and Manage Azure Storage**—Uses the Azure management libraries for working with the various Azure storage accounts

Azure Resource Group Deployment Projects

Previously in the chapter, you saw how you could create a Visual Studio ASP.NET project, link it to Azure, and deploy it when the time came. The two examples showed both the Azure setup and configuration required to host the site at the time of project creation and another example doing so post-project creation. This works great for working with web apps. However, a single Azure application might use many different Azure services, such as web app, SQL, and cache. In that case, you would like a means to build the entire Azure group of services for your application from within Visual Studio.

The Azure SDK includes the concept of Resource Groups. This is a method to manage the Azure resources that your application uses as a single group. This aids with deployment and management from within Visual Studio. You can even use PowerShell to further customize what get installed and configured inside Azure for your application environment.

To use resource groups, you first create a project using the Azure Resource Group project template. Figure 12.65 shows the project type for a new project and solution. Clicking the OK button on this dialog launches the Select Azure Template dialog, as shown in Figure 12.66. These are templates that can setup and configure the many services required for a common application. You can use these as a basis for your Azure resource group project.

As an example, suppose you wish to provision a resource group inside Azure for hosting a Web app. You might write custom configuration that you wish repeated on each deployment. In this case, you can create an Azure Resource Group project (as its own solution by adding it to an existing solution). When prompted for the Azure template, we select the "Web app" template shown at the top of Figure 12.66.

Figure 12.67 shows an example of the newly created Azure resource group project. Notice that the project contains a Windows PowerShell script for deploying the application to Azure (`Deploy-AzureResourceGroup.ps1`). There is also a deployment template (`WebSite.json`) and a deployment template parameters file (`WebSite.param.dev.json`).

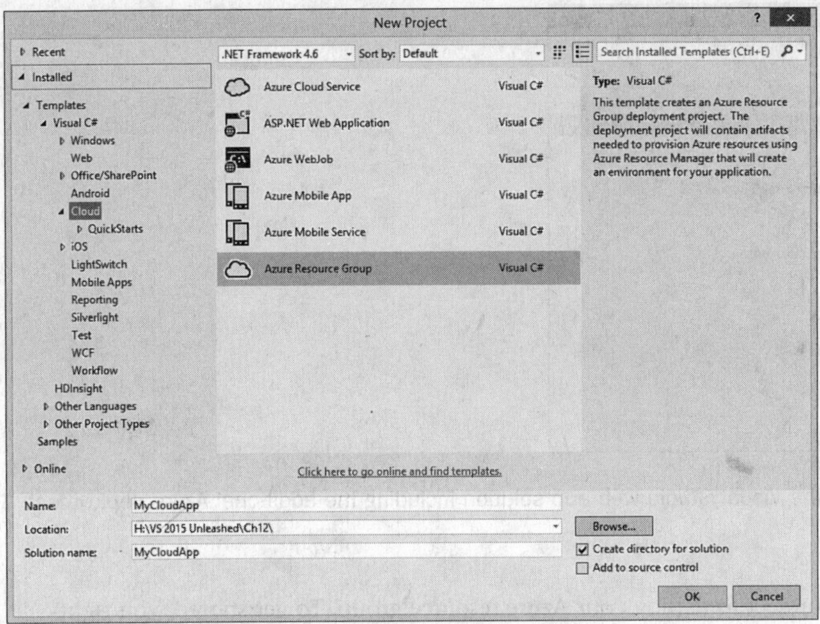

FIGURE 12.65 The Azure Resource Group template allows you to create resource group projects for deploying multiple Azure services in a single application.

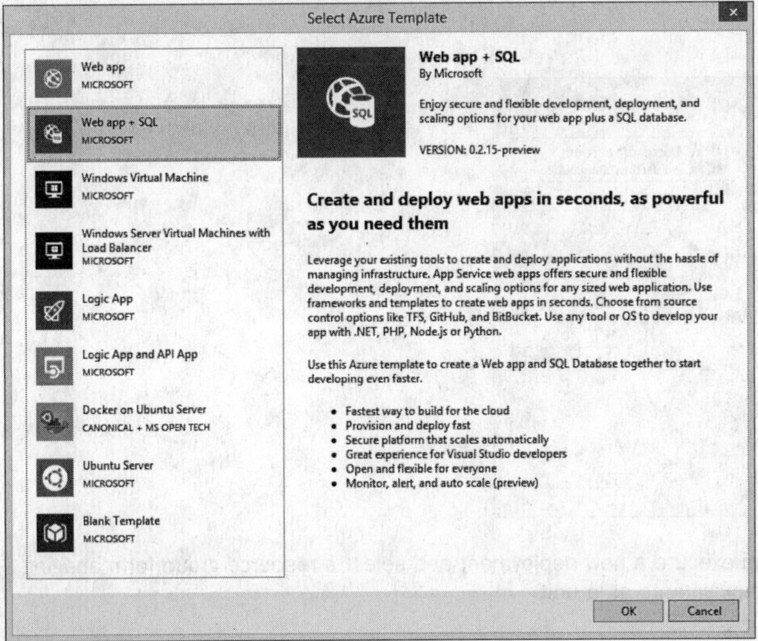

FIGURE 12.66 Select an Azure template to create a group of services for a single application.

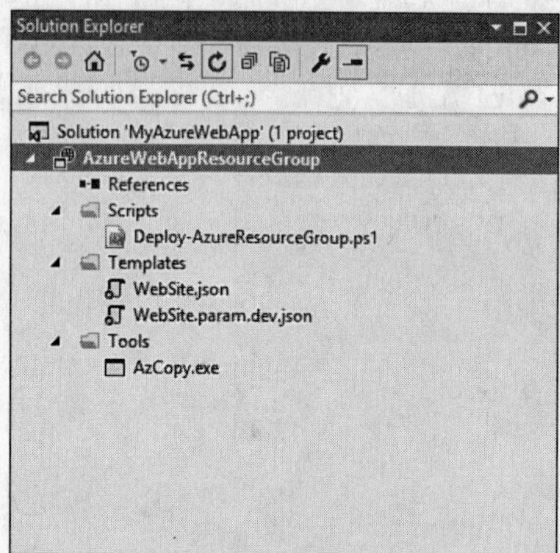

FIGURE 12.67 The Visual Studio web app solution including the additional Azure deployment project.

You can use the project to deploy your Azure resource group. To get started, you right-click the project in Solution Explorer and choose the Deploy option. This launches the New Deployment dialog, as shown in Figure 12.68. Here you can select your Azure account (upper-right). You then set your Azure subscription, the resource group, a deployment template (from the deployment project), deployment parameters, and a storage account (if required).

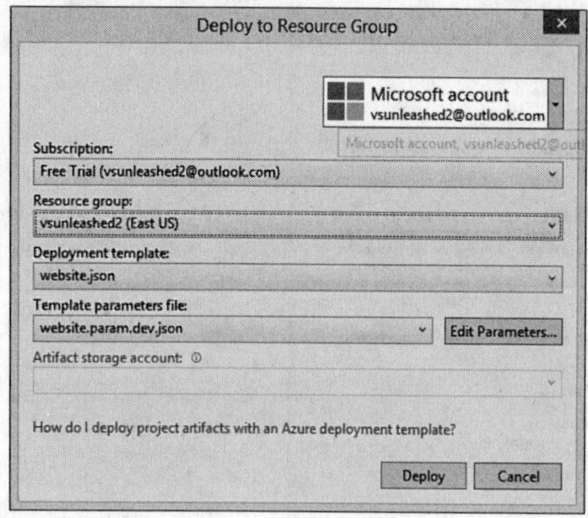

FIGURE 12.68 You can execute a new deployment and select a resource group for managing multiple Azure service deployments as a unit.

You must also set the deployment parameters to point to your site either inside the `website.param.dev.json` file or by using the Edit Parameters button in Figure 12.68. Figure 12.69 shows the parameter setup. The siteName parameter is the name of your site and new resource group. The hostingPlanName is your hosting plan as named inside Azure. The siteLocation is the Azure location you intend to use to host the resource group.

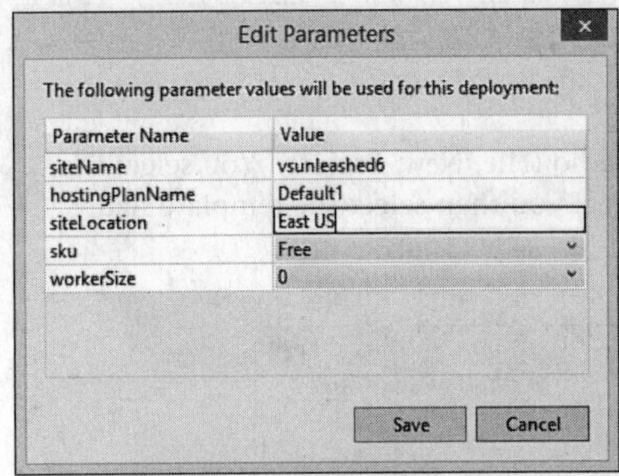

FIGURE 12.69 You configure your Resource Group deployment as a last step prior to final deployment to Azure.

The final step is to let Visual Studio deploy these resources to Azure on our behalf by hitting the Deploy button. You will see the progress of the deployment inside the Visual Studio Output window. You will also get a notification inside Azure once complete (success or failure). You can now use this project to make any changes to your hosting resource group and then simply redeploy as necessary.

Azure Cloud Services (PaaS)

The web applications we have created and deployed thus far are all running on Azure web apps. This is a hosting environment built to simplify website creation, deployment, and management. It is built on top of Azure Cloud Services to create an optimized approach for developers just looking to build and host a website.

You can, however, build and deploy directly to Azure Cloud Services. This is Microsoft's PaaS offering. You write and deploy applications on PaaS to provide reliability, free you from managing environments, and gain support for high scalability.

Recall that Azure web apps are built on Cloud Services. This makes the distinction a bit blurry. However, there are some key differences between hosting as an Azure website and using Cloud Services. With Cloud Services, for example, you can get access to the VMs that run your application. You have separate staging and production environments, and you can use networking to connect to on-premises servers. You should know that the VMs that run your Cloud Services are managed on your behalf (patched), which is unlike the Azure VM technology.

NOTE

For a great discussion on the various Azure hosting options, see the documentation "Azure Execution Models" at the link provided at the end of the Note. This includes a discussion of how VMs, websites, and Cloud Services differ. It also discusses how you might choose one over the other for your application: https://azure.microsoft.com/en-us/documentation/articles/fundamentals-application-models/

Creating a Cloud Service Project

You create a cloud service project from Visual Studio (File, New, Project). You select the Cloud option on the left of the New Project dialog; you then select the template Azure Cloud Service. Figure 12.70 shows an example.

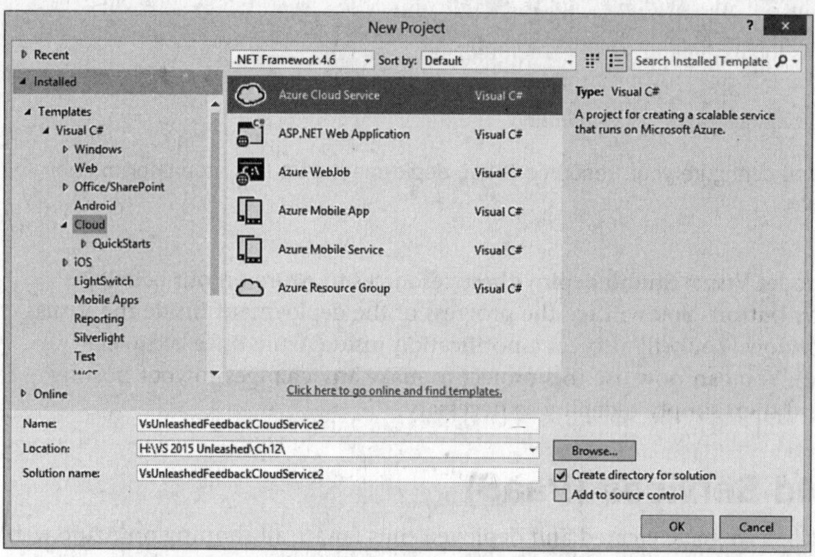

FIGURE 12.70 Select Azure Cloud Service to get started working with PaaS directly in Azure.

The Azure Cloud Service template then presents a few sub options, as shown in Figure 12.71. You use this dialog to select the type of cloud services you want to add to your solution. Your options include a web role for building a web user interface, the work role for creating web jobs that run in the background, a role for WCF services, and others. You can always add services at a later date. In this case, we added just the ASP.NET Web Role.

Visual Studio then prompts you on what type of ASP.NET application you want to create. You can choose between the standard site templates that are supported by the current version of Azure. Figure 12.72 shows options at the time of writing.

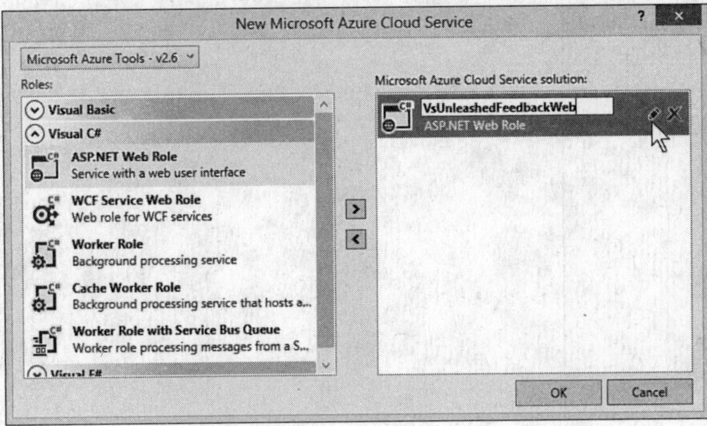

FIGURE 12.71 Choose various cloud services to add to your project.

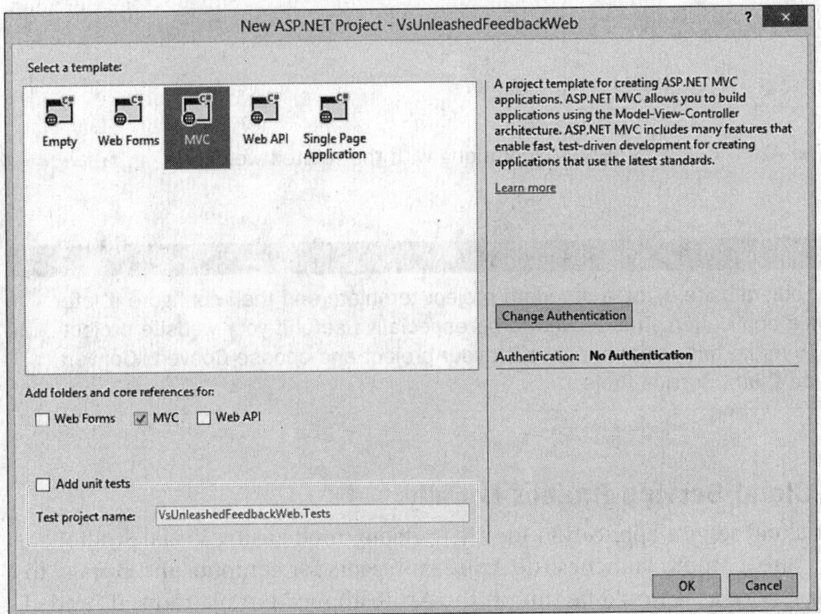

FIGURE 12.72 Select the remaining project parameters, such as ASP.NET template.

Visual Studio then creates two projects and adds them to a solution. The MVC Web role is simply an ASP.NET MVC website. The other project is an Azure configuration definition project for working with your Azure Cloud Service. Figure 12.73 shows an example inside Solution Explorer.

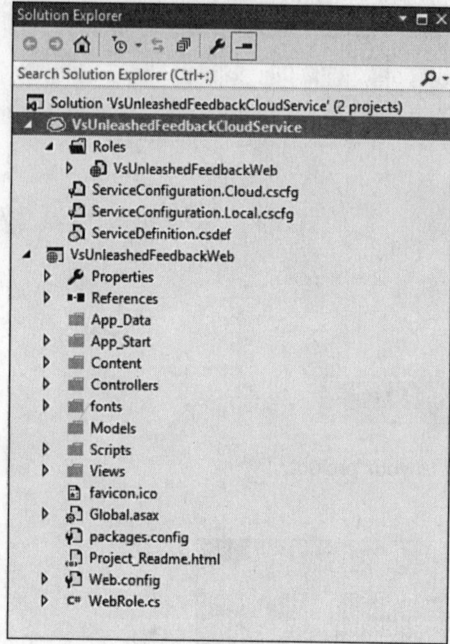

FIGURE 12.73 The Azure Cloud Service project along with the related website.

TIP

You can create your website using a standard project template and then configure it later as a cloud service application. This proves to be especially useful if your website project already exists. To make this happen, right-click your project and choose Convert, Convert to Microsoft Azure Cloud Service Project.

Running Your Cloud Service Project Locally

You can run your cloud service application locally in debug mode using Visual Studio. When debugging, Visual Studio launches the Azure emulators for compute and storage to host and run your service as it would be run on the Azure application platform. If needed, you can access these emulators from the system tray. Figure 12.74 shows the user interface (UI) for the Azure Compute Emulator.

Deploy the Cloud Service Project

You deploy your Azure Cloud Service project in a manner similar to that discussed for Azure websites. To get started, you right-click the cloud service project in Solution Explorer and choose Publish. This brings up the Publish Azure Application dialog shown in Figure 12.75. Here you can set the environment (staging or production), the build configuration (release or debug), and related configuration options.

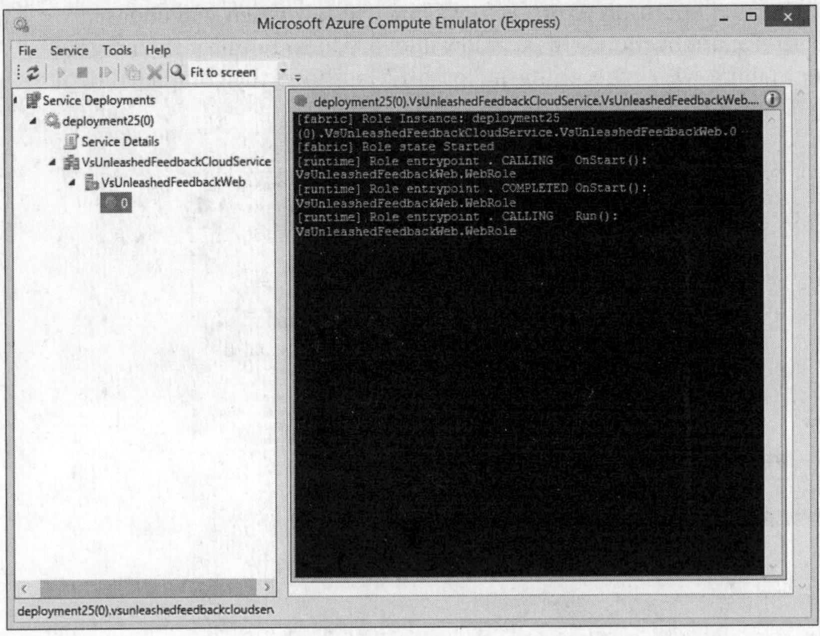

FIGURE 12.74 The Azure Compute Emulator runs your application locally as if it were running inside the Azure cloud.

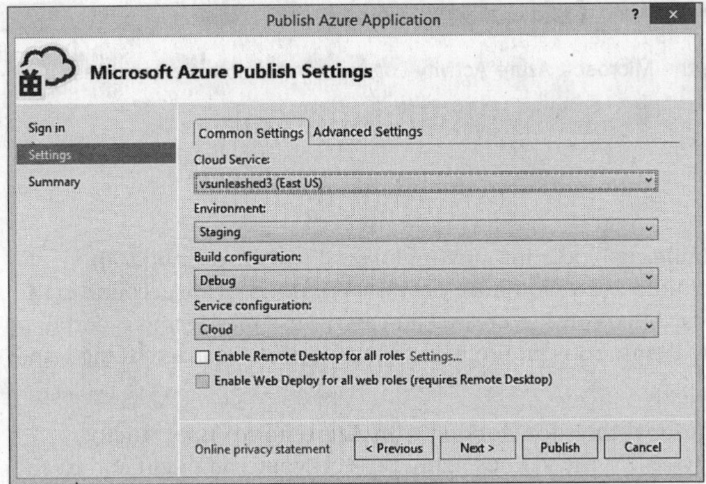

FIGURE 12.75 You can publish an Azure Cloud Service application directly from Visual Studio.

Visual Studio launches the Microsoft Azure Activity Log window when you choose to publish the cloud service application. This window allows you to monitor the progress of your deployment (along with other things). Figure 12.76 shows the completed deployment inside the IDE.

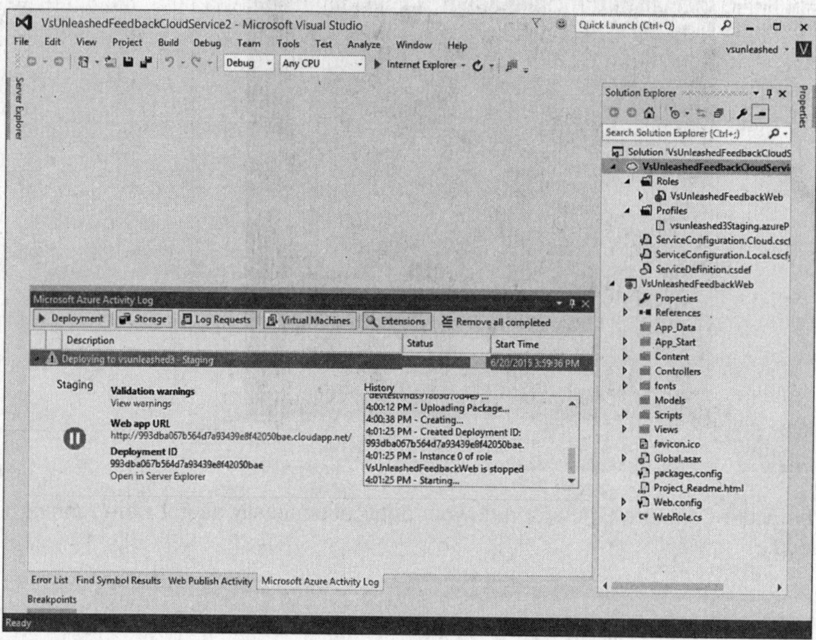

FIGURE 12.76 You can use the Microsoft Azure Activity Log to monitor activities such as deployments inside the IDE.

Summary

This chapter presented the building blocks for moving forward with Azure application development within Visual Studio 2015. You must create a Windows Azure account to use the many services. Thankfully, Microsoft has created an easy-to-use management portal for configuration of all Azure items. You can use it to create websites, manage storage, and monitor activity.

The Azure SDK provides additional tools for working with Azure from Visual Studio. With it, you can create templates for the various Azure project types you might add to an application, such as media services, table storage, queues, and service bus. The SDK also includes resource groups for working with a group of Azure items as a logical unit.

Finally, we discussed the differences between creating and deploying Azure websites and Azure Cloud Services. The former simplifies website hosting. However, the latter provides additional access and control of your hosting environment.

CHAPTER 13

Working with Databases

IN THIS CHAPTER

- ▶ Creating Tables and Relationships
- ▶ Working with SQL Statements
- ▶ Using Database Projects
- ▶ Creating Database Objects in Managed Code
- ▶ Binding Controls to Data
- ▶ Object Relational Mapping

This chapter is all about managing SQL Server databases and building data-aware applications using Visual Studio.

Six different Visual Studio tools enable you to interact with a database and assist with building applications that leverage data from a database:

- ▶ Solution Explorer
- ▶ Server Explorer
- ▶ SQL Server Object Explorer
- ▶ Database Diagram Designer
- ▶ Table Designer
- ▶ Query and View Designer

Collectively, they are referred to as the SQL Server Data Tools (SSDT). You first came across a few of these tools in Chapter 5, "Browsers and Explorers." Now this chapter explores how developers use these tools to create database solutions.

Project templates for database maintenance are also provided as part of the SQL Server Data Tools.

We start by examining how to build databases and database objects with the SSDT. From there, we can cover the specifics of creating data-aware applications with data-bound controls.

NOTE

Some tools may not be available or may function differently depending on the version of SQL Server you use. Here, we focus on using Visual Studio 2015 with SQL Server 2014.

Creating Tables and Relationships

The primary entities in any database are its tables. Tables are composed of a structure and data. Server Explorer and the new SQL Server Object Explorer are the Visual Studio instruments used to define or edit the structure or data of any table within a connected database. In fact, using either Explorer, it is possible to create a new SQL Server database instance from scratch. Because the functionality between these Explorer windows is nearly identical, we won't bother to illustrate every detail here within the context of both Explorers. The SQL Server Object Explorer (launched from the View menu, or by clicking the SQL Server Object Explorer button in the Server Explorer command bar) looks much more like the management console that ships with SQL Server itself and may be preferable to some people. Other than that, it will largely be a matter of preference in terms of which tool you use. For a quick side-by-side comparison of the two windows, see Figure 13.1.

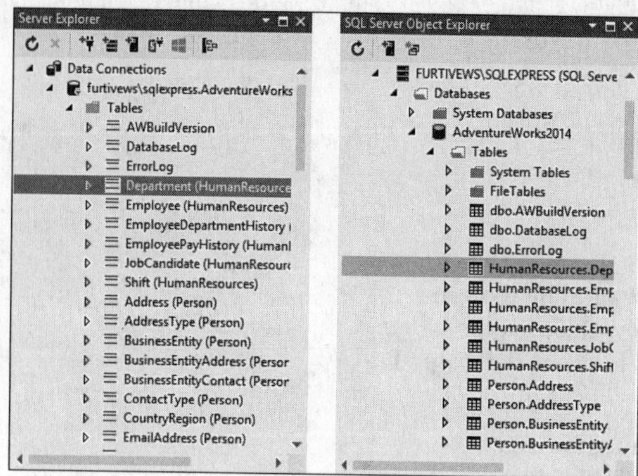

FIGURE 13.1 The Server Explorer versus the SQL Server Object Explorer.

We focus here on using the Server Explorer because most Visual Studio users are already familiar with it.

Creating a New SQL Server Database

Data connections are physical connections to a database. In Server Explorer, the Data Connections node has a list of every established database connection. To start the database creation process, right-click the Data Connections node and select the Create New

SQL Server Database option. In the resulting dialog box (see Figure 13.2), you need to provide a server name, login credentials, and a name for the new database.

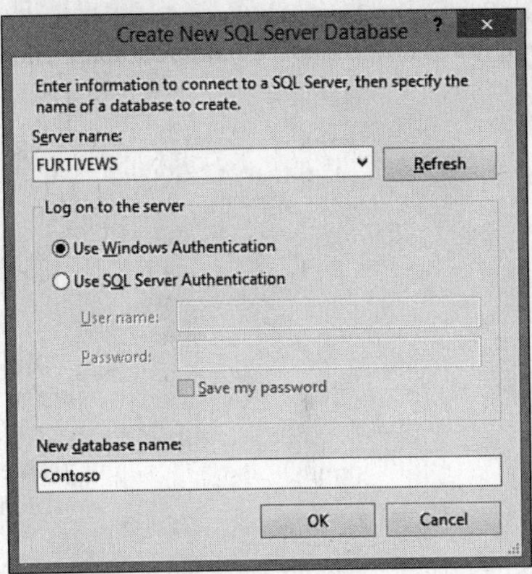

FIGURE 13.2 Creating a new SQL Server database.

This immediately creates the indicated database and adds a connection to the new database under the Data Connections node. Figure 13.3 shows the newly created Contoso database added to the list of connections.

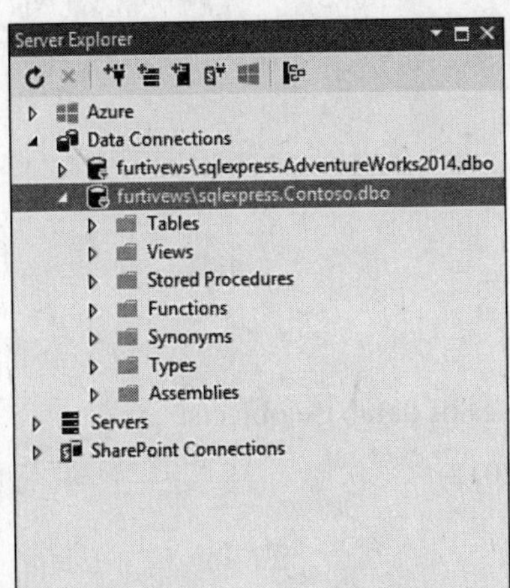

FIGURE 13.3 The new database added to the data connections.

Connecting to an Existing Database

You can also establish a connection to an existing database. Again, you right-click the Data Connections node; this time, though, you select the Add Connection option. The Add Connection dialog box (see Figure 13.4) is similar to the New Database dialog box. You specify a data source, server name, login credentials, and database name/database filename to connect to the database.

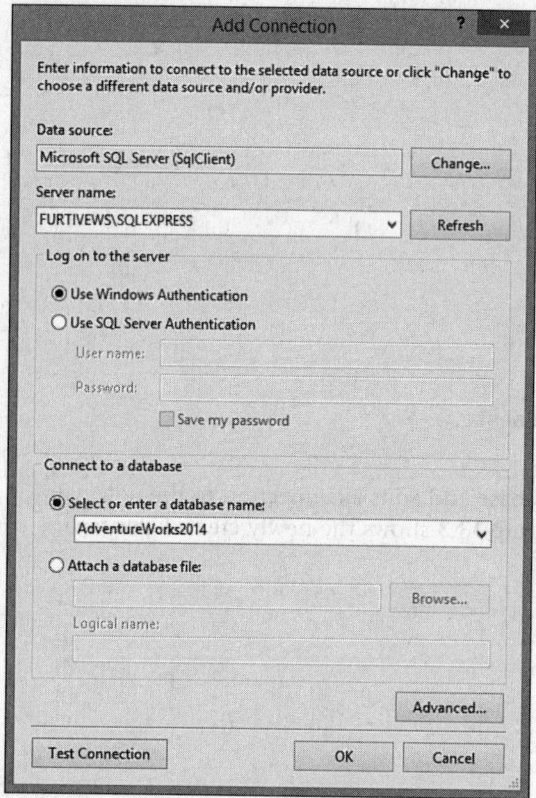

FIGURE 13.4 Connecting to an existing database.

Under each connection are folders for the following classes of database objects:

- Database diagrams (not available with SQL Server 2012)
- Tables
- Views
- Stored procedures
- Functions

- Synonyms
- Types
- Assemblies

These folders are the launching point for creating corresponding objects within the database.

Defining Tables

The table designer is the SQL Server data tool you use to define or edit the definition for a table. Using the Server Explorer window, right-click the `Tables` folder under an existing connection and select Add New Table.

The designer (see Figure 13.5) is implemented with two panes: a design pane that allows you to define the table in a "point and click" fashion, and a script pane that lets you work directly with the T-SQL syntax that defines the table. Within the design pane itself, there is a tabular presentation of the table columns. Adding a table column is as simple as adding a row to this definition matrix and setting the datatype using the in-grid drop-down. There is also a section within the designer that allows you to view, create, and edit the table's keys, constraints, indexes, and so on.

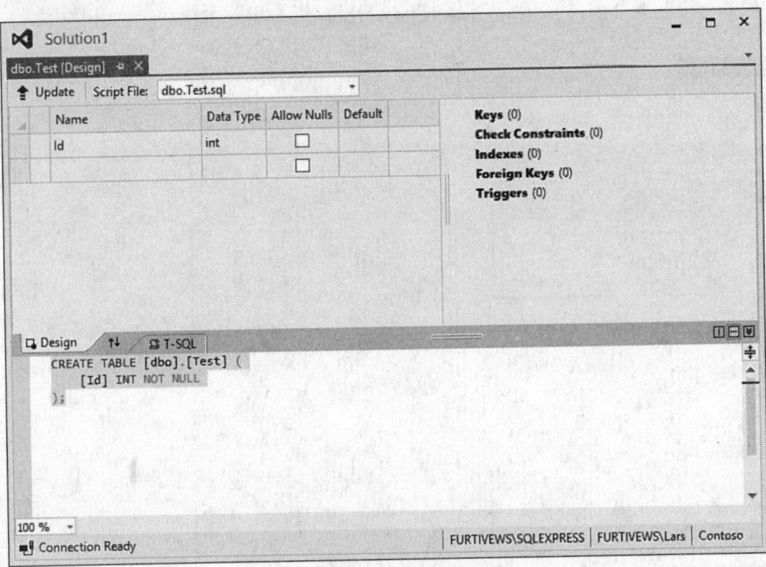

FIGURE 13.5 The Table Designer interface.

Setting a Primary Key

Creating a primary key for a table is a simple process: in the design pane, select the column or columns that constitute the key, right click, and then select Set Primary Key from the shortcut menu. A key icon indicates any primary keys defined in the table.

Creating Indexes, Foreign Keys, and Check Constraints

Indexes, foreign keys, and check constraints are all created using the same interface and process. Using the index tree to the right of the table definition, right-click on the type of object you want to create or edit, and then select Add New from the pop-up menu. This will immediately create a placeholder for that object; you can now right-click on the object, select Properties from the context menu, and then edit the properties (including column membership) using the standard property page within Visual Studio.

Let's put these moving parts together and see how this works end to end by creating a table within our database to hold course content for an online school.

- We will start with an existing database residing within a SQL Server 2014 instance. Open the Server Explorer, select the target database, right-click on the Tables node, and select Add Table (see Figure 13.6). Note that, by default, the tool has created a default primary key field for us named `Id`.

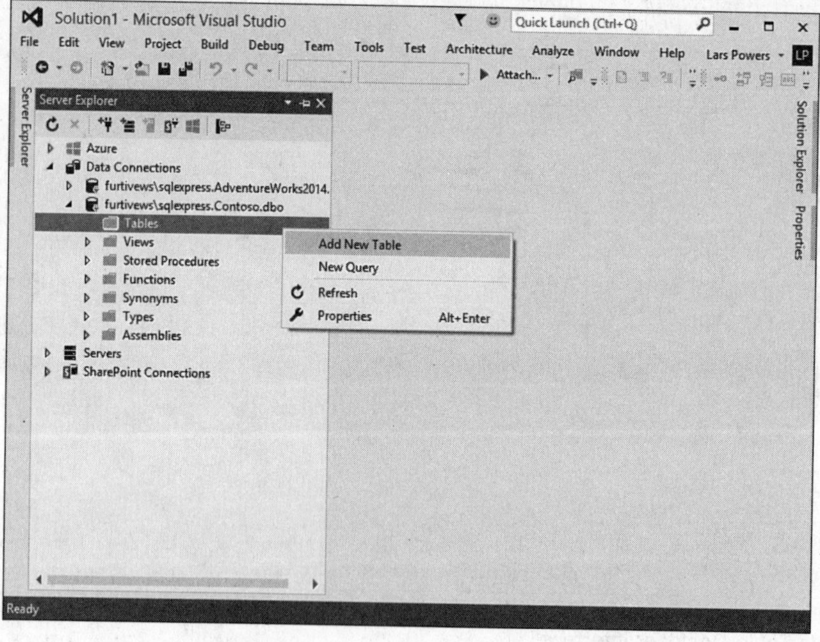

FIGURE 13.6 Adding a table.

- Let's name the table `Course`, which is best done using the SQL pane. Select the current `[Table]` name and type the name `Course` instead (see Figure 13.7).

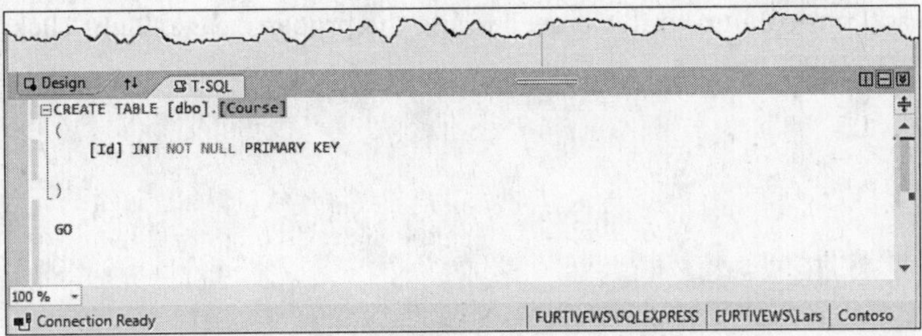

FIGURE 13.7 Renaming the table in the SQL pane.

▶ We now need to add the other columns to the table. Each of these can be added in turn just by typing their name and selecting their datatype within the designer. We'll add a `CourseCode` int, a `Title` varchar, and a `Description` varchar column. In the empty table designer row, type the name, select the data type from the drop-down, check the `Allow Nulls` column as appropriate, and then press the Tab key to create another row for defining your next column. In Figure 13.8, we have already added the `CourseCode` column and are working on the `Title` column.

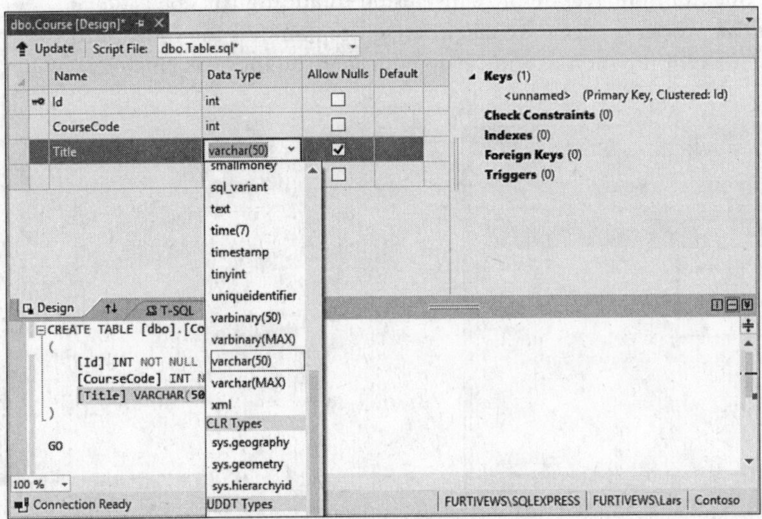

FIGURE 13.8 Adding columns to the table definition.

▶ Once the columns are added, we can worry about any check constraints, indexes, foreign keys, or triggers. For this example, we want to make sure that `CourseCode` is indexed. To create an index for this column, we will move our attention to the indexes/keys area of the design pane. Right-click on the Indexes node there and select Add New, Index (see Figure 13.9). The index will be created with a default name and will immediately show under the Indexes node. To change the name of the index and to add our column to it, we need to use the property page. Right-click the index and select Properties.

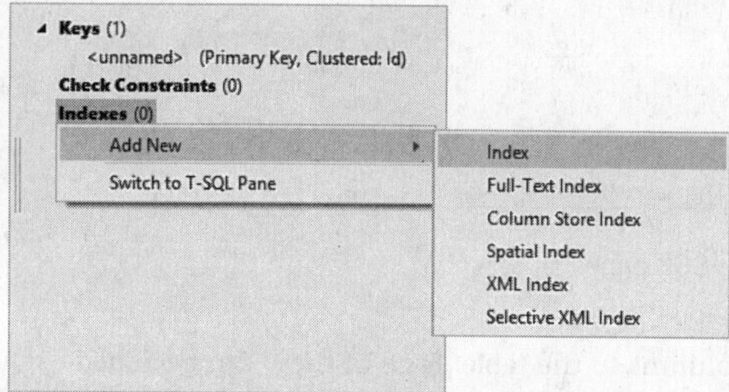

FIGURE 13.9 Defining an index.

- In the Property sheet, use the `Columns` property to add or remove columns to the index. Clicking the ellipses on this property will launch the Index Columns dialog (see Figure 13.10). In this dialog, one or more columns can be selected and added to the index. For our example, we are only interested in adding the `CourseCode` column. Back on the property sheet, we can change the name of the index and perform other useful actions, such as indicating whether the index is clustered.

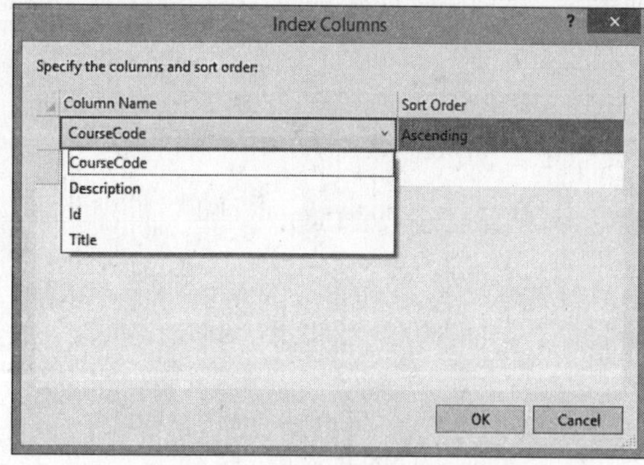

FIGURE 13.10 Adding columns to the index.

- Now that we have successfully defined our table, the last step is to update the database with the definition and physically create the table within the database. In the table designer, click on the Update button at the top/left of the designer (see Figure 13.11). We have the option to either generate a script with the table definition or update the database directly. In this case, we'll update directly. Once we kick off the process, progress and results of the operation will be reported back to us within the IDE (see Figure 13.12).

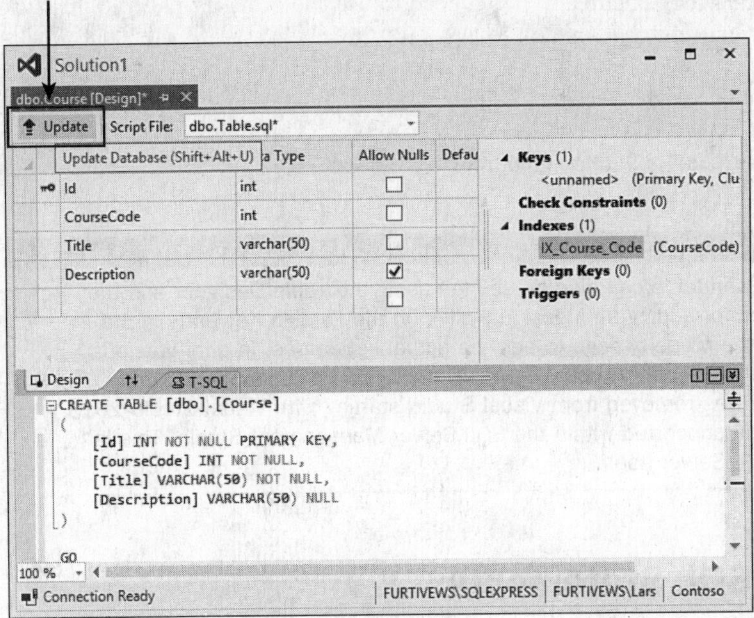

FIGURE 13.11 Updating the database.

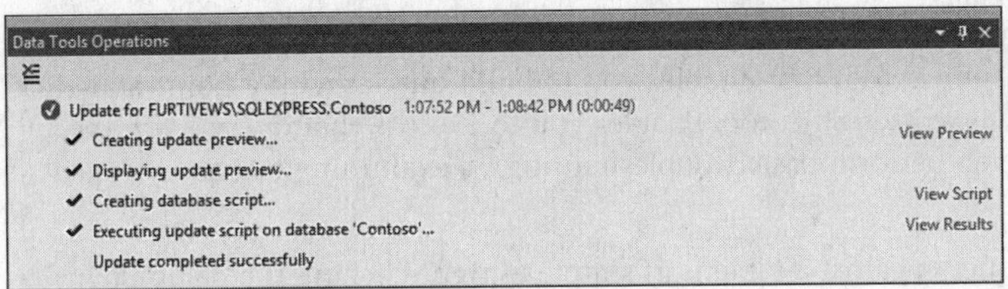

FIGURE 13.12 The results of the update.

Note that as we have been designing our table, Visual Studio has been keeping pace by writing all the necessary T-SQL in the T-SQL pane. This works the same way that the web page designer and XAML/WPF designers do within the tool. We are free to work with the design surface or write the necessary code directly. The two panes are automatically kept in sync. Therefore, we could create our table's columns and set the primary key by simply writing the necessary SQL in the SQL pane.

```
CREATE TABLE [dbo].[Course]
(
      [Id] INT NOT NULL PRIMARY KEY,
   [CourseCode] INT NOT NULL,
   [Title] VARCHAR(50) NOT NULL,
```

```
    [Description] VARCHAR(50) NULL
)

GO

CREATE INDEX [IX_Course_Code] ON [dbo].[Course] ([CourseCode])
```

NOTE

Foreign keys for any given table can also be defined using the Table Designer and the same process we used for adding an index: just click on the Foreign Key entry in the design page and use the property page to edit the actual key values. In prior versions of Visual Studio, table relationships could be easily built using a Database Diagram Designer. This feature was removed from Visual Studio starting with Visual Studio 2013, although the tool is still supported within the SQL Server Management Studio. This is installed as part of SQL Server itself.

Working with SQL Statements

There is full support within the SQL Server Data Tools set for crafting and executing SQL statements against a connected database.

Writing a Query

The primary tool that facilitates the development of SQL statements is the query/view designer, which is a graphical tool that enables you to build queries with a point-and-click interface. After a query is written, this tool enables you to execute that query, view the returned results, and even perform basic troubleshooting by examining the query execution plan.

Creating a new select query against a table is as simple as right-clicking the database in Server Explorer and then selecting New Query. An initial prompt gathers a list of the tables, views, functions, and synonyms to use as the target of the query (see Figure 13.13).

TIP

The visual query design tools we are discussing are, for some reason, only available when you have established a connection to SQL Server using the .NET Framework Provider for OLE DB. If you are trying to follow along with the instructions here and find that you are stuck with only the SQL editor (no visual tools), it is likely that your data connection in Server Explorer is using the native .NET Framework Provider for SQL Server. Conversely, you can only add or edit stored procedures if your data connection is using the native client and not the OLE DB client.

So, to recap: to use the visual tools, make sure your database connection is configured using the OLE DB Provider. To edit/create stored procedures, make sure you are using a connection that leverages the native SQL Server provider.

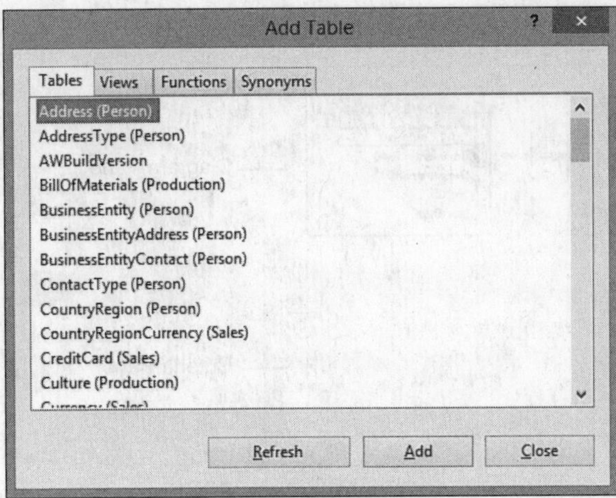

FIGURE 13.13 Adding tables to the query.

After you have selected the objects you want the query to target, the query designer opens. As Figure 13.14 illustrates, the designer has four panes:

- **Criteria pane**—This pane enables you to select, via a point-and-click diagram, the data columns to include in the select statement, sorting, and alias names.
- **Diagram pane**—This pane is similar to the diagram in the database diagram designer; it graphically depicts the database object relationships. This makes creating joins a simple action of using existing relationships or creating new ones right within this tool.
- **Results pane**—After the query is executed, this pane holds any data returned as a result. Note that this pane is equipped with navigation controls to enable you to page through large resultsets.
- **SQL pane**—The SQL pane holds the actual SQL syntax used to implement the query. You can alter the statement manually by typing directly into this pane, or you can leverage the designer and let it write the SQL for you based on what you have entered into the diagram and criteria panes.

You can show or hide any of these panes at will. Right-click anywhere in the designer and select the Pane fly-out menu to select or deselect the visible panes.

Fine-Tuning the SQL Statement

To flesh out the `select` statement, you can indicate which columns from which tables you want returned by placing a check next to the column in the diagram pane. You use the criteria pane to specify a sort order, provide alias names for the return columns, and establish a filter for the resultset. As you select these different options, the designer turns them into SQL, visible in the SQL pane.

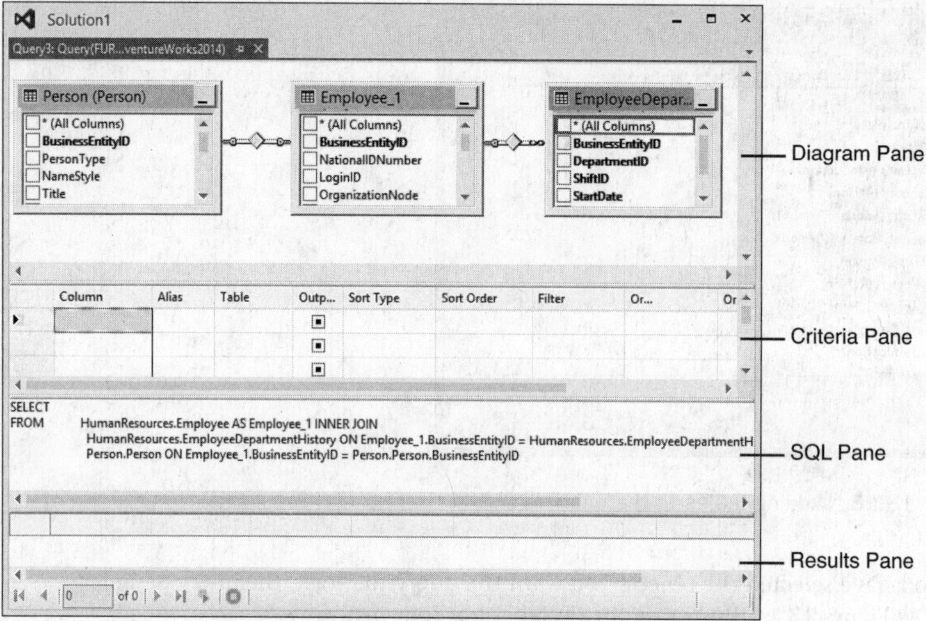

FIGURE 13.14 The Query Designer.

NOTE

We are using the `AdventureWorks` sample database in a SQL Server Express 2014 instance for most of this chapter. If you want to follow along, you can download a copy of this database and others by visiting http://MSFTDBProdSamples.codeplex.com/. `AdventureWorks` is also the sample database used by the SQL Server 2014 Books Online help collection.

Figure 13.15 shows the completed "Employee" query, with results visible in the bottom pane.

Specifying Joins and Join Types

When you add multiple related tables to the query designer, the designer uses their foreign key relationships to automatically build a `JOIN` clause for the query. You also have the option to create joins on table columns that don't have an existing relationship. You do this the same way that you specify relationships in the database diagram designer: you select and drag the column from one table to another within the diagram pane. The columns to be joined must be of compatible data types; for instance, you can't join a `varchar` column with an `integer` column.

Joins are created using a comparison operator. By default, this is the equal operator; in other words, return rows where the column values are equal across the join. But you have control over the actual comparison operation used in the join. For example, perhaps you want the resultset to include rows based on a join where the values in Table A are greater than the values in Table B on the joined columns. You can right-click the join relationship line in the diagram pane and select Properties to see the properties for the join; clicking the ellipsis button in the Join Condition and Type property reveals the Join dialog box, shown in Figure 13.16.

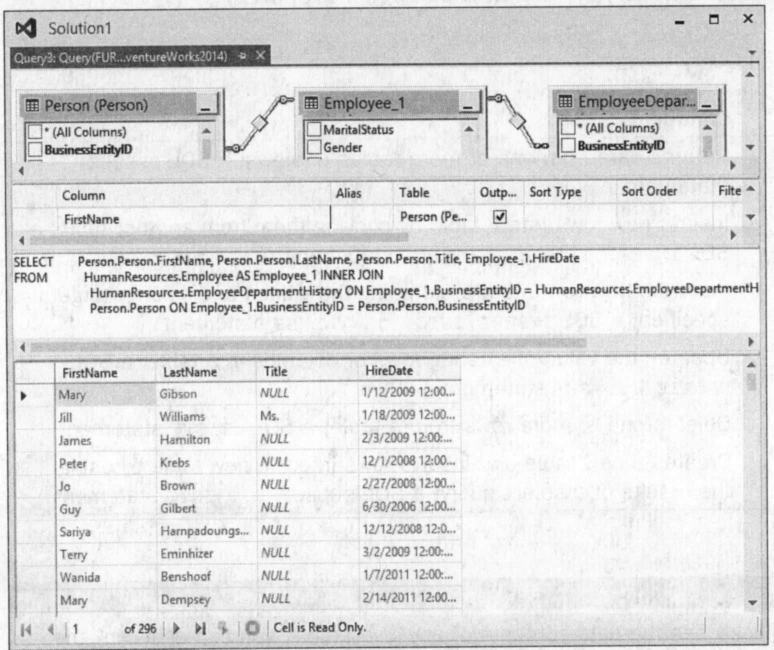

FIGURE 13.15 Querying for employee information in the `AdventureWorks` database.

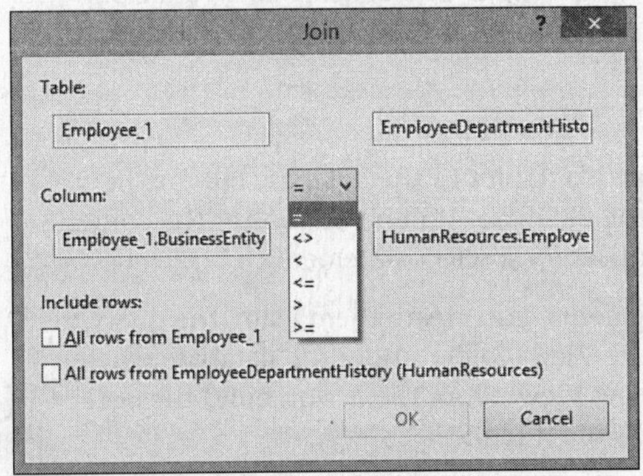

FIGURE 13.16 Setting join properties.

Other Query Types

By default, creating queries from the Server Explorer results in a select query. But the query designer is equally adept at building other query types. If you want, for instance, an insert query, you can change the type of the query loaded in the designer by selecting Query Design, Change Type.

Table 13.1 shows the different query types that the designer supports.

TABLE 13.1 Supported Query Types

Query Type	Comments
Select	Returns data from one or more tables or views; a SQL `SELECT` statement
Insert Results	Inserts new rows into a table by copying them from another table; a SQL `INSERT INTO ... SELECT` statement
Insert Values	Inserts a new row into a table using the values and column targets specified; a SQL `INSERT INTO ... VALUES` statement
Update	Updates the value of existing rows or columns in a table; a SQL `UPDATE ... SET` statement
Delete	Deletes one or more rows from a table; a SQL `DELETE` statement
Make Table	Creates a new table and inserts rows into the new table by using the results of a select query; a SQL `SELECT ... INTO` statement

TIP

If you just want to quickly see the data contents of any given table, you can right-click the table within the Server Explorer and then select Show Table Data. This initiates a new query/view designer with a `SELECT *` statement for the given table. By default, only the results pane is visible. This functionality is ideal for testing scenarios in which you need to quickly edit data in the database or observe the effects of SQL statements on a table.

Creating Views

Views are virtual tables. They look and act just like tables in the database but are, in reality, `select` statements that are stored in the database. When you look at the content of a view, you are actually looking at the resultset for a select statement.

Because views are implemented as select statements, you create them using the query/view designer tool. In Server Explorer, right-click the Views folder under the database where you want to create the view and select Add New View. From there, you build the `select` statement just as you would for any other SQL statement.

Clicking the Update button creates (or updates) the view in the database.

Developing Stored Procedures

A stored procedure is a SQL statement (or series of statements) stored in a database and compiled. With SQL Server, stored procedures consist of Transact-SQL (T-SQL) code and have the capability to involve many coding constructs not typically found in ad hoc queries. For instance, you can implement error-handling routines within a stored procedure and even call into operating-system functions with so-called extended stored procedures.

For a given database, right-click the stored procedures folder in Server Explorer and select Add New Stored Procedure. A template for a stored procedure will open in the query designer. The SQL Editor is a close sibling to Visual Studio's Code Editor; it includes support for IntelliSense, syntax coloring, breakpoints, and the more general text-editing features (cut-copy-paste, word wrapping, and so on).

TIP

Remember: if you don't see the `Stored Procedures` folder within Server Explorer, you are likely not connecting to the data source using the native SQL Server provider. If that is the case, just add another connection to the database using the SQL Server provider.

Figure 13.17 shows the beginnings of a stored procedure in the SQL Editor window.

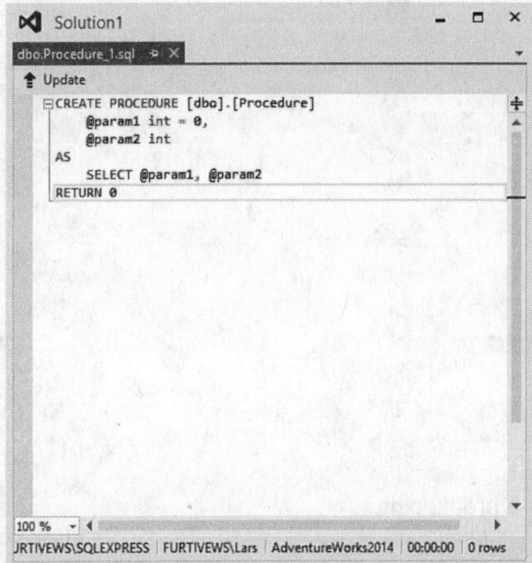

FIGURE 13.17 Writing a stored procedure.

With the template loaded into the SQL Editor, writing a stored procedure involves typing in the lines of code and SQL that perform the required actions.

NOTE

The capability to create and edit stored procedures is supported only in Microsoft SQL Server. You cannot use the Visual Studio tools to create a procedure in, say, an Oracle database.

Debugging Stored Procedures

In addition to coding stored procedures, you can leverage Visual Studio to help you debug them. With the stored procedure open in the SQL Editor window, set a breakpoint in the procedure by clicking in the Indicator Margin. (For more details on the indicator margin and general editor properties, see Chapter 6, "Introducing the Editors and Designers.") With a breakpoint in place, right-click the stored procedure's name in the Server Explorer tree and select Execute (see Figure 13.18).

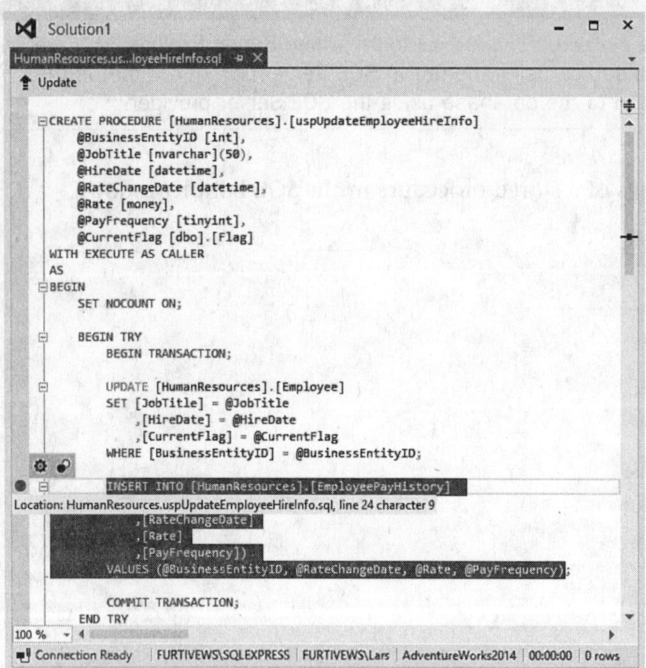

FIGURE 13.18 Running a stored procedure with a breakpoint.

The SQL Debugger is also parameter friendly. If the stored procedure uses any parameters, the debugger shows a dialog box to capture values for the parameters (see Figure 13.19).

You can quickly cycle through the list of parameters, supplying appropriate values. After you click OK, the stored procedure is executed. If you have set a breakpoint, execution pauses on the breakpoint. (A yellow arrow indicates the current line of execution within the editor, just the same as with the code editor window.) With execution stopped, you can use the Locals and Watch windows to debug the procedure's code. See Chapter 10, "Debugging Code," for a more thorough treatment of the Locals and Watch windows as debugging tools in Visual Studio.

Execute Stored Procedure

The stored procedure [HumanResources].[uspUpdateEmployeeHireInfo] requires the following parameters:

Name	Data Type	Out	Null	Default	Value
@BusinessEntityID	int	No			14
@JobTitle	nvarchar(50)	No			Manager
@HireDate	datetime	No			
@RateChangeDate	datetime	No			
@Rate	money	No			
@PayFrequency	tinyint	No			
@CurrentFlag	bit	No			

OK Cancel

FIGURE 13.19 Entering parameter values.

The Debug menu is used to control execution and flow. If you select Continue, the procedure continues running up to the next breakpoint (if present).

Creating Triggers

Triggers are a type of stored procedure designed to run when the data in a table or view is modified. Triggers are attached to an individual table; when a query (an update, insert, or delete query) affects data in the table, the trigger executes.

Because a trigger is really a stored procedure with a controlled execution time (hence the name trigger), it can have quite complex SQL statements and flow execution logic.

To create a trigger, use Server Explorer and locate the table to which the trigger is to be attached. Right-click the table name, select Add New Trigger, and then use the SQL Editor to write the SQL for the trigger. When the trigger is saved to the database, it shows up under its related table in Server Explorer (alongside the columns in the table). Figure 13.20 shows a simple trigger designed to raise an error if an update statement changes the Availability column in the Location table.

Creating User-Defined Functions

User-defined functions are bodies of code/SQL designed to be reusable across a variety of possible consumers: stored procedures, applications, or even other functions. In that respect, they are no different from functions written in C# or Visual Basic. They are routines that can accept parameters and return a value. User-defined functions return scalar values (for example, a single value) or a resultset containing rows and columns of data.

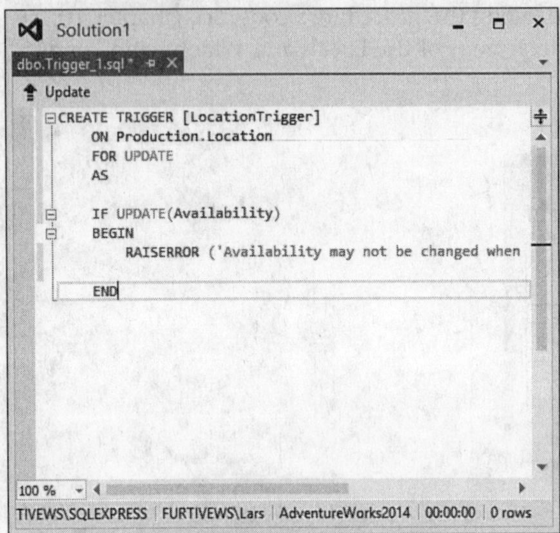

FIGURE 13.20 Creating a trigger.

One example of a user-defined function might be one that accepts a date and then determines whether the day is a weekday or weekend. Stored procedures or other functions in the database can then use the function as part of their processing.

Because user-defined functions are T-SQL statements with a format similar to stored procedures, the SQL Editor again is the primary tool for writing them. For each data connection visible in Server Explorer, a `Functions` folder contains any existing functions. To create a new function, you can right-click this folder, select Add New, and then select the type of function to create. You have three options:

- **Inline Function**—Returns values as a resultset; the resultset is built from the results of a `SELECT` query.
- **Table-Valued Function**—Returns values as a resultset; the resultset is built by programmatically creating a table within the function and then populating the table using `INSERT INTO` queries.
- **Scalar-Valued Function**—Returns a single value.

After selecting the appropriate function type, template code for the function is delivered inside a new SQL Editor window. Feel free to use the query/view designer to construct any required lines of SQL within the function.

For the specifics on how to write a function and put it to best use within the database, consult your database's documentation.

Using Database Projects

Up to this point, we have discussed the use of the Visual Database Tools outside of the context of a Visual Studio solution/project. Now let's investigate the role of the Database project type. Database projects in Visual Studio are used to manage the development and deployment of databases. They essentially represent an offline version of a database. It mirrors a database through a set of SQL files that contain the schema and object definitions for things such as tables, indexes, and stored procedures. With database projects, Visual Studio enables an end-to-end database development workflow that typically goes something like this:

- The DBA, who is typically the only person on a project team with access to the production database, uses Visual Studio to create an initial database project and reverse engineer a production database into that project.
- The DBA is also typically responsible for generating test data sets for use in nonproduction databases.
- From there, the database developer gets involved. The database developer works within the confines of the database project to write the database code, changes schema items as needed to implement the required functionality, and writes unit tests that validate those changes.
- When done with a set of changes, the database developer checks the schema changes into the Team Foundation Server source control system.
- The DBA is then reinjected into the process. The DBA reviews the changes, compares the changes to the schema and data already in production, builds a deployment package containing those changes, and then oversees the deployment of those changes in a moderated way into production.

NOTE

Scripts are nothing more than SQL statements stored in a file. They are useful because they can be executed in batch to do such things as create tables in a new database or add a canned set of stored procedures to a database. Because they are merely files, they can be transferred from computer to computer, enabling you to duplicate database structures across machines with ease.

The SQL scripts in the database project can create many of the database objects that we have already discussed: tables, views, triggers, stored procedures, and so on. Queries developed using the query/view designer can also be directly saved into a database project. In short, you use the Visual Database Tools in conjunction with a database project to create and save SQL scripts and queries.

Creating a Database Project

Database projects use the same project template system and "new project" process as all other Visual Studio project types. This means that we launch the creation process by selecting File, New and then selecting one of the templates located in the Other Languages/SQL Server category on the New Project dialog box (see Figure 13.21).

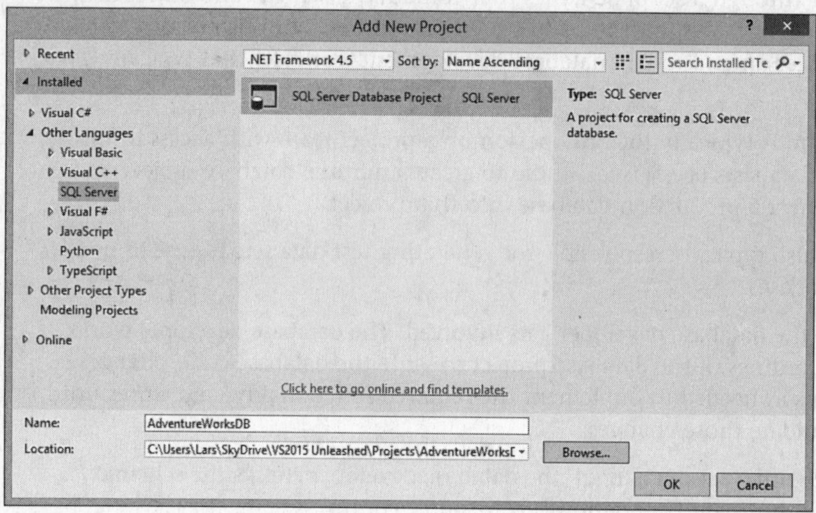

FIGURE 13.21 Selecting the database project template.

NOTE

If you are coming to Visual Studio 2015 as a prior user of Visual Studio 2010 or earlier, note the fundamental changes that have taken place with regard to the database tools. There is no longer a wizard that is launched when you create a new database project, and the number of project templates has shrunk to just the single SQL Server Database Project that comes in the currently shipping version of the SQL Server Data Tools.

NOTE

To be able to parse and validate the objects within a database project, Visual Studio needs to communicate with a local instance of SQL Server: this can be the Express Edition, Developer Edition, or Enterprise Edition of the particular database version you are targeting. If you do not have a local instance of SQL Server running, you see a dialog box at the start of the new project process prompting you to supply the path to a valid SQL Server local instance.

Importing a Database

After the project has been created, we are left with a rather sparse and empty solution tree (see Figure 13.22). We have two basic options at this point. We can create items within the project and configure the properties of the database by right-clicking the project name and running the Properties dialog, or we can import an existing database, thus pulling all of its attendant information into the project. Most database developers will want to build their initial project from an existing database. This preserves the concept of a production database being the "one version of the truth." This is a recognition of the fact that we really want our test and development database environments to mirror the production environment in terms of structure. By reverse engineering a database into its component objects, Visual Studio enables us to create copies of a database, and that, in turn, enables developers to work in their own private sandboxes without worrying about affecting the production data store.

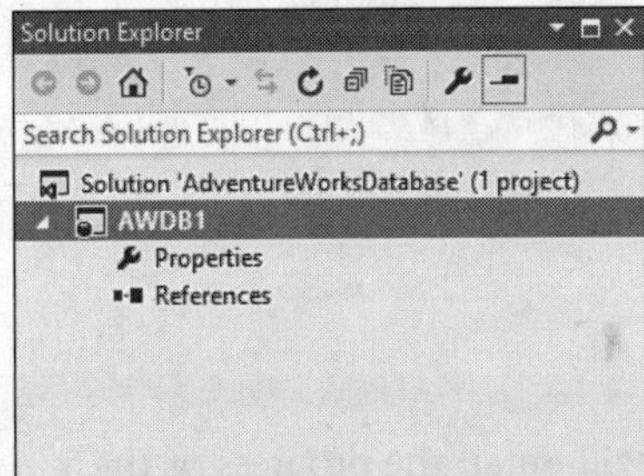

FIGURE 13.22 The initial, empty database project structure.

Let's import a database. Right-click the project, select Import, and then select Database. This launches the Import window.

The Import tool (see Figure 13.23) captures the database connection to use (effectively answering the question, "Which database should be imported?") and the various items to be imported.

At the bottom of the screen is a drop-down labeled Folder structure; the value set here dictates exactly how Visual Studio structures the project around the imported items. There are two approaches: organizing by object type and organizing by schema. For the object type approach, Visual Studio creates a schema objects folder with subfolders for your database objects such as tables and stored procedures. This is similar to the way that the Server Explorer represents a database in its tree view. The schema approach will group your project objects by the schema type that they belong to. There is also a hybrid approach, Schema/ObjectType, which will first organize by schema and then, within each schema folder, by object type. For most database implementations, the object type setting is the most useful. The exception is those cases where the database itself has multiple schemas. In those scenarios, the hybrid Schema/ObjectType option will likely be best. Because our sample `AdventureWorks` database contains multiple schemas, this is the option we will select.

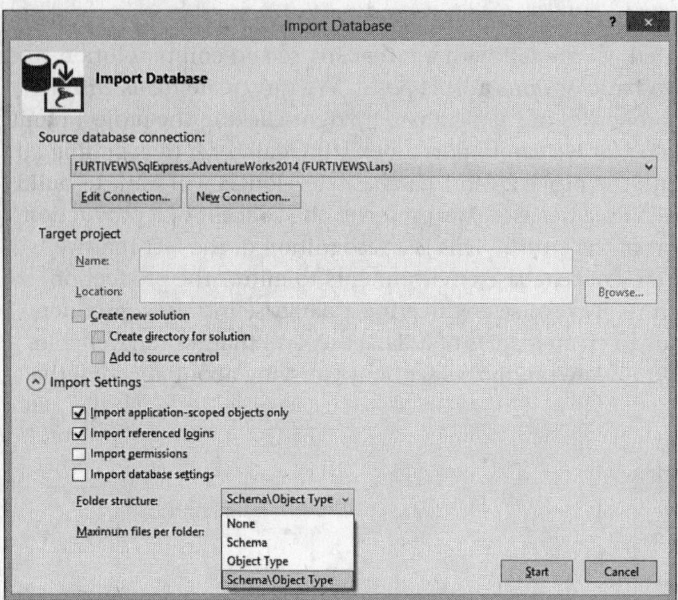

FIGURE 13.23 Importing a SQL Server database.

Click the Start button to start the import. A Status dialog will detail the progress of the import (see Figure 13.24).

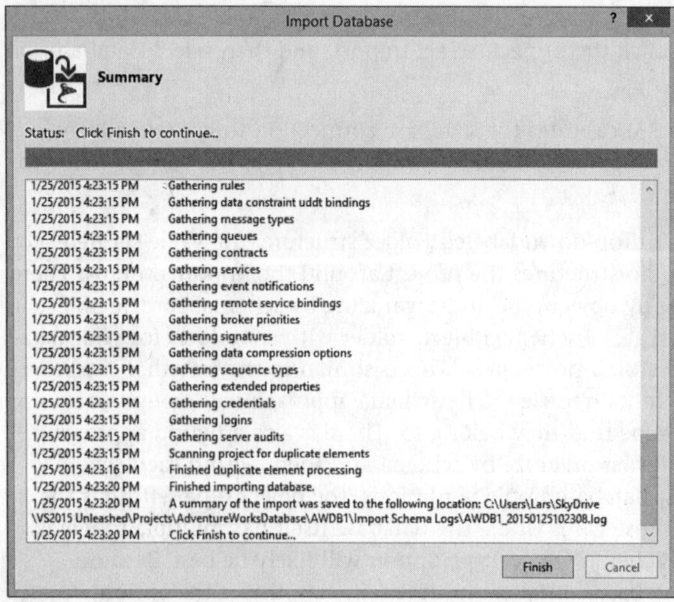

FIGURE 13.24 Importing the AdventureWorks2014 database.

At its conclusion, project items (which correspond to all the database schema items) will now exist in the project (see Figure 13.25). Note that each object in the database (be it a table, a stored procedure, an index, a key, or a constraint) is represented by a single `.sql` file. In addition to the schema files, we have folders for holding data generation plans (more on these in a bit) and pre- and post-deployment scripts. Scripts placed into the pre- and post-folders are executed just before or immediately after deployment.

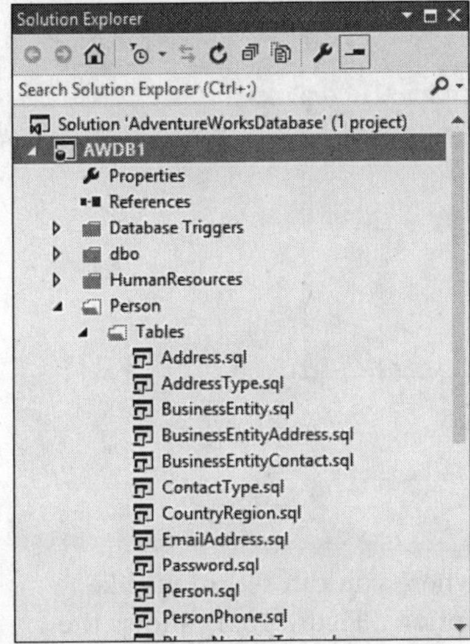

FIGURE 13.25 A database project after importing a database.

Changing the Database

With a fully populated database project, you can now make any desired changes by opening any of the generated `.sql` files and editing the file. This works the same way that object editing works using the Server Explorer or the SQL Server Object Explorer: you can edit the raw SQL commands using the SQL editor or, if you opened a table's `.sql` file, for instance, you can edit the table definition by using the designer or the SQL editor.

You can control a number of database and server options via the database project. You can access all these via the Project Properties dialog. These would rarely need to be changed by a developer (they are more likely to be within the database administrator's scope of work), but let's briefly cover what is available. First, launch the dialog by right-clicking the project, and then select Properties. The Project Settings page (see Figure 13.26) is where you can set the target deployment platform (in other words, the version of SQL Server) and general scripting options. This is also where you can set more fine-grained database options via the Database Settings button.

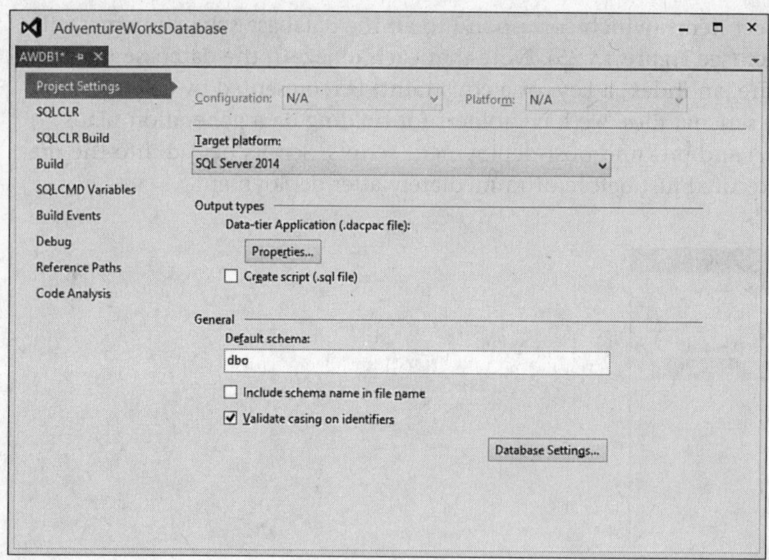

FIGURE 13.26 Database project properties.

Database Settings

Clicking the Database Settings button launches a dialog where you can set things like collation, filegroup, transaction, cursor, and text search options. Figure 13.27 shows the Operational tab of this dialog for a SQL Server 2008 database.

Building and Deploying

The final item we haven't covered is the actual act of updating a schema in a database with the schema in a database project. You use the familiar build-and-deploy paradigm leveraged by other Visual Studio project types. In the context of a database project, the build process parses all the SQL files and identifies any files that have SQL syntax errors. If the build is clean, you can now publish the database by right-clicking the project within Solution Explorer and selecting Publish (see Figure 13.28). This actually updates the target database with the schema (or creates a new database if the target database doesn't exist).

NOTE

You don't have to use Visual Studio to do the actual schema deployment to the server. By building the database project, you are generating a SQL script file with all the necessary SQL commands. You can execute that script file from within any tool that understands T-SQL (including SQL Server Management Studio itself). This is useful when the actual schema change is implemented by someone in the DBA role, who might or might not have Visual Studio installed, or who might have a specific tool that he is required to use for schema propagation.

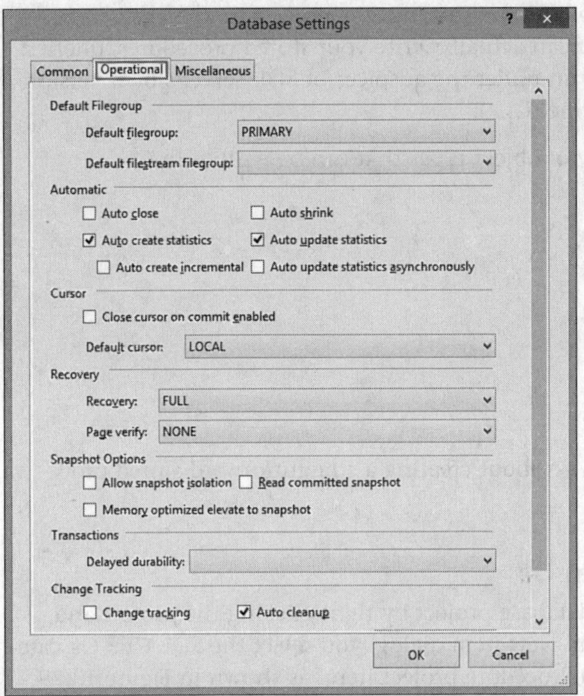

FIGURE 13.27 Setting database options.

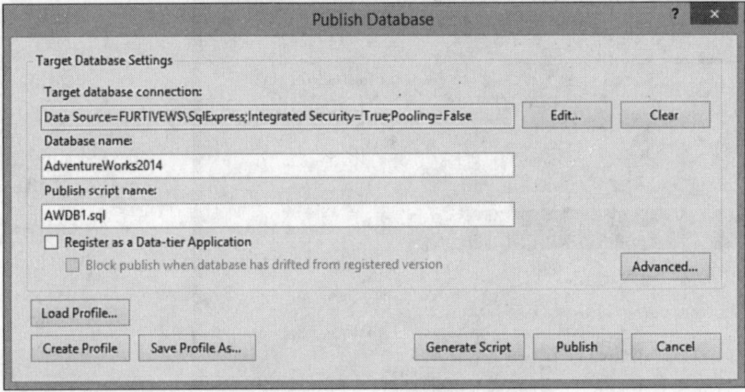

FIGURE 13.28 Publishing a database.

Creating Database Objects in Managed Code

Database objects are commonly implemented using some dialect of the SQL language. This is true with SQL Server as well, and as we have just reviewed, the Visual Studio database project allows you to craft your database objects using SQL. But using that same project, you can also design database objects using C#.

SQL Server 2005 introduced the capability of authoring SQL objects in managed code. So, instead of using Transact SQL, you can actually write your stored procedures, queries, views, and so on using C#. These are run under the auspices of SQL Server's own version of the .NET Common Language Runtime (CLR).

The SQL Server CLR supports a variety of object types that can be written in C#:

- Stored procedures
- Triggers
- Aggregates
- User-defined functions
- User-defined types

The following sections look at how to go about creating a straightforward stored procedure using C# instead of T-SQL.

Creating a Stored Procedure in C#

Add a stored procedure item to your database project by right-clicking the project and selecting Add, New Item. From the Add New Item dialog, you select the SQL CLR C# category and then the SQL CLR C# Stored Procedure project item, as shown in Figure 13.29. Let's name the stored procedure `UpdateEmployeeLogin`.

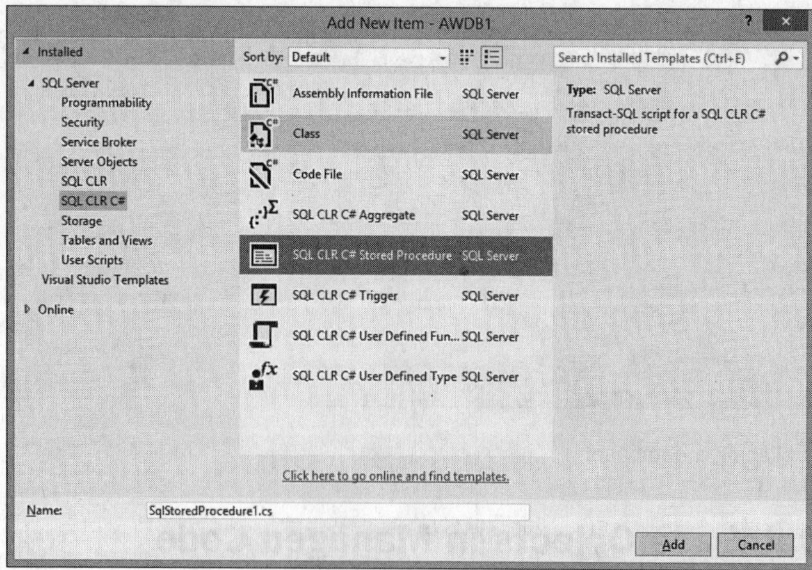

FIGURE 13.29 Adding a C# stored procedure.

A new class is added to the project. Listing 13.1 shows the base code that shows up within the new class file. You can add your custom code to the static void routine `UpdateEmployeeLogin`.

NOTE

Earlier versions of Visual Studio had a separate project type (SQL Server Project) that was used to write managed code SQL objects. With Visual Studio 2012 and the new SQL Server Data Tools, this functionality is now available directly from within the database project template. There is no need for a separate project. The single database project template will allow you to write and deploy your SQL CLR objects right alongside the more traditional T-SQL script files.

LISTING 13.1 The Start of a Managed Code Stored Procedure

```
using System;
using System.Data;
using System.Data.SqlClient;
using System.Data.SqlTypes;
using Microsoft.SqlServer.Server;


public partial class StoredProcedures
{
    [Microsoft.SqlServer.Server.SqlProcedure]
    public static void UpdateEmployeeLogin()
    {
        // Put your code here
    }
}
```

Managed code objects in SQL Server leverage the .NET Framework data classes (that is, ADO.NET) to do their work. This means that stored procedures you write will instantiate and use classes such as `SqlConnection` and `SqlCommand`. The code you write is identical to data access code that you would write from within any other .NET project type: class libraries, web projects, and Windows Forms projects. Because the common denominator is the use of ADO.NET classes, developers don't need to learn another language (such as T-SQL) to perform work in the database.

NOTE

It's beyond the scope of this chapter to cover the relative merits or disadvantages of writing your database objects in managed code as opposed to T-SQL. Check out the white-paper available on Microsoft Developer Network (MSDN) titled "Using CLR Integration in SQL Server 2005." Although it's fairly old (it was written in November 2004), it is a great treatment of this subject and is highly recommended reading.

Listing 13.2 shows a fleshed-out C# routine that updates the `AdventureWorks` Employee table with login information. None of this code is complicated, and it can be easily understood (and written) by anyone with C# data access experience.

LISTING 13.2 Managed Code for Updating Employee Login Values

```
using System;
using System.Data;
using System.Data.SqlClient;
using System.Data.SqlTypes;
using Microsoft.SqlServer.Server;


public partial class StoredProcedures
{
  [Microsoft.SqlServer.Server.SqlProcedure]
  public static void UpdateEmployeeLogin(SqlInt32 employeeId,
  SqlInt32 managerId, SqlString loginId, SqlString title,
  SqlDateTime hireDate, SqlBoolean currentFlag)
  {
      using (SqlConnection conn =
          new SqlConnection("context connection=true"))
      {
        SqlCommand UpdateEmployeeLoginCommand =
          new SqlCommand();

        UpdateEmployeeLoginCommand.CommandText =
            "update HumanResources.Employee SET ManagerId = " +
         managerId.ToString() +
            ", LoginId = '" + loginId.ToString() + "'" +
            ", Title = '" + title.ToString() + "'" +
            ", HireDate = '" + hireDate.ToString() + "'" +
            ", CurrentFlag = " + currentFlag.ToString() +
            " WHERE EmployeeId = " + employeeId.ToString();

        UpdateEmployeeLoginCommand.Connection = conn;

        conn.Open();
        UpdateEmployeeLoginCommand.ExecuteNonQuery();
        conn.Close();

      }
  }
};
```

One line of code, however, deserves a more detailed explanation. The `SqlConnection` object is created like this.

```
SqlConnection conn = new SqlConnection("context connection=true")
```

The connection string `"context connection=true"` tells the data provider engine that the connection should be created in the same context as the calling application. Because this routine is running inside a database, that means you are connecting to the host database and running within the context (transactional and otherwise) of the calling application. Because you are piggybacking on the context of the database that the routine is running in, you don't need to hard-code a full SQL connection string here.

For comparison purposes, Listing 13.3 shows the same update query implemented in T-SQL.

LISTING 13.3 T-SQL for Updating Employee Login Values

```
ALTER PROCEDURE [HumanResources].[uspUpdateEmployeeLogin]
    @EmployeeID [int],
    @ManagerID [int],
    @LoginID [nvarchar](256),
    @Title [nvarchar](50),
    @HireDate [datetime],
    @CurrentFlag [dbo].[Flag]
WITH EXECUTE AS CALLER
AS
BEGIN
    SET NOCOUNT ON;

    BEGIN TRY
        UPDATE [HumanResources].[Employee]
        SET [ManagerID] = @ManagerID
            ,[LoginID] = @LoginID
            ,[Title] = @Title
            ,[HireDate] = @HireDate
            ,[CurrentFlag] = @CurrentFlag
        WHERE [EmployeeID] = @EmployeeID;
    END TRY
    BEGIN CATCH
        EXECUTE [dbo].[uspLogError];
    END CATCH;
END;
```

Building and Deploying the Stored Procedure

When you build your SQL Server project, the typical compilation process takes place. Assuming that your code will build, you can now deploy the resulting assembly to the database, as we have already seen by using the Publish command on the project.

After the assembly has been deployed, you can test it by calling it from an application or from a query window. For detailed information on how to call and write managed assemblies, consult the SQL Server Books Online.

Binding Controls to Data

You have now seen all the various ways you can use Visual Studio to create and manage databases. The following sections look at the tools available for consuming data within Windows forms, WPF, or web applications.

An Introduction to Data Binding

There is a common problem and solution pattern at hand with applications that front databases. Typically, data has to be fetched from the database into the application, and the application's user interface has to be updated to display the data in an appropriate manner. For large data sets, the concept of paging comes into play. Because it is inefficient to load in, say, a 100MB data set, a paging mechanism needs to be pressed into action to enable the user to move forward and back through the data "stream." After the data has safely made it into the application's UI, the application-to-database flow needs to be handled. For any pieces of data that have been changed, those changes have to be reconciled and committed back into the database.

Data binding is the term given to the implementation of a design pattern that handles all facets of this round trip of data from a data structure, into an application's controls, and back again. Although the data structure is most commonly a database, it could be any sort of container object that holds data, such as an array or a collection. .NET further stratifies the concepts of data binding into simple data binding and complex data binding. Both of these terms refer to a control's intrinsic capabilities in the larger context of the data-binding process.

Simple Data Binding

Simple data binding is the capability for a control to bind to and display a single data element within a larger data set. A TextBox control is a great example of a control commonly used in simple data-binding scenarios. You might use a TextBox, for example, to display the last name of an employee as it is stored within the employee table of a database.

Support for simple data binding is widespread throughout both the Windows and web forms controls. When you use the built-in capabilities of the Windows and Web Forms Designer, it is trivial to add a group of controls to a form and simple-bind them to a data set (more on this in a bit).

Complex Data Binding

The term *complex data binding* refers to the capability of a control to display multiple data elements at one time. You can think of this as a "multirow" capability. If a control can be leveraged to view multiple rows of data at one time, it supports complex data binding.

The DataGridView control (for Windows forms) and DataGrid control (for web forms) are premier examples of controls that were purpose-built to handle tabular (multirow and multicolumn) data.

Although the internals necessary to implement data binding are messy, complex, and hard to understand, for the most part the Visual Studio tools have abstracted the cost of implementing data binding out to a nice and easy drag-and-drop model. Now let's look at how to rapidly build out support for round-trip data binding.

Autogenerating Bound Windows Forms Controls

Although there are various ways to approach and implement data-bound controls with Visual Studio, they all involve the same basic two steps:

1. Establish a data source.
2. Map the data-source members to controls or control properties.

From there, the Visual Studio Form Designers can generate the correct controls and place them on the form. All the data-binding code is handled for you; you just need to worry about the layout, positioning, and UI aspects of the controls.

As you might imagine, your form can have controls that use simple data binding or complex data binding or a mix of both. Now you're ready to look at the steps involved with creating a series of controls that leverage both simple and complex data binding to display information from the `AdventureWorks` Employee table. In this scenario, you work with the Windows Forms Designer. The ASP.NET Web Forms Designer works in a similar fashion, and you have a chance to investigate drag-and-drop approaches for data binding in the web environment in just a bit. As we have already established, the first step is selecting a data source.

Selecting a Data Source

In Visual Studio, make sure you are working inside a Windows Forms Application project and use the Data Sources window to select a data source. If this window isn't already visible, select View, Other Windows, Data Sources. If your current project doesn't have any defined data sources, you need to create one. Click the Add New Data Source button in the toolbar of the window to start the Data Source Configuration Wizard. On the first page of this wizard (see Figure 13.30), select the type of the data source. There are four options here:

- **Database**—The data source resides as a table within a relational database.
- **Service**—The data source is a web service that returns the data to be bound to the form controls.
- **Object**—The data source is an object that provides the data. (This is useful when a business object from another layer of the application is responsible for delivering the data to the form.)
- **SharePoint**—The data source is an object that is hosted within a SharePoint site.

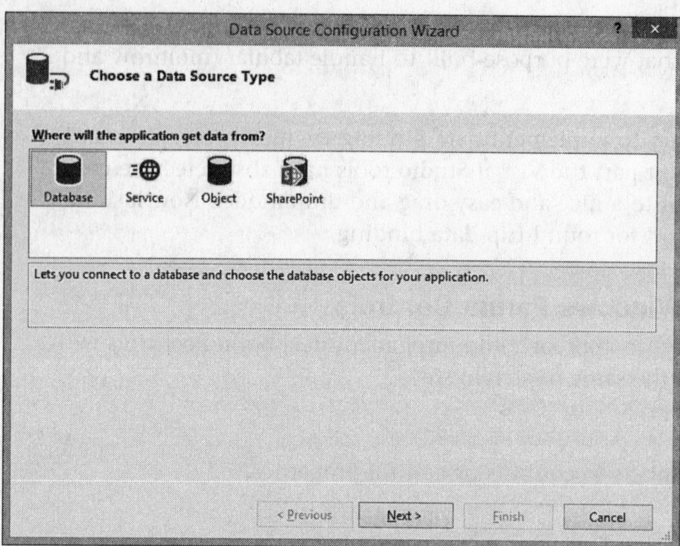

FIGURE 13.30 Choosing the data source type.

Because the concepts of data binding are most easily understood within the context of a database, we use the database data-source type as the underpinning for our walk-throughs in this chapter.

If you have selected the database data source type, the second page of the wizard focuses on selecting the type of data model you use. Prior versions of Visual Studio simply enabled you to model your data using data sets. Visual Studio now also enables you to build an Entity Data Model and use that as a data source for your binding. Entity Data Models are a feature of the Entity Framework, which we discuss later in this chapter. Regardless of the model you select, you need to indicate where the model gets its data (via connection string, and so on) and what data should be pulled into the model from the source database.

Select DataSet, and then click through the next two pages of the wizard, which will capture the connection and connection string to use. The final page of the wizard enables you to select which of the objects in the database should be used for the source data. You can select from any of the data elements present in any of the various tables, views, stored procedures, or user-defined functions in the database. For the purposes of this example, we have selected a DataSet model that pulls its data from the `AdventureWorks` database, and we have selected a few employee table data columns that are of interest: `BusinessEntityID`, `LoginID`, `HireDate`, `rowguid`, `BirthDate`, `Gender`, `SalariedFlag`, `VacationHours`, `SickLeaveHours`, and `CurrentFlag`.

At the conclusion of the wizard, your selected data source is visible in the Data Sources window (see Figure 13.31).

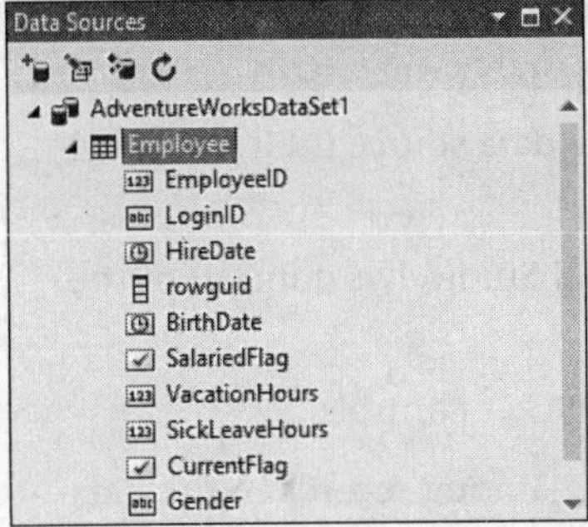

FIGURE 13.31 The Data Sources window.

NOTE

If you have chosen to use a DataSet as your data model, behind the scenes Visual Studio is really just using the data source information collected in the Data Source Configuration Wizard to create a typed data set. This data set is then stored as a project item in the current project.

With the data source in place, you're ready to move on to the next step: mapping the data-source elements to controls on your form.

Mapping Data Sources to Controls

The really quick and easy way to create your data-bound controls is to let Visual Studio do it for you. From the Data Sources window, click the drop-down button on the data-source name to reveal a menu (see Figure 13.32).

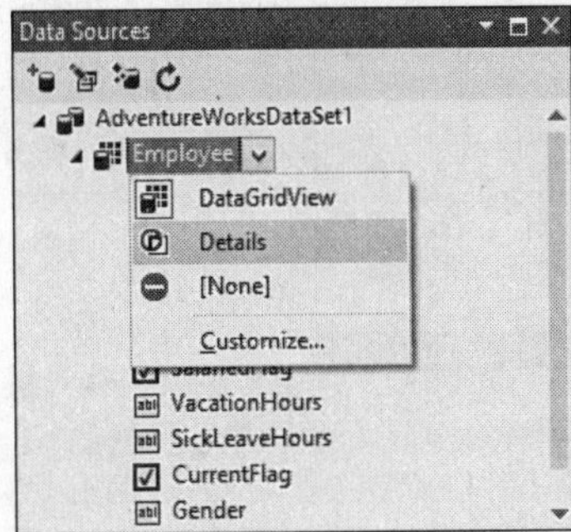

FIGURE 13.32 Changing the data table mapping.

This menu enables you to set the control generation parameters and really answers the question of which controls you want generated based on the table in the data source. By setting this to DataGridView, you can generate a DataGridView control for viewing and editing your data source. The Details setting enables you to generate a series of simple data-bound controls for viewing or editing data in the data source.

For this example, select Details, and then drag and drop the data source itself from the Data Sources window and onto a blank form.

Figure 13.33 shows the results. In just two short steps, Visual Studio has done all of the following for you:

- Autogenerated a set of Label, TextBox, and DataTimePicker controls
- Autogenerated a tool strip with controls for navigating among records in the data source, saving changes made to a record, deleting a record, and inserting a new record
- Created all the necessary code behind the scenes to establish a connection to the data source, read from the data source, and commit changes to the data source

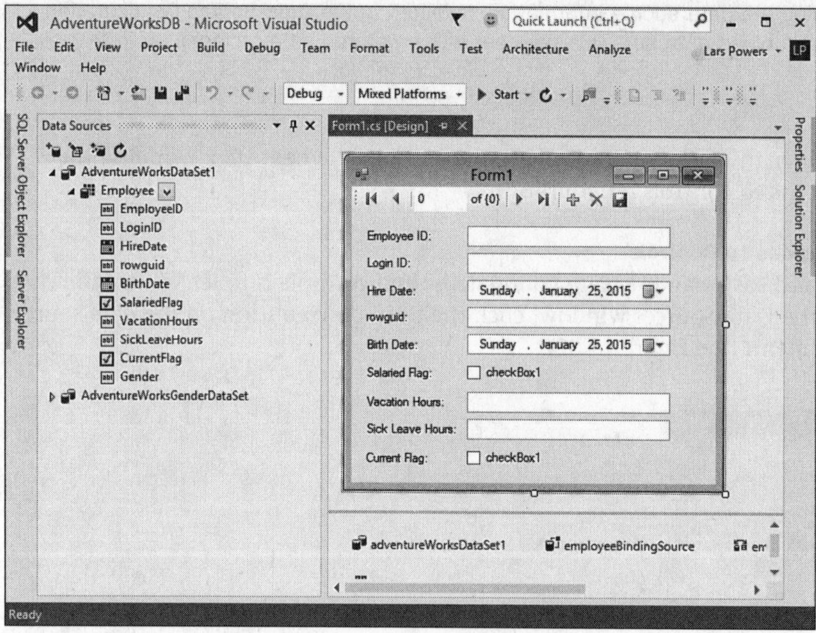

FIGURE 13.33 Auto-generated controls: viewing Employee data.

You have essentially created an entire data-enabled application from scratch with absolutely no coding on your part.

The approach of using simple data binding might not fit into the user interface design, so you always have the option of working in the complex data-binding world and using the DataGridView as an alternative. Figure 13.34 shows the results of autogenerating a DataGridView instance using this same process.

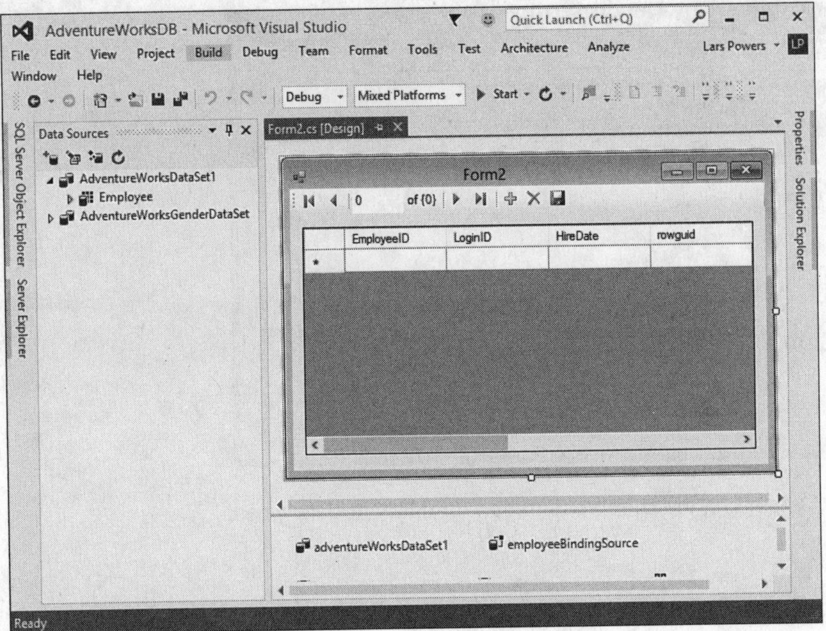

FIGURE 13.34 An autogenerated DataGridView.

Customizing Data-Source Mappings Refer again to Figure 13.31 and look at the individual data elements that show up under the Employee data source. Each of these is displayed with a name and an icon. The name is, of course, the name of the data element as defined in the database. The icon represents the default mapping of that data type to a .NET control. For example, the `Title` field maps to a TextBox control, and the `BirthDate` field maps to a DataTimePicker control. Visual Studio actually attempts to provide the best control for any given data type. But feel free to manually indicate the specific control you want used. If you want to display the value of the `EmployeeID` column in a label instead of a text box (in recognition of the fact that you cannot edit this value), it would be easy enough to change this before generating the controls by selecting the `EmployeeID` column in the Data Sources window and then clicking the drop-down arrow to select Label instead of TextBox.

In addition to changing the control to data type mapping on an individual level, you can affect the general default mappings that are in place by selecting the Customize option from that same drop-down menu. The Visual Studio Options dialog box opens with the Windows Forms Designer page selected. Using the settings there (see Figure 13.35), you can specify the default control type that you want to apply for each recognized data type.

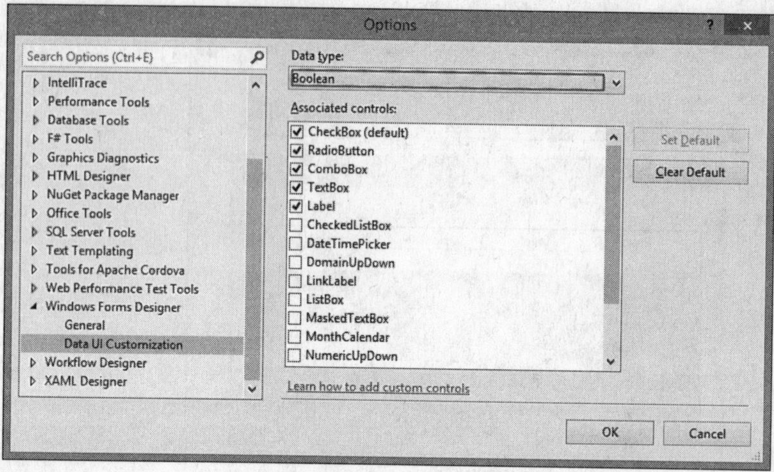

FIGURE 13.35 Customizing the UI representation for different data types.

Editing Typed Data Sets

There is a designer provided solely for editing (and creating) typed data sets within Visual Studio: the data set designer. This designer launches automatically when you open a DataSet project item such as the `AdventureWorksEmployeeDataSet.xsd` file that we just created when investigating data binding.

NOTE

Typed `DataSet` objects can be huge productivity enhancers over a normal data set: instead of using indexes into collections, you can reference tables and columns by their actual names. In addition, IntelliSense works with typed `DataSet` members, making coding against large data hierarchies much easier.

You can use the data set designer to easily tweak data sets by changing any of the various constituent parts, including the queries used to populate the data set. Figure 13.36 shows the previously created `AdventureWorksEmployeeDataSet` open in the data set designer.

Note that each piece of the data set is visually represented here, and we can interact with those pieces to effect changes. For instance, if we want to alter the query we originally constructed using the Data Set Configuration Wizard, we right-click the `Employee` table on the design surface and select Configure to relaunch the query editor.

In the scenario we have been discussing, we are wiring the data set directly to the results from a SQL query, but we can also use the data set designer to create "unbound" new data sets. Adding a DataSet project item to our project enables us to start with a blank slate, adding tables, queries, and so on to the data set to satisfy any storage requirements (or data retrieval requirements) that our application might have. This is especially useful for applications that read and write data but don't necessarily interact with a database. These data set files can be used as simple file storage that you can easily bind later to a relational database.

FIGURE 13.36 The data set designer.

Manually Binding Windows Forms Controls

In many situations, you don't want Visual Studio to create your data-bound controls for you, or you might need to bind existing controls to a data source. Data binding in these cases is just as simple and starts with the same step: creating or selecting a data source. Some controls, such as the DataGridView, have smart tag options for selecting a data source. Others don't have intrinsic data dialog boxes associated with them but can be bound to data just as easily by working, again, with the Data Sources window.

Binding the DataGridView

Grab a DataGridView from the Toolbox and drag it onto the form's surface. After you've created the control, select its smart tag glyph and use the drop-down at the top of the task list to select the data source to bind to (see Figure 13.37).

With a data source selected, you have again managed to develop a fully functional application with two-way database access. All the code to handle the population of the grid and to handle committing changes back to the database has been written for you.

Customizing Cell Edits The power of the DataGridView lies in its capability to both quickly bind to and display data in a tabular format and provide a highly customized editing experience. As one small example of what is possible in terms of cell editing, follow through with the `Employee` table example. When you auto-generated form controls to handle `Employee` table edits, you ended up with DateTimePicker controls to accommodate the date- and time-based data in the table. With the DataGridView, the cell editing experience is a simple text box experience. Each cell contains text, and you can edit the text and save it to the database. But you can provide a more tailored editing experience. You can use various stock controls (such as the DataGridViewButtonColumn, DataGridViewComboBoxColumn, and others that inherit from DataGridViewColumn; see Chapter 20, "Building Windows Forms Applications") to display data within the columns of the grid.

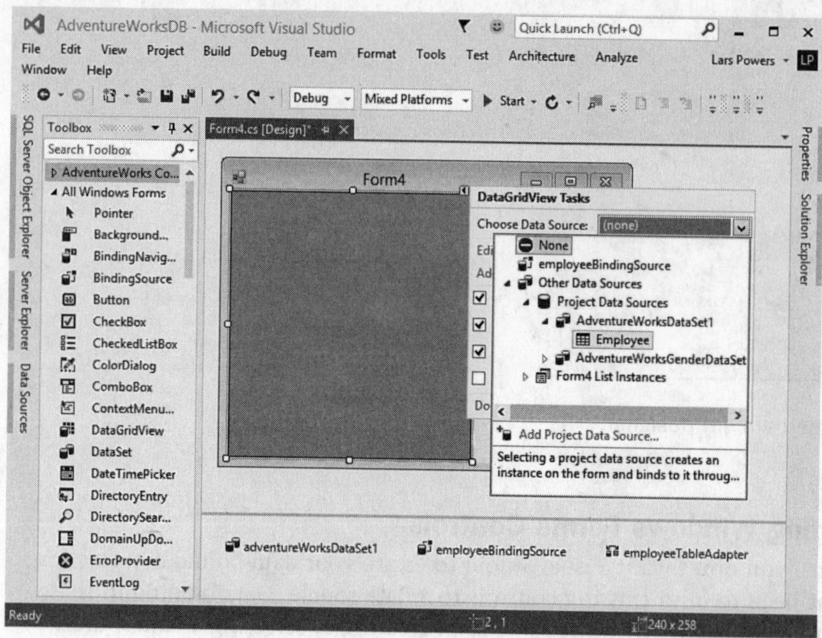

FIGURE 13.37 Selecting a data source for a DataGridView.

For example, you can use the `DataGridViewComboBoxColumn` class to provide a drop-down edit for the Gender column in the grid. To do this, you first need to change the default column type. Select the grid control, open the smart tag glyph, and select the Edit Columns action. In the Edit Columns dialog box, find the column for the employee gender data and change its column type to `DataGridViewComboBoxColumn` (see Figure 13.38).

With the column type changed, you now need to specify how the grid should retrieve the list of possible values to display in the drop-down; the grid is smart enough to already know to use the underlying gender values from the table to select the one value to display in the grid. To handle the list of possible values, you could hard-code them in the column, or you could wire up a separate query (something along the lines of `SELECT DISTINCT(Gender) FROM Employees`) and have that query provide the list of possible values. Because constructing another query or data source is easy and doesn't lead to a brittle hard-coded solution, that's the approach we investigate here. To create a query to feed the combo-box column, you can visit the Data Sources window, select the Add New Data Source action, and follow the same steps you followed before to add the original Employee data source. This time, though, select only the Gender column.

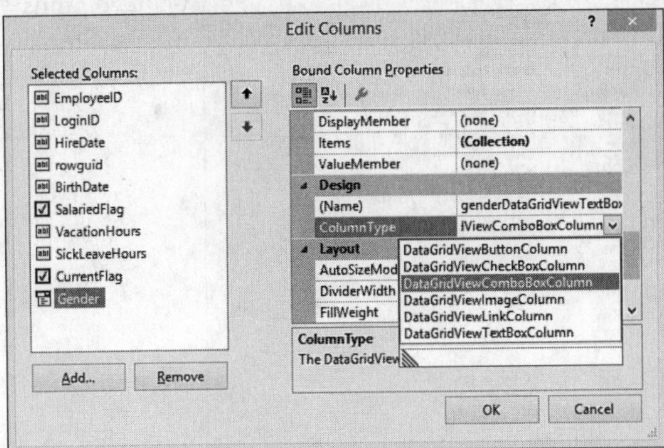

FIGURE 13.38 Changing the column type.

After the data source is created, right-click the data source and select Edit DataSet with Designer. We use the data set designer to modify our query appropriately. In the designer (see Figure 13.39), you can see the Fill query and TableAdapter used to populate the data set. If you click the query (that is, click the last row in the table graphic in the designer window), you can use the Properties window to directly edit the SQL for the query. By modifying this to reflect `SELECT DISTINCT` syntax, you can return the valid gender values for inclusion in the grid.

There are two more steps needed. We need a new binding source to connect to our gender data set, and then we need to set our gender column drop-down to point to that binding source. We already have one binding source that was automatically added to our form when we added the DataGridView and connected it to a data set. Now we need another binding source to connect to the new data set that is retrieving the distinct gender values. From the Toolbox window, under the Data category, select the BindingSource component and drag it onto your form. This will add a new binding instance to the component tray. Click the binding source, and in the property window set its data source to the gender data set that we just created.

Last step: go back to the GridView control, use the smart tag to select the Edit columns option, go back to the `Gender` column, and then set the `DataSource`, `DisplayMember`, and `ValueMember` properties. The `DataSource` will be set to the binding source we just configured (here, we have called it simply `genderBindingSource`), as shown in Figure 13.40.

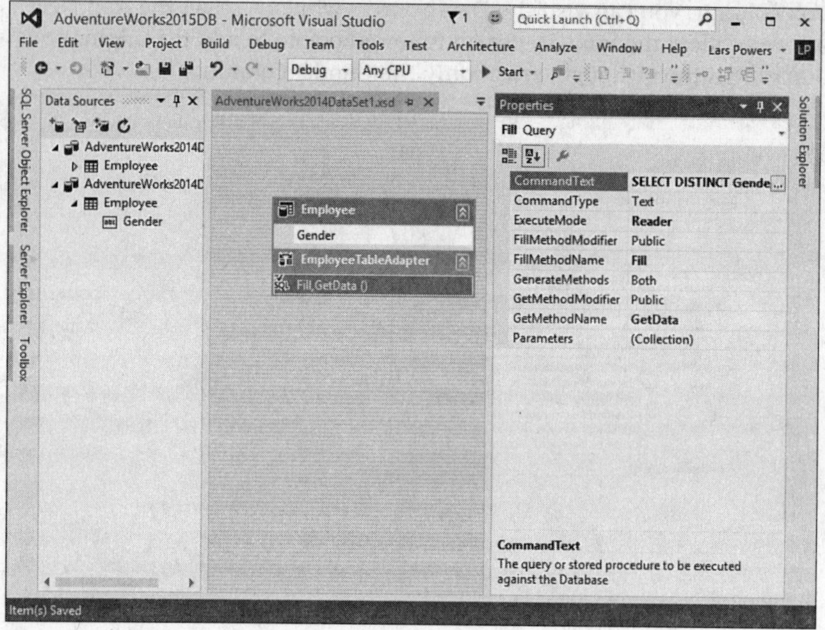

FIGURE 13.39 Changing the query for a data source.

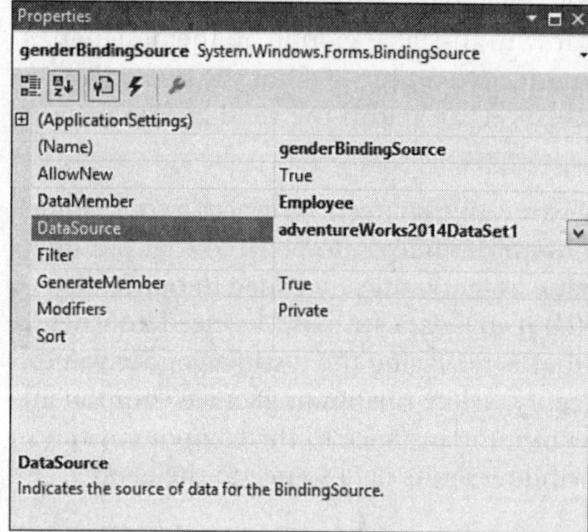

FIGURE 13.40 Configuring the binding source.

Figure 13.41 shows the results. If you need to implement a cell edit control that doesn't currently exist, you can create your own by inheriting from the DataGridViewColumn base control. This employee grid could benefit from a DateTimePicker control for the date- and time-based data, such as birth date and hire date.

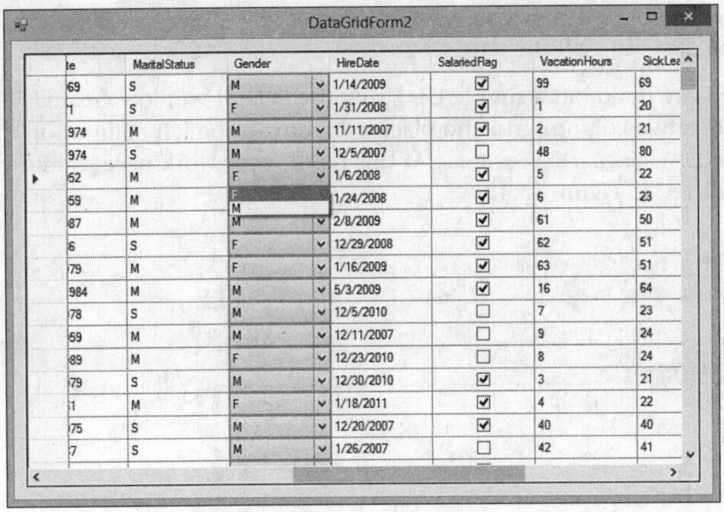

FIGURE 13.41 A data bound drop-down within a DataGridView.

NOTE

If you look in the MSDN documentation, there is a specific example of creating a DataGridViewDateTimePickerColumn control and then wiring it up within the grid. Search for "How to: Host Controls in Windows Forms DataGridView Cells."

Binding Other Controls

For other controls that don't have convenient access to binding via their smart tag, you can leverage the Data Sources window. Drag a data source from the Data Sources window and drop it onto an existing control. The designer creates a new binding source, sets it appropriately, and then makes an entry in the control's `DataBinding` collection. If you try to drag a data element onto a control that doesn't match up (for instance, dragging a character field onto a check box), the drop operation isn't allowed.

Data Binding in WPF Applications

Just as with Windows Forms applications, Visual Studio supports drag-and-drop data binding with WPF projects. The process is identical to the one we just covered for binding Windows Forms controls; we first need a data source added to our project. To change things up a bit, let's quickly build out a form that shows purchase orders and their detail line items.

First, create a new WPF project. Refer to Chapter 21, "Building WPF Applications," if you want to first refresh your knowledge of the WPF project type and its designers/editors. Add the data sources in the same fashion as we did previously by using the Data Sources Wizard. This time, instead of employee data, let's focus on purchase order data. From the

`AdventureWorks` database, select both the `PurchaseOrderHeader` and `PurchaseOrderDetail` tables to be included in the data set. Call the data set `AdventureWorksPurchasingDataSet`.

With the data source added, we build out a simple UI. Using the default window created for us, MainWindow, create a two-column grid and place a list box in the left column of the grid. Name the list box `listBoxPurchaseOrders`. At this point, your workspace should look similar to the one depicted in Figure 13.42.

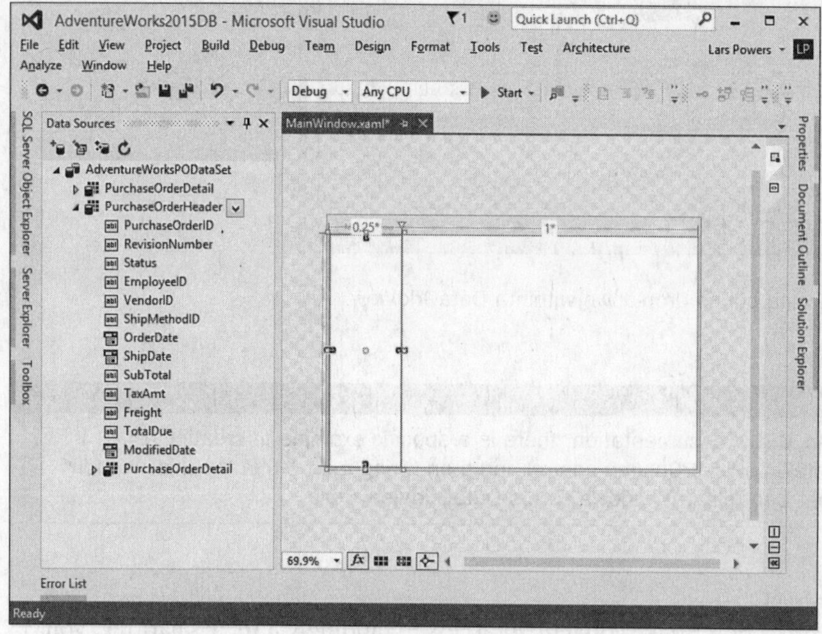

FIGURE 13.42 Working with a WPF window and data sources.

Now drag the `PurchaseOrderID` field from the `PurchaseOrderHeader` data source to the list box. Although nothing appears to have changed visually, the list box has actually been bound with a few lines of XAML:

- First, our data source has been referenced as a resource with the key `adventure-WorksPurchasingDataSet` (picking up from the name we gave the data set in the wizard).
- Additionally, a `CollectionViewSource` has been added with the appropriate binding path into the data set to pick up the `Department` table data.
- Finally, the `DisplayMemberPath` and `ItemsSource` properties have been set on the list box itself.

Besides the XAML modifications that we made, a series of statements have been added to the code file, within the `Window_Loaded` event handler. These statements are responsible for loading the data from the database via a table adapter object.

Listing 13.4 shows the current state of our XAML.

LISTING 13.4 XAML with Visual Studio-Generated Data Binding

```
<Window x:Class="AdventureWorksWPF.MainWindow"
        xmlns="http://schemas.microsoft.com/winfx/2006/xaml/presentation"
        xmlns:x="http://schemas.microsoft.com/winfx/2006/xaml"
        Title="MainWindow" Height="350" Width="525"
        xmlns:my="clr-namespace:AdventureWorksWPF"
        Loaded="Window_Loaded">
    <Window.Resources>
        <my:AdventureWorksPurchasingDataSet
            x:Key=" adventureWorksPurchasingDataSet" />
        <CollectionViewSource x:Key="purchaseOrderHeaderViewSource"
                              Source="{Binding Path=PurchaseOrderHeader,
            Source={StaticResource  adventureWorksPurchasingDataSet}}" />
    </Window.Resources>
    <Grid DataContext="{StaticResource purchaseOrderHeaderViewSource}">
        <Grid.ColumnDefinitions>
            <ColumnDefinition Width="150" />
            <ColumnDefinition Width="*" />
        </Grid.ColumnDefinitions>
        <ListBox Grid.Column="0" Margin="5"
                 X:Name="listBoxPurchaseOrders"
                 VerticalAlignment="Stretch"
                 DisplayMemberPath="PurchaseOrderID" ItemsSource="{Binding}"

        />
    </Grid>
</Window>
```

If we run the application at this stage, we see that we have a list of all the purchase order IDs displayed in our list box (see Figure 13.43).

Now every time we select a purchase order ID in the list box, we want to see its line items in the right column of our window. This is another, easy drag-and-drop operation requiring no hand-coding on our part. Grab the `PurchaseOrderDetail` data source column that sits under the `PurchaseOrderHeader` data source, and drag it over into the rightmost column of our WPF window. (Figure 13.44 shows the result within our WPF designer of this drag-drop action.) This has the net effect of creating a DataGrid control bound to the `PurchaseOrderDetail` rows that correspond to the currently selected `PurchaseOrderHeader` object in the list box.

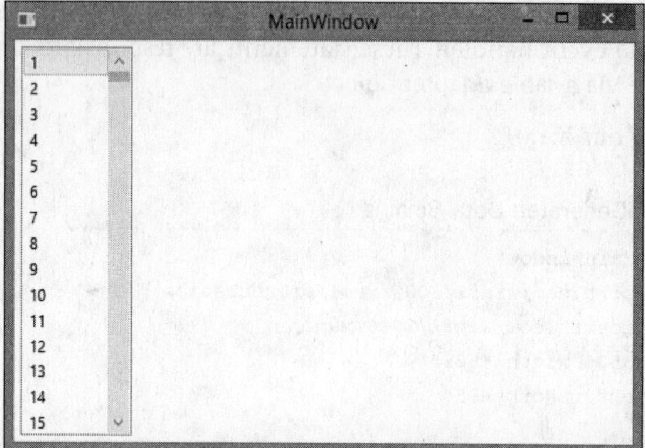

FIGURE 13.43 A data bound drop-down within a DataGridView.

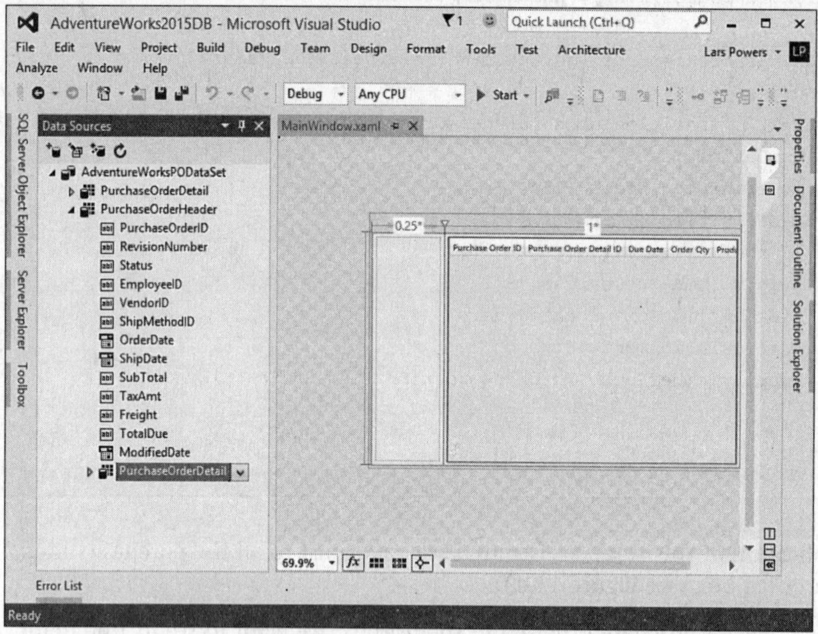

FIGURE 13.44 Adding a master-detail data source to the WPF window.

It's important that you grab the correct `PurchaseOrderDetail` column object from the Data Sources window; by selecting the one that lies *under* the `PurchaseOrderHeader`, you are also grabbing the foreign key relationship between those two tables in the database, and that provides the context necessary for the WPF designer and editor to wire up the correct code to respond to selections in the list box and display related records in the `DataGrid`.

Figure 13.45 shows the complete app that was accomplished with absolutely no coding required!

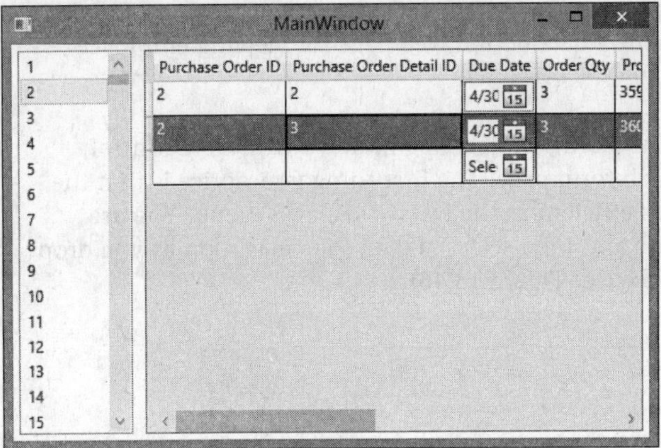

FIGURE 13.45 A master-detail window built entirely by dragging and dropping data sources.

Data Binding with Web Controls

Although the general concepts remain the same, data-binding web-based controls is a slightly different game than in the Windows Forms or WPF world. The first obvious difference is that data sources for web forms are implemented by data-source controls in the `System.Web.UI.WebControls` namespace; there is no concept of the Data Sources window with web applications. Because of this, instead of starting with a data source, you need to start with a data control and then work to attach that control to a data source.

Selecting a Data Control

You work with five primary controls in a web application to deliver data-bound functionality:

- **GridView control**—Provides a tabular presentation similar to the DataGridView control.
- **DetailsView control**—Displays a single record from a data source; with a DetailsView control, every column in the data source shows up as a row in the control.
- **FormView control**—Functions in the same way as the DetailsView control with the following exception: it doesn't have a built-in "default" for the way that the data is displayed. Instead, you need to provide a template to tell the control exactly how you want the data rendered onto the web page.
- **Repeater control**—Simply renders a list of individual items fetched from the attached data source. The specifics of how this rendering looks are controlled via templates.

- **DataList control**—Displays rows of information from a data source. The display aspects are fully customizable and include header and footer elements.

For demonstration purposes, let's go back to working with the `AdventureWorks` Employee table and see how you can implement a data-bound web page for viewing employee records.

Using the GridView First, with a Web Forms project open, drag a GridView control from the Toolbox onto an empty web form page. The first thing you notice is that the GridView's smart tag menu is just as efficient as the DataGridView's menu. You are directly prompted to select (or create and then select) a data source as soon as you drop the control onto the web page surface (see Figure 13.46).

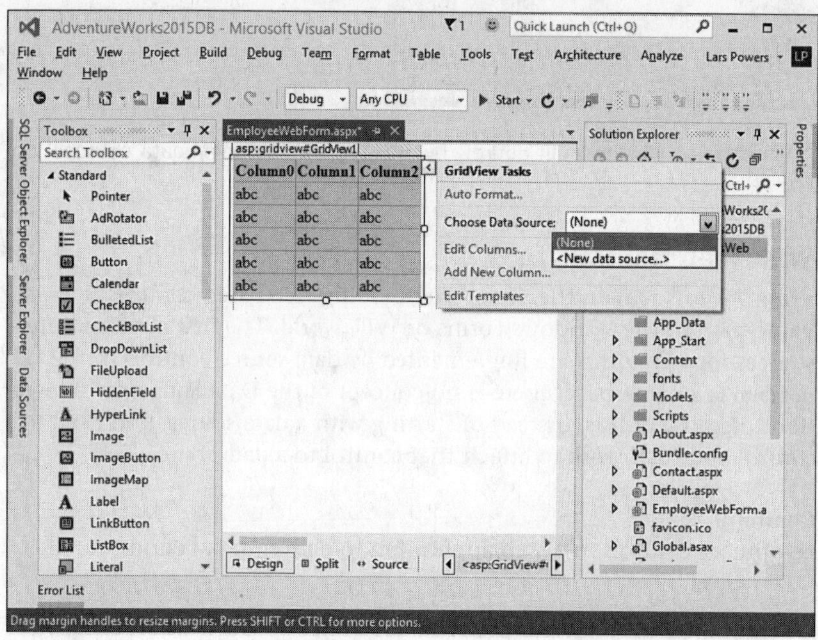

FIGURE 13.46 Adding a GridView to a blank web page.

The <New Data Source...> option uses a similar data-source wizard to collect information about your data source and add it to the project.

Once again, because of the data-binding support in the designer, you now have a fully functional application without writing a line of code. Figure 13.47 shows this admittedly ugly web page with live employee data.

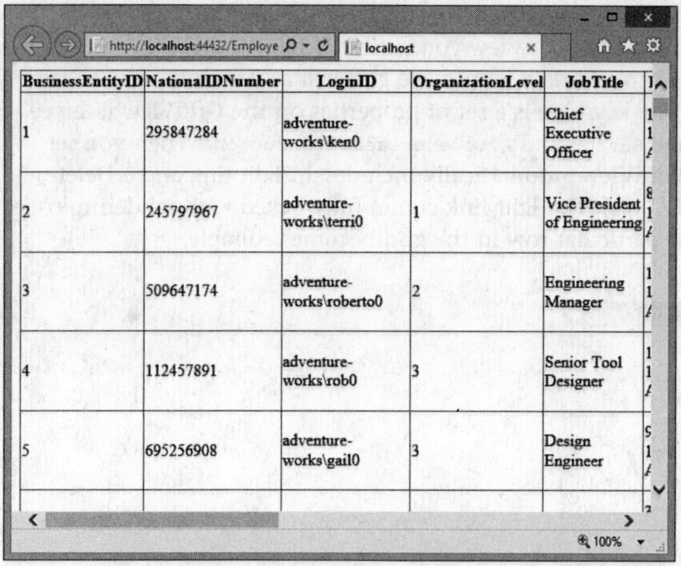

FIGURE 13.47 Live employee records in the GridView.

Thankfully, you can just as easily put some window dressing on the table and make it look nice. By using the GridView's smart tag menu again, you can select the Auto Format option to apply several flavors of window dressing to the table (see Figure 13.48). And, of course, by applying a style sheet, you can really affect the look and feel of the page.

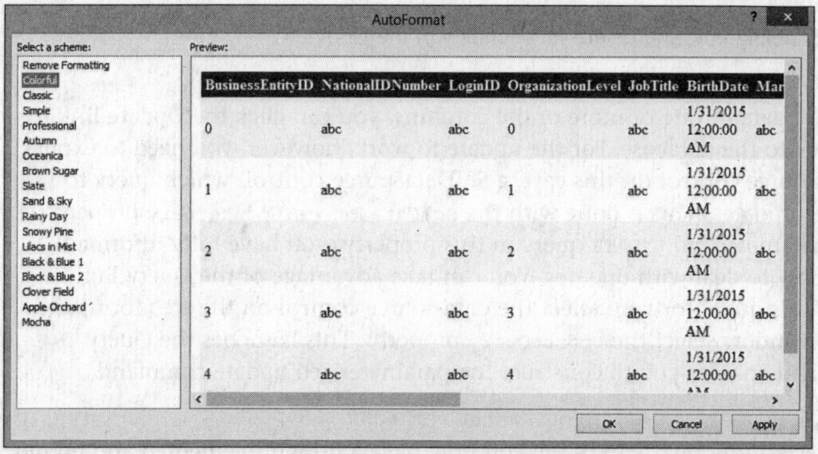

FIGURE 13.48 Auto-formatting options for the GridView control.

Updating Data with the GridView Creating the web grid was easy, and no data access coding was required on your part. The GridView you currently have is great for static reporting, but what if you want to edit data within the grid just as you did earlier in the Windows forms application? The key here is a set of properties on the GridView (see Figure 13.49): `AutoGenerateEditButton` and `AutoGenerateDeleteButton`. When you set these properties to `True`, the GridView automatically includes an Edit link and a Delete link (shown on the previous figures). The Edit link comes fully baked with rendering code so that when it is clicked, that particular row in the grid becomes editable.

FIGURE 13.49 Enabling edit and delete functionality in the GridView.

After changing the data in one or more of the columns, you can click the Update link to send the data back to the database. For the update to work, however, you need to explicitly tell the data-source control (in this case, a SqlDataSource control) which query to use for processing updates. This is done with the `SqlDataSource.UpdateQuery` property. By specifying a parameterized `UPDATE` query in this property, you have fully informed the data source how to deal with updates. You can take advantage of the Query Builder window to write this query for you: select the data-source control on the web form, and in the Properties window select the `UpdateQuery` property. This launches the Query Builder window and enables you to construct the parameterized update command (see Figure 13.50).

With that last piece of the puzzle in place, you now have a fully implemented and bound grid control that pages data in from the database and commits changes back to the database.

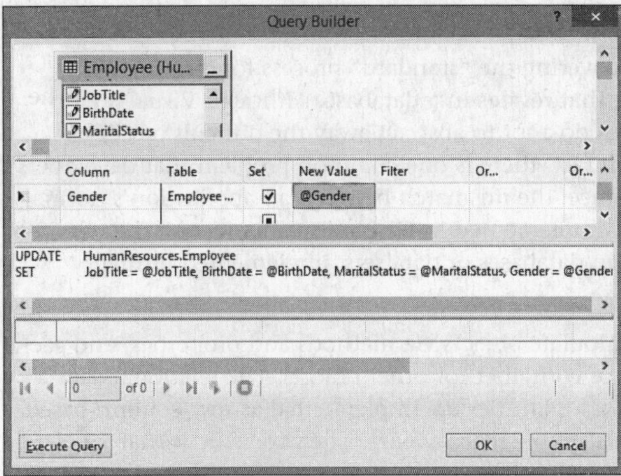

FIGURE 13.50 Setting the `UpdateQuery` property using the Query Builder dialog.

NOTE

To implement delete capabilities for a record, you perform the same steps using the `DeleteQuery` property and setting the `AutoGenerateDeleteButton` to `True`.

Data-Source Controls

As mentioned, data sources are surfaced through one or more data-source controls placed onto the web form. In the GridView example, the designer actually adds a SqlDataSource control to the form for you (based on your creation of a new DB-based data source). But there is nothing preventing you from adding one or more data-source controls to a web page directly. Just drag the control from the Toolbox onto the form surface. Table 13.2 itemizes the available data-source controls.

TABLE 13.2 Data-Source Controls

Control	Description
ObjectDataSource	Exposes other classes as data sources.
SqlDataSource	Exposes a relational database as a data source. Microsoft SQL Server and Oracle databases can be accessed natively; ODBC and OLE DB access is also supported.
AccessDataSource	Exposes a Microsoft Access database as a data source.
XmlDataSource	Exposes an XML file as a data source.
SiteMapDataSource	Exposes an ASP.NET site map as a data source.

After configuring the data source, you can visit any data-aware control and bind it to the source.

Object Relational Mapping

We have spent most of this chapter covering the "standard" process for creating .NET applications that read and write data that resides in a database. Although Visual Studio and the ADO.NET libraries themselves do a lot to abstract away the difficult pieces of that process, problems still remain. In fact, there is one common problem that developers writing database-driven applications face: the mismatch between an application's normal object-oriented programming model, implemented in C# or Visual Basic, and the relational programming model surfaced in databases or data sets, implemented primarily with SQL.

In the object-oriented world, we manipulate objects via methods and properties, and each object can be (and often is) a parent or container for other objects. The relational database world is much more straightforward: Entities are implemented as row/column-based tables, and each "cell" in a table holds simple scalar values. The core issue is that you must change programming models when dealing with an application's internal framework or the relational database used as its data store (and translating from one to the other isn't a straightforward task).

As a simple example, rows from an invoice table are easily fetched into a `DataSet` object using the various data-binding tools and classes discussed previously. But deriving a "native" `Invoice` object from the data set involves two-way manual translation and manipulation to get the core values to translate across this object/relational barrier. This highlights several issues. Do you abandon the data set approach and read directly from the database into your applications' objects? Do you eschew the object approach and try to use the DataSet component throughout all layers of your application? Or is a hybrid approach best, maintaining strongly typed object collections in addition to the data sets?

Ideally, application developers would be free to work with and manipulate objects within the program's object model and have those objects and changes automatically stored in the database with little or no intervention. Not only does this keep the focus on core well-understood object design patterns, but it lets the individual developer work with his core language strength without having to learn or become expert in SQL. Pursuit of this goal obviously requires some sort of standard approach and tooling support for mapping objects to and from their equivalents within the relational database. This is exactly what object/relational mapping tools do.

The term *object/relational mapping* (or *O/R mapping*) refers to this general process of translating objects to and from databases. O/R mapping tools have been on the market for years now, and Microsoft has finally delivered O/R mapping support directly in the .NET Framework and in Visual Studio through two different but similar technologies: LINQ to SQL and Entity Framework. Let's briefly discuss both of these technologies and their Visual Studio tooling, starting with LINQ to SQL.

An Overview of LINQ

LINQ is an acronym for Language Integrated Query. It is a component introduced as a framework component with .NET Framework 3.5 that adds SQL-like querying capabilities to .NET objects. Specifically, it extends the core .NET languages (Visual Basic and C#) and the runtime to try to erase the object-to-database-entity barrier. Both Visual Basic and C# support new query operators that operate over objects similar to the way SQL operates over tables in a database.

For example, you could query for all approved invoice objects like this.

```
var approved =
    from invoice in invoices
    where (invoice.Approved) == true
    select invoice;

foreach (Invoice invoice in approved)
{
    // do some work here
}
```

Runtime support is introduced for physically translating objects and methods to and from their database equivalents (primarily through the use of code attributes, as you see in a moment). This is a simple example of a class method mapped to a SQL Server stored procedure.

```
[Function(Name="HR.uspDeleteEmployee")]
public int uspDeleteEmployee([Parameter(Name="EmployeeID", DbType="Int")]
                              System.Nullable<int> employeeID)
{
   IExecuteResult result = this.ExecuteMethodCall(this,
           ((MethodInfo)(MethodInfo.GetCurrentMethod())), employeeID);
   return ((int)(result.ReturnValue));
}
```

LINQ comes in several flavors, each targeted at a specific mapping problem:

- **LINQ to SQL**—This enables you to map objects to database entities.
- **LINQ to XML**—This enables you to query XML documents and map objects to XML document elements.
- **LINQ to Objects**—This specifically refers to the inclusion of .NET language syntax that enables queries to be written over collections of objects (as in our previous example with the approved invoices).

You need to be aware of one important fact regarding LINQ to SQL: although Microsoft fully supports the technology, it has been deprecated in favor of the Entity Framework. Some developers might still prefer to use LINQ to SQL because it is a lighter weight and simpler object-relational mapping (ORM) to implement.

NOTE

In 2007, Microsoft released a technology preview of a version of LINQ designed specifically for parallel execution. This technology, called PLINQ (for Parallel LINQ), has now been officially released. In essence, PLINQ builds on the LINQ concepts by accepting any LINQ to XML or LINQ to Objects query and executes those queries by optimizing for multiple CPU or multiple core scenarios.

If you are interested more in PLINQ or parallel programming in general, the Parallel Computing Center on MSDN is a great start: http://msdn.microsoft.com/en-us/concurrency/default.aspx.

LINQ is a fairly broad and deep set of technology pieces, and covering even one in depth is beyond the scope of this book. We do, however, dig into the primary Visual Studio tool used when writing LINQ to SQL applications: the O/R designer.

Mapping Using the O/R Designer

The first step in creating a LINQ to SQL application is typically the construction of an object model that is based on a given database definition. This is the exact function of the O/R designer. It enables you to select a database and generate an object model that maps to the database's structure. Table 13.3 shows how the database components are mapped to object components.

TABLE 13.3 Default Database to Object Mappings

Database	Application Object
Table	Class
Table Column	Class Property
Foreign Key Relationship	Association
Stored Procedure/Function	Class Method

Adding Database Entities

The O/R designer is the design surface for project items known as LINQ to SQL Classes, so the first step in using the designer is to add a new LINQ to SQL Classes project item to a project. Figure 13.51 shows where this project item lives in the Add New Item dialog box.

After you've selected the LINQ to SQL Classes item and added it to the project, the O/R designer immediately launches.

There isn't much to see yet because we haven't selected which database entities we want to represent within our object model. This involves the use of the second primary tool for performing the O/R mapping: Server Explorer.

By selecting a valid data source in Server Explorer, we can simply drag and drop a table onto the left side (the "data class" side) of the O/R designer (see Figure 13.52).

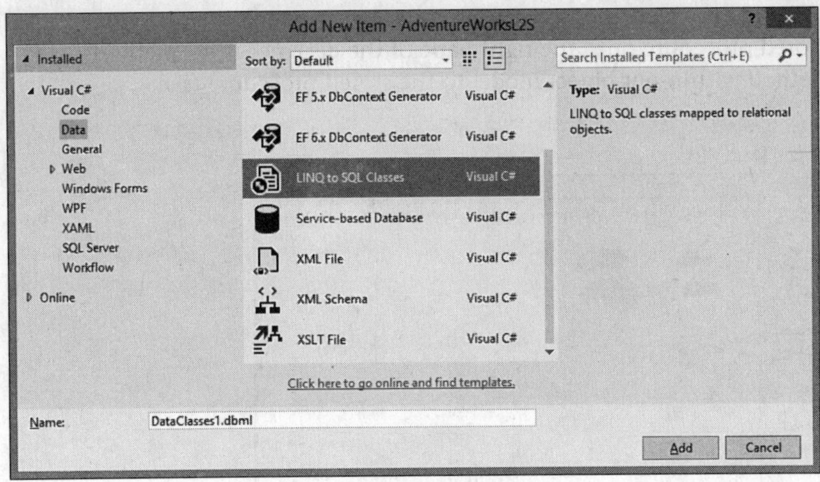

FIGURE 13.51 Adding a LINQ to SQL Classes item to an existing project.

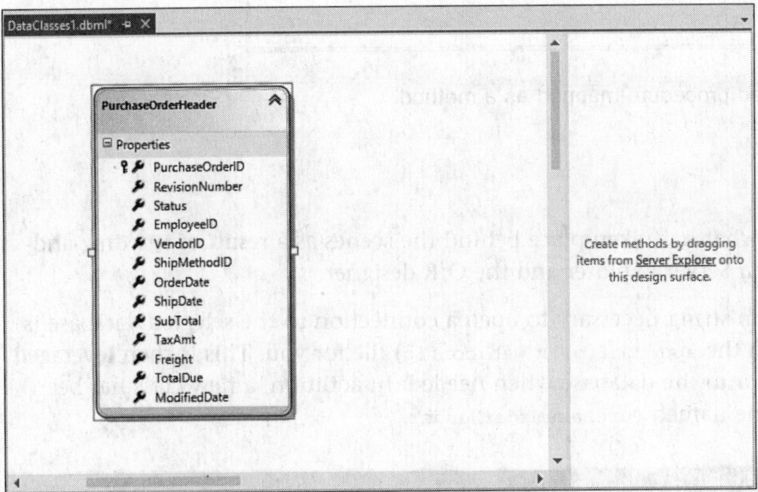

FIGURE 13.52 The `AdventureWorks` `PurchaseOrderHeader` table added to the O/R design surface.

Although nothing obvious happens after the table is dragged onto the data class pane (beyond having its visual representation in the designer), in reality potentially thousands of lines of code have been automatically generated to implement a class structure that mimics the table structure. In addition, all the attribute-based wiring has been implemented so that the LINQ engine can understand and process updates between the class object and the table's rows and columns.

This exact process is used to create methods within our object model. We can, for instance, drag a stored procedure onto the right pane of the designer (the "methods" pane) to map a method within our object model to the stored procedure (see Figure 13.53).

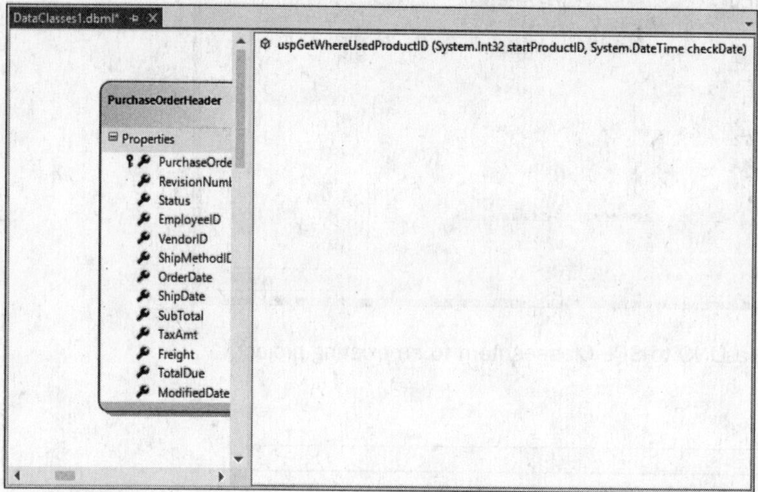

FIGURE 13.53 A stored procedure mapped as a method.

LINQ Code

Let's examine exactly what has taken place behind the scenes as a result of the drag-and-drop operation between Server Explorer and the O/R designer.

For one, the connection string necessary to open a connection to the selected database is automatically stored in the `app.config` (or `web.config`) file for you. This is then leveraged by LINQ to make calls into the database when needed. In addition, a new class has been defined, in this case one named `PurchaseOrderHeader`.

NOTE

The O/R designer actually "depluralizes" entity names for you automatically. Many HR databases, for instance, choose to implement an employee table and call it `Employees` because it stores the data records for more than one worker. In an attempt to further push through the object model to data model impedance mismatch, the O/R designer actually creates a class called `Employee` and *not* `Employees`; this correlates much better with the true intent of the class (which is to contain a single row/instance from the table and not the entire table).

If you look at the resulting LINQ code (in our example, by viewing the code inside the file `DataClasses1.designer.cs`), you will see that LINQ marks up the object model with attributes to perform the magic linking between the objects and the database. Via the `Table` attribute, this class has been identified as a direct map to the `Purchasing.PurchaseOrderHeader` table.

Each column in the `PurchaseOrderHeader` table has also been implemented as a property on the `Employee` class. This snippet shows the `PurchaseOrderID` property:

```
[global::System.Data.Linq.Mapping.ColumnAttribute(Storage="_PurchaseOrderID",
AutoSync=AutoSync.OnInsert, DbType="Int NOT NULL IDENTITY", IsPrimaryKey=true,
IsDbGenerated=true)]
public int PurchaseOrderID
{
        get
        {
                return this._PurchaseOrderID;
        }
        set
        {
                if ((this._PurchaseOrderID != value))
                {
                        this.OnPurchaseOrderIDChanging(value);
                        this.SendPropertyChanging();
                        this._PurchaseOrderID = value;
                        this.SendPropertyChanged("PurchaseOrderID");
                        this.OnPurchaseOrderIDChanged();
                }
        }
}
```

Beyond the `PurchaseOrderHeader` class, there has also been code generated for the data context. Here is a snippet of the class definition created automatically for us.

```
[global::System.Data.Linq.Mapping.DatabaseAttribute(Name="AdventureWorks2008")]
public partial class DataClasses1DataContext : System.Data.Linq.DataContext
{
   private static System.Data.Linq.Mapping.MappingSource mappingSource
      = new AttributeMappingSource();
#region Extensibility Method Definitions
partial void OnCreated();
partial void InsertPurchaseOrderHeader(PurchaseOrderHeader instance);
partial void UpdatePurchaseOrderHeader(PurchaseOrderHeader instance);
partial void DeletePurchaseOrderHeader(PurchaseOrderHeader instance);
#endregion
        public DataClasses1DataContext() :
             base(global::AWL2S.Properties.Settings.Default.
             AdventureWorks2008ConnectionString, mappingSource)
           {
```

```
            OnCreated();
        }
    public DataClasses1DataContext(string connection) :
        base(connection, mappingSource)
        {
            OnCreated();
        }
    public DataClasses1DataContext(System.Data.IDbConnection connection) :
        base(connection, mappingSource)
        {
            OnCreated();
        }
    public DataClasses1DataContext(string connection,
        System.Data.Linq.Mapping.MappingSource mappingSource) :
        base(connection, mappingSource)
        {
            OnCreated();
        }
    public DataClasses1DataContext(System.Data.IDbConnection connection,
        System.Data.Linq.Mapping.MappingSource mappingSource) :
        base(connection, mappingSource)
        {
            OnCreated();
        }
    public System.Data.Linq.Table<PurchaseOrderHeader>
        PurchaseOrderHeaders
    {
        get
        {
            return this.GetTable<PurchaseOrderHeader>();
        }
    }
}
```

You can think of DataContext as the LINQ manager: it handles the connection back to the database, manages the in-memory entities, and marshals the calls necessary for data updates and any issues that might arise from concurrency and locking conflicts. In total, more than 500 lines of functioning code were emitted to make all this work. So how do you actually use a LINQ object within your application? Read on.

Working with LINQ Objects

The goal with LINQ, again, is simplicity; LINQ classes look and behave just like any other class in our object model. If we wanted to add a new employee to the system, we would create a new `Employee` object and set its properties like this.

```
Employee emp = new Employee();

emp.BirthDate = new DateTime(1965, 4, 4);
emp.Gender = 'F';
emp.LoginID = "templogin";
emp.MaritalStatus = 'M';
emp.Title = "Project Resource Manager";
...
```

To commit this new `Employee` object to the `Employee` table, we need to add the object to the `Employees` collection held by our data context and then call the `SubmitChanges` method. Remember that the type is simply the default name given by the O/R designer to our data context class; we can change this to anything we want.

```
DataClasses1DataContext db = new DataClasses1DataContext();
db.Employees.InsertOnSubmit(emp);
db.SubmitChanges();
```

In a similar fashion, employees can be removed from the collection (and then from the database).

```
db.Employees.DeleteOnSubmit(emp);
db.SubmitChanges();
```

We have really just scratched the surface here with regard to the intricacies and complexities of O/R application development using LINQ; but hopefully this overview of the O/R designer can be used as a starting point for your O/R explorations in Visual Studio. Let's move on to the Entity Framework.

Working with the Entity Framework

Like LINQ to SQL, Entity Framework (EF) is a technology that enables you to program against objects that are backed by tables within a relational database. And because they share that same overall goal, most of the concepts we covered with LINQ to SQL apply to EF-based applications as well. The notable difference with EF is the level of abstraction it provides. Whereas LINQ to SQL is a direct map of objects to database tables, EF maps database tables to an Entity Data Model (EDM). From there, you can map objects to the EDM.

Within an EF's EDM, there are actually two discrete models that are maintained by Visual Studio: the conceptual model (think application objects) and the storage model (the database that stores those application objects).

In Visual Studio, the EF models are used by adding an ADO.NET EDM item to your project. Just like our previous look at the LINQ to SQL Data Classes project item, the EF project item is located under the Data category in the Add New Item dialog box (see Figure 13.54).

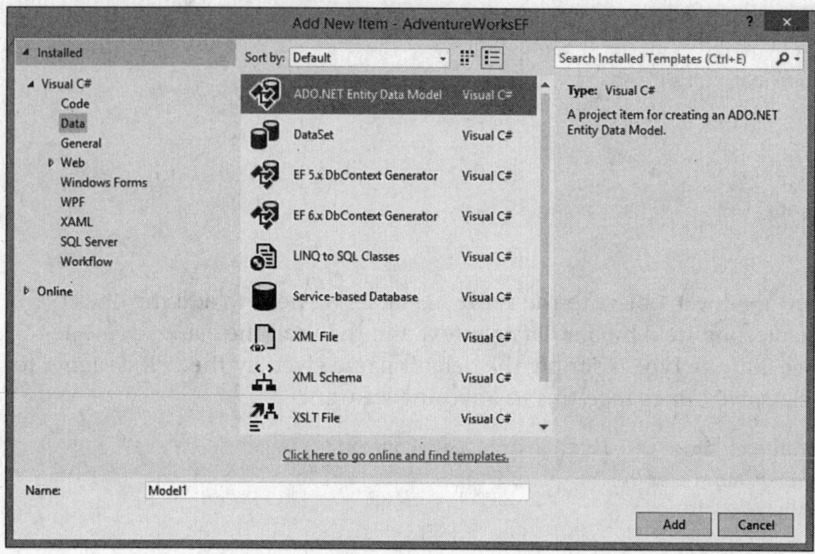

FIGURE 13.54 Adding the Entity Data Model item to a project.

When you add an entity model to your project, a wizard launches (see Figure 13.55). There are three primary approaches of development with the entity framework: code first, model first, and database first. In the code first approach, you start your application design by writing code to define your classes. With model first, you start your application design by visually "drawing" the design of your application using Visual Studio. Finally, with database first, you are allowing the EF tools to build out your application structure by creating it based on an existing data model. Regardless of your starting approach, once an application has been initially constructed, EF will keep the code and data models in sync. In our case, we continue our walk-through by selecting the EF Designer from Database option (the database first approach). We will again use the `AdventureWorks` database.

Editing the Entity Data Model

After the entity model is added to your project, you can make changes to it using the Entity Data Model designer. This is the visual design surface for your model. There are also two other windows displayed in conjunction with the model designer. The Model Browser provides a Solution Explorer-like view of both the conceptual model and the storage model for your entities, and the Mapping Details window shows exactly how objects in the conceptual model are mapped and linked to tables in the storage model. Figure 13.56 shows all three windows open within the IDE. Note that when we added the entity model to our project, we opted to build out the model using every existing table within the `AdventureWorks` database, under the Human Resources schema. Let's take a closer look at each of these windows.

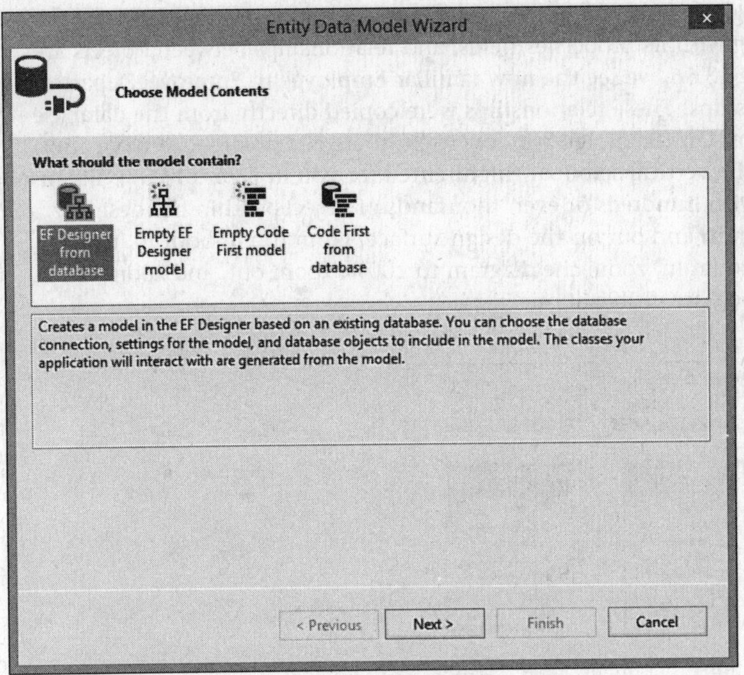

FIGURE 13.55 The Entity Data Model Wizard.

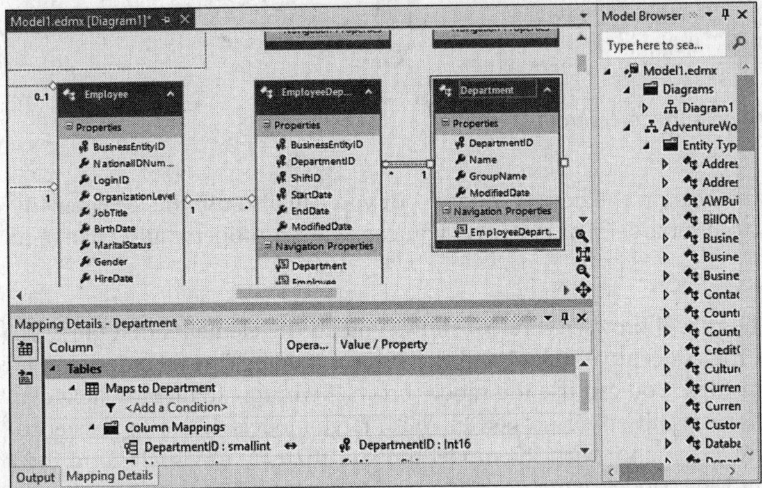

FIGURE 13.56 Editing an Entity Data Model.

The Designer The designer shows a familiar, visual view of the conceptual model. Each object is depicted, along with its properties/fields, and relationships between objects are clearly visible. In Figure 13.56, we see the now familiar Employee to EmployeeDepartment to Department relationships. These relationships were copied directly from the database foreign key relationships. On the design window itself, there is a small set of navigation buttons set just under the vertical scrollbar (highlighted for you in Figure 13.57). Because you might be dealing with hundreds or even thousands of objects within the designer, you need a way to zoom in and out on the design surface. From top to bottom, these buttons enable you to zoom in, zoom the diagram to 100%, zoom out, and zoom the diagram so that all objects are visible at once.

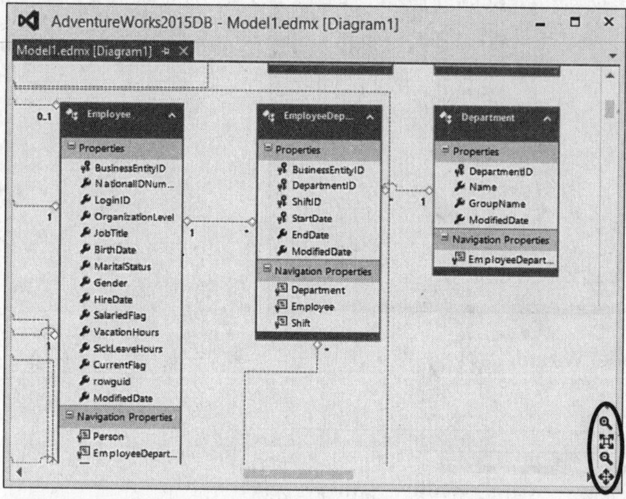

FIGURE 13.57 The design surface controls.

You can move around objects on the design surface, but you can also use the designer to directly make changes to the model. For instance, you can select a property and change its name.

The Model Browser The model browser window shows you all the elements that are contained within both the conceptual model and the storage model. This includes entities, tables, and relationships. You can use the model browser window to directly delete items from your models or modify their properties. With large models, it is often easier to locate the entity you are looking for with the model browser than try to visually find the object within the Entity Data Model designer pane.

TIP

You can immediately show any model element within the designer by right-clicking the element within the Model Browser and selecting Show in Designer.

One of the coolest things about the Model Browser window is its search functionality. By typing a search term into the search box at the top of the window, you can see every instance of that term anywhere within the model. The vertical scrollbar actually graphically depicts everywhere within the models that a search hit was found. If you examine Figure 13.58 closely, you see the results of a search for "Employee"; 74 matches were found. Within the vertical scrollbar, you see "blocks" that represent where the match was found within the model hierarchy. Hovering over those blocks gives you a ToolTip that identifies the exact name that contains the match. This enables you to quickly jump around your search matches within large models.

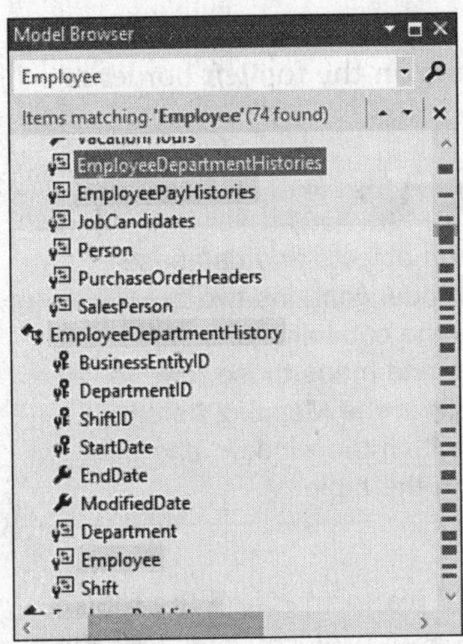

FIGURE 13.58 Searching within the Model Browser window.

The Mapping Details Window We have discussed the idea of the conceptual model and the storage model. But if these models lived in isolation, EF wouldn't be able to achieve its ultimate goal of linking code objects to database tables because there wouldn't be a way to map between the two models. The Mapping Details window is the tool within the IDE that lets you view and edit all the conceptual-to-storage model mappings.

Figure 13.59 shows the mapping details for the `Employee` object. All the mapping properties were preset for us because we chose to build out our conceptual model based on an existing database. When you select an entity with the designer, the mapping window will show an alphabetic list of all of the table columns. To the right of each column is displayed the property that the column maps to on the object.

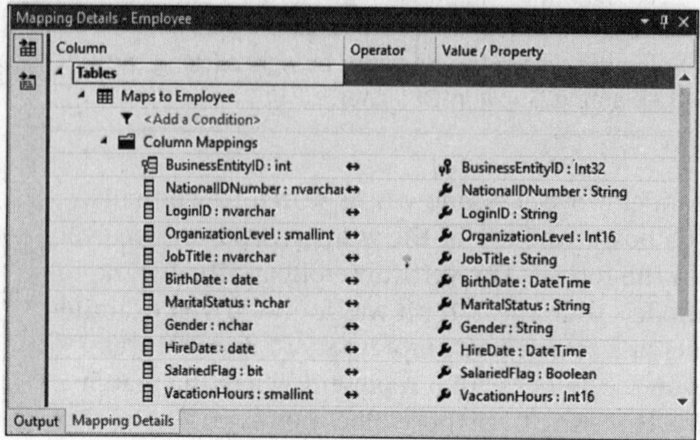

FIGURE 13.59 Mapping details for the `Employee` object/table.

The Mapping Details window is also used to map an object to your own, custom functions for performing inserts, updates, or deletes. Click the two icons on the top-left border of the Mapping Details window to change between these two modes.

NOTE

You aren't limited to performing just a one-to-one map between objects and database tables. You could decide, for instance, that your conceptual model contains two `Employee` classes: `HourlyEmployee` and `SalariedEmployee`. You have the capability to create a function that filters the rows in the underlying `Employee` table and maps those rows to one or the other of these two objects. This is done quite easily in the Mapping Details window by adding a condition. Click the Add a Condition link within the window, and then specify a condition to apply against the `SalariedFlag` field on the table.

We have now covered the high-level overview of what the EF platform is and the tools and project items you use within Visual Studio to create EF-based projects. Now let's dig a bit deeper to see how we would use these tools to perform common EF tasks.

Querying Against the Entity Data Model

The real power of EF is the ability to perform SQL-like operations against a set of objects (for example, the objects you have defined in your entity data model) using a variety of different methods.

Because every object in EF is LINQ enabled, we could use LINQ to Entities to query for a list of salaried employees, like this.

```
using (AdventureWorksEntities entities = new AdventureWorksEntities())
  {
    List<Employee> employees =
        (from e in entities.Employees
        where e.SalariedFlag == true select e).ToList();
  }
```

The `AdventureWorksEntities` object seen on the first line of code above represents our conceptual model; LINQ provides the syntax we need to iterate over those objects within the `AdventureWorksEntities` object.

EF also supports the ability to construct queries using the `ObjectQuery` class. This class lives within the `System.Data.Objects` namespace and enables us to use standard SQL-like syntax for generating queries. Here is that same query, rewritten using the `ObjectQuery` class.

```
using (AdventureWorksEntities entities = new AdventureWorksEntities())
  {
    ObjectQuery<Employee> query =
      entities.Employees.Where("it.SalariesFlag=@flag");

      query.Parameters.Add(new ObjectParameter("flag", "True"));

      List<Employee> employees = query.ToList();

  }
```

We could even query our objects using nothing more than standard stored procedures. This would be a two-step process. First, we create a stored procedure in our underlying database (and thus our store model). Second, we map that stored procedure to a function within our model. With the function in place (here we have named it `GetSalariedEmployees`), we can call that function like this.

```
using (AdventureWorksEntities entities = new AdventureWorksEntities())
  {
    List<Employee> employees = entities.GetSalariedEmployees().ToList();
  }
```

Updating Data in the Entity Data Model

Because we are simply programming against standard .NET objects within the entity data model, updating data that resides in those objects is as simple as setting the object properties.

We can create a new employee like this.

```
Employee newEmp = new Employee();
```

We can set its properties like we would for any other object.

```
newEmp.SalariedFlag = true;
newEmp.HireDate = DateTime.Today;
newEmp.Title = "HR Manager";
```

We then add the new employee to the Entity Data Model like this.

```
entities.Employees.AddObject(newEmp);
```

Finally, we would need to tell the Entity Data Model to persist these changes to the database.

```
entities.SaveChanges();
```

In a similar fashion, we can delete an object by first referencing it and then calling the `DeleteObject` method from our `entities` object. This code deletes the first employee in the `Employee` table.

```
Employee firstEmp = entities.Employees.First();
entities.DeleteObject(firstEmp);
```

NOTE

We have discussed how to change data within the Entity Data Model, but what happens if either the database schema changes or you want changes within your conceptual model to be made at the storage level as well? If you right-click the Entity Data Model designer, you see two options that essentially sync schema of the database with the object model or vice versa: Generate Database from Model and UpdateModelFromDatabase.

As you have probably guessed by now, Entity Framework is a vast and deep ORM platform. We have really only been able to scratch the surface here. If you intend to leverage EF inside your applications, we wholeheartedly recommend a book dedicated to the subject, such as Julia Lerman's *Programming Entity Framework* from O'Reilly.

Summary

In this chapter, you read about the broad and deep support that Visual Studio has for building and managing databases and for creating applications that access data in a database. We discussed the suite of SQL Server Data Tools, available right within the IDE, that function in synergy with one another and with the various Visual Studio designers to provide a seamless experience for writing queries, creating table structures, and crafting stored procedures. We also investigated the newfound support for writing SQL Server database procedures and functions using entirely managed code.

We spent some time discussing the basics of data binding: how it is a core problem space with many application development efforts and how the Visual Studio web, Windows Form Designers, and WPF Designers and controls provide first-class support for simple to complex data-binding scenarios. In particular, we examined the role that these Visual Studio designers play in the data-binding world by enabling developers to rapidly build forms-based applications with sophisticated data needs without writing a single line of code.

Finally, we examined the built-in support that Visual Studio provides for mapping entire object models to a database using two different technologies: LINQ2SQL and Entity Framework.

Hopefully, by exposing you to all these great built-in tools, we have started you on the road to becoming even more efficient in leveraging Visual Studio across a range of database interactions.

CHAPTER 14

Introducing the Automation Object Model

IN THIS CHAPTER

- An Overview of the Automation Object Model
- Solution and Project Objects
- Working with Windows
- Command Bars
- Documents
- Command Objects
- Debugger Objects

Visual Studio is built to be extensible. It ships with its own application programming interface (API) to enable you, the developer, to control many of the pieces of the IDE.

This API is called the Visual Studio automation object model, and understanding its capabilities is the key to unlocking your ability to program and control the IDE itself by writing code in the form of "packages" (discussed in Chapter 15, "Extending the IDE").

This is a reference chapter. It discusses the layout and structure of the automation object model and provides details on their properties and methods. As such, it is light on code. To truly understand the step-by-step process of extending the IDE, you may want to skip ahead to the next chapter and refer back here for object reference information.

For now, don't worry too much about the mechanics of writing a package; concentrate instead on understanding the automation objects and how they are referenced and used.

An Overview of the Automation Object Model

The automation object model is a structured class library with a top-level root object called DTE (or DTE2; more on this in a bit), which stands for Development Tools Environment. By referencing the assembly that defines the

DTE/DTE2 types, you can write code that instances this root object and use its members and child classes to access the IDE components.

Object Model Versions

The automation object model is actually defined across four different, complementary primary interop assemblies (PIAs): EnvDTE, EnvDTE80, EnvDTE90, and EnvDTE100. EnvDTE is the original automation assembly distributed with Visual Studio .NET 2003. EnvDTE80 was the library distributed with Visual Studio 2005. EnvDTE90 is distributed with Visual Studio 2008. (Yet another assembly, EnvDTE90a is installed with Visual Studio 2008 Service Pack 1.) Finally, EnvDTE100 made its first appearance with Visual Studio 2010. Each version of Visual Studio ships with the cumulative set of libraries. Starting with Visual Studio 2012, no new versions of the interop assembly have been introduced. Visual Studio 2012 and beyond ships with all four PIAs.

The reason for multiple assemblies is simple: they help balance the need for new features against the need to preserve backward compatibility. For instance, with Visual Studio 2008, Microsoft was faced with a common design decision: replace or upgrade the previous assembly shipped with Visual Studio 2005 (EnvDTE80) and risk introducing incompatibilities with current macros and add-ins, or ship a new assembly that could be leveraged when the new functionality was desired. (Existing code would still target the previous, unchanged library.)

The latter path was chosen; thus, EnvDTE100 (100 represents version 10.0) contains automation types and members that are new to Visual Studio 2010, while EnvDTE90 (for Visual Studio 2008) and EnvDTE80 (for Visual Studio 2005) provide the base level of functionality and backward compatibility.

Within the EnvDTE100 assembly, you find types that supersede their predecessors from the EnvDTE90 assembly. The same is true for types within EnvDTE90 that supersede types implemented in EnvDTE80, all the way back to the original EnvDTE assembly. In these cases, the type name has been appended with a number to indicate the revised version. Therefore, we have `DTE` and `DTE2`; `Solution`, `Solution2`, and `Solution3`; and so on.

Table 14.1 provides a side-by-side listing of some of the most important types implemented in the EnvDTE libraries. This type list is incomplete and should be considered for reference only. This table is useful, however, for identifying some of the newly minted types in the new automation assembly; in the next section, we see how these types can be organized into broad Visual Studio automation categories and how they map onto physical IDE constructs.

TABLE 14.1 Partial List of Automation Types

Type	Description
`AddIn`	Represents a Visual Studio add-in.
`Breakpoint`, `Breakpoint2`	Represents a debugger breakpoint.

Type	Description
BuildDependencies	For the selected project, represents a collection of BuildDependency objects.
BuildDependency	For the selected project, represents the projects that it depends on for a successful build.
BuildEvents	Exposes a list of events relevant to a solution build.
Command	Represents a command action in the IDE.
Commands, Commands2	Represents a collection of all commands supported in the IDE.
CommandWindow	Represents the command window.
Configuration	Represents a project's configuration properties.
Debugger, Debugger2, Debugger3, Debugger4, Debugger5	Represents the Visual Studio debugger.
DebuggerEvents	Exposes events from the debugger.
Document	Represents an open document in the IDE.
Documents	Represents a collection of all open documents in the IDE.
DTE	Represents the IDE; this is the top-level, root object for the automation object model.
EditPoint	Represents a text operation point within a document.
Events	Exposes all automation events.
ExceptionGroups	Represents the exception grouping categories supported by Visual Studio.
Find	Represents the Find capability for text searches in the IDE.
HTMLWindow, HTMLWindow3	Represents an HTML document window.
OutputWindow	Represents the Output window.
Program, (Process2)	Represents a program running within the IDE; useful for examining processes and threads within the program. EnvDTE80 functionality is provided by the Process2 object.
Project	Represents a project loaded in the IDE.
ProjectItem	Represents an item contained within a given project.
ProjectItems	Represents a collection of all items contained within a project.
Property	Represents a generic property for an object. (This can be used across various objects in the automation library.)
SelectedItem	Represents projects or project items that are currently selected in the IDE.
Solution, Solution2, Solution3, Solution4	Represents the solution currently loaded in Visual Studio.

Type	Description
SourceControl, SourceControl2	Represents the source control system of record within Visual Studio.
TaskItem	Represents an item in the Task List window.
TaskItems, TaskItems2	Represents a collection of all items in the Task List window.
TaskList	Represents the Task List window.
Template	Represents a Visual Studio template.
TextDocument	Represents a text file open in the IDE.
TextPane, TextPane2	Represents a pane within an open text editor window.
TextWindow	Represents a text window.
ToolBox	Represents the Toolbox window.
ToolBoxItem, ToolBoxItem2	Represents an item within the Toolbox window.
ToolBoxTab, ToolboxTab2, ToolboxTab3	Represents a tab of items on the Toolbox window.
Window, Window2	Represents, generically, any window within the IDE.
Windows, Windows2	Represents a collection of all windows within the IDE.

Automation Categories

Because any automation effort with Visual Studio starts with the object model, you should first understand how it maps onto the IDE constructs and determine the exact capabilities it exposes.

In general, you can think of the object model classes as being organized into categories that directly speak to these IDE concepts:

- Solutions and projects
- Windows and command bars (toolbars and menu bars)
- Documents
- Commands
- Debugger
- Events

Each of the objects in these categories touches a different piece of the IDE, and access to each object is typically through the root-level DTE2 object.

The DTE/DTE2 Root Object

The DTE/DTE2 object represents the tip of the API tree. You can think of it as representing Visual Studio itself, with the objects under it mapping to the various constituent parts of the IDE.

As mentioned previously, DTE2 is the most current version of this object, with DTE providing compatibility with earlier versions. In this chapter, unless we specifically need to differentiate between their capabilities, we generically refer to the DTE and DTE2 objects as simply DTE.

The DTE properties are used to gain a reference to a specific IDE object (or collection of objects). Methods on the object are used to execute commands in the IDE, launch wizards, or close the IDE.

Table 14.2 shows the major properties and methods defined on the DTE2 object; they have been organized within the six object categories itemized in the preceding section.

TABLE 14.2 DTE2 Properties and Methods for IDE Access

Category	Property	Description
Commands	`Commands`	Returns a collection of `Command` objects; in general, a command is an action that can be carried out within the IDE, such as opening or saving a file.
Debugger	`Debugger`	Returns the `Debugger` object.
Documents	`ActiveDocument`	Returns a `Document` object representing the currently active document.
Documents	`Documents`	Returns a collection of `Document` objects representing all open documents.
Event Notification	`Events`	Returns the `Events` object for handling event notifications.
Solutions and Projects	`ActiveSolutionProjects`	Returns a collection of the `Project` objects representing the projects that are currently selected within the Solution Explorer.
Solutions and Projects	`Solution`	Returns the `Solution` object for the currently loaded solution.
Windows and Command Bars	`ActiveWindow`	Returns a `Window` object representing the window within the IDE that currently has focus.
Windows and Command Bars	`CommandBars`	Returns a collection of `CommandBar` objects representing all the toolbars and menu bars.
Windows and Command Bars	`MainWindow`	Returns a `Window` object representing the IDE window itself.

Category	Property	Description
Windows and Command Bars	`StatusBar`	Returns a `StatusBar` object representing Visual Studio's status bar.
Windows and Command Bars	`ToolWindows`	Returns a `ToolWindows` instance, which in turns provides access to a few of the most prominent tool windows: the Command window, Error List, Output window, Solution Explorer, Task List, and Toolbox.
Windows and Command Bars	`WindowConfigurations`	Returns a collection of `WindowConfiguration` objects; these objects represent the various window layouts in use by Visual Studio.

Category	Method	Description
Commands	`ExecuteCommand`	Executes an environment command.
—	`LaunchWizard`	Starts the identified wizard with the given parameters.
—	`Quit`	Closes Visual Studio.

In summary, the DTE object is a tool for directly interacting with certain IDE components and providing access to the deeper layers of the API with its property collections. If you move one level down in the API, you find the major objects that form the keystone for automation.

Solution and Project Objects

The `Solution` object represents the currently loaded solution. The individual projects within the solution are available via `Project` objects returned within the `Solution.Projects` collection. Items within a project are accessed in a similar fashion through the `Project.ProjectItems` collection.

As you can see from Figure 14.1, this hierarchy exactly mirrors the solution/project hierarchy that we first discussed in Chapter 4, "Solutions and Projects."

There are some mismatches here (solution folders, for instance, are treated as projects), but for the most part, the object model tree closely resembles the solution project tree that you are used to.

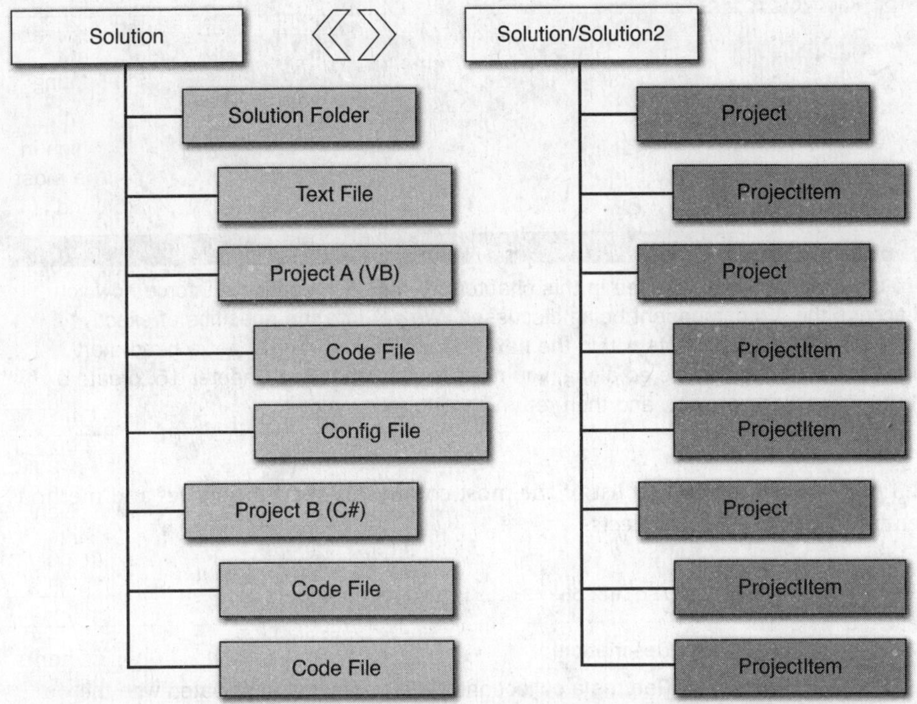

FIGURE 14.1 Mapping the solution/project hierarchy.

The `Solution` object and members enable you to interact with the current solution to perform common tasks such as these:

- Determining the number of projects in the solution (`Count` property)
- Adding a project to the solution based on a project file (`AddFromFile` method)
- Creating a new solution or closing the current one (`Create` and `Close` methods)
- Saving the solution (`SaveAs` method)
- Removing a project from the solution (`Remove` method)

You can directly retrieve a reference to any of the projects within the currently loaded solution by iterating over the `Solution.Projects` collection. As an example of interacting with the `Solution` and `Project` objects, this C# code snippet removes the first project from the current solution.

```
Solution solution = _applicationObject.Solution;
Project project = solution.Projects.Item(0) as Project;

if (project.Saved)
{
```

```
    solution.Remove(project);
}
else
{
    //
}
```

> **NOTE**
>
> Most of the code snippets you see in this chapter are merely meant to reinforce how you would access the API component being discussed. We get into the specifics of exactly how to leverage these concepts within the next chapter. If you want to get a head start by playing with the code as we go along, you need to skip ahead to Chapter 15, create a Visual Studio package project, and then return here to follow along.

Table 14.3 provides the combined list of the most commonly used properties and methods implemented by the `Solution` objects.

TABLE 14.3 Primary `Solution/Solution2/Solution3` Type Members

Property	Description
`AddIns`	Returns a collection of `AddIn` objects associated with the current solution.
`Count`	Indicates the count of the project within the solution.
`DTE`	Refers to the parent DTE object.
`FullName`	Indicates the full path and name of the solution file.
`Globals`	Returns the `Globals` object, a cache of variables used across the solution.
`IsOpen`	Indicates whether a solution is open.
`Projects`	Returns a collection of `Project` objects representing all the projects within the solution.
`Properties`	Returns a collection of `Property` objects that expose all the solution's properties.
`Saved`	Indicates whether the solution has been saved since the last modification.
`SolutionBuild`	Returns a reference to a `SolutionBuild` object. This is the entry point to the build automation objects applicable for the current solution.
Method	**Description**
`AddFromFile`	Adds a project to the solution using an existing project file.
`AddFromTemplate`	Takes an existing project, clones it, and adds it to the solution.

Method	Description
AddFromTemplateEx	Adds an existing project to a solution using the solution name.
AddSolutionFolder	Creates a new solution folder in the solution.
Close	Closes the solution.
Create	Creates an empty solution.
FindProjectItem	Initiates a search for a given item in one of the solution's projects.
GetProjectItemTemplate	Returns the path to the template used for the referenced project item.
GetProjectTemplate	Returns the path to the template used for the referenced project.
Item	Returns a Project instance.
Open	Opens a solution (using a specific view).
Remove	Removes a project from the solution.
SaveAs	Saves the solution.

Controlling Projects in a Solution

One of the things that the Solution object is good for is retrieving references to the various projects that belong to the solution. Each Project object has its own set of useful members for interacting with the projects and their items. By using these members, you can interact with the projects in various, expected ways, such as renaming a project, deleting a project, and saving a project.

See Table 14.4 for a summary of the most common Project members.

TABLE 14.4 Primary Project Object Members

Property	Description
CodeModel	Returns the CodeModel object associated with this project.
Collection	Returns a collection of Project objects for the current Solution.
DTE	Provides a reference to the parent DTE object.
FullName	Provides the full path and name of the solution file.
Kind	Returns a string globally unique identifier (GUID) indicating the type of project. Each project type is registered with Visual Studio using a GUID; consult the Visual Studio software development kit (SDK) documentation for a list that maps the project type GUIDs to their text description.
Name	Returns the name of the project.

Property	Description
`ParentProjectItem`	Returns an instance of the parent `Project`. Some project types within Visual Studio are able to host or contain other project types; this property can be used to identify the host project for the current project (if there is one).
`ProjectItems`	Returns a `ProjectItems` collection containing each object within the current project.
`Properties`	Returns a collection of `Property` objects that expose all the project's properties.
`Saved`	Indicates whether the project has been saved since the last modification.

Method	Description
`Delete`	Removes the current project instance from the solution.
`Save`	Saves the project.
`SaveAs`	Saves the project. This method enables you to provide a new name for the project.

Accessing Code Within a Project

Beyond the basic project attributes and items, one of the cooler things that can be accessed via a `Project` instance is the actual code within the project's source files. Through the `CodeModel` property, you can access an entire line of proxy objects representing the code constructs within a project. For instance, the `CodeClass` interface enables you to examine and edit the code for a given class in a given project.

NOTE

Support for the different `CodeModel` entities varies from language to language. The Microsoft Developer Network (MSDN) documentation for each `CodeModel` type clearly indicates the source language support for that element.

After grabbing a `CodeModel` reference from a `Project` instance, you can access its `CodeElements` collection (which is, not surprisingly, a collection of `CodeElement` objects). A `CodeElement` is nothing more than a generic representation of a certain code structure within a project. The `CodeElement` object is generic, but it provides a property: `Kind`. This property is used to determine the exact native type of the code object contained within the `CodeElement`.

The `CodeElement.Kind` property is an enumeration (of type `vsCMElement`) that identifies the specific type of code construct lurking within the `CodeElement` object. Using the `Kind` property, you can first determine the true nature of the code element and then cast the `CodeElement` object to its strong type. Here is a snippet of C# code that does just that.

```
if (element.Kind == vsCMElement.vsCMElementClass)
 {
           CodeClass myClass = (CodeClass)element;
 }
```

For a better grasp of the code model hierarchy, consider the C# code presented in Listing 14.1; this is a "shell" solution that merely implements a namespace, a class within that namespace, and a function within the class.

LISTING 14.1 A Simple Namespace and Class Implementation

```
using System;
using System.Collections.Generic;
using System.Text;

namespace MyNamespace
{
    class MyClass
    {
        public string SumInt(int x, int y)
        {
            return (x + y).ToString();
        }
    }

}
```

If you map the code in Listing 14.1 to the code object model, you end up with the structure shown in Figure 14.2.

To get an idea of the complete depth of the code model tree that can be accessed through the `CodeElements` collection, consult Table 14.5; this table shows all the possible `vsCMElement` values, the type they are used to represent, and a brief description of the type.

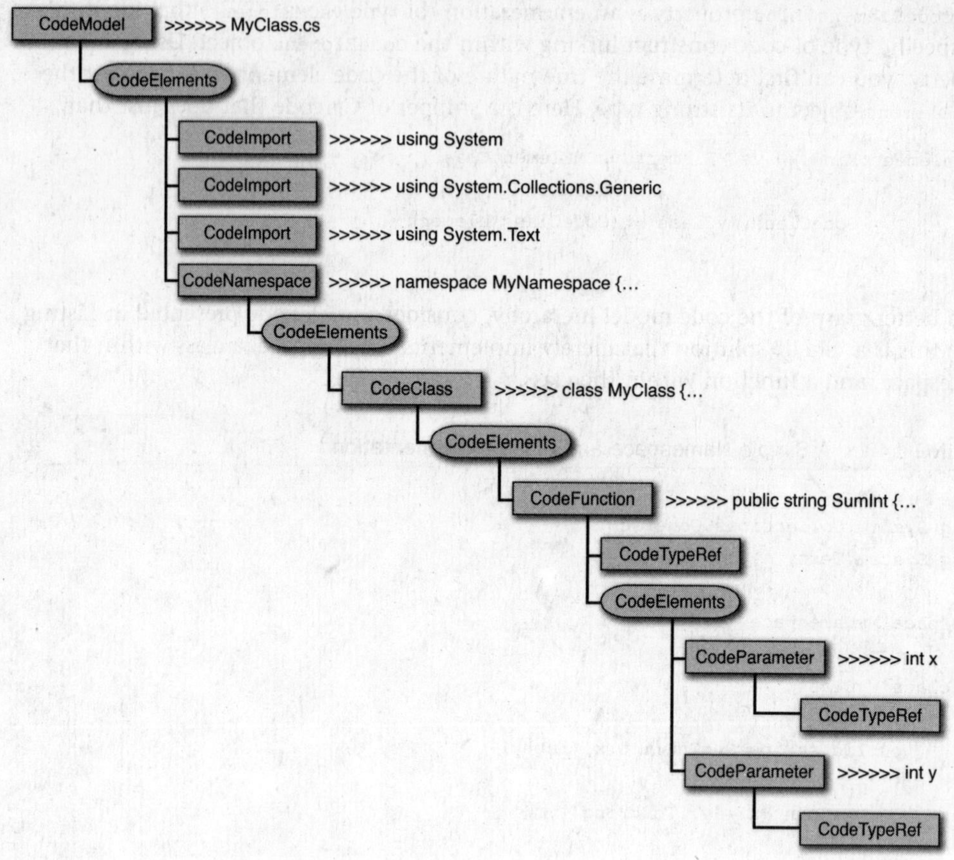

FIGURE 14.2 A simple code model object hierarchy.

TABLE 14.5 Mapping the `vsCMElement` Enumeration Values

Enumeration Value	Type	Description
`vsCMElementAssignmentStmt`		An `assignment` statement
`vsCMElementAttribute`		An attribute
`vsCMElementClass`	`CodeClass`	A class
`vsCMElementDeclareDecl`		A declaration
`vsCMElementDefineStmt`		A `define` statement
`vsCMElementDelegate`	`CodeDelegate`	A delegate
`vsCMElementEnum`	`CodeEnum`	An enumeration
`vsCMElementEvent`	`CodeEvent`	An event
`vsCMElementEventsDeclaration`		An event declaration

Enumeration Value	Type	Description
vsCMElementFunction	CodeFunction	A function
vsCMElementFunctionInvokeStmt		A statement invoking a function
vsCMElementIDLCoClass		An IDL co-class
vsCMElementIDLImport		An IDL import statement
vsCMElementIDLImportLib		An IDL import library
vsCMElementIDLLibrary		An IDL library
vsCMElementImplementsStmt		An implements statement
vsCMElementImportStmt	CodeImport	An import statement
vsCMElementIncludeStmt		An include statement
vsCMElementInheritsStmt		An inherits statement
vsCMElementInterface	CodeInterface	An interface
vsCMElementLocalDeclStmt		A local declaration statement
vsCMElementMacro		A macro
vsCMElementMap		A map
vsCMElementMapEntry		A map entry
vsCMElementModule		A module
vsCMElementNamespace	CodeNamespace	A namespace
vsCMElementOptionStmt		An option statement
vsCMElementOther	CodeElement	A code element not otherwise identified in this enum
vsCMElementParameter	CodeParameter	A parameter
vsCMElementProperty	CodeProperty	A property
vsCMElementPropertySetStmt		A property set statement
vsCMElementStruct	CodeStruct	A structure
vsCMElementTypeDef		A type definition
vsCMElementUDTDecl		A user-defined type
vsCMElementUnion		A union
vsCMElementUsingStmt	CodeImport	A using statement
vsCMElementVariable		A variable
vsCMElementVBAttributeGroup		A Visual Basic attribute group
vsCMElementVBAttributeStmt		A Visual Basic attribute statement
vsCMElementVCBase		A Visual C++ base

Working with Windows

The visible content portion of Visual Studio is represented by `Window` objects, which are instances of open windows within the IDE, such as the Solution Explorer, the Task List window, an open Code Editor window, and so on. Even the IDE itself is represented by a `Window` object.

Any given window is either a document window or a tool window. Document windows host documents that are editable by the Text Editor. Tool windows contain controls that display information relevant to the current context of the IDE; the Solution Explorer and Task List windows are examples of tool windows, and a VB source code file open in an editor is an example of a document window.

Referencing Windows

If you need to retrieve an instance of a specific window, you have a few different options, each optimal for a given situation. For starters, the main IDE window is always available directly from the `DTE` object.

```
Window IDE = _applicationObject.MainWindow;
```

Obviously, if you need to perform a specific action against the IDE window, this is your quickest route.

The `DTE.ActiveWindow` property also provides direct and quick access to a `Window` object, in this case the currently active window.

```
Window currentWindow = _applicationObject.ActiveWindow;
```

The tool windows within the IDE (that is, the Command window, the Error List window, the Output window, the Solution Explorer, the Task List window, and the Toolbox) also have a direct way to retrieve their object model instances: you use the `DTE.ToolWindows` property. This property returns a `ToolWindows` object that exposes a separate property for each of the tool windows.

This code grabs a reference to the Task List window and closes it.

```
Window taskwin = _applicationObject.ToolWindows.TaskList;
taskwin.Close();
```

Finally, the fourth way to access an IDE window is through the `DTE.Windows` collection; this collection holds an entry for each IDE window. You can access a window from the collection either by using an integer representing the window's position within the collection or by providing an object or a string that represents the window you are trying to retrieve.

The following code grabs a handle to the Solution Explorer window.

```
Windows windows = _applicationObject.Windows;
Window window = windows.Item(Constants.vsWindowKindSolutionExplorer);
```

Interacting with Windows

Table 14.6 itemizes the properties and methods available on each Window object.

TABLE 14.6 Window Object Members

Property	Description
AutoHides	A Boolean flag indicating whether the window can be hidden (applies only to tool windows).
Caption	The title/caption of the window.
Collection	The Windows collection that the current Window object belongs to.
CommandBars	A CommandBars collection of the command bars implemented by the window.
ContextAttributes	A collection of ContextAttribute objects; they are used to associate the current context of the window with the Dynamic Help window.
Document	If the Window object is hosting a document, this returns a reference to the document.
DTE	A reference to the root DTE object.
Height	The height of the window in pixels.
IsFloating	A Boolean flag indicating whether the window is floating or docked.
Left	The distance, in pixels, between the window's left edge and its container's left edge.
Linkable	A Boolean flag indicating whether the window can be docked with other windows.
LinkedWindowFrame	Returns a reference to the Window object that is acting as the frame for a docked window.
LinkedWindows	A collection of Window objects representing the windows that are linked within the same frame.
Object	Returns an object proxy that represents the window and can be referenced by name.
ObjectKind	A GUID indicating the type of the object returned from Window.Object.
Project	A Project instance representing the project containing the Window object.
ProjectItem	A ProjectItem instance representing the project item containing the Window object.
Selection	An object representing the currently selected item in the window. (For document windows, this might be text; for tool windows, this might be an item in a list; and so on.)
Top	The distance, in pixels, between the window's top edge and its parent's top edge.

Property	Description
`Visible`	A Boolean flag indicating whether the window is visible or hidden.
`Width`	The width of the window in pixels.
`WindowState`	The current state of the window (via a `vsWindowState` enum value: `vsWindowStateMaximize`, `vsWindowState-Minimize`, `vsWindowStateNormal`).
Method	**Description**
`Activate`	Gives the window focus.
`Close`	Closes the window; you can indicate, with a `vsSaveChanges` enum value, whether the window's hosted document should be saved or not saved or whether the IDE should prompt the user to make that decision.
`SetSelectionContainer`	Passes an array of objects to the Properties window when the `Window` object has focus. This property is mainly used for custom tool windows where you need to control what is displayed in the Properties window.
`SetTabPicture`	Specifies an object to use as a tab image; this image is displayed whenever the window is part of a tab group within the IDE.

Beyond the basics (such as using the `Height` and `Width` properties to query or affect a window's dimensions or setting focus to the window with the `SetFocus` method), a few properties deserve special mention:

- The `Document` property gives you a way to programmatically interact with the document that the window is hosting (if any).
- The `Project` and `ProjectItem` properties serve to bridge the `Window` portion of the API with the `Project/Solution` portion; in a similar vein to the `Document` property, you can use these properties to interact with the project that is related to the window or the project item (such as the Visual Basic code file, text file, or resource file).
- If you are dealing with a tool window, the `SetTabPicture` method provides a way to set the tab icon that is displayed when the tool window is part of a group of tabbed windows. (For instance, the Toolbox window displays a wrench and hammer picture on its tab when part of a tabbed group.)
- Again, specifically for tool windows only, the `SetSelectionContainer` can be used to supply one or more objects for display within the Properties window. This capability is useful if you have a custom window where you need to control what is displayed in the Properties window when the window has focus. (All the standard VS windows already do this for you.)

Listing 14.2 contains an excerpt from a C# package; the method `QueryWindows` illustrates the use of the `Window` object. In this example, each window is queried to determine its type, and then a summary of each window is output in a simple message box.

LISTING 14.2 A C# Routine for Querying the `Windows` Collection

```
using System;
using Extensibility;
using EnvDTE;
using EnvDTE80;
using Microsoft.VisualStudio.CommandBars;
using System.Resources;
using System.Reflection;
using System.Globalization;
using System.Windows.Forms;

public class Connect : IDTExtensibility2, IDTCommandTarget
{
   public void QueryWindows()
   {
      Windows windows = _applicationObject.DTE.Windows;
      Window window;
      int count = windows.Count;

      string results =
         count.ToString()  + " windows open..." + "\r\n";

      //Iterate the collection of windows
      for (int index = 1; index <= count; index++)
         {
            window = windows.Item(index);

            string title = window.Caption;

            //If the window is hosting a document, a valid Document
            //object will be returned through Window.Document
            if (window.Document != null)
            {
               //Write this out as a document window
               string docName = window.Document.Name;
               results =
                  results + "Window '" + title + "' is a document window" + "/r/n";
            }
            else
            {
               //If no document was present, this is a tool window
```

```
            //(tool windows don't host documents)
            results =
                results + "Window '" + title + "' is a tool window" + "/r/n";
        }

    }

    //Show the results

    MessageBox.Show(results, "Window Documents",
       MessageBoxButtons.OK, MessageBoxIcon.Information);

  }

}
```

NOTE

If you want to embed your own custom control inside a tool window, you have to write a package and use the `Windows.CreateToolWindow` method. We cover this scenario in Chapter 15.

Text Windows and Window Panes

Text windows have their own specific object abstraction in addition to the generic `Window` object: the `TextWindow` object is used to represent text editor windows. To obtain a reference to a window's `TextWindow` object, you retrieve the `Window` object's value and assign it into a `TextWindow` type.

```
TextWindow textWindow = DTE.ActiveWindow.Object;
```

The `TextWindow` object doesn't provide much functionality over and above the functionality found in the `Window` type; its real value is the access it provides to window panes.

Text editor windows in Visual Studio can be split into two panes; with a text editor open, simply select Split from the Window menu to create a new pane within the window. The `TextWindow.ActivePane` property returns a `TextPane` object representing the currently active pane in the window, and the `TextWindow.Panes` property provides access to all the panes within a text window.

```
//Get pane instance from collection
TextPane2 newPane = textWindow.Panes.Item(1);


//Get currently active pane
TextPane2 currPane = textWindow.ActivePane;
```

One of the more useful things you can do with the `TextPane` object is to scroll the client area of the pane (for example, the visible portion of the document within the pane) so that a specific range of text is visible. This is done via the `TextPane.TryToShow` method.

Here is the definition for the method.

```
bool TryToShow( [InAttribute] TextPoint Point,
        [OptionalAttribute] [InAttribute] vsPaneShowHow How,
        [OptionalAttribute] [InAttribute] Object PointOrCount)
```

The `TextPoint` parameter represents the specific location within the text document that you want visible in the text pane. (We discuss `TextPoint` objects in depth later in this chapter, in the section "Editing Text Documents.") The `vsPaneShowHow` value specifies how the pane should behave when scrolling to the indicated location:

- `vsPaneShowHow.vsPaneShowCentered` causes the pane to center the text/text selection in the middle of the pane (horizontally and vertically).
- `vsPaneShowHow.vsPaneShowTop` places the text point at the top of the viewable region in the pane.
- `vsPaneShowHow.vsPaneShowAsIs` shows the text point as is with no changes in horizontal or vertical orientation within the viewable region in the pane.

The last parameter, the `PointOrCount` object, is used to specify the end of the text area that you want displayed. If you provide an integer here, this represents a count of characters past the original text point; if you provide another text point, the selection is considered to be that text that resides between the two text points.

The `TextPane` object is also used to access the Incremental Search feature for a specific window pane. Listing 14.3 provides code that demonstrates one approach to searching a text window using the `TextPane` and `IncrementalSearch` classes.

LISTING 14.3 Controlling Incremental Search

```
using System;
using Extensibility;
using EnvDTE;
using EnvDTE80;

public class Connect : IDTExtensibility2
{

        private DTE2 _applicationObject;
        private AddIn _addInInstance;

        public void IncrementalSearchDemo()
        {
            //Grab references to the active window;
```

```
        //we assume, for this example, that the window
        //is a text window.
        Window window = _applicationObject.ActiveWindow;

        //Grab a TextWindow instance that maps to our
        //active window
        TextWindow txtWindow = (TextWindow)window.Object;

        //Get the active pane from the text window
        TextPane2 pane = (TextPane2)txtWindow.ActivePane;

        //Using the active pane, get an IncrementalSearch object
        //for the pane
        IncrementalSearch search = pane.IncrementalSearch;

        //Try to find our IMessageMapper interface by looking
        //for the string "IM"
        //Configure the search:
        //   search forward in the document
        //   append the chars that we are searching for
        //   quit the search

        search.StartForward();
        search.AppendCharAndSearch((short)Strings.Asc('I'));
        search.AppendCharAndSearch((short)Strings.Asc('M'));


        //To remove us from incremental search mode,
        //we can call IncrementalSearch.Exit()...
        search.Exit();

    }

}
```

The Tool Window Types

In addition to having a `Window` object abstraction, each default tool window in the IDE (the Command window, Output window, Toolbox window, and Task List window) is represented by a discrete type that exposes methods and properties unique to that tool window. Table 14.7 lists the default tool windows and their underlying types in the automation object model.

TABLE 14.7 Tool Windows and Their Types

Tool Window	Type
Command window	`CommandWindow`
Output window	`OutputWindow`
Task List window	`TaskList`
Toolbox window	`ToolBox`

To reference one of these objects, you first start with its `Window` representation and then cast its `Window.Object` value to the matching type. For instance, this C# snippet starts with a `Window` reference to the Task List window and then uses that `Window` object to obtain a reference to the `TaskList` object.

```
Windows windows = _applicationObject.Windows;
Window twindow =
   _applicationObject.Windows.Item(EnvDTE.Constants.vsWindowKindTaskList);
```

Tasks and the Task List Window

The `TaskList` object enables you to access the items currently displayed in the Task List window; each item in the window is represented by its own `TaskItem` object. The `TaskItem` object exposes methods and properties that enable you to manipulate the task items. For instance, you can mark an item as complete, get or set the line number associated with the task, and change the priority of the task.

You remove tasks from the list by using the `TaskItem.Delete` method and add them by using the `TaskItems.Add` method. The `Add` method allows you to specify the task category, subcategory, description, priority, icon, and so on.

```
TaskList tlist = (TaskList)twindow.Object;

tlist.TaskItems.Add("Best Practices", "Coding Style",
   "Use of brace indenting is inconsistent",
   vsTaskPriority.vsTaskPriorityMedium,
   vsTaskIcon.vsTaskIconUser, True,
   "S:\ContosoCommonFramework\Contoso.Fx.Common\Class1.cs", _
   7, True, True);
```

Table 14.8 provides an inventory of the `TaskItem` members.

TABLE 14.8 `TaskItem` Members

Property	Description
`Category`	The category of the task.
`Checked`	A Boolean flag indicating whether the task is marked as completed. (A check mark appears in the check box next to the task.)

Property	Description
`Collection`	The `TaskList` collection that the current `TaskItem` object belongs to.
`Description`	The description of the task.
`Displayed`	A Boolean flag indicating whether the task is currently visible in the Task List window.
`DTE`	A reference to the root DTE object.
`FileName`	The name of the file associated with the task (if any).
`IsSettable`	By passing in a `vsTaskListColumn` enum value to this property, you can determine whether that column is editable.
`Line`	The line number associated with the task.
`Priority`	A `vsTaskPriority` value indicating the task's priority level. Possible values include `vsTaskPriorityHigh`, `vsTaskPriorityMedium`, and `vsTaskPriorityLow`.
`SubCategory`	The subcategory of the task.
Method	**Description**
`Delete`	Removes the task from the Task List window.
`Navigate`	Causes the IDE to navigate to the location (for example, file and line) associated with the task.
`Select`	Selects or moves the focus to the task within the Task List window.

The Toolbox

Four objects are used to programmatically interface with the Toolbox:

- **`ToolBox`**—An object representing the Toolbox itself
- **`ToolBoxTabs`**—A collection representing the tab panes on the Toolbox
- **`ToolBoxItems`**—A collection representing the items within a tab on the Toolbox
- **`ToolBoxItem`**—A discrete item displayed within a Toolbox tab

Figure 14.3 illustrates the `Toolbox` object hierarchy.

These objects are used primarily to add, remove, or alter the items hosted by the Toolbox. For instance, you can easily add a custom tab to the Toolbox by using the `ToolBoxTabs` collection.

```
ToolBox tbox;
ToolBoxTab myTab;
tBox = _applicationObject.Windows.Item(Constants.vsWindowKindToolbox).Object;
myTab = tBox.ToolBoxTabs.Add("My TBox Tab");
```

You can also add items to a tab with the `ToolBoxItems.Add` method, which accepts a name for the item to add, a "data" object representing the item, and a `vsToolBoxItemFormat` enum, which specifies the format of the item. The `Add` method uses the `vsToolBoxItemFormat` to determine how to interpret the data object value. For instance, if you want to add a .NET control to the tab created in the preceding code snippet, you can accomplish that with just one line of code.

```
myTab.ToolBoxItems.Add("ContosoControl",
     "C:\Contoso\Controls\CalendarControl.dll",
     vsToolBoxItemFormat.vsToolBoxItemFormatDotNETComponent);
```

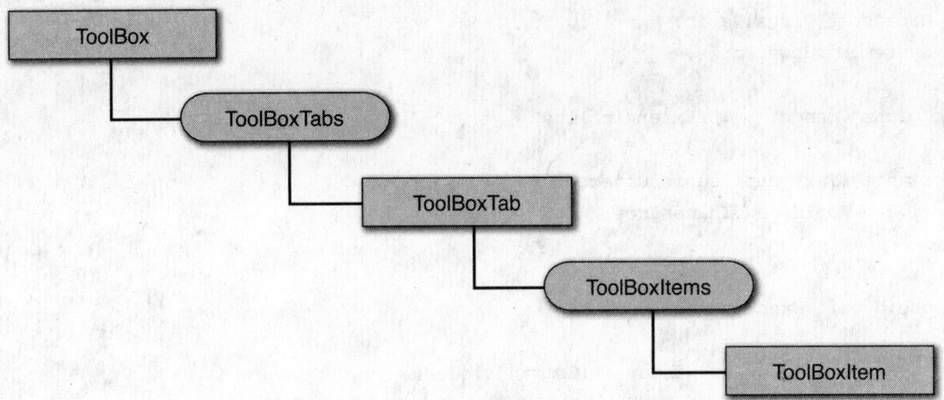

FIGURE 14.3 Mapping the solution/project hierarchy.

Notice that the item, in this case, is represented by a path to the assembly that implements the control, and it has an item format of `vsToolBoxItemFormatDotNETComponent`.

Executing Commands in the Command Window

The command window is a tool window used to execute IDE commands or aliases. IDE commands are essentially ways to tell the IDE to perform some action. Some commands map directly to menu items (such as File Open), whereas others don't have menu equivalents.

The `CommandWindow` object permits you to programmatically pipe commands into the command window and execute them. You can also output a text string (for informational purposes) to the window and clear its current content.

```
//Get a reference to the command window
CommandWindow cmdWindow =
   _applicationObject.Windows.Item(
   Constants.vsWindowKindCommandWindow).Object;

//Display some text in the command window
cmdWindow.OutputString("Hello, World!");

//Clear the command window
cmdWindow.Clear();
```

Listing 14.4 shows how to programmatically execute commands in the `CommandWindow` object.

LISTING 14.4 Executing Commands in the Command Window

```
using System;
using Extensibility;
using EnvDTE;
using EnvDTE80;
using Microsoft.VisualBasic;
using System.Windows.Forms;

public class Connect : IDTExtensibility2
{
    private DTE2 _applicationObject;
    private AddIn _addInInstance;

    public void ExecCommandWindow()
    {
        CommandWindow cmdWindow = (CommandWindow)
        _applicationObject.Windows.Item(
            EnvDTE.Constants.vsWindowKindCommandWindow).Object;

        //Display some text in the command window
        cmdWindow.OutputString("Executing command from the automation OM...");

        //Send some command strings to the command window and execute
        //them...

        //This command will start logging all input/output in the
        //command window to the specified file
        cmdWindow.SendInput("Tools.LogCommandWindowOutput cmdwindow.log", true);

        //Open a file in a code editor:
        //  1. We use an alias, 'of', for the File.OpenFile command
        //  2. This command takes quote-delimited parameters (in this case,
        //     the name of the editor to load the file in)
        string cmd = @"of ";
        cmd = cmd + @"""C:\Contoso\ContosoCommonFramework\Integration.cs""";
        cmd = cmd + @"/e:""CSharp Editor""";

        cmdWindow.SendInput(cmd, true);

        cmdWindow.SendInput("Edit.Find MessageTrxId", true);
```

```
        //Turn off logging
        cmdWindow.SendInput("Tools.LogCommandWindowOutput /off", true);
    }

}
```

Output Window

The Output window displays messages generated from various sources in the IDE. A prime example is the messages generated by the compiler when a project is being built. For a deeper look at the functionality provided by the Output window, see Chapter 10, "Debugging Code."

The Output window is controlled through three objects:

- `OutputWindow` is the root object representing the Output window.
- `OutputWindowPanes` is a collection of `OutputWindowPane` objects.
- `OutputWindowPane` represents one of the current panes within the Output window.

Using these objects, you can add or remove panes from the Output window, output text to any one of the panes, and respond to events transpiring in the window.

The following C# code fragment retrieves a reference to the Output window and writes a test string in the Build pane.

```
OutputWindow outWindow = (OutputWindow)
  _applicationObject.Windows.Item(Constants.vsWindowKindOutput).Object;

OutputWindowPane pane = (OutputWindowPane)
  outWindow.OutputWindowPanes.Item("Build");

pane.OutputString("test");
```

Using the `OutputWindowPane` object, you can also add items simultaneously to a specific output pane and the Task List window. The `OutputWindowPane.OutputTaskItemString` method writes text into the Output window and simultaneously adds that text as a task to the Task List window.

```
string output = "Exception handler not found";
string task = "Add exception handler";
pane.OutputTaskItemString(output,
  vsTaskPriority.vsTaskPriorityMedium,
  "", vsTaskIcon.vsTaskIconNone,
  "", 0, task, true);
```

Because most of the Output window actions are conducted against a specific pane, most of the useful methods are concentrated in the `OutputWindowPane` object. For your reference, the `OutputWindowPane` members are itemized in Table 14.9.

TABLE 14.9 `OutputWindowPane` Members

Property	Description
`Collection`	The `OutputWindowPanes` collection that the current `OutputWindowPane` object belongs to
`DTE`	A reference to the root DTE object
`Guid`	The GUID for the Output window pane
`Name`	The name of the Output window pane
`TextDocument`	A `TextDocument` object representing the window pane's content
Method	**Description**
`Activate`	Moves the focus to the Output window
`Clear`	Clears the contents of the window pane
`ForceItemsToTaskList`	Writes all task items not yet written to the Task List window
`OutputString`	Writes a string to the Output window pane
`OutputTaskItemString`	Writes a string to the Output window pane and simultaneously adds a task to the Task List window

Linked Windows

Tool windows can be positioned in various ways within the IDE: you can float tool windows around within the overall IDE container, you can dock a tool window to one of the sides of the IDE, you can join windows and pin and unpin them, and so on. (See the section "Managing the Many Windows of the IDE" in Chapter 2, "The Visual Studio IDE," for an introduction to window layout.)

A linked window refers to two or more tool windows that have been aggregated together. Figure 14.4 shows one common example of this; the Toolbox window and the Solution Explorer window have been joined in a common frame. You can view each window that is part of the frame by clicking its tab.

By joining two or more tool windows, you actually create an additional window object (called a linked window or window frame) that functions as the container for its hosted tool windows and is available as part of the `DTE.Windows` collection.

By using the `Window.LinkedWindows` and `Window.WindowFrame` properties and the `Windows2.CreateLinkedWindowFrame` method, you can programmatically link and unlink any available tool windows. The C# code in Listing 14.5 demonstrates this process by doing the following:

1. Selecting the window objects for the Toolbox window and the Solution Explorer window.

2. Programmatically joining these two windows, effectively creating the linked window shown in Figure 14.4.

3. Obtaining a reference to the newly created linked window and using its `LinkedWindows` property to unlink the windows that were previously linked.

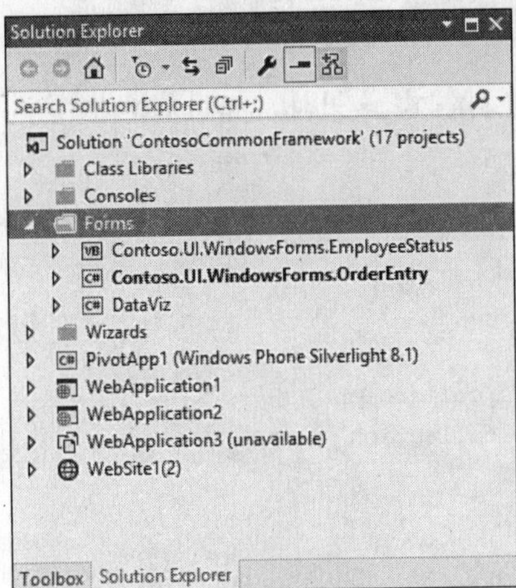

FIGURE 14.4 Linked windows.

LISTING 14.5 Linking and Unlinking Tool Windows

```
using System;
using Extensibility;
using EnvDTE;
using EnvDTE80;
using Microsoft.VisualBasic;
using System.Windows.Forms;

public class Connect : IDTExtensibility2
{

    private DTE2 _applicationObject;
    private AddIn _addInInstance;

    public void LinkUnLink()
    {
        Windows windows = _applicationObject.Windows;

        //Grab references to the Solution Explorer and the Toolbox
        Window solExplorer =
            windows.Item(EnvDTE.Constants.vsWindowKindSolutionExplorer);
```

```
        Window toolbox = windows.Item(EnvDTE.Constants.vsWindowKindToolbox);

        //Use the Windows2 collection to create a linked window/window
        //frame to hold the Toolbox and Solution Explorer windows
        Window windowFrame;
        windowFrame = windows.CreateLinkedWindowFrame(solExplorer,
           toolbox, vsLinkedWindowType.vsLinkedWindowTypeTabbed);

        //At this point, we have created a linked window with two tabbed
        //"interior" windows: the Solution Explorer, and the Toolbox...

        MessageBox.Show("Press OK to Unlink the windows", "LinkUnLink",
           MessageBoxButtons.OK, MessageBoxIcon.None);

        //To unlink the windows:
        //   - Use the window frame's LinkedWindows collection
        //   - Remove the window objects from this collection

        windowFrame.LinkedWindows.Remove(toolbox);
        windowFrame.LinkedWindows.Remove(solExplorer);

    }

}
```

Command Bars

A command bar is a menu bar or toolbar; from an object model perspective, these are represented by `CommandBar` objects. Because menu bars and toolbars are hosted within a window, you reference specific `CommandBar` objects via the `Window` object through the `Window.CommandBars` property. In turn, every `CommandBar` plays host to controls such as buttons and drop-downs. Figure 14.5 shows the Solution Explorer tool window with its command bar highlighted.

NOTE

Unlike the `Windows` collection, which holds only an instance of each open window, the `CommandBars` collection holds instances for every registered command bar, regardless of whether the command bar is currently being shown in the window. Also note that working with the `CommandBar` and `CommandBars` objects will require a reference to `Microsoft.VisualStudio.CommandBars`. This `using` statement is not included by default with add-in project class templates.

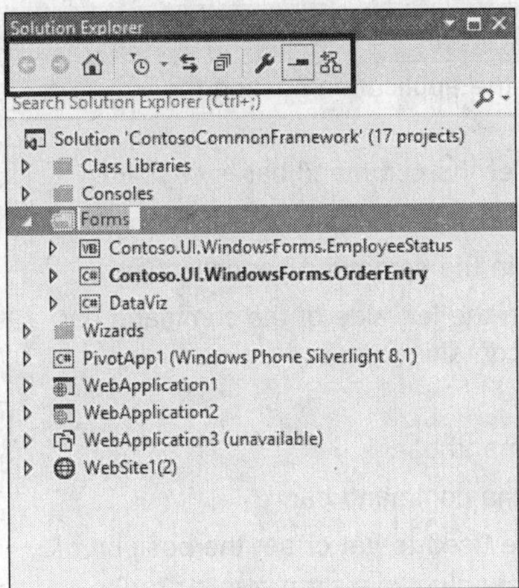

FIGURE 14.5 The Solution Explorer's command bar.

TIP

Use the `CommandBar.Type` property to determine whether a command bar is a toolbar or a menu bar. A value of `MsoBarType.msoBarTypeNormal` indicates that the command bar is a toolbar, whereas a value of `MsoBarType.msoBarTypeMenuBar` indicates that the command bar is a menu bar.

The `CommandBar` object properties and methods are documented in Table 14.10.

TABLE 14.10 `CommandBar` Members

Property	Description
`AdaptiveMenu`	For menu bars, this Boolean flag indicates whether the command bar has *adaptive menus* enabled. (Adaptive menus, sometimes referred to as *personalized menus*, are menus that alter their drop-down content based on projected or actual usage by the user; the intent is to display only those commands that are useful on the menu and hide the other nonessential commands.)
`Application`	An object representing the parent application to the command bar.
`BuiltIn`	A Boolean flag used to distinguish between built-in and custom command bars.
`Context`	A string indicating where the `CommandBar` is saved. (The format and expected content of this string are dictated by the hosting application.)
`Controls`	A `CommandBarControls` collection containing `CommandBarControl` objects; each of these objects represents a control displayed by the command bar.

Property	Description
`Creator`	An integer value that identifies the application hosting the `CommandBar`.
`Enabled`	A Boolean flag indicating whether the command bar is enabled.
`Height`	The height of the command bar in pixels.
`Index`	The index of the command bar in the command bar collection.
`Left`	The distance, in pixels, between the left side of the command bar and the left edge of its parent container.
`Name`	The name of the command bar.
`NameLocal`	The localized name of the command bar.
`Parent`	An object that is the parent of the command bar.
`Position`	An `MsoBarPosition` enum value used to get or set the position of the command bar (for example, `MsoBarPosition.msoBarTop`).
`Protection`	An `MsoBarProtection` enum value that identifies the protection employed against used modification (for example, `MsoBarProtection.msoBarNoMove`).
`RowIndex`	An integer representing the docking row of the command bar.
`Top`	The distance, in pixels, between the top of the command bar and the top edge of its parent container.
`Type`	The type of the command bar (as an `MsobarType` enum value; for example, `MsoBarType.msoBarTypeNormal`).
`Visible`	A Boolean flag indicating whether the command bar is currently visible.
`Width`	The width of the command bar in pixels.

Method	Description
`Delete`	Removes the command bar from its parent collection.
`FindControl`	Enables you to retrieve a reference to a control hosted by the command bar that fits various parameters such as its type, ID, tag, and visibility.
`Reset`	Resets one of the built-in command bars to its default configuration.
`ShowPopup`	Displays a pop-up representing a command bar.

NOTE

Earlier versions of Visual Studio actually relied on a Microsoft Office assembly for the `CommandBar` object definition (`Microsoft.Office.Core`). Visual Studio 2005 and later versions provide their own implementation of the `CommandBar` object that is defined in the `Microsoft.VisualStudio.CommandBars` namespace, although you will find some types that carry their nomenclature over from the Microsoft Office assembly, such as the various `MsoXXX` enums.

Documents

Document objects are used to represent an open document in the IDE. To contrast this abstraction with that provided by the Window object, a Window object is used to represent the physical UI aspects of a document window, whereas a Document object is used to represent the physical document that is being displayed within that document window.

A document could be a designer, such as the Windows Forms Designer, or it could be a text-based document such as a ReadMe file or a C# code file open in an editor.

Just as you get a list of all open windows using the DTE.Windows collection, you can use the DTE.Documents collection to retrieve a list of all open documents.

```
Dim documents As Documents = DTE.Documents
```

The Documents collection is indexed by the document's Name property, which is, in effect, the document's filename without the path information. This makes it easy to quickly retrieve a Document instance.

```
Dim documents As Documents = DTE.Documents

Dim readme As Document = documents.Item("ReadMe.txt")
Documents documents = DTE.Documents;
Document readme = documents.Item["ReadMe.txt"];
```

Using the Document object, you can do the following:

- Close the document (and optionally save changes)
- Retrieve the filename and path of the document
- Determine whether the document has been modified since the last time it was saved
- Determine what, if anything, is currently selected within the document
- Obtain a ProjectItem instance representing the project item that is associated with the document
- Read and edit the contents of text documents

Table 14.11 contains the member descriptions for the Document object.

TABLE 14.11 Document Members

Property	Description
ActiveWindow	The currently active window associated with the document. (A null or Nothing value indicates that there is no active window.)
Collection	The collection of Document objects to which this instance belongs.
DTE	The root-level DTE object.
Extender	Returns a Document extender object.

Property	Description
`ExtenderCATID`	The extender category ID for the object.
`ExtenderNames`	A list of extenders available for the current `Document` object.
`FullName`	The full path and filename of the document.
`Kind`	A GUID representing the kind of document.
`Name`	The name (essentially, the filename without path information) for the document.
`Path`	The path of the document's file excluding the filename.
`ProjectItem`	The `ProjectItem` instance associated with the document.
`Saved`	An indication of whether the solution has been saved since the last modification.
`Selection`	An object representing the current selection in the document (if any).
`Windows`	The `Windows` collection containing the window displaying the document.
Method	**Description**
`Activate`	Moves the focus to the document.
`Close`	Closes the document. You can indicate, with a `vsSaveChanges` enum value, whether the window's hosted document should be saved or not or whether the IDE should prompt the user to make that decision.
`NewWindow`	Opens the document in a new window and returns the new window's `Window` object.
`Object`	Returns an object proxy that represents the window and can be referenced by name.
`Redo`	Re-executes the last user action in the document.
`Save`	Saves the document.
`Undo`	Reverses the last used action in the document.

Text Documents

As previously mentioned, documents can have textual or nontextual content. For those documents with textual content, a separate object exists: `TextDocument`. The `TextDocument` object provides access to control functions specifically related to text content.

If you have a valid `Document` object to start with, and if that `Document` object refers to a text document, then a `TextDocument` instance can be referenced from the `Document.Object` property like this:

```
TextDocument doc;
Document myDocument;

doc = myDocument.Object;
```

Table 14.12 contains the `TextDocument` members.

TABLE 14.12 `TextDocument` Members

Property	Description
`DTE`	The root-level DTE object.
`EndPoint`	A `TextPoint` object positioned at the end of the document.
`Parent`	The parent object of the text document.
`Selection`	A `TextSelection` object representing the currently selected text in the document.
`StartPoint`	A `TextPoint` object positioned at the start of the document.
Method	**Description**
`ClearBookmarks`	Removes any unnamed bookmarks present in the document.
`CreateEditPoint`	Returns an edit point at the specific location. (If no location is specified, the beginning of the document is assumed.)
`MarkText`	Bookmarks lines in the document that match the specified string pattern.
`ReplacePattern`	Replaces any text in the document that matches the pattern.

TIP

A text document is represented by both a `Document` instance and a `TextDocument` instance. Nontext documents, such as a Windows form, open in a Windows Forms Designer window and have a `Document` representation but no corresponding `TextDocument` representation. Unfortunately, there isn't a great way to distinguish whether a document is text based during runtime. One approach is to attempt a cast or assignment to a `TextDocument` object and catch any exceptions that might occur during the assignment.

Two `TextDocument` methods are useful for manipulating bookmarks within the document: `ClearBookmarks` removes any unnamed bookmarks from the document, and `MarkText` performs a string pattern search and places bookmarks against the resulting document lines. A simple package to bookmark `For` loops in a Visual Basic document is presented in Listing 14.6.

LISTING 14.6 Bookmarking `For` Loops in a Visual Basic Document

```
using System;
using Extensibility;
using EnvDTE;
using EnvDTE80;
using Microsoft.VisualBasic;
using System.Windows.Forms;
using Microsoft.VisualStudio.CommandBars;
```

```
public class Connect : IDTExtensibility2
{

    private DTE2 _applicationObject;
    private AddIn _addInInstance;

    public void BookmarkFor()
    {
        Document doc;
        TextDocument txtDoc;

        //Reference the current document
        doc = _applicationObject.ActiveDocument;

        //Retrieve a TextDocument instance from
        //the document
        txtDoc = (TextDocument)doc.Object();

        //Call the MarkText method with the 'For' string
        bool found =
           txtDoc.MarkText("For", (int)vsFindOptions.vsFindOptionsFromStart);

        //MarkText returns a Boolean flag indicating whether or not
        //the search pattern was found in the TextDocument
        if (found)
        {
           MessageBox.Show("All instances of 'For' have been bookmarked.");
        }
        else
        {
           MessageBox.Show("No instances of 'For' were found.");
        }

    }

}
```

The other key functionality exposed by the `TextDocument` object is the capability to read and edit the text within the document.

Editing Text Documents

From a Visual Studio perspective, text in a text document actually has two distinct "representations": a virtual one and a physical one. The physical representation is the straight and unadulterated code file that sits on disk. The virtual representation is what Visual

Studio presents on the screen; it is an interpreted view of the text in the code file that takes into account various editor document features such as code outlining/regions, virtual spacing, and word wrapping.

Figure 14.6 shows this relationship. When displaying a text document, Visual Studio reads the source file into a text buffer, and then the text editor presents one view of that text file to you (based on options you have configured for the editor).

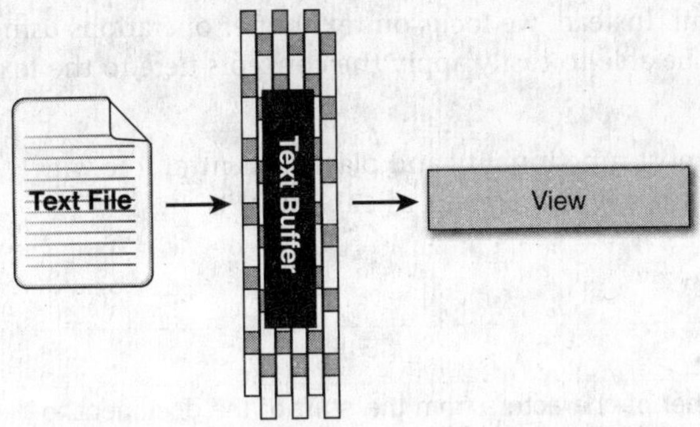

FIGURE 14.6 Presentation of text documents within the IDE.

Text in a document is manipulated or read either on the buffered text or on the "view" text that you see in the editor. Four different automation objects enable you to affect text; two work on the text buffer, and two work on the editor view.

For the text buffer:

- `TextPoint` objects are used to locate specific points within a text document. By querying the `TextPoint` properties, you can determine the line number of the text point, the number of characters it is offset from the start of a line, the number of characters it is offset from the start of the document, and its display column within the text editor window. You can also retrieve a reference to a `CodeModel` object representing the code at the text point's current location.
- The `EditPoint` object inherits from the `TextPoint` object; this is the primary object used for manipulating text in the text buffer. You can add, delete, or move text using edit points, and you can move the edit points around within the text buffer.

And, for the editor view:

- The `VirtualPoint` object is equivalent to the `TextPoint` object except that it can be used to query text locations that reside in the "virtual" space of the text view. (Virtual space is the whitespace that exists after the last character in a document line.) `VirtualPoint` instances are returned through the `TextSelection` object.
- The `TextSelection` object operates on text within the text editor view as opposed to the text buffer and is equivalent to the `EditPoint` interface. When you use the

TextSelection object, you are actively affecting the text that is being displayed within the text editor. The methods and properties of this object, therefore, end up being programmatic approximations of the various ways that you would manually affect text: you can page up or page down within the view; cut, copy, and paste text; select a range of text; or even outline and expand or collapse regions of text.

Because the VirtualPoint object is nearly identical to the TextPoint object, and the TextSelection object is nearly identical to the EditPoint object, we won't bother to cover each of these four objects in detail. Instead, we focus on text buffer operations using EditPoint and TextPoint. You should be able to easily apply the concepts here to the text view.

Because EditPoint objects expose the most functionality and play the central role with text editing, we have provided a list of their type members in Table 14.13.

TABLE 14.13 EditPoint2 Members

Property	Description
AbsoluteCharOffset	The number of characters from the start of the document to the current location of the edit point
AtEndOfDocument	Boolean flag indicating whether the point is at the end of the document
AtEndOfLine	Boolean flag indicating whether the point is at the end of a line in the document
AtStartOfDocument	Boolean flag indicating whether the point is at the beginning of the document
AtStartOfLine	Boolean flag indicating whether the point is at the start of a line in the document
CodeElement	The code element that maps to the edit point's current location
DisplayColumn	The column number of the edit point
DTE	The root automation DTE object
Line	The line number where the point is positioned
LineCharOffset	The character offset, within a line, of the edit point
LineLength	The length of the line where the edit point is positioned
Parent	The parent object of the EditPoint2 object
Method	**Description**
ChangeCase	Changes the case of a range of text
CharLeft	Moves the edit point to the left the specified number of characters
CharRight	Moves the edit point to the right the specified number of characters
ClearBookmark	Clears any unnamed bookmarks that exist on the point's current line location

Method	Description
`Copy`	Copies a range of text to the Clipboard
`CreateEditPoint`	Creates a new `EditPoint` object at the same location as the current `EditPoint` object
`Cut`	Cuts a range of text and places it on the Clipboard
`Delete`	Deletes a range of text from the document
`DeleteWhitespace`	Deletes any whitespace found around the edit point
`EndOfDocument`	Moves the edit point to the end of the document
`EndOfLine`	Moves the edit point to the end of the current line
`EqualTo`	A Boolean value indicating whether the edit point's `AbsoluteCharOffset` value is equal to another edit point's offset
`FindPattern`	Finds any matching string patterns in the document
`GetLines`	Returns a string representing the text between two lines in the document
`GetText`	Returns a string representing the text between the edit point and another location in the document
`GreaterThan`	Returns a Boolean value indicating whether the edit point's `AbsoluteCharOffset` value is greater than another edit point's offset
`Indent`	Indents the selected lines by the given number of levels
`Insert`	Inserts a string into the document, starting at the edit point's current location
`InsertFromFile`	Inserts the entire contents of a text file into the document starting at the edit point's current location
`LessThan`	Returns a Boolean value indicating whether the edit point's `AbsoluteCharOffset` value is less than another edit point's offset
`LineDown`	Moves the point down one or more lines
`LineUp`	Moves the point up one or more lines
`MoveToAbsoluteOffset`	Moves the edit point to the given character offset
`MoveToLineAndOffset`	Moves the edit point to the given line and to the character offset within that line
`MoveToPoint`	Moves the edit point to the location of another `EditPoint` or `TextPoint` object
`NextBookmark`	Moves the edit point to the next available bookmark in the document
`OutlineSection`	Creates an outline section between the point's current location and another location in the document
`PadToColumn`	Pads spaces in the current line up to the indicated column number

Method	Description
`Paste`	Pastes the contents of the Clipboard to the edit point's current location
`PreviousBookmark`	Moves the edit point to the previous bookmark
`ReadOnly`	Returns a Boolean flag indicating whether a text range in the document is read-only
`ReplacePattern`	Replaces any text that matches the provided pattern
`ReplaceText`	Replaces a range of text with the provided string
`SetBookmark`	Creates an unnamed bookmark on the edit point's current line in the document
`StartOfDocument`	Moves the edit point to the start of the document
`StartOfLine`	Moves the edit point to the beginning of the line where it is positioned
`TryToShow`	Attempts to display the point's current location within the text editor window
`Unindent`	Removes the given number of indentation levels from a range of lines in the document
`WordLeft`	Moves the edit point to the left the given number of words
`WordRight`	Moves the edit point to the right the given number of words

Now let's look at various text manipulation scenarios.

Adding Text `EditPoint` objects are the key to adding text. You create them by using either a `TextDocument` object or a `TextPoint` object.

A `TextPoint` instance can create an `EditPoint` instance in its same location by calling `TextPoint.CreateInstance`. With the `TextDocument` type, you can call the `CreateEditPoint` method and pass in a valid `TextPoint`.

Because `TextPoint` objects are used to locate specific points in a document, a `TextPoint` object is leveraged as an input parameter to `CreateEditPoint`. In essence, the object tells the method where to create the edit point. If you don't provide a `TextPoint` object, the edit point is created at the start of the document.

This code snippet shows an edit point being created at the end of a document.

```
Document doc = _applicationObject.ActiveDocument;
TextDocument txtDoc = (Textdocument)doc.Object();
TextPoint tp = txtDoc.EndPoint;
EditPoint2 ep = txtDoc.CreateEditPoint(tp);
//This line of code would have the same effect
ep = tp.CreateEditPoint();
```

After creating an edit point, you can use it to add text into the document. (Remember, you are editing the buffered text whenever you use an `EditPoint` object.) To inject a string into the document, you use the `Insert` method:

```
//Insert a C# comment line
ep.Insert("// some comment");
```

You can even grab the contents of a file and throw that into the document with the `EditPoint.InsertFromFile` method:

```
//Insert comments from a comments file
ep.InsertFromFile("C:\Contoso\std comments.txt");
```

Editing Text The `EditPoint` object supports deleting, replacing, cutting, copying, and pasting text in a document.

Some of these operations require more than a single point to operate. For instance, if you want to cut a word or an entire line of code from a document, you need to specify a start point and end point that define that range of text (see Figure 14.7).

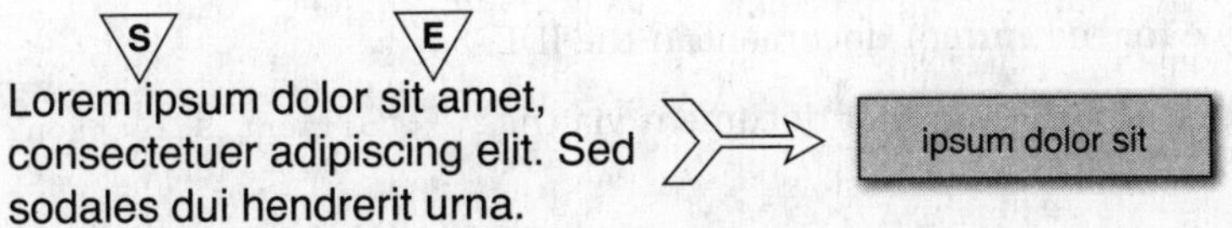

FIGURE 14.7 Using points within a document to select text.

This snippet uses two end points—one at the start of a document and one at the end—to delete the entire contents of the document.

```
Document doc = _applicationObject.ActiveDocument;
TextDocument txtDoc = (TextDocument)doc.Object();

TextPoint tpStart = txtDoc.StartPoint;
TextPoint tpEnd = txtDoc.EndPoint;

EditPoint2 epStart = txtDoc.CreateEditPoint(tpStart);
EditPoint2 epEnd = txtDoc.CreateEditPoint(tpEnd);
epStart.Delete(epEnd);
```

Besides accepting a second `EditPoint`, the methods that operate on a range of text also accept an integer identifying a count of characters. This has the effect of defining a select. For example, this snippet cuts the first 10 characters from a document.

```
epStart.Cut(10);
```

Repositioning an EditPoint After establishing an `EditPoint`, you can move it to any location in the document by using various methods. The `CharLeft` and `CharRight` methods move the point any number of characters to the left or right, and the `WordLeft` and `WordRight` methods perform the same operation with words.

```
// Move the edit point four words to the right
epStart.WordRight(4);
```

The `LineUp` and `LineDown` methods jog the point up or down the specified number of lines. You can also move `EditPoints` to any given line within a document by using `MoveToLineAndOffset`. In addition, this method positions the point any number of characters into the line.

```
// Move the edit point to line 100, and then
// in 5 characters to the right
epStart.MoveToLineAndOffset(100, 5);
```

To illustrate some of these text editing concepts, consider the task of programmatically adding a comment "flower box" immediately preceding a routine open in a code editor. To accomplish this, we would need to go through the following process:

1. Obtain a reference for the current document in the IDE.
2. Get the active cursor location in that document via the `TextDocument.Selection.ActivePoint` property.
3. Create an `EditPoint` using the `VirtualPoint` object.
4. Create a second `EditPoint` to act as the other "book end" for the text. In other words, these two edit points will represent the start and the end of the routine definition line (`ex: public void DoSomething(int someArg)`).
5. Parse the routine definition text (encapsulated by the endpoints) to try to ferret out items such as its name, return value, and parameter list.
6. Build a string using the routine information and then insert that string into the code editor/text document using an `EditPoint`.

Listing 14.7 demonstrates the preceding actions.

LISTING 14.7 Inserting Comments into a Text Window

```
using System;
using Extensibility;
using EnvDTE;
using EnvDTE80;
using Microsoft.VisualBasic;
using System.Windows.Forms;
```

```
using Microsoft.VisualStudio.CommandBars;
public class Connect : IDTExtensibility2
{

    private DTE2 _applicationObject;
    private AddIn _addInInstance;

    //This routine demonstrates various text editing scenarios
    //using the EditPoint and TextPoint types. If you place your
    //cursor on a Visual Basic subroutine or function, it will build
    //a default "flower box" comment area, insert it immediately
    //above the sub/function, and outline it.
    //
    //To use:
    //  1) put cursor anywhere on the Sub/Function line
    //  2) run add-in command
    //  This will fail silently (e.g., will not insert any
    //  comments) if it is unable to determine the start
    //  of the Sub/Function
    //
    public void  InsertVBTemplateFlowerbox()
    {
        //Get reference to the active document
        Document doc = _applicationObject.ActiveDocument;
        TextDocument txtDoc = (TextDocument)doc.Object();
        bool isFunc;

        try
        {
            EditPoint2 ep = (EditPoint2)txtDoc.Selection.ActivePoint.
➥CreateEditPoint();

            ep.StartOfLine();
            EditPoint2 ep2 = (EditPoint2)ep.CreateEditPoint();
            ep2.EndOfLine();

            string lineText = ep.GetText(ep2).Trim();

            if (lineText.IndexOf(" Function ") > 0)
            {
                isFunc = true;
            }
            else
            {
                if (lineText.IndexOf(" Sub ") > 0)
                {
```

```
                isFunc = false;
            }

            else
            {
                throw new Exception();
            }
        }

        //Parse out info that we can derive from the routine
        //definition: the return value type (if this is a function),
        //the names of the parameters, and the name of the routine.
        string returnType = "";

        if (isFunc)
        {
            returnType = ParseRetValueType(lineText);
        }


        string[] parameters = ParseParameters(lineText);
        string name = ParseRoutineName(lineText);
        string commentBlock = BuildCommentBlock(isFunc, name,
           returnType, parameters);

        //Move the edit point up one line (to position
        //immediately preceding the routine)
        ep.LineUp(1);

        //Give us some room by inserting a new blank line
        ep.InsertNewLine();

        //Insert our comment block
        ep.Insert(commentBlock.ToString());
    }
    catch (Exception ex)
    {

    }


}

private string BuildCommentBlock(bool isFunc,
    string name,
    string returnType,
```

```
        string[] parameters)
    {
        try
        {
            string comment = "";

            //Build up a sample comment block using the passed-in info
            comment += "////////////////////////////////////////////////\r\n";
            comment += "// Routine: " + name;
            comment += "\r\n";
            comment += "// Description: [insert routine desc here]";
            comment += "\r\n";
            comment += "//";
            comment += "\r\n";

            if (isFunc)
            {
                comment += "// Returns: A " +
                    returnType +
                    "[insert return value description here]";
            }

            comment += "\r\n";
            comment += "//";
            comment += "\r\n";
            comment += "// Parameters:";
            comment += "\r\n";

            for (int i = 0; i <= parameters.GetUpperBound(0); i++)
            {
                comment += "//      ";
                comment += parameters[i];
                comment += ": [insert parameter description here]";
                comment += "\r\n";
            }

            comment += "////////////////////////////////////////////////\r\n";

            return comment;

        }
        catch (Exception ex)
        {
            return "";
        }
```

```
}

private string ParseRetValueType(string code)
{
    try
    {
        //Parse out the return value of a function (VB)
        //Search for //As', starting from the end of the string
        int length = code.Length;
        int index = code.LastIndexOf(" As ");

        string retVal = code.Substring(index + 3, length - (index + 3));
        return retVal.Trim();

    }

    catch (Exception ex)
    {
        return "";
    }


}

private string[] ParseParameters(string code)
{
    try{
        //Parse out the parameters specified (if any) for
        //a VB sub/func definition
        int length = code.Length;
        int indexStart = code.IndexOf("(");
        int indexEnd = code.LastIndexOf(")");

        string parameters = code.Substring(indexStart + 1, indexEnd -
         (indexStart + 1));

        return parameters.Split(',');

    }
    catch (Exception ex)
    {
        return null;
    }
```

```
    }

    private string ParseRoutineName(string code)
    {
        try
        {
            string name;
            int length = code.Length;
            int indexStart = code.IndexOf(" Sub ");
            int indexEnd = code.IndexOf("(");

            if (indexStart == -1)
            {
                indexStart = code.IndexOf(" Function ");
                if (indexStart != -1)
                {
                    indexStart = indexStart + 9;
                }

            }
            else
            {
                indexStart = indexStart + 5;
            }

            name = code.Substring(indexStart, indexEnd - indexStart);

            return name.Trim();
        }
        catch (Exception ex)
        {
            return "";
        }

    }

}
```

Command Objects

Every action that is possible to execute through the menus and toolbars in Visual Studio is generically referred to as a command. For example, pasting text into a window is a command, as is building a project, toggling a breakpoint, and closing a window.

For each command supported in the IDE, there is a corresponding `Command` object; the `DTE.Commands` collection holds all the valid `Command` object instances. Each command is keyed by a name that categorizes, describes, and uniquely identifies the command. The Paste command, for instance, is available via the string key `"Edit.Paste"`. If you want to retrieve the `Command` object mapping to the Paste command, you pull from the `Commands` collection using that string key.

```
Commands2 commands = (Commands2)_applicationObject.Commands;
Command cmd = commands.Item["Edit.Paste"];
```

You can query a command's name via its `Name` property.

```
//name would = "Edit.Paste"
string name = cmd.Name;
```

Table 14.14 contains the members declared on the `Command` interface.

TABLE 14.14 Command Members

Property	Description
Bindings	The keystrokes that can be used to invoke the command
Collection	The `Commands` collection that the `Command` object belongs to
DTE	A reference to the root-level DTE object
Guid	A GUID that identifies the command's group
ID	An integer that identifies the command within its group
IsAvailable	A Boolean flag that indicates whether the command is currently available
LocalizedName	The localized name of the command
Name	The name of the command
Method	**Description**
AddControl	Creates a control for the command that can be hosted in a command bar
Delete	Removes a named command that was previously added with the `Commands.AddNamedCommand` method

The list of all available commands is extremely long (nearly 3,000 total), so it is impossible to cover every one of them, or even a large portion of them, here. To get an idea of the specific commands available, however, you can use the dialog box used that customizes the Visual Studio toolbars. If you select the Customize option from the View, Toolbars menu and then click the Commands tab, you can investigate all the various commands by category (see Figure 14.8). Another alternative is to programmatically iterate the `DTE.Commands` collection and view them that way.

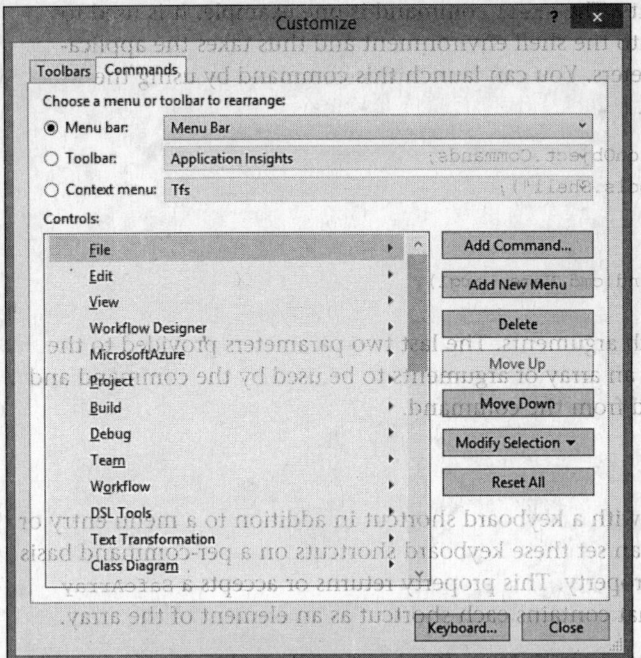

FIGURE 14.8 Using the Customize dialog box to view commands.

So, although we can't cover all the commands, you can learn how to perform common tasks with the `Command` objects, such as executing a command, checking on a command's current status, and even adding your own commands to the command library.

Executing a Command

You can execute commands in two ways. The `DTE` object has an `ExecuteCommand` method you can use to trigger a command based on its name.

```
_applicationObject.ExecuteCommand("Window.CloseDocumentWindow");
```

The `Commands` collection is also a vehicle for launching commands through its `Raise` method. Instead of using the command's name, the `Raise` method uses its GUID and ID to identify the command.

```
Commands2 commands = (Commands2)_applicationObject.Commands;
Command cmd = commands.Item["Window.CloseDocumentWindow"];
object customIn;
object customOut;

commands.Raise(cmd.Guid, cmd.ID, customin, customout);
```

Some commands accept arguments. The `Shell` command is one example. It is used to launch an external application into the shell environment and thus takes the application filename as one of its parameters. You can launch this command by using the `ExecuteCommand` method like this.

```
Commands2 commands = _applicationObject.Commands;
Command cmd = commands.Item("Tools.Shell");
string arg1 = "MyApp.exe";

_applicationObject.ExecuteCommand(cmd.Name, arg1);
```

The `Raise` method also works with arguments. The last two parameters provided to the `Raise` method are used to specify an array of arguments to be used by the command and an array of output values returned from the command.

Mapping Key Bindings

You can invoke most commands with a keyboard shortcut in addition to a menu entry or button on a command bar. You can set these keyboard shortcuts on a per-command basis by using the `Command.Bindings` property. This property returns or accepts a `SafeArray` (essentially an array of objects) that contains each shortcut as an element of the array.

Key bindings are represented as strings with the following format:
`[scopename]::[modifier+][key]`.

`Scopename` is used to refer to the scope where the shortcut is valid, such as `Text Editor` or `Global`. The `modifier` token is used to specify the key modifier, such as Ctrl+, Alt+, or Shift+. (Modifiers are not required.) And the `key` is the keyboard key that is pressed (in conjunction with the modifier if present) to invoke the command.

To add a binding to an existing command, you need to retrieve the current array of binding values, add your binding string to the array, and then assign the whole array back into the `Bindings` property like this.

```
Commands2 commands As = (Commands2)_applicationObject.Commands;
Command cmd =
   commands.Item("File.SaveSelectedItems");

object[] bindings;

bindings = cmd.Bindings;

// Increase the array size by 1 to hold the new binding
Array.Resize<object>(ref bindings, bindings.GetUpperBound(0) + 1);

// Assign the new binding into the array
bindings(bindings.GetUpperBound(0)) = "Global::Shift+F2";
```

```
// Assign the array back to the command object
cmd.Bindings = bindings;
```

NOTE

You can create your own named commands that can be launched from a command bar in the IDE (or from the command window for that matter). The `Command` object itself is added to the `Commands` collection by calling `Commands.AddNamedCommand`. The code that runs when the command is executed has to be implemented by an add-in. We cover this scenario in Chapter 15.

Debugger Objects

The automation object model provides a `Debugger` object that enables you to control the Visual Studio debugger. You can obtain a `Debugger` instance through the `DTE.Debugger` property.

```
Dim debugger As EnvDTE.Debugger
debugger = DTE.Debugger
```

With a valid `Debugger` object, you can do the following:

- Set breakpoints
- Start and stop the debugger for a given process
- Control the various execution stepping actions supported by the debugger, such as Step Into, Step Over, and Step Out
- Issue the Run to Cursor command to the debugger
- Query the debugger for its current mode (for example, break mode, design mode, or run mode)

The following code starts the debugger if it isn't already started.

```
Debugger2 debugger = (Debugger2)_applicationObject.Debugger;

If (debugger.CurrentMode != dbgDebugMode.dbgRunMode)
{
    debugger.Go();
}
```

Summary

The Visual Studio automation object model is a deep and wide API that exposes many of the IDE components to managed code running as an add-in in the IDE. This chapter documented how this API is organized and described its capabilities in terms of controlling the Visual Studio debugger, editors, windows, tool windows, solutions, and projects.

We also discussed the eventing model exposed by the API and looked at the API's capabilities with regard to accessing the underlying code structure for a project, issuing commands inside the IDE, and editing text documents programmatically.

Using the methods and properties expressed on the automation objects, you can automate common tasks in the IDE and extend Visual Studio in ways that address your specific development tool needs.

In the next chapter, we directly build on the concepts discussed here and specifically walk you through the process of writing Visual Studio add-ins.

CHAPTER 15

Extending the IDE

IN THIS CHAPTER

- Creating Your First Extension
- The Structure of an Extension
- A Sample Extension: Color Selector

As robust as Visual Studio is in terms of features and capabilities, its designers cannot anticipate every possible scenario. Nor can Microsoft move at a fast enough clip to deliver enough versions of Visual Studio to satisfy all the various requirements that individual developers or companies might have. So Visual Studio has been constructed in a way that allows .NET developers to reach out and customize the behavior of the IDE or even add new behaviors. This is done via extensions: compiled and deployable modules that are capable of hooking into the Visual Studio IDE to provide new functionality. You can craft your extensions using Visual Basic, Visual C#, or even Visual C++. Extensions have a variety of potential uses and allow you to surface your own custom forms, tool windows, and designers within the IDE. Here are just a few of the things possible with add-ins:

- Create and display custom tool windows
- Expose a custom user interface to end users
- Implement a property page hosted in the Visual Studio Options dialog box
- Publish new commands onto one or more Visual Studio menus
- Add a debugger visualizer
- Dynamically enable or disable menu and toolbar items in the IDE

Creating Your First Extension

Before getting started, you will need to take care of one prerequisite: installing the Visual Studio software development kit (SDK). The SDK provides the VSIX project template, along with various project item templates, that we will use to build our extension. To start, create a new project; with the SDK installed, you will see a VSIX Project entry under the Extensibility category of your language of choice. Select the project template, and click OK in the New Project dialog (see Figure 15.1).

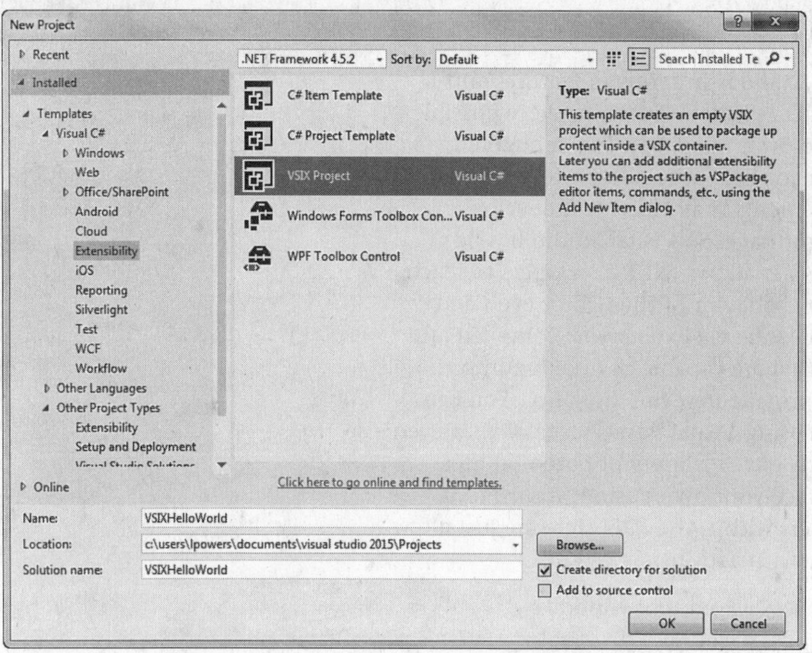

FIGURE 15.1 Selecting the VSIX project type.

NOTE

VSIX is simply the name for the deployable package that contains the components of one or more Visual Studio extensions. Physically, they are created as `.vsix` files. Each file, in addition to its extension payload, will contain metadata that is recognized by the Visual Studio Extension Manager, allowing the extension to be properly installed.

Once the project has been created, the first thing you will notice is the relative lack of content. In fact, initial VSIX projects contain only a single file: the manifest file. This manifest will open by default inside a property editor (see Figure 15.2).

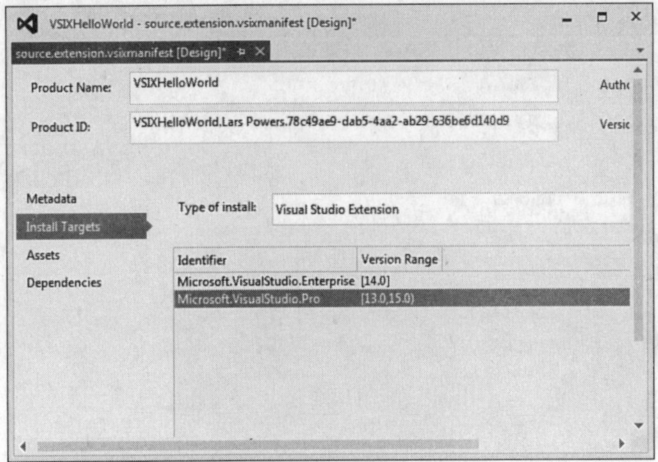

FIGURE 15.2 Editing the project manifest information.

Setting Package Parameters

Using the manifest editor, we can set various pieces of metadata for our extension, including its description, version level, supported languages, author, and so on. Most of this information will show up in your extension's About box. Others are used for true packaging and labeling information.

Packages (and their contained extensions) can target, and run within, a wide range of Visual Studio version and SKU levels. You can explicitly call out the target versions using the Install Targets tab in the manifest editor (see Figure 15.2).

For example, we could elect to target only Visual Studio 2015 Pro users, or we could support a range of all SKUs from Visual Studio 2010 and later. The decision is ours; the desire to reach a large number of potential users by targeting a range of Visual Studio versions is typically tempered by the need to exploit extension features that are only available in a new version of the IDE.

The real content for any extension is created through the use of project item templates. For this first `"Hello, World"` type sample, we can leave all our manifest details with default values and get on to the business of writing our extension's functionality.

Adding Project Items

Every major piece of potential extension capability is represented by its own project item. As we discussed earlier, creating a command that can be triggered from a custom Visual Studio menu selection is one potential way to surface an extension inside of the IDE. And this would be crafted and added into our VSIX project by using a tool window project item. Figure 15.3 shows the available project items.

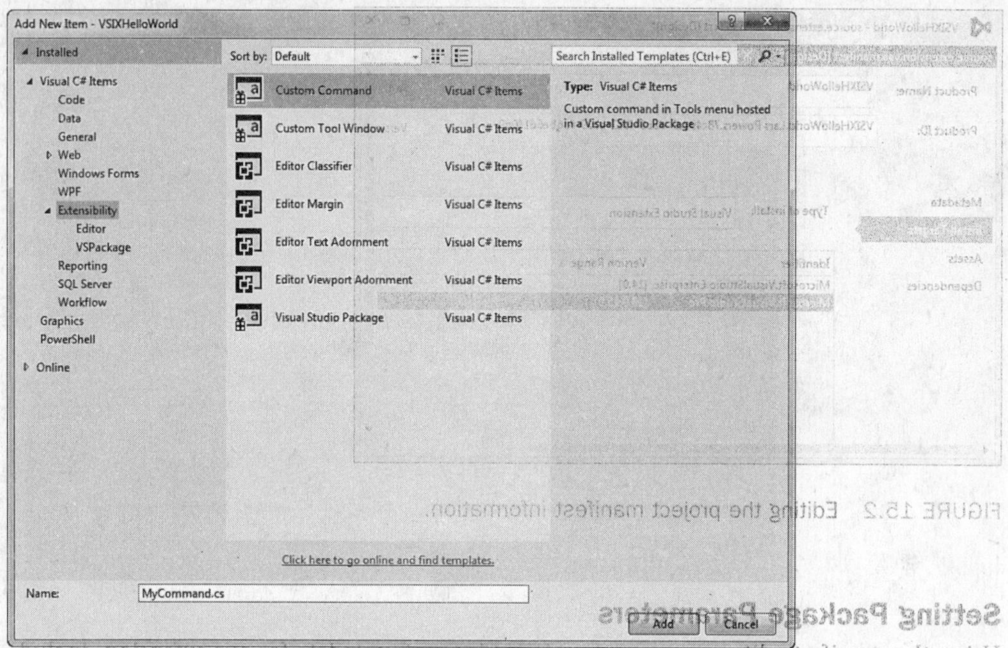

FIGURE 15.3 VSIX project items.

The available project items prefixed with `Custom` are the traditional Visual Studio extension items. You will see others in the list prefixed with `Editor`. These are project items that leverage a slightly different framework (the Managed Extensions Framework, MEF) to allow you to customize the code editor inside of Visual Studio. We cover those types of extensions in the next chapter.

Let's add a custom command item.

Custom Commands

A custom command is nothing more than a menu or toolbar item that kicks off a specific piece of code. To implement a traditional `Hello World` application, we can first create a menu command within the IDE and then, in response to someone clicking on that command, we can show a MessageBox with our `"Hello World"` text.

Select the Custom Command project item from the Add New Item dialog (see Figure 15.3), give it a name, and then click OK to add it to the project.

The first thing you will notice is that this one project item template actually creates multiple files for us: a command class file that implements the specifics of our command, image files to use as menu icons, and various package files that integrate and map our command into the IDE. (We'll talk more about these in a bit.)

To implement our command logic, we simply need to write code within the command C# code file. Specifically, because the command class already has plumbing in place to write the command to an event handler, we will add our code to the event handler.

```
private void ShowMessageBox(object sender, EventArgs e)
{
    //Show a MessageBox to prove we were here
    IVsUIShell uiShell = (IVsUIShell)Package.GetGlobalService(typeof(SVsUIShell));
    Guid clsid = Guid.Empty;
    int result;
    Microsoft.VisualStudio.ErrorHandler.ThrowOnFailure(uiShell.ShowMessageBox(
        0,
        ref clsid,
        "MyCommand1Package",
        "Hello, World!",
        string.Empty,
        0,
        OLEMSGBUTTON.OLEMSGBUTTON_OK,
        OLEMSGDEFBUTTON.OLEMSGDEFBUTTON_FIRST,
        OLEMSGICON.OLEMSGICON_INFO,
        0,        //false
        out result));
}
```

At this stage, the package doesn't actually do anything. You still have to implement your custom logic. What the project item template has done, however, is implement much (if not all) of the tedious plumbing required to do the following:

- Wire the extension into the IDE
- Expose it via a menu command
- Intercept the appropriate extensibility events to make the extension work

Our VSIX project is actually ready to run at this stage because all the required integration and wrapper code is included for you within files that the project item template created.

Debugging the extension project launches a separate instance of Visual Studio (called the "experimental instance"); the extension will be registered and installed into that instance. We are free to then test our extension.

By default, menu commands will show up under the IDE's Tools menu. Figure 15.4 shows our new menu command displayed within the experimental Visual Studio instance. And Figure 15.5 shows the results of clicking on that menu item.

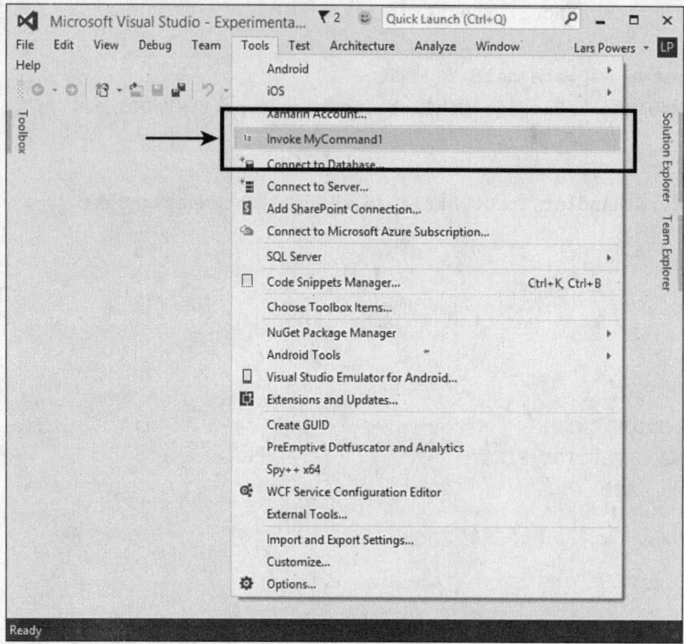

FIGURE 15.4 A custom command entry in the Tools menu.

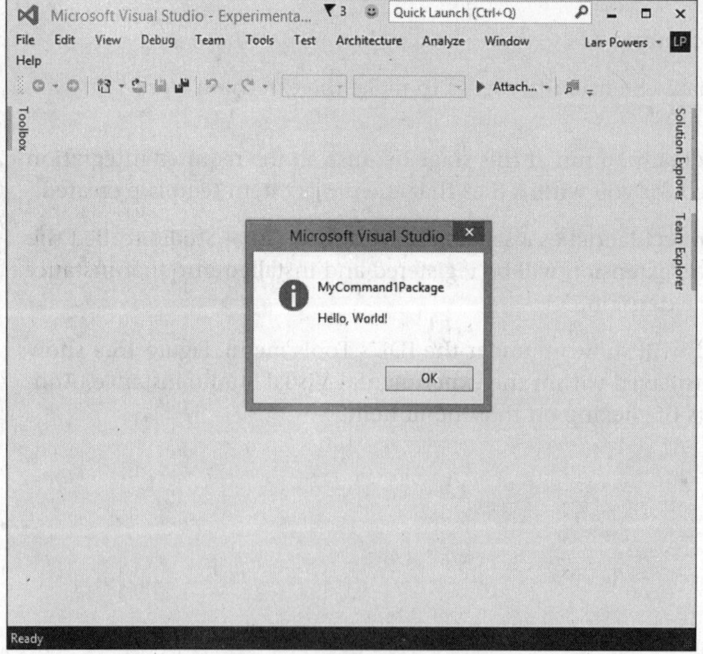

FIGURE 15.5 A custom command triggered message box.

Tool Windows

Creating a custom tool window is just as easy as creating a custom command: just add the custom tool window project item to your project.

Figure 15.6 shows a new VSIX project after adding the tool window project item. Just as with our prior command example, this project item template adds all the various, required files to your project. In addition to the plumbing and integration code and the class that implements the tool window's user interface (UI), you get a custom command added to the project that will, by default, display the tool window.

Tool windows are nothing more than user controls that implement their UI using XAML. (We introduce the core concepts of XAML in Chapter 21, "Building WPF Applications," and in Chapter 23, "Developing Windows Store Applications."

FIGURE 15.6 VSIX project implementing a custom tool window.

Figure 15.7 shows the default tool window running as an extension in the IDE. Custom tool windows are, by default, launched through the View, Other Windows menu.

To change the tool window UI, edit the user control class (in this case, `ToolWindow1Control` is defined within the `ToolWindow1Control.xaml` and `ToolWindow1Control.xaml.cs` files).

Now that you have a baseline of code to work with, you're ready to examine the source to understand the overall structure and layout of an extension.

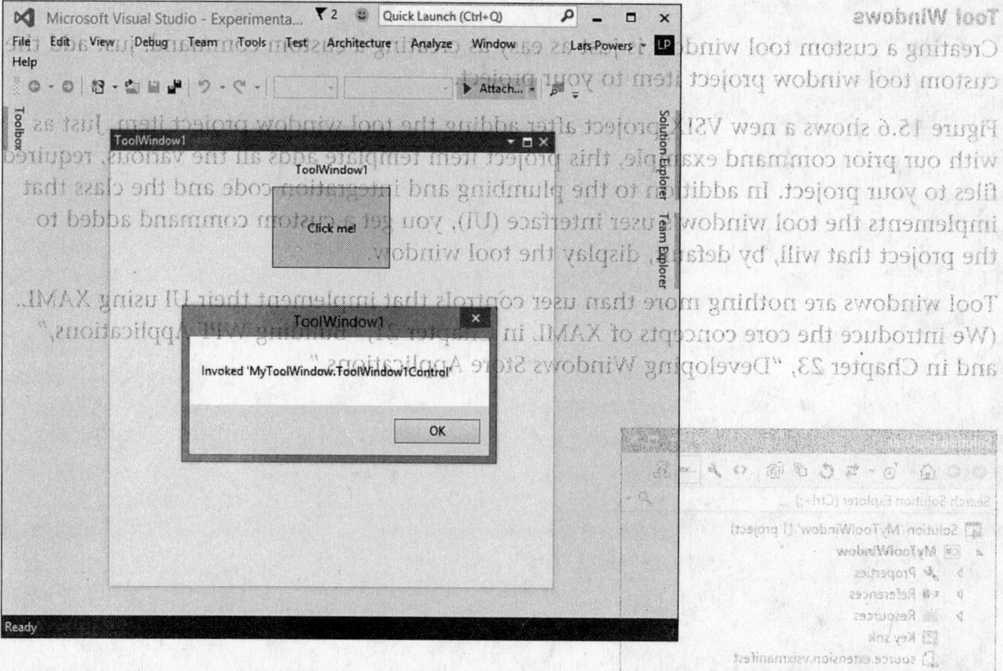

FIGURE 15.7 A basic custom tool window running as an extension in Visual Studio.

The Structure of an Extension

As we've seen, the VSIX extension project is composed of a few different files, all paved down by adding an extensibility project item. The core package class file contains the logic for our package.

Because packages are dynamic link libraries (DLLs), VSIX projects are class library projects. The core code file that is created implements a class called `Microsoft.VisualStudio.Shell.Package`. This class contains all the necessary interfaces to make the package work within the context of the IDE.

Referring back to our `"Hello, World"` example of a custom command, Listing 15.1 shows the `core Package` class as it was generated by the custom command project item template.

LISTING 15.1 Package Code Generated by the Custom Command Project Item

```
using System;
using System.Diagnostics;
using System.Globalization;
namespace HelloWorldExtension
{
    /// <summary>
    /// This is the class that implements the package exposed
    /// by this assembly.
    /// </summary>
```

```
/// <remarks>
/// <para>
/// The minimum requirement for a class to be considered a
/// valid package for Visual Studio is to implement the
/// IVsPackage interface and register itself with the shell.
/// This package uses the helper classes defined inside the
/// Managed Package Framework (MPF) to do it: it derives from
/// the Package class that provides the implementation of the
/// IVsPackage interface and uses the registration attributes
/// defined in the framework to register itself and its
/// components with the shell. These attributes tell the
/// pkgdef creation utility what data to put into the .pkgdef file.
/// </para>
/// <para>
/// To get loaded into VS, the package must be referred by
/// &lt;Asset Type="Microsoft.VisualStudio.VsPackage" ...&gt;
/// in .vsixmanifest file.
/// </para>
/// </remarks>
[PackageRegistration(UseManagedResourcesOnly = true)]
// Info on this package for Help/About
[InstalledProductRegistration("#110", "#112", "1.0",
    IconResourceID = 400)]
[ProvideMenuResource("Menus.ctmenu", 1)]
[Guid(MyCommand1PackageGuids.PackageGuidString)]
[SuppressMessage("StyleCop.CSharp.DocumentationRules",
    "SA1650:ElementDocumentationMustBeSpelledCorrectly",
    Justification = "pkgdef, VS and vsixmanifest are valid VS terms")]
public sealed class MyCommand1Package : Package
{
    /// <summary>
    /// Initializes a new instance of the <see cref="MyCommand1"/> class.
    /// </summary>
    public MyCommand1Package()
    {
        //Inside this method you can place any initialization
        //code that does not require any Visual Studio service
        //because at this point the package object is created but
        //not sited yet inside Visual Studio environment.
        //The place to do all the other initialization is the
        //Initialize method.
    }

    #region Package Members

    /// <summary>
```

```
        /// Initialization of the package; this method is called right
        /// after the package is sited, so this is the place
        /// where you can put all the initialization code that relies
        /// on services provided by Visual Studio.
        /// </summary>
        protected override void Initialize()
        {
            MyCommand1.Initialize(this);
            base.Initialize();
        }

        #endregion
    }
}
```

The first thing to notice is that your package class (which will, by default, be named after the project item that you added) inherits from the `Package` class:

```
public sealed class MyCommand1Package : Package
```

The `Package` class, in turn, implements the `IVsPackage` interface that provides the functionality necessary to expose the package and its functionality within the IDE.

This interface provides the eventing glue for packages. It is responsible for all the events that constitute the life span of an add-in.

Beyond the `Package` class itself, there are other files created within the package project. There are resource files for defining string and bitmap resources and a `.vsct` file and code files that define important commands for your package.

Defining and Reacting to Commands

One of the primary ways you interact with a package-based extension is by issuing it a command (perhaps via a Visual Studio menu, or a toolbar button press event). A command, in the VSPackage environment, is nothing more than a message to the extension that triggers an action. For example, if we have an extension that computed the total lines of executable code within a code editor window, we would probably trigger that computation via a command. Or, if our extension was capable of printing out a file loaded into Visual Studio, we would initiate the printing via a `print` command.

Listing 15.2 shows the command file code that was generated with our `"Hello, World"` custom command project.

LISTING 15.2 Command Class Generated by the Custom Command Project Item

```
using System;
using System.ComponentModel.Design;
using System.Globalization;
using Microsoft.VisualStudio.Shell;
```

```
using Microsoft.VisualStudio.Shell.Interop;

namespace HelloWorldExtension
{
    /// <summary>
    /// Command handler
    /// </summary>
    internal sealed class MyCommand1
    {
        /// <summary>
        /// Command ID.
        /// </summary>
        public const int CommandId = 0x0100;

        /// <summary>
        /// Command menu group (command set GUID).
        /// </summary>
        public static readonly Guid MenuGroup =
            new Guid("00527dbc-b05f-4ba5-b30b-b780795bbcf6");

        /// <summary>
        /// VS Package that provides this command, not null.
        /// </summary>
        private readonly Package package;

        /// <summary>
        /// Initializes a new instance of the <see cref="MyCommand1"/>
        /// class.
        /// Adds our command handlers for menu (commands must exist
        /// in the command table file)
        /// </summary>
        /// <param name="package">Owner package, not null.</param>
        private MyCommand1(Package package)
        {
            if (package == null)
            {
                throw new ArgumentNullException("package");
            }

            this.package = package;

            OleMenuCommandService commandService =
                this.ServiceProvider.GetService(
                    typeof(IMenuCommandService)) as OleMenuCommandService;
            if (commandService != null)
            {
```

```
            CommandID menuCommandID =
                new CommandID(MenuGroup, CommandId);
            EventHandler eventHandler =
                this.ShowMessageBox;
            MenuCommand menuItem =
                new MenuCommand(eventHandler, menuCommandID);
            commandService.AddCommand(menuItem);
        }
    }

    /// <summary>
    /// Gets the instance of the command.
    /// </summary>
    public static MyCommand1 Instance
    {
        get;
        private set;
    }

    /// <summary>
    /// Gets the service provider from the owner package.
    /// </summary>
    private IServiceProvider ServiceProvider
    {
        get
        {
            return this.package;
        }
    }

    /// <summary>
    /// Initializes the singleton instance of the command.
    /// </summary>
    /// <param name="package">Owner package, not null.</param>
    public static void Initialize(Package package)
    {
        Instance = new MyCommand1(package);
    }

    /// <summary>
    /// Shows a message box when the menu item is clicked.
    /// </summary>
    /// <param name="sender">Event sender.</param>
    /// <param name="e">Event args.</param>
    private void ShowMessageBox(object sender, EventArgs e)
    {
        //Show a MessageBox to prove we were here
```

```
            IVsUIShell uiShell =
                (IVsUIShell)Package.GetGlobalService(typeof(SVsUIShell));
            Guid clsid = Guid.Empty;
            int result;
            Microsoft.VisualStudio.ErrorHandler.ThrowOnFailure(
                uiShell.ShowMessageBox(
                0,
                ref clsid,
                "MyCommand1Package",
                "Hello, World!",
                string.Empty,
                0,
                OLEMSGBUTTON.OLEMSGBUTTON_OK,
                OLEMSGDEFBUTTON.OLEMSGDEFBUTTON_FIRST,
                OLEMSGICON.OLEMSGICON_INFO,
                0,         //false
                out result));
        }
    }
}
```

Looking at Listing 15.2: within the constructor routine, there is a block of code that effectively links a callback event to our command, allowing us to respond when the command menu item is clicked.

First, a command handler is created via the `OleMenuCommandService`. You can find more info on this object in MSDN, but it is essentially a managed class that shell extensions use to add menu command handlers and define "verbs" for those menu commands. Let's look at the code:

```
//Add our command handlers for menu
//(commands must exist in the .vsct file)
OleMenuCommandService mcs = GetService(
  typeof(IMenuCommandService)
  ) as OleMenuCommandService;
```

Assuming that we have managed to obtain a valid `OleMenuCommandService` object, the routine then creates a reference to the menu command itself with the following code:

```
//Create the command for the menu item.
CommandID menuCommandID = new CommandID(
  GuidList.guidMyFirstPackageCmdSet,
  (int)PkgCmdIDList.cmdidMyCommand);
```

The `CommandID` object is created using a GUID and an ID that uniquely represent that command. In other words, the GUID and ID used in conjunction are a key that uniquely identifies the command; the `CommandID` object is best understood as a wrapper for that key.

To define a command for our package, we need to modify something called the Visual Studio Command Table (VSCT).

Editing the VSCT

As we have already discussed, a command is nothing more than a trigger that causes the extension to do something. The VSCT shows a list of the commands supported by the extension and their corresponding definitions. Commands are fairly useless without a way to trigger them. The VSCT also contains information about how commands are exposed within the IDE (typically as a menu item or a toolbar button).

Physically, the VSCT is implemented as an XML file with a `.vsct` extension. This file is created automatically when you use the package wizard to generate your project. Listing 15.3 contains the command table XML that was generated for us as a result of completing the package wizard.

LISTING 15.3 A VSCT File Generated by the Package Wizard

```
<?xml version="1.0" encoding="utf-8"?>
<CommandTable xmlns="http://schemas.microsoft.com/VisualStudio/2005-10-18/
CommandTable"
              xmlns:xs="http://www.w3.org/2001/XMLSchema">

  <!--This is the file that defines the actual layout and type
      of the commands. It is divided in different sections
      (e.g. command definition, command placement, ...), with
      each defining a specific set of properties. See the
      comment before each section for more details about how to
      use it. -->

  <!--The VSCT compiler (the tool that translates this file
      into the binary format that Visual Studio will consume)
      has the ability to run a preprocessor on the vsct file;
      this preprocessor is (usually) the C++ preprocessor, so
      it is possible to define includes and macros with the
      same syntax used in C++ files. Using this ability of the
      compiler here, we include files defining some of the
      constants that we will use inside the file. -->

  <!--This is the file that defines the IDs for all the commands
  exposed by Visual Studio. -->
  <Extern href="stdidcmd.h"/>

  <!--This header contains the command ids for the menus provided
  by the shell. -->
  <Extern href="vsshlids.h"/>
```

```
<!--The Commands section is where the commands, menus, and menu
   groups are defined. This section uses a Guid to identify
   the package that provides the command defined inside it. -->
<Commands package="guidMyFirstPackagePkg">

  <!--Inside this section we have different subsections: one
  for the menus, another  for the menu groups, one for the
  buttons (the actual commands), one for the combos, and the last
  one for the bitmaps used. Each element is identified by a
  command id that is a unique pair of guid and numeric identifier;
  the guid part of the identifier is usually  called "command set"
  and is used to group different commands inside a logically related
  group; your package should define its own command set in order to
  avoid collisions  with command ids defined by other
  packages. -->


  <!--In this section you can define new menu groups. A menu group
     is a container for other menus or buttons (commands);
     from a visual point of view you can see the group as the
     part of a menu contained between two lines. The parent of a
     group must be a menu. -->
  <Groups>

    <Group guid="guidMyFirstPackageCmdSet" id="MyMenuGroup"
          priority="0x0600">
      <Parent guid="guidSHLMainMenu" id="IDM_VS_MENU_TOOLS"/>
    </Group>

  </Groups>

  <!--Buttons section. -->
  <!--This section defines the elements the user can interact with,
     like a menu command or a button or a combo box in a toolbar. -->
  <Buttons>
    <!--To define a menu group you have to specify its ID, the parent
        menu, and its display priority. The command is visible and enabled
        by default. If you need to change the visibility, status, etc., you
        can use the CommandFlag node.
        You can add more than one CommandFlag node e.g.:
            <CommandFlag>DefaultInvisible</CommandFlag>
            <CommandFlag>DynamicVisibility</CommandFlag>
        If you do not want an image next to your command, remove the Icon
        node /> -->
```

```
    <Button guid="guidMyFirstPackageCmdSet" id="cmdidMyCommand"
            priority="0x0100" type="Button">
      <Parent guid="guidMyFirstPackageCmdSet" id="MyMenuGroup" />
      <Icon guid="guidImages" id="bmpPic1" />
      <Strings>
        <ButtonText>My First Package Command</ButtonText>
      </Strings>
    </Button>

  </Buttons>

  <!--The bitmaps section is used to define the bitmaps that are used for
     the commands.-->
  <Bitmaps>
    <!--The bitmap id is defined in a way that is a little bit
        different from the others: the declaration starts with a guid
        for the bitmap strip, then there is the resource id of the
        bitmap strip containing the bitmaps and then there are the
        numeric ids of the elements used inside a button definition.
        An important aspect of this declaration is that the element id
        must be the actual index (1-based) of the bitmap inside the
        bitmap strip. -->
    <Bitmap guid="guidImages" href="Resources\Images.png"
           usedList="bmpPic1, bmpPic2, bmpPicSearch, bmpPicX, bmpPicArrows"/>

  </Bitmaps>

</Commands>


<Symbols>
  <!--This is the package guid. -->
  <GuidSymbol name="guidMyFirstPackagePkg"
             value="{4f99ea1f-b906-4e30-a40a-26f217a6b9ab}" />

  <!--This is the guid used to group the menu commands together -->
  <GuidSymbol name="guidMyFirstPackageCmdSet"
             value="{25e4d809-1d51-4bc4-b35c-d54e82d71907}">

    <IDSymbol name="MyMenuGroup" value="0x1020" />
    <IDSymbol name="cmdidMyCommand" value="0x0100" />
  </GuidSymbol>
```

```
<GuidSymbol name="guidImages"
            value="{e1e9e76f-29b9-43b0-b2e2-80d7cdea6bc3}" >
  <IDSymbol name="bmpPic1" value="1" />
  <IDSymbol name="bmpPic2" value="2" />
  <IDSymbol name="bmpPicSearch" value="3" />
  <IDSymbol name="bmpPicX" value="4" />
  <IDSymbol name="bmpPicArrows" value="5" />
  <IDSymbol name="bmpPicStrikethrough" value="6" />
</GuidSymbol>
</Symbols>
</CommandTable>
```

The Symbols and the Commands nodes are the two important parts of the file to pay attention to. Within the Symbols node, we set up the unique globally unique identifiers (GUIDs) and IDs that are used to refer to various elements of our commands. Each of these is represented using an `IDSymbol` element within the VSCT. In Listing 15.2, you can clearly see multiple `IDSymbol` entries created for a variety of things including icons, menu groups, and actual commands.

The Commands node defines the commands themselves, including how they are displayed within the Visual Studio UI.

Because the Symbols node ends up defining the keys to our commands (and to other items referenced within the file), we have to start the processing of adding a command by first adding its compound key to the Symbols node.

Then we add corresponding entries into the Commands node to configure menus, buttons (which are best thought of as menu items), combos (combo boxes), bitmaps (icons to be associated with the command), and groups (logical groupings of different commands).

We'll tie all this together in the sample extension project later in the chapter. For now, understand that adding a command to your extension will always involve the following steps:

1. Define the GUID/ID composite key for your command by adding an `IDSymbol` element into the VSCT file. You will need a separate IDSymbol entry for every command, menu, group, and so on.
2. Define the UI for the command by adding an appropriate entry in the Commands node within the VSCT file. For example, to expose your command via a button (for example, a menu item or button on a toolbar), create a `Button` element. If you also want to attach an icon to your command UI, you would define a `Bitmap` element within the Bitmaps node.
3. Implement the code to execute the command. Add code to the `MenuItemCallback` routine.

A Sample Extension: Color Selector

To cap this discussion of add-ins, let's look at the process of developing a functioning package from start to finish. This extension is a color picker. It enables users to click an area of a color palette, and the package emits code to create an instance of a color structure that matches the selected color from the palette. Here is a summary list of requirements for the add-in:

- In a tool window, it displays a visual color palette representing all the possible colors.
- As the mouse pointer is moved over the palette, the control displays the Red, Green, and Blue values for the point directly under the mouse pointer.
- If a user clicks the palette, it takes the current RGB values and copies the correct C# code to implement a matching Color struct onto the clipboard so that it can be easily pasted into an open code window.

Getting Started

To start the development process, you create a new solution and a VSIX project called `ColorSelector`.

Once it's created, as we saw earlier, we will be left with a basic, essentially empty, project.

Creating the User Control

We start by creating a `User Control` class that encapsulates the user interface for our tool window and the processing logic for the extension. Add a Custom Tool Window project item to the project; call it `MyToolWindow`.

The first thing to note is that the project item has already created the shell of our user control for us. After we added this project item, the design surface of the user control is loaded and ready to go (see Figure 15.8). As we noted before, the user control is a XAML-based user interface. If you need to familiarize yourself with Windows Presentation Foundation (WPF)/XAML development concepts, you may want to skip ahead and read Chapter 21 or Chapter 23.

Within the user control, there is already a StackPanel container created for us inside a grid. It currently contains a TextBlock and a Button control. We won't need the Button control, so delete it. We want to add an Image control (within the StackPanel, after the TextBlock) to display the palette of colors, stored as a simple `.jpg` file. In this case, we're using a color palette from a popular Paint program as our source for the bitmap; grab your own palette "picture" from wherever you like, copy it over into your project folder, and add it to your project. Set the `Source` property of the Image control to the relative path of your image file. Our path looks like this: `color-spectrum.jpg`.

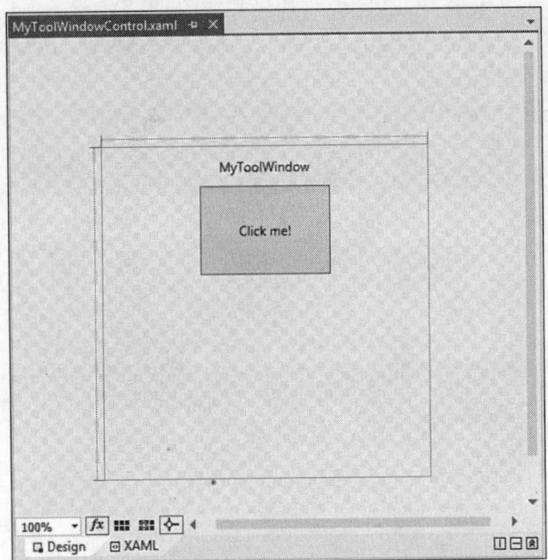

FIGURE 15.8 The default user control.

With the palette in place, you now need a TextBlock control to display the RGB values. (Set its name property to `TextBlockRGB`). This can be added directly into the existing StackPanel container immediately after the Image control. Finally, in the finest tradition of gold-plating, you also add a Border control (named `BorderSelectedColor`) that will have its background color set to the current color selection and another TextBlock control (`TextBlockCode`) that shows the code you would generate to implement that color in a color structure. Both of these can be added, one after another, to the StackPanel.

Figure 15.9 provides a glimpse of the user control after these controls have been situated on the design surface.

Handling Movement over the Palette

With the UI in place, you can now concentrate on the code. First, you can add an event handler to deal with mouse movements over the top of the palette picture box. Within the `MouseMove` event handler, we will update the TextBlock control and the Border control background as the pointer roves over the palette bitmap. This is easily accomplished by first establishing the event within the XAML markup, like this:

```
<Image Name="ImagePalette" Source="color-spectrum.jpg" Margin="10"
MouseMove="ImagePalette_MouseMove" />
```

If you let Visual Studio do the work for you and select `<New Event Handler>` as you are typing the `MouseMove` property into the XAML, you will get the C# event handler created for you for free. Within the handler, the code will need to look something like this:

```
private void ImagePalette_MouseMove(object sender, MouseEventArgs e)
{
    //Get the color under the current pointer position
    UIElement SelectedObject = e.Source as UIElement;

    Color color = GetPointColor();

    DisplayColor(color);
    DisplayCode(color, false);

}
```

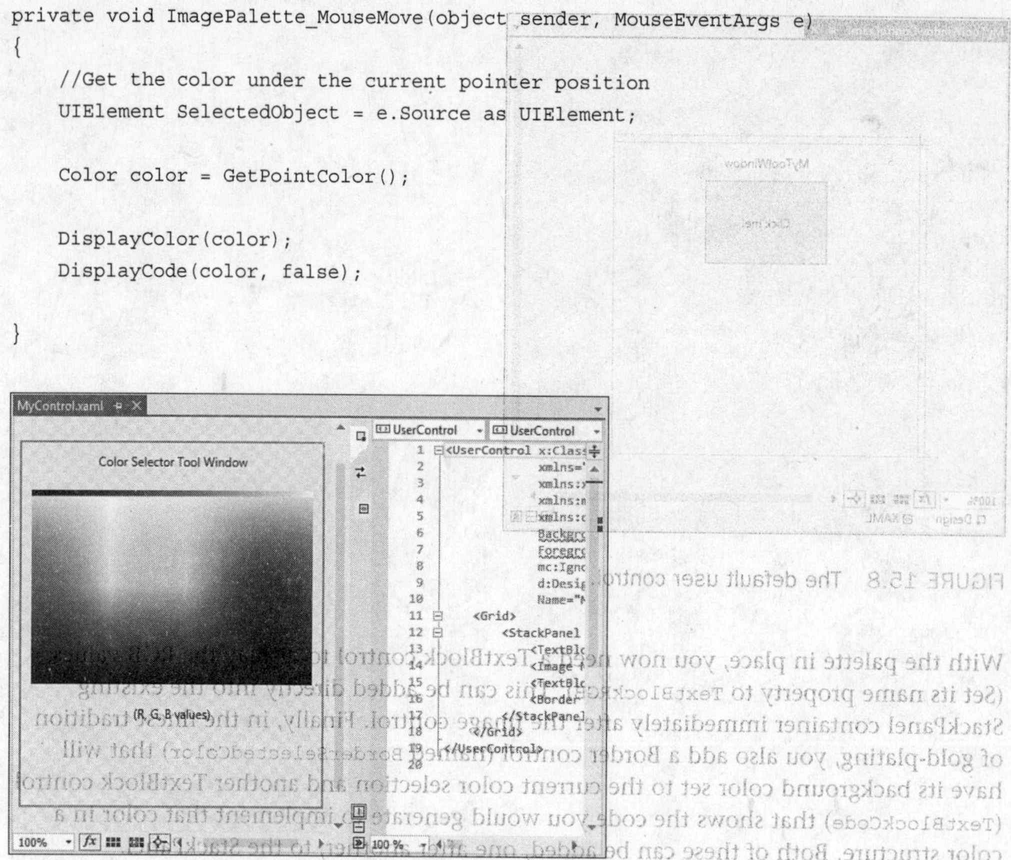

FIGURE 15.9 Designing the user control.

We also need a way to react when the user clicks on the palette (triggering a copy of the code to the Clipboard). So in the same fashion, add a new event handler in the XAML for the `MouseDown` event so that the `Image` element now looks like this:

```
<Image Name="ImagePalette" Source="color-spectrum.jpg" Margin="10"
MouseMove="ImagePalette_MouseMove" MouseDown="ImagePalette_MouseDown" />
```

And within the event handler C# code, write the clipboard action:

```
private void ImagePalette_MouseDown(object sender, MouseButtonEventArgs e)
{
   //On mouse click within the palette, copy
   //the Color code to the Clipboard
   Clipboard.Clear();
   Clipboard.SetText(TextBlockCode.Text);
}
```

We haven't implemented the `GetPointColor`, `DisplayColor`, or `DisplayCode` routines yet; let's do that now.

Implementing the Helper Routines

Whenever the mouse pointer moves over the picture box region, you need to capture the color components of the point directly below the cursor (`GetPointColor`), update the label controls and the border control to reflect that color (`DisplayColor`), and then generate the code to implement a matching color structure (`DisplayCode`). Here are the implementations of these routines.

```
/// <summary>


/// Returns a Color structure representing the color of
/// the pixel at the current mouse x and y coordinates.
/// </summary>
/// <returns>A Color structure</returns>
private Color GetPointColor()
{
    //Retrieve the relative coordinate of the mouse position \
    //in relation to the current window.
    Point point = Mouse.GetPosition(this);

    //Grab a bitmap of the current window
    var renderTargetBitmap =
        new RenderTargetBitmap((int)this.ActualWidth,
                               (int)this.ActualHeight,
                               96, 96, PixelFormats.Default);
    renderTargetBitmap.Render(this);

    //Determine if we are in bounds
    if ((point.X <= renderTargetBitmap.PixelWidth) &&
        (point.Y <= renderTargetBitmap.PixelHeight))
    {
        //Crop a pixel out of the larger bitmap.
        var croppedBitmap =
            new CroppedBitmap(renderTargetBitmap,
                               new Int32Rect(
                               (int)point.X,
                               (int)point.Y, 1, 1));

        //Copy the pixel to a byte array.
        var pixels = new byte[4];
        croppedBitmap.CopyPixels(pixels, 4, 0);
```

```
            //Convert the RGB byte array to a Color structure.
            Color SelectedColor = Color.FromRgb(pixels[2],
                pixels[1],
                pixels[0]);

            //Return the Color struct
            return SelectedColor;
        }
        else
        {
            //Return black if we are out of bounds
            return Colors.Black;
        }

    }

    /// <summary>
    /// Given a Color struct, update the UI controls
    /// to show the RGB values, and repeat the selected
    /// color within the BorderSelectedColor control.
    /// </summary>
    /// <param name="color">The current color under
    /// the mouse cursor.</param>
    private void DisplayColor(Color color)
    {
        //Set the border color to match
        //the selected color
        SolidColorBrush brush =
                new SolidColorBrush(color);

        BorderSelectedColor.Background = brush;

        //Display the RGB values
        string rgb = color.R.ToString() + ", "
                + color.G.ToString() + ", "
                + color.B.ToString();

        TextBlockRGB.Text = rgb;

    }

    /// <summary>
    /// Display the VB or C# code to implement the
    /// provided Color
    /// </summary>
```

```
/// <param name="color">The color to implement</param>
/// <param name="isVB">True to generate VB; false
/// for C#</param>
private void DisplayCode(Color color, bool isVB)
{

    string code = "";

    if (isVB)
    {
        code = "Dim color As Color = ";
    }
    else
    {
        code = "Color color = ";
    }

    code = code + @"Color.FromArgb(" + color.R.ToString() + ", " +
        color.G.ToString() + ", " +
        color.B.ToString() + ");";

    TextBlockCode.Text = code;

}
```

TIP

To isolate and test the user control, you might want to add a WPF project to the solution and host the control within a XAML window for testing. Just drop the control onto the design window and run the project.

With the user control in place, you are ready to proceed to the second stage of the add-in's development: wiring the user control into the IDE.

Finishing the Package

The `package` class already has all the basic code we need; with the user control/tool window UI and code finished, we are essentially done. If we run our package at this stage, a sandbox copy of Visual Studio will start up with the package loaded. We just need to know how to trigger our tool window to display. The launching code is already there inside the `ShowToolWindow` routine.

NOTE

A tool window, in Visual Studio parlance, is nothing more than a simple window that can be docked or floated within the IDE.

The custom tool window project item has already provided us with a straightforward routine that will display a tool window. This routine is already wired up to a menu command, and it is already configured to display our custom user control within the tool window. For reference, here is the default implementation you'll find within the package class.

```
/// <summary>
/// This function is called when the user clicks the
/// menu item that shows the tool window. See the
/// Initialize method to see how the menu item is
/// associated to this function using the
/// OleMenuCommandService service and the MenuCommand class.
/// </summary>
private void ShowToolWindow(object sender, EventArgs e)
{
    //Get the instance number 0 of this tool window.
    //This window is single instance, so this instance
    //is actually the only one.
    //The last flag is set to true so that if the tool
    //window does not exist, it will be created.
    ToolWindowPane window = this.FindToolWindow(typeof(MyToolWindow), 0, true);

    if ((null == window) || (null == window.Frame))
    {
        throw new NotSupportedException(Resources.CanNotCreateWindow);
    }

    IVsWindowFrame windowFrame = (IVsWindowFrame)window.Frame;
    Microsoft.VisualStudio.ErrorHandler.ThrowOnFailure(windowFrame.Show());
}
```

The VSCT file has been built for you; here is the snippet inside the .vsct file that wires the command to show the tool window to a menu item and places it inside the Other Windows menu.

```
<Button guid="guidColorSelectorCmdSet" id="cmdidColorSelectorToolWindow"
      priority="0x0100" type="Button">
  <Parent guid="guidSHLMainMenu" id="IDG_VS_WNDO_OTRWNDWS1"/>
  <Icon guid="guidImages" id="bmpPic1" />
  <Strings>
    <ButtonText>Color Selector Tool Window</ButtonText>
  </Strings>
</Button>
```

If you examine the Parent element, you will see an id attribute set to IDG_VS_WNDO_OTRWNDWS1. This is a constant that references the standard Other Windows menu within

Visual Studio. There are predefined GUIDs and IDs for every standard Visual Studio menu. Visit MSDN and search for "GUIDs and IDs of Visual Studio Menus" for the full reference.

Our package is fully functional. Figure 15.10 shows the package UI running as a tool window within an instance of Visual Studio. Listings are provided next for the key components of the tool window: Listing 15.4 provides the tool window extension code, and Listings 15.5 and 15.6 provide the XAML and code-behind (respectively) for the tool window control itself.

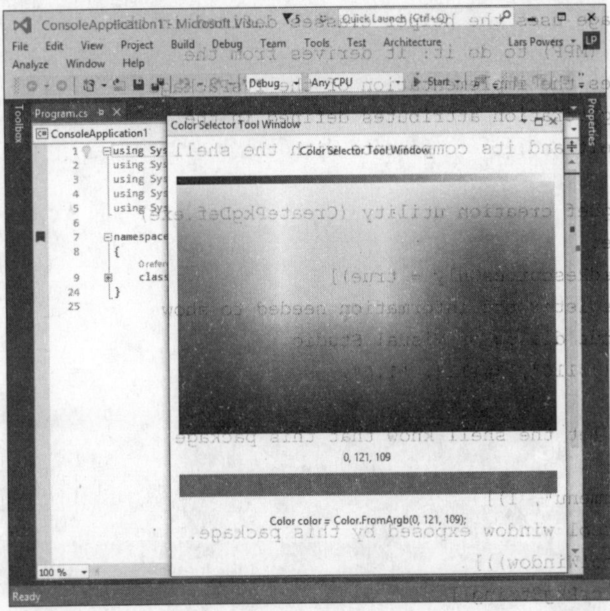

FIGURE 15.10 The `ColorSelector` package running in Visual Studio.

LISTING 15.4 The `ColorSelectorPackage` Class

```
using System;
using System.Diagnostics;
using System.Globalization;
using System.Runtime.InteropServices;
using System.ComponentModel.Design;
using Microsoft.Win32;
using Microsoft.VisualStudio;
using Microsoft.VisualStudio.Shell.Interop;
using Microsoft.VisualStudio.OLE.Interop;
using Microsoft.VisualStudio.Shell;
```

```
namespace VisualStudioUnleashed.ColorSelector
{
    /// <summary>
    /// This is the class that implements the package exposed by this
    /// assembly.
    ///
    /// The minimum requirement for a class to be considered a valid package
    /// for Visual Studio is to implement the IVsPackage interface and register
itself
    /// with the shell. This package uses the helper classes defined in the
    /// Managed Package Framework (MPF) to do it: it derives from the
    /// Package class that provides the implementation of the IVsPackage
    /// interface and uses the registration attributes defined in the
    /// framework to register itself and its components with the shell.
    /// </summary>
    //This attribute tells the PkgDef creation utility (CreatePkgDef.exe)
    //that this class is a package.
    [PackageRegistration(UseManagedResourcesOnly = true)]
    //This attribute is used to register the information needed to show
    //this package in the Help/About dialog of Visual Studio.
    [InstalledProductRegistration("#110", "#112", "1.0",
        IconResourceID = 400)]
    //This attribute is needed to let the shell know that this package
    //exposes some menus.
    [ProvideMenuResource("Menus.ctmenu", 1)]
    //This attribute registers a tool window exposed by this package.
    [ProvideToolWindow(typeof(MyToolWindow))]
    [Guid(GuidList.guidColorSelectorPkgString)]
    public sealed class ColorSelectorPackage : Package
    {
        /// <summary>
        /// Default constructor of the package.
namespace ColorSelectorExtension
{
    using System;
    using System.Runtime.InteropServices;
    using Microsoft.VisualStudio.Shell;

    /// <summary>
    /// This class implements the tool window exposed by this package
    /// and hosts a user control.
    /// </summary>
    /// <remarks>
    /// In Visual Studio, tool windows are composed of a frame
    /// (implemented by the shell) and a pane,
    /// usually implemented by the package implementer.
```

```
/// <para>
/// This class derives from the ToolWindowPane class provided
/// from the MPF in order to use its
/// implementation of the IVsUIElementPane interface.
/// </para>
/// </remarks>
[Guid("a320ef24-e22a-41de-9d6b-7eece4f50e61")]
public class ColorSelectorToolWindow : ToolWindowPane
{
    /// <summary>
    /// Initializes a new instance of the
    /// <see cref="ColorSelectorToolWindow"/> class.
    /// </summary>
    public ColorSelectorToolWindow() : base(null)
    {
        this.Caption = "ColorSelectorToolWindow";

        //Set the image that will appear on the tab of the
        //window frame when docked with another window.
        //The resource ID corresponds to the one defined
        //in the resx file, while the Index is the offset
        //in the bitmap strip. Each image in the strip
        //is 16x16.
        this.BitmapResourceID = 301;
        this.BitmapIndex = 1;

        //This is the user control hosted by the tool
        //window; note that, even if this class implements
        //IDisposable, we are not calling Dispose on this object.
        //This is because ToolWindowPane calls Dispose on
        //the object returned by the Content property.
        this.Content = new ColorSelectorToolWindowControl();
    }
  }
}
```

LISTING 15.5 The `UserControl` XAML

```
<UserControl x:Class="ColorSelectorExtension.ColorSelectorToolWindowControl "
   xmlns="http://schemas.microsoft.com/winfx/2006/xaml/presentation"
   xmlns:x="http://schemas.microsoft.com/winfx/2006/xaml"
   xmlns:mc="http://schemas.openxmlformats.org/markup-compatibility/2006"
   xmlns:d="http://schemas.microsoft.com/expression/blend/2008"
   Background="{DynamicResource VsBrush.Window}"
   Foreground="{DynamicResource VsBrush.WindowText}"
```

```
    mc:Ignorable="d"
    d:DesignHeight="350" d:DesignWidth="300"
    Name="MyToolWindow">
     <Grid>
         <StackPanel Orientation="Vertical">
             <TextBlock Margin="10" HorizontalAlignment="Center">
             Color Selector Tool Window</TextBlock>
             <Image Name="ImagePalette" Source="color-spectrum.jpg"
              Margin="10" MouseMove="ImagePalette_MouseMove"
              MouseDown="ImagePalette_MouseDown" />
             <TextBlock Name="TextBlockRGB" HorizontalAlignment="Center"
             Margin="10">(R, G, B values)</TextBlock>
             <Border Name="BorderSelectedColor" Height="25"
              Margin="10,0,10,10" Background="Transparent" />
             <TextBlock Name="TextBlockCode" HorizontalAlignment="Center"
              Margin="10">(code goes here)</TextBlock>
         </StackPanel>

     </Grid>
</UserControl>
```

LISTING 15.6 The `UserControl` Code Behind (C#)

```
using System;
using System.Collections.Generic;
using System.Linq;
using System.Text;
using System.Windows;
using System.Windows.Controls;
using System.Windows.Data;
using System.Windows.Documents;
using System.Windows.Input;
using System.Windows.Media;
using System.Windows.Media.Imaging;
using System.Windows.Navigation;
using System.Windows.Shapes;

namespace VisualStudioUnleashed.ColorSelector
{
    /// <summary>
    /// Interaction logic for MyControl.xaml
    /// </summary>
    public partial class MyControl : UserControl
    {
```

```
        public MyControl()
        {
            InitializeComponent();
        }

        [System.Diagnostics.CodeAnalysis.SuppressMessage("Microsoft.Globalization",
"CA1300:SpecifyMessageBoxOptions")]

        private Color GetPointColor()
        {
            //Retrieve the coordinate of the mouse position in relation to
            //the window.
            Point point = Mouse.GetPosition(this);

            //Use RenderTargetBitmap to get the visual, in case the
            //image has been transformed.
            var renderTargetBitmap =
                new RenderTargetBitmap((int)this.ActualWidth,
                    (int)this.ActualHeight,
                    96, 96, PixelFormats.Default);
            renderTargetBitmap.Render(this);

            //Make sure that the point is within the dimensions of the
            //image.
            if ((point.X <= renderTargetBitmap.PixelWidth)
                && (point.Y <= renderTargetBitmap.PixelHeight))
            {
                //Create a cropped image at the supplied point coordinates.
                var croppedBitmap =
                    new CroppedBitmap(renderTargetBitmap,
                        new Int32Rect((int)point.X, (int)point.Y, 1, 1));

                //Copy the sampled pixel to a byte array.
                var pixels = new byte[4];
                croppedBitmap.CopyPixels(pixels, 4, 0);

                //Assign the sampled color to a SolidColorBrush and
                //return as conversion.
                Color SelectedColor =
                    Color.FromRgb(pixels[2], pixels[1], pixels[0]);

                return SelectedColor;
            }
            else
            {
                return Colors.Black;
```

```
        }

    }

    private void ImagePalette_MouseMove(object sender, MouseEventArgs e)
    {
        //Get the color under the current pointer position
        UIElement SelectedObject = e.Source as UIElement;

        Color color = GetPointColor();

        DisplayColor(color);
        DisplayCode(color, false);

    }

    /// <summary>
    /// Given a Color struct, update the UI controls
    /// to show the RGB values, and repeat the selected
    /// color within the BorderSelectedColor control.
    /// </summary>
    /// <param name="color">The current color under
    /// the mouse cursor.</param>
    private void DisplayColor(Color color)
    {
        //Set the border color to match
        //the selected color
        SolidColorBrush brush =
                  new SolidColorBrush(color);

        BorderSelectedColor.Background = brush;


        //Display the RGB values
        string rgb = color.R.ToString() + ", "
                  + color.G.ToString() + ", "
                  + color.B.ToString();


        TextBlockRGB.Text = rgb;

    }

    /// <summary>
    /// Display the VB or C# code to implement the
    /// provided color
    /// </summary>
```

```
    /// <param name="color">The color to implement</param>
    /// <param name="isVB">True to generate VB; false
    /// for C#</param>
    private void DisplayCode(Color color, bool isVB)
    {

        string code = "";

        if (isVB)
        {
            code = "Dim color As Color = ";
        }
        else
        {
            code = "Color color = ";
        }

        code = code + @"Color.FromArgb(" + color.R.ToString() + ", " +
            color.G.ToString() + ", " +
            color.B.ToString() + ");";


        _code = code;
        TextBlockCode.Text = _code;


    }

    private void ImagePalette_MouseDown(object sender, MouseButtonEventArgs e)
    {
        //On mouse click within the palette, copy
        //the Color code to the Clipboard
        Clipboard.Clear();
        Clipboard.SetText(TextBlockCode.Text);
    }
  }
}
```

NOTE

If you have previously written Visual Studio add-ins, it is a relatively straightforward conversion process to turn those into package extensions. Search MSDN for the article titled "Converting Add-Ins to VSPackage Extensions."

Summary

This chapter described how to leverage the power of Visual Studio extensions to functionally add to Visual Studio's features.

You investigated the custom command project item and how to use the project item to quickly and easily define a new menu command.

You also saw how to use XAML UI technologies to create a completely custom user control from the ground up and surface that control as a tool window hosted by Visual Studio.

In the next chapter, we explore another way to extend Visual Studio by using the same VSIX project techniques with the code editor and a technology called the Managed Extensibility Framework.

CHAPTER 16

Extending the Code Editor

IN THIS CHAPTER

- The Extensibility Problem
- MEF Architecture
- The Visual Studio Editor and MEF
- Creating Your Own MEF-Based Editor Extension

You have seen in the preceding chapter that Visual Studio Extension (VSIX) projects provide an easy way to extend the capabilities of the IDE with custom commands, custom tool windows, and overall broad and deep integration points into the Visual Studio shell. There is another set of options available to us with VSIX projects that target customizations and extensions of the code editor. These project items leverage something called the Managed Extensibility Framework (MEF).

MEF is actually a generic architecture pattern, application programming interface (API), and .NET class library for enabling easy "plug-in" extensions for any .NET application. Visual Studio allows for MEF-based extensions in the code editor and will likely embrace MEF more broadly across the entire IDE as time goes on.

This chapter introduces Microsoft's MEF and how the framework can be applied to extend the Visual Studio code editor.

The Extensibility Problem

Before getting into the architecture and code-level details of MEF, it is useful to understand the problem or question that MEF is trying to answer. Put simply, that question is this: how can developers allow their applications to be easily extended by others, or conversely how can developers extend existing applications in a simple way?

A variety of hurdles have to be overcome in this space. For instance, how can an application be open for extensions yet closed so that its core functionality cannot be usurped against the intentions of its designers? What developers are really after is a consistent solution that enables dynamic applications to be created and thus enables other developers to extend those dynamic applications using well-known and understood mechanisms.

Creating Dynamic Applications

Prior to MEF, the work required to create a so-called open-ended .NET application (that is, an application that allows others to contribute code and alter or add to its functionality) was far from a trivial effort. The main issue here is one of discovery and instantiation. The "host" application (the application that supports extensions) needs to have a standard way of identifying and validating code meant to extend the host. And there needs to be a runtime activation approach: how is the plug-in code executed, and what portions of the host app can be affected by the plug-in?

This is where MEF enters the scene. It provides an architecture pattern and framework/API that host application developers and plug-in developers can use to enable these dynamic application scenarios.

In fact, MEF explicitly targets developers who are creating any of three different classes of applications:

- **Extensions**—Chunks of compiled code that enhance the functionality of an existing application. Extension developers need to be able to implement their components without having access to the host applications' source or even specialized knowledge of that source.
- **Extensible frameworks/host applications**—Applications that need to support the dynamic addition of functionality via extensions.
- **Programming model**—The least common scenario; in this case, a developer is interested in creating a potentially new way of developing against an application platform. In this case, MEF can provide the building blocks that developers need to build their own extensible application platform.

Visual Studio is merely one example of a host application that clearly benefits from its ability to support rich add-ins that add value to the core feature areas that Microsoft delivers out of the box.

MEF Architecture

MEF achieves its goals through three different, but related, mechanisms:

- Dependency injection
- Structural matching
- Naming and activation

Let's walk through each of these concepts in an abstract sense and then see how they are physically implemented with MEF.

MEF Principles

Dependency injection is a software architecture term that refers to the concept of a framework or runtime "injecting" an external dependency into another piece of software. Handling this process is a core requirement for an extensibility framework.

Structural matching, also sometimes referred to as *duck typing*, is a style of feature discovery and typing in which a host determines the type of an object based on the properties and methods it exposes as opposed to its actual type in the object-oriented sense.

Finally, *naming and activation* is the "last-mile" feature that puts all the pieces together and enables an application to load and run the plug-in code predictably.

When all three of these mechanisms are in place, you have a reasonable platform for building applications that can be dynamically composited at runtime. In other words, by exploiting an extensibility framework, you can deliver a flexible application that is capable of leveraging new features that are added dynamically over time—functionality that does not, in fact, require a wholesale replacement or upgrade of a core, monolithic executable.

Working with MEF

MEF applications are based around a small set of core concepts: the composition container, catalog, and parts. These are both abstract concepts and a physical API that you can interact with from managed code. All the MEF classes live within the `System.ComponentModel.Composition` namespace and its children namespaces, such as `System.ComponentModel.Composition.Hosting`.

Parts

An MEF *part* is the primary unit of functionality. Parts have a set of features they provide (called exports); parts might also depend on features that other parts provide (termed imports).

Parts verbalize their exports and imports through contracts. At the code level, contracts are specified by using declarative attributes to declare their imports and exports (`System.ComponentModel.Composition.ImportAttribute` and `System.ComponentModel.Composition.ExportAttribute`, respectively).

Here is an example of a C# class declaring an export.

```
[Export(typeof(IMyExtensionProvider))]
internal class TestExtensionProvider
```

Composition Container

The *composition container* is the core of an MEF application that does all the heavy lifting. It holds all the available parts, handles the instantiation of those parts, and is the primary composition engine in MEF. In this context, composition can be thought of as the process of matching required services (imports) with published services (exports).

Host applications can instantiate a container via the `System.ComponentModel.Composition.Hosting.CompositionContainer` class like this:

```
private CompositionContainer _container;
```

Catalog

The *catalog* is a sort of Registry and discovery mechanism for parts that the composition container uses. MEF provides a default set of catalogs, each one designed to discover parts from a particular source or target. There is a type catalog for discovering parts from a given .NET type (via the `TypeCatalog` class), an assembly catalog for discovering parts from an assembly (via the `AssemblyCatalog` catalog), and a directory catalog (via the `DirectoryCatalog` class) for discovering parts that exist in a specified folder.

A fourth class, `AggregateCatalog`, enables you to combine multiple catalogs so that parts from multiple catalog sources can be combined into one master catalog.

A catalog instance can be passed into the constructor for a `CompositionContainer` object. You could write the following code to both create a new composition container and specify a catalog of parts that are to be discovered from within the specific assembly.

```
var catalog = new TypeCatalog(typeof(MyExtension));

CompositionContainer container =
   new CompositionContainer(catalog);
```

Figure 16.1 shows a diagram of the abstract MEF architecture.

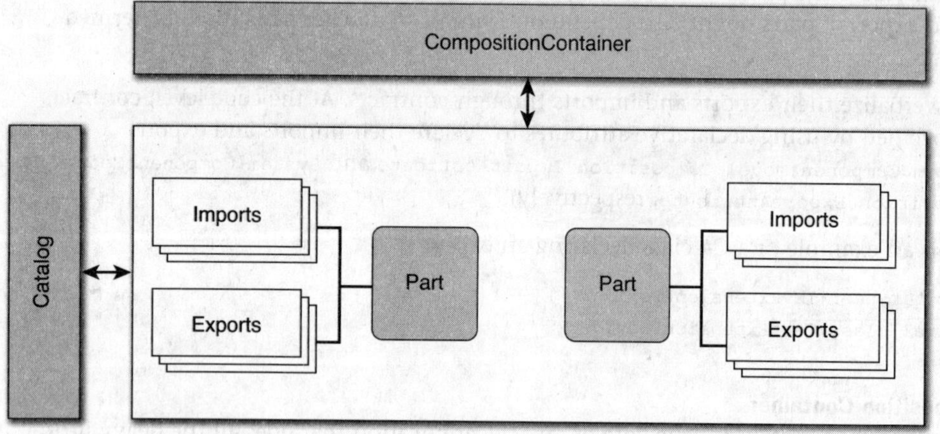

FIGURE 16.1 A simplified view of the MEF architecture.

The Visual Studio Editor and MEF

Although the MEF is a general-purpose extensibility framework applicable across a wide range of application scenarios, it is particularly applicable to extending the Visual Studio code editor for one simple reason: the editor itself was built by Microsoft using MEF. In other words, the code editor consists of a series of MEF parts. Adding additional parts to extend and change editor behavior is simply a matter of using the MEF design patterns and writing your own MEF parts to be discovered and used by the editor.

If you want to extend the editor, you need to know the exact editor extensibility points; in other words, you need to know which editor feature areas can be easily replaced or enhanced using your own MEF parts.

With our basic primer on MEF out of the way, it's time to examine how to create an MEF-based project within Visual Studio and review the numerous extension points the editor exposes.

Editor Extension Points

The Visual Studio code editor has its own sort of API that it exposes via MEF. In MEF terms, the editor publishes a set of exports that you can then use within your own MEF parts to extend the editor in virtually unboundless ways.

With nearly 100% coverage of the editor's features, the following feature areas are valid extension points that the Visual Studio editor exposes:

- **Content types**—A content type in the context of a Visual Studio code editor is the type of text and syntax that the editor can parse and understand. If you think about this from a languages perspective, Visual Studio content types map directly to the various syntax and text formats that Visual Studio understands, such as C#, plain text, Hypertext Markup Language (HTML), XML, XAML, and so on.
- **Classification types and classification formats**—Classification types are the types of text, appearing within a document, that the Visual Studio editor understands and looks for. In a typical C# file, for example, the editor recognizes numerical and string instances within the document because those are default classification types built in to Visual Studio. For each classification type, a format can be defined as well. A classic example of this is the highlighting and text coloring that you see within the editor for things like string literals or comments.
- **Margins and scrollbars**—If you think of the physical layout of a code editor, its visual surface is dominated by the text area where the code actually lives, and this is surrounded by scrollbars and by a margin area (for instance, the area where you see breakpoint information). Both the margins and scrollbars are artifacts that can be customized with MEF parts.
- **Tags**—Tags are objects that enable you to associate data with different recognized types of text within an editor. For instance, the SquiggleTag is implemented by Visual Studio to associate things like syntax errors with a chunk of text that is unrecognized. In this case, the data associated with the squiggle is the actual syntax error

generated by the compiler; this data is manifested as a tooltip when you hover the mouse over the squiggle.

- **Adornments**—Adornments are visual objects that can appear within an editor. Physically, they are implemented as Windows Presentation Foundation (WPF) objects, and they can exist at several different "layers" within the editor, so the adornment can actually occupy the same physical space as the text within the editor or float above text within the editor.

- **Mouse processors**—Mouse processors are extension points that enable you to capture and handle mouse input.

- **Drop handlers**—Drop handlers enable you to react to different types of objects as they are dropped on the editor surface. Visual Studio has a library of stock format types that it recognizes, including files, pen data, XAML, and TIFF or bitmap images.

- **Options**—Using MEF, it is possible to define, store, and react to your own set of custom options within the editor.

- **IntelliSense**—Chapter 7, "Working with Visual Studio's Productivity Aids," discusses IntelliSense extensively. You can write your own IntelliSense functionality using MEF.

Using the Visual Studio SDK

In Chapter 15, "Extending the IDE," we introduced the concept of VSIX projects and Visual Studio extensions. We discussed the fact that extensions are built by adding different project item types to a VSIX project. Code Editor extensions are built the same way: we add project items to a VSIX project. This means that code editor extensions also require the Visual Studio software development kit (SDK) to be installed.

NOTE

The Visual Studio SDK, generally speaking, is a collection of tools and project templates that help developers customize the IDE. The SDK is particularly germane to the topic of editor extensions because it ships with a set of project templates and code samples that help kick-start your extension development efforts.

The SDK download links for Visual Studio 2015 are located at the Visual Studio Extensibility center on MSDN: https://www.visualstudio.com/integrate/explore/explore-vside-vsi.

To review from Chapter 15: after downloading and installing the SDK, you see a new set of project templates—including the VSIX project type—available (under the Extensibility category) when you launch the New Project dialog box (see Figure 16.2).

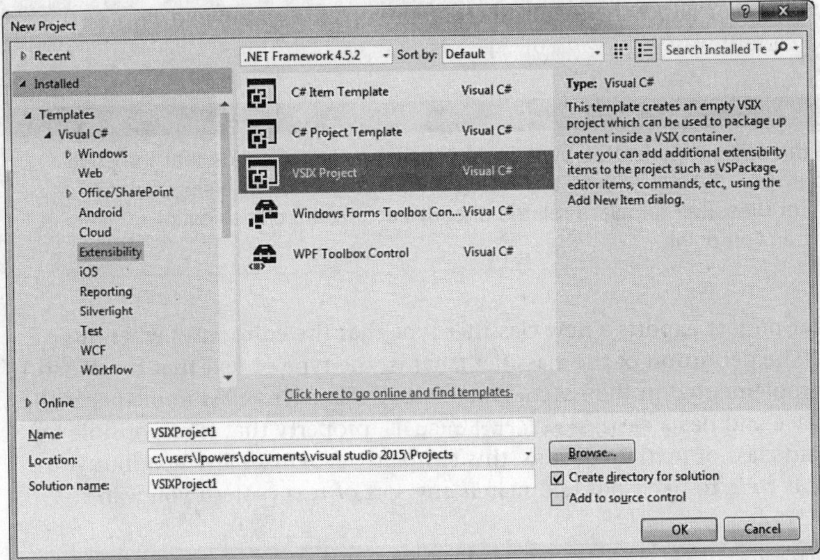

FIGURE 16.2 The VSIX Project template added by the Visual Studio SDK.

Once a VSIX project has been created, editor extensions are built by adding specific project items (which also live under the Extensibility category in the Add New Item dialog).

There are four MEF-centered project types: the Editor Classifier, Editor Margin, Editor Text Adornment, and Editor Viewport Adornment.

Based on their names and the prior list of extension points, you can get a good idea for the specific capabilities of each template. Seeing the extensions in action is as simple as running the template project; just as we saw with general extensions in Chapter 15, a new instance of Visual Studio launches with the extension running.

Keep in mind that extensions can be deployed by simply copying their binaries; they do not need to be deployed to the Global Assembly Cache (GAC) or otherwise registered. The default mechanism for deployment of extensions is the VSIX file. (To refresh your memory on what VSIX is, see Chapter 11, "Deploying Code.") The VSIX file, when run, automatically creates the correct folder in the correct location and copies the extension binaries.

After an extension has been deployed in this fashion, you can manage via the Extensions and Updates window (located under the Tools menu), discussed later in this chapter.

Editor Classifier

The Editor Classifier template creates an MEF part that exports a classifier; this classifier handles syntax highlighting within the editor. This is implemented with a set of default classes that can be customized to implement your own classifier. By using this project as a starting point, you can direct the editor to recognize certain syntax and display the matching text in a certain way.

NOTE

As you examine the content generated by these extension projects, notice that the code generated for you maps directly back to the extension points previously discussed. For example, the Editor Classifier template relates directly back to the classification types/formats extension point.

The Editor Classifier project exports a new classifier type that the editor uses when it's loaded in the IDE. The definition of the classifier (that is, the type of text that the classifier recognizes) is implemented in the `EditorClassifier1` class. This class implements the `IClassifier` interface and has a `GetClassificationSpans` property that is responsible for recognizing a certain class of text. By default, this template recognizes any text, but you are free to tweak this code to parse out and match any sort of text pattern you want.

NOTE

All these MEF extension templates end up creating classes and types that are named after the project. By using the default `EditorClassifier1` project name, you end up with classes such as `EditorClassifier1`, `EditorClassifier1Form`, and so on. If you have used a different name for your project, your type names should look different from those presented here.

Besides recognizing a class of text, a classifier is responsible for how that text is displayed within the editor. For instance, keywords are shaded a different color, comments are colored, and so on. All this work is performed within the `EditorClassifier1Format` class. The code generated for us sets the background color to blue violet and underlines the text, but you can change those details to whatever you want.

```
/// <summary>
/// Defines an editor format for the EditorClassifier1 type
/// that has a purple background
/// and is underlined.
/// </summary>internal sealed class EditorClassifier1Format
    : ClassificationFormatDefinition
    {
        /// <summary>
        /// Initializes a new instance of the
        /// <see cref="EditorClassifier1Format"/> class.
        /// </summary>
        public EditorClassifier1Format()
        {
            // human readable version of the name
            this.DisplayName = "EditorClassifier1";
```

```
            this.BackgroundColor = Colors.BlueViolet;
            this.TextDecorations =
                System.Windows.TextDecorations.Underline;
        }
    }
```

Editor Margin

The Editor Margin template creates a project that exports a margin displayed on one of the editor's borders. The main class here is `EditorMargin1`, which derives from the WPF `Canvas` class and places a canvas with a child text box (with the text `"Hello World!"`) at the bottom of the editor window (see Figure 16.3).

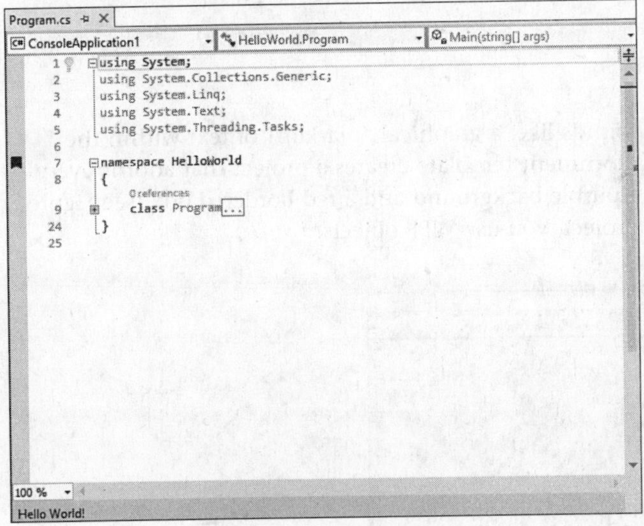

FIGURE 16.3 A `"Hello World"` margin added to the bottom of the code editor.

Here is the code responsible for displaying the margin. Again, if you had a need to display meaningful data within a margin (code review comments? bug counts?), you could easily use the code here as a building block.

```
/// <summary>
/// Creates a <see cref="EditorMargin1"/> for a given
/// <see cref="IWpfTextView"/>.
/// </summary>
/// <param name="textView">The <see cref="IWpfTextView"/> to
/// attach the marginto.</param>
public EditorMargin1(IWpfTextView textView)
```

```
{
    _textView = textView;

    this.Height = 20;
    this.ClipToBounds = true;
    this.Background = new SolidColorBrush(Colors.LightGreen);

    //Add a green colored label that says "Hello World!"
    Label label = new Label();
    label.Background = new SolidColorBrush(Colors.LightGreen);
    label.Content = "Hello world!";
    this.Children.Add(label);

}
```

Editor Text Adornment

A text adornment is just what it sounds like: a graphical "markup" of text within the editor window. The Editor Text Adornment template creates a project that adorns every instance of the character *A* with a purple background and a red bordered box (see Figure 16.4). As with the editor margin project, you use WPF objects.

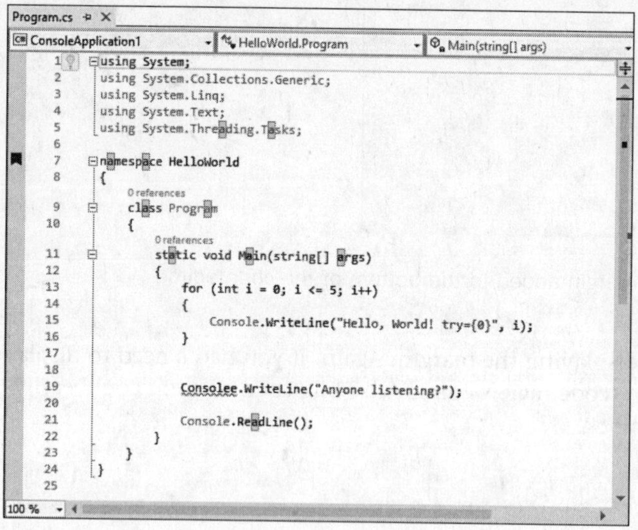

FIGURE 16.4 Creating a text adornment in the editor.

Adornments reside on different "layers" within the editor. In this case, the adornment is implemented on the same layer that the text is rendered in, and that's what makes this specifically a text adornment implementation. Note that this isn't actually a case of the editor changing the font of those *A*'s to include the background decoration. The adorner uses WPF to paint a red block behind the text. This block is then synced to any movements of the text within the editor (by re-creating its visuals every time the layout of the editor window changes).

```
public TextAdornment1(IWpfTextView view)
{
    _view = view;
    _layer = view.GetAdornmentLayer("TextAdornment1");

    //Listen to any event that changes the layout (text changes, scrolling,
    //etc.)
    _view.LayoutChanged += OnLayoutChanged;

    //Create the pen and brush to color the box behind the A's
    Brush brush = new SolidColorBrush(Color.FromArgb(0x20, 0x00,
        0x00, 0xff));
    brush.Freeze();
    Brush penBrush = new SolidColorBrush(Colors.Red);
    penBrush.Freeze();
    Pen pen = new Pen(penBrush, 0.5);
    pen.Freeze();

    _brush = brush;
    _pen = pen;
}
```

Editor Viewport Adornment

The viewport adornment project is similar to the text adornment project, but it applies to a different layer of the editor (one where the text does not reside, which is a small but important distinction). Adorning the viewport in this fashion enables you to introduce visuals within the editor that aren't tied to any particular piece of text and can float in front of or in back of the text layer.

The sample effect produced by this template places a simple purple box in the upper-right corner of the editor (see Figure 16.5).

```
Program.cs ⊕ X
ConsoleApplication1 | HelloWorld.Program | Main(string[] args)
using System;
using System.Collections.Generic;
using System.Linq;
using System.Text;
using System.Threading.Tasks;

namespace HelloWorld
{
    0 references
    class Program
    {
        0 references
        static void Main(string[] args)
        {
            for (int i = 0; i <= 5; i++)
            {
                Console.WriteLine("Hello, World! try={0}", i);
            }


            Consolee.WriteLine("Anyone listening?");

            Console.ReadLine();
        }
    }
}
100 %
```

FIGURE 16.5 Example of Editor Viewport Adornment

Structurally, the code differs only slightly from the code for the text adornment sample. The adornment class (`ViewportAdornment1`) uses the same WPF brush objects to paint its adornment. The key difference is the visual layer used by the factory class (`ViewportAdornment1Factory`). To compare and contrast the two, first examine the previous project's factory.

```
[Export(typeof(IWpfTextViewCreationListener))]
[ContentType("text")]
[TextViewRole(PredefinedTextViewRoles.Document)]
internal sealed class TextAdornment1Factory : IWpfTextViewCreationListener
{
    /// <summary>
    /// Defines the adornment layer for the adornment. This layer is ordered
    /// after the selection layer in the Z-order
    /// </summary>
    [Export(typeof(AdornmentLayerDefinition))]
    [Name("TextAdornment1")]
    [Order(After = PredefinedAdornmentLayers.Selection,
        Before = PredefinedAdornmentLayers.Text)]
    [TextViewRole(PredefinedTextViewRoles.Document)]
    public AdornmentLayerDefinition editorAdornmentLayer = null;
```

```
    /// <summary>
    /// Instantiates a TextAdornment1 manager when a textView is created.
    /// </summary>
    /// <param name="textView">The <see cref="IWpfTextView"/> upon which the
    /// adornment should be placed</param>
    public void TextViewCreated(IWpfTextView textView)
    {
        new TextAdornment1(textView);
    }
}
```

And now, here is the viewport adornment factory.

```
[Export(typeof(IWpfTextViewCreationListener))]
[ContentType("text")]
[TextViewRole(PredefinedTextViewRoles.Document)]
internal sealed class PurpleBoxAdornmentFactory : IWpfTextViewCreationListener
{
    /// <summary>
    /// Defines the adornment layer for the scarlet adornment. This layer is ordered
    /// after the selection layer in the Z-order
    /// </summary>
    [Export(typeof(AdornmentLayerDefinition))]
    [Name("ViewportAdornment1")]
    [Order(After = PredefinedAdornmentLayers.Caret)]
    [TextViewRole(PredefinedTextViewRoles.Document)]
    public AdornmentLayerDefinition editorAdornmentLayer = null;

    /// <summary>
    /// Instantiates a ViewportAdornment1 manager when a textView is created.
    /// </summary>
    /// <param name="textView">The <see cref="IWpfTextView"/> upon which the
    ///     adornment should be placed</param>
    public void TextViewCreated(IWpfTextView textView)
    {
        new ViewportAdornment1(textView);
    }
}
```

Note the different layer order defined by each via the Order attribute (`[Order(After = PredefinedAdornmentLayers.Caret)]` versus `[Order(After = PredefinedAdornmentLayers.Selection, Before = PredefinedAdornmentLayers.Text)]`).

Managing Extensions and Updates

Before we detailed the editor extension points, we briefly mentioned the Extensions and Updates window. This dialog is launched via the Tools menu, Extensions and Updates.

The user interface (UI) used by the extension manager is clean and simple (see Figure 16.6).

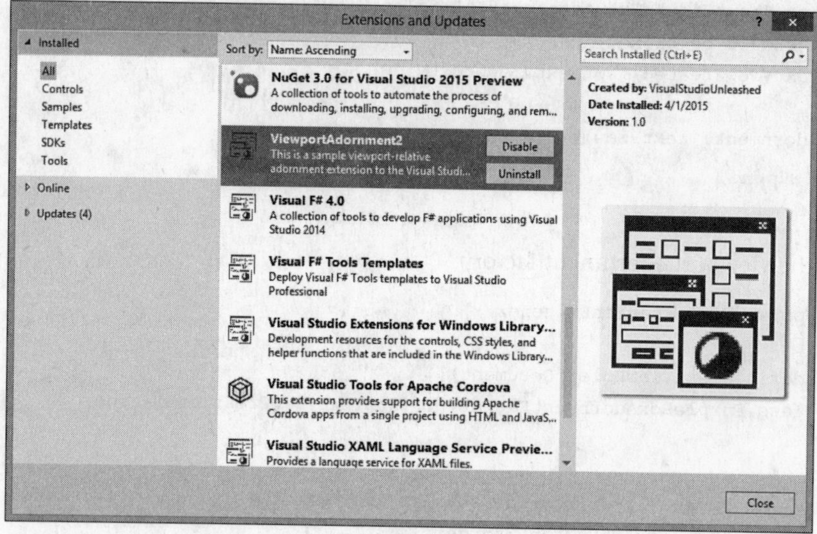

FIGURE 16.6 The Visual Studio Extension and Updates Manager.

You can manage installed extensions, browse extensions available online, or view updates available to any currently installed extensions. The left pane selects the location/category of the extensions or updates you want to manage. The center pane provides a list of the appropriate extensions; from here you can disable or enable an extension and install or uninstall an extension. In Figure 16.6, you can clearly see all the extensions that were installed as a result of running the four different extension template projects. The right pane provides general information about the currently selected extension.

Selecting Online in the left pane enables you to browse and install extensions that are hosted online (see Figure 16.7). You can post your own extensions online as well by visiting http://visualstudiogallery.msdn.microsoft.com/.

NOTE

The Visual Studio gallery and Visual Studio only fully support extensions packaged with VSIX. MSI-based extensions can be viewed here and installed, but Visual Studio can't enable or disable them through this UI. VSI-based extensions are not supported at all via the Extensions and Updates window.

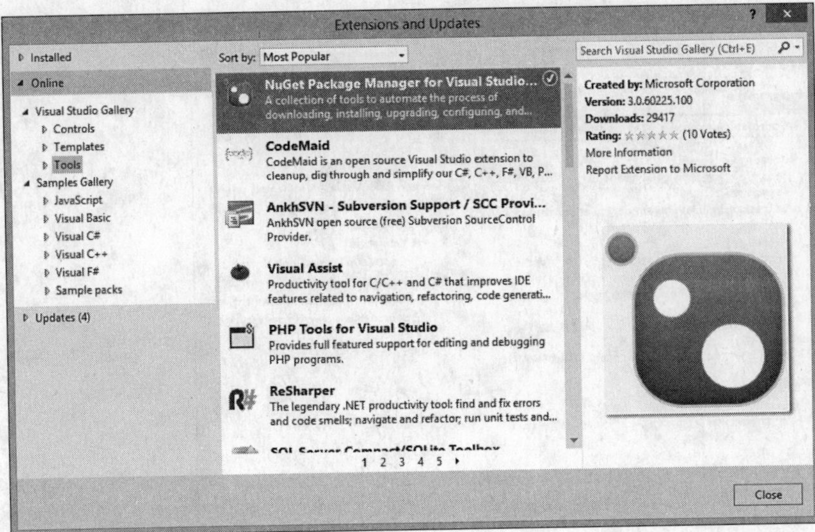

FIGURE 16.7 Finding extensions online.

Creating Your Own MEF-Based Editor Extension

You have now learned all the ingredients necessary to build your own extension. Let's walk through a simple example, end to end, and build an extension that displays some basic code metrics in a window in the corner of the editor. Functionally, you need to accomplish the following:

- Compute the required code stats by parsing the currently loaded code file
- Expose a set of properties on a WPF user control to hold those metrics (and which also displays those metrics)
- Display the WPF user control as an editor viewport adornment

Because this involves creating a new adornment pegged to the editor's viewport, you have the luxury of starting with the code produced for us by the Viewport Adornment template.

Create a new project called `CodeMetricAdornment` using the VSIX project template. Then add a new Editor Viewport Adornment item to the project and call it `CodeMetricViewportAdornment`. Finally, you will add a WPF user control titled `CodeMetricDisplayControl`. (If you are unfamiliar with WPF or XAML development in general, you may want to read through portions of Chapter 21, "Building WPF Applications.")

Your baseline project structure should look like Figure 16.8.

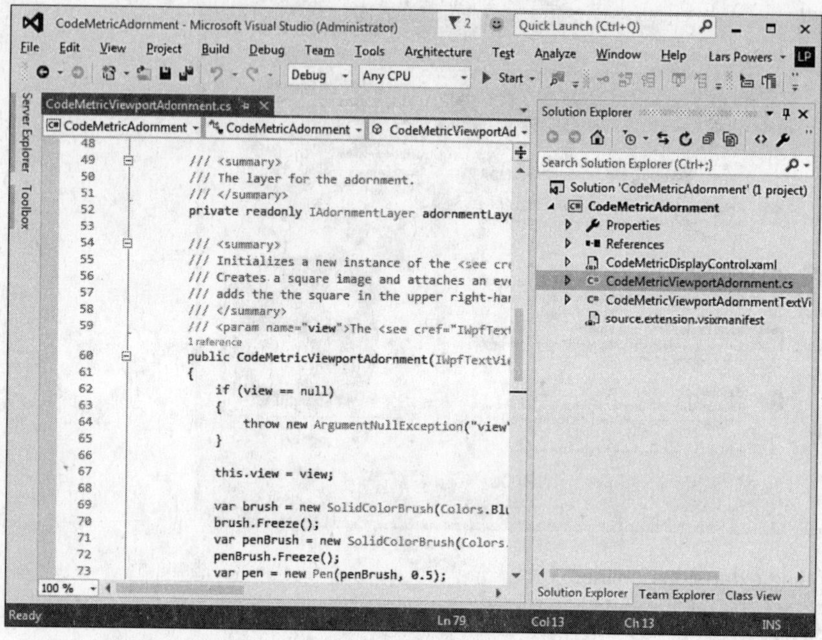

FIGURE 16.8 Creating a new adornment project.

Now open the `CodeMetricViewportAdornment` class itself. Within the class, you add a field to hold a WPF user control object, and you get rid of the current `Image` field that the template code uses.

```
private CodeMetricDisplayControl _displayControl =
        new CodeMetricDisplayControl();
```

We'll get to our code counting algorithm in a bit. Let's first focus on creating the content within our user control (`CodeMetricDisplayControl`). We need to display the three metrics and their three labels within the control; a grid works nicely for this.

Because the grid is already included by default as the root arrangement element of the control, you just need to tweak its display a bit. Add three rows and two columns to the grid.

```
<Grid>
    <Grid.ColumnDefinitions>
        <ColumnDefinition Width="auto" />
        <ColumnDefinition Width="*" />
    </Grid.ColumnDefinitions>
    <Grid.RowDefinitions>
        <RowDefinition />
        <RowDefinition />
        <RowDefinition />
```

```
    </Grid.RowDefinitions>
</Grid>
```

Within the grid, add six `TextBlock` objects—three to hold the labels, and three to hold the actual counts.

```
<TextBlock Grid.Column="0" Grid.Row="0"
           VerticalAlignment="Center"
           x:Name="TextBlockLOC"
           Padding="5">Total Lines of Code:</TextBlock>
<TextBlock Grid.Column="0" Grid.Row="1"
           x:Name="TextBlockComments"
           VerticalAlignment="Center"
           Padding="5">Comment Lines:</TextBlock>
<TextBlock Grid.Column="0" Grid.Row="2"
           x:Name="TextBlockWhitespace"
           VerticalAlignment="Center"
           Padding="5">Whitespace Lines:</TextBlock>

<TextBlock Grid.Column="1" Grid.Row="0"
           VerticalAlignment="Center">0</TextBlock>
<TextBlock Grid.Column="1" Grid.Row="1"
           VerticalAlignment="Center">0</TextBlock>
<TextBlock Grid.Column="1" Grid.Row="2"
           VerticalAlignment="Center">0</TextBlock>
```

Within the `CodeMetricDisplayControl` class, add a property for each of these integers as well.

```
public partial class CodeMetricDisplayControl : UserControl
{
    private int _loc = 0;  //total lines of code
    private int _whitespace = 0; //whitespace (empty) lines
    private int _comments = 0; //total lines that are comments

    public int LinesOfCode
    {
        get { return _loc; }
        set { _loc = value; Refresh(); }
    }


    public int CommentLines
    {
        get { return _comments; }
```

```
        set { _comments = value; Refresh(); }
    }

    public int WhitespaceLines
    {
        get { return _whitespace; }
        set { _whitespace = value; Refresh(); }
    }

    public CodeMetricDisplayControl()
    {
        InitializeComponent();
    }

}
```

Note that, in each setter, you are calling a `Refresh` routine. Let's write that routine, which updates the value of our `TextBlocks` to the current value held by our field for each of the code metrics.

```
private void Refresh()
{
    this.TextBlockComments.Text = _comments.ToString();
    this.TextBlockLOC.Text = _loc.ToString();
    this.TextBlockWhitespace.Text = _whitespace.ToString();
}
```

Disregarding any look and feel refinements, the WPF user control is now ready to go. Let's turn our attention back to the adorner class and write the code to actually count our lines of code, comments, and whitespace lines.

In `CodeMetricViewportAdornment`, strip out all the current drawing code from the constructor. In its place, add three lines that set the user control's properties based on the return values from a few private routines (which we implement next). The constructor should now look like this:

```
public CodeMetricAdornment(IWpfTextView view)
{
    _view = view;

    _displayControl.LinesOfCode = CountLOC(view);

    _adornmentLayer =
        view.GetAdornmentLayer
        ("CodeMetricAdornment");
```

```
    _view.ViewportHeightChanged += delegate { this.onSizeChange(); };
    _view.ViewportWidthChanged += delegate { this.onSizeChange(); };
}
```

The code to actually count our lines of code is straightforward. We take the `IWpfTextView` object provided by our adorner and get the string representation for all the current text in the editor window like this:

```
string code = view.TextSnapshot.GetText();
```

Now we can parse that string and return the various counts.

```
private int CountLOC(IWpfTextView view)
{
    string code = view.TextSnapshot.GetText();

    int count = 1;
    int start = 0;
    while ((start = code.IndexOf('\n', start)) != -1)
    {
        count++;
        start++;
    }

    return count;

}

private int CountWhitespaceLines(IWpfTextView view)
{
    string code = view.TextSnapshot.GetText();
    int count = 0;

    using (StringReader reader = new StringReader(code))
    {
        string line;

        while ((line = reader.ReadLine()) != null)
        {
            if (line.Trim() == "")
                count++;
        }

        return count;
    }
}
```

```
private int CountCommentLines(IWpfTextView view)
{
    string code = view.TextSnapshot.GetText();
    int count = 0;

    using (StringReader reader = new StringReader(code))
    {
        string line;

        while ((line = reader.ReadLine()) != null)
        {
            if (line.TrimStart().StartsWith("//"))
                count++;
        }

        return count;
    }
}
```

We are almost done. The final piece that we need to change from the template code is to rewrite a piece of the `OnSizeChange` event handler. This was wired to position and display the WPF Image control originally used by the template. Instead, we want this code to position and place our WPF user control. Change the code within `OnSizeChange` to this:

```
public void onSizeChange()
    {
        //Clear the adornment layer of previous adornments
        _adornmentLayer.RemoveAllAdornments();

        //Place the image in the top-right corner of the viewport
        Canvas.SetLeft(_displayControl,
            _view.ViewportRight - _displayControl.ActualWidth);
        Canvas.SetTop(_displayControl,
            _view.ViewportTop + _displayControl.ActualHeight);

        //Add the image to the adornment layer and make it relative to the
        //viewport
        _adornmentLayer.AddAdornment(
            AdornmentPositioningBehavior.ViewportRelative,
            null, null, _displayControl, null);
    }
```

Now the control is positioned and is in the adornment view layer. If you run the project and then open a code file from within the IDE instance that is launched, you should immediately see the fruits of your labor in the upper-right corner of the editor.

There is still one problem with this implementation. Although the code stats are displayed correctly, they aren't updated when we change the text within the editor. To fix this, we need to react to the adornment layer's `IWpfTextView LayoutChanged` event. We can hook this event inside our `CodeMetricViewportAdornment` constructor like this.

```
_view.LayoutChanged += this.OnLayoutChanged;
```

And then we create the event handler that updates our counts.

```
private void OnLayoutChanged(object sender, TextViewLayoutChangedEventArgs e)
{
    _displayControl.LinesOfCode = CountLOC(_view);
    _displayControl.CommentLines = CountCommentLines(_view);
    _displayControl.WhitespaceLines = CountWhitespaceLines(_view);
}
```

We can make our WPF user control more compelling to look at by tweaking the XAML to add things like a background gradient and text coloring.

Figure 16.9 shows the final product, and Listing 16.1 contains the viewport adornment class code. The full source listing for this project is available at this book's website: http://informit.com/title/9780672337369.

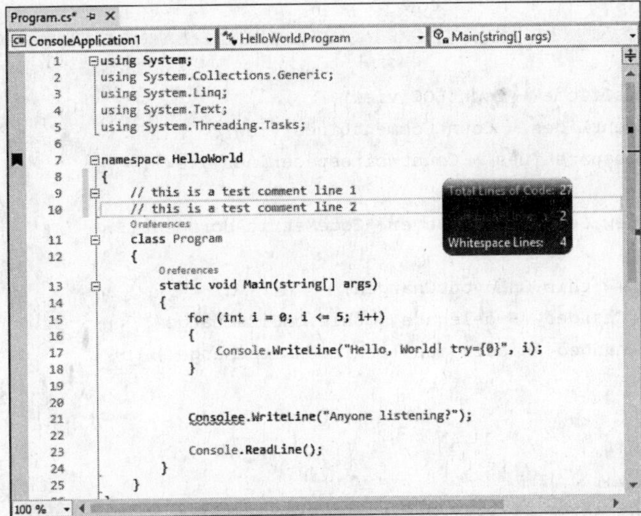

FIGURE 16.9 A simple code metric adornment in the editor.

LISTING 16.1 The `CodeMetricViewportAdornment` Class

```
using System.IO;
using System.Windows.Controls;
using System.Windows.Media;
using Microsoft.VisualStudio.Text.Editor;

namespace CodeMetricViewportAdornment
{
    /// <summary>
    /// Adornment class that draws a square box in the top-right corner of
    /// the viewport
    /// </summary>
    class CodeMetricAdornment
    {
        private IWpfTextView _view;
        private IAdornmentLayer _adornmentLayer;
        private CodeMetricDisplayControl _displayControl =
            new CodeMetricDisplayControl();

        public CodeMetricAdornment(IWpfTextView view)
        {
            _view = view;

            _displayControl.LinesOfCode = CountLOC(view);
            _displayControl.CommentLines = CountCommentLines(view);
            _displayControl.WhitespaceLines = CountWhitespaceLines(view);

            _adornmentLayer = view.GetAdornmentLayer("CodeMetricAdornment");

            _view.LayoutChanged += this.OnLayoutChanged;
            _view.ViewportHeightChanged += delegate { this.onSizeChange(); };
            _view.ViewportWidthChanged += delegate { this.onSizeChange(); };
        }

        public void onSizeChange()
        {
            //Clear the adornment layer of previous adornments
            _adornmentLayer.RemoveAllAdornments();

            int buffer = 50;

            //Place the image in the top-right corner of the viewport
            Canvas.SetLeft(_displayControl,
                _view.ViewportRight - (_displayControl.ActualWidth
```

```
            + buffer));
        Canvas.SetTop(_displayControl,
            _view.ViewportTop + (_displayControl.ActualHeight
            + buffer));

        _adornmentLayer.AddAdornment(
            AdornmentPositioningBehavior.ViewportRelative,
            null, null, _displayControl, null);
    }

    private void OnLayoutChanged(object sender, TextViewLayoutChangedEventArgs
e)
    {
        _displayControl.LinesOfCode = CountLOC(_view);
        _displayControl.CommentLines = CountCommentLines(_view);
        _displayControl.WhitespaceLines = CountWhitespaceLines(_view);
    }

    private int CountLOC(IWpfTextView view)
    {
        string code = view.TextSnapshot.GetText();

        int count = 1;
        int start = 0;
        while ((start = code.IndexOf('\n', start)) != -1)
        {
            count++;
            start++;
        }

        return count;

    }

    private int CountWhitespaceLines(IWpfTextView view)
    {
        string code = view.TextSnapshot.GetText();
        int count = 0;

        using (StringReader reader = new StringReader(code))
        {
            string line;

            while ((line = reader.ReadLine()) != null)
            {
                if (line.Trim() == "")
```

```
                    count++;
                }

                return count;

            }
        }

        private int CountCommentLines(IWpfTextView view)
        {
            string code = view.TextSnapshot.GetText();
            int count = 0;

            using (StringReader reader = new StringReader(code))
            {
                string line;

                while ((line = reader.ReadLine()) != null)
                {
                    if (line.TrimStart().StartsWith("//"))
                        count++;
                }

                return count;

            }
        }
    }
}
```

Summary

This chapter covered the Managed Execution Framework and illustrated how you can use it to write extensions for the Visual Studio code editor. You learned the overall architecture of MEF, including its extension discovery mechanisms and the core concepts of parts and imports/exports.

This chapter also examined all the specific Visual Studio 2015 editor extension points and outlined the value that the Visual Studio SDK provides with its prestocked set of extension templates that target those editor extension points.

Finally, this chapter provided a walk-through of the creation of an editor extension that exploits the editor's adornment layer to display a running total of three different code metrics, all through the use of a WPF-based user control.

CHAPTER 17

Building Modern Websites with ASP.NET 5

IN THIS CHAPTER

- ASP.NET Website Fundamentals
- Introducing ASP.NET 5
- Creating a Web Application with ASP.NET 5/MVC 6
- Writing ASP.NET Server Code (Models and Controllers)
- Coding for the UI (Views and Related Web UI Elements)

Modern website development is about building applications that take advantage of the client device using common client-side frameworks; render the UI appropriately based on screen size; and help developers build solutions for corporate websites, collaboration portals, enterprise business solutions, and mobile apps/games. Visual Studio 2015 and ASP.NET 5 give developers the flexibility to build all types of these web-based solutions. This includes support for the traditional ASP.NET Web Forms model, the Razor Web Pages approach, sites built on the Model-View-Controller (MVC) pattern, service applications built on Web API, single-page applications (SPAs) that leverage client-side frameworks such as AngularJS, and mobile solutions that use HTML5 and Cordova to run natively on a device.

Visual Studio supports all these various models, approaches, and templates for building web applications. We cover a number of these in this book. This chapter is about web fundamentals, ASP.NET 5, and MVC sites. Chapter 18, "Using JavaScript and Client-Side Frameworks," covers client-side frameworks used to build single-page applications (SPA). We cover Web API (and WCF) services in Chapter 19, "Building and Consuming Services with Web API and WCF." The final chapter in the book, Chapter 25, "Writing Cross-Platform Mobile Applications with Apache Cordova," covers building mobile applications with HTML5 and Cordova.

NOTE

The ASP.NET/web topic is huge. We are not able to dig in on its every aspect. Instead, we choose to concentrate on areas where modern web development happens, including ASP.NET 5, client frameworks, web services, and mobile.

One notable omission is ASP.NET Web Forms. Microsoft continues to invest in this approach; it is very much part of Visual Studio 2015. However, we have observed that, like ASP before it, Web Forms is becoming a legacy technology. There are great resources available on the web (as well as prior editions of this book) should you need to work with Web Forms.

We also expect that, as you build your ASP.NET applications, you will discover places that require further exploration. Again, this is a large topic with many twists and turns. To that end, we point out some of these as we move through these web chapters. Some additional examples include user membership, caching, website administration, and more.

ASP.NET Website Fundamentals

For those just starting to build web applications, we thought it useful to provide a high-level overview of how ASP.NET works to service user requests. Web development is a large and diverse topic. However, at its core, it is just Hypertext Markup Language (HTML) web pages pushed to browsers from web servers over Hypertext Transfer Protocol (HTTP) request/response. Understanding these fundamental concepts makes it easier to work with the greater complexities of web development (which we cover throughout this chapter). If you are familiar with writing web applications, we expect you to glance at Figure 17.1 and skip this section.

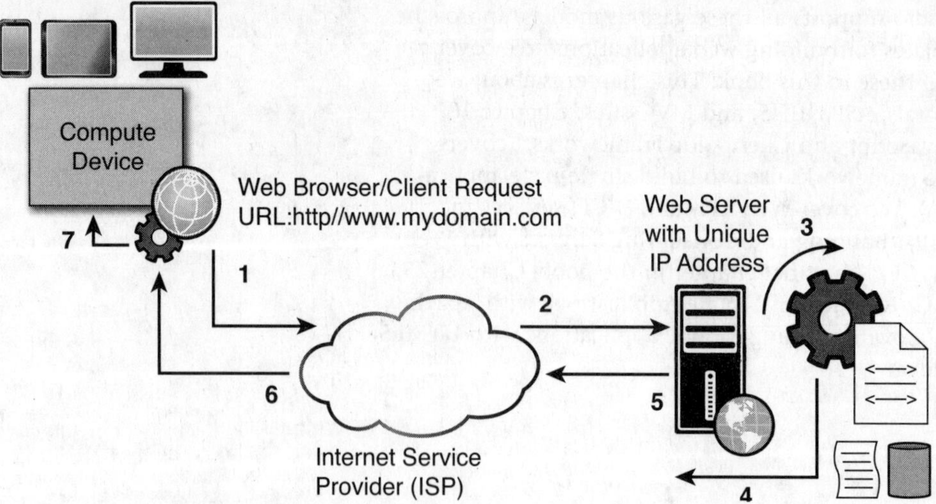

FIGURE 17.1 A high-level overview of how ASP.NET uses the various .NET web components (such as the HTTP stack) and protocols to handle user requests routed to the server, process them, and return the results to the user's browser.

Web development is about writing code to respond to a user request by first processing that request on the server, packaging a result back to the user, and allowing that result to execute on the client and ultimately render text, graphics, and behavior to the user. The code we write includes code for server-side processing of data and logic and client-side code to make the application dynamic and responsive to the user. Most of the other items we develop focus on making things look nice using HTML markup and Cascading Style Sheets (CSS). The following outlines how a web request is processed and results are rendered through the numbered items shown in Figure 17.1.

1. A compute device such as a PC, phone, tablet, or game console presents a web client application to the user. This could be a web browser or a native client application that speaks HTTP. The user then triggers a request to your web application. This request is defined by a unique uniform resource locator (URL).
2. The request is sent from the compute device network adapter using HTTP (Hypertext Transfer Protocol), typically through a local network/router, and then on to the user's Internet service provider (ISP). The URL is looked up against a DNS (domain name server) in order to find a unique IP (internet protocol) address that maps to the domain name. The ISP then forwards the HTTP request on to your web server based on the IP address.
3. A web server receives the request (typically via a network at the hosting provider). The server is typically running a web server host application, such as Microsoft Internet Information Server (IIS). This application sits waiting for HTTP requests and is ready to route them to the right web application that will process them and prepare a response to the web server.

   The request typically goes through an HTTP pipeline processer. This pipeline will validate the request and authorize user credentials (if any). The request is then routed to your code.

   As you will see shortly, in an ASP.NET MVC application, the request is routed to a controller class library you write. The controller processes the request. This processing typically includes reaching out to a database server to get requested data, selecting a view for the HTML markup, executing any data to view binding, applying any other server-side code to build the response, and then returning the results to the server to be sent to the requesting client. These results include the view (as HTML) to be rendered, JavaScript to be run on the client, and images to be sent back to the client.
4. The web server bundles the response for a return trip to the user's compute device (browser or native client application).
5. The response is routed back through the user's ISP to the compute device. This routing is also done through the IP address.
6. The response is received by the user's network and routed to the compute device's network adapter. Ultimately, the response is sent to the HTTP handler (typically a web browser but could be a native client application) that made the request.

7. The HTTP handler (typically a web browser) on the compute device receives the results, processes them, and renders the visual representation of the markup to the user. Processing includes interpreting styles, loading images, executing JavaScript code, and more. Of course, the client application then stands ready to process any additional client-side JavaScript based on user action (and to generate the corresponding next request).

This fundamental understanding of web requests, processing, and response is meant to provide a high-level overview to orient web developers as they start working with ASP.NET 5. There are, of course, many additional complexities that make this work, such as caching, routers, load balancers, and the like. We hope to provide a general overview for developers. The sections (and other web chapters) that follow illustrate how ASP.NET 5 leverages these concepts to enable developers to build great things.

Introducing ASP.NET 5

In late 2014, Microsoft released all of .NET to open source under the MIT license. Visual Studio 2015 and ASP.NET 5 (previously referred to as vNext) represent the first released versions of the products since Microsoft open sourced ASP.NET and the .NET Core framework. This includes the core .NET base class libraries, the Common Language Runtime (CLR), the Just-In-Time compiler (JIT), and the Garbage Collector (GC). This new approach has resulted in many exciting changes to the product, including these:

- Cross-platform support for both developing and hosting ASP.NET website on non-Windows machines
- ASP.NET allowing self-hosting (also called host-anywhere) of a web application on any device (in addition to web server hosting such as IIS)
- Cloud-ready, modular versions of the framework that can ship with your application as packages; can run side-by-side other versions; require only portions of the framework you intend to use (or no framework at all); and do not require machine upgrades to work
- A new, unified, open-source ASP.NET compiler (Roslyn) that supports C# and Visual Basic languages and works in the background (dynamic compilation) to save you time during debug and eliminate slow startups for users following site updates
- Adoption of many popular third-party client frameworks like jQuery, AngularJS, Ember, Knockout, and others
- Client-side packaged management using popular web tools like Bower and Gulp
- Support for responsive design with Twitter Bootstrap
- Support for developing using additional code editors (like Sublime Text, Vi, and others) on different operating systems such as Mac and Linux
- Cloud-ready configuration for environment variables, session, and cache

ASP.NET OPEN SOURCE

You can view the source code for ASP.NET at https://github.com/aspnet/home.

ASP.NET CODE EDITORS

.NET is coming to additional code editors (like Sublime Text, Vi, Emacs, and the new Visual Studio Code) thanks to the work done by a group of open source projects. To learn more, check out the site http://www.omnisharp.net/.

ASP.NET 5 also unifies the programming and execution models of MVC 6, Web Pages, Web API, caching, SignalR, and Entity Framework. In prior versions, many of these programming models overlapped, resulting in duplicate features that were implemented separately. This often meant unexpected behavior from similar classes. Thankfully, all these technologies are now merged, duplication has been removed, and you can write your code against a single framework.

THE .NET FOUNDATION

The .NET Foundation is an independent organization that manages the open source projects for .NET. To get more information and to access these projects, check out their website at http://www.dotnetfoundation.org/.

The .NET Core Framework and Execution Environment

Microsoft continues to evolve the .NET Framework; in doing so, it is now tackling the significant issue of the full framework being required (and installed machine wide) to get your applications to run properly. This has presented many problems over the years. For one, to take advantage of a new framework's features, you needed to upgrade the entire machine and thus anything else on that machine that relied on the .NET Framework. You also did not have a choice in the amount of the framework you wanted to use; instead, it was all or nothing. This added unnecessary overhead (and sometimes performance hits) to your application. With the latest version, the .NET Framework has answers for these dilemmas. It is moving from a single, machine-wide framework for all Windows programming to a framework that can be specialized (and optimized) to an application's needs. The following outlines the versions of the framework available to ASP.NET developers:

- **.NET Framework**—This is the full version of the .NET Framework that we have all been using to-date. It runs on Windows; it supports all existing applications without modification, and it includes ASP.NET. You can write ASP.NET 5 applications that target the full, NET Framework (version 4.6 at current release). This is also the default runtime for nearly all new projects created in Visual Studio.
- **.NET Core Framework**—This is the new, modular, cloud-optimized version of the framework and CLR runtime. This is referred to as .NET Core 5. Developers can pick and choose only the components and features (packages) on which their

application depends. You do so using the familiar NuGet package manager. You can then ship those features along with your application (instead of requiring a full machine install). This provides a couple advantages: you can run various versions of .NET Core 5 and the .NET Framework side by side on a single machine; and, individual components of the .NET Core can be upgraded, installed, and used separately without requiring a full revision of the framework (or patching on the server).

The .NET Core consists of a subset of .NET libraries called CoreFX. It also includes an optimized runtime called CoreCLR. The CoreFX libraries can be installed as individual NuGet packages (as `System.[module]`).

The .NET Core has a much smaller footprint (11 MB instead of nearly 200), and its memory requirements are also much smaller. It has been specifically optimized for running ASP.NET applications in the cloud by requiring lower memory consumption and higher throughput.

- **.NET Core 5 on other platforms**—Microsoft is also releasing the .NET Core 5 framework for both Linux and Mac OS X. This gives developers the ability to develop and execute .NET applications on these platforms. Microsoft has worked with the Mono community to develop these versions of the framework.

The .NET Execution Environment (DNX)

Microsoft has created the .NET Execution Environment (DNX) to bundle versions of the framework, the CLR, and an SDK to provide the necessary bits to build and execute ASP.NET applications on Windows, Mac, and Linux. DNX simplifies the packaging of these items. It also allows you to build on one platform and run the application on another platform, provided you are using the same DNX version.

Upcoming sections will examine targeting various versions of the framework and runtime using DNX while developing, debugging, and releasing code. We will also cover using NuGet to select the right modular framework packages for your application.

PORTING EXISTING WEB APPS

Your web applications built on prior versions of ASP.NET including Web Forms, Web API 2, MVC 5, Entity Framework 6, Web Pages 3, and so on will all still work in Visual Studio 2015 and the latest version of the .NET Framework, without modification. Of course, you likely will have to use the full .NET Framework (and not the new .NET Core Framework) because it maintains backward compatibility.

You can, of course, take advantage of the newer features of ASP.NET 5 and the Core Framework with your existing sites. To do so, you will need to port your applications to the new framework. Porting does not mean rewriting; it typically only involves fixing specific issues in the app.

Choosing an ASP.NET Project Template

Websites in Visual Studio start with a project template. The website project represents a connection between Visual Studio, the source code of your website, and a web server (be it local or otherwise). What the project template contains, however, continues to evolve and expand to support multiple web application scenarios.

Simple Hypertext Markup Language (HTML) sites with just text, hyperlinks, and a few images are rarely created anymore or even discussed seriously as websites. Instead, ASP.NET along with HTML 5, CSS 3, and various client-side JavaScript libraries have pushed the definition of website well beyond the original ASP (active server pages) model that combined HTML with some server-side script.

Today, we build websites (and web applications) that mimic user interactivity previously possible only with native code. This means client-side code interacting with compiled code on the server, database connectivity and binding, configurable user membership, responsive user interfaces, and so on. The Visual Studio 2015 tooling brings these concepts together to enable you to create these rich, modern web applications.

WEB APPLICATION VERSUS WEBSITE PROJECTS

Visual Studio enables you to create both websites (File, New, Web Site) and web application projects (File, New, Project). Both are represented by project templates that define default directories, configuration, pages, and other related files and settings. Both are nested in a solution. Both allow you to control properties and manage external references. A website works well for developers who typically deploy their site as a set of files. A web application project should be used when you want to deploy compiled code and need specialized control over compilation and output assemblies. Presently, you can only create ASP.NET 5, MVC, and Web API sites as web applications. They are the preferred option for the majority of ASP.NET developers. Therefore, this chapter focuses on web application templates.

You create a new ASP.NET web application using the New Project dialog (File, New, Project). You start by selecting the Web node under your chosen language. From there, you select the template titled ASP.NET Web Application, given your project a name and location, and hit the OK button. This brings up the New ASP.NET Project dialog, as shown in Figure 17.2. It allows you to refine your ASP.NET project type selection. Notice the templates are grouped by those that target ASP.NET 4.6 and those that are built on ASP.NET 5. Of course, you pick a template based on your specific needs. The following list provides an overview of many of the ASP.NET web application templates.

The Empty Project Templates

There are two empty project templates shown in Figure 17.2 (one for ASP.NET 4.6 and one for ASP.NET 5). Like they sound, these templates are used to create projects that are free of the basic template files and configuration. The Empty template for ASP.NET 4.6 targets the full .NET framework and follows that approach for development. It contains a `web.config` file for managing configuration. You use the template to create applications based on MVC 5, Web Forms, or similar web development approaches from prior versions.

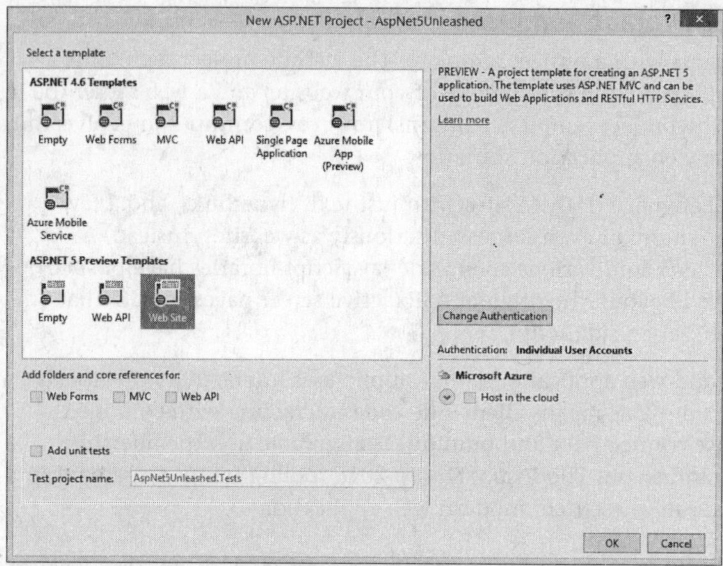

FIGURE 17.2 You can select from one of the many ASP.NET project templates in Visual Studio 2015.

The ASP.NET 5 Empty template can target different versions of DNX (dnx451 for the full .NET Framework or dnxcore50 for the .NET Core 5 Framework). It includes the `.json` JSON style configuration files and the new package managers (see upcoming section), and it can be used to create MVC 6 or Web API projects.

Web Forms

The ASP.NET Web Forms template has been around for a long while and offers developers ease of use, a strong set of controls, and a rich framework to extend. You build Web Forms using HTML and the ASP.NET controls using markup and a design-time editor. Each file has a code-behind class that includes server-side code executed in response to events on the page (such as page load and form postback).

The template includes a directory for storing data (`App_Data`), a default page (`Default.aspx`), a configuration file (`web.config`), a master page (`Site.master`), a style sheet (`Content/Site.css`), a page for intercepting application events (`Global.asax`), code for managing which scripts are loaded (`BundleConfig.cs`), and more. The template also includes an `Account` directory that contains pages for managing login and user accounts. The jQuery library is also provided by default in this template (inside the `Scripts` folder). Of course, additional folders and files can be added as you build out your site.

Web Forms tends to abstract the basic HTML and JavaScript from the developer, leaving us to work with controls that do much of the work for us. In addition, Web Forms combines UI code with presentation, making it difficult to test your UI code or to get good reuse of many of your UI methods. ASP.NET MVC was created as an alternative to get developers back in control of their HTML (the view) and to separate this view from the actual logic (the controller) and the data (the model). As a result, MVC (and related client frameworks) has become the preferred choice of ASP.NET developers over Web Forms.

NOTE

Your Web Forms 4.6 applications will still run in Visual Studio 2015 without modifications. They do require the full .NET Framework/Runtime. Microsoft continues to evolve the technology. You will see new features including the implementation of HTTP 2 for better request handling, async model binding, and the Roslyn compilers for code-behind files.

Web Pages

The ASP.NET Web Pages technology and project template were created the same time Microsoft introduced the Razor syntax for working with server-side code and basic HTML in the same page. This is the way MVC sites work. However, with Web Pages, you do not need the complexities of the MVC pattern. Instead, you create a URL-addressable page as a `.cshtml` page (no controller or models required). You then write basic HTML (no server-side controls) and embed C# code directly within the page itself. You use the Razor syntax throughout your HTML to display variable values, do conditional checks, loop through collections, and similar activities.

The ASP.NET Web Pages with Razor syntax gives developers a simple, easy-to-learn model for creating web pages. By contrast, ASP.NET Web Forms is largely based on controls that render their HTML and JavaScript to the browser at runtime. This is feature-rich but also carries with it a steep learning curve and some heavyweight pages. Web Pages with Razor eliminates these controls in favor of just HTML (including HTML 5). You can still add server-side code to your page to affect how the HTML is written to the browser and to respond to user requests. The results are web pages that are easier to understand, a technology that is faster to learn, and a lightweight processing engine.

You create a Web Pages template in Visual Studio from the File, New, Website menu and then select ASP.NET Web Site (Razor v3) as your template. This template includes a few `.cshtml` pages to get you started. Like the MVC template, it also defines a master layout called `_SiteLayout.cshtml`. This page contains common elements for your page, such as navigation, style sheet links, jQuery inclusion script tags, and a footer. You then need only add your specific page content to the new pages you create.

We cover the details of the Razor syntax later in this chapter. These details apply to Web Pages and MVC sites.

MVC

The ASP.NET MVC template leverages the MVC design pattern to separate the view (your HTML), the model (your data), and the logic that combines data with the right view (the controller). This separation increases opportunities for code reuse, makes your code more understandable, and supports unit testing of controller code.

The MVC template is based on a prior versions of ASP.NET and thus includes a web.config file and is set to target the full .NET Framework. However, outside of configuration and package management, the majority of development concepts and programming techniques are the same between the MVC template of old and the new ASP.NET 5 template. We cover the latter in depth later in this chapter. However, much of what we cover is also applicable to the MVC template.

Web API

There are two Web API templates: one targeting ASP.NET 4.6 and the other for ASP.NET 5. Both templates allows you to easily create HTTP REST-based services. The 4.6 template requires the full .NET Framework and is backward compatible with prior versions of the framework.

Microsoft has unified the technologies of Web API and MVC within ASP.NET 5. Therefore, you can use the Web API 5 template or simply build HTTP services with one of the other ASP.NET 5 templates. We cover creating services with Web API in Chapter 19.

Single-Page Application (SPA)

The SPA template focuses on building a rich web client that uses HTML 5 and JavaScript to provide an interactive user experience. This template is based on the MVC template. However, it focuses on client-side libraries of Knockout, jQuery, Twitter Bootstrap, and others. It was created to help you build a site using these client frameworks, HTML 5, CSS 3, and JavaScript.

You can create a SPA using any of the templates; you need only include the right client-side libraries and be ready to write JavaScript. We cover more on building SPAs in Chapter 18.

ASP.NET 5 Web Site

The ASP.NET 5 Web Site is the new template for building ASP.NET 5 applications. This template is also focused squarely on the MVC pattern. However, it uses the new versions of the .NET Framework and includes tools for working with client-frameworks. That makes it a great candidate for a new website, Web API projects, and SPAs.

This template (along with the DNX and ASP.NET 5) is the focus of this chapter; thus, the primary details are covered within.

Understanding the ASP.NET 5 Project Template and Related Files

A typical website contains a number of different files including web pages, class files, scripts, style sheets, configuration files, images, JavaScript client libraries, and more. Visual Studio works to keep these many files organized and grouped together so that you may focus on building your site. As an example, the ASP.NET 5 Web Site project template (created as shown back in Figure 17.2) has a default structure in Solution Explorer, including many special directories and file types. Figure 17.3 show the default structure and contents when using this template.

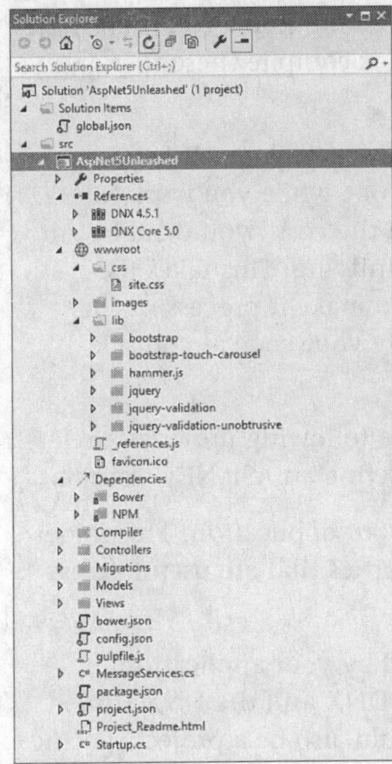

FIGURE 17.3 The ASP.NET 5 Web Site template contains folders, client libraries, configuration, and related structure for your website.

The many folders, special directories, configuration files, and web pages come together at runtime to provide a response to a user's browser request. The following walks you through the key elements shown in Figure 17.3. Later in the chapter we walk through using these file types and directories to build an actual site.

`wwwroot` and Other Significant Directories

An ASP.NET website groups files using conventions and "special" directories (as shown in Figure 17.3). The regular folders such as `Controllers`, `Models`, and `Views` allow you to easily organize your code. The special directories represent a convention on how ASP.NET works and where it stores required items that are outside your project code.

One such directory is `wwwroot`, which is new to ASP.NET 5. It represents the actual root of your site as in http://mydomain/. It is used for the static files in your project, such as images, style sheets, JavaScript files, and the like. Putting static files in this common location makes referencing them easier; it also allows ASP.NET to serve these static files directly to clients (knowing it does not need to process or compile them).

The `wwwroot` of the default ASP.NET 5 Web Site template already contains your style sheet (`css/site.css`) as well as key client-side JavaScript frameworks such as Bootstrap and jQuery in the `lib` folder (placed there at compile time by a Gulp task). Other items will end up in the `wwwroot` folder, too. This includes processed CSS files, minified JavaScript, optimized images, compiled TypeScript to JavaScript, and more. Typically, the source for these items sits outside of `wwwroot` while you create, edit, and refine them. You then write tasks (using tools like Gulp, as you will see shortly) to process or compile these files and put the results in the `wwwroot` for serving to clients.

For example, you may have a JavaScript library that you have written yourself for your specific website. You would keep that code outside of the `wwwroot` while you work to edit and refine it over time. When it is time to run (or release) the code, you would want to optimize it for faster processing through a process called minifying. This takes the JavaScript file and removes whitespace (among other things) to make it process much faster. To do so, you would write a Gulp task to tell it to minify your code at compile time and push the results to `wwwroot`.

ASP.NET includes a number of special folders like `wwwroot`. The following provides a reference for the many directories that are used as convention to define an ASP.NET website:

- **`Properties`**—Used to define settings and properties for your application. This folder contains a class, `AppSettings`. Here you can define properties that are useful across your site.
- **`References`**—Controls the other .NET libraries referenced by your application. By default, the ASP.NET 5 templates reference both the full DNX and the DNX Core. References are typically managed through NuGet but could also be a project specific reference or a connected service reference.
- **`wwwroot`**—The root of your website. Used for containing and serving up static files. (See earlier discussion.)
- **`Dependencies`**—Groups the client-side libraries that your application depends on and their build tasks. These dependencies are managed in the `bower.json` configuration file; the tasks are managed in the Task Runner Explorer. See the upcoming section, "ASP.NET 5 Dependencies and Package Managers."
- **`Compiler`**—Store compilation configuration code. In the current release, this is a file that enables pre-compilation of Razor views to cut down on compile time for the first use.
- **`Migrations`**—Works with the Entity Framework and contains code used to migrate changes and updates to your database as your code evolves.
- **The MVC folders (`Models`, `Views`, and `Controllers`)**—Folders for grouping the key code items in your website. The `Models` folder contains class files that represent your data model. The `Views` folder is where you store `.cshtml` markup pages for rendering your user interface. The `Controllers` folder is used for writing code to intercept web requests and return the response (usually by working with Models and Views). See the upcoming section, "Creating a Web Application with ASP.NET 5/MVC 6."

Project Files

Numerous files and file types define a typical ASP.NET website. You need only look at the Add New Item dialog (right-click Website in Solution Explorer and choose Add, New Item) to see the many file types you can add to your site. There are files that you use often, such as web views/partial views and classes. You might also work with configuration files and write a lot of JavaScript. Table 17.1 lists some of the more common files that might exist in any given ASP.NET 5/MVC 6 web application. The table includes the given item template name (from the Add New Item dialog), the file extension, and a short description.

TABLE 17.1 ASP.NET Files

Item Template(s)	Extension	Description
HTML Page	`.html`	A standard HTML web page.
Style Sheet	`.css`	A cascading style sheet for defining your visual style and behaviors.
MVC View Page	`.cshtml`	Similar to an HTML page in that it includes HTML Markup but also contains server-side processed code.
JavaScript File AngularJS Controller AngularJS Directive AngularJS Module Grunt Configuration File Gulp Configuration File	`.js`	A file containing client-side JavaScript, including those written against the frameworks of AngularJS, Grunt, and Gulp.
ASP.NET Configuration File Bower JSON Configuration File NPM Configuration File JSON File	`.json`	A JSON file contains data described using the JavaScript Object Notation. ASP.NET also uses this notation for various configuration files.
Class MVC Controller Class Web API Controller Class Startup Class	`.cs.vb`	Contains C#/VB code that gets compiled and runs on the server. Used for defining MVC Controllers, class libraries, and other types.
CoffeeScript File	`.coffee`	A file containing CoffeeScript (a language that compiles into JavaScript). CoffeeScript makes writing JavaScript easier and cleaner.
LESS Style Sheet	`.less`	A file for defining LESS CSS. LESS is an extension of CSS that includes features like variables and is processed as CSS when sent to the browser.
SCSS Style Sheet (SASS)	`.scss`	A file for writing Sass style sheets. Sass is a scripting language that is output to a CSS.

The Configuration Files

ASP.NET 5 introduces the JSON configuration files. JSON stands for JavaScript Simple Object Notation and is used by developers to exchange data. It replaced XML for most HTTP web services because XML is viewed as too large and complex. Microsoft has now replaced the `.config` files that were based on XML with new `.json` files for doing configuration. The section that follows ("ASP.NET 5 Dependencies and Package Managers") illustrates working with and editing these various configuration files. The following provides a reference for some of the many `.json` configuration files you will encounter in an ASP.NET 5.0 site:

- **`global.json`**—Used to define settings at the solution level (file is inside the Solution Items folder); it also allows for project-to-project references.
- **`project.json`**—This is the primary configuration file for your project. Here you define the version of the framework on which your site depends, other dependent packages (from NuGet), your intended web host, your web root, client package managers, and more.
- **`config.json`**—A configuration file you can use for your project configuration items, such as database connection strings. This relies on `Microsoft.Framework.ConfigurationModel.Json` for reading values from your configuration file.
- **`bower.json`**—Used to manage the client-side JavaScript packages on which your site might depend, such as jQuery and Bootstrap.
- **`package.json`**—Configures NPM (Node Package Manager) packages. NPM is another JavaScript client-side library package manager. It is used for libraries like Node, AngularJS, and Gulp.
- **`gulpfile.js`**—A JavaScript file used by Gulp to define and configure automated processing tasks. Gulp tasks are used for processing client files for deployment, such as minifying JavaScript or processing Sass into CSS.
- **`Startup.cs`**—This is not a `.json` file but an actual class file that is compiled with your application. That said, the class file is used to define various configuration elements through code. You use `Startup.cs` to configure the ASP.NET request pipeline. This includes defining your application host, configuring application services (such as MVC), setting URL routing conventions, and more.

Given that so many of the configuration files are written as JSON, it is important that you have a feel for how this notation works. At its most basic level, you define an object using curly brackets {}. Inside the brackets you define properties of that object using name and value pairs separated by a colon, as in `"name": "value"`. Each of these properties could also define another object following the same semantics. Each property is separated by a comma. The following shows a basic example of a customer object in JSON notation. Notice the email property inside the customer contact object; its values are defined by an array enclosed with square brackets ([ ]).

```
{
  "customer": {
    "name": "Jane Smith",
    "id": 123456,
    "age": 38,
    "contact": {
```

```
            "street": "One Microsoft Way",
            "city": "Redmond",
            "state": "Washington",
            "postalCode": "98052",
            "email": [
              "jsmith@contoso.com",
              "jane@fabrikam.com"
            ]
        }
    }
}
```

ASP.NET 5 Dependencies and Package Managers

Visual Studio 2015 and ASP.NET 5 make it easier to manage the many libraries and code packages on which a modern web application depends. This includes compiled server code libraries such as the .NET Framework itself (see the earlier section "The ASP.NET Framework") using NuGet. Microsoft has also added support for handling client-side libraries using the popular, open source projects Bower, NPM, and Gulp. This section takes you through using each of these package managers to add features and functionality to your site.

Framework Dependencies and References (Using `project.json` and NuGet)

As discussed in "The ASP.NET Framework," you can configure your web application to target the full, machine-wide .NET Framework using DNX 4.5.1. Or you can decide to target the more modular, application-specific .NET Core using DNX Core 5.0. The ASP.NET 5 Web Site template is set to dual-compile to both versions by default. This enables you to verify that your application supports both scenarios. Of course, you can change this behavior and only target the framework version (and packages) on which your application is intended to depend.

You manage your .NET Framework configuration using `project.json`, the `References` folder in Solution Explorer, project properties, and the NuGet package manager. Let's start by examining configuration with `project.json`.

The `project.json` file replaces assembly references in favor of this new, lightweight approach to managing dependencies through references to NuGet packages. Recall that a NuGet package represents a server-side code library on which your application depends. The packages could be from a third party or created and available directly from Microsoft (EntityFramework and AspNet.WebApi, for example). Figure 17.4 shows an example of the default `project.json` file inside Visual Studio (for a Web Site set to no authentication).

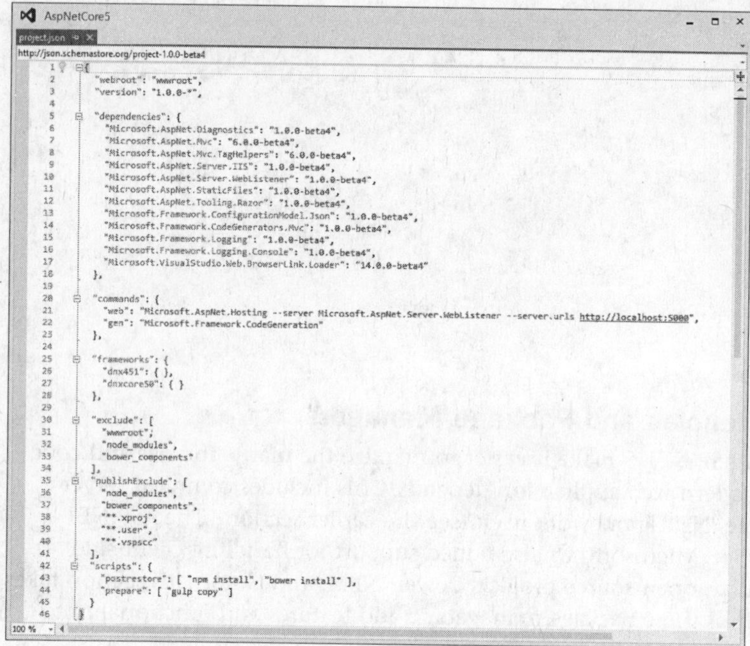

FIGURE 17.4 The `project.json` file is used to configure the frameworks, package dependencies, and compile options for your web application.

Package dependencies are defined inside the "dependencies" data element. Notice in Figure 17.4 this section includes dependency references to AspNet.Mvc, the ConfigurationModel.Json, and many others. The `project.json` file includes many additional configuration sections; the following list provides an overview of many of these:

- **Dependencies**—Used to define the NuGet packages on which your application depends. These are defined by package name : version. You can edit this list, and NuGet will work behind the scenes in Visual Studio to update your installed packages accordingly.

- **Frameworks**—Indicates the target frameworks against which your application should be built. By default, this includes both the full, machine-wide .NET Execution Environment (dnx451) and the core version (dnxcore50).

  Note that the dependencies you add to the "dependencies" element discussed earlier apply to both DNX versions. You can also add framework-specific dependencies here. Recall that the core framework is highly modular; therefore, should you target just the core framework, you would then need to add package dependencies for the base class libraries you intend to leverage, such as `System.Linq`, `System.Collections`, and the like.

- **Commands**—Used to indicate command-line tasks that should be run when your application executes. This could be a host server for the application, unit tests, or any other commands you need executed to run your application.

- **WebRoot**—Indicates the root of the webserver; by default, this is `wwwroot`.
- **Scripts**—Allows you to run scripts when the project is built. This includes events for pre-build, post-build, pre-pack, post-pack, and more. These events are used by tools such as NPM and Gulp to install client-side packages and execute tasks to prepare these scripts for release.
- **Exclude**—Used to indicate folders for the compiler to ignore when building your application.

Let's look at an example of adding a package dependency to `project.json`. We start with the default ASP.NET 5 Web Site template. In this case, however, we are going to configure `project.json` to only support DNX Core 5. The following walks you through this process:

1. Create a new web application based on the ASP.NET 5 Web Site template. You can run the application and click around to see how things work by default (including registering as a new user).
2. Inside Solution Explorer, expand the References node and both the DNX 4.5.1 and DNX Core 5.0 folders. Notice that both contain similar references. These are the ones defined at the top of `project.json` in the Dependencies section.

   However, notice that the core reference does not include the system references. That is because the core framework is modular and only needs the portions required for your site. Should you need something inside those frameworks, you would add just it specifically (instead of adding the full framework).
3. Open the `project.json` file. Find the Frameworks section and remove the dnx451 reference. Save the file; when you do, notice the References node in Solution Explorer. It should now include the text `(Restoring...)`. You will see this a lot as edits to `project.json` kick off NuGet to update your package. Figure 17.5 shows an example.

   When complete, you should now only see DNX Core 5.0 under the References node in Solution Explorer.
4. The last thing you need to do is to set the appropriate runtime version for your application. It will no longer run against the full .NET Framework (because you removed this dependency). Instead, it needs you to select a version of the core runtime.

   The .NET runtimes are referred to as a DNX version. By default, the template sets your project to run against the x86 version of the.NET Framework. This is the full version of the .NET Framework and Runtime.

   To change the runtime, right-click the project node in Solution Explorer and choose Properties. This will bring up the Properties window for the application, as shown in Figure 17.6. Here you can set the target DNX version to the .NET Core as shown.

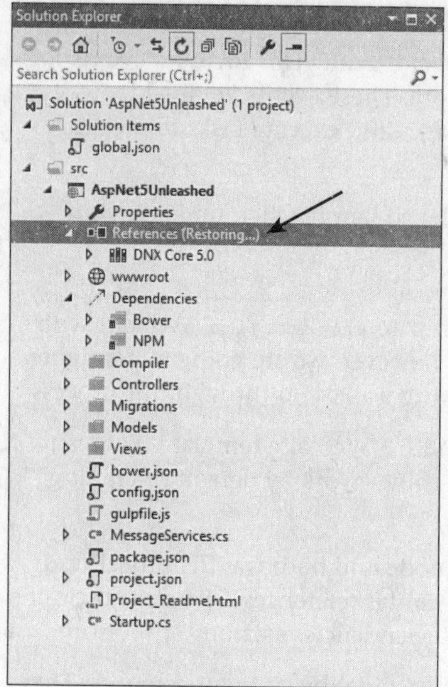

FIGURE 17.5 Edits to `project.json` will kick off NuGet to update your references and installed assemblies accordingly.

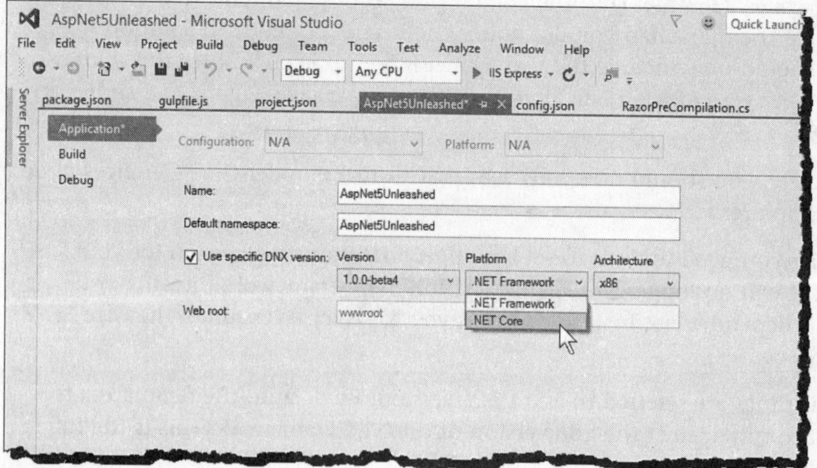

FIGURE 17.6 Use project properties to select the target runtime (DNX version) for your application (in this case, the .NET CORE).

5. You can now build and run your application. Notice that, by default, the template code works against the core. Should you need additional libraries, you can add them as you need them (as you will see next).

The application is now ready for cloud deployment. (It targets only the core framework.) Recall that one of the key benefits of the core is that it will install and run along with your application. It does not require your server admins to upgrade and patch a machine (and thus potentially break other things). This includes cloud-ready for Azure.

The dependencies shown in Figure 17.4 may not look like enough to allow your application to execute. However, it is important to note that these are packages (and not namespace imports). A package contains everything required for the package to run. The `project.json` file does not show these additional dependencies (in order to keep things cleaner). If you expand the packages in Solution Explorer, you will see just how much of the framework you depend on by using these packages. Figure 17.7 shows an example. Note that if you uninstall a given package, the subitems under the package are uninstalled as well (unless another package is also using it).

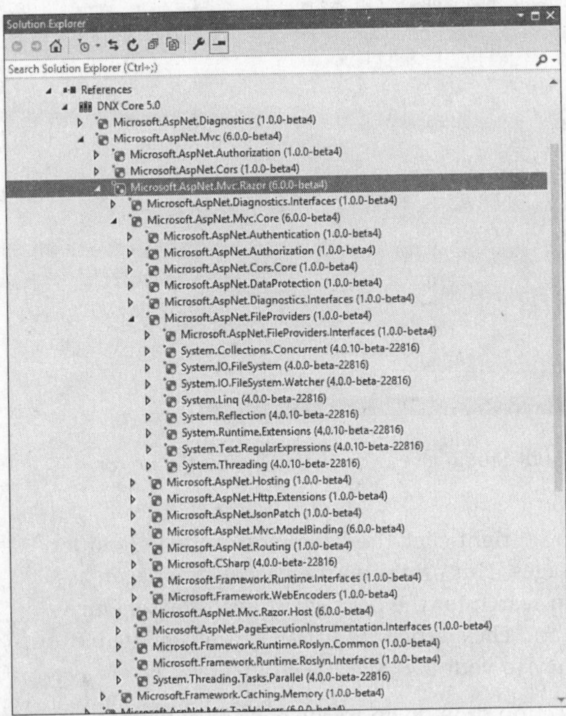

FIGURE 17.7 Each dependent package includes the other portions of the framework on which the package depends.

You can add dependencies directly to the `project.json` file. This is the equivalent of using NuGet to select a package and install it. Visual Studio provides IntelliSense to make setting these dependencies easier. As an example, suppose you want to add support for the popular SignalR package. (SignalR allows you to push content real-time from your web server to a client using WebSockets.) To add this support, you open `project.json` and start typing in either the full set of dependencies at the top of the file or the framework-specific dependencies near the middle of the file. Figure 17.8 shows the latter. Notice that you get IntelliSense as you peruse packages. Once you select the package, you get IntelliSense on the various versions available. When you save `project.json`, NuGet will install the package and add the reference to your project.

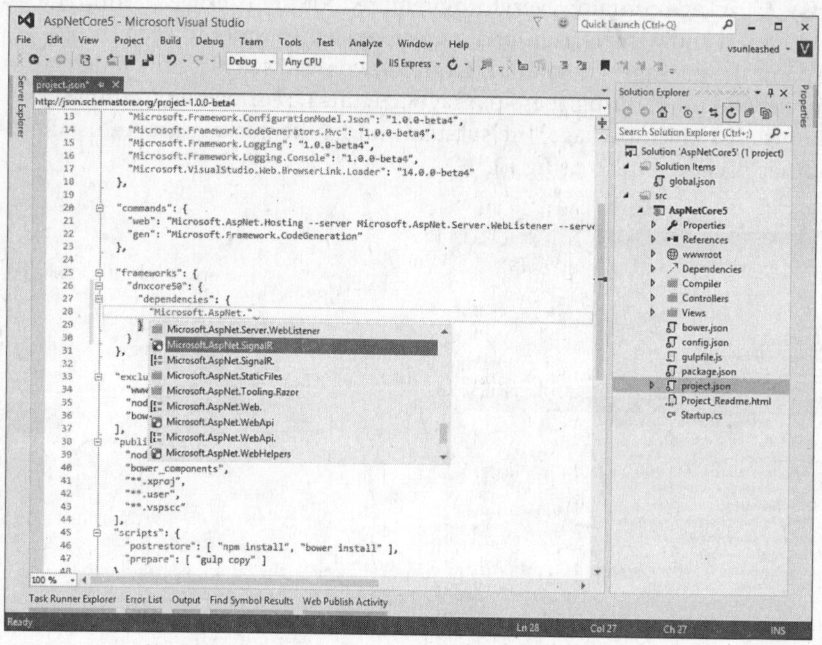

FIGURE 17.8 The `project.json` file in Visual Studio gives you `NuGet` inside the editor.

You can, of course, still use NuGet. To do so, right-click the References node in Solution Explorer and choose Manage NuGet Packages. This brings up the package manager, as shown in Figure 17.9. Notice that you can search for the package or just browse. Once you've selected it, you indicate a version and click either the Install or the Update button. Visual Studio will then add the dependency to your `project.json` file.

Visual Studio has added a Framework Selection drop-down to the code editor in the event you do need to program against multiple versions of the .NET Framework. Figure 17.10 shows an example. If you select the DNX Core 5.0 framework, for example, any code that would not work under this condition is compiled as an error and shown in the editor. The Debug tab allows you to switch which version of the framework you are targeting.

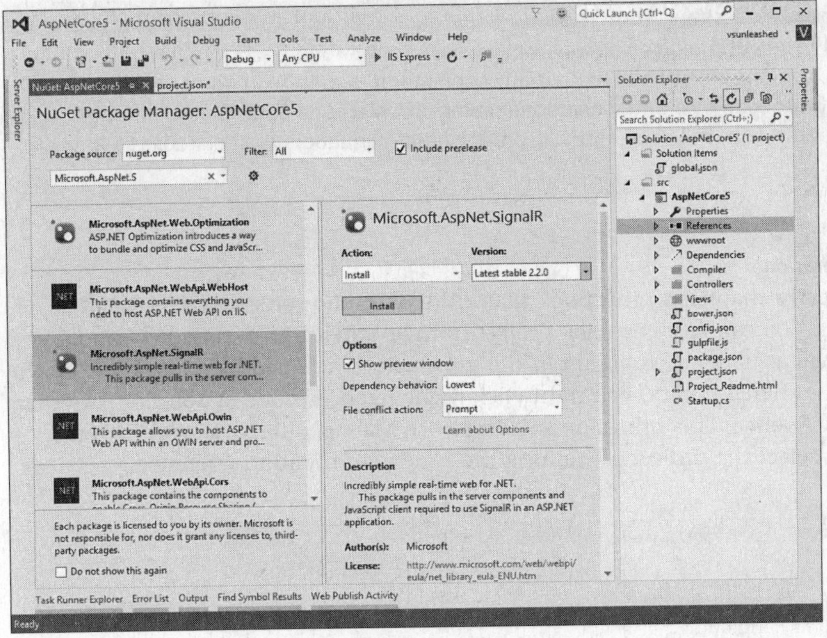

FIGURE 17.9 You can use NuGet to add project dependencies to `project.json`.

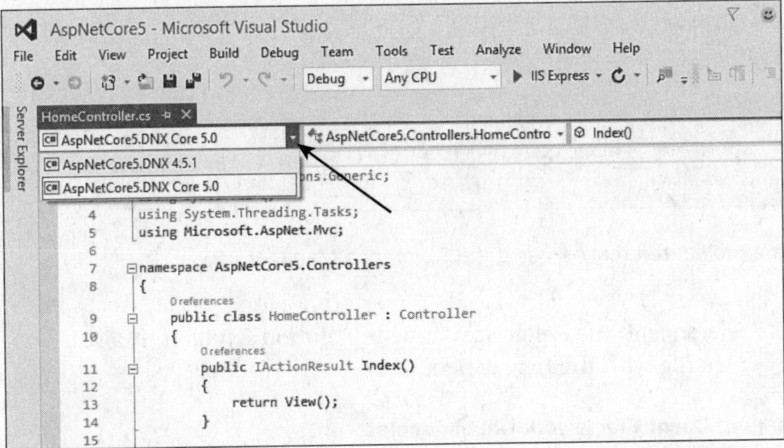

FIGURE 17.10 The code editor allows you to set a target framework against which your code will be debugged.

TIP: SUPPORTING MULTIPLE FRAMEWORK VERSIONS

If you do need to target multiple versions of the .NET Framework, each with different dependencies, you can often code around any conflicts or issues. You do so using `#if` statements in your code to create conditional compilation around code that is different between framework versions. You can use the configuration labels `#if DNXCORE50` and `#if DNX451`.

Add Project Reference

Recall from the early chapters in this book that a Visual Studio solution can support multiple projects. You can reference one project from another. As an example, you may have your web and a shared class library in the same solution. To add a reference from the web project to the shared library, you right-click the References node in Solution Explorer and select Add Reference. This brings up the Reference Manager dialog shown in Figure 17.11. Here, you select the project containing the code you intend to reference.

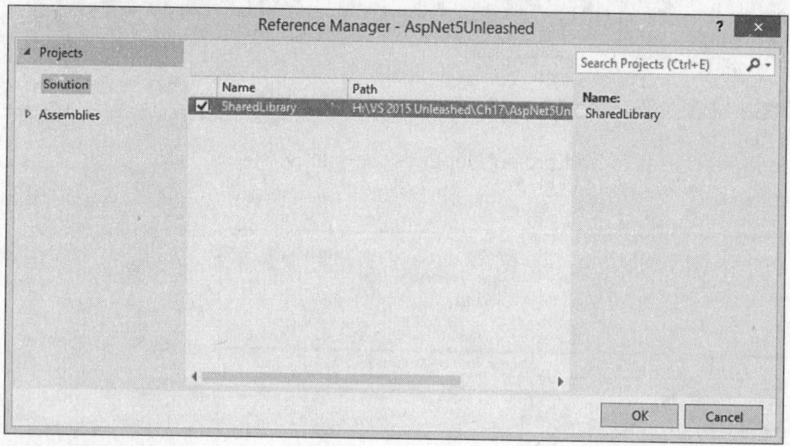

FIGURE 17.11 Adding project references using the Reference Manager.

Visual Studio adds the reference to the References node in Solution Explorer. It also updates your `project.json` file with the new dependency.

Using Bower for Managing Client Framework Dependencies

Visual Studio and ASP.NET 5 have embraced developing with popular open source client frameworks such as Bootstrap, AngularJS, and jQuery. You can also write your own project-specific JavaScript libraries. These libraries have their own package and task managers: Bower, NPM, and Gulp. Like NuGet, these package managers make the business of installing and updating shared frameworks much easier. The following provides a high-level overview of each:

- **NPM**—NPM stands for Node Package Manager because it was originally designed for Node.js. It is a JavaScript package manager used by Visual Studio for installing Bower and Gulp.
- **Bower**—Bower is a package manager for web libraries and client-side frameworks. Visual Studio uses Bower like NuGet for installing client-side frameworks. The `bower.json` file works in a similar way to `project.json` (including IntelliSense).
- **Gulp**—Gulp executes tasks to automate the packaging of your JavaScript code, CSS, and related items for release. Tasks include minification of JavaScript, compilation of CoffeeScript to JavaScript, conversion of Sass to CSS, and many others. Visual Studio provides the Task Runner Explorer for working with Gulp.

Let's look at a couple of examples. First, we will add a JavaScript library to our project using Bower. In this example, we will add the CoffeeScript JavaScript library to our project. This library makes writing JavaScript easier. The CoffeeScript code is output as actual JavaScript when sent to a client. Of course, we could use any of the dozens of libraries available through Bower for our example:

1. To get started, open the `bower.json` file from Solution Explorer.
2. Inside the dependencies group, add a line for coffee-script. Notice that the editor uses IntelliSense to reach out to the Bower library and show you what is available.
3. Once coffee-script is selected, type a colon (`:`), and you will get a drop-down showing available versions. Figure 17.12 shows an example. Select version ~1.9.3.

   Notice that all three versions have the same version number. These versions are marked with upgrade symbol options. The version is written as `major.minor.patch`. The use of the caret (^) indicates that you want to at least match to the latest major version specified. The use of the tilde (~) indicates that you want to at least match the minor version. Omitting the caret and tilde indicates that you want to use the exact version.
4. Next, save `bower.json`. This will instruct Bower to reach out and install CoffeeScript. You can verify installation by opening Solution Explorer and navigating to the `Dependencies/Bower` folder. You should see the new library here. You can also right-click this entire folder and choose Restore Packages. Figure 17.13 shows an example.

   Note that you can use this same method to remove an installed package (right-click the package and choose Uninstall Package). Also, should you remove a reference from `Bower.json`, your installed package will now be marked "extraneous" indicating you can uninstall.

   You can now work with CoffeeScript in your application.

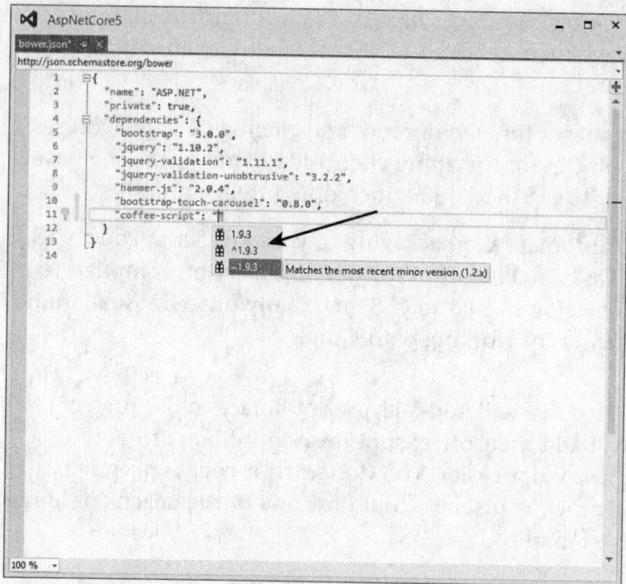

FIGURE 17.12 Editing the `bower.json` file provides IntelliSense on available JavaScript packages.

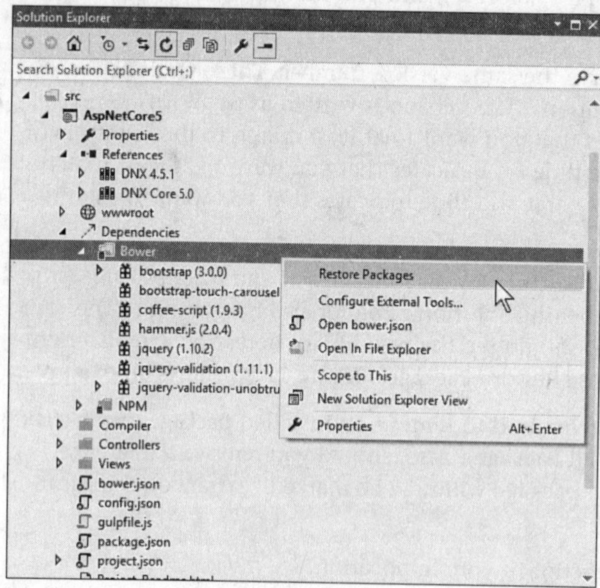

FIGURE 17.13 You can open the `Bower` folder and choose Restore Package to force install of a new package or version.

Note that Visual Studio automatically restores packages when you open the solution. This includes getting updates based on your version numbers. Bower libraries are stored in your website directory under the folder `bower_components`. This folder is not in your solution because it is updated for you. You would not typically check in Bower components to source code control. Instead, these components are managed for you by Bower via the checked-in file `bower.json`.

Using Gulp to Manage Client Build Tasks

Let's take a look at using Gulp for creating and executing an automated build task in our application. These tasks are not about building your server code. Instead, Gulp tasks help you with your client-side code, such as JavaScript and CSS. The following walks you through creating a style sheet using LESS and then creating a Gulp task to output that styles sheet as standard CSS:

1. To get started, we will add a LESS style sheet to our project. Recall that static files like a style sheet should exist inside `wwwroot`. LESS, however, is a preprocessor language for writing style sheets using variables and other constructs. The LESS file must be processed to a CSS file before being stored in `wwwroot`. Therefore, we will create a folder in which to store our LESS file until Gulp processes it and outputs it to `wwwroot`.

   Right-click your project in Solution Explorer and choose Add, New Folder. Name the folder `Assets`.

   Right-click the new `Assets` folder and choose Add, New Item. Select the item template LESS Style Sheet. Name your style sheet `site.less`.

2. Open `site.less` in the editor. One of the features of LESS is the ability to define variables and use those variables in your style definitions. The following shows a simple example of declaring the variable `@light-gray` and using it as the background color for the body tag.

   ```
   @light-gray: #d5d5d5;
   body {
     background-color: @light-gray;
   }
   ```

3. You now need to output this `.less` file to a `.css` file so you can use it with your application. This is where Gulp helps. Gulp allows you to create a processing task and bind the task to the Visual Studio build event.

   You could write a custom Gulp task. However, there are already Gulp tasks for preprocessing LESS files into CSS. To include the Gulp task, open `package.json` from Solution Explorer. This file manages the NPM (Node Package Manager) libraries. Under devDependencies, type `gulp-less` to select the LESS task for Gulp, as shown in Figure 17.14 (current version is 3.0.3).

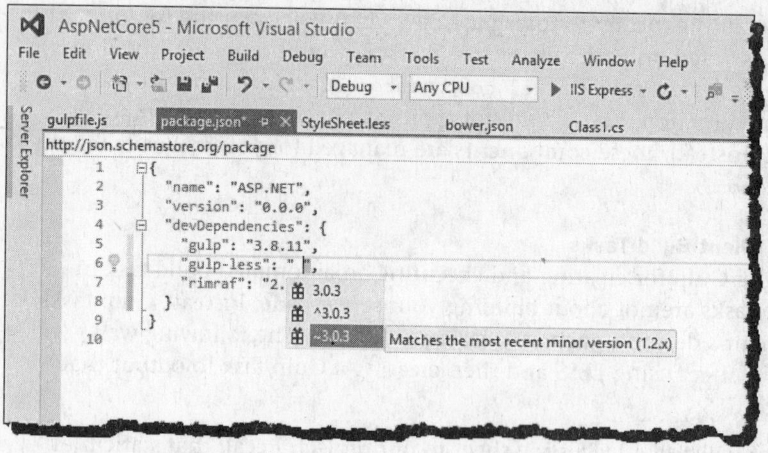

FIGURE 17.14 The `package.json` file is used to install NPM packages such as Gulp.

4. Saving the `package.json` file will automatically install the gulp-less library under Dependencies/NPM. Like the `Bower` package folder, you can right-click NPM and select Restore Packages to force an install.
5. The next step is to define the Gulp task. To start, open the file `gulpfile.js` from Solution Explorer. This is a JavaScript file for defining Gulp task information and Gulp task plug-in options.

   To start, add the `less` definition line to the top of the code. This sets a variable pointing to the gulp-less plugin. The code is as shown below:

```
var gulp = require("gulp"),
  rimraf = require("rimraf"),
  fs = require("fs"),
  less = require("gulp-less");
```

   Next, you add configuration options to the Gulp task by defining the Gulp task for the `less` object. Listing 17.1 shows the full contents of `gruntfile.js` after this addition. Notice the `gulp.task('less',...` code; it indicates that the file `site.less` should be output to the `wwwroot/css` folder as part of the preprocessing of LESS to CSS.

TIP

Listing 17.1 also shows the clean and copy Gulp tasks. These tasks are for cleaning out your `wwwroot/lib` folder and then copying the appropriate JavaScript files from the `bower_components` folder to the `wwwroot/lib` folder. Should your site stop behaving (and looking right) you can execute these tasks in Task Runner Explorer to clean things up and copy over fresh files.

LISTING 17.1 The `gulpfile.js` Configuration to Use a LESS Preprocessing Task

```
var gulp = require("gulp"),
  rimraf = require("rimraf"),
  fs = require("fs"),
  less = require("gulp-less");

eval("var project = " + fs.readFileSync("./project.json"));

var paths = {
  bower: "./bower_components/",
  lib: "./" + project.webroot + "/lib/"
};

gulp.task('less', function () {
  return gulp.src('./Assets/site.less')
    .pipe(less())
    .pipe(gulp.dest('./wwwroot/css'));
});

gulp.task("clean", function (cb) {
  rimraf(paths.lib, cb);
});

gulp.task("copy", ["clean"], function () {
  var bower = {
    "bootstrap": "bootstrap/dist/**/*.{js,map,css,ttf,svg,woff,eot}",
    "bootstrap-touch-carousel": "bootstrap-touch-carousel/dist/**/*.{js,css}",
    "hammer.js": "hammer.js/hammer*.{js,map}",
    "jquery": "jquery/jquery*.{js,map}",
    "jquery-validation": "jquery-validation/jquery.validate.js",
    "jquery-validation-unobtrusive": "jquery-validation-unobtrusive/jquery.
➥validate.unobtrusive.js"
  }

  for (var destinationDir in bower) {
    gulp.src(paths.bower + bower[destinationDir])
      .pipe(gulp.dest(paths.lib + destinationDir));
  }
});
```

6. The next step is to run the Gulp task. Visual Studio provides the Task Runner Explorer for doing so. To access it, right-click `gulpfile.js` in Solution Explorer and choose Task Runner Explorer. Figure 17.15 shows an example. You may have to use the refresh button on the left side of the window pane to update the Gulp tasks.

Notice that you can right-click the `less` element defined in `gulpfile.js`. Here you can choose to run the processor now or bind it to run based on IDE events of Before Build, After Build, and more. Select After Build from the context menu.

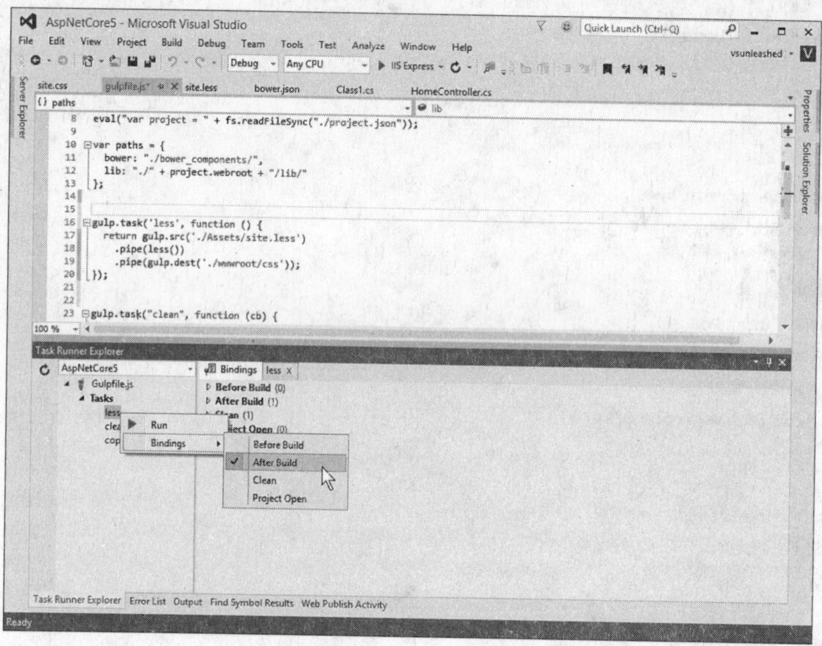

FIGURE 17.15 The Task Runner Explorer is used to manage and execute Gulp tasks.

7. You can now run your application. When you do so, the Task Runner Explorer shows the output from the various tasks (including our less task).

   After running the application, you can open the `site.css` file under `wwwroot/css`. The contents of the `site.less` file is now output to `site.css` as follows.

   ```
   body {
     background-color: #d5d5d5;
   }
   ```

   You should also see the results by running the application in your browser window. (You may need to refresh if styles were cached.)

This section has illustrated the many features of package management and project settings in ASP.NET 5 applications. As you will see, these skills are useful when building ASP.NET 5/MVC 6 websites, JavaScript SPA clients, and Web API projects. As we discuss these application types in the next sections and chapters, we will point back to configuration items discussed herein.

Creating a Web Application with ASP.NET 5/MVC 6

The MVC design pattern is at the core of most of the ASP.NET templates. If you have worked with it in past editions, you find that it works in a similar way under Visual Studio 2015 and ASP.NET 5/MVC 6. In fact, some of the bigger changes (those surrounding the framework and project structure) have been discussed already. This section takes a look at the MVC pattern and illustrates creating websites using it with ASP.NET.

Understanding the MVC Pattern

The ASP.NET MVC application template works to separate your code and markup into three distinct layers: the model represents your application domain objects (or data), the view is how you render data to the user and request their input, and the controller is where you write logic to handle user requests and combine model data with the right view when responding to users. Putting code into layers has been a good practice for many years. Layered separation increases opportunities for code reuse, makes your code more understandable, and supports test-driven development. The ASP.NET MVC framework requires this separation. Figure 17.16 shows an illustration of the ASP.NET MVC implementation.

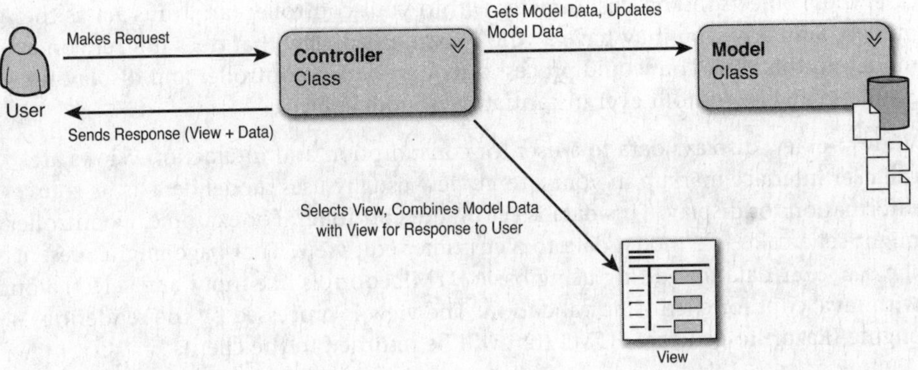

FIGURE 17.16 An ASP.NET MVC application abstracts the model (data) from the view (user interface markup) and the controller (code to connect the model and view).

NOTE

If you are used to Web Form development, you will quickly notice that ASP.NET MVC does not use the ASP.NET Web Forms control model. Instead, it gives developers greater control of their HTML output using standard HTML `<input/>` and related tags. This ensures lightweight, simple markup that is easier to write, understand, and test.

The following provides additional details on the three layers that make up an ASP.NET MVC web application:

- **Model**—A model represents the code that is used for managing the domain model (or data) of your application. A modern model is defined by simple classes that represent your domain objects and the Entity Framework for persisting those classes to, and retrieving them from, a data store. Note that model state is referred to as the actual data stored in a relational database (or similar data store).

  As an example, you might create a `Customer` class that is used to represent a customer in your application. This class would define business rules surrounding a customer along with field-level validation. To round out your model, you need code to persist the `Customer` instance to a data store and retrieve it when required. You could, of course, write this code yourself or leverage a data access layer that already knows how to work with your data store.

  A more common scenario for ASP.NET MVC sites is to leverage the Entity Framework as the data access layer for the model. We will look at such an example later in this chapter. You may also refer to Chapter 13, "Working with Databases," for more information about using Entity Framework with databases.

  The ASP.NET MVC framework does not require a model. If you do not have (or need) domain objects, you might not write a lot of code in the model. For example, you may rely on arrays or other collections for working with information. In that case, these objects might exist directly within your controller (and thus act as the model). Similarly, you may have a wholly contained view that does not rely on a model. In this case, you would process a request with a controller and display the results in a view without ever instantiating a model object.

- **View**—A view displays data to a user for consumption and interaction. Views are the user interface markup in your site. A view usually uses model data as its source information for display. This data is set by the controller. For example, a controller might set a `Customer` model data to a customer edit view. That page might present the `Customer` data for editing using basic HTML controls like input and select, along with JavaScript for client-side validation. The view is processed by the rendering engine (Razor) to generate HTML that will be returned to the client.

- **Controller**—A controller is code you write to handle the user interaction and events inside an MVC application (often called input logic). Requests to your site are routed to a controller class via a routing engine based on the URL. Your controller code knows how to handle a user's request, work with the model, and connect results to the right view. For example, when a user request a page for editing customer details, a method of the controller is called. This method works with the model to get the customer details, selects the appropriate view, and provides the model data to that view. When the user clicks the Save button, the controller again takes over to move the data back into the model (and the model moves it to the database). The controller then sends the results (as another view) back to the user.

The Execution Model of an ASP.NET MVC Request

An application written using the ASP.NET MVC framework has a different processing model than that of an ASP.NET Web Form or Web Page. One of the biggest differences is how user requests are mapped to your pages. For example, Web Forms maps a user request via a URL directly to a folder and file on the web server. A request for http://www.*[mydomain]*.com/customer/edit.aspx would map to your web root, the `Customer` folder, and a page actually called `edit.aspx`.

That is not the case with MVC. Instead, an MVC request goes through a routing engine (that uses a routing table to define routing convention), which maps the request to a method on your controller class (and not a web page in a folder). Your controller method then processes the request. It understands the user's requested action, works with the model, and selects the appropriate view to display back to the user. The view and model are processed on the server and output as HTML (and JavaScript, CSS, and so on) to be sent back to the user's browser for rendering. The following provides an overview of the ASP.NET MVC processing model:

1. Your application is deployed and started on the web server. When this happens, the configuration code inside your `Startup.cs` file is executed. This includes the hosting environment (as `IHostingEnvironment`). It also includes configuring services (as `IServiceCollection`) and the services you add to the startup pipeline (such as a data context and MVC itself), including the routing definition.

2. A user sends a request via a URL to the server (see fundamentals above). The web server (typically IIS) understands the request is meant for your application and ASP.NET, so it sends the request to the `UrlRoutingModule` class. This is an HTTP module that serves as the front controller for routing requests.

3. The `UrlRoutingModule` parses the request and performs route selection, ultimately using the `MvcRouteHandler` class to select one of the controller objects in your site to receive the request.

   You can manage the way requests are mapped to your controllers by editing the `Startup.cs Configure` method in your project (more on this later).

NOTE

If no route is found, the request passes to ASP.NET. This enables you to mix both MVC and standard ASP.NET code in a single site.

4. After a controller class is identified, the MVC framework creates an instance of the controller and calls its `Execute` method.

5. An action method (a method you write in your controller to handle the request and connect the model with the view) inside your controller is identified based on the request URL and the routing definition. The request URL is mapped to the controller method via the HTTP verb (such as `GET` or `POST`). Also, any parameters sent with the request URL (on the query string or in the `POST` message) are mapped to the parameters of the action method.

   The ASP.NET MVC framework then calls the identified action method.

6. An action method receives user input from the request (query string or POST data) as a parameter, connects that information to the model, and then passes any response back as a specific MVC return type. The most common return types implement `Microsoft.AspNet.Mvc.IActionResult`. Using this interface allows you to return one of many result types, including `ViewResult`, `RedirectResult`, `JsonResult`, `ObjectResult` (for Web API services), and more. (See "The Result Objects" later in this chapter.)

NOTE

ASP.NET Web Forms and ASP.NET MVC can coexist; neither excludes the other. If you build on ASP.NET MVC, there still might be times you create a standard ASP.NET page, perhaps to use a specific server control.

Creating a New ASP.NET 5 MVC 6 Project

You can create an ASP.NET 5 MVC 6 application using the Visual Studio template ASP.NET 5 Web Site. You can access this application template from File, New, Project. You select the Web node in the template tree. You then select ASP.NET Web Application. Figure 17.17 shows an example.

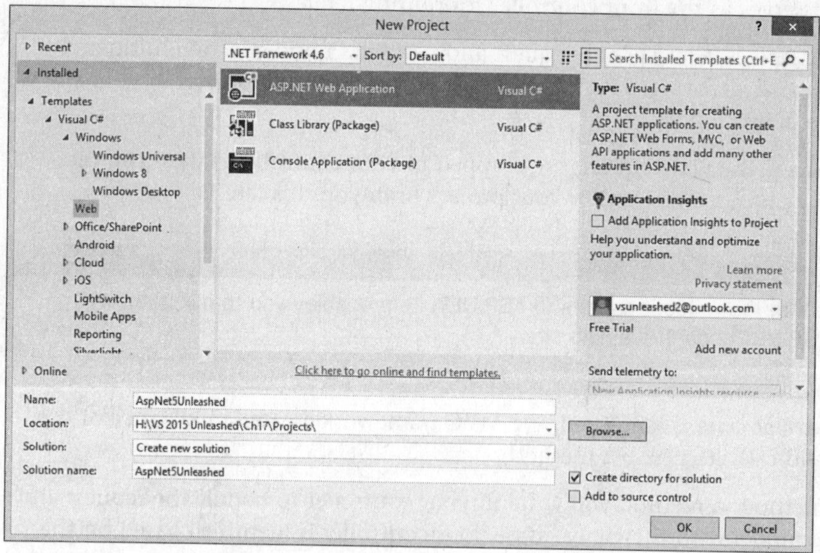

FIGURE 17.17 You first select ASP.NET Web Application as your project template.

The next step is to select from one of the many ASP.NET project templates (refer to Figure 17.2). These templates were covered in the section "Choosing an ASP.NET Project

Template." Here we focus on the ASP.NET 5 Web Site template. However, much of what is discussed is applicable to the templates: MVC, ASP.NET 5 Empty, SPA, and the Web API.

One additional option you may notice when selecting an ASP.NET template is the button Change Authentication (refer back to Figure 17.2). Most of these templates include code for user membership and account management. You use this button to configure how you want to handle this in your application. Figure 17.18 shows an example. Notice that you have four options for site authentication:

- **No Authentication**—Used for public sites that do not require user authentication.
- **Individual User Account**—Used for forms-based authentication against a SQL Server database store. This also supports using Facebook, Twitter, Google, Microsoft, and other providers.
- **Organizational Accounts**—Allows you to create applications that rely on Active Directory (AD) for authentication. This includes on-premises AD as well as cloud AD services in Azure and Office 365. You can use this screen to configure an AD connection and domain.
- **Windows Authentication**—Used for local intranet applications.

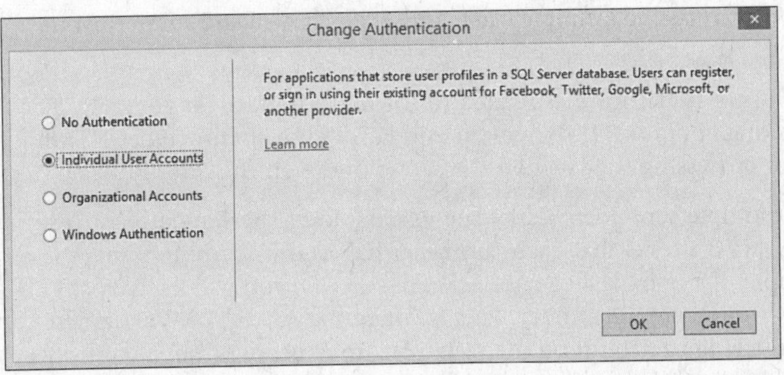

FIGURE 17.18 Use Change Authentication when creating your ASP.NET application to set the way your site intends to authenticate users.

Notice, too, in Figure 17.2 that Visual Studio gives you the option to create a related unit test project for your MVC site. Recall that one of the advantages of ASP.NET MVC is that you can more easily unit test your web logic (controllers). Therefore, we suggest you select this option and allow Visual Studio to create a test project that references your web application. We are not going to re-cover unit testing in this chapter. For more information, refer to Chapter 8, "Testing Code."

The ASP.NET MVC template organizes your code into a different structure. Recall this structure was discussed in the section "Understanding the ASP.NET 5 Project Template and Related Files." That section showed the structure in Figure 17.3. This includes the folders where you write most of the code for your website: `Models`, `Views`, and `Controllers`. The following provides additional details on each of these key folders inside your ASP.NET MVC site:

- **Models**—Use the `Models` folder for class files that define your business logic and work with your database. For example, you might write a `Customer.cs` class and store it here. You might also define an Entity Framework Code First `DbContext` class for working between your model and data store and keep it in the root of `Models`. You are not bound to this folder; you may choose to create your model as a separate class library (`.dll`) and reference it from your website.
- **Controllers**—Use this folder for all controller classes in your application. Controller classes contain action code that connects user actions to the model and selects the appropriate response (typically a view). The ASP.NET MVC framework uses the convention of appending the word *Controller* to the end of each controller class, such as `CustomerController.cs`.

  An ASP.NET 5 controller class inherits `Microsoft.AspNet.Mvc.Controller` by default. (Note the namespace has changed with this latest release and the unification of Web API, Web Pages, and MVC.) With ASP.NET 5, you are not required to inherit from `Controller`. However, the class does provide a number of benefits, such as access to session state, user context, `ViewBag` data, request data, and more. If you do not need these benefits, you can define a simple class, and ASP.NET will still route to your class and method.
- **Views**—Use the `Views` folder for files related to the user interface for your site. These are `.cshtml` files that contain HTML markup and Razor code that includes HTML helper objects for processing the view on the server (more on this shortly).

  A site will have multiple subfolders under the `Views` folder. The standard convention for ASP.NET MVC sites is that each controller has its own corresponding `Views` folder. For example, if you have a `CustomerController.cs`, you will likely have a corresponding `Views\Customer` folder. This is where the ASP.NET MVC framework looks when trying to determine the view you are returning from a controller method.

  The `Views` folder also contains the `Shared` folder for defining partial views that are shared throughout the site. A partial view is typically reused within multiple pages (and thus shared). This folder also contains the primary layout page for the site, `_Layout.cshtml`. This page defines the overall layout for your site (header, navigation, footer, styles, scripts, and so on).

  Another convention is to name your views the same as you name the action methods in the corresponding controller. As an example, the `Account` controller has the method `Register`. There is a corresponding `Register.cshtml` view inside the `Account view` folder. In this way, the MVC framework will try to map requests to http://www.*[mydomain]*.com/account/register to the `Account` controller's `Register` method. When you return a view from this method, it will look first for a view in the `Views\Account` folder with the same name as the method (`Register`) unless, of course, you specify otherwise.

An ASP.NET MVC Request in Action

Let's take a look at an MVC page in action. To start, we will examine the files the ASP.NET 5 Web Site template generated. This will provide a feel for how an ASP.NET MVC application processes a web request.

We will start by looking at the `HomeController.cs` class file. The `HomeController` class in the template has four methods: `Index`, `About`, `Contact`, and `Error`. None of these methods actually rely on a model, so no model is required in this example. Each method return an `IActionResult`.

The `IActionResult` interface is implemented by the many action result types in the Framework. This allows you to return a result that the ASP.NET pipeline will process accordingly. This includes the common `ViewResult` for returning a view page, a `JsonResult` instance to return a JSON message in the case of a Web API call, the `HttpStatusCodeResult` to return a HTTP status, or one of the many other result objects. (See "The Result Objects" later in this section.)

Listing 17.2 shows the code. Notice that each of these methods returns a `ViewResult` object using the `Controller.View()` method. `ViewResult` inherits from `ActionResult`. (`ActionResult` implements `IActionResult`.)

LISTING 17.2 The `HomeController.cs` Class and Related Action Methods

```
using System;
using System.Collections.Generic;
using System.Linq;
using System.Threading.Tasks;
using Microsoft.AspNet.Mvc;

namespace AspNet5Unleashed.Controllers
{
  public class HomeController : Controller
  {
    public IActionResult Index()
    {
      return View();
    }

    public IActionResult About()
    {
      ViewBag.Message = "Your application description page.";

      return View();
    }
```

```
    public IActionResult Contact()
    {
      ViewBag.Message = "Your contact page.";

      return View();
    }

    public IActionResult Error()
    {
      return View("~/Views/Shared/Error.cshtml");
    }
  }
}
```

Only the `Error()` action method explicitly specifies the cshtml to process via `ViewResult`. The other methods rely on ASP.NET MVC naming conventions to return the expected view. For example, a call to http://www.contoso.com/home/index will be routed to the `HomeController.Index` method (based on the URL); the method will return an empty `ViewResult` understood by MVC as the `Index.cshtml` view stored in the `Home` folder (again, based on the name taken from the URL convention—controller name and action method).

Note that the `Index` page in a folder and the `HomeController` are special in the MVC routing engine. MVC will look for an Index method (and page) if you simply send the URL http://www.contoso.com/home/ (regardless of which controller you are specifying). Similarly, the home controller is routed in a special way; a call to the domain such as http://www.contoso.com/ will route to the `HomeController.Index` method. Note that you can control how MVC handles routing inside the `Startup.cs` class using the `asp.UseMvc(routes)` method call.

Notice that the `About` and `Contact` methods are settings values to `ViewBag.Message`. This is a simple means for the controller to set data that the view will use to display this data. The `ViewBag` is a dynamic container used as a key/value pair dictionary.

Again, the `HomeController` does not use a `Model`. So the only item left to discuss for this template-driven example is the views themselves. (We will discuss models shortly.) We cover views in the section "Coding for the UI (Views and Related Web UI Elements)."

The `Index.cshtml` view in the template is a lengthy listing of HTML and Razor code. We suggest that you peruse this in the IDE to familiarize yourself with the HTML. To round out this example, however, let's take a quick look at the much shorter `About.cshtml`. Listing 17.3 shows an example.

LISTING 17.3 The `About.cshtml` View Page

```
@{
  ViewBag.Title = "About";
}
<h2>@ViewBag.Title.</h2>
<h3>@ViewBag.Message</h3>

<p>Use this area to provide additional information.</p>
```

The `About.cshtml` includes simple markup that displays the `@ViewBag.Message` content as set by the controller (Listing 17.2, `About()` method). It does so using the `@` symbol. This is ASP.NET Razor syntax indicating that this bit of code should execute on the server before returning the final HTML to the requestor. (We cover Razor in the subsection "The Razor Syntax.")

You run the application like you would any other .NET project. Just click the Run (or Play) button on the toolbar. You can see the requested URL and the result in Figure 17.19.

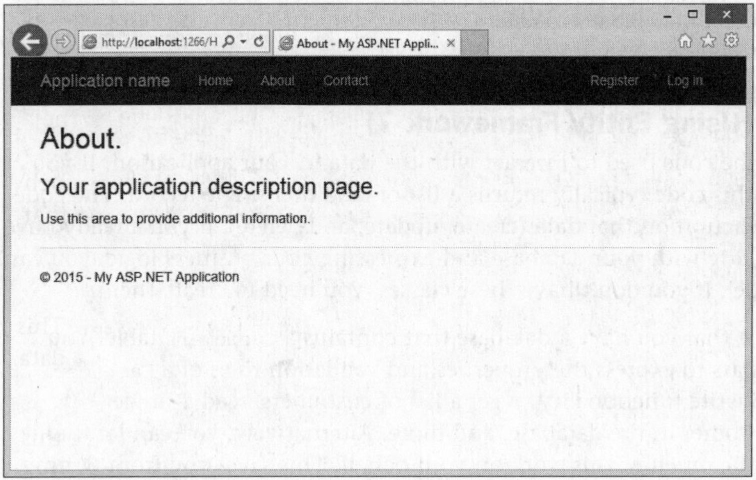

FIGURE 17.19 The `About.cshtml` view rendered in a browser.

As you can see from Figure 17.19, the markup in Listing 17.3 is not a lot compared to the output of the page. This is because pages in this site are set to work with a shared content page called `_Layout.cshtml`. The layout page provides the header, footer, navigation, style sheet, and default JavaScript libraries for pages in the site. (To see how this works, read the upcoming subsection "Page Layout with Razor.")

TIP

Visual Studio 2015 and ASP.NET now use the new Roslyn compiler. This compiler speeds debugging as it builds your application and changes. Thus, you can often make a change in your code and simply refresh your browser to see the results. (No recompile step is necessary.)

You can test this by making a change to one of the `ViewBag.Message()` calls in the `HomeController` while your application is running. Save the change and refresh the browser to see the results.

Writing ASP.NET Server Code (Models and Controllers)

You've now looked at the basics of creating, running, and working with an ASP.NET 5/MVC 6 application. It's time to dig a little deeper. This section explores implementing a model for a sample application (a model that works with a database). We then discuss handling requests and returning results using controllers and the many action methods available in the framework. For views, however, we created a separate section that follows this one. "Coding for the UI (Views and Related Web UI Elements)" covers many aspects of building a web UI inside ASP.NET MVC.

Defining a Model (Using Entity Framework 7)

Recall that a model is the code used to interact with the data in your application. If you work with a database, this code typically returns a list of data or a single record. The code also supports user interaction on that data (create, update, and delete). If you already have a set of classes for working with your database and expressing your business logic, you can use them for your model. If you don't have these classes, you need to create them.

As an example, imagine that you have a database that contains a `Customers` table. You could write a custom class to express the properties and validation rules of a `Customer` object. You might also write functionality to get a list of customers, read a single customer, update a customer in the database, and more. Alternatively, you can let the Entity Framework handle much of this work on your behalf. This saves you from writing the data access, update, storage, and delete code from scratch. In this example, we use the Entity Framework 7 Code First. (See Chapter 13 for more details on working with databases.)

Creating a Simple Class

With Code First, you write very little code, and you do not have a bunch of generated code in your solution. Instead, you write plain old CLR objects (POCOs) classes to represent your model. These classes define objects, properties, and business rules. The database access is taken care of for you with Entity Framework. The following walks you through building the `Customer` model.

1. Start by creating a new project (File, New Project) based on the ASP.NET 5 Web Site template (or, if you've been following along, you can use the project you've already created for the other examples earlier in the chapter).

   The examples assume your site is named, `AspNet5AppSample`. This name is used in the namespace definitions for class files.

2. Inside Visual Studio Solution Explorer, right-click the `Models` folder and choose Add, New Item. Select the Class template from the Add New Item dialog. Name the class `Customer.cs`.

3. Create the properties to represent a simple `Customer` instance. Listing 17.4 shows an example.

LISTING 17.4 The `Customer.cs` POCO Model Class

```
using System;

namespace AspNet5AppSample.Models
{
  public class Customer
  {
    public int Id { get; set; }

    public string Name { get; set; }

    public string Email { get; set; }

    public bool OptInEmail { get; set; }

    public string Notes { get; set; }
  }
}
```

Adding Model Validation Rules

ASP.NET includes support for data annotations. A data annotation is metadata that you assign to the properties of your class using data attributes. This metadata is then interpreted by ASP.NET at runtime as validation rules for the properties in your class. For example, you might annotate a property with the `RequiredAttribute`. ASP.NET will then validate your model both on the client (using JavaScript) and on the server. If the model state is not valid, the object is not valid and the user should be notified.

The data attributes are found in the `System.ComponentModel.DataAnnotations` namespace. There are dozens of attribute classes available to you. However, the following provides an overview of many of the common data attribute classes. (The word *Attribute* is omitted from the class name for clarity.)

- `Association`—Used to indicate the property works as a data relationship (or foreign key).
- `Compare`—Used to compare the values of two properties (such as password and password match).
- `CreditCard`—Used to indicate that a given property should be a credit card number.
- `DataType`—Used to mark a property as a specific data type. This is useful if the actual type you intend is different from the one stored in your database. For example, you may have a `PostalCode` property you store as a string in the database but want to validate it as numeric.
- `Editable`—Used to indicate if a given property should be allowed to be changed by a user. You can use this attribute to mark a property read only or allow an initial value.
- `Email`—Validates a property as containing an email address.
- `Key`—Used to indicate if a property represents a primary key for the item.
- `MinLength`, `MaxLength`—Used to validate against a min or max length of a property that represents a string or array.
- `Phone`—Validates a given property contains a valid phone number.
- `Range`—Used to validate against an allowable numeric range for the property.
- `RegularExpression`—Allows you to write a regular expression against which the property should be validated.
- `Required`—Used to mark a property as requiring a value.
- `StringLength`—Used to set the min and max length of characters in a property of type `string`.
- `Url`—Validates a property as a URL.

The attribute classes just listed all work in a similar way. You use them to annotate properties of your object. A simple validation attribute will require no additional configuration and will include a default message to be displayed when the validation fails. However, some data annotation attributes require additional configuration to work properly, such as setting the `maximumLength` on `StringLength`. Each attribute also includes the `ErrorMessage` property that allows you to set a custom error message if validation fails.

Let's add a few data annotations to the `Customer` class created previously. The following walks you through this process:

1. Add a `using` statement at the top of `Customer.cs` for `System.ComponentModel.DataAnnotations`.
2. Annotate the `Name` property with the `Required` attribute.

3. Add both the `Required` and the `EmailAddress` to the `Email` property. You can do so by separating them with a comma.

   Configure the `ErrorMessage` property for the `EmailAddress` attribute to set a custom message to be displayed when the property is not valid.

4. Mark the `Id` property with the `Key` attribute to indicate this is the primary key for the object.

5. Constrain the `Notes` property using `StringLength`. Set the `maximumLength` to 250.

Listing 17.5 shows an example of what your model should now look like following the addition of these data annotations.

LISTING 17.5 The `Customer.cs` Model with Data Annotations

```
using System;
using System.ComponentModel.DataAnnotations;

namespace AspNet5AppSample.Models
{
  public class Customer
  {
    [Key]
    public int Id { get; set; }

    [Required]
    public string Name { get; set; }

    [Required, EmailAddress(
      ErrorMessage ="Please use email format, name@domain.com")]
    public string Email { get; set; }

    public bool OptInEmail { get; set; }

    [StringLength(maximumLength:250)]
    public string Notes { get; set; }
  }
}
```

ASP.NET will use these data annotations to execute validation on the client (using the `jQuery.validate` plug-in). They will also be part of the model state validation on the server (inside your controller). You will see these in action later in the chapter as we round out this sample.

Creating the Data Context

The next step with Entity Framework 7 (EF7) is to create a database context class that derives from `Microsoft.Data.Entity.DbContext`. Entity Framework uses the database context class to get enough information about your objects so it can work with the entities in your database. You can do a lot with `DbContext` and related Entity Framework code (including handling object to data entity migrations/updates). However, this example simply uses this approach for writing `Customer` objects to a database.

Recall that EF7, like ASP.NET Core 5, is now modular. The project template in our sample already includes a reference to EF7 for SQL Server. You can open the `project.json` file to see this (`"EntityFramework.SqlServer": "7.0.0-beta4"`). You could replace this, for example, with SQLite using NuGet and installing EntityFramework.SQLite. For our example, however, we will stick to the SQL Server version. The following walks you through this process of creating the `DbContext` object:

1. Add a class to the `Models` folder called `CustomerDbContext.cs`. To do so, right-click the `Models` folder in Solution Explorer and choose Add, New Item. Select the Class template.
2. Add a `using` statement at the top of the class for `Microsoft.Data.Entity`.
3. Update the `CustomerDbContext` class definition to inherit from `DbContext`.
4. Create a public property of type `DbSet<Customer>` called `Customers`.

Listing 17.6 shows the new `CustomerDbContext` class.

LISTING 17.6 The Data Context Class

```
using System;
using Microsoft.Data.Entity;

namespace AspNet5AppSample.Models
{
  public class CustomerDbContext : DbContext
  {
    public DbSet<Customer> Customers { get; set; }
  }
}
```

Connecting to the Database

Of course, we need a database with which to work. EF7 supports working with an existing database or using the tools to create one based on your model. In past versions of the Entity Framework, you could simply run your application; if EF did not find the database, it automatically created one for you. However, this database generation at project runtime was problematic and difficult to keep in synch beyond the initial database generation. EF7 addresses these issues. You no longer get a database just by running some code. Instead, you can use console commands to generate a database migration script based on your model. You can then execute that script to create your database. These migration scripts are code files stored in the `Migrations` folder of an ASP.NET MVC project. You can use these files to keep your database and model in sync during development and deployments.

To get started, we will define a connection string for working with the database. There are many places we can put the database connection. For this example, we will use the `config.json` file for storing a database connection string for our project. The following walks you through the process:

1. Open the `config.json` file from Solution Explorer. Notice there is already a `Data` group with a `DefaultConnection` item. This was created by the template for working with the ASP.NET user profile and membership services.

In the example, however, we plan to store membership data and application data in the same database. Therefore, edit the connection in the file to point at a new database named `AspNet5Unleashed`. (`Database=AspNet5Unleashed`). We will generate this database in a moment.

Note that you may also have to change your server name in the connection string depending on your installation. To get your server name, open SQL Server Object Explorer in Visual Studio (View, SQL Server Object Explorer). Your local database server should show in the tree (along with its name).

You can also right-click the server and choose Properties. Here you can find the "Connection string" property to use as a guide. For example, you can use the first section, `Data Source=(localdb)\\ProjectsV12;` to get the server name, `(localdb)\\ProjectsV12` and update the default connection string to `Server=(localdb)\\ProjectsV12;`.

When complete, your connection string should look similar to the one shown at the top of Figure 17.20.

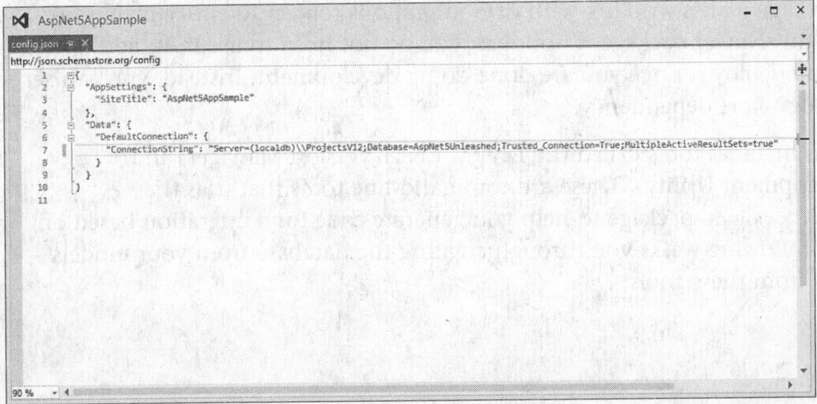

FIGURE 17.20 Create a database connection string inside `config.json`.

2. Now open `Startup.cs` from Solution Explorer. Recall that this is where you configure the ASP.NET request pipeline. Navigate to the `ConfigureServices` method.

   You should see a call to `services.AddEntityFramework()`. There are methods on this object that use dependency injection to add additional dependent services at runtime. Use this call to add registration for the `CustomerDbContext` instance as shown here.

```
services.AddEntityFramework()
   .AddSqlServer()
   .AddDbContext<ApplicationDbContext>(options =>
     options.UseSqlServer(Configuration
       ["Data:DefaultConnection:ConnectionString"]))
   .AddDbContext<CustomerDbContext>(options =>
          options.UseSqlServer(Configuration
       ["Data:DefaultConnection:ConnectionString"]));
```

Creating the Database Using EF7 Migrations

Now that you have defined a connection to the database, you need to actually create the database. You can do so manually using SQL Server Object Explorer. You can also use the EF7 migration commands in Visual Studio to generate your database from your model. You will see an example of both scenarios. Some developers like to use the SQL tools and create the database manually. Others prefer to keep their database in synch with their models using tools.

Let's start by looking at how you would automate database schema updates using EF migration. To do so, you will use commands that are part of the `EntityFramework.Commands` package installed by the default template. You can see this package in the `References` folder in Solution Explorer and in `project.json`. In the latter, these commands get mapped to the `ef` variable. You will use this in the command window to generate a migration file and execute it.

The `Commands` package makes working with data migrations (object to entity mapping) easier. However, this NuGet package is optional; you do not need to use it. In addition, there is no need to deploy it once you are done doing development. Instead, you can set the package as a dev-time dependency.

Visual Studio also includes tools called the DNVM (.NET Version Manager) and DNU (.NET Development Utility). These are command-line tools that uses the `EntityFramework.Commands` package to help you generate code for a migration based on your model. The following walks you through creating the database from your models using commands from these tools:

NOTE

The EF7 code was in beta (beta 4) at the time of writing. In addition, the supporting tools were also in development. This section walks you through what was available at the time of writing: the command line approach to creating and applying a migration based on your model. However, it is possible the tooling will also be integrated directly into the Visual Studio IDE. That said, this command line approach should still operate as outlined.

---

1. Open the Developer Command Prompt for VS2015 (Windows Start, Developer Command Prompt for VS 2015). This opens a command window setup to work with Visual Studio command line tools.

2. To get started, you need to change the active directory in the command prompt to folder that contains your `project.json` file. In our example, you use the cd command to navigate to the project folder. You then use the following to get to the folder containing `project.json`:

```
cd .\src\aspnet5appSample
```

3. Next, you need to use DNVM to add a .NET runtime for use by the command window. You can do so using the `use` command. To see a list of available runtimes, type `dnvm list`. To bind a runtime to the path, use the following command at the prompt (where your version number matches that found in the `dnvm list`):

```
dnvm use 1.0.0-beta4 coreclr
```

4. You may also have to use the DNU to restore NuGet packages before continuing. You can do so using the following command:

```
dnu restore
```

5. You are now ready to execute a command to create an EF7 migration. You do so using the DNX tool and the `ef` command. The `ef` command is defined inside `project.json` under Commands to point to `EntityFramework.Commands`.

   The first step is to generate migration code based on your data context object. The following command does so. You can see that we name the migration `InitialSchema`; the migration class will contain this name. We also explicitly indicate which class (`CustomerDbContext`) we want to use as a basis for the generated migration code (as there may be more than one in your project).

```
dnx . ef migration add InitialSchema -c CustomerDbContext
```

6. Upon success, return to Visual Studio and navigate to the `Migrations` folder for your project. You should now have two new files in the folder: one that ends with the name, `_InitialSchema.cs`; and another with the name, `CustomerDbContextModelSnapshot.cs`.

7. The DNX tool will use these classes to apply this migration to your database. The database connection will be gleaned from your project file, `config.json`. Enter the following `apply` command inside the command window.

```
dnx . ef migration apply -c CustomerDbContext
```

You can now return to Visual Studio and open the database (View, SQL Server Object Explorer). You may have to use the refresh button on the tool pane window. You should then see the AspNet5Unleashed database and the `dbo.Customer` table.

This EF7 migration method can be used to keep your model and database in synch. As you make changes to the model, you can use the commands discussed here to create migration scripts. You can then apply these scripts as required to various environments in order to deploy your database changes.

Creating the Database Manually

Some developers prefer to create the database manually using script or the tools themselves to generate script. Visual Studio and EF7 support this scenario. The following walks you through creating the database manually using Visual Studio:

1. Open SQL Server Object Explorer from the View menu; navigate to your database and the `Databases` folder.

   Right-click the `Databases` folder and choose Add New Database. Name the database `AspNet5Unleashed`.

2. Expand the node that represents your newly created database. Navigate to the `Tables` folder and right-click it. Select Add New Table.

3. Use the table designer to create fields for the `Customers` table. Use the T-SQL script editor to change the name of the table to `Customer` (singular).

   Figure 17.21 shows an example of what your table should look like.

4. Right-click the `Id` property and choose Properties. Set this primary key as an `Identity` column with an Identity Seed of 1 and an Identity Increment of 1. See the right side of Figure 17.21 as an example.

5. Click the Update button on the table designer to update the database. This brings up the Preview Database Updates dialog. If all looks right, click the Update Database button to submit your changes. You should see the changes as they are being made inside the Data Tools Operations window. Note that Visual Studio will ask you if you want to save the `.sql` script file. This is not necessary for most workflows as you can always regenerate this if necessary.

You should now have a database, a data context class, and a class that represents your data model. Entity Framework should also now be configured to connect to and work with your database. The next step is to write a controller for handling requests for customer data and views.

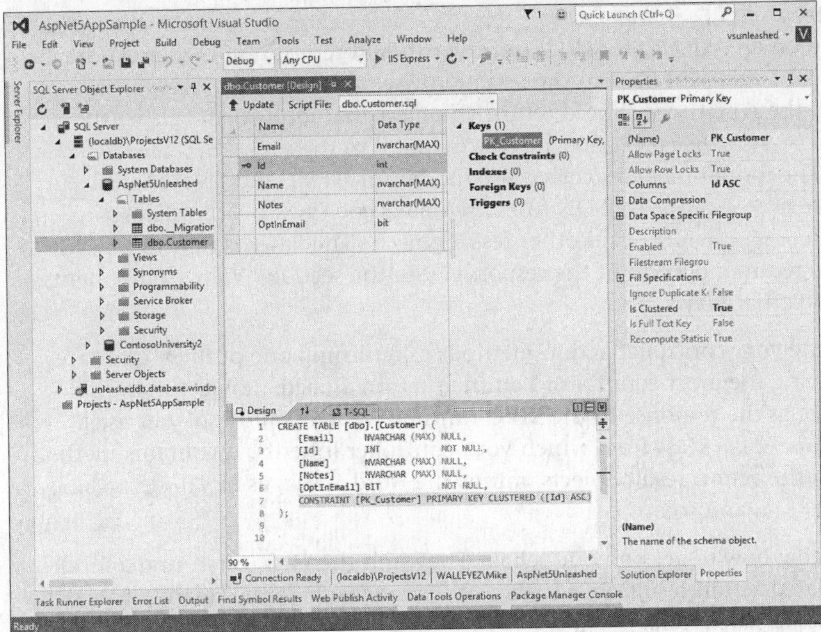

FIGURE 17.21 Use the database tools to create the `AspNet5Unleashed` database and the `Customer` table.

Developing Controllers

An ASP.NET 5 MVC controller handles user requests to your site. Recall that the routing engine uses the URL convention to route a request to your controller and on to a method on that controller. For example, a request for `./customer/edit/5` will, by default, route to your `CustomerController.Edit(id)` method; the value 5 will be passed as the `id` parameter.

The controller method is then responsible for connecting the request to your model and returning the appropriate view result. The `Edit(id)` method, for example, will likely use a `DbContext` (created in the prior section) to find a specific customer from the database.

The controller would pass the `Customer` instance from the model to the Customer/Edit view page and return a `ViewResult`. Finally, the runtime would then likely look for a view called Edit inside the `Views/Customer` folder. As part returning results, ASP.NET would generate on the server, based on the view code, the appropriate HTML and JavaScript to be sent back as the response to the user machine.

This section covers creating controllers, working with the model, and returning an `IActionResult` to let MVC generate the right web response.

The Result Objects

An action method on an ASP.NET 5 MVC controller should return results that can be processed by ASP.NET and sent back to the user's browser as a valid HTTP response. For the most part, these methods should return an object that implements either the `IActionResult` or `IViewComponentResult` interface (found in the `Microsoft.AspNet.Mvc` namespace). The former includes classes used to return HTML and JavaScript (`ViewResults`, `PartialViewResult`), JSON formatted messages (`JsonResult`), Files (`FileResult`, `FileContentResult`), and other result objects. The latter is new to ASP.NET 5 MVC. It is used to return a portion of the response. (See the section "View Components, View Models, and Partial Views.")

You typically define your controller action methods as returning one of these interfaces (`IActionResult` being the most common). You then return an actual object that implements the interface as the response to the MVC runtime. When you do so, you use a method on the `Controller` class from which your controller inherits. It contains method names that match the action result objects, minus the word *Result*, as in `View()`, `Json()`, `Redirect()`, `Content()`, and so on.

These methods know how to act on your behalf. They find the view, often find a model, and return the related action result object. The MVC framework defines many of these action result classes as listed here:

- `ContentResult`—Used to return a custom content type as the result of the action method. This is an HTTP content type, such as text/plain.
- `EmptyResult`—Used to return nothing (void) as the result.
- `FileResult (FileContentResult, FilePathResult, FileStreamResult)`—Used to send back binary output (and files) as the response.
- `HttpNotFoundResult`—Used to send an HTTP status indicating that the requested resource was not found.
- `HttpStatusCodeResult`—Used to send a specific HTTP status code (from the many available) as the result.
- `JsonResult`—Used to return a message formatted as JSON.
- `NoContentResult`—Used to indicate that the response has no actual content.
- `ObjectResult`—Used to return an object as the result. (See Chapter 19.)
- `RedirectResult`—Used to redirect to another URI.
- `RedirectToRouteResult (RedirectToActionResult)`—Used to redirect to another action method.
- `PartialViewResult`—Used to send a section of a partial view (portion of HTML) to be rendered inside another view.
- `ViewViewcomponentResult`—Used to return a view component (portion of the response) as a result (implements `IViewComponentResult`).
- `ViewResult`—Used to return a web page generated from a view.

Let's now take a look at using these action result objects inside a controller.

Creating the Controller

Visual Studio 2015 provides an ASP.NET 5 MVC template for adding a controller to your project. This template already derives from `Controller`. You store controllers in the `Controllers` folder. When creating a new controller, you use the naming standard `FeatureAreaController`, where `FeatureArea` is the name of your feature (in our example, `CustomerController`). The following walks you through creating a controller:

1. Right-click the `Controllers` folder in Solution Explorer. Choose Add, New Item.
2. From the Add New Item dialog (see Figure 17.22), select MVC Controller Class. Name your controller `CustomerController.cs`. Click the Add button to continue.
3. Visual Studio creates a basic controller with an `Index()` method that returns an `IActionResult` (in this case, a `ViewResult`). Listing 17.7 shows an example.

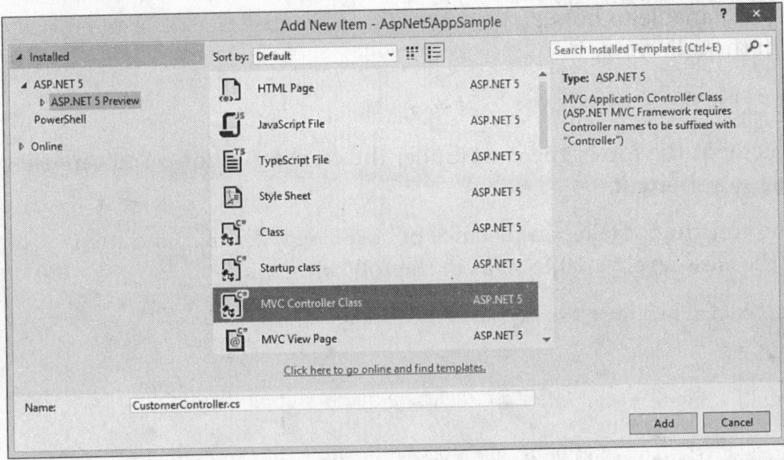

FIGURE 17.22 You add a new controller to an ASP.NET MVC project using the Add New Item dialog box.

LISTING 17.7 The `CustomerController.cs` Class Generated by the Controller Template

```
using Microsoft.AspNet.Mvc;

namespace AspNet5AppSample.Controllers
{
  public class CustomerController : Controller
  {
    //GET: /<controller>/
    public IActionResult Index()
    {
```

```
            return View();
        }
    }
}
```

Adding a DbContext

The `CustomerController` class will work closely with the model (your data access classes) to handle requests to read and write customer data. Therefore, the class needs an instance of your `DbContext` object, `CustomerDbContext`. Recall that you added this to the request pipeline earlier using the `Startup.cs` file `ConfigureServices` method. ASP.NET will pass this content to your controller provided you request it in the constructor. The following walks you through creating this code:

1. Open the `CustomerController` class file from Solution Explorer.
2. Add a `using` statement at the top of the class file for `AspNet5Unleashed.Models`.
3. Define a class-level variable to hold an instance of `CustomerDbContext`. Name this variable `db`, as in the following:

   ```
   private CustomerDbContext db;
   ```

4. Create a constructor at the top of the class (under the class definition). You can use the snippet `ctor` as a shortcut.

   Indicate that the constructor takes an instance of `CustomerDbContext` and then assigns that to the class-level variable `db` as in the following:

   ```
   public CustomerController(CustomerDbContext context)
   {
     db = context;
   }
   ```

ASP.NET will now provide the database context object as part of the request when creating an instance of your controller. The next step is to define actual action methods on the controller for returning, editing, creating, and deleting customers. The following sections examine each in turn.

Returning a List of Customers

We will use the `Index` action method of the controller to return a list of customers from the model and pass it to a view page called `Index.cshtml` (which we will create later). This is a simple method. Remember, we already set up the database context inside a variable called `db`. Therefore, the following is all that is needed for the `Index()` action method.

```
public IActionResult Index()
{
  return View(db.Customers);
}
```

This method is set to return an IActionResult instance. This is common for most of your action methods (see the "The Result Objects" section) and indicates the result should be an action. In this case, the action will be to create a view. Therefore, the code uses the Controller.View() method to return a ViewResult instance. The actual view page is not named because you can rely on the framework to follow convention and look for a view called Index in the Views/Customer folder.

Notice that a list of customers is passed to the view using the model and data context. The view, as you'll see later, will be strongly typed to expect a list of customers.

Returning a New Customer Page

Likely, the most simplistic controller method is one that only returns a view. In our example, a user requests to create a new customer. The data context is not needed for this (until the form is filled out and posted back to the server anyway). Therefore, you simply return a View. The following shows an example.

```
public IActionResult Create()
{
  return View();
}
```

In this case, ASP.NET will look for a view called Create.cshtml in the Views/Customer folder. The view itself will know to bind to the Customer class for outputting validation rules and error messages. It will then return a view with essentially a blank customer so the user can enter new customer information.

Returning a Single Customer for Edit

We will now create an Edit(id) method to find a customer in the database using the Id property and return an Edit.cshtml view page (which we will also create later). This id parameter is passed to the action method from the URL using the ASP.NET routing engine convention. For example, a user may the request ./customer/edit/2. The value 2 will be passed to CustomerController.Edit(id) as a parameter.

The first step is to add a using statement to the top of the CustomerController class to add support for the LINQ query engine. The following shows an example.

```
using System.Linq;
```

Next, we write the method. The method should use LINQ to look up a customer from the DbContext. If it exists, it will return a ViewResult object. If not, it returns the HttpNotFound error (resulting in an HTTP 404 error page). An example of the code is shown here.

```
public IActionResult Edit(int id)
{
  Customer customer =
    db.Customers.FirstOrDefault(x => x.Id == id);
```

```
  if (customer == null)
  {
    return HttpNotFound();
  }
  return View(customer);
}
```

Accepting a Customer Edit (POST)

So far we have looked at action methods that simply return views. These action methods are called as part of HTTP `GET` requests. In the case of `Edit(id)` and `Create()`, a user must fill out a form. The form is then sent back to the server as an HTTP `POST`. What is needed then are action methods to handle these `POST` requests.

The convention is to define these action methods with the same name as their corresponding request action method. The difference is that these action methods include the attribute `HttpPost` to indicate the method should be called as part of an HTTP `POST` request. These action methods also take different parameters. The `Create` and `Edit` methods, for example, take a `Customer` object.

The following code shows an example of the additional `Edit` method.

```
[HttpPost]
[ValidateAntiForgeryToken]
public IActionResult Edit(
  [Bind(new string[] { "Id", "Name", "Email", "OptInEmail", "Notes"})]
  Customer customer)
{
  if (ModelState.IsValid)
  {
    db.Customers.Update(customer);
    db.SaveChanges();
    return RedirectToAction("Index");
  }
  return View(customer);
}
```

The `Edit` method uses the `Bind` model binder attribute to map form post fields to the `Customer` instance properties explicitly. This is a security precaution to prevent something called *over posting*. Over posting occurs when you maintain a property on your object that you do not expose on the form. This allows someone to post extra data to your form and, if lucky enough, set properties on your object you did not intend for him to be able to set. Using `Bind` is essentially whitelisting which properties you allow to be set; only those form fields will be bound to the `Customer` instance passed as a parameter to the `action` method. That is not required in this case because we allow all properties to be written. However, it is a good practice, and consistency is key. You may add a property later you do not want to bind, for example.

Notice that inside the method we first check to confirm the model state is valid. This executes the business rules you added to the model class as data annotations. If not valid, the `Edit.cshtml` view is returned and the errors are shown to the user. If the model is valid, we use the `Update` method to mark the customer for update and `SaveChanges` to commit the update to the database. Finally, upon completion, we return the user to the `Customer/Index.cshtml` page using the `RedirectToAction` action method.

CROSS SITE REQUEST FORGERY

Notice that the `Edit` method is decorated with the `ValidateAntiForgeryToken` attribute. This is to help prevent the security threat Cross Site Request Forgery (CSRF). CSRF is when another application tries to post to your controller. This attribute, along with the `AntiForgeryToken()` HTML helper in the view, helps validate calls to your controller.

Accepting a New Customer (POST)

Handling a HTTP POST for a new customer is nearly the same as handling a POST for customer edit. In fact, the only difference is the call to the `DbContext`; instead of `Update`, we use `Add`. The following shows the `Create` method for the `Customer` controller.

```
[HttpPost]
[ValidateAntiForgeryToken]
public IActionResult Create(
  [Bind(new string[] { "Name", "Email", "OptInEmail", "Notes"})]
  Customer customer)
{
  if (ModelState.IsValid)
  {
    db.Customers.Add(customer);
    db.SaveChanges();
    return RedirectToAction("Index");
  }
  return View(customer);
}
```

Processing a Customer Delete Request

The last method we will add to the `CustomerController` is a method to handle a request to delete a customer. The method is similar to the one that simply returns a customer based on `Id`. In this case, the call will take an `id` parameter, use it to find the customer instance, and then use the `DbContext` to remove this customer. The following shows the code.

```
public IActionResult Delete(int id)
{
  Customer customer =
    db.Customers.FirstOrDefault(x => x.Id == id);
```

```
    db.Customers.Remove(customer);
    db.SaveChanges();

    return RedirectToAction("Index");
}
```

Note that in an actual application, you may not want to make it this easy to delete data. Instead, you might require this via a form submit (and HTTP POST), only by an authorized user, and provide an "are you sure" message for committing the data deletion.

You now have a model, a database, and a controller for working with customer objects. We have not, however, created views yet. Therefore, you cannot simply run this code and see your results. Let's take a look at creating the views.

Coding for the UI (Views and Related Web UI Elements)

Writing a UI view can seem like a complex endeavor. You need to know a lot of different server-side and web technologies to make everything work. This includes client-side JavaScript, HTML markup, CSS for visual styling, server-side Razor code, multiple client-side JavaScript libraries, page layouts and partial views, and even more. Thankfully, Visual Studio and ASP.NET help to abstract a lot of this complexity so we can focus on building our actual pages for rendering.

This section starts with the basics of building a view in ASP.NET 5 MVC, including HTML, Razor, helper methods, page layout, and the like. We then look at using these basics to build the sample pages based on the `CustomerController` (and related model) created in the previous section. Of course, if you are already familiar with many of these concepts, you can skip this section and go to "Creating the Customer Example Pages." We cover JavaScript in more detail in the coming chapters.

The HTML Tags

It all starts with HTML. The ASP.NET MVC template gives developers control again of HTML markup (contrasted with web server controls). We assume that most readers will have a basic understanding of HTML. However, we cover a few core concepts here should you need a brush-up or are new to web development and need to understand how to use HTML to build views as discussed later in this chapter.

LEARNING HTML AND CSS

If you are starting at the beginning, there are many good books, videos, and tutorials on learning the basics of HTML and CSS. These cover layout and styling. (Here we only cover forms and input controls.) You should not have to look far for good material. For example, you might check www.w3schools.com; they have been helping with HTML for years and include tutorials on HTML and CSS.

The HTML controls start with the ubiquitous `<input>` tag. This tag is used to define text boxes, buttons, check boxes, radio buttons, and more. The following shows an example of the `<input>` tag and a few key attributes.

```
<input type="text" name="Notes" maxlength="250" value="Some notes ..." />
```

Notice that the `<input>` tag uses the name property to name the element. This allows you to refer to the tag using jQuery selectors. It also helps ASP.NET MVC map the form element back to the object when working on the server. The tag also sets the initial value attribute. The key attribute, however, is `type`. The `type` here is set to `text`. Therefore, this will render as a text box for user input. You use `<input>` and `type` to define many different HTML form controls. The following lists the most common `type` attribute definitions:

- `button`—Used to create a button object. A button, by default, does not submit the form. Instead, use it to call some JavaScript or something similar. Use the Submit type to create a button that posts the form back to the controller.
- `checkbox`—Used to create a check box for the user to click. Use the `checked` attribute to indicate whether the check box should be checked or not upon display.
- `file`—Used to create a file upload input element. Allows a user to select a file and have it uploaded to the server.
- `hidden`—Used to create a hidden form field. You might do so if you do not want user input but do want the form field passed as part of the form submit.
- `password`—Used to create a text box for entering passwords. (Text is blanked out with bullets.)
- `radio`—Used to provide users with a selection of choices as radio buttons. A user is expected to select only one. You name each of these input items the same but set the values differently.
- `reset`—Used to create a button for resetting a form on the client. This erases any user input and sets things back to default values.
- `submit`—Used to define a button that will submit the form back to the server when it's pressed.
- `image`—Used to create a Submit button whose visual is an image.
- `text`—Used to create a single-line text box for user entry.

HTML 5 defines many, newer input types. However, most of these newer types are not supported in earlier browsers. This includes types like `URL`, `DateTime`, `Search`, `Email`, `Color`, and many more. If you are targeting browsers that support these types, you can use them. Otherwise, you will have to provide an alternative. As you will see shortly, the HTML helpers can help handle this decision on your behalf.

Outside of the `<input>` tag, there are many other markup elements you are likely going to encounter when creating views and user input forms. The following provides a high-level overview of some of these additional tags:

- `<div>`—Used to group other markup into sections within your page. In general, everything goes within one `<div>` tag or another. You can also nest `<div>` tags within each other. CSS often uses `<divs>` to apply styles to various sections of your page.
- `<table>`—Used to create a table of columns and rows within your HTML page. You use the `<thead>` tag to define a table head (top row); the `<th>` tag to define columns within your table head. You use `<tr>` to indicate a table row; `<td>` is used to indicate table data for the given column in the row.
- `<a>`—Called an anchor tag, `<a>` is used to define a hyperlink from one page to another. You can also use an anchor tag and some JavaScript to submit a form (like a button might).
- `<select> / <option>`—Used to create a drop-down list of options for the user. You use the `<option>` tag within `<select>` to present each option.
- `<textarea>`—Used to create a larger text entry form field. You use the attributes `rows` and `cols` to indicate how big the text area should be (`rows` = height based on rows text; `cols` = width based on width of characters).
- `<label>`—Used for defining a label for a form element. The `<label>` tag does not render any differently than just text in HTML, by default. However, using a `<label>` can make styling easier and gives you something to leverage should you need to reference the `<label>` in JavaScript.
- `<fieldset>, <legend>`—Used to group related HTML elements (typically form input fields). The `<legend>` tag provides a name for the grouping. Both fields are useful for styling a section with CSS.

The last HTML tag we want to discuss in this overview is the `<form>` element. You nest your user input elements inside a `<form>` tag. The `<form>` tag is used to define how your input elements should be sent to the server (HTTP `GET` or `POST`) and where they are to be sent. The following shows an example of a `<form>` element.

```
<form id="form-create" action="create" method="post">
```

Notice that you use the `action` attribute to indicate what should receive the action of the form. This is typically something in your site (such as a page or a controller method). You use the `method` attribute to indicate how that data is to be sent to your site—in this case as a `POST`. There are many other options when working with a form, such as processing JavaScript and submitting as JSON (as you will see in Chapter 19).

Now that you have a basic refresher on working with HTML, let's take a look at how the ASP.NET Razor syntax and the related HTML helper classes make creating and working with HTML views even easier.

CSS / RESPONSIVE DESIGN

The ASP.NET 5 template includes a basic style sheet, `site.css`, under the `wwwroot/css` folder. It also leverages Twitter Bootstrap for a basic theme and what is called responsive design. Responsive design leverage styles and JavaScript to render your pages correctly regardless of device size (see Chapter 18). The Bootstrap files are also under the `bower_components` folder (hidden by default in Solution Explorer). CSS and responsive design is a big topic, and we do not have the space to cover it here. However, you will notice that we touch on this (and styles in general) throughout this chapter and the next.

The Razor Syntax

The Razor syntax refers to how you write code mixed inside your view markup. Remember that this code is meant to run on the server. The Razor syntax strives to make it easy to embed code throughout your page. If you have done this in earlier versions of ASP, you will recall things like brackets and percent signs (`<% ... %>`) to indicate code start and end blocks. These statements were painful to write and hard to read. Razor makes it much easier.

Razor uses the at sign, `@`, to indicate an inline expression of code. Typically, this is all you need to tell the engine that you intend it to process some code on your page. If you have just a single line of code, you can embed it right within your HTML. The following markup with Razor shows an example. Here you can see markup (the `div` and `p` tags) combined with code as written using the `@` character. This code simply uses the server-side object, `DataTime`, to get the current year and add it to the output, as in © 2015 – VS Unleashed.

```
<div class="float-left">
  <p>&copy; @DateTime.Now.Year - VS Unleashed</p>
</div>
```

NOTE

Note that in the example, `@DateTime.Now.Year`, we are using the Razor syntax to indicate the year should be written to the page. ASP.NET makes sure to HTML-encode this output before displaying it to the user. This protects you from inadvertently sending HTML or script to the page from an object. Of course, if this is your intent, you can use an HTML helper, `@Html.Raw`, to send unencoded content to the browser.

If you have code that runs across multiple lines, you can use brackets `{}`. (VB developers can go without the brackets and simply use things like `End If` and `Next`.) You can, of course, still mix markup with this code. Consider the following markup and code from the default template partial view, `_LoginPartial.cshtml`.

```
@using System.Security.Principal

@if (User.Identity.IsAuthenticated)
{
  using (Html.BeginForm("LogOff", "Account", FormMethod.Post,
    new { id = "logoutForm", @class = "navbar-right" }))
  {
    @Html.AntiForgeryToken()
    <ul class="nav navbar-nav navbar-right">
      <li>
        @Html.ActionLink("Hello " + User.Identity.GetUserName() +
          "!", "Manage", "Account", routeValues: null,
          htmlAttributes: new { title = "Manage" })
      </li>
      <li><a href="javascript:document.getElementById('logoutForm').submit()">
        Log off</a></li>
    </ul>
  }
}
else
{
  <ul class="nav navbar-nav navbar-right">
    <li>@Html.ActionLink("Register", "Register", "Account", routeValues: null,
     htmlAttributes: new { id = "registerLink" })</li>
    <li>@Html.ActionLink("Log in", "Login", "Account", routeValues: null,
     htmlAttributes: new { id = "loginLink" })</li>
  </ul>
}
```

There is a lot going on in this partial view. However, notice that the page starts out with code that uses Razor to call an `@if` statement. This `@if` statement's true portion is then defined inside brackets. However, the brackets contain markup and more code (including HTML helpers, which you will read about in a moment). The Razor engine can parse all this just fine. This leaves developers free to easily express server-side code and client markup on the same page.

For longer sections of code, you can declare the `@` character followed directly by a bracket. This is typically used when you only want to write code (no markup). Inside the brackets, you can make server-side calls, declare variables to be used later, run other code, create loops; pretty much anything you can write in C# or VB can be added to your web page using the Razor syntax.

```
@{
  ViewBag.Title = "Home Page";
  var requestTime = DateTime.Now.TimeOfDay;
}
```

Notice that in the previous examples, all the code and markup combinations include markup inside of HTML tags (like `<p>` and `<ul>`). This makes it easy for the Razor engine to distinguish between what is code and what is markup. Sometimes, however, you might want to output text to the page from within your code that is not surrounded by tags. In this case, you need to use the `@` sign with a colon, also called the `@:` operator. The following code shows an example.

```
@if(WebSecurity.IsAuthenticated) {
  @: Current time: <br /> @DateTime.Now
}
```

Another key part of the Razor syntax is the `@Html` helper objects. Let's take a look at these next.

HTML Helpers

HTML helpers are lightweight methods that execute on the server and return a string to be used as standard HTML on your page. They are accessed using `@Html`, which is essentially a property on your view. The HTML helper classes and related methods are found in the namespace `Microsoft.AspNet.Mvc.Rendering`.

These helper methods generate UI markup and should only be used on your pages (and not in the controller). Of course, you do not need to use HTML helpers. You can code all your view as actual HTML markup. In addition, many of the HTML Helpers have evolved into TagHelpers (see next section). However, these methods can simplify writing a lot of repetitive, basic HTML markup. The methods run on the server, but they are also lightweight. (Unlike web form controls, they do not have an event model or view state.)

As an example, consider the following `@Html` helper inside a view page. Its job is to generate a drop-down list for user input based on a list of name-value pairs.

```
@Html.DropDownList(name: "Confirmed", selectList: confirmOptions)
```

Running this inside a view page outputs the following HTML to the browser.

```
<select id="Confirmed" name="Confirmed">
  <option value="1">Yes</option>
  <option value="2">No</option>
  <option value="3">Maybe</option>
</select>
```

Note that the preceding example requires a list of `SelectListItems`. You can either return them from your controller (most likely scenario) or embed the list in your page. The following shows an example of the latter just to clarify the example.

```
@{
  List<SelectListItem> confirmOptions = new List<SelectListItem>();

  confirmOptions.Add(new SelectListItem { Text = "Yes", Value = "1" });
```

```
    confirmOptions.Add(new SelectListItem { Text = "No", Value = "2" });
    confirmOptions.Add(new SelectListItem { Text = "Maybe", Value = "3" });
}
```

The HTML helper methods include one that maps to each of the form input (and related) tags covered in the earlier section, "The HTML Tags." This includes the following helper methods: `@Html.CheckBox`, `@Html.DropDownList`, `@Html.Hidden`, `@Html.Label`, `@Html.ListBox`, `@Html.Password`, `@Html.RadioButton`, and `@Html.TextArea`. Each of these helper methods also defines a similar method that includes the word *For* appended to the end, as in `@Html.TextBoxFor`. You use the "For" HTML helper methods for model binding—that is, when you want to have ASP.NET output-specific HTML for a given property in your model. The following shows an example.

```
@Html.EditorFor(model => model.Email,
  new { htmlAttributes = new { @class = "form-control" } })
```

Notice that this example uses model binding inside a strongly typed view (more on this in a moment). Notice, too, that you can use one of the additional overloads of the helper method to set specific HTML attributes on the HTML to be output (in this case, the style class name).

There are many additional HTML helpers designed to take advantage of the server-side ASP.NET engine and make writing HTML easier. The following provides a list of some of these key helper methods you are likely to encounter:

- `@Html.BeginForm`—Used to create a `<form>` tag inside your view.
- `@Html.AntiForgeryToken`—Used to generate an anti-forgery key to be validated back on the controller (provided you decorate your controller method with the `ValidateAntiForgeryToken` attribute). See the example later in this section.
- `@Html.ValidationSummary`—Used to create an error on your page to display a summary of field validation errors on the page.
- `@Html.LabelFor`—Used to generate a label for one of your input items.
- `@Html.EditorFor`—Used to create an editor (typically an `<input>` tag) for a given property of your model. This allows the framework to select the editor on your behalf (based on data type).
- `@Html.ValidationMessageFor`—Used to create messages that display when a field has an error (and hide when it does not).
- `@Html.ActionLink`—Used to create a hyperlink on your page that can also call your controller (including using HTTP POST).
- `@Html.Encode`—Used to convert a value to an HTML-encoded string for output.

You will use these helper methods throughout the remainder of this section to write sample view pages for the customer example discussed earlier.

CREATE CUSTOM HTML HELPERS

You can build your own Razor HTML helpers. You create these helpers to make writing markup easier for you or your team of developers. A custom helper can contain both code and markup. It will show up in IntelliSense and work the same way as other HTML helpers to generate markup for you.

ASP.NET MVC TagHelpers

ASP.NET MVC 6 introduces TagHelpers to provide a more markup-based approach to extending HTML with server-side code processing. Like HTML Helpers, TagHelpers process on the server and simplify the writing of repetitive code. What makes them different is that they look and feel more like HTML markup. There is no need for the `@Html` signal in your markup to indicate a server-side helper method is being called. Instead, the TagHelpers add custom attributes to existing HTML tags. This makes them look and feel like HTML markup (but can be color coded for easy identification in the IDE). These attributes then execute on the server much the same way a HTML helper would. The TagHelper classes are found in the namespace `Microsoft.AspNet.Mvc.TagHelpers`.

Let's look at an example. The following is a call inside markup to an HTML Helper for creating a hyperlink that works with the `CustomerController` (based on convention of the URL) and the `Edit` action method. This looks and acts like code inside of markup.

```
@Html.ActionLink("Edit", "Edit", new { id = item.Id })
```

The same link can be written as follows using a TagHelper:

```
<a asp-controller="Customer" asp-action="Edit"
  asp-route-id="@item.Id">Customer</a>
```

Notice this is just HTML markup with two custom attributes: `asp-controller` and `asp-action`. This can be easier to write and to read for developers used to writing and working with markup. This also includes the optional, `asp-route-id` to append an id parameter to the controller request. There are additional attributes as well, such as `asp-fragment`, for pointing to a section of the page being linked.

There are many such TagHelpers available in the new ASP.NET MVC 6. They can be identified easily in markup by their default attribute color, purple. The following outlines the TagHelpers available. We will use TagHelpers throughout the rest of this chapter and in some upcoming chapters.

- **Anchor**—Used to create hyperlinks using the `<a/>` tag as shown above.
- **Cache**—A special tag that supports partial page caching.
- **Environment**—A special tag that allows you to control the page rendering based on runtime environments such as development, staging, and production.
- **Form**—Augments the `<form/>` tag for creating forms bound to MVC models.

- **Input**—Extends the `<input/>` tag for creating input elements based on strongly typed model data.
- **Label**—Used on the `<label/>` tag to create labels for model elements.
- **Link**—Used to process link elements.
- **Option**—Used to work with individual options in a select list.
- **Script**—Simplifies writing script tags.
- **Select**—Extends the `<select/>` tag to generate dropdown lists.
- **TextArea**—Augments the `<textarea/>` tag for model elements.
- **ValidationMessage**—Used to display validation messages inside a `<span/>` for individual model elements.
- **ValidationSummary**—Used to show a validation summary of validation issues for a given model.

CREATE CUSTOM TAG HELPERS

You can write your own TagHelpers for ASP.NET to generate code based on markup. This is very similar to creating HTML Helpers. You will also see TagHelpers available from various control vendors.

Page Layout with Razor

Much of your page markup is common across views such as navigation, header, footer, general look and feel, and more. You want to write this markup once and use it everywhere. ASP.NET MVC provides `_ViewStart.cshtml` and `_Layout.cshtml` for this purpose. Note that the underscore used in the name of a page is a common way to indicate that the page is shared (and not accessed directly by a user).

The default `_ViewStart.cshtml` page sits inside the root of your `Views` folder in Solution Explorer. The ASP.NET runtime knows to look there to find a common layout for your pages. The following shows an example of the content in this page.

```
@{
  Layout = "_Layout.cshtml";
}
```

Notice that this default view start page simply points to the actual layout page, `_Layout.cshtml`, that is stored in the `/Views/Shared` directory. You might also define different view start pages inside your `Views` folders. This is helpful if a given set of views should render with a different layout. ASP.NET will look in your `Views` folders first; if not found, it will look for this default view start page. Note that you can also explicitly define your layout page at the top of a specific view.

AREAS

You can further group your code inside what are called areas. These are useful when your site changes based on a specific area such as Shopping and Account. Inside this area, you would have folders for models, views, and controllers. You would likely use a separate `_ViewStart.cshtml` page as well to define the layout for the area.

The `_Layout.cshtml` page inside the `Views/Shared` folder works as the master layout page for your site. It includes your opening `<html>`, `<head>`, and `<body>` tags. It links to style sheets, loads any default JavaScript files, and defines your navigation. The layout page is then combined with a view at runtime to render a full set of HTML to the browser. We suggest that you open the page in Visual Studio and examine the markup.

The page uses the Razor call `@RenderBody()` to tell ASP.NET to embed the view in this exact section of the page. The following shows an example from within the markup for `_Layout.cshtml` with the integration of the current year.

```
<div class="container body-content">
  @RenderBody()
  <hr />
  <footer>
    <p>&copy; @DateTime.Now.Year - @AppSettings.Options.SiteTitle</p>
  </footer>
</div>
```

Similarly, there is another Razor call near the bottom of the layout: `@RenderSection("scripts", required: false)`. This tells ASP.NET to render your scripts inside a section called `"scripts"`. The following shows how you would use this in a view page. (will see an example of this in moment.)

```
@section Scripts {
  <script src="..."></script>
}
```

Strongly Typed Views

A strongly typed view is one that is designed to work with an object from your model (or view model, as discussed later in this chapter). You create a strongly typed view by adding the `@model` definition at the top of your view page. For example, you would add the following line to the top of view that works with a `Customer` instance.

```
@model AspNet5Unleashed.Models.Customer
```

This definition at the top of your page indicates to the MVC framework that the view expects a `Customer` object when the controller creates it. The controller passes this model data to the view and the runtime will assign this object to the view's `@model` definition. It will also post this same customer object back to your `POST` action method on the controller when a user submits the form.

A strongly typed view allows you to use the model inside your markup (and with the @Html helper classes). For example, the following markup shows creating a label, text box, and validation message for the Name field from a model.

```
<div class="editor-label">
  @Html.LabelFor(model => model.Name)
</div>
<div class="editor-field">
  @Html.EditorFor(model => model.Name)
  @Html.ValidationMessageFor(model => model.Name)
</div>
```

User Input Validation

Pages written using the Razor syntax can take advantage of both client-side and server-side validation. This validation is actually provided by the jQuery.validate.js plug-in (script files) included with the default project template. Recall that the model already includes field-level validation rules using data annotations. These rules will be applied to the client code by ASP.NET when binding the model fields to the view. Of course, these same rules will process on the server, too.

The HTML helper methods and TagHelpers can be used to define validation; they require the jquery.validate plug-in to be added to the view. Recall that the shared _Layout.cshmtl page defined a section called scripts for adding script files to the page. You can use that section to add these validation scripts. Note that if you intend to use these on all the pages in your site, you might add them directly to the layout page.

The following shows the markup required to add the two validation scripts to a single view page.

```
@section Scripts {
  <script src="@Url.Content("~/lib/jquery-validation/jquery.validate.js")">
  </script>
  <script src="@Url.Content(
    "~/lib/jquery-validation-unobtrusive/jquery.validate.unobtrusive.js")">
  </script>
}
```

The ASP.NET 5 template includes a file that makes adding these scripts to a view even easier. This file is in the Views/Shared directory; it is called _ValidationScriptsPartial.cshtml. This file makes use of the <environment/> TagHelpers to deploy a version of these scripts that can be debugged during development and minified (think optimized) versions for staging and production. These scripts can be included in your view page using Html.RenderPartialAsync as follows:

```
@section Scripts {
  @{await Html.RenderPartialAsync("_ValidationScriptsPartial"); }
}
```

The next step is to reserve a spot within the view for any validation message. To do so, you can use the `@Html.ValidationMessageFor` HTML helper. The following shows an example of creating a validation message for the model's `Email` property:

```
@Html.ValidationMessageFor(model => model.Email, "",
  new { @class = "text-danger" })
```

You can also use a TagHelper to add validation for a field. The validation information above would be written as follows using a TagHelper:

```
<span asp-validation-for="Email" class="text-danger"></span>
```

In addition to the message that is added to each field, we can add an overall summary message to the page using the `@Html.ValidationSummary` helper method. This will also allow you to show a message to the user should the form post to the server and result in errors that were not trapped on the client. The following shows an example of this Razor call.

```
@Html.ValidationSummary(true, "", new { @class = "text-danger" })
```

This summary can also be written using a TagHelper. The following shows an example.

```
<div asp-validation-summary="ValidationSummary.All" class="text-danger"></div>
```

Creating the Customer Example Pages

The prior sections should have given you a good overview of writing ASP.NET 5 MVC 6 views. We will now use this information (helper methods, TagHelpers, Razor syntax, HTML input tags, layout, and the like) to create views using the customer example model and controller created previously.

This section steps you through writing each of the customer sample views. It contains complete listing for the two views. It then walks you through the salient points for creating the final view. Of course, the code for all this is available from the download for this book.

Add Basic Navigation

The first thing we are going to do is add navigation support for customers to the menu bar. The following walks you through this process:

1. With the project open in Visual Studio, use Solution Explorer to open the `_Layout.cshtml` page from the `Views/Shared` folder.

2. Find the menu items inside the page markup. They are near the middle inside a `<ul>` tag nested inside a `<div>` tag whose class is set to `navbar-collapse collapse`.

3. Add a navigation menu item using the anchor TagHelper. This helper allows you to write a simple `<a/>` tag but include the controller and action name. The following shows an example of navigating to the `Index()` action of the `CustomerController`.

```
<li><a asp-controller="Customer" asp-action="Index">Customers</a></li>
```

You should now see the menu link within your site (top navigation). You can run the application; it should look similar to Figure 17.23.

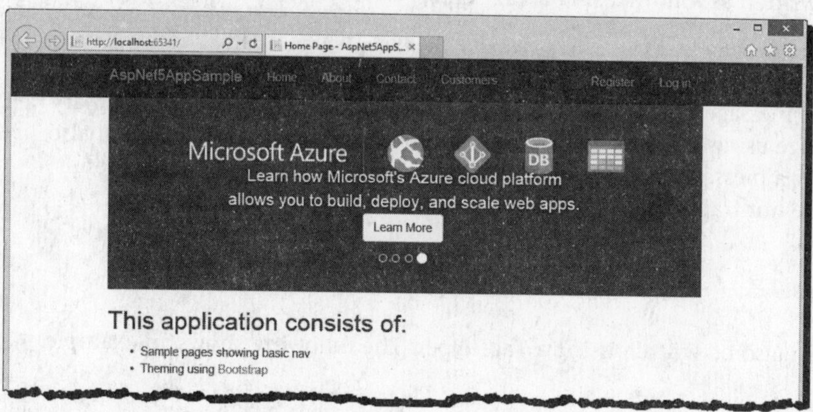

FIGURE 17.23 The `Customers` action link added to the page-level navigation layout.

Display a List of Customer

When a user clicks the `Customers` link, the `Index` method of the `CustomerController` will fire. Recall that this method returns a view with a list of customer objects. What is needed now is to create that view. The following walks you through the process:

1. Right-click the `Views` folder in Solution Explorer and choose Add, New Folder. Name the folder `Customer`.
2. Right-click the newly created `Customer` folder and choose Add, New Item.

   From the Add New Item dialog, select the MVC View Page template. Name the page `Index.cshtml` and click the Add button.
3. Remove the default contents of `Index.cshtml`.
4. Strongly type the view by adding a model reference to the top of the page. This should be for a list of `Customer` objects. The following shows an example.

```
@model IEnumerable<AspNet5AppSample.Models.Customer>
```

5. Use a TagHelper to create a link that takes the user to the new customer page. This should look as follows.

```
<a asp-controller="Customer" asp-action="Create">Create New</a>
```

6. Use HTML to define a table for holding customer data. This should include a table head for each of the columns (excluding `Id`).

For the rows, use Razor HTML Helpers to write a `For...Each` statement to loop through the model as you create a row, as in: `@foreach (var item in Model)`. Use the HTML Helper, `@Html.DisplayFor` inside the loop to show each field the data set.

Add a final column to the table rows to include a link using TagHelpers for both editing and deleting a customer.

Listing 17.8 shows an example of what a completed `Index.cshtml` page might look like. You can now run the application and click the `Customers` link in the navigation bar at the top of the page. This should bring up the view as shown in Figure 17.24.

LISTING 17.8 The `Index.cshtml` Page Used to Display a List of Customers

```
@model IEnumerable<AspNet5Unleashed.Models.Customer>

@{
  ViewBag.Title = "Customers";
}

<h2>@ViewBag.Title</h2>

<a asp-controller="Customer" asp-action="Create">Create New</a>

<table class="table">
  <thead>
    <tr>
      <th>Name</th>
      <th>Email</th>
      <th>Opt In</th>
      <th>Notes</th>
    </tr>
  </thead>
  @foreach (var item in Model)
  {
    <tr id="row-@item.Id">
      <td>
        @Html.DisplayFor(modelItem => item.Name)
      </td>
      <td>
        @Html.DisplayFor(modelItem => item.Email)
      </td>
      <td>
        @Html.DisplayFor(modelItem => item.OptInEmail)
      </td>
      <td>
```

```
        @Html.DisplayFor(modelItem => item.Notes)
      </td>
      <td>
        <a asp-controller="Customer" asp-action="Edit"
          asp-route-id="@item.Id">Edit</a> |
        <a asp-controller="Customer" asp-action="Delete"
          asp-route-id="@item.Id">Delete</a>
      </td>
    </tr>
  }
</table>
```

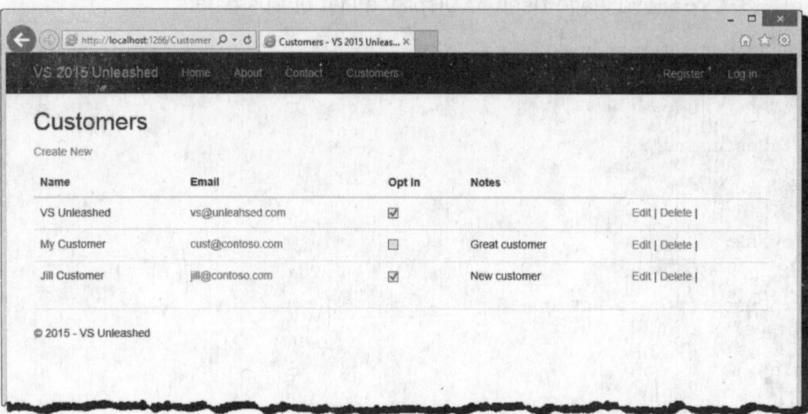

FIGURE 17.24 The list of customers returned from the model, processed by the `Index` method on the controller, and shown in the `Index.cshtml` view.

Create a New Customer

We can now build a view to allow a user to create a new customer. The prior example embedded a hyperlink TagHelper on the customer list page for calling the `Create` method on the controller. The following walks you through key steps of building this view:

1. Right-click the `Views/Customer` folder and choose Add, New Item.

   From the Add New Item dialog, select the MVC View Page template. Name the page `Create.cshtml` and click the Add button.

2. Remove the default contents of `Create.cshtml`.

3. Strongly type the view by adding a model reference to the top of the page. This should be for a single `Customer` object that will be created. We need the model to help build and validate the form. The following shows an example.

   ```
   @model AspNet5AppSample.Models.Customer
   ```

4. Use the TagHelper for `<form/>` to help define the form for the page, as in the following. Notice you set the controller and action method for the form using TagHelper attributes.

```
<form asp-controller="Customer" asp-action="Create" method="post"
  class="form-horizontal" role="form">
```

5. Use a TagHelper on a `<div/>` tag to add a section at the top of the form to display any client-side validation errors or those sent back by the server. The following shows an example.

```
<div asp-validation-summary="ValidationSummary.All"
  class="text-danger"></div>
```

6. Add a `<div>` tag for each customer field on the page. Inside the `<div>` tag, use the TagHelpers for creating a label, an HTML input, and a validation message. The following shows one such field. Repeat this process for each field of `Customer` (except `Id`).

```
<div class="form-group">
  <label asp-for="Name" class="col-md-2 control-label"></label>
  <div class="col-md-10">
    <input asp-for="Name" class="form-control" />
    <span asp-validation-for="Name" class="text-danger"></span>
  </div>
</div>
```

7. At the bottom of the form, add a button for submitting the form as in the following markup:

```
<div class="form-group">
  <div class="col-md-offset-2 col-md-10">
    <input type="submit" value="Create" class="btn btn-default" />
  </div>
</div>
```

8. After the form, add an anchor tag using a TagHelper to allow navigation for cancelling the request, as in the following.

```
<div>
  <a asp-controller="Customer" asp-action="Index">Back to List</a>
</div>
```

9. Finally, include the `jQuery.validate` plug-in script to the page using the Scripts section (see the example in the earlier section "User Input Validation"). The following shows an example.

```
@section Scripts {
  @{await Html.RenderPartialAsync("_ValidationScriptsPartial"); }
}
```

Your page should be complete. Listing 17.9 shows a full example of the page.

LISTING 17.9 The `Create.cshtml` Page Used to Create a New Customers

```
@model AspNet5AppSample.Models.Customer

@{
  ViewBag.Title = "Create Customer";
}

<h2>@ViewBag.Title</h2>
<form asp-controller="Customer" asp-action="Create" method="post"
  class="form-horizontal" role="form">

  <h4>Create a new customer.</h4>
  <hr />
  <div asp-validation-summary="ValidationSummary.All" class="text-danger"></div>

  <div class="form-group">
    <label asp-for="Name" class="col-md-2 control-label"></label>
    <div class="col-md-10">
      <input asp-for="Name" class="form-control" />
      <span asp-validation-for="Name" class="text-danger"></span>
    </div>
  </div>

  <div class="form-group">
    <label asp-for="Email" class="col-md-2 control-label"></label>
    <div class="col-md-10">
      <input asp-for="Email" type="email" class="form-control" />
      <span asp-validation-for="Email" class="text-danger"></span>
    </div>
  </div>

  <div class="form-group">
    <label asp-for="Notes" class="col-md-2 control-label"></label>
    <div class="col-md-10">
      <input asp-for="Notes" class="form-control" />
      <span asp-validation-for="Notes" class="text-danger"></span>
    </div>
  </div>
```

```
    <div class="form-group">
      <label asp-for="OptInEmail" class="col-md-2 control-label"></label>
      <div class="col-md-10">
        <input asp-for="OptInEmail" class="form-control" />
        <span asp-validation-for="OptInEmail" class="text-danger"></span>
      </div>
    </div>

    <div class="form-group">
      <div class="col-md-offset-2 col-md-10">
        <input type="submit" class="btn btn-default" value="Create" />
      </div>
    </div>

</form>

<div>
  <a asp-controller="Customer" asp-action="Index">Back to List</a>
</div>

@section Scripts {
  @{await Html.RenderPartialAsync("_ValidationScriptsPartial"); }
}
```

Run the application and click the Customers link. From the customer list page, select the Create New link (upper left). This should show the view as displayed in Figure 17.25. Enter a customer and click the Create button. You should be returned to the list of customers and should see your newly created customer in the list. You can also verify client-side validation by filling out an invalid form and trying to submit it to the server.

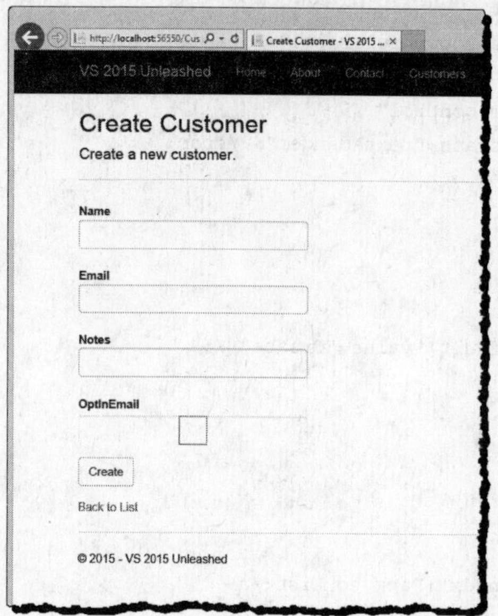

FIGURE 17.25 The `Create.cshtml` view for creating a new customer and posting it back to the controller.

Edit an Existing Customer

The Edit view is pretty much the same as the Create view. In fact, you can copy the markup inside the `Create.cshtml` page created in the prior example, add a line of code, change a couple cosmetic things, and you will have an `Edit.cshtml` page. The following walks you through this simple process (assuming you built the Create view earlier):

1. Right-click the `Customer` folder and choose Add, New Item.

   From the Add New Item dialog, select the MVC View Page template. Name the page `Edit.cshtml` and click the Add button.

2. Remove the default contents of `Edit.cshtml`.

3. Open the file you created in the prior example, `Create.cshtml`. Copy all the markup for the view. Paste this markup inside `Edit.cshtml`.

4. At the top of the page, change the page title (`ViewBag.Title`) to "Edit Customer." You can also change the contents of the `<h4/>` tag to "Edit an existing customer."

5. Edit the `<form/>` tag to point to the `Edit` action of the `Customer` controller as in the following.

```
<form asp-controller="Customer" asp-action="Edit" method="post"
  class="form-horizontal" role="form">
```

6. Add a hidden field inside the form for working with the `Customer.Id` property. You can use the TagHelper for `<input/>` to do so as in the following example.

```
<input asp-for="Id" type="hidden" />
```

7. Near the bottom of the markup, edit the Submit button value attribute to read Save (instead of Create).

The `Edit.cshtml` page is now complete. Run the application, and then click the `Customers` link at the top of the page. Select a customer from the list and click the Edit link. This brings up the page shown in Figure 17.26. Make a few changes and click the Save button.

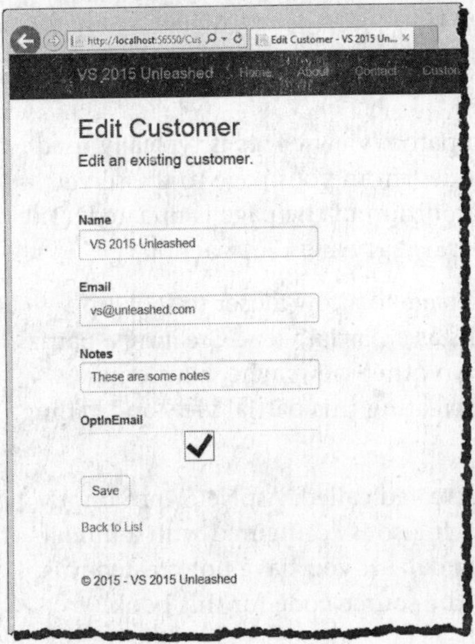

FIGURE 17.26 The `Edit.cshtml` view for editing an existing customer and saving the results to the database via the controller.

Delete a Customer

There is nothing more you need to do to process a delete request. Recall that the customer list view already includes an `ActionLink` for `Delete`. The controller accepts a `GET` request using a customer `Id` as a parameter. Simply run the code and select a customer you want to delete.

View Components, View Models, and Partial Views

The customer example presented thus far shows working with a complete model class (`Customer`) and single views (`Index`, `Create`, `Edit`) that represent a full page. However, there are times when you need to reuse part of a view across different pages. For these occasions, ASP.NET allows you to create partial views and the new view components.

Similarly, you may find yourself needing only a portion of a model class or a mix of a couple different objects and their properties. This is often the result of a specific view that does not map well to your individual model classes. In this case, you can create a view model. Let's take a look at each of these modular components.

Partial View

A partial view is markup that does not represent a full body section of your page. Instead, the markup is meant to be used inside another view. This solves the problem of view reuse across multiple pages in your site. Partial views can also be strongly typed to a model (or a view model). The convention for creating partial views is using the underscore in front of the file name, as in `_LoginPartial.cshtml`.

A common way that partial views are added to a page is using an `@Html` helper inside the parent page's markup. The helpers for displaying partial views are `@Html.Partial` and `@Html.RenderPartialAsync`.

An action method on your controller can also return partial views. This is typically used when sending an AJAX (asynchronous JavaScript) request from your page to the server (controller). The partial result is returned, and only a portion of the page is updated. (The page does not fully refresh.) In this case, you use the `PartialViewResult` action.

Let's consider an example. Suppose you are writing a page to allow a user to look up a customer by name. You might then display the results as a partial view. Creating a partial view that shows customer details may also be useful on other views where customer details are needed. The following walks you through creating this partial view and calling it asynchronously from the client.

1. This walkthrough builds on the site previously created called, AspNet5AppSample. It uses an ASP.NET 5 MVC 6 Web Site template. It also is configured with a model, controller, and views for working with customer data. If you have not created this site, you can also download this example from the source code for this book.
2. You can store all your partial views in the `Shared` folder as a common convention. Or you can reserve this folder just for site-wide partial views. In this case, the partial view is specific to the customer domain; therefore, we will store it in the Customer folder.

   Right-click the Customer folder and choose Add, New Item.

   From the Add New Item dialog, select the MVC View Page template. Name the page `_DetailsPartial.cshtml` and click the Add button.

   Remove the default contents from the view.
3. The markup for this partial view is straightforward. You start by strongly typing the partial view to a `Customer` instance. You then use the `@Html` helpers to create labels and values for the customer object. You can wrap the results in an `If` statement to verify a valid customer. Listing 17.10 shows an example.

LISTING 17.10 The `_DetailsPartial.cshtml` Partial View

```
@model AspNet5AppSample.Models.Customer

<hr />
<h3>Customer Details:</h3>

@if (Model != null)
{
  <div>
    @Html.LabelFor(model => Model.Name): @Html.DisplayFor(model => Model.Name)
    <br />
    @Html.LabelFor(model => Model.Email): @Html.DisplayFor(model => Model.Email)
    <br />
    @Html.LabelFor(model => Model.Notes): @Html.DisplayFor(model => Model.Notes)
  </div>
}
else
{
  <div>Customer not found.</div>
}
```

4. Next, create a view for entering a customer name and looking up the results. Create the view as an `MVC View Page` inside the Customer folder; name it `Lookup.cshtml`.

   The markup should include a text box for entering a customer name, a button for submitting a request, and a `<div>` tag to be a placeholder for the partial view. Listing 17.11 shows an example.

   Notice that the button is set to `<input type="button" ... />` instead of Submit. This is to prevent the form from submitting to the server. Instead, we will add some JavaScript code to load the partial view when the button is pressed.

LISTING 17.11 The `Lookup.cshtml` View

```
@{ ViewBag.Title = "Lookup Customer"; }

<h2>Lookup Customer</h2>

<form id="form-lookup">
  <div class="form-horizontal">
    <hr />
    <div class="form-group">
      @Html.Label("LookupName", "Customer name",
        htmlAttributes: new { @class = "control-label col-md-2" })
      <div class="col-md-10">
        @Html.TextBox("LookupText", "",
          htmlAttributes: new { @class = "form-control" })
```

```
      </div>
    </div>
    <div class="form-group">
      <div class="col-md-offset-2 col-md-10">
        <input type="button" id="buttonLookup" value="Lookup"
               class="btn btn-default" />
      </div>
    </div>
  </div>
</form>

<!--placeholder for the customer details-->
<div id="CustomerDetails">
</div>
```

5. Add a Scripts section to the bottom of `Lookup.cshtml`. Here you will use jQuery to trap the button click event. (jQuery is covered in greater detail in the following two chapters.) The jQuery load event will also be used to call the controller and load the partial view into the tag `<div id="CustomerDetails">`. Listing 17.12 shows an example.

   Notice the use of `@Url.Action`. This is server-side Razor code to create a URL for the partial view. The jQuery load event takes this URL along with any parameters you want to send. In this case, the parameters come from a jQuery selector for the text box. The parameter is defined as an object in the load method. Therefore, the jQuery method will send the request as an HTTP `POST` to the controller.

   This call maps to the controller method `DetailsPartial(string lookupText)`, which you will create in a moment. This method returns a partial view to be loaded into the `<div>` tag asynchronously (thanks to jQuery).

LISTING 17.12 The Button Click Event Loads the Partial View into the `<div>` Tag

```
@section Scripts {
  <script type="text/javascript">
    $('#buttonLookup').click(function () {

      //clear customer details
      $('#CustomerDetails').html("");

      $('#CustomerDetails').load(
        '@Url.Action("DetailsPartial", "Customer")',
        { lookupText: $('#LookupText').val() }
      );
    });
  </script>
}
```

6. Now let's add a method to the `CustomerController` to return the customer lookup page. This method is named `Lookup` and is straightforward, as shown here.

```
public IActionResult Lookup()
{
  return View();
}
```

7. Next, add another controller method for returning the partial view. Name this method `DetailsPartial`. It should take a string parameter to hold the text to look up from the customer database.

   Decorate the method with `HttpPost` to indicate it should be called using a `POST` method.

   After looking up the customer, use `PartialView` as the return value. This method can take the name of the partial view (`_DetailsPartial`) and the object you want to bind to this view (a `Customer` instance).

   The following shows an example of this controller method.

```
[HttpPost]
public IActionResult DetailsPartial(string lookupText)
{
  //get customer based on name
  Customer customer =
    db.Customers.FirstOrDefault(n => n.Name == lookupText);

  //return partial view
  return PartialView("_DetailsPartial", customer);
}
```

   This partial view example is now complete. Run the application and navigate to http://localhost:[your-port]/Customer/lookup (you can also add a link to this page). Type a name in the text box and click the Lookup button. Figure 17.27 shows the results.

View Component

ASP.NET 5 MVC introduces the concept of view components. A *view component* is a class that is responsible for rendering a portion of the response. This is similar to a partial view as discussed in the prior section. However, a view component has its own class that works like a controller. This keeps the code for the component separate from your regular controllers and self-contained. In addition, the class derives from `ViewComponent`, which makes coding and using these component views for complex tasks a bit easier.

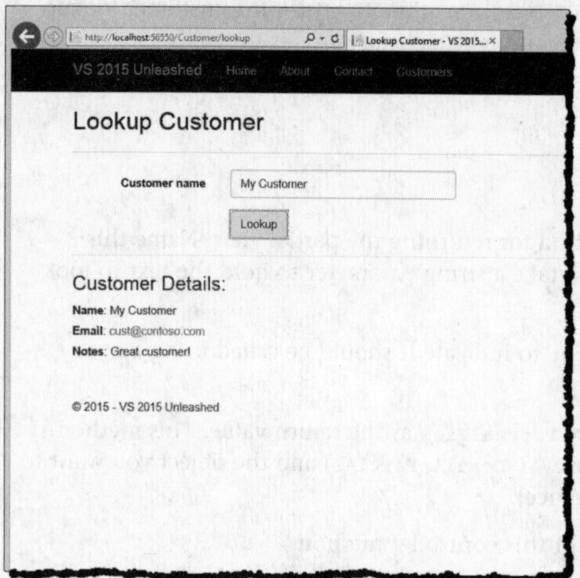

FIGURE 17.27 The `_DetailsPartial.cshtml` view being rendered inside the `Lookup.cshtml` view via the `jQuery.load` call to the controller.

Let's look at an example. The following builds on the customer example we created previously. Here, we will add a view to confirm the user's request to delete a customer. This page will use a view component we create. The view component consists of a class that derives from `ViewComponent` and a Razor view. The view can be any markup; in this case, we will leverage the `_DetailsPartial.cshtml` created in the earlier partial view example. Let's get started:

1. You can store your view components anywhere in your project. You might create a separate folder in which you store all of them, for example. In this case, we will simply store it inside the existing `Controllers` folder.

   Right-click the `Controllers` folder and choose Add, New Item.

   From the Add New Item dialog, select the class template. Name the class file `CustomerDetailsViewComponent.cs` and press the Add button.

2. Add `using` statements to the top of the class file for all of the following.

```
using Microsoft.AspNet.Mvc;
using System.Linq;
using AspNet5AppSample.Models;
```

3. Mark the class as inhering from `ViewComponent`, as in the following.

```
public class CustomerDetailsViewComponent : ViewComponent
```

4. Like the `CustomerController`, this `ViewComponent` will require a database context. Add a local variable to hold the `CustomerDbContext` instance and a constructor to set this instance. Listing 17.12 includes this code.

5. The `ViewComponent` class uses the methods `Invoke` and `InvokeAsync` to create and return an instance of the view.

   Add an `Invoke` method that takes an `id` parameter as `int`. The method should return the `IViewComponentResult` interface.

   Listing 17.13 shows the completed `ViewComponent` class.

LISTING 17.13 The `CustomerDetailsViewComponent` Class

```
using Microsoft.AspNet.Mvc;
using System.Linq;
using AspNet5Unleashed.Models;

namespace AspNet5AppSample.Controllers
{
  public class CustomerDetailsViewComponent : ViewComponent
  {
    private CustomerDbContext db;

    public CustomerDetailsViewComponent(CustomerDbContext context)
    {
      db = context;
    }

    public IViewComponentResult Invoke(int id)
    {
      Customer customer =
        db.Customers.FirstOrDefault(x => x.Id == id);
      return View("_DetailsPartial", customer);
    }
  }
}
```

6. You can use the `_DetailsPartial.cshtml` created in the prior example as the actual view markup. However, this page must be placed in a specific directory for ASP.NET to find your view based on the view component.

   Add a `Components` folder under `Views/Customer`. Then add a folder called `CutomerDetails` under the newly created `Components` folder.

   Copy a version of `_DetailsPartial.cshtml` into the `CustomerDetails` folder. We make a copy so as not to break the prior example. Figure 17.28 shows what Solution Explorer should look like.

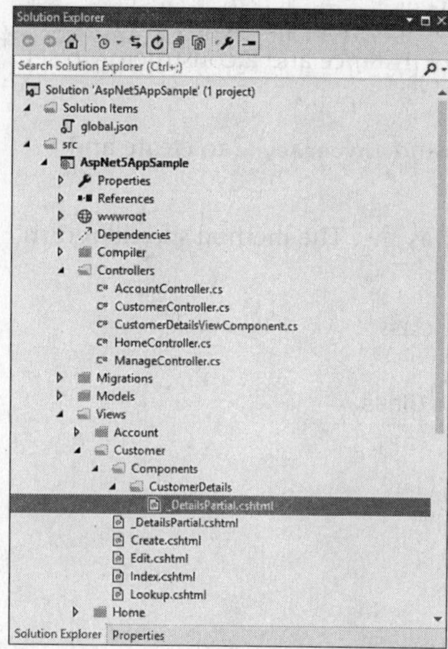

FIGURE 17.28 Place your view components in a folder named the same as your actual view component class (minus the words `ViewComponent`). This folder should itself be in a `Components` folder.

7. Add a new MVC View Page to the Views/Customer folder. Name the page `ConfirmDelete.cshtml`. This will serve as a confirmation page for deleting a customer (and not a view component or partial view).

   This view can be strongly typed to an `int` (customer ID). The customer ID will be bound to this page. The page will then use `Component.Invoke` method to call the view component, pass the customer ID, and display the partial view. Listing 17.14 shows an example of this view page.

   Note also that this page used an `ActionLink` to delete the customer. This calls the `CustomerController.Delete` method discussed earlier in the chapter.

LISTING 17.14 The `ConfimDelete.cshtml` File

```
@model int?

<hr />
<h3>Confirm Delete</h3>

@if (Model != null || Model != 0)
{
  <p>Are you sure you wish to delete this customer?</p>
  @Component.Invoke("CustomerDetails", Model)
  <br/>
```

```
  <b>@Html.ActionLink("Delete", "Delete", new { id = Model })</b>
}
else
{
  <div>Customer not found.</div>
}
```

8. Open the `CustomerController` class and add a method to show the ConfirmDelete.cshtml page. This method should take an `id` parameter and pass that `id` parameter to the page (which will then pass it to the view component). The following shows an example.

```
public IActionResult ConfirmDelete(int id)
{
  return View(id);
}
```

9. Open the Customer\Index.cshtml page and add another link to the navigational elements inside the table rows (near the bottom). This will be for the Confirm Delete view. You can leave the other Delete link in the table as a reference to the prior example. This markup should look like this:

```
<a asp-controller="Customer" asp-action="ConfirmDelete"
  asp-route-id="@item.Id">Confirm Delete</a>
```

Run the application to see the results. Select Customers from the top-level navigation. Select Confirm Delete for one of the existing customers. You should be presented with the page, as shown in Figure 17.29. Click the Delete button to delete the selected customer.

View Models

Not all your models will align directly to your views as they have thus far in the `Customer` model sample. Many times, you will have a page that needs to use multiple model classes to show a complete picture to the user. In this case, you create a view model with one property for each required model. It is called a view model because it only exists to service your views (and is not a representation of your data domain).

A view may also need page-specific values or calculations that have little to do with your model. Again, the approach here is to create a view model with properties specific to the requirements of the view.

View models are typically stored in their own folder in the solution called `ViewModels`. You create a view model by simply defining a class file (like other POCO models). This class will contain the properties for your view-specific model. These properties often extend one or more existing models from your regular model classes. You can then use that view model (in lieu of your actual model classes).

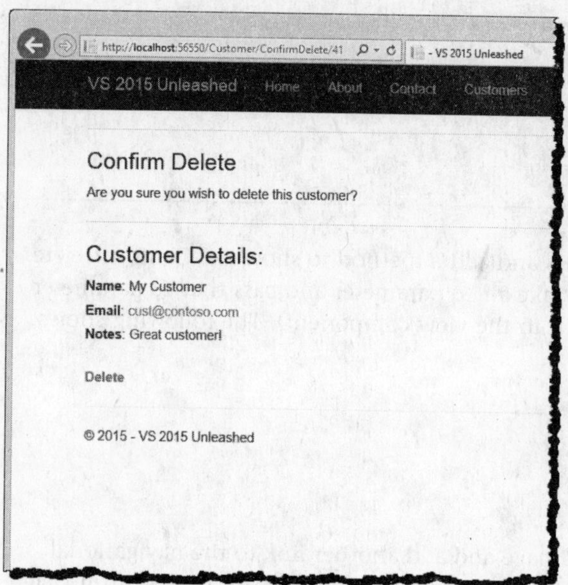

FIGURE 17.29 A view component showing customer details on the Confirm Delete page.

Using a view model involves strongly typing your view (as you have seen in the other examples) to this view model class. You then pass it to the view inside your controller method that handles the request. When the data is posted back to the controller, the controller is responsible for dealing with the model and making sure any database records are updated accordingly.

Using Scaffolding to Generate a Controller and Views

This chapter has presented the details of building a controller and views manually. However, Visual Studio 2015 ASP.NET 5 MVC 6 include a tool for generating a controller class and a set of basic views (create, delete, details, edit, and index) based on your model. This tool is found in the DNX command line (discussed previously) and is called `gen`. This can save a lot of time generating the basics. You can then adapt these files to your specific needs.

You can use `dnx . gen` from the Developer Command Prompt for VS2015 console. The following walks you through this process using the `Customer` and `CustomerDbContext` model classes created previously:

1. Start by creating a new project based on the ASP.NET 5 MVC 6 Web Site template. Name the project `DNXGenControllerViews`.

   You can open `project.json` and scroll to the "commands" section. There you will see the `gen` command definition for your project as, `"gen": "Microsoft.Framework.CodeGeneration"`.

2. Use Windows File Explorer to copy the `Customer` and `CustomerDbContext` classes from the prior model example (or the code download for this book) into the `Models` folder. Open each file and change the namespace definition to match your new project name.

3. Recall that in the prior model example you then set the database connection string inside `config.json`. You should repeat this process here. You should also have created the AspNet5Unleashed database in the prior model example. You will use that here too.

   The `dnx . gen` tool will need you to set the connection string in your DbContext class as well (at least until the code gen is complete). We will look at that in a moment.

4. As in the prior model example, open `Startup.cs` and add the `CustomerDbContext` to the `ConfigureServices` method as in the following.

```
services.AddEntityFramework()
   .AddSqlServer()
   .AddDbContext<ApplicationDbContext>(options =>
     options.UseSqlServer(Configuration
       ["Data:DefaultConnection:ConnectionString"]))
   .AddDbContext<CustomerDbContext>(options =>
     options.UseSqlServer(Configuration
       ["Data:DefaultConnection:ConnectionString"]));
```

5. Open `CustomerDbContext`. Add an override for the `DbContext OnConfiguring` method. Here use the `DbContextOptionsBuilder.UseSqlServer` method to pass a connection string to the generator during configuration. This is a viable approach. However, post code generation you can remove this method. The following shows an example of this override.

```
protected override void OnConfiguring(
  DbContextOptionsBuilder optionsBuilder)
{
  optionsBuilder.UseSqlServer(@"Server=(localdb)\ProjectsV12;
Database=AspNet5Unleashed;Trusted_Connection=True;
MultipleActiveResultSets=true");
}
```

6. You can now use `dnx . gen` to generate your controller and views from the `CustomerDbContext` object and related `Customer` model. To get started, open the Developer Command Prompt for VS2015 console (accessed from Windows Start, Developer Command Prompt for VS2015).

   Use the `cd` command to Navigate the prompt to the folder that contains your project.json file.

7. Next, you need to use DNVM to add a .NET runtime for use by the command window. You can do so using the `use` command. To see a list of available runtimes, type `dnvm list`. To bind a runtime to the path, use the following command at the prompt (where your version number matches that found in the `dnvm list`):

```
dnvm use 1.0.0-beta4
```

8. Next, execute the `dnx . gen` command. You tell the command to create a controller (views come along for the ride) by specifying the `-name` parameter. You then use `--model` parameter to set your model class. Finally, use `--dataContext` to point to your data context object. The following shows an example.

```
dnx . gen -name CustomerController --model Customer -dataContext
CustomerDbContext
```

You should now have a `CustomerController` class in the Controllers folder and a set of views in the Views/Customer folder. Figure 17.30 shows an example of the new files in Solution Explorer.

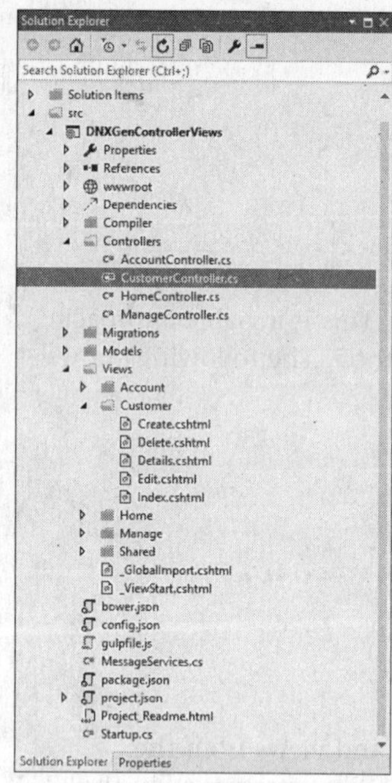

FIGURE 17.30 The generated controller and views for the `Customer` model.

Note that at the time of writing, the DNX tools generated scaffolding using the HTML Helper classes (and not the TagHelpers). These templates also require some cleanup for use with the ASP.NET 5 MVC 6 project template. The following walks you through this process (for the templates at the time of writing). You can also download this code from the book's source.

1. Each template includes a call to Layout at the top of the page. This is already in _ViewStart.cshtml and thus needs to be removed from each generated page.
2. Each view generated includes markup for `<html>` and `<body>`. All of this needs to be removed from each page (as it is already defined by _Layout.cshtml. Only the actual page elements and related Razor code should remain.
3. The Create.cshtml page is generated with an edit field for the `Id` property. This needs to be removed.
4. The pages do not include references to the validation script files. You need to add these to both Create.cshtml and Edit.cshtml at the bottom of the page. The following shows an example:

```
@section Scripts {
  @{await Html.RenderPartialAsync("_ValidationScriptsPartial"); }
}
```

Future versions may improve on the templates generated. In addition, this is an extensible framework. Therefore, look for additional templates to become available. You can now run the application and navigate to `/customer` to see the results.

Summary

This chapter started by showing the basics of a website processing from client to server using ASP.NET. We then introduced the new ASP.NET 5, which works with both the full .NET Framework and the new .NET Core. You can use it to build and run applications on Windows, Mac/iOS, and Linux/Android.

The new project template for ASP.NET 5 includes package managers for both server and client libraries. The server libraries are managed through the familiar NuGet. Client libraries now use the open source package manager, Bower (along with NPM and Gulp for related tasks).

ASP.NET 5 MVC 6 projects provide a powerful programming model for handling user requests. This includes a controller for processing a routed request, selecting a model object, and combining model with view to return to the user. We also looked at reuse with partial views, component views, and view models.

Visual Studio provides tooling that makes adding ASP.NET MVC features straightforward. You can use the Razor syntax and `@Html` helper methods for easily creating page markup. There is support for generating your database using EF7 migrations and the `dnx . ef` commands. You can also use the `dnx . gen` tool to create a controller and set of views based on your data model.

In the end, web developers should be excited by this latest release—the first since Microsoft open sourced ASP.NET.

CHAPTER 18

Using JavaScript and Client-Side Frameworks

IN THIS CHAPTER

- JavaScript Fundamentals
- Developing with jQuery
- Building Single-Page Applications (SPAs) with Client-Side JavaScript Frameworks

JavaScript has become the key language for client-side development of web applications. It runs in all browsers on all platforms on all device types, and it delights users with the increased interactivity, responsiveness, animations, and native-like feel it allows us to produce. JavaScript is required for writing client applications for ASP.NET or any other web server platform (PHP, Ruby, Python, and so on) because it runs on the client—all clients. JavaScript even extends to mobile applications, including Windows Store (WinJS) and cross-platform apps built with Cordova (see Part VII, "Creating Mobile Apps"). It's fair to say that if there is a Hypertext Transfer Protocol (HTTP) call involved, there is a good chance you'll need JavaScript skills to write a portion of the user interface.

There was a time when web developers all but ignored JavaScript. These developers wrote a lot of code that ran on the server, spent time making things look nice with Hypertext Markup Language (HTML) and Cascading Style Sheets (CSS), but used JavaScript sparingly for two reasons. First, JavaScript seemed complex because it is a dynamic language (and not very object-oriented). Second, the implementation of JavaScript to work with an HTML document object model (DOM) was different across browsers. This meant writing code for one browser and then fallback code to support other browsers and older versions. This was too much work. However, it resulted in the rise of JavaScript client frameworks.

JavaScript client frameworks ease the burden of writing cross-browser compliant JavaScript. They unlock the power of the ubiquitous nature of the language. These frameworks (such as the popular jQuery) make it easy to work with the

DOM for partial-page updates, animations, touch, responsive design based on screen size, client-side data interactivity, and similar. These frameworks continue to evolve and make developers more productive.

This chapter is not as much about Microsoft Visual Studio features as it is about using Visual Studio to write client-side code. Our intent is to give Visual Studio web developers a foundation for using these technologies in their applications to delight their users.

JavaScript Fundamentals

JavaScript and jQuery have become synonymous with web development. You use HTML to define content, CSS for presentation, and JavaScript for client-side behavior. We assume you have a good understanding of the first two; this section covers some of the key fundamentals of using the JavaScript language. We then cover what is now a key framework: jQuery.

Visual Studio, of course, supports client-side web development with JavaScript, jQuery, and many related client frameworks. Following these introductory sections, we explore building applications with Visual Studio that leverage JavaScript and some of the key client frameworks.

Storing and Using Scripts

JavaScript can be embedded directly inside a web page or stored as a separate script file. Before getting started with the language, let's look at where you can write JavaScript, how you store it, and how you can include it in your pages.

Embed Script on a Page

You can embed JavaScript code directly inside a page. This is true of `.html` pages and `.cshtml` views (and other .NET pages). The JavaScript will execute where it is found within the page. Later in this chapter, you will see how you can use events to determine when your JavaScript code should execute.

The JavaScript code placed inside a page should be contained within a `<script>` tag. The `<script>` tag looks like this.

```
<script type="text/javascript">
  //my client-side code
</script>
```

This `<script>` tag can sit anywhere within your HTML markup. However, it is recommended that you place the `<script>` tag (and JavaScript it contains) at the end of your page just before the closing `</body>` tag. Placing it elsewhere in the page makes the page load slower. This also ensures the DOM is loaded before your script is executed.

Code encountered by the browser's JavaScript parser that is not within a function (see "Functions" later in this chapter) will be executed as it is found. For example, the following alert will pop up as the page loads or is refreshed.

```
<script type="text/javascript">
  alert('hello world');
</script>
```

Code should be placed in functions and then called as part of a page or user event. We cover both functions and events later in the chapter. In fact, if you do need to run code when the page loads, there is an event for that purpose.

Create a Script File

If you are writing more than a few lines of JavaScript for your pages, it is often a best practice to store this code in its own file. This keeps your view markup separate from your code. It also increases the likelihood that you may be able to write some reusable JavaScript.

You create a JavaScript code file as any text file using the `.js` extension. Visual Studio allows you to create a JavaScript file for your project by right-clicking the project in Solution Explorer and choosing File, New Item. You can store your JavaScript files anywhere in your solution. It is common to create a directory named `src` (for source) to do so.

To use a JavaScript file on a web page, you can again use the `<script>` tag. In this case you use the `src` attribute of `<script>` to indicate the location of the script you want to use. The following shows an example. Again, be sure to place this at the end of your HTML markup, before the closing `</body>` tag.

```
<script src="~/lib/jquery/jquery.js"></script>
```

Visual Studio is not required for anything we discuss in this section. You can create everything here in a standard `.html` page, edit it in Notepad, add your JavaScript, and open the page in a browser. Of course, Visual Studio makes it easier to write JavaScript; this includes IntelliSense for the language. JavaScript is also part of the ASP.NET Model-View-Controller (MVC) projects you write using Visual Studio.

Writing JavaScript

JavaScript is not unlike C#. In fact, they both have their roots in Java. Hence, you will find many similarities—if you can read and write C#, you can read and write JavaScript. They both use brackets to group sections of code; end lines with semicolons; concatenate strings with +; use the logic operators `&&` (and), `||` (or), `!` (not); call properties and methods with dot notation; and use `this` as a keyword. The similarities continue from there: global and local scoping rules, `switch` statements, looping constructs (`for...next`, `do ...while`), conditions (`If...Else`), objects with properties and methods, functions with parameters, events, comments, operators, variables, functions, and more.

JavaScript does simplify data types using only numeric, string, and Boolean for simple types. Of course, you can create complex objects that include these types (and other objects). JavaScript also simplifies collections using only an array. However, all these items pretty much work the same as they do in C#. In fact, take a look at the following two code segments: one C# and one JavaScript. Notice that they are essentially the same; the primary exception is that the C# code is written inside a class (in this case, a Console application with the `Main()` method). The JavaScript code is just script (a class definition is not required). The other difference is that C# requires a delegate for a lambda expression (`findBike`). JavaScript simplifies this by allowing you to assign the function to a variable. In general, however, you should be able to read and write using both languages with a few semantic differences.

C#

```
delegate int search(string text);

static void Main(string[] args)
{
  string[] bikes = new string[]
    { "BMX", "10-Speed", "Cruiser", "Road", "Mountain" };
  var searchBike = "Road";

  //Lambda expression using a delegate
  search findBike = (string text) => {
    for (int i = 0; i < bikes.Length; i++)
    {
      if (text == bikes[i])
      {
        return i;
      }
    }
    return -1;
  };

  Console.WriteLine("Bike found at: " + findBike(searchBike).ToString());
  Console.ReadLine();
}
```

JavaScript

```
var bikes =
  [ "BMX", "10-Speed", "Cruiser", "Road", "Mountain" ];
var searchBike = "Road";

//Assign a function to a variable.
var findBike = function(text) {
  for (i = 0; i < bikes.length; i++)
  {
    if (text == bikes[i])
    {
      return i;
```

```
    }
  }
  return -1;
};

alert("Bike found at: " + findBike(searchBike));
```

The power of JavaScript is not necessarily the language; it is what you are able to do with the language. These tasks include manipulating the browser window and the document object model (DOM) on the user's computer running your page. This is the true power of JavaScript.

There are many ways to write functions, create objects, and manipulate the DOM; this variety is what makes JavaScript sometimes difficult to read and understand. The core language, however, should be pretty familiar. First, let's start with a deeper overview of some of the unique elements of JavaScript that make it different to C# developers. We will then look at harnessing some of the power to work with web pages inside a client's browser. Once you have adapted to working with JavaScript, you should become effective very quickly.

NOTE

If you really do need to start at the beginning with JavaScript, we hope you use this chapter as a primer. There are many other great resources out there, such as *Sams Teach Yourself Java in 24 Hours*.

Functions

We start with functions as that is the primary script code that JavaScript developers write. C# developers will notice that functions are not bound by namespaces or classes. Instead, they are just defined as script. You can then call these functions inside your page as a response to a user action or similar.

A JavaScript declarative function is code you write to execute an action and possibly return a value(s). Again, this should be familiar to server-side developers. Functions can be declared anywhere in your script, including as a method of a JavaScript object (more on this in a moment). You declare a function with the keyword `function`. You then name it, set any parameters inside parentheses, and use the `return` keyword to return a value from the function.

As an example, the following JavaScript function calculates the average speed (as miles/hour). Notice that it takes two parameters and uses the `return` keyword to provide the results.

```
//Calculate average speed using named function.
function averageSpeed(distanceMiles, timeMinutes) {
  return distanceMiles / (timeMinutes / 60)
}
```

You can call this function (inside the same script file or web page) by name. The following shows an example. Of course, in most cases a call to this function happens as the result of user action (clicked a button, navigated away from a field, etc.). And, the values you pass into the function would likely come from user input. We will see that shortly.

```
var speed = averageSpeed(22, 90);
```

Note that functions can return more than one value. You can do so using an array as the return type. However, if you need to return more than one value, it is often cleaner to return an object with multiple properties (see the "Objects" section later in this chapter).

The `averageSpeed` function is known as a *named function*. It has a name; can exist anywhere in your script; and can be called from anywhere in your script or on the web page. JavaScript interpreters look for named functions before executing any code. The interpreter finds these functions and loads then. It then looks for any script that is meant to be executed immediately (including those that call a named function) and then begins executing your code line by line as we will see next. Some functions are only called based on user action (click a button, select a value, etc.). The browser works with the JavaScript interpreter to execute those functions too.

Anonymous Functions

You will often write functions without names; a function without a name is known as an *anonymous function*. You write anonymous functions when you need the power of a function but do not intend to reuse that function throughout your code. These functions can also help prevent name conflict between multiple scripts used in the same page (as there is less likely a conflict if the function is unnamed).

For example, assigning a function to a variable uses an anonymous function. However, this creates a *function expression*. A function expression is when a function is used where the interpreter might normally expect to see an expression. The interpreter does not find these in advance of running your script. Instead, the interpreter encounters them as it executes your code, line by line. Therefore, you must declare your function expression (using an anonymous function) first, before calling it. The following shows the prior example now written (and executed) using a function expression.

```
//Calculate average speed with function expression.
var speed = function(distanceMiles, timeMinutes) {
  return distanceMiles / (timeMinutes / 60)
}
var mySpeed = speed(22, 90);
```

Immediately Invoked Function Expressions (IIFE)

There are also times when you will need the power of an anonymous function directly inside a line of executing code. These type of functions are known as *immediately invoked function expressions*, or IIFE (pronounced "iffy"). You write an IIFE by enclosing the function in parentheses, as in `(myFunction(){});`. You call the function directly using parentheses after the declaration, as in `(myFunction(){}());`.

The following shows the average speed calculation as an IIFE. In this case, the function is immediately executed by the interpreter when it encounters the line of code. It returns the value to the variable `bikeSpeed`. This value is then used in the alert message. (The function is not and cannot be called a second time.)

```
var bikeSpeed = (function (distanceMiles, timeMinutes) {
  return distanceMiles / (timeMinutes / 60)
}(22, 90));

alert(bikeSpeed);
```

Functions are everywhere in JavaScript. It is important that you understand these few key differences to work with them effectively. Functions can also be assigned to an object. In doing so, the function becomes a *method* of that object. Let's look at that next.

Objects

JavaScript can be used to define objects. These objects act like classes in that they contain properties and methods. Like other languages, you use objects in JavaScript to make your code more readable, easier to understand, and thus more maintainable. There are two primary ways to create objects in JavaScript: using the literal notation, and using the object construction notation. Let's look at each.

Literal Notation

You create an object using the literal notation by assigning a variable as the object name and then using brackets to contain the properties and method for the object. Each property and method is defined using a colon and separated by a comma. The methods are defined as a function. The following shows an object created in JavaScript using literal notation.

```
var ride = {
  bikeType: 'Road',
  weather: 'Clear',
  distanceMiles: 22,
  timeMinutes: 90,
  averageSpeed: function () {
    return this.distanceMiles / (this.timeMinutes / 60);
  }
}
```

Notice that in this example, the method `averageSpeed` used the `this` keyword to reference properties of the object.

You can also assign properties and methods directly to a blank object (or add properties and methods to an existing object). You do so with the dot notation. The following code starts by defining an object using empty brackets. It then adds properties and a method using assignment (=).

```
var ride = { };

ride.bikeType = 'Road';
ride.weather = 'Clear';
ride.distanceMiles = 22;
ride.timeMinutes = 90,
ride.averageSpeed = function () {
  return this.distanceMiles / (this.timeMinutes / 60);
};
```

Object Constructor Notation

The constructor notation allows you to create objects using a constructor (a method that is used to define an object). You can do so in two ways. First, you can create an instance of an `Object` type using the `new` keyword. You can then add your properties and methods to that object. The following shows an example.

```
var ride = new Object();

ride.bikeType = 'Road';
ride.weather = 'Clear';
ride.distanceMiles = 22;
ride.timeMinutes = 90,
ride.averageSpeed = function () {
  return this.distanceMiles / (this.timeMinutes / 60);
};
```

Second, you can use a function to write a named constructor for an object. This function will take the object values as parameters. It then uses the `this` keyword to define properties and methods. You can then use this constructor to create one or more instances of your object using the `new` keyword. The following shows this example.

```
function Ride(bikeType, weather, distanceMiles, timeMinutes) {
  this.bikeType = bikeType;
  this.weather = weather;
  this.distanceMiles = distanceMiles;
  this.timeMinutes = timeMinutes,
  this.averageSpeed = function () {
    return this.distanceMiles / (this.timeMinutes / 60);
  };

}
var myRide = new Ride('Road', 'Clear', 22, 90);
```

JAVASCRIPT AND INTELLISENSE

Visual Studio provides IntelliSense when working with JavaScript in the IDE. Figure 18.1 shows an example calling the `Ride` function with constructor notation.

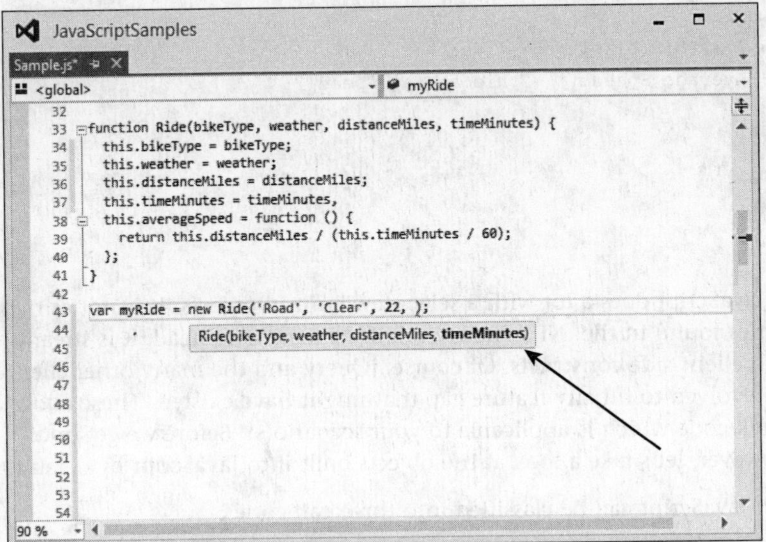

FIGURE 18.1 Visual Studio provides IntelliSense when working with JavaScript.

Using, Adding, and Removing Items

You can use an object's properties in methods with the dot notation. For example, to get the weather property for the ride object, you would write this.

```
var w = ride.weather;
```

You can also access this property using braces, as in the following.

```
var w = ride['weather'];
```

You can follow this same syntax for writing values like this:

```
ride.weather = 'Cloudy';
```

You can clear a property by setting it to a blank string as in this example.

```
ride.weather = '';
```

Alternatively, you can remove a property from an object. You do so using the `delete` keyword, as in the following.

```
delete ride.weather;
```

Finally, you can add new properties and methods to an object simply by defining them using the dot notation. The following shows an example of adding a method to an existing instance of `Ride` created using the constructor notation (last example of the prior subsection).

```
myRide.ToString = function () {
  return 'Bike type: ' + this.bikeType + ' Weather: ' +
    this.weather + ' Average Speed: ' + this.averageSpeed();
};

alert(myRide.ToString());
```

Built-In Objects

As you will discover, JavaScript does a lot with a select few built-in objects. It is not as rich as the base class libraries found in the .NET Framework, for example. Instead, it is streamlined for working with client-side constructs. Of course, jQuery and the many other client-side frameworks have evolved to fill any feature gap that might have existed. These allow you to select framework code which is applicable to your scenario(s). Before we get into those frameworks, however, let's take a look at the objects built into JavaScript by default.

The built-in objects in JavaScript can be classified into three categories:

- **Global JavaScript Objects**—These include a set of objects for handling data types (string, number, Boolean) and for processing real-world concepts (date, math, and regex).
- **Browser Object Model (BOM)**—An object that represents the user's browser (or tab). The topmost object is `window`. From there you can access `window.document`, `window.history`, `window.location`, `window.navigator`, and `window.screen`.
- **Document Object Model (DOM)**—A built-in object for working with the active web page in which your script is running. You use the `document` object for accessing the portions of the page, such as `body`, `head`, and `forms`.

In this section we cover the global objects. The section that follows discusses working with the BOM and DOM.

Working with Data Types

You have already encountered the JavaScript built-in objects representing data types of `String`, `Number`, `Boolean`, and `Object`. JavaScript is not typed, however. It is only when you assign a variable a string or numeric value does it know the variable is of a specific, built-in object. These are global objects in JavaScript. As such, they contain properties and methods for working with them. For example, the `String` object includes the property `length` for returning the number or characters in the string. Of course, it also contains many methods for doing basic string manipulation. Table 18.1 lists the properties and methods of the JavaScript `String` type.

TABLE 18.1 The Javascript `string` Object Properties and Methods

Property/Method	Description
`charAt()`	Method used to return a given character within the string based on a numeric index parameter.
`indexOf()`	Method used to get the numeric index value where a given character (or group of characters) passed as a parameter is first found within the string.
`lastIndexOf()`	Method used to get the numeric index value where a given character (or group of characters) passed as a parameter is last found within the string.
`length`	Property that returns the number of characters in the given string.
`replace()`	Method to search a string for a set of characters and replace them with another set.
`substring()`	Method used to return a portion of a string. Takes two parameters: start and end.
`split()`	Method used to split a string into an array of substrings based on a separator character (or regular expression).
`toUpperCase()`	Method used to change the characters in a given string to all uppercase.
`toLowerCase()`	Method used to change the characters in a given string to all lowercase.
`trim()`	Method used to remove whitespace from the start and end of a given string.

The `Number` object also has a few methods you can use. Table 18.2 lists these for reference.

TABLE 18.2 The Javascript `Number` Object Methods

Method	Description
`isNaaN()`	Method to verify that the value is a number.
`toExponential()`	Method to return a string representation of a given number showing the number using exponential notation.
`toFixed()`	Method to return a string representation of a given number rounded to a specified number of decimal points.
`toPrecision()`	Method to return a string representation of a given number rounded to a set number of places.

JavaScript also includes the data type definitions of `Undefined` and `Null`. `Undefined` indicates that a variable has been declared but has not been assigned a value. `Null` indicates that the given variable had a value at one time but currently does not.

Working with `Math`, `Date`, and `Regex`

JavaScript defines actual, global objects of `Date`, `Math`, and `Regex` for working with these concepts. The `Math` object, for example, contains properties and methods for doing math inside your JavaScript. Table 18.3 lists these items.

TABLE 18.3 The Javascript `Math` Object

Property/Method	Description
`Math.ceil()`	Method used to round a number up to the nearest integer.
`Math.floor()`	Method used to round a number down to the nearest integer.
`Math.PI`	Property to return the value of PI.
`Math.random()`	Method used to generate a random number between 0 and 1 (with decimal places).
`Math.round()`	Method used to round a number to the nearest integer.
`Math.sqrt()`	Method used to return the square root of a positive number.

As an example, suppose you needed to use the `Math` object to return random numbers between 1 and 10. The `Math.random()` method returns a number between 0 and 1 but with many decimal places. You can use the returned value, multiply it by 10, and then use `floor()` to round down the result. This will give you a number between 0 and 9. You can add 1 to get a number between 1 and 10. The following shows an example.

```
var rnd = Math.floor((Math.random() * 10) + 1);
```

The `Date` object is used to create an instance of a date (either the current date on the user's computer or a date you specify). The date is represented as the number of milliseconds since midnight on January 1, 1970. Of course, you can format this date to appear as you like.

For example, the following code create a `Date` instance based on the current date. The result is an alert box showing `Sun Mar 08 2015`.

```
var today = new Date();
alert(today.toDateString());
```

Table 18.4 lists the many methods of the `Data` object. You can, of course, use these in your code when working with a date concept.

TABLE 18.4 The Javascript `Date` Object

Method	Description
`getDate(), setDate()`	Used to get/set the day of the month.
`getDay()`	Returns the day of the week as a number (0 as Sunday to 6 as Saturday) for the given date/time.
`getFullYear(), setFullYear()`	Used to get/set the year.

Method	Description
`getHour(), setHours()`	Used to get/set the hour (0–23) of the given date/time.
`getMilliseonds(), setMilliseconds`	Used to get/set the milliseconds portion of the given date and time.
`getMinutes(), setMinutes()`	Used to get/set the minutes for the given date and time.
`getMonth(), setMonth()`	Used to return the month (0–11) for the given date and time.
`getSeconds(), setSeconds()`	Used to return the second (0–59) for the given date and time.
`getTime(), setTime()`	Used to get/set the time.
`getTimezoneOffset()`	Returns the time zone offset for a locale.
`toDateString()`	Returns the given date in a readable format.
`toTimeString()`	Returns the given time in a readable format.
`toString()`	Returns a string for the given date.

The `Regex` object is used to creating and executing regular expressions with JavaScript. These expressions help with pattern-matching and doing search and replace functions on text. For example, you can write a regular expression to determine if a given string matches a valid email address. `Regex` uses its own notation for describing patterns. This is a specialized notation of its own. Therefore, we do not cover it here. However, there are many good regular expression references available on the Web.

Working with the Browser Object Model (BOM)

One of the key purposes of JavaScript is to work with the BOM and the DOM. You use these objects to change your application inside the user's browser. This includes manipulating look and feel, navigating to other pages, modifying content on the page, and more. Let's start by looking at what you can do with the BOM.

The browser object model is a model of the current browser or tab in which your page is running. You access this model using the object `window`. This object gives you access to many of the features of the actual browser. For example, the JavaScript code `window.print();` will launch the browser's print dialog from your page. There are many such methods and properties of `window`—too many to list them all here. However, the following walks you through a few examples of using `window` in various scenarios.

Alert the User

You may have noticed that we've used the `alert` method a few times already in this chapter. This method allows you to display text to the screen. This can often be helpful when you're debugging JavaScript. The `alert` method is off the `window` object. You send an alert dialog as follows.

```
window.alert('Hello World');
```

Confirm User Action

You can use the confirm method to confirm whether a user wants to take a given action. This displays a dialog with an OK and Cancel button. The results are returned as `true` if the user presses OK. The following shows an example.

```
var isConfirmed = window.confirm('Are you sure?');
if (isConfirmed) {
  //Do something on true.
}
```

Open (and Close) a New Window

The `window.open` method allows you to create a new browser window. When you do so, you can load a page in the window. You can also set properties of the window itself, such as height and width. The following shows opening a new window and loading an About page.

```
var newWin = window.open("home/about", "newWin",
  "width=400, height=500", false);
newWin.focus();
```

You can then close the window using the `window.close` method. For example, you might add an anchor tag to the About page (as loaded in the prior example). This anchor tag can get set to call the `window.close` method, as in the following.

```
<a href="javascript:this.window.close();">Close</a>
```

Open a Window Relative to Another Window

The `window` object provides information on positioning. This includes determining the active windows left and top coordinates relative to the current screen. The following code shows an example of using this information to open a new window slightly offset inside the parent window.

```
var winWidth = 400;
var winHeight = 500;

var left = (window.screenLeft + 50);
var top = (window.screenTop + 50);

window.open('home/about', 'newWin', 'resizable=no,' +
  'width=' + winWidth + ', height=' + winHeight +
  ', top=' + top + ', left=' + left, false);
```

These are just a few of the things you can do using the `window` object. The `window` object also provides access to a number of child objects. These objects offer even more core features for manipulating the browser. For example, the screen object allows you to get the height and width of the screen, excluding the user's task bar (as `availHeight` and `availWidth`). Figure 18.2 shows the child objects of `window` and a brief description of each.

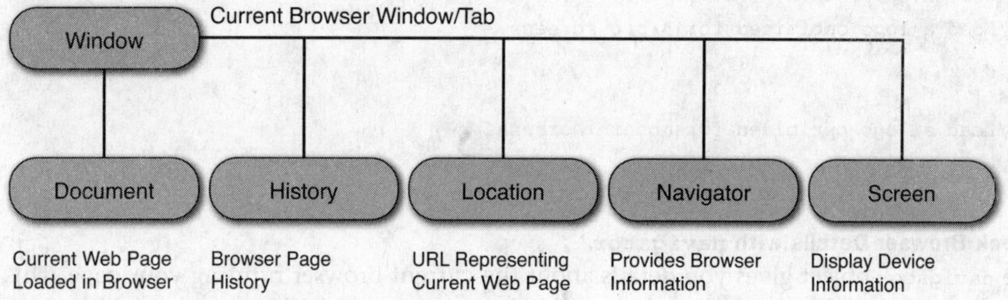

FIGURE 18.2 The Browser Object Model.

Let's look at a few more examples. Each of the following uses the `window` object along with its child objects shown in Figure 18.2.

Navigate with `history`

This `history` object allows you to work with URLs navigated by the user in the current browser, current session. This includes the `back` and `forward` methods for going to the previous URL and the next one in history. It also includes the `go` method for moving to a specific item in history.

The following example creates a back and forward link on your page. This is the equivalent of using the browser's Back and Forward buttons. If there is no page to go back or forward to, nothing happens.

```
<a href="javascript:this.window.history.back();">< Back</a>
<a href="javascript:this.window.history.forward();">Forward ></a>
```

Control the URL with `location`

The `window.location` object allows you to get information for the current URL as well as navigate to new URLs. You can use the `href` property to return the full URL, for example. You can also use it to send the user to a new URL. The following shows using the `reload` method to refresh a page when a user hits a link. (Of course, you could do the same for a button.)

```
<a href="javascript:window.location.reload();">Refresh</a>
```

Use the `screen` Object

The `screen` object gives you details about height (`height` and `availHeight`), width (`width` and `availWidth`), color resolution (`pixelDepth`), and color palette depth (`colorDepth`). You can use these properties to size make decisions about colors and window sizes. For example, the following shows using the `colorDepth` property to load a logo optimized for a user's screen.

```
if (screen.colorDepth <= 8) {
  //Load a logo optimized for 8-bit screens.
}
else {
  //Load a logo optimized for modern screens.
}
```

Check Browser Details with `navigator`

The `navigator` object gives you details about the current browser running your page. This includes whether the user has cookies enabled (`cookieEnabled`), the name of the browser (`appName`), the version of the browser (`appVersion`), the computer platform running the browser (`platform`), and more.

A common use of `navigator` is browser detection. All browsers are different; they all support the HTML, CSS, JavaScript standards in different ways. Sometimes you will have to program your JavaScript and HTML around the version of a given browser. You may also expect cookies to be enabled to run your application. With `navigator`, you can check in advance and notify the user if there are unmet constraints for using your application.

The previous BOM examples illustrate using the child objects of `window`. That is, with one notable exception: `document`. The `document` object gives you access to the actual document object model of the page. This is a much bigger (and widely used) object. Let's look at it next.

Document Object Model (DOM)

The DOM is created by a browser to represent the HTML of your current web page. You can then use this model in your JavaScript code to update elements. This includes changing values, updating styles, adding content to various sections of your page, and more.

Every browser implements the DOM differently. This inconsistent implementation gave rise to jQuery. In fact, most web developers now rely on jQuery where they would have previously used DOM methods. The jQuery framework takes these different DOM implementations into account and abstracts them from the developer. That said, it is still important to understand the DOM and be able to work with it either directly or with jQuery. This section presents an overview of working with the DOM before we dig into jQuery.

The DOM is represented by an object (`window.document`) with a standard set of methods for accessing nodes in the model. The model is the markup for a web page that is broken down into a hierarchy of nodes called a DOM tree. These nodes consist of four main types:

- **document node**—The topmost node representing the entire page of markup. All other nodes for the page are under the document node.
- **element nodes**—Nodes that represent elements in your HTML, such as `<h1>`, `<div>`, `<a>`, and `<p>`. Element nodes contain other element nodes. They can also contain attributes and text nodes.

- **attribute nodes**—An attribute node provides descriptive information about the element that contains the attribute. In the markup `<div id="header">`, for example, the DOM creates a node for `<div>` that contains an attribute, `id`.
- **text nodes**—Node representing the text contained within the element node. For example, `<h1>My Page Title</h1>` contains the text node "My Page Title" inside the element node for `<h1>`.

Let's look at how a DOM is built form a standard web page. Listing 18.1 show a simple HTML page.

LISTING 18.1 Markup of an HTML Page

```
<!DOCTYPE html>
<html>
<head>
  <meta charset="utf-8" />
  <title>Biking Ride Log - Home</title>
</head>
<body>
    <div id="header"
      style="background-color: lightgray; padding: 20px 20px 20px 20px;">
    <a href="Index.html" class="hlink">VS Unleashed</a> | 
    <a href="About.html" class="hlink">About</a>
  </div>
  <div id="content">
    <hr />
    <h1 class='pageTitle'>Biking Ride Log</h1>
    <ul id="navbar">
      <li><a href="Index.html" class="hlink">View logs by month</a></li>
      <li><a href="Rides.html" class="hlink">Log new ride</a></li>
      <li><a href="About.html" class="hlink">
        Edit ride options / metadata</a></li>
    </ul>
  </div>
  <div id="footer">
    <hr />
    <footer>
      <p>&copy; 2015 - VS Unleashed</p>
    </footer>
  </div>
</body>
</html>
```

The markup for this page is broken into DOM nodes. Figure 18.3 shows a hierarchical tree representation of the HTML markup in Listing 18.1. (A few attributes are omitted from the diagram for clarity.) These nodes are then accessible to your code using the `document` object. Each node has its own set of properties and methods for working with the node. You use these properties and methods to make changes to the content of the node and thus update the browser's rendering of your page. There are also methods for traversing the DOM via child nodes of an element, sibling nodes, and going back to parent nodes if needed.

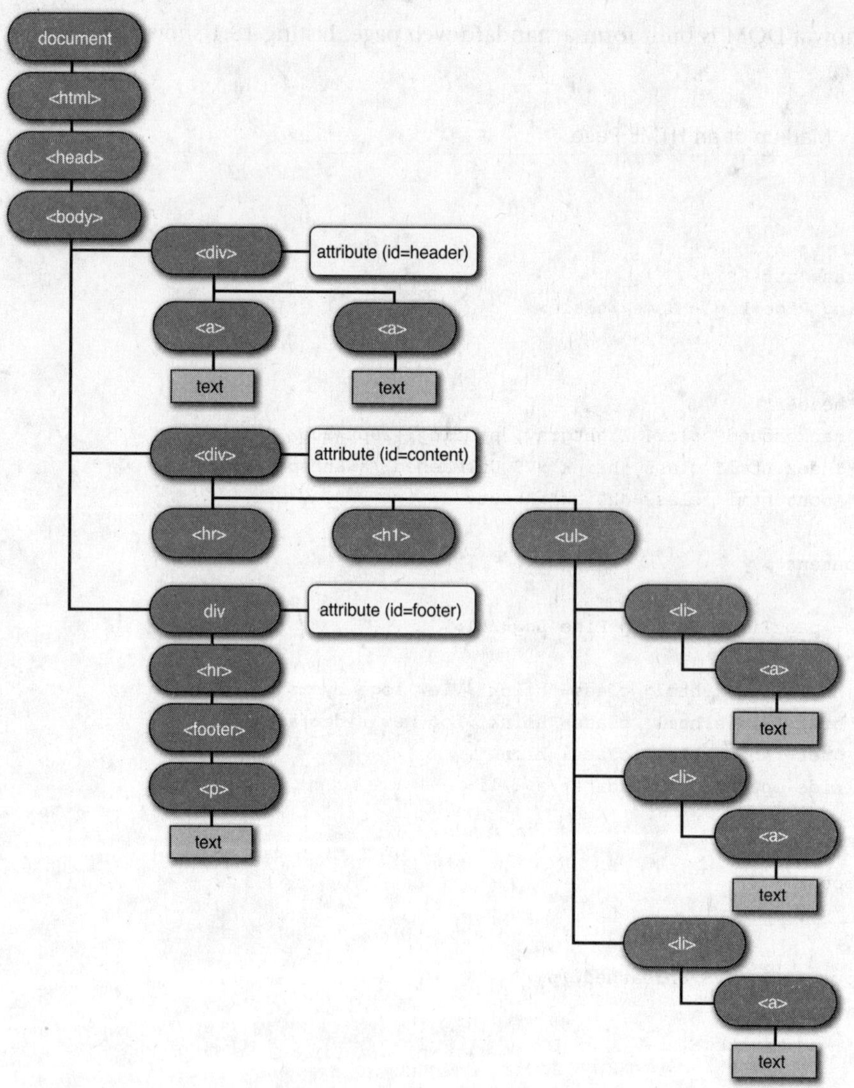

FIGURE 18.3 The DOM as a visual tree.

Accessing Elements (and Subnodes)

You use the many methods of the document object to access the items in the DOM tree. The method you should use depends on how you intend to access the node. You might query the DOM for a single element (`getElementById`), or you might be searching for a group of elements (`getElementByTagName`). Once you have a node, you can use other methods to traverse its child/sibling nodes. Let's look at a few examples.

NOTE

Everything discussed here is supported in the current version of modern browsers. However, there are some spotty support issues through the years. If you are using DOM methods, you should determine your target browsers fist. You should then verify support for your usage and test against your targets.

Select a Single Node

There are two primary methods for selecting a single node from the DOM. The first, `getElementById`, uses the unique nature of the `id` attribute to find an element based on its ID value. This is often the easiest method for finding a single node in the DOM. For example, the following JavaScript returns the node representing `<div id="header">` from Listing 18.1.

```
var divh = document.getElementById('header');
```

The second method for accessing a single node is `querySelector`. This method allows you to write specific CSS selectors to find the first matching element in the DOM. There may be more than one matching element, however, this method returns the first (if you need them all, see `querySelectorAll`). For example, to find a node using its ID, you can use the hash (#), as in the following.

```
var divh = document.querySelector('#header');
```

There are many such query selectors. Let's examine a few more. To get the `<h1>` in Listing 18.1 by CSS class name, you would write the following.

```
var hTitle = document.querySelector('.pageTitle');
```

You can use `querySelector` to get even more specific in your selection. For example, the following looks for an `<h1>` tag with the CSS class `.pageTitle` inside a `<div>` tag.

```
document.querySelector('div > h1.pageTitle')
```

You can also find a form element on your page. For example, if you were searching for the `<input>` of type `checkbox` that is checked, you might write this.

```
document.querySelector('#myform input[type="checkbox"]:checked')
```

You can use document.querySelector to select against the entire document. However, you can also use this method from a node to search only within that node. For example, the following uses getElementById to find the header node. You can then use querySelector to search within that node—in this case, to find the first anchor tag within the node (<div>).

```
var divh = document.getElementById('header');
var anchor = divh.querySelector('a');
```

Select a List of Nodes

There are times when you want to select all the nodes that match certain criteria. You may want to highlight certain required form fields on a page by changing their style, for instance. For these occasions, the document object includes methods that return all nodes that match a given criteria.

Nodes are returned as a NodeList, which is a special JavaScript collection object (not an array) containing nodes. Some objects return a static version of NodeList, which is essentially a snapshot of the list at the time the query was run. Others return a live NodeList. The live NodeList is updated as nodes inside your code change, are added, or are removed. The live NodeList has better performance, so be sure to choose a selection method accordingly.

You use the getElementByClassName method to return a live NodeList of elements that have the same CSS class. The following returns a list of nodes with the same CSS class named hlink. In Listing 18.1, this would be all the anchor tags. You might then use this list to disable some of these elements or change their style to highlight them in some way.

```
var cssList = document.getElementByClassName('hlink');
```

The getElementByTagName method allows you to select a live NodeList of elements based on the same HTML tag. You can use this to select a group of <img>, <div>, <a>, or any HTML element. Like the other node selection methods, you can use this method from document or from a given node. For example, the following selects a table by its ID. It then uses getElementByTagName to select each row in the table. You can then loop through each row and take action as required.

```
var tbl = document.getElementById('bikes-table');
var rws = tbl.getElementByTagName('tr');
for (var i = 0; i < rws.length; i++) {
  //Take some action with the row.
}
```

The querySelectorAll method works like the querySelector method but returns a NodeList (as a snapshot, not live). For example, the following returns the list items (<li>) under the <ul> tag, inside the <div> tag with the ID of content.

```
var listItems = document.querySelectorAll('#content > ul > li');
```

There are other object properties and methods that return `NodeList`, such as `childNodes` (which is a live `NodeList`). We look at some of this in the next section when discussing traversing elements (or nodes).

Traverse Nodes

Once you have selected a node, you may need to access its child nodes, sibling nodes, or parent. For example, you might search for a list definition such as `<ul>`; you can then access its children nodes as list items `<li>`. The DOM exposes methods for traversing your HTML model from one node to the other. Let's take a look.

WHITESPACE NODES

Most browsers treat whitespace (spaces or carriage returns) between nodes in your markup as actual text nodes. This means they are child nodes and siblings. You must take this into account in your DOM JavaScript. This is another reason libraries like jQuery exist; they take care of this issue on your behalf.

The following shows the code for the example just discussed. This code using the markup in Listing 18.1. It finds the `<ul>` by its ID and then loops through each child node using the `childNodes` property. We use `nodeName` to verify that the child node is a list item. Note that nodeName uses uppercase to reference nodes. We can then take action on that item (in this case, sending an alert to the user).

```
var list = document.getElementById('navbar');

for (var i = 0; i < list.childNodes.length; i++) {
  var listItem = list.childNodes[i];
  if (listItem.nodeName == 'LI') {
    //Do something with each list item ...
    alert(listItem.textContent);
  }
}
```

Many similar properties allow you to traverse the DOM based on its hierarchical structure. The `parentNode` property can be used to reference the containing element of a node, such as the `<ul>` element for a given `<li>` element. The `nextSibling` and `previousSibling` properties allow you to move from one node in a group to the next. For instance, if you have selected the first `<li>` item, a call to `listItem.nextSibling` would give you the next `<li>` item in the list. Finally, you can use the `firstChild`/`lastChild` properties to access a node's child nodes. This is similar to the `childNodes` mentioned earlier. However, it simply takes you directly to the first child in the group (or the last one).

Working with Elements (and Subnodes)

Once you have selected a node or a `NodeList`, you likely want to take action on that element (or elements). The JavaScript DOM provides methods for accessing the text of an element, the value, an attribute within the element, or the actual HTML contained within the element. There are also methods for adding and removing elements to the DOM. Let's take a look at working with selected nodes.

Update Text of a Node

The `textContent` property gives you the actual text contained within a given node. You can use this property to both read and write text. As an example, the following finds the `<h1>` in Listing 18.1. It then uses `textContent` to change the title of the page.

```
var titleNode = document.querySelector('div > h1');
titleNode.textContent = "Bike Page Title";
```

Change a Node Attribute

Sometimes you will need to look within a given element at its attributes. The DOM exposes methods for checking attributes (`hasAttribute`), reading attributes (`getAttribute`), writing/adding new attributes (`setAttribute`), and removing attributes (`removeAttribute`).

As an example, the following uses `getAttribute` to verify that the given element has a class defined as `pageTitle`. It then uses `setAttribute` to add a `style` definition to the `<h1>` element. Notice that when it does so, it sets parameters as `name, value`.

```
var titleNode = document.querySelector('div > h1');
if (titleNode.getAttribute('class') == 'pageTitle') {
  titleNode.setAttribute('style', 'font-size: xx-large; color: red;');
}
```

Edit the HTML Content of a Node

The DOM provides the `innerHtml` property to get, set, and even replace the entire contents of an element with new HTML you expect the browser to render. A common use is to replace a portion of your page based on an AJAX call to your server. You use the `innerHtml` property (or the equivalent `jQuery.html` property) to do so.

However, `innerHtml` can be used to execute code you did not intend for your site (cross-site scripting attack). Therefore, be sure to only insert strings obtained from a trusted source. Untrusted strings include the query string, cookies, or user input (forms). If you use content that a user can manipulate, you must escape that content using an encoding method. We will look at using `innerHtml` (and `jQuery.html`) in coming sections.

> **NOTE**
>
> A common mistake is using `innerHtml` when you only need to insert plain text within your page. In this instance, the `textContent` property is more secure because the parser does not interpret the text as HTML but just as raw text. Use `innerHtml` when you are in full control of the string to be output to the page (see earlier).

There are other ways to add HTML to your page more specifically. We look at those next.

Add/Remove Elements from the DOM

You can use specific methods for adding nodes to the DOM. These methods include `createElement` and `createTextNode`. When you use these methods, you add the created node to the DOM. You then tell the DOM where you want the items to be placed within the DOM tree using `insertBefore` or `appendChild`.

As an example, the following creates a new hyperlink to be used in the `navbar` list, as defined in Listing 18.1. It uses `createElement`, `createTextNode`, `setAttribute`, and `appendChild` to do so.

```
//Add an HREF to the DOM.
var hlink = document.createElement("a");
hlink.href = "Map.html";
hlink.setAttribute('class', 'hlink');

//Create text for the link.
var linkTxt = document.createTextNode("Map new ride");

//Add text to the link.
hlink.appendChild(linkTxt);

//Create a list item and add the HREF.
var listItem = document.createElement("li");
listItem.appendChild(hlink);

//Find the list on the page.
var list = document.getElementById('navbar');

//Add the li link to the list.
navbar.appendChild(listItem);
```

You can also use `removeChild` to remove a given node from the DOM. Every node in the DOM is a child of another node (the outermost node being document). Therefore, every child can be removed.

TIP: EXPLORING THE DOM

You can explore the DOM generated for your web page from within most modern web browsers. Internet Explorer (IE) allows you to access the DOM via the F12 debug tools. Figure 18.4 shows an example of the DOM Explorer for the page shown back in Listing 18.1. Here you can select an element and view information such as styles and layout.

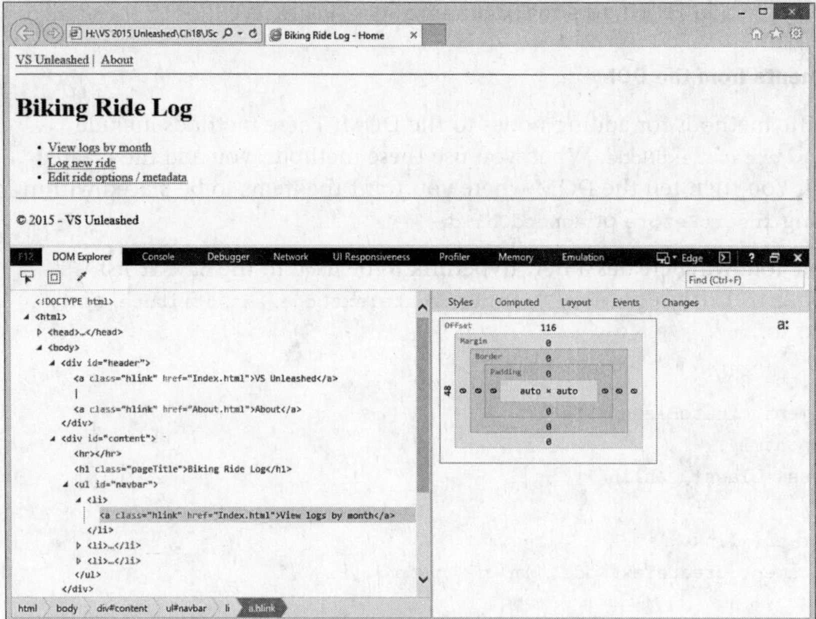

FIGURE 18.4 Use IE's F12 tools to explore the DOM.

Events

JavaScript is used to run client code in the browser as a reaction to a user taking action or something on the page happening. These actions are triggered events to which you can subscribe by writing event-handling functions. There are dozens of events, such as the page loading, the user clicking a button, the Tab key being pressed, a hyperlink being selected, and the browser being resized.

Events are based on a publisher-subscriber pattern. Objects already expose events that will be triggered when certain things happen. You can then write code to subscribe to these events. In doing so, your code will then be called when the event bubbles up.

Let's take a look at an example. Imagine that you have the markup shown in Listing 18.2. This page provides a text box to enter a distance (miles) and a text box to enter time (in minutes).

NOTE

This code can be found in the download for the book in the JavaScriptSamples project, VsUnleashedSampleCode folder, average-speed-dom.html page.

LISTING 18.2 HTML Markup for a Calculator Page for Average Speed

```
<!DOCTYPE html>
<html>
<head>
  <meta charset="utf-8" />
  <title>Biking Ride Log - Average Speed</title>
</head>
<body>
    <div id="header"
      style="background-color: lightgray; padding: 20px 20px 20px 20px;">
    <a href="Index.html" class="hlink">VS Unleashed</a> | 
    <a href="About.html" class="hlink">About</a>
  </div>
  <div id="content">
    <hr />
    <h1 class='pageTitle'>Calculate Average Speed</h1>
    <form action="/" method="post">
      <label>Distance:</label>
      <input id="distance" type="text" name="distance" value="" />
      <br />
      <label>Time (minutes):</label>
      <input id="time" type="text" name="time" value="" />
      <br /><br />
      <div id="calculation">
        <label>Average speed (miles/hour): </label>
        <label id="averageSpeed"></label>
      </div>
    </form>
  </div>
  <div id="footer">
    <hr />
    <footer>
      <p>&copy; 2015 - VS Unleashed</p>
    </footer>
  </div>
</body>
</html>
```

Now suppose you want to add client-side code to calculate average speed anytime a user enters a new value into one of the text boxes. You can do so using events. The following walks you through this process:

1. Add an event listener to the page to respond to the page load event. When the page loads, you want a custom function you will write called `winLoad` to execute. The following shows an example.

```
window.addEventListener('load', winLoad);
```

2. Inside the `winLoad` function, you want to add event listeners to both the Distance and the Time text box. The event you want to trap is lost focus. This event is called *blur* in JavaScript. When you trap this event, you plan to call another custom function you will write called `calculateSpeed`. The following shows an example of `winLoad`.

```
function winLoad() {
  var distTxt = document.getElementById('distance');
  var timeTxt = document.getElementById('time');

  distTxt.addEventListener('blur', calculateSpeed);
  timeTxt.addEventListener('blur', calculateSpeed);
}
```

3. You need to write the `calculateSpeed` event handler function. This event handler will look up the values from the text boxes. It then verifies that each value is numeric using `!isNaN` (which means "not is not a number"). The following shows an example.

```
function calculateSpeed(e) {

  var dist = document.getElementById('distance').value;
  var time = document.getElementById('time').value;

  if (!isNaN(dist) && !isNaN(time)) {
    var avg = document.getElementById('averageSpeed');
    avg.textContent = (dist / (time / 60));
  }
}
```

You can now run this sample in the browser. When you enter valid numbers into both the Distance and Time text boxes, notice that the average speed is updated on the page as soon as focus changes from one of the text boxes to anything else on the page.

The prior example used the `addEventListener` method for adding events to a given object. This is the explicit (and often preferred) method for registering your events. However, you can also use what is called *inline event subscription* to register an event. This simply means attaching the event as an attribute of the markup or as a property of the object. For example, you could register the text box blur events for Listing 18.2 directly in the markup as follows.

```
<input id="distance" type="text" name="distance" value=" "
  onblur="javascript: calculateSpeed();" />
```

```
<input id="time" type="text" name="time" value=" "
  onblur="javascript: calculateSpeed();" />
```

Alternatively, you could register these events using the object. The following shows edits to the `winLoad` method written previously.

```
distTxt.onblur = calculateSpeed;
timeTxt.onblur = calculateSpeed;
```

Stopping Events

There are a few more things you can do when working with events. First, you can remove an event handler you have already registered using `removeEventListener`. This method works just like `addEventListener` (but has the opposite result).

Next, most events have a default action. For example, if you trap the click event of an `<input>` whose type is check box, the default action is to check the box. You can cancel default event actions using the method `preventDefault`. Recall that the event handler we wrote in the example `calculateSpeed(e)` took the argument `e`. JavaScript sends you the `event` object should you need it in your handler. In this case, a call to `e.preventDefault();` will stop the event's default action.

Finally, events are said to "bubble up" the event chain and thus call any subscribers in the chain. For example, you may have an event handler subscribing to a button click. You may have another global event defined at the document level for handling such actions. You can use the `stopPropagation` method of the `event` object if you need to cancel an event from bubbling up the chain.

The Many DOM Events

There are events for nearly everything that can happen on a given web page. These events are connected to the window object, the form, the mouse, and the keyboard. The following lists just some of the many events to which you might need to subscribe. (This is not a complete reference.)

- **Window events**—`load, beforeonload, blur, error, focus, resize, unload`
- **Form events**—`blur, contextmenu, focus, invalid, submit`
- **Keyboard events**—`keydown, keypress, keyup`
- **Mouse events**—`click, dblclick, drag` (and related), `drop, mouseover, scroll`
- **Media events (such as video playback)**—`canplay, durationchange, ended, pause, playing, progress, volumechange`

Developing with jQuery

The jQuery client-side framework simplifies the tasks of working with the DOM as described in the prior section. This includes providing easier access to elements and their attributes using the jQuery CSS-style selectors. It also makes working with these selected elements easier. For example, you can act on a group of selected items with a single line of code; no looping code is required. jQuery also makes creating event listeners easier. And it provides methods for calling the server asynchronously from the client (AJAX). Best of all, it makes the DOM code you write compliant with both new and older browsers—without the need to write fallback code.

It is important that you also understand the default JavaScript DOM selectors, events, and actions discussed in the prior section. These traditional techniques make you even more effective when writing JavaScript and working with jQuery.

jQuery is by far the single most used client-side framework on the Web. It is estimated that nearly one-third of all websites use jQuery. This number is much higher for newly created sites. If you are doing web development today, it is highly likely that you are writing JavaScript using the jQuery framework.

NOTE

There is a lot you can do with jQuery. We cover the core concepts here. You can also use it to quickly build small controls like panels, centered model dialogs, accordions, image rotators, and more. There are also jQuery plug-ins available. For a full reference, see the site, jQuery.com.

jQuery in Your Visual Studio Project

The jQuery framework is part of nearly all the Visual Studio web project templates. This includes the readable version of the file (useful for debugging) `jquery.js` and the minified version (for faster processing in production) `jquery-min.js`. Recall from Chapter 17, "Building Modern Websites with ASP.NET 5" that these files are stored in the `bower_components` folder of the ASP.NET 5 Web Site template and end up in the `wwwroot/lib/jquery` folder. Chapter 17 also introduced Bower and the `bower.js` file for including client scripts in your project. The ASP.NET 5 template uses this approach to include jQuery in the project.

Recall from the prior section that you need to add a reference to your page for any JavaScript files you intend to use. Again, you do this using the `<script>` tag at the bottom of your HTML markup, before the closing `</body>` tag.

Of course, adding this reference to every page in your site can be tedious. Chapter 17 also introduced the concept of the `_Layout.cshtml` page in your project. Recall that this page controls common layout items for each page in the ASP.NET 5 MVC 6 template. Thankfully, this page also includes the jQuery `<script>` tags based on deployment environment, as shown in Figure 18.5. This means all your pages in the site that use `_Layout.cshtml` already have access to jQuery.

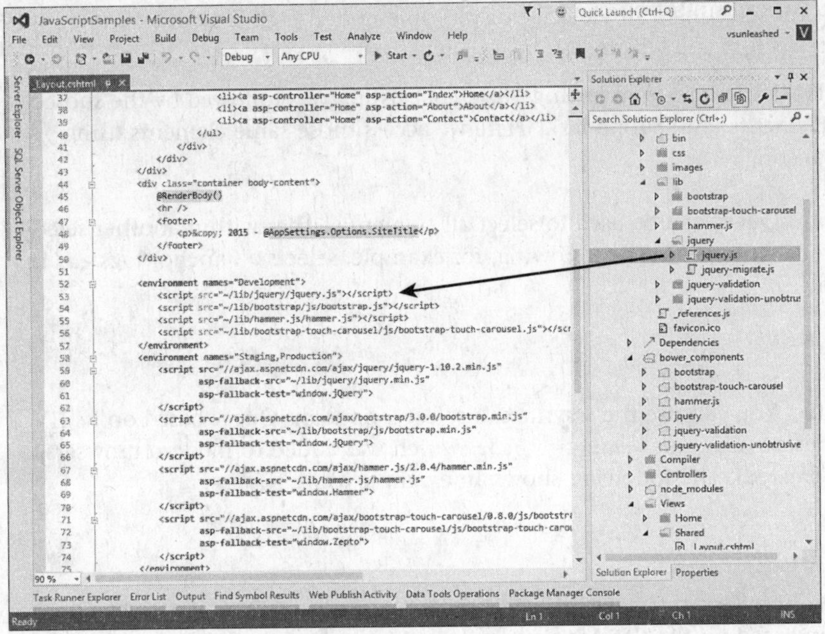

FIGURE 18.5 The jQuery library is included in all your pages by default when using the ASP. NET 5 MVC 6 project template (and others).

Selecting Elements

As you saw in the prior section, the DOM provides methods such as `getElementById` and `querySelector` for accessing element nodes. jQuery exposes similar methods but with a more straightforward and powerful syntax for doing DOM selection. It allows more finite selection based on element, ID, class, or CSS. It also allows you to filter your selection. Finally, it allows you to select a single node or multiple nodes using the same selection syntax.

THE JQUERY OBJECT AND $

Like the JavaScript `document` object for working with the DOM, jQuery provides the object `jquery` for calling the many methods of jQuery. This includes doing selection. jQuery also provides the shortcut `$` as a replacement for `jquery`. This means that `jquery.hide()` and `$.hide()` are equivalent.

Basic Selectors

The jQuery framework includes a single method for doing selection, `$('')`. This method is flexible with respect to what you pass as your selection. It also returns a jQuery object that includes a reference to each node in your selection. You do not, therefore, need to use separate methods for selecting a single node or multiple nodes. Let's look at examples of a few basic jQuery selectors you will use often.

First, recall the HTML markup from Listing 18.1. That listing was followed by the subsection "Accessing Elements (and Subnodes)." Here we access those same elements using jQuery for comparison.

Select an Element jQuery can be used to select all elements either within another selection or within your entire page. The following, for example, selects all anchor tags `<a>` in a given document.

```
var sel = $('a');
```

Select Based on ID You can use the # syntax to select a node in jQuery based on its ID. This is similar to using `document.querySelector` (which was added to modern browsers after jQuery was created). The following shows an example using jQuery.

```
var sel = $('#header');
```

Select Using CSS The jQuery framework selection is made especially powerful by allowing finite selection based on the CSS for a given item. You can select all items with the same CSS class. However, many times you are looking for a specific element within other elements. The following example selects an `<h1>` tag with the CSS class `pageTitle` nested inside a `<div>` tag.

```
var sel =  $('div > h1.pageTitle');
```

Combination Selections You can use jQuery to return a group of items that match more than one single selection. To do so, you simply separate your selections by a comma. The following selects all `<a>` tags and the `<title>` tag with the class name `.pageTitle` (from Listing 18.1).

```
var sel = $('a, .pageTitle');
```

Selection Filters

The jQuery selectors allow you to filter your selection by a variety of criteria. This allows you to further narrow your selection to the item for which you are seeking. Selection filters are created with a colon, as in `:filter`. For example, the following selects an anchor tag using the `:contains()` filter to find only elements containing the given text.

```
var sel = $('a:contains("ride")');
```

There are many jQuery filters you can add to your selectors—more than we can list here. However, Table 18.5 lists some common filters you might find yourself using. Some of these use the colon notation inside the selector; others are written using the dot notation following the actual selector. Note that form item filters are listed in Table 18.6.

TABLE 18.5 The jQuery Selection Filter

jQuery Filter	Description
`:not(selector).not()`	Selects all elements in the selector but filters out those in the "not" sub selection. You can use as part of the selector (using a colon) or as a method after the selector (using the dot notation).
`:first, :last`	Selects the first or the last element in the selection.
`:focus`	Filters the selection for the items that have the current focus in the browser.
`:animated`	Finds elements in the selection that are currently being animated.
`:has(selector).has()`	Provides a subselection on the given elements selected. For example, `div:has(a)` finds all the `<div>` tags that contain at least one `<a>` tag.
`:hidden`	Filters the selection for only items that are hidden in the markup.
`.filter()`	Allows you to further filter your selection, as in `$('a').filter('.hlink');`.
`.find()`	Used to find decedents in the selected elements based on another selector.

Form Selectors

Another common use of jQuery selectors is finding form elements. You often need to work with these as the user is working with them. For example, the following finds all the input tags on the page inside the `<div>` tag with the ID of `userForm`.

```
var sel = $('#userForm :input')
```

You can refine your form searches further with other filters. Table 18.6 lists a number of additional form-based jQuery select filters.

TABLE 18.6 The jQuery form Element Selection Filters

jQuery Filter	Description
`:text`	Filters the selection for `<input>` tags of type text
`:password`	Filters the selection for `<input>` tags of type password
`:radio`	Filters the selection for `<input>` tags of type radio
`:checkbox`	Filters the selection for `<input>` tags of type checkbox
`:submit`	Filters the selection for `<input>` tags of type submit
`:image`	Filters the selection for `<input>` tags of type image
`:button`	Filters the selection for `<input>` tags of type button

jQuery Filter	Description
`:selected`	Filters the selection for selected items in a drop-down list
`:checked`	Filters the selection for all checked items in a group of radio buttons or check boxes
`:disabled`	Filters the selection for all disabled input elements

Acting on Your Selection

You can act on your selection results immediately, within the same line of code. jQuery allows you to simply call a method of the returned selection (or another jQuery method) directly from the selection. Alternatively, you can store the results in a variable for use later in your code (as the preceding examples have shown).

This example finds the selection and then acts on it immediately, as a group, using the jQuery `addClass` method to add a CSS class to each item in the selection.

```
$('a').addClass('alink');
```

You can also store your selection for later use. When you do so, jQuery stores a reference (not a copy) to the elements in the selection. You can then use the returned jQuery object to call other jQuery methods, as in the following:

```
var sel = $('a');
sel.addClass('alink');
```

The examples in the following sections will use both approaches to acting on your jQuery selections.

Traversing Your Selections

As with the DOM, you can traverse jQuery selected results based on child, sibling, or parent nodes. In fact, traversing your jQuery results is nearly the same as the DOM but with a few more methods at your disposal. The methods for traversing jQuery object nodes include `.parent()`, `.parents()`, `.children()`, `.siblings()`, `.next()`, and `.prev()`.

As an example, the following shows finding all child nodes of `<li>` inside the `navbar` `<ul>` shown back in Listing 18.1. Recall that this example in the "Document Object Model (DOM)" section of the chapter was more than five lines of code to get this selection.

```
var sel = $('#navbar').children('li');
```

Looping Through Your Selection

As you saw previously, you do not often need to loop through items in your results. Instead, you can act on them as a whole using the jQuery methods. However, there are times when you do need to access each item in your results. The jQuery framework provides the `.each()` method for this purpose.

The `.each()` method takes a function as a parameter. This function is executed for each item in your selection. You can access each item inside the function using `$(this)`.

The following shows an example (again from Listing 18.1). Here, a selection is made for all the items in a list. We then loop through each item in the list. If the text contained within the `<li>` item (in this case, the anchor text) starts with the substring `View`, we add a class to the given anchor tag (child of the `<li>`).

```
var sel = $('#navbar').children('li');

sel.each(function () {
  if ($(this).text().substring(0, 4) == 'View') {
    $(this).children().addClass('alink');
  }
});
```

You can also access specific items within your selected results by index value in the collection. To do so, you use the `.eq(0)` method and pass the index of the item you want to access as an argument.

Accessing Selection Content

Your selected objects in jQuery are returned as a jQuery object that maintains a reference to the DOM node. This is different from objects returned by the `document` selectors. Therefore, jQuery provides its own methods for working with your selected results. Chief among them are `.html()`, `.text()`., and `.val()`.

The `.html()` method returns the HTML inside the selected element. If more than one element is in your results, only the HTML contained inside the first element is returned. As an example, the following selection returns all the `<li>` items inside the `<ul>` in Listing 18.1.

```
var sel = $('#navbar').children('li');
var ht = sel.html();
```

However, the call to `.html()` in the preceding code returns only the markup that follows. Of course, you can use `.each()` to return each item in the given selection, one by one.

```
<a href="Index.html" class="hlink">View logs by month</a>
```

The jQuery `.text()` method returns all the text found within your selection. This means if you select more than a single element with text, you will get all the text appended to each other with no spaces. Consider the following example.

```
$('#navbar').children('li').text();
```

This example returns the string `View Logs by monthLog new rideEdit ride options / metadata`. This is useful if you intend to search this string or work with it as a whole.

However, you can refine your selection (or use `.each()`) if you intend to work with just a single element's text.

You use the `.val()` method to get at the content contained in a form element or `<input>` tag. For example, the following returns the value entered in the `<input id='distance' />` from Listing 18.2.

```
var val = $('#distance').val();
```

You can use the selected HTML, text, and value methods to change your content, too. You do so simply by passing the new value into the given method. The following shows a couple examples.

```
$('.pageTitle').text('New Page Title');
$('#distance').val('50');
```

Changing Elements/Attributes

You can replace or modify your HTML using `.html()`. However, the more likely scenarios is to add more information to the HTML, remove something, or append other elements. Let's look at these examples next.

Append/Remove Items

jQuery supports building parts of your HTML using code. Once you have a selection, you can use the methods `.remove`, `.replaceWith()`, `.before`, `.after`, `.prepend`, and `.append`. This is true if your selection is an element node or the HTML content.

For example, the following code appends an additional `<li>` item to the `navbar` list from Listing 18.1.

```
$('#navbar').append('<li>Import ride date from race computer</li>');
```

As another example, suppose you want to work with each HTML element within a selection. You can do so by defining a function as an argument to the `.html()` method. This will cause jQuery to work in each child node found within the selection. The following shows the code. Within the function we set the `<a>` tag between a `<strong>` tag using `$(this).html()` for the given `<a>` tag.

```
$('#navbar').html(function () {
  return '<strong>' + $(this).html() + '</strong>';
});
```

Changing Element Attributes

You can use the jQuery framework to change element attributes in your markup. This includes getting and setting attribute values using `.attr()` and `.addClass()`, as well as adding and removing attributes with `.removeAttr()` and `.removeClass()`. Let's view an example.

The following adds an id attribute to the <h1> tag (the only tag in Listing 18.1 with the class of .pageTitle). It then uses the id attribute to access the text contained within the tag.

```
$('.pageTitle').attr('id', 'page-title');
alert($('#page-title').text());
```

As another example, suppose you have the following style defined on your page (or in your .css file).

```
<style>
  .danger { border: 1px solid #ff0000; }
</style>
```

You can use this style to highlight an element within your page. You might use the style to turn the border of an input element of type text to the color red. You might do so if you validate the form and want to highlight input items with bad values. You use the .addClass() method to add the CSS class to the element.

The code that follows is an example based on the HTML in Listing 18.2. Recall that the sample code associated with Listing 18.2 used the event model to validate input based on the blur event (lost focus) for each text box. We replaced the calculateSpeed() method with the following code. We also added an isErr method to validate each text box (and use the .addClass method with the .danger style if the text box input is in error). Note, too, the use of the jQuery function $.isNumeric() as a more usable form of the DOM style !isNaN().

```
function calculateSpeed(e) {

  var dist = $('#distance');
  var time = $('#time');
  var avg = $('#averageSpeed');

  //Clear average speed.
  avg.text('');

  //Validate each text object and store it in an error array.
  var err = [false, false];
  err[0] = isErr(dist);
  err[1] = isErr(time);

  if (!err[0] && !err[1]) {
    avg.text((dist.val() / (time.val() / 60)));
  }
}
```

```
function isErr(inputCheck) {
  inputCheck.removeClass('danger');
  if ($.isNumeric(inputCheck.val()) == false) {
    inputCheck.addClass('danger');
    return true;
  }
  return false;
}
```

CSS Rules

jQuery provides the `.css()` method for accessing CSS styles and making updates to them. You use this method for specific CSS styles and not the entire CSS class (as in `.addClass()`). As an example, the following gets the background style value associated with `header` in Listing 18.1.

```
var clr = $('#header').css('background-color');
```

You can then add a CSS style (or change an existing one) using name-value as arguments to `.css()`. The following uses the selected value in the preceding code to apply it to the page footer `<div>` tag.

```
$('#footer').css('background-color', clr);
```

Handling Events

jQuery helps you add event listeners to the objects you select. These are similar to the DOM events but are somewhat easier to work with and provide greater flexibility. In addition, jQuery defines its own events for animating the display of information. These animations make your page more appealing to users.

Let's start by looking at the `.ready()` function. This is a key jQuery event that can be used to wrap code you want to execute when the DOM has fully loaded and is ready for work. You write this event as `$(document).ready(function(){...})`. There is also a shorthand version of this method written as `$(function(){...})`. The following shows an example.

```
$(document).ready(function () {
  $('#footer').css('background-color', 'lightgray');
});
```

WAIT FOR AN ASSET TO LOAD

Note that the `$(document).ready()` method will execute once the DOM tree has loaded. It will not wait for other assets such as images to finish loading. Typically, this is preferred. However, if you need to run your code only after a certain asset is loaded (such as checking the size of an image), you can attach your event directly to the image load using either `$('#my-img').load(function(){...})` or the similar `$('#my-img').on('load', function(){...})`.

jQuery, like the DOM, allows you to listen for events raised by elements of the page. The biggest difference, however, is that jQuery abstracts all the cross-browser issues that can often make working with events difficult. It handles these issues on your behalf.

Recall that there are a few options for adding events from the DOM: using `addEventListener()` (preferred), adding to the selected element using dot notation (`distTxt.onblur = calculateSpeed`), and adding directly inside the HTML (`<input id="distance" onblur="javascript: calculateSpeed();" />`. Each approach is applicable to jQuery, too.

First, jQuery uses `.on()` to explicitly add an event listener method to an event. Consider the Event sample from the "Document Object Model (DOM)" section that used Listing 18.2. The following registers events for both input elements once the DOM has loaded.

```
$('document').ready(function () {
  $('#distance').on('blur', calculateSpeed);
  $('#time').on('blur', calculateSpeed);
});
```

This explicit event registration can be replaced with a less formal version using jQuery, as in the following.

```
$(function () {
  $('#distance').blur(calculateSpeed);
  $('#time').blur(calculateSpeed);
});
```

jQuery defines its own events for working with a web page and its actions. Most of these map to a similar DOM event. The following lists just some of the many events to which you might need to subscribe. (This is not a complete reference.)

- **Window (browser) events**—`error, resize, scroll`
- **Document events**—`ready, load, unload`
- **Form events**—`select, change, submit, blur`
- **Keyboard events**—`keydown, keypress, keyup, focusout`
- **Mouse events**—`click, dblclick, mouseover, hover, toggle`
- **Media events (such as video playback)**—`canplay, durationchange, ended, pause, playing, progress, volumechange`

Animations and Effects

Users like a fluid user interface (UI) that quickly responds to their actions. The jQuery framework provides a set of animations and effects for enhancing the way your UI transitions based on user input. As these effects happen, the other markup on the page moves in response. If you slide a new bullet into a list, for example, the other bullets move to make space for the new one. The jQuery animations and effects are an easy way to add more "feel" to the look of your UI.

A simple example is to use the `.hide()` and `.show()` methods of jQuery. Recall the average speed calculator example markup (refer to Listing 18.2). You can mark the `<div id='calculation'>` with the `hidden` attribute. You can then add the following line to `calculateSpeed` to hide the results by default.

```
$('#calculation').hide();
```

Next, you can use `.show()` to animate the display of the `<div>` tag if the user input is valid. You would add this line under the actual calculation inside the `if` statement. The `.show()` method can be used without arguments; or, it can take the number of milliseconds it should use to fade the item into display. It can also take a named speed such as `fast` or `slow` (as in the following).

```
$('#calculation').show('slow');
```

You need only run this once to notice the improvement this gives to the "feel" of the page. There are many similar effects to `.show()` and `.hide()` available. The following provides an overview of these standard effects. Again, most of these take the milliseconds as the duration you want the animate to spread over. You can also use named speeds like `slow` and `fast`. Of course, there are many other parameters available should you want to really customize some of these effects:

- **Basic effects**—`.show()`, `.hide()`, `.toggle()`
- **Fading effects**—`.fadeIn()`, `.fadeOut()`, `.fadeTo()`, `.fadeToggle()`
- **Sliding effects**—`.slideDown()`, `.slideToggle()`, `.slideUp()`

You can also use jQuery to create custom animations. The framework provides the method `.animate()` (and similar supporting methods) for doing custom animations. Generally, you create a custom animation using specific CSS styles on a selection. You then tell jQuery the speed at which you want to make the changes, how you want to see the changes (linear or swing), and what to do when the animation completes.

As an example, we add the following animation to the `calculateSpeed` example after the call to `.show()`. This animates the text moving left to right from small to large. Note that once you animate something, you may have to reset the CSS if you want to reanimate the item the next time the user takes an action.

```
$('#calculation').animate(
  {
    width: "50%",
    opacity: 0.4,
    marginLeft: "0.25in",
    fontSize: "2em"
  }, 1000, 'swing');
```

jQuery and AJAX

The jQuery framework includes methods that make writing Asynchronous JavaScript (AJAX) much easier. These methods are used to call a service on the server and receive the results (typically as a JSON message or an HTML partial view). You then use these results to update sections of your page.

The jQuery AJAX methods are key components of building applications that are perceived as responsive to the user's eyes. A lot of your code has to execute on the server to get data, save results, and more. Typically, this means page refresh. With AJAX, you do not need to refresh an entire page on post. Instead, it can simply update a portion of the page much like a native application.

Writing and calling services are covered in Chapter 19, "Building and Consuming Services with Web API and WCF." jQuery is used throughout that chapter. The subsection "Use jQuery to Create a New Customer" covers the jQuery AJAX methods of `$.get()`, `$().post`, `$.getJson()`, and `$.ajax()`. You may want to scan that section of the chapter before continuing. Some of the techniques discussed in Chapter 19 are used throughout the rest of this chapter.

Building Single-Page Applications (SPAs) with Client-Side JavaScript Frameworks

JavaScript client frameworks have flourished primarily based on the initial success and popularity of jQuery. There are now dozens of quality frameworks you can use to solve all kinds of issues building websites, single-page applications (SPAs), and even mobile applications (see Chapter 25, "Writing Cross-Platform Mobile Applications with Apache Cordova"). Most of these frameworks simplify what are otherwise difficult tasks to accomplish with JavaScript.

Alongside the rise in JavaScript frameworks came the adoption of the SPA. An SPA by its strict definition is a web application that loads a single page and then responds to user activity to chunk or push page updates to the browser. This is akin to a native application that loads a primary screen and then shows subscreens or modal dialogs contained within the primary window.

In reality, however, most modern web applications use the techniques of an SPA and not its strict definition. You might, for instance, create a website based on various features for orders, customers, and shipments. Instead of one SPA to manage these items, you might write a more standard site and then use the techniques of SPA within a given subarea of the application (manage orders, for example).

This section introduces the rich set of client libraries available for building modern sites. We then show how to use a few of these frameworks inside of Visual Studio and ASP.NET to solve certain scenarios.

Selecting a Client Framework

Picking the right framework can be a challenge. Nearly all modern sites include jQuery and Bootstrap. ASP.NET sites also include .validate (among a few others). From there, you are left to review and pick which framework you might need for your given scenario. When picking a framework, we suggest you verify that the framework really solves your specific needs; pick one that has a large support base (and good documentation/samples).

The following is an overview of just some of the many client frameworks that have recently grown in popularity. We are certain that by the time you read this there will be more, and existing frameworks will be doing more.

ADDING CLIENT LIBRARY SUPPORT WITH BOWER

Visual Studio 2015 and ASP.NET 5 include Bower by default for managing the many client-side JavaScript frameworks. This is similar to NuGet, but for JavaScript. We cover using Bower in Chapter 17 (subsection "Using Bower for Managing Client Framework Dependencies").

AngularJS (angularjs.org)

This JavaScript framework allows you to write MVC inside the browser. It is similar to the MVC you might write on the server in an ASP.NET MVC application. However, it is all client-based and written as JavaScript. Of course, the client code can call back to the server to get and post data.

Google controls and supports Angular. However, Microsoft and Google have recently joined forces to bring the next version of AngularJS to market with TypeScript. (We introduce TypeScript later in this chapter.)

The AngularJS templates are included inside Visual Studio by default. These templates can be used for SPAs, WinJS store applications, and Cordova mobile solutions. We walk through an example of using this framework later in this chapter.

Bootstrap (getbootstrap.com)

Bootstrap combines CSS and JavaScript to allow you to create sites that are responsive to device size by default. Using Bootstrap correctly will ensure that your site works well on large screens down to small mobile devices such as phones.

Like jQuery, Bootstrap includes add-ins or derivatives. There are dozens of reusable components available to help with icons, controls, playing media, and more.

Bootstrap is included by default in many of the ASP.NET templates. We walk through an example of using this framework later in the chapter.

Knockout (knockoutjs.com)

This library uses the Model-View-ViewModel (MVVM) pattern inside the browser for creating models based on the given view (called a ViewModel) and then using declarative data binding to connect the ViewModel to the view. Knockout takes care of managing any dependencies. This way, if two or more items in your page are dependent on the same item in the ViewModel and an update occurs, all items automatically get the update.

Even more powerful, you can bind the ViewModel to any markup elements, including input tags. You can also write functions inside your ViewModel for handling various computed scenarios. You can then use the data binding features to bind these functions in your model to an element in your markup. We walk through an example of using this framework later in this chapter.

Sammy.js (sammyjs.org)

This is a small framework designed around making Representational State Transfer (REST)-based calls to the server (a route) using AJAX. Results (JSON or HTML) are then used to update the page.

Modernizer (modernizr.com)

A library that allows you to determine if a browser executing your code supports certain features of HTML, CSS, and JavaScript. It can be used to verify whether the executing browser supports your intent; if it doesn't, you can write fallback code to handle a certain scenario differently.

jQuery UI (jqueryui.com)

This is another library from the jQuery foundation; it contains jQuery plug-ins for specific user interface features such as widgets (tabs, accordion, slider, data picker, autocomplete, and more), new effects such as color animation, and interactions such as drag, drop, resize, and sort.

jQuery.validate (jqueryvalidation.org)

This is used for client-side form validation. ASP.NET uses this framework to handle form field validation on the client. This is included by default in most ASP.NET project templates.

Respond.js (Download from GitHub.com)

This provides a responsive CSS framework for browsers that do not support CSS3.

Hammer.js (hammerjs.github.io)

This is a JavaScript library for working with touch gestures in the browser. Hammer.js is included with the ASP.NET 5 Web Site template by default.

Backbone.js (backbonejs.org)

This is a JavaScript library for building MVC applications in the browser. Like Knockout and AngularJS, you create JavaScript models, and Backbone.js provides assistance with binding the model and calling back to the server.

Breeze (getbreezenow.com)

This is a JavaScript library for managing your database entities in JavaScript. It allows you to use JavaScript to write data queries against your objects persisted on the server. Breeze handles database updates on the server and data binding on the client. It works with Knockout, Backbone, and AngularJS (among others).

Ember.js (emberjs.com)
This is a framework for building client-side MVC applications in JavaScript. Ember defines a specific, repeatable pattern for building highly interactive web applications. It is similar to AngularJS, Backbone.js, and others.

Views in Ember are written as templates (using Handlebars.js). Models represent your data and are loaded using REST and JSON. A controller is used to store application state about a given template. As a model is updated, the template knows about the update and is responsible for updating itself.

Chart.js (chartjs.org)
This is a library of responsive, interactive, HTML5-based graphical charts you use when displaying data in your application.

Less (lesscss.org)
Less is not a JavaScript library. Instead, Less extends the capabilities of the CSS language to allow variables, functions, and other techniques. Less is preprocessor in that a Less file is ultimately output to a standard `.css` file. See Chapter 17 for a small example.

Sass (sass-lang.com)
Sass is another CSS language extension (see "Less" in the previous paragraph). It, too, adds features to your CSS, such as variables. It also works as a preprocessor and ultimately spits out `.css` files based on your Sass files.

Node.js (nodejs.org)
This is a JavaScript library for doing real-time, nonblocking input/output (I/O) between a browser and a server. Node uses Transfer Control Protocol (TCP) sockets to communicate real time with a server across the Web.

SignalR (signalr.net)
SignalR is a JavaScript library for ASP.NET that enables real-time, socket-based web development (similar to Node.js). This includes doing chat, auctions, or any real-time transaction with the server.

CoffeeScript (coffeescript.org)
CoffeeScript is a version of the JavaScript language that attempts to simplify common JavaScript development techniques. It cuts down on the amount of code you need to write by adding support for simplified syntax. A CoffeeScript file is preprocessed as JavaScript before being output to the browser.

TypeScript (typescriptlang.org)
TypeScript is a superset of JavaScript that allows you to write JavaScript as strongly typed code (whereas JavaScript does not enforce type checking). Think of TypeScript as its own language that is compiled into JavaScript for production code.

The TypeScript language was created and is supported by Microsoft as an open source language product. Microsoft has therefore added support inside the Visual Studio tools. This means you get IntelliSense, compiler type checking, code-refactoring, code navigation, and more. TypeScript simplifies writing large JavaScript libraries.

You can learn more about TypeScript, download the language, and get the TypeScript Visual Studio tools from their website. In addition, you can peruse the TypeScript source or even contribute thoughts to the product if you like. The TypeScript website can be found at typescriptlang.org.

Responsive Web Layout with Bootstrap 3

The Bootstrap framework is made up of CSS and JavaScript (using jQuery) that work together to create a mobile-first, responsive design for a website by default. Mobile-first means that Bootstrap is built to check the screen size of the device requesting your page and then only render the portions of the CSS that can be displayed by the device. This keeps the CSS lean based on the device. Of course, a larger device (with more processing power) will load the richer CSS.

Responsive design is part of this mobile-first strategy. It refers to the ability of the design to respond to screen real estate. This typically means collapsing the layout, simplifying the navigation (even moving it off the page into a foldout menu), and more. The mobile-first, responsive design allows your website to automatically adapt to phone, tablets, and larger screens without writing different HTML or CSS.

Bootstrap is extremely popular because it solves a key issue with websites. Users now expect this type of behavior from the sites they visit. Thankfully, Bootstrap makes it easy to implement mobile-first, responsive designs. Let's take a look.

The Bootstrap Files in the ASP.NET Templates

Bootstrap is included by default in many of the ASP.NET templates. This includes the ASP.NET 5 Web Site template. Recall from Chapter 17 that these files are installed in the `wwwroot/lib` folder under the folder named `bootstrap`. Figure 18.6 shows these files in Solution Explorer. Notice too the bower_component folder (accessed via the Solution Explorer, Show all Files option). This folder contains all of Bootstrap. Gulp then generates what is required for the given build and target environment.

The many files shown in Figure 18.6 make up the typical Bootstrap package for a given site. The following describes the files in each of the three folders:

- `css`—The files inside the `css` folder include the Bootstrap CSS in both readable form (`bootstrap.css`) and optimized-for-production form (`bootstrap-min.css`). There are also readable and minified Bootstrap theme files. This is the standard Bootstrap theme; however, you can download and create additional themes (more on themes to come).
- `fonts`—The `fonts` folder contains a number of common glyphs as common icons used for most sites and devices. For example, there is a down arrow for drop-down

lists, a "hamburger" icon for displaying a menu on small devices, and dozens more. There are multiple sizes of each to be used based on screen size.

- `js`—The `js` folder contains the readable and minified version of the Bootstrap JavaScript that works with the CSS for adaptive rendering.

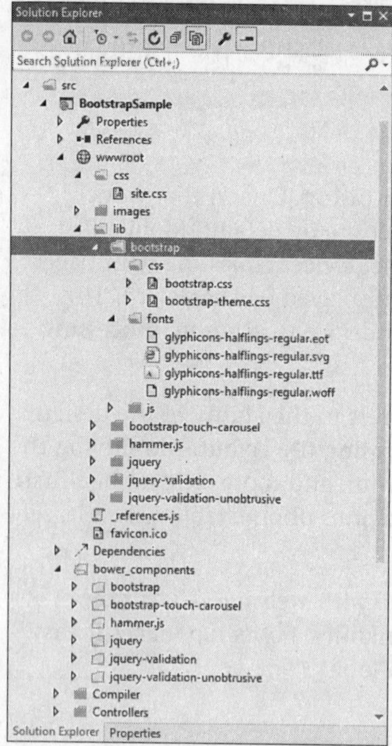

FIGURE 18.6 The Bootstrap files inside the standard ASP.NET 5 Web Site template in Visual Studio.

Recall from Chapter 17 that Bootstrap is installed in your project using the Bower package manager. You can see the dependency by opening `bower.json` from Solution Explorer. Bootstrap uses either Less or Sass as a processor for CSS. You can write your own files to override default Bootstrap and then compile it for your project (using Less or Sass and Gulp). More on this later in the chapter.

Bootstrap is included in your project via the `_Layout.cshtml` page. Inside the `<head>` tag of this page, you will find the following two references (among others).

```
<link rel="stylesheet" href="~/lib/bootstrap/css/bootstrap.css" />
<link rel="stylesheet" href="~/css/site.css" />
```

The first `<link>` tag indicates the Bootstrap style sheet. The second `<link>` tag is for your site-specific CSS, which often includes overrides for Bootstrap styles (more on this to come).

Near the bottom of `_Layout.cshtml` is where the Bootstrap JavaScript is included for pages within the site. (Note that Bootstrap requires jQuery.) This is done via that following call.

```
<script src="~/lib/bootstrap/js/bootstrap.js"></script>
```

For the most part, Bootstrap does not style much of your site by default. Instead, you use the many, many class definitions inside Bootstrap for your HTML elements. These style classes work to handle layout, responsiveness, and visual design of your site. We will examine some of these classes in the coming sections.

How the Bootstrap Grid Layout Works

It is important to understand how Bootstrap works to lay out your pages to maximize responsiveness and readability. Page layout is a key decision you will make when starting a Bootstrap site. You need to determine your target device displays and the way you intend to divide your pages into vertical and horizontal sections using the Bootstrap grid system.

The Bootstrap layout is built on a grid made up of columns and rows. There are 12 logical columns in the grid. However, you typically choose the number of columns in the grid to apply to a specific vertical section of your page. For example, you might define the primary content area of your page as a single row with 3 sections of equal width across the page when shown on larger displays. In this case, you would assign each section 4 columns of the grid. As your page narrows, Bootstrap will wrap each column underneath the others until ultimately you are showing only a single column of the row. (The other columns will wrap under each other, right to left.) It will then compress this single column (including fonts and images) as the screen further narrows. This is the page being responsive to the screen size and keeping the page readable and easy to navigate. (A user can scroll up and down versus having to scroll left and right to view your page.)

Figure 18.7 shows an example of the grid applied to the ASP.NET 5 Web Site template `Index.cshtml` page. The page is displayed on a desktop screen with the resolution of 1024 wide. The top and bottom of the page consist of sections that are meant to span the entire grid. The highlighted area is a Bootstrap row (defined as `<div class="row">`). Within the row, you can see the 12 columns across the page. Each section takes up four of these columns (defined as `<div class="col-md-4">`).

Bootstrap will wrap each column in the row under one another when the same page is displayed on a smaller screen (< 768 wide). However, it will maintain a single column section on the page and further shrink that section (through scaling) as the page narrows. The logical columns of each row are wrapped under one another. Each row is then stacked on the other. Figure 18.8 shows the same page with a width similar to a phone.

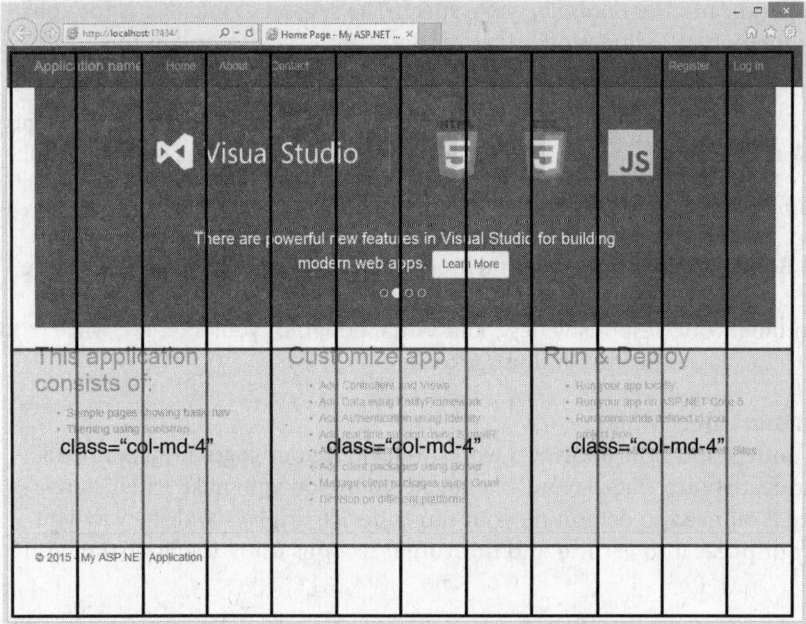

FIGURE 18.7 The Bootstrap logical grid applied to a page template.

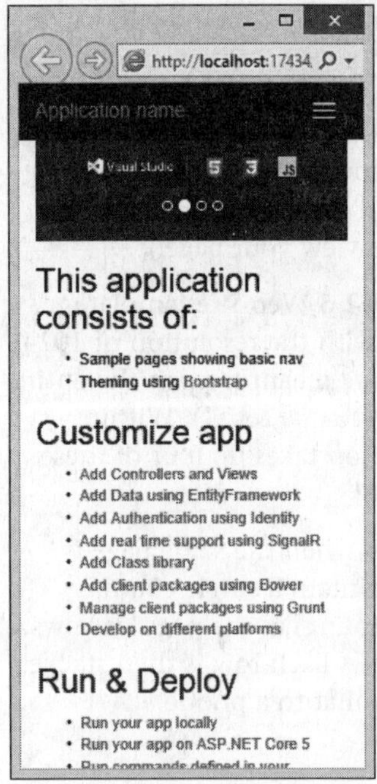

FIGURE 18.8 The Bootstrap grid wraps columns as the page narrows.

The Bootstrap 3 grid layout system always uses 12 columns; however, you specify a grid size and the way you intend your page to be displayed on that grid. You can target a single grid size and let Bootstrap do the work to render your site on the other sizes. You might develop and test against the one grid size you believe users will view your site with most often. Figure 18.7 targets the medium grid. In this case, the page shows all three sections of columns when viewed using this grid. Figure 18.8 shows the way the site renders using an extra-small grid; it wraps the columns. The Bootstrap grids are defined by screen resolution. The following lists the grids in Bootstrap by their style name. (`xx` refers to the number of columns you intend for the style definition.)

- `col-lg-xx`—screens >= 1200px, typically large desktop displays
- `col-md-xx`—screens >= 992px, typically standard desktops and tablets used in the landscape mode (held horizontally)
- `col-sm-xx`—screens >= 768px, typically tablets used in portrait mode (held vertically)
- `col-xs-xx`— screens < 768px, typically phones used in portrait mode

Page layout is a specific choice you will make for your site. It is not predetermined by Bootstrap. Instead, you use the grid system to define an overall layout for your page based on a given grid. The Bootstrap site does include a number of templates for various scenarios. However, these are easy enough to customize. Let's take a look at the Bootstrap-specific markup for the ASP.NET Web Site template.

Figure 18.9 shows the two primary files that make up layout for the ASP.NET 5 Web Site template home page: `_Layout.cshtml` and `Index.cshtml`. The former defines the overall layout shared across the site. The latter is layout specific to the home page. Let's walk through this layout using line numbers from the markup.

- `_Layout`, line 25—Uses the `navbar` class to indicate that `<div>` defines navigation for the site (more on `navbar`s to come).
- `_Layout`, line 26—Marks the `<div>` as a container. A Bootstrap container is meant to represent the full width of the page (the entire grid with padding). You typically stack containers on one another and use rows within containers. The container then scales based on page size.
- `_Layout`, line 45—Marks the `<div>` as another container—in this case, the body-container for styling the main body portion of your site.
- `_Layout`, line 46—ASP.NET Razor syntax indicating where the body of the page that uses the given layout will be rendered (in this case, `Index.cshtml`).
- `Index`, line 5—Uses the style class, carousel slide, to indicate the use of the Bootstrap carousel component (see "Component" section below).
- `Index`, line 68—Marks this `<div>` as a Bootstrap row in the grid system.

- Index, lines 69, 76, and 89—Each line indicates that the given `<div>` should be part of the grid system using the medium screen and targeting four columns when shown on that screen (`col-md-4`).

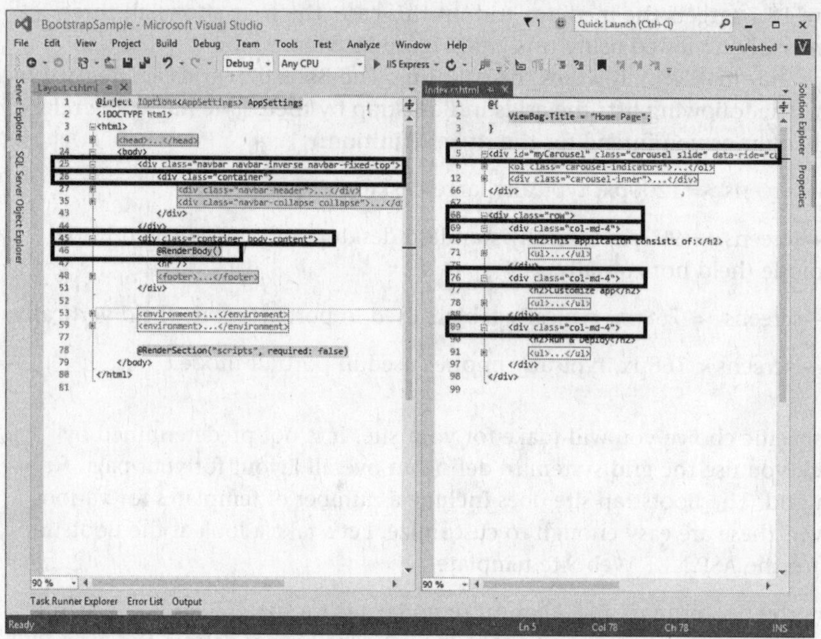

FIGURE 18.9 Bootstrap layout styles applied to the ASP.NET 5 Web Site template.

As you may have noticed in the earlier walk-through, each page can define its own layout in the grid system. It will then render inside the body container, which spans the full page width. In fact, for content that is meant to take the full page, you do not need to specify grid layout rendering. Grid layout is used when you need to show different sections of the page as vertical columns when rendered at the appropriate width.

You should test your site against each grid (or page size) you intend to target. As you have seen, Bootstrap will, by default, adjust your layout automatically for different screen sizes. However, you can also have fine control over how your page is laid out on the different screen sizes. You do so by specifying additional column styles for the given screen size.

As an example, the home page shown thus far shows three sections at the medium and large grid sizes. It wraps to a single section when rendered at the small and extra-small screen sizes. Figure 18.10 shows an example. However, you may want to change this to show two sections when at the small size (and leave the others as-is). You can do so by setting the style definition for the first two `<div>` tags as follows.

```
<div class="col-md-4 col-sm-6">
```

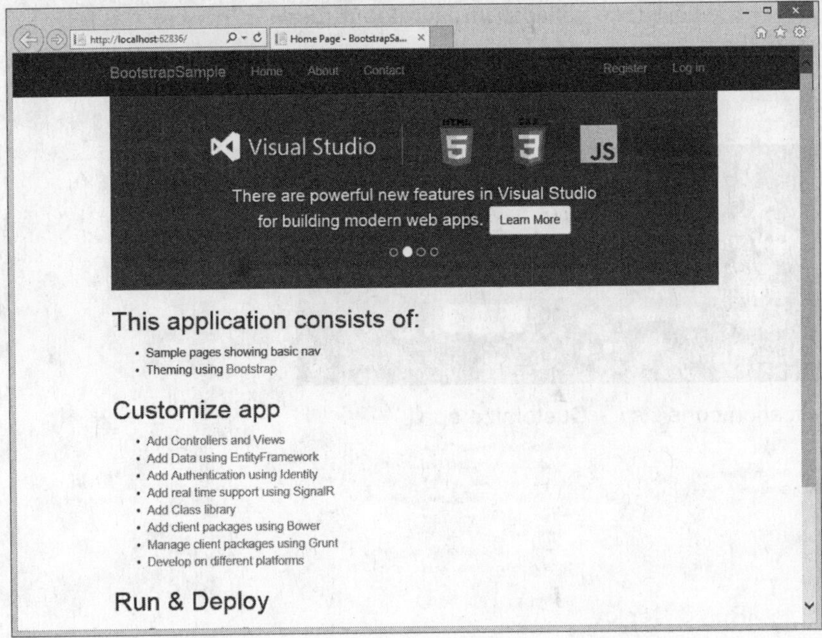

FIGURE 18.10 The template wraps all sections when rendered as small.

This definition tells Bootstrap that when the page is shown on the small grid, you want the first and second `<div>` sections to take up 6 columns each (and the third `<div>` can wrap). You might then indicate the third `<div>` to also render at the same width (6 columns) when shown on the small grid. Furthermore, you can use the offset style to indicate the third `<div>` should center by offsetting 3 columns to the left (3 left columns + 6 display columns + 3 remaining columns = 12). When you use offset, you will also need to indicate an offset for the medium grid (0 in this case). The following shows the markup for this third section.

```
<div class="col-md-4 col-md-offset-0 col-sm-6 col-sm-offset-3">
```

The page will now be displayed differently for small grids. Figure 18.11 shows the same page size as 18.9 with the new results.

How the Bootstrap Navigation Bars Work

A primary element of Bootstrap is the `navbar` class. This class indicates a form of navigation for your site. Typically, you have a single `navbar` for your page. However, you can use `navbar` anywhere a toolbar is needed on your site.

A `navbar` is made up of many elements, each with its own class definition. These elements and classes allow you to control the visual aspects and behavior of the `navbar`. This includes keeping the `navbar` at the top of the page regardless of how far down the user scrolls. You can also add a logo to your page and icons to the individual navigation elements. It also allows the `navbar` to collapse into a foldout menu if the screen is too small to reliably show the full `navbar`.

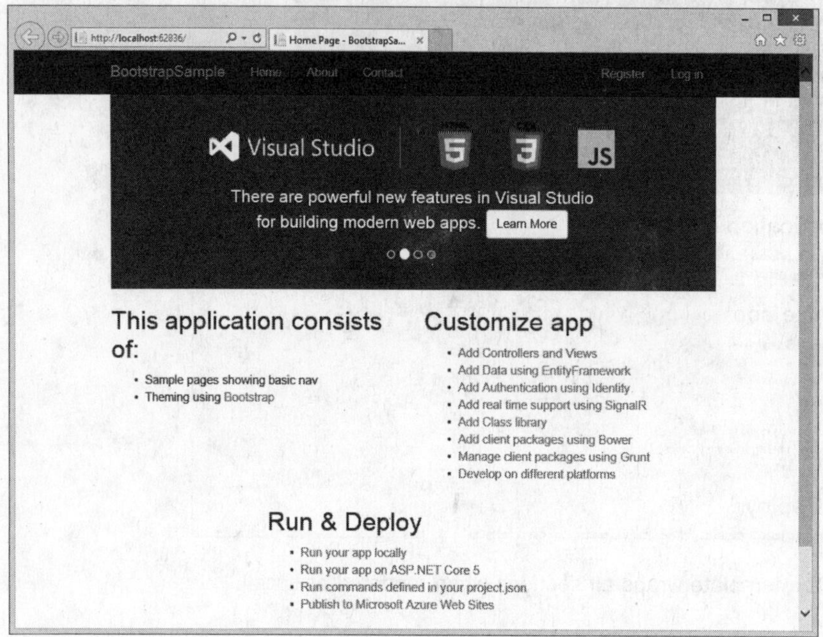

FIGURE 18.11 The template rendering differently for small grids.

Let's take a look at the markup for the `navbar` in the ASP.NET 5 Web Site template. This will help you understand the styles and resulting behavior when working with Bootstrap `navbars`. Figure 18.12 shows the markup.

Figure 18.2 shows specific markup lines highlighted. The following walks you through each of these lines by line number:

- Line 26—Indicates the `<div>` contains markup for a navigation bar using the style `navbar`. The style `navbar-fixed-top` indicates the given `navbar` should always be fixed to the top of the page.
- Line 30—Defines the `<div>` that contains the header information for the given `navbar`—in this case, a button (line 32) that will show navigation elements (line 44) and a logo (line 38).
- Line 32—Used to indicate a button for displaying navigation elements when the page width is small. The navigation elements themselves are referenced by line 44, `class="nav navbar-nav"`.

  The class definition, `class="navbar-toggle"`, indicates that this button should be shown as a toggle button (click to open/close). Toggle buttons for navigation are only shown when the navigation does not fit the width of the screen.

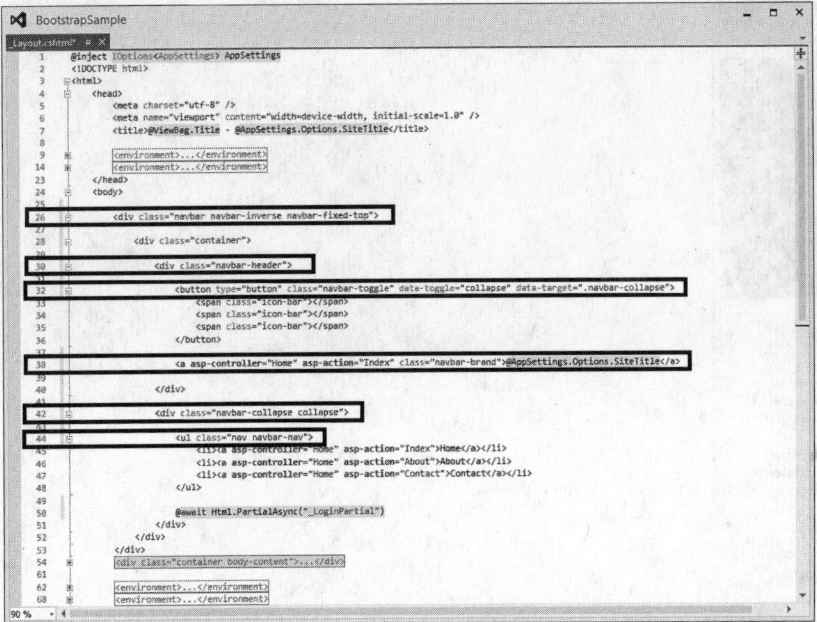

FIGURE 18.12 The markup for a Bootstrap `navbar`.

The button itself is rendered as glyphs. These glyphs are defined inside the `<span>` tags under button. In this case, three icon bars are shown. This is often referred to as a "hamburger" menu. You could, of course, use a different icon of your choosing.

The `data-toggle="collapse"` and `data-target=".navbar-collapse"` indicates that the content for the menu when toggled is contained in the element marked with these styles (line 42).

- Line 38—Represents the logo inside the `navbar`. This item uses the `navbar-brand` class to indicate that this item represents the brand for the site. It is also outside the collapsed region; it will therefore stay on the page as it shrinks.
- Line 42—Marks the `<div>` that contains the collapsed navigation items. This includes the list of items (line 44) and the Login link (line 50).
- Line 44—Marks the actual `navbar` list of navigation elements.

These styles allow you to show and hide navigation elements as the screen size changes. Refer to Figure 18.11 to see the navigation in full view. Figure 18.8 shows the navigation collapsed inside the hamburger menu with the application name still displayed. Clicking the menu icon shows the menu, as demonstrated by Figure 18.13.

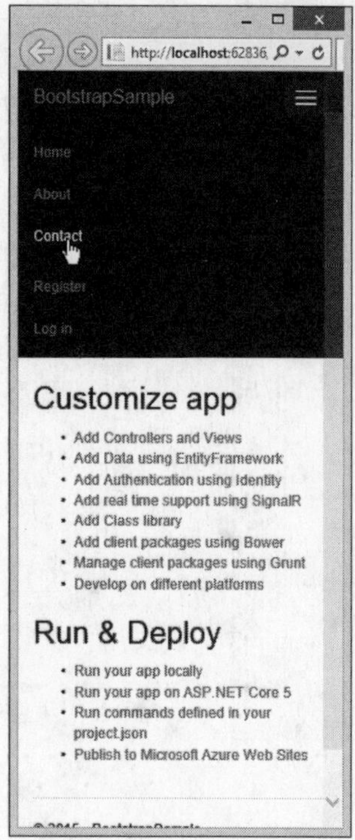

FIGURE 18.13 The navigation collapsed and toggled opened for a smaller screen.

MORE INFO

There is more you can do with a Bootstrap `navbar`. This includes supplying icons for navigation elements, creating drop-down menus for various top-level items, changing colors and fonts, and more. You can find details at the Bootstrap site http://getbootstrap.com/components/#navbar.

Bootstrap Components

The `navbar` discussed in the prior section is just one of the many Bootstrap components available to developers. A Bootstrap component is simply standard HTML markup with CSS class definitions in Bootstrap to help make your page visually appealing and responsive. Other components include buttons, drop-downs, input groups, alerts, badges, breadcrumbs, thumbnails, panels, progress bars, and more. We cannot cover them all here, but the following provides a brief overview of a few more of these components to give you an understanding of how to use them and their power.

The examples that follow are used to style the contact page in the ASP.NET 5 Web Site template. Figure 18.14 shows an example of what this page looks like by default. As we proceed along, you can use this for comparison.

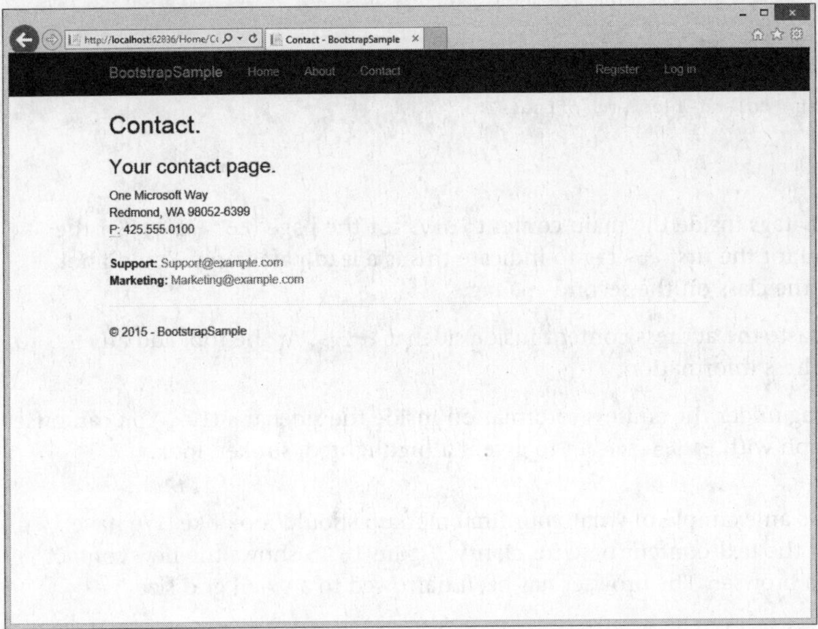

FIGURE 18.14 The default looks of the contact page with minor Bootstrap styling.

Working with Text Bootstrap provides a number of styles you can use to change the font and font size and draw your attention to text elements on the page. This includes the standard heading tags of `<h1>`, `<h2>`, and so on for defining titles, subtitles, and subsections of pages. However, there are many additional classes that help make the text of your page visually appealing and easy to consume. The following walk-through identifies a number of these:

1. Using the ASP.NET 5 Web Site template, open the `Contact.cshtml` page from Solution Explorer.

2. Replace the `<h3>` tag with a `<p>` tag under the `<h2>` title tag. Mark this tag with the Bootstrap CSS class, text muted. This will serve as a muted subtitle under the actual page title. The following shows an example.

```
<p class="text-muted">Contact us; we ...</p>
```

3. Create a new `<div>` tag with the class of `row`, as in `<div class="row">`.

4. Create two `<div>` tags inside the row `<div>` tag. The first tag will represent the main content of the page. The second will be a sidebar containing the address information. Set the class for each of these new `<div>` tags to work with the Bootstrap grid system as follows.

```
<div class="row">
  <div class="col-md-7">
  </div>
  <div class="col-md-4 col-md-offset-1">
  </div>
</div>
```

5. Add two `<p>` tags inside the main content `<div>` for the page (`col-md-7`). Set the class to `lead` for the first `<p>` tag to indicate this is a lead paragraph. You do not need to set the class on the second `<p>` tag.
6. Copy and paste the address content inside sidebar `<div>`. At the top, add an `<h3>` to title the address information.
7. Add a `<p>` tag under the address information inside the sidebar `<div>`. You can offset this paragraph with `class="well"` to give it a highlighted, sunken look.

Listing 18.3 shows an example of what your final markup should look like. We have excluded some of the text content here for clarity. Figure 18.15 shows the new contact page running in a browser. The browser has been narrowed to a small grid size.

LISTING 18.3 The Contact Markup Demonstrating Bootstrap Text Styling

```
@{
    ViewBag.Title = "Contact";
}
<h2>@ViewBag.Title</h2>
<p class="text-muted">Contact us; we love to speak with users.</p>

<div class="row">
  <div class="col-md-7">
    <p class="lead">Use this form to ...</p>
  </div>
  <div class="col-md-4 col-md-offset-1">
    <h3>Address, Phone, and Email</h3>
    <address>
      One Microsoft Way<br />
      Redmond, WA 98052-6399<br />
      <abbr title="Phone">P:</abbr>
      425.555.0100
    </address>
    <address>
      <strong>Support:</strong>
      <a href="mailto:Support@example.com">Support@example.com</a><br />
      <strong>Marketing:</strong>
      <a href="mailto:Marketing@example.com">Marketing@example.com</a>
    </address>
```

```
    <p class="well">Please use the contact form to ...</p>
  </div>
</div>
```

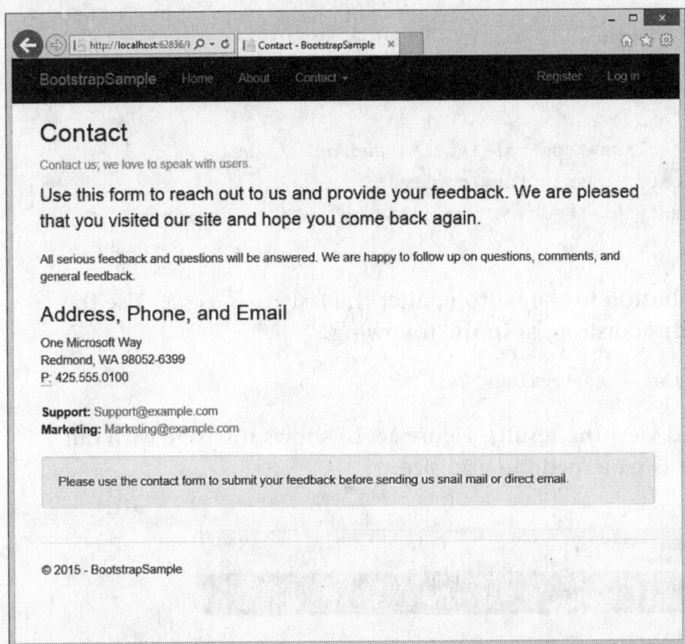

FIGURE 18.15 The Contact page using a few Bootstrap text styles to highlight specific areas of the page.

Standard Form Elements Bootstrap also helps you create good-looking user input forms. There are styles for labels, input controls, buttons, and more. The following walks you through adding and styling a few controls on the Contact form. You'll notice that ASP.NET MVC pages use these styles inside the Razor syntax. Here, however, we simply use the styles in standard markup:

1. Open the `Contact.cshtml` page you created in the prior section.
2. Form elements are grouped by Bootstrap using the class `form-group`. This class typically styles a `<div>` to indicate a group of controls such as a label and a text box. Start by adding this `<div>` to the page inside the main content area as follows: `<div class="form-group"></div>`.
3. Add a `<label>` and an `<input>` tag to the `<div>`. The `<label>` uses the class `control-label`. The `<input>` uses the class `form-control`. You can also set the `placeholder` attribute of the `<input>` tag to create default text for the user. The following shows an example.

```
<div class="form-group">
  <label for="name" class="control-label">Name</label>
  <input type="text" name="name" class="form-control"
         placeholder="your name" />
</div>
```

4. Repeat Steps 2 and 3 for a `<textarea>` control to allow the user to type her feedback. The following shows an example.

```
<div class="form-group">
  <label for="feedback" class="control-label">Feedback</label>
  <textarea name="feedback" class="form-control"
            placeholder="your feedback" rows="6" cols="40"></textarea>
</div>
```

5. Finally, add an `<input>` button to the bottom, after the last `form-group`. Use the class `btn` to stylize it with Bootstrap, as in the following.

```
<input type="submit" class="btn" value="Send" />
```

You can now run the page and view the results. Figure 18.16 shows the page with our developing form. The browser is set a medium grid size.

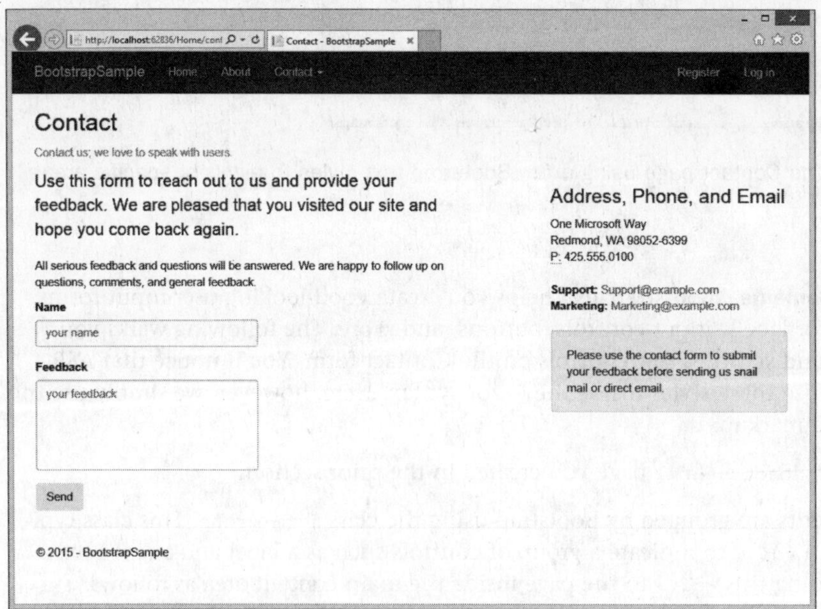

FIGURE 18.16 The Contact page with a basic form stylized by Bootstrap.

Button Drop-Downs You can use standard `<select>` tags to create drop-downs and have them stylized by Bootstrap. However, Bootstrap includes a more powerful drop-down component that allows a user to select from a menu of items based on a user clicking a button or an icon or taking some other action. The following walks you through using the Bootstrap drop-down component:

1. Open the `Contact.cshtml` page you created in the prior section.
2. Add a new `<div>` styled as a `form-group` class between the name and the feedback groups. Add a label and name it `Reason`. The following shows an example.

```
<div class="form-group">
  <label class="control-label">Reason</label>

</div>
```

3. Add another `<div>` under the `<label>` control. Style this `<div>` as `class="dropdown"`.
4. We will create a drop-down that consists of two buttons. The first button will tell the user to select an item. Once selected, this button will display the item selected. This button will be styled as `btn`. We give this button an ID because we will use it in some JavaScript we need to write. The following shows an example.

```
<button class="btn" id="selectedBtn">Select</button>
```

The second button uses a down arrow (or caret) to give the user a visual indication to click for selection. This caret is set using a `<span>` tag. We use the `data-toggle` attribute to reference the container for the actual menu when the user toggles the button. The following shows an example.

```
<button class="btn" data-toggle="dropdown">
  <span class="caret"></span>
</button>
```

5. We now add a list of items for the menu as a `<ul>`. We style that list as `class="dropdown-menu"`. We give this an ID as well to make it easy to select using jQuery. Each of the `<li>` items in the `<ul>` we make as `<a>` tags. This gives Bootstrap a way to style the items as a user hovers over them. The following shows the full group of controls for the drop-down component.

```
<div class="form-group">
  <label class="control-label">Reason</label>
  <div class="dropdown">
    <button class="btn" id="selectedBtn">Select</button>
    <button class="btn" data-toggle="dropdown">
      <span class="caret"></span>
    </button>
    <ul class="dropdown-menu" id="reasonsList">
      <li><a href="#">Question</a></li>
      <li><a href="#">Comment</a></li>
```

```
            <li><a href="#">Error</a></li>
        </ul>
    </div>
</div>
```

6. We now need to write a small JavaScript function that uses jQuery to update the Select button text based on the selected menu item. You can do so in a separate file or within the same page in a scripts section at the bottom of the page. The following shows the code added to the same page.

```
@section Scripts {
<script type="text/javascript">
  $('document').ready(function () {
    var resultBtn = $("#selectedBtn");
    $("#reasonsList li a").on("click", function () {
      var selected = $(this).text();
      resultBtn.text(selected);
    });
  });
</script>
}
```

You can now run the page and view the results. Figure 18.17 shows the page executing in a browser with the drop-down being selected.

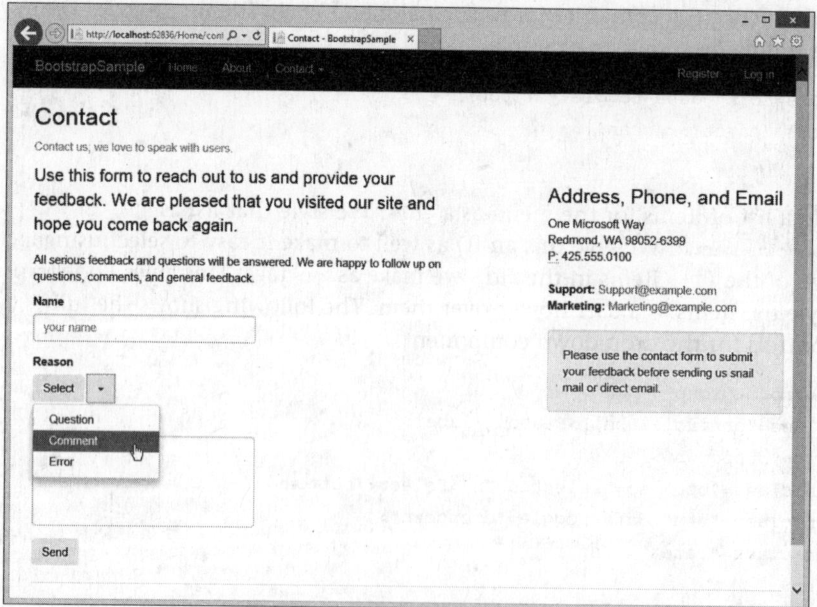

FIGURE 18.17 The Bootstrap drop-down component in action.

Note that the sample for the book uses the same technique to add a drop-down menu to the `navbar` (one for each of the contact pages listed in the examples).

MORE INFO

The preceding examples will get you started building stylized components in Bootstrap. However, there are many additional items with which you will likely need to work. For more information, see http://getbootstrap.com/components/.

Changing the Bootstrap Visual Design

At the time of writing this chapter, it is estimated that Bootstrap is used on nearly one-third of all websites. This number is significantly higher for new sites; nearly all of them use Bootstrap. You do not have to go far on the Internet to find a site built with Bootstrap. One drawback is that if not done right, many sites start to look the same. You can fix this. Bootstrap is meant to provide mobile-first, responsive design. However, the visual design (fonts, colors, look and feel) is still very much in your control. Here we take a look at ways to implement new designs for sites that use Bootstrap.

There are four primary ways you can change your default Bootstrap design. Each comes with its own trade-offs and support overhead. You may also decide to mix these approaches for various reasons. We explore each option here. But first, a warning: you do not want to simply overwrite your Bootstrap files. This will make it painfully difficult to upgrade to the latest version of Bootstrap in the future. Instead, follow any of the approaches listed next.

Override Styles Using site.css You can still write custom styles using a site-specific style sheet. The style sheet, site.css, is loaded after Bootstrap inside the `_Layout.cshtml` page. Therefore, any styles placed in site.css will override the themed styles of Bootstrap. This is the easiest (and most widely used) form of creating a custom look for Bootstrap.

There is a lot of guidance available on both the Bootstrap site and related blogs for writing custom CSS for Bootstrap. This includes making changes to fonts and colors, buttons, the `navbar`, and form elements. All you need is a good understanding of CSS, and you can write customizations.

As an example, suppose you wanted to modify the background of the `navbar`. You might start by switching from the `navbar-inverse` Bootstrap theme to the default. You would do so by editing the first `navbar <div>` in `_Layout.cshtml` as follows.

```
<div class="navbar navbar-default navbar-fixed-top">
```

Next, you can open site.css and add an override for the background color for the `navbar`. The following shows this style override along with an override for the logo text (`.navbar-brand`) to be black.

```
.navbar-default {
  background-color: azure;
}
```

```
.navbar-default .navbar-brand {
  color: black;
}
```

This simple change is shown in Figure 18.18. Of course, you can apply this process for more dramatic changes to the look of your site. The benefit of this approach is that you are not impacting your Bootstrap files and thus can upgrade at a later date. However, you now are maintaining multiple style definitions for the elements in your site.

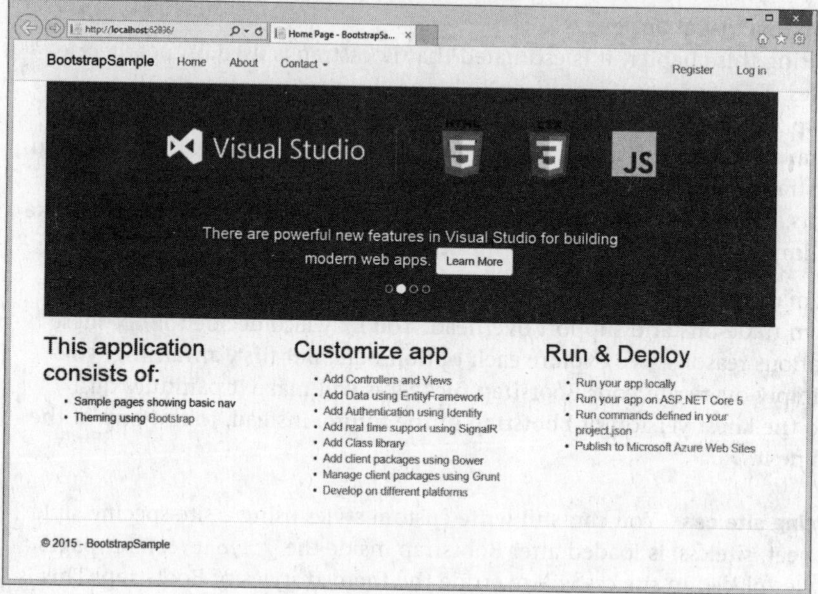

FIGURE 18.18 Use `site.css` to override Bootstrap style definitions (or create your own).

Download a Custom Theme There are many free and paid Bootstrap themes available for use. A good place to start is bootswatch.com. Here you will find more than a dozen Bootstrap themes. You can use these as is, or you can further customize them using the techniques listed in this section.

To use a theme from bootswatch.com, you simply download it and copy over your existing Bootstrap files (after backing them up, of course). This includes `bootstrap.min.css` and `bootstrap.css`.

There are also source files available for these themes. If you use Less, there are `variables.less` and `bootswatch.less` files used to compile a new version of Bootstrap. (See "Create Bootstrap Customizations and Compile with Less/Sass" later in this chapter). If you use Sass, the `_variables.scss` and `_bootswatch.scss` files can be used.

Create a Custom Build of Bootstrap The Bootstrap site provides a customization page (http://getbootstrap.com/customize/) that allows you to edit the many features of Bootstrap and then compile to a customized version. One of the features is setting the many variables used to define colors in your site. For example, Figure 18.19 shows the Less variables that define the gray and brand colors. You make changes here and then have them compiled and propagated throughout the CSS.

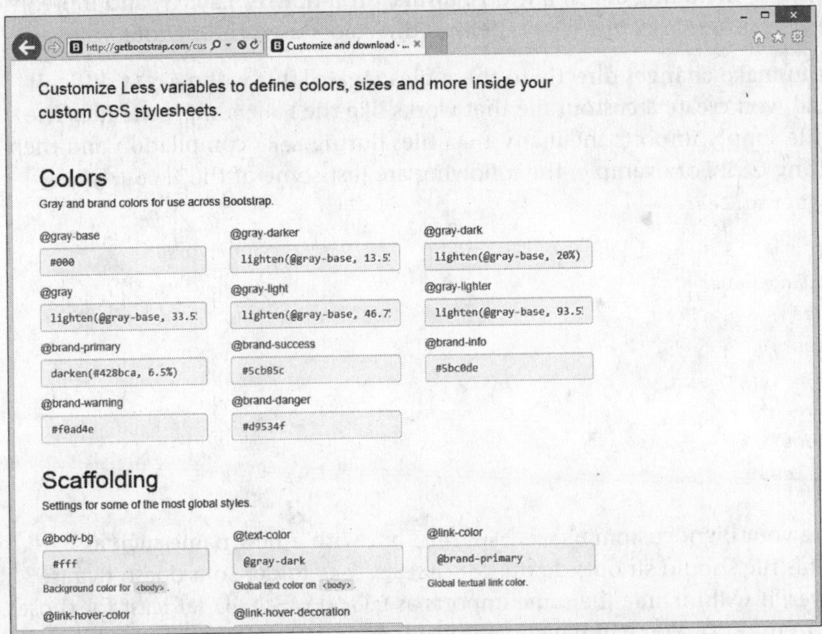

FIGURE 18.19 The Bootstrap customizer allows you to make changes and then generate a new Bootstrap file for your site.

Once you make customizations using this site, you will have to make them again the next time you upgrade. This is one of the drawbacks of this approach. The site does help you keep track of your changes. It generates a `config.json` file on your behalf. You can use this file in future compilations as a starting point.

In addition to custom variables (for colors), the site allows you to select which part of Bootstrap you want to include. You have options for portions of the CSS, the components you intend to use, and jQuery plug-ins you want to add to the site. This is great if you only intend to use a subset of Bootstrap. It then works to lower the overall download footprint of Bootstrap on your site.

Once you have completed making customizations, there is a button at the bottom of the page to compile and download. This provides a set of Bootstrap files you can use as a replacement for your current files.

Create Bootstrap Customizations and Compile with Less/Sass The last method for customizing Bootstrap is using the source files. This is similar to the customizer page from the Bootstrap site but puts you in control of the files and the compilation. This requires some setup and configuration using Less (or Sass) and Gulp tasks for compilation (see Chapter 17 for examples).

The primary folder in the source is the `less` folder. It contains files for all the many Bootstrap components, including alerts, buttons, forms, drop-downs, `navbar`, and more. It also includes the `variables.less` file, which defines the colors used throughout your site.

You do not want to make changes directly to these files. Again, this will make it difficult to upgrade. Instead, you create a custom file that works like the `bootstrap.less` file. The `bootstrap.less` file simply imports the many `less` files during `Less` compilation and then outputs the resulting CSS. For example, the following are just some of the `import` statements inside `bootstrap.less`.

```
//Core CSS
@import "scaffolding.less";
@import "type.less";
@import "code.less";
@import "grid.less";
@import "tables.less";
@import "forms.less";
@import "buttons.less";
```

You want to create your own, custom `bootstrap.less` but with a new name such as `my-theme.less`. This file should sit outside the `bootstrap.less` folder so it doesn't cause confusion. However, it will include the same imports as `bootstrap.less` (at least for those items you intend to import). You will have to edit the `import` statements to point `Less` to the `bootstrap` directory from your custom `my-theme.less` file.

Next, you create a copy of `variables.less` and move this outside the Bootstrap directory. This file defines the colors for the site. You will edit this custom version of this file for your needs. You need to then make sure your theme file `my-theme.less` points to this version of `variables.less`.

Finally, you can add your style overrides directly to the `my-theme.less` file. Or you can create another file for overrides and import that one, too. You can then set Gulp tasks in Visual Studio to compile your Less into a new style sheet. This gives you controlled customizations to Bootstrap without breaking upgrades.

Minify Your JavaScript with Gulp

We covered Gulp in Chapter 17 when discussing the ASP.NET 5 template. However, Gulp is a key component for working with your own, custom JavaScript files. You can use Gulp to copy, combine, and minify (and take similar actions) your development JavaScript files to files that will execute faster in production. We will use this approach through these remaining samples in this chapter. So let's take a look at how you configure Gulp to minify a JavaScript file.

1. Start with an ASP.NET 5 Web Site template in Visual Studio. You can also view this sample from the code download for this book.

2. Gulp uses NPM for package management. The NPM configuration file is `package.json`. Open this file from Solution Explorer.

3. We will use the Gulp plug-in uglify. The uglify plug-in can make a copy of your existing JavasScript files and then minify (or uglify) them for faster processing. This plug-in has many additional options. You can begin reviewing these details at: https://www.npmjs.com/package/gulp-uglify.

   Add the following highlighted line to `package.json` and save the file.

```
{
  "version": "0.0.0",
  "name": "",
  "devDependencies": {
    "grunt": "0.4.5",
    "grunt-bower-task": "0.4.0",
    "grunt-uglify": "~1.2.0"
  }
}
```

4. Visual Studio will install the plug-in upon save of the `package.json` file. To force Visual Studio to download and install this new packages, navigate to Dependencies/NPM in Solution Explorer. Right-click the NPM folder and choose Restore Packages. You should see the new packages installed under the NPM folder.

5. Open `gulpfile.js` to configure Gulp to use this new plug-in. Figure 18.20 shows the additional code. In this case, the Gulp task will be called `'compress'`. It will then look for `.js` files in the `assets` folder. It then will copy and uglify these files. The output will go to `wwwroot`.

   We will execute this new task using Task Runner Explorer in a moment.

6. Add a folder to the web project called `Assets` (under the solution name). This is where you will store your JavaScript files to be minified.

   Add a new JavaScript file to the folder and write some simple JavaScript in the file as an example.

7. Open Task Runner Explorer from View, Other Windows. Recall that this is the tool used for running Gulp tasks.

8. Inside Task Runner Explorer, select the compress task. Right-click it and choose Run to execute it now. You can also use Bindings, After Build to tell the IDE to run this task after a build of the project.

Figure 18.21 shows the results of the Gulp task inside Task Runner Explorer. Notice the two `.js` files in Solution Explorer. Both are also open in the IDE. The lower one contains the original `.js` source. The minified version is open at the top of the code editor.

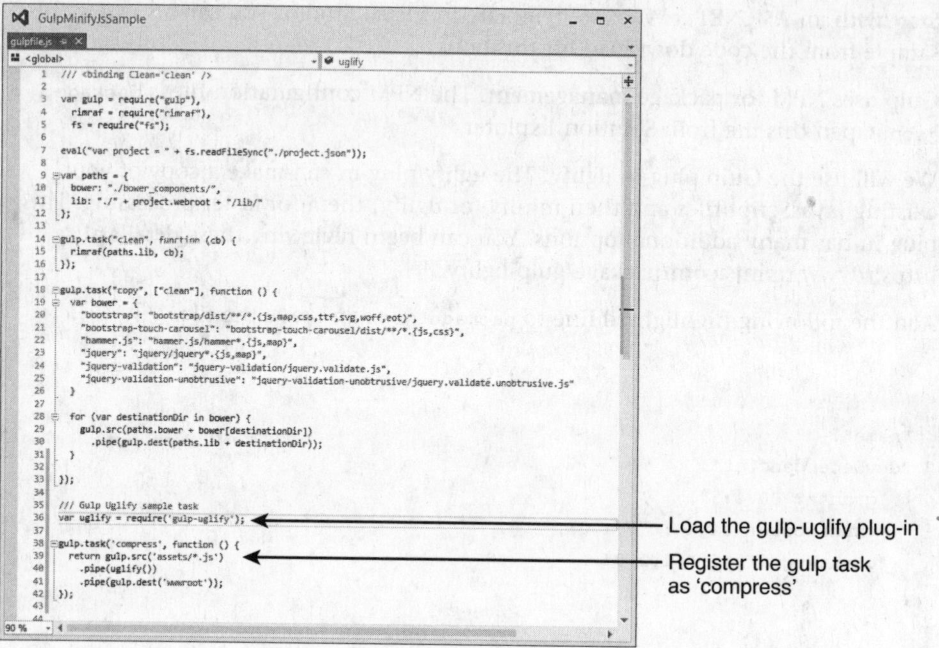

FIGURE 18.20 Use `gulpfile.js` to configure gulp-uglify NPM package.

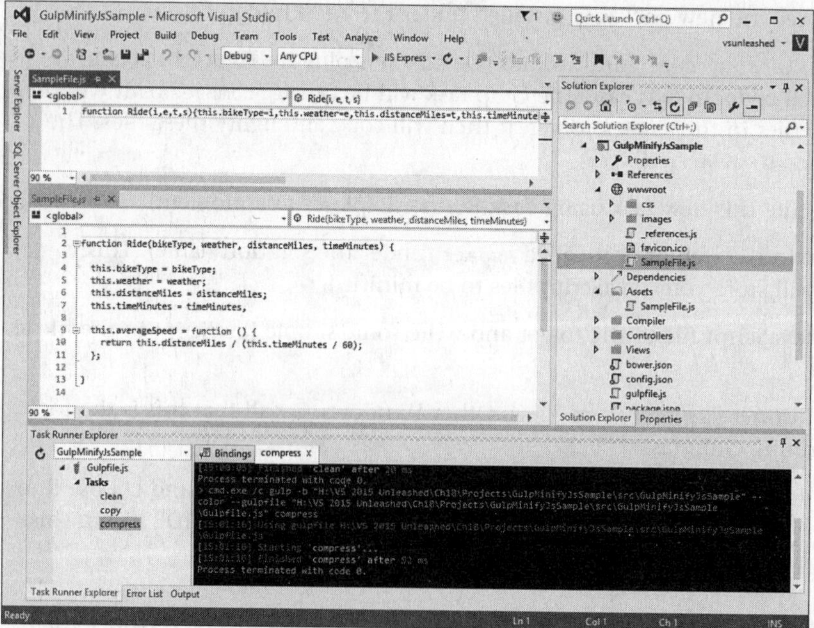

FIGURE 18.21 The Gulp Uglify plug-in executed inside the IDE using Task Runner Explorer.

Using Knockout

Knockout is a popular JavaScript library that simplifies writing dynamic web user interfaces that rely heavily on data. It provides client-side, declarative data binding that works to keep the user interface updated as data changes. This includes data that changes in response to a user action or an update from the server. Knockout works to keep your UI and data in sync.

Knockout is a small JavaScript library that all browsers support. You can use it with jQuery, but Knockout does not require jQuery. Instead, Knockout works using data binding to automatically keep your UI and data in sync (versus using jQuery to find DOM elements, track them, and update them for every action).

Understanding Knockout Basic

Knockout uses the MVVM pattern to keep your UI in synch with your data. This pattern splits your UI concerns from your data into three separate parts:

- **Model**—Like the MVC pattern, this is the model for the data in your application. The model works to retrieve and store data. In ASP.NET MVC, we typically create this model using Entity Framework (see Chapter 17). We may then expose this data through a Web API interface (see Chapter 19). Your client code makes AJAX calls to the Web API (and thus your model) for retrieving and storing data. Once the data is on the client, you convert it to a view model (see below) using JavaScript.
- **View**—The view is the actual UI markup as HTML. In Knockout, your view will contain declarative bindings to link the UI elements to the view model. The view will often send an event to the view model, such as a user entering a value or clicking a button. Knockout works to keep your view updated based on changes to the view model.
- **View Model**—The view model is a client-side JavaScript class representing the model required for the given view (user interface or page). The view model does not deal with the actual view, nor does it know how to retrieve and persist your data. Instead, it simply is a set of properties and methods for working with data as either a single item or a list of items.

One item not mentioned is Knockout itself. Knockout is a JavaScript library that keeps your data bound views in synch with your view models. There is no need to customize or extend Knockout. Instead, you call Knockout to apply your data binding on the client. Let's look at a basic example.

We will leverage the calculate speed example from the JavaScript and jQuery sections earlier in this chapter. Here, however, we will create the example inside an ASP.NET 5 site (see the next section for creating the site and adding Knockout) and use Knockout to do all the work. Let's start with a simple view page (called `BasicSample.cshtml`) as defined here.

```
@{
  ViewBag.Title = "Basic Knockout Sample";
}

<h2>@ViewBag.Title</h2>

<p>Distance (miles): <span data-bind="text: distance"></span></p>
<p>Time (minutes): <span data-bind="text: time"></span></p>
<hr />
<p><strong>Calculated pace (mins/mile): <span></span></strong></p>
```

This view uses `<span>` tags to set up data binding in Knockout using the Knockout text data binder, as in `<span data-bind="text: distance">`.

Next, we need to define a view model. A Knockout view model is defined as a JavaScript class typically using function/constructor notation. In this case, we need only two properties to start: `time` and `distance` (the properties bound to the view above). The following shows an example of the JavaScript embedded in the `BasicSample.cshtml` page.

```
@section Scripts {
<script type="text/javascript">
  function BasicViewModel() {
    this.time = '100';
    this.distance = '10';
  }

  //Activates knockout.js
  ko.applyBindings(new BasicViewModel());
</script>
}
```

Notice the `ko.applyBindings()` method call in the preceding JavaScript. This tells Knockout to apply the defined bindings for the page. You can now run this page in the browser (after adding a simple MVC controller and method for the page). When run, the page will display the model. However, we want to allow a user to enter both time and distance and see it automatically calculated and updated by Knockout. Let's do that next.

We start by updating the view markup to use `<input>` text boxes instead of `<span>` tags. This will allow a user to enter the time and distance on the page. The following shows an example.

```
<p>Distance (miles): <input type="text" data-bind="value: distance" /></p>
<p>Time (minutes): <input type="text" data-bind="value: time" /></p>
<hr />
<p><strong>Calculated pace (mins/mile):
  <span data-bind="text: pace"></span></strong>
</p>
```

Notice when using `<input>` tags that we switch from the Knockout text binder to its value binder. In addition, we added the binder for the calculated speed as a text binder inside a `<span>` tag.

The form is now bound to the view model. However, we need to modify the view model to add the pace (minutes/mile) attribute as a calculated value. We also need to understand another piece of Knockout called *observables*. An observable is a special Knockout property definition that works like an event to update any items that are bound to the property when the property value changes. To define an observable, you use `ko.observable()` as a method call. The following shows these changes to the view model along with the calculated field `pace`. Notice that the calculated field is defined using `ko.computed()`, which takes a function.

```
function BasicViewModel() {
  this.time = ko.observable('100');
  this.distance =  ko.observable('10');

  this.pace = ko.computed(function () {
    return (this.time() / this.distance()).toFixed(2);
  }, this);
}
```

Running this application results in an immediate update to the calculated pace as a user changes a value (and navigates off the input box as in lost focus or blur). Knockout handles all the binding from the view model to the view. Making the property observables ensures that updates occur as values change. Figure 18.22 shows an example running in the browser. We will look at a more detailed example in the coming sections.

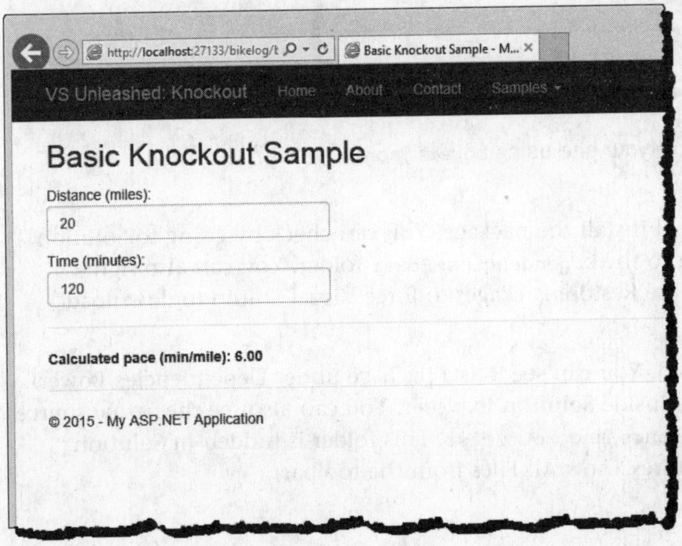

FIGURE 18.22 The Knockout calculate pace example running in the browser.

Adding Knockout to Your ASP.NET Project

Knockout is not installed by default in the ASP.NET Visual Studio templates. However, thanks to Bower support in ASP.NET, it is easy to add to your project. The following walks you through adding Knockout to an ASP.NET 5 MVC 6 template:

1. Start with a new or existing site built off the ASP.NET 5 Web Site template (which includes support for Bower, Gulp, and other items).
2. Open `bower.json` from Solution Explorer. Recall from Chapter 17 that this is where you can add client framework dependencies.
3. Inside the "Dependencies" section at the top of the file, add Knockout as a dependency. You should get IntelliSense here and see the Knockout framework as well as version 3.3.0 (latest at the time of writing). Figure 18.23 shows an example.

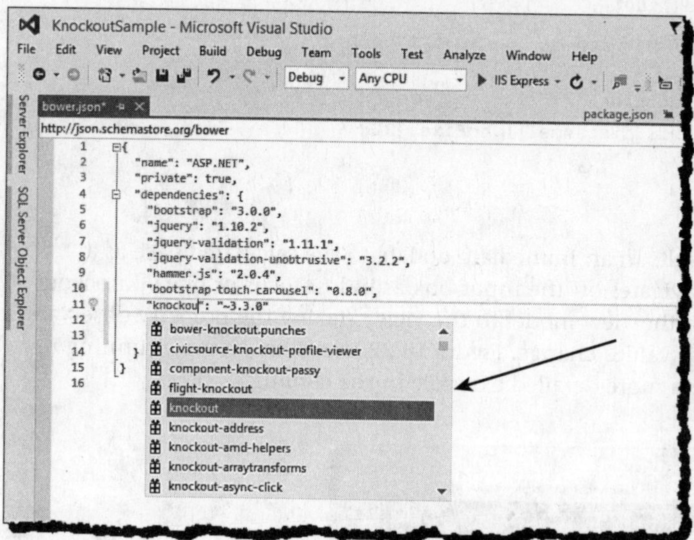

FIGURE 18.23 Add Knockout to your site using `bower.json`.

4. Saving `bower.json` should install the package. You can check by going to Solution Explorer and navigating to the `Dependencies`, `Bower` folder. You can also right-click the folder and choose Restore Packages to force Visual Studio to download Knockout.

   Knockout is now installed. You can see it as a package under Dependencies/Bower. Figure 18.24 shows both inside Solution Explorer. You can also see the actual source files inside `bower_components/knockout/dist`. This folder is hidden in Solution Explorer by default (requires Show All Files from the toolbar).

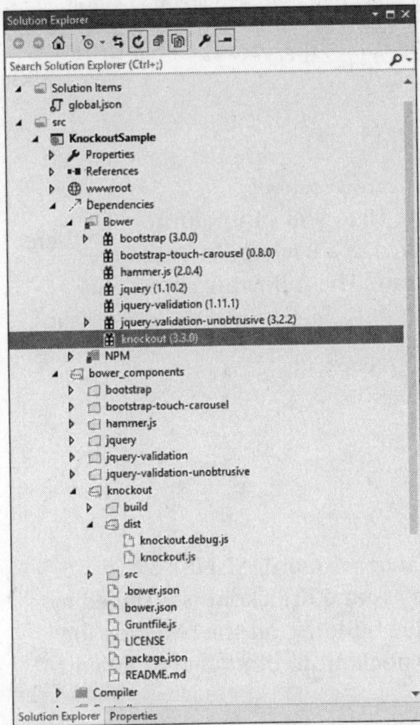

FIGURE 18.24 Knockout installed in the solution as a Bower dependency.

5. The next step is to add Knockout to the `copy` task in `gulpfile.js`. Gulp will use the copy task to move the `knockout.js` and `knockout.debug.js` files to the `wwwroot/lib` folder.

   Open `gulpfile.js` and find the code for `gulp.task("copy")...`; add the following to the end of the list in this method call:

   ```
   "Knockout": "knockout/dist/knockout*.js"
   ```

   This tells the Gulp task to copy the `knockout.js` source from the `bower_components` folder to the `wwwroot/lib`.

6. Open Task Runner Explorer and run the `clean` and `copy` tasks to move the `knockout.js` file into `wwwroot/lib`.

7. You also need to add Knockout to your page before you can use it. In ASP.NET MVC, this can be done site-wide inside the `_Layout.cshtml` page provided you intend to use the framework across your site. (Otherwise, you can add to specific pages where you intend to use it.).

Inside the `_Layout.cshtml`, scroll to near the bottom of the page. Find the `<environment names="Development">` tag. Add the following `<script>` tag inside this tag to include a reference to the Knockout library.

```
<script src="~/lib/knockout/knockout.debug.js"></script>
```

As an optional step, you can add Knockout to the `<environment names="Staging,Production">` section of the page. Here you can point to a CDN (content delivery network) and use your local source as a backup. In both cases, you should pint to the minified version of Knockout. The following shows this `<script/>` tag:

```
<script src="//ajax.aspnetcdn.com/ajax/knockout/knockout-3.3.0.js"
        asp-fallback-src="~/lib/knockout/knockout.js"
        asp-fallback-test="window.Knockout">
</script>
```

Creating an App with Knockout

Let's look at a larger example using Knockout. We will start with an ASP.NET 5 MVC 6 project based on the ASP.NET 5 Web Site Template. We assume Knockout is installed to start (see prior section). In this example, we will continue building on the bike ride log sample used earlier in the book. However, we will use Knockout to bind data to an editable list, allow new entries, and support delete.

Create the Model (on the Server) To get started, let's first create the code that runs on the server. This is an ASP.NET MVC project (see Chapter 17), so this code will include a model to represent the server-side data and a controller for displaying pages and exposing a Web API. Creating these classes should be familiar to you from the prior chapter, so we will not walk through each step here. Listing 18.4 shows the model for a bike log entry.

KNOCKOUT AND DESTROY

Knockout can add an additional property to your objects called `_destroy` to help you work with arrays of data. For example, suppose you are working with a list of data on the client and want to remove one or more items from the list. This works fine with the `.remove()` method. However, you may need to know these items were removed when submitted back to the server. For this case, Knockout provides the `.destroy()` method.

Knockout will add the property `_destroy: true` to your object when you call the `.destroy()` method on a Knockout collection. The Knockout binding knows to ignore these items in your collection. However, these items are passed back to the server for update.

You need to add a `_destroy` property to your server-side model to account for this instance (provided you need this functionality). You can do so by creating a view model on the client or by adding the property and marking it as `NotMapped` to indicate to Entity Framework that it should ignore this property when mapping to your database. Listing 18.4 takes this approach as this example uses bulk updates on the array (including deletes).

LISTING 18.4 The `BikeLog` Model Inside an ASP.NET MVC Application

```
using System;
using System.ComponentModel.DataAnnotations;
using System.ComponentModel.DataAnnotations.Schema;

namespace KnockoutSample.Models
{
  public class BikeLogModel
  {
    [Required, Key]
    public int Id { get; set; }

    [Required]
    public string Description { get; set; }

    public double TimeMinutes { get; set; }

    public double DistanceMiles { get; set; }

    [NotMapped]
    public bool _destroy { get; set; }
  }
}
```

Create the Controller

Next, we need to add a controller (called `BikeLogController`) to the application for working with the bike log pages. In this example, we will include all features on a single page called `Index.cshtml`. Therefore, we only need a single method in the controller to return this view: `Index()` (see Figure 18.25).

We can use Knockout with traditional `GET` and `POST` HTTP page calls or AJAX calls against web services (using Web API) for retrieving and saving data. Web API is covered in the next chapter; therefore, we do not cover it here. However, Figure 18.25 shows the `BikeLogController` where we have combined both page calls (`Index` and `BasicSample`) and the Web API methods `Get` and `Post`. This controller works with a static collection (instead of a database) to simulate working with the bike log data. The `Get` method returns the collection of bike log entries. The `Post` method takes a string formatted as JSON as an argument. It then uses the `Newtonsoft.Json` library (included with the ASP.NET 5 template) to deserialize the JSON string into an `IEnumerable<BikeLogModel>` list. The method then iterates over this list and makes the appropriate updates (add, remove, update). We do not cover these methods in detail here because Web API is covered in the next chapter. However, you can download the sample from this book's website for reference.

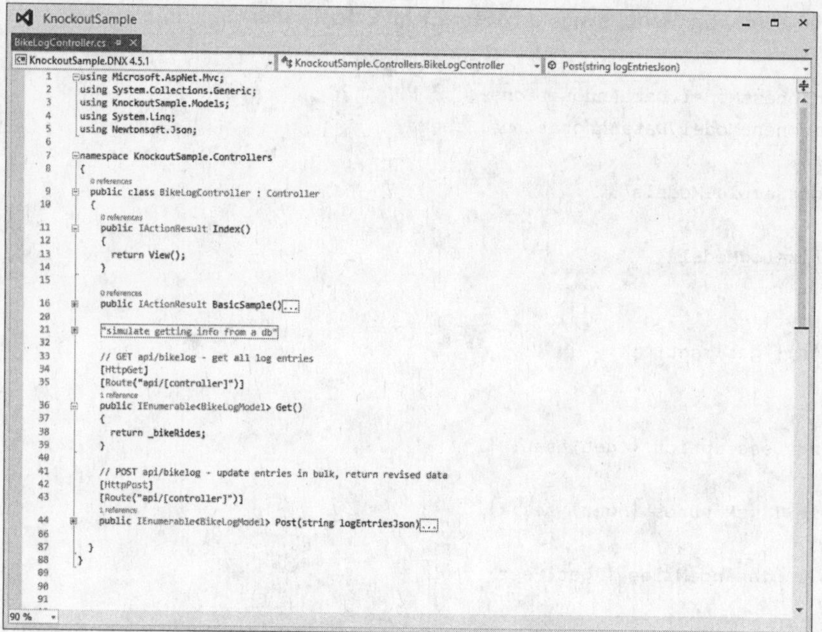

FIGURE 18.25 Use the `BikeLogController` to contain both methods to show pages as well as Web API methods for working with `BikeLogModel` data.

Create Bike Log List View Now that we have an ASP.NET MVC model and controller, let's look at creating the view and view model. The view will use Knockout and the MVVM pattern on the client. Recall that the model in MVVM is the model we created on the server (`BikeLog` and the collection class used to work with it). We will call this model through the Web API using AJAX and jQuery on the client. The view represents our page markup. We also need to create the view model as JavaScript that runs on the client. The following walks you through creating the initial view model and related view for displaying an editable list of bike log entries.

1. Create the view model. The view model will be JavaScript stored in a separate `.js` file. In Solution Explorer, right-click the project names and choose Add, New Folder. Name this folder `Assets`. We will use it to store our project source code for JavaScript files.

   Next, configure Gulp to copy the JavaScript files to `wwwroot` upon project build. See the prior section "Minify Your JavaScript with Gulp" for defining this exact configuration. Be sure to use Task Runner Explorer to bind the `compress` task to After Build.

2. Right-click the newly created `Assets` folder and choose Add, New Item. Select the JavaScript File template. Name this file `app.js`.

3. Create a JavaScript class with constructor notation called `BikeLog`. This class takes an argument that passes in data for creating a new instance of `BikeLog`. This object will be similar to the object created in the earlier sample.

   Add properties for `description`, `timeMinutes`, and `distanceMiles` as Knockout observables. Include an `id` property and the computed field `pace`. Listing 18.5 shows an example.

LISTING 18.5 The `BikeLog` Knockout Object

```
function BikeLog(logEntry) {
  this.id = logEntry.Id;
  this.description = ko.observable(logEntry.Description);
  this.timeMinutes = ko.observable(logEntry.TimeMinutes);
  this.distanceMiles = ko.observable(logEntry.DistanceMiles);

  this.pace = ko.computed(function () {
    return (this.timeMinutes() / this.distanceMiles()).toFixed(2);
  }, this);
}
```

4. Create the actual view model to work with the `BikeLog` class. Define a new class in the same `app.js` file; call this class `BikeLogListVm`.

   This class should include a Knockout array of `BikeLog` entries as a property; name this property `logItems`. Knockout defines the object `observableArray`. This allows you to create an array in which each item in the array is an observable.

   The view model should also include a jQuery call to `$.getJSON()`. This method will self-execute when a new instance of the class is created. It will use AJAX to call the Web API created previously in the controller class to return the current list of bike log entries.

   The results from `$.getJSON()` can be passed into a function for mapping the results to the Knockout array. Create this function as a separate method on the object called `mapRides`. You will need to reuse this function following a post to the server to update the data.

   The `mapRides` function should use the jQuery function `$.map()` to map each item returned from the Web API call to a `BikeLog` instance. This method maps JSON data to JavaScript objects. Finally, we will update the array `logItems` with these mapped objects.

Listing 18.6 shows the Knockout view model object.

LISTING 18.6 The BikeLogListVm Knockout View Model Object

```
function BikeLogListVm() {
  var self = this;
  self.logItems = ko.observableArray([]);

  //Get data from server.
  $.getJSON("/api/bikelog/", function (rides) {
    self.mapRides(rides);
  });

  self.mapRides = function(rideData){
    var mappedRides = $.map(rideData, function (item) {
      return new BikeLog(item)
    });
    self.logItems(mappedRides);
  };
}
```

NOTE

Note that JavaScript and the `$.map` jQuery function are case sensitive. Therefore, if your MVC model uses uppercase (as in `Id` and not `id`), your JSON data will be returned as uppercase. Also, your mapping will look for uppercase values in your JavaScript code. Notice that `BikeLog` (Listing 18.5) takes the `logEntry` parameter and then uses these uppercase values for mapping.

5. Add the Knockout call to `applyBindings` to the JavaScript file (outside the class definitions) as follows.

```
ko.applyBindings(new BikeLogListVm());
```

6. Define the actual view page, its markup, and Knockout binding. Inside Solution Explorer, navigate to the `Views` folder. Right-click this folder to add a new folder called `BikeLog`.

7. Right-click the `BikeLog` folder and choose Add, New Item. Select the template MVC View Page. Name this new page `Index.cshtml` and click the Add button.

8. Add a `<script>` tag pointing to the `app.js` file at the end of the page, inside a Scripts section. Recall that the file will be the one output to `wwwroot` by Gulp. The file will include the view model JavaScript created previously. This script section should look as follows.

```
@section Scripts {
  <script src="~/app.js"></script>
}
```

9. Next, create a `<table>` to hold each bike log entry as a row. We will use the Knockout `foreach` data binder. This binds to an array (`logItems`) and will loop for each item in the array. In this case, we will apply that binder to the `<tbody>` tag, which indicates that each row `<tr>` inside the `<tbody>` represents an item in the collection.

Next, we create the template row and its columns. Each column will use a Knockout binder to bind to the view model. For `id` and `pace`, use the `text` binder. We want to allow editing of other properties, so there you use `<input>` tags and the `value` binder.

Listing 18.7 shows the completed view page bound to the view model (minus a few style class definitions).

LISTING 18.7 The Markup for the Bike Log `Index.cshtml` Page Bound to the View Model Using Knockout

```
@{
  ViewBag.Title = "Bike Log Sample App";
}

<h2>@ViewBag.Title</h2>
<p>See the bike log data for recent rides and track new ones.</p>

<div class="row">
  <div class="col-md-12">
    <hr />
    <table>
      <thead>
        <tr>
          <td>Id</td>
          <td>Description</td>
          <td>Time (minutes)</td>
          <td>Distance (miles)</td>
          <td align="center">Pace (min/mile)</td>
        </tr>
      </thead>
      <tbody data-bind="foreach: logItems, visible: logItems().length > 0">
        <tr>
          <td data-bind="text: id"></td>
          <td>
            <input type="text" data-bind="value: description" />
          </td>
          <td>
```

```
          <input type="text" data-bind="value: timeMinutes" />
        </td>
        <td>
          <input type="text" data-bind="value: distanceMiles" />
        </td>
        <td align="center" data-bind="text: pace"></td>
        <td><a href="#" data-bind="click: $parent.removeEntry">delete</a></td>
      </tr>
    </tbody>
  </table>
  <hr />
</div>
</div>
@section Scripts {
  <script src="~/app.js"></script>
}
```

You can now run the application and view the results. Figure 18.26 shows an example. Notice that the computed field `pace` is automatically updated by Knockout as you change values in the grid. The next steps are to allow a user to add, edit, and delete items and then save their changes.

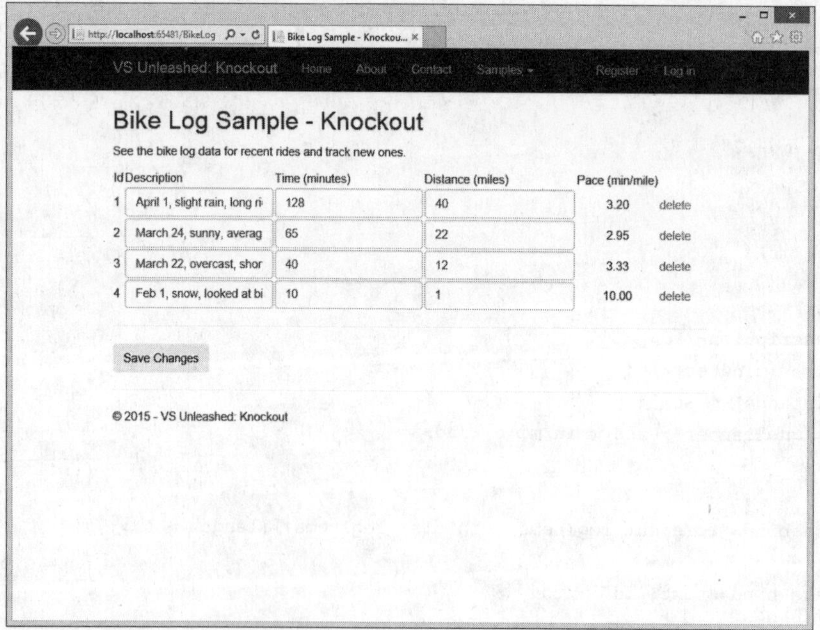

FIGURE 18.26 The bike log view page bound to model data from the server using an AJAX call and Knockout.

Add a New Ride Entry This sample will do all the adds, edits, and deletes in the memory of the browser. We will then ask the user to click the Save button to commit his changes. Of course, we could write this to work one data item at a time if we preferred. The following walks you through including support for adding an item.

1. Add a button near the top of the `Index` page (after the `<div>` tag). This button will allow a user to add a new item to the grid. Use the Knockout click binding to bind the button to a method on the view model called `addEntry` (which you will write next). The following shows an example of this markup.

```
<button type="button" data-bind="click: addEntry"
        class="btn">Add New Entry</button>
```

2. Open the `App.js` file and add the `addEntry` method to the `BikeLogListVm` object. This method will simply use the `.push` method of the array to add a new instance of the `BikeLog` class to the collection. Knockout binding will take care of the rest (adding the item to the bound grid on the page). The following shows this method.

```
//Add a new entry to the collection.
self.addEntry = function () {
  self.logItems.push(new BikeLog({
    Id: 0,
    Description: "",
    TimeMinutes: 0,
    DistanceMiles: 0
  }));
};
```

Run the code and view the results. You can now add entries to the grid by clicking the Add New Entry button. Figure 18.27 shows an example. Notice that these items work like the others in the list. However, they do not have a value for their ID. We will fix this when we add support for saving the view model updates back on the server.

Delete an Entry Deleting an entry with Knockout is just a matter of removing the item from the collection. Knockout will handle the rest. In this case we will use `.destroy` and not `.remove` (see the Knockout and Destroy sidebar above). The following walks you through adding this feature:

1. On the `Index` page, add a new column to the table to hold an `<a>` tag for allowing a user to delete a row. This will also use the Knockout click binder. Here we will point to a function named `removeEntry` that you will write in a minute. The following shows the markup.

```
<td><a href="#" data-bind="click: $parent.removeEntry">delete</a></td>
```

2. Open the `App.js` file and add the `removeEntry` method to the `BikeLogListVm` object. This method uses the Knockout destroy method to mark the item in the collection as removed. The Knockout binding takes care of keeping the UI up to date. The following shows this method.

```
//Remove item from collection.
self.removeEntry = function (bikeLog) {
  self.logItems.destroy(bikeLog);
};
```

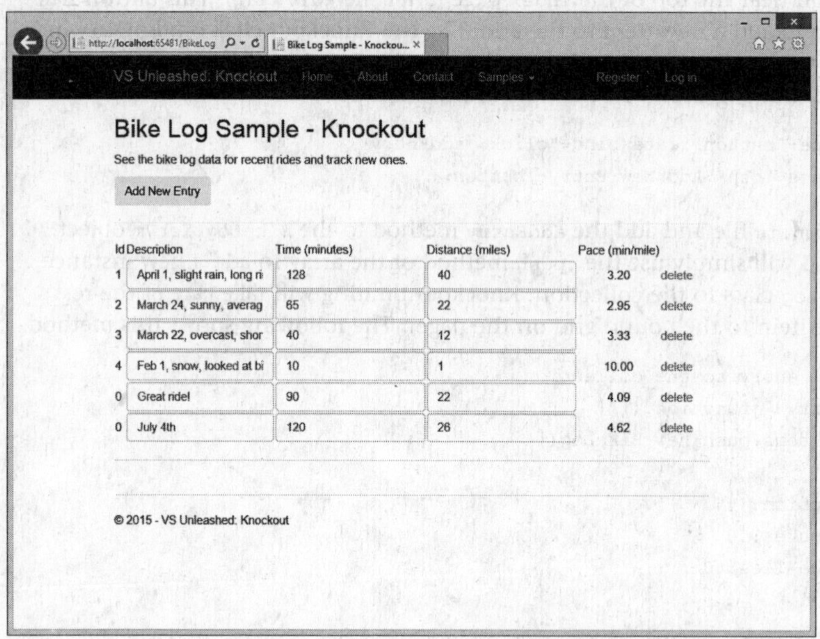

FIGURE 18.27 The bike log view page including the Add New Entry feature.

You can now run the code again and see the results. You should be able to add, edit, and delete records from the table. However, there is still no means for a user to save her changes. Let's add that feature now.

Save Changes Changes will be saved back to the server in bulk. Recall that the controller contains the method `Post` that takes a JSON string and deserializes it into bike log entries for processing. It then returns the updated collection as a result of the Web API call. Let's look at adding the save feature.

1. Add a button to the `Index` page after the `</table>` tag. This button should use the Knockout click binding to bind to a `saveChanges` method you will write in a moment.

   In addition, after the button, add a `<span>` tag to bind to a new property you will create called `saveResult`. This will show results to the user when saving the data.

The following shows these two additional markup elements.

```
<button type="button" data-bind="click: saveChanges"
        class="btn">Save Changes</button>
<span data-bind="text: saveResult"
      class="text-success" id="success"></span>
```

2. Open the `App.js` file and add the property `saveResult` to `BikeLogListVm` as follows:

```
self.saveResult = ko.observable('');
```

3. Add the `saveChanges` method to the `BikeLogListVm` object. This method will use `$.ajax` to call the Web API controller's `Post` method. When doing so, you pass the array data using Knockout's utility method `toJson`, which converts the array to JSON.

   After the call to the Web API succeeds, update the collection with the results from the server. This will add the `Id` field values for new entries and resynch the collection with the right data.

   Finally, write code to update `saveResult` upon success of saving the data. In the next example, we use the jQuery `show` and `fadeout` methods to first show `saveResult` to the user and then fade the message off the screen.

```
//Save data back to the server.
self.saveChanges = function () {
  self.saveResult('');
  $.ajax({
    type: "POST",
    url: "/api/bikelog/",
    data: { logEntriesJson: ko.toJSON(self.logItems) },
    success: function (response) {
      self.mapRides(response);
      self.saveResult('Saved');
      $('#success').show();
      $('#success').fadeOut(3000);
    }
  });
};
```

You can now run the completed application. Figure 18.28 shows the application in action. Notice that item 2 has been deleted; items 5 and 6 were added. Save Changes was executed (and is fading away in the image).

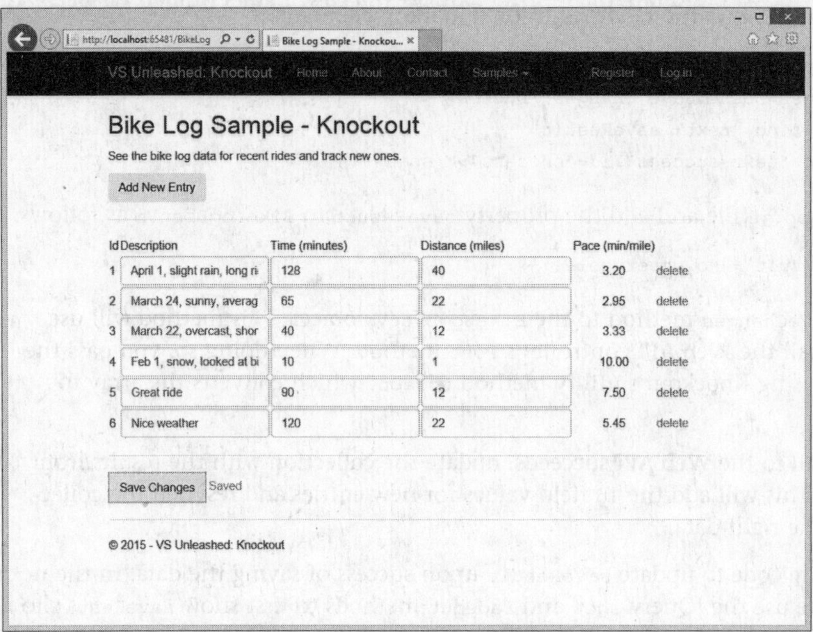

FIGURE 18.28 The completed bike log view page demonstrating a Knockout application working with JavaScript, jQuery, MVC, and the Web API.

Doing More with Knockout

You should now have a solid foundation on using the power of Knockout for form binding with MVVM. Knockout provides even more binding options. Thankfully, all the bindings work in a similar way to what you have seen thus far. The following lists a few additional Knockout bindings to go with those you have used thus far (`text`, `value`, `click`, `foreach`). This is not a complete reference, but an overview. See the Knockout documentation on its website for a complete reference to all other bindings.

- `visible`—This binding makes the element show or hide based on a Boolean value you pass to the binding from the view model. The values `false`, `0`, `null`, and `undefined` cause the element not to display.
- `css` **and** `style`—The `css` binding will bind a new class value to an estimate based on the data in your view model. Similarly, the `style` binder adds an inline to an element based on a view model binding. This is similar to using jQuery selectors in your JavaScript to change a style. However, it makes use of the binding in Knockout to do so.
- `attr`—The `attr` binding allows you to set an attribute of an element based on view model data.
- `if`/`ifnot`—The Knockout `if` binder works to display a section only if a certain value from your view model is `true`. You can apply it to a `<div>`, for example, to show

and hide the content contained in the <div> if the view model property is `true`. This is similar to visible. However, the `if` binding actually adds or removes the markup from the DOM based on binding (whereas `visible` simply uses CSS to show or hide an element).

- `enable/disable`—These bindings enable or disable elements based on the value of the bound item in the view model.
- `textInput`—Works like the value binding to bind an <input> element to a property of the view model. However, `textInput` will update the view model real time as a user types in the input. This is useful for situations such as real-time validation and autocomplete (among others).
- `hasFocus`—This binding will set focus to an item on the page when the value from the view model is `true`. In addition, should the user manually set focus to the element, the view model will update the property to `true` (and you may then take additional action if required, such as changing the items style).

There are additional bindings available beyond those just listed and shown thus far. Knockout also support creating your own custom bindings using its binding framework.

MORE INFO

This section introduced the core features of Knockout. However, there are more details about binding, control flow, and extensions with Knockout. To learn more, you can visit the Knockout site at knockoutjs.com, where you'll find good documentation of key techniques.

Creating a Site with AngularJS

The AngularJS client-side JavaScript framework is a powerful (and popular) library that allows you to more easily create SPAs that do not refresh for every user action. This provides a better user experience without the use of a browser plug-in.

AngularJS can be used with just an HTML page as your view. The JavaScript works to call the server Web API as needed to update the model and persist data. However, you can also combine Angular with ASP.NET MVC (and similar technologies). This section will walk you through the basics of AngularJS and a sample using it with an ASP.NET 5 MVC 6 project template.

Understanding AngularJS Basics

AngularJS leverages the MVC pattern on the client to keep your JavaScript code organized. It also provides a repeatable pattern for handling data and binding that data to views. This is similar to Knockout (shown in the prior section) but takes a different approach to organizing your code and binding your model and view.

The following outlines the basics of the MVC pattern in AngularJS. Each item is also shown with its AngularJS directive preceded with `ng`. (The `ng` is just a way to refer to the word "Angular.") A directive in Angular is markup that instructs Angular as to what you are trying to accomplish. You will see that there are a lot of directives in Angular.

- **Model** (`ng-model`)—The model is a JavaScript client representation of the data used by your view. You typically still maintain an API on the server for retrieving and persisting the data (also called a model). However, you work with that data on the client as a JavaScript model object. The model gets exposed by the controller (which is sometimes referred to as a view model).

  You use the `ng-model` directive to indicate that a given section (like a `<div>` tag) works with a specific model from your Angular application.

- **View** (`ng-app`)—The view represents your HTML markup for the page. You use Angular to bind items from your model to the view. This way, as the model updates, so does the view. Angular defines the view as a projection of your model using an HTML template.

  You use the directive `ng-app` to wire a specific application to your view. You can do so inside the `<html>` tag for the page or inside a specific page section, such as a `<div>`.

- **Controller** (`ng-controller`)—A JavaScript function that you write to create an instance of your model (typically defined as `$scope`). The controller works to bind properties of your model to the page and keep the page and model in sync. You can think of the controller like a view model. Angular does not use a strict version of MVC; rather, it is a variation designed for a specific purpose. The controller allows you to move your application logic out of the page and into code (where it belongs). This also makes your front end more testable.

  You use the `ng-controller` directive to attach a controller to your page. You can do so inside the `<body>` tag or another tag such as `<div>`. You cannot use items of the controller outside the scope of where the controller is used in the markup. You can add multiple controllers to a page, each within its own page section. You can also work with multiple controllers in the same page section.

Let's start by looking at a simple example. We will again leverage the "calculate pace" example from the prior sections to show comparison (between JavaScript, jQuery, Knockout, and now AngularJS). We will create the example inside an ASP.NET 5 site (see the next section for creating the site and adding AngularJS to your project), but we will use AngularJS to do most of the work.

The view page (called `BasicSample.cshtml`) uses AngularJS for binding to a model via a controller. The view page we are examining is an ASP.NET MVC view that uses a `_Layout.cshtml` page as its base (which includes a `<script>` tag pointing to the AngularJS library). This sample page is shown in Listing 18.8 (which includes line numbers for reference).

There are a number of AngularJS-specific directives to point out; the following walks you through each:

- **Line 07**—Use the ng-app directive to indicate the module (or AngularJS application) that this page is using (<div ng-app="basic-sample">). It is possible to register multiple modules on a page, each specific to an app and a section of the page.

- **Line 08**—The ng-controller directive indicates that the given <div> and (its contents) is to be used within the application's controller, BasicSampleCtrl. The controller is part of the module (ng-app="basic-sample"). You can have multiple controllers in an application and use multiple controllers within the same page for different purposes. (This helps keep your code clean and maintainable.)

- **Line 09 and 11**—This is a user form that uses <input> tags to be bound to the AngularJS model. There are a number of binding directives in AngularJS. The most used is one-way data binding. The syntax for this is as follows: <input type="text" value="{{ basicModel.distance }}" />.

  However, in this case, we want two-way data binding that updates the model as a user enters data into a given field. Therefore, we use the ng-model directive. This represents two-way data binding in Angular (from the code to the UI and from the UI back to the code). Without two-way data binding, we would have to scrape the input from the form elements after a user executes an action such as changing focus (blur) and using jQuery (or, we could process the data on the server via a POST, but that is not responsive).

- **Line 17**—This uses the ng-bind directive to bind a <span> to the results of the model's method, pace(). This is also a two-way binding. The method calculates based on user input. It will update real time given our use of ng-model binding and ng-bind.

- **Line 24**—This line simply includes the AngularJS script for the page. You will see that script in a moment. It includes definitions for the AngularJS module, controller, and a JavaScript model.

LISTING 18.8 A Simple Angular View That Uses Two-Way Data Binding

```
01  @{
02    ViewBag.Title = "Basic Angular Sample";
03  }
04
05  <h2>@ViewBag.Title</h2>
06
07  <div ng-app="basic-sample">
08    <div ng-controller="BasicSampleCtrl">
09      <p>Distance (miles): <input type="text" ng-model="basicModel.distance"
10                                  class="form-control" /></p>
11      <p>Time (minutes): <input type="text" ng-model="basicModel.time"
```

```
                       class="form-control" /></p>
    <hr />
    <p>
      <strong>
        Calculated pace (mins/mile):
          <span ng-bind="basicModel.pace()" ></span>
      </strong>
    </p>
  </div>
</div>

@section Scripts {
  <script src="~/app.js"></script>
}
```

The AngularJS code defines a module, a controller, and a model. This code is shown in Listing 18.9 (again, with line numbers for reference). The following highlights key areas within this code (by line number):

- **Line 05**—This line uses the angular object to register an angular module called `basic-sample`. Think of an Angular module as an application. You typically create a new module for each main feature of your application. Modules contain Angular controllers. You can also mark a given module as dependent on one or more other modules using the parameter array in the second argument.
- **Line 06**—This creates a controller called `BasicSampleCtrl` that is added to the module. You can also use the syntax `moduleName.controller()` to add a new module to a given controller.
- **Line 10**—The `$scope` for a given controller is used to represent the model (or view model). You can define `$scope` inside the controller. Alternatively, you can keep your models separate (as in this example) and instantiate an instance and assign it to `$scope`. The content of `$scope` is what can be bound to your page by Angular.
- **Lines 14–21**—This is the actual model. It is just the class we have used in previous examples.

LISTING 18.9 The AngularJS Code for the Page Inside a File Called `app.js`

```
01  (function () {
02    'use strict';
03
04    //The angular module definition
05    angular.module('basic-sample', [])
06      .controller(BasicSampleCtrl, BasicSampleCtrl);
07
08    //The controller defining the model as $scope
```

```
  function BasicSampleCtrl($scope) {
    $scope.basicModel = new BasicModel();
  }
})();

//The model
function BasicModel() {
  this.time = 100;
  this.distance = 10;
  this.pace = function () {
    return (this.time / this.distance).toFixed(2);
  };
};
```

When you run this application, you get the screen shown in Figure 18.29. Again, because we are using two-way binding, as a user types in the input fields, the pace is calculated and updated automatically by Angular binding. We will look at some of the concerns of building a larger Angular example with ASP.NET 5 next.

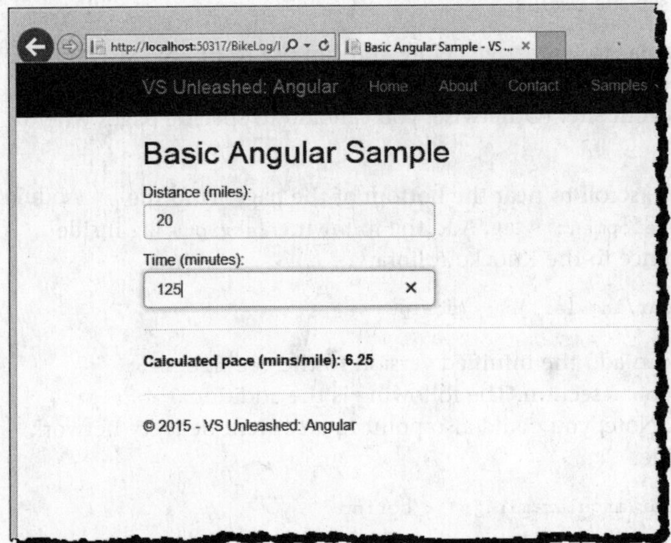

FIGURE 18.29 The basic pace sample running as an AngularJS project.

Adding AngularJS to Your Project

There are file templates for AngularJS built into Visual Studio. There is also IntelliSense by default. However, Angular is not installed by default as a client framework in the ASP.NET template. This is where Bower support in ASP.NET can again help. The following walks you through adding AngularJS to an ASP.NET 5 MVC 6 template:

1. Start with a new or existing site built off the ASP.NET 5 Web Site template (which includes support for Bower).
2. Open `bower.json` from Solution Explorer. Inside the Dependencies section at the top of the file, add Angular as a dependency. You should get IntelliSense here and see the framework as well as version 1.4.1 (latest at the time of writing). Refer to Figure 18.23 as an example (for Knockout).
3. The next step is to add Angular to the `copy` task in `gulpfile.js`. Gulp will use the copy task to move the `Angular.js` file to the `wwwroot/lib` folder.

   Open gulpfile.js and find the code for `gulp.task("copy")...`; add the following to the end of the list in this method call:

   ```
   "angular": "angular/angular*.{js,map}"
   ```

   This tells the Gulp task to copy the `.js` source files from the `bower_components` folder to the `wwwroot/lib`. This will include the debug version of Angular (`angular.js`) and the minified version (`angular.min.js`).
4. Open Task Runner Explorer and run the `clean` and `copy` tasks to move the Angular files into `wwwroot/lib`. After running the tasks, use Solution Explorer to navigate to `wwwroot/lib/Angular` to see the results.
5. You also need to add Angular to your page before you can use it. In ASP.NET MVC, this can be done site-wide inside the `_Layout.cshtml` page provided you intend to use the framework across your site. (Otherwise, you can add to specific pages where you intend to use it.).

   Inside the `_Layout.cshtml`, scroll to near the bottom of the page. Find the `<environment names="Development">` tag. Add the following `<script>` tag inside this tag to include a reference to the Knockout library.

   ```
   <script src="~/lib/angular/angular.js"></script>
   ```

   As an optional step, you can add the minified version to the `<environment names="Staging,Production">` section. The following is the additional `<script/>` tag to add to this section. Note, you could also point to a content delivery network (CDN) instead of a local file.

   ```
   <script src="~/lib/angular/angular.min.js"></script>
   ```

Creating an App with AngularJS

We will now look at building a larger application with AngularJS. We will stick with a similar application that we used in the Knockout sample to allow for comparison between the two frameworks. The application starts with an ASP.NET 5 starter web template. We assume that the project is set up to include the AngularJS library as shown in the prior section. We also assume you are using a Gulp task to output your script files to the `wwwroot` directory. (See the prior section, "Minify (or Copy) Your JavaScript with Gulp"). Once you've completed those tasks, it is time to get started.

Create the Model (on the Server) The model for the server-side MVC code will be the same as the model created in the Knockout example (`BikeLog`). Refer to Listing 18.4 for an example.

Create the Controller (on the Server) The ASP.NET MVC controller will be the same as the one used in the Knockout sample. Refer to Figure 18.25 for an example. You can get the details of this controller from the source code for the book.

Create the AngularJS Application, Controller, and Initial Service We will write the server-side elements by first focusing on the initial Angular JavaScript to define the application. The following walks you through these steps:

1. This example will need to call the Web API RESTful services inside the controller. Like many things in Angular, there are a few ways to do so. You can use the `$http` method that exists inside of Angular and works similarly to jQuery. Alternatively, you can use the Angular `$resource` service, which can make your code somewhat easier to understand and maintain.

   We will use this `$resource` approach to call our Web API services. This feature is part of a separate angular library called angular-resource. We need to include this library in our project.

   Open `Bower.json` and add `"angular-resource": "~1.4.1"` to the dependencies list (under the Angular dependency). Save the file. You should see the package under Dependencies/Bower.

   Open `gulpfile.js` and find the code for `gulp.task("copy")...`; add the following to the end of the list in this method call:

   ```
   "angular-resource": "angular-resource/angular-resource*.{js,map}"
   ```

   Finally, add this library to the markup inside the shared file `_Layout.cshtml`, `<environment names="Development">` section as in the following.

   ```
   <script src="~/lib/angular-resource/angular-resource.js"></script>
   ```

   You may also add the minified version of this file to the `<environment names="Staging,Production">` section as in the following.

   ```
   <script src="~/lib/angular-resource/angular-resource.min.js"></script>
   ```

2. Create an `Assets` folder inside your project. Add a JavaScript file called `app.js` inside this folder.

3. Next, we will configure Gulp to copy the JavaScript files from the Assets folder to the `wwwroot` upon project build. In this case, we will not minify the files. Instead, we will just copy them as the gulp-uglify plugin in its current version does not always work well with Angular (without customizations).

Start by opening gulpfile.js. Add the highlighted lines below to the paths object. This will setup paths for the Assets folder and the wwwroot.

```
var paths = {
  bower: "./bower_components/",
  lib: "./" + project.webroot + "/lib/",
  root: "./" + project.webroot + "/",
  assets: "./assets/"
};
```

Next, create a Gulp task inside gulpfile.js to copy files from Assets to wwwroot. This task should look as follows:

```
gulp.task("copyAssets", function () {
  var assets = {
    "assets": "*.js"
  }
  for (var file in assets) {
    gulp.src(paths.assets + assets[file])
      .pipe(gulp.dest(paths.root + file));
  }
});
```

Finally, use Task Runner Explorer to bind the new copyAssets to the After Build action. This will ensure this file is output upon a new build.

NOTE

We put all the Angular code for the project in this example inside a single file, app.js. You could, however, create separate folders under Assets for Controllers, Services, and the like. You can then use Gulp to either output these files separately at build or "uglify" them together as a single file. Each development group has a specific way it likes to organize its code, including the many JavaScript files used by an AngularJS application.

4. Open app.js and define an AngularJS module (application) as an anonymous function nested inside another anonymous function. Call this module rideLog-app, as in the code that follows. Notice that the module definition includes the dependency ngResource. This indicates that the module is dependent on angular-resource (for creating services).

```
//The rideLog-sample module, controller, and services
(function () {
  'use strict';

  //The angular application definition
  var app = angular.module('rideLog-app', ['ngResource']);

})();
```

5. Define an Angular service for calling the Web API `Get` method to return a list of ride log entries (defined back in Figure 18.25). We add this code to the same `app.js` file.

   The code uses the app reference created earlier when defining the module. It uses `app.factory` to add a service called `LogSrv` as a `$resource`. Notice that we pass the URL to `$resource`. We also define the service using the query argument. Here we state that the HTTP method is `GET`, there are no parameters, and we expect an array as a return value.

```
app.factory('LogSrv', ['$resource',
function ($resource) {
  return $resource('/api/bikelogsrv/', {}, {
    query: { method: 'GET', params: {}, isArray: true }
  });
}]);
```

6. We now need to define the controller for this page. We add the controller to the module again using the `app` reference. This controller will use `$scope` to set the model data (`logEntries`). It will also depend on the `LogSrv` created earlier to retrieve this data from the HTTP call (`query`). Angular automatically decodes JSON from the service into a JavaScript model (in this case, an array). The following shows an example of this code.

```
//The controller defining the model as $scope
app.controller('RideLogCtrl', ['$scope', 'LogSrv', function ($scope, LogSrv) {
  $scope.logEntries = LogSrv.query();
}]);
```

   The next step is to bind this application to an HTML view.

TIP

Visual Studio ships with item templates for key AngularJS features. These templates create new `.js` files stubbed to work with AngularJS. Templates include controller, controller using $scope, directive, factory (for working with services), and module. This example uses a single file, `app.js`. These templates are useful if you write a lot of AngularJS and maintain separate files.

Bind the AngularJS Application to a Bike Log List View Let's now look at how you can bind the angular module, controller, and data to an HTML view. The following walks you through this task:

1. Inside Solution Explorer, navigate to the `Views` folder. Right-click this folder to add a new folder called `BikeLog`.
2. Right-click the `BikeLog` folder and choose Add, New Item. Select the template MVC View Page. Name this new page `Index.cshtml` and click the Add button.

3. Add a `<script>` tag pointing to the `app.js` file at the end of the page, inside a Scripts section. Recall that the file will be the one that Gulp outputs to `wwwroot`. The file will include the JavaScript created previously. This Script section should look like this:

```
@section Scripts {
  <script src="~/assets/app.js"></script>
}
```

4. Indicate that the page uses the Angular application `rideLog-app` by adding the following `<div>` tag (also marks the tag as a Bootstrap row).

```
<div class="row" ng-app="rideLog-app">
```

5. Add another `<div>` tag inside the previous one for defining the controller, as in the following (also marks the tag width using Bootstrap).

```
<div class="col-md-12" ng-controller="RideLogCtrl">
```

6. Create a `<table>` to hold each bike log entry as a row. We will use the Angular directive `ng-repeat` to indicate a template for the table body. This directive will then repeat for each item (`entry`) in the array defined in our scope (`logEntries`).

   We will then use one-way binding to bind items (as `entry`) from the `logEntries` array. Angular creates and maps these objects to the array automatically when we call the service.

   Listing 18.10 shows the completed view page bound to view app, controller, and model (controller data).

LISTING 18.10 The Markup for the Bike Log `Index.cshtml` page Bound Using AngularJS

```
@{
  ViewBag.Title = "Bike Log Sample - Angular";
}

<h2>@ViewBag.Title</h2>
<p>See the bike log data for recent rides and track new ones.</p>

<div class="row" ng-app="rideLog-app">
  <div class="col-md-12" ng-controller="RideLogCtrl">
    <hr />
    <table>
      <thead>
        <tr>
          <td>Id</td>
          <td>Description</td>
          <td>Time (minutes)</td>
          <td>Distance (miles)</td>
```

```
        <td align="center">Pace (min/mile)</td>
        <td></td>
      </tr>
    </thead>
    <tbody ng-repeat="entry in logEntries">
      <tr>
        <td>{{entry.Id}}</td>
        <td>{{entry.Description}}</td>
        <td>{{entry.TimeMinutes}}</td>
        <td>{{entry.DistanceMiles}}</td>
      </tr>
    </tbody>
  </table>
  <hr />
 </div>
</div>
@section Scripts {
 <script src="~/app.js"></script>
}
```

You can now run the application and view the results. Figure 18.30 shows the page and its table bound to the Web API data by Angular.

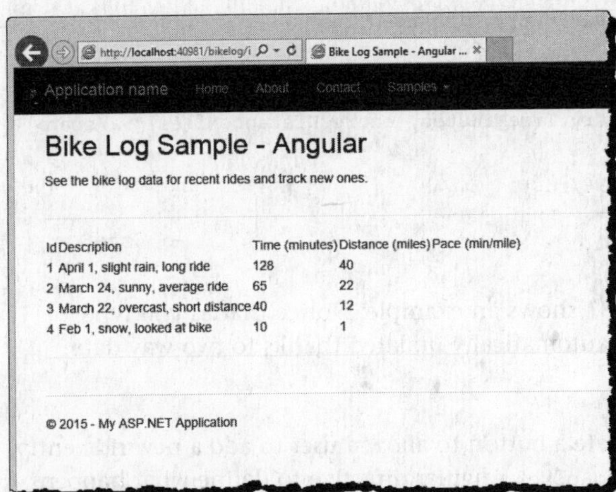

FIGURE 18.30 The Web API data bound to the page using Angular.

Turn the Page into a Form Let's now turn the view into a form using two-way data binding. We will also add the calculation for pace. The following walks you through this process:

1. Open app.js. Inside the app.controller definition, add the method setPace to the $scope. This method should take time and distance as parameters. The following shows an example.

```
$scope.setPace = function (t, d) {
  return (t / d).toFixed(2);
};
```

2. Next, open Index.cshtml. Change the data inside the <tr> template to use <input> tags and two-way binding using the directives ng-bind and ng-model. Add a new column that calls the setPace method for each entry in logEntries passing in both time and distance. This binding will allow the page to automatically update as a user changes a value. The following shows an example.

```
<tbody ng-repeat="entry in logEntries">
  <tr>
    <td><span ng-bind="entry.Id"></span></td>
    <td>
      <input type="text" ng-model="entry.Description" />
    </td>
    <td>
      <input type="text" ng-model="entry.TimeMinutes" />
    </td>
    <td>
      <input type="text" ng-model="entry.DistanceMiles" />
    </td>
    <td align="center">
      <span ng-bind="setPace(entry.TimeMinutes, entry.DistanceMiles)"></span>
    </td>
    @*<td><a href="#">delete</a></td>*@
  </tr>
</tbody>
```

You can again run the page. Figure 18.31 shows an example. Notice that as you type in the <input> fields, the Pace value is automatically updated thanks to two-way data binding in AngularJS.

Add a New Log Entry Next, we will create a button to allow a user to add a new ride entry to the form. To do so, we will use the ng-click Angular directive to define what happens when a user presses a button. Let's get started.

1. Inside app.js, add the method called addEntry() to the $scope inside the controller definition. This method should just push a new item on to the logEntries array (already bound to our form). The following shows an example.

```
$scope.addEntry = function () {
  this.logEntries.push(
    { Id: 0, Description: '', TimeMinutes: 0, DistanceMiles: 0 });
};
```

2. Add a button to the `Index.cshtml` page near the top (before `<table>`). Use the `ng-click` directive to set the `click` event of the button to the `addEntry` method of the `$scope`, as in the following.

```
<button type="button" class="btn"
        ng-click="addEntry()">Add New Entry</button>
```

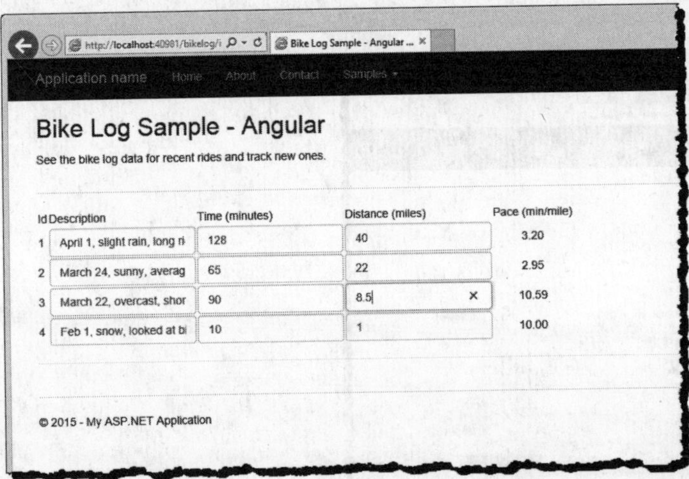

FIGURE 18.31 The Angular page turned into a form using two-way data binding.

Run the page and view the results. Figure 18.32 shows an example. Notice that you can add new items every time you click the Add New Entry button. These items are automatically bound to the form using the same template as the other items in the array.

Delete an Entry Let's now take a look at deleting an entry from the list of bike log items. Recall that Knockout used a special array to mark an item as `_destroy`. This allowed us to not show the item in the UI and have this information available to us when the data was posted to the server. Unfortunately, Angular does not have anything built in along those lines. However, we can create a similar feature to track an item as being deleted and filter the view accordingly. The following steps you through this process:

1. The model on the server already contains a property called `_destroy`. Therefore, the object sent to Angular by the service also includes this property. We will use it here.
2. Open `app.js` and add a function called `deleteEntry` to the `$scope` inside the controller. This function should take an entry item as a parameter. It then simply sets the `_destroy` property to `true`, as in the following.

```
$scope.deleteEntry = function (entry) {
  entry._destroy = true;
};
```

3. Inside the page markup of `Index.cshtml`, add a column with an `<a>` tag for deleting a row. This tag should use the `ng-click` directive to bind to the `deleteEntry` method, as in the following:

```
<td><a href="#" ng-click="deleteEntry(entry)">delete</a></td>
```

4. Next, use the `ng-hide` directive to show the row based on the value of `_destroy`. The following shows an example.

```
<tr ng-hide="entry._destroy">
```

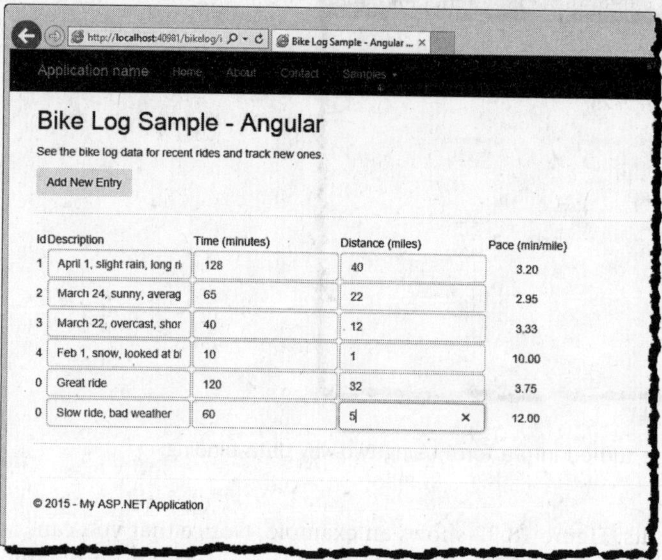

FIGURE 18.32 Adding new rows to the page using the `ng-click` directive to bind to a method defined in the model.

You can run the application and view the results, as shown in Figure 18.33. Notice that as you click Delete, the view is filtered to no longer show the deleted item. However, the item is still in the array so that the delete can be processed back on the server.

NOTE

Another option is to remove the item directly from the server using another service and calling it with HTTP `DELETE`. In that case, we would create an Angular service that knew how to pass an `id` parameter and call HTTP `DELETE`. The source code for this book includes this example as well; it is commented in the `app.js` file under the `deleteEntry` method.

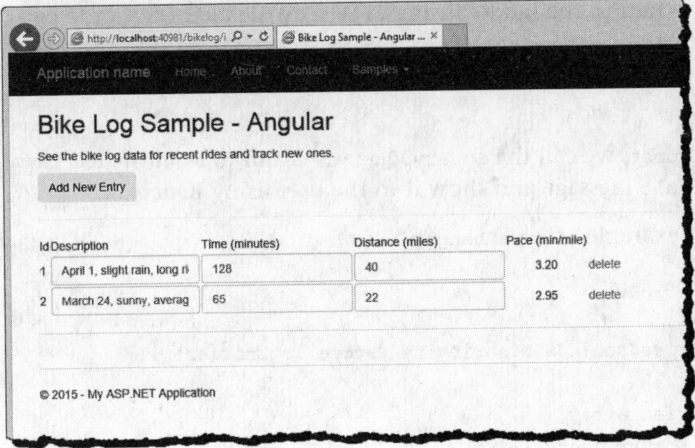

FIGURE 18.33 Use ng-hide to indicate that an item should be hidden based on a Boolean value in your model.

Save Changes Let's take a look at saving the form changes back to the database using the Web API. This is the same web service call we used in the Knockout sample. The following walks you through setting this up with Angular:

1. Start by adding a new button to the `Index.cshtml` form to allow a user to save changes. This button should use the directive `ng-click` to bind to a `saveChanges` method you will create in a moment. We will also include a `<span>` tag for displaying the results of the save action to the user.

```
<button type="button" class="btn"
        ng-click="saveChanges()">Save Changes</button>
<span class="text-success" id="success">{{ saveResult }}</span>
```

2. Inside `app.js`, extend the `app.factory` to include the additional service call to send a POST request to the Web API. This following shows this addition (along with an optional `remove` addition from the prior example).

```
app.factory('LogSrv', ['$resource',
function ($resource) {
  return $resource('/api/bikelogsrv/:id', {}, {
    query: { method: 'GET', params: {}, isArray: true },
    remove: { method: 'DELETE', params: { id: '@id' } },
    post: { method: 'POST',
            params: { logEntriesJson: '@logEntriesJson' } }
  });
}]);
```

3. Add the `saveChanges` method to the model (using `$scope`). This method should call the `post` service and pass the `logEntries` data as a JSON string. Recall that the Web API method will use `Newtonsoft.Json` to deserialize the string into strong types on the server.

   After making the call to `post`, we call the `LogSrv.query()` again to reset the list view. We then set the `saveResult` message and show it to the user using jQuery.

   The following shows an example of `saveChanges`.

```
$scope.saveChanges = function () {
  //Post the save data.
  LogSrv.post({ logEntriesJson: JSON.stringify($scope.logEntries) });

  //Update the log entries array.
  $scope.logEntries = LogSrv.query();

  //Update the UI to show value saved.
  $scope.saveResult = 'Saved';
  $('#success').show();
  $('#success').fadeOut(2000);
};
```

NOTE

Internet Explorer (IE) will cache the query call from Angular. (Chrome will not.) You can fix this by setting the `ResponseCache` attribute on the Web API service to not allow caching. We have done so here in the sample code for the book.

You can again run the application and view the results. You can now edit, delete, and add new items and then save the changes to the server.

TIP

Remember that when using Gulp to output your code to `wwwroot`, the code running in the client is the code pushed to `wwwroot` (not the code inside your `Scripts` folder). If you need to debug your JavaScript, you set a breakpoint in the code file in `wwwroot` (and not the one in Scripts).

Doing More with AngularJS

This section should give you a good grasp of using the power of the Angular client framework. However, there is a lot more to Angular than we are able to show here. This includes many additional directives and filters that make writing responsive user interfaces easier. The following provides a few additional areas for further exploration.

Form Validation Angular has built-in support for validating form field items. You can use Angular to set specific rules on `<input>` elements such as email, date, number, required, URL, and more. Angular will then validate these items on your behalf.

You can also tell Angular not to submit the form if it is not valid using the directive `ng-submit` on a `<form>` tag as in the following (where `submitMethod` is a method on your model that is called when the form is submitted).

```
<form name="myForm" ng-submit="myForm.$valid && submitMethod">
```

Angular also keeps track of each field using CSS classes that tell you if a value has not been changed (`ng-pristine`), has been changed and is not valid (`ng-dirty.ng-invalid`), or has been changed and is valid (`ng-dirty.ng-valid`). You can use these classes inside your `site.css` to create styles that highlight your form elements based on these validation conditions.

Angular Directives The examples thus far have presented many of the AngularJS directives such as `ng-app`, `ng-model`, `ng-controller`, `ng-bind`, `ng-repeat`, `ng-click`, and more. However, there are many more. In addition, Angular supports creating your own custom directives that allow you to write more expressive, easy-to-read HTML that shows behavior and intent.

The following lists additional Angular directives. (It is not a complete reference.)

- **`ng-model`**—Bind to form elements such as text box, check box, text area, and radio buttons.
- **`ng-submit`**—Allows you to bind an angular expression to an `onsubmit` event for a `<form>`.
- **`ng-show`**, `ng-hide`—Used to show and hide elements within your form based on a Boolean value from your model.
- **`ng-src`**—Used to map data in your model to the `src` attribute of an `<img>` tag.
- **`ng-click`, `ngChange`, `ngBlur`, `ngFocus` (and more)**—Used to bind user events to methods in your model.
- **`ng-class`**—Used to set the CSS class based on a value from your model or an expression.

Filters Angular includes a set of built-in filters that make displaying data in the UI much easier. These filters are used in your markup using the "pipe" style, as in `{{ data | filter:options }}`. There are filters for currency, date, number, orderby, uppercase, and more. The following shows a model binding that uses a filter to ensure the value is shown as currency format.

```
<span>{{price | currency}}</span>
```

NOTE

Microsoft and Google announced that they are going to leverage TypeScript as the new language for Angular development. Expect to see the next version of Angular made even easier to use with TypeScript.

Summary

This chapter covered a lot of ground around JavaScript and client-side development. This included writing basic JavaScript. We also covered using the popular client-framework, jQuery. From there, we presented the many other client frameworks that build on JavaScript and jQuery. These frameworks are available to help make developers more successful. Core frameworks discussed were as follows:

- **Bootstrap**—You can use Bootstrap to build fluid, responsive user interfaces. Bootstrap makes your web app work well on any device size. Bootstrap is part of the ASP.NET templates. You can customize Bootstrap to match any look and feel or design for your site.
- **Bower and Gulp**—Bower is the client-side package manager for web development. It allows you to easily install and maintain the many shared libraries that make up a modern web application. Gulp is a task manager for these libraries. You can use it to minify your code (among other things).
- **Knockout**—The Knockout library provides easy-to-use, declarative data binding to your JavaScript model. This binding is based on MVVM and is two-way binding by default. Knockout is easy to use and powerful.
- **AngularJS**—The AngularJS library allows you to create complex client code that works as MVC. Angular uses directives in your markup to make binding and showing/hiding data much easier. Angular is powerful. However, there is a steeper learning curve when trying to master Angular.

You can combine the many client-side techniques learned in this chapter for your own, project-specific web architecture. This will help you build mobile-first, responsive, and user-pleasing sites.

CHAPTER 19

Building and Consuming Services with Web API and WCF

IN THIS CHAPTER

- Service Fundamentals
- Use ASP.NET Web API to Build HTTP Services
- WCF Service Applications

Services have transformed the way we think of the Web and how we leverage it to build software. Prior to services, the Web was mostly a means to deliver content across platforms with low deployment costs. Of course, that was a huge deal (and remains so) for Internet websites and applications. Services, however, have harnessed the power and ubiquity of the web to change the way software is written. For example, it is common for developers to write rich, native clients on tablets, phones, and gaming consoles that leverage the Web via services. Services enable software that is highly distributed, interactive, and always available while making use of a device's power to render a great user experience.

At their core, services represent an interface (or set of methods) that provides black-box-like access to shared functionality using common formats and protocols. By this definition, a service should be loosely coupled with its clients and work across boundaries. These boundaries have, for a long time, prevented the true promise of reusable application components such as services. By working across boundaries such as process, machine, language, and operating system, services can truly be leveraged by the many potential clients that an organization might have today and tomorrow.

Visual Studio 2015 enables developers to create services that enable cross-platform applications and integration. In this chapter, we cover the two primary service technologies built into Visual Studio: the ASP.NET Web API (application programming interface) for creating Hypertext Transfer Protocol (HTTP) services and the Windows Communication Foundation (WCF) technology for building services that work over the Web, a network, or a related endpoint.

Service Fundamentals

A service defines a contract between a calling client and the service itself. In English, this contract states something like this: "If you send me data in this format, I will process it and return you the results in this other format." The format of this data and the communication parameters of these calls are based on open standards (such as HTTP, XML, JSON, SOAP, and WSDL). These service standards apply across technology boundaries and therefore make services attractive for exchanging data between heterogeneous environments.

To frame the benefits of services, it can be helpful to think of them within the context of the problems they were designed to solve. For example, many large companies have multiple applications that need to access and update similar information. They might, for instance, rely on customer data records inside a customer relationship management (CRM) system, an order-processing application, a logistics tool, an enterprise resource planning (ERP) system, and a reporting package. In this case, the customer record is duplicated per system. This means the data may be contradictory (or out of date) in any one system. Companies might have band-aids in place, such as batch processing that tries to keep the data in sync on a regular basis. Figure 19.1 illustrates this problem example.

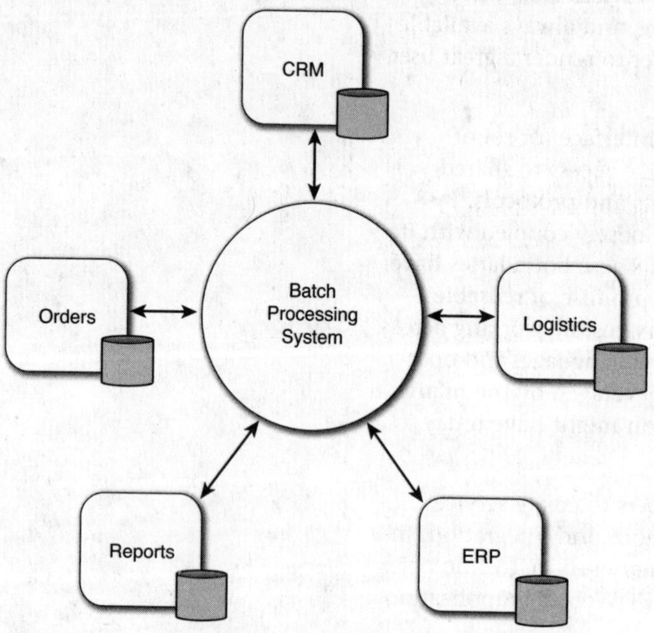

FIGURE 19.1 Heterogeneous applications often share data and have similar needs around that data. Nightly batch processing to update data across applications is not the best way to solve this dilemma.

What's worse, a company might have multiple systems that offer the same functionality (such as two CRM systems). This can happen if the company has grown through acquisition and merger activities or if each department has chosen its own technology. In fact, even if a company wrote all these applications from scratch, you often see duplicate (or similar) code in each application for doing the same thing. This code, of course, has to be maintained, and changes to it can often have unintended consequences on the other systems.

These problems are what service-oriented solutions are intended to solve. Consider that each of the applications in the earlier example might work on different servers running different code on different operating systems. They often even have different database technologies. Therefore, a reusable component that could be plugged into each application could not be easily created. Even if it did, the need to centralize this information into a common view would still exist. For example, an update to a customer record in one system needs to somehow be recorded in the other systems.

What is required to solve this problem (and problems like it) is a common shared interface into a centralized view of the data (in this example, customer data). This interface should be able to work across application boundaries such as protocols, data types, and processes. Architects recognized this problem but did not see a viable solution until the advent of the Web. With web technologies, the HTTP protocol was ubiquitous. Servers could talk to each other. Then along came the XML standard for describing messages and later the more lightweight JavaScript Object Notation (JSON). With a ubiquitous protocol such as HTTP and standard message formats like XML and JSON, applications running on different platforms had a way to communicate.

Why ASP.NET Web API and WCF

Before comparing the technologies of ASP.NET Web API and WCF, it is important to understand there are actually two styles/standards for creating web services: REST (Representational State Transfer) and SOAP/WSDL. The latter was the original standard on which web services were built. However, it was difficult to use and had bulky message formats (like XML) that degraded performance. REST-based services quickly became the alternative. They are easier to write because they leverage the basic constructs of HTTP (`GET`, `POST`, `PUT`, `DELETE`) and typically use smaller message formats (like JSON). As a result, REST-based HTTP services are now the standard for writing services that strictly target the Web.

ASP.NET Web API is Microsoft's technology for developing REST-based HTTP web services. (It long ago replaced Microsoft's ASMX, which was based on SOAP/WSDL.) The Web API makes it easy to write robust services based on HTTP protocols that all browsers and native devices understand. This enables you to create services to support your application and call them from other web applications, tablets, mobile phones, PCs, and gaming consoles. The majority of applications written today to leverage the ever-present Web connection use HTTP services in some way.

That said, communicating across the Internet is not always the most efficient means. For example, if both the client and the service exist on the same technology (or even the same machine), they can often negotiate a more efficient means to communicate (such as TCP/IP). Service developers found themselves making the same choices they were trying to avoid. They now would have to choose between creating efficient internal services and being able to have the broad access found over the Internet. And, if they had to support both, they might have to create multiple versions of their service or at least separate proxies for accessing their service. This is the problem Microsoft solved with WCF.

With WCF, you can create your service without concern for boundaries. You can then let WCF worry about running your service in the most efficient way, depending on the calling client. To manage this task, WCF uses the concept of endpoints. Your service might have multiple endpoints (configured at design time or after deployment). Each endpoint indicates how the service might support a calling client: over the Web, via remoting, through Microsoft Message Queuing (MSMQ), and more. WCF enables you to focus on creating your service functionality. It worries about how to most efficiently speak with calling clients. In this way, a single WCF service can efficiently support many different client types.

Consider the example from before. The customer data is shared among the applications. Each application might be written on a different platform, and it might exist in a different location. You can extract the customer interface into a WCF service that provides common access to shared customer data. This centralizes the data, reduces duplication, eliminates synchronization, and simplifies management. In addition, by using WCF, you can configure the service endpoints to work in the way that makes sense to the calling client. Figure 19.2 shows the example from before with centralized access of customer data in a WCF service.

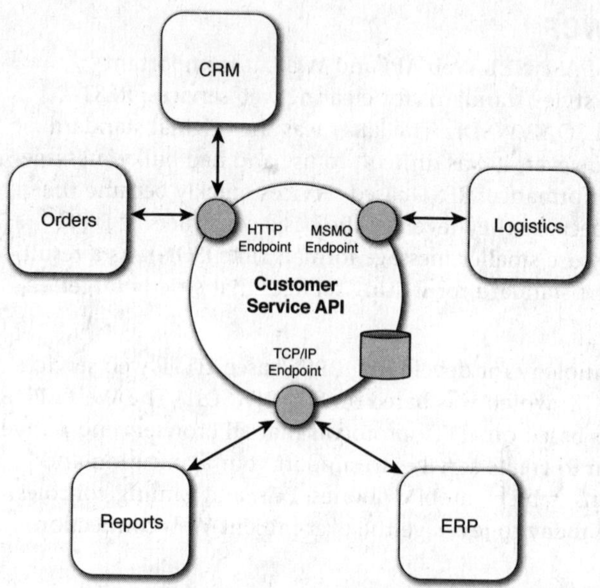

FIGURE 19.2 A centralized, service-oriented implementation of the customer data and service contract using WCF and multiple endpoints.

Choosing Between Web API and WCF

There is no denying that REST-based HTTP services like those created using ASP.NET Web API have become the standard for building web services. These services offer an easy, straightforward approach for web developers building services. Web developers understand HTTP `GET` and `POST` and thus adapt well to these types of services. Therefore, if you are writing services strictly targeted to HTTP, ASP.NET Web API is the logical choice.

The WCF technology is useful when you need to support multiple service endpoints based on different protocols and message formats. Products like Microsoft BizTalk leverage WCF for creating robust services that can be used over the Web as well via different machine-to-machine configurations. Web developers often view WCF as more difficult and complex to develop against. Therefore, if you do not foresee the need for multiprotocol services, you would likely stick with ASP.NET Web API. If, however, you do need to write an application that communicates over TCP/IP when connected to the local network and works over HTTP when outside the network, WCF is your answer.

In the coming sections, we cover both creating HTTP services using the ASP.NET Web API and creating services using WCF. Visual Studio 2015 and the .NET Framework do a lot to abstract the intricacies or "plumbing" of building services away from everyday programming tasks. The result is a more productive development experience. You spend less time worrying about how to negotiate content types or building communications channels and more time developing real business value.

Key Web Service Terms

It can be important for developers to understand the key concepts and standard terms around web services. This knowledge ensures that you know what is happening in your application. It also helps when you are reading the .NET documentation and articles related to building web service applications. Therefore, we have put together the following glossary of key terms related to web services:

- **Web service**—A web service represents a cohesive set of application logic that performs actions and provides data. A web service groups this logic as methods that can be called over HTTP. Not all services are web services; only those that work over the Internet are considered web services.
- **Web service method (or web method)**—A web service method represents a method exposed by a web service. A web method can take parameters and return a response.
- **XML (Extensible Markup Language)**—XML is used to both represent and describe data in a platform-neutral manner. XML can represent both simple and complex data elements and relationships. It is the XML standard that makes web services possible.
- **JSON (JavaScript Object Notation)**—JSON was created as a reaction to overly large XML messages. It is a lightweight data-interchange format that is human readable and built on simple collections of name-value pairs.

- **WSDL (Web Service Description Language)**—WSDL is used to describe the contents of a web service and its web methods. The WSDL provides the message data contracts that enable clients to work with a given service.
- **XSD (XML Schema Document)**—XSD contains a set of predefined types (string, decimal, and so on) and a standard language for describing your own complex types. An XML Schema Document (also referred to as an XSD) uses these types to describe (and restrict) the contents of an XML message.
- **SOAP**—SOAP is an XML-based protocol for communicating between the client and the web service. It is helpful to think of SOAP as representing the format of the messages as they pass over the wire. SOAP wraps XML messages (in envelopes) for communication across the Web. Most SOAP messages are sent over HTTP. However, they can also be sent with transport protocols such as Simple Mail Transfer Protocol (SMTP) and File Transfer Protocol (FTP).
- **HTTP (Hypertext Transfer Protocol)**—HTTP represents the communication protocol used by web services to transfer SOAP-formatted (or encoded) messages. HTTP is also the way standard web page requests (`GET` and `POST`) communicate.
- **UDDI (Universal Description, Discovery, and Integration)**—UDDI is used to define a registry of web services. This capability is useful for the publication of services for developers to find and consume.
- **URI (uniform resource identifier)**—URIs provide a means for locating items on the web. In most cases, URIs are URLs (uniform resource locators) that point to a given service.
- **DISCO (Discovery Document)**—A DISCO file provides information that links to other key elements of a web service. This includes links to XSDs, SOAP bindings, and namespaces. A program can use a DISCO file to determine how to work with a given web service.
- **WS-***—This term represents the overall standards for web services.

Use ASP.NET Web API to Build HTTP Services

Nearly all compute devices created these days speak HTTP. This includes computers, game consoles, and mobile devices running on all platforms, including Windows, iOS, Android, and more. These devices use HTTP because users want access to the Internet. In addition, HTTP is open on firewalls across nearly all networks. For this reason, HTTP web services based on REST have emerged as a default standard that is highly accessible on nearly all client devices and increases interoperability across platforms.

The Microsoft ASP.NET Web API eases the development of HTTP services. You can use the skills you learned in Chapter 17, "Building Modern Websites with ASP.NET 5," regarding web development with MVC (Model-View-Controller) to build service-oriented websites that work with nearly all clients.

The Web API framework takes care of all the plumbing code for you. For example, it includes features such as content negotiation, which allows a client and service to negotiate the right message format, including XML and JSON. Furthermore, ASP.NET Web API services are fully asynchronous and task based. They also have a lightweight hosting model, which gives you a lot of hosting options, including the cloud.

NOTE

We cover the new ASP.NET 5 Web API in this chapter. You can still use the older version of the ASP.NET application stack to create Web API applications in Visual Studio 2015. In fact, the prior versions work in a similar way, following the MVC pattern. They simply have a different project model and target different framework features (such as not supporting the new .NET Core CLR runtime). Please refer to Chapter 17 for a detailed discussion about the ASP.NET 5 application stack and prior versions.

Creating an ASP.NET Web API Project

The ASP.NET Web API services are built on the basic nature of HTTP: GET and POST. In this way, you can send a request to a service the same way you would type a uniform resource locator (URL) into your browser. This request can pass parameters on the query string. Of course, you can get a response from the service, too. You can also post data to a service, work with Secure Sockets Layer (SSL) for security, and do most of the basic web-like things you would do in any website.

You can add ASP.NET Web API services to any ASP.NET web application. The services can be hosted on the same server and domain as another website. (Of course, there are other hosting options, too.) This means you can define a Web API service inside your ASP.NET MVC sites, Razor web page sites, single-page applications (SPAs), and ASP.NET Web Form sites. To do so, you simply right-click the website in Solution Explorer and choose Add, New Item. From here, you select the Web API Controller Class template. The version of the Web API Controller template you use is dependent on the version of the ASP.NET application stack your project targets. If you're using the prior version of ASP.NET, for example, the template is called Web API Controller Class (v2.1). If you're using ASP.NET 5.0, the template is simply called Web API Controller Class. We leverage this template in a moment.

Microsoft has unified the MVC and Web API frameworks with ASP.NET 5.0. However, Visual Studio has a separate template for Web API projects based on the ASP.NET 5.0 framework application stack. This template is accessed by creating a new ASP.NET web application. Recall that you do so via File, New, Project and selecting ASP.NET Web Application. This brings up the secondary dialog for selecting a specific web template, as shown in Figure 19.3. In this case, you select the Web API template.

Notice in Figure 19.3 that there are a number of ASP.NET templates. You can create web services using all these templates. There is a Web API template targeted at using the ASP.NET 4.6 application stack to create HTTP services. There is another for ASP.NET 5. The ASP.NET 5 Web Site template includes everything you need to create Web API services that target the new 5.0 application stack. This template, as discussed in Chapter 17 and 18, includes the basics of a website, too.

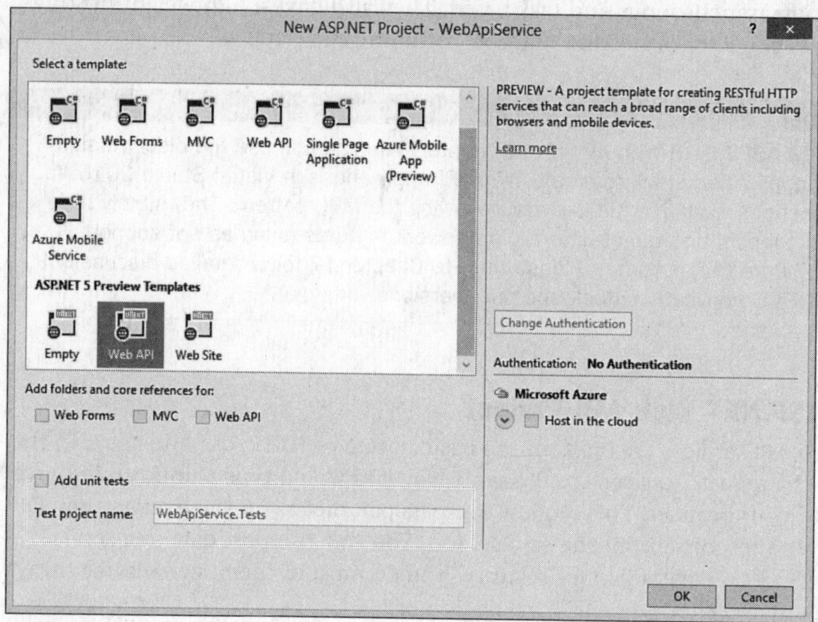

FIGURE 19.3 Select the ASP.NET 5 Web API template to create a project for writing REST-based services.

Figure 19.4 shows the Solution Explorer for a new project using the ASP.NET 5 Web API template. Notice that the project contains a Controllers folder; this is where you write your Web API methods following the ASP.NET MVC pattern. The figure also shows the referenced libraries of the DNX Core 5.0 framework relative to service applications. Not shown is `Startup.cs`; this includes the ASP.NET request pipeline configured for MVC and the HTTP request pipeline.

Defining a Model

Chapter 17 presented the ASP.NET MVC application. Recall that, in this pattern, there is a Model that represents your business objects and their persistence layer. The Controller is used to manage requests and response from the HTTP traffic to your site. Views, of course, allow you to render a user interface (UI) to the user. The ASP.NET Web API service model leverages this same pattern. You define models for your data and a controller for handling service requests and response. (There is no real UI, of course, and hence no views.)

The framework for the ASP.NET Web API handles the plumbing of turning your model objects into serialized data that can be embedded in the HTTP response message. This serialization is typically JSON or XML but can be other formats, too. In this way, clients that can make a basic HTTP GET or POST request and read the response as JSON, XML, or a related format can work with your service. In fact, a client call may indicate which format it needs (called content negotiation) as part of the Accept header in the HTTP request.

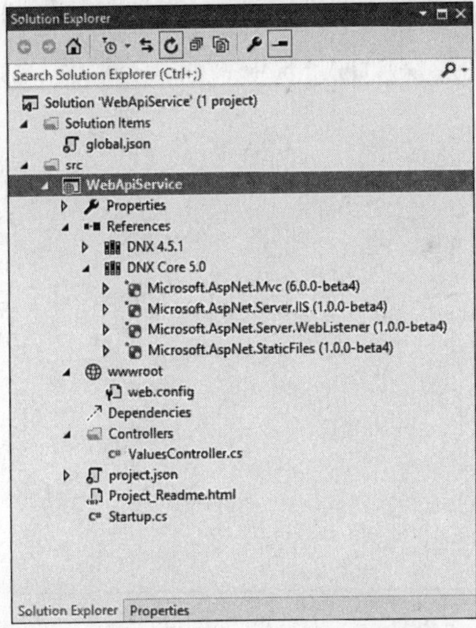

FIGURE 19.4 Start with the ASP.NET 5 Web API template for building a project for just REST-based services.

For example, let's work to create a set of services for managing customer objects. To get started, we will create a simple class to represent our model: in this case, a customer. To do so, we start with the ASP.NET 5 Web API template project called `WebApiService` and follow these basic steps:

1. Add a folder named `Models` to the project in Solution Explorer.
2. Add a class to the `Models` folder and name the class `Customer`.
3. Write a `using` statement at the top of `Customer` for `System.ComponentModel.DataAnnotations`.
4. Write simple properties to represent the customer.
5. Add data annotations to add field level validation.

Listing 19.1 shows an example of this simple `Customer` model class. Notice that this is similar to the model created back in Chapter 17. Next, we will use this model to create HTTP services.

LISTING 19.1 The `Customer.cs` Model Class

```
using System;
using System.ComponentModel.DataAnnotations;

namespace WebApiService.Models
{
  public class Customer
  {
    public int Id { get; set; }

    [Required]
    public string Name { get; set; }

    [Required, EmailAddress]
    public string Email { get; set; }

    public bool OptInEmail { get; set; }

    public string Notes { get; set; }
  }
}
```

Creating the Services (Controller)

We will start with an example of coding the service from scratch. For starters, we are going to add a controller class to the project we've been working with. The following walks you through this process:

1. Right-click the `Controllers` folder and choose Add, New Item. From the Add New Item dialog, select Web API Controller Class. Figure 19.5 shows an example. Notice the left side of the dialog that ASP.NET 5 is selected.

2. Name the file `CustomerController` and click the Add button.

Visual Studio will then create a `controller` class on your behalf, specifically configured for the Web API. Listing 19.2 shows an example. There are a few items to note. First, notice this class inherits from the new `Microsoft.AspNet.Mvc.Controller` (and not the previous namespace, `System.Web.Http.ApiController`). Also, notice that the class has default methods stubbed out for `Get`, `Post`, `Put`, and `Delete`. Finally, notice the `Route` attribute at the top of the class. This controls the way your URLs are routed to the controller and its methods (more on this in a moment).

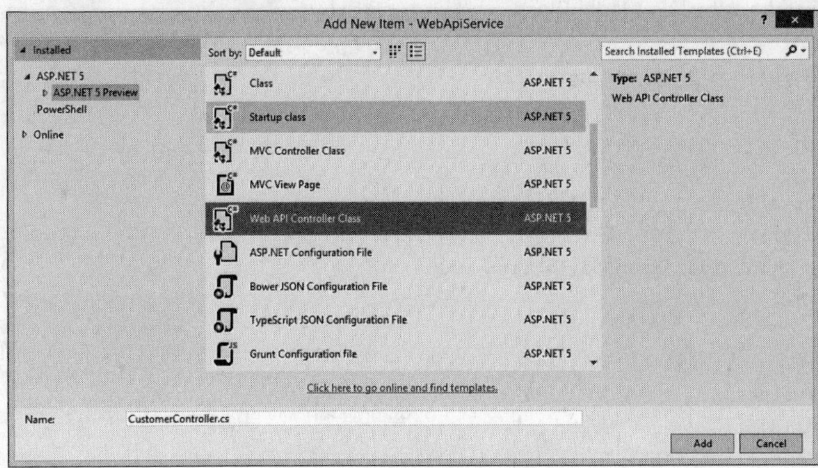

FIGURE 19.5 Select Web API Controller Class from the Add New Item dialog.

LISTING 19.2 The Default Web API Controller Template Class

```
using System;
using System.Collections.Generic;
using System.Linq;
using System.Threading.Tasks;
using Microsoft.AspNet.Mvc;

namespace WebApiService.Controllers
{
  [Route("api/[controller]")]
  public class CustomerController : Controller
  {
    //GET: api/values.
    [HttpGet]
    public IEnumerable<string> Get()
    {
      return new string[] { "value1", "value2" };
    }

    //GET api/values/5.
    [HttpGet("{id}")]
    public string Get(int id)
    {
      return "value";
    }
```

```
        //POST api/values.
        [HttpPost]
        public void Post([FromBody]string value)
        {
        }

        //PUT api/values/5.
        [HttpPut("{id}")]
        public void Put(int id, [FromBody]string value)
        {
        }

        //DELETE api/values/5.
        [HttpDelete("{id}")]
        public void Delete(int id)
        {
        }
    }
}
```

The next step is to write code inside these stubbed-out methods to service requests for `Customers` and return the appropriate results. Just like an MVC application, these methods can be called by addressing a URL and passing parameters in the query string as part of the request. The response will be sent as the body of the HTTP response message (more on all this in a moment). Before writing these methods, it is important to note a little more about our HTTP services written with ASP.NET 5.0.

HTTP web services leverage the standard HTTP verbs of `GET`, `PUT`, `POST`, and `DELETE`. These HTTP verbs indicate the required HTTP actions. For example, if a user is requesting a page, the browser issues an HTTP `GET` to the server; if the user posts data to the page, the browser issues an HTTP `POST`. Services work the same way: the calling client issues an HTTP request (`GET`, `POST`, and so on). The request is mapped to your code via a route (more on this in a moment). Your code then returns the HTTP results as a response.

NOTE

You can get by with just `GET` and `POST` for all your web service needs. In fact, there are many proponents of this approach. There was a time when not all browsers and corporate firewalls allowed `PUT` and `DELETE`. (All modern browsers do.) This chapter leverages all these HTTP verbs as Microsoft's template does the same. In fact, you can decorate a method as accepting both verbs (`POST` and `DELETE`, for example).

You use attributes to decorate methods in your controller with the appropriate HTTP verb. This allows ASP.NET to route the request appropriately. The following outlines these attributes and their usages:

- `[HttpGet]`—Indicates a request for data and is used to retrieve a single object instance (typically as JSON message) or a list of objects.
- `[HttpPost]`—Marks a method as `HttpPost` when you intend to post data to an existing URL/service. The method will receive the submitted data, and you can use it as you see fit within the method (typically adding or updating an item in your model).
- `[HttpPut]`—Can be used like `POST` (to send data to the server). Notice in the template (Listing 19.2) it is being used as the CRUD (create, read, update, and delete) operations. However, the `PUT` verb is more a part of the HTTP standard than anything else. `PUT` was meant for accessing a resource that does not exist (think page or image). If not found, the `PUT` will create the resource on the server (and thus the URL would be formed). If found, `PUT` simply was to replace the resource. You can still use `PUT` to do a CRUD update if that makes your code cleaner. However, you can also just use `POST`.
- `[HttpDelete]`—Used to indicate an item in your model should be deleted.

NOTE

If you used prior editions of ASP.NET Web API, you recall that methods were mapped to HTTP verbs primarily based on method naming conventions. For example, you would write `GetCustomer()` or `PostCustomer()`. Decorating the method with an attribute was optional. With ASP.NET 5.0 Web API, attributes are required to map HTTP verbs to method names (at least in the version used when writing this book).

The use of these HTTP verb-based attributes aligns your services clearly with the HTTP specification and makes the intent of your code clear. This makes the code easier to understand and work with. Let's look at writing a few of these service methods for accessing our `Customer` model.

TIP

When you're building a web service, it is best to group functionality into coarse-grained interfaces. You don't want web methods that do a number of fine-grained operations, such as setting properties. This chatty nature can be expensive when communicating across the Internet.

Of course, this approach is also contrary to most object-oriented application designs. Therefore, the use of a proxy object to bundle operations around a business object is ideal. The business object is serialized and passed across the wire. On the other side, it can be deserialized and then worked with in an in-process manner (in which chatty calls are not expensive).

Get a Customer (`HttpGet`)

The first method we will add to our service is `Get(int id)`. It will return a customer object and its values based on the `id` parameter passed on the URL. The customer will be returned from a collection of customers. This allows us to simulate looking up the customer from a database and thus extract that complexity. The following walks you through this first step:

1. Open `CustomerController.cs`.
2. Add a `using` statement to the top of the class for your model as follows: `using WebApiService.Models;`
3. Add a static variable as a generic collection of `Customer` objects to simulate data table results, as in the following:

```
//Simulate getting customers from a database.
static readonly List<Customer> _customers = new List<Customer>()
{
  new Customer { Id = 1, Name = "Customer 1", Email = "c1@contoso.com" },
  new Customer { Id = 2, Name = "Customer 2", Email = "c2@contoso.com" },
  new Customer { Id = 3, Name = "Customer 3", Email = "c3@contoso.com" }
};
```

Next up is the method itself. The generated method for `GET` that takes an `id` parameter returns a string. In our case, we want to return a `Customer` object. Therefore, we replace the `string` return type with `IActionResult`. We then write some LINQ to look up the customer by ID from the `collection` class created previously. If we don't find it, we return an instance of `HttpNotFoundResult`. Listing 19.3 shows the new web service method. Notice also that we added the type `(id:int)` to the `HttpGet` attribute to constrain (strongly type) the parameter passed. Passing a string value for the ID, for instance, would result in a 404 error (resource not found).

LISTING 19.3 The `Get` Method to Return a Customer from the Collection

```
[HttpGet("{id:int}")]
public IActionResult Get(int id)
{
  var customer = _customers.FirstOrDefault(x => x.Id == id);
  if (customer == null)
  {
    return HttpNotFound();
  }
  return new ObjectResult(customer);
}
```

You can now run this basic service and view the results. Before you do, you should configure what happens when Visual Studio launches the browser in debug mode. You can do so by right-clicking the project in Solution Explorer and choose properties. Here you will see the Debug node on the left. One of the configuration settings is Launch Browser.

Remember, this is a service and there is no UI to be shown in a browser. However, we will use the browser to call service methods as URLs and view the results. Use this screen to clear the URL for Launch Browser (removing the default, "api/values") as shown in Figure 19.6.

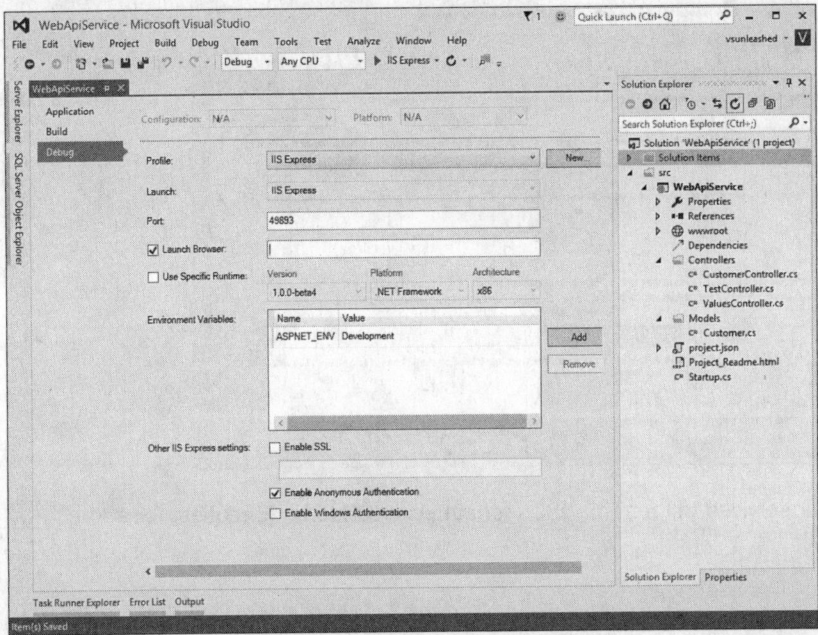

FIGURE 19.6 Use the project properties to indicate how a service application is launched by Visual Studio in debug mode.

Now, run the web application in debug mode (Start button set to IIS Express). This will launch a web browser pointed at your site (localhost). Again, because we have no pages in the site, a 403 (forbidden) error will display; the server thinks you are trying to list contents of the directory.

To invoke the service, you need to enter a URL that points to it. Recall from Listing 19.2 that comments above each service method actually describe the URL format required to invoke the method. These URL formats, like the rest of MVC, follow a routing convention that we will discuss momentarily.

To access the `Get` service by ID, you need to enter a URL in the form `http://localhost:xxxxx/api/customer/1`, where `xxxxx` is the random port number IIS Express has assigned to your site. The value 1 simply indicates a possible value for the `id` parameter.

Doing so invokes the service from Internet Explorer (IE). IE then asks you if you want to open or save the JSON result as a file. The lower part of Figure 19.7 shows an example.

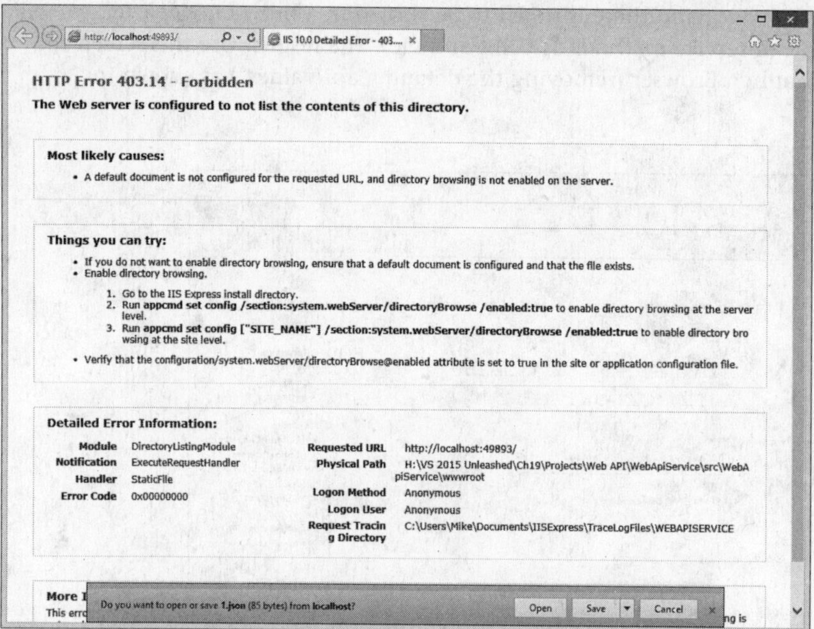

FIGURE 19.7 Your services will return a JSON-formatted result to an IE request for a Customer.

Clicking the Open option in Figure 19.7 will open the file inside of Visual Studio. The file contains the customer object as represented by JSON. The following shows the result (formatted with line breaks). You can now use this service from JavaScript, a mobile device, or a similar client.

```
{"Id":1,"Name":"Customer 1","Email":"c1@contoso.com","OptInEmail":false, "
OptInPhone":false,"Notes":null}
```

Note that the same request in Firefox and Chrome will, by default, return the message in the browser (versus a separate file). Figure 19.8 shows the result from Chrome.

When debugging HTTP services, it is useful to view the HTTP request and response messages sent to and from your service. You can use the F12 tools built in to IE 9 and later to help. Then click the Network tab and click the Enable Network Capturing button (green arrow). You can now call your web service, and IE will capture the messages for you. To view them, find the entry in the list and double-click it. You should now have tabs to view the request and response headers and bodies. Figure 19.9 shows an example.

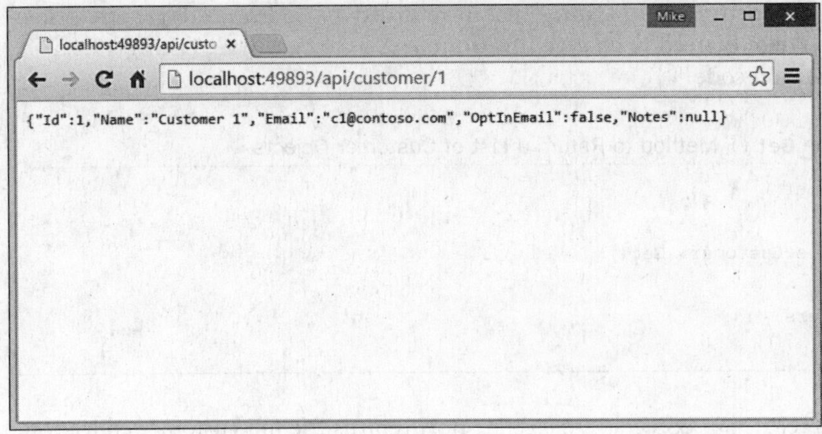

FIGURE 19.8 Chrome formats your service result as XML by default.

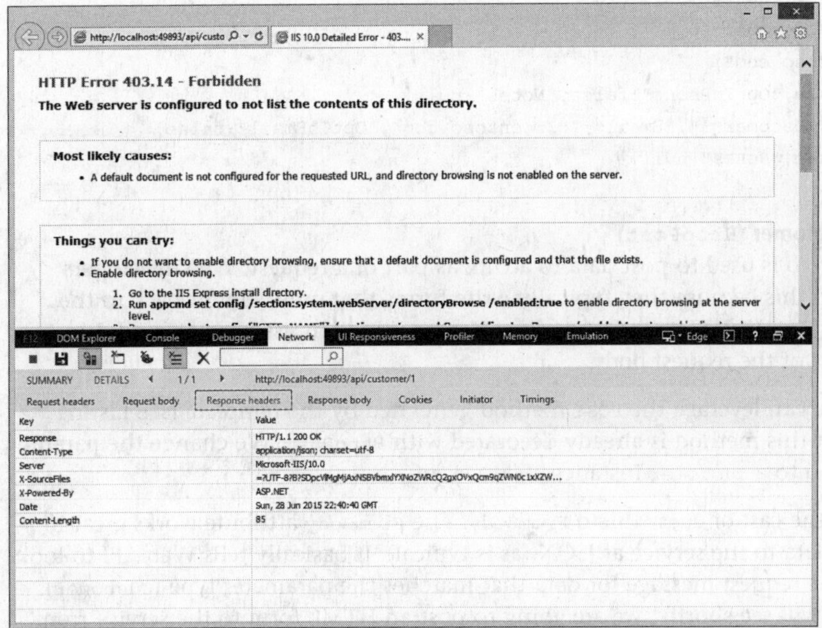

FIGURE 19.9 Use the F12 tools in IE to examine your service requests and response.

Get a List of Customers (`HttpGet`)

To return a list of customers, we simply need to return a collection of customers (in this case, based on the `collection` class used to simulate a data query). ASP.NET Web API takes care of wrapping this collection into an HTTP service response message format such as JSON or XML.

Recall the simple `Get` method from Listing 19.2. It returned an `IEnumerable` generic collection `string` type. We only need to change this from `string` to `Customer`. Listing 19.4 shows the new method code.

LISTING 19.4 The `Get()` Method to Return a List of Customer Objects

```
//GET: api/customer
[HttpGet]
public IEnumerable<Customer> Get()
{
  return _customers;
}
```

A call to `http://localhost:xxxxx/api/customer` now returns the full customer collection. The following shows the results (formatted with line breaks for spacing).

```
[{"Id":1,"Name":"Customer 1","Email":"c1@contoso.com","OptInEmail":false,
"OptInPhone":false,"Notes":null},
{"Id":2,"Name":"Customer 2",
"Email":"c2@contoso.com",
"OptInEmail":false,"OptInPhone":false,"Notes":null},
{"Id":3,"Name":"Customer 3","Email":"c3@contoso.com","OptInEmail":false,
"OptInPhone":false,"Notes":null}]
```

Create a New Customer (`HttpPost`)

The HTTP `POST` verb is used to post data to a URL as part of a request. Web developers should be used to this because they typically write forms that users submit back to the server for processing. An HTTP service works the same way. You use `POST` to send data to the service as part of the request body.

To get started, we can leverage the `POST` method generated by the template (see Listing 19.2). Notice that this method is already decorated with `HttpPost`. We change the parameter from a `string` to a `Customer` instance.

We also remove the cast of `Customer` to `FromBody`. The `FromBody` attribute works great if you are posting data to the service as JSON (as is typical). It basically tells Web API to look in the body of the request message for data that matches the parameter type (`Customer`). However, as you will see shortly, we are going to post an HTML form to the service from jQuery. The form would need to be converted into JSON (or similar) to comply with the `FromBody` attribute. Unfortunately, there is no method to convert form data directly to JSON (but you could write one or download one of the many that do exist). So, in this example, we will eliminate `FromBody` here and serialize the form for posting using jQuery.

Listing 19.5 shows the full method. Notice that the method does not return a value. Instead, it adds a code to the response (either `bad request` or `created`).

LISTING 19.5 The `Post()` Method to Add a New Customer Object

```
//POST api/customer.
[HttpPost]
public void Post(Customer customer)
{
  if (!ModelState.IsValid)
  {
    //Send 400 - bad request.
    Context.Response.StatusCode = 400;
  }
  else
  {
    //Get next customer id for collection.
    customer.Id = 1 + _customers.Max(x => (int?)x.Id) ?? 0;

    _customers.Add(customer);

    //Send 201 - created code.
    Context.Response.StatusCode = 201;
  }
}
```

The `Post` method uses the HTTP `POST` verb; therefore, you need a client capable of sending a `POST` to the server to call the method. This could be a web page with a form that posts data, JavaScript, a unit test, or a native application capable of sending an HTTP `POST`. Microsoft has also written a default ASP.NET Web API Help Page that you can use to call and test your service without writing additional code. We look at these client options in an upcoming section.

Update an Existing Customer (`HttpPut`)

You can send an update request to the server using the `PUT` verb. In our example, it would be an update to an existing customer record. The Web API Controller template assumes this approach. However, recall that `PUT` was not meant specifically for this purpose. Instead, the Web API has adopted it as a possible convention. You do not need to use `PUT` to process an update. In fact, if you were writing a web form, you would use the HTTP `POST` to update data to the server (and not use `PUT`).

If you intend to use `POST` for your Web API (instead of `PUT`), you could simply change the method signature to include both an ID and a `Customer` instance (as in the `PUT` method signature in the template shown in Listing 19.2). Or, you could use the same method created in Listing 19.5 but add logic to check whether a valid ID is passed on the given object; if so, look up the `Customer` instance from `_customers` and update; if not, create a new customer.

For our example, we will use `PUT`. Listing 19.6 shows the method. Later, you will see how to call the `PUT` method using the `HttpClient` library.

LISTING 19.6 Use `PUT` to Send an Update to a Customer

```
//PUT api/customer/1 to update a customer.
[HttpPut]
public void Put([FromBody]Customer customer)
{
  //Get customer to be updated.
  var customerToUpdate = _customers.FirstOrDefault(x => x.Id == customer.Id);

  if (customerToUpdate == null || !ModelState.IsValid)
  {
    //Send 400 - bad request.
    Context.Response.StatusCode = 400;
  }
  else
  {
    //Simulate updating the customer values.
    customerToUpdate.Name = customer.Name;
    customerToUpdate.Notes = customer.Notes;
    customerToUpdate.Email = customer.Email;
    customerToUpdate.OptInEmail = customer.OptInEmail;

    //Send 201 - created code.
    Context.Response.StatusCode = 201;
  }
}
```

> **NOTE**
>
> You can actually indicate a method that allows multiple HTTP verbs access. To do so, you use the attribute class `AcceptVerbs` and pass the verbs you want the method to accept. This would enable you to accept both `PUT` and `POST` on a single method, for example.

Delete a Customer (`HttpDelete`)

To delete an item using our service, we will leverage the HTTP `DELETE` verb. We do so by decorating the method with `HttpDelete`. The method takes an `id` parameter to indicate the customer to be deleted. We again constrain the parameter to an `int` value using the attribute definition at the top of the method. All that is left is to find the customer in the collection and remove it. Listing 19.7 shows the code. Notice that the code does not return anything. Instead, we just add the appropriate HTTP status code to the response. We will look at calling this method (along with `POST` and `PUT`) when we create a service client in an upcoming section.

LISTING 19.7 The `Delete()` Method to Delete a Customer from the Collection

```
//DELETE api/customer/1.
[HttpDelete("{id:int}")]
public void Delete(int id)
{
  var customer = _customers.FirstOrDefault(x => x.Id == id);
  if (customer == null)
  {
    //Send 404 - not found.
    Context.Response.StatusCode = 404;
  }
  else
  {
    //Remove customer.
    _customers.Remove(customer);

    //Sent 204 - no content (delete successful).
    Context.Response.StatusCode = 204;
  }
}
```

Understanding Service Routing

As you saw with the method `Get(id)` in the `CustomerController` class, service methods in ASP.NET Web API are accessed via a URL routing convention. This convention works in a similar way to the routing in ASP.NET MVC. The biggest difference is that Web API leverages the HTTP verb to select the appropriate action in your controller.

A request is sent to your website, parsed for the HTTP verb (`GET`, `POST`, `PUT`, `DELETE`), and processed through a routing engine. The routing engine uses conventions to find your controller and map the request based on verb and parameters to the appropriate action method. Recall that we set the route for the `CustomerController` class at the top of the class using the attribute `[Route("api/[controller]")]`. This is the default convention for Web API.

The `api/` portion of the construct is a convention indicating that this request is meant for a service. The `[controller]` portion of the route definition is used to find your controller based on the URL. In the example you have been creating, this is `customer`. (The word *controller* is not necessary.) You can then append parameter values to the request, as in `/api/customer/1`.

ASP.NET uses the `api/` portion of the route to avoid collision with your other controllers. For example, you might want to route requests for `/customer/1` to a web page to display a customer where the customer id=1. This allows a request to `/api/customer/1` on the same domain to service customer data interactions with your API. Of course, this is easily changed if you do not like the convention. Just mark your service controller route attribute as `[Route("[controller]")]`; this eliminate the `api/` portion of the convention.

Include the Action in the Route

Sometimes your service includes multiple definitions that use the same HTTP verb and accept the same parameter types. For example, you may have `GetCustomer(int id)` and `GetCustomerOrder(int id)` in the same service controller. In this case, using the default routing convention of `api/[controller]` will result in an error because the request is ambiguous and cannot be satisfied. Figure 19.10 shows the error in the browser.

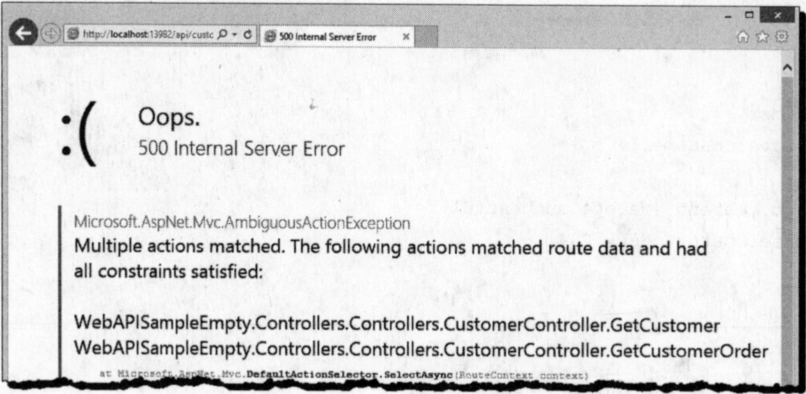

FIGURE 19.10 Two service methods in the same controller with the same HTTP verb and parameters will result in a server error (unless you change the route convention to include the action).

You can solve this problem by changing the route convention to include the action method. You do so by editing the `Route` attribute at the top of the class as follows: `[Route("api/[controller]/[action]")]`. This changes the convention to require the action name.

Notice that the route is now mapped to your method name. ASP.NET Web API also gives you control of your action names for the route. To change the action name (without renaming your methods), you add the `ActionName` attribute class. For example, you might use `[ActionName("Get")]` for the `GetCustomer` method and `[ActionName("GetOrder")]` for the `GetCustomerOrder` method. Doing so changes your URL route; now to get a customer, you would call `/api/customer/get/1`.

Consuming an ASP.NET Web API Service

ASP.NET Web API services can be consumed by any client capable of speaking HTTP. This means other websites as well as native client applications. In the case of a website, you can use standard HTTP `GET` and `POST` messages to work with the service. Typically, you do so using JavaScript and the helper library, jQuery. This helper library simplifies sending requests and receiving response messages from services.

For native clients such as iOS, Android, and Windows, you use an HTTP framework class library. In Windows, this is the `System.Net.Http` namespace (or `Microsoft.Net.Http` inside the DNX Core 5.0) and the `HttpClient` class. This framework lets you easily make a request to an HTTP service and consume the results. This section discusses both using jQuery and `System.Net.Http` to access Web API services.

TIP

Microsoft has created the ASP.NET Web API Help Page NuGet package to automatically generate help page content for your Web API services. You can add this package to your application from NuGet. You then use the help pages to exercise your methods without writing additional code. This library also uses jQuery to call your service methods. However, it automatically generates forms for posting data (among other things).

Create the Client Application

A website is a likely candidate for consuming Web API services. Websites run in the browser and thus already know how to send `GET` and `POST` requests to the server. In this example, we will use an ASP.NET MVC application for creating the web pages to call the services and process the results. We will look at doing so directly from the client using jQuery and AJAX. We will also show how to consume these services from your server-side code (inside your controller) to simulate how native clients might access the services. (For more information on ASP.NET MVC and JavaScript, see Chapter 17 and Chapter 18, "Using JavaScript and Creating Client-Side Frameworks").

NOTE

This example uses a website as a client for Web API services. However, if you do not have a need for services, you can simply create a website and embed the service logic there. You can even still use jQuery to call back to your server code the same way you might call a web service (see Chapters 17 and 18).

In addition, you might want to have a website that also exposes an API. In that case, there is a benefit to intermingling the website and service code in the same project. For example, you would only need to create a single model that could be shared by the website and the services. Other calling clients, of course, would have to handle the response (deserialize) in their own way.

Let's look at creating a sample website that uses the `Customer` service created previously. The following list steps you through creating the project.

1. We will start by adding a new project to the existing solution. Right-click the solution in Solution Explorer and choose Add, New Project. Add a new project.
2. Select the Web node on the left of the New Project dialog and find the ASP.NET Web Application template.
3. Name the project `WebApiClient` and click OK.
4. Select ASP.NET 5 Web Site as your project template and again click the OK button.

Visual Studio will create the new project template on your behalf. Notice under the Dependencies node in Solution Explorer (see Figure 19.11) that there is a folder called `Bower`. Recall from Chapter 17 that Bower is a package manager for web frameworks (and is used by Visual Studio). Notice here that jQuery (among other things) is an installed package for this template.

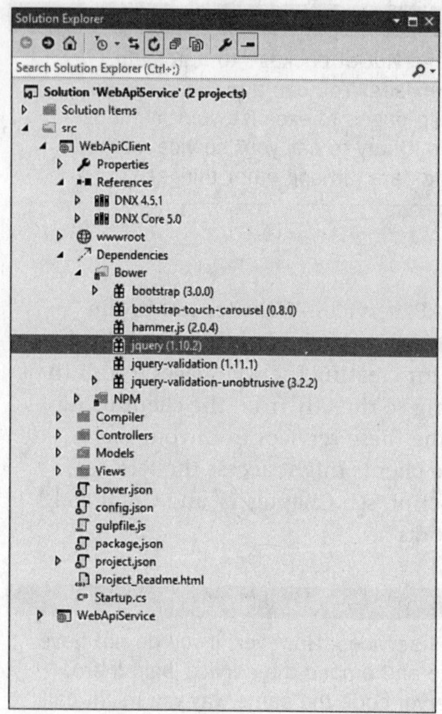

FIGURE 19.11 The web client project we intend to use for consuming our HTTP services.

We also need to make both the client and service projects execute correctly inside Visual Studio at startup. To do so, right-click the solution in Solution Explorer and choose Properties. Here you will see the Startup Project options as shown in Figure 19.12. Select Multiple startup projects as shown and set their Action to Start. Also, use Project Dependencies to indicate that the client project depends on the service project.

Create the Files for the Customer Views and Controller

The Web Site template includes a home and about page. We are going to ignore these items for now and create our own customer views and a related controller for handling requests. The following walks you through the process of creating the basic files you will need:

1. Using the `WebApiClient` project, open Solution Explorer, right-click the `Views` folder, and choose Add, New Folder. Name the new folder `Customer`.

2. Right-click the newly created folder and choose Add, New Item. From the Add New Item dialog, select ASP.NET 5 on the left. Select the template MVC View Page. Name the page `Index.cshtml` and click the Add button.

   Visual Studio will create and open this page. We will use this page momentarily to show a list of customers and allow access to the Create and Edit actions.

3. Repeat Steps 1–3 for adding pages for `Edit.cshtml` and `Create.cshtml`. We will enable the Edit page to allow a user to edit an existing customer or delete it. The Create page will allow a user to create a new customer.

4. Finally, add the controller. Right-click the `Controllers` folder in Solution Explorer and choose Add, New Item. From the Add New Item dialog, select the template MVC Controller Class. Name the class `CustomerController.cs`.

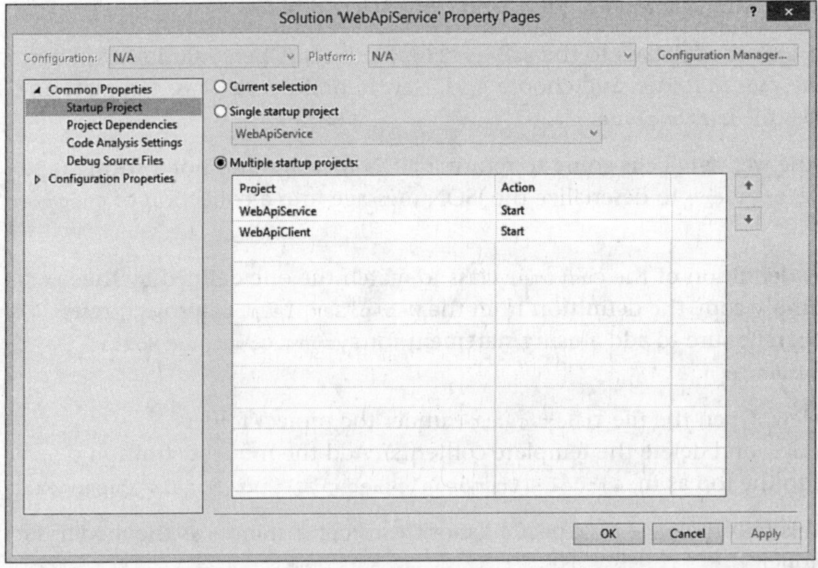

FIGURE 19.12 Use Solution Properties to set the startup projects for the Visual Studio solution.

The last step is to code the three views (Index, Create, Edit), the controller, and any related JavaScript we want to use. We discuss each view and the corresponding jQuery and controller code in the upcoming sections.

NOTE

The ASP.NET 5 Web Site template is based on MVC. MVC has its own pattern for calling a controller, getting model data, and associating that data with a view as part of the response (see Chapter 17). In this example, we are going to mix the MVC pattern with jQuery. We will show calling services from both the controller (using `System.Net.Http`) and directly from the client with jQuery AJAX calls.

You might prefer a cleaner approach that uses either all MVC controller calls or all jQuery client calls. You could, of course, also use standard HTML pages, Web Forms, or an SPA built on things like AngularJS (see Chapter 18).

Use `HttpClient` to Call the Web API Service and Display a List of Customers

The first example will be to call an HTTP service from the server using MVC. Think of the server like you would a native device (Windows phone or tablet). In the case of a native device, you use a library that knows how to send HTTP requests and process the results. In this case, we will use `Microsoft.Net.Http`.

We are going to leverage the ASP.NET MVC pattern for this example. This means creating a Model to represent the Customer, a View to display the customers, and logic in the controller to handle the request (and call the Web API customer services). The following walks you through creating the Model, View, and Controller.

1. Add the `Customer` model class to the `WebApiClient` project. Open Solution Explorer, right-click the `Models` folder, and choose Add, New Item. Select a Class template and name the class file `Customer.cs`.

   Remember, the web service is going to return a JSON message and not a strong type. We will use `HttpClient` to deserialize the JSON message into a collection of `Customer` instances.

2. Create a new definition of the `Customer` class to match the one defined by the service (or simply copy the definition from the `WebApiSampleEmpty` project; refer to Listing 19.1). Be sure to add a using statement for `System.ComponentModel.DataAnnotations`.

3. Define the view. Open the file `Index.cshtml` under the project folder `Views/Customer` (and delete the template contents). Add the model definition for the page to the top as in, `@model IEnumerable<WebApiClient.Models.Customer>`.

   Recall that this tells the page to expect a list of Customer instances as the model, set by the controller.

4. Add HTML markup and Razor syntax (or TagHelpers) that defines a table to hold the customer data. Listing 19.8 shows an example using Razor syntax (see Chapter 17 on how you could also use TagHelpers instead). Notice that the table body is enclosed by a `for each` loop to iterate over the model that contains the customer list.

LISTING 19.8 The Markup for the Index Page to Show a List of Customers

```
@model IEnumerable<WebApiClient.Models.Customer>
@{
  ViewBag.Title = "Customers";
}
<h2>Customers</h2>
<p>
```

```
  @Html.ActionLink("Create New", "Create")
</p>
<table class="table">
  <thead>
    <tr>
      <th>Name</th>
      <th>Email</th>
      <th>Opt In</th>
      <th>Notes</th>
    </tr>
  </thead>
@foreach (var item in Model)
{
  <tr>
    <td>
      @Html.DisplayFor(modelItem => item.Name)
    </td>
    <td>
      @Html.DisplayFor(modelItem => item.Email)
    </td>
    <td>
      @Html.DisplayFor(modelItem => item.OptInEmail)
    </td>
    <td>
      @Html.DisplayFor(modelItem => item.Notes)
    </td>
    <td>
      @Html.ActionLink("Edit", "Edit", new { id = item.Id }) |
      @Html.ActionLink("Delete", "Delete", new { id = item.Id })
    </td>
  </tr>
}
</table>
```

5. Open `_Layout.cshtml` and add a link in the navigation bar to `Customers` as in the following:

```
<li><a asp-controller="Customer" asp-action="Index">Customers</a></li>
```

6. Before we create the controller method to handle the request for the customer index view, we need to add a reference to the NuGet package `Microsoft.AspNet.WebApi.Client` to the `WebApiClient` project. To do so, right-click the References node in Solution Explorer under `WebApiClient` and choose Manage NuGet Packages.

   Search for `Microsoft.AspNet.WebApi.Client` and click the Install button. Figure 19.13 shows an example.

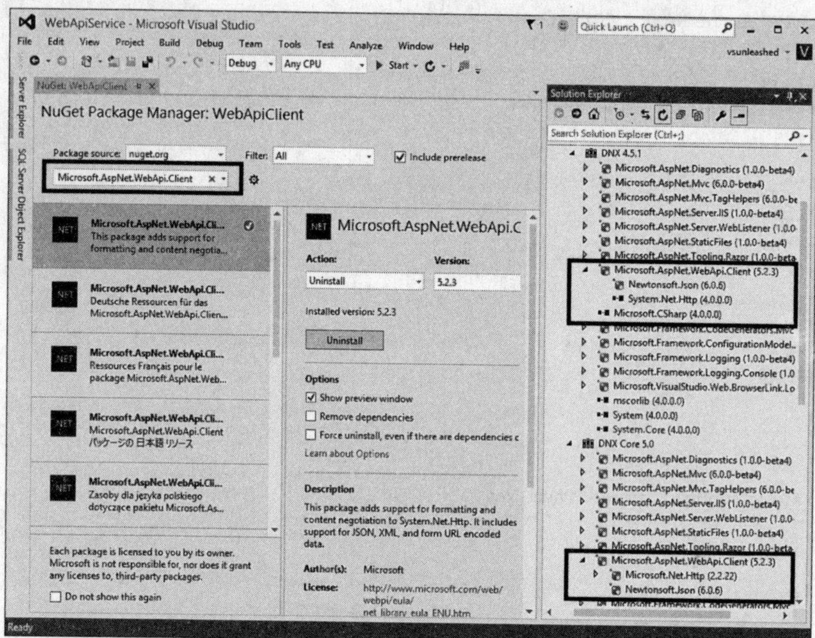

FIGURE 19.13 Install the NuGet package for `Microsoft.AspNet.WebApi.Client`.

Notice the package added to the DNX frameworks references. This package references `Microsoft.Net.Http` inside the DNX Core 5.0 framework and `System.Net.Http` inside DNX 4.51. The former is a newer package targeted at Core 5.0 development. The latter is a fuller version; we will use it in our examples (you could switch to the core version but would have to modify the code accordingly).

Notice too the reference to `Newtonsoft.json` (an open-source framework for working with JSON and .NET).

7. Because we are only using `System.Net.Http` in the client application you need to remove the reference to the DNX Core 5.0 framework. Open `project.json` and remove the reference, `"dnxcore50": { }` from the `"frameworks"` section.

8. Open the `CustomerController` class by double-clicking it in the Solution Explorer window and add a number of `using` statements to the top of the file. These will be for working with the `System.Net.Http` and `System.Net.Http.Headers` namespaces to call the service and the `WebApiClient.Models` namespace for working with the `Customer` model. The following shows an example.

```
using System;
using Microsoft.AspNet.Mvc;
using System.Net.Http;
using System.Threading.Tasks;
using WebApiClient.Models;
using System.Net.Http.Headers;
```

9. Add a line at the top of the class as a variable to store the service URL. You would likely store this in a configuration file. In this sample code, however, we are going to hard-code it at the top of the file, like this (where xxxxx represents to port number to the Web Api project).

```
string baseUri = "http://localhost:XXXXX/";
```

10. Edit the Index method signature to be called asynchronously. The following shows an example.

```
public async Task<IActionResult> Index()
{
}
```

11. Add code that tells `HttpClient` to call the URL to the customer service call, `api/customer`. Listing 19.9 shows the full code listing for the method. Notice that we tell the `HttpClient` instance to accept JSON headers. We then call `GetAsynch` to execute the Web API service call. The results are read into a list of `Customer` instances using `ReadAsAsync`. Finally, we send the `Customer` list to the view as the result of the request.

LISTING 19.9 The `CustomerController` Class `Index()` Method That Uses `HttpClient` to Call the Web API Service to Return a List of Customers and the Customer Index View

```
using System;
using Microsoft.AspNet.Mvc;
using System.Net.Http;
using System.Threading.Tasks;
using WebApiClient.Models;
using System.Net.Http.Headers;
using System.Collections.Generic;

namespace WebApiClient.Controllers
{
  public class CustomerController : Controller
  {
    string baseUri = "http://localhost:13982/";

    //Display list of customers.
    public async Task<IActionResult> Index()
    {
      //Call web service (/api/customer) and return result (view)
      using (var hClient = new HttpClient())
      {
        hClient.BaseAddress = new Uri(baseUri);
        hClient.DefaultRequestHeaders.Accept.Clear();
```

```
        hClient.DefaultRequestHeaders.Accept.Add(
          new MediaTypeWithQualityHeaderValue("application/json"));

        //Call HTTP GET api/customer to get all customers.
        HttpResponseMessage response = await hClient.GetAsync("api/customer");

        //Verify response and map JSON to Customer instance.
        if (response.IsSuccessStatusCode)
        {
          List<Customer> customers =
            await response.Content.ReadAsAsync<List<Customer>>();

          return View(customers);
        }
        else
        {
          ModelState.AddModelError("", response.ReasonPhrase);
          return View();
        }
      }
    }
  }
}
```

You can now use Visual Studio to run both projects and view the results. Navigate to the /customer page. You should be taken to a page similar to that shown in Figure 19.14.

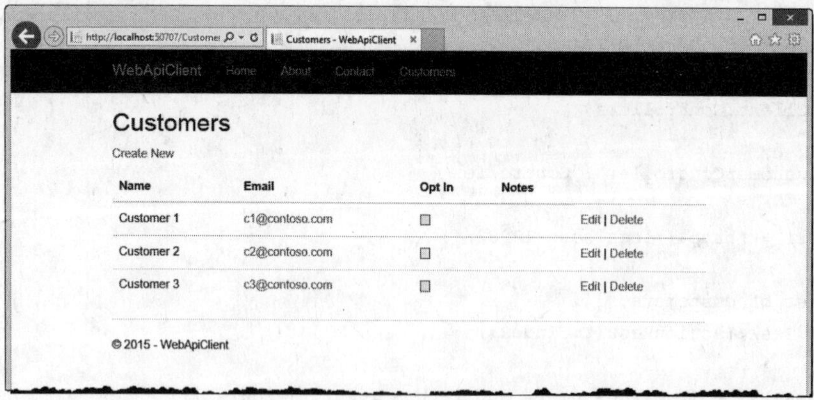

FIGURE 19.14 The ASP.NET Web Client calling the Web API service from the Controller and displaying the customer list results.

Use `HttpClient` to Get and Edit a Customer

We will now add a view for displaying a customer to edit. Recall that the customer index view included the Edit `ActionLink` for each row in the table (refer to Listing 19.8). This sends a request to the controller as `/customer/edit/1`. We will create an Edit method in the controller that takes an ID to handle this request by calling the Web API service. The View will then post back to the controller; we will use `HttpClient` to send a `PUT` request to the Web API to update the customer. Let's get started:

1. We need to define the `Edit.cshtml` view. Start by adding a model definition for the `Customer` class to the top of the page, as in: `@model WebApiClient.Models.Customer`.

   The rest of the view follows standard HTML/Razor syntax, including a form field and validation message for each property of Customer.

   Note: this markup is lengthy and thus omitted here. Please check the source code download for the book to examine this view more closely. You can also jump ahead to Figure 19.15 to see the view in action.

2. Open `CustomerController` and add an Edit method signature to be called asynchronously, return an action result, and take an `id` parameter. The following shows an example.

   ```
   public async Task<IActionResult> Edit(int? id)
   {
   }
   ```

3. Add code to call the web method, passing the `id` parameter (using the URL), casting the results into a Customer instance, and returning the Edit view. This code is similar to the code written previously to return a list of customers. Listing 19.10 shows an example.

LISTING 19.10 The `Edit(id)` Method in the Customer Controller to Call the Web API `Get(id)` Web Method Using `HttpClient`

```
public async Task<IActionResult> Edit(int? id)
{
  //Verify id parameter.
  if (id == null)
  {
    return new HttpStatusCodeResult(400); //bad request
  }

  //Call web service (/api/customer) and return result (view).
  using (var hClient = new HttpClient())
  {
    hClient.BaseAddress = new Uri(baseUri);
    hClient.DefaultRequestHeaders.Accept.Clear();
    hClient.DefaultRequestHeaders.Accept.Add(
      new MediaTypeWithQualityHeaderValue("application/json"));
```

```
    //Call HTTP GET api/customer/1.
    HttpResponseMessage response = await hClient.GetAsync(
      string.Format("api/customer/{0}", id.ToString()));

    //Verify response and map JSON to Customer instance.
    if (response.IsSuccessStatusCode)
    {
      Customer customer = await response.Content.ReadAsAsync<Customer>();
      return View(customer);
    }
    else
    {
      return HttpNotFound();
    }
  }
}
```

4. Write another Edit controller method to receive the form postback. The form itself is already set to post back to the controller. In this case, you mark the Edit method with the `HttpPost` attribute to indicate that the method should be called for a postback. The method signature can take a `Customer` instance. MVC will handle mapping the postback data to the `Customer` parameter. The following shows the method signature.

```
[HttpPost]
[ValidateAntiForgeryToken]
public async Task<IActionResult> Edit(Customer customer)
{
}
```

5. We now need to call the service to update the given customer. The code to call the service is again similar to the code shown to call the other two services thus far. The big difference is that this code calls the Web API `PUT` method; we therefore use the `HttpClient` call `PutAsJsonAsync`. Listing 19.11 shows the full method.

LISTING 19.11 The `Edit(customer)` Method in the Customer Controller to Call the Web API `Put([FromBody]Customer customer)` Web Method Using `HttpClient`

```
[HttpPost]
[ValidateAntiForgeryToken]
public async Task<IActionResult> Edit(Customer customer)
{
  if (ModelState.IsValid)
  {
```

```
using (var hClient = new HttpClient())
{
  hClient.BaseAddress = new Uri(baseUri);
  hClient.DefaultRequestHeaders.Accept.Clear();
  hClient.DefaultRequestHeaders.Accept.Add(
    new MediaTypeWithQualityHeaderValue("application/json"));

  //Post customer to the Web API service.
  HttpResponseMessage response =
    await hClient.PutAsJsonAsync("api/customer", customer);

  //Check response.
  if (response.IsSuccessStatusCode)
  {
    return RedirectToAction("Index");
  }
  else
  {
    ModelState.AddModelError("", response.ReasonPhrase);
  }

}

}
return View(customer);
}
```

We can now run the application. Again, make sure the Web API services application is running. You can click on a customer Edit link in the customer list (see Figure 19.14). This brings up the page shown in Figure 19.15. Clicking the Save button posts the page back to the controller, off to the service, and returns the customer list view with the updated change.

Use jQuery to Create a New Customer

The jQuery library is a JavaScript library that makes the business of using JavaScript to write AJAX calls much easier. It is a framework that wraps some repetitive, complex JavaScript for client-side programming. jQuery is included with all Visual Studio web templates. (For more details on jQuery, see jQuery.com and our discussion in Chapter 18.)

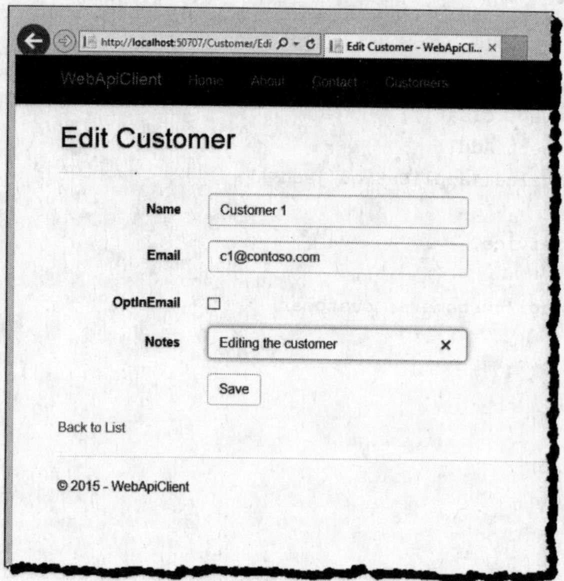

FIGURE 19.15 The customer edit page in action.

jQuery is especially useful because it contains helper methods that allow you to make HTTP GET and POST requests. These methods are part of the jQuery AJAX capabilities. The following are key methods here:

- `jQuery.get()` sends a GET request to a server and manages the results.
- `jQuery.post()` sends data via a POST to a server and handles the response.
- `jQuery.getJSON()` sends a GET request and processes the results as JSON-encoded data.
- `jQuery.ajax()` is the low-level method for performing asynchronous HTTP requests. Note that the methods just listed are shorthand methods that can be used in place of `jQuery.ajax()`. However, the `ajax` method can also be used for GET and POST requests. Its biggest benefit is that it can be used when sending requests using the HTTP verbs PUT and DELETE (for which there are no shorthand methods).

Notice that each of these methods is prefixed by a call to the jQuery object. The shorthand for this call is a dollar sign (`$`), as in `$.post`. The `post` method takes a URL to the service, data that is to be sent to the service, and a callback function that is executed when the request completes. The following outlines using the `$.post` method to call the Web API service to save a newly created customer:

1. Using the `WebApiClient` project, open the `Create.cshtml` page (created earlier) and remove the template content from the page.

2. Add a model definition for `Customer` at the top of the page as we did with the Edit page. This will make it easier to write the markup and validation for the form. The following shows an example.

```
@model WebApiClient.Models.Customer
```

3. Define the HTML form tag to nest the input controls. The following shows an example. In this case, we set the ID of the form so we can select it using jQuery. The action and the method are set. However, we are not going to write corresponding logic in the controller. Instead, we will intercept the post using our jQuery call.

```
<form id="form-create" action="create" method="post">
```

4. The rest of the view should be similar to the Edit view created earlier. This is again just standard HTML/Razor syntax for each property of `Customer`.

   Note: this markup is also lengthy and thus omitted here. Please check the source code download for the book to examine this view more closely. You can also jump ahead to Figure 19.16 to see the view in action.

5. Write the JavaScript that will call the service (`POST` to `/api/customer`) using jQuery. We will add the script to the bottom of the `Create.cshtml` file.

   For starters, mark the script section using the `@section Scripts` identifier. This tells ASP.NET that your script should be loaded in the Scripts section of the page. Recall that the `_Layout.cshtml` page in Views/Shared defines when and where page sections are rendered. Listing 19.12 shows an example of the section, the inclusion of the validation libraries for the form, and the newly created JavaScript code to call the service. (We will walk through this code in a moment.)

LISTING 19.12 The jQuery Code to Call the Web API `Post(customer)` Method

```
@section Scripts {
  <script src="@Url.Content(
    "~/lib/jquery-validation/jquery.validate.js")"></script>
  <script src="@Url.Content(
    "~/lib/jquery-validation-unobtrusive/jquery.validate.unobtrusive.js")">
  </script>

  <script type="text/javascript">

    var url = "http://localhost:xxxxx/api/customer";

    $('#form-create').submit(function () {

      //Clear result message.
      $('#result').html("");
```

```
        //Verify form is valid.
        if ($('#form-create').valid()) {

          //Serialize the form data and post to the web service.
          $.post(url, $('#form-create').serialize())
            .success(function () {
              window.location = "/customer";
            })
            .error(function () {
              $('#result').html("Error saving customer.");
            });
          return false;
        }
      });

    </script>
}
```

The JavaScript starts by defining the variable, `url`, that points to our service method (note you need to include your port number instead of xxxxx). Next, notice that the code is set to run when the form posts, `$('#form-create').submit`. This uses the jQuery to find the form and attach a method to the `submit` event.

Inside the form `submit` function, we use the jQuery `$.post` to call our web service. We pass in the URL and the form as serialized, `$.post(url, $('#form-create').serialize())`.

Upon success, we navigate back to the customer list page. If there is an error, we add a message to the top of the form using the jQuery selector call `$('#result').html`. (See the HTML for the page.)

6. Add a method to the `CustomerController` class to return the page, as in the following.

```
public IActionResult Create()
{
  return View();
}
```

You can now run the page and create new customers. Make sure to run the Web API services project first. Navigate your browser to `/customer` to see a list of customers. Click the `Create New` link (refer to Figure 19.14). This should bring up the form shown in Figure 19.16. Notice that the validation works without a post to the service. Enter valid form data and click Save. Your new record will be added to the collection associated with the Web API service.

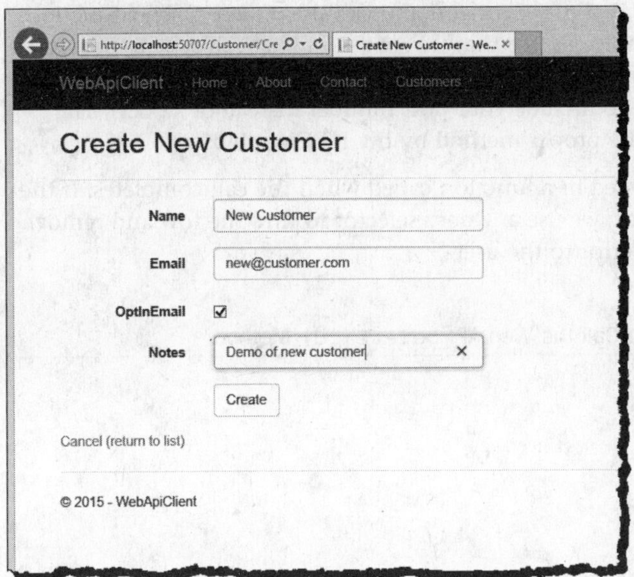

FIGURE 19.16 The Create New Customer page uses jQuery to call the Web API service to save a new customer.

Use jQuery to Delete a Customer

The last Web API client example is a call to the `Delete(id)` service (refer to Listing 19.7). Again, we have the choice of making this call from the client app's controller on the server using `HttpClient` or directly from the user's web browser using jQuery and AJAX. For this example, we will demonstrate the later. The following walks you through a few simple steps (assuming you have completed the prior tasks in this section).

1. Using the `WebApiClient` project, open the `Index.cshtml` page (created earlier to show a list of customers in a table).

2. Add markup at the top of the page as a container that displays an error if the web service delete call fails.

```
<div id="result" class="text-danger"></div>
```

3. Add an identifier for each table row. This will allow the row to be selected using jQuery and removed on a successful delete. The following shows the addition to the row definition inside the `foreach` loop.

```
<tr id="row-@item.Id">
```

4. Remove the `ActionLink` for Delete in the column at the bottom of the table row definition. Replace this with a standard anchor tag that calls a new JavaScript function you will write, `deleteCustomer(id)`. The following shows an example.

```
<a href="javascript:deleteCustomer(@item.Id)">Delete</a>
```

5. The last step is to write the JavaScript function and call the jQuery `$.ajax` function. Listing 19.13 shows an example. Notice that we set the `$.ajax` call type to `DELETE` to send the HTTP `DELETE` verb request. Notice too that the URL is simply a call to `/api/customer/id` (note you need to include your port number instead of xxxxx), The Web API routes this call to the proper method by the HTTP verb used.

Finally, the results are processed in a function called when the call completes. If the status code is 204 (no content, we use a jQuery selector to find the row and remove it. Otherwise, we display an error to the user.

LISTING 19.13 The jQuery Code to Call the Web API `Delete(id)` Method

```
@section Scripts {
  <script type="text/javascript">
    function deleteCustomer(id) {
      //Clear result message.
      $('#result').html("");

      //Send delete request to web service.
      $.ajax({
        url: "http://localhost:xxxxx/api/customer/" + id,
        type: 'DELETE',
        complete: function (response) {
          if (response.status == 204) {
            $('#row-' + id).remove();
          } else {
            $('#result').html("Error deleting customer.");
          }
        },
      });
    };
  </script>
}
```

WCF Service Applications

WCF services have become less prevalent because web developers prefer the more straightforward programming model of REST-based services (and the Web API). However, WCF still has its place for writing robust services that can be called by multiple clients using multiple endpoints/protocols.

Like web services, WCF services have their own set of terms. It is important that you have a baseline understanding of these before trying to understand the key concepts related to WCF service applications:

NOTE

It is not imperative that you understand all these terms to work with WCF. However, it can be helpful to have a cursory understanding when you are creating and configuring these services.

- **WCF service**—A WCF service is a set of logic that you expose to multiple clients as a service. A service might have one or more service operations (think methods). A WCF service is exposed to clients through one or more endpoints that you define. Each endpoint has a binding and behaviors (see the "Endpoint" entry in this list). In this way, you can create a single service and configure it to work efficiently with multiple clients (such as HTTP, TCP, and named pipes).
- **WCF client**—A WCF client is an application that Visual Studio generates to call a WCF service. You can create a WCF client by adding a service reference to a client application. The client application is the actual application that consumes the results of the WCF service. Think of the WCF client as the go-between or proxy that helps connect your client code to the WCF service.
- **Host**—A host is a process that runs (or hosts) the WCF service. This process controls the lifetime of the service. It's similar to the way ASP.NET provides a host for web services. You can write your own service host or allow a service to be self-hosted.
- **Contract**—Contracts define your WCF services. This is essentially the public contract you guarantee between your service and any clients. There is a service contract that defines the content of the service (such as its operations). There is also an operation contract for each service operation. This contract indicates the parameters and return type of the service operation. There are also message, data, and fault contracts.
- **Endpoint**—Endpoints are configured for each service operation. An endpoint is where messages for your service are sent and received. Each endpoint defines both an address and binding for communicating with a service. For example, you might have one endpoint that works with SOAP over HTTP. You might have another endpoint for the same service that enables the service to work with MSMQ. In this way, you can add and configure endpoints to your service independently of actually coding the service. This ensures that your service can be configured to work efficiently with both existing and new clients.
- **Address**—An address is a unique URI for a given service. The address is used by calling clients to locate the service. The URI also defines the protocol that is required to reach the address, such as HTTP or TCP. Each endpoint you define for your service can have its own address.
- **Behaviors**—A behavior defines the way an entire service, a specific endpoint, or a specific service operation behaves. You can define behaviors for such things as security credentials and service throttling.
- **Binding, binding element, and channel**—Endpoints have bindings that define the way the endpoint communicates. A binding includes information about transport,

encoding, and security. For example, you can configure an endpoint's binding to work with the HTTP transport encoded as text.

- A binding is made up of binding elements. Each element represents a single portion of the binding. You might, for example, have a binding element for the encoding and another for the transport. Binding elements and their configuration are implemented as channels. The binding elements are stacked together to create this channel. In this way, the channel represents the actual implementation of the binding.

Visual Studio provides various tools that make building WCF services easier. If you know that you intend to host your WCF service inside a website under IIS, you can actually add a WCF service to a website using the item templates. However, if you want to host outside of IIS or to decide on hosting at a different time, you can create a WCF project. In either case, you then define your service contract (as an interface). Next, you implement the service contract. Finally, you configure communication endpoints for the service. After your service is complete, you pick a hosting model and deploy it accordingly. Clients can then access the service. Let's take a look at each of these steps.

The WCF Project Template

You can use Visual Studio to create a WCF service project in much the same way as you define other projects (File, New, Project). From the Add New Project dialog box, you can select the WCF node under either C# or Visual Basic. This enables you to choose a WCF service project template. Figure 19.17 shows this dialog box.

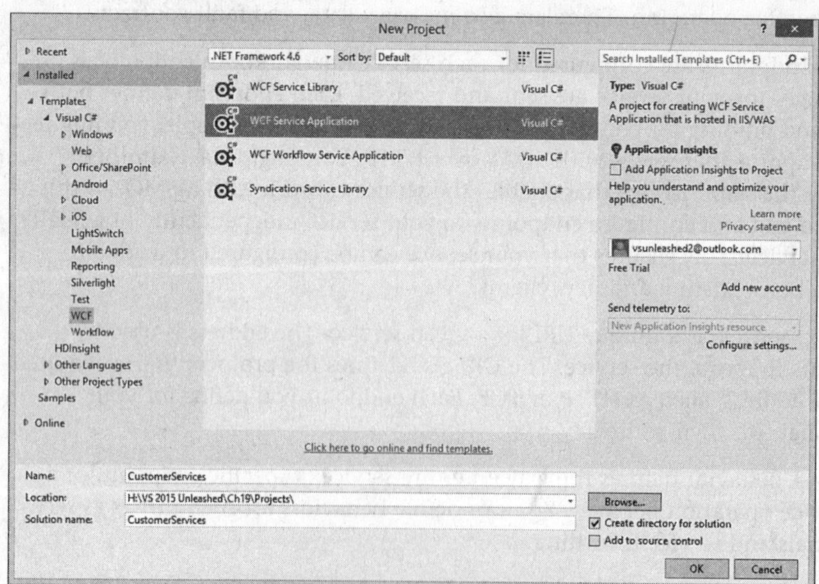

FIGURE 19.17 Use the WCF project templates to define your WCF service application.

Notice that there are a few WCF service templates from which to choose. These templates enable you to create WCF services based on your specific needs. There is a template for working with Windows workflow called WCF Workflow Service Application. The Syndication Service Library enables you to create a syndication service like an RSS feed. The template, WCF Service Library, enables you to create a basic WCF service and then deploy it to a host at a later time. (See "Hosting and Deploying a WCF Service," later in this chapter.) The final template, WCF Service Application, creates an ASP.NET website and a WCF service. This template provides a default host for the service (IIS). We use this template in the example.

NOTE

You can also create an ASP.NET web project and add WCF services to it. In that case, your host for the service has been determined by the website definition (and callers communicate with your service using IIS and ASP.NET).

WCF Service Application Files

The actual WCF Service Application project that is created through the Visual Studio template contains an interface for defining your service contract (`IService1.cs`), a file that represents the URI of your service (`Service1.svc`), and a related class file for implementing the service code (`Service1.svc.cs`). The project template also includes a `Web.config` file for configuring the service and the appropriate .NET references. Figure 19.18 shows a new project based on the template. Note that the default filenames have been changed from `Service1.svc` and `IService1.cs` to `CustomerProfile.svc` and `ICustomerProfile.cs`. The generated code for the start of the `ICustomerProfile` interface is depicted in the code window.

The service interface class (shown as `ICustomerProfile.cs` in the figure) is an interface you use to define your service contract. A contract includes the service operations and the data contract. Having the interface split into a separate file helps abstract all the WCF attributes and contract items away from your actual service logic.

The class is defined as a WCF service through the use of the `ServiceContract` attribute at the top of the class. In addition, the service operations (or service methods) are indicated as such through the `OperationContract` attribute applied to the method (`GetData`).

The actual service class (listed in the Solution Explorer as `CustomerProfile.svc.cs`) implements the service interface as follows.

```
namespace CustomerServices
{
  public class CustomerProfile : ICustomerProfile
  { ...
```

You place your application logic for the service inside the class that implements the service interface. You might decide to actually put business code here, or you might choose to call out to another library that contains the actual implementation code. Let's look at an example.

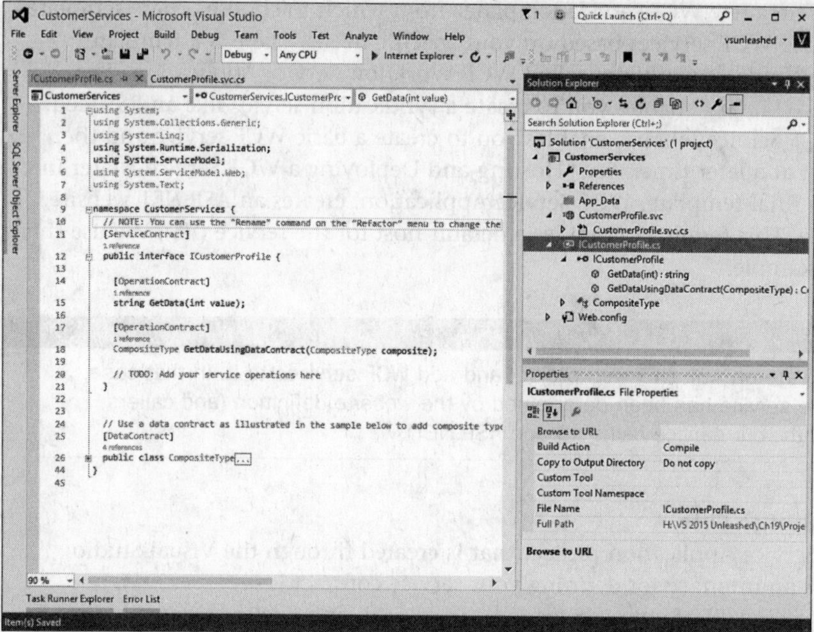

FIGURE 19.18 The WCF Service Application creates a service that can be hosted as a website.

Creating a WCF Service

This section illustrates creating an actual WCF service with Visual Studio 2015. We will develop an implementation for a WCF customer profile service. This example is similar to the Web API service example created earlier to allow comparison between the two methods for developing services. The following steps outline the process of exposing this functionality as a WCF service:

1. Start by creating a new WCF Service Application project. Name the project `CustomerServices`.

2. Use Solution Explorer to rename the interface and service files to `ICustomerProfile.cs` and `CustomerProfile.svc`, respectively.

   Note that the service also contains a markup file (not shown in Solution Explorer). You will need to right-click the service, `CustomerProfile.svc`, in Solution Explorer and choose View Markup. Here you need to change the `Service` attribute to point to your actual service name. Figure 19.19 shows an example.

3. Add a class to the project to represent the customer. (Consider this the model class for the customer, as you saw in the Web API example.) Name the class `Customer.cs`.

4. Define the `Customer` class as shown in Listing 19.14. Notice that this class uses the attribute `DataContract` to indicate that the class represents a WCF service data contract. Each property of the class must also be marked as `DataMember`.

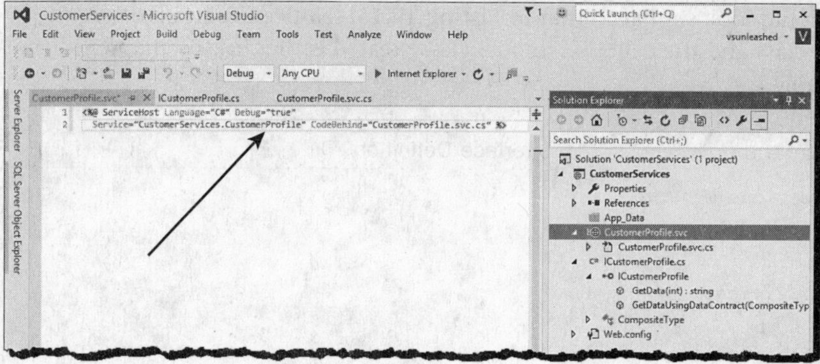

FIGURE 19.19 Change the markup in the `.svc` class after renaming.

LISTING 19.14 The `Customer` Class to Represent Our Data Model

```
using System.Runtime.Serialization;

namespace CustomerServices
{
  [DataContract]
  public class Customer
  {
    [DataMember]
    public int Id { get; set; }

    [DataMember]
    public string Name { get; set; }

    [DataMember]
    public string Email { get; set; }

    [DataMember]
    public bool OptInEmail { get; set; }

    [DataMember]
    public string Notes { get; set; }
  }
}
```

5. Open the `ICustomerProfile.cs` file and remove the template code in the file. Here you will define an interface for working with the customer profile service. Start by marking the interface with the `ServiceContract` attribute. Next, add method definitions for working with a `Customer` instance. Each method definition should be marked with the `OperationContract` attribute.

Your code should look similar to that in Listing 19.15. (Notice the similarities between this class and the `Customer` model class created earlier in this chapter in the Web API sample.)

LISTING 19.15 The `ICustomerProfile` Interface Definition

```
using System.Collections.Generic;
using System.ServiceModel;

namespace CustomerServices
{
  [ServiceContract]
  public interface ICustomerProfile
  {
    [OperationContract]
    IEnumerable<Customer> GetList();

    [OperationContract]
    Customer Get(int id);

    [OperationContract]
    void Delete(int id);

    [OperationContract]
    void Create(Customer customer);

    [OperationContract]
    void Update(Customer customer);
  }
}
```

6. Open the `CustomerProfile.svc.cs` class file. Here you implement the code for the interface defined in the preceding step. To start, remove the template code inside the class definition. Next, add a class definition that implements the `ICustomerProfile` interface. You should see a lightbulb in the code editor to help you stub out the implementation methods. Figure 19.20 shows an example.

7. Write code for each of the service methods to work with the data contract. Listing 19.16 shows the complete code. Notice that it looks a lot like the code created for the Web API sample. It, too, simulates database lookup by using a static list of customers in lieu of a database connection. It then just works with this collection through CRUD operations to get a customer, get a list of customers, create a new customer, update an existing customer, and delete a customer.

   Notice that neither the class nor method definitions need to be marked with attributes. Instead, the interface takes care of that on our behalf.

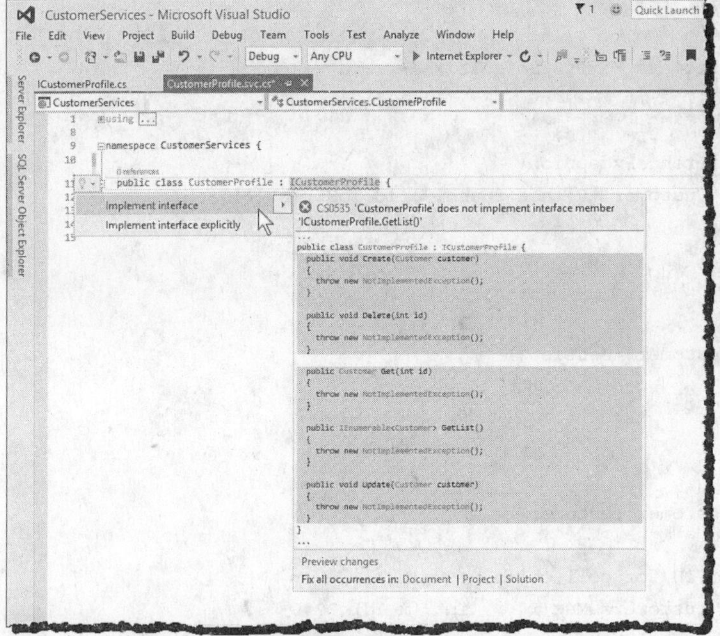

FIGURE 19.20 Use the lightbulb in the code editor to implement the service interface.

LISTING 19.16 The `CustomerProfile.svc.cs` Implementation

```
using System;
using System.Collections.Generic;
using System.Linq;
using System.Runtime.Serialization;
using System.ServiceModel;
using System.ServiceModel.Web;
using System.Text;

namespace CustomerServices
{
  public class CustomerProfile : ICustomerProfile
  {
    static readonly List<Customer> _customers = new List<Customer>()
    {
      new Customer { Id = 1, Name = "Customer 1", Email = "c1@contoso.com" },
      new Customer { Id = 2, Name = "Customer 2", Email = "c2@contoso.com" },
      new Customer { Id = 3, Name = "Customer 3", Email = "c3@contoso.com" }
    };
```

```
public Customer Get(int id)
{
  var customer = _customers.FirstOrDefault(x => x.Id == id);
  if (customer == null)
  {
    throw new NullReferenceException(
      string.Format("Customer {0} not found.", id.ToString()));
  }
  return customer;
}

public IEnumerable<Customer> GetList()
{
  return _customers;
}

public void Create(Customer customer)
{
  //Get next customer ID for collection.
  customer.Id = 1 + _customers.Max(x => (int?)x.Id) ?? 0;

  _customers.Add(customer);
}

public void Update(Customer customer)
{
  //Get customer to be updated.
  var customerToUpdate = _customers.FirstOrDefault(
    x => x.Id == customer.Id);

  if (customerToUpdate == null)
  {
    throw new NullReferenceException(
      string.Format("Customer {0} not found.", customer.Id.ToString()));
  }
  else
  {
    //Simulate updating the customer values.
    customerToUpdate.Name = customer.Name;
    customerToUpdate.Notes = customer.Notes;
    customerToUpdate.Email = customer.Email;
    customerToUpdate.OptInEmail = customer.OptInEmail;
  }
}
```

```
    public void Delete(int id)
    {
      var customer = _customers.FirstOrDefault(x => x.Id == id);
      if (customer == null)
      {
        throw new NullReferenceException(
          string.Format("Customer {0} not found.", id.ToString()));
      }
      _customers.Remove(customer);
    }

  }
}
```

Running and Testing Your WCF Service

Whether you create a WCF Service Application (hosted in a website) or a WCF Service Library (hosted independently of the service definition), Visual Studio provides a mechanism for running and debugging your services without your having to deploy them first or write your own service client.

In the example, we created a WCF Service Application. Visual Studio leverage IIS Express to host this service. Visual Studio provides you a test client to run and debug the service. To use this test client, select your service in Solution Explorer (`CustomerProfile.svc`) and, from the Debug menu, select Start Debugging (or just press F5). Visual Studio will run the code in debug mode using the WCF Test Client, as shown in Figure 19.21.

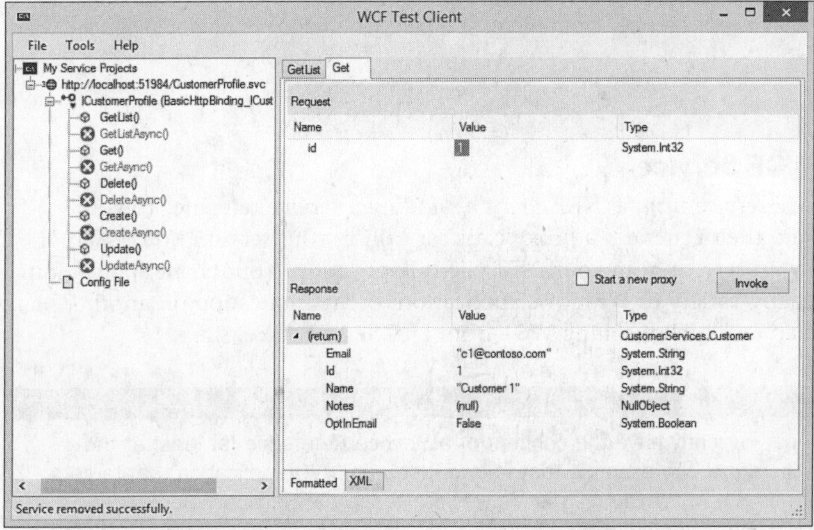

FIGURE 19.21 The WCF Test Client can help you test and debug your services.

Notice in Figure 19.21 that the WCF Test Client shows your service and all its operations. The operations marked with the red 'x' indicate the async versions of your service (which cannot be accessed by the test client).

You double-click a given service to go to the test client for that service (right-side of Figure 19.21). Notice that there are multiple tabs at the top of this form section. These are all the services currently being tested. You can also see the `Get(id)` service in action. Notice that the test client gives you a place to define parameters (Request section) and a button to invoke the service. The bottom section shows the response from the service.

Notice, too, that at the bottom of the form in the Response area, you can toggle between the formatted results and XML. The XML view shows both the Request and the Response as markup. This can be useful when debugging. To stop testing, select File, Exit in the WCF Test Client.

TIP: CONFIGURE ENDPOINTS

After your service exists, you can edit its configuration to support various clients. This means adding endpoints and related configuration information. Remember, the promise of WCF is that you can create a single service and then optimize it to work with multiple clients. One client might access via HTTP, another through TCP, and yet another with named pipes. You can support all of these clients (and more) through configuration.

The WCF Service Library template contains an `App.config` file. The WCF Service Application contains the file `Web.config`. Both files define your service configuration. Typically, you edit the `Web.config` file using the XML editor in Visual Studio. However, when dealing with Service Library projects and multiple endpoints, it can be easier to edit this information using the Service Configuration Editor tool. To access this tool, right-click the `config` file and choose Edit WCF Configuration.

If you're using `Web.config`, you want to click the Create a New Service link in this configuration editor. A wizard then walks you through the process to connect to configuration information about your service. From there, you can add endpoints and bindings as appropriate.

Consuming a WCF Service

You consume a WCF service from a .NET client by adding a service reference to your project. Visual Studio then generates a proxy class for calling your service. You use this proxy class to call your service from your .NET client application. Your client application could be a website, any variety of Windows application, or an application on another platform. Let's look at an example of calling WCF from an ASP.NET MVC site.

NOTE

ASP.NET 5 does not currently have the concept of a Service Reference (at least at the time of writing). Therefore, the example that follows uses an MVC application that targets ASP.NET MVC 6 (and not ASP.NET 5). This allows you to see the Service Reference concept in action.

You can also consume WCF services using `HttpClient` and jQuery (without a Service Reference proxy). This requires additional configuration on your services/endpoints to make them work as REST-based services.

1. Open a new instance of Visual Studio and create a new web project (File, New, Project). Select the ASP.NET Web Application, name the project `WcfClientMvc`, and click the OK button. Select the MVC template (and not an ASP.NET 5 template; we will use that later) and click OK again.

2. Make sure your customer services application is running in another instance of Visual Studio. (You can run in debug mode.)

   Inside the `WcfClientMvc` project, Right-click the References node in Solution Explorer and choose Add Service Reference to launch the Add Service Reference dialog box.

   Type the address to your running service in the Address line of the Add Service Reference dialog. You can get the address from the WCF Test Client, right-click the service and choose Copy Address. With the address in the Add Service Reference dialog, click the Go button. Visual Studio will find your service and display the methods, as shown in Figure 19.22.

   Set the Namespace to `CustomerProfile` and click the OK button to add the service reference to your project.

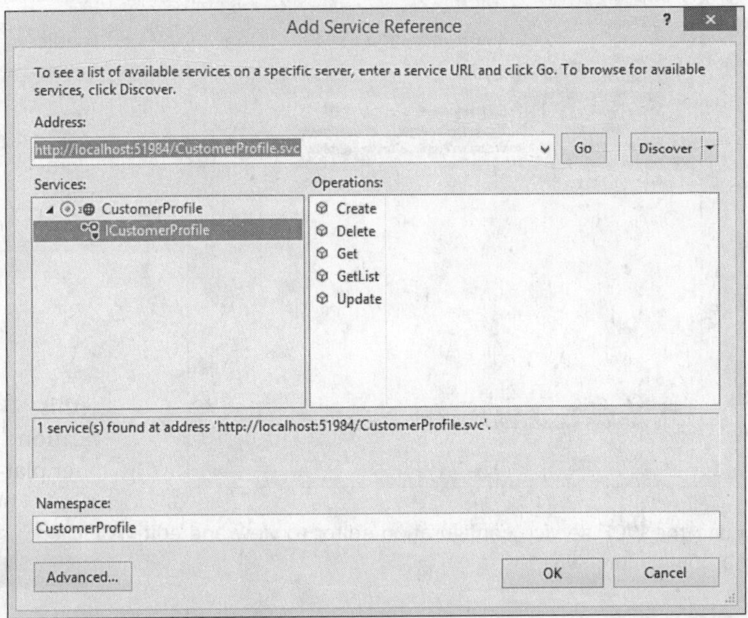

FIGURE 19.22 Use the Add Service Reference dialog to set a reference from your project to an existing WCF service.

3. Visual Studio will create a `Service Reference` folder in your solution and add the `CustomerProfile` reference (as a proxy class for working with the service). It will also add a reference to your project, including `System.NET.Http`, for working with `HttpClient`, as we did in the Web API client example. The proxy class generated on your behalf uses this to work with the WCF service.

   Note that if you double-click the CustomerProfile service reference, Visual Studio shows the Object Browser. Here, you can view the contents of the service reference proxy.

   In addition, if you open the `Web.config` file, you will see a node called `<system.serviceModel>`; this represents your service configuration data, including bindings and client endpoints.

   Right-click the `Web.config` file in Solution Explorer and choose Edit WCF Configuration to open the configuration (as shown in Figure 19.23). Select the `Client` folder, `Endpoints`, `BasicHttpBinding_ICustomerProfile`. Note the client endpoint name and address (as you use them shortly) and close the configuration editor.

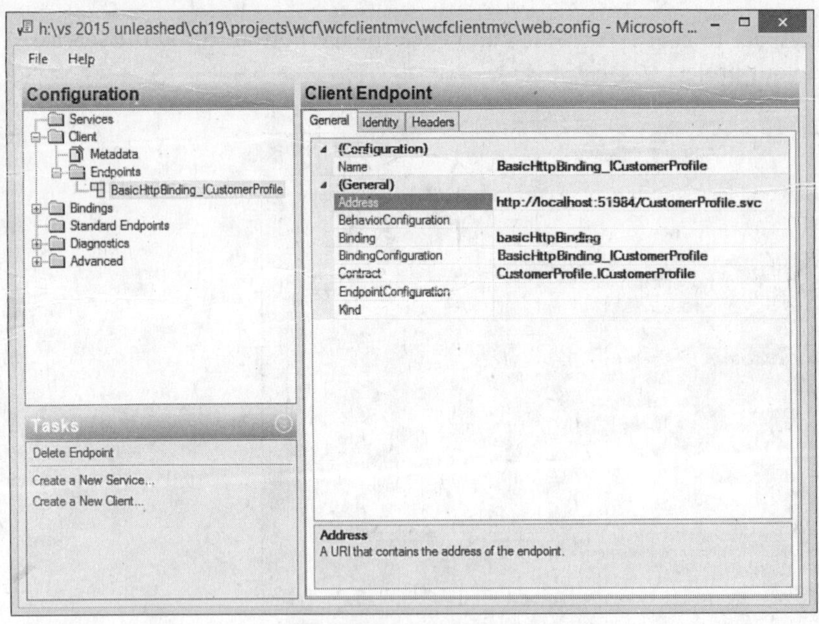

FIGURE 19.23 You can use the WCF service configuration editor to view and edit WCF client configurations for your web application.

4. Create the controller for handling requests to the WCF service and serving up views. Right-click the `Controllers` folder and choose Add, Controller. Select the MVC 5 Controller – Empty and click the Add button. When prompted, name your controller `CustomerController`.

5. Write the code for the `Index` method to call the WCF service, get a list of customers, and return the `Index` view with the customer data. Start by adding a `using` statement for `System.Threading.Tasks;` to the top of the `CustomerController.cs` file.

   Remove the `Index()` stubbed-out method in the template class. Replace it with code similar to Listing 19.17. Notice that we first create an instance of the proxy class, `CustomerProfile.CustomerProfileClient` as `custSrv`. We then use that class to get a list of customers by calling `custSrv.GetListAsync();`.

LISTING 19.17 The `CustomerController Index()` Method Used to Call the WCF Service via the Service Reference Proxy and Return the Corresponding Index View

```
public async Task<ActionResult> Index()
{
  CustomerProfile.CustomerProfileClient custSrv =
    new CustomerProfile.CustomerProfileClient(
    "BasicHttpBinding_ICustomerProfile");

  CustomerProfile.Customer[] customers =
    await custSrv.GetListAsync();

  return View(customers);
}
```

6. Create the view for showing a list of customers. Make sure you have a `Customer` folder under Views in Solution Explorer (if not, add one). Right-click the `Customer` folder and choose Add, View.

   In the Add View dialog (see Figure 19.24), set the view name to `Index`. Under template, choose List. Under `Model` class, find the `Customer` object that was generated when you created the service reference. Finally, select the layout page for the application and click Add.

   Visual Studio will generate a working view for `Index`. You need only to change the page title (optional).

You can now run the client application and navigate to the customer page. Make sure the WCF service application created earlier is also running (inside another instance of Visual Studio). Figure 19.25 shows the results.

SAMPLE CODE

We end the example here. However, the sample code for the book contains all the services in WCF (`Get`, `GetList`, `Create`, `Update`, and `Delete`) wired to the MVC client project.

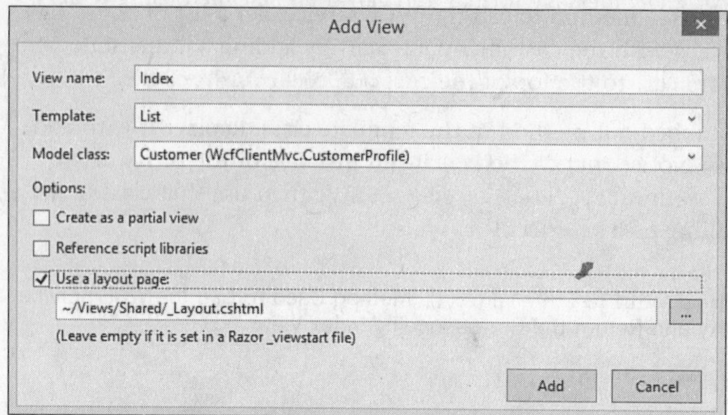

FIGURE 19.24 Use MVC scaffolding to generate a view based on the Customer model in the Service Reference proxy.

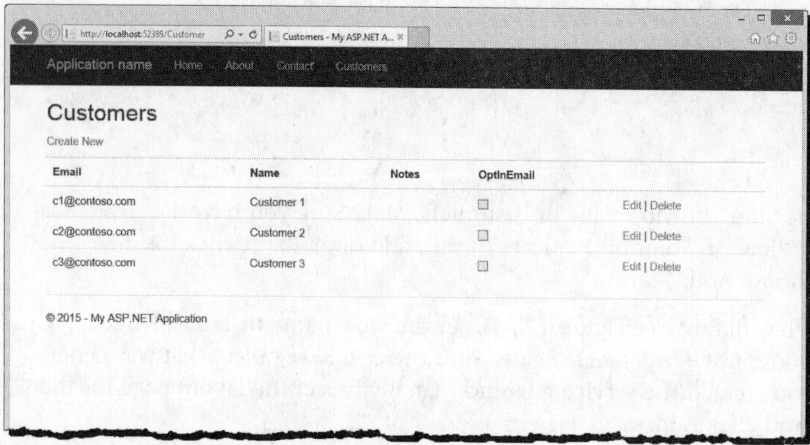

FIGURE 19.25 The MVC application running against the WCF services.

Other Windows .NET clients work the same way (WinForms and WPF, for example). You add a Service Reference to the project and then use the service reference to call the service from the client. Remember, WCF services can support multiple endpoint types. This includes REST-based HTTP services. The next section shows how to leverage this popular approach with WCF.

Creating/Calling REST-Based WCF Services

As discussed previously, REST-based services allow your services to be called by any device that communicates HTTP (which is nearly everything). We demonstrated this approach using Web API. However, WCF can also be configured to work as REST-based services. REST makes your services URL-accessible from HTTP requests using GET, POST, PUT, and

DELETE. They can also support JSON message format and can then be called using jQuery and AJAX.

You indicate support for REST through attributes on the WCF service methods. These attributes, WebGet and WebInvoke, are described as follows:

- WebGet—Indicates the service can be called using HTTP GET
- WebInvoke—Identifies the service as supporting the HTTP verbs of POST, PUT, and DELETE

Both of these attributes have the property UriTemplate. This property is used to route URL requests to a specific web-hosted, URL-addressable service and pass the appropriate parameters. This is just like the MVC and Web API routing with which you may be familiar. You define the UriTemplate property to your domain, a name to identify your service, and then the parameters you intend to pass. For example, the following interface method indicates a call to the Get method using the URL http://localhost/CustomerService.svc/Get/1 to return a Customer instance by the id parameter. You can indicate additional parameters with UriTemplate by appending them to the URL using /{parameter}.

```
[OperationContract]
[WebGet(UriTemplate = "Get/{id}")]
Customer Get(int id);
```

The WebGet and WebInvoke attributes also include the ResponseFormat property. This allows you to indicate the format (XML or JSON) you want to use when sending a response back to the request, as in ResponseFormat = WebMessageFormat.Json.

You must also configure an HTTP endpoint for the services to be called. You can do this in your service web.config file by editing the XML, or you can use the WCF Configuration editor. The example that follows walks you through both options.

Update WCF Services to Accept REST Requests

Let's look at an example. We are going to update the WCF project CustomerServices created earlier to support REST services. Recall that this project is a WCF Services Application and contains the Customer class as a DataContract, the ICustomerProfile interface for the service, and the CustomerProfile class that implements the interface. (Refer to Listings 19.15 through 19.17.)

We need to update the ICustomerProfile interface to indicate support for REST. Listing 19.18 shows the completed example. First, we added a using statement to the top for System.ServiceModel.Web (if it was not already there). Next, notice the use of WebGet and WebInvoke. We set the UriTemplate to work similar to a Web API request. The ResponseFormat is set to return JSON for those services that return customer data. Notice that WebInvoke includes the parameter Method to indicate the HTTP verb we want to respond to (POST, PUT, or DELETE).

LISTING 19.18 The ICustomerProfile Interface Definition

```
using System.Collections.Generic;
using System.ServiceModel;
using System.ServiceModel.Web;

namespace CustomerServices
{
  [ServiceContract]
  public interface ICustomerProfile
  {
    [OperationContract]
    [WebGet(ResponseFormat = WebMessageFormat.Json)]
    IEnumerable<Customer> GetList();

    [OperationContract]
    [WebGet(UriTemplate = "Get/{id}", ResponseFormat = WebMessageFormat.Json)]
    Customer Get(string id);

    [OperationContract]
    [WebInvoke(Method = "DELETE", UriTemplate = "Delete/{id}")]
    void Delete(string id);

    [OperationContract]
    [WebInvoke(Method = "POST", UriTemplate = "Create")]
    void Create(Customer customer);

    [OperationContract]
    [WebInvoke(Method = "PUT", UriTemplate = "Update")]
    void Update(Customer customer);
  }
}
```

Notice in Listing 19.18 that we changed the `Get` and `Delete` methods to accept a `string` value instead of an `int`. This is required by the WCF REST-based HTTP web services. We must also then edit the code in `CustomerProfile` for both these service methods to accept a string and not an `int`. Of course, we convert the `string` to `int` as a first step within the method.

The final step to set up the `CustomerProfile` WCF services as REST based is to add an HTTP binding to the `web.config` file. You can do so either by manually editing the XML in the `config` file or by using the WCF config editor. Let's look at the latter option first.

1. In Solution Explorer, right-click `Web.config` and choose Edit WCF Configuration.
2. Under the Configuration tree (left side), choose the `Advanced` folder, Endpoint Behaviors. Click the link `New Endpoint Behavior Configuration` (or right-click the folder and choose the same).

3. In the Behavior edit screen, name the behavior `web`. Click the Add button to add an element. From the Stack Element drop-down, choose `webHttp`. Figure 19.26 shows an example.

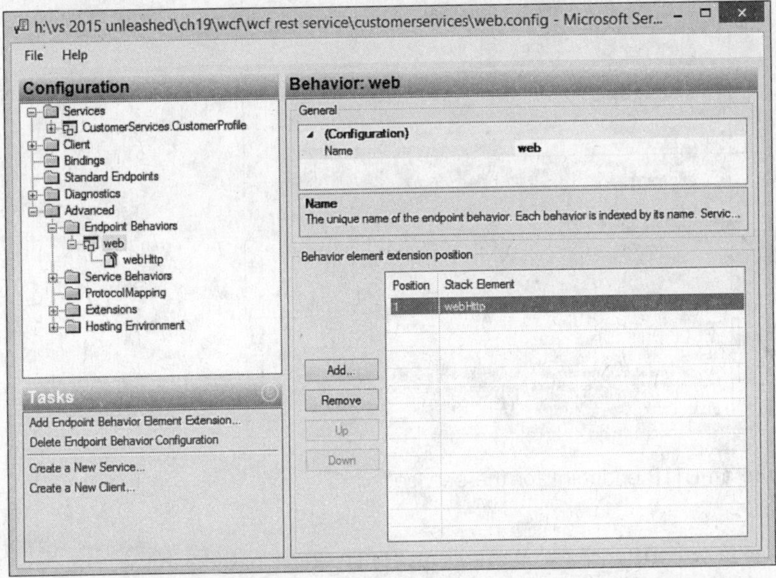

FIGURE 19.26 Add a `webHttp` behavior to the WCF configuration.

4. Navigate to the `Services` folder. If you do not see the `CustomerProfile` service, you will need to add it. Click the `Create a New Service` link. This will launch the New Service Element Wizard.

   For the first dialog, select `CustomerServices.CustomerProfile` (you can browse to this by selecting your compiled dll in the `bin` folder) and click Next.

   On the service contract page of the wizard, select `CustomerServices.ICustomerProfile` and click the Next button.

   Select the communication mode of HTTP and select Next.

   Select Basic Web Service interoperability and click Next.

   Set the address to your service endpoint as http://localhost:PORT#/CustomerProfile.svc and click Finish. You should now have the `CustomerServices.CustomerProfile` Service in the WCF configuration editor (see the left side of Figure 19.27).

5. If an endpoint exists, use it to configure as follows. If not, right-click Endpoints and choose New Service Endpoint. Configure the service as shown in Figure 19.27.

   This includes setting the Name to `REST-based`, the BehaviorConfiguration to `web` (the behavior you just created in the wizard), the Binding to `webHttpBinding`, and the Contract to `CustomerServices.ICustomerProfile`.

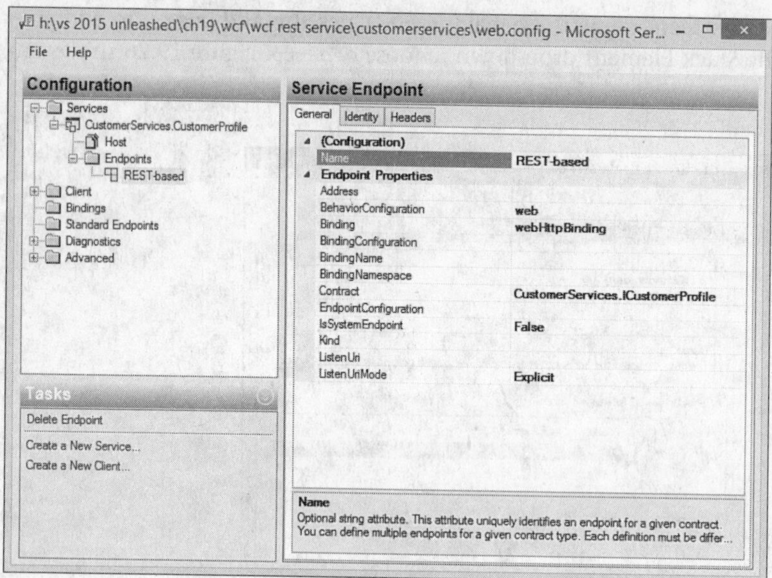

FIGURE 19.27 Configure an HTTP endpoint for the service.

The WCF service is now configured to work as an HTTP, REST-based service. You can review your configuration by opening `web.config`. The following shows the `system.serviceModel` section post-configuration. (Note that you can use this to simply edit the `web.config` file by hand.)

```
<system.serviceModel>
  <services>
    <service name="CustomerServices.CustomerProfile">
      <endpoint address="" behaviorConfiguration="web" binding="webHttpBinding"
        name="REST-based" contract="CustomerServices.ICustomerProfile" />
    </service>
  </services>
  <behaviors>
    <endpointBehaviors>
      <behavior name="web">
        <webHttp />
      </behavior>
    </endpointBehaviors>
    <serviceBehaviors>
      <behavior name="">
        <serviceMetadata httpGetEnabled="true" httpsGetEnabled="true" />
        <serviceDebug includeExceptionDetailInFaults="false" />
      </behavior>
    </serviceBehaviors>
  </behaviors>
```

```
  <protocolMapping>
      <add binding="basicHttpsBinding" scheme="https" />
  </protocolMapping>
  <serviceHostingEnvironment aspNetCompatibilityEnabled="true"
    multipleSiteBindingsEnabled="true" />
</system.serviceModel>
```

NOTE

Configuring your WCF service in this way will prevent the WCF Test Client from working with your services. However, you can now access them directly from a web browser. To do so, run the application and navigate to http://localhost:xxxxx/CustomerProfile.svc/GetList (where xxxxx represents your port number).

Update ASP.NET 5 Client to Call WCF Services Using REST

We can now write client code to call the REST-based WCF services using HTTP. As an example, consider the client application we wrote for consuming the REST-based Web API services using ASP.NET 5. (See the section, "Consuming an ASP.NET Web API Service.") We can create a similar site for working with these WCF services.

To get started, this example assumes you copy the `WebApiClient` project created earlier (or download the sample code for the book). To follow along reading, you might refamiliarize yourself with Listings 19.8 through 19.13.

The changes to the code are minimal and involve mostly updating the URL addresses for calling the services. The following steps you through the code changes for the `CustomerController` class:

1. Open the `CustomerController` class. At the top of the class, change the `baseUri` variable to point to the new `CustomerProfile` service as follows (your port number will likely differ). Note the slash (/) at the end of the Uri.

```
string baseUri = "http://localhost:6795/CustomerProfile.svc/";
```

2. In the `Index()` method, change the `GetAsync` call to use the new service path as the following illustrates.

```
HttpResponseMessage response = await hClient.GetAsync("GetList");
```

3. In the `Edit(int? id)` method, change the `GetAsync` method as follows.

```
HttpResponseMessage response = await hClient.GetAsync(
  string.Format("get/{0}", id.ToString()));
```

4. In the `Edit(Customer customer)` method, change the `PutAsJsonAsync` call as follows.

```
HttpResponseMessage response =
  await hClient.PutAsJsonAsync("update", customer);
```

That's it for the controller changes. Recall that the Web API project we used as a basis for this sample made the calls for creating a new customer and deleting an existing customer from the user's browser using JavaScript, jQuery, and AJAX. The following steps you through making these modifications:

1. Open the `Create.cshtml` page from the `Views/Customer` folder in Solution Explorer.
2. Navigate to the bottom of the page and edit the `url` variable as follows (your port number may vary).

   ```
   string url = "http://localhost:6795/CustomerProfile.svc/Create";
   ```

3. Open the `Index.cshtml` (shows a list of customers).
4. Rewrite the form `submit` function to use the jQuery method, `$.ajax` (instead of `$.post`). In this case, we need to send the data to the service as JSON (instead of a serialized form as we did with the Web API sample; note that this approach can also work with Web API `POST` requests).

   Listing 19.19 shows the full example. The JSON message is created by defining a type, `formData`, and adding the form values to the type. We then use `JSON.stringify(formData)` to convert the type to JSON.

LISTING 19.19 The `Create.cshtml` JavaScript and jQuery Code to Send a `POST` Message with Customer Form Data on Submit

```
<script type="text/javascript">
  $('#form-create').submit(function () {

    //Clear result message.
    $('#result').html("");

    //Verify form is valid.
    if ($('#form-create').valid()) {

      //Create formData to be converted to JSON.
      var formData = {
        "Name": $("#Name").val(),
        "Email": $("#Email").val(),
        "OptInEmail": $("#OptInEmail").val(),
        "Notes": $("#Notes").val()
      }

      //Post the data as JSON and verify response code 200 - OK.
      $.ajax({
        url: 'http://localhost:6795/CustomerProfile.svc/Create',
        type: 'POST',
        data: JSON.stringify(formData),
        dataType: 'json',
```

```
        contentType: 'application/json; charset=utf-8',
        processData: true,
        complete: function (response) {
          if (response.status == 200) {
            window.location = '/customer';
          } else {
            $('#result').html('Error saving customer.');
          }
        }
      });

      return false;
    }
  });
</script>
```

The final step is to run the application. Be sure to have the WCF REST-based service application running in a host. (A Visual Studio debug session using IIS Express will work.) Figure 19.28 shows the client running against the WCF, REST-based services. Notice the additional customer added to the default collection (using the client-side code in Listing 19.19).

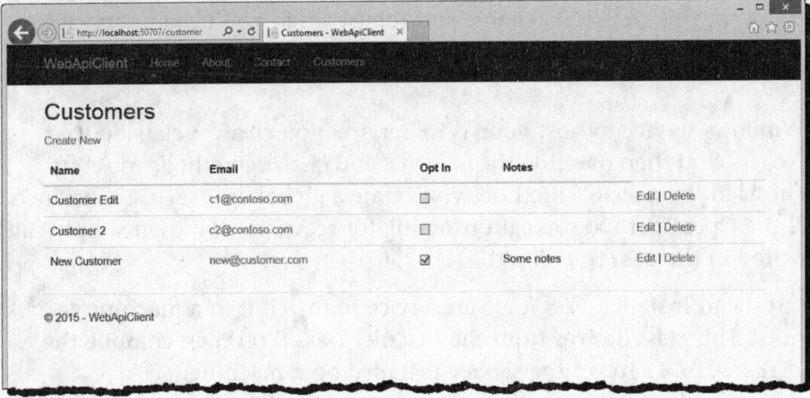

FIGURE 19.28 The ASP.NET 5 application running against the WCF services configured to support REST.

Hosting and Deploying a WCF Service

For your services to accept requests, they have to be active and running, which means they need to be hosted in some runtime environment. Recall that when we covered web services, they were hosted for us by IIS. You can host your WCF services there, too. However, you do have other options.

You want to pick your host based on your needs. For example, if you have a peer-to-peer application, you might already know that each peer can host its own services. You also need to consider issues such as deployment, flexibility, monitoring, process lifetime management, security, and more. Here is a brief overview of the WCF host options available to you:

- **Self-hosted**—A self-hosted service contains the service within a running executable. The executable is managed code you write. You simply embed one or more services within the executable. In this way, the service is self-hosted. It does not require an additional process to execute. Instead, its lifetime is managed by the lifetime of the executable. When the executable is running, the service is listening for requests and responding accordingly. If not, the service is out of commission.

  Self-hosted services are great when your clients need to communicate with one another. This is the case with peer-to-peer applications like Microsoft's Groove. Each client has services that can speak with the other clients.

  To create a self-hosted service, you create an instance of the `ServiceHost` class inside your application. This class is passed an instance of your service. You then call the `Open` method of `ServiceHost` to begin hosting the service. When you're finished, you call the `Close` method.

- **Windows service**—You can host your WCF service inside a Windows service application. A Windows service application is one that is installed as a service on a given machine. A Windows service can be configured to start, stop, and start up again on system reboot. In this way, it is reliable and robust when you need a service to simply stay up and running. It is also supported on all versions of Windows and Windows server.

  To create a Windows service to host your WCF service, you create a class derived from `ServiceBase`. You then override the `OnStart` and `OnStop` methods to set up your service host. In the `OnStart` method, you create a global `ServiceHost` instance and then call the Open method to begin listening for requests. You then simply call the Close method in the `OnStop` method.

  Finally, you create an Installer class for your service to install it in a machine's service directory. This class derives from the Installer class. You then compile the code and run `installutil` to get the service installed on a machine.

- **IIS**—IIS can host your WCF services. In this way, you can take advantage of the many features built in to this platform, including monitoring, high availability, high scalability, and more. You saw how to create services hosted in a website in the preceding section.

- **WAS (Windows Process Activation Service)**—WAS was introduced with Windows Server 2008. It gives you the benefits of IIS (health monitoring, process recycling, message-based activation, and so on) without the limitations of HTTP only. WAS works with HTTP, TCP, named pipes, and MSMQ. In addition, WAS does not require that you write hosting code (like the self-hosted and Windows Service options do). Instead, you simply configure WAS to be a host of your service (as you would IIS).

As you can see, you have many options for hosting your service. Each has its own plusses and minuses with respect to setup, coding, configuration, and deployment. Depending on your needs, spend some time learning more about your host options. You can find a how-to on each option inside the Microsoft Developer Network (MSDN). Simply search for "WCF hosting options."

Summary

This chapter presented both ASP.NET Web API services and those built on WCF. You saw how .NET abstracts the programming of services and provides tools to make your life easier. In this way, you can concentrate on building business functionality (and not writing plumbing code). Some key points in this chapter include the following:

- Web services are based on open standards. .NET adheres to these standards to ensure that heterogeneous applications can work together with web services.
- An ASP.NET Web API service helps you write REST-based HTTP services that can be called from any application that speaks HTTP, including web and native clients.
- The ASP.NET Web API is built on ASP.NET MVC and therefore includes a controller and routing engine for accessing your service methods. These service methods are written to leverage the HTTP verbs `GET`, `POST`, `PUT`, and `DELETE`.
- You can use jQuery to call an HTTP service asynchronously directly from a web browser on the client.
- A WCF service can be created with multiple endpoints to efficiently support multiple clients across different communication protocols. WCF services work across HTTP, TCP, named pipes, sockets, and more.
- Use `WebGet` and `WebInvoke` attributes to mark a WCF service as supporting REST-based HTTP verb calls.
- You consume a service by adding a service reference to a .NET application. This generates a local proxy client for your code to call. You can also consume a service by using other HTTP client libraries such as `System.Net.HttpClient`.

CHAPTER 20

Building Windows Forms Applications

IN THIS CHAPTER

- The Basics of Form Design
- Creating a Form
- Adding Controls and Components
- Creating Your Own Controls

One of the core goals for Visual Studio is enabling rapid Windows Forms construction. Using the Windows Forms Designer, the Controls Toolbox, and the various common controls provided by the .NET Framework, this chapter serves as your guide to the drag-and-drop creation of rich form-based applications. Specifically, we look at how best to leverage the built-in capabilities of the Forms Designer and the Visual Studio project system to quickly build a baseline form from scratch.

We don't worry about the code behind the form at this point; instead, the focus is on the user interface and Visual Studio's inherent rapid application development (RAD) capabilities with the Windows Forms Designer. In other words, this chapter's focus is on the design-time capabilities of the IDE as opposed to the runtime capabilities of the form and control classes.

The Basics of Form Design

Designing the appropriate user interface for a Windows application is still part art and part science. In the Windows Forms world, a user interface is a collection of images, controls, and window elements that work in synergy. Users absorb information through the user interface (UI) and use it as the primary vehicle for interacting with the application.

The task in front of any developer when creating a user interface is primarily one of balance: balancing simplicity of design with the features that the application is required to implement. Also thrown in the mix is the concept of standards, both formal and experiential.

NOTE

Although we use the term *developer* in this chapter, much of the UI design and layout process is squarely in the camp of the *designer*. Although many development teams don't have the luxury of employing a full-time UI designer (developers handle this area on many teams), this is rapidly becoming a key competitive differentiator as software development firms look to distinguish their applications and rise above their competitors at the "look and feel" level.

Considering the End User

You can't start the design process unless you understand how the application will be used and who its intended audience is. Even applications that surface similar feature sets might need to provide significantly different user experiences. An application designed to store medical information might have the same data points and functions but would likely have a different persona if it was designed for the ordinary consumer as opposed to a physician or registered nurse.

Use cases and actual usability labs are both great tools for understanding user expectations, and they provide great data points for preserving that function versus simplicity of design balance.

Location and Culture

Location and culture figure into the equation as well. The typical form application used in the United States caters to this culture's expectations by anticipating left-to-right, top-to-bottom reading habits. In this environment, the most important elements of the UI are typically placed in the most prominent position: top and left in the form. Other cultures require this strategy to change based on right-to-left and even bottom-to-top reading traits.

Most controls in Visual Studio directly support right-to-left languages through a `RightToLeft` property. By setting this property to an appropriate `RightToLeft` enum value, you can indicate whether the control's text should appear left to right or right to left or should be based on the setting carried on the parent control. Even the `Form` class supports this property.

Beyond the `RightToLeft` property, certain controls expose a `RightToLeftLayout` property. Setting this Boolean property affects the overall layout within the control. As an example, setting `RightToLeftLayout` to `True` for a `Form` instance causes the form to mirror its content.

TIP

Search for "Best Practices for Developing World-Ready Applications" in the Microsoft Developer Network (MSDN) for more detailed information on how to design an application for an international audience.

In addition, simple things such as the space allocated for a given control are affected by language targets. A string presented in U.S. English might require drastically more space when translated into Farsi. Again, many controls support properties designed to overcome this design issue; setting the `AutoSize` property on a control to `True` automatically extends the client area of the control based on its contained text.

Understanding the Role of UI Standards

Applications must also strive to adhere to any relevant standards associated with their look and feel. Some standards are documented for you by the platform "owner." Microsoft, for example, has a set of UI design guidelines documented within MSDN. The book *Microsoft Windows User Experience*, published by Microsoft Press, is included in its entirety within MSDN. By tackling topics such as data-centered design, input basics, and design of graphic images, this book provides a structured baseline of UI design collateral for Windows application developers.

Design guidelines and UI standards are often specific to a given platform. The current look and feel expected from a Windows application trace primarily back to the "new" design that debuted with Windows 95. Windows XP further refined those expectations. Windows Vista and Windows 7 offered a new set of design principals and now, Windows 8 and Windows 10 offer up the most radical set of changes in recent history with their focus on the touch experience and Modern UI/Windows Store-style applications.

Visual Studio surfaces some of these design guidelines and standards to make it easy to develop conforming interfaces. For instance, default button heights match the recommended standard, and Visual Studio assists developers with standard control positioning relative to neighboring controls by displaying snaplines as you move controls on the form surface. We cover this topic more fully later in this chapter.

De Facto Standards

Sometimes the influence of a particular application or suite of applications is felt heavily in the UI design realm. One example here is Microsoft Outlook. Various applications now in the wild mimic, for instance, the structure and layout of Microsoft Outlook even though they are not, per se, email applications. The Microsoft Outlook designers struck a vein of usability when they designed its primary form, and now other companies and developers have leveraged those themes in their own applications. A similar comment can be made about the appearance of the "ribbon" toolbar that debuted with Microsoft Office 2007.

Although there are limits, Visual Studio enables developers to achieve the same high-fidelity UIs used in Microsoft Office and other popular applications. In fact, if you look at the official Windows Forms website, you see demo applications written with Visual Studio showcasing how you can develop replicas of the Microsoft Outlook, Quicken, or even Microsoft Money facades. (Visit the Downloads page at http://www.windowsclient.net.)

Planning the User Interface

Before you embark on the design process in Visual Studio, it is probably a decent idea to first draft a mock-up of the form's general landscape. This can be a simple pen and paper sketch; what we are looking for is a simple, rough blueprint for the application.

As a sample scenario, consider a Windows Forms application written for Contoso customer service representatives. The application needs to expose a hierarchical list of orders placed with Contoso, and it should enable the reps to search on orders and edit data.

Preliminary Design

A few basic components have been established as de facto standards for a Windows form: menus, toolbars, and status bars are all standard fare and can certainly be leveraged within this fictional order application.

Beyond those staples, you know that you need to list orders on the screen and provide for a region that shows order details. By borrowing liberally from an existing layout theme à la Microsoft Outlook, you might arrive at a tentative form layout plan like the one shown in Figure 20.1.

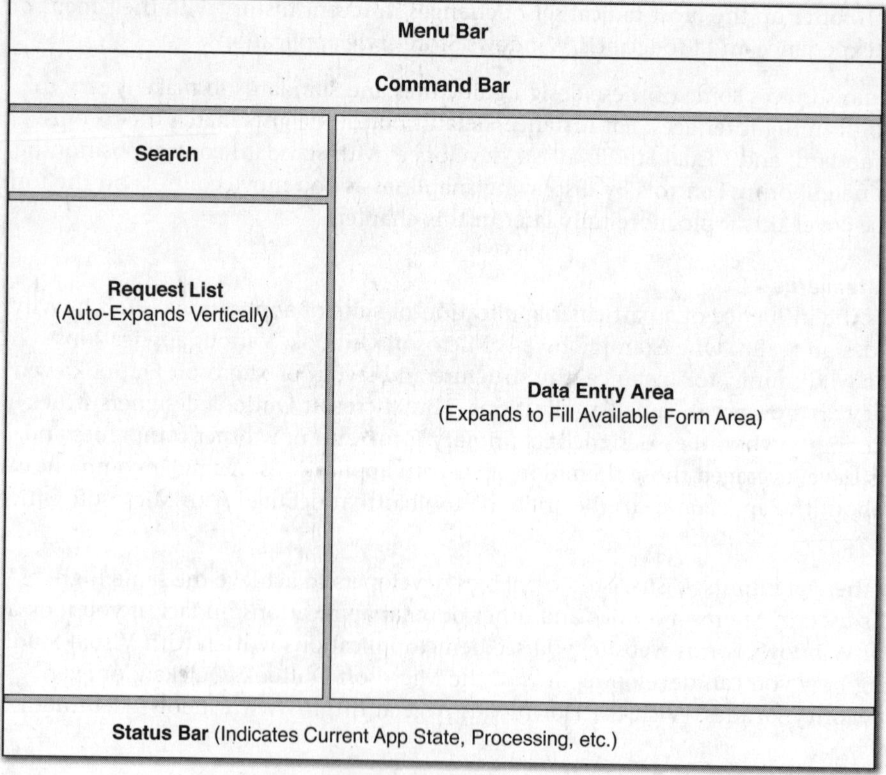

FIGURE 20.1 An initial layout plan.

It is important to pay some attention to the concept of resizing. How do the form's constituent controls respond relative to one another when a user resizes the form? What if a control element is resized because of a language change or a change in the underlying data? By fleshing out some of the resizing design intent now, you can save a mountain of work later. The prototype sketch in Figure 20.1 includes some simple text to remind you how to accommodate the different form regions during resizing.

Creating a Form

Although there are many different ways of approaching form design, the starting point for all of them within Visual Studio is the Windows Forms Application project template. From the New Project dialog box, select this template, give the project an appropriate name, and click OK (see Figure 20.2).

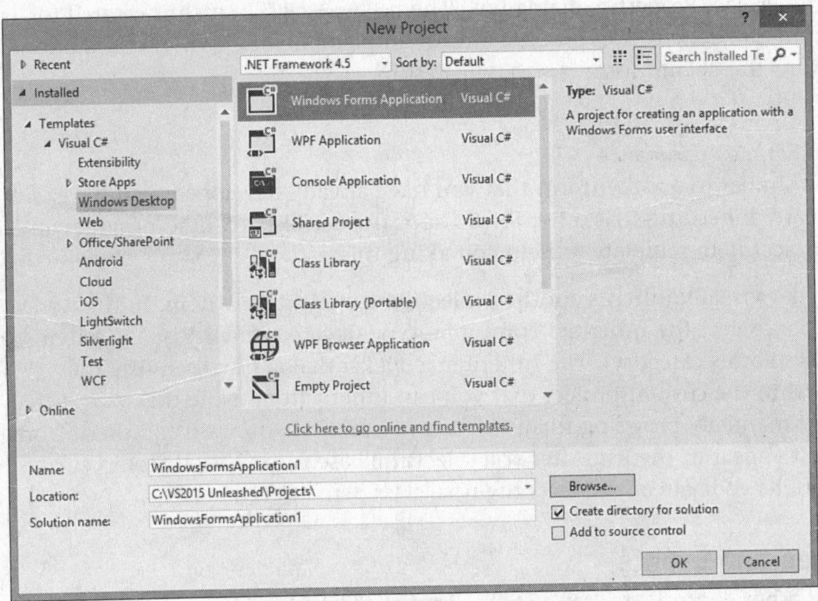

FIGURE 20.2 Creating a new Windows Forms project.

The Windows Forms Application Project Type

Windows Forms Application projects consist of a default form class and, in the case of C#, a default static `Program` class. After creating the project, you are immediately presented with a blank, default form opened in the Windows Forms Designer. For a refresher on the basic capabilities and components of the Windows Forms Designer, see Chapter 6, "Introducing the Editors and Designers."

Setting the Startup Form

Although the default project creates only a single form, you can add multiple forms at any time. This then raises the question of how to indicate at design time which form you initially want displayed at runtime (if any). There are two methods:

- For Visual Basic projects, the startup form is set using the Project Properties dialog box. The Startup Object drop-down in this dialog box contains a list of all valid form objects. You simply select the form you want launched on startup, and you're all set.
- For Visual C# projects, a slightly more complex approach is needed. The notion of a C# startup object is simply any class that implements a `Main()` method. Within the body of the `Main` method, you need to place a line of code that passes in a form instance to the `Application.Run` method, like this: `Application.Run(new OrderForm())`. Assuming that you have a class that implements `Main` and code that calls `Application.Run` in that `Main` method, you can then select the specific startup object via the Project Properties dialog box. The `Program` class, which is created for you during the project creation process, already implements the `Main` method and by default runs the default form (`Form1`) on startup.

Inheriting Another Form's Appearance

If your form looks similar to another form that you have already developed, you have the option of visually inheriting that other form's appearance. Visual Studio provides an Inherited Form project item template to help you along this path.

To create a form that visually inherits another, select Project, Add New Item. In the Add New Item dialog box, select the Inherited Form item type (located under Visual C# Items, under the Windows Forms category). The Inheritance Picker dialog box then lists the available forms within the current project that you can inherit from. Note that you also have the option of manually browsing to an existing assembly if you want to inherit from a form that doesn't appear in the list. After you select the base form, Visual Studio creates the new form class; its code already reflects the base class derivation.

Form Properties and Events

A form is like any other control: you can use the Properties window in the IDE to control its various properties. Although we don't touch on all of them here, you should consider a few key properties as you begin your form design process.

Startup Location

You use the form's `StartPosition` property to place the form's window on the screen when it is first displayed. This property accepts a `FormStartPosition` enumeration value; the possible settings are documented in Table 20.1.

TABLE 20.1 `FormStartPosition` Enumeration Values

Value	Description
`CenterParent`	This centers the form within its parent form.
`CenterScreen`	This centers the form within the current display screen.
`Manual`	The form positions itself according to the `Form.Location` property value.
`WindowsDefaultBounds`	This positions the form at the Windows default location; the forms bounds are also determined by the Windows default.
`WindowsDefaultLocation`	This positions the form at the Windows default location; the form's size is determined by the `Form.Size` property. (This is the default setting.)

Appearance

Given our discussion on the priority of UI design, it should come as no surprise that the appearance of the form is an important part of the overall application's user experience. For the most part, the default appearance property values are sufficient for the typical application. You should set the `ForeColor` and `BackColor` properties according to the color scheme identified for your application. Note that when you add controls to the form, most of them have their own `ForeColor` values set to mimic that of the form.

Some properties enable you to implement a more extravagant user interface. The `Opacity` property enables you to implement transparent or semitransparent forms. This capability might be useful when users want to see a portion of the screen that actually sits behind the form's window. In addition to the `Opacity` property, you use the `Form.BackgroundImage` property to set an image as the form's background. This property is best used to display subtle color gradients or graphics that are not possible with just the `BackColor` property.

In keeping with our goal of rapidly crafting the form, most of the activities within the designer described in this chapter consist of tweaking the form's properties and adding controls from the Toolbox to the form.

Form Events

Forms inherit the same event-driven architecture as other controls do. Certain public events defined on the `Form` class are useful as injection points across the continuum of a form's life.

Figure 20.3 shows the various stages (and corresponding events) from form inception to close. To react to a form event, you first need to create an event handler.

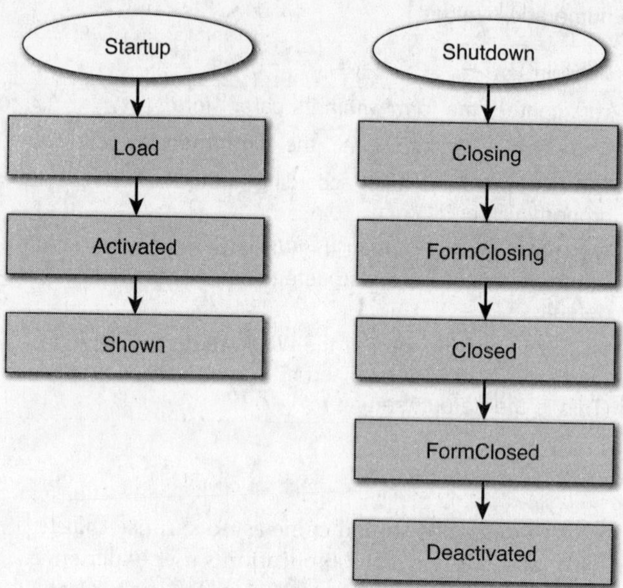

FIGURE 20.3 The events in the life of a Windows form.

Creating an Event Handler Visual Studio's Properties window provides a speedy mechanism for defining an event handler. First select the form of interest. Then click the Events button in the Properties window's toolbar. The window now shows a list of every event defined on the form. Double-clicking the event creates a blank event handler routine and opens it in the code editor for you. The event handler has the correct arguments list and follows established standards for event handler naming (typically, `classname_eventname`).

> **NOTE**
>
> The form needs to be opened in the IDE before the events can be accessed in the Properties window. If the form is selected in the solution explorer but not opened in the IDE, you can still edit the form properties, but you won't be able to access the events in this fashion.

Figure 20.4 depicts the form events within the Properties window.

With the form in place, you can start placing controls onto its surface.

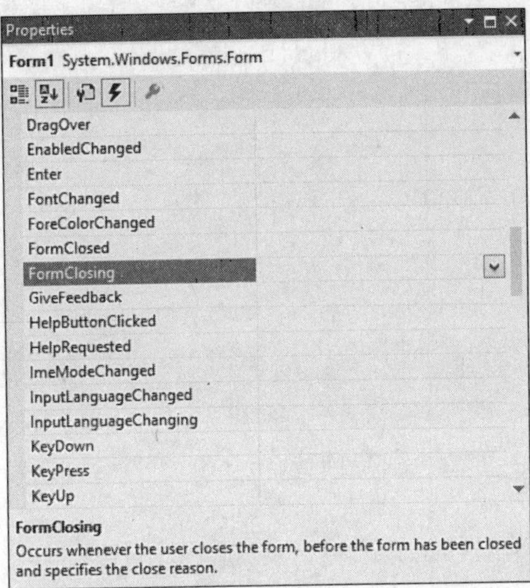

FIGURE 20.4 Accessing form events in the Properties window.

Adding Controls and Components

When you are building a form-based application, the user interface design really involves three separate tools within Visual Studio: the Forms Designer tool, which provides the canvas for the form; the Toolbox, which contains the controls to be placed onto the canvas; and the property browser, which is used to affect the form and its child controls, appearance, and behavior. This triad of IDE tools provides the key to rapid form construction with Visual Studio, especially as it relates to building a form's content.

The term *control* technically refers to any .NET object that implements the `Control` class. In practice, we use the term to refer to the visual controls hosted by a form. This is in contrast to a component, which has many of the same characteristics of a control but doesn't expose a visual interface. A button is an example of a control; a timer is an example of a component.

Controls and components alike live in the Toolbox window. (See additional coverage of the Toolbox in Chapter 6.) Adding either a control or a component to a form is as easy as dragging its likeness from the Toolbox and dropping it onto the form's surface.

After you place a control on a form, the Windows Forms Designer paints the control onto the form to give you a WYSIWYG view of how the form will look at runtime. As noted in Chapter 6, components are handled in a slightly different fashion. The Forms Designer has a special region called the component tray; any components placed onto the form are represented here. This enables you to interact in a point-and-click fashion with the component as you would with a control, but it doesn't place a representation onto the form itself because a component has no visual aspect to it.

Figure 20.5 highlights the component tray area of the Windows Forms Designer.

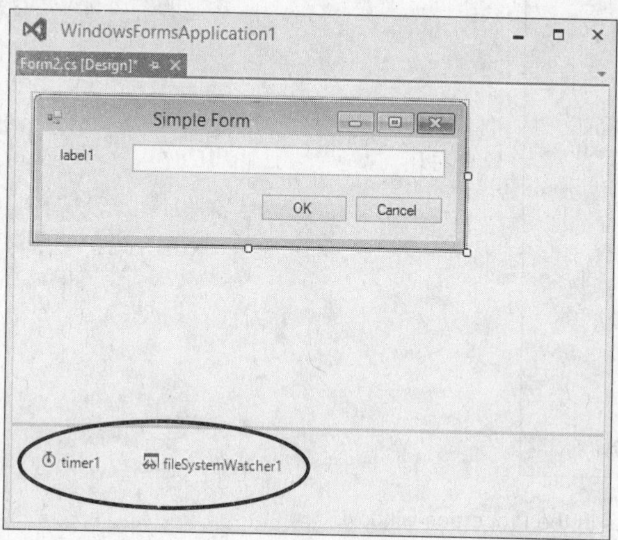

FIGURE 20.5 The component tray.

TIP

The Toolbox is customizable. You can add or remove controls from the Toolbox within any of the Toolbox tabs. Right-click anywhere in the interior of the Toolbox window and select Choose Items to launch the Choose Toolbox Items dialog box; from here, you can select or deselect the Toolbox control population. If a control doesn't show up in the .NET Framework Components tab or the COM Components tab of the dialog box, you can browse to the control's assembly and add it directly.

Control Layout and Positioning

When a few controls are on a form, the Windows Forms Designer can help automate some of the more common layout tasks, such as aligning a group of controls vertically to one another. Again, refer to Chapter 6 to see how you can leverage these productivity tools. But these layout functions, although nice from a design perspective, do nothing for you at runtime.

As previously noted, a control's runtime behavior within its parent form is an important area that needs attention if you are to implement your form according to your design intent. That is, you not only want controls to look a certain way; you also want them to act a certain way when the form is resized.

The simplest way to underscore the issue presented during a form resize is to look at a few figures. Figure 20.6 shows the simplest of forms: a label, a text box, and OK and Cancel buttons. The controls on the form have been carefully placed to maintain equal spacing; the controls are nicely aligned in the vertical and horizontal planes; and, in short, this form looks just like the developer intended it to look.

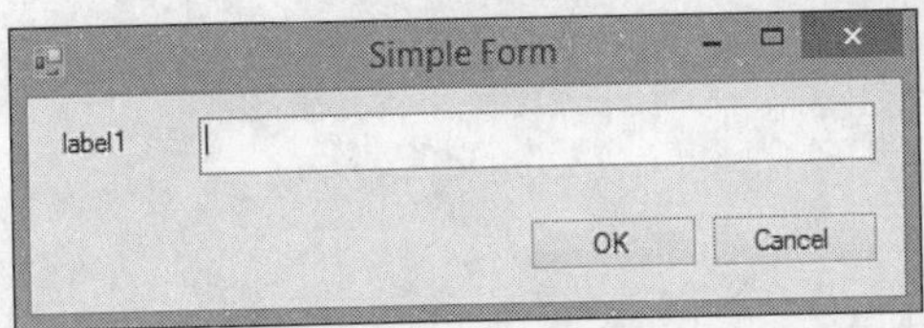

FIGURE 20.6 Controls aligned on a form.

But then a user becomes involved. Figure 20.7 shows the results of resizing the form horizontally and vertically.

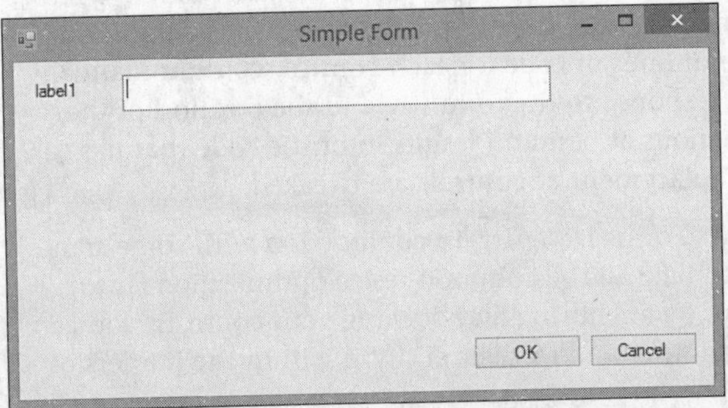

FIGURE 20.7 Form resize effects on design.

This appearance is clearly not what was intended; the nice clean design of the form has failed to keep up with the form's size. Perhaps the user resized the form in an attempt to get more room to type in the text box. Or perhaps the user tiled this application's window with other applications, causing its size to change. Whatever the reason, it is clear that further intervention by the developer is needed to keep the design "valid," regardless of the size of the form.

Just by viewing the before and after figures, you can decide on a strategy and answer the question, "What should happen when a user resizes the form?" Figure 20.8 is a snapshot of the ideal; the text box has "kept pace" with the resize by horizontally extending or shrinking its width. The command buttons have kept their alignment with one another and with the text box, but they have not altered their overall dimensions. Plus, the label has stayed in its original location.

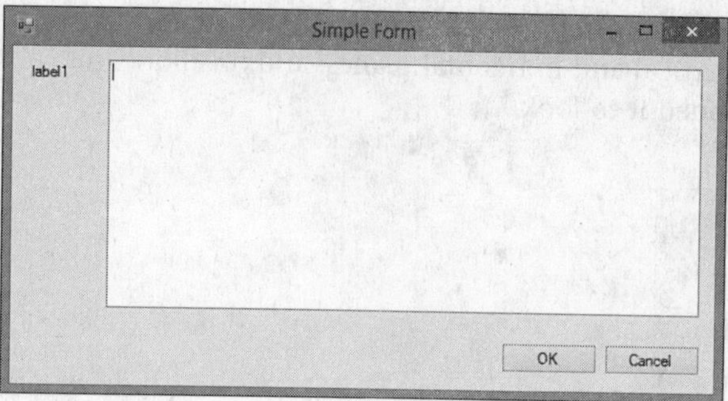

FIGURE 20.8 Reacting to a form resize.

Every form object has a resize event that fires whenever the form boundary size changes (most commonly as the result of a user dragging the form's border to increase or decrease the size of the form). Because every control has positioning properties such as `Top`, `Left`, `Height`, and `Width`, you could implement a brute-force approach to achieving the form shown in Figure 20.8. By writing several lines of code for each control, you can manually move or redimension the controls in response to the form size and the position of the other controls. But this approach is tedious at best and results in brittle code that has to be touched every time the layout and placement of controls are tweaked.

Thankfully, the Visual Studio Windows Forms Designer, in conjunction with some standard control properties, enables you to take all the common resize optimizations into account during the layout of the form. By anchoring and docking your controls, you can dictate their position relative to one another and to their position within the borders of the form.

Anchoring

Anchoring, as its name implies, is the concept of forcing a control's left, top, right, or bottom border to maintain a static, anchored position within the borders of the form. For instance, anchoring a label control to the top and left of a form (this is the default) causes the label to maintain its exact position regardless of how the form is resized. Each control's `Anchor` property can be set to any combination of Top, Left, Bottom, and Right. The control's property browser provides a convenient property editor widget, shown in Figure 20.9, which graphically indicates the sides of the control that are anchored.

Anchoring opposite sides of a control has an interesting effect. Because each side must maintain its position relative to the sides of the form, the control itself stretches either vertically or horizontally depending on whether the Top and Bottom or Right and Left anchors have been set. In fact, this is the exact behavior you want with the text box: you want its width and height to adjust whenever the form is resized. By anchoring all sides of the control, you get the behavior shown with the TextBox control in Figure 20.8; the control has automatically adjusted its dimensions (by stretching both horizontally and vertically) with no code required from the developer.

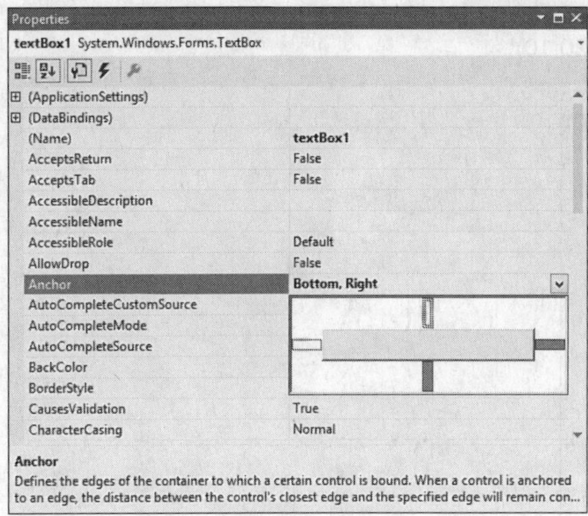

FIGURE 20.9 Setting the `Anchor` property.

NOTE

By default, controls are typically anchored on their top and left sides. You might be wondering what happens if no anchors are specified at all. In that case, the control maintains its exact position regardless of form resize actions. This is, in effect, the same behavior as top and left anchors would have because forms have their top-leftmost points as their "origin."

Anchoring also solves the positioning problem with the OK and Cancel buttons. If you change their `Anchor` properties to Bottom, Right, they anchor themselves to the bottom right of the form, which is consistent with their recommended placement on a form. Because you aren't anchoring opposing sides of the control, you aren't forcing the buttons to resize; the buttons are merely repositioned to keep station with the right and bottom edge of the form. Contrast this with the anchoring performed for the text box: because you anchored all sides, you are not only keeping a uniform border between the edge of the text box and the form but also causing the text box to stretch itself in both dimensions.

Docking

For the simple form in Figure 20.8, you can implement most of your layout logic using the Anchor property. But if you refer to the overall plan for the CSR screen (refer to Figure 20.1), you can see that you have some positioning needs that would be cumbersome to solve using anchors. For instance, the data entry region of the form should automatically expand vertically and horizontally to fill any space left between the list of requests, the status bar, and the command bar. This is where the concept of docking comes to the rescue. Docking is used either to stick a control to a neighboring control's edge or the form's edge or to force a control to fill all the available space not taken by other controls.

As with the Anchor property, the property browser provides a graphical tool to set a control's `Dock` property (shown in Figure 20.10).

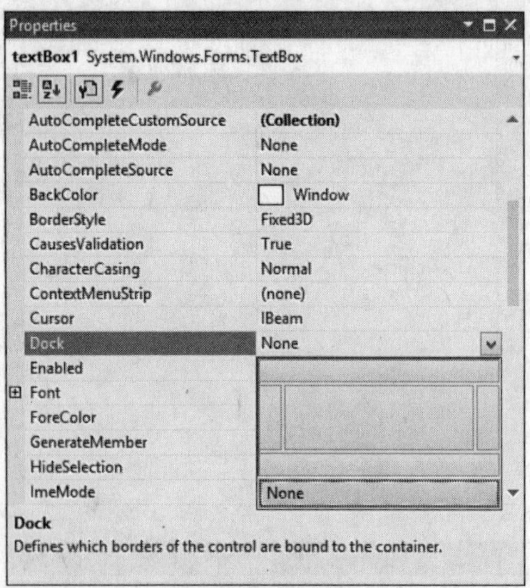

FIGURE 20.10 Setting the `Dock` property.

Control Auto Scaling

The Windows Forms engine supports the capability to dynamically adjust a control's dimensions to preserve its original design proportions. This capability is useful if the form or control is displayed at runtime on a system with different display characteristics (resolution, DPI, and so on) than the system the form or control was designed on.

A simple example of this occurs when an application that uses a reasonable 9-pt. font during design becomes almost unusable when displayed on a system whose default font size is larger. Because many UI elements auto-adjust based on the font of their displayed text (such as window title bars and menus), this can affect nearly every visual aspect of a form application.

Container controls (for example, those deriving from the `ContainerControl` class, including the `Form` class and `UserControl` among others) starting with .NET 2.0 support two properties that enable them to counter these issues automatically without a lot of developer intervention: `AutoScale` and `AutoScaleDimensions`. `AutoScaleMode` specifies an enumeration value indicating what the scaling process should use as its base reference (DPI or resolution). Table 20.2 shows the possible `AutoScaleMode` values.

TABLE 20.2 `AutoScaleMode` Enumeration Values

Value	Description
`Dpi`	Scale relative to the resolution (96 DPI, 120 DPI, and so on)
`Font`	Scale relative to the dimensions of the font being used
`Inherit`	Scale according to the base class `AutoScaleMode` value
`None`	No automatic scaling is performed

`AutoScaleDimensions` sets the dimensions (via a `SizeF` structure) that the control was originally designed to. This could refer to a font size or the DPI.

Using Containers

Containers are .NET controls designed to hold other controls. You can use containers in conjunction with the Anchor and Dock control properties to create intricate design scenarios. Although there are various container controls, the ones most applicable to control layout are `FlowLayoutPanel`, `TableLayoutPanel`, and `SplitContainer`.

Both the `TableLayoutPanel` and the `FlowLayoutPanel` containers derive from the more generic `Panel` class. The `Panel` class provides high-level capabilities for grouping controls. This is beneficial from a placement perspective because you can aggregate a bunch of controls into one group by positioning them within a panel. This way, you can act on them as a group; for instance, disabling a panel control disables all its child controls. The `TableLayoutPanel` and `FlowLayoutPanel` build on that functionality by also providing the capability to dynamically affect the positioning of their child controls.

The `TableLayoutPanel`

Consider a series of labels and text boxes for entering address information. They are typically arrayed in a column-and-row fashion. The `TableLayoutPanel` is ideal for implementing this behavior because it automatically forces the column and row assignment that you make for each of the controls. Figure 20.11 shows a series of Label and TextBox controls embedded within a `TableLayoutPanel`. Notice that resizing the form (and thus the panel, which is docked to fill the form interior) causes the panel's controls to auto-adjust their alignment.

If an item within one of the cells extends beyond the cell's boundaries, it automatically overflows within the cell. This provides you with the same layout capabilities that HTML offers for web browser-based interfaces.

NOTE

When a control is added to a `TableLayoutPanel`, it is decorated with five additional properties: `Cell`, `Column`, `Row`, `ColumnSpan`, and `RowSpan`. These properties can be used to change the control's row/column position within the layout panel at runtime. The `ColumnSpan` and RowSpan properties are used the same way as their namesakes in the HTML world. In .NET, controls that imbue other controls with additional properties are called *extender providers*.

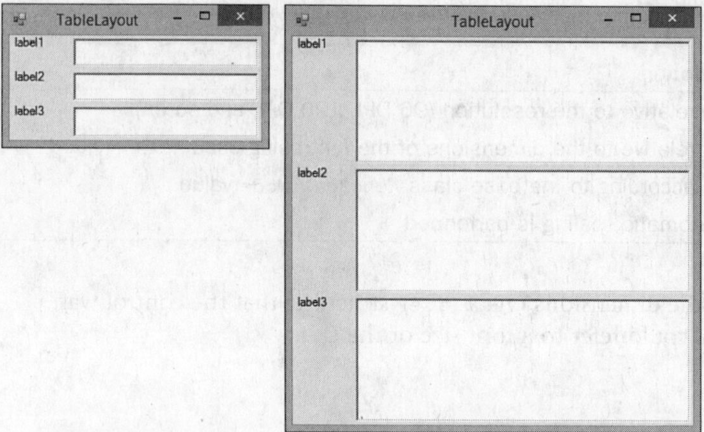

FIGURE 20.11 Using the `TableLayoutPanel`.

The `FlowLayoutPanel`

The `FlowLayoutPanel` has a simpler layout algorithm. Items are ordered either vertically or horizontally by wrapping control sets across rows or columns as needed. The two screens shown in Figure 20.12 illustrate the effect of resizing a flow layout panel containing a series of radio buttons.

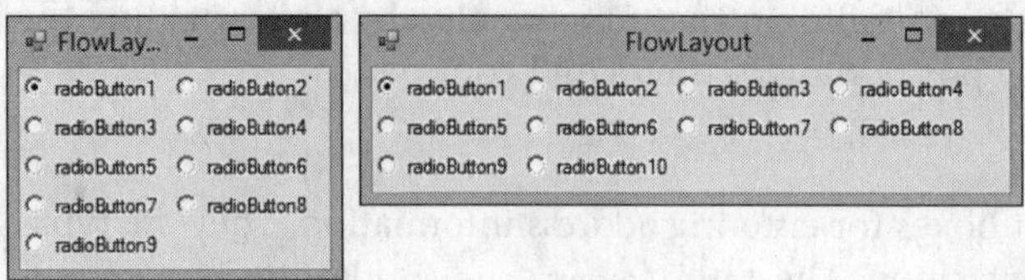

FIGURE 20.12 The `FlowLayoutPanel`.

The `SplitContainer`

The `SplitContainer` control is a much enhanced alternative to the original `Splitter` control that was included with .NET 1.0/1.1/Visual Studio 2003. This control represents the marriage of two panels and a splitter; the splitter separates the two panels either horizontally or vertically and enables a user to manually adjust the space (in the horizontal or vertical) that each panel consumes within the overall container.

Figure 20.13 shows the versatility of this control; two split containers, one embedded within a panel hosted by the other, are used to provide both vertical and horizontal resizing capabilities for the panels on a form. (Panel 2 isn't visible because it is the panel functioning as the container for the split container with panels 3 and 4.) By dragging the split line to the right of panel 1, you can increase or decrease the horizontal real estate it occupies on the form. The same is true for the split line between panel 3 and panel 4;

dragging this adjusts the ratio of space that both panels vertically occupy in relation to one another.

FIGURE 20.13 Resizing with the `SplitContainer`: a horizontal `SplitContainer` embedded in a vertical `SplitContainer`.

The `ToolStripContainer`

Many applications support the capability to drag and dock a toolbar, menu, and the like to any side of a form: top, bottom, left, or right. Visual Studio itself is an example of just such an application. By grabbing and dragging a Visual Studio toolbar, you can reposition it, for example, to the left side of the IDE. The ToolStripContainer control enables this functionality in your applications as well; it is a combination of four panels, each positioned on the four different edges of the containing form. These panels are used to host ToolStrip controls (more on these in a bit) and (at runtime) enable users to move tool strips within and between the four panels.

NOTE

Although the ToolStripContainer provides a convenient vehicle for snapping tool strips to the sides of a form, there is unfortunately no built-in support for "floating" tool strips.

The design experience is simple: you can shuffle controls around to the four different panels depending on where you want them positioned within the parent form. Figure 20.14 shows a `ToolStripContainer` in design mode. The smart tag offers up control over the visibility of the top, left, right, and bottom panels. Each panel is hidden by default. You can click any of the arrows on the sides of the container to expand the corresponding panel and give you room to place tool strips within the panel.

Although it is convenient to be able to place items in a `ToolStripContainer` within the designer, the real benefit that you get from the control is the automatic support for dragging and dropping between panels at runtime. This means that, without writing a single line of layout or positioning code, you have enabled functionality that lets users place their menus or toolbars wherever they want within the form. Figure 20.15 shows a toolbar, hosted in a `ToolStripContainer`, which has been redocked from the top panel to the left panel at runtime.

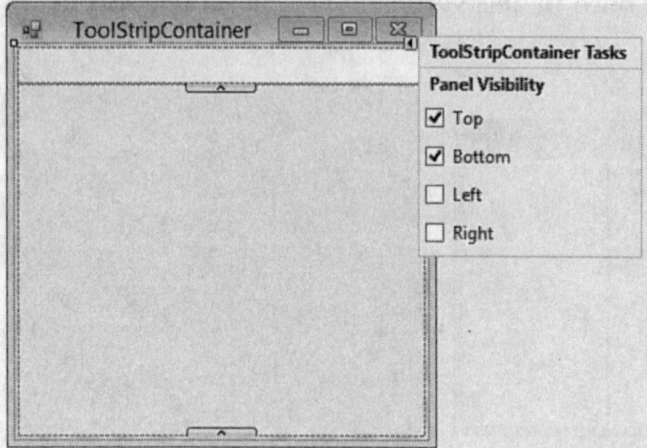

FIGURE 20.14 ToolStripContainer in design mode.

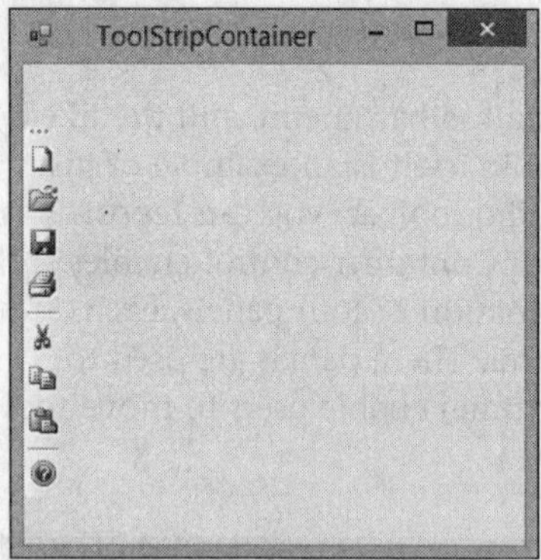

FIGURE 20.15 A toolbar positioned at runtime within a ToolStripContainer.

Multiple `ToolStrip` controls can also be stacked within any of the given panels in the `ToolStripContainer`. Figure 20.16 shows multiple command bars stacked within the right-most panel. As noted later in the chapter, a control's z-order dictates its place within the stack.

NOTE

The sharing of space (vertically or horizontally) within a ToolStripContainer is sometimes referred to as *rafting*. The ToolStrip controls are free to float anywhere within the panel.

A few other intricacies are involved with form/control layout and positioning, but we have now covered the basics. With these concepts in hand and a general design for your form, you can start using the Windows Forms Designer.

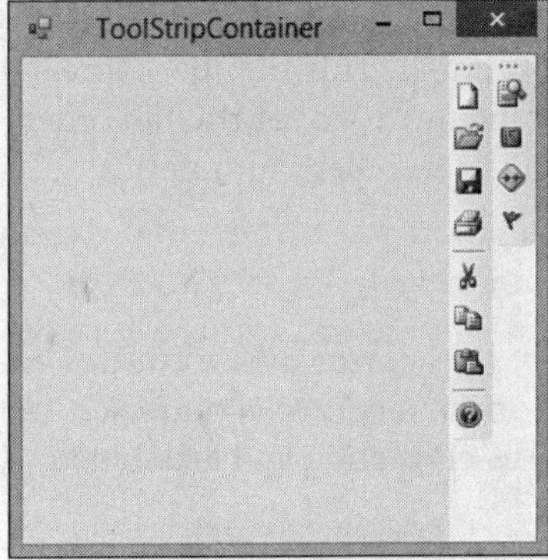

FIGURE 20.16 Multiple toolbars stacked within the same panel.

Control Appearance and Behavior

A control's appearance is set via the same set of basic properties used to control form appearance: Items such as `ForeColor`, `BackColor`, and `Font` make an appearance on most controls.

Visual Styles

One item of interest is the capability for a control to automatically alter its appearance to conform to the currently selected "Desktop Theme" if it's running on Windows XP, Windows Vista, Windows 7, or Windows 8. This capability is enabled by a call to the `Application.EnableVisualStyles` method. This line of code is automatically included for you by default as the first line in the `Main` method. This location is ideal because it must be called before the controls in the application are actually created. If you remove the call, you can easily compare the appearance with and without the effects enabled. Figure 20.17 shows a form without visual styles enabled (left) alongside one with visual styles enabled (right).

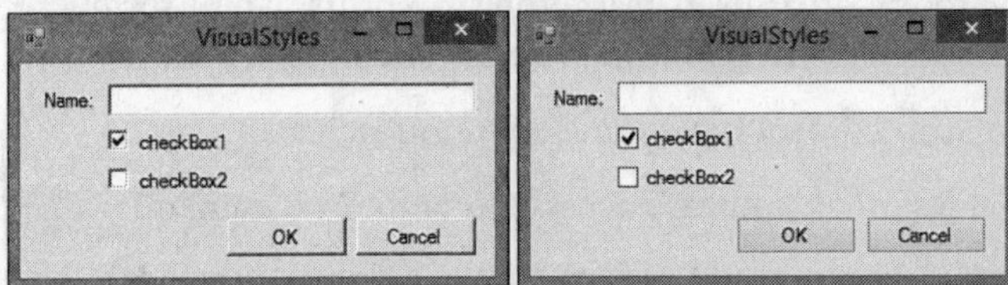

FIGURE 20.17 The effects of setting `Application.EnableVisualStyles`.

Tab Order

By default, the order in which the controls on a form receive focus (tab order) is the same as the order in which they were placed on the form. To explicitly set the tab order for all the controls on a form, the IDE has a tab order selection mode.

To enter tab order selection mode, select View, Tab Order from the menu. The Windows Forms Designer annotates every control on the form with a number. This number represents that control's position within the overall tab order for the form. To set the tab order that you want, click sequentially on the controls; their tab order numbers automatically change as you click.

ToolTips

ToolTips are small "balloons" that display text as a user moves his cursor over a control. Typically, they are used to provide helpful hints or descriptions of a control's purpose, action, and so on. ToolTips are implemented with the `ToolTip` class and can be assigned to controls at design time.

The `ToolTip` class is an example of an extender provider. (See the previous note on extender providers in our discussion on the TableLayoutPanel control.) When you add a ToolTip component to a form, every control on the form now implements a ToolTip property that is used to assign a ToolTip to that specific control.

For illustration, if you wanted to add a ToolTip to a ToolStrip button, you would first drag the ToolTip component over to the form from the Toolbox. You would then select the ToolStrip button that you want to add the ToolTip to, and you would set its `ToolTip` property to reference the ToolTip instance on your form.

Working with ToolStrip Controls

Many of the standard, core visual elements of a form are realized with ToolStrip controls. A ToolStrip control functions as a container for other controls that derive from ToolStripItem. It can host various types of controls: buttons, combo boxes, labels, separators, text boxes, and even progress bars. The `ToolStrip` class itself is used to directly implement toolbars on a form and functions as a base class for the StatusStrip control and the MenuStrip control.

ToolStrip controls come with an impressive list of built-in capabilities. They intrinsically support, for example, dragging an item from one tool strip to another, dynamically reordering and truncating items in the tool strip as users resize the strip or its parent form, and fully supporting different operating system (OS) themes and rendering schemes.

All the different flavors of the ToolStrip control have some common traits:

- A design-time smart tag provides quick and easy access to common commands.
- In-place editing of child controls is supported. (For example, a point-and-click interface is offered for adding, removing, and altering items within the ToolStrip, StatusStrip, or MenuStrip.)
- An Items Collection Editor dialog box enables you to gain more fine control over child control properties and enables add/reorder/remove actions against the child controls.
- Tool strips support a pluggable rendering model; you can change the visual renderer of a tool strip to a canned rendering object or to a custom object to obtain absolute control over the appearance of the tool strip.

From the initial form design, you know that you need menus, toolbars, and status bars, so the ToolStrip control and its descendants play a crucial role.

Creating a Menu

MenuStrip controls enable you to visually construct a form's main menu system. Dragging and dropping this control from the Toolbox onto the blank form automatically docks the menu strip to the top of the form (see Figure 20.18).

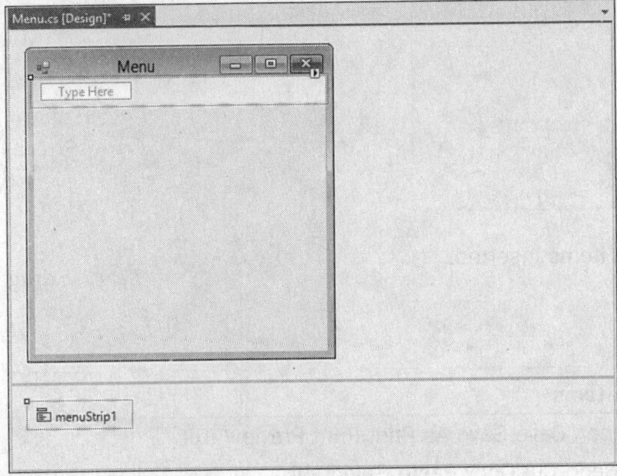

FIGURE 20.18 A menu positioned on the form.

After you place this control on the form, selecting the MenuStrip control activates the smart tag glyph. (Smart tags are covered in Chapter 7, "Working with Visual Studio's Productivity Aids.") Clicking the smart tag enables you to quickly do three things:

- Automatically insert standard items onto the menu
- Change the menu's `RenderMode`, `Dock`, and `GripStyle` properties
- Edit the menu items

Leveraging the capability to automatically equip a menu strip with a standard set of menus shaves a few minutes of design time off the manual approach. Figure 20.19 shows the result.

Not only has the designer inserted the standard File, Edit, Tools, and Help top-level menu items, but it also has inserted subitems below each menu. Table 20.3 indicates the exact menu structure that results from using the menu's Insert Standard Items feature.

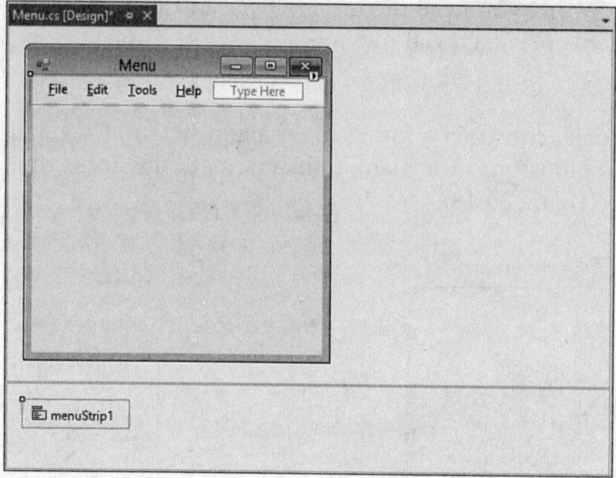

FIGURE 20.19 A menu with standard items inserted.

TABLE 20.3 Standard Menu Items

Main Menu	Menu Items
File	New Open Save Save As Print Print Preview Exit
Edit	Undo Redo Cut Copy Paste Select All
Tools	Customize Options
Help	Contents Index Search About

If you want to manually add menu items into the menu strip, you can use the placeholder block within the menu strip labeled with the text "Type Here." Every time you type in the placeholder block, additional placeholders become visible, and a menu item is added to the menu strip (see Figure 20.20).

Creating a Toolbar

The next item up for inclusion on the form is a toolbar. Toolbars in .NET 2.0 and later are implemented directly with ToolStrip controls. As mentioned before, ToolStrip controls can host various child controls; each inherits from the `ToolStripItem` base class. Figure 20.21 shows the controls that can be implemented inside a tool strip.

In fact, the interactive layout features of the tool strip work the same way as the menu strip: dragging the control onto the form will result in a blank ToolStrip control docked to the top of the form just under the existing menu control, and you can quickly add a roster of standard items to the tool strip by using its smart tag and selecting Insert Standard Items.

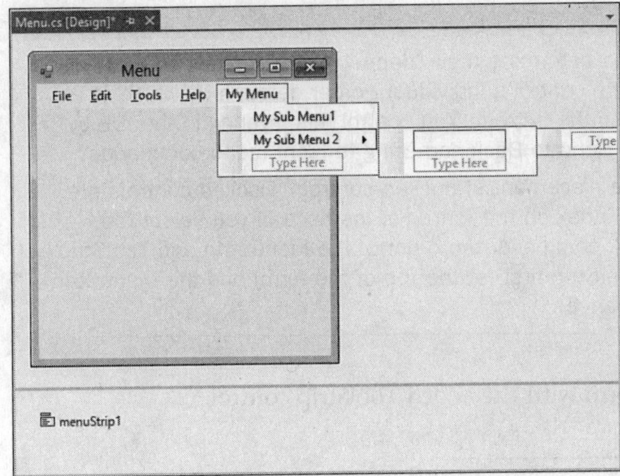

FIGURE 20.20 Manually adding menu items.

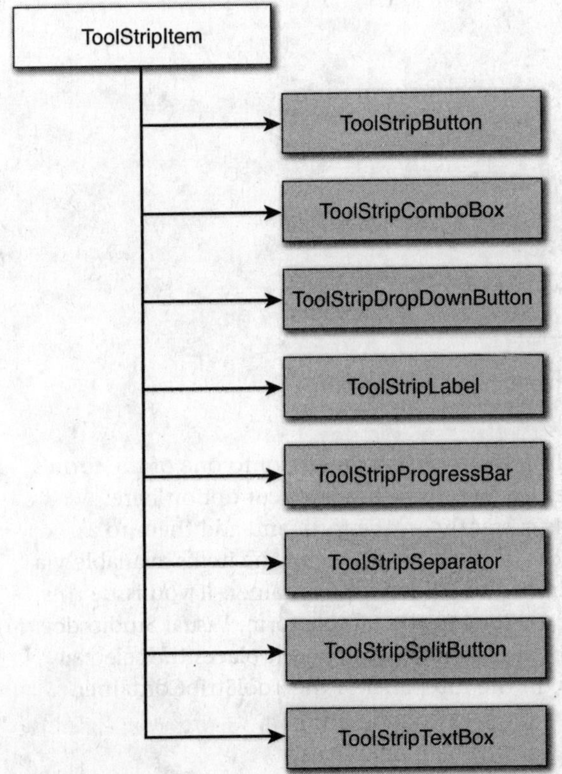

FIGURE 20.21 Classes inheriting from ToolStripItem.

NOTE

Controls use the concept of *z-order* to determine their "depth" on the form. If two controls occupy the same space on a form, the control's individual z-order determines which of the two controls is on top and which is on the bottom. You control this layering in the IDE by right-clicking a control and using the Send to Back and Bring to Front menu commands.

Z-order plays an important role in the placement of docked controls. Docked controls are arrayed in increasing order of their z index on the form. For instance, if you select the ToolStrip and issue the Send to Back command, the order of the MenuStrip and ToolStrip containers is altered to place the ToolStrip first (at the top of the form) and the MenuStrip second (just below the ToolStrip instance).

Figure 20.22 shows the in-progress form with the added ToolStrip control.

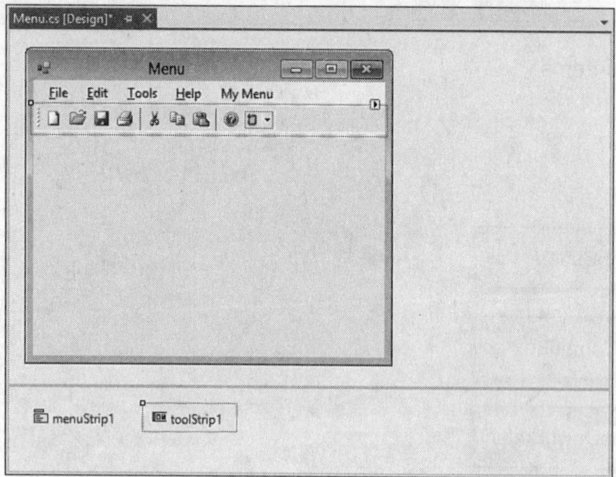

FIGURE 20.22 The main form with a complete menu and toolbar.

If you want to enable users to drag and drop the toolbar or menu onto one of the form's four sides, you use the ToolStripContainer. In fact, there is a shortcut option here: you can take any of the ToolStrip controls currently on the form and add them to a ToolStripContainer with just a couple clicks of the mouse. One of the items available via a tool strip's smart tag is the command Embed in a ToolStripContainer. If you issue this command against the toolbar that you just added to the sample form, Visual Studio does two things for you: it adds a ToolStripContainer to the form, and it places the selected ToolStrip into the container—specifically, in the top panel of the ToolStripContainer.

Creating a Status Bar

Status bars provide the user feedback on an application's current status, progress within an action, details in context with an object selected on a form, and so on. The StatusStrip control provides this functionality in starting with .NET 2.0/Visual Studio 2005, and it supplants the StatusBar control found in earlier versions.

As with the other ToolStrip descendants, the StatusStrip control functions as a container; its capability to host labels in addition to progress bars, drop-downs, and split buttons makes it a much more powerful control than the StatusBar.

Figure 20.23 shows the fictional Contoso CSR form with a StatusStrip docked at the bottom of the form. In design mode, you see a drop-down button that holds a selection for each of the four supported child controls. For the purposes of this demonstration prototype, add a label control to report general application status and an additional label and progress bar in case you run into any long-running retrieval or edit operations.

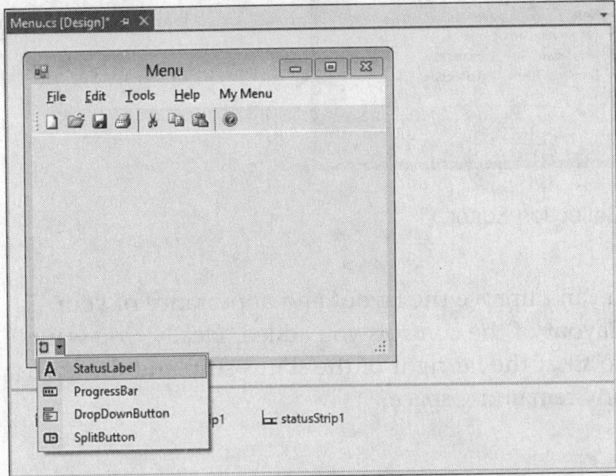

FIGURE 20.23 A StatusStrip in design mode.

By default, child controls are added in a left-to-right flow layout pattern within the StatusStrip pattern. With just six clicks (two per item), you can add these controls to the strip. The in-place editing capabilities are great for quickly building out the look and feel of the strip; for greater control of the strip's child controls, you can use the Items Collection Editor dialog box.

TIP

By right-clicking any of the StatusStrip child controls and selecting Convert To, you can quickly change the type of the control. For instance, if you have a label control currently on the strip but you really want a drop-down button, you right-click the label and select Convert To, DropDownButton. This saves you the hassle of deleting the control and adding a new one.

Editing the StatusStrip Items You use the StatusStrip's smart tag and select Edit Items to launch the Items Collection Editor dialog box. The editor provides direct access to all the hosted control's properties and enables you to edit, delete, and reorder items within the status strip (see Figure 20.24).

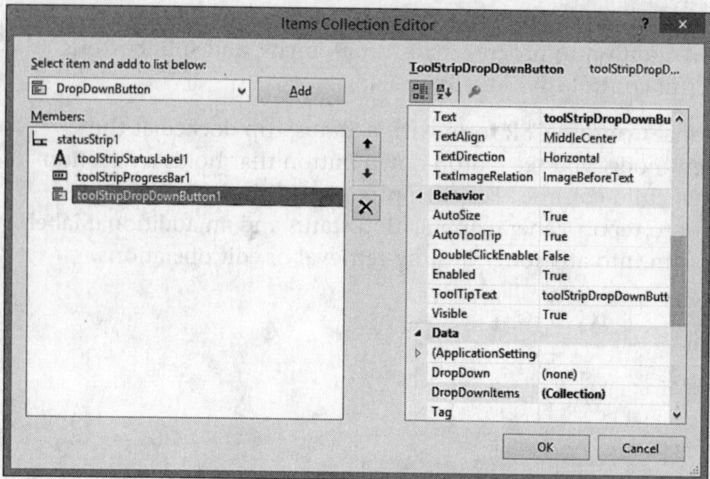

FIGURE 20.24 The StatusStrip Items Collection Editor.

By tweaking some properties here, you can improve the layout and appearance of your items. Figure 20.25 shows the default layout of the controls you added; ideally, you want the progress bar and its label control to sit at the far right of the status strip and the status label to sit at the far left to consume any remaining space.

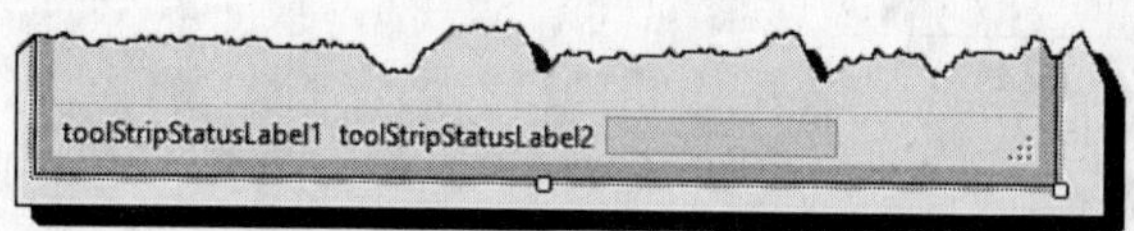

FIGURE 20.25 Default positioning of the StatusStrip items.

To make this happen, you need to set the `Spring` property to `True` for the leftmost label. This will cause the label to expand and contract to fill the available space on the status strip. Next, set its `TextAlignment` property to situate the text to the left of the label region and change the Text property to something more appropriate.

Figure 20.26 shows the fruits of our labor.

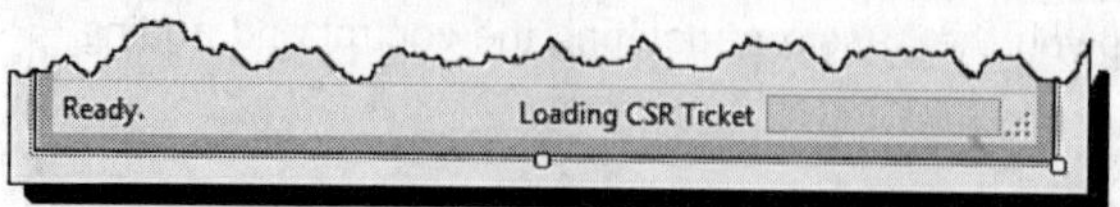

FIGURE 20.26 The final StatusStrip look and feel.

Displaying Data

So far, we have only touched on form elements that provide the basic framework user navigation, status, commands, and so on. However, the capability to access, display, and edit data from an underlying data store (relational or otherwise) is the real value of an application such as the fictional Contoso CSR application. We touch on the details of working with databases in the next chapter; here, we describe some of the basic controls used to display data in a form.

Hierarchical Data

The TreeView control is ideal for presenting data with hierarchical relationships and is thus a good candidate for housing the list of order records (which can be grouped by different criteria). First, add a SplitContainer control to partition the leftover interior space in the form into two discrete panels. Yet another panel houses the search function for orders; this is docked to the top of the left split panel. A TreeView dock fills the remainder of this leftmost panel, and the right panel houses the data fields (text boxes, labels, radio buttons, and so on) for an individual CSR record.

TreeView controls present data as a list of nodes; each node can serve as a parent for additional nodes. Typically, with applications that front a database, you build the contents of the TreeView by binding to a resultset from the database or by programmatically looping through the resultset and adding to the TreeView's node list through its application programming interface (API). But you also have control over the TreeView content in the designer by launching the TreeNode Editor.

The TreeNode Editor The TreeNode Editor (see Figure 20.27) is a dialog box that acts much the same as the Items Collection Editor examined previously. It enables you to add, edit, and remove items from the TreeView control. You launch the editor dialog box by selecting Edit Nodes from the TreeView's smart tag.

Using the Add Root and Add Child buttons, you can insert new nodes into the tree's data structure at any given nesting level. Figure 20.27 shows manually inserted nodes with test data so that you can get an idea of what the order list would look like using the company as a parent node and order instances as child nodes under the corresponding company. Each item, or node, in the TreeView consists of two parts: an image and text. The image is optional; if you want to attach an icon to a node, you start by assigning an ImageList control to the TreeView control.

Using an ImageList ImageList controls function as an image provider for other controls. They maintain a collection of `Image` objects that are referenced by their ordinal position or key within the collection. Any control that provides an `ImageList` property can reference an ImageList component and use its images. ListView, ToolStrip, and TreeView are some examples of controls that can leverage the ImageList component.

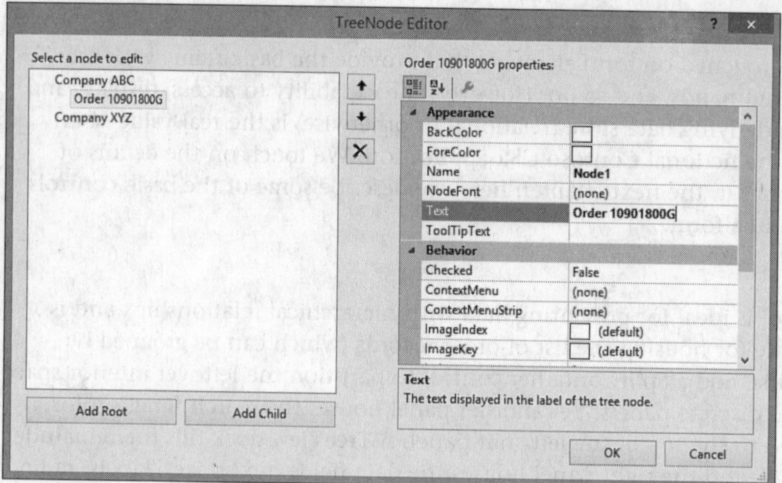

FIGURE 20.27 Using the designer to edit nodes in the TreeView control.

NOTE

Microsoft provides a large library of images that you can use with the TreeView or any other control that requires these types of standard graphics, such as toolbars and menus. Search msdn.microsoft.com for "Visual Studio Image Library."

An ImageList doesn't have a visual presence on a form; in other words, you can't see the ImageList itself. Its sole use is as a behind-the-scenes component that feeds images to other controls. Dropping an ImageList onto the designer puts an instance of the component in the component tray. You can then use the Images Collection Editor dialog box to add, edit, and remove the images hosted by the component. Changing the images associated with the image list automatically changes the images used by any controls referencing the ImageList.

Figure 20.28 shows a few images added within the Images Collection Editor. To enable the TreeView to use these images, you have to do two things:

1. Assign the `TreeView.ImageList` property to point to the instance of the ImageList component (in this case, ImageList1).
2. Set the image associated with a node either programmatically or via the TreeNode Editor dialog box.

With the ImageList component in place and the TreeView dropped in the SplitContainer's left panel, the form is almost there from a design perspective. The remaining piece is the series of fields that display the data for a record selected in the TreeView control.

You could add this piece just by dragging a bunch of text boxes and labels over into a TableLayoutPanel and then docking the whole mess in the open SplitContainer panel. But because you really want to treat this as one cohesive unit to simplify positioning, eventual data binding, and so on, you instead create a user control for displaying a CSR record.

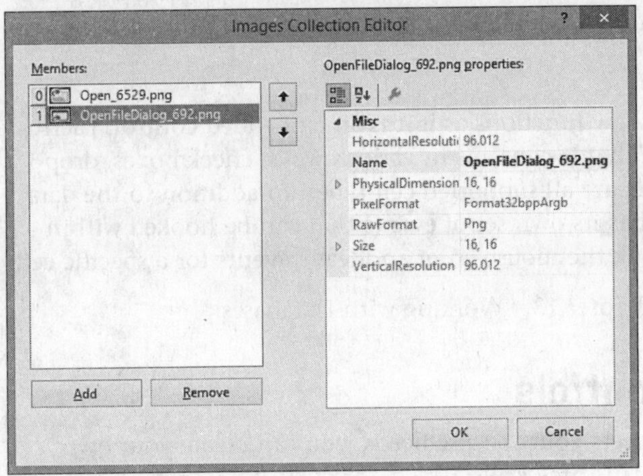

FIGURE 20.28 The Images Collection Editor.

Tabular Data
The DataGridView control is the premium Visual Studio control for displaying data in a tabular format. It provides a row/column format for displaying data from a variety of data sources. Figure 20.29 shows a DataGridView with its smart tag menu opened; the smart tag menu provides fast access to the column properties of the grid control and enables you to directly bind the DataGridView to a data source.

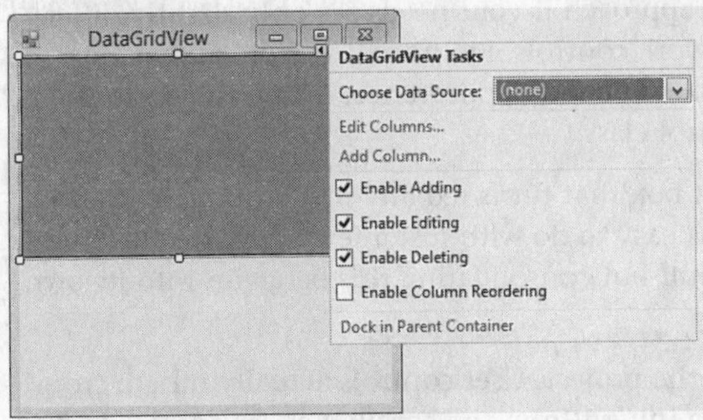

FIGURE 20.29 Configuring a DataGridView control with its smart tag.

Data Sources The DataGridView control supports various possible data sources. For instance, scenarios such as displaying name/value pairs from a collection are supported, in addition to datasets returned from a relational data store. If you select a data source for the grid, a column is added to the grid for every column that appears in the data source, and the row data is automatically provided inside the DataGridView control.

Data can be displayed in the grid control in an "unbound" mode as well; using the grid's row/column API, you can programmatically define the structure of the grid and add data to it at runtime.

Cell Types Each cell in a DataGridView functions as if it is an embedded control. Each cell can express the underlying data that it contains in various ways; check boxes, drop-downs, links, buttons, and text boxes are all supported cell types. In addition to the data visualization possibilities, each cell has its own set of events that can be hooked within your code. For example, you can hook the mouse enter and leave events for a specific cell.

We cover this control in depth in Chapter 13, "Working with Databases."

Creating Your Own Controls

If none of the stock .NET controls meets your specific needs, you can create your own controls for use on a Windows Form in three ways:

- You can subclass an existing control and modify or extend its behavior and appearance.
- You can create a user control by compositing together two or more existing controls.
- You can create a custom control from scratch, implementing your own visuals and behavior.

Subclassing an Existing Control

Subclassing an existing control is the best approach if your needs are only slightly different from one of the standard .NET Framework controls. By inheriting from an existing control class, you are riding on top of its behavior and appearance; it's up to you to then add the specialized code to your new control class.

For example, suppose that you want a text box that turns red anytime a numeric (that is, nonalphabetic) character is entered. This is easy to do with just a few lines of code sitting in the TextBox control's TextChanged event, but consolidating this behavior into its own class provides a reuse factor.

You start by adding a new user control to the project. User controls actually inherit from the UserControl class; because you want to inherit from the TextBox class, you need to change the class definition by using the code editor. After you do that, you can place the new component on a form and use its functionality.

Working with an Inherited Control

Because TextBox already has a UI, you don't need to do anything about the appearance of the control. In fact, it works just like any other text box control within the Windows Forms Designer (see Figure 20.30).

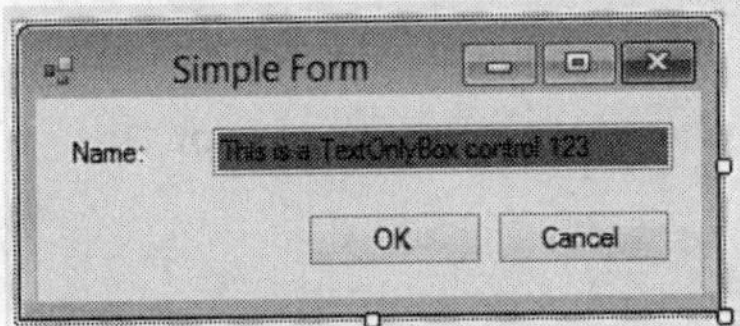

FIGURE 20.30 A control derived from TextBox.

The Properties window for the control behaves as expected, and double-clicking the control immediately takes you to an open code editor window. In short, the design-time experience remains fully functional and requires no effort on the part of the developer.

Designing a User Control

A user control is technically the same as any other class that you author as a developer. Because a user control has a visual aspect to it, Visual Studio provides a designer, just as with Windows Forms, to help in the drag-and-drop creation of the control.

User controls are composite controls; that is, they are constructed from one or more existing .NET controls. As with a derived control, their user interfaces inherit from the native controls they are composed of, making them simple to build and use in the designer.

There are two approaches to the user control creation process: you can create a separate Windows Control Library project, or you can simply add a user control class to an existing Windows Forms project.

Creating a separate project enables the user control to live in its own assembly. If it is a separate assembly, you can treat the user control as the quintessential black box, giving you greater flexibility from a source control perspective and enabling you to share the control among multiple projects. For production scenarios, this is clearly the best route. However, for simple prototyping work, as you are doing here with the CSR form application, the ease and simplicity of just adding a new class to the existing project make this approach preferable to using the separate project approach. The class lives inside the same namespace as the form class.

If you were ever in a position to transition from prototyping to actual production development, nothing would preclude you from refactoring the control by simply copying the user control class file and embedding it in a separate control library project.

As soon as you add the user control class to the project, you are presented with the User Control Designer. The designer works the same way as the Windows Forms Designer; to build the user control, you drag components or controls from the Toolbox onto its surface.

Adding Controls

Obviously, the controls that you use to build your composite control entirely depend on how you envision the control's functionality. As an example, to create an order display control, you need to think about the underlying data structure of an order. An order record might contain the following:

- An order number
- A series of dates that capture the date the order was placed, the date the order was shipped, and so on
- A list of items included on the order
- The billing information and shipping address
- Miscellaneous comments

Because this is a lot of information to try to cram onto one screen, you can turn to the TabControl. A tab control is another general-purpose container control that enables you to organize content across several pages that are accessed via tabs. Within each tab, you can leverage the TableLayoutPanel and implement most of the order fields with simple label and text box pairs.

As mentioned earlier, the whole process of getting these controls into the user control works identically to the Windows Forms Designer: You drag and drop the controls from the Toolbox onto the user control design surface. Figure 20.31 shows the OrderDisplay user control with its user interface completed.

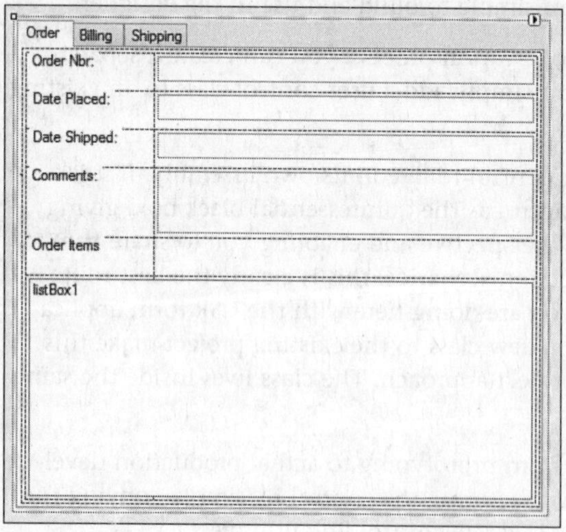

FIGURE 20.31 Designing a user control.

Embedding the User Control

Now that you have a completed design for your user control, the only remaining step is to embed the control into your primary form. If you compile the project, Visual Studio automatically recognizes the user control class and includes an entry for the control in the Toolbox. From there, you are just a drag and drop away from implementing the OrderDisplay control.

Creating a Custom Control

Custom controls represent the ultimate in extensibility because they are built from scratch. As a result, they are relatively hard to develop because they require you to worry not only about functionality but also about every single aspect of the control's visual appearance. Because the physical user interface of the custom control needs to be drawn 100% by custom code, a steep learning curve is associated with authoring a custom control.

Because much of the work that goes into creating a custom control is at the code level, we won't try to tackle this subject with any useful degree of detail in this book. You should note, however, that the process starts the same way as with other control options: Visual Studio has a custom control project item template; adding this to your project gives you a baseline of code to start with. From there, it's up to you.

NOTE

The Paint event is where you place the code to draw your control's user interface. Although so-called "owner draw" controls can involve complex drawing code, the good news is that the Windows Forms Designer leverages whatever code you place in the Paint event to render the control at design time. This means that you can still rely on the Windows Forms Designer to provide you with a WYSIWYG experience even with custom controls.

Summary

This chapter described the various design-time capabilities of the Windows Forms Designer tool. Windows Forms are a powerful presentation layer technology, and Visual Studio 2015 provides an array of tools for quickly building impressive, rich user interfaces based on this technology.

The role of the Windows Forms Designer, the Toolbox, and the Properties window were introduced in the context of delivering a modern, well-thought-out, standards-based user interface for a .NET Windows application. Using the tools documented here, you can wring the most out of your WinForm development experience.

Creating a Custom Control

Summary

CHAPTER 21

Building WPF Applications

IN THIS CHAPTER

- The Windows Presentation Foundation Platform
- Introducing the WPF Designer
- Programming with WPF
- Building a Simple Image Viewer Application

With .NET 3.0, Microsoft delivered a brand-new set of technologies for powering the presentation layer in your applications: the Windows Presentation Foundation (WPF). WPF was designed from the ground up to leverage the strengths of both the Windows Forms development world and the web forms development world. At the same time, WPF attempts to overcome many of the obstacles that developers face when trying to build rich, compelling user interfaces that involve media and highly customized user interfaces and that exploit all the horsepower available in modern CPUs and graphics processors.

WPF is intended to be a unifying platform with built-in, first-class support for data binding, audio, video, and both 2D and 3D graphics. Because WPF likely represents a significant learning curve for both new and experienced developers, we spend some time up front in this chapter discussing the basics before diving into the real target: how to use the Visual Studio WPF Designer tool (previously known by its code name Cider) to build high-octane user interfaces for your Windows applications.

The Windows Presentation Foundation Platform

WPF brings a lot of new concepts and new coding territory with it (and can represent a fairly significant learning curve for developers). But let's take a brief look at the overall architecture of the WPF platform and then dissect the programming model.

Physically, WPF is implemented with a series of three assemblies:

- `WindowsBase.dll`
- `PresentationFramework.dll`
- `PresentationCore.dll`

Every presentation layer framework has to eventually paint pixels onto a screen, and WPF is no different. Implemented within its binaries is a composition and rendering engine that talks to your hardware through DirectX. In addition to the rendering layers, there is obviously a rich programming model that is implemented with deep support for things such as layout, containership (the capability for one element to contain another), and events/message dispatches. In short, it does all the heavy lifting to ensure that some complicated user interface scenarios can be rendered on the screen with enough performance to appeal to a wide range of solution scenarios.

Figure 21.1 shows the logical architecture of the various WPF components. The actual rendering "engine" is contained within the Media Integration Layer component; `PresentationCore` handles interop with the Media Integration Layer, and `PresentationFramework` contains all the other magic necessary to make WPF successful as an end-to-end platform such as layout, data binding, and event notifications.

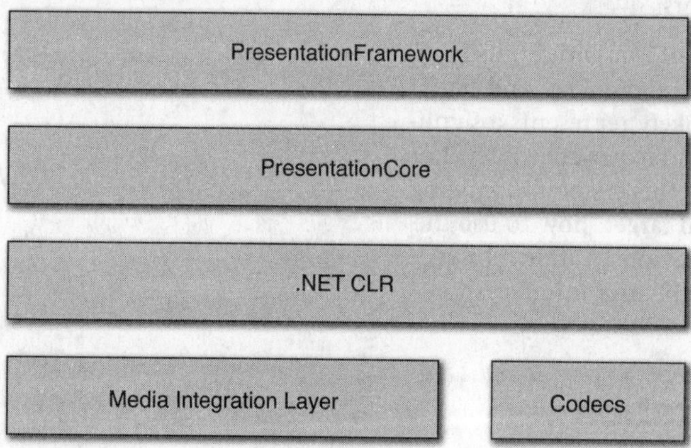

FIGURE 21.1 WPF logical architecture.

NOTE

Most of WPF itself is implemented in managed .NET code. The exception is the Media Integration Layer. When it comes to rendering the user interface (UI) to the screen, WPF needs to optimize for performance over nearly all other concerns; therefore, the Media Integration Layer is implemented as native code.

All these WPF components work in concert to deliver an impressive laundry list of improvements to the state of the art with regard to presentation layer design, construction, and runtime support with .NET. Here is a small sample:

- **Media**—WPF supports 2D and 3D graphics, as well as WMV, MPEG, and AVI video.
- **Data binding**—WPF was built from the start to fully support the entire spectrum of data-binding scenarios, up to and including LINQ and the Entity Framework.
- **Windows Forms interoperability**—WPF applications can host WinForms components and vice versa. This is comforting because it means developers won't need to abandon the hard-won knowledge that comes with programming WinForms for many years.
- **Document support**—WPF has several native constructs for building document-centric applications. For instance, there is a `DocumentReader` class for displaying fixed-format documents and a `FlowDocumentReader` class for displaying documents with a dynamic layout. Think of a newspaper article, for instance, that automatically repaginates while remaining true to the column structure.
- **Animation**—Developers can create storyboard-based animations and specify animation triggers and timers.
- **Control "look and feel"**—Controls in WPF have their appearance controlled by a template, which developers can replace or change to fully customize nearly every aspect of a control's "chrome."
- **Text**—There is rich typography support in WPF. Developers can manipulate a slew of font attributes (kerning; effects such as glow, drop-shadows, and motion blur; auto line spacing; and so on), and WPF developers can choose to have text rendered using ClearType technology or via two additional rendering modes introduced in WPF 4: aliased and grayscale.

During the initial beta cycles, Microsoft produced a series of prototype applications to showcase the new technologies in .NET 3.0, including WPF. Figure 21.2 shows a screenshot from one of those original prototypes (in this case, a healthcare application). Although a static shot like this doesn't do the application much justice, you can get a good sense for the possibilities. The UI for this application would have been extremely difficult to implement using Windows Forms technology.

For the most part, developers are free to not worry so much about the low-level architectural details of WPF; the programming model (and the tools which help us leverage that model) is where most developers will focus their energies.

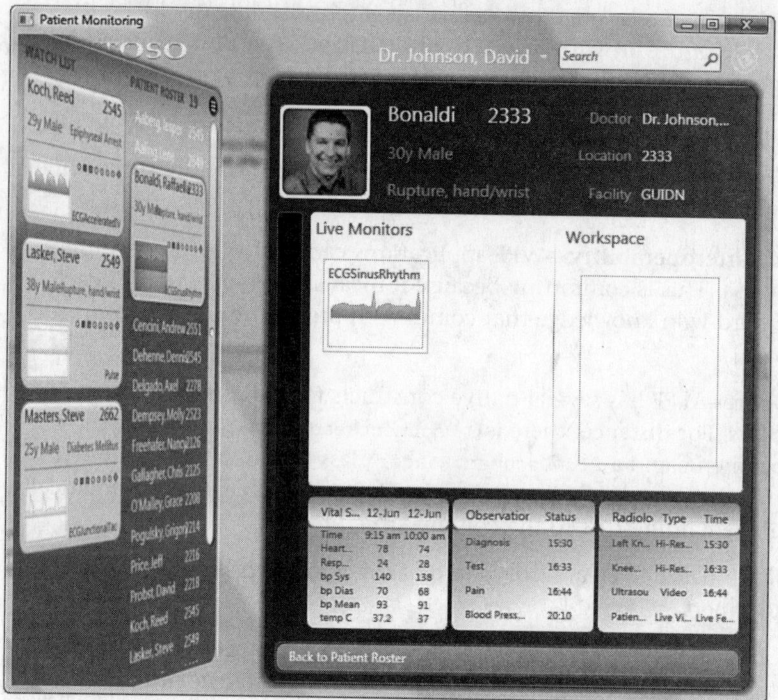

FIGURE 21.2 An early WPF-based healthcare application prototype.

Programming Model

The WPF class library consists of approximately 1,600 public types and more than 3,500 classes. As such, it has a considerably larger application programming interface (API) surface than either ASP.NET or Windows Forms. As you would expect from a .NET class library, all these classes can trace their ancestry back to `System.Object`. In addition, most WPF classes are based on so-called base elements: the `UIElement`, `FrameworkElement`, `ContentElement`, and `FrameworkContentElement` classes. These classes are responsible for basic item presentation and layout capabilities and are contained within the `System.Windows` namespace.

In addition to these four base element classes, a few other important base classes drive a lot of the functionality found in WPF:

- **Visual**—This class is the core rendering unit within WPF; `UIElement` inherits from Visual, as do the higher-level classes such as `Button`.
- **DispatcherObject**—This class supports the WPF threading model.
- **Control**—This is the base class for controls in WPF.

- **Application**—The `Application` class encapsulates all WPF applications; it provides application lifetime services, including the basic concepts of `Run` (to start an application) and `Exit` (to quit an application).

As you would expect, the WPF class library provides all the major controls that you would typically find in a Windows application, such as buttons, labels, list boxes, and text boxes.

The following snippet shows a WPF Button control being instantiated, and the text `Push Me` is assigned to the button. Note that the control constructs are familiar, but the actual object model is slightly different; the `Button` object in WPF does not have a `.Text` property as we would expect from an ASP.NET or WinForms button. Instead, it exposes a `.Content` property:

```
System.Windows.Controls.Button btn = new Button();
btn.Content = "Push Me";
```

Besides procedural code like that shown here, WPF enables us to create and manipulate objects in a declarative fashion using a markup syntax called XAML.

Extensible Application Markup Language

XAML is an XML dialect that can be used to describe the structure of a WPF application's presentation layer (for example, control instantiation, appearance, and layout).

XAML is the principal way in which the various WPF tools define objects and set properties in a declarative fashion. As such, it is tempting to compare XAML to HTML. It certainly fills a similar role in that both XAML and HTML are declarative ways to describe objects. But XAML is actually tightly coupled to the .NET Framework. In fact, XAML is really describing which .NET objects to create, plus setting their properties and attaching event handlers. WPF tools, such as the WPF Designer in Visual Studio, happen to leverage XAML, but strictly speaking, XAML is not a part of WPF. You can write an entire XAML application, for instance, using only the managed code language of your choice. Because XAML, as a programming model, brings several important advancements to the scene, it is heavily leveraged by all the Microsoft and non-Microsoft tools in the WPF world and beyond. For instance, Windows Workflow Foundation uses it to describe workflows. It is also one of the ways that you can create Windows Store applications in Windows 8/10 (and even Windows Phone).

Just as we did previously, let's create a `Button` object and assign some text to the button. But this time, let's define it with XAML.

```
<Button Content="Push Me"/>
```

Alternatively, we could write this code like this:

```
<Button>Push Me</Button>
```

Basically, when you define an element in XAML, the WPF engine will create an instance of the given type (`Button` in this example) for you. When you give a value to an attribute, it will be translated as setting this value to the property (`Content` here) with the same name as the attribute to the newly created object.

> **NOTE**
>
> XAML functionality is a subset of what is possible in .NET code. Or, to put it another way, anything you can define in XAML you can do in code, but not everything done in code can be defined in XAML.

In a typical WPF application, XAML coexists with managed code through the same partial class paradigm introduced with ASP.NET. In other words, we may have a `MainForm.xaml` file with the look and feel of a window and a `MainForm.xaml.vb` (or `.cs`) file that contains code that reacts to a user's input on that form. We see more of this in action a little later in this chapter when we take a close look at the WPF Designer.

If XAML isn't necessary to create a WPF application, why is it desired? Given the fact that you can accomplish the necessary tasks to create UI objects in XAML or in managed code, why is XAML even in the picture? There are a few areas where the declarative syntax becomes tremendously important.

Syntax Parsing Simplicity As is true with all XML-based languages, XAML is relatively easy for applications to parse and understand. Several developers have used this to their advantage and delivered lightweight tools for WPF development, such as XAMLPad. This has also enabled tool vendors, including Microsoft, to rapidly release products into the market that understand XAML. Adobe Illustrator, for example, has a XAML plug-in that enables you to emit XAML, and of course Microsoft has not one but two design tools that read and write XAML: Expression Design and Expression Blend.

The boundary between XAML and code also turns out to be a nice dividing line between appearance and behavior. In this scenario, XAML is used to define the UI objects and the general look and feel of the application, whereas procedural code is used to implement the business logic and to react to a user's input. This leads us directly to the other important advantage of XAML: collaboration.

Collaboration If we separate appearance and behavior, we can also reap the benefits of improved collaboration among project team members (specifically, collaboration between designers and developers). Before WPF, designers would rely on "flat" bitmaps created with drawing programs or would even rely on applications such as PowerPoint to mock up the user experience for an application. When that design is eventually handed off to the developer for implementation, there is an inherent disconnect: programming tools don't understand 2D bitmaps or PowerPoint storyboards. They understand code and objects. And in the reverse direction, we have the same problem: tools made for designers don't understand managed code. A developer can't implement a form in Visual Basic, for example, and hand it back to a designer for review and tweaking.

So developers are forced to re-create, as best they can, the vision delivered from the design team. This is a decidedly second-rate way to design and build applications. But with XAML, this situation changes dramatically. Because designers can now use highly visual tools that generate their design in XAML behind the scene (such as Microsoft Expression Blend), the developer can simply open that XAML file in Visual Studio and provide the coding "goop" necessary to flesh out the desired features in the code behind file. In the process, we have completely preserved the fidelity of the designers' original vision because the developer's tools are talking the same language. We also have full collaboration in the other direction: changes that a developer makes to the designer's XAML can be instantly reviewed and tweaked within the designer's tools. This simple concept—the sharing of a codebase and language between design and development roles and tools—proves to be a powerful argument for leveraging XAML in your applications.

Now that we have covered the basics of WPF, let's see how we can start writing WPF applications using Visual Studio.

Introducing the WPF Designer

We introduced the WPF Designer in Chapter 6, "Introducing the Editors and Designers." Let's recap the basics and then move on to a more involved discussion of the WPF Designer.

The WPF Designer is the tool in Visual Studio that provides the WYSIWYG design surface for building WPF windows. In many ways, it behaves just like the designers we use for web forms and Windows forms. But it is in fact a brand-new tool, with some subtle differences over its IDE brethren. To see the designer in action, let's create a new project in Visual Studio. The project template we want to select is WPF Application, and it is located in the Windows category on the New Project dialog box (see Figure 21.3).

This template takes care of adding the necessary WPF namespaces for us; the project also includes a file that implements the default window for the application: `MainWindow.xaml`. Double-clicking the `Window1.xaml` file launches the designer, which is shown in Figure 21.4.

XAML and Design Panes

The WPF Designer offers two different views: the visual representation of the window and the XAML that implements the window. You can make changes to the window and its controls by either editing the XAML or changing elements on the design surface. Either way, the designer keeps both panes in sync.

You can configure the position and layout of the XAML and design panes in the following ways:

- The Swap button swaps the positions of the XAML and design panes with one another.
- Vertical Split button tiles the panes vertically.
- The Horizontal Split button tiles the panes horizontally.

- The Collapse/Expand Pane button minimizes or restores the bottom or leftmost pane (depending on the view mode you are in).

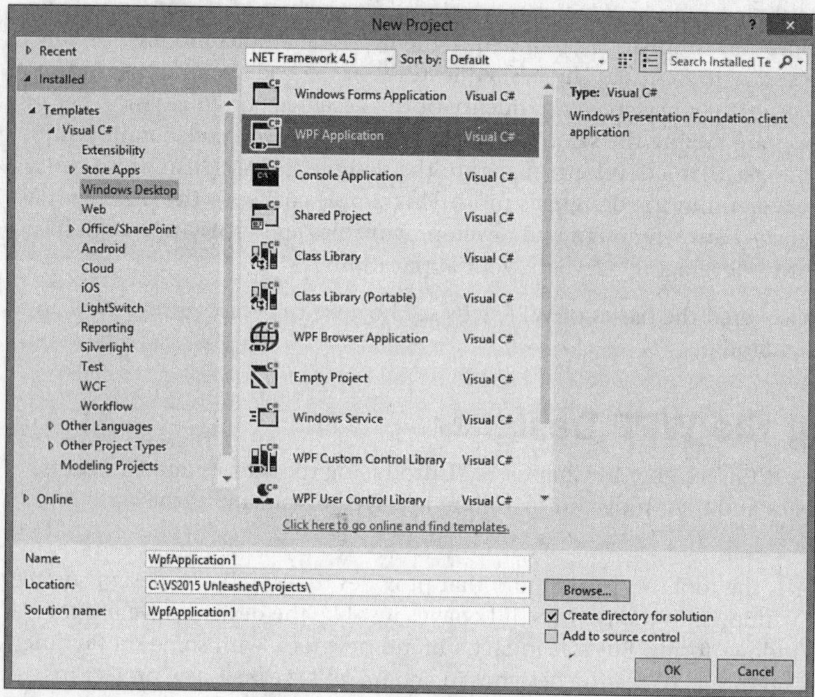

FIGURE 21.3 Creating a new WPF application.

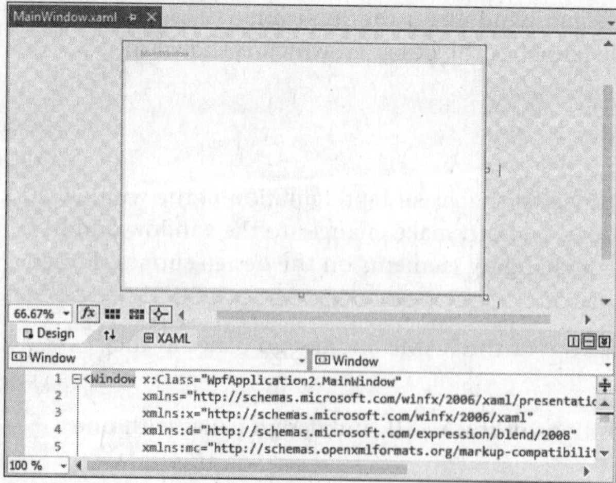

FIGURE 21.4 The WPF Designer.

Figure 21.5 shows the location of these pane management buttons on the designer.

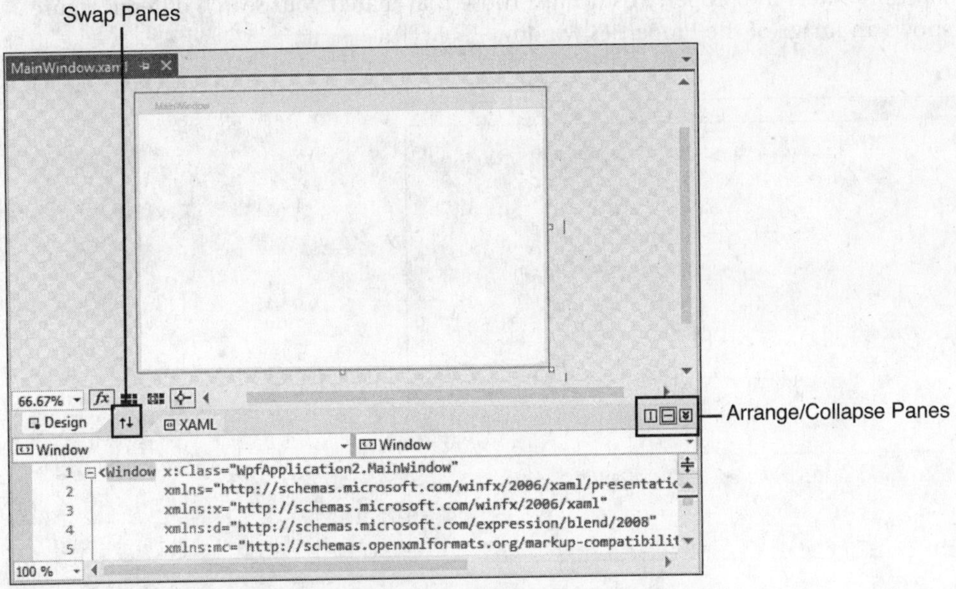

FIGURE 21.5 Controls for configuring the XAML and designer panes.

TIP

If you are lucky enough to have a multimonitor setup, the vertical split view is particularly helpful because you can display your XAML code on one screen and your visual design surface on another.

We interact with the designer in the same way we interact with other design surfaces or code editors: Controls can be placed on the design pane from the Toolbox and then manipulated, and we can use the XAML pane to handcraft or alter XAML (with complete IntelliSense and formatting).

For the most part, control placement and positioning works the same as it does in the Windows Forms designer. There are a few minor exceptions: the WPF Designer has some unique visualizations for displaying snap lines and control sizing (see Figure 21.6).

The Property Window

As expected, when you have a control selected in the designer, you can manipulate its attributes using the Properties window. The WPF Properties window has some significant differences over its Windows Forms sibling. It supports two unique ways for locating control properties. Besides the categorized and alphabetic display modes, you can group and sort properties by source. This is great for quickly looking at those properties, for instance, that have their value set explicitly in XAML or that have values that are currently being inherited down from a style. The WPF Properties window also enables you to search for properties of the control by typing in a search box. As you type, the window automatically filters the property list to just those that match your search criteria. Figure 21.7 shows an image of the Properties window.

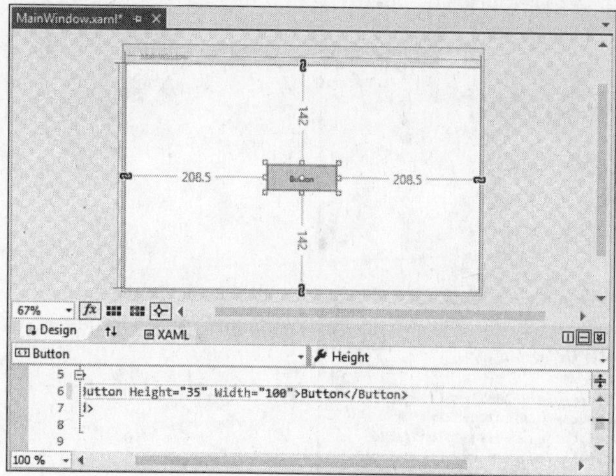

FIGURE 21.6 Sizing and positioning indicators.

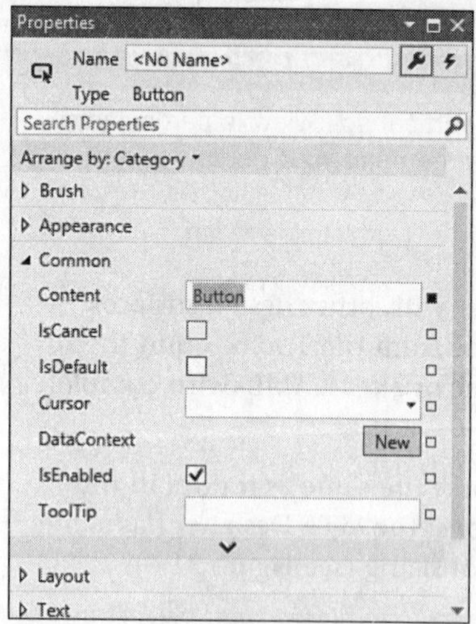

FIGURE 21.7 The WPF Designer Properties window.

The Zoom Control

One additional item is present with the WPF designer: a zoom control. Perched in the small toolbar at the bottom of the design page, this drop-down can be used to zoom in or out on the current window from 3% to 6400% of the window's actual size. Figure 21.8 shows the magnification control, and Figure 21.9 shows our Push Me button (and container window) at 8 times magnification.

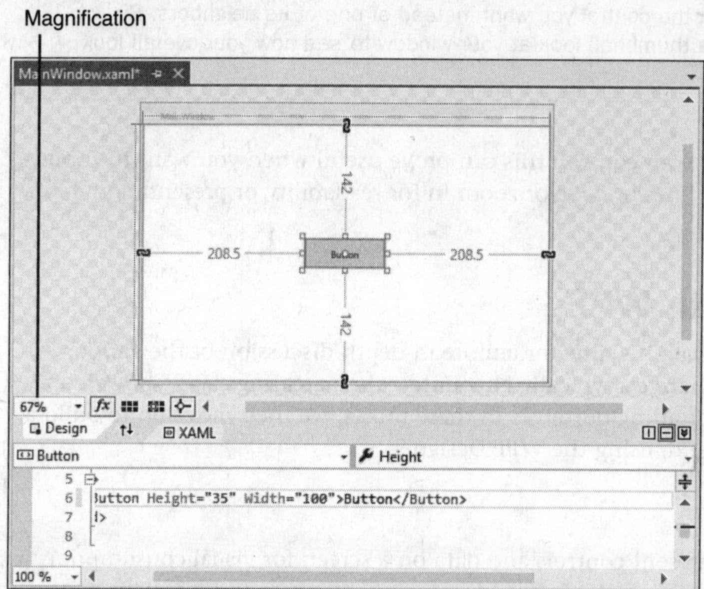

FIGURE 21.8 The zoom control.

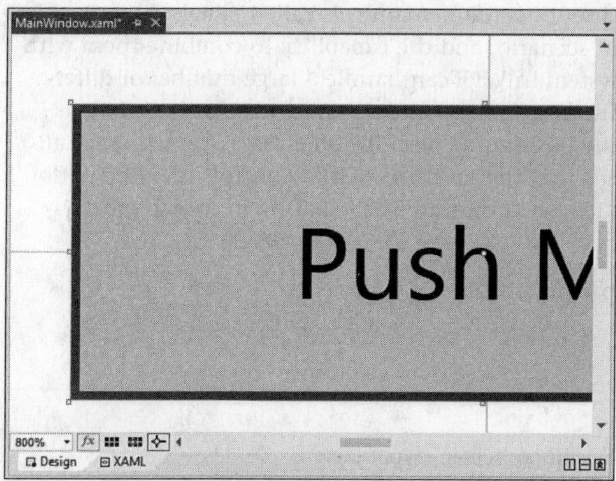

FIGURE 21.9 A button at 800% magnification.

TIP

The zoom control is particularly useful when you have a complex form layout with a lot of snap lines and nested/layered controls amassed in a certain area. By zooming in on the area, you can get a crisp view of where things are positioned, and it becomes much easier to select or position the control you want instead of one of its neighbors. By zooming out, you can get a thumbnail look at your window to see how your overall look and feel are shaping up.

The XAML pane also has a zoom control; this can prove useful when you want to zoom out to quickly drill through lines or code or zoom in for readability or presentation purposes.

Programming with WPF

With the basics out of the way, it's time for a more in-depth discussion of the various controls and technologies that you typically encounter when creating a WPF-powered application. After firmly grounding ourselves in these topics, we then move on to build a simple application, end to end, using the WPF Designer.

Layout

Because software needs to present controls and data on a screen for visual consumption by users, the layout (or how things are arranged onscreen) becomes an important design feature. Good layout systems not only have to enable developers to structure controls in a coherent fashion, but also need to be robust in terms of how they handle things such as window resizing and flow.

In WPF, layout is exercised through a set of container controls called panels. Each panel is uniquely suited for a specific layout scenario, and the capability to combine them with one another means that the layout system in WPF can handle a large number of different control organization scenarios. The key point to understand with panels is that, as containers, they are responsible for the positioning (and in some cases, the sizing) of all the controls placed within. This means that the individual child controls themselves don't need to be aware of the specific layout system they are participating in, which greatly simplifies the code and architecture.

Table 21.1 lists the available layout panel controls.

TABLE 21.1 The WPF Layout Panels

Class	Description
`Canvas`	A container control with no built-in layout logic
`DockPanel`	Panel that enables docking of its child elements
`Grid`	A container control that allows child objects to be positioned within columns and rows

Class	Description
StackPanel	A container control that implements horizontal and vertical stacking behavior for its child controls
WrapPanel	Panel that will automatically wrap elements to a new row as needed

Let's examine these controls and their subtypes one by one.

The Canvas Control

The Canvas control is unique among all the layout controls because it is the only one that actually performs no layout at all. It is functionally similar to the GroupBox control that you might have used with a Windows Forms project: child objects that are placed within a Canvas control are placed using coordinates relative to the canvas itself. No automatic resizing, flow layout, or positioning is done on behalf of the child controls by the canvas. If any such logic is needed, you need to implement it yourself. This highlights the purpose of the Canvas control: providing the developer with the absolute control to position things as desired.

In Figure 21.10, we have a Canvas control with four buttons in a unique arrangement. They are all positioned relative to the sides of the Canvas container.

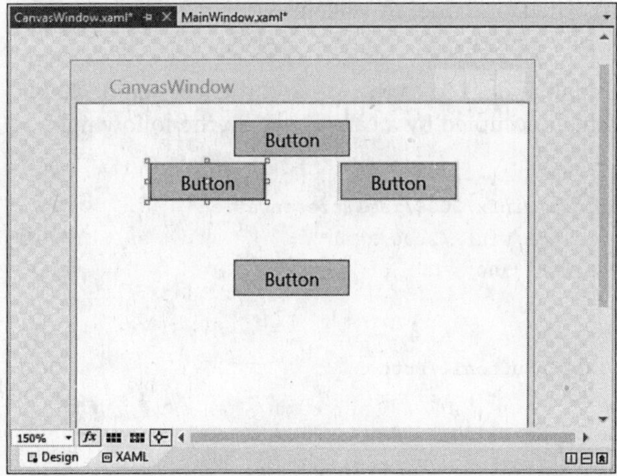

FIGURE 21.10 Four buttons in a Canvas.

Here is the XAML.

```
<Window x:Class="ContosoAvalon.Canvas"
    xmlns="http://schemas.microsoft.com/winfx/2006/xaml/presentation"
    xmlns:x="http://schemas.microsoft.com/winfx/2006/xaml"
    Title="Canvas" Height="300" Width="300">
    <Canvas>
```

```
        <Button Canvas.Left="102" Canvas.Top="11" Height="23" Name="button1"
         Width="75">Button</Button>
        <Button Canvas.Left="47" Canvas.Top="38" Height="23" Name="button2"
         Width="75">Button</Button>
        <Button Canvas.Right="46" Canvas.Top="38" Height="23" Name="button3"
         Width="75">Button</Button>
        <Button Canvas.Left="102" Canvas.Top="99" Height="23" Name="button4"
         Width="75">Button</Button>
    </Canvas>
</Window>
```

Note that we have provided coordinates that are relative to a specified side of the canvas. If we resize the window, the buttons move accordingly. Unless you absolutely need to manually specify control positions (as may be the case, for instance, if you are arranging controls in a nonstandard way or using controls to "draw" something in a window), it is recommended that you use one of the other panels that automatically perform the layout you need.

The DockPanel Control

Modern lines of business applications typically use some kind of docking arrangement for their controls. Toolbars may be docked at the top or sides of the window, a status bar may be docked at the bottom, and so forth. The DockPanel in WPF provides the capability to dock controls to one of the four sides of a window.

If we need to create a window with a toolbar docked to the top and the left side of the window, with the remainder of the screen occupied by a canvas, we do the following:

```
<Window x:Class="ContosoAvalon.DockPanel"
    xmlns="http://schemas.microsoft.com/winfx/2006/xaml/presentation"
    xmlns:x="http://schemas.microsoft.com/winfx/2006/xaml"
    Title="DockPanel" Height="300" Width="300">
    <DockPanel Name="dockPanel1">
        <ToolBar DockPanel.Dock="Top">
            <Button BorderBrush="Black">Button1</Button>
        </ToolBar>
        <ToolBar DockPanel.Dock="Left" MaxWidth="75">
            <Button BorderBrush="Black">Button2</Button>
        </ToolBar>
        <Canvas>
            <TextBlock>Canvas</TextBlock>
        </Canvas>
    </DockPanel>
</Window>
```

With the DockPanel, you can place more than one element in a certain dock position. Figure 21.11 shows six regions docked in a window: three of them are docked to the left, and three of them are docked to the top.

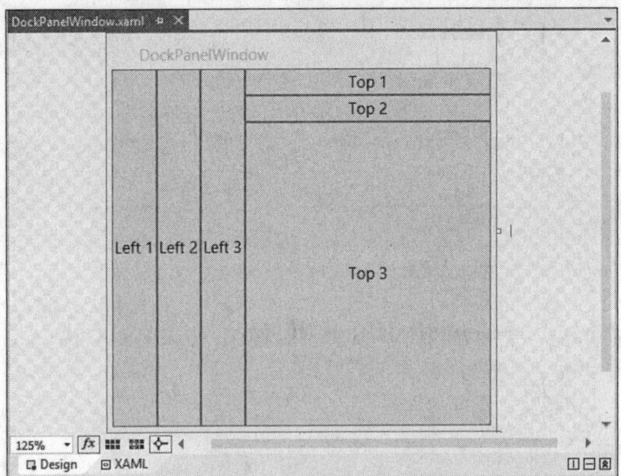

FIGURE 21.11 Docking controls within a DockPanel.

And here is the matching XAML.

```
<Window x:Class="ContosoAvalon.DockPanel"
    xmlns="http://schemas.microsoft.com/winfx/2006/xaml/presentation"
    xmlns:x="http://schemas.microsoft.com/winfx/2006/xaml"
    Title="DockPanel" Height="300" Width="300">
    <DockPanel Name="dockPanel1">
        <Button DockPanel.Dock="Left">Left 1</Button>
        <Button DockPanel.Dock="Left">Left 2</Button>
        <Button DockPanel.Dock="Left">Left 3</Button>
        <Button DockPanel.Dock="Top">Top 1</Button>
        <Button DockPanel.Dock="Top">Top 2</Button>
        <Button DockPanel.Dock="Top">Top 3</Button>
    </DockPanel>
</Window>
```

All the elements within a DockPanel are resized such that they stay docked in their designated position, and they entirely “fill” the window edge that they are docked to.

The Grid Control

The Grid panel is used for row and column arrangements, similar to an HTML table or the TableLayoutPanel control in WinForms.

One common use for the Grid control is with dialog boxes or data-entry forms where labels and values exist side by side and row by row; we can use the columns in the grid to align items horizontally and the rows to align items vertically.

Columns are created in a grid through the use of the `Grid.ColumnDefinitions` element. For example, this XAML snippet would create a grid with three columns.

```
<Grid>
    <Grid.ColumnDefinitions>
        <ColumnDefinition></ColumnDefinition>
        <ColumnDefinition></ColumnDefinition>
        <ColumnDefinition></ColumnDefinition>
    </Grid.ColumnDefinitions>
</Grid>
```

In a similar fashion, the `Grid.RowDefinitions` element defines the rows within a grid.

```
<Grid>
    <Grid.RowDefinitions>
        <RowDefinition></RowDefinition>
        <RowDefinition></RowDefinition>
        <RowDefinition></RowDefinition>
    </Grid.RowDefinitions>
</Grid>
```

The WPF Designer also has interactive features that allow for row and column addition, deletion, and sizing. Figure 21.12 shows a three-column, eight-row grid placed in a window. Note that the designer shows the grid lines demarcating the rows and columns, and there is a shaded border area to the top and to the left of the Grid control. This border area shows us the current size (width or height) of a column or row and is used to create new rows or columns in the grid. Moving the mouse cursor into the top border area of the grid or to the left border area of the grid results in a visual "caret" and a line; this provides the visual clue for inserting new rows or columns into the grid. Just click, and Visual Studio will create the new row or column for you.

We can also drag the row or column lines to increase or decrease the size of the row or column, and we can use the sizing drop-down box (again, refer to Figure 21.12) to change between star, pixel, and auto-sizing modes. (We cover these in more detail when we do a sample application walk-through later in this chapter.)

The dialog box shown in Figure 21.13 is easily achieved using a Grid panel; the XAML is shown in Listing 21.1. Arguably, the Grid control is the most flexible and relevant of the panel controls for almost all layout scenarios. For this reason, when you add a new window project item to a WPF project, the window by default already contains a Grid control.

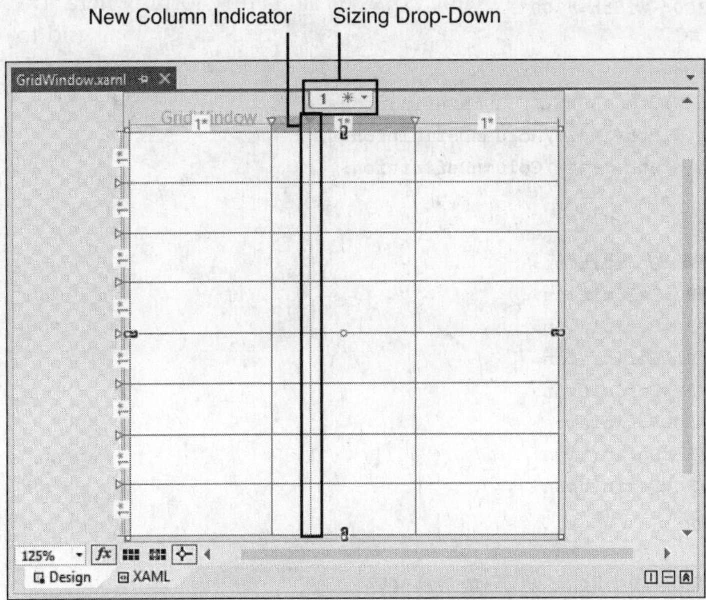

FIGURE 21.12 Working with a Grid control in the designer.

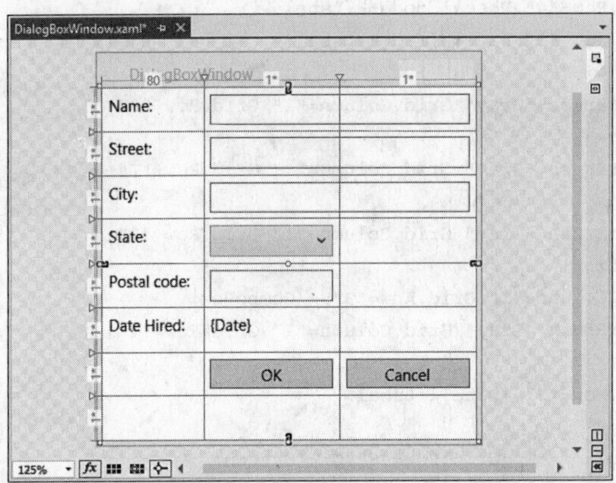

FIGURE 21.13 Implementing a dialog box using the rows and columns of a Grid control.

LISTING 21.1 Implementing a Dialog Box with a Grid Panel

```
<Window x:Class="ContosoAvalon.Grid"
    xmlns="http://schemas.microsoft.com/winfx/2006/xaml/presentation"
    xmlns:x="http://schemas.microsoft.com/winfx/2006/xaml"
```

```
    Title="Grid" Height="300" Width="300">
  <Grid>
    <Grid.ColumnDefinitions>
      <ColumnDefinition Width="80"></ColumnDefinition>
      <ColumnDefinition Width="*"></ColumnDefinition>
      <ColumnDefinition Width="*"></ColumnDefinition>
    </Grid.ColumnDefinitions>
    <Grid.RowDefinitions>
      <RowDefinition></RowDefinition>
      <RowDefinition></RowDefinition>
      <RowDefinition></RowDefinition>
      <RowDefinition></RowDefinition>
      <RowDefinition></RowDefinition>
      <RowDefinition></RowDefinition>
      <RowDefinition></RowDefinition>
      <RowDefinition></RowDefinition>
    </Grid.RowDefinitions>

    <Label Grid.Column="0" Grid.Row="0">Name:</Label>
    <Label Grid.Column="0" Grid.Row="1">Street:</Label>
    <Label Grid.Column="0" Grid.Row="2">City:</Label>
    <Label Grid.Column="0" Grid.Row="3">State:</Label>
    <Label Grid.Column="0" Grid.Row="4">Postal code:</Label>
    <Label Grid.Column="0" Grid.Row="5">Date Hired:</Label>

    <TextBox Margin="5,5" BorderBrush="Gray" Grid.Column="1" Grid.Row="0"
    Grid.ColumnSpan="2"></TextBox>
    <TextBox Margin="5,5" BorderBrush="Gray" Grid.Column="1" Grid.Row="1"
    Grid.ColumnSpan="2"></TextBox>
    <TextBox Margin="5,5" BorderBrush="Gray" Grid.Column="1" Grid.Row="2"
    Grid.ColumnSpan="2"></TextBox>
    <ComboBox Margin="5,5" Grid.Column="1" Grid.Row="3"></ComboBox>
    <TextBox Margin="5,5" BorderBrush="Gray" Grid.Column="1" Grid.Row="4">
    </TextBox>
    <Label Grid.Column="1" Grid.Row="5">{Date}</Label>

    <Button Margin="5,5" Grid.Column="1" Grid.Row="6">OK</Button>
    <Button Margin="5,5" Grid.Column="2" Grid.Row="6">Cancel</Button>
  </Grid>
</Window>
```

There are three things to note in this XAML:

- We have used the concept of column spanning to get our controls to line up the way we want.
- We are using the `Margin` property on the child elements to give each label, text box, and so on some room. Without a margin specified, each control automatically fills the bounds of the cell it resides in, meaning that we have absolutely no border or gap between the controls (either horizontally or vertically).
- In the grid's column definitions, we use an asterisk to denote a proportional size. In other words, the second and third columns equally share whatever space is left over after the first column has been rendered. We can adjust the proportion "ratio" by including a number as well (for example, `ColumnDefinition.Width="2*"`). We cover the details on grid sizing later in this chapter when we build a sample application.

The StackPanel Control

StackPanel controls implement a vertical or horizontal stack layout for their child elements. Compared with the Grid control, this is a simple panel that supports little tweaking. You can select to stack children horizontally or vertically using the `Orientation` property, and then the panel takes care of everything else. Each element within the StackPanel is resized/scaled to fit within the height (if stacked vertically) or width (if stacked horizontally) of the panel. Owing to the control's simplicity, the XAML is straightforward as well. Here, we are vertically stacking several check boxes, labels, a button, and a text box (see Figure 21.14).

```
<StackPanel>
   <Label>Format Options:</Label>
   <CheckBox Margin="4" Height="16" Name="checkBox1">Perform Fast Format</CheckBox>
   <CheckBox Margin="4" Height="16" Name="checkBox2">Verify After Format</CheckBox>
   <CheckBox Margin="4" Height="16" Name="checkBox3">Enable Large Partition
    Support</CheckBox>
   <Label>Drive Label:</Label>
   <TextBox Margin="10,0" BorderBrush="Gray" Height="23" Name="comboBox2" />
   <Button Margin="80,20" Height="23" Name="button1" >Format</Button>
</StackPanel>
```

Another similar panel is the WrapPanel. This is essentially a StackPanel with additional behavior to wrap its children into additional rows or columns if there isn't enough room to display them within the bounds of the panel. See Figure 21.15 to see how the WrapPanel has auto-adjusted a series of buttons when its window is sized smaller.

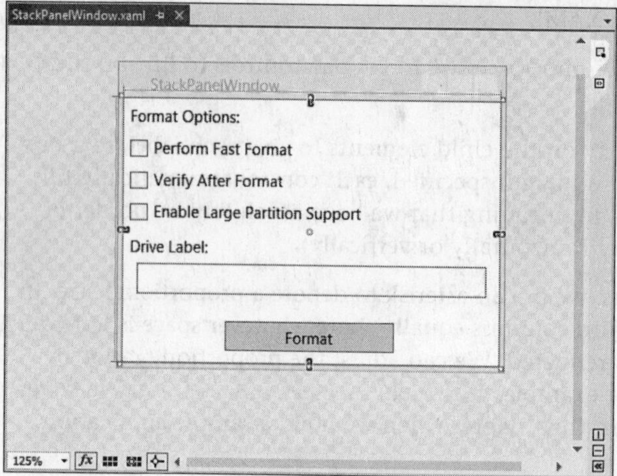

FIGURE 21.14 The StackPanel in action.

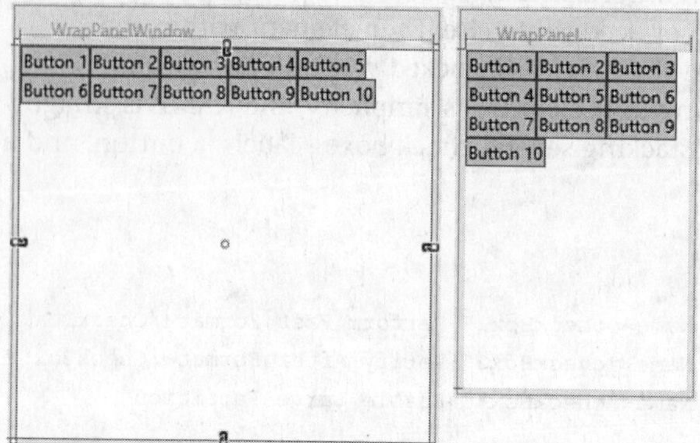

FIGURE 21.15 The WrapPanel.

Styles and Templates

The capability to customize the look of a control in WPF, without losing any of its built-in functionality, is one of the huge advantages that WPF brings to the development scene. Consider the two slider controls in Figure 21.16. The top is the default style, and the bottom represents a restyled slider. Functionality is identical. We have simply changed the appearance of the control.

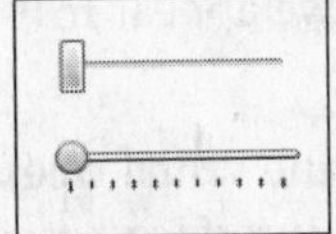

FIGURE 21.16 The standard slider (top) and a restyled slider (bottom).

`Style` is an actual class (in the `System.Windows` namespace) that is used in association with a control; it groups property values together to enable you, as a developer, to set them once and have them applied to controls en masse instead of having to set them individually on each control instance. Suppose, for instance, that your application uses a nice grayscale gradient for its button backgrounds. In addition, each button has a white border and renders its text with the Segoe UI font. We can manipulate each of these aspects using `Button` properties, but it would quickly become laborious to do this on every button. A `Style` class enables us to set all these properties once and then refer each Button control to these properties by assigning the style to the button.

Here is the `Style` class defined within a window in XAML.

```
<Window.Resources>
   <Style x:Key="GradientButton" TargetType="Button">
      <Setter Property="Margin" Value="2"/>
      <Setter Property="BorderBrush" Value="White" />
      <Setter Property="FontFamily" Value="Segoe UI"/>
      <Setter Property="FontSize" Value="12px"/>
      <Setter Property="FontWeight" Value="Bold"/>
      <Setter Property="Foreground" Value="White" />
      <Setter Property="Background" >
         <Setter.Value>
            <LinearGradientBrush StartPoint="0,0" EndPoint="0,1" >
               <GradientStop Color="Gray" Offset="0.2"/>
               <GradientStop Color="DarkGray" Offset="0.85"/>
               <GradientStop Color="Gray" Offset="1"/>
            </LinearGradientBrush>
         </Setter.Value>
      </Setter>
   </Style>
</Window.Resources>
```

Assigning this style to any button within the window is as simple as this:

```
<Button Style="{StaticResource GradientButton}" Height="38" Name="button1"
Width="100">OK</Button>
```

This works well for simplifying property sets. But what happens when we want to customize an attribute that isn't surfaced as a property? To continue with our Button control, what if we wanted an oval shape rather the standard rectangle? Because the `Button` class doesn't expose a property that we can use to change the background shape, we appear to be out of luck.

Enter the concept of templates. Templates enable you to completely replace the visual tree of any control, giving you full control over every aspect of the control's user interface. A visual tree in WPF is the hierarchy of controls inheriting from the `Visual` class that provide a control's final rendered appearance. You can find a good overview of WPF visual trees and logical trees at http://www.msdn.microsoft.com. Search for the article "Trees in WPF."

NOTE

Earlier we mentioned that controls in WPF were "lookless"; templates are evidence of that fact. The functionality of a control exists separately from its visual tree. The default look for all the controls is provided through a series of templates, one per each Windows theme. This means that WPF controls can automatically participate in whatever operating system (OS) theme you are running.

Templates are created via the `ControlTemplate` class. Within this class (or element, if you are implementing the template in XAML), you need to draw the visuals that represent the button. The `Rectangle` class in WPF can be used to draw our basic background shape. By tweaking the `RadiusX` and `RadiusY` properties, we can soften the normal 90-degree corners into the desired elliptical shape.

```
<Rectangle RadiusX="25" RadiusY="25" Width="100" Height="50"
Stroke="Black" StrokeThickness="1" />
```

We can also add some more compelling visual aspects, such as a gradient fill, to the button.

```
<Rectangle.Fill>
   <LinearGradientBrush>
      <LinearGradientBrush.GradientStops>
         <GradientStop Offset="0" Color="Gray" />
         <GradientStop Offset="1" Color="LightGray" />
      </LinearGradientBrush.GradientStops>
   </LinearGradientBrush>
</Rectangle.Fill>
```

TIP

To test the look and feel so far, type your "shape" XAML into the XAML editor, and tweak it as desired. When you are satisfied, you can copy and paste the XAML into the template. A better tool for designing user interfaces is Microsoft Blend for Visual Studio, but hand-crafting the XAML or relying on Visual Studio's designer should be sufficient for simple design scenarios.

The text within the button is easily rendered using a `TextBlock` object.

```
<TextBlock Canvas.Top="5" Height="40" Width="100" FontSize="20"
TextAlignment="Center">OK</TextBlock>
```

Once we are happy with the look and feel, we can "template-ize" this appearance by nesting everything within a `ControlTemplate` element. Because we need to refer to this template later, we associate it with a key.

```
<ControlTemplate x:Key="OvalButtonTemplate">
```

Finally, we embed the whole thing as a resource. A resource is simply a .NET object (written in XAML or code) that is meant to be shared across other objects via its key. In this specific case, we want to be able to use this template with any button we want. Resources can be declared at any level within a WPF project. We can declare resources that belong to the overall window or to any element within the window (such as a Grid panel), or we can store all our resources in something known as a `ResourceDictionary` and allow them to be referenced from any class in our project. For this example, we stick to a simple resource defined in our parent window. (For reference, this is the `Window.Resources` element that you see in the following code.)

Listing 21.2 pulls this all together, and Figure 21.17 shows the resulting button.

LISTING 21.2 Replacing a Button's Template

```
<Window x:Class="ContosoAvalon.CustomLook"
    xmlns="http://schemas.microsoft.com/winfx/2006/xaml/presentation"
    xmlns:x="http://schemas.microsoft.com/winfx/2006/xaml"
    Title="CustomLook" Height="300" Width="300"
    Background="#F8F8F8">
  <Window.Resources>
    <ControlTemplate x:Key="OvalButtonTemplate">
      <Canvas Width="100" Height="25" Margin="2">
        <Rectangle x:Name="BaseRectangle" Canvas.Top="0" RadiusX="25"
          RadiusY="25" Width="100" Height="40" Stroke="DarkGray"
          StrokeThickness="1">
            <Rectangle.Fill>
              <LinearGradientBrush>
                <LinearGradientBrush.GradientStops>
                  <GradientStop Offset="0" Color="Gray" />
                  <GradientStop Offset="1" Color="LightGray" />
                </LinearGradientBrush.GradientStops>
              </LinearGradientBrush>
            </Rectangle.Fill>
        </Rectangle>
        <TextBlock Canvas.Top="5" Height="40" Width="100" FontSize="20"
          TextAlignment="Center">OK</TextBlock>
      </Canvas>
```

```
    </ControlTemplate>
  </Window.Resources>
  <Canvas>
  <Button Canvas.Left="49" Canvas.Top="44" Height="38" Name="button1"
   Width="93" Template="{StaticResource OvalButtonTemplate}" />
  </Canvas>
</Window>
```

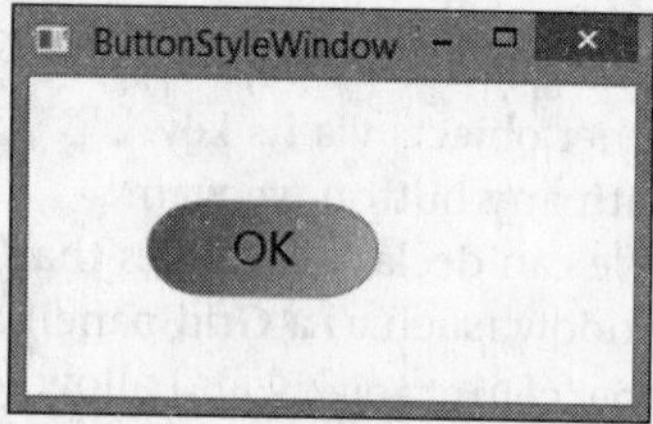

FIGURE 21.17 A custom button template assigned to a button.

Debugging the Visual Tree

Although the ability to replace portions of the visual tree via templates and styles is a powerful feature, it does come with a downside. Depending on the depth of the visual tree and the number of properties and attributes overridden at various levels by templates, it can become exponentially difficult to actually understand and debug issues that might arise somewhere within the tree.

Consider a template that overrides a few properties on a button and then a series of additional templates that override different properties on the base button and within the other templates themselves. Trying to unwind those dependencies by simply looking at the XAML can be difficult if not impossible. For instance, simply locating all the XAML can be a challenge because a template could live in a multitude of places within the project. Second, any errors within a given template may not produce a readily identifiable exception or stack trace that tells the whole story.

Enter the Live Visual Tree window, brand new with Visual Studio 2015. The Live Visual Tree, as its name implies, is a hierarchical view of the running XAML application and all its elements. The "live" moniker stems from the fact that it is reactive to changes within the visual tree as the application is running.

You access the Visual Tree window under the Debug, Windows menu. Figure 21.18 shows the visual tree associated with Listing 21.2. You will notice that the Live Visual Tree window provides information on every element within the visual tree, including child counts for each element. You can also click on any element and, when possible, the IDE will immediately navigate to the XAML that implements that element.

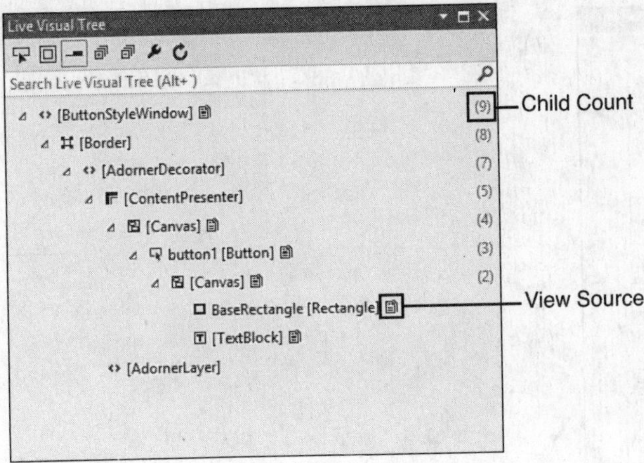

FIGURE 21.18 The Live Visual Tree window.

If you right-click on an element and select Show Properties, you will see the Live Property Explorer. The Live Property Explorer works as a companion window to the Live Visual Tree. It provides current property information for any given element within the running application. This window has a few attributes that make it extremely useful for debugging a running WPF application. For one, it shows an element's properties grouped on the scope in which they were set. This window also lets you change properties on an element and see those changes immediately take effect within the running application.

Let's see how this works using our button template example. Using Listing 21.2, run the WPF application, and then launch the Live Visual Tree window. With the window open, expand all the nodes within the tree and locate the node that corresponds to the button itself (button1). Right click that node, select Show Properties, and then examine the details within the Live Property Explorer window (see Figure 21.19).

Because you see those properties displayed within the Local section of the Explorer window, it's easy to determine that the `Height` and `Width` properties of the button are being set within the Local scope. You can also quickly see those attributes of the button that are being overridden by the template that we attached to the button. For example, the default style for a button would use the system default template. We have replaced that with our own template, so that property within the Live Property Explorer has a line through it, showing that we have overridden with another value.

As mentioned, you can change any of these elements right within the window. For example, select the `BaseRectangle` element within the Live Visual Tree. In the Live Property Explorer, locate the `RadiusX` and `RadiusY` properties. (You can search for the properties using the Search Properties text box at the top of the window.) If you recall from Listing 21.2, we tweaked these properties in our template to create the oval structure for our button. In the Property Explorer, change both of these values to 0, and you should see the button instantly change to a rectangle with no rounded corners (see Figure 21.20).

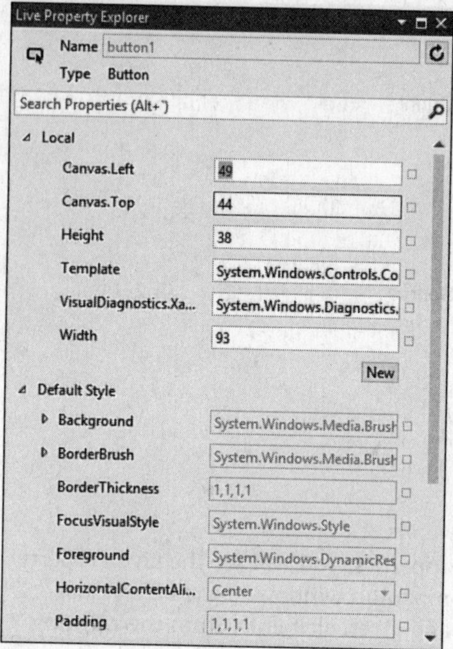

FIGURE 21.19 The Live Property Explorer window.

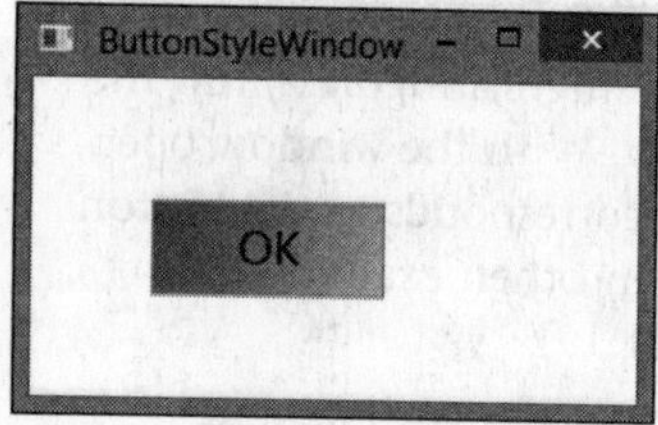

FIGURE 21.20 Changing visual elements at runtime using the Live Property Explorer.

Data Binding

Data binding, in its purest sense, is the capability of a control to be wired to a data source such that the control (a) displays certain items from that data source and (b) is kept in sync with the data source. After the connection is made, the runtime handles all the work necessary to make this happen. It doesn't really matter where or how the data is stored. It could be a file system, a custom collection of objects, a database object, and so on.

Let's look briefly at how we can establish a data binding connection using WPF. The key class here is `System.Windows.Data.Binding`. This is the mediator in charge of linking a control with a data source. To successfully declare a binding, we need to know three things:

- What UI control property do we want to bind?
- What data source do we want to bind to?
- And, within the data source, what specific element or property or such holds the data we are interested in?

We can bind to either single objects (such as binding a string property on an object to a text box) or to collections of objects (such as binding a `List<>` collection to a list box). Either way, the mechanics remain the same.

```
Binding binding = new Binding();
binding.Source = _stringList;

listBox1.SetBinding(ListBox.ItemsSourceProperty, binding);
```

The preceding code snippet creates a `Binding` object, sets the source of the `Binding` object to our `List<string>` collection, and then calls `SetBinding` on our control (a list box), passing in the exact property on the control we want to bind to our data source and the `Binding` object instance.

We can also assign data sources into a special object called the data context. Every `FrameworkElement` object, and those that derive from that class, implements its own `DataContext` instance. You can think of this as a global area where controls can go to get their data when participating in a data binding arrangement.

This ends up simplifying our data binding code quite a bit. We can set the context in our Window constructor like this:

```
this.DataContext = _stringList;
```

Now, we just point our `ListBox` to this data context using a tag within the `ListBox`'s XAML element.

```
<ListBox Name="listBox1" ItemsSource="{Binding}" />
```

The `Binding` object in this case automatically hunts for objects stashed within a data context somewhere within the object tree. When it finds one, it automatically binds the objects.

This works great for our simple `List<string>` example, but what if we are trying to bind a collection of custom objects to the list box? If we have a simple `Employee` class with a `Name` property and a `PhoneNbr` property, how could we bind to a collection of those objects and show the employee name? Our process would actually remain the same. If we create an `Employee` class and then create a `List<Employee>` collection, all this code still works. But there is a problem. Figure 21.21 highlights an issue we have to solve.

We haven't yet told the binding engine how exactly we want our data to be represented within the list box. By default, the binding process simply calls `ToString` on every object.

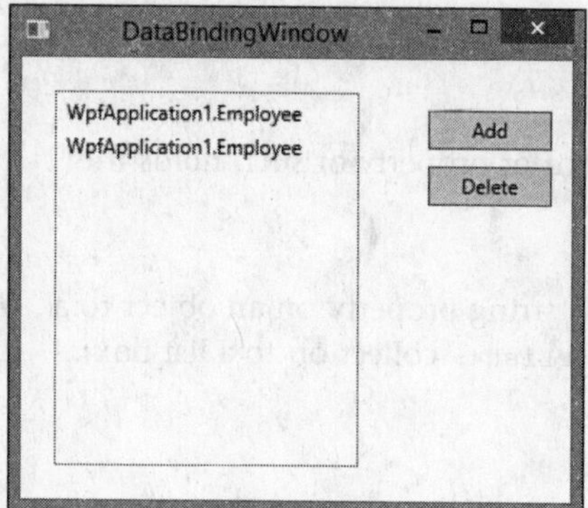

FIGURE 21.21 Binding a ListBox to a collection of custom objects.

One quick remedy is to simply override the `ToString` method.

```
public override string ToString()
{
    return _name;
}
```

This corrects the problem in this instance. But a more robust approach involves the use of a `DataTemplate`. We cover that approach a little later, in the section "Building a Simple Image Viewer Application."

Routed Events

The standard way that .NET classes and controls raise and handle events is essentially the way that you perform these tasks in WPF. But the WPF libraries bring an important improvement to standard events. We call these routed events.

Consider a simple scenario. You have a Button control that consists of a background image and some text (see Figure 21.22). If you recall from our discussion of a controls template and visual tree, this means we actually have a few discrete elements that make up the button: a `TextBlock`, an `Image`, and the basic frame and background of the button.

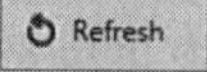

FIGURE 21.22 A button made of multiple elements.

These are separate objects/elements unto themselves. So the event situation becomes a little complex. It isn't enough to react to a click on the button background; we also have to react to a click on the button's text or the button's image. This is where routed events come into play. Routed events are capable of calling event handlers up or down the entire visual tree. This means we are free to implement an event handler at the `Button` level and be confident that a click on the button's image or text will bubble up until it finds our event handler.

Routed events in WPF are broken down into three categories: bubbling events, tunneling events, and direct events:

- **Bubbling events**—These events travel up the visual tree starting at the initial receiving element.
- **Tunneling events**—These events start at the top of the control's visual tree and move down until they reach the receiving element.
- **Direct event**—These are the equivalent of "standard" .NET events: Only the event handler for the receiving element is called.

Events themselves, like nearly everything else in WPF, can be declared in XAML or in code. Here we have a Button control with a `MouseEnter` event defined.

```
<Button MouseEnter="button1_MouseEnter" Name="button1"
>OK</Button>
```

The event handler itself, in C#, looks like any other .NET event handler.

```
private void button1_MouseEnter(object sender, MouseEventArgs e)
{
  MessageBox.Show("MouseEnter on button1");
}
```

We have only scratched the surface on many of the basic programming concepts within WPF, but you should now be armed with enough knowledge to be productive writing a simple WPF application. Let's do just that, using the tools available to us in Visual Studio.

Building a Simple Image Viewer Application

To illustrate the role that Visual Studio plays in WPF application development, let's build a sample application from scratch. In the tradition of "experience first," let's select something that can benefit from WPF's strong suits—namely, visualizations and robust control layouts and templating.

Consider an image viewer application. We can use this application to view a list of image thumbnails and, after selecting a thumbnail, we can view the image itself and even make changes to it.

We target the rough design shown in Figure 21.23.

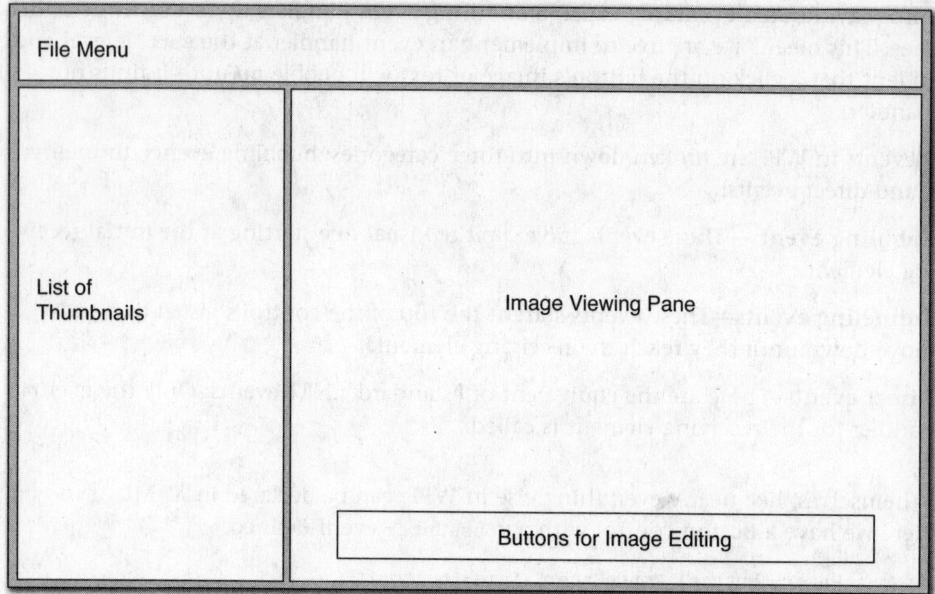

FIGURE 21.23 A sketch of an image viewer UI.

Here are our base requirements:

- When the application loads, it parses the images contained in the specified folder.
- Every image is listed in a list box; the list box shows image thumbnails and no text.
- When the user clicks one of the items in the list box, the image viewing area is populated with the selected image.
- The user can then choose to manipulate the image: a black-and-white effect can be applied, the image can be rotated clockwise or counterclockwise, the image can be flipped, and it can be mirrored.
- In general, we try to use WPF's capabilities when possible to make the application more visually compelling; a standard battleship gray application is not what we are looking for here.

Starting the Layout

After creating a new WPF project, we double-click the `MainWindow.xaml` file and start designing our user interface. To start, a `Grid` panel and some nested `StackPanel` or `WrapPanel` containers provide the initial layout. Referring to the sketch design (see Figure 21.23), one can envision a `Grid` with two rows and two columns to start. The top row holds the Menu control (which should span both columns). The bottom row holds the list box of images in the left column, and another parent control in the right column displays the image and the editing buttons.

To get started on this layout, we can use the grid control that has been automatically placed on our window during project creation. We could use the XAML pane for our window to quickly enter some XAML tags for the right elements, but let's see how quickly the WPF Designer enables us to create a layout without typing anything. Select the grid within the designer; you can do this by either clicking within the designer or clicking within the `<Grid>` element in the XAML pane. With the grid control selected, notice two shaded border areas to the top and to the left side of the grid control. These are known as grid rails. The grid rails enable you to quickly create columns and rows within the grid. If you move the mouse cursor over one of the grid rails, the cursor changes to cross-hairs. A grid splitter also appears; this visually indicates where the exact column or row divider is positioned within the grid. By clicking within the top grid rail, you can add a column; clicking in the left grid rail adds a row. Figure 21.24 shows an example of a grid selected in the designer, with the grid rails visible to the top and to the left of the grid.

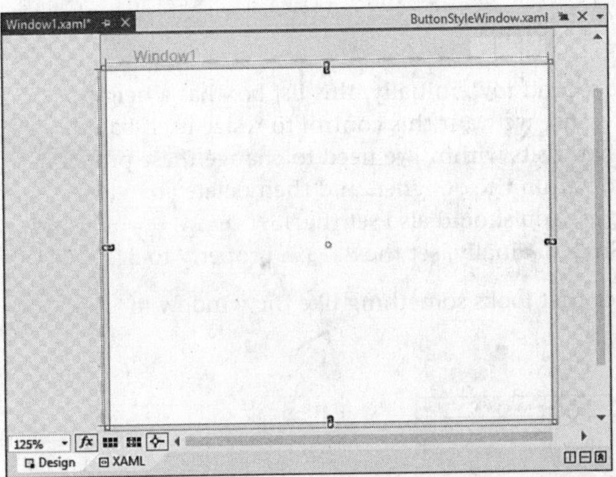

FIGURE 21.24 Grid with grid rails visible to the top and left.

For this project, move your cursor over the top grid rail and move the resulting column splitter so that it is approximately one-third of the way through the Grid's width. Now click within the rail to create the two columns. Note that the designer shows us the exact width, in pixels, for each column (see Figure 21.25).

Now do the same within the left grid rail. Position the row splitter so that the top row has a height of about 30 pixels. Don't worry about getting this exact; we tweak the sizing a little later.

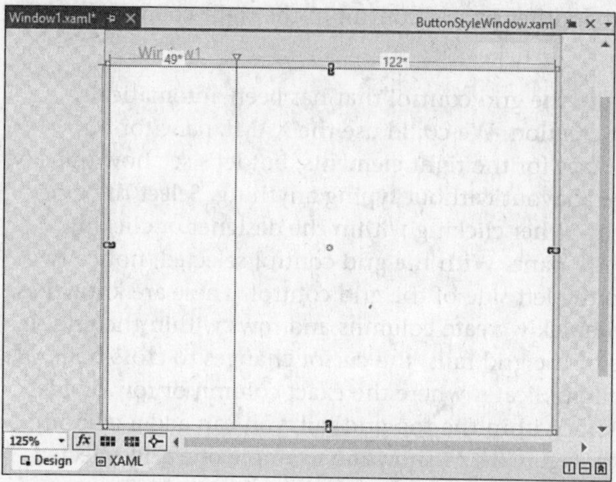

FIGURE 21.25 Sizing columns within a grid.

Add the List of Images

Drag a list box into the first column, second row. Initially, this list box has a height, width, and margin value set for it. Because we want this control to resize itself based on the size of the column and row that it sits within, we need to change these properties. Make sure the list box is selected within the designer, and then delete any values within the `Height` and `Width` properties. You should also set the `VerticalAlignment` and `HorizontalAlignment` properties to Stretch. Finally, set the `Margin` property to 5.

You should now have a design surface that looks something like the window in Figure 21.26.

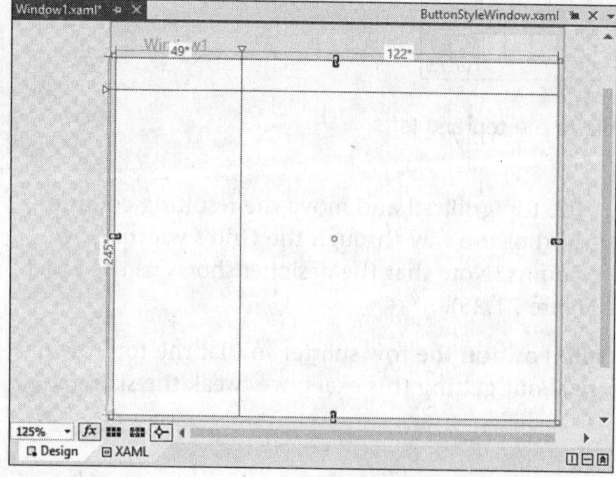

FIGURE 21.26 Our UI in progress.

Add the Top Menu

The top Menu control in our application will be used to open a folder selection dialog box. Drag a Menu control into the first column and first row. This control needs to span both of the columns in our grid, so resize it within the designer so that it crosses the border between column one and column two. We can now make adjustments similar to those we made for our list box. Using the property window, remove any `Height` value, and set the `Width` to Auto. Set the `HorizontalAlignment` and `VerticalAlignment` properties to Stretch, and set the `Margin` to 5.

We know we need to provide folder selection capabilities, so we title a main menu item as `Folder` and include a subitem under that titled `Open`. To implement this design, use the property window and edit the `Items` property; a collection editor dialog box opens that enables us to add the Folder menu items. Via the `Header` property, we need to specify the text that is displayed for the menu (see Figure 21.27) and the name: `FolderOpenMenuItem`.

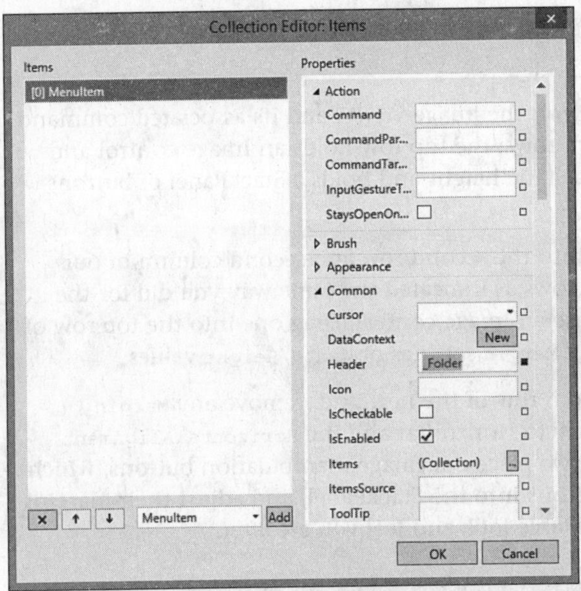

FIGURE 21.27 Properties of a MenuItem.

After the Folder menu item has been created, select it and use the property window to edit its Items collection to add the final Open menu item. For this menu item, we also want to specify an event handler for its `Click` event. Make sure you have the Events tab selected in the property window, and then enter `FolderOpenMenuItem_Click` in the `Click` event (see Figure 21.28). Visual Studio automatically creates a stub for the event handler and opens it within the code editor for you. Because we aren't ready to implement this event yet, you can simply click back to the WPF Designer within the IDE.

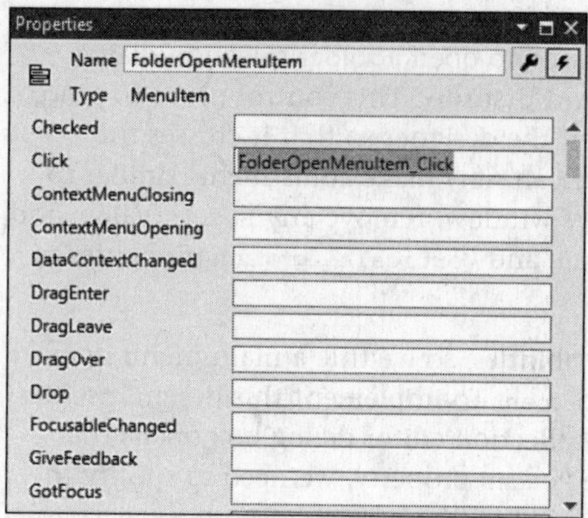

FIGURE 21.28 Wiring the `Click` event for our FolderOpenMenuItem.

Add the Image Viewer

The main screen area for this application is the image viewer and its associated command buttons. This consists of a grid with two rows: the top row holds an Image control and grows as we resize. The bottom row is a static height and holds a StackPanel of buttons oriented horizontally.

Drag a Grid control from the Toolbox into the second row and second column of our original parent grid. You configure the rows as indicated the same way you did for the root grid. For the image view box, we use an Image control. Drag one into the top row of the new grid and, as before, remove any `Margin` settings or `Width/Height` values.

Finally, drag a StackPanel into the bottom row of the new grid, remove any `Margin` settings, and set its `Orientation` property to Horizontal and the `HorizontalAlignment` property to Center. This panel is where we place our image manipulation buttons, which you can add now as well. Drag four buttons into the StackPanel, and adjust their margins and height/width until you get the workable look and feel you are after.

NOTE

While building this app, we have mostly relied on the WPF Designer's property window to tweak our control properties. But because the XAML code editor supports IntelliSense, and because XAML is fairly readable, you might find it faster and more productive to make the changes directly within the XAML. The bottom line here is that the IDE enables you to choose how you are most productive.

Grid Sizing Details

With all our grids, columns, and rows now in place, we can think about how we want to handle sizing. In other words, how do we want our columns and rows to resize themselves if a user happens to resize the parent window? To configure the grid correctly, we need to understand the concepts of fixed, auto, and proportional sizing.

Proportional sizing, also sometimes referred to as *star sizing*, is used to apportion row height or column width as a proportion of all available space. XAML-wise, proportional sizing is expressed with an asterisk inside of the `Row.Height` or `Column.Width` properties. With star sizing, you indicate the proportional "weight" that you want the column to occupy. For instance, for a grid with two columns, if we specified a width on both columns of `".5*"`, we would end up with both columns taking up half of the available space (width-wise) of the grid. Figure 21.13 shows some example column sizes using proportional sizing. If we just specify an asterisk with no weight (for example, `Width="*"`), we are instructing that column to take all the remaining space.

Auto sizing causes the row height or width to grow or shrink as necessary to exactly fit whatever is currently placed within the row or column. So a row that is auto sized would be as tall as the tallest control it hosts. Note that in addition to the control height, other things can affect the space reserved for a control, such as margins and padding.

Finally, *fixed sizing* works exactly like you think it would. You specify a width or height in pixels, and the column or row snaps to that dimension regardless of how the grid's parent control or window is sized.

With these details exposed, we can formulate a strategy for our layout. Figure 21.29 shows a revised sketch indicating our sizing scheme.

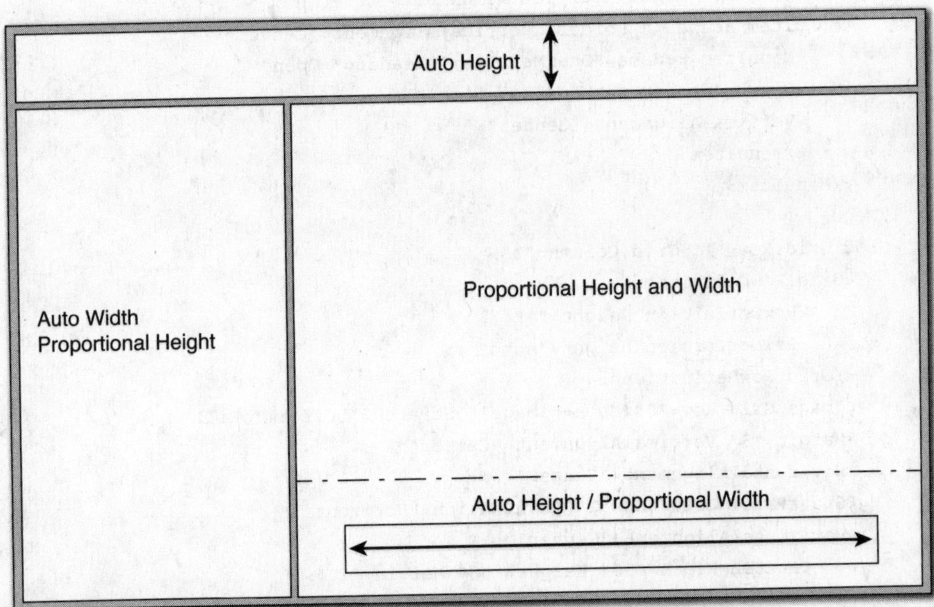

FIGURE 21.29 UI sketch with resizing notes.

The WPF Designer provides a way to directly indicate the sizing type for each row and column. Using the grid rails again, hover the mouse over the rail space for a column.

A small toolbar pops up directly above the rail with three buttons. These three buttons correspond to the three sizing modes. Go ahead and cycle through all the rows and columns in the designer, setting the height and width properties using the designer toolbar.

Here is a look at the current XAML with all the basic elements in place.

```
<Grid>
    <Grid.RowDefinitions>
        <RowDefinition Height="Auto" />
        <RowDefinition Height="*" />
    </Grid.RowDefinitions>
    <Grid.ColumnDefinitions>
        <ColumnDefinition Width="Auto" />
        <ColumnDefinition Width="*" />
    </Grid.ColumnDefinitions>
    <ListBox Grid.Row="1" HorizontalAlignment="Stretch"
     Margin="5" Name="listBox1" VerticalAlignment="Stretch"
     ItemsSource="{Binding}"
     Width="175" />
    <Menu Grid.ColumnSpan="2" HorizontalAlignment="Stretch"
     Margin="0" Name="menu1" VerticalAlignment="Stretch">
        <MenuItem Header="_Folder" VerticalAlignment="Center">
            <MenuItem x:Name="OpenMenuItem" Header="_Open"
             Click="FolderOpenMenuItem_Click"
             VerticalAlignment="Center">
            </MenuItem>
        </MenuItem>
    </Menu>
    <Grid Grid.Row="1" Grid.Column="1">
        <Grid.RowDefinitions>
            <RowDefinition Height="*" />
            <RowDefinition Height="Auto" />
        </Grid.RowDefinitions>
        <Image Grid.Row="0" Name="image1" Stretch="UniformToFill"
         Margin="5" VerticalAlignment="Center"
         HorizontalAlignment="Center" />
        <StackPanel Grid.Row="1" Orientation="Horizontal"
         HorizontalAlignment="Center" >
            <Button Width="50" Height="50" Margin="10">
             Button</Button>
            <Button Width="50" Height="50" Margin="10">
             Button</Button>
            <Button Width="50" Height="50" Margin="10">
             Button</Button>
            <Button Width="50" Height="50" Margin="10">
             Button</Button>
```

```
        </StackPanel>
    </Grid>
</Grid>
```

Storing the Images

With the UI elements in place, we can move on to the data binding implementation. We'll come back later and give the UI more polish. The first task is to store the files in a collection of some sort. It turns out that there is a class in the `System.Windows.Media.Imaging` namespace that is suitable for our needs: `BitmapSource`. For a collection, a `List<BitmapSource>` object should work for the moment, but we need some way to populate the list. So let's create a wrapper class that both loads the list and exposes it as a property.

Add a new class to the project with the following code.

```
public class DirectoryImageList
{
   private string _path;
   private List<BitmapSource> _images = new List<BitmapSource>();

   public DirectoryImageList(string path)
   {
      _path = path;
      LoadImages();

   }

   public List<BitmapSource> Images
   {
      get { return _images; }
      set { _images = value; }
   }

   public string Path
   {
      get { return _path; }
      set
      {
         _path = value;
         LoadImages();
      }
   }

   private void LoadImages()
   {
      _images.Clear();
```

```
        BitmapImage img;

        foreach (string file in Directory.GetFiles(_path))
        {
            try
            {
                img = new BitmapImage(new Uri(file));

                _images.Add(img);
            }
            catch
            {
                //empty catch; ignore any files that won't load as
                //an image...
            }
        }
    }
}
```

The LoadImages method in the preceding code is where most of the important logic is found; it enumerates the files within a given directory and attempts to load them into a BitmapImage object. If it succeeds, we know that this is an image file. If it doesn't, we just ignore the resulting exception and keep on going.

Back in our MainWindow class, we need to create some private fields to hold an instance of this new class and to hold the currently selected path. This is something we let the user change through a common dialog box launched from the Folder, Open menu item.

Here are the fields.

```
private DirectoryImageList _imgList;
private string _path =
  Environment.GetFolderPath
          (Environment.SpecialFolder.MyPictures);
```

Note that we have defaulted our path to the Pictures folder. To load the list object, we write a ResetList method in our MainWindow class.

```
private void ResetList()
{
   _imgList = new DirectoryImageList(_path);
}
```

Referring to our earlier discussion on data binding, we round things off by adding a few lines of code to the MainWindow constructor: an initial call to ResetList and a call to assign the data context to the Images property from the DirectoryImageList instance.

```
public MainWindow()
{
   InitializeComponent();
   ResetList();
   this.DataContext = _imgList.Images;
}
```

If we run the application now, we see a familiar sight (as in Figure 21.30): the data binding is working but isn't quite the presentation format we want.

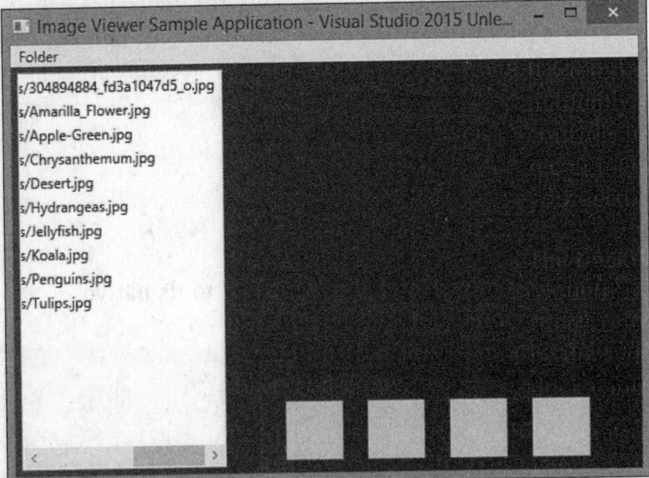

FIGURE 21.30 Initial data binding results.

Binding to the Images

Because our earlier trick of overriding `ToString` won't give us the right data presentation (an image, after all, is not a string), we need to turn to data templates. The `DataTemplate` class is used to tell a control specifically how you want its data to be displayed. By using a data template within the visual tree of the control, you have complete freedom to present the bound data in any fashion you want.

For this application, we are looking for images in the `ListBox`. This turns out to be quite easy. Create a `Window1.Resources` element in XAML, and create a `DataTemplate` that sets up the exact visualization we need.

```
<Window.Resources>
   <DataTemplate x:Key="ImageDataTemplate">
      <Image Source="{Binding UriSource.LocalPath}" Width="125"
       Height="125" />
   </DataTemplate>
</Window.Resources>
```

Then assign the `DataTemplate` to the `ListBox`.

```
<ListBox Grid.Row="1" Name="listBox1" ItemsSource="{Binding}"
 ItemTemplate="{StaticResource ImageDataTemplate}"/>
```

In our data template, the `Image` element is expecting a source uniform resource indicator (URI) for each image. So we use the `UriSource.LocalPath` that is provided on the `BitmapSource` object. If you rerun the application, you should immediately see that our `ListBox` is now displaying thumbnail-sized images (125×125) for every picture it finds in our local `Pictures` directory.

We aren't done yet; clicking a thumbnail in the list box should cause the central `Image` control to display the indicated picture. By creating a `SelectionChanged` event handler and wiring it to the `ListBox`, we can update our `Image.Source` property accordingly.

The event is declared as expected within the `ListBox` XAML element.

```
<ListBox SelectionChanged="listBox1_SelectionChanged" Grid.Row="1"
 Name="listBox1" ItemsSource="{Binding}"
 ItemTemplate="{StaticResource ImageDataTemplate}"/>
```

And for the event handler, we cast the `SelectedItem` from the `ListBox` to its native `BitmapSource` representation and assign it to our image control.

```
private void listBox1_SelectionChanged(object sender,
   SelectionChangedEventArgs e)
{
   image1.Source = (BitmapSource)((sender as ListBox).SelectedItem);
}
```

Button Event Handlers and Image Effects

With the images successfully loaded into the list box and displayed in the central Image control, we can turn our attention to our four image editing/effects features:

- Black-and-white filter
- Image blur
- Rotate
- Flip

Because these four functions are controlled by the four buttons, we need to add some appropriate button images and events; we don't cover the button stylings here because they involve external graphics resources, but you can see how they turn out in the final screenshot (at the end of this chapter) or by downloading the source from this book's website.

The code for the events, however, is fair game. First, here are the XAML event declarations on each button.

```
<Button Click="buttonBandW_Click" Margin="20,0,0,0" Height="23"
 Name="buttonBandW" Width="30"/>

<Button Click="buttonBlur_Click" Margin="20,0,0,0" Height="23"
 Name="buttonBlur" Width="30"/>

<Button Click="buttonRotate_Click"  Margin="20,0,0,0" Height="23"
 Name="buttonRotate" Width="30"/>

<Button Click="buttonFlip_Click" Margin="20,0,20,0" Height="23"
Name="buttonFlip" Width="30"/>
```

Notice as you type these click events into the XAML pane that the XAML editor intervenes with IntelliSense pop-ups that not only complete our `Click` declaration but also create the corresponding event handler in our code-behind class!

Changing the image to grayscale is accomplished via the class `FormatConvertedBitmap`, which allows you to specify the color depth and format of your palette.

```
private void buttonBandW_Click
    (object sender, RoutedEventArgs e)
{
    BitmapSource img = (BitmapSource)image1.Source;
    image1.Source =
        new FormatConvertedBitmap
            (img, PixelFormats.Gray16,
            BitmapPalettes.Gray256, 1.0);
}
```

To perform the image manipulations, we use something known as a transform: the manipulation of a 2D surface to rotate, skew, or otherwise change the current appearance of the surface. We can handle our rotation feature directly with `RotateTransform` like this:

```
private void buttonRotate_Click(object sender, RoutedEventArgs e)
{
   CachedBitmap cache = new CachedBitmap((BitmapSource)image1.Source,
      BitmapCreateOptions.None, BitmapCacheOption.OnLoad);
   image1.Source = new TransformedBitmap(cache, new RotateTransform(90));
}
```

Our flip action ends up being just as easy but uses a `ScaleTransform` instead.

```
private void buttonFlip_Click(object sender, RoutedEventArgs e)
{
   CachedBitmap cache = new CachedBitmap((BitmapSource)image1.Source,
```

```
        BitmapCreateOptions.None, BitmapCacheOption.OnLoad);
    ScaleTransform scale = new ScaleTransform(-1, -1, image1.Source.Width / 2,
        image1.Source.Height / 2);
    image1.Source = new TransformedBitmap(cache, scale);
}
```

The image-blurring action is provided through a different mechanism known as an effect. By creating a new `BlurBitmapEffect` instance and assigning that to our image control, WPF applies the appropriate algorithm to the bitmap to blur the picture.

```
image1.Effect = new BlurEffect();
```

Path Selection with a Common Dialog Box

The last item on our to-do list is allowing the user to change the path of the picture files. WPF itself doesn't have built-in dialog box classes to manage this, but the `System.Windows.Forms` namespace has just what we need: the `FolderBrowserDialog` class. This is launched from within the event handler for our `FolderOpenMenuItem Click` event.

```
private void FolderOpenMenuItem_Click(object sender, RoutedEventArgs e)
{
    SetPath();
}

private void SetPath()
{
    FolderBrowserDialog dlg = new FolderBrowserDialog();
    dlg.ShowDialog();
    _path = dlg.SelectedPath;
    ResetList();
}
```

When a user selects a folder, we update our internal field appropriately, reload the `DirectoryImageList` class with the new path, and then reset our window's `DataContext` property to reflect the change. This is a perfect example of how seamless it is to use other .NET technologies and class libraries from within WPF. By adding the appropriate namespace and reference to our project, we just instantiate this class like any other class in our solution.

TIP

Because there are a fair number of controls that share the same name between WPF and WinForms (the ListBox control is one example), if you find yourself using classes from the `System.Windows.Controls` and the `System.Windows.Forms` libraries, you inevitably need to fully qualify some of your object names to avoid operating against the wrong class.

And with that, the application is functionally complete. For reference, we have provided the current state of the XAML and the code-behind listings in Listing 21.3 and Listing 21.4, respectively. If you really want to dissect this application, however, you should download the source code from this book's website. This enables you to see the improvements made with graphics resources and general look and feel, producing the final polished version shown in Figure 21.31.

FIGURE 21.31 The final app after finishing touches have been applied.

LISTING 21.3 The Image Viewer XAML Code

```
<Window x:Class="WpfImageViewer.MainWindow"
        xmlns="http://schemas.microsoft.com/winfx/2006/xaml/presentation"
        xmlns:x="http://schemas.microsoft.com/winfx/2006/xaml"
        Title="Image Viewer Sample Application"
        Height="400" Width="550"
        Background="{DynamicResource BackgroundGradientBrush}">

    <Window.Resources>
        <DataTemplate x:Key="ImageDataTemplate">
            <Image Source="{Binding UriSource.LocalPath}"
                   Width="125" Height="125" />
        </DataTemplate>
    </Window.Resources>

    <Grid>
        <Grid.RowDefinitions>
            <RowDefinition Height="Auto" />
```

```
        <RowDefinition Height="*" />
    </Grid.RowDefinitions>
    <Grid.ColumnDefinitions>
        <ColumnDefinition Width="Auto" />
        <ColumnDefinition Width="*" />
    </Grid.ColumnDefinitions>
    <ListBox Grid.Row="1"
             HorizontalAlignment="Stretch"
             Margin="5" Name="listBox1"
             VerticalAlignment="Stretch"
             Width="175"
             ItemsSource="{Binding}"
             ItemTemplate="{StaticResource ImageDataTemplate}"
             SelectionChanged="listBox1_SelectionChanged" />
    <Menu Grid.ColumnSpan="2"
          Background="{DynamicResource MenuBackgroundGradientBrush}"
          HorizontalAlignment="Stretch"
          Margin="0"
          Name="menu1"
          VerticalAlignment="Stretch">
        <MenuItem Header="_Folder"
                  VerticalAlignment="Center">
            <MenuItem x:Name="OpenMenuItem"
                      Header="_Open"
                      Click="FolderOpenMenuItem_Click"
                      VerticalAlignment="Center">
            </MenuItem>
        </MenuItem>
    </Menu>
    <Grid Grid.Row="1" Grid.Column="1">
        <Grid.RowDefinitions>
            <RowDefinition Height="*" />
            <RowDefinition Height="Auto" />
        </Grid.RowDefinitions>
        <Image Grid.Row="0"
               Name="image1"
               Stretch="UniformToFill"
               Margin="5"
               VerticalAlignment="Center"
               HorizontalAlignment="Center" />
        <StackPanel Grid.Row="1" Orientation="Horizontal"
                    HorizontalAlignment="Center" >
            <Button Name="buttonBandW"
                    Style="{DynamicResource BWImageButtonStyle}"
                    Click="buttonBandW_Click"
                    Width="50"
```

```
                    Height="50"
                    Margin="10" />
            <Button Name="buttonBlur"
                    Style="{DynamicResource BlurImageButtonStyle}"
                    Click="buttonBlur_Click"
                    Width="50"
                    Height="50"
                    Margin="10" />
            <Button Name="buttonRotate"
                    Style="{DynamicResource RotateImageButtonStyle}"
                    Click="buttonRotate_Click"
                    Width="50"
                    Height="50"
                    Margin="10" />
            <Button Name="buttonFlip"
                    Style="{DynamicResource FlipImageButtonStyle}"
                    Click="buttonFlip_Click"
                    Width="50"
                    Height="50"
                    Margin="10" />
        </StackPanel>
    </Grid>
  </Grid>
</Window>
```

LISTING 21.4 The Image Viewer Code Behind C#

```
using System;
using System.Collections.Generic;
using System.Linq;
using System.Text;
using System.Windows;
using System.Windows.Controls;
using System.Windows.Data;
using System.Windows.Documents;
using System.Windows.Input;
using System.Windows.Media;
using System.Windows.Media.Effects;
using System.Windows.Media.Imaging;
using System.Windows.Navigation;
using System.Windows.Shapes;
```

```
namespace WpfImageViewer
{
    /// <summary>
    /// Interaction logic for MainWindow.xaml
    /// </summary>
    public partial class MainWindow : Window
    {
        #region Private fields

        private DirectoryImageList _imgList;
        private string _path =
            Environment.GetFolderPath(
            Environment.SpecialFolder.MyPictures);

        #endregion

        #region Ctor

        public MainWindow()
        {
            InitializeComponent();
            ResetList();
            this.DataContext = _imgList.Images;
        }

        #endregion

        #region Event handlers and delegates

        private void FolderOpenMenuItem_Click
            (object sender, RoutedEventArgs e)
        {
            SetPath();
        }

        private void listBox1_SelectionChanged
            (object sender, SelectionChangedEventArgs e)
        {
            this.image1.Source = (BitmapSource)
                            ((sender as ListBox).SelectedItem);
            this.image1.Effect = null;
        }

        private void buttonBandW_Click
            (object sender, RoutedEventArgs e)
        {
            BitmapSource img = (BitmapSource)image1.Source;
```

```
        image1.Source =
            new FormatConvertedBitmap
                (img, PixelFormats.Gray16,
                BitmapPalettes.Gray256, 1.0);
}

private void buttonBlur_Click
    (object sender, RoutedEventArgs e)
{
    if (image1.Effect != null)
    {
        //if blur is current effect, remove
        image1.Effect = null;
    }
    else
    {
        //otherwise, add the blur effect to the image
        image1.Effect = new BlurEffect();
    }
}

private void buttonRotate_Click
    (object sender, RoutedEventArgs e)
{
    CachedBitmap cache =
        new CachedBitmap((BitmapSource)image1.Source,
            BitmapCreateOptions.None,
            BitmapCacheOption.OnLoad);
    image1.Source =
        new TransformedBitmap(cache,
            new RotateTransform(90));

}

private void buttonFlip_Click
    (object sender, RoutedEventArgs e)
{
    CachedBitmap cache =
        new CachedBitmap((BitmapSource)image1.Source,
            BitmapCreateOptions.None,
            BitmapCacheOption.OnLoad);
    ScaleTransform scale =
        new ScaleTransform(-1, -1, image1.Source.Width / 2,
            image1.Source.Height / 2);
    image1.Source =
        new TransformedBitmap(cache, scale);
}
```

```
    .

    #endregion

    #region Implementation

    private void SetPath()
    {
        System.Windows.Forms.FolderBrowserDialog dlg =
            new System.Windows.Forms.FolderBrowserDialog();
        dlg.ShowDialog();
        _path = dlg.SelectedPath;
        ResetList();
    }

    private void ResetList()
    {
        if (IsValidPath(_path))
        {
            _imgList = new DirectoryImageList(_path);
        }

        this.DataContext = _imgList.Images;

    }

    private bool IsValidPath(string path)
    {

        try
        {
            string folder =
                System.IO.Path.GetFullPath(path);
            return true;
        }
        catch
        {
            return false;
        }
    }

    #endregion

  }

}
```

Summary

This chapter briefly introduced the Windows Presentation Foundation (WPF). We investigated the overall framework architecture and its programming model, including the new concept of using declarative markup to design and lay out a WPF client application's user interface. You saw how the Visual Studio WPF Designer can be used to quickly craft compelling user interfaces using the same development processes you use when building Windows Forms or even ASP.NET applications.

We spent some time discussing the basics of control layout (a central theme in WPF) and covering the first-class data binding support that WPF enjoys.

As mentioned, developers trying to learn WPF and XAML-based development in general will find that it is both a broad and a deep subject. It is highly recommended that you spend some time with Microsoft Developer Network (MSDN) resources (such as the WPF developer center at www.msdn.microsoft.com/wpf) and then revisit this chapter to get a full sense of the skills and knowledge required to come up to speed on WPF development. Spending time with the design tools is also highly recommended; free trials are available. See www.microsoft.com/expression for more information.

CHAPTER 22

Developing Office Business Applications

IN THIS CHAPTER

- ▶ An Overview of Office Extension Features
- ▶ Creating an Office Add-In
- ▶ Creating an Office Document Extension
- ▶ Extending Office with Webpages

Microsoft Office is the well-known, best-selling suite of information worker productivity applications. We are all familiar with the word processing, spreadsheet, email, and form features provided by Microsoft Word, Microsoft Excel, Microsoft Outlook, and Microsoft InfoPath. But these applications are capable of more than just their stock features. They are a development platform unto themselves, a platform that can be extended and customized to build out line-of-business applications that leverage and build on the best-of-breed features offered by each application.

For instance, a purchase-order application could leverage the end user's familiarity with Microsoft Word to allow for data entry using a Word form, and reports and charts can be generated against purchase-order history using Excel.

In the past, the primary tool for extending Microsoft Office applications has been Visual Basic for Applications (VBA). With VBA, developers and even end users could create a broad range of solutions from simple macros to more complicated features that implement business logic and access data stored in a database. VBA offers a simple "on ramp" for accessing the object models exposed by every application in the extended suite of Microsoft Office: Project, Word, Outlook, InfoPath, PowerPoint, Publisher, and so on.

But starting with the first release of the Visual Studio Tools for Office (VSTO), Microsoft gave developers a robust way to create Office solutions in managed code (Visual Basic and Visual C#) from directly within Visual Studio.

Visual Studio 2010 was released with the fourth generation of VSTO, and it enabled you to target both Microsoft Office 2007 and Microsoft Office 2010 applications. Visual Studio 2015 has continued its support for Office application development. "VSTO" is now referred to simply as Office Developer Tools for Visual Studio. The topic of using Visual Studio for Office development is a large one that has entire books devoted to it; in this chapter, we hope to simply introduce the concepts involved with Office development and show how the Visual Studio Office project types can be used to quickly create powerful applications that leverage the existing power of Word, Excel, and Outlook. Subjects we cover include these:

- Creating custom actions panes
- Creating custom task panes
- Customizing the Office ribbon

We specifically do not attempt to cover the object automation models for any of the Office applications, beyond the minimum necessary to understand the preceding concepts. For a more complete treatment of Office as a development platform, we recommend the VSTO team blog at http://blogs.msdn.com/b/vsto/ and, of course, the various MSDN sections that cover development for Office.

Let's start with a quick run-through of the various Office features that are available for customization.

An Overview of Office Extension Features

Because each Office application has a unique and specialized function, it should come as no surprise that the ways in which you can customize an Office application depend on the Office application. Although they all share a common, general layout for their user interface, there are intricacies involved with each of them that dictate different capabilities from within Visual Studio.

For instance, both Excel and Word deal with files as their central work piece, whereas Outlook deals with emails (which might be stored locally, on a server, or both). We can apply document-level extensions to Excel and Word, but this is not possible in Outlook. Conversely, the Outlook object model supports the concept of form regions, a concept absent in Excel and Word.

Office Features

Table 22.1 provides a matrix of the various features available for customization or extension within each Office application. We discuss each of these in the next section.

TABLE 22.1 Microsoft Office Extension Points

Application	Feature
Microsoft Excel	Actions pane Task pane Data cache Ribbon
Microsoft InfoPath	Task pane
Microsoft Outlook	Task pane Outlook form regions
Microsoft PowerPoint	Task pane
Microsoft Word	Actions pane Task pane Data cache Ribbon

Some of these features are document-level features, and others are application-level features. The detailed difference between the two is largely one of scope. Document-level customizations are attached to, and live with, a specific document, whether a Word `.doc/.docx` file or an Excel spreadsheet file. In contrast, application-level features are more global in reach and are implemented as add-ins to a specific Office application in much the same way that packages are created and implemented for Visual Studio itself. (See Chapter 15, "Extending the IDE.")

We look at the mechanics of how document-level and application-level solutions are differentiated in just a bit when we overview the Office project types. First, let's examine the features mentioned in Table 22.1. Understanding these features is key to determining how you might leverage Office in your solutions.

Task Panes and Actions Panes

Task panes in Office are used to expose commands and features that are central to the task at hand without disrupting the user from focusing on the currently loaded document. See Figure 22.1 for a screenshot of a Microsoft Word 2013 task pane for merging form letters. This task pane is able to guide the user through a series of steps while still allowing the loaded letter document to be visible. Task panes exist at the application level. Actions panes, in contrast, are a type of task pane implemented at the document level.

Data Cache

A data cache refers to the capability of Office to store data locally within a document. This cache is also sometimes referred to as a data island. Because Visual Studio can read and write to the data cache, it is a useful tool for storing information needed by your Office add-in or for shadowing data that resides in a database but is needed in certain disconnected scenarios.

Ribbon

The ribbon is a user interface element that premiered with Microsoft Office 2007. It represents a new way to present features to users without using the traditional toolbars and menus. Commands in the ribbon are grouped by task category, and within each task category commands are visually grouped with other similar commands. So with Word, for instance, we have a Review tab that consolidates all the commands related to document review. Because the ribbon makes the most-used commands immediately visible and available, the ribbon attempts to avoid the problems caused by the menu bar paradigm in which items could be grouped and nested several layers deep (and thus, out of sight) within the menu system.

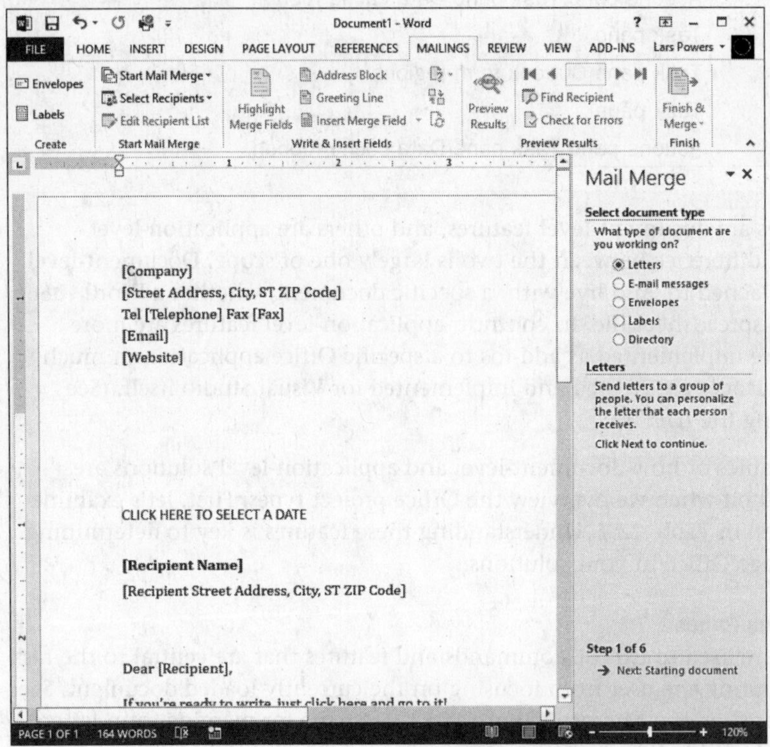

FIGURE 22.1 A Microsoft Word 2013 actions pane.

The tabs of the ribbon and the command groupings within a tab are free to change from application to application depending on the context. Figure 22.2 compares the ribbon home tab for Word and PowerPoint.

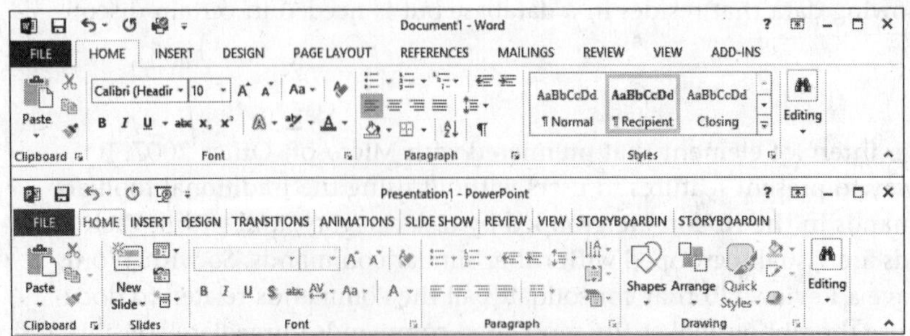

FIGURE 22.2 The Microsoft PowerPoint 2013 and Word 2013 ribbons.

Visual Studio Office Project Types

In general, each Office application has a project type or family of project types available. Figure 22.3 shows the various project types available by expanding your chosen language node and then the Office node within the New Project dialog box.

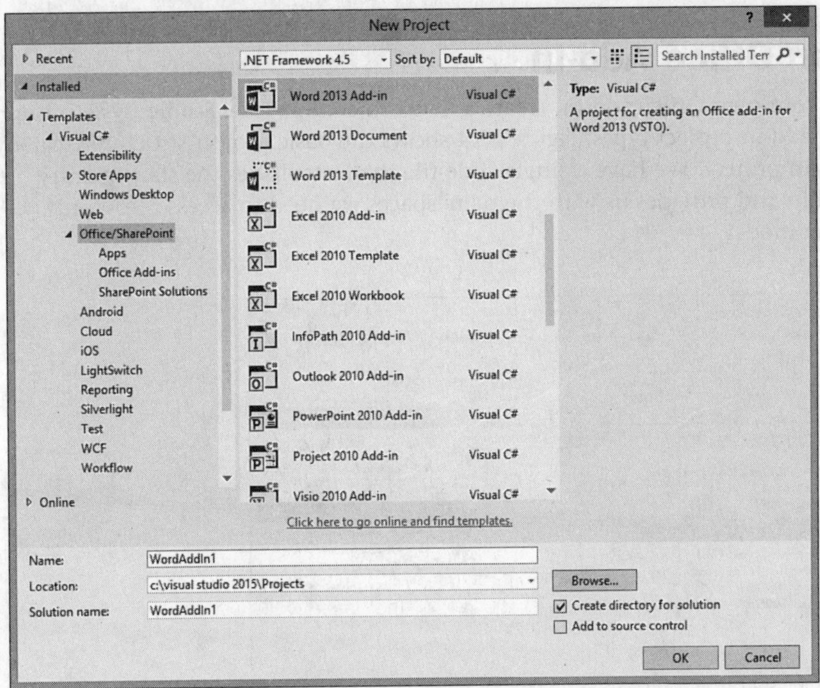

FIGURE 22.3 The available Office project types in Visual Studio.

For each version of Word and Excel, you see three project types: an add-in template and two document-level templates. The document-level templates enable you to target either document files (for Word, this is referred to as the Word Document project template, and for Excel, this is referred to as the Excel Workbook project template) or Office template files (for example, you can customize a Word template).

As previously discussed, the difference between an application-level add-in and a document extension is one of scope. When you compile an Office project, just as with every other project type in Visual Studio, a managed code assembly is generated. That assembly can be attached or linked to an Office application (for example, Word or Excel) or to an Office document (for example, a `.doc`/`.docx` file or an `.xls`/`.xlsx` file). Document-level assemblies are loaded only when the document is loaded and are limited in scope to the document. Application-level add-ins are loaded during application startup (although this can be controlled by the user) and are more global in their reach.

NOTE

Although Visual Studio fully supports Microsoft Office projects right out of the box (at least with the Visual Studio Professional version), you also need to have a copy of Microsoft Office and potentially various other components installed on your computer.

Creating an Office Add-In

To start creating your own Office add-in, create a new project in Visual Studio by selecting any of the Office add-in project types. Figure 22.4 shows the basic project structure created with a Word add-in project. We have a single code-file that establishes the startup entry point for the add-in and provides us with the namespaces we need to access the Word automation object model.

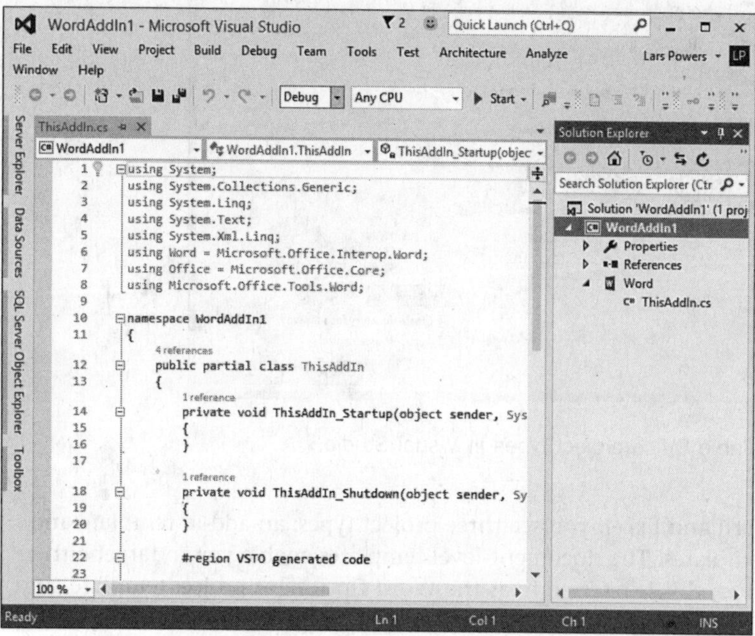

FIGURE 22.4 A Microsoft Word 2013 add-in project.

There isn't anything terribly compelling about the developer experience so far. But Visual Studio does provide a set of visual designers you can use to craft your Office solution just as you would any other project in Visual Studio. To access these, we need to add a project item that has an associated designer. To start, let's see how to create a customized ribbon.

Customizing the Ribbon

Ribbon support within an Office project is enabled by adding a ribbon project item to the project. Right-click the project within Solution Explorer and select Add New Item. In the

Add New Item dialog box (see Figure 22.5), you see two different ribbon templates available for selection: Ribbon (Visual Designer) and Ribbon (XML). As their names suggest, the Visual Designer template provides you with a what-you-see-is-what-you-get (WYSIWYG) design surface for creating your ribbon customizations. Because this design surface can't be used to build certain types of more advanced ribbon features, the Ribbon (XML) item template is provided to enable you to handcraft ribbon features in XML. You need to use the Ribbon (XML) item if you want to do any of the following:

- Add a built-in (as opposed to custom) group to a custom tab
- Add a built-in control to a custom group
- Customize the event handlers for any of the built-in controls
- Add or remove items from the Quick Access toolbar

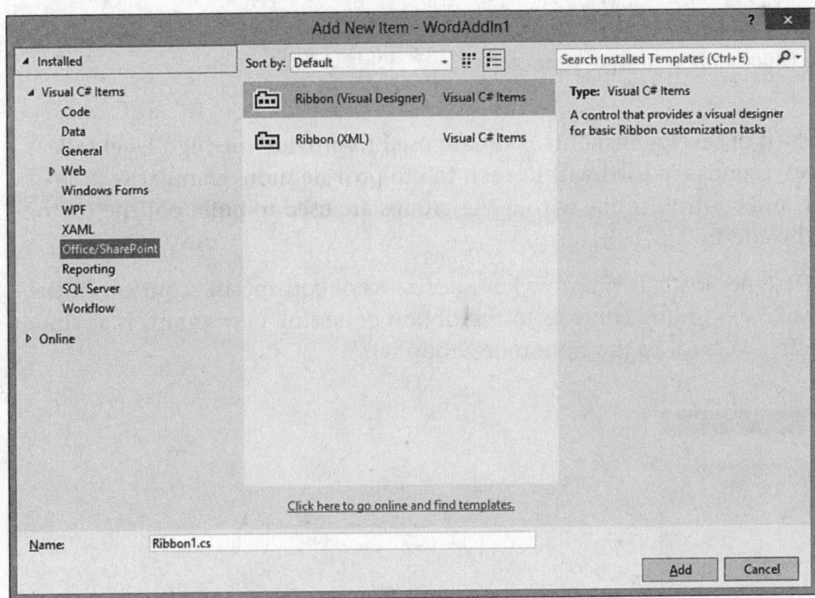

FIGURE 22.5 Adding a Ribbon project item.

For our purposes, let's select the Ribbon (Visual Designer) item and add it to our project. This adds the `Ribbon1.cs` file to our project. In a fashion similar to the other Visual Studio project types, this file has a designer and a code-behind file attached to it.

The design surface you are presented with is an exact replica of an empty ribbon (see Figure 22.6).

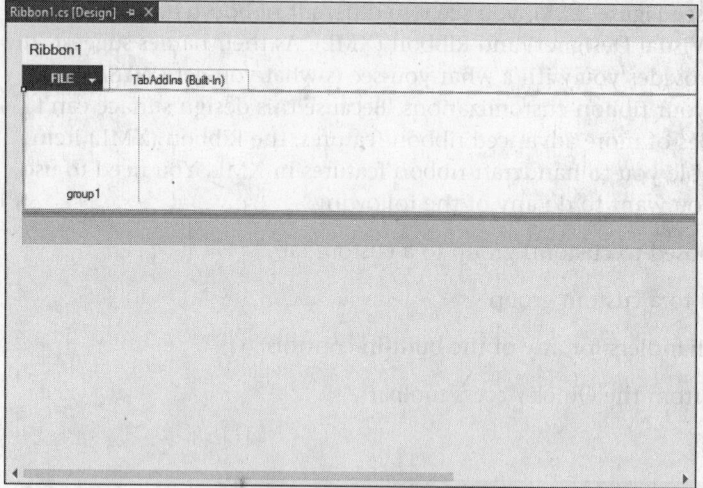

FIGURE 22.6 The Office ribbon design surface.

Ribbons are composed of several elements. Tabs are used to provide the high-level task grouping of features, groups are used within each tab to provide more granular sectioning of the features, and controls reside within the groups are used to build out the custom user interface for the add-in.

With the Ribbon Designer loaded, you now have access to ribbon-specific controls in the Toolbox (see Figure 22.7). Adding controls to the ribbon or adding new groups is as simple as dragging the desired control to the ribbon or Group tab.

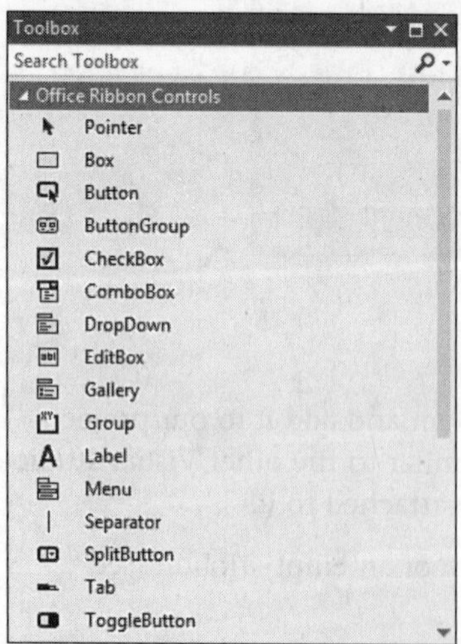

FIGURE 22.7 Office ribbon controls in the IDE toolbox.

Adding Items to the Ribbon

To demonstrate, you can create our own custom group within the Add-Ins tab. Because you are presented with one group already by default, you can rename it to something more appropriate for your add-in. All the items in the ribbon are modified via the Properties window, just as with all other Visual Studio project types. We just click the group and then set its label property.

Groups act as containers on the design surface, enabling us to drag and drop a button into the group. Figure 22.8 shows the beginnings of a custom ribbon for a purchasing system integration add-in. To duplicate this, drag three buttons into the existing group on the ribbon, change their `ControlSize` property to `RibbonControlSizeLarge`, set their label properties to the appropriate text you want displayed on the button, and add some images of your choosing to the buttons by setting the `Image` property.

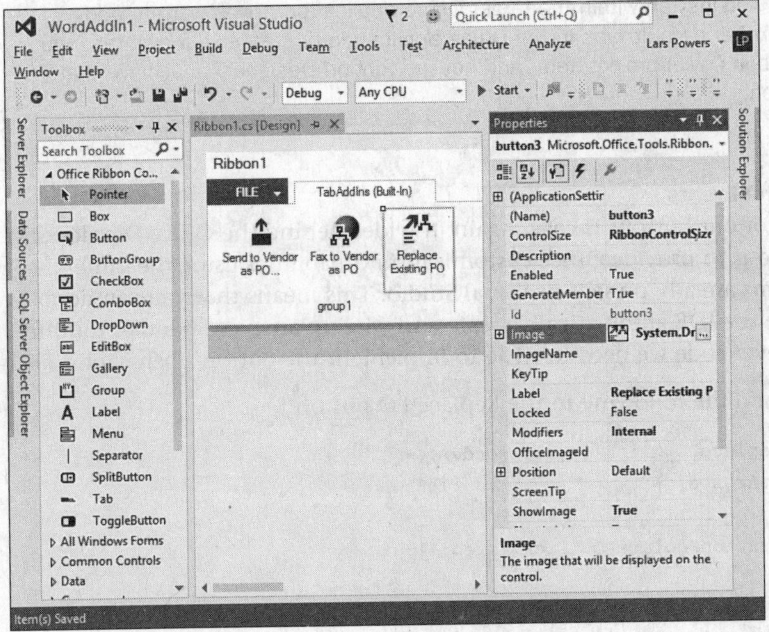

FIGURE 22.8 Creating a custom ribbon.

TIP

The images used in this example were taken from the Visual Studio 2015 Image Library, but there is actually a cool way to reuse any of the icons that you see within Office. First, download the Icons Gallery add-in from the Microsoft Download Center. (Search for "Office 2010: Icons Gallery.") This download places a Word document file on your drive. Open the file, and then click the File tab at the top of the ribbon. Down the column on the left, you should see two entries labeled `ImageMso 0` and `ImageMso 1`. Click either of these to see the gallery of icons.

Each icon has an accompanying label—a string that you can plug directly into a ribbon button's OfficeImageId property. As long as an image isn't already set for the button, the identified Office icon is used. This is a real boon for UI design, given the hundreds and hundreds of high-quality icons already available within Office. The image doesn't show in design time but does display correctly at runtime.

Adding more groups to your ribbon involves more of the same drag-and-drop action from the Toolbox. You can change the order of the groups in the ribbon by selecting and then dragging a group to the left or right of any other existing groups.

NOTE

Notice that there is already a default tab implemented in the ribbon called TabAddIns (Built-In). When you're creating a ribbon for your add-in, its groups are automatically displayed under the Add-Ins tab within the target Office application. If you want to add items to one of the other default tabs in the Office application or create your own tab, you have to use the Ribbon (XML) project item, and not the Ribbon Designer, to achieve that level of customization.

Handling Ribbon Control Events

Handling the events for our buttons is easy. Again, the idea behind the Office Developer Tools for Visual Studio is to provide Office customization capabilities using the same development paradigms already present in Visual Studio. This means that you can double-click a button to have the IDE automatically create and wire up an event-handler routine, ready to accept whatever code we need to write to implement the button's behavior.

To test this out, let's add the following to the Replace PO button.

```
private void buttonReplacePO_Click(object sender,
    RibbonControlEventArgs e)
{
    MessageBox.Show("buttonReplacePO_Click fired!");
}
```

If you run the project now by pressing F5, Word automatically launches; you can see your ribbon customizations by clicking the Add-Ins tab. Clicking the Replace PO button yields the results shown in Figure 22.9.

Customizing the Task Pane

Task panes don't have a dedicated visual designer because they are implemented through the creation of a user control, which already has a design surface. To add a custom task pane to your Word add-in, right-click the project, select Add New Item, and then select the Windows Forms User Control item.

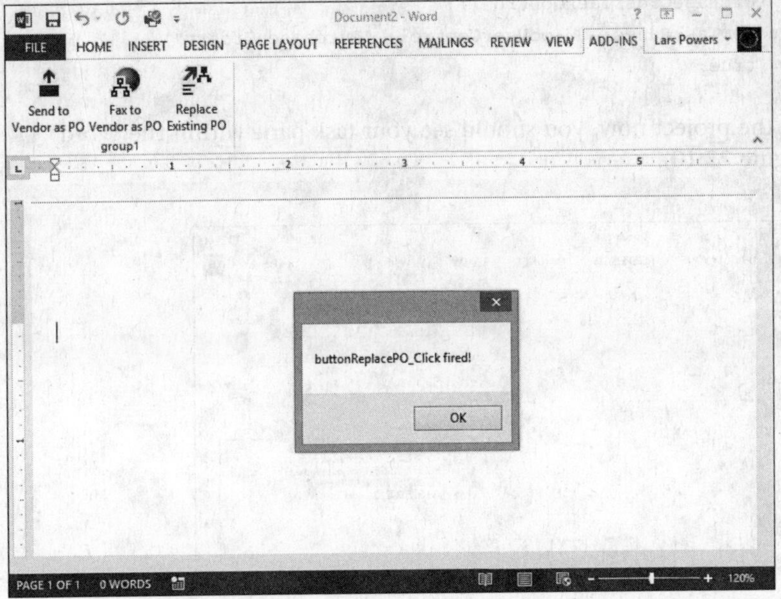

FIGURE 22.9 Testing a ribbon button.

NOTE

Because actions panes are document-level concepts, you'll read about those separately in the section "Creating an Office Document Extension," later in this chapter. You follow the same general development process.

After the user control is added and the designer is loaded, you can set about creating the UI and code-behind for the task pane. The only Office-specific action item here is wiring the task pane user control into Word's object model. All that work is accomplished in code within the add-in class. First, to make life a bit easier, you add a `using` statement to your add-in class (in this case, the `ThisAddIn` class).

```
using Microsoft.Office.Tools;
```

Then you declare two local objects—one for the task pane and one for the user control.

```
private PurchaseOrderTaskControl poUserControl;
private CustomTaskPane poTaskPane;
```

Finally, you need the code to add the custom task pane to the application instance. You put this in the `Startup` event (for this example, `ThisAddIn_Startup`) so that the task pane is immediately available and visible when you run the add-in.

```
poUserControl = new PurchaseOrderTaskControl();
poTaskPane = this.CustomTaskPanes.Add(poUserControl, "Purchase Orders");
poTaskPane.Visible = true;
```

If you build and run the project now, you should see your task pane within the Word environment (see Figure 22.10).

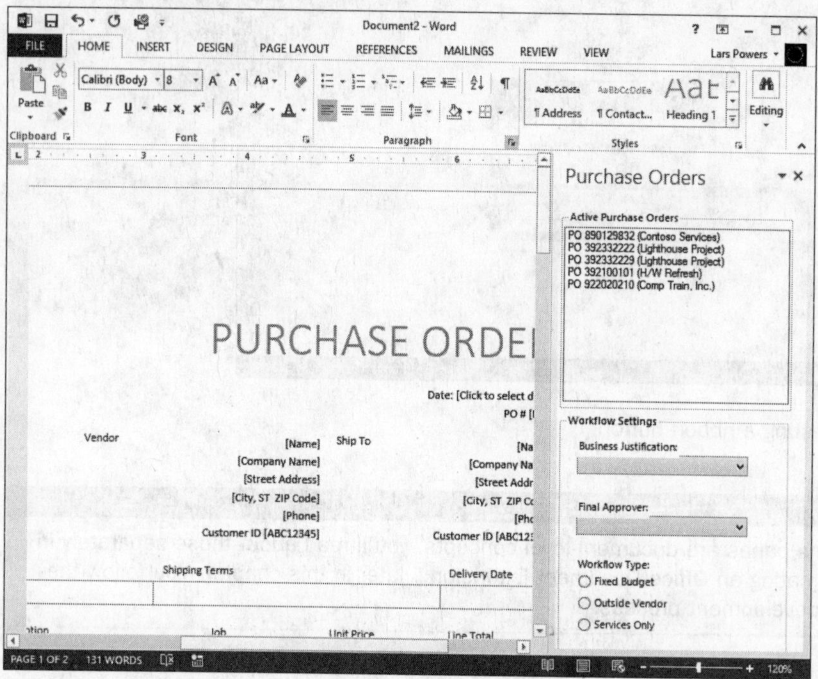

FIGURE 22.10 A custom task pane in Microsoft Word.

TIP

The preceding example uses a Windows Forms user control. If you want to create your task pane using Windows Presentation Foundation (WPF) instead, you simply add a WPF user control to the project. Everything from a design and coding experience would work the same. Behind the scenes, Visual Studio will automatically create a `System.Windows.Forms.Integration.ElementHost` object and use that to parent/host your WPF controls within the targeted Office application.

Creating Outlook Form Regions

Let's turn our attention now to Outlook. As previously mentioned, Outlook has a unique extension point that is not available or relevant in Word or Excel; Outlook add-ins are capable of implementing form regions to any message class within Outlook. A message class is best thought of as the various entities that Outlook defines. These include notes, tasks, email, and so on. Put simply, a form region is the principal mechanism for developers to implement custom form fields within an existing form (for example, email, contact, or other custom forms not included in Outlook by default). To continue with the purchase order example from Word, perhaps a purchase order sent by email should have a set of editable fields and another user interface (UI) associated with it. You can implement those fields and UI in Outlook as a form region. The best way to really understand form regions is to jump right into the task of creating one.

Form regions are implemented by first creating an Outlook add-in project and then adding an Outlook Form Region item. This triggers the Form Region Wizard, which captures the information necessary to autogenerate a region class file. The first screen in the wizard is used to indicate whether you want to create a brand-new form region or use an existing one that was designed in Outlook. For this example, select the Design a New Form option.

The second page in the wizard, shown in Figure 22.11, specifies where the region presents itself. There are four options here, with a graphic that illustrates the positioning behavior of the region. Select Adjoining to create the purchase order UI at the bottom of the Outlook email form.

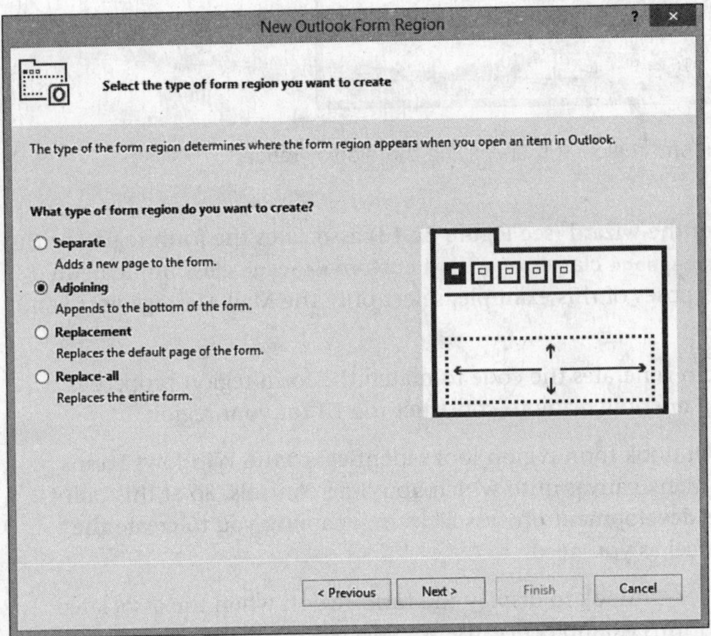

FIGURE 22.11 Selecting the Outlook form region type.

The third page of the wizard (see Figure 22.12) queries for the name of the region and which inspector display modes the region should support. Inspector is the Outlook term for the window used to view and edit a specific message class. For instance, when you compose a new email message in Outlook, you are actually seeing the email inspector in action.

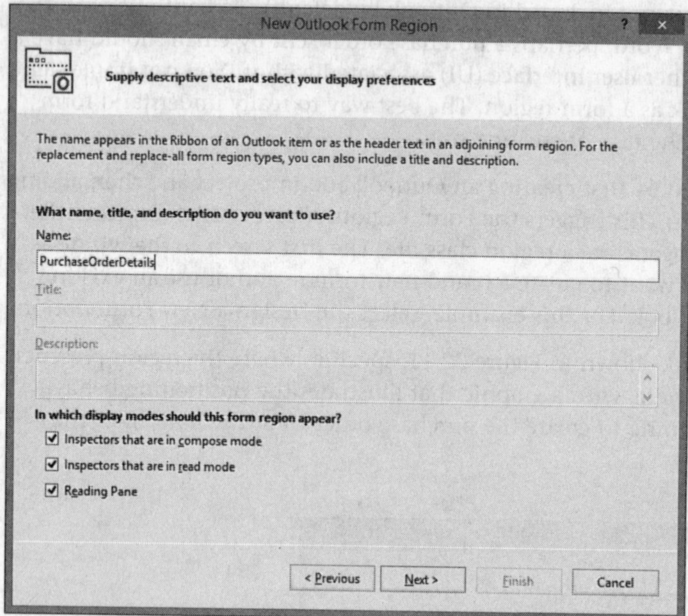

FIGURE 22.12 Naming the form region and specifying the display mode.

The fourth and final page of the wizard (see Figure 22.13) associates the form region with any of the built-in Outlook `message` classes or with a custom `message` class implemented by a third party. For the purposes of this example, select only the Mail Message entry and click the Finish button.

When finished, Visual Studio generates the code to match the form region properties provided in the wizard. You are now ready to construct the UI for your region.

The visual designer for an Outlook form region looks identical to the Windows Forms Designer: It is essentially a blank canvas onto which you drag controls. So at this point, the typical Windows Forms development process kicks in, enabling you to create the behavior and the look and feel as you need.

No other code is necessary for Outlook to display the form region when the associated message class is invoked. For this example, because we selected the mail message class earlier when we executed the Form Region Wizard, the region automatically shows up anytime we create a new email item (as shown in Figure 22.14).

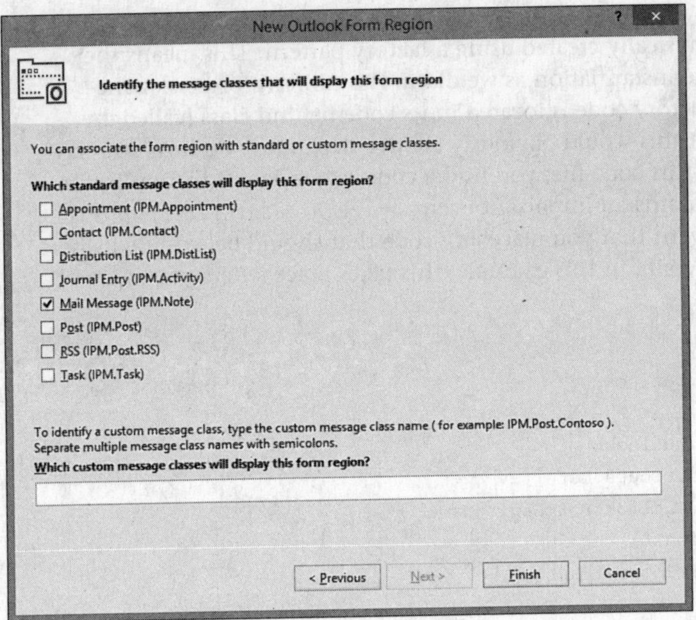

FIGURE 22.13 Associating the form region with a message class.

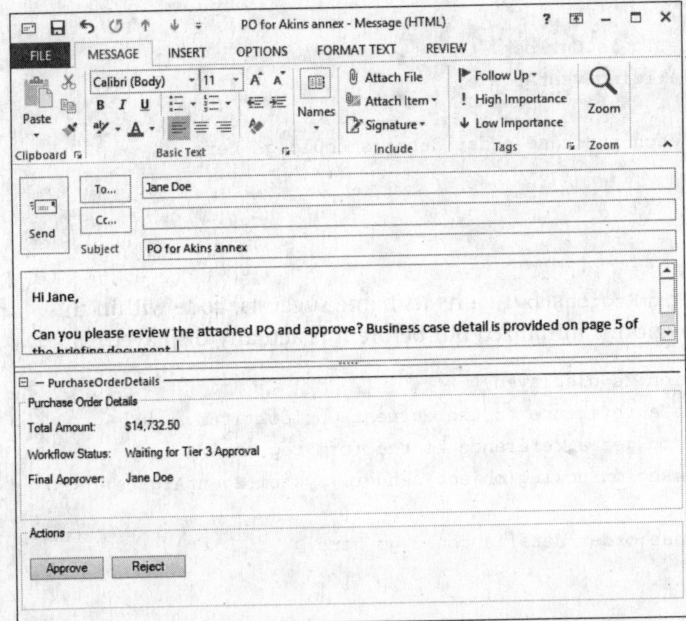

FIGURE 22.14 An Outlook form region at runtime.

Runtime Events

Outlook form regions are physically created using a factory pattern. This means they aren't "newed up" via simple instantiation as we did in the earlier Word task pane example. The form region factory code is located in its code-behind class (called, by default, `FormRegion1.cs`, but this would obviously change depending on how you have named the project item). In this code file, you find a code region labeled Form Region Factory. And that region contains an important event: `FormRegionInitializing`. It is within the context of this event that you place any code that should be executed when the form region first loads. Again, in this example, this takes place whenever an email item is displayed.

```
#region Form Region Factory
    [Microsoft.Office.Tools.Outlook.
    FormRegionMessageClass
    (Microsoft.Office.Tools.Outlook.
    FormRegionMessageClassAttribute.Note)]
    [Microsoft.Office.Tools.Outlook.FormRegionName
    ("OutlookAddIn2.FormRegion1")]
    public partial class FormRegion1Factory
        {
            //Occurs before the form region is initialized.
            //To prevent the form region from appearing, set e.Cancel to true.
            //Use e.OutlookItem to get a reference to the current Outlook item.
            private void FormRegion1Factory_FormRegionInitializing
            (object sender,
             Microsoft.Office.Tools.Outlook.
             FormRegionInitializingEventArgs e)
            {
                //Code to fetch purchase order details could go here.
            }
        }
#endregion
```

The other important event is `FormRegionShowing`. As its name suggests, code within this event executes after the form region is initialized but before it is actually displayed.

```
//Occurs before the form region is displayed.
//Use this.OutlookItem to get a reference to the current Outlook item.
//Use this.OutlookFormRegion to get a reference to the form region.
private void FormRegion1_FormRegionShowing(object sender, System.EventArgs e)
  {
      //Code to format purchase order details could go here.
  }
```

Creating an Office Document Extension

You can customize Office documents in various ways. You can host controls in a document, create actions panes specific to a document, and store data within a document.

A document-level project is created using the same process we used for add-ins. This time, however, you select an Excel Workbook or Word Document project type. These project types use designers that represent the look and feel of an Excel workbook or a Word document.

Hosting Controls

Both Word and Excel have host items that function as containers for controls and code. A host item is essentially a proxy object that represents a physical document within either application. These are key to document-level customizations. For Word, we have the `Microsoft.Office.Tools.Word.Document` object, and for Excel, we have the `Microsoft.Office.Tools.Excel.Worksheet` object. Within Visual Studio, we build functionality using these host items through the use of designers. Each host item can host both Windows Forms controls and native Office controls.

NOTE

There is actually a third host item that represents an Excel workbook: `Microsoft.Office.Tools.Excel.Workbook`. It is a host item for enabling workbook-level customization, but it is not an actual controls container. Instead, `Workbook` functions as a component tray and can accept components such as a DataSet.

Windows Forms Controls

You can add Windows Forms controls onto the document design surface just as if you were designing a Windows Forms application. In this example, we use an Excel workbook. The Excel 2010 Workbook project template automatically adds an `.xslx` file to our project, which includes three worksheets, each represented by its own class. (These are the host items we discussed previously.) These sheets have defined events for startup and shutdown, enabling us to perform work as the worksheet is first opened or closed.

The design surface for the worksheet looks identical to the worksheet in Excel. From here, we can add Windows Forms controls to the worksheet by using the Visual Studio Toolbox, and we can implement code in the code-behind file to customize the action of those controls. Figure 22.15 shows a workbook designer in the IDE with a few controls added.

NOTE

Creating an Office document project requires that your system allow access to the Microsoft Office Visual Basic for Applications project system. Normally, this type of access is disabled for security reasons. If access is disabled, Visual Studio prompts you to enable it before creating your Office project.

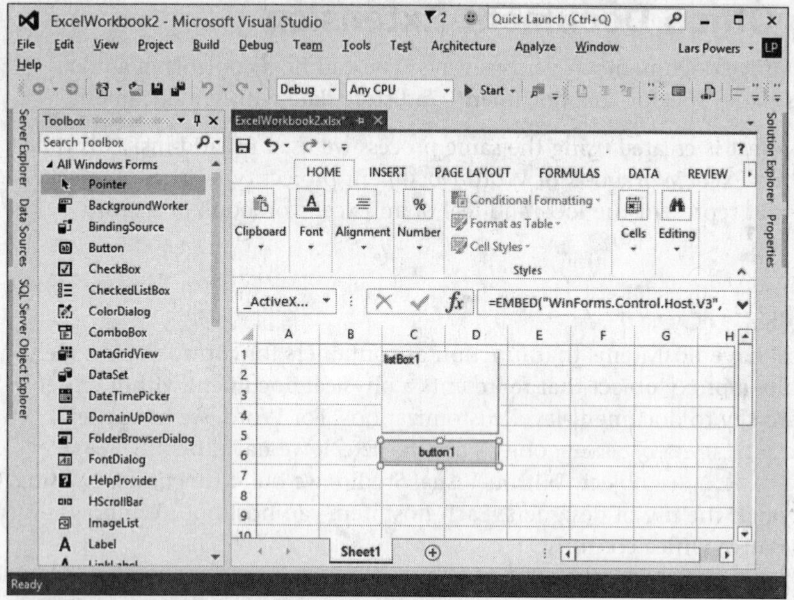

FIGURE 22.15 Adding controls to an Excel spreadsheet.

Host Controls

Host controls is the term applied to native Office controls. These controls actually extend objects found in the Word or Excel object models to provide additional capabilities such as event handling and data binding. Building out a document using host controls follows the same process as with Windows Forms controls. With a document-level project loaded, you see a tab in the Visual Studio Toolbox that stores the host controls for the specific application that is targeted. For Excel, there is an Excel Controls tab, and for Word, there is a Word Controls tab.

Table 22.2 itemizes the available host controls for both Excel and Word.

TABLE 22.2 Microsoft Office Extension Points

Project Type	Host Control	Function
Excel workbook	`ListObject`	Displays data in rows and columns.
Excel workbook	`NamedRange`	Represents an Excel range; can be bound to data and expose events.
Word document	`Bookmark`	Represents a Word bookmark.

Project Type	Host Control	Function
Word document	`BuildingBlockGalleryContentControl`	Document building blocks are pieces of a document meant to be reused (a cover page, header, and so on). This control displays a list of building blocks that users can insert into a document.
Word document	`ComboBoxContentControl`	A standard combo box.
Word document	`DatePickerContentControl`	A standard date picker control.
Word document	`DropDownListContentControl`	A drop-down list of items.
Word document	`PictureContentControl`	Represents a document region that displays an image.
Word document	`PlainTextContentControl`	Represents a block of text.
Word document	`RichTextContentControl`	Represents a block of text; can contain rich content.

Creating an Actions Pane

In addition to customizing the interaction with users within a document, Windows Forms controls are used to craft custom actions panes. Actions panes should be used to provide contextual data and command options to users as they are editing/viewing a document (either a Word document or an Excel workbook file).

There are several reasons why you would elect to implement your document interface using an actions pane. One reason is that the actions pane is "linked" to the document but is not an actual part of the document; the contents of the actions pane won't be printed when the document is printed. Another reason to implement an actions pane is to preserve the application's document-centric focus: you can read and page through an entire document while keeping the information and commands in the actions pane in full view at all times.

Physically, actions panes are created with user controls and are represented by an Actions Pane Control item. Adding this item to your document project creates a user control class; you simply build out the UI of the control as normal. In general, though, you likely want to dynamically add or remove controls from the actions pane depending on what the user is doing within the document that is open in Word or Excel. Providing this level of contextual relevance is the strong point and target of the actions pane in the first place.

Controlling Stacking Behavior

Because the actions pane functions as a toolbar container that can be docked and moved around by the user, there is a complete control layout engine for dictating how the controls within the actions pane should be displayed. The `ActionsPane.StackOrder` property works with a `StackStyle` enum to control layout behavior. The various `StackStyle` values are documented for you in Table 22.3.

TABLE 22.3 `StackStyle` Values

Value	Description
`FromBottom`	Controls are stacked starting from the bottom of the actions pane.
`FromLeft`	Controls are stacked starting from the left of the actions pane.
`FromRight`	Controls are stacked starting from the right of the actions pane.
`FromTop`	Controls are stacked starting from the top of the actions pane.
`None`	No stacking is performed. (Order and layout are manually controlled.)

As we did with the custom task pane, after you have assembled a user control that you want to surface within the actions pane, you need to create a field variable to hold an instance of the control and then add the control to the actions pane.

So in the `ThisWorkbook` class, we add the following declaration.

```
private ActionsPaneControl1 approvalPane = new ActionsPaneControl1();
```

And the following line of code, inserted into the `ThisWorkbook_Startup` event, adds our user control to the workbook's actions pane.

```
this.ActionsPane.Controls.Add(approvalPane);
```

Figure 22.16 shows a custom actions pane alongside its worksheet.

Storing Data in the Data Cache

The data cache is a read/write location within an Office Word document or Excel workbook that can be leveraged by your Office application to store needed data. One common scenario is to bind host controls or Windows Forms controls in an actions pane or on a document surface to a data set stored in the document's data island.

Physically, this data island is implemented as an XML document that is embedded within the Office document. This XML container can host any data type that meets the following two requirements:

- It has to be implemented as a read/write public field on the host item (for example, the Word `ThisDocument` or Excel `ThisWorkbook` class).
- It must be serializable (the runtime uses the `XmlSerializer` to verbalize the object within the data island).

Most of the built-in .NET types meet these requirements. If you have written a custom type that also adheres to these requirements, it, too, can be stored within the data island.

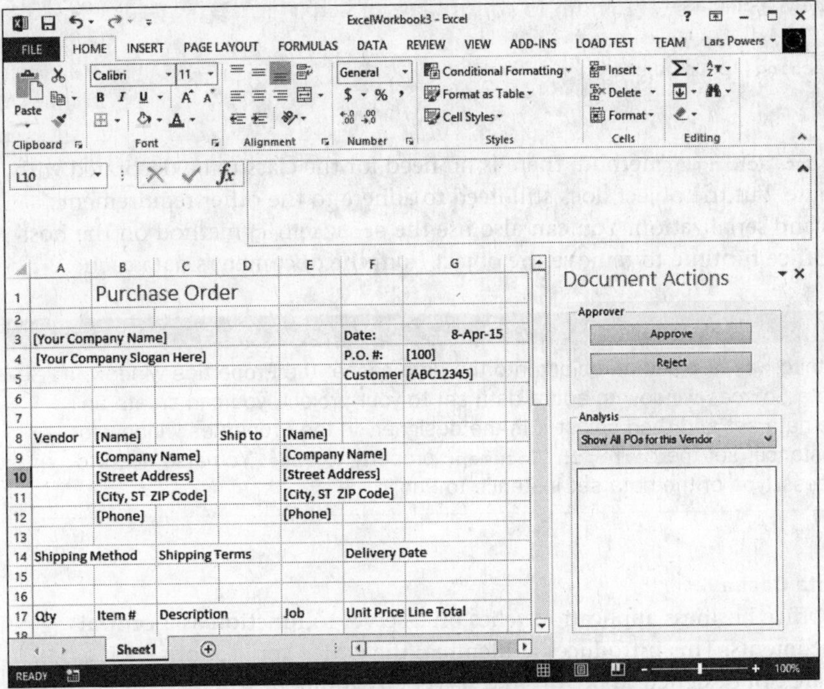

FIGURE 22.16 A custom actions pane in Excel.

Adding data to the data cache is easy. You mark the data type you want to store with the `CachedAttribute` attribute; assuming that the type meets the data cache requirements and that you have created an instance of the type within your document-level project, it is automatically added to the data island.

`DataSet` objects turn out to be useful for conveyance within a data island. To declare a `DataSet` as cached, we write the following.

```
[Microsoft.VisualStudio.Tools.Applications.Runtime.Cached()]
public DataSet poDataSet;
```

This declaratively instructs the Office runtime to serialize the object and add it to the current document's data cache. The `DataSet` itself can be populated any way you see fit.

There is also a way to imperatively cache an object in a document. Each host item exposes an `IsCached` method and a `StartCaching` method. By combining the two, you can check to see whether an object is already in the cache, and, if it isn't, add it. Using these two methods, we might end up with the following code to store our `poDataSet` object in a document.

```
if (!this.IsCached("poDataSet"))
{
   this.StartCaching("poDataSet ");
}
```

If you use the `StartCaching()` method, there is no need for the class to be decorated with the `Cached` attribute, but the object does still need to adhere to the other requirements for Office data island serialization. You can also use the `StopCaching` method on the host item to tell the Office runtime to remove the object from the document's data cache.

TIP

There is yet a third way to place an object into the data cache: the Properties window. If you use the Data Sources window to add a data set to your project, you can create an instance of the data set and then select it in the designer. In the Properties window for the data set instance, set the `Cache in Document` property to `True`. You also need to change the access type of the data set instance to Public.

Accessing the Data Cache

Many times, an Office business application relies on a server to function as a central repository for documents. This introduces a dilemma: the Office applications such as Word and Excel are not designed to be run in a server environment where many instances might need to be spooled up to serve multiple requests for document-level extensions. So far, we have been using objects within the Office object model to extend Office. And this implies that Office is installed on the machine running your assembly (something that is certainly not the case for typical server installations). Thankfully, one of the primary goals for document-level Office architecture is to enable the clean separation of data from the view of the data. Or, put another way, the Office architecture defines a way to access a document without actually using the Office client application. Instead, the Office runtime itself is used.

The key to accessing a document server side is the `ServerDocument` class. This class, which is part of the Office Developer Tools and lives in the `Microsoft.VisualStudio.Tools.Applications` namespace, allows programmatic access to a document's data cache on machines that do not have Office installed. The process running on the server passes the path for the needed document into the `ServerDocument`'s constructor and then uses the `CachedDataHostItem` class and the `CachedDataItem` class to obtain either the schema or the XML or both from the document's data island.

As long as the target computer has the VSTO runtime installed, the following code could be used to access the purchase order data from a server-side purchase order spreadsheet.

```
string poFile = @"C:\ServerData\po39233202.xls";
ServerDocument poDoc = null;
poDoc = new ServerDocument(poFile);
CachedDataHostItem dataHostItem =
   sd1.CachedData.HostItems["ExcelWorkbook1.DataSheet1"];
```

```
CachedDataItem dataCache = dataHostItem.CachedData["CachedPO"];
//The dataCache.Xml property will contain the XML
//from the specified data island
```

Using the `dataCache.Xml` property, you can now deserialize back into the source data type, view the data, and so on.

Extending Office with Webpages

We have so far focused on writing extensions to the Office client applications through the traditional "add-in" notion: you use the usercontrol/Office project Item approach to design a user interface and code logic that is hosted within the target Office client app. In this last section, we cover a final project type—"App for Office"—that follows the same solution pattern but instead of using client technology allows you to write webpages that are then hosted within Office.

Starting with the App for Office Project Template

The first step to getting started with an App for Office project is to create a new project and select the App for Office project template (see Figure 22.17).

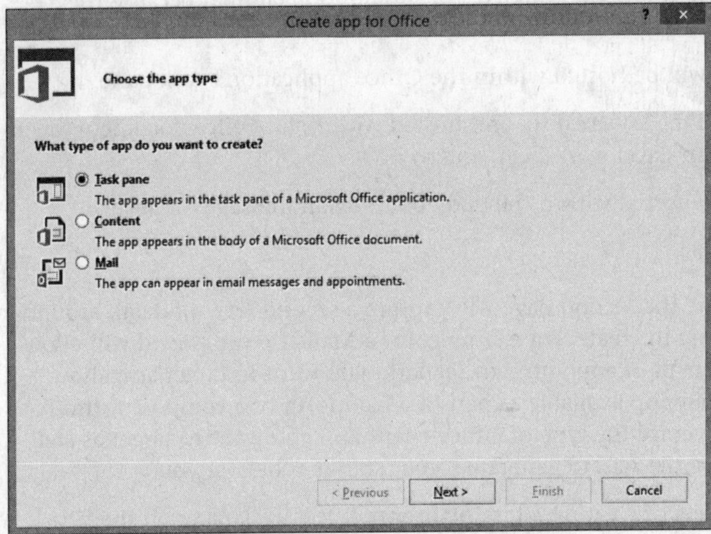

FIGURE 22.17 The App for Office project templates.

Unlike the add-in projects that are broken out by specific applications such as Excel or Word, there is only a single App for Office project template. After you select the project template and create the new project, a two-page wizard will launch. The first page will capture the type of the extension (see Figure 22.18).

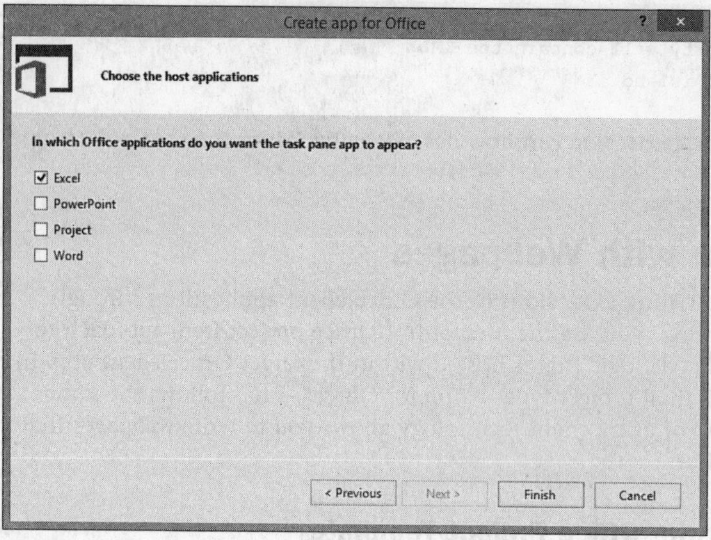

FIGURE 22.18 The starting page of the App for Office Wizard.

There are three different extension types offered. All should look familiar because they represent the same types of extension functionality covered earlier in this chapter:

- **Task pane**—The app will be hosted within the Office application's task pane.
- **Content**—The app will be attached to, and hosted within, an Office document (a Word document file, an Excel worksheet, and so on)
- **Mail**—The app will be hosted within the body of an email message (or an appointment).

Based on your selection here, the second page will capture a second level of detail around the type of app you are trying to create. For example, for a Mail app the wizard will allow you to fine-tune the exact email or appointment scenario you want to target and allow you to select if you want your app available as part of a read form or a compose form. For a content app, you can customize the type of Office client app you want to target as well as whether you want to have the wizard generate some "starter code" for you.

Let's walk through the process of creating a task pane app. Select Task pane on the first page of the wizard (refer to Figure 22.18). On the second screen, we'll constrain our solution down to Excel (see Figure 22.19).

After clicking Finish on the wizard, the project will load. The first thing you will notice is that two projects have been created: a "manifest" project and a web project (see Figure 22.20).

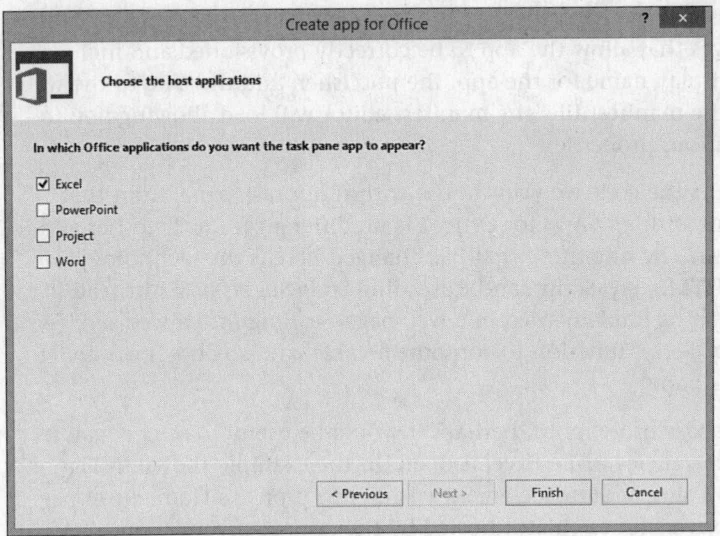

FIGURE 22.19 Selecting the target application for a task pane app.

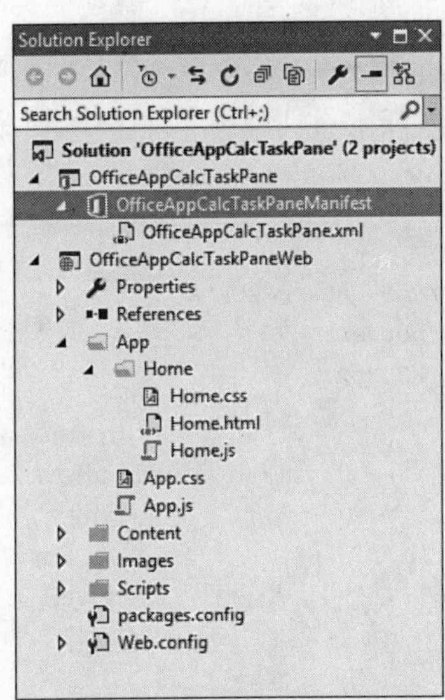

FIGURE 22.20 An App for Office solution.

The manifest project holds a single XML file that is our project's manifest. This is nothing more than a set of directives that allow the app to be correctly provisioned and include information such as the display name for the app, the publisher, and the URL to the web page. If you double-click the manifest file, the manifest editor will load allowing you to inspect and change the various properties.

The web project implements the code we want to use within our task pane; from that point of view, development with an "App for Office" is no different from the other add-in projects we discussed earlier. The one thing that has changed here is the technology: we will write our code using HTML, JavaScript, and Cascading Style Sheets (CSS) instead of using C#. Anything that can be implemented in a web page—calling into a web service to retrieve values, calling a JScript function to compute a value, and so on—is possible to implement within our task pane.

To continue with our purchase order motif, perhaps it would be useful to offer a way to quickly convert between currencies while Excel is open. In the example shown in Figure 22.21, we have embedded a simple `iframe` element within our project's Home.html page. This embeds a currency conversion calculator hosted by themoneyconverter.com.

```
<body>
    <div id="content-header">
        <div class="padding">
            <h1>Currency Converter</h1>
        </div>
    </div>
    <div id="content-main">
        <div class="padding">
            <iframe id="tmcmini"
➥src="http://themoneyconverter.com/MoneyConverter.aspx?from=USD&to=EUR"
➥marginwidth="0" marginheight="0" scrolling="no" style="border:
➥currentColor; border-image: none; width: 175px; height: 202px;
➥background-color: rgb(255, 255, 255);"></iframe>
        </div>
    </div>
</body>
```

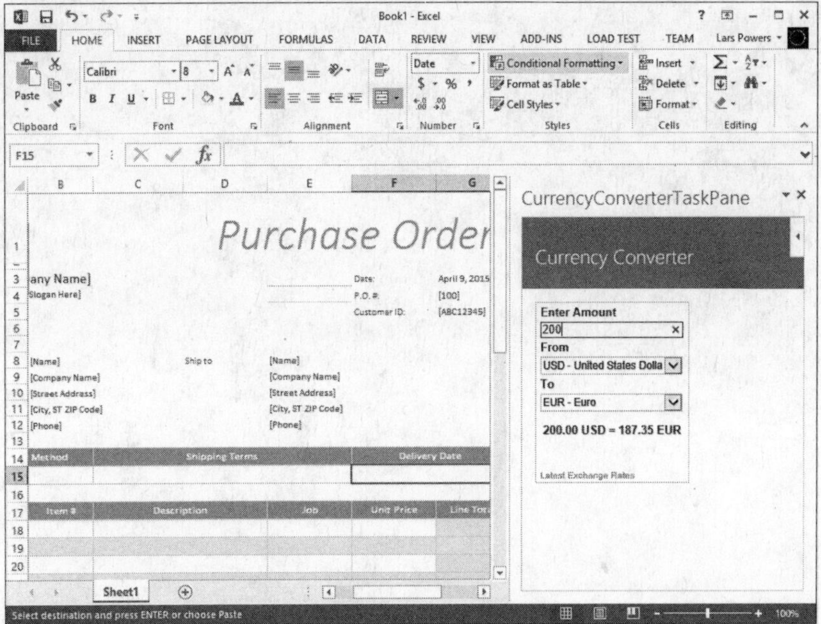

FIGURE 22.21 A web page based task pane within Excel.

Summary

This chapter covered the capabilities present in Visual Studio 2015 for building on top of Microsoft Office applications and customizing their behavior at both the application level and the document level. The discussion about Office add-ins covered the capability to add your own items, tabs, and groupings to the ribbon; the construction of Outlook forms regions; and the development of custom task panes. The discussion about Office document-level extensions illustrated the concepts behind hosting Windows Forms controls and native Office controls on a document's surface, building custom actions panes to provide context-aware actions and information to users, and using the data cache architecture to both read and write data to Office documents on the client and server side. Finally, we concluded with a brief walk-through illustrating the process of creating an Office app by hosting a web page within an Excel task pane.

Although this chapter focused on only a few of the Office applications that can be customized using the Office Developer Tools for Visual Studio, you should now have enough information about these project types and designers to get you started on your own investigation into Visual Studio and Office as a development platform.

CHAPTER 23

Developing Windows Store Applications

IN THIS CHAPTER

- ▶ Introducing the Modern UI
- ▶ The Windows Runtime Library
- ▶ Building a Windows Store Application

Windows 8 represented a significant departure from Windows releases of the past. For the first time in many, many years, the core development model, application design approach, and operating system fundamentals have all undergone a major shift. With touch-enabled devices abounding, Microsoft needed an operating system that could cater equally well to mainstream desktop, tablet and mobile form factors, and everything in between.

Therefore, Windows 8 ships with two distinct personalities: a desktop personality that looks and behaves somewhat similarly to Windows 7, and a new touch-focused and mobile device-targeted personality. This new personality (which has been variously referred to as Metro, Immersive, Modern UI, and most recently, simply "Windows applications") is backed by a Windows Store: an app store that serves as the single install source for all such applications.

This chapter introduces you to the Visual Studio tools that enable you to write applications that can be published into that Windows Store—applications that leverage the technical capabilities of Windows 8 and beyond while conforming to the new look and feel and behavior expectations that users will have on the new UI platform. We examine the new Windows Runtime library, also known as WinRT, and we do a deep dive into the Windows Store project types and project item templates. Finally, we put these concepts into action by writing a Windows Store application.

NOTE

Before getting into the material here, please know that to develop Windows Store applications, you must be running Windows 8/8.1 on your development machine. And of course, you need a copy of Visual Studio. Visual Studio 2012 is required if you need to target Windows 8 specifically, Visual Studio 2013 and Visual Studio 2015 can target Windows 8.1 applications.

Introducing the Modern UI

To start to understand the differences between the two Windows 8 UI personalities and the change in design approach from Windows 7 to Windows 8, one needs look no further than the Windows 8 start screen (see Figure 23.1). As you can see, this looks nothing like the Windows of old. It has more in common, in fact, with the tile-based UI introduced on the Windows Phone platform. (See Chapter 24, "Creating Windows Phone Applications," for our coverage of Windows Phone development.) We see that applications are now represented as tiles. The tiles themselves are not simple, static icons; they are alive and animated, providing up-to-date information surfaced from the prospective application. Thus, at a glance, we have information about our email, our calendar, the weather, current sports scores, and anything else we care to pin to our start screen.

FIGURE 23.1 The Windows 8 start screen.

The work surface can be panned, scrolled, and flicked using touch interactions. In fact, everything on the start screen works without the need for a keyboard or mouse if you have a touch-enabled screen/device.

System-level and application-level settings are controlled via charms. Charms show to the right side of the screen as a sort of toolbar that slides into view when the mouse or touch input is directed to the top-right corner of the screen (see Figure 23.2).

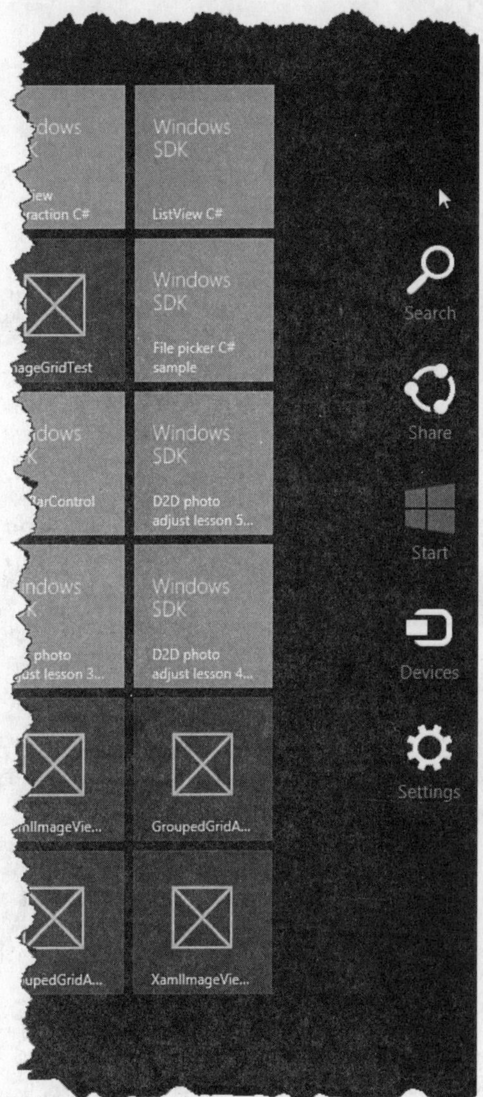

FIGURE 23.2 The Windows 8 charms bar.

Within each application, commands may also be accessed via a bottom app bar that appears on right-click or via the swipe-up gesture on the screen. Figure 23.3 shows the app bar for the Windows 8 Messaging application. Note the Status and Invite command buttons.

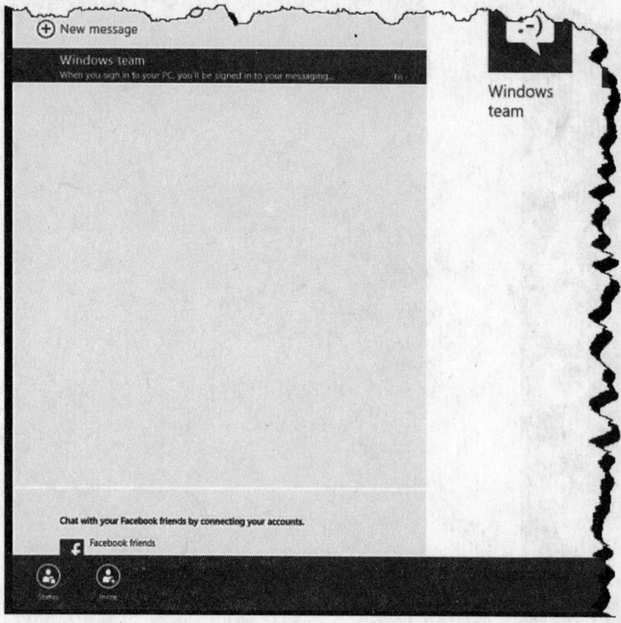

FIGURE 23.3 An app bar at the bottom of the Messaging app.

You can likely infer many of the design characteristics of Windows Store applications by looking at these figures. But let's examine in some detail the principles to which every Windows Store application is expected to adhere.

Modern UI Attributes

A Windows Store application is built on a core set of principles:

- **Pride in craftsmanship**—Windows Store applications should be ruthless in their attention to detail and their level of fit and polish presented to the end user.
- **Fast and fluid**—Applications should be responsive, should fully embrace touch and gesture-driven interactions, and should be visually engaging for users.
- **Authentically digital**—Skeuomorphism is eschewed in favor of simple colors, typography, and connections to the digital world.
- **Do more with less**—Content is king; more content, less chrome is the mantra here. Don't let applications get between users and their content.
- **Win as one**—Your applications should be subtly woven into the overall user experience. This implies sharing data with other applications, conforming to the overall UI model, and innovating within a common framework to provide consistency.

Compare and contrast Figures 23.4 and 23.5, which show a common Windows application, the Media Player, in both its standard and Modern UI variants. Note how the Modern UI version (see Figure 23.5) very clearly places an emphasis on content (songs and artists) over the presence of chrome and application-level UI elements. The desktop Media Player (see Figure 23.4) looks positively cluttered by comparison.

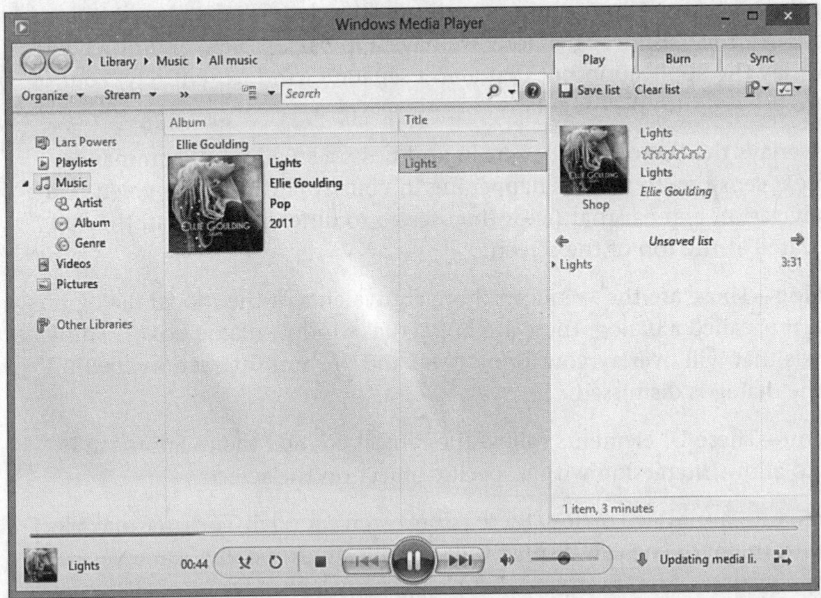

FIGURE 23.4 The Windows desktop version of the Windows Media Player.

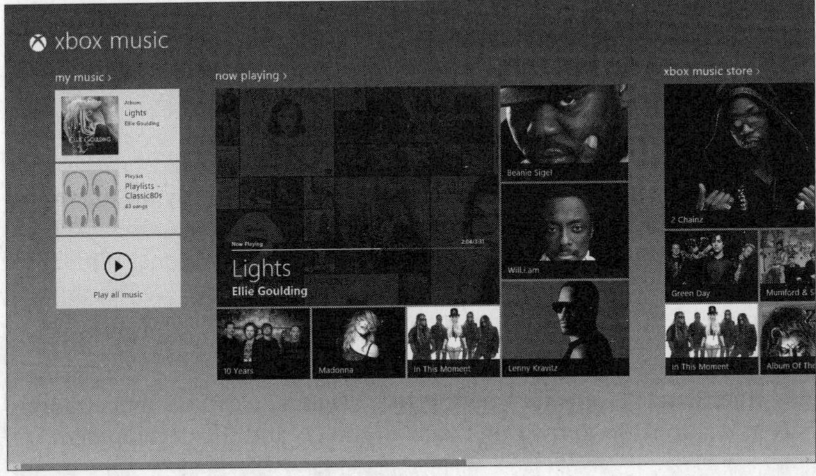

FIGURE 23.5 The updated, Modern UI version of the Media Player.

Controls

It is important to note that a Windows Store application doesn't just look different; it also behaves differently from a traditional desktop application. As a developer, this means that there is a different set of expectations and requirements placed on any Modern UI application you may write. For instance, standard desktop applications usually make liberal use of dialog boxes, pop-up windows, and even multiple windows within the same application. This is not true of the Modern UI app, where everything UI-wise will take place within the same chunk of screen real estate. Therefore, we have app bars, panels, and other constructs that overlay the application but that aren't separate windows entirely. Four of these constructs are pressed into play regularly:

- **App bar**—Overlays the bottom of the screen and hosts a small set of commands that are context sensitive to what is happening in your application at a given point in time. A navigation app bar that helps the user go to different places in the app should be located at the top of the screen.
- **Message dialog**—These are the Windows Store equivalents of the modal dialog box. Even though it is called a dialog, these are not actual window dialog boxes. Think of them as panels that will overlay your primary UI and prevent interaction "behind" them until the dialog is dismissed.
- **Context menu**—These UI elements follow the typical context menu approach by popping up to allow interaction with a specific object on the screen.
- **Fly-out**—Similar to a message dialog, these panels aren't modal. The user may elect to interact with them, or she can dismiss them by clicking/touching someplace else within the application.

These, and others, make up a standard control set that you can use in your applications. Figure 23.6 shows some of the many new XAML controls loaded into the Visual Studio Toolbox.

Along with the Windows Store design paradigm, Windows 8 brings a completely new programming model and set of APIs: the Windows Runtime library (WinRT).

The Windows Runtime Library

WinRT, distilled to its simplest definition, is a Windows API that sits directly on top of the core Windows 8 services. As such, it is actually a direct peer of the previous Win32 API. Microsoft invested in a new runtime library for a few different reasons. For one, Win32 APIs weren't the easiest to access and develop against from a .NET perspective. The impedance mismatch between the .NET Framework surface and the Win32 API/COM surface made for sometimes confusing, and sometimes impossible, development tasks.

Figure 23.7 shows the traditional "layer cake" architecture diagram, clearly demonstrating where the WinRT sits in relationship to the other parts of the OS and the development platform.

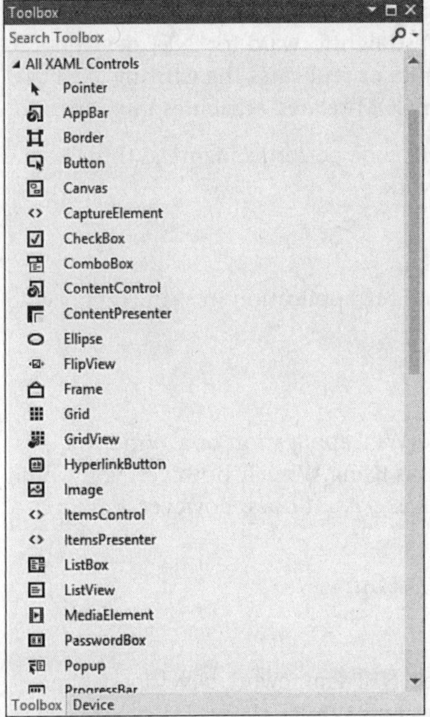

FIGURE 23.6 The WinRT controls for XAML projects.

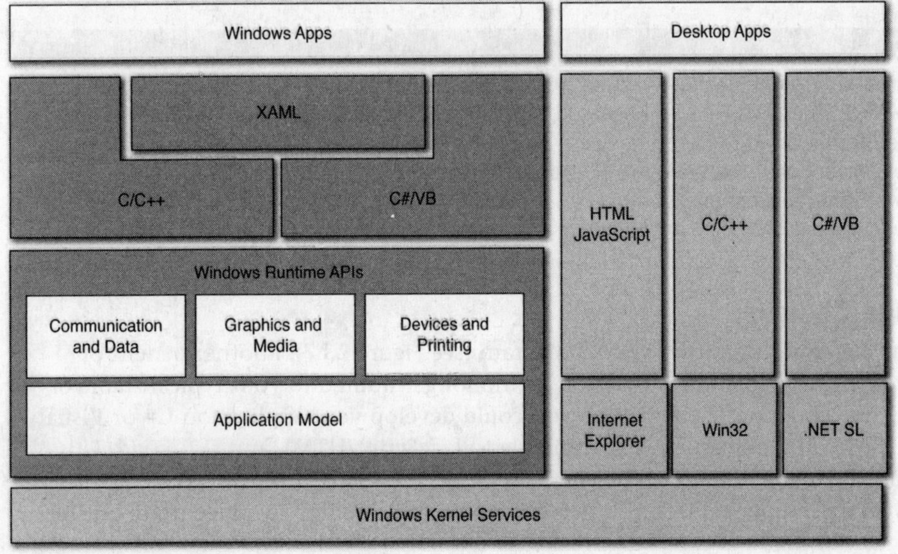

FIGURE 23.7 The WinRT architecture.

With WinRT, Microsoft has gone to great lengths to wrap all the underlying Windows behavior and surface functionality in a way that is a) straightforward for .NET developers to understand, and b) in many cases directly mimics or replicates the existing .NET Framework objects. This means no more `P/Invoke` or COM-related attributes in your code.

Here is a simple example. The following line of XAML code performs identical things when compiled against WinRT and the .NET Framework.

```
<Button Click="Button_Click_1" Content="OK" />
```

Conversely, if we were to set out to write a `Hello, World!` application in WinRT, we might be tempted to write this.

```
MessageBox.Show("Hello, World!");
```

That line of C# would work great in either a standard WPF application or a Windows Forms application. If you were to try to implement this using WinRT, however, you would quickly discover that WinRT doesn't have a `MessageBox` class. It does, however, have a `MessageDialog` class.

```
MessageDialog dialog = new MessageDialog("Hello, World!");
Dialog.ShowAsync;
```

So, although the approach and syntax are familiar for .NET Framework developers, there is not a 100% match between .NET Framework classes and WinRT classes. Also note that the WinRT XAML stack has been rewritten without .NET, and you might find some differences with advanced features of the WPF version of XAML presented in Chapter 21, "Building WPF Applications."

NOTE

WinRT, as shorthand for the Windows Runtime library, should not be confused with Windows RT. Windows RT was Microsoft's product name for the version of Windows 8 designed to run on ARM-based devices (as opposed to Intel- or AMD-based machines). With few exceptions, the Windows RT operating system is only capable of running Windows Store applications.

Language Choices

As you can see from the earlier WinRT diagram (see Figure 23.7), another benefit of having WinRT in the picture is that you are no longer limited to your typical stable of managed code languages. So although you could develop your application C# or Visual Basic, all the WinRT objects are also available to JavaScript/HTML and C++ code. This widens the playing field quite a bit. There are no second-class citizens in the equation: WinRT is an equal-opportunity API. As a developer, you are free to concentrate on the toolset that you feel most comfortable with from a skill set and background perspective. The tooling and the API are there to support you.

With WinRT, you can develop a Modern UI application using DirectX, HTML/JavaScript/CSS, C#, Visual Basic, or C++. Each language will have a set of common and a set of unique project types.

HTML and JavaScript and CSS

For developers coming from the web side of the business, Hypertext Markup Language (HTML), JavaScript, and Cascading Style Sheets (CSS) are familiar and capable technologies. Building a WinRT application using these languages results in a structure that is similar, if not identical, to a website/application:

- ▶ CSS is used for the presentation (that is, the layout and styling of the user interface).
- ▶ JavaScript is used to code the behavior (the way the app handles interactions, events, business rules, and so on).
- ▶ HTML is used for the structure of the content within the UI.

To create a JavaScript application, click File, New Project, and then locate the JavaScript language selection to the left (see Figure 23.8).

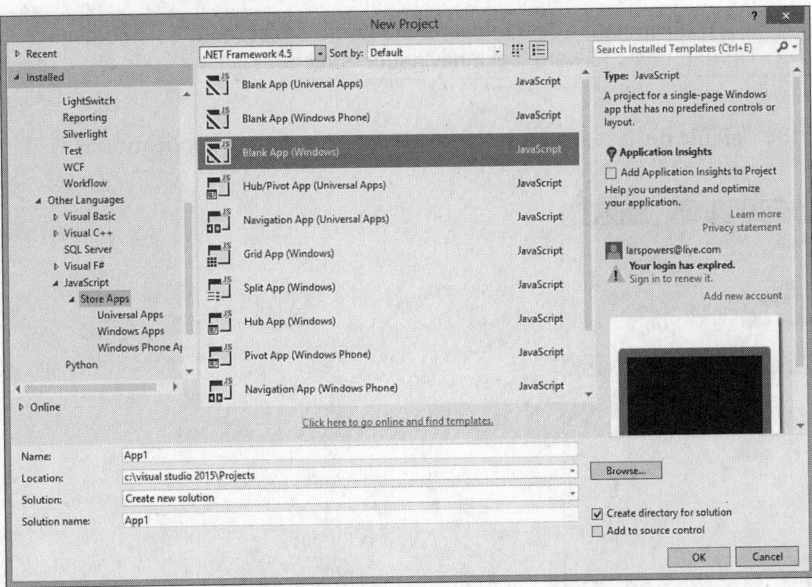

FIGURE 23.8 Creating a JavaScript application.

Note that there are five selections to choose from, as described in Table 23.1.

TABLE 23.1 The JavaScript Project Choices

Project Type	Description
Blank App	This is the expected empty project. There are a handful of default files added for you, including a `default.html` file and a `default.js` file.
Grid App	The Grid App template will create a project containing three separate pages: a grid-based selection page containing groups of items, and then two details pages meant to display details of an item selected on the grid page.
Split App	The Split App template creates projects with two pages: a group selection page to display a list of grouped items, and then a details page that will show details of the selected item along with a list of other items.
Fixed Layout App	As its name implies, Fixed Layout Apps are those that do not dynamically scale for different views, screen sizes, or positions on the screen. In general, these types of apps should not be created because they violate one of the fundamental principles of Modern UI, but there could be unique circumstances where they are necessary.
Navigation App	The Navigation App template creates a project with a home page and basic forward/back navigation structures.

Figure 23.9 shows the default project structure for an HTML/JavaScript application.

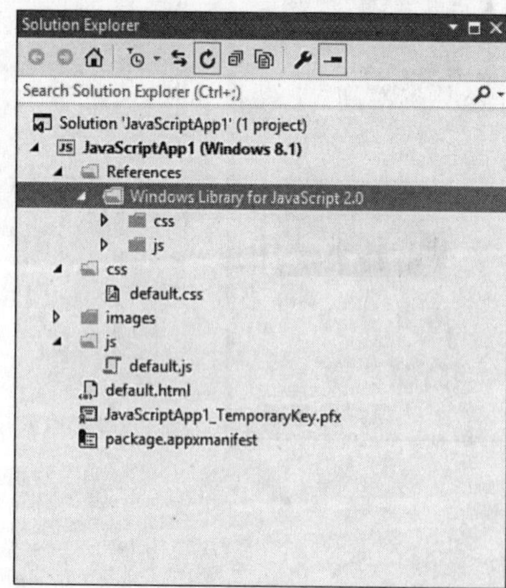

FIGURE 23.9 The project structure of an HTML/JavaScript application.

C#/Visual Basic/XAML

Developers more familiar with WPF or Silverlight will benefit from using the XAML with C# or Visual Basic project templates, with this choice:

- XAML styles are used for the presentation.
- C# or Visual Basic is used to code the behavior.
- XAML is used for the structure of the content within the UI.

To create a XAML application, click File, New Project, and then locate the C# or Visual Basic language selection to the left (see Figure 23.10); then select Windows, and then Windows 8.

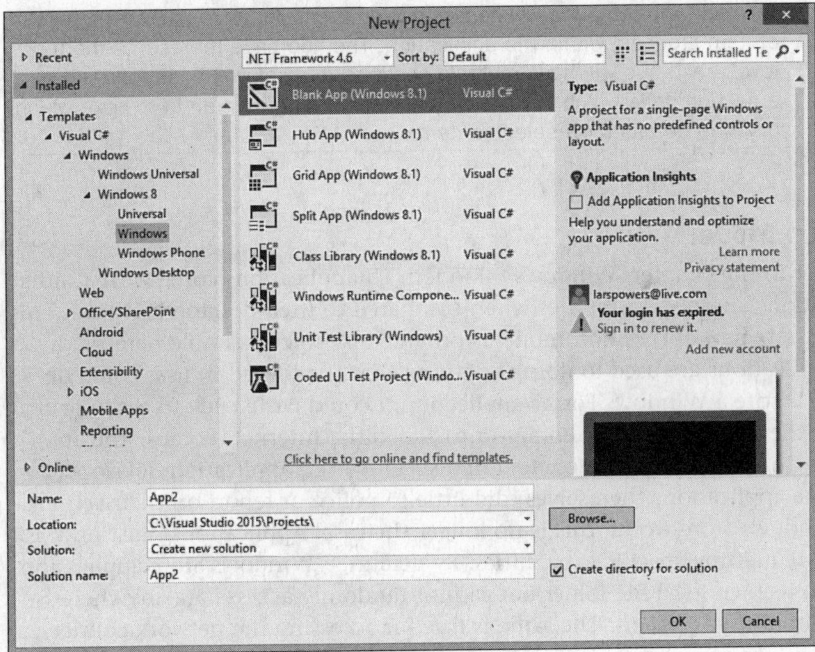

FIGURE 23.10 Creating a C# XAML application.

With C# XAML projects, note that there are four primary UI project selections to choose from, as described in Table 23.2.

TABLE 23.2 The XAML Project Choices

Project Type	Description
Blank App	An essentially empty project; represents a blank slate for development. There are a handful of default files added for you, including a `MainPage.xaml` file.
Grid App	The Grid App template will create a project containing three separate pages: a grid-based selection page containing groups of items, and then two details pages meant to display details of an item selected on the grid page.
Split App	The Split App template creates projects with two pages: a group selection page to display a list of grouped items, and then a details page that will show details of the selected item along with an item list of other items.
Hub App	The Hub App template will generate 3 different pages to allow for 3 levels of item grouping within the application. The hub page represents the top level; each hub will have multiple sections to display. This is followed by a section page which in turn contains items, and then an item page which displays details for a selected item.

The Application Model

As discussed earlier in the chapter, Windows 8 Modern UI applications come with a different set of expectations and responsibilities when compared to their desktop brethren. This means that an entirely new application model is provided. A quick example here: traditional desktop applications are used to doing anything that the logged-in user could do. In other words, if I write a Windows Forms application, I could write code to easily read a document from the user's document library or to access the Internet. Because the application was running under the security context of a specific user, application developers (and, therefore, the applications themselves) did little to police or report on their actions. In the WinRT/Windows Store world, this is no longer the case. Applications must now ask for permission by requesting specific capabilities. By default, a Windows Store application will have access to its own local file folder but cannot randomly access data anywhere else in the OS without user consent. The same is true for accessing the network connection, interacting with the camera or microphone, and so forth. These are referred to in the Windows 8/WinRT world as capabilities, and applications must be given explicit permission at install time to use the capabilities they are requesting but also, for some of them, the first time they are used.

Another difference involves the concept of application lifecycles. Desktop applications would generally be launched and, barring an application crash, would stay there, chewing up UI real estate, memory, and CPU cycles until the user explicitly closed them. Again, there is a big change with Modern UI applications. To provide an application model that would work effectively under adverse memory or processing conditions (as you might find on low-powered tablets, for instance), Windows Store applications are carefully managed by the OS. If an application isn't in the foreground (that is, has focus and is receiving user interaction), the application will be suspended.

A suspended application's threads are no longer running, although it is kept loaded into memory. Once suspended, the OS may elect to actually terminate the application at any point in time without notification. This frees the OS to do what it needs to do to optimize system resources and frees the user from ever having to worry about physically closing an application.

Implied in this lifecycle is the concept of implicit data storage. With desktop applications, data is typically stored when the user issues the Save command, and not before. But if the OS could suspend or terminate an application at any time, it would lead to severe data loss potential (or at the very least, an intrusive message to the user along the lines of "this app is about to be killed, do you want to save your data?"). So Modern UI applications must embrace the concept of implicit saves. That is, the application will take full responsibility for persisting whatever data has been entered; this includes things such as current page/navigation state.

Lifecycle States

Figure 23.11 shows the various lifecycle states that a WinRT Modern UI application can progress through. Note that although the OS could terminate an application at any time and for any reason (but mostly when memory is needed), the intent is to keep apps in suspended mode for as long as possible.

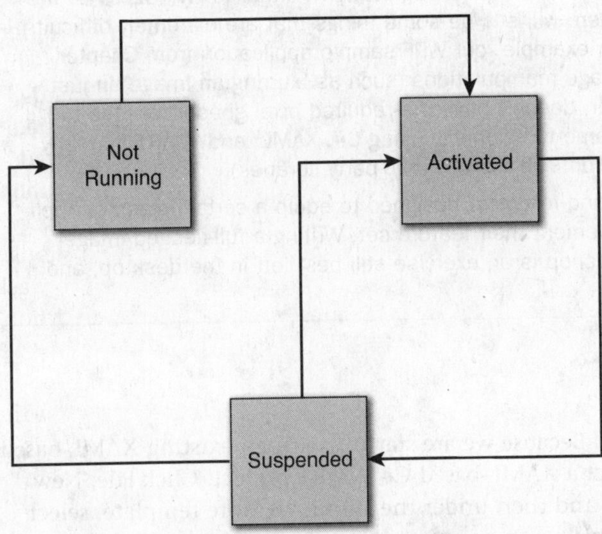

FIGURE 23.11 The application lifecycle.

Building a Windows Store Application

As with most concepts in the IDE, the best way to truly understand how the Visual Studio tools work is to go through the process of creating an application using those tools. Our inspiration will be the WPF image viewer application that we built in Chapter 21. But instead of just constructing the same image editor, we'll create an application that enables you to rate pictures. We'll try to reuse as many of the concepts and actual code as we can from our earlier WPF effort, but we'll have some unique constructs to deal with in the WinRT world.

As a base set of requirements, here are the capabilities we will try to deliver:

- Display a list of pictures from the user's `Pictures` library.
- Click a photo that will provide details about it.
- Edit the picture's rating value and save it back to disk.
- Make everything inherently usable on touch-enabled devices. (That is, the application will work as well for touch only as it will for keyboard and mouse setups.)

The application will make use of the `GridView` and the app bar and will use capabilities to tie into the `Pictures` library. With the end goal now in sight, let's get started.

NOTE

It is worthwhile to reinforce the fact that the Windows Runtime Library (WinRT), although powerful in many different ways, is not a complete replacement either for Win32 or for the .NET Framework. In other words, there will still be some things that are extremely difficult or impossible to do with WinRT. For example, our WPF sample application from Chapter 21 was able to do some simple image manipulations (such as blurring an image) in just a few lines of code. WinRT, however, doesn't have the required pixel shader classes to do this. Trying to implement that same functionality using C#, XAML, and WinRT is nearly impossible (or at best, prohibitively difficult without third-party libraries).

Keep in mind that WinRT was first and foremost designed to equip a certain class of applications with what they need to implement their feature set. Writing a full-fledged image-editing application like Adobe Photoshop is an exercise still best left in the desktop, and not Windows Store, world.

Selecting the Project Type

The language selection for us is easy. Because we are starting with an existing XAML-based C# WPF application, we should select a XAML-based C# WinRT project. Click File, New Project, Visual C# (as the language), and then under the Windows Store template, select the Blank App template. We'll call this `XamlImageViewer` (see Figure 23.12). Click OK to create the project structure.

As mentioned previously, the only way to install Windows Store applications is via the Windows Store itself. Each application published to the Windows Store is actually validated, verified, and then certified by Microsoft before it is made available. This has some ramifications. One is that you need a developer license to even deploy things to your own Windows 8 device as part of the normal code and debug process.

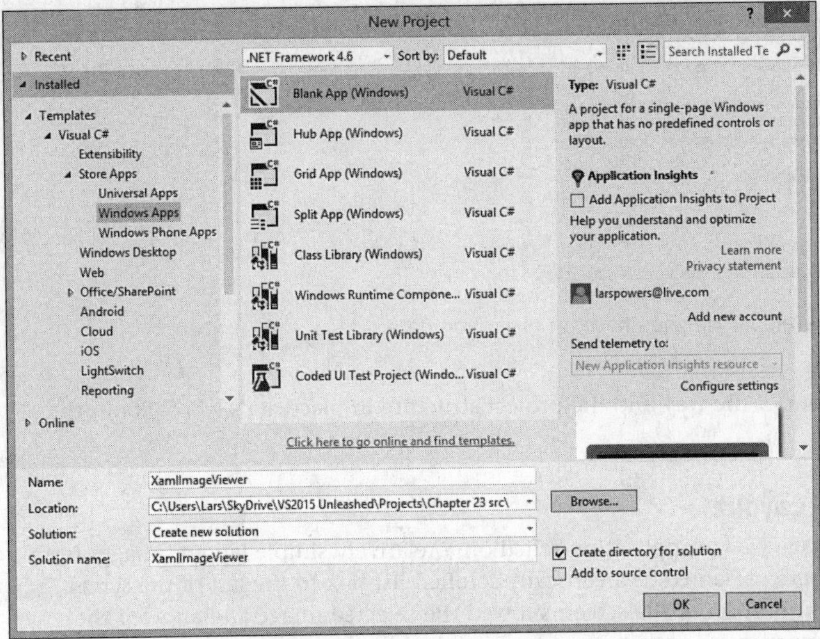

FIGURE 23.12 Creating the new project.

During the new project operation, if you don't have an existing and valid developer license, you are prompted to get one (see Figure 23.13). The process itself is automated; you merely need to click through a series of dialogs before your project will be created. These culminate in a notification dialog (see Figure 23.14) that indicates if your request for a license was successful or not and what the expiration date is for that license.

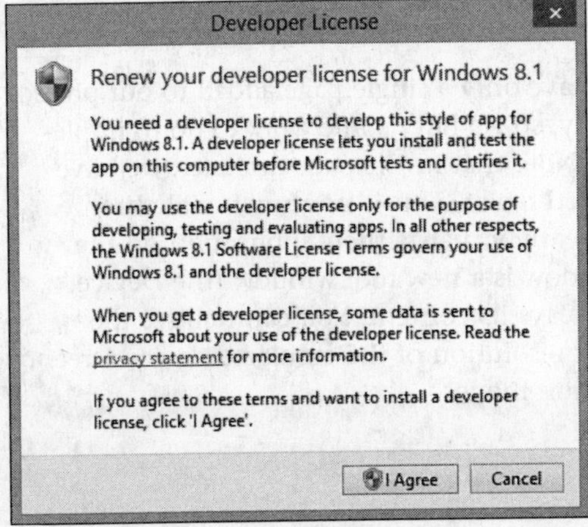

FIGURE 23.13 Obtaining a developer license.

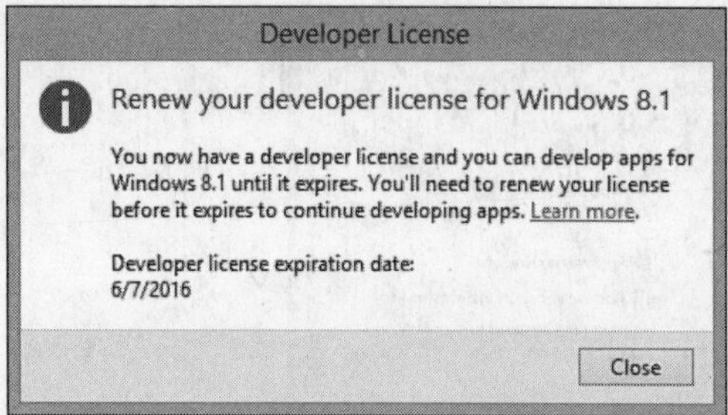

FIGURE 23.14 Developer licenses have an expiration date.

With the license out of the way and the project structure in place, let's worry about the design and layout.

Designing the Layout

Our prior WPF image viewer application relied on a relatively simple layout. Images from a selected folder were presented in a vertically scrolled list box to the left of the screen, and the right, main portion of the screen showed the selected image and allowed the user to alter the image in four basic ways: you could make the image grayscale, you could apply a blur effect to the image, you could rotate the image, and you could flip the image vertically.

Instead of using a single-page approach as we did with the original application, we now use two pages: a grid page that shows all the available images in the targeted folder (grouped by their rating value), and an edit/details page that shows the image selected from the grid and allows us to apply a new rating.

Figure 23.15 shows a sketch of the new application starting page, and Figure 23.16 shows the editing page.

Implementing the Grid Page UI

Because we chose the Blank App template, we have only a single page added to our project at this stage: `MainPage.xaml`. It's currently empty, so we have some work to do to implement our initial grid display (see Figure 23.17). Note that in the page designer, we have a graphical representation of a landscape-oriented tablet. This is nonfunctional chrome added to the window to enable developers to clearly visualize their application on the intended device. To the left of the designer window is a new tool window (the Device window) that changes the way the designer displays its content. You can remove the device border chrome, change the screen size or resolution of the emulated device screen, and even put the display into different orientation modes.

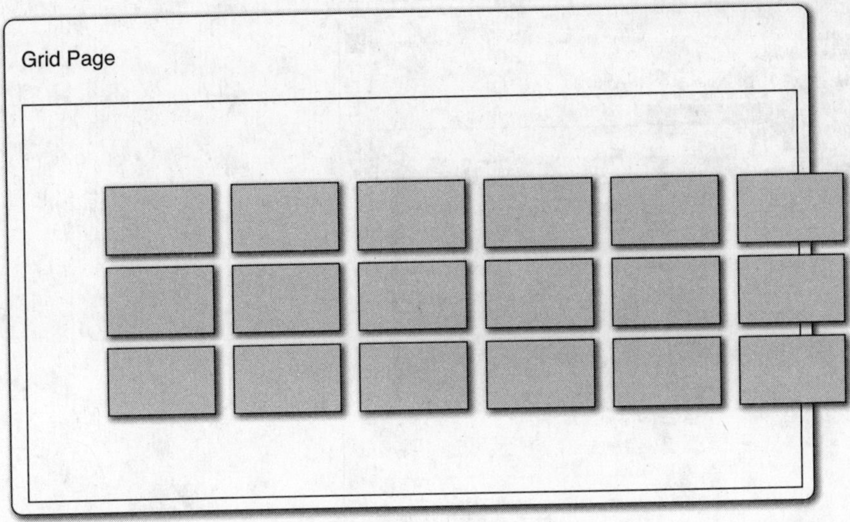

FIGURE 23.15 The grid of images.

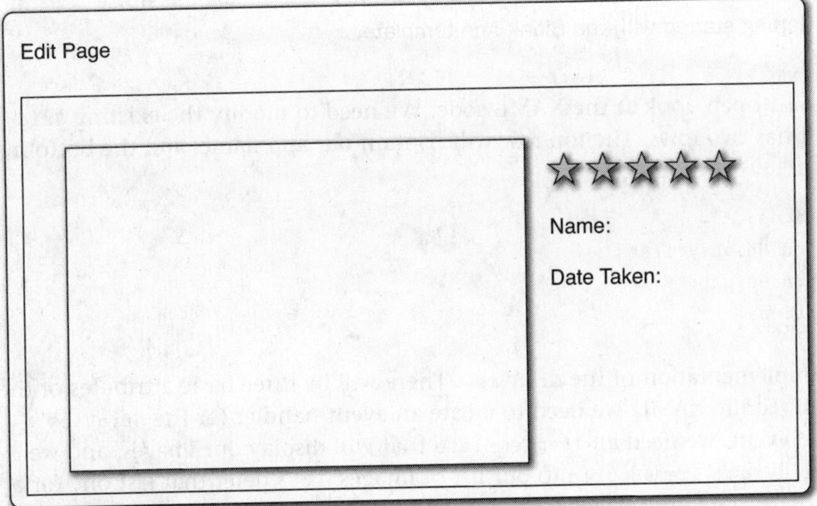

FIGURE 23.16 The image detail page.

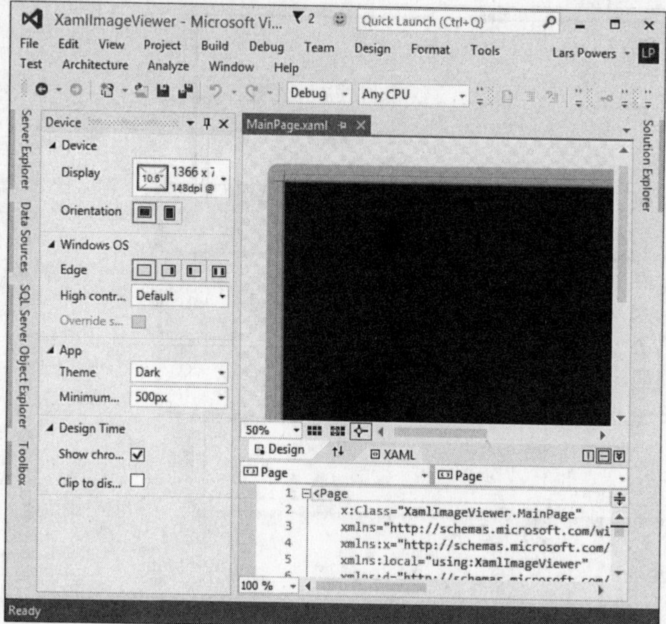

FIGURE 23.17 Getting started with the Blank App template.

With `MainPage.xaml` open, look at the XAML code. We need to modify the existing `Grid` element so that it has two rows. The top row will contain our app name, and the bottom will contain the `GridView` of images.

```
<Grid.RowDefinitions>
    <RowDefinition Height="140" />
    <RowDefinition Height="*" />
</Grid.RowDefinitions>
```

Next comes the implementation of the `GridView`. There will be three basic attributes of the `GridView` that will require XAML: we need to create an event handler for the `GridView`'s `SelectionChanged` event, we need an `ItemTemplate` that will display our images, and we need to set the `GridView`'s `ItemsSource` to our list of images. Let's defer that last one for a bit and instead concentrate on the event handler and the item template.

Create a `GridView` element inside the existing `Grid` and name it `ImagesGridView`; now let Visual Studio do the work for you on the event handler side by adding the `SelectionChanged` event and selecting New Event Handler (see Figure 23.18). Visual Studio will stub out the code for us in the code-behind file.

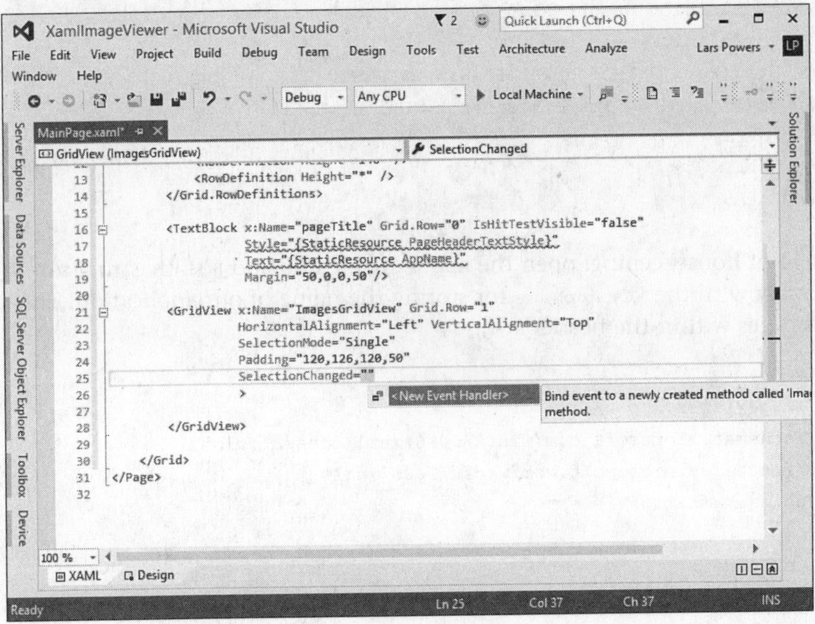

FIGURE 23.18 Creating the `SelectionChanged` event handler.

Also within the `GridView` element, we need to establish the link to our data model. Set the `ItemsSource` property to bind to an object called `Images`. (This object doesn't exist yet, but we will get around to creating it in a short while.)

```
ItemsSource="{Binding Images}"
```

Your `GridView` declaration should now look like this:

```
<GridView x:Name="ImagesGridView" Grid.Row="1"
    HorizontalAlignment="Left" VerticalAlignment="Top"
    SelectionMode="Single"
    Padding="120,126,120,50"
    SelectionChanged="ImagesGridView_SelectionChanged"
    ItemsSource="{Binding Images}"
    />
```

An item template is now needed. Templates provide the structure around the way data is displayed within the `GridView`. In our case, we are simply showing an image, and XAML has an `Image` element designed to do just that. To embed an `Image` element within the `GridView`, the syntax looks like this:

```
<GridView.ItemTemplate>
    <DataTemplate>
        <Grid HorizontalAlignment="Stretch">
            <Grid.RowDefinitions>
```

```
                <RowDefinition Height="175"/>
            </Grid.RowDefinitions>
            <Image Grid.Row="0" Height="175" Width="275"
                Source="{Binding Image}" Stretch="UniformToFill"/>
        </Grid>
    </DataTemplate>
</GridView.ItemTemplate>
```

One last minor piece of housekeeping: open the `App.xaml` file and add a static string to the resource dictionary with the key `AppName` for storing the name of our application. This will be used across pages within the header area.

```
<Application
    x:Class="XamlImageViewer.App"
    xmlns="http://schemas.microsoft.com/winfx/2006/xaml/presentation"
    xmlns:x="http://schemas.microsoft.com/winfx/2006/xaml"
    xmlns:local="using:XamlImageViewer">

    <Application.Resources>
        <ResourceDictionary>
            <ResourceDictionary.MergedDictionaries>

                <!--
                    Styles that define common aspects of the platform look
                    and feel.
                    Required by Visual Studio project and item templates
                -->
                <ResourceDictionary Source="Common/StandardStyles.xaml"/>
            </ResourceDictionary.MergedDictionaries>

            <x:String x:Key="AppName">Xaml Image Viewer</x:String>
        </ResourceDictionary>
    </Application.Resources>
</Application>
```

We will reference the application name within the header area of the page (in other words, the top row of our outermost `Grid`) by using a simple `TextBlock` bound to that static string.

```
<TextBlock x:Name="pageTitle" Grid.Row="0"
    IsHitTestVisible="false"
    Style="{StaticResource PageHeaderTextStyle}"
    Text="{StaticResource AppName}"
    Margin="50,0,0,50"
    />
```

And with that, the structure of our main page's UI is in place.

Creating the Data Model

With our base UI in place, we turn our attention to the classes that will hold our image information. We need two of them: one to store the list of images (obtained from the `Pictures` library) and a second to wrap each image file.

Add a new class to the project and call it `ImageFile`. To this class, add three properties: a `string` property called `FileName`, an `ImageSource` property called `Image`, and an `integer` property called `Rating`. All of these should be backed by private fields (called `_fileName`, `_image`, and `_rating`, respectively) and should implement getters and setters.

```
string _fileName;
private ImageSource _image = null;
private int _rating = 0;

public string FileName
{
    get { return _fileName; }
    set {_fileName = value; }
}

public int Rating
{
    get { return _rating; }
    set {_rating = value; }
}

public ImageSource Image
{
    get { return this._image; }
    set { this._image = value; }
}
```

Because this object will be contained within a collection and we will want to know if properties change so that they can be signaled back to the parent collection, we will use the `INotifyPropertyChanged` pattern here.

First inherit the `ImageFile` class from `INotifyPropertyChanged`. Then declare an event handler called `PropertyChanged`.

```
public event PropertyChangedEventHandler PropertyChanged;
```

Next, implement an `OnPropertyChanged` routine.

```
private void OnPropertyChanged(string propertyName)
{
    if (PropertyChanged != null)
        PropertyChanged(this, new PropertyChangedEventArgs(propertyName));
}
```

In each of the property sets, include a call to `OnPropertyChanged`, passing in the name of the property.

```
public string FileName
{
    get { return _fileName; }
    set { _fileName = value; OnPropertyChanged("FileName"); }
}

public int Rating
{
    get { return _rating; }
    set {_rating = value; OnPropertyChanged("Rating"); }
}

public ImageSource Image
{
    get { return this._image; }
    set { this._image = value; OnPropertyChanged("Image"); }
}
```

The actual bitmap that is the image file is assigned via the `Image` property. Let's write a `SetImage` routine that will take in the file, create a bitmap object from that file, and then assign it to our `Image` property.

```
public async void SetImage(StorageFile file)
{
    IRandomAccessStream fileStream =
        await file.OpenAsync(Windows.Storage.FileAccessMode.Read);
    BitmapImage bitmap = new BitmapImage();
    bitmap.SetSource(fileStream);
    Image = bitmap;
}
```

Before moving on, there is one last piece of functionality to add: a method that will examine the file's `Rating` property, transform it from its `0-100` value into a `0-5` value, and then assign that to our `ImageFile`'s `Rating` property. `Image` properties are held in the WinRT class `ImageProperties`, which we populate directly from the `StorageFile` instance via its `GetImagePropertiesAsync` method.

```
public async void SetRating(StorageFile file)
{
    //Get the image properties for the file.
    ImageProperties imageProps =
        await file.Properties.GetImagePropertiesAsync();
```

```
    //We are looking for the Rating property.
    uint rating = imageProps.Rating;

    //Rating is a number 0-100.
    //We need to factor this down to a 0-5 rating.

    //0 == 0
    //1-24 = 1
    //25-49 = 2
    //50-74 = 3
    //75-98 = 4
    //99 = 5
    if (rating == 0)
    {
        Rating = 0;
    }
    else if (rating > 98)
    {
        Rating = 5;
    }
    else if (rating >= 75)
    {
        Rating = 4;
    }
    else if (rating >= 50)
    {
        Rating = 3;
    }
    else if (rating >= 25)
    {
        Rating = 2;
    }
    else
    {
        Rating = 1;
    }

}
```

NOTE

We are making liberal use of the new `async` and `await` C# keywords in our code to reinforce app responsiveness via async processing. We touch on these keywords a bit in Chapter 3, "The .NET Languages," but it will be well worth your while to understand these patterns in detail to support your WinRT development efforts. Here is the best place to start: http://msdn.microsoft.com/en-us/library/hh191443(v=VS.140).aspx.

Creating the Collection Class

Now on to the class that will hold our collection of images. Add a new class to the project, called `ImageList`. This class is simple in structure. It will hold an internal `ObservableCollection` of type `ImageFile` and expose this collection via a property called `Images`. Just as with the `ImageFile` class, we want to implement the `INotifyPropertyChanged` pattern here.

```
private ObservableCollection<ImageFile> _imageList =
    new ObservableCollection<ImageFile>();

public ObservableCollection<ImageFile> Images
{
    get { return _imageList; }
    set
    {
        _imageList = value;
        OnPropertyChanged("ImageList");
    }
}
```

We also need a method to actually load the collection with `ImageFile` instances. File and folder access in WinRT is accomplished via the `StorageFile` and `StorageFolder` classes. There is also a handy helper class, `KnownFolders`, that can be used to get a reference to specific libraries such as the `Music` library or the `Pictures` library. We will get a reference to the `Pictures` library and then iterate through its collection of `StorageFile` instances. For each, we create a new `ImageFile` instance and populate its properties accordingly.

```
public async void LoadImages()
{
    //Folder and file objects
    StorageFolder folder;
    ImageFile imageFile;
    IReadOnlyList<IStorageFile> files;

    //Get reference to Pictures library.
    folder = KnownFolders.PicturesLibrary;

    //Get the files within the Pictures library.
    files = (IReadOnlyList<IStorageFile>)await folder.GetFilesAsync();

    //Iterate each file and create a new ImageFile to wrap it.
    foreach (StorageFile file in files)
    {
        imageFile = new ImageFile();
        var stream = await file.OpenAsync(FileAccessMode.Read);
```

```
        imageFile.FileName = file.Name;
        imageFile.SetImage(file);
        imageFile.SetRating(file);
        this.Images.Add(imageFile);
    }
}
```

Binding the Data

We should have a fully functioning set of data objects at this stage. But we have to bind those images to our UI. First create an instance of our data model within the `MainPage.xaml.cs` file. Open the code-behind and add a private field to the page class for our `ImageList` object.

```
private ImageList _imageList;
```

In the page constructor, we need to set the data context for our page to the `ImageList` and make the call to load the image list.

```
public MainPage()
{
    this._imageList = new ImageList();
    this.DataContext = this._imageList;
    this.InitializeComponent();
}
```

At this stage, our data model should be functionally complete. However, if you try to run the application now, you will get the error message shown in Figure 23.19.

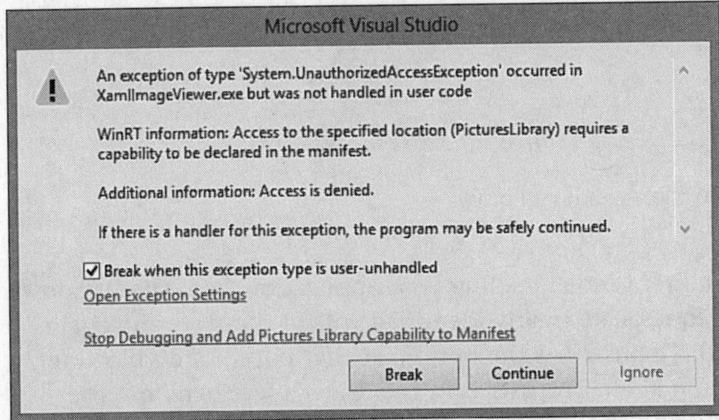

FIGURE 23.19 An unauthorized access exception.

If you recall from our earlier discussion around the concept of capabilities, Windows Store applications do not, by default, have permission to access file directories. We need to request that permission. And that is done via *capabilities*.

Requesting Capabilities

Capabilities, put simply, are access categories that an application must first be granted permission to. This includes file system access, network access, and access to hardware devices such as cameras and microphones. Capabilities are requested via the applications package `manifest` file. Find this file in Solution Explorer, and double-click it to open the manifest editor (see Figure 23.20). For our application to work, we need to place a check mark next to the Pictures Library entry on the Capabilities tab.

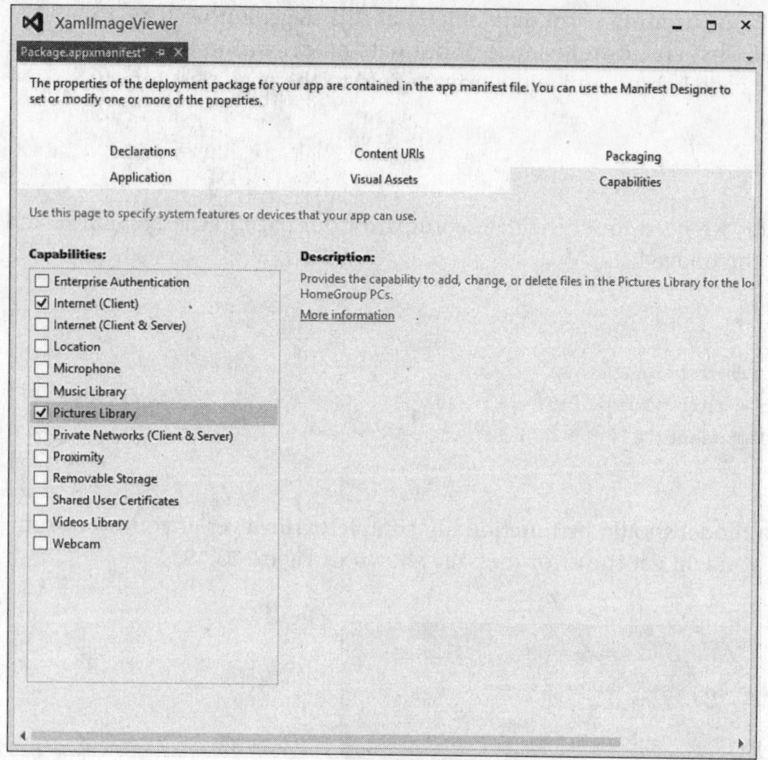

FIGURE 23.20 Gaining access to the `Pictures` library.

In a normal situation in which a user is downloading your application from the Windows Store, these special permission requests are clearly identified within the store and again when the application is installed. The user has the option, at that point, of disallowing the access or not installing the app at all. The user is in the driver's seat here, not the application. When you are debugging applications under Visual Studio, the access is automatically granted at runtime provided you have checked the appropriate box and saved the manifest file.

With that done, run the application. Assuming you have images in the root of your `Pictures` library, the application should look like Figure 23.21.

FIGURE 23.21 The main page with images loaded.

Now we can focus on the second page, which will allow us to view and change the rating for the selected image.

Implementing the Image Editor Page

Right-click the project in the Solution Explorer window and select Add, New Item. From the Templates list, we want to add an Items Detail page, as shown in Figure 23.22. Name the page `ImagePage`.

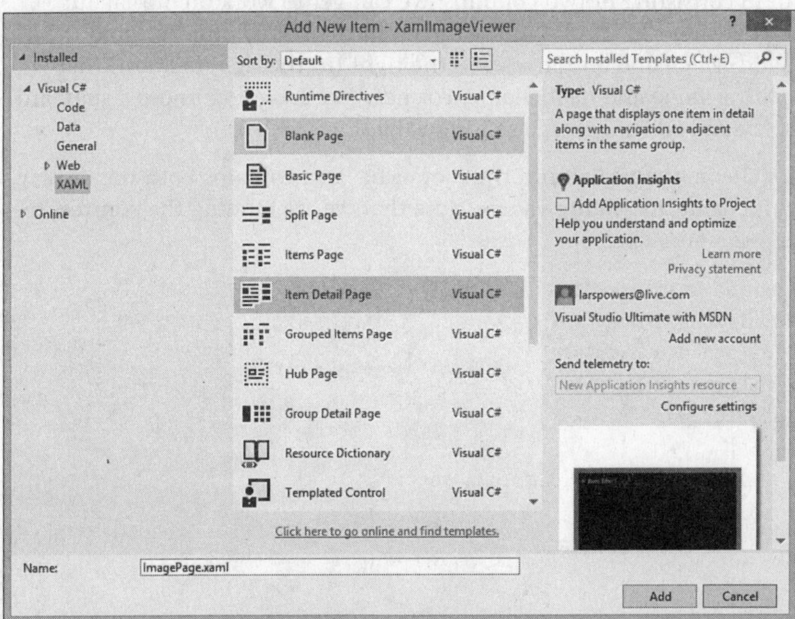

FIGURE 23.22 Adding the Image Detail page.

When you add this page to your project, you will see a warning dialog (see Figure 23.23). The template for this page is preplumbed to do a variety of things for you, the developer. To do those things, it relies on a bunch of standard helper classes and XAML constructs. These are normally placed within the `Common` folder of your project and in the project root. Because we haven't added these yet (remember, we started with a basic blank project), Visual Studio has detected that they are missing and offers to add them for you. Click Yes.

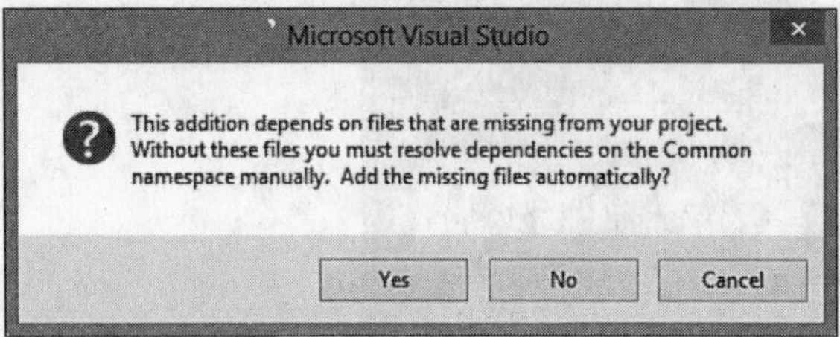

FIGURE 23.23 Automatically adding common dependencies.

The first thing we do in this page is fix up the app name header (find the `TextBlock` with the name `pageTitle` and bind its `Text` to `"{StaticResource AppName}"` just as we did on `MainPage`). Then we clear out everything sitting within the outermost `Grid` element except for the `VisualStateManager` markup you will see; we won't be using any of those default UI elements, although we will keep some of the code structure that was created as part of the items detail template.

So, with an empty `Grid` consisting of two columns, we can get to work on our layout. We want a large `Image` element to the left of the screen in the left column (to hold the selected image from `MainPage`) and a form area to the right (in the right column) that will display the image's rating value and its filename. For now, we are going to use a standard slider control to display and edit the image's rating value.

Here is the XAML for the image area within the root `Grid`. This contains both the display of the image and its filename and rating values. Note that we are binding the controls to properties off of our `ImageFile` class.

```
<Grid x:Name="ImageGrid" Grid.Row="1">
    <Grid.ColumnDefinitions>
        <ColumnDefinition Width=".65*" />
        <ColumnDefinition Width=".35*" />
    </Grid.ColumnDefinitions>

    <Image x:Name="SelectedImage" Grid.Column="0"
           Margin="50,0,25,25"
           Source="{Binding Image}"/>

    <Grid Grid.Column="1">
```

```
        <Grid.ColumnDefinitions>
            <ColumnDefinition Width="100" />
            <ColumnDefinition Width="*"/>
        </Grid.ColumnDefinitions>
        <Grid.RowDefinitions>
            <RowDefinition Height="auto" />
            <RowDefinition Height="auto" />

        </Grid.RowDefinitions>

        <!--Image rating and filename display -->
        <Slider Grid.Row="0" Grid.Column="1" Grid.ColumnSpan="2"
                x:Name= "RatingSlider"
                Style="{StaticResource RatingSliderStyle}"
                TickPlacement="Inline" TickFrequency="1" Minimum="0"
                Maximum="5"
                HorizontalAlignment="Left" Orientation="Horizontal"
                Width="300"
                Margin="15,0,0,0"
                Value="{Binding Rating}"
                SnapsTo="Ticks"/>

        <TextBlock Grid.Column="0" Grid.Row="1" Margin="5,5,0,5"
                   Style="{StaticResource BasicTextStyle}"
                   HorizontalAlignment="Left" VerticalAlignment="Center"
                   Height="20">File name:</TextBlock>

        <TextBlock Grid.Column="1" Grid.Row="1" x:Name="FileNameTextBlock"
                   Style="{StaticResource BasicTextStyle}" Margin="5,5,0,5"
                   HorizontalAlignment="Left" Text="{Binding FileName}"
                   Width="auto"/>

    </Grid>
</Grid>
```

This page isn't done yet. We have two major areas to work on: passing the selected image into the page, and then saving the rating information back to the image file. Let's tackle these in that order.

Page Navigation and Passing State

If you examine the code in `ImagePage.xaml.cs`, you will notice a routine called `LoadState`. This was stubbed out for us as part of this page's template. This routine is called when the page is navigated to and provides something crucial: a navigation parameter that enables us to pass objects around between pages. To make this work, we have to take a quick trip back to `MainPage.xaml.cs` and write some code in our `SelectionChanged` event handler to navigate to the details page and pass along the `ImageFile` object we need.

```
private void ImagesGridView_SelectionChanged(object sender,
    SelectionChangedEventArgs e)
{
    //Navigate to the next page, passing the selected image along.

    //Cast selected item to ImageFile.
    ImageFile image = (ImageFile)ImagesGridView.SelectedItem;
    this.Frame.Navigate(typeof(ImagePage), image);
}
```

With that code in place, we are ready to fill out the `LoadState` routine in `ImagePage.xaml.cs`. Add a private field and property in the page to hold the passed-in `ImageFile`.

```
private ImageFile _imageFile;

public ImageFile ImageFileInstance
{
    get { return _imageFile; }
    set { _imageFile = value; }
}
```

Now assign `ImageFileInstance` within the `LoadState` routine. Because we have bound our UI controls to the `ImageFile` properties, we also need to update our page's data context to point to the `ImageFileInstance` property.

```
protected override void LoadState(Object navigationParameter,
     Dictionary<String, Object> pageState)
{
    ImageFileInstance = navigationParameter as ImageFile;
    this.DataContext = ImageFileInstance;
}
```

As a quick check, let's run the app. With the navigation state passing and data binding working, we have a page that does everything but save rating information back to the file (see Figure 23.24).

Creating an App Bar

Even though we have discussed the fact that Windows Store applications will generally save data implicitly and not explicitly, in this case we want our users to actively tell the application that they want a changed rating value to be saved back to the file. So we start by implementing a simple app bar with a single Save button to execute that process.

App bars can appear at either the top of the page or the bottom. The convention is that navigation-related commands go on top and application commands go on the bottom. Our app bar with its solitary Save button will live at the bottom.

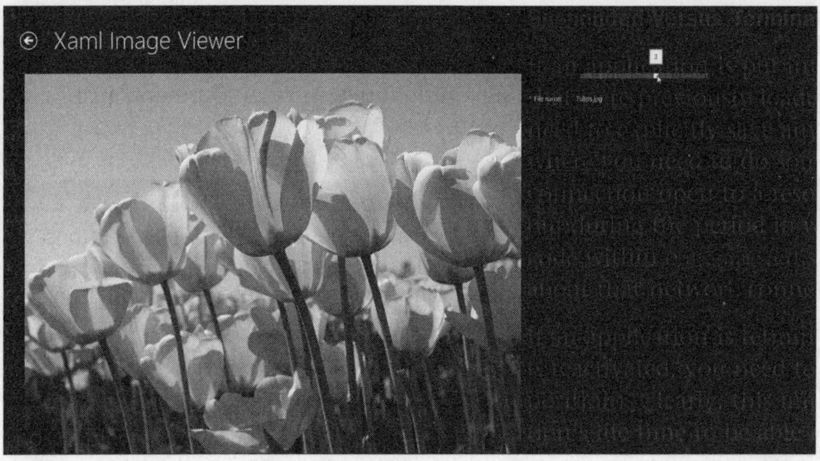

FIGURE 23.24 The image detail page.

In the ImagePage.xaml, create a Page.BottomAppBar element outside the outermost layout grid but within the page itself. Within that element, we want to nest an actual AppBar element. AppBar objects are typically structured using a simple StackPanel containing your app bar buttons. Remember that our UI should work well with touch devices, including tablets. For that reason, we want to actually avoid centering our button in the middle of the bar. With a tablet device, a user will want to be able to press the button using only the thumbs of the hands gripping the tablet. And that means that buttons should be placed to the far right or far left of the app bar. We'll go to the right with ours.

```
<Page.BottomAppBar>
    <AppBar x:Name="BottomAppBar1" Padding="10,0,10,0"
        AutomationProperties.Name="Bottom App Bar">
        <Grid>
            <StackPanel x:Name="AppBarStackPanel"
                Orientation="Horizontal"
                Grid.Column="0" HorizontalAlignment="Right">
                <Button x:Name="SaveButton"
                    Style="{StaticResource SaveAppBarButtonStyle}"
                    Tag="Edit"
                    Click="SaveButton_Click"/>
            </StackPanel>
        </Grid>
    </AppBar>
</Page.BottomAppBar>
```

If you carefully examine the Button that we have defined, you will notice a style reference to SaveAppBarButtonStyle. With WinRT XAML projects, a StandardStyles.xaml resource dictionary is included for you by default. And within that XAML file are many, many style resources for a wide spectrum of app bar buttons for commands ranging from save to search to rename to volume. They are all commented out to start; simply pick the ones you need, copy them into your page, or uncomment them.

That's all the XAML we need. The app bar is now fully functioning. We are now just missing the save routine.

TIP

The app bar button styles use a unique approach to their embedded icons. These buttons are intrinsically aware of the Segoe UI Symbol character set. By setting their `Content` property to an offset value, WinRT will automatically grab the appropriate glyph/icon from that character set and use it. Because that font has hundreds of basic Metro-style icons, it is a perfect match and is simple to implement. The best way for you to find icons this way is to fire up the `charmap.exe` program on Windows 8. Select Segoe UI Symbol in the top drop-down, and then click the icon you want. Its offset will display in the status bar. For instance, a "star" icon is located at offset E113. Therefore, we would have a content tag set to ``.

We'll call the save routine from the `SaveButton_Click` event; the routine itself will retrieve the file property information, change the `Rating` property to whatever the current value of the rating slider is, and then save the properties back out using the `SavePropertiesAsync()` method call.

```
private void SaveButton_Click(object sender, RoutedEventArgs e)
{
    SaveRating();
}

private async void SaveRating()
{
    var file =
        await KnownFolders.PicturesLibrary.GetFileAsync(_imageFile.FileName);

    var fileProperties = await file.Properties.GetImagePropertiesAsync();

    fileProperties.Rating = (uint)this.RatingSlider.Value;

    await fileProperties.SavePropertiesAsync();
}
```

Reacting to Lifecycle Events

We have already discussed the application model and its attendant lifecycle. Refer to Figure 23.11. We have three possible application states:

- Activated
- Suspended
- Not Running

At the application level, you are notified of app changes via a series of events that correspond to the arrows you see in Figure 23.11. Handling these events and reacting appropriately means you need to write some event handlers; your project's `App` class is your vehicle for hooking these events. In fact, the standard `App.xaml.cs` file created for you already contains code to wire up the `Suspending` event.

```
public App()
{
    this.InitializeComponent();
    this.Suspending += OnSuspending;
}

private void OnSuspending(object sender, SuspendingEventArgs e)
{
    var deferral = e.SuspendingOperation.GetDeferral();
    //TODO: Save application state and stop any background activity
    deferral.Complete();
}
```

The use of the `deferral` object may seem confusing at first, but its job is fairly simple. While running your program, when the end of the `OnSuspending` routine is reached, the runtime will assume that you have taken care of everything that needs to be taken care of and will promptly suspend the application. But if your application has followed good practice, your state saving activity will be executed asynchronously. And that means that the `OnSuspending` routine could conclude before your async activity has actually completed.

The `SuspendingDeferral` object, which is returned from the call shown above to `e.SuspendingOperation.GetDeferral`, is used to signal to Windows that you want to explicitly tell the runtime when you are done with your state housekeeping. There is a caveat here: Windows will suspend your application regardless of your deferral object if you take longer than approximately 5 seconds to complete your work. So in essence, having the deferral object created means "don't suspend the application until I tell you to, or until my 5 seconds are up, whichever comes first."

The flip side of the `Suspending` event, when an application is being resumed, is the `Resuming` event, which looks similar. (You need to add this yourself; it isn't included automatically.)

```
this.Resuming += OnResuming;
```

Finally, the `OnLaunched` routine is called when your application is launched. This could be by a user clicking/tapping the app tile, or it could be because a user is going back to your app after it has been suspended and then terminated.

```
protected override void OnLaunched(LaunchActivatedEventArgs args)
{
    Frame rootFrame = Window.Current.Content as Frame;
```

```
    //Do not repeat app initialization when the Window already has content,
    //just ensure that the window is active.
    if (rootFrame == null)
    {
        //Create a frame to act as the navigation context and
        //navigate to the first page
        rootFrame = new Frame();

        if (args.PreviousExecutionState == ApplicationExecutionState.Terminated)
        {
            //TODO: Load state from previously suspended application.
        }

        //Place the frame in the current window.
        Window.Current.Content = rootFrame;
    }

    if (rootFrame.Content == null)
    {
        //When the navigation stack isn't restored navigate to the first page,
        //configuring the new page by passing required information as a
        //navigation parameter.
        if (!rootFrame.Navigate(typeof(MainPage), args.Arguments))
        {
            throw new Exception("Failed to create initial page");
        }
    }
    //Ensure the current window is active.
    Window.Current.Activate();
}
```

Storing State

Once your application is aware of these events, you can react to them appropriately. There is no stock answer here in terms of how you should read and write your applications state. But the simple high-level pattern is this: when your application is suspending, do a final save of its state, and when it is restarted after termination, restore the state. One attractive option is the use of local storage. Each application has default permissions to access the local storage area. (In other words, it isn't a capability that needs to be explicitly declared.) For our image viewing app, if we wanted to store the page name of the current page, along with the filename of any currently loaded image, we could do that quite easily by a) creating a general object to store those items and b) serializing that object into local storage.

Saving into the application storage area can be accomplished via the familiar `StorageFile` class and serializer (commonly, `DataContractSerializer`). A great way to bootstrap your application state storage development is to take a look at a helper class delivered by Microsoft, called `SuspensionManager`. This class maintains a `Dictionary` object that in turn contains the objects making up your application's state. If you add your state information to its dictionary, you can then call a `SaveAsync` method on the class, which will take care of serializing everything to disk:

```
//Save the current session state.
static async public Task SaveAsync()
{
    //Get the output stream for the SessionState file.
    StorageFile file = await
        ApplicationData.Current.LocalFolder.CreateFileAsync(filename,
        CreationCollisionOption.ReplaceExisting);

    using (StorageStreamTransaction transaction = await
        file.OpenTransactedWriteAsync())
    {
        //Serialize the session state.
        DataContractSerializer serializer = new
            DataContractSerializer(typeof(Dictionary<string, object>),
               knownTypes_);

        serializer.WriteObject(transaction.Stream.AsStreamForWrite(),
            sessionState_);

        await transaction.CommitAsync();
    }
}
```

Similarly, you can rehydrate your state information via its `RestoreAsync` method.

```
//Restore the saved session state.
static async public Task RestoreAsync()
{
    //Get the input stream for the SessionState file.
    try
    {
        StorageFile file = await
           ApplicationData.Current.LocalFolder.GetFileAsync(filename);
```

```
        if (file == null) return;

        using (IInputStream inStream = await file.OpenSequentialReadAsync())
        {
            //Deserialize the session state.
            DataContractSerializer serializer = new
               DataContractSerializer(typeof(Dictionary<string, object>),
                  knownTypes_);

            sessionState_ = (Dictionary<string,
               object>)serializer.ReadObject(inStream.AsStreamForRead());
        }
    }
    catch (Exception)
    {
        //Restoring state is best-effort. If it fails, the app will
        //just come up with a new session.
    }
}
```

As mentioned previously in this chapter, remember that if you are dealing with anything more than a moderate amount of data in your application, you should consider saving that data regardless of whether any of the lifecycle events have been triggered. You don't want to get into a scenario in which the time it takes to save your data is longer than the allotted window for either application startup or suspension. In the case of the former, Windows will assume that the app is hung and will kill it. And in the case of the latter, you might not get all your data committed before the application process disappears. If the application is then subsequently terminated, you have now permanently lost data.

Publishing to the Windows Store

When your application is complete and you want to share it with the rest of the world (for profit or not), it is time to publish it into the Windows Store. That means you will need a developer's account. The process itself is straightforward. Using your Microsoft Account, you register for access to the store as a developer. After your registration has been approved, you can reserve your application's name, establish a price, and upload your packaged application into the store.

Once again, Visual Studio makes this process seamless with development. From within the IDE, you can select Store under the Project menu and execute all the activities needed to go from no account to published application (see Figure 23.25).

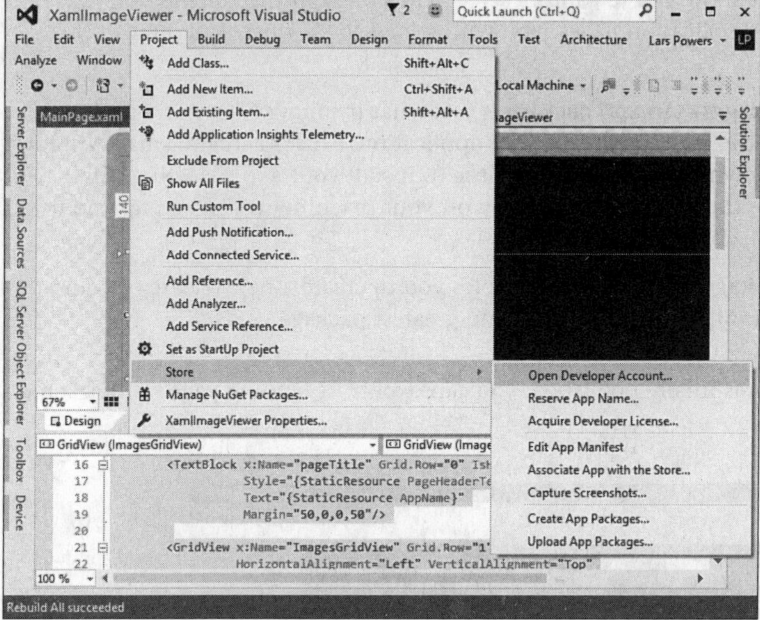

FIGURE 23.25 Using the Store menu.

There are several actions available to us from the Store menu:

- **Open Developer Account**—To publish into the Windows Store, you'll need a developer account to get you started.
- **Reserve App Name**—All applications within the Windows Store are required to have a unique name. Because the app name may be featured prominently in various pieces of your UI, it is wise to settle on and reserve a name before you even begin development. (You can always change things down the road.)
- **Acquire Developer License**—As you build out your application, you will need to run that application within one or more development environments to construct and test your code. And that requires a developer license for each machine that you want to deploy your "in progress" code to.
- **Edit App Manifest**—This opens the package manifest window (refer to Figure 23.20).
- **Associate App with the Store**—This launches a wizard that will automatically download details from your store account (including your publisher ID, publisher name, and so on) and then include those details into your local app manifest file.
- **Capture Screenshots**—Applications should have screenshots included in their Window Store entries to enable potential users/purchasers to see what the app is like before downloading. Selecting this option will run the current project within

the emulator and allow you to capture screenshots on your machine as you navigate through the application pages. You will upload them when you publish the application.

- **Create App Packages**—An app package is just what it sounds like: it is a package that contains all the components of your application. This is actually what Windows Store users will download when they choose to install your app. Selecting this option will create the appropriate package on your machine so you can upload it to the store later.
- **Upload App Packages**—This option enables you to create a new release of your app into the Windows Store with the latest and greatest package.

When your application is finally published, you can expect its landing page to look something like Figure 23.26.

FIGURE 23.26 The Kindle app in the Windows Store.

As a final word, please visit this book's download site (http://informit.com/title/9780672337369 or just search for the book title on InformIt.com) to get the complete source code for the XAML image viewer application. The final application adds some fit and finish to the walk-through presented here, including an app tile and a restyled rating slider control. Listings 23.1 and 23.2 provide the XAML and C# code for the MainWindow page, and Listings 23.3 and 23.4 provide the XAML and C# code for the ImageDetails page.

LISTING 23.1 The Image Viewer XAML Code: MainPage.xaml

```
<Page
    x:Class="XamlImageViewer.MainPage"
    xmlns="http://schemas.microsoft.com/winfx/2006/xaml/presentation"
    xmlns:x="http://schemas.microsoft.com/winfx/2006/xaml"
    xmlns:local="using:XamlImageViewer"
    xmlns:d="http://schemas.microsoft.com/expression/blend/2008"
    xmlns:mc="http://schemas.openxmlformats.org/markup-compatibility/2006"
    mc:Ignorable="d">

    <Grid Background="{StaticResource ApplicationPageBackgroundThemeBrush}">
        <Grid.RowDefinitions>
            <RowDefinition Height="140" />
            <RowDefinition Height="*" />
        </Grid.RowDefinitions>

        <TextBlock x:Name="pageTitle" Grid.Row="0" IsHitTestVisible="false"
                   Style="{StaticResource PageHeaderTextStyle}"
                   Text="{StaticResource AppName}"
                   Margin="50,0,0,50"/>

        <GridView x:Name="ImagesGridView" Grid.Row="1"
                  HorizontalAlignment="Left" VerticalAlignment="Top"
                                              SelectionMode="Single"
                  Padding="120,126,120,50"
                  SelectionChanged="ImagesGridView_SelectionChanged"
                  ItemsSource="{Binding Images}"
                  >
            <GridView.ItemContainerStyle>
                <Style TargetType="GridViewItem">
                    <Setter Property="HorizontalContentAlignment"
                     Value="Stretch"/>
                    <Setter Property="VerticalContentAlignment" Value="Top"/>
                    <Setter Property="HorizontalAlignment" Value="Stretch"/>
                    <Setter Property="VerticalAlignment" Value="Top"/>
                </Style>
            </GridView.ItemContainerStyle>
            <GridView.ItemTemplate>
                <DataTemplate>
                    <Grid HorizontalAlignment="Stretch">
                        <Grid.RowDefinitions>
                            <RowDefinition Height="175"/>
                        </Grid.RowDefinitions>
                        <Image Grid.Row="0" Height="175" Width="275"
                               Source="{Binding Image}"
```

```
                                Stretch="UniformToFill"/>
                    </Grid>
                </DataTemplate>
            </GridView.ItemTemplate>

        </GridView>

    </Grid>
</Page>
```

LISTING 23.2 The Image Viewer XAML Code: `MainPage.xaml.cs`

```
using System;
using System.Collections.Generic;
using System.IO;
using System.Linq;
using Windows.Foundation;
using Windows.Foundation.Collections;
using Windows.UI.Xaml;
using Windows.UI.Xaml.Controls;
using Windows.UI.Xaml.Controls.Primitives;
using Windows.UI.Xaml.Data;
using Windows.UI.Xaml.Input;
using Windows.UI.Xaml.Media;
using Windows.UI.Xaml.Navigation;


namespace XamlImageViewer
{
    /// <summary>
    /// An empty page that can be used on its own or navigated to within a frame.
    /// </summary>
    public sealed partial class MainPage : Page
    {
        private ImageList _imageList;

        public MainPage()
        {
            this._imageList = new ImageList();
            this.DataContext = this._imageList;
            this._imageList.LoadImages();

            this.InitializeComponent();
        }
```

```
        /// <summary>
        /// Invoked when this page is about to be displayed in a frame.
        /// </summary>
        /// <param name="e">Event data that describes how this page was reached.
        /// The Parameter property is typically used to configure the page.</param>
        protected override void OnNavigatedTo(NavigationEventArgs e)
        {
        }

        private void ImagesGridView_SelectionChanged(object sender,
            SelectionChangedEventArgs e)
        {
            //Navigate to the next page, passing the selected image along.

            //Cast selected item to ImageFile.
            ImageFile image = (ImageFile)ImagesGridView.SelectedItem;
            this.Frame.Navigate(typeof(ImagePage), image);

        }
    }
}
```

LISTING 23.3 The Image Viewer XAML Code: `ImagePage.xaml`

```
<common:LayoutAwarePage
    x:Name="pageRoot"
    x:Class="XamlImageViewer.ImagePage"
    DataContext="{Binding DefaultViewModel,
        RelativeSource={RelativeSource Self}}"
    xmlns="http://schemas.microsoft.com/winfx/2006/xaml/presentation"
    xmlns:x="http://schemas.microsoft.com/winfx/2006/xaml"
    xmlns:local="using:XamlImageViewer"
    xmlns:common="using:XamlImageViewer.Common"
    xmlns:d="http://schemas.microsoft.com/expression/blend/2008"
    xmlns:mc="http://schemas.openxmlformats.org/markup-compatibility/2006"
    mc:Ignorable="d">

    <Page.Resources>
        <ResourceDictionary Source="SliderStyle.xaml"/>
    </Page.Resources>

<Page.BottomAppBar>
    <AppBar x:Name="BottomAppBar1" Padding="10,0,10,0"
➥AutomationProperties.Name="Bottom App Bar">
        <Grid>
```

```
            <StackPanel x:Name="AppBarStackPanel" Orientation="Horizontal"
                  Grid.Column="0" HorizontalAlignment="Right">
                <Button x:Name="SaveButton"
                      Style="{StaticResource SaveAppBarButtonStyle}"
                      Tag="Save"
                  Click="SaveButton_Click" />
            </StackPanel>
        </Grid>
    </AppBar>
</Page.BottomAppBar>
    <!--
        This grid acts as a root panel for the page that defines two rows:
        * Row 0 contains the back button and page title
        * Row 1 contains the rest of the page layout
    -->
    <Grid Style="{StaticResource LayoutRootStyle}">
        <Grid.RowDefinitions>
            <RowDefinition Height="140"/>
            <RowDefinition Height="*"/>
        </Grid.RowDefinitions>

        <!-- Back button and page title -->
        <Grid>
            <Grid.ColumnDefinitions>
                <ColumnDefinition Width="Auto"/>
                <ColumnDefinition Width="*"/>
            </Grid.ColumnDefinitions>
            <Button x:Name="backButton" Click="GoBack"
                    IsEnabled="{Binding Frame.CanGoBack, ElementName=pageRoot}"
                    Style="{StaticResource BackButtonStyle}"/>

            <TextBlock x:Name="pageTitle" Grid.Column="1"
                       Text="{StaticResource AppName}"
                       Style="{StaticResource PageHeaderTextStyle}"/>

        </Grid>

        <Grid x:Name="ImageGrid" Grid.Row="1">
            <Grid.ColumnDefinitions>
                <ColumnDefinition Width=".65*" />
                <ColumnDefinition Width=".35*" />
            </Grid.ColumnDefinitions>

            <Image x:Name="SelectedImage" Grid.Column="0"
                   Margin="50,0,25,25"
                   Source="{Binding Image}"/>
```

```
<Grid Grid.Column="1">

    <Grid.ColumnDefinitions>
        <ColumnDefinition Width="100" />
        <ColumnDefinition Width="*"/>
    </Grid.ColumnDefinitions>
    <Grid.RowDefinitions>
        <RowDefinition Height="auto" />
        <RowDefinition Height="auto" />

    </Grid.RowDefinitions>

    <!--Image rating and filename display -->
    <Slider Grid.Row="0" Grid.Column="1" Grid.ColumnSpan="2"
            x:Name="RatingSlider"
            TickPlacement="Inline" TickFrequency="1"
            Minimum="0" Maximum="5"
            HorizontalAlignment="Left"
            Orientation="Horizontal" Width="300"
            Style="{StaticResource RatingSliderStyle}"
            Margin="15,0,0,0"
            Value="{Binding Rating}"
            SnapsTo="Ticks"/>

    <TextBlock Grid.Column="0" Grid.Row="1" Margin="5,5,0,5"
               Style="{StaticResource BasicTextStyle}"
               HorizontalAlignment="Left" VerticalAlignment="Center"
               Height="20">File name:</TextBlock>

    <TextBlock Grid.Column="1" Grid.Row="1"
               x:Name="FileNameTextBlock"
               Style="{StaticResource BasicTextStyle}"
               Margin="5,5,0,5"
               HorizontalAlignment="Left" Text="{Binding FileName}"
               Width="auto"/>


  </Grid>
</Grid>


<VisualStateManager.VisualStateGroups>

    <!--Visual states reflect the application's view state -->
    <VisualStateGroup x:Name="ApplicationViewStates">
        <VisualState x:Name="FullScreenLandscape"/>
```

```
            <VisualState x:Name="Filled"/>

            <!--The entire page respects the narrower 100-pixel margin
➥convention for portrait -->
            <VisualState x:Name="FullScreenPortrait">
                <Storyboard>
                    <ObjectAnimationUsingKeyFrames
                     Storyboard.TargetName="backButton"
                     Storyboard.TargetProperty="Style">
                        <DiscreteObjectKeyFrame KeyTime="0"
                            Value="{StaticResource PortraitBackButtonStyle}"/>
                    </ObjectAnimationUsingKeyFrames>
                </Storyboard>
            </VisualState>

            <VisualState x:Name="Snapped">
                <Storyboard>
                    <ObjectAnimationUsingKeyFrames
                        Storyboard.TargetName="backButton"
                        Storyboard.TargetProperty="Style">
                        <DiscreteObjectKeyFrame
                            KeyTime="0"
                            Value="{StaticResource SnappedBackButtonStyle}"/>
                    </ObjectAnimationUsingKeyFrames>
                    <ObjectAnimationUsingKeyFrames
                        Storyboard.TargetName="pageTitle"
                        Storyboard.TargetProperty="Style">
                        <DiscreteObjectKeyFrame
                            KeyTime="0"
                            Value="{StaticResource
                            SnappedPageHeaderTextStyle}"/>
                    </ObjectAnimationUsingKeyFrames>
                </Storyboard>
            </VisualState>
        </VisualStateGroup>
    </VisualStateManager.VisualStateGroups>
  </Grid>
</common:LayoutAwarePage>
```

LISTING 23.4 The Image Viewer C# Code: `ImagePage.xaml.cs`

```
using System;
using System.Collections.Generic;
using System.IO;
using System.Linq;
```

```
using Windows.Foundation;
using Windows.Foundation.Collections;
using Windows.Storage;
using Windows.UI.Xaml;
using Windows.UI.Xaml.Controls;
using Windows.UI.Xaml.Controls.Primitives;
using Windows.UI.Xaml.Data;
using Windows.UI.Xaml.Input;
using Windows.UI.Xaml.Media;
using Windows.UI.Xaml.Navigation;


namespace XamlImageViewer
{
    /// <summary>
    /// A page that displays details for a single item within a group while
    /// allowing gestures to flip through other items belonging to the
    /// same group.
    /// </summary>
    public sealed partial class ImagePage :
        XamlImageViewer.Common.LayoutAwarePage
    {
        private ImageFile _imageFile;

        public ImageFile ImageFileInstance
        {
            get { return _imageFile; }
            set { _imageFile = value; }
        }

        public ImagePage()
        {
            this.DataContext = ImageFileInstance;
            this.InitializeComponent();
        }

        /// <summary>
        /// Populates the page with content passed during navigation.
        /// Any saved state is also provided when re-creating a
        /// page from a prior session.
        /// </summary>
        /// <param name="navigationParameter">The parameter value
        /// passed to
        /// <see cref="Frame.Navigate(Type, Object)"/> when this page was
        /// initially requested.
```

```
        /// </param>
        /// <param name="pageState">A dictionary of state preserved
        /// by this page during an earlier session.  This will be null
        /// the first time a page is visited.</param>
        protected override void LoadState(Object navigationParameter,
            Dictionary<String, Object> pageState)
        {
            ImageFileInstance = navigationParameter as ImageFile;
            this.DataContext = ImageFileInstance;
        }

        /// <summary>
        /// Preserves state associated with this page in case the
        /// application is suspended or the page is discarded
        /// from the navigation cache.  Values must conform to
        /// the serialization
        /// requirements of <see cref="SuspensionManager.SessionState"/>.
        /// </summary>
        /// <param name="pageState">An empty dictionary to be
        /// populated with serializable state.</param>
        protected override void SaveState(Dictionary<String, Object> pageState)
        {
            //TODO: Derive a serializable navigation parameter
            //and assign it to pageState["SelectedItem"]
        }

        private void SaveButton_Click(object sender, RoutedEventArgs e)
        {
            SaveRating();
        }

        private async void SaveRating()
        {
            var file = await
                KnownFolders.PicturesLibrary.GetFileAsync(_imageFile.FileName);
            var fileProperties = await
                file.Properties.GetImagePropertiesAsync();

            fileProperties.Rating =
                (uint)this.RatingSlider.Value;

            await fileProperties.SavePropertiesAsync();
        }

    }
}
```

Summary

This chapter introduced you to the new Windows Runtime library (WinRT) and the new Visual Studio project and item templates for creating Windows Store applications for Windows 8. We discussed the fundamentals of WinRT, including its goals, its high-level architecture, its programming model, and the Application Lifecycle Model for WinRT applications.

We visited the primary design principles that underlie Modern UI applications and discussed how those principles are enabling a new class of applications to run on the Windows 8 operating system.

The various language choices for doing WinRT development were explored, and the basics of control layout were bridged from the existing WPF world to the XAML/WinRT world.

Finally, we explored in depth the construction of a WinRT/Windows Store application from the ground up, expanding on XAML concepts first explored in Chapter 21.

Although WinRT will look familiar and be comfortable, for .NET developers at large, the devil is in the details. Before you embark on any serious WinRT development projects, we highly recommend that you start your journey with the Windows Dev Center website, located at dev, windows.com.

In the next chapter, as we discuss Windows Phone development, we will further explore Windows Store applications with the concept of a "universal app," capable of running on multiple Windows devices.

CHAPTER 24

Creating Windows Phone Applications

IN THIS CHAPTER

- ▶ Windows Phone Fundamentals
- ▶ Moving from Silverlight to WinRT
- ▶ Building a Universal App

In November 2010, Microsoft introduced a new platform to compete in the fast-moving mobile device market: Windows Phone 7. This was an all-new hardware and software platform for Microsoft at the time; this new platform represented a whole new set of application development opportunities, and challenges, for developers. Today, the Microsoft mobile platform has matured with version 8.1 of its mobile operating system and application development framework. Over the years, the platform has grown in depth and breadth and shares many synergies today with the Windows Store app platform that we covered in the previous chapter.

In this chapter, we examine the fundamental concepts associated with Windows Phone applications and the Visual Studio project types, tools, and controls that you will use to design, construct, test, and deploy Windows Phone 8.1 applications. We will also introduce the concept of Universal apps: applications that can be written and structured in a way to enable them to run on many different device formats from tablets, to phones, to desktop computers.

Windows Phone Fundamentals

Like other phone platforms, Windows Phone consists of an operating system and an application development framework. Both clearly reflect the constraints typically found with mobile devices: memory, storage, and battery life are all precious resources that need to be conserved and balanced, and screen size is a driving factor in terms of application design. It should come as no surprise, then, that the Windows Phone development model can be very different from the other development technologies that we have discussed in this book. But as we mentioned in the introduction to this chapter, it is also tightly related to Window Store development. Consider the following shared characteristics of Windows Phone and Windows Store apps:

- Applications can be written using either XAML + C#/Visual Basic or by using Hypertext Markup Language (HTML) stack technologies
- Applications have an operating system (OS)-governed execution model and lifecycle
- Application development is fully supported through the use of specific project types and project items in Visual Studio
- Applications can be packaged and published into a store for download and install by end users

Let's first focus on some of the unique aspects of Windows Phone applications.

The UI Basics

The Windows Phone user experience is centered on the concept of tiles. Tiles are chunks of UI real estate that can either be static representations of an app or dynamic tiles that show live, useful information related to an app. Figure 24.1 shows the Windows Phone start screen; here you see tiles pinned to the start screen. Some of them are functioning merely as icon-based app launchers. Others are displaying useful, contextual information (such as the calendar tile, which is showing live appointments for the day). You can clearly see that this tile-based UI joins together the user experience between Windows 8 and Windows Phone 8. Refer back to Figure 23.1 in Chapter 23, "Developing Windows Store Applications," for the Windows 8 comparative screen shot.

Applications themselves are composed of a few basic user interface elements. There is a system tray at the top of the device screen that displays global information about signal strength, wireless signal strength, remaining battery, and so on. Toward the bottom of the screen is an optional application bar; this is where some applications will host buttons and menu items for issuing commands to the application. And then, between the system tray and the application bar, there is the client/frame area that hosts an application's page-based UI (see Figure 24.2).

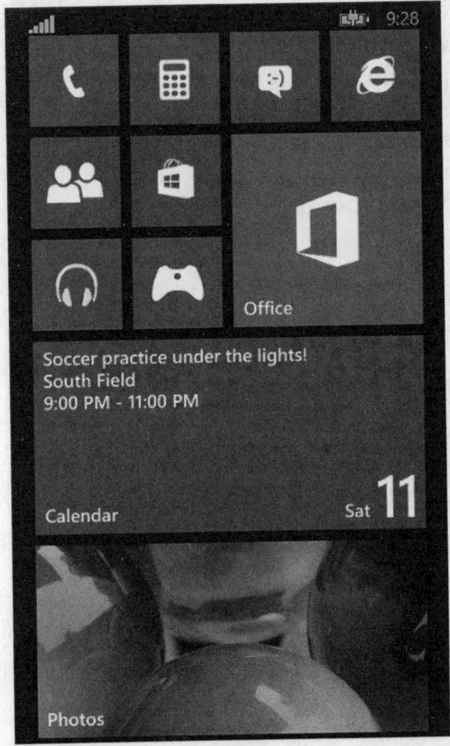

FIGURE 24.1 The Windows Phone start screen.

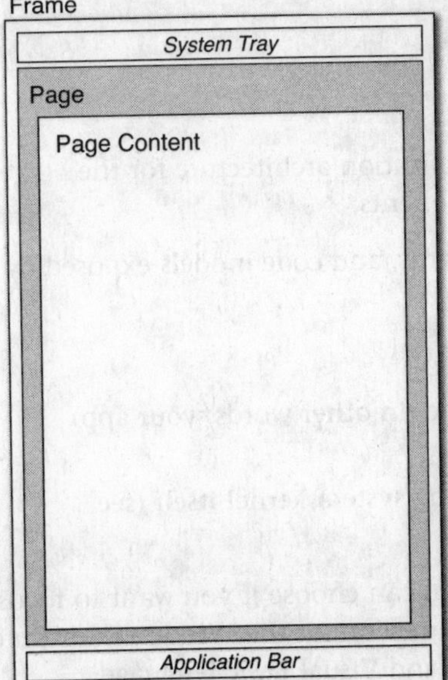

FIGURE 24.2 The UI structure of a Phone app.

Device Orientation

The UI is capable of changing its layout based on the orientation of the device (landscape versus portrait). For those applications that expose an app bar, this will typically migrate to the right side of the screen, and the system tray will occupy the left strip of screen real estate. Applications can also react intelligently to orientation changes. For instance, in the case of the built-in calculator app, the app will switch to a scientific mode when used in the landscape orientation, offering more computation buttons using the available screen area (see Figure 24.3).

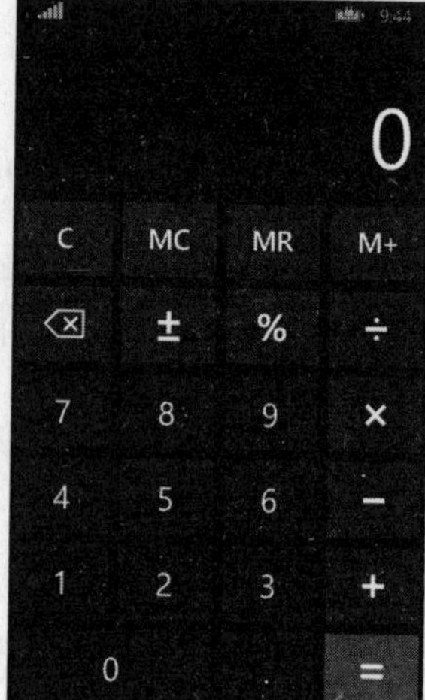

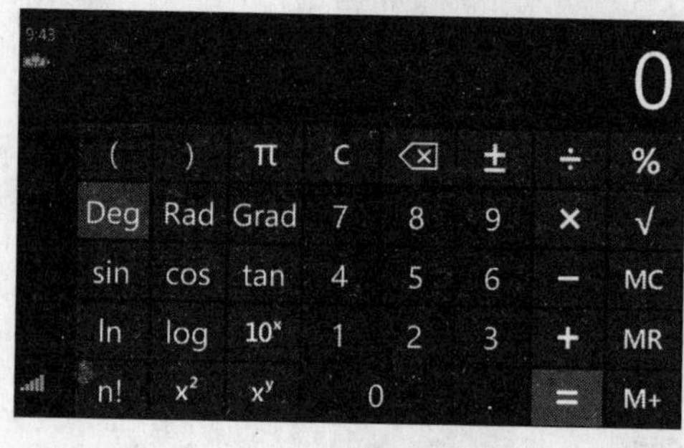

FIGURE 24.3 Portrait versus landscape orientation modes.

The Programming Model

Just like other Visual Studio development scenarios, application architecture for the Windows Phone platform consists of three major components:

- Events, application user interfaces (APIs), UI elements, and code models exposed by the operating system
- The runtime libraries for implementing functionality
- Logic, custom code, and UI elements that you write (in other words, your app)

All those components are running on top of the operating system kernel itself (see Figure 24.4).

For Phone apps, there are two different runtimes that you can choose if you want to focus on managed code, XAML applications: the Silverlight framework or the Windows Runtime Library (WinRT). For either, you have the traditional C# and Visual Basic language options.

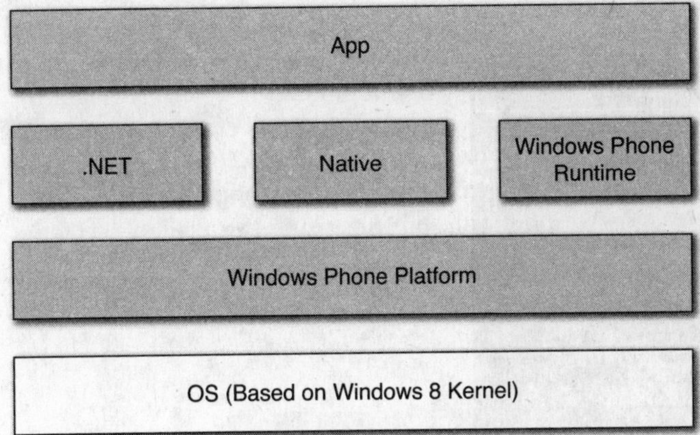

FIGURE 24.4 Windows Phone architecture.

We focus this chapter on C#/XAML applications built using WinRT. Silverlight was the only framework option available for .NET developers with Windows Phone 7 through Windows Phone 7.5 and will be familiar to developers who have prior exposure to those platforms. However, WinRT is the roadmap focus for device development going forward given its cross-platform nature (Windows 8 and Windows Phone 8). This is also a crucial change point if you want to write Universal apps (applications that are capable of running on either Windows or Windows Phone).

NOTE

Silverlight started life as a modernized version of the Windows Presentation Framework, specifically designed for rich Internet application development. As a sort of WPF "light," it was an ideal development framework for Windows Phone, which required extensive capabilities (including immersive UI elements) all while running in a resource-constrained device environment. WinRT is coming from the opposite direction: it was first delivered as a core component of Windows 8 and is now moving downstream to Windows Phone and other devices such as HoloLens.

Applications that target the Windows Phone runtime have unique attributes and a unique structure.

Application Anatomy

Windows Phone applications, just like a website, consist of one or more pages. Each of these pages (which are physically instances of `System.Windows.Controls.Page`) will have a XAML file and a code-behind file. They all run within the context of a "frame" (an instance of `System.Windows.Controls.Frame`). This is analogous to a web browser: it provides the system tray and application bar regions, and it displays the application page and page content (see Figure 24.5).

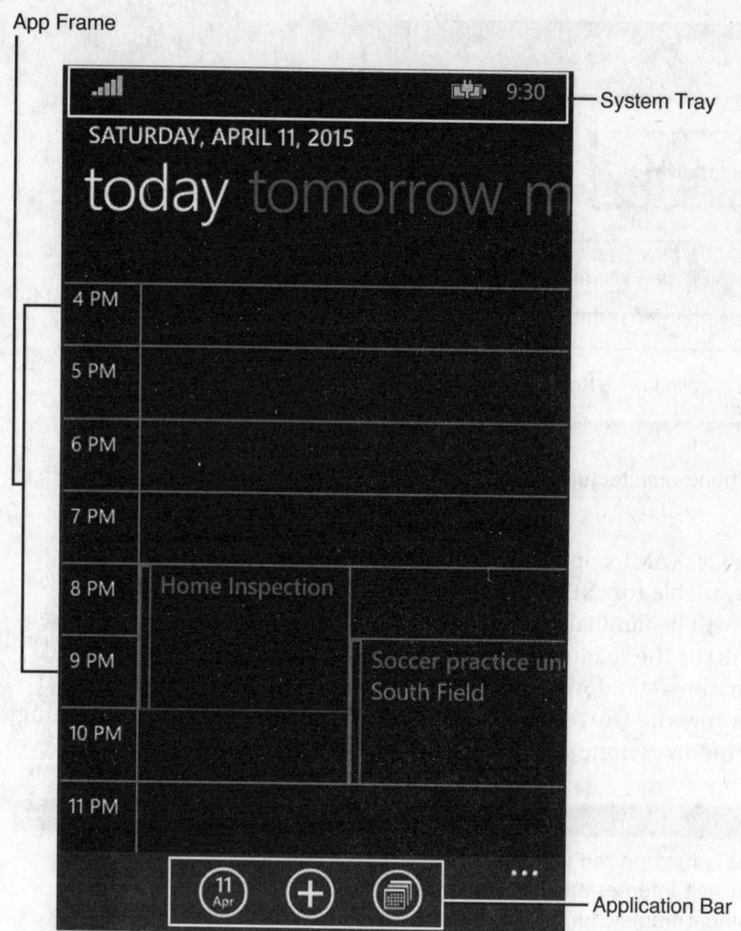

FIGURE 24.5 An application's frame, page, and page content areas.

Page Navigation

Users (or logic within your app) can navigate forward and backward through the pages of the app. As navigation happens, a stack of pages (called the back stack) is built up, in just the same way that your web browser maintains history when you browse the web. Clicking the Back button (a Back button is required on all Windows Phone devices) will cause the Windows Phone runtime to page back through that stack of pages.

As discussed in Chapter 23, you can also programmatically navigate between pages by using the Navigate method on the Frame class. For example, consider an application that helps you to file expense reports. The application may allow you to navigate from the main list of expense reports directly to a page that allows you to input notes. In this case, we might want to wire up the click event of a button to load that next page like this:

```
private void ButtonEditNotes_Click(object sender, RoutedEventArgs e)
{
    this.Frame.Navigate(typeof(ReportDetailPage));
}
```

You can also pass data between pages using an alternate form of the Navigate method. By supplying an object as a second parameter into Navigate, the target page can retrieve that object and act on it. We saw this in action with our sample Windows Store application from the previous chapter: selecting an image on the main page caused that image to be loaded onto a detail page. The image itself was passed as an object using the following code.

```
this.Frame.Navigate(typeof(ImagePage), image);
```

If we needed to pass a collection of objects, we would simply add those objects to a container collection object. (Any will do: `List`, `Collection`, `Array`, and so on.)

In the destination page, the passed object is available in the `OnNavigatedTo`. Retrieving it is as simple as pulling it from the `NavigationEventArgs` object.

```
protected override void OnNavigatedTo(NavigationEventArgs e)
{
    base.OnNavigatedTo(e);

    //Retrieve the passed-in object, and cast as necessary.
    var myObject = e.Parameter as MyObject;
}
```

App Lifecycle

WinRT applications on the phone participate in the same, common lifecycle of WinRT Windows applications (Chapter 23); at any time, a Windows Phone application will be in one of three different states: Activated, Suspended, or Not Running:

- **Activated**—The application is currently executing, although it may be idle.
- **Suspended**—Applications reach this state when they are deactivated. This could happen as the result of many different actions. For example, the user may navigate out of the application. Suspended apps aren't executing code, but they are still loaded into memory and can thus be quickly reactivated.
- **Not Running**—Applications that have been terminated completely are, of course, not running.

Events are defined on the `Windows.UI.Xaml.Application` class (in other words, the `App.Xaml` and `App.Xaml.cs` code files) that correspond to these state changes. See Figure 24.6 for a visual map of the various states and the events that correspond to the state transitions.

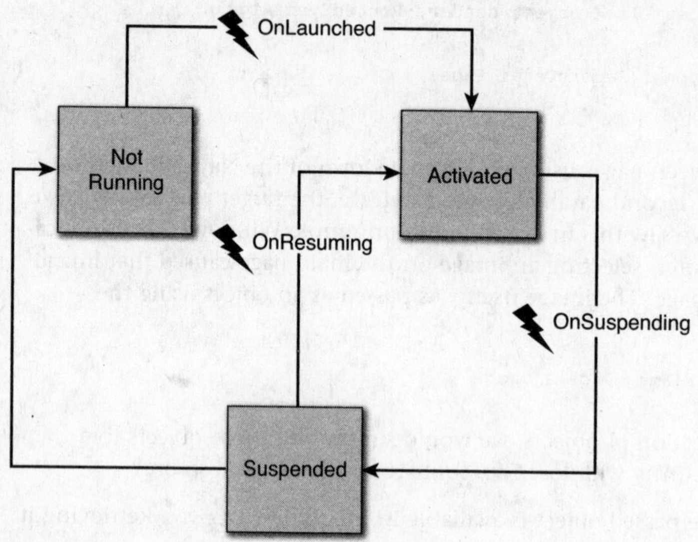

FIGURE 24.6 Application lifecycle and Application events.

NOTE

If you look at Figure 24.6, you will notice that there isn't an event associated with the application moving to the Not Running state. The operating system will not notify your application that it is being terminated. This means that you have to take care of all state persistence when the application is suspended. In other words, you have to react as if the application is actually being terminated every time it is suspended because you have no control over that state transition.

Understanding the lifecycle is important because you will need to react to changes between states within your code. It is also important to recognize that you, the developer, are not in control of when your application moves between these states. The Windows Phone OS itself may choose to suspend or terminate an application based on memory conditions or other application activity. One simple example of this is the OS taking control and suspending the currently running app when a phone call comes in.

Reacting to State Change Events

Defensive programming is in order here. You need to know when these various state transitions happen; this, again, is a topic we covered in Chapter 23. The Windows Phone environment exposes the same set of state change events in `App.Xaml.cs`. The Suspending event handlers are connected for you by default within the App constructor, and you have to manually add the handler for `Resuming`.

```
public App()
{
    this.InitializeComponent();
    this.Suspending += OnSuspending;
    this.Resuming += OnResuming;
}
```

Note that the `Resuming` event handler is stubbed out with an exception that you must replace by your own implementation.

```
void OnResuming(object sender, object e)
{
    throw new NotImplementedException();
}

/// <summary>
/// Invoked when the application is launched normally by the end user.
/// </summary>
/// <param name="args">Details about the launch request and process.</param>
protected override void OnLaunched(LaunchActivatedEventArgs args)
{
}

/// <summary>
/// Invoked when application execution is being suspended.  Application state is
/// saved without knowing whether the application will be terminated or resumed
/// with the contents of memory still intact.
/// </summary>
/// <param name="sender">The source of the suspend request.</param>
/// <param name="e">Details about the suspend request.</param>
private void OnSuspending(object sender, SuspendingEventArgs e)
{
    var deferral = e.SuspendingOperation.GetDeferral();
    //TODO: Save application state and stop any background activity
    deferral.Complete();
}
```

NOTE

As a reminder: keep in mind that the two different frameworks, Silverlight and WinRT, will have different lifecycles, APIs, events, and more. We are explicitly covering WinRT in this chapter.

Suspended Versus Terminated

If an application is put into the Suspended state and then reactivated, all of the objects that were previously loaded in memory will be automatically restored for you. There is no need to explicitly save any of their state information. There will be exceptions, however, where you need to do some extra lifting here. For example, you may have had a network connection open to a resource somewhere, and that network connection may have timed out during the period in which the app was dormant. Your reactivation code (for example, code within `OnResuming`) should try to correct this scenario before making assumptions about that network connection.

If an application is terminated, it is officially unloaded from memory. If the application is reactivated, you need to explicitly repopulate your app's state (including navigation position). Clearly, this implies the need to "save state" at various points within an application's life time to be able to restore it.

Application State and the Model-View-ViewModel Pattern

Windows Phone applications deal with both transient data (control state and "work in progress" un-saved data) and data that is meant to be persisted long term. Applications need to implement their own logic to save both types of data.

How and when to save transient data and persistent data is tightly reliant on the lifecycle events that we just discussed. Your app will need to be smart enough to store transient data along the way. If we have a list of string entries within our application, for example, we would want to save the state (contents) of that list when the app is suspended. In a similar fashion, when we move between pages, we want to save the transient data that might be represented within the page. For example, users will expect the contents of a text box that they just typed in to still be there if they navigate away from, and then back to, a page in your application. We also need to write persistent data so that the next time the app is launched, it will read in the prior saved data.

There is an architecture pattern that helps significantly with application data loading, saving, and binding: the Model-View-ViewModel (MVVM) pattern. MVVM is a terrific pattern for binding data within application pages and centralizing an application's state so that it can be easily persisted and loaded. MVVM, as its name implies, consists of three different (but related) constructs:

- **Model**—This represents a data entity used within an application. For an expense report application, one of the models would likely be an expense report. There is generally no logic contained within a model, and it is sometimes best implemented as a simple class with some properties.
- **View**—This is the user interface for the application; for Windows Phone applications, this is manifested as the page `.xaml` files that define the various UI control elements on each page.
- **ViewModel**—This is the glue that holds everything together in the MVVM architecture. Code within the ViewModel is responsible for handling events, performing data binding, encapsulating any business logic in the app, and encapsulating our Models.

MVVM (see Figure 24.7) is relevant to the state discussion with Windows Phone because it allows us to wrap up all the data entities that our app cares about (in other words, all the Models) into a single ViewModel. We can then load/save that single ViewModel in reaction to the various lifecycle events.

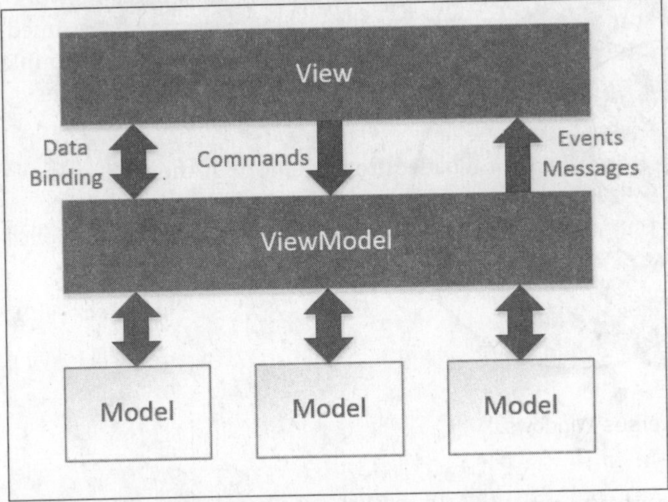

FIGURE 24.7 The Model-View-ViewModel architecture.

We'll pull all this together in a bit when we build our first sample application.

NOTE

Although its core concepts are simple, it can take some active development time with MVVM before you fully understand its moving parts. It's beyond the scope of this chapter to furnish a full and in-depth treatment of MVVM, although it is core to Windows Phone—and XAML/WinRT development—in general. We recommend that you watch the brief video "Practical MVVM for Windows Phone" available on the Microsoft Channel 9 website (channel9.msdn.com).

Moving from Silverlight to WinRT

Moving onto the new WinRT platform is not a zero-cost exercise for existing applications. The UI controls that you interact with are just one example of the API change between Windows Phone Silverlight and Windows Phone WinRT applications. Silverlight controls live within the Microsoft.Phone.Controls namespace, whereas WinRT components live under Windows.UI.Xaml. The UI elements are similar, but not the same.

There is another fact that is important to understand: WinRT for Windows and WinRT for Windows Phone are very similar APIs, but they are *not* identical. Although there is considerable overlap, there are items that exist in the phone library that don't exist in the windows library, and vice versa. You can envision the Venn diagram (see Figure 24.8). This is not unexpected. Device capabilities will be different between laptops and desktops and tablets and large format phones and small format phones. This sliding window of capabilities is a core focus of Microsoft as it tries to homogenize its OS and deliver a core environment that scales across all devices.

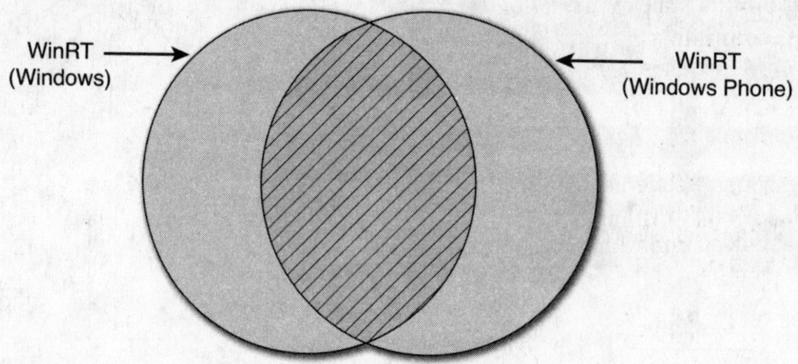

FIGURE 24.8 WinRT for Phone versus Windows.

There are, of course, other differences to consider. WinRT offers you the ability to build your applications using HTML. So one decision you will be faced with is whether to continue down the XAML path or adopt an HTML/JavaScript-centric view of the world. Page navigation and lifecycle events are similar but certainly changed. And there are a score of equivalent, but different, classes residing in different areas of both the Phone class libraries and .NET proper. The MSDN dev center offers up an article titled "Windows Phone Silverlight to Windows Runtime Namespace and Class Mappings" that is highly suggested reading.

We've covered some of these controls already in our Chapter 23 coverage of building a Windows Store application. We'll cover some more here and review some of the new WinRT control equivalents to their "old" Silverlight counterparts.

Porting a Simple Silverlight Phone App to WinRT

Windows Phone and its corresponding Silverlight platform introduced a handful of new controls that formed an essential part of its user experience. These controls represented new approaches that didn't have stock equivalents in the WPF or Windows Forms or Web worlds. As the development platforms and operating systems have started to converge, WinRT replacement controls have come onto the scene. This represents new work on the part of the developer who wants to move his current Silverlight application to WinRT.

Building a Universal App

With the basics out of the way, let's put our combined knowledge of Windows Phone apps (covered in the first part of this chapter) and Windows Store apps (covered in Chapter 23) and build a simple Universal app. To demonstrate the Visual Studio project templates and the core concepts of lifecycle management, data persistence, and the MVVM approach, we'll build a simple master-detail application that allows you to keep track of restaurant bills, compute a tip, and determine the total for each party if you decide to "split the tab."

NOTE

Although we provide extensive code listings in this chapter and walk through the major pieces of this project, we explicitly do not cover every little element or line of code needed to assemble the full, cross-platform, Universal app. Our recommendation is that you open the full sample application from this book's website and then use that as a backdrop as you work through this Universal app content: www.informit.com/title/9780672337369.

The application should support the following three end user requirements:

- A meal bill/tab can be split equally among two or more parties; the app should also be able to handle a single party.
- The app will generate the grand total by adding a specific tip (percentage) onto the total; the app will also compute the total owed by each party.
- Once the meal cost has been allocated and computed, the details will be added to the master list of meal bills.

And for our purposes here, we'll cater to the following nonfunctional requirements:

- The app should use an MVVM approach to simplify maintenance of the code and optimize the built-in data binding features in XAML apps.
- The app will save the meal data to a form of persistent storage.
- The app will run equally well, with no loss of functionality, between Windows 8.1 and Windows Phone 8.1.

The goal is to have a similar look and feel across devices but also to cater to each device. If we were to sketch out a quick design for both the phone version and the Windows 8 version, we would quickly see that we likely need two pages to make this work on the phone: the master list page and then a details page for each entry. For the Windows version, with additional screen real estate available (and with a common landscape orientation to that real estate), we will likely find it better to create just a single page. Figures 24.9 through 24.11 show our quick and dirty prototype.

FIGURE 24.9 Windows Phone design—master list page.

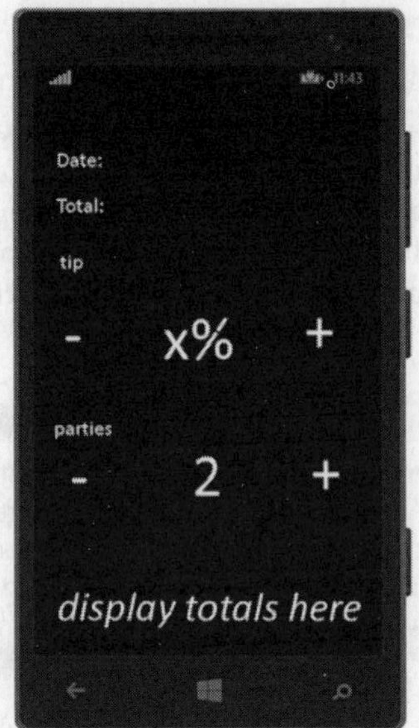

FIGURE 24.10 Windows Phone design—details page.

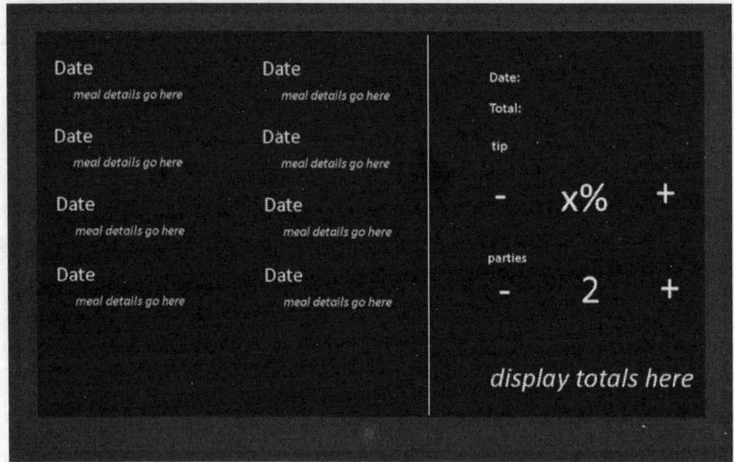

FIGURE 24.11 Windows design.

As always, we start the adventure by selecting a project type in Visual Studio.

The Universal Project Types

There are four different Universal app project templates that ship with Visual Studio 2015: Blank App, Hub App, Class Library, and Windows RunTime Component.

The Blank App is self-explanatory. It creates blank phone and Windows pages for you without any predefined layout or control set. The Hub App is used to create multilevel hub-type user experiences where multiple items can be grouped in different ways, and drilling down on an item will allow you to view the item detail. This is similar to the approach we adopted with the XAML Image Viewer app. Class Library is also self-explanatory; it is meant for creating a standard `.dll`/class library with no UI components.

Finally, the Windows Runtime Component template allows you to create components that can be reused across C++ and HTML/JavaScript in addition to the managed frameworks.

For our purposes, the Hub app comes closest to our design intent, but it is also overkill. We'll start with the Blank App template. With Visual Studio open, select New Project, and then select the Universal App category. Then select the Blank App template from the list, name the project, and click OK (see Figure 24.12).

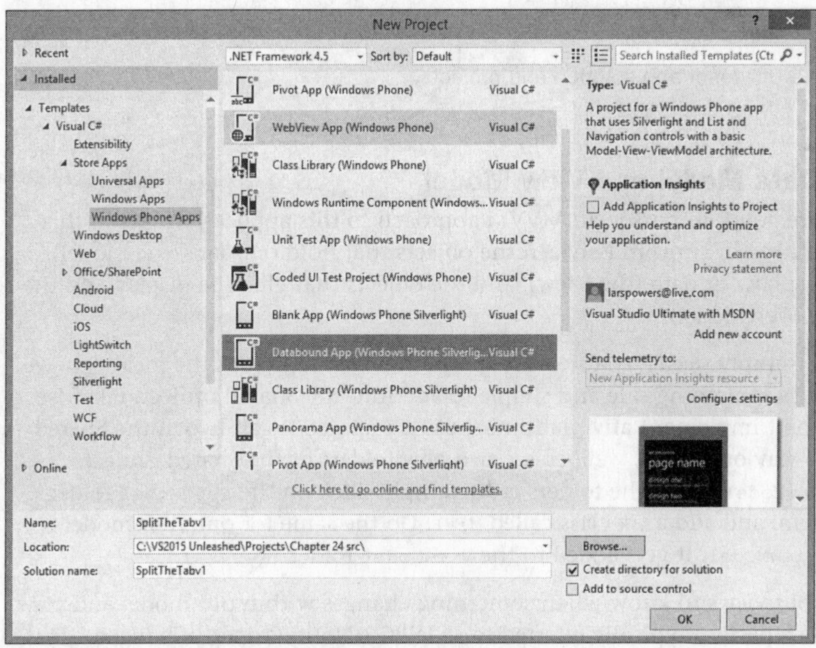

FIGURE 24.12 The Universal app templates.

When Visual Studio is done processing the template, you should have a single solution with three different projects: a Windows 8.1 project for our Windows UI, a Windows Phone 8.1 project for our phone UI, and a "shared" project that will contain as much logic (and XAML) as possible for sharing between the two target platforms (see Figure 24.13).

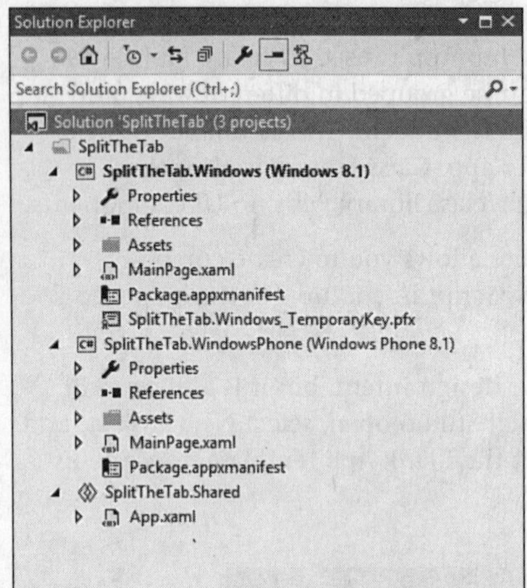

FIGURE 24.13 The Universal app solution and projects.

Creating the Data Model and View Model

As discussed, we are going to pursue an MVVM approach to this application. Recall that this means a separation of concern between the objects that hold our data (the Model), the objects that display our data (the View), and the objects that glue the display and the data together (the ViewModel).

Because our model simply needs to store a few properties that represent the meal data we want to track, this is something safe and simple to add into the Shared project. Likewise, the ViewModel won't implement any platform-specific logic, so it can live in the Shared project as well. To stay organized, we'll create two new folders in the Shared project: `DataModel` and `ViewModel`. With the folders created, right-click on the `DataModel` folder, select Add New Item, and add a C# class called `Meal`. Do the same for our view model class, called `MainViewModel`. It gets added to the `ViewModel` folder.

Because we want our views to know when something changes within our model and view model, we will use a pattern typically referred to as INPC (INotifyPropertyChanged). This is an interface that we can implement within our classes that will send a notification to the visual tree and any bound pieces of the view to let them know that they need to redisplay the data.

First we inherit from the interface.

```
public class Meal : INotifyPropertyChanged
```

Then we implement the required event and event handler.

```
public event PropertyChangedEventHandler
    PropertyChanged;

private void NotifyPropertyChanged(String propertyName)
{
    PropertyChangedEventHandler handler =
        PropertyChanged;
    if (null != handler)
    {
        handler(this,
            new PropertyChangedEventArgs(propertyName));
    }
}
```

Now we are all set to be able to notify any of the views that care when a property changes. From within every property "setter" in our class, we will include a call out to `NotifyPropertyChanged`, like this:

```
NotifyPropertyChanged("SubTotal");
```

We need a handful of read/write properties on the `Meal` class: `SubTotal`, `Date`, `Parties`, `TipPercent`. We will also need to expose a few read-only properties. These will be computed internal to the class: `GrandTotal`, `PerPartyGrandTotal`, `DateString`, and `Description`. `Description` and `DateString` are convenience properties; we can generate those internal to the model class and get our UI/view to quickly display the information we are looking for without having to do any necessary conversion activities within our view or the view model. You can see how we will use both of these properties within the view by referring back to Figure 24.9.

Our view model class is nothing more than a holder for a collection of `Meal` objects. The class can hold an `ObservableCollection` instance of meals and thus function as our data source for our list of meals.

```
private ObservableCollection<Meal> _meals;

public ObservableCollection<Meal> Meals
{
    get { return _meals; }
    set
    {
        _meals = value;
        NotifyPropertyChanged("Meals");
    }
}
```

Because our view model and model objects live in their own, separate project, we have to have a way for something durable to instantiate them and make them available to our other UI projects. To make this happen, we'll create an app-level field called `ViewModel` that will create the view model and hold its instance. Because this is an app-level property, it is defined within the Shared project's `App.xaml.cs` file.

```
private static ViewModel.MainViewModel viewModel = null;

/// <summary>
/// A static ViewModel used by the views to bind against.
/// </summary>
/// <returns>The MainViewModel object.</returns>
public static ViewModel.MainViewModel ViewModel
{
    get
    {
        //Delay creation of the view model until necessary
        if (viewModel == null)
            viewModel = new ViewModel.MainViewModel();

        return viewModel;
    }
}
```

With that final piece in place, we can turn our attention to the UI projects.

Creating the Windows Phone UI

Thinking back to our prototype, we know that we need two pages within our Phone app: a master "list" page and a details page. When Visual Studio created the Windows Phone 8 project, it added a `MainPage.xaml` by default. We'll make that our master list page.

We have a few options for controls to display our list of meals. ListView is a great choice; it's easy to work with but still provides enough flexibility for multiple line templates, and so on.

The Master Page

With the `MainPage` open, create a new ListView control within the XAML. You can handcraft the code or drag the control over from the toolbox. With the control in place, we need to tweak a few things. First, we need to bind the control to the view model that we previously created. We also need to react when the user selects an item in the list, so we have to wire up an event for that. And we have to provide a quick set of data templates for showing the data.

Here is an initial declaration for our ListView.

```
<ListView x:Name="ListViewMeals"
        ItemsSource="{Binding Meals}"
        SelectionChanged="ListViewMeals_SelectionChanged"
        Tapped="ListViewMeals_Tapped" >
    <ListView.ItemTemplate>
        <DataTemplate>
            <StackPanel Margin="0,0,0,17">
                <TextBlock Text="{Binding DateString}"
                        TextWrapping="Wrap"
                        Style="{StaticResource ListViewItemTextBlockStyle}" />
                <TextBlock Text="{Binding Description}"
                        TextWrapping="Wrap"
                        Margin="12,-6,12,0"
                        Style="{StaticResource GroupHeaderTextBlockStyle}"
                        FontSize="14" />
            </StackPanel>
        </DataTemplate>
    </ListView.ItemTemplate>
</ListView>
```

Note that we have added an event handler for the `Tapped` event on the ListView control. We'll use that later to start the editing process for that selected meal. The styles we are using are built-in, WinRT styles. Because IntelliSense is supported inside of XAML, you can get the list of available styles by starting to fill out the syntax for the Style property; then just select from the available list of `StaticResource` entries.

If you look at our binding syntax within the DataTemplate elements, you will see that we are referencing the `DateString` and `Description` property. But in order for the view to pick up on that binding, we have to set an overall data context to our page. That is done in the code-behind file like this:

```
public MainPage()
{
    this.InitializeComponent();

    this.NavigationCacheMode = NavigationCacheMode.Disabled;

    DataContext = App.ViewModel;
}
```

When everything is wired up and working, our collection of meals (for example, our view model) will automatically connect to the ListView, which will automatically display all the `Meal` objects contained within the collection.

We need one more piece of functionality to allow users to add a new meal to the list. We'll trigger that action via an app bar placed at the bottom of the page. Dragging and dropping a Command Bar control from the toolbox will add the initial XAML to our page, which we can then tweak.

```
<Page.BottomAppBar>
    <CommandBar x:Name="BottomAppBar1" Padding="10,0,10,0">
        <AppBarButton x:Name="AddButton"
                      Icon="Add"
                      Label="Add"
                      Click="AddButton_Click" />
    </CommandBar>
</Page.BottomAppBar>
```

The `AddButton_Click` event handler simply creates a new `Meal` instance and adds it to our view model.

```
private void AddButton_Click(object sender, RoutedEventArgs e)
{
    Meal newMeal = new Meal();
    newMeal.Date = DateTime.Today;
    newMeal.Parties = 1;
    newMeal.TipPercent = .20;
    newMeal.SubTotal = 50.00;

    App.ViewModel.Meals.Add(newMeal);

    this.Frame.Navigate(typeof(MealPage), newMeal);

}
```

Now we have to worry about how we will deal with a user clicking on an item in the ListView and adding a new item to the ListView. Both require the details page to be in place, so let's build that next.

The Details Page

Right-click on the Windows Phone 8.1 project and select Add New Item. Then select a blank XAML page. Name the page `MealPage`, and click OK. Your solution/project tree should now look similar to Figure 24.14.

On the details page, we need to build out a series of controls for displaying, and allowing the editing of, the data from a selected `Meal` object. A Grid offers an easy way to position the items on the page. Within the Grid, we'll need items like TextBlock, TextBox, and Button controls to implement our UI design (refer to Figure 24.10). We also need a DatePicker control to allow us to display and edit the date. All the controls that are meant to display dynamic data associated with the selected will have to have the appropriate binding setup within the XAML.

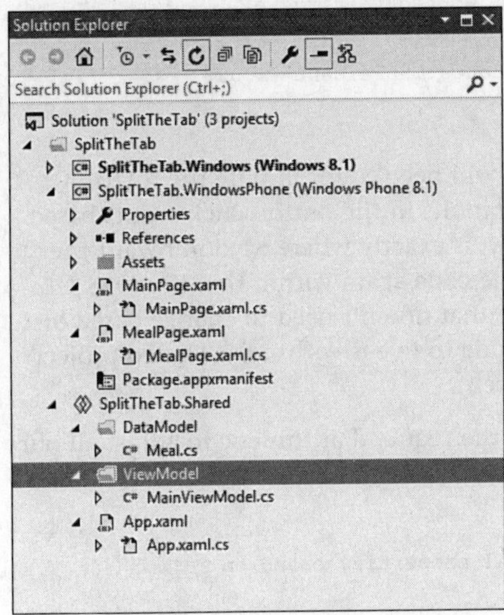

FIGURE 24.14 The Universal app solution and projects.

For instance, the TextBox that holds the subtotal amount will look something like this:

```
<TextBox x:Name="TextBoxTotal"
        Grid.Column="1"
        Grid.Row="2"
        VerticalAlignment="Center"
        Text="{Binding SubTotal}"/>
```

The bindings that we establish are a direct link back to the model and view model properties that are exposed.

The Button controls need to have their click events wired up to enable the end user to change the values for `SubTotal` and `TipPercent`. That is a straightforward effort. Add the event handler in the XAML, and let Visual Studio create the code-behind C# routine for you automatically. Then add the code in the event handler to increment or decrement the property. Here is the “decrease tip” code.

```
<Button x:Name="ButtonDownTip"
               Grid.Row="4"
               Grid.Column="0"
               VerticalAlignment="Center"
               HorizontalAlignment="Center"
               FontSize="60"
               Click="ButtonDownTip_Click"
               >-
</Button>
```

```
private void ButtonDownTip_Click(object sender, RoutedEventArgs e)
{
    this.MealInstance.TipPercent = this.MealInstance.TipPercent - .05;
}
```

When the user adjusts any of these properties, we will need to recompute the totals. A brute force approach would just make those calculations in the button click events based on the adjusted values. But here, inside of the view, is exactly where we don't want the code to live. That would mean re-implementing the code again within the Windows UI project. Because this is simple arithmetic and code that doesn't need to change based on the deployment platform, the best place for this code to live is within the Shared project as part of our data model (part of the `Meal` class itself).

First add a routine to the `Meal` class that performs the required arithmetic to adjust all our read-only properties anytime one of our writable properties changes.

```
/// <summary>
/// Update the GrandTotal and PerPartyGrandTotal properties based on
/// changes to either subtotal or tip percent.
/// </summary>
private void ComputeGrandTotals()
{

    _grandTotal = _subTotal + (_subTotal * _tipPercent);
    _grandTotal = Math.Round(_grandTotal, 2);
    _perPartyGrandTotal = _grandTotal / _parties;
    _perPartyGrandTotal = Math.Round(_perPartyGrandTotal, 2);

    NotifyPropertyChanged("GrandTotal");
    NotifyPropertyChanged("PerPartyGrandTotal");

}
```

Note that we are raising the property changed event via `NotifyPropertyChanged` for our two properties. Because this routine needs to be called every time we touch `SubTotal`, `TipPercent`, or `Parties`, we will add a call to the routine from each of the property setters.

Here is the example for `SubTotal`.

```
public double SubTotal
{
    get
    {
        return _subTotal;
    }
    set
    {
        if (value != _subTotal)
```

```
        {
            _subTotal = value;
            ComputeGrandTotals();
            NotifyPropertyChanged("SubTotal");
        }
    }

}
```

With the UI for the detail page in place, we now need to ensure that our page is being passed the correct object from the master page. As we mentioned previously in the chapter, data can be passed from one page to another using the `Frame.Navigate` method. This is how we will capture the currently selected `Meal` object from the master page and display its details on the detail page.

Revisit `MainPage.xaml`, and put the appropriate `Navigate` call into the previously created `ListView_Tapped` event.

```
private void ListViewMeals_Tapped(object sender, TappedRoutedEventArgs e)
{
    //Cast selected item to Meal.
    Meal meal = (Meal)ListViewMeals.SelectedItem;
    this.Frame.Navigate(typeof(MealPage), meal);
}
```

This will pull the `Meal` object from the item in the list that was clicked/tapped and pass it onto the details page by way of the second `Navigate` parameter.

Then, within the `MealPage.xaml`, we add the code within `OnNavigatedTo` to pull the passed `Meal` object out and then bind it to the data context of the page (thus making all our bound controls "live").

```
protected override void OnNavigatedTo(NavigationEventArgs e)
{
    base.OnNavigatedTo(e);

    var mealInstance = e.Parameter as Meal;
    MealInstance = mealInstance;
    DataContext = MealInstance;
}
```

Barring some minor clean-up and debugging here and there, the Windows Phone project should now be complete. Figures 24.15 and 24.16 show the project running in the Phone emulator. We won't provide all the code here, but Listing 24.1 shows the `MainPage.xaml` content, and Listing 24.2 has the `MainPage.xaml.cs`. The other code files are available at this book's website.

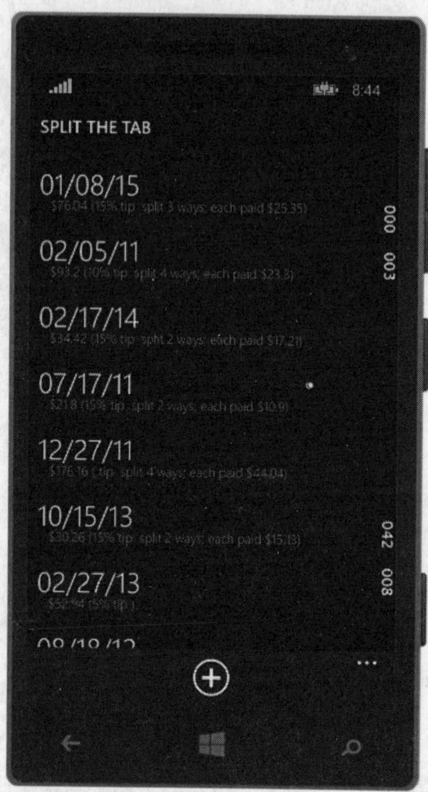

FIGURE 24.15 The app running in the Phone emulator.

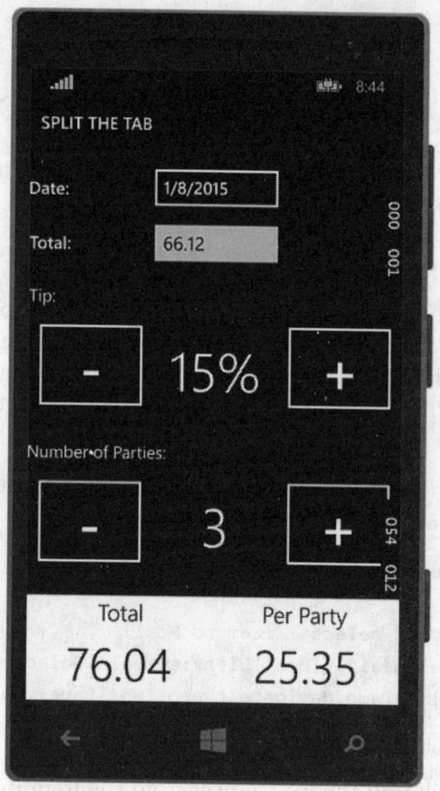

FIGURE 24.16 The detail page in the Phone emulator.

LISTING 24.1 The `MainPage.xaml` Code

```
<Page
    x:Class="SplitTheTab.MainPage"
    xmlns="http://schemas.microsoft.com/winfx/2006/xaml/presentation"
    xmlns:x="http://schemas.microsoft.com/winfx/2006/xaml"
    xmlns:local="using:SplitTheTab"
    xmlns:d="http://schemas.microsoft.com/expression/blend/2008"
    xmlns:mc="http://schemas.openxmlformats.org/markup-compatibility/2006"
    mc:Ignorable="d"
    Background="{ThemeResource ApplicationPageBackgroundThemeBrush}">

    <Grid x:Name="LayoutRoot" Background="Transparent">
        <Grid.RowDefinitions>
            <RowDefinition Height="Auto"/>
```

```
            <RowDefinition Height="*"/>
        </Grid.RowDefinitions>

        <!--TitlePanel contains the name of the application and page title-->
        <StackPanel Grid.Row="0"
                    Margin="12,17,0,28">
            <TextBlock Text="SPLIT THE TAB"
                       Style="{StaticResource TitleTextBlockStyle}" />
        </StackPanel>

        <!--ContentPanel contains ListView and its data templates -->
        <Grid x:Name="ContentPanel"
              Grid.Row="1"
              Margin="12,0,12,0">
            <ListView x:Name="ListViewMeals"
                      ItemsSource="{Binding Meals}"
                      Tapped="ListViewMeals_Tapped" >
                <ListView.ItemTemplate>
                    <DataTemplate>
                        <StackPanel Margin="0,0,0,17">
                            <TextBlock Text="{Binding DateString}"
                                       TextWrapping="Wrap"
                                       Style="{StaticResource ListViewItemTextBlock
                                              Style}" />
                            <TextBlock Text="{Binding Description}"
                                       TextWrapping="Wrap"
                                       Margin="12,-6,12,0"
                                       Style="{StaticResource GroupHeaderTextBlock
                                              Style}"
                                       FontSize="14" />
                        </StackPanel>
                    </DataTemplate>
                </ListView.ItemTemplate>
            </ListView>
        </Grid>
    </Grid>
</Page>
```

LISTING 24.2 The `MainPage.xaml.cs` Code

```
using System;
using Windows.ApplicationModel;
using Windows.ApplicationModel.Activation;
using Windows.UI.Xaml;
using Windows.UI.Xaml.Controls;
```

```
using Windows.UI.Xaml.Media.Animation;
using Windows.UI.Xaml.Navigation;

//The Blank Application template is documented at
//http://go.microsoft.com/fwlink/?LinkId=234227.

namespace SplitTheTab
{
    /// <summary>
    /// Provides application-specific behavior to supplement
    /// the default Application class.
    /// </summary>
    public sealed partial class App : Application
    {
#if WINDOWS_PHONE_APP
        private TransitionCollection transitions;
#endif
        private static ViewModel.MainViewModel viewModel = null;


        /// <summary>
        /// Initializes the singleton application object.
        /// This is the first line of authored code
        /// executed, and as such is the logical equivalent of
        /// main() or WinMain().
        /// </summary>
        public App()
        {
            this.InitializeComponent();
            this.Suspending += this.OnSuspending;
        }

        /// <summary>
        /// A static ViewModel used by the views to bind against.
        /// </summary>
        /// <returns>The MainViewModel object.</returns>
        public static ViewModel.MainViewModel ViewModel
        {
            get
            {
                // Delay creation of the view model until necessary
                if (viewModel == null)
                    viewModel = new ViewModel.MainViewModel();
```

```
            return viewModel;
        }
    }

    /// <summary>
    /// Invoked when the application is launched normally by the end user.
    /// Other entry points will be used when the application is launched
    /// to open a specific file, to display search results, and so forth.
    /// </summary>
    /// <param name="e">Details about the launch request and process.</param>
    protected override void OnLaunched(LaunchActivatedEventArgs e)
    {
#if DEBUG
        if (System.Diagnostics.Debugger.IsAttached)
        {
            this.DebugSettings.EnableFrameRateCounter = true;
        }
#endif

        Frame rootFrame = Window.Current.Content as Frame;

        //Do not repeat app initialization when the window already has
        //content; just ensure that the window is active.
        if (rootFrame == null)
        {
            //Create a frame to act as the navigation context and
            //navigate to the first page.
            rootFrame = new Frame();

            //TODO: Change this value to a cache size that is appropriate
            //for your application.
            rootFrame.CacheSize = 1;

            if (e.PreviousExecutionState ==
                ApplicationExecutionState.Terminated)
            {
                //TODO: Load state from previously suspended
                //application.
            }

            //Place the frame in the current window.
            Window.Current.Content = rootFrame;
        }

        if (rootFrame.Content == null)
        {
```

```
#if WINDOWS_PHONE_APP
                //Removes the turnstile navigation for startup.
                if (rootFrame.ContentTransitions != null)
                {
                    this.transitions = new TransitionCollection();
                    foreach (var c in rootFrame.ContentTransitions)
                    {
                        this.transitions.Add(c);
                    }
                }

                rootFrame.ContentTransitions = null;
                rootFrame.Navigated += this.RootFrame_FirstNavigated;
#endif

                //When the navigation stack isn't restored navigate to the
                //first page,
                //configuring the new page by passing required information
                //as a navigation parameter.
                if (!rootFrame.Navigate(typeof(MainPage),
                    e.Arguments))
                {
                    throw new
                        Exception("Failed to create initial page");
                }
            }

            //Ensure the current window is active.
            Window.Current.Activate();
        }

#if WINDOWS_PHONE_APP
        /// <summary>
        /// Restores the content transitions after the app has launched.
        /// </summary>
        /// <param name="sender">The object where the handler is attached.</param>
        /// <param name="e">Details about the navigation event.</param>
        private void RootFrame_FirstNavigated(object sender, NavigationEventArgs e)
        {
            var rootFrame = sender as Frame;
            rootFrame.ContentTransitions = this.transitions ??
                new TransitionCollection() { new NavigationThemeTransition() };
            rootFrame.Navigated -= this.RootFrame_FirstNavigated;
        }
```

```
#endif

        private void OnSuspending(object sender, SuspendingEventArgs e)
        {
            var deferral = e.SuspendingOperation.GetDeferral();

            // TODO: Save application state and stop any background activity.
            deferral.Complete();
        }
    }
}
```

Creating the Windows UI

Now we're ready to tackle the Windows UI project. As specified in our prototype, our goal is to provide a single-page experience with the Windows project; we won't need a details page—just a single main page that allows us to both list and edit details of an item in the list.

Because of the overlap in the XAML control library for Windows and for Windows Phone, we can quickly assemble much of the Windows user interface by copying what we have already implemented within the phone project.

The Master and Detail Regions

Open the `MainPage.xaml` file in the Windows project. Using the blank canvas of the design surface, we'll first establish the separate regions for our list of meals and then detail edit/display controls. Within the existing grid, use the XAML designer to drop a column into the existing Grid control. (Refer to Chapters 21, "Building WPF Applications" and 23 for guidance on the XAML design surface.) We want the rightmost column to use auto width sizing, whereas the leftmost column will use star-sizing to occupy the remaining area of the screen.

```
<Grid Background="{ThemeResource ApplicationPageBackgroundThemeBrush}">
        <Grid.ColumnDefinitions>
            <ColumnDefinition Width="*" />
            <ColumnDefinition Width="Auto" />
        </Grid.ColumnDefinitions>
```

Due to slight differences in the way we want to present our data and inconsistencies between the ListView control between the two different platforms, we are going to use a GridView control instead of a ListView control here. This will enable the more standard horizontal display that you would typically see on a larger screened device.

Our GridView will share many attributes, however, with our phone UI. It will still use a two-line data template to display the meal information, and it will implement a Tapped event handler. Other than that, our bindings stay the same.

```
<GridView x:Name="GridViewMeals"
          Grid.Column="0"
          ItemsSource="{Binding Meals}"
          Tapped="GridViewMeals_Tapped" >
    <GridView.ItemTemplate>
          <DataTemplate>
               <Grid HorizontalAlignment="Stretch">
                    <Grid.RowDefinitions>
                         <RowDefinition Height="auto"/>
                         <RowDefinition Height="auto"/>
                    </Grid.RowDefinitions>
               <Grid.ColumnDefinitions>
                    <ColumnDefinition Width="250" />
               </Grid.ColumnDefinitions>
               <TextBlock Text="{Binding DateString}"
                          Grid.Row="0"
                          TextWrapping="Wrap"
                               HorizontalAlignment="Left"
                          Style="{StaticResource HeaderTextBlockStyle}"
                               FontSize="32"/>
               <TextBlock Text="{Binding Description}"
                     Grid.Row="1"
                     TextWrapping="Wrap"
                               HorizontalAlignment="Left"
                          Margin="12,-6,12,0"
                          Style="{StaticResource SubtitleTextBlockStyle}"
                          FontSize="14" />

               </Grid>
          </DataTemplate>
      </GridView.ItemTemplate>
</GridView>
```

Over in the right column, add a Border control. This will be the parent control of our editing region of the screen (functioning as a sort of replacement for the Phone page that implemented this in the phone project). Set the background color to white.

```
<Border x:Name="DetailsPaneBorder"
      Width="450"
      Background="White"
      Grid.Column="1"
      >
```

Inside the Border parent container, you can go back to the phone project and copy and paste the entire Grid object that contained our editing controls. We'll want to make some tweaks to account for the white background (setting border brushes to black, setting Foreground properties to black, and so on), but by and large the entire chunk of XAML can come over intact. We also want to copy over all our eventing code-behind for the plus and minus buttons.

The remaining item on the to-do list is fixing the data context for our XAML page. In the Phone world, we set the context of our main page to the main view model and then passed in the selected `Meal` object (using Navigate); then, in the detail page we set our data context from the passed-in `Meal` object within the `OnNavigatedTo` event. In the Windows project, we have only the single page. So there is no need to pass data around. But we still need to maintain two different data contexts: the main view model and the selected item. Within the `MainPage.Xaml.cs` code, place a member field to hold our `Meal` object.

```
private Meal _mealInstance;


public Meal MealInstance
{
    get { return _mealInstance; }
    set { _mealInstance = value; }

}
```

Then we can use the phone ListView's `Tapped` code as a starting point. In the `Tapped` event in the `Window's MainPage.xaml.cs`, copy over the ListView `Tapped` code and remove the `Navigate` command. Then set the `MealInstance` object to the object pulled from the `SelectedItem` property.

```
//Cast selected item to Meal.
Meal MealInstance = (Meal)GridViewMeals.SelectedItem;
this.DetailsPaneBorder.DataContext = MealInstance;
```

With that final data context mapping in place, our app should be fully data aware and ready to run. To test the app, we will want to change the startup project to the Windows project and then make sure we have the Windows 8.1 simulator selected in the IDE (see Figure 24.17).

Figure 24.18 shows our app now running in the Windows 8 simulator.

The application is now fully functional, and ready to be deployed to either a Windows Phone 8.1 or Windows 8.1.

The Windows `MainPage.xaml` listing is provided in Listing 24.3, and the `MainPage.xaml.cs` listing is provided in Listing 24.4.

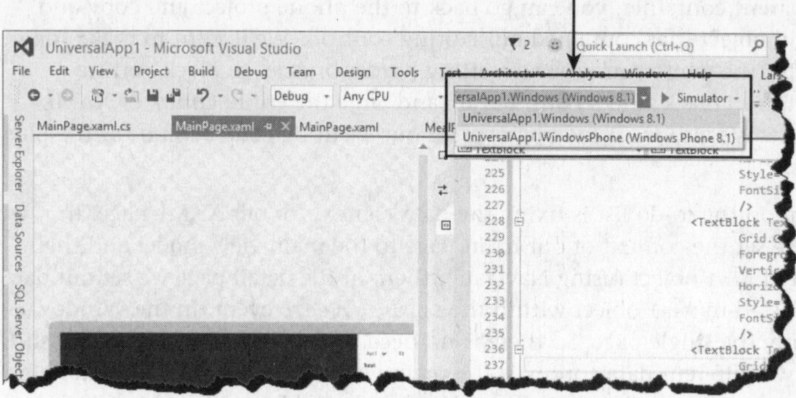

FIGURE 24.17 Switching between the Windows Phone emulator and the Windows simulator.

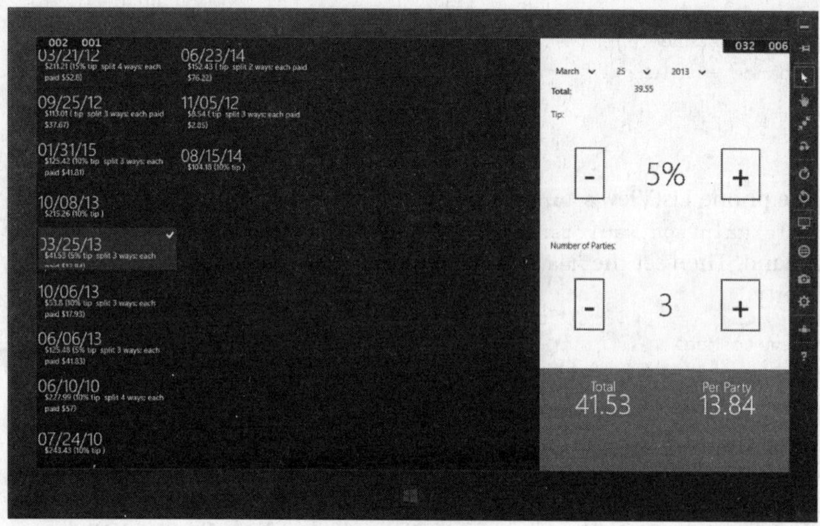

FIGURE 24.18 The app running in the Windows 8.1 simulator.

LISTING 24.3 The `MainPage.xaml` Code (Windows)

```
<Page
    x:Class="SplitTheTab.MainPage"
    xmlns="http://schemas.microsoft.com/winfx/2006/xaml/presentation"
    xmlns:x="http://schemas.microsoft.com/winfx/2006/xaml"
    xmlns:local="using:SplitTheTab"
    xmlns:d="http://schemas.microsoft.com/expression/blend/2008"
    xmlns:mc="http://schemas.openxmlformats.org/markup-compatibility/2006"
```

```
mc:Ignorable="d"
>

<Page.Resources>
    <local:DateTimeToDateTimeOffsetConverter
        x:Key="DateTimeToDateTimeOffsetConverter"/>
</Page.Resources>
<Page.BottomAppBar>
    <CommandBar x:Name="BottomAppBar1" Padding="10,0,10,0">
        <AppBarButton x:Name="AddButton"
                        Icon="Add"
                        Label="Add"
                        Click="AddButton_Click" />
    </CommandBar>
</Page.BottomAppBar>

<Grid Background="{ThemeResource ApplicationPageBackgroundThemeBrush}">
    <Grid.ColumnDefinitions>
        <ColumnDefinition Width="*" />
        <ColumnDefinition Width="Auto" />
    </Grid.ColumnDefinitions>

    <GridView x:Name="GridViewMeals"
            Grid.Column="0"
            ItemsSource="{Binding Meals}"
            Tapped="GridViewMeals_Tapped" >
        <GridView.ItemTemplate>
            <DataTemplate>
                <Grid HorizontalAlignment="Stretch">
                    <Grid.RowDefinitions>
                        <RowDefinition Height="auto"/>
                        <RowDefinition Height="auto"/>
                    </Grid.RowDefinitions>
                <Grid.ColumnDefinitions>
                    <ColumnDefinition Width="250" />
                </Grid.ColumnDefinitions>
                <TextBlock Text="{Binding DateString}"
                        Grid.Row="0"
                        TextWrapping="Wrap"
                            HorizontalAlignment="Left"
                        Style="{StaticResource HeaderTextBlockStyle}"
                            FontSize="32"/>
                <TextBlock Text="{Binding Description}"
                    Grid.Row="1"
                    TextWrapping="Wrap"
                        HorizontalAlignment="Left"
```

```
                                Margin="12,-6,12,0"
                                Style="{StaticResource SubtitleTextBlockStyle}"
                                FontSize="14" />

                    </Grid>
                </DataTemplate>
            </GridView.ItemTemplate>
</GridView>

<Border x:Name="DetailsPaneBorder"
        Width="450"
        Background="White"
        Grid.Column="1"
        >
    <Grid Margin="20,0,20,0">
        <Grid.ColumnDefinitions>
            <ColumnDefinition />
            <ColumnDefinition />
            <ColumnDefinition />
        </Grid.ColumnDefinitions>
        <Grid.RowDefinitions>
            <RowDefinition Height="15" />
            <RowDefinition Height="Auto" />
            <!-- Date -->
            <RowDefinition Height="Auto" />
            <!-- Sub Total -->
            <RowDefinition Height="Auto" />
            <!-- Tip -->
            <RowDefinition />
            <!-- Tip -->
            <RowDefinition Height="Auto" />
            <!-- Parties -->
            <RowDefinition />
            <!-- Parties -->
            <RowDefinition />
            <!-- Final totals -->
        </Grid.RowDefinitions>

        <StackPanel Grid.Row="0" Margin="12,17,0,28">
            <TextBlock Text="SPLIT THE TAB"
            Style="{StaticResource TitleTextBlockStyle}" />
        </StackPanel>

        <!-- Date -->
        <DatePicker x:Name="DatePickerMeal"
```

```
            Header="Date:"
        Grid.Column="0"
            Grid.ColumnSpan="3"
        Grid.Row="1"
        VerticalAlignment="Center"
        Foreground="Black"
            BorderBrush="Black"
        Date="{Binding Date,
        Converter={StaticResource
        DateTimeToDateTimeOffsetConverter}, Mode=TwoWay}"/>


<!-- Sub Total -->
<TextBlock Text="Total:"
       Grid.Row="2"
       Grid.Column="0"
       Style="{StaticResource TitleTextBlockStyle}"
       VerticalAlignment="Center"
           Foreground="Black" />
<TextBox x:Name="TextBoxTotal"
     Grid.Column="1"
     Grid.Row="2"
     VerticalAlignment="Center"
     Text="{Binding SubTotal}"
         Foreground="Black" />

<TextBlock Grid.Row="3"
       Style="{StaticResource BodyTextBlockStyle}"
       Text="Tip:"
       Margin="0,15,0,0"
           Foreground="Black" />


<!-- Tip -->
<Button x:Name="ButtonDownTip"
    Grid.Row="4"
    Grid.Column="0"
    VerticalAlignment="Center"
    HorizontalAlignment="Center"
    FontSize="60"
    Click="ButtonDownTip_Click"
        Foreground="Black"
        BorderBrush="Black"
    >-
```

```
</Button>
<TextBlock x:Name="TextBlockTip"
       Grid.Column="1" Grid.Row="4"
       VerticalAlignment="Center"
      HorizontalAlignment="Center"
      Style="{StaticResource HeaderTextBlockStyle}"
      Text="{Binding TipPercentString}"
          Foreground="Black"/>

<Button x:Name="ButtonUpTip"
    Grid.Row="4"
    Grid.Column="2"
    HorizontalAlignment="Center"
    VerticalAlignment="Center"
    FontSize="60"
    Click="ButtonUpTip_Click"
       Foreground="Black"
       BorderBrush="Black"
    >+
</Button>

<!-- Number of Parties -->
<TextBlock Grid.Row="5"
      Grid.ColumnSpan="2"
      Grid.Column="0"
      Style="{StaticResource BodyTextBlockStyle}"
      Text="Number of Parties:"
      Margin="0,15,0,0"
          Foreground="Black" />

<Button x:Name="ButtonDownParties"
    Grid.Row="6"
    Grid.Column="0"
    VerticalAlignment="Center"
    HorizontalAlignment="Center"
    FontSize="60"
    Click="ButtonDownParties_Click"
       Foreground="Black"
       BorderBrush="Black"
    >-
</Button>

<TextBlock x:Name="TextBlockParties"
      Grid.Column="1"
      Grid.Row="6"
```

```
        VerticalAlignment="Center"
        HorizontalAlignment="Center"
        Style="{StaticResource HeaderTextBlockStyle}"
        Text="{Binding Parties}"
            Foreground="Black"/>
<Button x:Name="ButtonUpParties"
    Grid.Row="6"
    Grid.Column="2"
    HorizontalAlignment="Center"
    VerticalAlignment="Center"
    FontSize="60"
    Click="ButtonUpParties_Click"
        Foreground="Black"
        BorderBrush="Black"
    >+
</Button>

<Border Background="Gray"
    Grid.Row="7"
    Grid.Column="0"
    Grid.ColumnSpan="3"
    Margin="-20,15,-20,0"
    >
    <Grid>
        <Grid.ColumnDefinitions>
            <ColumnDefinition />
            <ColumnDefinition />
        </Grid.ColumnDefinitions>
        <Grid.RowDefinitions>
            <RowDefinition Height="Auto" />
            <RowDefinition />
        </Grid.RowDefinitions>
        <TextBlock Text="Total"
                Grid.Column="0"
                Foreground="White"
                VerticalAlignment="Bottom"
                HorizontalAlignment="Center"
                Style="{StaticResource HeaderTextBlockStyle}"
                FontSize="24"
                />
        <TextBlock Text="Per Party"
                Grid.Column="1"
                Foreground="White"
                VerticalAlignment="Bottom"
                HorizontalAlignment="Center"
                Style="{StaticResource HeaderTextBlockStyle}"
```

```
                    FontSize="24"
                    />
            <TextBlock Text="{Binding GrandTotal}"
                    Grid.Column="0"
                    Grid.Row="1"
                    Foreground="White"
                    VerticalAlignment="Top"
                    HorizontalAlignment="Center"
                    Style="{StaticResource HeaderTextBlockStyle}"
                    FontSize="48"
                    />
            <TextBlock Text="{Binding PerPartyGrandTotal}"
                    Grid.Column="1"
                    Grid.Row="1"
                    Foreground="White"
                    VerticalAlignment="Top"
                    HorizontalAlignment="Center"
                    Style="{StaticResource HeaderTextBlockStyle}"
                    FontSize="48"
                    />
                </Grid>
            </Border>
        </Grid>
    </Border>

  </Grid>
</Page>
```

LISTING 24.4 The `MainPage.xaml.cs` Code (Windows)

```
using System;
using System.Collections.Generic;
using Windows.UI.Xaml;
using Windows.UI.Xaml.Controls;
using Windows.UI.Xaml.Controls.Primitives;
using Windows.UI.Xaml.Data;
using Windows.UI.Xaml.Input;
using Windows.UI.Xaml.Media;
using Windows.UI.Xaml.Navigation;
using SplitTheTab.DataModel;

namespace SplitTheTab
{
```

```
public sealed partial class MainPage : Page
{
    private Meal _mealInstance;

    public Meal MealInstance
    {
        get { return _mealInstance; }
        set { _mealInstance = value; }

    }
    public MainPage()
    {
        this.InitializeComponent();

        this.NavigationCacheMode =
            NavigationCacheMode.Disabled;

        DataContext = App.ViewModel;
    }

    private void AddButton_Click(object sender,
        RoutedEventArgs e)
    {
        Meal newMeal = new Meal();
        newMeal.Date = DateTime.Today;
        newMeal.Parties = 1;
        newMeal.TipPercent = .20;
        newMeal.SubTotal = 50.00;

        App.ViewModel.Meals.Add(newMeal);
    }

    private void ButtonDownTip_Click(object sender,
        RoutedEventArgs e)
    {
        this.MealInstance.TipPercent =
            this.MealInstance.TipPercent - .05;
    }

    private void ButtonUpTip_Click(object sender,
        RoutedEventArgs e)
    {
        this.MealInstance.TipPercent =
            this.MealInstance.TipPercent + .05;
    }
```

```
        private void ButtonDownParties_Click(object sender,
            RoutedEventArgs e)
        {
            this.MealInstance.Parties =
                this.MealInstance.Parties - 1;
        }

        private void ButtonUpParties_Click(object sender,
            RoutedEventArgs e)
        {
            this.MealInstance.Parties =
                this.MealInstance.Parties + 1;
        }

        private void GridViewMeals_Tapped(object sender,
            TappedRoutedEventArgs e)
        {
            //Cast selected item to Meal.
            Meal MealInstance =
                (Meal)GridViewMeals.SelectedItem;
            this.DetailsPaneBorder.DataContext =
                MealInstance;
        }
    }
}
```

Summary

This chapter built on the foundational concepts of XAML and the Visual Studio designers that were covered in Chapter 21, and the Windows Store application development concepts in Chapter 23, to enable you to write XAML applications for Windows Phone. We discussed the various components of the Windows Phone application and system architecture, including a brief comparison between the "old" Silverlight approach to Phone development and the new roadmap, which relies heavily on WinRT XAML libraries. We discussed the Windows Phone application lifecycle and some of the subtle differences between the Phone and Windows version of the XAML components. Finally, we pulled the phone information together with the prior WPF and Windows Store information in this book and pressed that into play to build a fully functional "Universal app" that compiles and runs against either Windows Phone 8.1 or Windows 8.1.

In the next chapter, the last in the book, we take the cross-platform device development story to the next stage with a discussion of Cordova and writing for non-Windows platforms.

CHAPTER 25

Writing Cross-Platform Mobile Applications with Apache Cordova

IN THIS CHAPTER

- ▶ Fundamentals of Cordova Development
- ▶ Using Cordova Frameworks and Plug-Ins
- ▶ Developing a Cordova App with Ionic and Angular

Cordova is a set of device application programming interfaces (APIs) that allow you to build mobile apps for iOS, Android, and Windows. These applications run natively on the device. However, they are built using the web technologies Hypertext Markup Language (HTML), Cascading Style Sheets (CSS), and JavaScript. This includes support for client frameworks such as Angular, Bootstrap, and Knockout. A mobile app, like a website, also typically calls backend services such as those built with the Web API. Cordova allows you to adapt your web skills to mobile development. (See Chapters 17, "Building Modern Websites with ASP.NET 5," 18, "Using JavaScript and Client-Side Frameworks," and 19, "Building and Consuming Services with Web API and WCF," for a discussion on web technologies.)

As native applications, they can access features of the native device such as the camera, the file system, the accelerometer, and local storage (to allow the application to work offline). Cordova supports APIs written in JavaScript for working with the device. A native application also means you can build for the mobile app store and thus monetize your creations.

Cordova also solves the big problem of building a mobile application targeted at a single device (such as iOS) and then having to completely rebuild it to support other device types (such as Android and Windows). Building native mobile applications often means writing an app three times, in three different languages, on three different platforms. This is time consuming and expensive to create, maintain, and evolve. With Cordova, you write once and deploy to multiple platforms. This decreases your development and maintenance costs significantly.

Microsoft has made a big investment in supporting Cordova with tools built into Visual Studio 2015. These tools simplify getting an environment up and running (and keeping it that way). For example, Cordova requires more than a dozen tool chain dependencies to set up and start developing. Thankfully, Visual Studio has built-in support to solve this problem for developers. This chapter introduces you to building cross-platform mobile applications using Cordova and Visual Studio.

NOTE

Microsoft is not only including Apache Cordova in Visual Studio; it is also contributing back to the community with numerous updates that help all developers on all platforms. This includes security improvements, support for Windows 8.1 / 10 Universal Apps, and platform-specific configuration.

Fundamentals of Cordova Development

If you are a web developer, you will be happy to know that your CSS, HTML, and JavaScript client framework skills all come into play when building Cordova apps. This means you do not have to work with multiple languages such as Objective C, C++, Java, Swift, and C# to build a single application. Instead, you can build with the web development tools with which you are already familiar.

Apache Cordova is an open-source, top-level project from the Apache Software Foundation (http://www.apache.org/). This foundation is committed to building open-source software products for the public good. They manage the project and ensure it remains free and open source. Microsoft has also become a key contributor to the project.

How Cordova Works

Cordova is an application container that runs natively on supported mobile devices. The container wraps a web application that you write using standard HTML, CSS, and JavaScript. Figure 25.1 provides an overview of how Cordova works.

The Cordova application container wraps a web view that takes up the entire screen of the application. This web view uses the native operating system's web view container (`UIWebVew` in iOS, `android.webkit.WebView` in Android, and `WebView` in Windows and Windows Phone). Each of these web views provides different web view rendering engines based on operating system and version. This means that building a Cordova application is similar to building a website targeted to a mobile device. You must account for differences in the DOM implementation within your HTML, JavaScript, and CSS. The good news is, like website development, you can take advantage of the frameworks that help you do this already, such as Bootstrap, jQuery, Angular, and more (see Chapter 18).

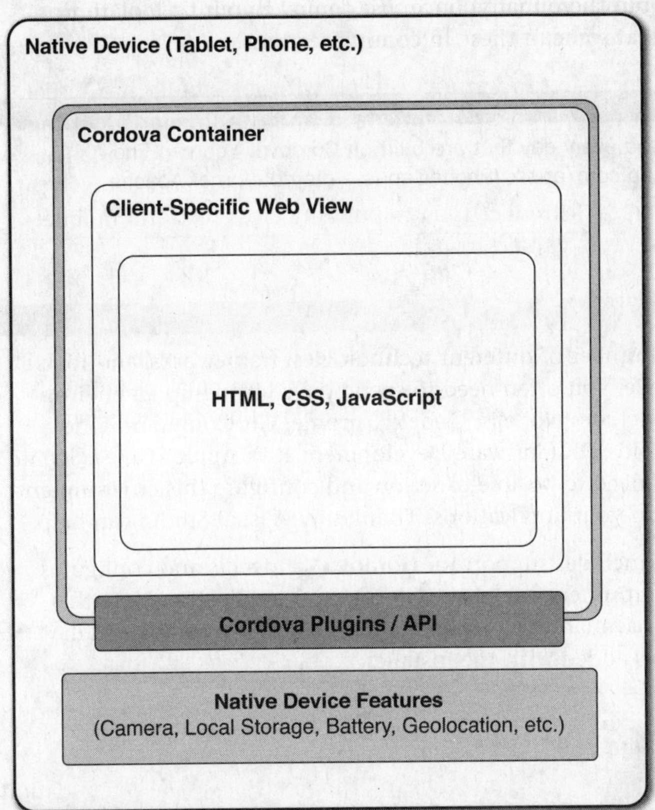

FIGURE 25.1 Cordova is a native application container for a web application. It provides access to the native device capabilities through plug-ins.

Your Cordova app gets compiled to a native application on the target device. For iOS, this is an `.ipa` (iPhone Application Archive), for Android an `.apk` (Android Application Package), and for Windows an `.xap` (x-Application Package). Cordova packages your application as a native app that can then be installed as any other native application. Remember, this native application wraps a web view and then runs your application like a hosted web page.

Cordova provides plug-ins that work as native device APIs for calling on device-specific features such as the camera, GPS, network, and sound. These plug-ins work to abstract the per-device complexity and serve as an interface between your application and the native device. Cordova ensures the APIs are consistent across device. This means you can write your code (as JavaScript) once, and it will work on each device thanks to the Cordova APIs.

The Cordova framework does not provide special user interface (UI) components for building your applications. Instead, you get the browser's HTML rendering. However, like a website, there are many tools out there that you can use to make your UI look more native on a device. We will look at some of these in coming sections.

CORDOVA APPS

There are hundreds of apps used every day that are built on Cordova. You can find a sample list at http://phonegap.com/app/. (PhoneGap is a distribution of Apache Cordova.)

Cordova Dependencies

Cordova applications rely on a number of different technologies, frameworks, and tools. Just to get started developing code, you often need to spend days setting up an environment. The Cordova tool chain includes Node.js, Google Chrome, Git Command-Line Tools, Apache Ant, Java 7, Android SDK (Software Development Kit), Apple iTunes, SQLite, WebSocket4Net, and more. You need to be able to set up and configure this environment so you can build, deploy, and run your applications. Thankfully, Visual Studio can help.

The Visual Studio 2015 installer includes support for Cordova. It installs and configures the baseline set of tools and environments needed to develop an application Note that these Visual Studio tools are also available for Visual Studio 2013 as a separate install. Figure 25.2 shows the many tools added with the installer.

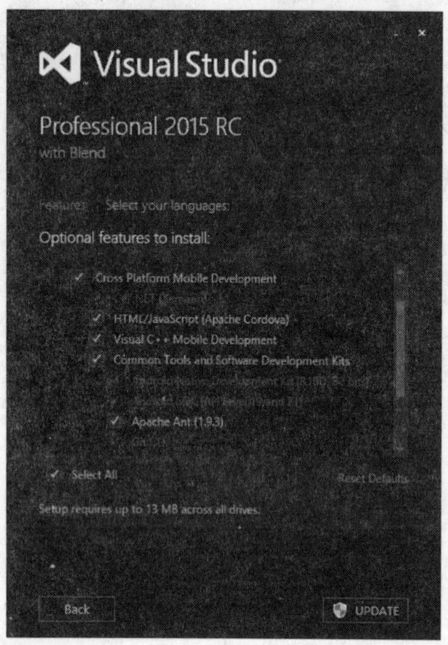

FIGURE 25.2 The Visual Studio 2015 installer includes support for installing and configuring the many tool chain dependencies required for Cordova applications.

The Cordova Project Template

Visual Studio 2015 ships with two project templates for creating Cordova applications. These templates provide full IntelliSense in the JavaScript code editor, special tools such as a plug-in manager, and support for your application markup with tools like the DOM Explorer and CSS editor. Cordova applications in Visual Studio also get the full debugging experience across emulators, simulators, and test devices; this means breakpoints, watch windows, the immediate window, and more. It all starts with the project template; let's take a look.

Creating a New Cordova Project

You can develop Cordova applications with Visual Studio using either JavaScript or TypeScript. Recall that TypeScript is a superset of JavaScript that allows you to develop strongly typed applications that are ultimately processed (compiled) to JavaScript when executed. This chapter focuses on the more familiar JavaScript. However, the two are similar.

To create a Cordova project in Visual Studio, you start with File, New Project. This brings up the New Project dialog, as shown in Figure 25.3. Notice the project type is under either the JavaScript or the TypeScript language. Note that when you create a Cordova application, Visual Studio may ask you to create or renew your Windows Developer license for creating apps for the Windows Store.

When the project launches in the IDE, you are shown a getting started page. This provides helpful information and links on developing with Cordova. This page is actually the `Project_Readme.html` file inside Solution Explorer.

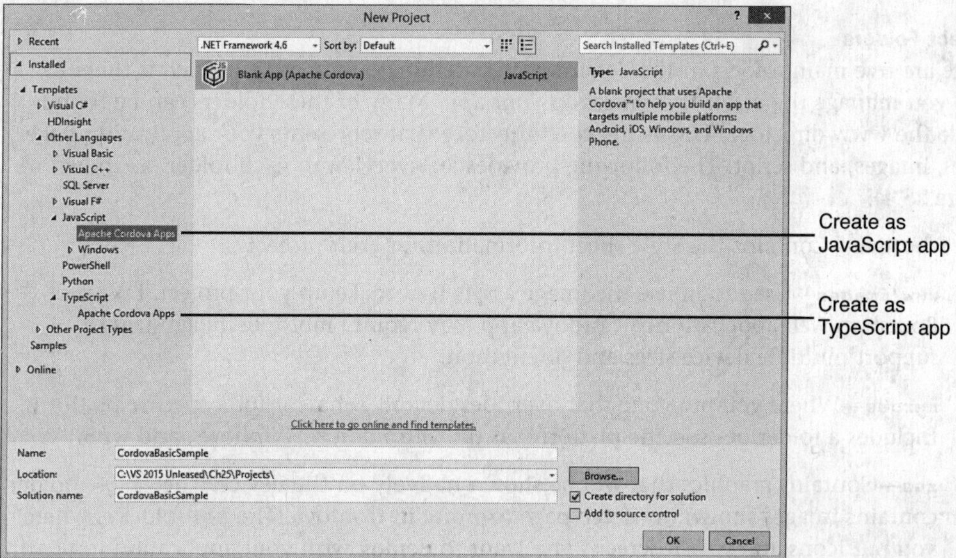

FIGURE 25.3 Use the Add New Project dialog to create a Cordova application based in either the JavaScript or the TypeScript language.

Like all projects in Visual Studio, Solution Explorer offers you access to the elements that make up the code for your Cordova application. Figure 25.4 shows a blank app template inside the IDE. Let's take a look at the folders and files of the solution.

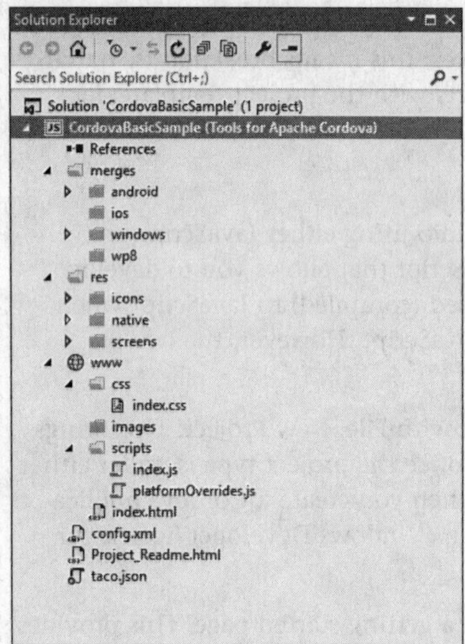

FIGURE 25.4 A blank Cordova application inside Solution Explorer.

Project Folders

There are five main folders in the default project template for Cordova. Each is there to help you manage the assets that make up your app. Many of these folders can be found inside the www directory. This is the core directory that represents your application pages, styles, images, and script. The following provides an overview of each folder (as shown in Figure 25.4):

- **`www/css`**—Contains the style sheet information for your project.
- **`www/images`**—Used to house the image assets that make up your project. Like a Bootstrap web application, a Cordova app may require multiple image sizes to support multiple device sizes and orientation.
- **`merges`**—Where you put code that overrides default behavior for a specific platform. Includes a folder per specific platform, as in Android, iOS, Windows, and wp8.
- **`res`**—Contains graphics that will be shown natively on the device. The `Images` folder contains images shown on a web page running in Cordova. The `Res` folder is where you put icons and splash screens you want to deploy with your application to be run locally (by the native device versus through a web view).

- `www/scripts`—Contains the JavaScript code you write to enable the features of your application.

Project Files

The files inside a Cordova project are similar to those found in a website. These files make up your user interface, the code required to make the UI execute, and configuration information. The following highlights key files in a Cordova app:

- `.html`—These are your UI pages. Your UI pages typically sit at the root of the special www folder. The main page for a Cordova application is `index.html`. It shows the first screen in your app and then works with your code (or a client library such as Angular) to load additional views.
- `index.css`—Represents the styles used to define the look of your application. This file can be found in the www/css folder.
- `config.xml`—The `config.xml` file provides the configuration information for your app. This includes defining common elements such as start page, version, splash screen, default orientation, and more. This file is stored in the root of your app (see Figure 25.4). Visual Studio ships with a designer for editing `config.xml`. The common application properties are shown in this designer in Figure 25.5.

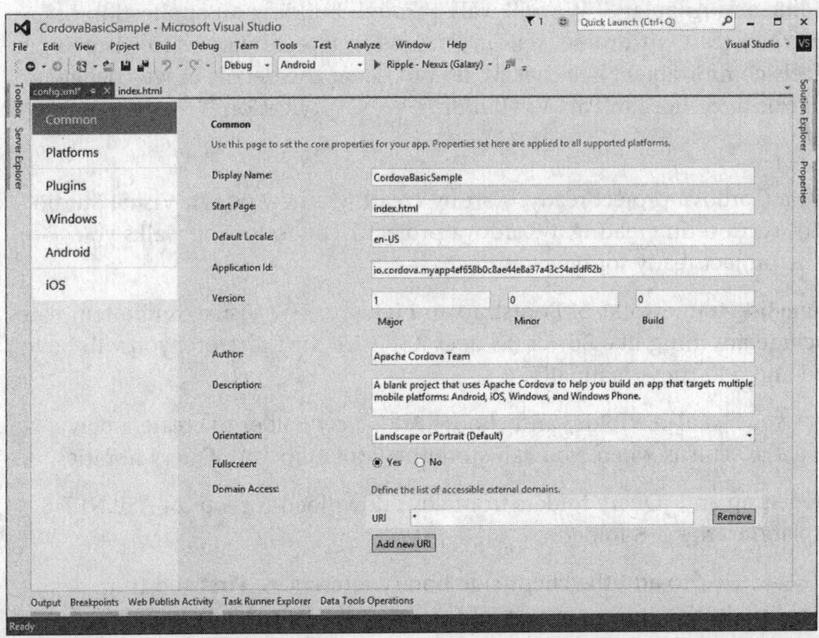

FIGURE 25.5 Use the Common section of the `Config.xml` designer to change basic properties of your application.

The `.config` designer for Cordova also enables adding plug-ins to your project. (See the "Cordova Plug-Ins (for Accessing Native Device Capabilities)" section later in this chapter.) Finally, this designer supports setting platform-specific properties of your application. Notice the links on the left side of Figure 25.5. Each exposes a form for setting properties for the selected platform (such as target version/device).

- **index.js**—This file (stored in the www/`scripts` directory) provides special Cordova events that execute code when the application starts (`onDeviceReady`), is paused (`onPause`), and is resumed (`onResume`). You can use the events to initialize parts of your application on startup, save state on pause, and restore state on resume. We demonstrate using this file later in this chapter.
- **taco.json**—This file is used by Visual Studio to specify the version of the Cordova CLI used to build your application. This is useful when building on a remote machine.

Creating a Basic Cordova App

One of the best ways to understand Cordova (or any new technology) is to walk through writing that first application to get moving with the basics. We are going to start with what should be familiar to web developers looking to do mobile: HTML, CSS, JavaScript, Bootstrap, and jQuery. We are aware that the current popular frameworks for Cordova applications are Ionic and AngularJS. We will walk through building an application on those, too. However, we start with these well-understood web technologies to ensure your first application feels comfortable. Note that we do not cover the details of web development because you can find those in Part V, "Building Web Applications."

Project Setup

If you do not have a Cordova project ready, start by creating a new one in Visual Studio 2015. (See the prior section on creating a Cordova project.) The following walks you through getting the project ready for development:

1. Add the client-side frameworks of Bootstrap and jQuery. The Visual Studio template does not include anything like Bower (as does ASP.NET 5). Therefore, you will have to download and add these manually.

   Right-click the `www/scripts` folder and choose Add, New Folder to create a new folder named `lib`. This is where you can store the Bootstrap and jQuery libraries.

   Copy the Bootstrap and jQuery folders from your download (or a prior ASP.NET 5 project template) to the `lib` folder.

2. Open `www/index.html` to add the client-side library references. First add the `Boostrap.css` link in the `<head>` section of the page. (Make sure it comes before `index.css` because this is where you typically put your Bootstrap overrides, so it must come second). The following shows an example.

```
<link rel="stylesheet"
     href="scripts/lib/bootstrap/css/bootstrap.css" />
<link href="css/index.css" rel="stylesheet" />
```

3. At the bottom of `Index.html`, add the `<script>` tags to include jQuery and the Bootstrap script file. Remember to keep the reference to your custom script for the page (`index.js`) last in this list. (It will likely rely on the other scripts being loaded first.) The following shows an example of this complete section (including the default items in the template).

```
<!-- script references -->
<script src="cordova.js"></script>
<script src="scripts/platformOverrides.js"></script>
<script src="scripts/lib/jquery/jquery.js"></script>
<script src="scripts/lib/bootstrap/js/bootstrap.js"></script>
<script src="scripts/index.js"></script>
```

The project and initial page should now be set up. We will look at building the user interface next.

Creating the Main App Page

The mobile application you create here is based on the samples from Chapter 18. It allows a user to log data related to a bike ride or run. Here, however, we are going to log each entry using a mobile device running Cordova. There is one primary page for this application: `index.html`. The following walks you through creating this user interface:

1. Start with the `index.html` page you used in the prior walk-through (where you added the client-side scripts). The markup for this page will include five primary sections between the opening and closing `<body>` tags. These sections are shown in Listing 25.1 highlighted with a preceding, bold comment tag, as in `<!-- comment -->`. Notice that we are using Bootstrap styles throughout the markup. We will look at each section of the markup as we proceed.

LISTING 25.1 The <body> of the `Index.html` Page

```
<!-- the header + navigation -->
<div id="navbar"></div>

<div class="container body-content">
  <h2>Track My Pace</h2>

  <!-- user input form -->
  <div class="row">
    <div class="col-md-4">
      <label class="control-label">Distance (miles): </label>
      <input type="text" id="distance" class="form-control" />
      <label class="control-label">Time (minutes): </label>
      <input type="text" id="time" class="form-control" />
```

```
      <button type="button" class="btn" id="btnCalc">calculate</button>
    </div>
  </div>

  <div class="row col-md-4">

    <!-- pace calculation results -->
    <div id="paceDisplay" style="display: none;">
      <hr />
      <p><strong>Calculated pace (mins/mile):</strong></p>
      <span class="pace" id="pace"></span>
      <button type="button" class="btn btnSave" id="btnSave">save</button>
    </div>

    <!-- results log -->
    <div id="logDisplay" style="display: none;">
      <hr />
      <p><strong>Pace log (date, dist, time, pace):</strong></p>
      <ul id="logData"></ul>
      <button type="button" class="btn" id="btnClear">clear</button>
    </div>
  </div>

  <!-- the footer -->
  <div id="footer"></div>

</div>
```

2. The header and footer `<div>` tags in Listing 25.1 are empty. This is because our app is being designed to work like a website in that it will contain multiple pages. Each page will have a common header and footer. (We will look at building a single-page application with Cordova in a coming section.) We will write some simple jQuery to add the header and footer to these `<div>` sections.

   Start by adding a new page to the application for the navigation. You can do so by right-clicking the www folder in Solution Explorer and choosing Add, New Item. Select the HTML Page template. Name the page `navbar.html`.

   Repeat this process for a page named `footer.html`.

3. Open `navbar.html` and add a standard Bootstrap `navbar`. This will contain the main header for the application as well as three navigational elements (Home, About, Contact). The following shows an example.

```
<div class="navbar navbar-inverse navbar-fixed-top">
  <div class="container">
    <div class="navbar-header">
```

```
        <button type="button" class="navbar-toggle"
                data-toggle="collapse" data-target=".navbar-collapse">
          <span class="icon-bar"></span>
          <span class="icon-bar"></span>
          <span class="icon-bar"></span>
        </button>
        <a href="index.html" class="navbar-brand">My Run / My Ride</a>
      </div>
      <div class="navbar-collapse collapse">
        <ul class="nav navbar-nav">
          <li><a href="index.html">Home</a></li>
          <li><a href="about.html">About</a></li>
          <li><a href="contact.html">Contact</a></li>
        </ul>
      </div>
    </div>
  </div>
```

4. Open `footer.html` and add the following simple content to represent the footer in our application. (Note that the app does not require a footer.)

```
<footer>
  <hr />
  <p>&copy; VS 2015 Unleashed</p>
</footer>
```

5. Make sure the header and footer are displayed on each page in the application. Open `index.js` from the `www/scripts` folder. Inside the main closure function, add the following jQuery calls just before the end of the function (after `onResume`). These two lines of code find the given `<div>` tag for either the header or the footer and load the contents of the appropriate file.

```
//Load the HTML common to all pages.
$("#navbar").load("navbar.html");
$("#footer").load("footer.html");
```

6. Notice that the sections from Listing 25.1, "pace calculation results" and "results log," are marked with a style to hide these `<div>` tags and their contents. We do not want to show these sections unless the user adds content to them.

7. You can add a page to the application for `about.html` and `contact.html`. Simply use the markup created earlier in Listing 25.1 as a basis. Replace the content within the `<body>` tags with a simple title for these pages. We are showing them here just to illustrate navigation and page refresh using a standard web model to build a Cordova application.

We also added a few overrides to `www/css/index.css`. These are styles to make the application look a bit nicer. We do not cover those here, but you can review these style changes from the code download for this book.

Writing the JavaScript for the App

The last step is to create some basic JavaScript (also using jQuery) to wire up the application to user input. The following walks you trough each of these steps:

1. **Calculate the pace**—The UI contains a button called Calculate that should calculate and show the user her pace based on her entered time and distance. You need to wire the click event for this button to a JavaScript function you will write. Open `index.js` and add the following two lines to the `onDeviceReady()` function:

```
var btnCalc = document.querySelector('#btnCalc');
btnCalc.addEventListener('click', onCalculate);
```

   Also inside `index.js`, add the following method to get the input values, calculate `pace`, and display the information to the user (provided `pace` is numeric). You should add this method inside the main closure of the page (under the `onResume()` function).

```
function onCalculate() {
  var paceDisplay = $('#paceDisplay');
  paceDisplay.hide();

  //Get values from input fields.
  var time = $('#time').val();
  var dist = $('#distance').val();

  var pace = (time / dist);

  if (!isNaN(parseFloat(pace)) && isFinite(pace)) {
    //Update UI.
    $('#pace').text(pace.toFixed(2));
    paceDisplay.fadeIn();
  }
};
```

2. **Save log data**—After a user has calculated her pace, she either calculate another pace or save her calculation to the log. The UI contains a button called Save inside the Pace Calculation Results section. Again, add the click event to the button inside the `onDeviceReady()` function of `index.js`. The following shows an example.

```
var btnCalc = document.querySelector('#btnSave');
btnCalc.addEventListener('click', onSave);
```

   Add a method to `index.js` called `onSave()` (under the prior method) to handle the save button click event. This method should create an entry as a list item (`<li>`) and prepend that item to the list in the application. The list should include the date of the entry, the actual time and distance, and the calculated pace. The following shows an example.

```
function onSave() {
  var pace = $('#pace').text();
  if (!isNaN(parseFloat(pace)) && isFinite(pace)) {
    //Get values from input fields.
    var time = $('#time').val();
    var dist = $('#distance').val();

    //Build string to add to <li>.
    var date = (new Date()).toDateString();

    var list = $("#logData");
    list.prepend('<li>' + date + ' - D: ' + dist +
      ', T: ' + time + ', P: ' + pace + '</li>');
    $('#logDisplay').fadeIn();
  }
};
```

3. **Clear log data**—The Results Log section of the UI contains a Clear button. Use `index.js` and the `onDeviceReady()` function to bind to this click event as you did the prior two buttons. The following is an example.

   ```
   var btnCalc = document.querySelector('#btnClear');
   btnCalc.addEventListener('click', onClear);
   ```

   Add a method inside `index.js` to clear the log when the user presses the Clear button. The following is an example.

   ```
   function onClear() {
     $("#logData").empty();
     $('#logDisplay').fadeOut();
   };
   ```

The application is now complete. We can run and debug using Visual Studio. Of course, Cordova requires emulators, simulators, or actual devices to execute your code properly. We look at these features of the tool next.

Running and Debugging Your App

Visual Studio works with the Cordova command-line interface (CLI) to allow you to build an application for deployment to a native device. You configure the build process to target a specific platform such as Windows, iOS, or Android, and Visual Studio and the CLI create the appropriate app package for the device. You can then run your app on a device tethered to your machine, an emulator, or a simulator. We will look these scenarios next.

Visual Studio uses MSBuild to call out to the CLI through a layer called vs-mda. These tools then deliver the appropriate Cordova package (along with your app) that the native device can execute. When developing on a Windows machine, this works great for building Windows Phone/Store apps and apps for Android. However, iOS requires Xcode components that only work on a Mac. Visual Studio include the vs-mda-remote agent to get past this problem. You can set a Mac as a build server, target it from Visual Studio, execute the build, and then debug on the same device, a tethered device, or an emulator running on a Mac. Of course, you can develop the same Cordova apps directly on a Mac.

NOTE

For more details on the Cordova build process inside Visual Studio, see "How the Cordova Build Process Works in Visual Studio" on msdn.microsoft.com.

Selecting Your Target Run Environment

There are a large number of options in Visual Studio for deploying your device for debugging and verification. These many options mimic the variety of devices, sizes, versions, and types available on the market. You will want to run and debug your application on each platform you intend to support, the version of the operating system (OS) you intend to support, and the device type (phone, tablet, PC).

Figure 25.6 illustrates the run options for Cordova applications in Visual Studio. The Debug menu should be familiar; this is where you select what type of compilation you want to execute. Debug is used for debugging because it allows you to step through your code. Release allows you to run your code in a full release mode. Distribution creates the packages required to distribute your application to an app store.

Notice the second menu option in Figure 25.6. This is where you pick your target platform. The options are Android, iOS, and the many configurations of Windows. The Windows options are there to support both Phone 8 and Phone 8.1 (universal apps) as well as Windows 10 universal apps. The other Windows options are there to support apps written for the Windows Store on the Win8 desktop or table (such as the Surface).

The third option in Figure 25.6 shows the options available for deployment and debugging your application based on your selected platform. In this instance, the platform selected is iOS. Notice the many Ripple simulators available. Ripple, like Cordova itself, is an open source project from Apache. It creates native device simulators that run in a browser for the many platforms and device types out there (more on Ripple in a moment). The other options in this list include Local Device and the simulators available for iOS. If targeting iOS, Visual Studio supports targeting the many Ripple simulators (currently through iPhone 5). However, if you want to use a local device or one of the many simulators available, you need to configure a Mac as a build server to work with Visual Studio. (See the following Note.)

BUILD AND DEBUG FOR MAC

To configure a Mac as a build server and to run your simulators on the same machine or a tethered device, you use the Visual Studio Options dialog (Tools, Options). Under the section Tools for Apache Cordova, you will find Remote Agent Configuration. Here you set the Host, Port, and Security PIN properties to enable a remote configuration on a Mac.

You must also install and configure the vs-mda-remote agent on the same Mac and set your Security PIN. For a walk-through of this scenario, see the MSDN article, "Install Tools to Build for iOS." This walk-through illustrates setting up the vs-mda-remote build on a Mac and connecting it to Visual Studio for the debug experience.

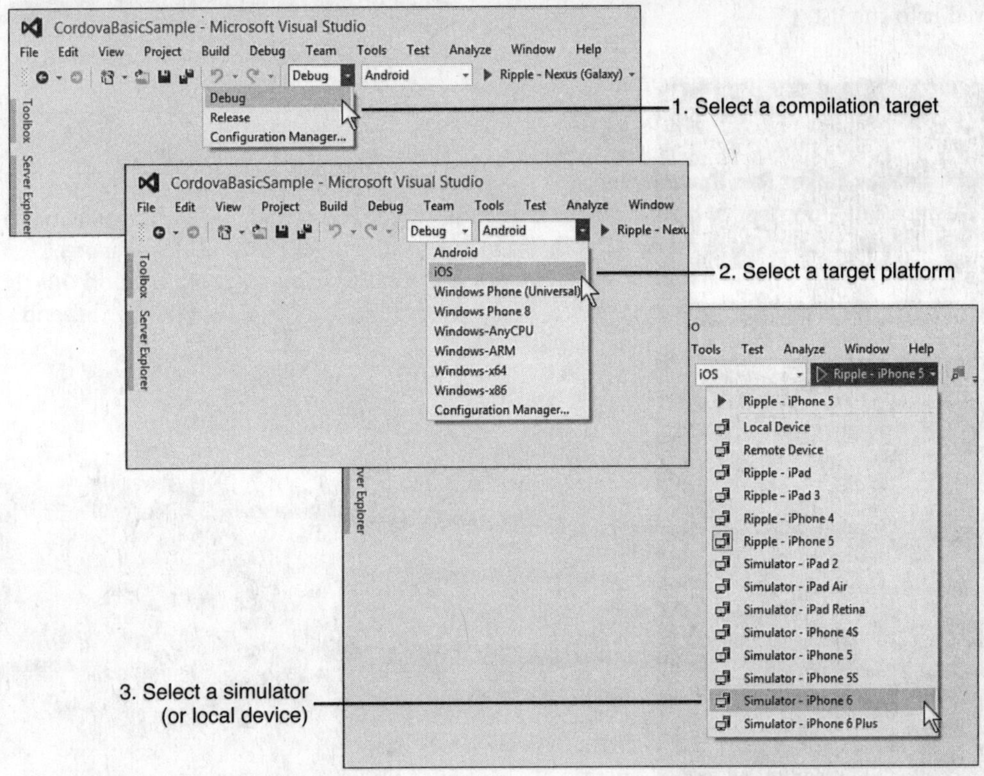

FIGURE 25.6 Use the debug options to select a compilation, target platform, and target device/simulator when running your application in debug mode.

Selecting a different environment (Windows or Android) from the second drop-down in Figure 25.6 changes your options for emulators and devices. There are currently no Ripple simulators for Windows. However, Microsoft ships with multiple emulator environments for phones. You can also tether a device to your PC or even use the local machine (for Windows 8 store). Your Android options also include a tethered device, Ripple simulators, and the two new Android emulators created by Microsoft that ship with Visual Studio (one for phone, one for tablet).

Debugging with Apache Ripple

We will start by running the basic sample application created earlier in this chapter using Apache Ripple. We use the drop-downs shown in Figure 25.6 to select Debug, iOS, and Ripple iPhone 5. You then press the Play button (green arrow) or F5. This will build the application, deploy it to the Ripple simulator, and open it within a browser window. It also binds the Visual Studio debugger to the running application.

Figure 25.7 shows the application running in the Ripple iPhone 5 simulator. Notice the menu bar at the top right. Clicking this "hamburger" button drops down the menu options (because this uses Bootstrap). Also notice that here we have calculated a pace and saved it to the list.

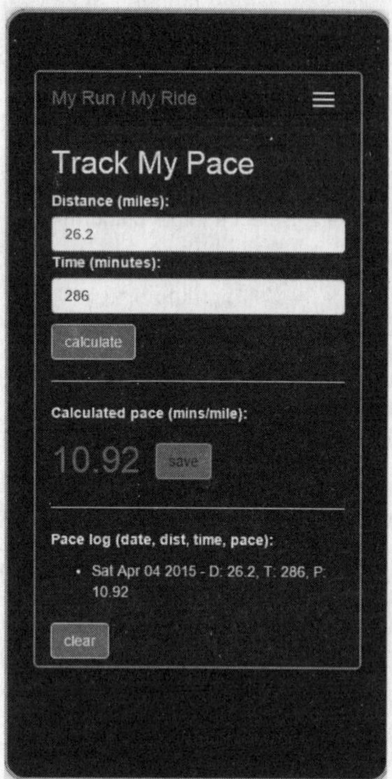

FIGURE 25.7 The Cordova sample running in the iPhone 5 simulator from Ripple.

The Ripple simulators use Chrome as the default browser. Figure 25.7 shows just the application. However, Ripple provides a number of options for simulating a user working with the device. These options are available in the actual browser window, as shown in Figure 25.8. The following highlights some of these many options:

- **Devices**—Allows you to select a different device. You should stay with the device selected if running in debug mode. However, you can also run inside of Ripple without debugging (Ctrl+F5) in Visual Studio. In that scenario, you can easily flip devices and see how your application may look and behave on those devices.

  You can also change the orientation of the screen from this section. This will show how your application behaves in Portrait and Landscape mode. Recall that you can choose if you intend to support both modes from the `config.xml` file in your project.

- **Information**—Provides detailed information about the environment of the simulator including versions and screen size information. It also provides details on the actual native browser used in the web view (user agent).
- **Accelerometer**—Allows you to mimic what happens when a user activates the device's accelerometer by tilting, rotating, and shaking the device. You may expect certain behavior in different scenarios (such as a driving game).
- **Batter Status**—Supports simulating what happens when the device is running low on battery. You may have code you expect to run in this scenario.
- **Settings, Device and Network Settings**—Allow you to set various options for the simulated device.
- **Geo Location**—Supports changing the user location on the device. This is helpful if you are using geo location in your application for various scenarios.
- **Config**—Illustrates how your application configuration is seen by the device.
- **Events**—Allows you to fire events on the device and then see the results. Events include Back button, Pause, Resume, Online/Offline, and more.

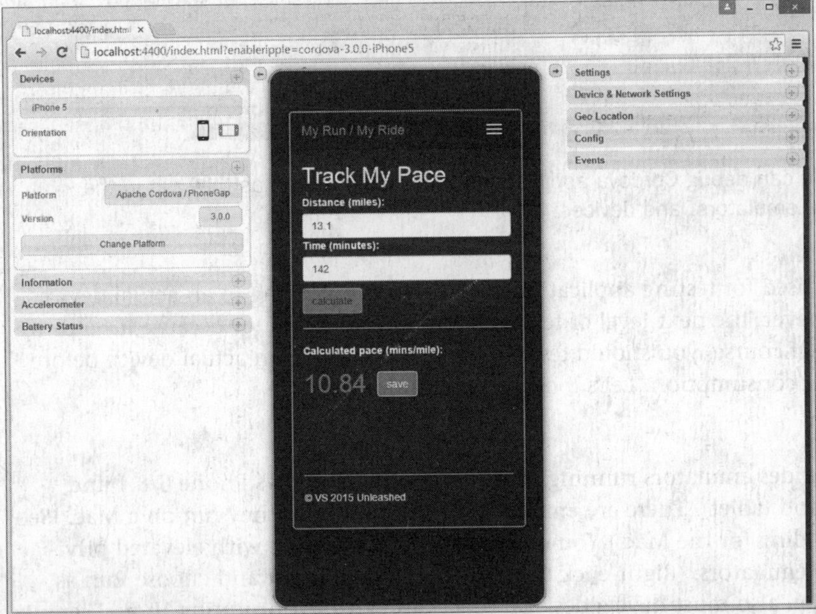

FIGURE 25.8 Use the Ripple simulators to mimic working with a device.

Remember that you can set breakpoints in Visual Studio and have them fired from the simulators, devices, and emulators. Figure 25.9 shows a breakpoint inside `index.js` for the `onAdd()` method. Notice that the Ripple application is running in the browser (background of the image). The Locals window (bottom left) allows you to interrogate variables. The JavaScript Console (bottom right) provides a log of JavaScript activities in your application.

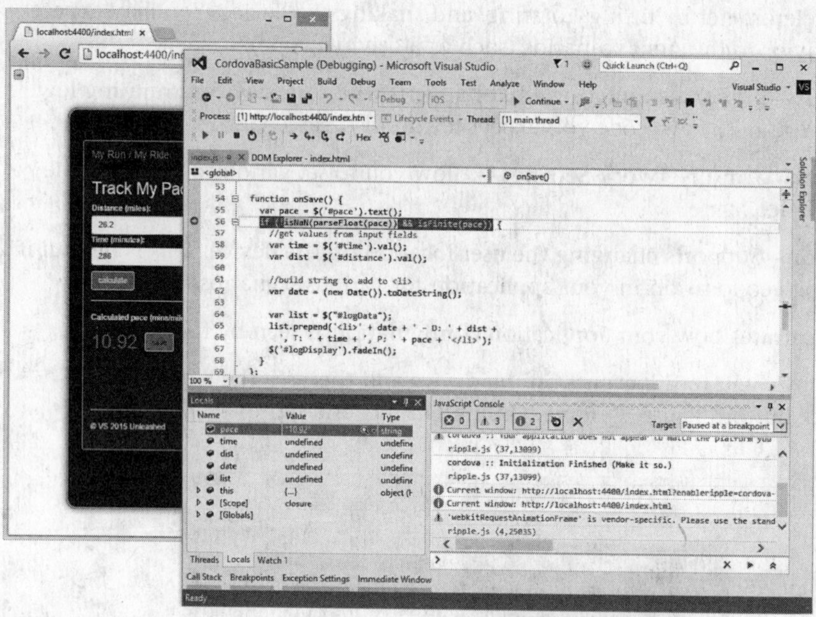

FIGURE 25.9 You can debug Cordova applications with Visual Studio as they run in the various simulators, emulators, and devices.

Ripple should be used for testing applications quickly without going to an actual device or emulator. However, the next level of testing should be an emulator because it tends to be more precise. Of course, you should test all applications using an actual device before deploying for user consumption. Let's look at these options next.

Emulators

Visual Studio provides emulators running in Windows for Windows Phone 8/8.1 and Android (phone and tablet). There are emulators for iOS, too, but they run on a Mac. (See prior note on building for the Mac.) You need to run Visual Studio with elevated privileges to use these emulators. (Right-click the Visual Studio shortcut and choose Run as Administrator.) You also must have a desktop processor capable of running HyperV emulations. Finally, you should have sufficient memory (4GB+) and available disk space (2GB+).

NOTE

Older processors do not always support the emulators. If you are getting errors when trying to run an emulator, it is likely that your processor does not support the technology required to run the emulator or your BIOS has not enable this feature. There is guidance online for checking your processor's support for running emulation.

You select an emulator using the drop-downs, as shown in Figure 25.6. Visual Studio launches the selected emulator at debug time. It then packages your application and deploys it to the emulator. Figure 25.10 shows the sample application running in a Windows Phone 8.1 emulator, with the Additional Tools window open.

FIGURE 25.10 The Windows Phone 8.1 emulator works to closely mimic user interaction with an actual device.

You can work with the emulator as you would an actual device. This means the buttons and other applications all work as if it were an actual device. Notice that in Figure 25.10 the keyboard shows when the user navigates to a text box (as it would in an actual device). The thin vertical toolbar in the emulator (middle of Figure 25.10) allows you to simulate touch (hand icon), rotate the view (circle arrows), zoom (magnifying glass), and open the Additional Tools menu (double arrows icon).

The Additional Tools work in a similar fashion to the extra tools in Ripple (see prior section). You can use the Accelerometer tab, for instance, to simulate moving the device side to side or shaking it. The Location tab allows you to set geo location. The Screenshot tab supports taking a screenshot of your device (useful when debugging). The other tabs inside the Additional Tools window provide even more options for working with the emulated device.

Local Device

Visual Studio supports debugging against actual devices. You can do so using tethering (with a USB connection). You can also communicate with the device remotely (over a network). You select the device option from the same options you saw back in Figure 25.6. Figure 25.11 shows the application being debugged on an actual Windows Phone. Note that you can do the same for Windows tablets, Android devices, and iOS devices.

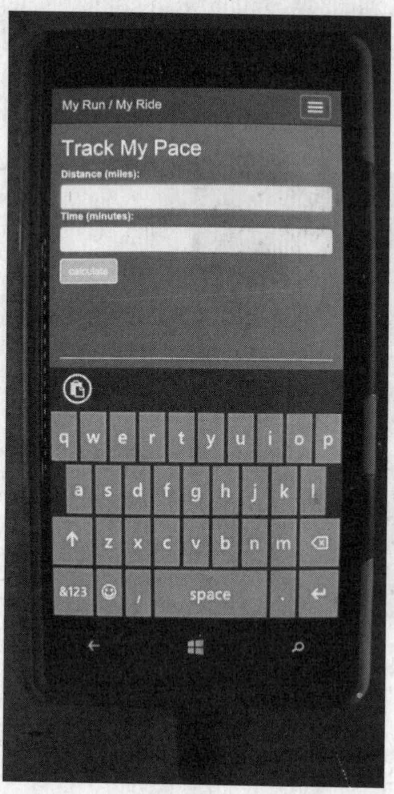

FIGURE 25.11 You can debug your applications directly on connected devices.

Visual Studio also supports running your application as a Windows Store app (see Chapter 23, "Developing Windows Store Applications") that runs directly on your machine, a remote machine, or a simulation of your current machine. You again use the drop-downs shown in Figure 25.6 to configure this scenario. Figure 25.12 shows the app running as a store app in the Windows-x64 simulator. The toolbar on the right allows you to work with the device for capturing screenshots, simulating touch, and more. Also, notice that Bootstrap spreads out the menu when using a wider screen.

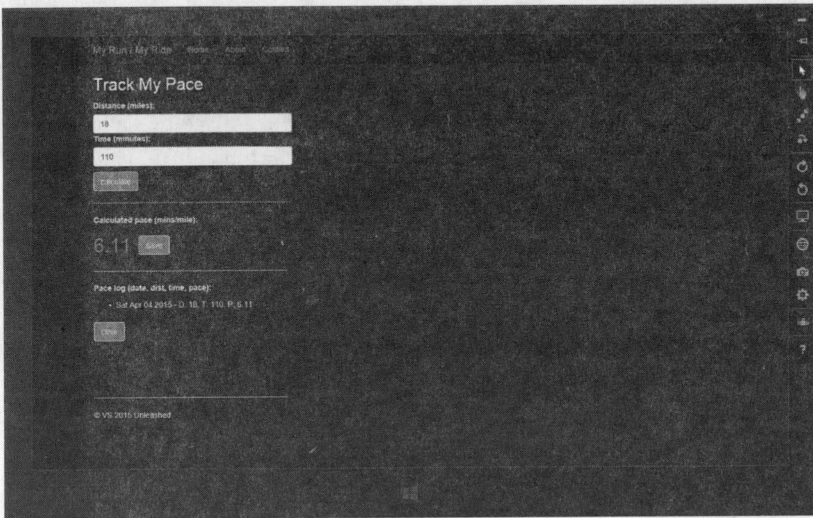

FIGURE 25.12 Visual Studio supports debugging your Cordova applications as Windows Store applications.

TIP

Remember, Cordova apps work like web pages running inside a native container using the device's web view. Like debugging web pages, it can often be useful to access the browser tools (F12 in IE) for inspecting the DOM and related styles. This is hard to do on a device. Thankfully, Visual Studio includes the DOM Explorer window to help. You access this window from Debug, Windows, DOM Explorer. (It also works for websites.) Figure 25.13 shows an example. Notice here that the Bootstrap `background-color` and `color` styles for the `<body>` tag are being overridden by `index.css`.

Next Steps

So far we have looked at building, running, and debugging a basic Cordova application using standard web technologies. This works great and is an option for building your application. However, there are some issues with apps like this. They tend to feel to the user more like a webpage and less like a native application. For example, when you click a new page in the sample app, the screen reloads and thus flickers like navigating to a new web page. Also, the application is currently not storing any data locally (or on a server). There are no icons or splash screens. The application does not take advantage of native device features. Thankfully, we can solve a lot of these issues with Cordova. We will look at using Angular and Ionic along with Cordova plug-ins for help.

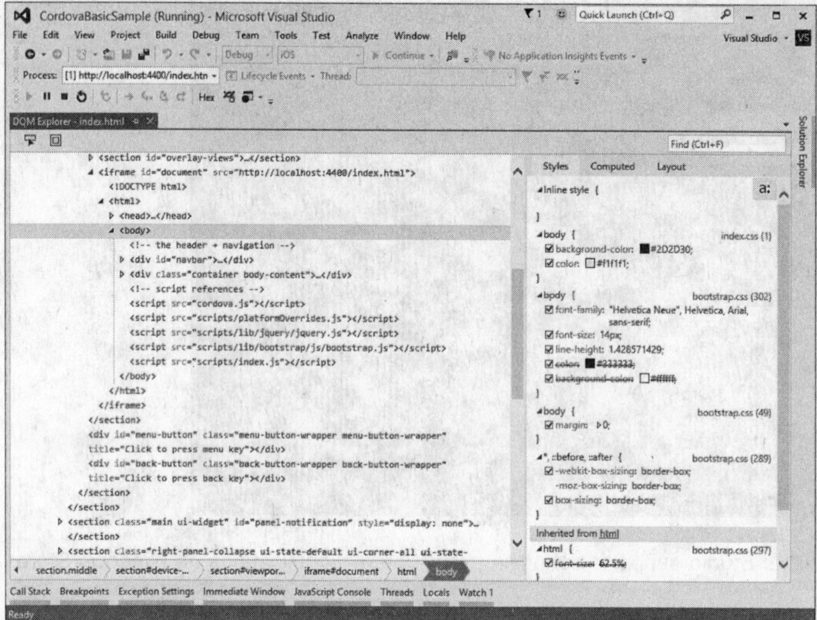

FIGURE 25.13 Use the DOM Explorer to debug DOM and style issues in your Cordova application.

Using Cordova Frameworks and Plug-Ins

JavaScript client-side frameworks increase your productivity when building a Cordova app. They are not required but, as in building a website, they can be very useful. We covered many of these framework back in Chapter 18; they help with data binding, responsive UI, look and feel, organizing code, and more. The prior sample used Bootstrap and jQuery. Here we highlight a few more of the frameworks common to Cordova applications.

Choosing Cordova Client Frameworks

The JavaScript framework choices are similar between a Cordova app and a website. These choices are split between frameworks that help you build a better user experience and those that define application framework structure. The following discusses each group of frameworks:

- **User experience (UX) frameworks**—Bootstrap is often used to provide better-looking and responsive UIs on Cordova. Web developers are comfortable using it and often leverage it for mobile web development. However, earlier versions of Bootstrap were seen as too heavy and slow for mobile. Later versions have made great improvements.

  Ionic is a mobile-first UI framework. It is typically not used by websites but often has become the popular framework for building mobile apps on Cordova. It provides a more native user experience on a device. It includes UI elements and "formulas" for tackling common design problems. Ionic also relies on AngularJS for UI logic such as loading pages, data binding, gestures, animations, and other user interactions. Ionic + AngularJS has become a popular set of frameworks for building Cordova apps. (We look at using this approach later in this chapter.)

There are other great UX frameworks out there, such as jQuery mobile and Sencha Touch. Nearly all of them provide great components based on HTML5 and user interaction with JavaScript.

- **Application frameworks**—The frameworks are created to help manage how your pages load, events fire, and data is bound. They are often referred to as SPA (single-page application) frameworks. Popular application frameworks for Cordova include these:
  - AngularJS provides an MVC pattern on the client. It supports two-way data binding and page loading through a routing engine. See Chapter 18 for more details on building with AngularJS.
  - Backbone is another MVC, client-side framework. It, too, supports databinding and custom events. Learn more at backbonejs.org.
  - WinJS is an open-source project from Microsoft that eases building JavaScript client-side apps. It combines both UI controls and an application framework. You can use it to build Cordova apps, websites, and Windows native applications. You can learn more at http://try.buildwinjs.com/#get.

All the frameworks mentioned here are open source. However, there are also commercial options available. Of course, you are not limited to any specific framework and may combine more than one for your solution. This chapter explores building a Cordova app with AngularJS and Ionic.

Cordova Plug-Ins (for Accessing Native Device Capabilities)

Recall the Cordova plug-in layer from Figure 25.1. This layer represents native plug-ins you can use in your application that serve as a bridge between the native web view and the actual device features (such as the camera, audio, geo-location, and even the app status bar).

There are nearly 1,000 plug-ins available from the Apache Cordova Plugins Registry (plugins.cordova.io). It can be hard to sort through that many options. Thankfully, Microsoft has vetted a number of great Cordova plug-ins and has made them available right from within Visual Studio. These are plug-ins Microsoft has tested for compatibility and use.

You add a plug-in to your application from the config.xml designer. You access this designer simply by double-clicking the app's `config.xml` file inside Solution Explorer. Figure 25.14 shows an example. Notice the many plug-ins available under the Core heading. Currently there are 25 listed here (out of nearly 1,000 possible).

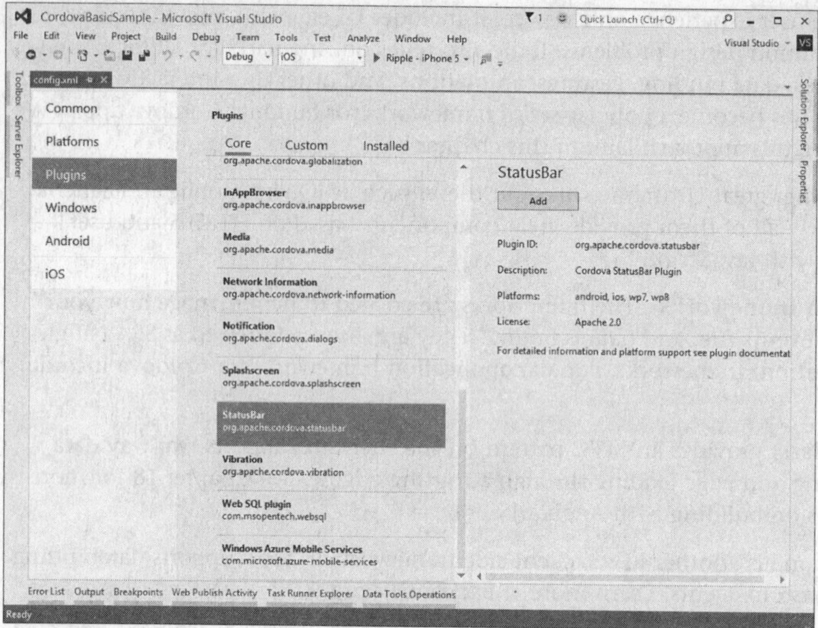

FIGURE 25.14 The config.xml designer provides access to installing the Cordova plug-ins to your application.

You click the Add button to add the plug-in to your open application. We will look at doing so in the next section.

> **TIP**
>
> You can find more information (and documentation) about each plug-in from the Cordova Plugins Registry at plugins.cordova.io.

Developing a Cordova App with Ionic and Angular

Ionic is a SDK for developing hybrid mobile applications using Cordova. It is not required (as we saw in the prior example). There are many similar products and open-source project out there. However, Ionic has become a popular (and powerful) way to build Cordova applications that have a more native look at feel.

This section illustrates the setup and configuration of Ionic inside a Visual Studio project. We then look at rebuilding an app written in the prior sample using Ionic and Angular (covered in Chapter 18). This should provide a good comparison. We also extend the features of our app to include a few more common items (like local storage). Let's get started.

NOTE

Ionic requires AngularJS (and includes it as part of its package). It also requires Cordova, of course. Ionic makes use of Node.js, NPM, Gulp, and Bower (among other things). Thankfully, most of these items also ship with Visual Studio 2015 as part of ASP.NET 5 and are thus likely already installed and configured on your machine.

Set Up Your Project

You have a few options for creating applications with Ionic. You can start with a blank Cordova template in Visual Studio and then add Ionic into your project as you would any other JavaScript library. You then hand-code your UI and JavaScript from scratch following the examples they set forth in their documentation. This is not a bad route to follow if you are building a custom application from the ground up.

Alternatively, you can start with an Ionic sample project. Ionic ships with three project templates for Cordova: blank, tabs based, and side menu. Blank is similar to the Visual Studio blank project (with Ionic installed). Tabs provides a tab-based user interface with a header and buttons at the bottom of the application. The header and button toolbar are fixed at the top and bottom of the application, but the content area will scroll (like a web page). Side menu uses a foldout menu pattern for navigation. You can start with one of these project templates and customize it to your needs. Each template is already set up to work and illustrate how to use common features. Or you can simply create your own user interface paradigm from scratch.

For our example, we are going to start with the tabs project template. However, this template is designed to work with the Ionic Cordova tools (and not necessarily the Visual Studio blank template). We can fix this. The following walks you through creating the Ionic tabs template and then stealing what you need for the Visual Studio default template to work as a tabs project template.

1. Start by launching a command prompt on your Windows machine. Remember, Node.js, NPM, Bower, and more all ship with Visual Studio 2015. We can use these tools to install Ionic and create a project based on their templates.

2. Inside the command prompt, type the following to do a global install of Ionic on your machine.

   ```
   npm install - g ionic
   ```

3. Next, create a new project based on the tabs Ionic template.

   Make sure you first use the command prompt to navigate to a folder where you want the application created. Then type the following to create a new Cordova tabs project with Ionic.

   ```
   ionic start yourAppName tabs
   ```

4. Launch Visual Studio and create a new Cordova project based on JavaScript (using the blank template).

5. We now walk through a series of steps to align the Ionic template structure to structure defined in Visual Studio. Start by first creating a folder called `lib` in the `www/scripts` directory.

6. In File Explorer, navigate to the Ionic generated tabs project created earlier. Copy the `ionic` folder from `www/lib/` to the new `www/scripts/lib` directory just created. This folder includes Ionic and Angular.

   If you use the file system to copy and paste, be sure to use the Solution Explorer toolbar to show all files, find the `ionic` folder, right-click, and choose Include in Project.

7. Copy the application code (written for AngularJS) from the Ionic tabs template project directory `www/js`. Paste these three files (`app.js`, `controller.js`, and `services.js`) into the root of the `www/scripts` directory of your project.

   You can delete the `index.js` file in the `scripts` directory. This sample will rely on AngularJS, so this file is not needed.

8. The Ionic template uses the AngularJS routing system for page navigation. This navigation is based on page templates (more on this to come). From the Ionic generated project, copy the `www/templates` folder and paste it into the `www` folder of the Cordova app.

9. The Ionic template includes a working shell for the application inside the file `index.html`. This file loads all of Ionic, the CSS, AngularJS, and more. Copy this page from the `www` folder in the Ionic template and overwrite `www/index.html` inside the Visual Studio Cordova sample.

10. Finally, open the newly pasted `index.html` file in Visual Studio. There are a number of references here you now have to edit to point to the new directory structure in Visual Studio. Figure 25.15 shows the modifications. (Modified lines are highlighted with the bookmark icon.) You can also see Solution Explorer, which includes the new directories and files for the project.

You can now run the application to see the results. Figure 25.16 shows the default Ionic tabs template being run from Visual Studio. We will now make use of this default template as we rebuild the sample application.

IONIC VISUAL STUDIO TEMPLATES

The code download for this book includes the three Ionic templates (blank, tab, and sidemenu) in both their default state (as generate by Ionic using the command-line) and as Visual Studio projects. We converted each template to its own Visual Studio 2015 Cordova project, including a shim for working with Ionic and Windows Phone/Store. (See "Running on Windows Phone" later in this section.)

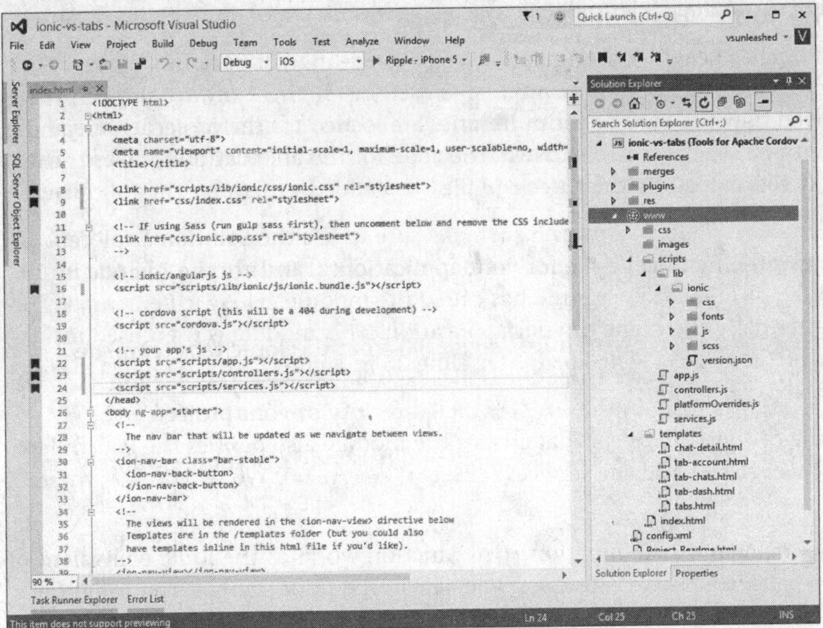

FIGURE 25.15 Edit `index.html` from the Ionic template to point to the items now in the new directory structure inside Visual Studio.

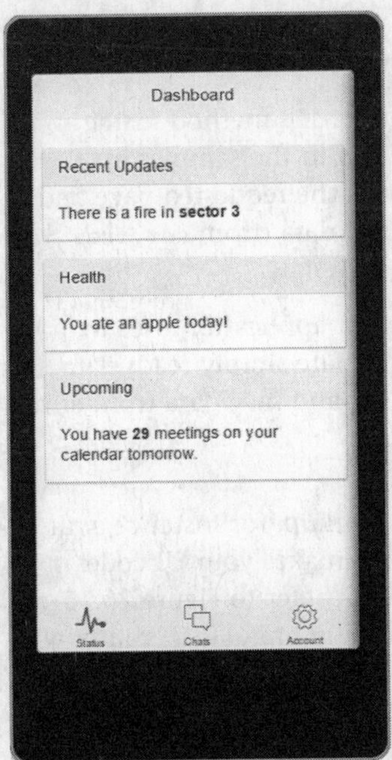

FIGURE 25.16 The Ionic Cordova tabs template running from Visual Studio.

Anatomy of the Ionic-Angular-Cordova App

The Ionic template relies heavily on AngularJS. We covered Angular back in Chapter 18; however, we want to illustrate here how Angular is used inside this Cordova project. First, Figure 25.15 showed how the various script libraries are loaded for the project. Ionic and Angular are loaded by `ionic.bundle.js`. Next, the code for the application follows the Angular pattern. It gets loaded by the three `.js` files you added to scripts. The following provides a refresher on each of these:

- `app.js`—This is the main code file for your application. It defines the Angular module (as `angular.module()`); Ionic has called the module `starter`. Remember, the module is essentially the name of your application. This module is then used inside the markup of `index.html`. The `<body>` tag (line 26 in Figure 25.15) includes the directive `ng-app="starter"`.

  The same line of code in `app.js` that creates the module also defines the controllers (`starter.controllers`) and the services (`starter.services`). We will look at these files next.

  This file also includes a `.run` function. This function works as the Ionic equivalent of the Cordova `onDeviceReady()` function you saw in the prior sample. You use it for app initialization code.

  The `.config` function uses the Angular UI router to load partial pages (called templates in Angular) as a user navigates through the app.

- `controllers.js`—This file contains the AngularJS controllers for the application. Recall that controllers work to bind the model data, or `$scope`, to the views (or templates). In this case, the model data is served by calling methods of `services.js`.

  Controllers are bound to your page templates using the `.config` method inside `app.js` (and not through a directive on the page as you saw in the samples in Chapter 18). This is how the Angular router works. It loads the requested page and its controller. The controller then loads the required model data (from `services.js` as `$scope`).

- `services.js`—This `script` file defines the services that your application uses to retrieve and save data for your application. This Ionic template simply reads data from an array. However, your applications would likely get and save data from either device local storage or from a Web API service (or both).

All the Ionic UI elements are built as Angular directives. Your markup, for instance, will use these directives such as `<ion-view>` and `<ion-content>`. This makes your UI code much easier to write, read, and maintain. Notice that `index.html` (refer to Figure 25.15) includes the line near the bottom of the page: `<ion-nav-view>`. The Angular UI router will load the pages from the `templates` directory into this container.

The `Template` files themselves represent just the markup required for the requested view. This markup is loaded into `index.html`. Listing 25.2 shows an example. Notice the use of the many Ionic Angular directives (`<ion...>`). You can also see that this template takes advantage of Angular binding using the syntax `{{chat.name}}`. In addition, the template uses the Angular directive `ng-click` to bind code from the button to a method in the app.

LISTING 25.2 The `tab-chats.html` Template Page Built with Angular-Ionic

```
<ion-view view-title="Chats">
  <ion-content>
    <ion-list>
      <ion-item class="item-remove-animate item-avatar item-icon-right"
                ng-repeat="chat in chats" type="item-text-wrap"
                href="#/tab/chats/{{chat.id}}">
        <img ng-src="{{chat.face}}">
        <h2>{{chat.name}}</h2>
        <p>{{chat.lastText}}</p>
        <i class="icon ion-chevron-right icon-accessory"></i>
        <ion-option-button class="button-assertive" ng-click="remove(chat)">
          Delete
        </ion-option-button>
      </ion-item>
    </ion-list>
  </ion-content>
</ion-view>
```

The page shown in Listing 25.2 is loaded by the Angular UI router found inside `app.js`. The code for loading this page is as follows. Notice that it uses a `url` route (`/chats`) to point to the actual page using `templateUrl`. It then uses `controller` to bind the controller to the template.

```
.state('tab.chats', {
  url: '/chats',
  views: {
    'tab-chats': {
      templateUrl: 'templates/tab-chats.html',
      controller: 'ChatsCtrl'
    }
  }
})
```

This is the standard way most Angular and Ionic Cordova apps are built. We will further examine this application pattern as we build on the tabs template throughout the rest of this chapter.

Rebuild the Sample App

We will now discuss building out the basic sample application created in the prior section. Recall that this app allows a user to enter details about a run or a ride and then track those details. You will see that we can quickly build a more full-featured version of this application using Ionic, Angular, and Cordova.

Develop the Overall App Structure

The app structure is provided by the tab template in Ionic. However, we want to replace the pages, icons, and navigation used by the template with our own application-specific content. Once we have this structure, we can start building the application. The following walks you through this process:

1. Start with the Visual Studio project as set up in the prior section (Visual Studio Cordova Blank project converted to use the Ionic tabs template).

   In Solution Explorer, navigate to the `www/templates` directory. This directory contains view templates that are loaded by Angular UI routing. Delete each `.html` file in this directory with the exception of `tabs.html`. We are going to create our own pages.

2. Add the following pages to the `templates` directory by right-clicking the directory in Solution Explorer and choosing Add, New Item: `tab-about.html`, `tab-calculate.html`, `tab-log.html`.

   Open each of the new pages and delete the contents. Add simple Ionic directives in the markup to show the page title when running a test of the application. This tag might look like this. (Replace `[PageName]` with the actual name of the template.)

```
<ion-view view-title="My Run / My Ride - About">
  <ion-content class="padding">
    <div class="item item-body">
      <h1>[PageName]</h1>
    </div>
  </ion-content>
</ion-view>
```

3. Open the `tabs.html` file. This file defines the icons on the bottom of the screen (see Figure 25.16) and sets up the navigation between tabs. It does so using the Ionic-created Angular directive `<ion-tab>`. Edit this file as shown next to point to the names for our tabs and use new icons. (See the following Tip on Ionic icons and colors.)

```
<ion-tabs class="tabs-icon-top tabs-dark">
  <!-- calculate tab -->
  <ion-tab title="Calculate" icon-off="ion-ios-calculator-outline"
           icon-on="ion-ios-calculator" href="#/tab/calculate">
    <ion-nav-view name="tab-calculate"></ion-nav-view>
  </ion-tab>
  <!-- log tab -->
  <ion-tab title="Log" icon-off="ion-ios-analytics-outline"
           icon-on="ion-ios-analytics" href="#/tab/log">
    <ion-nav-view name="tab-log"></ion-nav-view>
```

```
  </ion-tab>
  <!-- about tab -->
  <ion-tab title="About" icon-off="ion-ios-information-outline"
           icon-on="ion-ios-information" href="#/tab/about">
    <ion-nav-view name="tab-about"></ion-nav-view>
  </ion-tab>
</ion-tabs>
```

4. Notice in the prior markup that each tab includes an `href` attribute pointing to a named page. This name is translated by the Angular UI router to load the correct template. Open `scripts/app.js` and modify the contents of the `.config` method to point to the current template based on the tab `url`. The following shows an example.

```
.config(function ($stateProvider, $urlRouterProvider) {

  //Ionic uses the AngularUI router, which uses the concept of states.
  //Learn more here: https://github.com/angular-ui/ui-router.
  //Set up the various states where the app can be.
  //Each state's controller can be found in controllers.js.
  $stateProvider

  //Set up an abstract state for the tabs directive.
    .state('tab', {
      url: "/tab",
      abstract: true,
      templateUrl: "templates/tabs.html"
    })

  //Each tab has its own nav history stack:

  .state('tab.calculate', {
    url: '/calculate',
    views: {
      'tab-calculate': {
        templateUrl: 'templates/tab-calculate.html',
        controller: 'CalculateCtrl'
      }
    }
  })

  .state('tab.log', {
    url: '/log',
    views: {
      'tab-log': {
        templateUrl: 'templates/tab-log.html',
        controller: 'LogCtrl'
```

```
          }
        }
      })

      .state('tab.about', {
        url: '/about',
        views: {
          'tab-about': {
            templateUrl: 'templates/tab-about.html',
            controller: 'AboutCtrl'
          }
        }
      });

      //If none of the above states is matched, use this as the fallback.
      $urlRouterProvider.otherwise('/tab/calculate');
```

5. Set up the default controllers for use by the application. Open the `controller.js` file from the `scripts` folder. Delete the contents and replace them with the following JavaScript. You now have one AngularJS controller per page template. Note that we are not using these controllers yet; we are simply defining them for later.

```
angular.module('starter.controllers', [])

.controller('CalculateCtrl', function ($scope) {
})

.controller('LogCtrl', function ($scope) {
})

.controller('AboutCtrl', function ($scope) {
});
```

6. Open `services.js` and delete the sample contents. Add the following JavaScript to this file. Remember that an AngularJS service typically works to get and save data for the application. We will use it later to define the data for the actual run/ride log.

```
angular.module('starter.services', [])

.factory('Log', function() {
});
```

You can now run the revised application template. Your app should look like Figure 25.17. We can now start building the actual content for each page template. In doing so, we will walk through building the application one template view at a time. However, as we discuss a specific view (or tab in our template), we will also cover the supporting controller and service code (if required). Let's get started.

FIGURE 25.17 The newly defined application structure for the Cordova sample.

TIP: IONIC ICONS AND COLORS

Ionic provides an icon library. You can view the icons available to you from ionicons.com. You can search this library by name. Of course, you can use another icon library (there are many out there) or create your own custom icons.

Notice, too, that we changed the overall color scheme for the tabs.html template by setting the `tabs-dark` style class on the outer element: `<ion-tabs>`. Ionic ships with a number of default styles for items such as tabs, buttons, and more. You can find more info on these at ionicframework.com/docs/components/.

Calculate Tab

We now have the application basic structure. We can start building features with the main page of the application, `tab-calculate.html`. This page uses Ionic to build a form to allow the user to enter his date. It has a Calculate button to calculate the pace. The user can then decide to save the data to his log. Upon save, we show an Ionic pop-up dialog indicating that the data has been saved. The following walks you through this template and related code:

1. Start with the project template as built thus far in the chapter. Alternatively, the source for this book includes a template configured to this starting point in the folder `Cordova Ionic Sample - App Structure`.

2. Open the `tab-calculate.html` page (from `www/templates`) and replace the markup with that shown in Listing 25.3. Notice the use of Ionic markup elements combined with standard HTML. We have included line numbers to make it easy to point out a few things in the markup.

   Line 03—Notice the Angular controller definition `ng-controller="CalculateCtrl"`.

   Lines 10 and 14—The `<input>` tags use the Angular ng-model to bind to a `$scope.entry` object you will define inside the `CalculateCtrl`.

   Note that Ionic gives you many options for how the form is built. Here we use the "Stacked Labels" approach by setting the class of the `<label>` element in Lines 8 and 12 to `item item-input item-stacked-label`.

   Line 17—The Calculate button is bound to a method you will write in `CalculateCtrl` called `calculatePace()`. It uses the Angular `ng-click` directive to do so.

   Ionic has a number of options for creating buttons of various sizes, shapes, and colors. Here we set the `button` class in Line 18 to `button button-block button-calm`. The first style indicates this it has the look of a button. The second style, button-block, indicates the button should fill up the width of the container. The last style, button-calm, sets the color of the button based on the Ionic theme. Of course, we could use a small button instead (or any number of button types).

   Line 21—The `<div>` identified as `paceDisplay` is set to be hidden by default. This element will be shown when a user calculates a valid pace.

   Line 22—The markup here is bound to `$scope.pace` from the `CalculateCtrl` using `{{ pace }}`.

   Line 23—The Save to Log button uses `ng-click` to bind to the `addEntry()` event you will create inside `CalculateCtrl`.

LISTING 25.3 The tab-calculate.html Template Page

```
01  <ion-view view-title="My Run / My Ride">
02    <ion-content class="padding">
03      <div class="item item-body" ng-controller="CalculateCtrl">
04        <h1>Track My Pace</h1>
05
06        <!-- user input form -->
07        <div class="list">
08          <label class="item item-input item-stacked-label">
```

```
        <span class="input-label">Distance</span>
        <input type="text" placeholder="miles" ng-model="entry.distance">
      </label>
      <label class="item item-input item-stacked-label">
        <span class="input-label">Time</span>
        <input type="text" placeholder="minutes" ng-model="entry.time">
      </label>
    </div>
    <button id="btnCalc" ng-click="calculatePace()"
            class="button button-block button-calm">calculate</button>

    <!-- pace calculation results -->
    <div id="paceDisplay" style="display: none;">
      <div class="pace">Your Pace: {{ pace }}</div>
      <button type="button" ng-click="addEntry()"
              class="button button-block button-calm">save to log</button>
    </div>
  </div>
 </ion-content>
</ion-view>
```

3. Write the supporting code required to make the tab-calculate page operate. This code will go inside the `CalculateCtrl` definition inside `www/scripts/controllers.js`. Listing 25.4 shows the code with line numbers.

   The following walks you through this code:

   Line 01—Initializes the controller using `$ionicPopup`, which is part of the Ionic AngularJS extensions (ionicframework.com/docs/api/) for showing a pop-up modal dialog to a user. Notice, too, that the Log service is being loaded with this controller.

   Lines 04–06—These lines initialize the `$scope` items used by the page. Line 06 calls the Log service to get the list of saved entries.

   Line 08—This is the method for `calculatePace()` that fires based on the calculate button click. Notice that it uses binding to get the values for `time` and `distance`. It then shows the `paceDisplay` `<div>` provided the calculation is valid.

   Line 22—The `addEntry()` method fires when the user clicks the Add button for the given item to log. Notice that we have not fully implemented this method here. We will do so in a coming section. It will call the `Log` service to get the data from storage. The method then resets the form for the user to add another entry. Finally, it calls `showAlert()` to give a user the message that the item was added to the log.

   Line 33—The `showAlert()` method shows an alert message to the user after adding an item to the log.

LISTING 25.4 The `CalculateCtrl` Controller Inside `controller.js`

```
.controller('CalculateCtrl', function ($scope, $ionicPopup, Log) {

  //Define overall scope.
  $scope.entry = { distance: '', time: '' };
  $scope.pace = '';
  $scope.log = Log.all();

  $scope.calculatePace = function () {
    $scope.pace = '';
    document.getElementById('paceDisplay').style.display = 'none';

    //Get data from .entry and calculate.
    var pace = ($scope.entry.time / $scope.entry.distance);

    //If a number, show results.
    if (!isNaN(parseFloat(pace)) && isFinite(pace)) {
      $scope.pace = pace.toFixed(2);
      document.getElementById('paceDisplay').style.display = 'block';
    }
  };

  $scope.addEntry = function () {
    //TODO: add the item to the log scope.

    //Clear form; show success.
    $scope.pace = '';
    $scope.entry = { distance: '', time: '' };
    document.getElementById('paceDisplay').style.display = 'none';
    $scope.showAlert();

  };

  $scope.showAlert = function () {
    var alertPopup = $ionicPopup.alert({
      title: 'My Run / My Ride',
      template: 'Item saved to log!'
    });
  };
})
```

4. Finally, open `services.js` from the `scripts` folder. Replace the contents with code to create the Log service. For now, this service should return a simple array of log items. It should also support clearing the log (which we will use on the tab-log.html

page). Listing 25.5 shows an example. Note that we will replace this sample code in a coming section to save and retrieve this data from storage.

LISTING 25.5 The `services.js` File Contents

```
angular.module('starter.services', [])
.factory('Log', function() {
  //Fake data.
  var log = [
    { date: "Date: Sun Apr 05 2015",
      data: "Distance: 24, Time: 345, Pace: 14.38",
    },
    {
      date: "Date: Sun Apr 05 2015",
      data: "Distance: 24, Time: 345, Pace: 14.38"
    },
    {
      date: "Date: Sun Apr 05 2015",
      data: "Distance: 24, Time: 345, Pace: 14.38"
    },
    {
      date: "Date: Sun Apr 05 2015",
      data: "Distance: 24, Time: 345, Pace: 14.38"
    },
  ];

  return {
    all: function() {
      return log;
    },
    clear: function () {
      this.log = [];
    }
  };
});
```

You can now run the application and start working with the first page. Figure 25.18 shows the form in action. Be sure to click the Save to Log button to see how the Ionic pop-up behaves.

NOTE

Right now our application simply hides or shows elements based on user interaction. Recall that jQuery includes the ability to animate these transitions. We could, of course, include jQuery in our project to make use of these features. However, Ionic is working to provide an animations library. It was in beta at the time of writing this chapter.

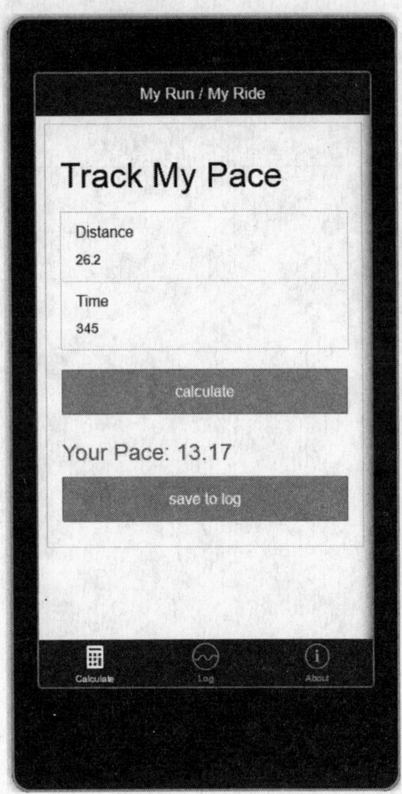

FIGURE 25.18 The tab-calculate.html view working inside a Ripple simulator.

Log Tab

The `tab-log.html` page will give a user a list of all her saved run/ride entries. Ionic provides many options for showing items in a list because this is a common feature of most mobile applications. These options include lists with icons, lists with buttons, clickable lists, organized lists, and much more. Here we create a simple list with an icon next to each element. The following walks you through creating this page template.

1. Open `tab-log.html`. Add markup to the page for showing an Ionic list using Angular binding. Listing 25.6 shows an example. Line numbers are included for reference:

   Line 02—The view is connected to `LogCtrl` from `controllers.js`.

   Line 03—The "clear log" button is connected to the `LogCtrl.clear()` method using `ng-click`.

   Line 07—Here we use `ng-repeat` to iterate over each item inside of `logItems` (from the `$scope` defined inside `LogCtrl`).

   Lines 11 and 12—These lines bind to properties of the `logItem` objects using `ng-bind`.

LISTING 25.6 The tab-log.html Markup

```
<ion-view view-title="My Run / My Ride - View Log">
  <ion-content class="padding" ng-controller="LogCtrl">
    <button type="button" ng-click="clear()"
            class="button button-block button-calm">
      clear log
    </button>
    <div class="list" ng-repeat="item in logItems">
      <div class="item item-icon-left">
        <p>
          <i class="icon ion-ios-calendar"></i>
          <span ng-bind="item.date"></span></p>
        <p span ng-bind="item.data"></p>
      </div>
    </div>
  </ion-content>
</ion-view>
```

2. Add the code to the `controller.js` file to support the log view template. Listing 25.7 shows an example. The following walks you through this code by highlighted line number:

   Line 01—The controller is initialized using the `$ionicPopup` Angular extension and the `Log` service.

   Line 02—The controller loads by setting the `$scope.logItems` to the result of the service call, `Log.all()` (see Listing 25.5).

   Line 04—The `clear()` method uses a confirm dialog to verify that the user wants to clear the form. If he does, we call the service `Log.clear()` method.

LISTING 25.7 The `LogCtrl` Code Inside the `controller.js` File

```
01 .controller('LogCtrl', function ($scope, $ionicPopup, Log) {
02   $scope.logItems = Log.all();
03
04   $scope.clear = function () {
05     var confirmPopup = $ionicPopup.confirm({
06       title: 'My Run / My Ride',
07       template: 'Are you sure you want to clear your entire log?'
08     });
09     confirmPopup.then(function (res) {
10       if (res) {
11         //Clear the log.
12         $scope.logItems = Log.clear();
13       } else {
14         //Do nothing.
```

```
        }
      });
    }
  })
```

You can now run the app and click the Log item from the tab bar at the bottom of the application. Notice that the form loads with some default data (from the data defined in Listing 25.5). Figure 25.19 shows an example. This is showing the confirm pop-up after a user has asked to clear the form. Notice the log in the background.

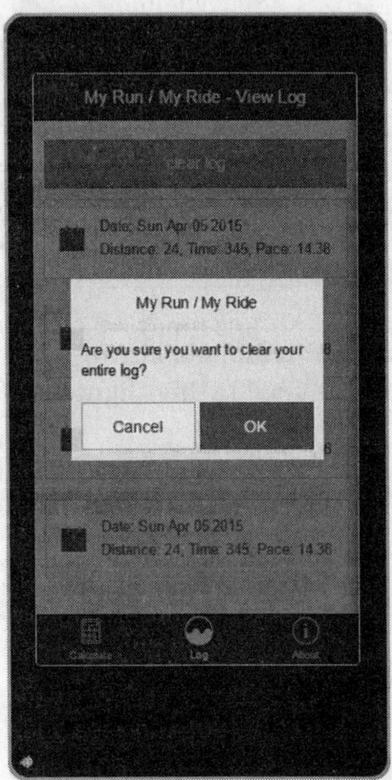

FIGURE 25.19 The Log tab after the Clear Log button has been pressed.

About Tab

The `tab-about.html` page is there just to add a simple About page to the application and show navigation with the tab layout. Open this page and change the markup as follows. (No additional changes are required.)

```
<ion-view view-title="My Run / My Ride - About">
  <ion-content class="padding">
    <div class="item item-body">
      <h1>About</h1>
      <p>Sample for the book, Microsoft Visual Studio 2015 Unleashed.</p>
    </div>
  </ion-content>
</ion-view>
```

NOTE

Like Bootstrap, you can customize the look at feel of Ionic using Sass. It also provides a variables file listing the many colors in the application. This file is called `Variables.scss`. You change these values and then recompile the Ionic theme to meet your needs. Of course, you can also override Ionic styles using your own CSS inside `index.css`.

Support Storage

You saw back in Chapters 17 through 19 that we can create a Web API for storing data and accessing it with web code. The same is true for mobile applications. They can connect to your Web API (running on Azure or another cloud platform). This API can then save data to a database or some other storage mechanism. You can make further API calls to retrieve the data.

Here, however, we are going to look at storing data locally on the device. We have a couple options to do so. First, we can use HTML5 Web Storage (localStorage). Alternatively, we could use a small database that is pushed to the device, such as SQLite. We are going to work with the former approach (HTML 5 Web Storage). Of course, you might consider a hybrid approach in which users can work offline (local storage) and then synch through a Web API (cloud storage). This is a popular model for many applications.

We are going to add storage support to the application created to this point. If you have not been following along, you can start with a version of the application to this point from the download for this book. This version is inside the folder `CordovaIonicSample - BeforeStorage`. The following walks you through adding local storage to an application:

1. Clean up the `addEntry()` method inside the `CalculateCtrl` to make it add a real item to the log. Open `controllers.js` and navigate to `addEntry()`. Change the method to mimic the code that follows.

   Notice that the only difference here is that we create a real item based on the bound `$scope`. We then call the `Log` service to add the item.

```
$scope.addEntry = function () {
  //Add the item to the log scope.
  var item = {
    date: (new Date().toDateString()),
    data: 'Distance: ' + $scope.entry.distance +
        ', Time: ' + $scope.entry.time +
        ', Pace: ' + $scope.pace
  };

  Log.addItem(item);

  //Clear the form; show success.
  $scope.pace = '';
  $scope.entry = { distance: '', time: '' };
```

```
    document.getElementById('paceDisplay').style.display = 'none';
    $scope.showAlert();

  };
```

2. Modify the `services.js` file to work with HTML Web Storage. Listing 25.8 shows an example with line numbers for reference. The following walks through this code:

   Line 07—We set a key to be used by this application for storing and retrieving data from the HTML Web Storage.

   Line 10—The `loadFromStorage` method uses Angular to load JSON into an array. The data is loaded from the `localStorage.getItem` method of `$window` (passed into the service by Angular).

   Line 15—The `saveToStorage` method uses `$window.localStorage` to save the data as JSON (`angular.toJson`).

   Line 23—The `Log.all()` method simply calls `loadFromStorage` to return all items from local storage.

   Line 28—The `Log.addItem()` method takes an item as a parameter. It then loads the data from local storage, adds an item, and saves the data back.

   Line 35—The `Log.clear()` method loads the data from storage, removes all items in the array (using JavaScript splice) and then saves the empty results back to local storage.

LISTING 25.8 The Log Service Code Inside the `services.js` File

```
01  angular.module('starter.services', [])
02
03  .factory('Log', ["$window", function ($window) {
04
05    //Init objects and methods.
06    var log = [];
07    var storageKey = "appMyRunMyRide";
08
09    //Load from local storage.
10    var loadFromStorage = function () {
11      return angular.fromJson($window.localStorage.getItem(storageKey)) || [];
12    };
13
14    //Save all to local storage.
15    var saveToStorage = function (items) {
16      $window.localStorage.setItem(storageKey, angular.toJson(items));
17    }
18
19    //Define services.
20    return {
```

```

    //Get all items from storage.
    all: function() {
      return loadFromStorage();
    },

    //Add an item to storage and save.
    addItem: function (item) {
      var items = loadFromStorage();
      items.push(item);
      saveToStorage(items);
    },

    //Delete the local storage and save.
    clear: function () {
      var items = loadFromStorage();
      items.splice(0, items.length);
      saveToStorage(items);
    }
  };
}]);
```

3. IMPORTANT: By default, Ionic caches views in your application to help make performance better. However, this can often cause issues such as adding a new item to the Log, navigating to the log, and not seeing the item. Thankfully, you can control the Ionic cache inside the AngularUI router code found in `app.js`. Edit the tab.log state call as follows in order to add `cache: false` to the parameters list.

```
.state('tab.log', {
  cache: false,
  url: '/log',
  views: {
    'tab-log': {
      templateUrl: 'templates/tab-log.html',
      controller: 'LogCtrl',
    }
  }
})
```

You can again run the application to see the changes. You should now have a persistent log of items. Figure 25.20 shows the app after some actual items have been logged. You should be able to close the app and return to it and find that your logged items are still stored locally.

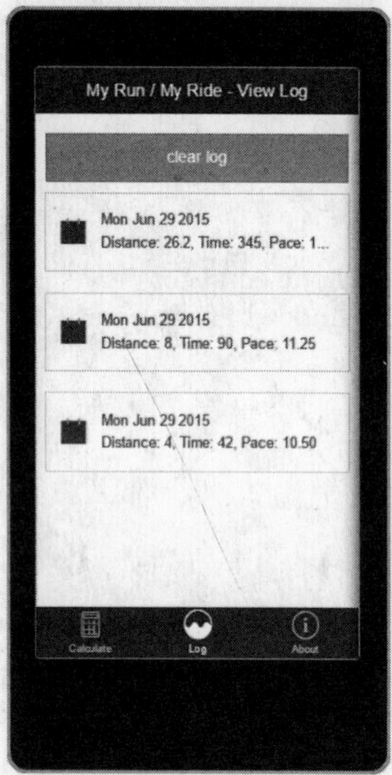

FIGURE 25.20 The sample app storing and retrieving data from the HTML Web Storage (local storage).

Running on Windows Phone

The application created to this point runs fine inside the iOS and Android simulators and emulators. However, you will get an error if you try to run it on Windows Phone. This is because frameworks such as AngularJS, EmberJS, and KnockoutJS (among others) use properties of JavaScript that Microsoft has flagged as unsafe because they can cause common security issues (properties such as `innerHTML` and `outerHTML`). Thankfully, there is a fix.

The Microsoft Open Technologies (MS Open Tech) group has released a JavaScript shim called the Dynamic Content shim for Windows Store apps. It is a JavaScript file you run to mitigate the errors when using client-side scripts. The shim still achieves the fundamental goal set by the security model, but it allows your client side framework code to run.

The following walks you through using this shim.

1. Start by downloading the shim from the Git repository. It is a single file called `winstore-jscompat.js`. You can download it from the following URL:

   `https://github.com/MSOpenTech/winstore-jscompat.git`

2. Open your project in Visual Studio. Copy the `winstore-jscompat.js file` into the `scripts/lib` directory.

3. Open the `index.html` file from the root of your project. Add a `<script>` tag near the top of the file (inside the `<head>` tag) before any other `.js` scripts are executed. This `<script>` tag should look like this.

```
<!-- dynamic content shim for Windows Store apps -->
<script src="scripts/lib/winstore-jscompat.js"></script>
```

You should now be able to run your application on a Windows Phone emulator or an actual device. Figure 25.21 shows the application running on a Windows Phone emulator.

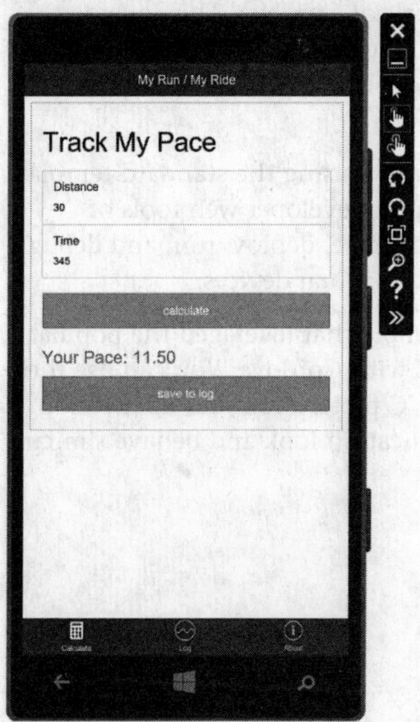

FIGURE 25.21 Use the `winstore-jscompat.js` shim to run your AngularJS (and related frameworks) on a Windows Phone.

At the time of writing, Ionic mentions that Windows Phone is on its roadmap. Most of it works. (It is just HTML5 and JavaScript.) However, Ionic does not currently support Windows Phone. This should change in the near future (and likely has already since this book was written). Therefore, you might run into anomalies with their controls. You can work through most of these.

Additional Items to Consider

The application created thus far is a great start to building a Cordova mobile application. However, it is just a start. There are many additional things to consider when building commercial application. These include loading data on pause and resume, handling user accounts, creating push notifications, storing your data in the cloud, creating custom icons for the app and a splash screen, and more. Thankfully, Microsoft, Cordova, Ionic, and Angular all have prescriptive guidance on adding these features to your application.

Summary

Visual Studio 2015 and the tools for Apache Cordova allow you to write mobile applications that run on iOS, Android, Windows, and other mobile platforms. This approach provides native applications that can be deployed to (and sold through) the various app stores.

We started this chapter by going through the fundamentals of Cordova. This included discussing how HTML, CSS, and JavaScript can be used to create apps that run on native devices. Visual Studio provides tool support, application dependencies, and project templates to get you started.

This chapter presented building a simple Cordova application using the standard template in Visual Studio. In this example, we leveraged the common developer web tools of Bootstrap and jQuery. We then examined how you can package, deploy, run, and debug Cordova applications using simulators, emulators, and even actual devices.

Finally, we wrapped up the chapter by building a rich sample that leveraged the popular Ionic and AngularJS frameworks for creating mobile apps with Cordova. You can use these frameworks inside Visual Studio. Angular provides an MVC pattern for your application logic. Ionic provides UI components that make your application look and behave similar to a native app.

Index

Symbols

A

B

C

F

G

H

I

J

K

L

M

N

O

Q

R

S

T

U

V

W

X-Y

Z